the handbook of
INTERNATIONAL DIRECT AND e-MARKETING

fifth edition

published in association with

KOGAN PAGE

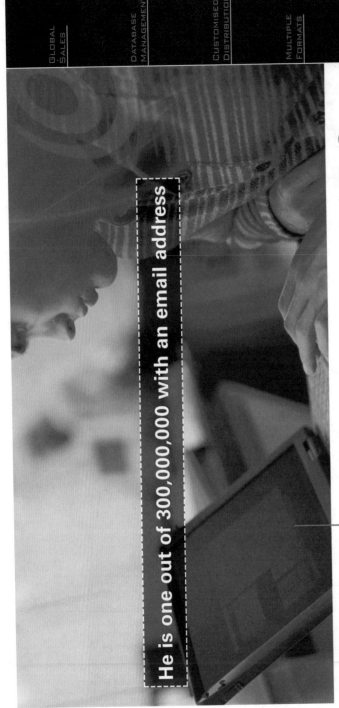

He is one out of 300,000,000 with an email address

Would you like an introduction?

With 24/7 Media's email marketing services, you can precisely target your email campaign to reach just the right audiences — wherever they may be.

You can choose from dozens of demographic and lifestyle options from the world's largest email database, with over 29 million names. Compared with traditional direct mail, email campaigns cost less than

half, and provide two to three times the redemption rate. With 24/7 Media's email services, your campaign is faster, more cost-effective and far more responsive.

At 24/7 Media our promise to you is service, quality and innovation. Call our experienced team at 24/7 Media today — because we don't just get your message out, we get your message heard.

Contact: David Woodrow, Director of Sales, email Europe Phone:+ 44 207 355 4447 Fax:+ 44 207 355 4448 dwoodrow@247europe.com

Made-to-measure services for international direct marketing.

Organising a direct mail campaign can be difficult enough but when it's an international mailing, there's even more to think about. No one's better placed to understand the complexities than TNT International Mail, one of the world's most successful delivery companies. For example, with our International Reply Service we can increase your response rates by creating the impression that your company has a local presence, even if it is on the other side of the globe. For more information give us a call on +31 20 500 8005. We'll be round to measure up your business right away!

Global Express, Logistics & Mail (T)(N)(T)

CONTENTS

CONTENTS

CONTENTS

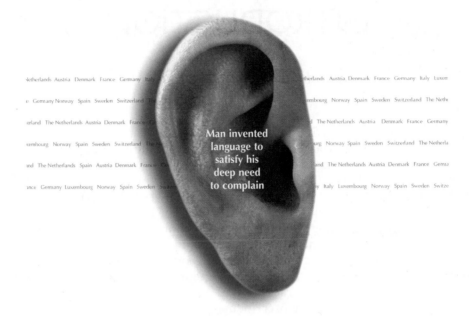

Man invented
language to
satisfy his
deep need
to complain

NOBODY KNOWS IT BETTER THAN WE DO –
A COMPLAINING CUSTOMER IS BETTER THAN
A LOST CUSTOMER. HOWEVER, WE AT
TRANSCOM DO A LOT MORE THAN
RECEIVING COMPLAINS. WE BUILD THE
CUSTOMER RELATIONSHIPS THAT BUILD
YOUR BUSINESS. WHATEVER YOUR NEED IS:
AQUISITION, SALES, CUSTOMER CARE,
TECHNICAL SUPPORT AND HELPDESK –

LET US LISTEN TO YOUR CUSTOMERS

THE CALL CENTER NETWORK
00352 40 14 21 000

INTRODUCTION

Ivan Hodac, Chairman of FEDMA

It is a great pleasure for me to write the introduction to the 'Handbook of International Direct Marketing', and this way continue FEDMA's close relationship with Kogan Page. The emphasis of this year's edition is interactive marketing, hence the new title 'Handbook of International Direct and E-Marketing', a topic close to my heart as FEDMA Chairman. The year 2000 saw the publication of the FEDMA Code of Practice on eCommerce and Interactive Marketing, which is the most comprehensive European code of good practice for this new business sector.

Direct marketing has become increasingly popular as a marketing strategy over the last decade, due to the development of sophisticated databases, telemarketing and now interactive marketing. For direct marketing this development has meant a closer focus on new media, e-commerce and interactive marketing.

Since the Handbook was last published in 1999, Europe has seen a tremendous change in the use of Internet. Over the last decade, the explosion of new telecommunications and Internet technologies has transformed the European communications landscape. The number of private Internet connections has gone up all over Europe, and countries such as Denmark, Sweden and the Netherlands now have more private Internet users, proportionally speaking, than the United States. At the same time, last year proved problematic for the dot.coms with many of them having to close down or downsize their operations. However, the Christmas period, a crucial one for our industry, gave positive results compared to previous years and this might be an indication that the Internet and eCommerce will keep growing rapidly. Competition between ISPs, lower telephone costs and greater involvement by SMEs in the e-world can explain this trend.

The Handbook of International Direct and E-Marketing is a complete guide to the direct marketing industry and a publication we highly recommend to our members. FEDMA is proud to contribute to the new Handbook with a reference to our Code of Conduct, our new '2000 Survey of DM Activities in the European Union', and our Legal Fact Pack. Publications are one of FEDMA's core activities in the year 2001, and we are therefore happy to present summaries of our publication in this edition of the Handbook. In addition to the section on industry statistics and chapter on European regulatory regimes, the Handbook also offers the readers an extensive country-by-country directory, including information on demographics, economy, language and cultural considerations, legislation and consumer protection, postal services, and an overview of national Direct Marketing Associations around the world.

The last two years have also seen positive policy initiatives at European level for the service industries in general and direct marketing specifically. On 11 January this year, the European Commission presented its new cross-border strategy for the service industries, which FEDMA, as the European voice of the direct marketing industry, fully supports. The strategy stresses that service companies established in one EU Member State will be able to operate from and within any other EU country as well. This is the start of the Commission's programme to remove barriers to services in the Internal Market, and is part of the target to develop the EU into the most competitive and dynamic knowledge-based economy in the world.

By the end of 2002, the Commission wants to remove all unnecessary regulatory and administrative barriers currently preventing service providers from expanding into new EU markets. FEDMA welcomes the Commission's new emphasis on a horizontal approach to the service industries, as opposed to its previous concentration on specific sectors. Many direct marketers use more than one direct marketing medium, such as mail, Internet and telephone, in their marketing campaigns. They have so far had to deal with various EU initiatives for their different strategies, with duplication of rules and inconsistent national applications as a common result. A comprehensive framework for free movement of services will more closely reflect the way the real economy works and make it easier for direct marketing to develop within the EU Internal Market.

The previous two years have also seen a major development in self-regulatory schemes for interactive marketing. FEDMA represents one of the major European players in the development of several initiatives to generate consumer confidence for e-commerce ('The Ring of Confidence'), such as codes of conduct on good business practice, Alternative Dispute Resolution (ADR) systems and trustmarks. These initiatives emphasise the importance of a combination of private sector schemes and a clear, consistent and predictable European legal framework in order to generate consumer confidence. All agree that a legal framework, provided by the eCommerce Directive, adopted in record time last year by the EU, is necessary to achieve this. However, the global nature of the Internet challenges existing national and regional legal frameworks. It is therefore important to develop programmes that offer consumers fast, fair and effective solutions to a conflict where the legal system might take years.

FEDMA plays an important role in the development of the International Federation of Direct Marketing Associations (IFDMA), of which Colin Lloyd, DMA UK president and FEDMA Board Member, was appointed president during the DMA (US) annual congress in New Orleans in October last year. This federation was set up in 1995 to promote direct marketing at the global level and to co-ordinate DMA activities worldwide. The global aspect of our industry is reflected in the Handbook as well, specifically in the directory, in which the readers can search information from different continents.

To conclude, the future looks bright for direct marketing in light of recent expenditure figures and policy initiatives. One of FEDMA's responsibilities towards direct marketing is to inform its members and press contacts about the latest developments. This Handbook is an essential tool. It provides a wealth of information and readers will find the necessary information about global direct marketing markets to help them conduct business everywhere.

Ivan Hodac, Chairman of FEDMA
17 January 2001

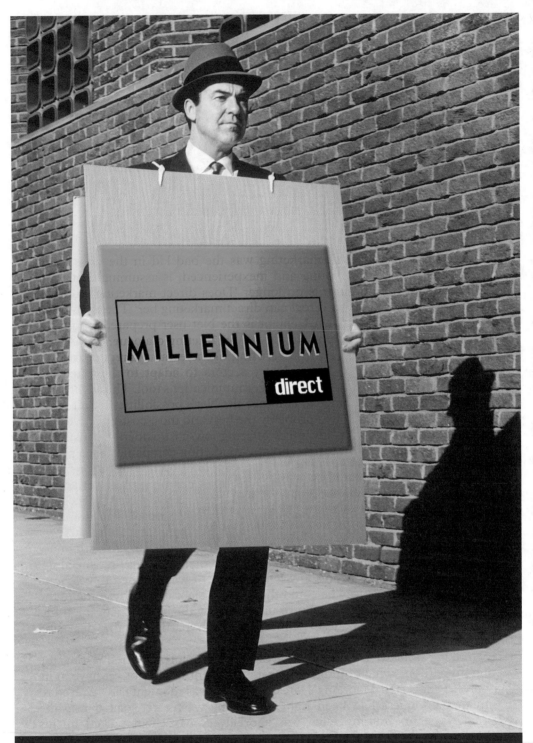

Millennium Direct is <u>the</u> advertising agency for the mature market.

Advertising to maturity?

Millennium ADMP. Plc. Windhill Manor, Leeds Road, Shipley, West Yorkshire BD18 1BP.
Tel: 01274 53 88 88   Fax: 01274 53 88 99   Email: info@millenniumdirect.co.uk

1

Direct marketing agencies: use the right side of your brain!

Martin Lindstrom, BT LookSmart

Some ten years ago, direct marketing was the bad kid in the class. Now direct e-marketing, new, young and inexperienced, is assuming that same reputation and the question is no longer 'Does direct marketing work?' It does. The question is 'How direct can direct marketing be?' The answer lies in consumer tolerance: to what extent is the Net user prepared to use the Web if doing so means joining the direct e-marketing dialogue?

It's an ironic fact that both advertising agencies and direct marketing agencies were among the last industry sectors to adapt to the Internet's philosophy and adopt the Internet as a communications tool. The advertising industry's seeming reluctance to embrace the Net's possibilities didn't make sense: the new digital tool was probably the best and most cost-effective one-to-one tool that's yet been invented, offering low-cost, superior consumer-targeting opportunities. But new direct e-marketing companies have mush-roomed and managed to capture the highly lucrative online direct business. Over the next couple of years we're likely to see opportunities and rewards in the business growing with mobile Internet access untying consumers from their desk-bound PCs and cross-platform strategies broadening the spectrum of consumer exposure to direct e-marketing communications.

So, what's in the direct marketing future? Well, let me share with you a couple of firsthand experiences. I have Japan to thank for this first anecdote.

After concluding a meeting, my Japanese client was inclined to celebrate the deal. And the best way he could think of to celebrate was by going to the nearest karaoke bar. In case you're unfamiliar with the practice, it's tradi-tional among some Japanese people that both parties to the deal sing together – in Japanese!

Thinking quickly, I thought I'd avoid embarrassment by requesting the song myself, one which I judged the establishment might not yet have in its archive. I suggested Madonna's latest song and was momentarily relieved to find that my guess had been right. The song wasn't yet loaded into the karaoke system. But my relief was short-lived. My client picked up his I-Mode phone and requested that the song be downloaded! Within five minutes the song was available on the karaoke system, having been down-loaded via the mobile phone. And so I was forced to sing the latest Madonna song, in Japanese no less.

So, what am I illustrating by sharing this experience with you? The rapidly changing face of consumer demand, that's what. Customer demand is entering a new dimension and direct marketing is entering a new and parallel one. Let me explain why and how.

I-Mode has introduced a technology to Japan that allows, among other valuable facilities, I-Mode phone holders to be warned of a friend's approach. If an individual whose data is entered into the virtual phonebook hoves into the I-Mode phone holder's vicinity, a message appears on the screen informing the I-Mode owner of the fact. What's more, once the message has been accepted, information on, say, a special offer at the nearest coffee shop will appear on the screen by way of an invitation to the establishment. The coffee shop has, of course, paid for the messages and takes the opportunity of offering a special discount to its guests.

This is not the future of direct marketing. This is the current reality! None of this presages the disappearance of letters and brochures from the direct marketing agencies' deliverables. But it does indicate that considering direct marketing's mix of tools is going to be more important than ever.

We can think about this all-important tool mix in terms of direct channel strategy.

What will be the mix between direct mail, catalogues, phone-canvassing, mobile Internet messaging systems and direct e-mails? The role of direct marketing agencies will change, not only because communication tools have expanded to include electronic devices, but because we are now able to monitor and measure consumer behaviour in more reliable detail than has ever been possible before. And the cost for this dream scenario? Almost nil. On the other hand, the availability of electronic media to direct marketing agencies will place a burden of responsibility on them to understand the new media, to understand the tools so well that they can compose the right channel strategies and to be even more result-driven.

What do I mean by 'understanding' the new media? I mean that direct marketers must develop a comprehensive appreciation of Net-based communications as a truly interactive direct communications opportunity.

Some years ago I was involved in developing a Website for girls that promoted a feminine hygiene product. The site was built on simple objective: to create a space for girls to seek information, capture and explore it and express whatever they wanted. The site's ostensible job was to communicate with the young clients and to do so in the most intimate of contexts. For example, one of the site's sections offered its young visitors the opportunity of revealing the dates of their two last periods in order that the system might calculate when the individual's next period was due and send an e-mail two days beforehand reminding them of the fact.

More than 400,000 girls signed up for the service. But more impressively, over 95% maintained contact with the service for more than twelve months. This allowed the company not only to capture very valuable information about the consumer group concerned, but also to develop a relationship of trust with this market sector through trustworthy dialogue. The result was a highly loyal consumer group, one which didn't consider using any feminine hygiene brand other than the one they'd heard from every month via e-mail. This direct communication, data capturing and marketing would never have been possible six years ago. Without the Internet being available as the communication tool, any process to achieve these results would have been too expensive and impossible to justify: the marketing budget would over-reach the potential revenue return any non-electronic one-to-one strategy would generate. The cost of the campaign I've described was less than £40,000.

This example not only shows that interactivity means more than sending e-mails in order to promote a product or a service. Of course, interactivity is about dialogue. But it also depends on creativity. Effective direct e-marketing depends on the marketer's ability to think differently and beyond the frames of presumed function: beyond the expectation of e-mail function, beyond the presumptions of mobile phone use, beyond the assumed capacities of the palm pilot, and so on.

And all this leads me to a simple conclusion. New technology will never make advertising and direct marketing agencies redundant. Almost the opposite is likely as the more technology we have available to us, the more creativity is needed to optimise its use and achieve the strongest possible consumer attention.

That's why direct marketing agencies will always survive, as long as they don't forget to use their right brain now and then.

Chief Operating Officer of BT LookSmart, Martin Lindstrom is an international marketer with leading expertise in the analysis and development of global Internet brands and operations. Lindstrom founded BBDO Interactive/Europe in 1995, one of the world's first advertising/Internet agencies and in 1997 established Clemenger Interactive, renamed ZIVO in 1998, and now the largest Internet development player in Australasia.

Martin Lindstrom co-authored *Brand Building on the Internet* and is the author of the soon-to-be-released *Clicks, Bricks & Brands*. *Brand Building on the Internet has become an international best-seller*, is available in twelve countries and is now in its third edition.

For years business people have been writing to their customers.

Today, with our help, they're finally getting the message.

Each time we work with a company or marketing agency, we try to ensure their direct mail campaign is received as a personal *communication* rather than a 'circular', whereby their selling message has true relevance to their customers' needs. People are individual and unique, not merely anonymous decision makers.

"We'll keep you posted"

We also understand the time constraints of marketing professionals who need to concentrate on developing strategic direct mail campaigns, rather than worry about how they will be sent out. Our business is to understand the client's objectives and work with them to realise those goals.

How can we help?

Through our experience and expertise, we can advise you on how direct mail can reinforce the message of new and existing integrated campaigns and so help build the brand, increase sales and develop long term relationships with customers.

What can we do for you?

Very simply, we can clean your database, print and personalise your letters, fold them along with your creative elements, matchmail personalised items, insert them and despatch finished items directly to An Post.

A solution that isn't a problem...

Mail Marketing
Together we can Communicate

Call Eddie Sharpe. Tel: 01 8680577. Fax: 01 868 0594.
Email: eddie.sharpe@mailmarketing.ie

2
Industry Statistics:
a FEDMA survey

INTRODUCTION

The '2000 Survey on Direct Marketing activities in the European Union' is the 6th consecutive study of statistics FEDMA has published on the direct marketing industry in Europe. This continuity allows us accurately to follow the development of the sector. The study is sponsored by Royal Mail, which has also contributed most of the figures on direct mail.

Since this survey was last published in April 1999, Europe has seen a rapid increase in the use of the Internet. Over the last decade, the explosion of new telecommunications and Internet technologies has transformed the European communications landscape. The number of private Internet connections has gone up all over Europe. Competition between ISPs, lower telephone costs and greater involvement by the small and medium-sized enterprises in the e-business can explain this trend, which does not look likely to stop in the immediate future.

For direct marketing this development has meant a closer focus on new media, e-commerce and interactive marketing, a development clearly shown in this Handbook. Online marketing, however, is only one of many direct marketing strategies growing fast. Another sector is telephone marketing (in-bound and out-bound) while more traditional direct marketing tools, such as direct mail, have continued to experience a steady growth since 1998.

As a whole, direct marketing has become increasingly popular as a marketing strategy over the last decade, mainly due to the development of sophisticated databases, telemarketing and now interactive marketing. These changes stimulate the need for more data on the size and influence of the sector within marketing communications.

One of the main aims of the FEDMA survey is to publish direct marketing expenditures (investments) and employment by country and media (mail, telephone and Internet). Statistics are still difficult to get in some markets, however, improvements have been made, and some markets have regular professional data.

Methodology
FEDMA collected data from various sources for this publication. National Direct Marketing Associations were asked to send a 2-page questionnaire to national member companies in order to compile the requested data. The

questionnaire is based on a set of definitions which serves as a European standard for DM statistics. In addition to national direct marketing associations (DMAs), research companies such as Datamonitor and Forrester, the Danish Post, and Royal Mail, have kindly allowed us to use their valuable figures. The market research company NTC, which also produces an annual analysis of advertising expenditure data, completed the report with these data.

It is important to stress that the data which appear in these charts may vary from that published by each direct marketing association nationally due to the fact that we have used a common set of definitions which are not always similar to those in use in the national markets.

It will be noted that some countries lack figures for a certain medium for one or more years. This sometimes reflects badly on the total spend figures of the EU. This, in our opinion, does not represent the correct picture of the DM industry in Europe, and in order to give the most accurate overview, we prefer to refer to a country breakdown for each medium rather than the European total.

Direct Mail
The latest direct mail figures represent a steady consolidation of the '97 figures and show that direct mail remains the most important direct marketing strategy. The largest European markets, such as France, the UK, the Netherlands, and Germany, all experienced an increase from 1997 throughout 1998 to 1999. Direct mail is still the largest DM sector and is constantly renewing itself as a medium for communication; it is not only used as a separate direct marketing tool, but also recently has been a means to drive people to the Internet, i.e. as part of an integrated marketing strategy.

Telemarketing
Regarding this medium, we have more information on employment than expenditure. Only Germany, Ireland and France have delivered expenditure figures since 1997, and in all these markets the increase in telemarketing spend is significant. The UK and the Netherlands have delivered estimated figures which also indicate a solid growth. Further development in the management of databases will most probably encourage continued growth in the telemarketing sector. There is no reason why software companies will not continue their on-going development of new and increasingly sophisticated programmes for the call centre industry. The variety of verbal/textual use within a call centre and the challenges of new CRM techniques, such a eCRM, constantly create new challenges for call centre software providers.

According to a Datamonitor study on the call centre industry in Europe, Middle-East and Africa 1999-2005, both the numbers of centres and agents has increased between 1999 and 2000, and a further growth is estimated for the next 5 years. The vertical market which sees the most significant growth of call centres in France, Germany, Ireland, Italy, the Netherlands, Spain, and the UK, is Financial Services, which counted for 22.1% of the call centres in 2000.

Online marketing

Regarding interactive marketing, further rapid development seems less clear. We still lack comprehensive figures from the different markets, and despite the rapid growth of online marketing, the last two years have seen uncertainty regarding dot.com start-ups, and consumer confidence. However, FEDMA is convinced consumer confidence <u>will</u> increase, thanks to the effort put into various self-regulatory systems by the industry, and it hopes to see more initiatives for collecting statistical data on interactive on-line marketing by the next edition of these statistics.

The '2000 Survey on Direct Marketing Activities in the European Union' is the product of the industry's continued efforts, under the guidance of FEDMA and the DMAs, to produce a full statistical picture that shows the true size and importance of direct marketing in Europe.

Table 1: Direct Mail summary (EUR m)

	Austria	Belgium	Denmark	Finland	France	Germany	Greece	Ireland	Italy	Netherlands	Portugal	Spain	Sweden	UK
1987	–	–	–	–	–	–	–	–	–	784	–	–	–	686
1988	–	–	–	–	–	3,321	–	–	–	914	–	–	–	798
1989	–	–	–	–	–	–	–	–	–	982	–	–	–	1,126
1990	855	–	–	272	2,879	3,952	–	–	–	1,027	–	–	–	1,371
1991	–	–	–	276	–	–	–	–	–	1,143	9	–	–	1,277
1992	–	–	385	344	–	5,192	–	24	1,316	1,255	15	–	524	1,281
1993	–	–	427	293	3,789	5,727	–	70	1,466	1,383	20	1,764	523	1,163
1994	–	–	448	329	4,472	5,404	–	78	1,462	1,516	23	1,727	545	1,353
1995	825	–	543	387	4,685	6,137	5	85	1,413	1,705	27	1,777	577	1,369
1996	–	–	568	407	5,136	6,335	–	97	1,634	1,767	31	1,836	622	2,050
1997	988	913	726	428	5,160	6,567	–	112	1,161	1,802	36	1,886	663	2,872
1998	–	655	–	444	5,673	8,078	–	–	–	1,978	37	–	671	2,464
1999	1,101	655	–	460	5,844	8,385	–	53	–	2,147	42	–	706	3,193

Table 2: Telemarketing summary

	Austria	Belgium	Denmark	Finland	France	Germany	Greece	Ireland	Italy	Netherlands	Portugal	Spain	Sweden	UK
1987	–	–	–	–	–	–	–	–	–	–	–	–	–	–
1988	58	–	–	–	–	689	–	–	–	–	–	–	–	–
1989	–	–	–	–	712	–	–	–	–	–	–	–	–	–
1990	–	–	–	–	752	867	–	–	–	340	–	–	–	64
1991	–	–	–	–	–	–	–	–	–	469	–	–	–	66
1992	–	–	–	–	–	1,287	–	–	188	528	–	–	–	66
1993	183	–	–	–	304	1,549	–	10	326	688	–	78	–	769
1994	–	–	4	–	336	1,455	–	11	339	917	–	82	–	–
1995	–	–	11	–	396	1,761	0	12	338	1,139	–	86	–	1,297
1996	–	–	17	–	496	1,937	–	15	404	1,310	–	91	–	1,418
1997	–	–	22	–	521	2,240	–	18	287	1,507	–	104	–	–
1998	–	–	–	–	554	2,352	–	–	–	–	–	–	–	1,604
1999	–	–	–	–	598	2,556	–	22	–	–	–	–	–	2,506

8

Table 3: Total direct marketing

	Austria	Belgium	Denmark	Finland	France	Germany*	Greece	Ireland	Italy*	Netherlands*	Portugal	Spain*	Sweden	UK*
1987	–	–	–	–	–	–	–	–	–	784	–	–	–	686
1988	58	–	–	–	–	4,059	–	–	–	914	–	–	–	798
1989	–	–	–	–	712	–	–	–	–	982	–	–	–	1,126
1990	855	–	–	272	3,631	4,873	–	–	–	1,367	–	–	–	1,436
1991	–	–	–	276	–	–	–	–	–	1,612	9	–	–	1,342
1992	–	–	385	344	–	6,628	–	24	1,504	1,783	15	–	524	1,348
1993	183	–	427	293	4,093	7,447	–	80	1,792	2,071	20	1,842	523	1,932
1994	–	–	452	329	4,808	7,067	–	89	1,802	2,433	23	1,809	545	2,650
1995	825	–	554	387	5,081	8,538	6	97	1,751	2,844	27	1,863	577	2,787
1996	–	–	585	407	5,632	9,319	–	112	2,224	3,160	31	1,934	622	3,731
1997	988	913	747	428	5,681	10,080	–	131	1,662	3,467	36	2,003	663	5,509
1998	–	655	–	444	6,227	11,657	–	–	–	1,978	37	–	671	2,464
1999	1,101	655	–	460	6,442	12,271	–	75	–	2,147	42	–	706	3,193

Table 4: Total direct marketing per capita (1999)

	EUR per capita		EUR per capita
Austria	136.0	Ireland	20.0
Belgium	64.0	Italy	0.0
Denmark	0.0	Netherlands	136.3
Finland	89.0	Portugal	4.2
France	109.2	Spain	0.0
Germany	149.6	Sweden	79.7
Greece	0.0	UK	0.0

Table 5: Volume, Total direct mail, million items

	Austria	Belgium	Denmark	Finland	France	Germany	Greece	Ireland	Italy	Netherlands	Portugal	Spain	Sweden	UK
1987	–	533	200	197	2,407	3,352	–	20	–	680	82	–	2,384	1,626
1988	–	556	215	216	2,684	3,609	–	30	–	780	96	647	2,076	1,766
1989	–	750	230	236	2,985	3,704	–	40	–	4,878	100	786	2,190	2,117
1990	–	780	240	355	3,084	3,852	–	40	–	5,035	113	902	2,377	2,272
1991	–	800	250	365	3,261	4,487	–	49	–	5,332	52	680	2,474	2,212
1992	–	850	257	370	3,490	5,138	–	56	–	5,924	89	883	2,284	2,246
1993	–	860	229	370	17,662	5,451	–	57	–	6,409	113	807	2,511	2,436
1994	–	865	209	385	19,751	5,548	–	70	–	7,098	125	807	2,633	5,730
1995	3,332	870	218	1,474	20,843	18,064	–	172	–	7,700	135	1,218	2,763	6,405
1996	–	1,095	241	1,556	21,902	21,605	–	191	1,300	8,183	138	1,186	2,793	7,104
1997	3,930	1,122	270	1,620	21,296	21,834	–	214	1,200	8,947	677	852	3,077	7,792
1998	–	1,117	292	1,651	21,878	21,298	–	300	–	10,128	746	921	3,183	4,014
1999	4,297	1,091	263	1,621	22,240	21,898	–	322	–	10,539	826	918	3,430	4,345

Table 6: Total volume per capita 1999

	Addressed	Unaddressed	Total	Direct mail	TM	Total
Austria	83.3	447.7	531.0	136.0	–	136.0
Belgium	106.6	–	106.6	64.0	–	64.0
Denmark	49.3	–	49.3	–	–	–
Finland	98.8	214.7	313.5	89.0	–	89.0
France	70.0	307.2	377.2	99.1	10.1	109.2
Germany	78.0	188.9	266.9	102.2	31.2	133.4
Greece	0.0	–	–	–	–	–
Ireland	27.0	59.0	86.0	14.2	5.9	20.0
Italy	0.0	–	–	–	–	–
Netherlands	92.0	577.1	669.1	136.3	–	136.3
Portugal	18.9	63.7	82.6	4.2	–	4.2
Spain	21.7	1.6	23.3	–	–	–
Sweden	68.4	318.7	387.1	79.7	–	79.7
UK	73.0	–	73.0	53.7	–	53.7
EU total*	83.0	295.7	378.8	111.0	37.0	148.1

Table 7: Internet/On-line expenditure

	Germany	Italy	Netherlands	Spain	UK	EU Total
1987	–	–	–	–	–	–
1988	48	–	–	–	–	48
1989	–	–	–	–	–	-
1990	54	–	–	–	–	54
1991	–	–	–	–	–	–
1992	148	–	–	–	–	148
1993	170	–	–	–	–	170
1994	208	–	–	–	–	208
1995	640	–	–	–	–	640
1996	1,047	186	83	7	77	1,400
1997	1,273	215	159	13	131	1,789
1998	1,227	–	–	–	–	1,227
1999	1,329	–	–	–	–	1,329

Table 8: Agent positions in EMEA, 1999–2005

Millions at year-end	1999	2000	2001	2002	2003	2004	2005
Number of APs	0.88	1.03	1.19	1.36	1.53	1.72	1.93
Number of new APs		0.15	0.16	0.17	0.18	0.19	0.20
Growth		16.5%	15.4%	14.3%	13.1%	12.3%	11.8%

Source: Datamonitor

Table 9: Call centers in EMEA, 1999–2005

000s at year-end	1999	2000	2001	2002	2003	2004	2005
Call centers	19.2	22.5	26.1	30.1	34.5	39.1	44.2
New call centers		3.3	3.7	4.0	4.3	4.7	5.1
Growth		17.0%	16.3%	15.3%	14.3%	13.5%	13.0%

Source: Datamonitor

Figure 1: Vertical markets in 7 EMEA countries, 2000

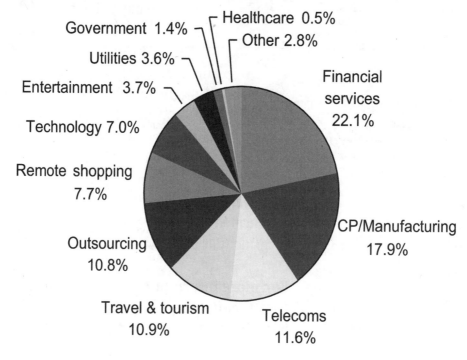

Government 1.4%
Healthcare 0.5%
Other 2.8%
Utilities 3.6%
Entertainment 3.7%
Technology 7.0%
Remote shopping 7.7%
Outsourcing 10.8%
Travel & tourism 10.9%
Telecoms 11.6%
Financial services 22.1%
CP/Manufacturing 17.9%

3

The Regulation of Direct Marketing

Alastair Tempest, Director General, FEDMA

Over the last decade direct marketing strategies have become increasingly popular worldwide. The introduction of on-line services has provided yet more communication vehicles for the use of direct marketing concepts. Together with this growth in the availability and popularity of direct marketing has come greater interest by international and national authorities in regulating the business. This article looks at the main trends from an admitted Euro-centric point of view, and poses the question – what can the sector do to ensure that direct marketing strategies are not over-regulated?

In Europe throughout the 1980s, many countries developed data protection legislation based on a Convention set down by the Council of Europe in 1981. Although this Convention provided a basic framework, national laws developed in significantly different ways, and used the vocabulary of data protection differently. For example, the concept of consent by the data subject can be interpreted by some national laws to mean explicit (often written) consent, whereas in other national legislation implicit consent can be accepted.

By 1990, some countries were preventing personal data from being exported to other countries without equivalent national laws, and the European Commission (EC) was asked to produce a framework directive to ensure free flow of personal data throughout the European Union (EU). Over the next five years the EC prepared its directive, which was finally adopted on 24 October 1995. The 15 EU Member States were given three years to bring their national laws into line with the provisions of the directive. Few of them managed to do this, within the deadline, and even now, five and a half years on three EU Member States still fail to have implemented the directive.

The directive is a complex legal text, which is unclear on a number of important aspects – for example, on the question of when and how to provide information to the citizen that his/her data have been passed on from one company/organisation to another. However, it does provide a legal framework which will slowly converge the existing differences in national approaches, and it set up two committees (one of national government experts and the other of the national data commissioners) whose task is *inter alia* to ensure that national laws and practices in the future will slowly but

14

surely become similar within the European Union. The Committee of national data commissioners has issued many recommendations or opinions on how the directive should be applied. This has started the slow process of converging national interpretations, however these opinions are not legally binding.

The directive has already had a considerable impact outside the EU. It is one of the directives, which must be applied by any Central and Eastern European country (CEECs), which wishes to join the Union. Most of the five front-runners (Czech Republic, Estonia, Hungary, Poland and Slovenia) have quickly introduced national data protection laws, and other CEECs are considering whether to do so.

Other countries as far flung as Australia, New Zealand, Brazil, Argentina, Taiwan, Canada and Hong Kong have also been encouraged to prepare national data privacy laws based on the principles of the EU directive and the OECD Guidelines (which pre-date the directive).

The influence of the EU's data protection initiative has, therefore, spread far and wide, and its insistence on adequate regulation for any transfers of personal data from the EU to non-EU countries is certain to continue to influence its trading partners around the world. In 2000 the EU concluded a 'Safe Harbor' agreement with the USA. This sets down specific rules for US-based companies wishing to import personal data from Europe. Individual companies, if they decide to join the Safe Harbors, must register with the US authorities. In addition, the EU is concluding bilateral agreements with non-EU countries which already have 'adequate' national laws (e.g. Switzerland, Norway, Iceland, Hong Kong).

The directive puts some emphasis on the benefits of self-regulation. The direct marketing sector in Europe, represented by FEDMA, has started to negotiate a code of practice with the EC's committee of national data commissioners (the Art. 29 Working Party) which will be the first European sectoral code. This code intends to put the requirements of the directive into the context of direct marketing, as a guide to European direct marketers on how they must conduct their data processing as required by the directive. Certainly this code will, like the directive, have a considerable impact outside the EU. The most essential aspect of the EU directive is that commercial use of personal data (except sensitive data) does *not* require explicit consent. Commercial use specifically includes direct marketing use.

Opting out of direct marketing lists is also to be found in a number of other EU directives, which put additional restrictions on direct marketing. Both the Telecommunications and Data Privacy Directive, and the Distance Selling Directive, require that direct marketers must provide consumers with an *opt out* mechanism, except in the case of fax marketing and the use of automated calling units (recorded messages without human intervention) where the consumer must *opt in*.

Consumers must, therefore, be able to opt out either by requiring that their name by put on a company's suppression list, or by subscribing to a general preference service (or Robinson List). Most direct marketing associations in the EU operate a mail preference service (MPS); some telephone preference services (TPS) or no-call lists already exist, and an e-mail preference service (EPS) has been launched by the US DMA, which is locally managed but global in scope. The alternative, in Europe, to a self-regulatory approach with preference services/Robinson lists, is inevitably a government operated system. The Swedish government, for example, has operated such an official system through its national databanks for some time.

The latest entry to the European regulatory stable is the directive on Electronic Commerce. This directive, which just over one year to adopt, leaves it up to the Member States to decide whether or not to demand explicit consent for any form of unsolicited on-line approach (which could be e-mail, individually addressed web-sites or other push technologies). Recently, however, the European Commission has introduced a revision of the Telecoms and Data Privacy Directive, which calls for opt-in for e-mail marketing. This draft is now before the European Parliament. Already five EU Member States have introduced forms of opt-in for email (although not all require explicit consent). This follows a trend in the USA where a number of states (e.g. California) have passed laws requiring opt-in for email in response to consumer pressure to ban email spamming.

This demonstrates the European approach to regulation. In Europe, legislation is seen as a mean to prevent perceived problems from developing, whereas in the USA regulation is the last ditch reaction to stop unacceptable behaviour once other means, such as self-regulation, have failed.

Typically, therefore, the European authorities decided to produce a directive on distance selling (adopted in 1997, which should have been implemented by all the Member States by 2000) as a preventative measure, and when they did so they used existing direct marketing codes of conduct as the basis of the directive.

This directive lays down the information, which must be given at the time of the offer and when the order is fulfilled; it provides a cooling off period of seven working days, and it bans inertia selling. It also strongly encourages self-regulation by industry. A second part to that directive, on the distance selling of financial services, is now under preparation.

Some of the basic concepts on contractual requirements that are set out in that directive can be found back in the Electronic Commerce Directive. Electronic Commerce is one of the most popular subjects at present in the EC. It is also the issue that has made many policy makers realise just how different national legislation remains within the EU, despite the EC's efforts to complete the Single European Market, and it has encouraged a number of EU Member States to reconsider their national restrictions – for example, Germany has now announced that it is reconsidering its laws restricting the use of sales promotions, which have become and embarrassment when German consumers can benefit from sales promotion offers on foreign websites.

The EU's new Electronic Commerce Directive should become one of the most influential pieces of legislation because it establishes country of origin control. This concept is a fundamental cornerstone of the EU – products legally produced in one Member State should be able to flow freely through the rest of the EU. In terms of Electronic Commerce, obviously, such a concept is the most pragmatic approach to cut through the Gordian knot of vastly different national regulations on trade in goods and services. (The data protection directive, for example, is based on this concept – if the collector and processor of personal data meet the legal requirements of its country of origin, other EU Member States cannot put barriers in the way when that data is transferred to or from their territory. Many other EU laws, such as the Television without Frontiers Directive, are also based on this concept.)

Obviously, without the guiding principle of country of origin control, traders will find it extremely difficult to operate in a global market place. Instead of applying one set of national rules to their commercial communications, to their contractual arrangements, and for the contents of their web sites, they could find themselves having to apply the national rules of *all* the countries from which consumers can access their services and purchase their products (the 'country of destination' concept). If the country of destination rules applied, a European direct marketer, for example, could find himself liable to the US system of private actions brought by individuals to the courts. In the USA these have resulted in vast damages being awarded by juries. Since there are not only variations in national laws, but even direct conflicts and contradictions between the regulations of some countries, control by the county of destination put electronic marketers in a particularly difficult position.

The EU's country of origin approach, therefore, would seem a sensible basis and a pragmatic solution to real legal problems on the global as well as the EU level. However, unfortunately this cornerstone of EU law is one of the most shaky and insecure principles.

There are, obviously, a number of exceptions to the concept – country of origin control does not apply in cases of national security; libel and slander of individuals; political, racial or religious intolerance; pornography; or protection of public health. To this list many opinion formers would like to add consumer protection. A country would therefore be able to stop or prosecute incoming Electronic Commerce on the basis of any national regulations, which could claim to be based on the loose terms 'consumer protection' or 'protection of public health'. In effect, this could reverse the whole basis of the Single European Market from that of country of origin control to country of destination control for most commercial communications.

A marketer would therefore have to craft its website in such a way as to meet with the wide variations in national laws within Europe; and, in FEDMA's view, if Europe were to embrace country of destination control, the Electronic Commerce 'global market' would soon find itself faced with major trade barriers and would simply fail to materialise. Country of destination control is, of course, a concept favoured by many politicians (and quite a large number of businesses) who want to have the ability to prevent, or at least control, imports of foreign goods and services. For the business which has no ambitions to sell across frontiers, or which has to apply strict national rules, there is no attraction in Electronic Commerce which offers competing products, probably at very competitive prices, and which does so without being hampered by the regulations of the receiving country.

In 2000 the EU adopted a resolution on the competent court which should deal with a cross-border consumer complaint for either on- or off-line distance sales. This resolution states that the court in the consumer's country of residence should be competent to ruling on any complaint. This is a major move towards *de facto* country of origin control, although *de jure* the court can apply either its own or the country of the e-merchant's (country of origin) laws. However, a new proposal, now in the pipe line, seeks to close this gap by ensuring that country of destination (the consumer's country of residence) law will apply. This proposal is extremely worrying, in FEDMA's view, both because it will seriously undermine the E-Commerce Directive, and also because it deals with pre-contractual terms (i.e. not the contract, but any claims made in the offer which can be considered as a promise and therefore part of the contract – e.g. 'these shoes last a lifetime').

Within the EU, at least, there are legal mechanisms for ensuring that national legislation is proportionate (that is, that the law does not apply unduly restrictive requirements), and that it is in line with the spirit of the Single European Market. Those legal mechanisms do not exist outside the EU, with the exception of the World Trade Organisation's regulations on free trade, but the WTO lacks the clout of the EU.

An example of the approach taken by the EU to disproportionate national legislation is the work of the European Court of Justice and the 'infringement' cases, which it deals with. In one complaint, Polygram Music Club wanted to extend into Germany. Its mailing from the Netherlands offered an introductory '3 for the price of 2' promotion, which is a normal sales promotion offer in the Netherlands. It is, however, forbidden in Germany because German unfair competition practice considers that promotions become unfair if they exceed a small monetary equivalent (about 0.80 DM). The German Courts therefore condemned Polygram, which was forced to stop its promotion and to leave the German market. The European Commission took up Polygram's case and wrote to the German authorities to demand that they allow foreign marketers to use such sales promotion techniques. As we have seen, above, the German government is now due to change its laws.

The European Commission is not only relying on the European Court to tackle disproportionate national restrictions for marketing communications. It has also set up a system whereby national government officials from the 15 Member States meet regularly to review specific national laws, which are considered to distort the Single European Market. It is hoped that that debate will lead to the dismantling of these regulations before industry has to start the expensive, and lengthy, process of infringement cases before the European Court.

The EU is, therefore, actively pursuing a policy of de-regulation of commercial communications, and the removal of specific national regulations that prevent businesses from using advertising, direct marketing, sales promotion or sponsorship in some Member States.

A close and coordinated approach is being sought at the global level through the International Federation of Direct Marketing Associations (IFDMA), which groups DMAs from 29 countries (and FEDMA) to developing self-regulation. The IFDMA has already agreed to cooperate on email, mail and telephone preference services (eMPS, MPS and TPS) and has prepared Conventions on both these services to ensure smooth exchange of national MPS and TPS lists.

IFDMA also strongly supports the work of the International Chamber of Commerce (ICC), with its model contract for transfers of personal data, and its marketing codes, including the recently updated and revised code on Direct Marketing. IFDMA will go a step further with a code for on-line marketing to children. IFDMA also has a system for handling consumer complaints across frontiers. In Europe such a system is operated by the European Advertising Standards Alliance (EASA) for all marketing communications.

One of the major problems that plague direct marketing is the ease by which unscrupulous operators can mail (and now use the Internet) to offer sub-standard or non-existent goods, or to send unacceptable products (pornography, or racist propaganda, etc.) to consumers. Their activities blight the name of direct marketing, and they threaten the 99.9 per cent of direct marketers who follow ethical good practices. In particular, their activities attract strong criticism by politicians and government officials and a negative press. They threaten to undermine the essential trust between the consumer and business.

Public figures often (deliberately or not) combine their criticism for the 'intrusiveness' of direct marketing with tales of mail, telephone, teleshopping or internet fraud. Self-regulation codes help by setting down the guidelines and parameters for good business practice. They are designed to improve consumer trust in the direct marketing process. However, fraudulent behaviour is not going to be stopped by self-regulation – it is not stopped by laws condemning fraud. The direct marketing sector must face this problem by cooperating with national authorities to identify and root out fraud. There is also a need for education both of practitioners, to ensure that they know and respect national laws and self-regulation, and also of the consumer to help them recognise and reject fraud.

E-commerce poses specific problems, particularly in terms of trust and confidence. Recent studies are showing that consumers view the e-commerce with suspicion. There have been disappointments over delivery dates; irritation over lack of information and extra costs added to those publicised on the website; and fears of privacy intrusions and financial transaction security. FEDMA has recognised that these concerns must, rapidly, be addressed, and that a multi-layered approach is called for. General codes of practice, either supporting or in place of legislation, must be accompanied by sector-by-sector codes and practices (such as the preference services; on-line trustmarks or seals of good practice and privacy enhancing technologies; codes for specific forms of direct marketing, etc.). This gives a flow-chart of measures which should be reflected at the national, EU and international levels to ensure that contradictions do not occur. There is now more co-ordination at global level thanks to the Global Business Dialogue on e-commerce (GBDe) and (as yet) an informal network of self-regulatory code/trustmark and alternative dispute resolutions systems (ADRs) which was set up in September 2000.

Direct marketing will continue to become increasingly popular as part of the marketing mix of companies, organisations and governments. It is subject to regulation, particularly in Europe, and is able to self-regulate. In order to continue to prosper and grow, it needs to ensure consumer trust. How best to ensure that direct marketing continues to serve the consumer, and avoids being instructive and badly behaved, will continue to dominate the legal and self-regulatory debates in Europe and elsewhere for the foreseeable future.

Finally, it is important to add a short word of the EC's latest ideas on regulations (the so-called 'new governance'). The processes for adopting an EU directive are notoriously slow. Directives have been known to take over 10 years from the start to finish, not including the time given to the Member States to apply the directive in their national law. The EC has looked with envy at some national proceedings, for example the tradition in Australia to co-regulation. The government passes basic framework legislation and then calls the industry, consumers and any other relevant parties together to negotiate 'codes' which are legally binding. In the USA, the Federal Trade Commission acts as the guardian for industry codes. This allows the Federal government to rely on industry codes, rather than detailed regulation.

The EC believes that co-regulation is particularly apt for a number of issues, where details are important, but EU legislation would be difficult (or too slow) to apply. Healthy and safety, environment, financial services, commercial communications (which include direct marketing advertising and sales promotion) are considered by the EC as suitable cases for co-regulatory approaches. The process has already started (e.g. particularly for environmental controls, health and safety – or, of course, FEDMA negotiations on a code on data protection and direct marketing, which we discussed above). The EC plans to build on these experiences. One plan which is being spoken out at time of writing is a framework directive on the 'duty to trade fairly' which would then be amplified by co-regulatory codes and negotiated between the European Commission, the industry and consumers.

Royal Mail

introduction

Despite the widely predicted bursting of the dotcom bubble, the world is in the grip of a digital revolution - and it's changing irrevocably the way we do business.

But whilst the technical improvements may be hard to keep up with, no-one can fail to understand the benefits that e-commerce brings. New technology is enabling businesses to become more efficient, reduce costs, and communicate more effectively with their customers. And e-commerce opens up the world - businesses can now more easily sell products and services around the globe, as well as around the clock.

For the consumer it means that their TVs are set to become the gateway to a global shopping mall. And e-commerce is already affecting the way people buy goods - with the advent of companies such as Amazon, Jungle, and thetrainline.com customers are choosing to buy certain items through the Web or TV, and are making outdoor shopping an event for special purchases.

So what does this mean for the direct marketer? Does the digital age mean the death of direct mail? Well in the UK the pattern has been growth rather than decline. In the last seven years volumes of direct mail have almost doubled, and with experts forecasting that relationship marketing is the key to success in the digital age, the opportunities for direct mail in this marketing mix look set to increase.

Most organisations are realising now that whilst the internet is a good channel in which customers can buy, it's not a good channel for businesses to' sell. Businesses that are going to survive the dotcom explosion are ones that will employ multi channel marketing – targeting consumers through a variety of media, from catalogues to on-line activity.

Companies are rushing to invest in on-line facilities, but it's not just about setting up a website. Experience has shown that investing in up-front marketing activity, customer care and logistics can make all the difference – and integrating new technology with existing systems is critical.

The direct marketing techniques that have been the bedrock of any marketing plan are more than ever relevant to today's marketers. Catalogues will continue to be vital to the home shopping market, and direct mail is being seen as a key method of driving consumers to the web – after all, you may have the best site in the world, but it's no good if your consumers don't know about it.

Royal Mail has responded to the opportunity and challenges that businesses face in the future with its Media Markets business unit, which has been set up to manage Royal Mail's interest in direct mail. We're well placed to help our business customers understand the need for multi-channel marketing and to develop a distance selling capacity.

We have a wealth of experience and information which we're passing on to both start-ups and established businesses, via a comprehensive series of guides and packs, such as our recently launched *Know How* pack – a comprehensive guide to producing, designing and targeting advertising mail. We also have a hugely informative website, which can advise on how to set up successful international mail media campaigns.

And of course Royal Mail continues to strive to provide the best delivery service for its customers. Fulfilment is already becoming a major issue for start-up dotcoms, but it's not just about the reliable delivery of goods. For the distance seller, the delivery can be the only physical interface with their customers. In effect their reputation is carried along with the goods – so brand compatibility is vitally important.

Royal Mail has an enviable reputation for integrity and trust, which can positively enhance the brand of our customers – Amazon for example use the term 'goods delivered by Royal Mail' as a positive selling benefit.

E-commerce is here to stay – and with it direct marketing. They have a natural fit that will help many companies survive the dotcom boom – and Royal Mail is here to help deliver the best campaigns, as well as the goods themselves.

convert clicks to customers

At Royal Mail we aim to go far beyond our established position as a first-class supplier with a trusted reputation among consumers. By providing up-to-date information, education and practical solutions to help grow the home shopping sector, we can offer real support to the direct marketing industry. We see this role as being especially important in the e-commerce sphere.

It's a fairly damning statistic, but recent research undertaken by Royal Mail revealed that 97% of people who visit websites are just there to browse. The challenge currently facing all e-tailers then is clear – converting this volume of passing traffic into loyal customers.

To meet that challenge it's vital that businesses develop a relationship with potential buyers away from the site. This relationship is not only about getting people to go to the site in the first place, but also keeping in contact with them once you've got them there, and ending with the point of delivery.

In order to develop this customer relationship, off-line e-commerce propositions need communication support that is complementary. Research carried out by advertising agency CDP has shown that ads alone are not working hard enough for dotcoms. In spite of high investment in advertising, awareness of specific sites is low, and one third of people with Internet access don't recall seeing any website ads.

Direct marketing works really well alongside new media as it further enhances the one-to-one relationship. This personalisation is key as it empowers the consumer, and is a far better trigger for action than blanket advertising. Direct marketing is now an essential tool for web sites trying to attract customers to their site, whether by mailshot of a brochure, direct response press or TV ads, or on-line activity.

The success of direct mail lies in the precision of its targeting, and again this is an area in which Royal Mail has essential information and experience. Syndicated databases are revolutionising the direct marketing industry, and are set to transform the way businesses target new customers on the Internet. These become especially important in light of new legislation which is set to restrict use of Electoral Roll (ER) by giving the public the right to opt out of having personal data passed to companies, and a threatened increase in fees of as much as 400% for ER use.

A growing number of players are realising that the value they get from sharing information is much greater than the perceived risk. A recent forum of more than 30 financial firms produced useful ideas on approaches improving and growing the industry as a whole. This type of knowledge pooling can only benefit retailers and consumers, and Royal Mail sees its role as crucial in facilitating and promoting such ways of working.

For firms acknowledging that no customer is theirs alone, typically buying from a variety of suppliers of products and services, the benefits of combining customer-buying information with other players makes it possible to build a dynamic model of customers in the UK. This will allow customised models to begin to be generated that will help predict future buying habits. In turn this will help improve targeting for customer acquisition, retention and cross selling, allow firms to cut down on wastage and eliminate unnecessary marketing activity to unresponsive consumers.

But perhaps the greatest strength of direct marketing, including mail media, lies in its potential to maintain and build the customer relationship, helping to create a brand reputation and increasing awareness of promotions. This can all help to reactivate lapsed customers or cross-sell to current ones. An Internet user visiting a web site with knowledge of its proposition and purpose is much more likely to be converted into a customer than a casual surfer.

delivery crucial to the distant retailer

For the distance seller, whose only physical interface with their customers is at the point of delivery, it is more than a logistical matter and is instead a vital time when the reputation of the brand is at stake. Good service above all else will make the difference between success and failure for web ventures. Royal Mail and Parcelforce Worldwide recognise that this is an opportunity and a responsibility for us and are strengthening our offer to businesses accordingly.

Royal Mail's extensive delivery network reaches 25 million addresses across the UK, and can access over 280 international gateways. Serving over 95 per cent of the Times top 100 companies, Parcelforce Worldwide is a leading player in the next-day market and a growing force in the expanding home shopping sector. Parcelforce Worldwide has recently invested more than £40 million in technology which will provide greater reliability, damage-free delivery, improved communication with vehicles and the road, and therefore accurate tracking to inspire trust and confidence in its customers.

But we are also offering much more than delivery – we can develop an entire fulfilment and logistics package for companies. Parcelforce Worldwide's logistics capabilities enable it to integrate with clients' existing supply chains and offer home shopping companies a personal service. This may be anything from customer management at call centres, to storing of goods in warehouses, from packing and delivery of merchandise to integrated IT tracking systems meaning that packages can be tracked in real time by retailers and customers. For on-line transactions we can also ensure financial security through Royal Mail's recently developed Via Code service.

In the e-tail environment customers' demands are making speed of delivery and choice when and where goods are delivered key to the new way operating. That is why Parcelforce Worldwide has spent the last two years researching new channels and are improving distribution accordingly, with evening deliveries between 5 and 9pm and on Saturday mornings. Work is also being planned to include the collection of returned goods at similar times, and requests for items to be handed over at another address or dropped off at the local Post Office.

For the dotcom world excellent customer service is paramount – if last minute tickets don't arrive exactly on time or at the right location, then the whole company's raison d'etre disappears, and with it its future. Electronic shoppers are notoriously fickle, and one bad experience will have them changing to the competition at the click of a mouse

royal mail offers the whole package to the direct marketing industry

The e-commerce era has endless possibilities for us all, and with proper planning companies tapping into the potential offered by the Internet will not only survive but will prosper when the dotcom consolidation begins. Royal Mail is well placed to help deliver customers to their site and keep them there as well as deliver the goods to their customers' doors.

For more information please call:

Media Markets – if you want more details of Royal Mail's direct marketing expertise please call **0345 950950,** or visit our website www.royalmail.co.uk

4

A New Framework for Postal Services

Caroline Kostka, Legal Advisor, FEDMA

Postal markets are changing rapidly throughout the world, partly as the result of increasing competition from telecommunications-related correspondence which has replaced the mail in a number of important segments of the postal market, and partly as the result of new technical developments which have improved the processing of mail.

In order to provide better services and meet competition, public postal operators or governments have developed different strategies. In some cases this has led to the opening up of the monopoly, and even to complete privatisation (for example in the Argentine). Deregulation is usually combined with greater freedom for the public postal operator to become involved in other competitive services. A number of postal operators have therefore been launched on the financial markets (e.g. Deutsche Post, KPN in the Netherlands) and have started to purchase postal support services (for example, Deutsche Post's purchase of DHL).

Thus the market is moving fast to change postal operators into competitive businesses operating in an increasingly competitive market, particularly for international mail.

The European debate has been particularly interesting in this respect, because the postal market in each of the 15 Member States varies in some cases significantly in terms of structure, quality of service, pricing policies, flexibility to deal with bulk mailers, etc. Attempts to introduce a common European approach have, therefore, been only partially successful, with the adoption of a European Union directive last year.

The EU directive on postal services will enter into force in January 1999. At present, EU countries are reviewing their national legislation and most of the postal services in European Union countries are going through significant changes. However, a large number of uncertainties remain for the development of cross-border mail.

Access to the information

The first uncertainty comes from the lack of information to be given to the users on the commercial services available from the post and on the criteria to be filled to get specific services. The directive defines direct mail as 'a

25

communication consisting solely of advertising, marketing or publicity material and comprising an identical message, ... which is sent to a number of significant addressees ...'. The notion of 'identical message' and 'number of addressees' can then be defined very differently by the national authorities. In order to facilitate the circulation of information, FEDMA made a specific pack for its members, compiling all national requirements[1]. Two elements were noticed: first, the information is not easy to understand, since postal offices usually only publish their details in their national language; and the criteria differ a lot.

Quality of the services

Secondly, the development of cross-border direct mail campaigns is directly related to the quality of the services given. It is essential that the customers are sure that the mailing will be delivered within a certain time, even to non-urban areas; however, there are significant disparities in the quality of service between EU countries.

It is important that the new postal regulations provide incentives to encourage the postal operators to ameliorate their services. There is a common agreement that these incentives should exist and postal operators in Europe have put in place an independent measurement system to measure the delivery performance, called UNEX. The results are regularly published and constitute an important factor for users to get data and to enhance delivery performance.

It is clearly crucial when good quality service is achieved that postal operators receive adequate remuneration for the delivery and the processing of incoming bulk mail. Cross-border mail is usually handled by at least two postal operators, the sending operator in the country where the item is mailed to the receiving country's postal operator. Article 27 of the EU Directive states that terminal dues must provide an incentive to improve the quality of cross-border service through the use of quality of service targets. It is essential that the payment fully reflects the costs of the processing and delivery, and the country of destination is adequately compensated.

Non-discriminatory access to the receiving market

On the basis of the REIMS II draft agreement, the postal operators must grant each other access to the domestic rates, which is a positive step. It is in fact crucial that non-domestic users benefit from the same conditions and price access to the market for their commercial items as the domestic users, and there should be a strong commitment from the postal operators to achieve this level. Non-domestic users will therefore benefit from the same tariffs as domestic users, but will also have the possibility to access the services available in the local market receiving the mail, and to access information more easily on the existing postal services.

Liberalisation of the postal market

A number of other important aspects, dealt with by the first EU Directive on postal services, also should be considered.

One of the most important aspects of the directive is its definition of the postal services, which must be provided by the public postal operators (the Universal areas), and the part of that area which the public postal operators may consider reserved for them. Recognising the competitive nature of the market, the EU has also set out rules for transparency and cost accounting to prevent the postal operators from cross-subsidising their loss-making services from the profitable areas.

Article 7 of the EU Directive on postal services is a key precursor to the complete postal liberalisation. Paragraphs 3 and 4 provide that the Commission would table a proposal by the end of 1998 on the further liberalisation of the postal market, particularly of cross border and direct mail, to take effect from January 2003. A deadline for liberalisation would be crucial since it would give the consumers more choice and would encourage the postal operators to modernise their activities.

In fact, the Commission only fulfilled this obligation in 2000, in a proposal to reduce the 'reserved area' for 350 gms to 50 gms. This proposed directive is now under discussion, but it looks unlikely that it will be adopted soon, or intact.

Standardisation of postal services

Finally, but of great importance for the mailers, the EU is supporting a process of standardising a wide range of specific aspects of postal services, including address formats, bar-coding, hybrid mail systems, quality of measurement statistical models, etc.

This initiative is certain to impact across the global postal market in numerous ways. Just to take one very practical example, this process of standardisation proposes that all international mail received or sent from Europe will, in future, be carried in trays and not in bags. Such detailed and specific agreements between the public postal operators in Europe are certain to be taken up to some extent by non-European postal operators.

Conclusions

We have seen that the postal market is developing, in some countries very fast. Direct mail is becoming increasingly important for all postal carriers. It is the only significant segment of the postal market that is growing on a regular basis. The introduction of on-line media has not reduced direct mail postal volumes. In fact, it appears from research that postal volumes have increased as the result of Electronic Marketing.

Whether European legislation will force liberalisation on the 15 EU countries (as it did in the case of the telecommunications market), or whether it will not be possible to reach a common European solution, the most important factor is the real and obvious change at the national level to the postal markets. Major players are now slowly but surely moving out of their national markets and taking on a new role as international businesses whose product is the mail, and related services.

1. Postal rules in the European Union, FEDMA, September 1998

5

The United States of America: Land of Opportunity. An Overview of Direct Marketing

Charles Prescott
Vice President, International Business Development & Government Affairs, Direct Marketing Association, USA

A Brief History

The United States has earned the name 'Land of Opportunity'. In the 19th century, the nation's borders expanded, stretching further and further west – the growth driven by an increasing flow of immigrants from around the world, especially Europe. A network of crude log roads first carried the adventurous and the ambitious across the Appalachian Mountains, which separated the eastern seaboard from the interior. Subsequently, a growing network of canals, and finally railroads, spread across the Midwest prairies, through the mighty Rocky Mountains, stopping at the Pacific Ocean. A nation, with a diversity of cultural roots, committed to free enterprise, self-determination, and personal liberty and responsibility, was born.

Between the 19th and 20th centuries, the United States experienced phenomenal growth: from a population of more than 5 million to one of almost 100 million. From a 94% rural, 6% urban population to one that was 51% rural, 49% urban. From a nation of subsistence agriculture with modest craft capacities to the largest manufacturing economy in the world.

In the late 1800s, Richard W. Sears, a railroad clerk in North Redmond, Minnesota, acquired an abandoned case of pocket watches. Using his list of other railroad clerks throughout the Midwest, he marketed his watches with great success. Sears recognised immediately that an entrepreneur with a list of accurate names and addresses, and a stock of quality merchandise, no longer needed a store. He only needed a good message delivery vehicle and first-rate customer service. And so was born an American institution, one of the first and most successful direct marketing stories of all time: Sears Roebuck. The business grew to be the largest direct mail order company in the world. It wasn't until 1931 that its retail store sales surpassed mail order sales.

And many, many more mail order business success stories followed. In fact, because distances between suppliers and consumers throughout the newly forming territories were so vast, and the increasing variety of

29

merchandise being produced was in such demand, mail order opportunities seemed endless. A robust network of railroads connected countless small towns and cities, many without stores. And each community, no matter how small, was served by the US Postal Service, a system established by the farsighted authors of the Constitution of the United States in 1787 to help knit the young nation together.

Now and into the Future

The opportunities in this vast market are still vast, and new success stories unroll – and will continue to unroll every day, as men and women of courage, vision, and energy grasp new ideas, or remake old ones, and find profitable niches, and consumers. Old companies remake themselves; new ones appear and thrive.

Today, the US boasts a US$1.5 trillion market for direct marketers. This is without a doubt the largest and richest single market in the world – and growing at an unprecedented 8.6% per year. With over 10,000 different catalogues alone being mailed in the US, there is a niche for every player and every project and service.

In the discussion that follows, The Direct Marketing Association (DMA) gives our direct marketing colleagues from overseas, who are considering buying or establishing a business here, a look at the many elements of US direct marketing.

The Legal Environment – Federal and State

The legal environment for business is dominated by statutes passed by the Federal Government and by the 50 states. In addition, cities and counties (subdivisions of states) have codes relating to subjects within their power – such as land use, building codes, and other local concerns.

The FTC

One of the most important enforcement agencies for direct marketers is the Federal Trade Commission (FTC), which enforces federal consumer protection and fair trade (anti-trust) laws passed by Congress, and which has the authority to adopt regulations and rules interpreting and implementing those laws. There are FTC rules on marketing to children online, regulating distance selling delivery requirements, telemarketing, and many other subjects. Each of the states has similar powers and authority, usually under the office of the state's attorney general, who is the chief law enforcement officer of the state.

The Courts

A second major source of law is the courts that interpret and enforce both statutory law and the common law. The common law is the body of judicial decisions built up over years, which interprets statutes and searches for justice where there are no laws. For the most part, a businessperson who has been educated in Europe and worked there will find nothing particularly unusual in this. Here, there are federal and state codes, which are enforced and interpreted by agencies and courts. Due to the widespread adoption of administrative codes in the United States, laws and regulations are easily accessible and publicly available.

However, unlike many other systems, the legal process in the United States is a major factor in business. Lawyers can bring lawsuits on behalf of clients 'on contingency,' which means without cost to the client. If the claim succeeds, the lawyer is entitled to a fee from the proceeds. With only a few modest exceptions, each side of the lawsuit pays its own lawyer, regardless of the outcome. In addition, the United States invented the 'class action,' which enables a plaintiff and his or her lawyer to sue on behalf of a class of people with a common claim if that group of people is too numerous to be individually named or represented. The class action system has resulted in judgements and settlements of surprising size.

Consequently, most companies, even of modest size, have counsel to advise them, generally on an hourly rate basis. It is not unusual for even modestly sized companies to have a lawyer permanently on staff, or a staff of lawyers. Many risks can be insured against, of course. To protect against misguided legislation, The DMA has a staff of 30 professionals in its Washington DC office who actively lobby in Washington and state capitals to make the voice of the industry heard on important issues in legislatures and regulatory agencies.

The National Market

The United States is a Common Market, which means that marketing, packaging, labelling, and promotion campaigns can be planned and implemented in one language throughout all 50 states. There are local exceptions to this generalisation, of course, that would be familiar to people working in a particular business, as well as to their counsel. In some states, for example, sweepstakes promotions are subject to licensing, or to disclosure requirements, and have received federal treatment. In a similar vein, some states have confronted telemarketing by establishing 'do not call' list use requirements and setting permissible hours of contact. Sales of alcoholic beverages at both the retail and wholesale levels are subject to state-level control, including licensing, making this business one for direct marketing specialists, not novices!

Pharmaceuticals and similar products obtaining Federal Government approval need no further approvals for sale and distribution in the United States; however, there may be advertising limitations with respect to prescription drugs, which may be sold by licensed pharmacists only.

Taxes

The tax system is complex and highly developed. Corporate income is taxed at the federal level, in most states, and in some cities and counties. Credits for state and local taxes on income may be applied against federal tax liability. Depreciation schedules for property used in business are relatively clear and straightforward.

The United States does not have a valued-added tax (VAT) system at either the state or the federal level. However, sales tax systems are in place in most states and in many localities. Under current law, a direct marketing company must collect sales taxes only from residents in those states and localities in which it has a 'nexus,' which is generally understood to mean a 'physical presence' such as an office, warehouse, or other physical facility. This situation also applies to the Internet. Thus, a cataloguer with its office in New York need not collect sales tax on a mail order from a resident in California. This factor makes purchasing through catalogues attractive to consumers in high tax states.

As a general rule, get legal advice whenever you are contracting for services – e.g., telemarketing or warehouse services – because the service provider's location might obligate you to collect state and/or local sales tax from consumers within that locality.

Corporate Formalities

Formation of a company with limited liability, or one of the other limited liability legal entities developed in recent years, is relatively straightforward, inexpensive, and quick. If standard forms are used and the investors do not require special provisions, a corporation can be formed within three days. Corporate formation and governance matters are the subject of state laws. While there is wide variation in the corporation laws of the 50 states, in general, they provide for much more flexibility in matters of internal governance than most European codes. For example, a company's board of directors can usually be empowered to meet by telephone or video conference and adopt resolutions in writing without formally meeting. The accounts of corporations that are not subject to Securities and Exchange Commission (SEC) regulations usually do not need to be made public. However, states' corporation laws all share common protections for minority shareholders. The two states generally considered to provide directors and management with the most flexibility are Delaware and New York. The Supreme Court of the State of Delaware is generally acknowledged to be the most sophisticated court in the United States on company law, as many large companies are incorporated there and the court hears numerous complex cases involving corporate governance and control, often arising out of tender offers and merger-related litigation.

Data Protection and Privacy

In the United States, there is currently no omnibus federal or state legislation like the European Union Data Protection Directive. However, consumers' personal data is subject to a sophisticated network of laws at the federal level concerning the collection, use, retention, and transfer of certain kinds of data. Two examples are the Federal Fair Credit Reporting Act, governing the use and disclosure of information affecting an individual's creditworthiness, and the Video Rental Privacy Protection Act, which forbids disclosure of the rental records of customers without their express consent.

At the state level, telemarketers are subject to diverse laws regulating when and who, they may call, some of which require telemarketers to use 'do not call' lists. Rules regarding the recording of business calls differ state to state. A recently adopted federal law would forbid states from disclosing information from a driver's license and automobile purchase records without the individual's express consent. Because driver's license and automobile registration information is critical to a wide variety of businesses, including banks, insurance companies, credit agencies, and direct marketers, The DMA is continuing its efforts to have this law changed.

The DMA's Privacy Promise

The US Direct Marketing Association requires members marketing to consumers to run their files against The DMA's mail and telephone preference lists on a quarterly basis on pain of expulsion from membership. These marketers must also run e-mail lists against the e-mail preference service list prior to any use. Members must also inform their customers of their right to opt out of having their information disclosed to other marketers.

Because consumers, and thus legislators, are increasingly concerned about privacy (especially on the Internet) and the pace of legislative activity has quickened, a number of new laws in this subject area are expected. Much of the protection of information that enters the commercial sphere is protected and used pursuant to various self-regulatory initiatives by different voluntary organizations such as The DMA. Legislators reviewing this subject find that The DMA has generally been successful in advocating for 'notice and opt-out' provisions. For more detailed information about particular elements of the network of privacy protections in the United States, contact Charles Prescott at cprescott@the-dma.org.

Databases and Lists

The United States has a tradition of information-sharing that goes back as far as the founding of Dun & Bradstreet in the early 19th century. Government makes much data publicly available – sometimes free of charge. Companies also frequently share information about their customers. Consequently, consumer information is robust and deep.

Direct marketing companies outside the United States are astonished at the quality and variety of consumer and business lists available here. The list brokerage and list rental business in this country is highly developed and responsive to direct marketing customers' needs. The diversity of demographics and the consumer interests represented by the lists available are as wide as the range of the country itself. Besides company customer lists, compiled lists meeting a bewildering array of criteria are available: hobby interests, financial status, profession, marital status, religion, race, etc.

An important tool for many marketers is the co-operative database. A group of companies will contribute the names and addresses of recent purchasers to a common database from which contributors may draw. Thus, for example, a catalogue company selling home decorative items that knows from experience that purchasers of furniture respond well to its offers, will have a ready source of potential clients from the contributions by the furniture cataloguers of their customers' names and addresses.

And, supporting all of these players, and providing useful selection tools and data enhancement capabilities, are the data aggregators, who collect and make available publicly available information such as real estate and automobile ownership, recent births and deaths, lawsuit reports, and so forth. All major list and data firms in the United States are members of The DMA.

Databases and lists are considered 'property' in the United States, which is not the case in some civil law countries. In the United States, the theft or misuse of a database may incur criminal as well as civil penalties. Lists are seeded with decoy names as standard practice to detect misuse.

Most marketers, publishers, and list compilers in the United States who rent lists do so through list management companies, which handle many lists and are in a position to provide valuable advice on which lists will most closely meet a renter's needs. Many list owners will permit limited testing before a large-scale mailing. Generally, rentals are for one-time use, but other arrangements can be made. Net-name arrangements – either de-duplication against an existing database or net of undeliverables – are common practice. For the most part, although there are exceptions, list owners do not object to a renter using its own data processor or mailing house, as they fully appreciate that their business depends on their reputation for integrity as well as service.

The DMA has set the standards for the list industry through development of its Guidelines for List Practices, which may be downloaded from www.the-dma.org/library/guidelines/index.shtml

The US DMA's List Council membership comprises many reputable list companies and their executives. The International Department of The DMA will be happy to put you in contact with the leadership of the Council, which can provide valuable introductions and information.

Telemarketing and Telefaxing

Inbound and outbound telemarketing are highly advanced in the United States. These areas of the direct marketing industry generate some $460 billion in sales of goods and services and employ approximately 8.7 million people. Usually, direct mail pieces, catalogs, and direct response TV ads include a toll-free number for customers. Numerous telemarketing firms provide strategic planning in using telemarketing, as well as the telemarketing services themselves, and are highly specialised in the industries they serve or the techniques they employ. For example, they may offer multi-language and international services or have sophisticated programs linking the Internet, faxes, e-mail, direct mail, and the telephone. The DMA membership includes many telemarketing firms; our Teleservices Council can advise you in pre-selecting which ones to interview if you anticipate outsourcing this function.

Recently the use of predictive dialling equipment has resulted in increased consumer concerns. As a consequence, The DMA has issued guidelines on the use of this equipment. The Federal Government has issued a regulation limiting the hours during which a consumer may be contacted at home (that is, between 8 a.m. and 9 p.m.), and requires telemarketers to maintain in-house suppression lists of consumers requesting that they not be contacted. In addition, some states have adopted laws requiring the use by telemarketers of state 'do not call' lists, and all DMA members marketing to consumers are required to run their files against the DMA's telephone preference service list of consumers who have requested not to be contacted.

Unsolicited telefax solicitation is illegal, both to consumers and to businesses. The civil penalty is fixed by statute at $500 per completed fax.

Consumer Protection

There is an extensive system of protections for consumers at both the state and federal levels. The FTC and the attorneys general of the 50 states are extremely aggressive in enforcing anti-fraud statutes, product safety laws, and other protections. Many state statutes provide for the award of statutory damages to consumers, sometimes of significant amounts, for violations. The US DMA provides guidance for compliance with most consumer protection laws through both subject-specific booklets, such as that concerning the Mail Order Rules and through its ethical codes. The DMA has practice guidelines and discussions of these and related regulations at www.the-dma.org/library/guidelines/index.shtml

Advertising and Promotion

European marketers may be surprised at the degree of flexibility available to them in the United States. However, the overriding principle that advertising must be fair and not misleading applies here as well as abroad. Comparative advertising is legal, provided the comparisons are supportable with evidence. Marketers here use numerous promotional devices such as giveaways, sweepstakes (provided no purchase is necessary), discounts, premiums, and gifts. Loyalty programmes are popular here.

Most advertising and direct marketing agencies in the United States are members of The DMA, and we can arrange appointments and introductions to help you preselect a list of potential agency partners from among our 540 agency members.

Further data and help

If you are interested in researching the U.S. market in detail, you will need an exhaustive compendium of data about direct marketing in the United States. This is available in two works published annually by the Direct Marketing Association: *The Factbook* and the *Economic Impact of Direct Marketing* study produced in conjunction with WEFA (Wharton Economic Forecasting). You will find data about every aspect of direct marketing in these works, which are updated annually.

The DMA has many resources available to help you research our market. We also can help you enter the wider web of information and assistance provided by the U.S. Government and state and city agencies. These agencies have a diverse variety of valuable information available. In addition, many states and localities have investment project programs and assistance programs that can be especially attractive to new companies. For more information, contact: international@the-dma.org

6

E-commerce and Outsourcing in a European Context

Bob Bischof, Chairman, McIntyre & King Ltd

The spectacular failures of a handful of Internet companies are believed by many to be an omen that the Internet revolution is about to come to a grinding halt.

Just as the Internet was hugely oversold in its early stages, the critics and doom-mongers are now just as far off the mark in the opposite direction. The Internet is set to become part of everyday life for the developed world as one of many channels of communication and trade between businesses and customers and between suppliers and purchasers of all kinds of goods and services.

Lessons learnt

The difficulties Internet companies have encountered should, however, serve as a lesson to the business world. E-commerce is a business model that requires more than just specific technical skills; it is not a surrogate for market knowledge, logistical competence and financial awareness.

The main lesson that can be drawn is that e-commerce is here to stay, albeit at a less dramatic volume, and it will not replace traditional trading channels such as mail order. Rather, it should be used alongside these traditional methods to enhance them and so better to serve the customer.

In home or distance shopping terms, the Internet itself will be strongly challenged in the future by digital TV, which already offers a more comfortable shopping experience. The Internet will be most successful in business-to-business solutions and in business-to-consumer marketing beyond national borders.

Consumers' needs vary according to their particular circumstances and they will choose the most convenient option for themselves from the whole range of sales channels available at the moment they want to make a purchase. For them, shopping becomes easier. For the trader, things become more competitive and much more complex.

As home markets are threatened by foreign, Internet-based invaders, the need to fight back and serve other European markets increases and this adds even more to the complications. Different payment methods, trading standards, VAT rates and currencies have to be dealt with.

Outsourcing

An obvious solution to overcome these difficulties is to outsource. The UK has long been aware of the benefits of outsourcing: the acquisition of specialist expertise, simplification of processes and increased economies of scale. In home shopping fulfilment terms, outsourcing offers a low risk, highly cost-effective way to service customers. The fulfilment aspects of e-commerce have much in common with traditional home shopping, and forward looking mail order fulfilment houses have combined their distance shopping skills with Internet capabilities to provide Internet traders with the back-end expertise and resources they may lack.

Logistics

A fundamental rule of distance shopping is making sure that your orders are processed efficiently and the goods are delivered on time, every time. On the Internet, it is even more important as your customer is only a few clicks away from your competitor's site. Repeat custom is the lifeblood of any business. People who shop on the net expect quick and efficient service. Get it right and they'll come back for more. Get it wrong and you'll lose them for good.

Delivering this requires every aspect of your logistics operation to go like clockwork, from bulk storage to order picking and despatch of individual orders. Linking your web shopping site online to the back-end processes will help to achieve this goal by ensuring the data entered on your site is used right up to the point of despatch. It brings numerous benefits not only in customer service but also in operational efficiency and accuracy. Using real-time stock levels at the time of order ensures the customer's expectations can be properly managed; for example, if an item is out of stock they can be immediately informed of a delay in delivery.

Issues such as handling returns, reinstating them into stock and refunding via credit cards -either partially or in total - are not uncommon in distance shopping and complicate the logistics task. These are all day to day routines of a mail order fulfilment house with a home shopping software to match but for newcomers to this game they are an organisational nightmare. Close partnerships with delivery companies are essential to effect seamless trace-ability and tracking.

These are just a few examples of the issues an e-tailer faces. Dedicating the necessary management attention to address these in-house can often mean diverting focus from core business activities.

Finding the right partner

Outsourcing is therefore the answer for virtually all start ups. Finding the right partner is then the next question. The outsourcing service provider needs a fitting infrastructure and needs to remain at the forefront of technical development in its field. This is absolutely essential at a time when new communication tools seem to emerge and evolve by the day. Digital TV is a good example. WAP (Wireless Application Protocol) is another. It is well know that WAP is only the first stage in the mobile commerce era, and a partner's ability to accommodate the next phase, 3G, and subsequent developments of m-commerce will be vital if a company wants to exploit this channel to the full.

Handling communications from every channel and recording details on a central database will support an integrated Customer Relationship Management (CRM) strategy. It ensures that through whichever method a customer chooses to make contact, details of their previous orders can be viewed and updated and new orders can be effected quickly and easily. The ability to use the most appropriate mix of sales channels could be the difference between becoming a leader or a follower.

7

Getting your marketing message across the language divide: some keys to multilingual copy adaptation

Ursula Grüber, President, and Judith Harris, International Director
Ursula Grüber Communication Internationale S.A.

Direct marketing provides us with the means to establish a direct and ongoing relationship with the customer. Now Internet marketing and e-commerce have opened up the perspectives even further. Here is a medium that is truly one-to-one in terms of interactivity, and truly global in terms of accessibility and reach.

But with the opportunity to contact Internet users across the globe comes the need to speak to this vast market spectrum not only in their language, but also in a style adapted to today's new media. Making a quick translation of your web site or e-mail pieces will not automatically ensure strong international presence or impact online. Building image and relationships via the Net means adapting your copy to vastly – or subtly – different markets, using the skills of professional copywriters who live and work in the target market and who are familiar with the techniques of Internet marketing.

Good management of the language adaptation process is a key component of any successful multilingual campaign, both online and off. A number of important issues need to be considered at the outset. Is the basic copy entirely suitable for all markets? Are the foreign language writers fully familiar with DM techniques? Are they e-literate? Is the style appropriate for the market in question? Should your local marketing teams be involved in the copy adaptation process? How to be sure that your foreign language copy truly reflects your strategy?

By working with a professional copy adaptation specialist, you can settle these questions before the actual writing process begins. Here are some principles and precautions that can make a vital difference to your foreign language communications.

Choose the right language adaptation partner

Any company setting up a web site becomes, by the very nature of the Internet, an international marketer. But while the reach of the Net may be global, the need will soon be felt to target more specifically, addressing customers and prospects in their own language. This stage should not be rushed. The Net abounds in poorly translated sites, which can only do a disservice to the marketer. Choosing professional copy adapters for your foreign language versions is therefore an essential first step. They should be experienced mother-tongue writers living in their own country – because people who live abroad for any length of time grow rusty in their own language and lose touch with the markets you want to reach. Your writers should be experienced in DM and online copy techniques. Check that they have a thorough understanding of the source language, and see that the copy is reviewed by a competent reader or second writer to ensure nothing has been incorrectly interpreted. If your communications contain technical information, you'll need a writer who knows the specific terminology of your sector.

Brief the writers

Don't presume that your Spanish, Italian or Chinese writers will know enough about your communication objectives simply because they are adapting your brochure, or your web site, or your mailing – however detailed and informative this material may be. Ensure that they are properly briefed on the operation in hand. In the case of a multilingual campaign, spell out the global strategy, but be sure to highlight any local particularities that they should take into account. And always supply a layout so that they can adjust their copy to design constraints.

Provide background material

Your foreign language writers will work more confidently if you give them full background material on your business, preferably in their own language. Provide them, for example, with an annual report, existing brochures, catalogues, mailings and any other above- or below- the-line material which can give them further insight into your world. And ask your subsidiaries abroad to provide any local literature that's available to ensure that specific company terminology is respected.

Build a consistent image

A direct marketing campaign establishes an ongoing dialogue with the customer. All the more reason therefore when organising your foreign language campaigns to stay with the same team of writers to ensure maximum continuity in terms of style and terminology. Have your adaptation specialists create a glossary of frequently used terms in each language, so that from one project to another the same key expressions are used. Provide your writers with copies of your current above-the-line communications, so that there is no discrepancy between the corporate terminology used in, say, a print advertisement and a direct mail piece.

If your customer services are handled through a call centre, be sure that your copywriters and call centre operators are using the same key terms. It is confusing for a customer to receive printed information based on one set of terms, and then to have to talk on the phone with a service contact who is using significantly different vocabulary.

Don't hesitate to pass on feedback from your call centre to the foreign language writing teams. Call centre staff are an invaluable source of information for copywriters. They can help them assess what are sensitive issues for customers, what words or expressions may be best avoided, what mail pieces got a particularly enthusiastic response, etc. Since their comments are based on real-time, everyday dealings with their customers, they contain useful indicators that allow the copywriter to adjust and fine-tune his or her copy.

Involve local management

Generally speaking, local marketing managers wish to be involved in the translation/adaptation of their communications, however busy they may be. Enlist their assistance from the outset by asking them to pinpoint any areas in the original text that they feel may be inappropriate for their own local market. In this way you can adjust the copy before giving it to the foreign language writers for translation.

Ask each subsidiary to appoint a person whom the writer can contact if he or she needs information or wishes to check on specific company terminology. This liaison facility helps to create goodwill for the campaign at local level and adds value to your translated material.

Proofreading – last but definitely not least

In the matter of proofreading, electronic data transmission has unfortunately lulled us into a false sense of security. Certainly, there are far less errors now that we can email files straight to the studio or printer, but mistakes will still occur when specific items are displaced, enlarged, or otherwise manipulated. So vigilance should be the byword.

Have the proofs checked by at least two people for each country: by the copywriter who wrote the copy, and by a second native reader not actually involved in the writing. This second person will have more distance from the copy and may see something the more familiar eye has missed.

After initial corrections have been made, have the proofs checked again – and yet again if necessary – until no errors remain.

Send the corrected copy to a local manager in each country for the final sign-off. Do not rely on your copywriters for this. There may be errors that only the local offices can spot – for example the wrong photo next to a caption, or a recently changed phone number.

Finally, a word on proofreading the web site. Many a great-looking site is riddled with mistakes you would never find in a print brochure from the same company. A bout of rigorous checking before the copy goes online can protect your image – and promote the cause of e-literacy in our new economy!

Ursula Grüber is President of *Ursula Grüber Communication Internationale*, the world specialist in foreign language copy adaptation. Born in Germany, she spent 10 years in advertising, including several in the Bates Group. In 1972 she opened her own agency specialising in foreign language copy adaptation, a concept she originated and developed. The agency has an international network of 200 copywriters and technical specialists, all living in their own country and working in their native language. Adaptation of DM campaigns, press campaigns, brochures and PR material is handled by the agency's team of project managers in the Paris headquarters.

President of the French Chapter of the IAA (International Advertising Association) from 1997 to 1999, Ursula Grüber is a member of the World Board and holds the IAA Medal for Merit in Advertising.

Judith Harris is International Director of Ursula Grüber Communication Internationale. Born in London, she pursued a copywriting career in Montreal and Paris before joining the agency, where she heads the team of multicultural project managers.

Ursula Grüber Communication Internationale S.A.
83, rue Saint Honoré
F – 75001 Paris
Tel.: +33 (0)1 42 33 57 61 Fax: +33 (0)1 42 21 41 14
www. ursulagruber.com

Part Two:
Country-by-Country Directory

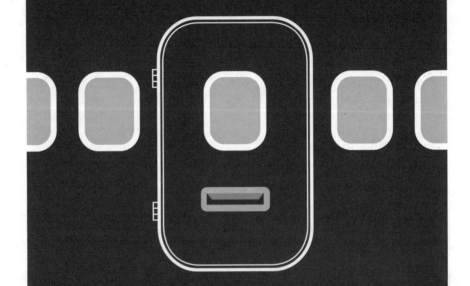

We can get your business mail onto more scheduled flights than anyone else.

Royal Mail

WESTERN EUROPE

FEDERATION OF EUROPEAN DIRECT MARKETING (FEDMA)

Over the last decade direct marketing as a strategy has become increasingly popular worldwide. The introduction of on-line services has provided yet more communication vehicles for the use of direct marketing concepts. But, together with this growth in the availability and popularity of direct marketing has come greater interest by international and national authorities in regulating the business.

FEDMA was created to represent this growing sector on a European scale: an association dedicated to promoting and defending the interests of its members and to advancing the image, status and prestige of direct marketing in Europe. Through its many activities, FEDMA is the single voice dedicated to building the business of cross-border direct marketing, both through its vast network of contacts and businesses within Europe and beyond, and by representation within the institutions of the European Union.

Some of the legal issues FEDMA is dealing with at the moment include the European Commission's package of proposals for regulation to develop further the Single European Market. This package includes a Directive, announced on 18 November, which will ensure that within the EU the country of origin should be responsible for control of Electronic Commerce that originates from it. There are also proposals for on-line copyright, digital signatures, on-line taxation, and a mechanism, which has been agreed, to ensure that the Member States have to consult with the EC and with other Member States before adopting their own national laws regulating the on-line environment. Other EU initiatives of vital importance to direct marketers include data protection, distance selling and postal issues. FEDMA plays a key role in each of these.

FEDMA, supported by the expertise of its corporate members and the national direct marketing associations, plays a central role in ensuring that European legislative and policy initiatives are positive, and do not restrict the further development of direct marketing. Your membership will ensure that you are well informed in these matters and will help reinforce our voice within the European Union institutions.

As a member of FEDMA you will also have access to a range of exclusive services, which are essential for staying up-to-date in the direct marketing business. Here are just some of the benefits you can gain from FEDMA membership:

Free publications:

- *DM in Europe: an examination of the statistics* – a guide to the state of the industry;
- *Legal Council Fact Pack* – a summary of the important national legislation in Europe affecting direct marketers in 13 countries;
- *List Council Fact Pack* – essential reference for all working in the list broking sector in Europe;
- *Postal Fact Pack* – complete review of the postal services in the EU.

Events:

- The FEDMA Forum is entering its 10th year as the truly pan-European DM conference, giving an update on what is happening in Europe and what are the future trends.
- The Council Day, a one day conference to boost your DM know-how and to network with fellow European colleagues.

Other benefits include:

- Exclusive access to the FEDMA pan-European information services
- Access to a pan-European network of independent DM legal experts
- Information on success stories via the Best of Europe competition
- Savings on entry to DM trade shows, magazines and key information resources in the FEDMA vouchers booklet
- A FEDMA membership plaque, and exclusive use of the FEDMA logo, both designed to convey commitment and adherence to best practice in direct marketing.

Membership of FEDMA is the best way to benefit from all these advantages and the only way to guarantee access to pan-European direct marketing information into the new millennium.

To find out more, contact membership services at +32 2 779 4269 or membership@fedma.org

AUSTRIA

> *Population*: 8.0 million
> *Capital*: Vienna
> *Language*: German
>
> *GDP*: $213 billion
> *GDP per capita*: $26,625
> *Inflation*: 1.0 per cent
>
> *Currency*: Austrian Schilling (ATS) = 100 groschen
> *Exchange rate*: ATS12.82 : $1 (ATS 13.77 : 1 euro)
>
> *Time*: GMT +1 hour

OVERVIEW

Austria has a long history of trade with its European neighbours, and in January 1995 became a full member of the EU. Combined with a return to economic growth, European trading prospects are considerably enhanced.

The Austrian direct mail market is well developed, displaying many similarities with that of its German neighbour, not only in terms of the range of lists and DM services available, but also in terms of the legislative environment. The industry is highly regulated and, while a wide range of business and consumer lists are available, swaps are prohibited and strict privacy legislation prevents the development of geodemographic and lifestyle databases.

However, the Austrian direct marketing industry works well within these constraints, and has developed a modern and sophisticated infrastructure. Direct marketing accounts for over 35 per cent of total advertising expenditure, suggesting a thriving industry with no signs yet that the market has reached saturation point.

LANGUAGE AND CULTURAL CONSIDERATIONS

Business language interpreting and translation assistance are available through the Interpreters' Institute of Vienna University. Commercial firms can usually find interpreters easily.

51

LEGISLATION AND CONSUMER PROTECTION

Austria has a well-established Mailing Preference Service (MPS). All data relating to individuals are protected by law. It is illegal to make any correlation between name, address and any special interest. The exportation or swapping of lists is prohibited.

THE DIRECT MARKETING ASSOCIATION

Name:	Direct Marketing Verband Osterreich (DMVO)
Address:	Linzer Strasse 357, A-1144 Vienna
Tel:	+43 1 911 43 00
Fax:	+43 1 911 29 72
Email:	office@dmvoe.at
Website:	www.dmvoe.at
Year founded:	1986
President:	Juergen Memedetter
Total staff:	2
Members:	380
Contact:	Joseph Hamberger
	Secretary General

DM agencies	35	DM consultants	10
List brokers	25	Handling houses	25
Mailing houses	25	Mail order companies	5
Printers	15	Database agencies	20
Telemarketing agencies	30	Advertisers	30

Facilities for overseas users of direct mail

Membership: overseas members can join the DMVO, and there are no minimum standards for membership. The annual fees stand at ATS 4,100.

Newsletter: there is a newsletter, which was first published in March 1992.

Library: there is currently no library.

Legal advice: the DMVO cannot, at this stage, advise on local legislation.

Business liaison service: the DMVO will put prospective mailers in touch with business partners. This service is available to members and non-members alike.

Other facilities: the DMVO publishes a highly informative, 70-page market research document on addressed direct mail and bulk mail (1999).

POSTAL SERVICES

The Austrian postal service, Postdienst, does not publish a general guide to its services. As a major international postal operator, however, it does offer the full range of specialist DM services including:

- bulk, discounted rates for addressed mail;
- bulk, discounted rates for unaddressed mail;
- rapid delivery overseas (EMS).

There are no deliveries on Saturday and only larger post offices are open on Saturday mornings, with the exception of main station offices in main cities which are open 24 hours a day, seven days a week.

Details of the Postdienst can be obtained from the annual report (available free on request). This provides a very useful analysis of volumes, mailing trends and wider industry issues (150 pages, German language).

For details of individual services, rates and procedures, contact:

Post & Telecom Austria AG
Postgasse 8
A-1011 Vienna
Austria
Tel: +43 1 515 51 (1601)
Fax: +43 1 513 41–24
Email: info@post.at
Website: www.post.at

PROVIDERS OF DM SERVICES

A LOHS GESMBH & CO KG DRUCK + DIREKTWERBUNG
A-6960 Wolfurt
Albert Loacker Strasse 8
Austria
Tel: +43 5574 72 1500
Fax: +43 5574 72 15081
lohshart@lohs.vol.at
Harmuth Lohs (GF), Manager

Services/Products:
Database consultant; Lettershop

AGG WERBEAGENTUR
A-5020 Salzburg
Reichenhaller Strasse 10B
Austria
Tel: +43 662 669 550
office@agg.at
Andreas G. Gressenbauer (GF),
Manager

Services/Products:
Telemarketing agency; Database
consultant; Fulfilment and sampling
house; List broker

AKUV GMBH DIREKTMARKETING
A-1232 Wien
Mosetiggasse 1
Austria
Tel: +43 1 667 2730
Fax: +43 1 667 273075
Adolf Haden (GF), Manager

Services/Products:
Lettershop

ASSET MARKETING GMBH
A-1020 Wien
Praterstrasse 31
Austria
Tel: +43 1 213 12222
Fax: +43 1 213 12265
Andreas E. Gaiser (GF), Manager

Services/Products:
Telemarketing agency

AZ DIRECT MARKETING BERTELSMANN
A-1210 Wien
Richard Neutra G. 9
Austria
Tel: +43 1 25 96505
Fax: +43 1 25 91885
gustav-cattarozzi@bdirect.at
Gustav Cattarozzi, Manager

Services/Products:
Telemarketing agency; Database
consultant; Lettershop; List broker;
Database management; Direct
marketing agency; Fulfilment and
sampling house

BOZELL KOBZA
A-1030 Wien
Landstrasser Haupstraße 146/7A
Austria
Tel: +43 1 37 9110
office@bozell-kobza.at
Rudolf Kobza (GF), Manager

Services/Products:
Telemarketing agency; Database
consultant; Lettershop; List broker

CALL & MAIL TELEFONMARKETING UND DIREKTWERBUNG GMBH
8010 Graz
Conrad von Hötzendorfstrasse 127/I
Austria
Tel: +43 316 42 20 00
Fax: +43 316 42 20 00 40
callumail@styria.com
Ferdinand Reichmann

Services/Products:
Creative agency; Database
management; Fulfilment and sampling
house; Lettershop; Printing services;
Telemarketing agency

CALL-MARKETINGSERVICE GMBH
1090 Wien
Rossauer Lände 25/7
Austria
Tel: +43 1 315 66 60
Fax: +43 1 315 66 60 150
callmarketing@callmarketing.com
www.callmarketing.com/
Richard Funder

Services/Products:
Creative agency; Electronic media/
internet services/website design

CHICAGO ADVERTISING
A-1060 Wien
Linke Wienzeile 8
Austria
Tel: +43 1 586 9626
Fax: +43 1 587 1963
chicago.advertising@eunet.at
Thomas Braun (GF), Manager

Services/Products:
Telemarketing agency; Database
consultant; Lettershop; List broker

CO+CO DIALOGMARKETING
A-1130 Wien
Konrad Duden Gasse 65
Austria
Tel: +43 1 804 8144
Fax: +43 1 804 814433
co+co@dialoguemarketing.co.at
Cornelius Veith (GF), Manager

Services/Products:
Telemarketing agency; Database
consultant; Fulfilment and sampling
house; Lettershop; List broker

CONNEX MARKETING- UND WERBEAGENTUR GMBH
A-4600 Wels
Linzer Strasse 28–30
Austria
Tel: +43 7242 2025 0
Fax: +43 7242 2025 44
office@connex.co.at
Ernst Haslinger (GF), Manager

Services/Products:
Telemarketing agency; Database
consultant; Direct marketing agency;
Database management; Creative
agency

CREDITREFORM WIRTSCHAFTSAUSKUNFTEI KUBICKI KG
A-1050 Wien
Lasallestrasse 7, PF335
Austria
Tel: +43 1 218 62 20
Fax: +43 1 218 62 204
creditreform@acw.at
Rainer Kubicki (GF), Manager

Services/Products:
Database consultant; Database
management

DAS AGENTURHAUS, WERBE- UND MARKETING GMBH
9020 Klagenfurt
Völkermarkter-Ring 25
Austria
Tel: +43 463 50 27 12
Fax: +43 463 27 12 630
agenturhaus@agenturhaus.com
www.agenturhaus.com/
Gerhard Hochmüller

Services/Products:
Creative agency; Database consultant;
Database management; Direct
marketing agency; Fulfilment and
sampling house; Telemarketing agency

DIESTLER WERBEMITTELVERTEILUNG GES.M.B.H
1050 Wien
Schwarzhorngasse 7
Austria

Tel: +43 1 544 31 11
Fax: +43 1 545 74 16
Kurt Diestler (GF)

Services/Products:
Door-to-door distribution

DIRECT TEAM, LILIANE MIKULEC
A-1140 Wien
Matznergasse 10-12
Austria
Tel: +43 1 985 46600
Fax: +43 1 985 466025
direct_team@compuserve.com
Liliane Mikulec (Inh), Manager

Services/Products:
Telemarketing agency; Database consultant; Fulfilment and sampling house; List broker; Database management; Printing services; Lettershop; Creative agency

DIREKTA DRUCKEREI & DIRECTMARKETING GMBH & CO KG
A-4020 Linz
Petzoldstrasse 6
Austria
Tel: +43 732 78 49490
Fax: +43 732 78 4441
directa@magnet.at
Dr Elfi Fraunschiel-Richter v. Pröeck, Manager

Services/Products:
Database consultant; Fulfilment and sampling house; Lettershop; List broker; Database management; Printing services

DIREKTWERBUNG SCHWÖLBERGER
A-2120 Wolkersdorf
Johann Gallerstraße 10
Austria
Tel: +43 1 2245 38 100
Fax: +43 1 2245 3737
schwölberger@netway.at
Kurt Schwölberger (Inh), Manager

Services/Products:
Telemarketing agency; Database consultant; Fulfilment and sampling house; List broker

DMB MARKETING BERATUNG
A-1070 Wien
Kirchengasse 3
Austria
Tel: +43 1 52 1470
Fax: +43 1 52 147400
dmb_marketing@vip.at
Dkfm Walter Mika (GF), Manager

Services/Products:
Telemarketing agency; Database consultant; Fulfilment and sampling house; List broker; Database management; Printing services; Lettershop; Direct marketing agency

DMI INSTITUT FÜR DIREKTMARKETING, ÖSTERREICH
1050 Wien
Mittersteig 22
Austria
Tel: +43 1 587 20 95
Fax: +43 1 587 71 36
suppandmi@magnet.at
Wolfgang Suppan

Services/Products:
Creative agency; Database consultant; Database management; Direct marketing agency; Fulfilment and sampling house; Lettershop; List broker

DMR DIRECT MAIL REALISATION GMBH
A-1140 Wien
Moßbachergasse 10
Austria
Tel: +43 1 535 7711
dmr@dmr.at
Peter Landrichter (GF), Manager

Services/Products:
Fulfilment and sampling house; Lettershop

DR FIRZINGER & PARTNER
A-4202 Kirchschlag bei Linz
Birkenweg 5
Austria
Tel: +43 1 7215 34030
Fax: +43 1 7215 3775
firzinger_partner@compuserve.com
Dr F. Firzinger (GF), Manager

Services/Products:
Telemarketing agency; Database consultant; Fulfilment and sampling house; List broker

DR KOSSDORFF WERBEAGENTUR GMBH
A-1130 Wien
Melchartgasse 9
Austria
Tel: +43 1 803 2770
Fax: +43 1 803 27721
ad@kossdorff.at
Ucki Kossdorff, Manager

Services/Products:
Telemarketing agency; Database consultant; Fulfilment and sampling house; List broker

DUN & BRADSTREET, INFORMATION SERVICES GMBH
1015 Wien
Opernring 3–5
Austria
Tel: +43 1 588 61 0
Fax: +43 1 586 33 59
dun-bradstreet@apanet.at
www.dbaustria.com/
Michael Höher, Business Marketing Services Manager

Services/Products:
List broker

EUROCOM SALES PROMOTION
A-1040 Wien
Argentinierstrasse 26/5
Austria
Tel: +43 1 505 6200
Fax: +43 1 504 3812
eurocom@eurorscg.at
Armin Fehle

Services/Products:
Telemarketing agency; Database consultant; Fulfilment and sampling house; List broker

EUROMARKETING BERATUNGS GMBH
1010 Wien
Gonzagagasse 12
Austria
Tel: +43 1 533 46 15
Fax: +43 1 532 76 78
sylvia.steindl@euromarketing.at
www.euromarketing.at/
Sylvia Steindl

Services/Products:
Advertising agency; Creative agency; Database consultant; Database management; Direct marketing agency; Fulfilment and sampling house; Lettershop; Telemarketing agency; List broker

FEIBRA VERTRIEBS GMBH
2640 Gloggnitz
Wiener Strasse 65
Austria
Tel: +43 2662 456 53 0
Fax: +43 2662 456 53 11
feibra.gltz@feibra-vertrieb.co.at
Roland Tauchner

Services/Products:
Door-to-door distribution

FEIBRA WERBUNG GESMBH.
1170 Wien
Halirschgasse 16
Austria

Tel: +43 1 488 88 0
Fax: +43 1 488 88 286
feibra@aktiv.co.at
www.feibra.co.at/
Anton Feistl

Services/Products:
Door-to-door distribution

FEIPRO VERTRIEBS GMBH
2191 Gaweinstal
In Lüssen 3
Austria
Tel: +43 2574 38 88 0
Fax: +43 2574 38 88 19
feipro@magnet.at
www.members.co.at/feipro
Robert Holy

Services/Products:
Door-to-door distribution

FOLLOW-UP
A-1140 Wien
Penzinger Strasse 69
Austria
Tel: +43 1 894 2050
Fax: +43 1 894 3230
followup@via.at
Elisabeth Knall, Manager

Services/Products:
Telemarketing agency; Database
consultant; Fulfilment and sampling
house; List broker

GEMM BERATUNGS GMBH
5020 Salzburg
Innsbrucker Bundes Strasse 40
Austria
Tel: +43 662 441 317
Fax: +43 662 4413 47
gemm@gemm.co.at
Richard Leitner

Services/Products:
Creative agency; Database consultant;
Database management; Direct
marketing agency; Telemarketing
agency

**GFW GESELLSCHAFT FÜR
   WERBEMITTELVERTEILUNG
   GMBH**
A-1220 Wien
Percostrasse 15
Austria
Tel: +43 1 259 6900
Fax: +43 1 259 69009
prospect@gfw.vienna.at
www.gfw-werbung.co.at/
Andreas Reinisch, Manager

Services/Products:
Telemarketing agency; Database
consultant; Door-to-door distribution;

Fulfilment and sampling house; List
broker

GLAVAN + PARTNER
5020 Salzburg
Vogelweiderstr.61
Austria
Tel: +43 662 87 39 33 0
Fax: +43 662 87 39 33 25
100601.3542@compuserve.com
Wolfgang Glavan

Services/Products:
Creative agency; Database consultant;
Database management; Direct
marketing agency; Lettershop; Printing
services; Telemarketing agency

GLOBEMAIL SERVICES GMBH
A-2362 Biedermannsdorf
Josef Ressel Strasse 8
Austria
Tel: +43 2236 736080
Fax: +43 2236 73615
service@globemail.via.at
Peter Gosch (GF)

Services/Products:
Fulfilment and sampling house;
Lettershop

**GOESSLER KUVERTS GMBH
   KUVERTFABRIK**
A-2514 Traiskirchen
Eugen Dahmstraße 5
Austria
Tel: +43 1 2252 53186
Fax: +43 1 2252 5352222
Felix Goessler, Manager

GRÖTZL GMBH & COKG
4690 Schwanenstadt
Linzerstrasse, 39
Austria
Tel: +43 7673 2294 0
Fax: +43 7673 2294 4
www.groetzlwlwonline.at
Ludwig Grötzl

Services/Products:
Creative agency; Database consultant;
Direct marketing agency; Fulfilment
and sampling house; Lettershop;
Printing services; Telemarketing
agency

HAHN & PARTNER GMBH
A-1070 Wien
Lindengasse 43
Austria
Tel: +43 1 521 480
Fax: +43 1 521 4811
feedback@hahn-partner.at
Roland Hahn (GF), Manager

Services/Products:
Telemarketing agency; Database
consultant; Fulfilment and sampling
house; List broker

**HARTINGER CONSULTING
   GMBH**
A-8340 Kaindorf
Römerstrasse 18
Austria
Tel: +43 3452 855 56
Fax: +43 3452 855 5622
hc.office@hartinger.at
Sepp Hartinger (GF), Manager

Services/Products:
Database consultant; Fulfilment and
sampling house; Lettershop; List
broker

**HEROLD BUSINESS DATA
   GMBH**
2340 Mödling
Guntramsdorfer Strasse 105
Austria
Tel: +43 2236 401 0
Fax: +43 2236 401 8
kundendienst@herold.co.at
Jon Martinsen

Services/Products:
Database management

**HOLZHUBER MARKETING
   UND WERBEGESMBH**
A-2342 Giesshübl
Franz Schubert Gasse 5
Austria
Tel: +43 1 797 600
Fax: +43 1 797 6010
office@impaction.at
Dr Thomas Holzhuber (GF), Manager

Services/Products:
Telemarketing agency; Database
consultant; Fulfilment and sampling
house; List broker

**HOSSE & PARTNER AGENTUR
   FÜR MARKETING GMBH**
A-1040 Wien
Wiedner Hauptstrasse 61
Austria
Tel: +43 1 503 5600
Fax: +43 1 503 5622
office@hosse.at
Walter M. Hosse, Managing Director

Services/Products:
Advertising agency; Telemarketing
agency; Database consultant;
Fulfilment and sampling house; List
broker

HUMANMEDIA, MARKETING AND VERLAG GMBH

A-2500 Baden
Austria
Tel: +43 2252 23 230
office@humanmedia.at
Edith Wanka (GF), Manager

Services/Products:
Telemarketing agency; Database consultant; Fulfilment and sampling house; List broker

INSTITUTE FOR INTERNATIONAL RESEARCH GMBH

1150 Wien
Linke Wienzeile 234
Austria
Tel: +43 1 891 59 0
Fax: +43 1 891 59 300
conference@iir.at
www.iir.at/
Anita Samek, Marketing Director

Services/Products:
List broker

IQ-M GMBH

A-1100 Wien
Favoritner Gewerbering 6
Austria
Tel: +43 1 600 1010
Fax: +43 1 600 10106
office@iq-m.co.at
http://iq-m.co.at/iq-m
Heike Reiseing (GF)

Services/Products:
Telemarketing agency; Database consultant; Fulfilment and sampling house; List broker; Lettershop; Database management

KB-ENDLOS KROISS+BICHLER GMBH

A-4840 Vöcklabruck
Gutenbergstraße 2
Austria
Tel: +43 1 7672 7050
Fax: +43 1 7672 78 860
kb@kb-endlos.com
Ing Martin Kroiss (GF), Manager

Services/Products:
Telemarketing agency; Database consultant; Fulfilment and sampling house; List broker

KÜMMERLY + FREY WIEN

1050 Wien
Nikolsdorfer Gasse 8
Austria
Tel: +43 1 545 14 45
Fax: +43 1 545 10 80 83

kuemmerly_frey@xpoint.at
Gerhard Kogel

Services/Products:
Creative agency; Database consultant; Database management; Direct marketing agency; List broker

KUNZ DIRECT MARKETING

A-1160 Wien
Feßtgasse 16
Austria
Tel: +43 1 484 0303
Fax: +43 1 484 03033
kunz_direct@magnet.at
Wolfgang Kunz (Inh), Manager

Services/Products:
Creative agency; Database consultant; Lettershop; List broker

LE-DIREKT LOSSIE, ERTL & CO GMBH

A-1150 Wien
Sechshauser Gürtel 3
Austria
Tel: +43 1 893 95 58
Fax: +43 1 893 95 5827
le-direkt@le-direkt.at
Manfred Lossie, Manager

Services/Products:
Database consultant; List broker; Direct marketing agency; Creative agency

LEMBACHER DIREKTMARKETING

A-1100 Wien
Favoritner Gewerbering 6
Austria
Tel: +43 1 600 10990
Fax: +43 1 600 10996
lmdirekt@ping.at
Martin Lembacher (GF), Manager

Services/Products:
Telemarketing agency; Database consultant; Lettershop; List broker; Direct marketing agency; Creative agency; Fulfilment and sampling house

LUSTIG DIRECT MARKETING GMBH

A-2000 Stockerau
Schießstattgasse 10
Austria
Tel: +43 2266 61601
Fax: +43 2266 61612
office@ldm.at
Norbert Lustig (GF), Manager

Services/Products:
Telemarketing agency; Database consultant; Lettershop; List broker

M&H VERSANDHANDEL GMBH

A-6923 Lauterach
Reitschulstrasse 7
Austria
Tel: +43 1 5574 8010
Fax: +43 1 5574 8016
mh@mhdirek.at
Hanns Schindler, Business Intelligence

Services/Products:
Lettershop; Mailing house

M-S-B+K WERBEAGENTUR FÜR DIRECT MARKETING GMBH

A-1190 Wien
Grinzinger Strasse 22
Austria
Tel: +43 1 321388
Fax: +43 1 3271910
cs@msbk.co.at
Christian Spiegelfeld (GF), Manager

Services/Products:
Database consultant; Fulfilment and sampling house; Lettershop; List broker

MAG WERBEAGENTUR MICHAEL A GÖRTZ GMBH

A-1160 Wien
Wilhelminenstraße 174
Austria
Tel: +43 1 489 55500
Fax: +43 1 480 9500
mag-ad@mag-ad.at
Michael A. Görtz (GF), Manager

Services/Products:
Telemarketing agency; Database consultant; Fulfilment and sampling house; Lettershop

MARIC & RINALDIN

A-1090 Wien
Austria
Tel: +43 1 315 290 200
office@maric.at
Ing Konrad Maric (GF), Manager

Services/Products:
Telemarketing agency; Database consultant; Lettershop; List broker

MARSCHALL & HARFMANN OHG

A-5280 Braunau
Lederergasse 5
Austria
Tel: +43 7722 66506
Fax: +43 7722 665064
office@m-h.at
Erich Marschall, Manager

Services/Products:
Direct marketing agency; Creative agency

MASTER MANAGEMENT
A-1210 Wien
Franz Jonas Platz 3/2
Austria
Tel: +43 1 275 25250
Fax: +43 1 275 2525 100
direct@master.co.at
www.telenetz.com
Andreas Hutflesz (GF), Manager

Services/Products:
Telemarketing agency; Database
consultant; Lettershop; List broker;
Fulfilment and sampling house; Direct
marketing agency

MEDIENSERVICE & WERBERECHTGMBH & CO KG
4010 Linz
Promenade 23–25
Austria
Tel: +43 732 7805 301
Fax: +43 732 79 41 44
k.winkler@oon.at
www.oon.at/
Karl Winkler

Services/Products:
Door-to-door distribution;
Telemarketing agency

MEILLER DRUCK GMBH ÖSTERREICH
A-4100 Ottensheim
Schlagberg 15
Austria
Tel: +43 7234 847 11
Fax: +43 7234 847 1120
Manfred Kefer, Manager

Services/Products:
Direct marketing agency; Database
consultant; Lettershop; List broker

MERCURBANK (GE CAPITAL BANK)
1220 Wien
Donau-City Straße 6
Austria
Tel: +43 1 260 70 9181
Fax: +43 1 260 70 9469
Gerlinde Thurner

Services/Products:
Creative agency; Database consultant;
Direct marketing agency;
Telemarketing agency

MICHAEL OPPL – MASSENSENDUNGEN
3441 Baumgarten
Doppelnstraße 2
Austria

Tel: +43 2274 4001 0
Fax: +43 1 4001 2
mail@oppl.at
Michael Oppl

Services/Products:
Creative agency; Database consultant;
Database management; Direct
marketing agency; Fulfilment and
sampling house; Lettershop; Printing
services; Telemarketing agency

MOORE GMBH
A-1034 Wien
Paragonstraße 2 (Erdbergstrasse 218)
Austria
Tel: +43 1 740 510
Fax: +43 1 740 51281
info@moore.at
Günter Bollmann (Inhaber), Manager

Services/Products:
Telemarketing agency; Database
consultant; Lettershop; List broker

MPS MARKETING & PRODUKTION SERVICE GMBH
1230 Wien
Altmannsdorferstr 309
Austria
Tel: +43 1 667 83 13
Fax: +43 1 667 83 13 6
mps@aon.at
Gabriele Cinibulk-Reisenauer,
Manager

Services/Products:
Creative agency; Database consultant;
Database management; Direct
marketing agency; Fulfilment and
sampling house; Lettershop; List
broker; Telemarketing agency

MS MAIL SERVICE GMBH
A-6923 Lauterach
Scheibenstrasse 3
Austria
Tel: +43 5574 65310
Fax: +43 5574 65313
Peter Stössel (GF), Manager

Services/Products:
Telemarketing agency; Database
consultant; Lettershop; List broker

MULTIBUS GMBH
A-3400 Klosterneuburg
Inkustraße 1–7/7
Austria
Tel: +43 1 2243 34455
Fax: +43 1 2243 34459
office@multibus.at
Leo Tongits (GF), Manager

Services/Products:
Telemarketing agency; Lettershop

NAGY & ZWINZ WERBEAGENTUR
A-1010 Wien
Plankengasse 6
Austria
Tel: +43 1 512 9790
Fax: +43 1 512 979011
nagys@via.at
Thomas J. Nagy (GF), Manager

Services/Products:
Telemarketing agency; Database
consultant; List broker

OGILVY ONE
A-1230 Wien
Austria
Tel: +43 1 717 520
one@ogilvy.co.at
Wolfgang Hafner (GF), Manager

Services/Products:
Telemarketing agency; Database
consultant; Direct marketing agency;
Lettershop; List broker

OMNITEL AGENTUR FÜR TELEFON-MARKETING UND DIREKTWERBUNG GMBH
A-1200 Wien
Hochstädtplatz 3
Austria
Tel: +43 1 332 4213
Fax: +43 1 332 421421
jonke@ins.at
Oliver Jonke (GF), Manager

Services/Products:
Telemarketing agency; Database
consultant; List broker

OTTO VERSAND GMBH
8021 Graz
Weinerstrasse 286
Austria
Tel: +43 316 606 0
Fax: +43 316 606 424
dieter.uphoff@ottoversand.at
Anton Windisch

Services/Products:
Creative agency; Database consultant;
Database management; Direct
marketing agency; Fulfilment and
sampling house; Lettershop;
Telemarketing agency

PALLA KOBLINGER & PARTNER
A-1020 Vienna
Praterstr. 31
Austria
Tel: +43 1 214 87 96

Fax: +43 1 214 97 96 96
office@pkp.at
Alfred Koblinger, Managing Director

Services/Products:
Advertising agency; Direct marketing
agency; Sales promotion agency;
Database consultant; Response analysis
bureau; Electronic media/internet
service/website design

**PLANK WERBEGESMBH (DIE
    AGENTUR PLANK)**
A-1150 Wien
Preysinggasse 29
Austria
Tel: +43 1 985 7192
Fax: +43 1 985 719218
hp@plank.co.at
Hans Plank (GF), Manager

Services/Products:
Database consultant

**PLM
    VERTRIEBSGESELLSCHAFT
    MBH**
4020 Linz
Zamenhofstrasse 9
Austria
Tel: +43 732 6964 20
Fax: +43 732 6964 21
redaktion@correct.co.at
Prok. Dietrich Haas

Services/Products:
Door-to-door distribution; Lettershop

**PRESSE MEDIEN SERVICE
    GMBH**
A-1030 Wien
Faradaygasse 6
Austria
Tel: +43 1 79500
Fax: +43 1 7950033
pms@pms.vienna.at
Kurt Schügerl (GF), Manager

Services/Products:
Telemarketing agency

PRESSEL DIREKTWERBUNG
A-1235 Wien
Ed. Kittenberger-Gasse 56
Obj. 10
Austria
Tel: +43 1 86 3780
Fax: +43 1 86 378100
pressel@aon.at
Peter Vostrovsky (GF), Manager

Services/Products:
Telemarketing agency; Database
consultant; Lettershop; List broker;
Direct marketing agency; Database
management; Creative agency;

Fulfilment and sampling house

**PROWERB –
    WERBEMITTELVERTEILUNG**
8020 Graz
Waagner-Biro-Strasse 125
Austria
Tel: +43 316 58 40 40
Fax: +43 316 58 40 40 20
Josef Perl

Services/Products:
Door-to-door distribution

**RADIO AUSTRIA AUDIOTEX
    GMBH**
1060 Wien
Lehargasse 9/II/18
Austria
Tel: +43 1 586 10 63
Fax: +43 1 586 10 64
raag@telecom.at
www.telecom.at/raag
Gernot Erber

Services/Products:
Fax mailings; Fulfilment and sampling
house; Telemarketing agency

**RBC DIREKTMARKETING
    SERVICE GMBH**
6923 Lauterach
Reitschulstrasse 7
Austria
Tel: +43 5574 8010
Fax: +43 5574 8016
rbc@mhdirekt.at
Hanns Schindler

Services/Products:
Database consultant; Database
management; Fulfilment and sampling
house; List broker; Telemarketing
agency

**RECHENZENTRUM
    VOSTROVSKY**
A-1230 Wien
Deutschstrasse 25
Austria
Tel: +43 1 616 3606
Fax: +43 1 616 5323
rz.vostrovsky@aon.at
Peter Vostrovsky (GF), Manager

Services/Products:
Telemarketing agency; Database
consultant; Lettershop; List broker;
Fulfilment and sampling house;
Printing services

**REED MESSE SALZBURG
    GMBH**
5021 Salzburg
Am Messegelände
Austria

Tel: +43 662 4477 0
Fax: +43 662 4477 161
info@reedexpo.at
www.reedexpo.at/
Rudolf Stadler

Services/Products:
Database consultant; Fulfilment and
sampling house; Lettershop

REICHL & PARTNER WIEN
A-1010 Wien
Dr Karl-Lueger-Ring 10
Austria
Tel: +43 1 535 4838
Fax: +43 1 535 48388
Michael Braun (GF-Wien), Manager

Services/Products:
Telemarketing agency; Database
consultant; Lettershop; List broker

**REICHL + PARTNER
    WERBEAGENTUR GMBH**
A-4020 Linz
Rainerstrasse 6–8
Austria
Tel: +43 732 666 222
Fax: +43 732 666 444
reichl.linz@reichl.co.at
Rainer Reichl (GF), Manager

Services/Products:
Telemarketing agency; Database
consultant; Lettershop; List broker

**ROCK & PARTNER
    WERBEAGENTUR**
A-1130 Wien
Larochegasse 21
Austria
Tel: +43 1 877 74920
Fax: +43 1 877 74929
agentur@rock.co.at
Peter M. Rock (GF), Manager

Services/Products:
Telemarketing agency; Database
consultant; Lettershop; List broker

**SAZ MARKETING SERVICES
    GMBH**
A-1100 Wien
Favoritenstrasse 93
Austria
Tel: +43 1 602 39 12
Fax: +43 1 602 39 12 33
werner.zednicek@saz.net
Werner Zednicek, Managing Director

Services/Products:
Direct marketing agency; Database
consultant; Database management;
Response analysis bureau; Service
bureau; Telemarketing agency

SCHOBER SUPPAN DIREKTMARKETING GMBH

A-1100 Wien
Hebbelplatz 5
Austria
Tel: +43 1 605 100
Fax: +43 1 606 3770
schober.info@schober.co.at
Anton Jenzer (GF), Manager

Services/Products:
Telemarketing agency; Database
consultant; Database management;
Lettershop; List broker; Fulfilment and
sampling house; Printing services

SCHWARZINGER – ADRESSEN GMBH & COKG

1020 Wien
Fugbachgasse 4
Austria
Tel: +43 1 218 03 09
Fax: +43 1 218 03 09 20
schwarzinger-adressen@netway.at
Vera Steinweg

Services/Products:
Creative agency; Database
management; Direct marketing agency;
Fulfilment and sampling house;
Lettershop

SERY DM & PR GMBH

4060 Leonding
Ruflingerstrasse 155
Austria
Tel: +43 732 68 00 86
Fax: +43 732 68 00 86 38
serydirect@sdm-pr.at
www.sery.co.at/advertising
Martin Wazek

Services/Products:
Creative agency; Database consultant;
Direct marketing agency;
Telemarketing agency

SKOPIK TELEFONMARKETING

1020 Wien
Praterstrasse 66/37
Austria
Tel: +43 1 214 24 67
Fax: +43 1 214 24 67
traintelecom@netway.at
Peter Skopik

Services/Products:
Telemarketing agency; Training/
recruitment

STURM MARKETING DIREKT GMBH

A1010 Wien
Austria
Tel: +43 1 513 78 70
Fax: +43 1 513 78 77

office@smd.co.at
Barbara Sturm, Manager

Services/Products:
Database consultant; Lettershop;
Direct marketing agency; Creative
agency

SÜDDRUCK KALENDERHERSTELLGS-, BUCHBINDEREI- UND VERARBEITGSGMBH

A-2512 Tribuswinkel
Süddruckgasse 4
Austria
Tel: +43 2252 80 5340
Fax: +43 2252 23 025
Christian Menzel (GF), Manager

Services/Products:
Fulfilment and sampling house;
Lettershop

TCS-DIRECTMARKETING DIETMAR HEURITSCH

A-4020 Linz
Mozartstrasse 43
Austria
Tel: +43 732 7822770
Fax: +43 732 782276
tcs.heuritsch@telecom.at
Dietmar Heuritsch (GF), Manager

Services/Products:
Telemarketing agency; Database
consultant; Lettershop; Fulfilment and
sampling house

TELE CONSULT TELEFON-MARKETING & UNTERNEHMENSBERAT-UNGS GMBH

A-4600 Wels
Beethovenstraße 15
Austria
Tel: +43 7242 52 3010
Fax: +43 7242 52 30133
Andrea Manner-Hössl, Manager

Services/Products:
Telemarketing agency; Database
consultant; Fulfilment and sampling
house; Lettershop; List broker

TELEMARK MARKETING GEBHARD ZUBER GMBH

A-1140 Wien
Austria
Tel: +43 1 892 85 850
telemark@stg.co.uk
Gebhard Zuber (GfGS), Manager

Services/Products:
Telemarketing agency; Database
consultant

TELEPERFORMANCE MARKETING-UND UNTERNEHMENSBERATUNG GESMBH

A-1050 Wien
Siebenbrunnengasse 21
Austria
Tel: +43 1 54 555 540
Fax: +43 1 54 555 53
tp.info@teleperformance.at
www.teleperformance.vienna.at/tele-performance
Martina Tobianah (GF), Manager

Services/Products:
Telemarketing agency; Database
consultant; Lettershop; List broker

TUNE IN COMMUNICATION SERVICES FÜR MARKETING & PROMOTION GMBH

1070 Wien
Zollergasse 13/3
Austria
Tel: +43 1 524 41 80
Fax: +43 1 524 41 80 25
office@cybercafe.co.at
www.cybercafe.co.at/cybercafe
Stefan Ashton

Services/Products:
Database consultant; Database
management; Fulfilment and sampling
house; Lettershop

TWISTER COM GMBH, TECHNOLOGIEZENTRUM

7000 Eisenstadt
Marktstr. 3
Austria
Tel: +43 2682 704 6300
Fax: +43 2682 704 6310
sales@twistercom.at
www.twistercom.at/
Johann Vogl

Services/Products:
Creative agency; Database consultant;
Database management; Direct
marketing agency; Fulfilment and
sampling house; Lettershop; Printing
services; Telemarketing agency

UP DATE MARKETING SERVICE GMBH

A-1130 Wien
Austria
Tel: +43 1 878 550
michaela.pany@update-marketing.com
Gilbert Hödl (GF), Manager

Services/Products:
Database consultant

**UTE DAMISCH
ÖFFENTLICHKEITSARBEIT**
A-1210 Wien
Carabelligasse 5/117
Austria
Tel: +43 1 292 7566
Fax: +43 1 292 7566
Ute Damisch, Manager

Services/Products:
Telemarketing agency; Database
management; Lettershop; Fulfilment
and sampling house; Creative agency;
Printing services

**VSG DIREKTWERBUNG
VERSAND SERVICE GMBH**
A-1232 Wien
Perfektastrasse 86
Austria
Tel: +43 1 86 540547
Fax: +43 1 86 5405720
vsg@vsg-direkt.at
Helmut Moser (GF), Manager

Services/Products:
Database consultant; Fulfilment and
sampling house; Lettershop; List
broker

**WELLDONE MARKETING- UND
KOMMUNIKATIONSBERAT-
UNGS GMBH**
A-1090 Wien
Mariannengasse 14/12
Austria
Tel: +43 1 402 1341
Fax: +43 1 402 134118
office@welldone.at
Wolfgang Maierhofer, Manager

Services/Products:
Telemarketing agency; Database
consultant; Database management;
Lettershop; List broker; Creative
agency; Direct marketing agency;
Fulfilment and sampling house

WERBESERVICE GMBH
A-1120 Wien
Darnautgasse 13
Austria
Tel: +43 1 812 2211
Fax: +43 1 813 0977
office@werbeservice.at
Martin Hlavacek, Manager

Services/Products:
Database consultant; Fulfilment and
sampling house

**WIERINGER
DIRECTMARKETING**
A-1170 Wien
Weidmanngasse 19
Austria

Tel: +43 1 407 0547
Fax: +43 1 407 504775
office@wieringer-direkt.co.at
Monika Poltner (GF), Manager

Services/Products:
Telemarketing agency; Database
consultant; Lettershop; List broker

**WIESMÜLLER & PARTNER
GMBH**
A-1090 Wien
Nussdorfer Strasse 3
Austria
Tel: +43 1 317 3407
Fax: +43 1 310 21 4522
wpartner@via.at
Erich Wiesmüller, Manager

Services/Products:
Database consultant; Fulfilment and
sampling house; Lettershop; List
broker

WIGEO-GIS GESMBH
A-1030 Wien
Hansalgasse 3
Austria
Tel: +43 1 715 19870
Fax: +43 1 715 198799
office@wigeogis.at
www.wigeogis.at
Georg Magenschab (GF), Manager

Services/Products:
Database consultant; List broker

**WIRTSCHAFTSKAMMER
ÖSTERREICH,
FACHVERBAND WERBUNG
UND
MARKTKOMMUNIKATION**
A-1045 Vienna
Wiedner Hauptstrasse 63
Austria
Tel: +43 1 50105 3539
Fax: +43 1 50206 285
Herbert Bachmeier, Executive Director

Services/Products:
Media buying agency; Training
recruitment

WUNDERMAN CATO JOHNSON
A-1010 Wien
Sterngasse 13
Austria
Tel: +43 1 533 58580
Fax: +43 1 533 585881
erika_walker@wcj.com
Erika Walker

Services/Products:
Telemarketing agency; Database
consultant; Lettershop; List broker

ZMG DIREKTWERBUNG GMBH
A-1140 Wien
Mossbachergasse 10
Austria
Tel: +43 1 914 7614
Fax: +43 1 914 761442
Margarete Zadina (GF), Manager

Services/Products:
Telemarketing agency; Database
consultant; Database management;
Lettershop; List broker; Direct
marketing agency; Creative agency;
Fulfilment and sampling house

SERVICES/PRODUCT LISTING

Advertising agency
Euromarketing Beratungsgesellschaft
  MBH
Hosse & Partner Agentur Für
  Marketing GMBH
Palla Koblinger & Partner

Creative agency
CALL & MAIL Telefonmarketing und
  DirektwerbunggmbH
Call-Marketingservice GmbH
Connex Marketing- Und
  Werbeagentur GmbH
Das Agenturhaus, Werbe- und
  Marketing GmbH
Direct Team, Liliane Mikulec
DMI Institut für Direktmarketing,
  Österreich
Euromarketing Beratungsges.m.b.H.
GEMM BeratungsgmbH
Glavan + Partner
Grötzl GmbH & CoKG
Kümmerly + Frey Wien
Kunz Direct Marketing
Le-Direkt Lossie, Ertl & Co GMBH
Lembacher Direktmarketing
Marschall & Harfmann OHG
Mercurbank (GE Capital Bank)
Michael Oppl – Massensendungen
MPS Marketing & Produktion Service
  GMBH
MPS Marketing & Produktion Service
  GmbH
Otto Versand GmbH
Pressel Direktwerbung
Schwarzinger – Adressen GmbH &
  CoKG
Sery DM & PR GmbH
Sturm Marketing Direkt GMBH
TWISTER COM GmbH,
  Technologiezentrum
Ute Damisch Öffentlichkeitsarbeit
Welldone Marketing- Und

Kommunikationsberatungs GMBH
ZMG Direktwerbung GMBH

Database consultant

A Lohs Gesmbh & Co Kg Druck +
  Direktwerbung
AGG Werbeagentur
AZ Direct Marketing Bertelsmann
Bozell Kobza
Chicago Advertising
Co+Co Dialogmarketing
Connex Marketing- Und
  Werbeagentur GmbH
Creditreform Wirtschaftsauskunftei
  Kubicki Kg
Das Agenturhaus, Werbe- und
  Marketing GmbH
Direct Team, Liliane Mikulec
Direkta Druckerei & Directmarketing
  GMBH & Co Kg
Direktwerbung Schwölberger
DMB Marketing Beratung
DMI Institut für Direktmarketing,
  Österreich
Dr Firzinger & Partner
Dr Kossdorff Werbeagentur GMBH
Eurocom Sales Promotion
Euromarketing Beratungsges.m.b.H.
Euromarketing Beratungsgesellschaft
  MBH
Follow-Up
GEMM BeratungsgmbH
GFW Gesellschaft Für
  Werbemittelverteilung GMBH
Glavan + Partner
Grötzl GmbH & CoKG
Hahn & Partner GMBH
Hartinger Consulting GMBH
Holzhuber Marketing Und
  Werbegesmbh
Hosse & Partner Agentur Für
  Marketing GMBH
Humanmedia, Marketing and Verlag
  GMBH
IQ-M GMBH
KB-Endlos Kroiss+Bichler GMBH
Kümmerly + Frey Wien
Kunz Direct Marketing
Le-Direkt Lossie, Ertl & Co GMBH
Lembacher Direktmarketing
Lustig Direct Marketing GMBH
M-S-B+K Werbeagentur Für Direct
  Marketing GMBH
Mag Werbeagentur Michael A Görtz
  GMBH
Maric & Rinaldin
Master Management
Meiller Druck GMBH Österreich
Mercurbank (GE Capital Bank)
Michael Oppl – Massensendungen
Moore GMBH
MPS Marketing & Produktion Service
  GMBH

MPS Marketing & Produktion Service
  GmbH
MS Mail Service GMBH
Nagy & Zwinz Werbeagentur
Ogilvy One
Omnitel Agentur Für Telefon-
  Marketing Und Direktwerbung
  GMBH
Otto Versand GmbH
Palla Koblinger & Partner
Plank Werbegesmbh (Die Agentur
  Plank)
Pressel Direktwerbung
RBC Direktmarketing Service GmbH
Rechenzentrum Vostrovsky
Reed Messe Salzburg GmbH
Reichl & Partner Wien
Reichl + Partner Werbeagentur
  GMBH
Rock + Partner Werbeagentur
Saz Marketing Services GMBH
Schober Suppan Direktmarketing
  GMBH
Sery DM & PR GmbH
Sturm Marketing Direkt GMBH
TCS-Directmarketing Dietmar
  Heuritsch
Tele Consult Telefon-Marketing &
  Unternehmensberatungs GMBH
Telemark Marketing Gebhard Zuber
  GMBH
Teleperformance Marketing-Und
  Unternehmensberatung GESMBH
tune in Communication Services für
  Marketing & Promotion GmbH
TWISTER COM GmbH,
  Technologiezentrum
Up Date Marketing Service GMBH
VSG Direktwerbung Versand Service
  GMBH
Welldone Marketing- Und
  Kommunikationsberatungs GMBH
Werbeservice GMBH
Wieringer Directmarketing
Wiesmüller & Partner GMBH
Wigeo-Gis GESMBH
Wunderman Cato Johnson
ZMG Direktwerbung GMBH

Database management

AZ Direct Marketing Bertelsmann
CALL & MAIL Telefonmarketing und
  DirektwerbunggmbH
Connex Marketing- Und
  Werbeagentur GmbH
Creditreform Wirtschaftsauskunftei
  Kubicki Kg
Das Agenturhaus, Werbe- und
  Marketing GmbH
Direct Team, Liliane Mikulec
Direkta Druckerei & Directmarketing
  GMBH & Co Kg
DMB Marketing Beratung

DMI Institut für Direktmarketing,
  Österreich
Euromarketing Beratungsges.m.b.H.
GEMM BeratungsgmbH
Glavan + Partner
Herold Business Data GmbH
IQ-M GMBH
Kümmerly + Frey Wien
Michael Oppl – Massensendungen
MPS Marketing & Produktion Service
  GmbH
Otto Versand GmbH
Pressel Direktwerbung
RBC Direktmarketing Service GmbH
Saz Marketing Services GMBH
Schober Suppan Direktmarketing
  GMBH
Schwarzinger – Adressen GmbH &
  CoKG
tune in Communication Services für
  Marketing & Promotion GmbH
TWISTER COM GmbH,
  Technologiezentrum
Ute Damisch Öffentlichkeitsarbeit
Welldone Marketing- Und
  Kommunikationsberatungs GMBH
ZMG Direktwerbung GMBH

Direct marketing agency

AZ Direct Marketing Bertelsmann
Connex Marketing- Und
  Werbeagentur GmbH
Das Agenturhaus, Werbe- und
  Marketing GmbH
DMB Marketing Beratung
DMI Institut für Direktmarketing,
  Österreich
Euromarketing Beratungsges.m.b.H.
GEMM BeratungsgmbH
Glavan + Partner
Grötzl GmbH & CoKG
Kümmerly + Frey Wien
Le-Direkt Lossie, Ertl & Co GMBH
Lembacher Direktmarketing
Marschall & Harfmann OHG
Master Management
Meiller Druck GMBH Österreich
Mercurbank (GE Capital Bank)
Michael Oppl – Massensendungen
MPS Marketing & Produktion Service
  GMBH
MPS Marketing & Produktion Service
  GmbH
Ogilvy One
Otto Versand GmbH
Palla Koblinger & Partner
Pressel Direktwerbung
Saz Marketing Services GMBH
Schwarzinger – Adressen GmbH &
  CoKG
Sery DM & PR GmbH
Sturm Marketing Direkt GMBH
TWISTER COM GmbH,

Technologiezentrum
Welldone Marketing- Und
  Kommunikationsberatungs GMBH
ZMG Direktwerbung GMBH

Door-to-door distribution
Diestler Werbemittelverteilung
  Ges.m.b.H
feibra VertriebsgmbH
feibra werbung gesmbh.
feipro Vertriebs gmbH
gfw Gesellschaft für
  Werbemittelverteilung GesmbH
Medienservice & WerberechtgmbH &
  Co KG
PLM Vertriebsgesellschaft mbH
Prowerb – Werbemittelverteilung

Electronic media/internet services/website design
Call-Marketingservice GmbH
Palla Koblinger & Partner

Fax mailings
Radio Austria Audiotex GmbH

Fulfilment and sampling house
AGG Werbeagentur
AZ Direct Marketing Bertelsmann
CALL & MAIL Telefonmarketing und
  DirektwerbunggmbH
Co+Co Dialogmarketing
Das Agenturhaus, Werbe- und
  Marketing GmbH
Direct Team, Liliane Mikulec
Direkta Druckerei & Directmarketing
  GMBH & Co Kg
Direktwerbung Schwölberger
DMB Marketing Beratung
DMI Institut für Direktmarketing,
  Österreich
DMR Direct Mail Realisation GMBH
Dr Firzinger & Partner
Dr Kossdorff Werbeagentur GMBH
Eurocom Sales Promotion
Euromarketing Beratungsges.m.b.H.
Euromarketing Beratungsgesellschaft
  MBH
Follow-Up
GFW Gesellschaft Für
  Werbemittelverteilung GMBH
Globemail Services GMBH
Grötzl GmbH & CoKG
Hahn & Partner GMBH
Hartinger Consulting GMBH
Holzhuber Marketing Und
  Werbegesmbh
Hosse & Partner Agentur Für
  Marketing GMBH
Humanmedia, Marketing and Verlag
  GMBH
IQ-M GMBH
KB-Endlos Kroiss+Bichler GMBH

Lembacher Direktmarketing
M-S-B+K Werbeagentur Für Direct
  Marketing GMBH
Mag Werbeagentur Michael A Görtz
  GMBH
Master Management
Michael Oppl – Massensendungen
MPS Marketing & Produktion Service
  GmbH
Otto Versand GmbH
Pressel Direktwerbung
Radio Austria Audiotex GmbH
RBC Direktmarketing Service GmbH
Rechenzentrum Vostrovsky
Reed Messe Salzburg GmbH
Schober Suppan Direktmarketing
  GMBH
Schwarzinger – Adressen GmbH &
  CoKG
Süddruck Kalenderherstellgs-,
  Buchbinderei- Und
  Verarbeitgsgmbh
TCS-Directmarketing Dietmar
  Heuritsch
Tele Consult Telefon-Marketing &
  Unternehmensberatungs GMBH
tune in Communication Services für
  Marketing & Promotion GmbH
TWISTER COM GmbH,
  Technologiezentrum
Ute Damisch Öffentlichkeitsarbeit
VSG Direktwerbung Versand Service
  GMBH
Welldone Marketing- Und
  Kommunikationsberatungs GMBH
Werbeservice GMBH
Wiesmüller & Partner GMBH
ZMG Direktwerbung GMBH

Lettershop
A Lohs Gesmbh & Co Kg Druck +
  Direktwerbung
Akuv GMBH Direktmarketing
AZ Direct Marketing Bertelsmann
Bozell Kobza
CALL & MAIL Telefonmarketing und
  DirektwerbunggmbH
Chicago Advertising
Co+Co Dialogmarketing
Direct Team, Liliane Mikulec
Direkta Druckerei & Directmarketing
  GMBH & Co Kg
DMB Marketing Beratung
DMI Institut für Direktmarketing,
  Österreich
DMR Direct Mail Realisation GMBH
Euromarketing Beratungsges.m.b.H.
Glavan + Partner
Globemail Services GMBH
Grötzl GmbH & CoKG
Hartinger Consulting GMBH
IQ-M GMBH
Kunz Direct Marketing

Lembacher Direktmarketing
Lustig Direct Marketing GMBH
M&H Versandhandel GmbH
M-S-B+K Werbeagentur Für Direct
  Marketing GMBH
Mag Werbeagentur Michael A Görtz
  GMBH
Maric & Rinaldin
Master Management
Meiller Druck GMBH Österreich
Michael Oppl – Massensendungen
Moore GMBH
MPS Marketing & Produktion Service
  GMBH
MPS Marketing & Produktion Service
  GmbH
MS Mail Service GMBH
Multibus GMBH
Ogilvy One
Otto Versand GmbH
PLM Vertriebsgesellschaft mbH
Pressel Direktwerbung
Rechenzentrum Vostrovsky
Reed Messe Salzburg GmbH
Reichl & Partner Wien
Reichl + Partner Werbeagentur
  GMBH
Rock + Partner Werbeagentur
Schober Suppan Direktmarketing
  GMBH
Schwarzinger – Adressen GmbH &
  CoKG
Sturm Marketing Direkt GMBH
Süddruck Kalenderherstellgs-,
  Buchbinderei- Und
  Verarbeitgsgmbh
TCS-Directmarketing Dietmar
  Heuritsch
Tele Consult Telefon-Marketing &
  Unternehmensberatungs GMBH
Teleperformance Marketing-Und
  Unternehmensberatung GESMBH
tune in Communication Services für
  Marketing & Promotion GmbH
TWISTER COM GmbH,
  Technologiezentrum
Ute Damisch Öffentlichkeitsarbeit
VSG Direktwerbung Versand Service
  GMBH
Welldone Marketing- Und
  Kommunikationsberatungs GMBH
Wieringer Directmarketing
Wiesmüller & Partner GMBH
Wunderman Cato Johnson
ZMG Direktwerbung GMBH

List broker
AGG Werbeagentur
AZ Direct Marketing Bertelsmann
Bozell Kobza
Chicago Advertising
Co+Co Dialogmarketing
Direct Team, Liliane Mikulec

Direkta Druckerei & Directmarketing
   GMBH & Co Kg
Direktwerbung Schwölberger
DMB Marketing Beratung
DMI Institut für Direktmarketing,
   Österreich
Dr Firzinger & Partner
Dr Kossdorff Werbeagentur GMBH
Dun & Bradstreet, Information
   Services GmbH
Eurocom Sales Promotion
Euromarketing Beratungsgesellschaft
   MBH
Follow-Up
GFW Gesellschaft Für
   Werbemittelverteilung GMBH
Hahn & Partner GMBH
Hartinger Consulting GMBH
Holzhuber Marketing Und
   Werbegesmbh
Hosse & Partner Agentur Für
   Marketing GMBH
Humanmedia, Marketing and Verlag
   GMBH
Institute for International Research
   GmbH
IQ-M GMBH
KB-Endlos Kroiss+Bichler GMBH
Kümmerly + Frey Wien
Kunz Direct Marketing
Le-Direkt Lossie, Ertl & Co GMBH
Lembacher Direktmarketing
Lustig Direct Marketing GMBH
M-S-B+K Werbeagentur Für Direct
   Marketing GMBH
Maric & Rinaldin
Master Management
Meiller Druck GMBH Österreich
Moore GMBH
MPS Marketing & Produktion Service
   GMBH
MPS Marketing & Produktion Service
   GmbH
MS Mail Service GMBH
Nagy & Zwinz Werbeagentur
Ogilvy One
Omnitel Agentur Für Telefon-
   Marketing Und Direktwerbung
   GMBH
Pressel Direktwerbung
RBC Direktmarketing Service GmbH
Rechenzentrum Vostrovsky
Reichl & Partner Wien
Reichl + Partner Werbeagentur
   GMBH
Rock + Partner Werbeagentur
Schober Suppan Direktmarketing
   GMBH
Tele Consult Telefon-Marketing &
   Unternehmensberatungs GMBH
Teleperformance Marketing-Und
   Unternehmensberatung GESMBH
VSG Direktwerbung Versand Service

GMBH
Welldone Marketing- Und
   Kommunikationsberatungs GMBH
Wieringer Directmarketing
Wiesmüller & Partner GMBH
Wigeo-Gis GESMBH
Wunderman Cato Johnson
ZMG Direktwerbung GMBH

Mailing house
M&H Versandhandel GmbH

Media buying agency
Wirtschaftskammer Österreich,
   Fachverband Werbung Und
   Marktkommunikation

Printing services
CALL & MAIL Telefonmarketing und
   DirektwerbunggmbH
Direct Team, Liliane Mikulec
Direkta Druckerei & Directmarketing
   GMBH & Co Kg
DMB Marketing Beratung
Glavan + Partner
Grötzl GmbH & CoKG
Michael Oppl – Massensendungen
Rechenzentrum Vostrovsky
Schober Suppan Direktmarketing
   GMBH
TWISTER COM GmbH,
   Technologiezentrum
Ute Damisch Öffentlichkeitsarbeit

Response analysis bureau
Palla Koblinger & Partner
Saz Marketing Services GMBH

Sales promotion agency
Palla Koblinger & Partner

Service bureau
Saz Marketing Services GMBH

Telemarketing agency
AGG Werbeagentur
Asset Marketing GMBH
AZ Direct Marketing Bertelsmann
Bozell Kobza
CALL & MAIL Telefonmarketing und
   DirektwerbunggmbH
Chicago Advertising
Co+Co Dialogmarketing
Connex Marketing- Und
   Werbeagentur GMBH
Das Agenturhaus, Werbe- und
   Marketing GmbH
Direct Team, Liliane Mikulec
Direktwerbung Schwölberger
DMB Marketing Beratung
Dr Firzinger & Partner
Dr Kossdorff Werbeagentur GMBH
Eurocom Sales Promotion

Euromarketing Beratungsges.m.b.H.
Euromarketing Beratungsgesellschaft
   MBH
Follow-Up
GEMM BeratungsgmbH
GFW Gesellschaft Für
   Werbemittelverteilung GMBH
Glavan + Partner
Grötzl GmbH & CoKG
Hahn & Partner GMBH
Holzhuber Marketing Und
   Werbegesmbh
Hosse & Partner Agentur Für
   Marketing GMBH
Humanmedia, Marketing and Verlag
   GMBH
IQ-M GMBH
KB-Endlos Kroiss+Bichler GMBH
Lembacher Direktmarketing
Lustig Direct Marketing GMBH
Mag Werbeagentur Michael A Görtz
   GMBH
Maric & Rinaldin
Master Management
Medienservice & WerberechtgmbH &
   Co KG
Mercurbank (GE Capital Bank)
Michael Oppl – Massensendungen
Moore GMBH
MPS Marketing & Produktion Service
   GMBH
MPS Marketing & Produktion Service
   GmbH
MS Mail Service GMBH
Multibus GMBH
Nagy & Zwinz Werbeagentur
Ogilvy One
Omnitel Agentur Für Telefon-
   Marketing Und Direktwerbung
   GMBH
Otto Versand GmbH
Presse Medien Service GMBH
Pressel Direktwerbung
Radio Austria Audiotex GmbH
RBC Direktmarketing Service GmbH
Rechenzentrum Vostrovsky
Reichl & Partner Wien
Reichl + Partner Werbeagentur
   GMBH
Rock + Partner Werbeagentur
Saz Marketing Services GMBH
Schober Suppan Direktmarketing
   GMBH
Sery DM & PR GmbH
Skopik Telefonmarketing
TCS-Directmarketing Dietmar
   Heuritsch
Tele Consult Telefon-Marketing &
   Unternehmensberatungs GMBH
Telemark Marketing Gebhard Zuber
   GMBH
Teleperformance Marketing-Und
   Unternehmensberatung GESMBH

TWISTER COM GmbH,
Technologiezentrum
Ute Damisch Öffentlichkeitsarbeit
Welldone Marketing- Und
Kommunikationsberatungs GMBH
Wieringer Directmarketing
Wunderman Cato Johnson
ZMG Direktwerbung GMBH

Training/recruitment
Skopik Telefonmarketing
Wirtschaftskammer Österreich,
Fachverband Werbung Und
Marktkommunikation

Association
DMA (USA)
DMB Marketing Beratung
Hosse & Partner Agentur Für
Marketing GMBH
M&H Versandhandel GmbH
RBC Direktmarketing Service GmbH

DMVÖ
A Lohs Gesmbh & Co Kg Druck +
Direktwerbung
AGG Werbeagentur
Akuv GMBH Direktmarketing
Asset Marketing GMBH
AZ Direct Marketing Bertelsmann
Bozell Kobza
CALL & MAIL Telefonmarketing und
DirektwerbunggmbH
Call-Marketingservice GmbH
Chicago Advertising
Co+Co Dialogmarketing
Connex Marketing- Und
Werbeagentur GmbH
Creditreform Wirtschaftsauskunftei
Kubicki Kg
Das Agenturhaus, Werbe- und
Marketing GmbH
Diestler Werbemittelverteilung
Ges.m.b.H
Direct Team, Liliane Mikulec
Direkta Druckerei & Directmarketing
GMBH & Co Kg
Direktwerbung Schwölberger
DMB Marketing Beratung
DMI Institut für Direktmarketing,
Österreich
DMR Direct Mail Realisation GMBH
Dr Firzinger & Partner
Dr Kossdorff Werbeagentur GMBH
Dun & Bradstreet, Information
Services GmbH
Eurocom Sales Promotion
Euromarketing Beratungsges.m.b.H.
Euromarketing Beratungsgesellschaft

MBH
feibra VertriebsgmbH
feibra werbung gesmbh.
feipro VertriesgmbH
Follow-Up
GEMM BeratungsgmbH
gfw Gesellschaft für
Werbemittelverteilung GesmbH
GFW Gesellschaft Für
Werbemittelverteilung GMBH
Glavan + Partner
Globemail Services GMBH
Goessler Kuverts GMBH Kuvertfabrik
Grötzl GmbH & CoKG
Hahn & Partner GMBH
Hartinger Consulting GMBH
Herold Business Data GmbH
Holzhuber Marketing Und
Werbegesmbh
Hosse & Partner Agentur Für
Marketing GMBH
Humanmedia, Marketing and Verlag
GMBH
Institute for International Research
GmbH
IQ-M GMBH
KB-Endlos Kroiss+Bichler GMBH
Kümmerly + Frey Wien
Kunz Direct Marketing
Le-Direkt Lossie, Ertl & Co GMBH
Lembacher Direktmarketing
Lustig Direct Marketing GMBH
M&H Versandhandel GmbH
M-S-B+K Werbeagentur Für Direct
Marketing GMBH
Mag Werbeagentur Michael A Görtz
GMBH
Maric & Rinaldin
Marschall & Harfmann OHG
Master Management
Medienservice & WerberechtgmbH &
Co KG
Meiller Druck GMBH Österreich
Mercurbank (GE Capital Bank)
Michael Oppl – Massensendungen
Moore GMBH
MPS Marketing & Produktion Service
GMBH
MPS Marketing & Produktion Service
GmbH
MS Mail Service GMBH
Multibus GMBH
Nagy & Zwinz Werbeagentur
Ogilvy One
Omnitel Agentur Für Telefon-
Marketing Und Direktwerbung
GMBH
Otto Versand GmbH
Palla Koblinger & Partner

Plank Werbegesmbh (Die Agentur
Plank)
PLM Vertriebsgesellschaft mbH
Presse Medien Service GMBH
Pressel Direktwerbung
Prowerb – Werbemittelverteilung
Radio Austria Audiotek GmbH
RBC Direktmarketing Service GmbH
Rechenzentrum Vostrovsky
Reed Messe Salzburg GmbH
Reichl & Partner Wien
Reichl + Partner Werbeagentur
GMBH
Rock + Partner Werbeagentur
Saz Marketing Services GMBH
Schober Suppan Direktmarketing
GMBH
Schwarzinger – Adressen GmbH &
CoKG
Sery DM & PR GmbH
Skopik Telefonmarketing
Sturm Marketing Direkt GMBH
Süddruck Kalenderherstellgs-,
Buchbinderei- Und
Verarbeitgsgmbh
TCS-Directmarketing Dietmar
Heuritsch
Tele Consult Telefon-Marketing &
Unternehmensberatungs GMBH
Telemark Marketing Gebhard Zuber
GMBH
Teleperformance Marketing-Und
Unternehmensberatung GESMBH
tune in Communication Services für
Marketing & Promotion GmbH
TWISTER COM GmbH,
Technologiezentrum
Up Date Marketing Service GMBH
Ute Damisch Öffentlichkeitsarbeit
VSG Direktwerbung Versand Service
GMBH
Welldone Marketing- Und
Kommunikationsberatungs GMBH
Werbeservice GMBH
Wieringer Directmarketing
Wiesmüller & Partner GMBH
Wigeo-Gis GESMBH
Wirtschaftskammer Österreich,
Fachverband Werbung Und
Marktkommunikation
Wunderman Cato Johnson
ZMG Direktwerbung GMBH

FEDMA
Palla Koblinger & Partner
Saz Marketing Services GMBH
Wirtschaftskammer Österreich, Fach-
verband Werbung Und Marktkom-
munikation

BELGIUM

Population: 10.2 million
Capital: Brussels
Languages: Dutch, French and German

GDP: $269 billion
GDP per capita: $26,440
Inflation: 1.4 per cent

Currency: Belgian Franc (BFr) = 100 centimes
Exchange rate: BFr37.53 : $1 (BFr40.36 : 1 euro)

Time: GMT +1 hour

OVERVIEW

Belgium holds a unique position in Europe. Located in the centre of Europe's industrial heartland, its capital city houses the headquarters of both NATO and the European Union. Its culturally diverse and multilingual population mirrors with startling accuracy the European averages in terms of population and consumption profiles; as such, it is seen by many as a 'micromarket' of Europe and hence an ideal test ground for direct marketers approaching Europe for the first time.

With four national borders and a large contingent of temporary and permanent foreign residents, the Belgian population is constantly subject to outside influences, and is consequently not averse to absorbing new products and approaches. The Belgians are the second most heavily mailed population in Europe, receiving 87 items per capita in 1994. Direct marketing in Belgium has shown rapid growth in recent years and, with a well-developed infrastructure and sophisticated consumer base, growth looks set to continue.

LANGUAGE AND CULTURAL CONSIDERATIONS

There are three languages in Belgium: Dutch, French and German. It is important to be sensitive to the distinct linguistic communities and understand why one language will be preferred in an area more than another. In Brussels, French is the main language.

LEGISLATION AND CONSUMER PROTECTION

There is some important legislation on consumer privacy and commercial practices which relates to DM. The December 1992 law on the protection of privacy is being progressively implemented. There are three main points of concern for the Belgian Direct Marketing Association:

1. The obligation to inform the data subject when collecting data;
2. The obligation to inform the data subject at first registration for list makers;
3. The declaration concerning 'treatments', ie the use of information which may fall under the supervision of a commission.

The Belgian Direct Marketing Association is fighting to obtain a change in the law which presently prevents a vendor from asking for advance payment made before the expiration of the trial period (which is seven working days).

In October 1998, the Belgian DMA presented the new code of conduct for the Direct Marketing Industry. This code contains chapters on commercial practices, telemarketing, address transactions, DM agencies, the preference services and the surveillance committee. Consumers can contact the BDMA for information on and registration in the Robinson lists. Three lists are available: Robinson (Mail), Robinson Phone and Robinson Fax.

Furthermore, the BDMA has launched its Direct Marketing label. This label shows to consumers that the company is member of the Belgian DMA, that the company respects the code of conduct of the BDMA and, when encountering problems with DM, the consumer can count on the BDMA to solve the problem. It also shows to the other companies the professionalism of the company-member.

THE DIRECT MARKETING ASSOCIATION

Name: (French):	Association Belge du Marketing Direct
Name (Dutch):	Belgisch Direct Marketing Verbond
Address:	Buro & Design Center, Heizel Esplanade 346, B-1020 Brussels
Tel:	+32 2 477 1797
Fax:	+32 2 479 0679
Email:	info@bdma.be
Website:	www.bdma.be
Year founded:	April 1994
President:	Michiel Casters
Contact:	Patrick Marck (Public Relations)
Total staff:	5
Members:	500 companies (250 service providers, 250 advertisers, a total of 4,000 contacts)

DM agencies	75	Printers	15
List brokers	15	Telemarketing agencies	25
Advertisers	250	DM consultants	12
Mailing houses	25	Handling houses	20
Mail order companies	46	Database agencies	20

Facilities for overseas users of direct mail

Membership: effective membership depends on company turnover (60,000 BF to 350,000 BF). Supporting membership is 30,000 BF per company. Every company can join, but candidature must be approved by the Management Council. There are no other conditions.

Newsletter: the magazine for members is *Interactive*. It is published every two weeks. There is no subscription rate: it is free for members only.

Library: The BDMA has a library – access to which is free.

On-line information service: the BDMA has an on-line information service. Their website address is www.bdma.be (info on Belgian DMA) or www.marketing.be (info on Belgian marketing community).

Legal advice: free for effective members. For others the rate is fixed on the amount of work.

Business liaison service: for members and non-members alike, the DMA will supply details of local suppliers, but insists on taking a strictly neutral line and will not recommend any suppliers in particular.

Other facilities: the DMA publishes a number of other circulars, and publishes the excellent *DM Directory*. The *DM Directory* is in both Dutch and French and contains details of some of the best campaigns in the market and details of the spectrum of suppliers who created them. The directory offers a highly informative snapshot of the local industry.

POSTAL SERVICES

The Belgian Post Office and Postcheque are independent state enterprises. Together they offer the direct marketer an impressive range of specialist services, including:

- several bulk mailing services;
- express service comprising Taxipost, Express Mail Service and bureau-fax;
- financial services: Giro service money transfers in US$, cash on delivery and home services;
- pre-franked replies;
- international business reply service facilitates response from 40 countries;
- IDM: favourable rates for exports;

- discount mailing rates: rebates for letters, postcards and printed matter start at 500 items, with a weight limit of 350g. The same quantity applies for pre-sorting promotional samples (up to 350g). For small parcels, rebates are available from 1000 items, with a weight limit of 2kg. For parcels in excess of this weight, rebates are available on request.

- postage paid by addressee: payment of postage on pre-addressed envelopes or cards. There is a small surcharge for this service;

- PO box: any individual or company established in Belgium can have one or more PO boxes, not necessarily at their place of residence;

- reply number: a service combining the advantages of the 'postage paid by addressee' system, and the PO box. This type of service is ideally suited for returns from coupon advertisements. There is a small surcharge for this service.

For more information on post office services, contact:

French address:

La Poste
Service Commercial
Centre Monnaie
B-1000 Brussels
Belgium

Dutch address:

De Post
Commerciële Dienst
Muntzentrum
B-1000 Brussels
Belgium
Tel: +32 2 226 2243
Fax: +32 2 226 2141
www.post.be

PROVIDERS OF DM AND E-M SERVICES

2-SIGMA
Morgensterpad 3
Knokke-Heist
8500
Belgium
Tel: +32 5062 8149
Fax: +32 5062 8148
Email: info@2-sigma.be
Alain Van Buyten, Director

Services/Products:
Consultancy services

E-Services:
E-Marketing consultant

Member of:
FEDMA; National DMA

4REAL
Brogniestraat 54
Rue Brogniez
Brussels
1070
Belgium
Tel: +32 2 523 19 11
Fax: +32 2 523 83 11
Email: katy.vancoillie@forrcal.be
Katy Vancoillie, Director

Services/Products:
Direct marketing agency

Member of:
BDMV

AB-CREATIONS & COMMUNICATIONS
Stationstraat 140
Waregem
8790
Belgium
Tel: +32 56 61 00 70
Fax: +32 56 61 00 37
Email: info@abcreations.be
Web: www.abcreations.be
Tina Fabry

Services/Products:
Direct marketing agency; Electronic media; Internet services

Member of:
BDMV

ABC & D, BOOMERANG COLLARD & DETAEYE, DIRECT COMMUNICATION
Waterkasteelstraat
Rue de Château d'Eau 43
Brussels
1180
Belgium
Tel: +32 2 376 00 06
Fax: +32 2 332 12 44
Email: abc&d@pophost.eunet.be
Jean-Luc Collard, Director

Services/Products:
Direct marketing agency

Member of:
BDMV

AMAZING ADVERTISING
Stadsvest 25
Wilsele
3012
Belgium
Tel: +32 16 29 24 20
Fax: +32 16 29 50 25
Email: kristien.hansebaut@ping.be
Kristien Hansebaut, Director

Services/Products:
Direct marketing agency

Member of:
BDMV

ANDRé WINANDY COMMUNICATION
Eikenlaan 4
Herentals
B-2200
Belgium
Tel: +32 1421 7921
Fax: +32 1422 1817
Email: andrewinandy@glo.be
André Winandy, Director

Services/Products:
Translation services

Member of:
National DMA

ARTEX
Roeselaarsestraat 594
Izegem
8870
Belgium
Tel: +32 51 33 54 00
Fax: +32 51 33 54 11
Email: artex@artex.be
Geert Neutens, Director

Services/Products:
Direct marketing agency

Member of:
BDMV

ASSOCIATION GREGOIRE
Rue Camille Lemonnier 68
Brussels
1050
Belgium
Tel: +32 2 3456807
Fax: +32 2 3436678
Email: avocats@gregoire.be
Alain Guilmot

Services/Products:
Legal services

Member of:
FEDMA

B & C
Grote- Reukens 1
Destelbergen
9070
Belgium
Tel: +32 9 231 45 96
Fax: +32 9 231 45 96
Email: buscom@glo.be
Philippe Delodder, Director

Services/Products:
Direct marketing agency

Member of:
BDMV

B.I.C.
Molièrelaan
Avenue Molière 64
Brussels
1190
Belgium
Tel: +32 2 340 33 00
Fax: +32 2 346 03 62
Email: b.i.c.@euronet.be
Claire van den Branden

Services/Products:
Direct marketing agency

Member of:
BDMV

BBDO/DIRECT
De Beaulieulaan 25
Av. de Beaulieu 25
Brussels
1160
Belgium
Tel: +32 2 673 99 00
Fax: +32 3 672 47 92
Email: ulbe.jelluma@bbdo.bee
Ulbe Jelluma, Director

Services/Products:
Direct marketing agency; Market research agency

Member of:
BDMV

BEBOP DIRECT CREACTIVITIES
Bondgenotenstraat 68
Brussels
1190
Belgium
Tel: +32 2 346 +55 11 50
Fax: +32 2 344 20 52

Email: bebop@bebop.be
Jan Vierstraete, Managing Director

Services/Products:
Direct marketing agency; Media
buying agency; Service bureau

Member of:
FEDMA; BDMV

BELGIAN DMA
Buro & Design Center
Heizel Esplanade B46
Brussels
B-1020
Belgium
Tel: +55 32 2477 1797
Fax: +55 32 2479 0679
Email: info@bdma.be
Web: www.bdma.be
Patrick Marck, PR Manager

Services/Products:
Direct marketing agency

Member of:
DMA (US); European Mail Order &
Trade Association (EMOTA)

BELGIAN MAILHOUSE NV
Building 709
Brucargo
Zaventem
1931
Belgium
Tel: +32 2 7523213
Fax: +32 2 7523215
Email: borisk@belgianmailhouse.be
Boris Knops

Services/Products:
Lettershop; Mailing/Faxing services;
Personalisation

Member of:
FEDMA; BDMV

BINPAC
Groenstraat 68
Sint-Truiden
3800
Belgium
Tel: +32 +55 11 69 22 20
Fax: +32 11 69 41 30
Wido Bourel

Services/Products:
Labelling/envelope services

Member of:
BDMV

BONGS ENVELTEC
rue de la Guelenne, 20
Soignies
7060
Belgium
Tel: +32 67 34 76 76

Fax: +32 67 33 95 94
Patrick Machiels, Sales Director

Services/Products:
Labelling/envelope services

Member of:
FEDMA

BRIDGE MARKETING
Tervuursevest 11
bus 51
Heverlee
3001
Belgium
Tel: +32 16 31 95 80
Fax: +32 16 31 95 85
Email: bridge.marketing@tvd.be
Web: http://home.tvd.be/ws35499/
   index.htm
Ludovic Depoortere

Services/Products:
Database services; Telemarketing
agency

Member of:
BDMV

BRUCALL
Leuvensesteenweg
Chaussée de Louvain 658
Brussels
1030
Belgium
Tel: +32 2 744 22 11
Fax: +32 2 744 22 16
Valérie Godin

Services/Products:
Telemarketing agency

Member of:
BDMV

BRUYNEEL
Rivierstraat 54
Beervelde
9080
Belgium
Tel: +32 9 355 52 70
Fax: +32 9 355 14 36
Email: info@bruyneel.be
Eric D'Hooge

Services/Products:
Mailing/Faxing services; Print services

Member of:
BDMV

CALLCENTER INSTITUTE
Winninglaan 3
Temse
9140
Belgium
Tel: +32 3 710 89 89

Fax: +32 3 710 82 83
Dirk Van de Walle

Services/Products:
Telemarketing agency; Training/
recruitment; Call centre services/
systems

Member of:
BDMV

CALLMETRICS
Onderstraat 36
Gent
9000
Belgium
Tel: +32 9 234 20 10
Fax: +32 9 234 29 08
Email: info@callmetrics.be
Bart Ghesquière

Services/Products:
Telemarketing agency; Call centre
services/systems

Member of:
BDMV

**CARIBOU CREATIVE
   BUSINESS**
Vrijwilligerslaan 21
Av. des Volontaires 21
Brussels
1160
Belgium
Tel: +32 2 732 61 41
Fax: +32 2 733 64 07
Email: caribou@skynet.be
Jean-Luc Aubry

Services/Products:
Direct marketing agency

Member of:
BDMV

CARLSON MARKETING GROUP
Pater Eudore Devroyestraat 47
Rue Père Eudore Devroye 47
Brussels
1040
Belgium
Tel: +32 2 736 89 25
Fax: +32 2 736 53 28
Email: gkeg@carlson-marketing-co.uk
Gertjan Keg

Services/Products:
Direct marketing agency

Member of:
BDMV

COMMUNICATION CENTER
Graslei 17
Gent
9000
Belgium

Tel: +32 9 266 05 11
Fax: +32 9 266 05 19
Email: info@c-center.com
Trui Beel

Services/Products:
Telemarketing agency; Direct marketing agency

Member of:
BDMV

CONSULTANTS IN SPORTS (CIS)
Schoebroekstraat 8
Beringen
3583
Belgium
Tel: +32 +55 11 45 99 00
Fax: +32 11 45 99 10
Email: info@cis.be
Bernard Polet

Services/Products:
List services; Direct marketing agency

Member of:
BDMV

COPYWISE
Jan Van Rijswijcklaan 164
bus 22
Antwerpen
2020
Belgium
Tel: +32 3 238 88 02
Fax: +32 3 238 91 57
Email: info@copywise.be
Web: www.copywise.be
Johan Verschueren

Services/Products:
Direct marketing agency; Copy adaptation

Member of:
BDMV

COPYWRITING WOUTERS
Thaliastraat 32
Antwerpen
2600
Belgium
Tel: +32 3 366 54 87
Fax: +32 3 366 54 89
Email: joris.wouters@glo.be
Joris Wouters

Services/Products:
Copy adaptation

Member of:
BDMV

CPP-COMMUNICATIE PERS PRODUCTIE - COMMUNICATION PRESSE PRODUCTION
Huart Hamoirlaan 109
Avenue Huart Hamoir 109
Brussels
1030
Belgium
Tel: +32 2 245 56 91
Fax: +32 2 241 97 67
Email: cpp.be@skynet.be
Jean-Gilles Massard

Services/Products:
Database services; Direct marketing agency

Member of:
BDMV

CREA
Diksmuidesteenweg 388
Roeselare
8800
Belgium
Tel: +32 51 22 77 74
Fax: +32 51 22 72 30
Email: crea@innet
Web: http://www.crea.be
Bob David

Services/Products:
Print services

Member of:
BDMV

DACOTEAM
Stallestraat
Rue de Stalle 65
Brussels
1180
Belgium
Tel: +32 2 370 16 70
Fax: +32 2 332 11 39
Email: jls@sopres.be
Jean-Luc Schellens

Services/Products:
Software supplier

Member of:
BDMV

DATASCOPE
Kapelanielaan 1–5
Temse
9140
Belgium
Tel: +32 3 710 07 40
Fax: +32 3 710 08 06
Web: www.ketels.be
Luc Robbens

Services/Products:
List services; Database services; Response analysis bureau; Software supplier

Member of:
BDMV

DDB GROUP BELGIUM
17 rue Saint-Hubert
Brussels
1150
Belgium
Tel: +32 2 761 1900
Fax: +32 2 761 1901
Email: info@ddb.be
Web: www.ddb.be
Xavier Caytan, New Business Manager

Services/Products:
Advertising Agency; Catalogue producer; Direct marketing agency; Media buying agency; Sales promotion agency; Fully integrated communication agency

E-Services:
E-Marketing consultant

Member of:
National DMA; BBA

DE WITTE & CO
Chrysantenlaan 14
Heusden-Zolder
3550
Belgium
Tel: +32 +55 11 87 25 74
Fax: +32 11 87 27 92
Email: bart@dewitte.be
Web: dewitte.be
Bart De Witte

Services/Products:
Direct marketing agency

Member of:
BDMV

DELABIE S.A.
Bld. De l'Eurozone 9
ZI La Martinaire
Mouscron
7700
Belgium
Tel: +32 5684 1000
Fax: +32 5684 0962
Email: willem.mandeville@delabie.be
Willem Mandeville

Services/Products:
Catalogue producer; Print services

DENIS BODDEN SA
Chaussée de Neerstalle 91–105
Brussels
1190

Belgium
Tel: +32 2 332 32 40
Fax: +32 2 376 44 37
Jean-Marie Taroli

Services/Products:
List services; Fulfilment and sampling
house; Direct marketing agency;
Service bureau; Print services

Member of:
FEDMA

DHU COMMUNICATION
Rue du Chevalet 2
Louvain-la-Neuve
1348
Belgium
Tel: +32 10 45 68 69
Fax: +32 10 45 68 08
Email: dhu@euronet.be
Benoit David

Services/Products:
Fulfilment and sampling house;
Response analysis bureau

Member of:
BDMV

DIABOL'O
Rue de la Vignette 179
b 1
Brussels
1160
Belgium
Tel: +32 2 689 08 20
Fax: +32 2 679 08 28
Email: diabolo@mail.interpac.be
Valérie Van Lembergen

Services/Products:
Direct marketing agency

Member of:
BDMV

DIRACT
Gouvernementstraat 32
Gent
9000
Belgium
Tel: +32 9 233 20 00
Fax: +32 9 233 30 17
Stein Schoemans

Services/Products:
Telemarketing agency

Member of:
BDMV

DIRECT CALL
Parnassusgaarde 13b
clos du Parnasse 13b
Brussels
1050
Belgium

Tel: +32 2 503 33 13
Fax: +32 2 503 33 23
Email: directc@arcadis.be
Chris Van den Broeck

Services/Products:
Telemarketing agency

Member of:
BDMV

DIRECT CREATIONS
Vorstlaan 100
Boulevard du Souverain 100
Brussels
1170
Belgium
Tel: +32 2 675 32 35
Fax: +32 2 675 50 31
Email: info@directcreations.be
André Van der Stappen

Services/Products:
Direct marketing agency

Member of:
BDMV

DIRECT MARKETING ATELIER
Hoogkamerstraat 296
Temse
9140
Belgium
Tel: +32 3 771 55 83
Fax: +32 3 771 40 55
Email: jenny.dierickx@club.innet.be
Jenny Dierickx

Services/Products:
Direct marketing agency

Member of:
BDMV

DIRECT MARKETING KNOW-HOW INSTITUTE
Beekstraat 22
Mariakerke (Gent)
9030
Belgium
Tel: +32 9 216 66 00
Fax: +32 9 216 66 06
Email: info@vanvooren.be
Kathleen Bruggeman

Services/Products:
Consultancy services; Training/
recruitment

Member of:
BDMV

DIRECT PARTNER INTERNATIONAL
De Dreef van Hertebos 24
Gravenwezel
2970
Belgium

Tel: +31 3 293 0040
Fax: +31 3 293 0041
Email: margret@knoware.nl
Margret Ressang, Managing Partner

Services/Products:
Consultancy services

Member of:
FEDMA; DMA (US)

DIRECT PRODUCTION
Stallestraat
Rue de Stalle 65
Brussels
1180
Belgium
Tel: +32 2 370 17 70
Fax: +32 2 332 00 64
Email: michel.bruyr@sopres.be
Michel Bruyr

Services/Products:
Print services

Member of:
BDMV

DIREXIONS
Rue de l'Aurore, 4
Brussels
1000
Belgium
Tel: +32 2 537 6960
Fax: +32 2 537 9984
Email: contact@direxions.be
Irene Allanson, Managing Director

Services/Products:
Advertising Agency; Consultancy
services; Database services; Direct
marketing agency; Interactive media;
Electronic media

E-Services:
Website design; Online/e-marketing
agency

Member of:
FEDMA; DMA (US); National DMA

DISTRIMAIL
Begoniastraat 18a
Eke
9810
Belgium
Tel: +32 9 385 86 44
Fax: +32 9 385 86 47
Email: distrimail@alo.be
Eric Buggenhoudt

Services/Products:
Mailing/Faxing services

Member of:
BDMV

DMA
Kastanjebosstraat 2a
Veltem-Beisem
3020
Belgium
Tel: +32 16 48 94 06
Fax: +32 16 48 98 62
Jos Bex

Services/Products:
Mailing/Faxing services

Member of:
BDMV

DRUKKERIJ DE COKER
Industrieterrein Polderstad
Boombekelaan 12
Hoboken
2660
Belgium
Tel: +32 3 830 30 00
Fax: +32 3 830 33 89
Email: luc@decoker.be
Luc De Coker

Services/Products:
Print services

Member of:
BDMV

DRUKKERIJ STROBBE
Kasteelstraat 1
Izegem
8870
Belgium
Tel: +32 51 33 32 11
Fax: +32 51 31 33 42
Jan Roels

Services/Products:
Labelling/envelope services; Print
services

Member of:
BDMV

**DSC - DIRECT SOCIAL
COMMUNICATIONS**
Montoyerstraat 18b
Rue Montoyer 18b
Brussels
1000
Belgium
Tel: +32 2 280 00 74
Fax: +32 2 280 04 17
Email: dsc@arcadin.be
Marcel De Kock (NL), David
Vanderbiest (FR)

Services/Products:
Direct marketing agency

Member of:
BDMV

DUN & BRADSTREET
Plejadenlaan 73
avenue des Pléiades 73
Brussels
1200
Belgium
Tel: +32 2 778 72 11
Fax: +32 2 778 72 72
Email: blommaert@mail.dnb.com
Web: www.dbbelgium.com
Johan Blommaert

Services/Products:
List services

Member of:
BDMV

**DVN – DE VISSHER & VAN
NEVEL**
Kasteellaan 160
Gent
9000
Belgium
Tel: +32 9 224 43 60
Fax: +32 9 224 01 69
Email: dvn@skypro.be
Georges Van Nevel, Managing Partner

Services/Products:
Advertising Agency; Direct marketing
agency; Consultancy services; Sales
promotion agency

Member of:
FEDMA; BDMV

**EAAA - EUROPEAN
ASSOCIATION OF
ADVERTISING AGENCIES**
5 Rue St. Quentin
Brussels
B-1000
Belgium
Tel: +32 2 280 16 03
Fax: +32 2 230 09 66
Ronald Beatson, Director General

Member of:
BDMV

**EASA - EUROPEAN
ADVERTISING STANDARDS
ALLIANCE**
10A Rue de la Pépinière
Brussels
B-1000
Belgium
Tel: +32 2 513 7806
Fax: +32 2 513 28 61
Email: library@easa-alliance.org
Web: www.easa-alliance.org
Dr. Oliver Gray, Director General

Services/Products:
NGO promoting and supporting
advertising self-regulation

Member of:
BDMV

**EAT - EUROPEAN
ADVERTISING TRIPARTITE**
267 Avenue de Tervuren
Brussels
B-1150
Belgium
Tel: +32 2 779 21 30
Fax: +32 2 772 89 80
David Hanger, Chairman

Member of:
BDMV

EFFECTS
Edingsesteenweg 122
Asse
1730
Belgium
Tel: +32 2 453 1430
Fax: +32 2 453 1426
Email: effects@effects.be
Web: www.effects.be
Jan Deelen, Managing Partner

Services/Products:
Consultancy services; Direct marketing
agency

E-Services:
E-Marketing consultant; Website
design

Member of:
BDMV

ELEP
Kerkhovensesteenweg 92
Lommel
3920
Belgium
Tel: +32 +55 11 55 01 11
Fax: +32 11 54 26 86
Jean-Claude Mertens

Services/Products:
Labelling/envelope services

Member of:
BDMV

ENVELBAG
G. Callierlaan 231
Gent
9000
Belgium
Tel: +32 9 233 32 84
Fax: +32 9 224 32 84
Philippe Sys

Services/Products:
Labelling/envelope services

Member of:
BDMV

EURO DB SA
Place de l'Université 16
Louvain-la-Neuve
B-1348
Belgium
Tel: +32 10 476711
Fax: +32 10 476767
Email: info@eurodb.be
Web: www.eurodb.be
Didier Jurfest, Sales Manager

Services/Products:
List services; Database services

Member of:
National DMA

EUROCALL.NET
Rue de la Borne 14
Brussels
B-1080
Belgium
Tel: +32 2413 4911
Fax: +32 2413 4900
Email: info@eurocall.be
Web: www.eurocall.be

Services/Products:
Call centre services/systems; Sales
promotion agency; Telemarketing
agency

Member of:
National DMA

EXPERIAN BELGIUM
Kortrijksesteenweg 400D
Gent
9000
Belgium
Tel: +32 9 244 63 40
Fax: +32 9 244 63 41
Email: experian@ping.be
Web: www.experian.com
Laurence Machiels

Services/Products:
Database services; Response analysis
bureau; Software supplier

Member of:
BDMV

EXPERTLIST
Kapelanielaan 1–5
Temse
9140
Belgium
Tel: +32 3 710 07 00
Fax: +32 3 710 08 06
Web: www.ketels.be
Michèle Grangé

Services/Products:
List services; Database services;
Response analysis bureau

Member of:
BDMV

**FAMILY SERVICE (NDPK/
SNPME)**
Wijngaardenstraat 16
Rue de Vignes 16
Brussels
1020
Belgium
Tel: +32 2 478 48 40
Fax: +32 2 478 49 26
Chris Meyers

Services/Products:
List services

Member of:
BDMV

**FAST COMMUNICATION
GROUP**
St. Michielslaan 47
Boulevard St. Michel 47
Brussels
1040
Belgium
Tel: +32 2 736 60 96
Fax: +32 2 736 50 84
Email: fast@mail.interpac.be
Jan Boschmans

Services/Products:
Direct marketing agency; Electronic
media; Internet services

Member of:
BDMV

FAST MOVERS/PROMO-POST
Avenue des Pâquerettes 55
Waterloo
1410
Belgium
Tel: +32 2 352 01 70
Fax: +32 2 352 01 80
Email:
    francodufays@promocontrol.com
Web: http://www.promocontrol.com
Franois Dufays

Services/Products:
Fulfilment and sampling house;
Database services

Member of:
BDMV

FCB
Gulledell 98
Brussels
1200
Belgium
Tel: +32 2 777 01 70
Fax: +32 2 777 01 79
Email: phcallens@fcb.be
Philippe Callens

Services/Products:
Direct marketing agency

Member of:
BDMV

FEDMA
439 avenue de Tervuren
Brussels
1150
Belgium
Tel: +32 2 779 42 68
Fax: +32 2 779 42 69
Carel Rog, Chairman

Member of:
FEDMA

FEED BACK
Henri Wafelaertsstraat 36
Rue Henri Wafelaerts 36
Brussels
1060
Belgium
Tel: +32 2 534 91 05
Fax: +32 2 534 95 15
Email: feedback@feedback.be
Vinciane Croonenberghs

Services/Products:
Direct marketing agency

Member of:
BDMV

**FIDELITY DIRECT
MARKETING**
Vorstsesteenweg 168
Ruisbroek
1601
Belgium
Tel: +32 2 331 26 41
Fax: +32 2 331 27 69
Email: fidelity@fidelity.be
Web: www.fidelity.be
Veronique Deville

Services/Products:
List services; Fulfilment and sampling
house; Database services; Mailing/
Faxing services; Direct marketing
agency

Member of:
BDMV

FILLAD
Ottergemsesteenweg 703
Gent
9000
Belgium
Tel: +32 9 243 99 29
Fax: +32 9 221 18 65
Email: filad@cci.be
Dirk Onderdonck

Services/Products:
Telemarketing agency; Training/
recruitment

Member of:
BDMV

FRANK ANTHONI
Meidoornlaan 15
Brecht
2960
Belgium
Tel: +32 3 636 45 15
Fax: +32 3 636 47 39
Email: frank@anthoni.bvba.be
Frank Anthoni

Services/Products:
Copy adaptation

Member of:
BDMV

GOOD FOR YOU
Vrijwilligerslaan
Av. des Volontaires 21
Brussels
1160
Belgium
Tel: +32 2 732 59 58
Fax: +32 2 733 64 07
Email: good.for.you@skynet.be
Michel De Schauwers

Services/Products:
Copy adaptation; Creative agency

Member of:
BDMV

GRAPHIC GROUPS SPARKS
Roeselaarsestraat 594
Izegem
8870
Belgium
Tel: +32 51 33 54 10
Fax: +32 51 33 54 11
Email: kris.pieters@sparks.be
Kris Pieters

Services/Products:
Database services; Direct marketing
agency; Print services

Member of:
BDMV

GRAYDON BELGIUM, DIV.
Marktselect
Meir 21
b10
Antwerpen
2000
Belgium
Tel: +32 3 231 96 36
Fax: +32 3 231 96 99
Email: markselect@graydon.be

Web: http://www.graydon.be
Michel Wyckaert

Services/Products:
List services; Database services

Member of:
BDMV

GREY DIRECT
Vandenhovenstraat 3
Rue Vandenhoven 3
Brussels
1200
Belgium
Tel: +32 2 772 45 45
Fax: +32 2 771 76 25
Email: rene.henrion@grey.be
René Henrion

Services/Products:
Direct marketing agency

Member of:
BDMV

HAGEMAN VERPAKKERS BELGIË
Industriepark West 57
Sint-Niklaas
9100
Belgium
Tel: +32 3 776 15 36
Fax: +32 3 766 68 78
Werner Boes

Services/Products:
Mailing/Faxing services

Member of:
BDMV

HARTE-HANKS RESPONSE MANAGEMENT EUROPE
Bedrijfsstraat 10
Hasselt
3500
Belgium
Tel: +32 +55 11 300 300
Fax: +32 11 300 310
Email: jvs@harte-hanks.be
Jo Van Samang, Managing Director

Services/Products:
Fulfilment and sampling house;
Mailing/Faxing services; Telemarketing
agency; Direct marketing agency;
Response analysis bureau; Electronic
media; Internet services

Member of:
FEDMA; DMA (US); BDMV

HIGHWAY PRODUCTIONS
Bospleinlaan 3
av. de la Clairière 3
Brussels
1000

Belgium
Tel: +32 2 373 95 00
Fax: +32 2 373 95 01
Email: virginie-highway@skynet.be
Virginie Van Haeren

Services/Products:
Database services; Software supplier

Member of:
BDMV

HOLIDAY INNS OF BELGIUM NV
Woluwe Office Park 1
Rue Neerveld 101
Brussels
1200
Belgium
Tel: +32 2 777 55 11
Fax: +32 2 777 56 04
Email: peter.pal@basshotels.com
Web: www.holidayinn.com
Peter Pal, Brand Marketing Director

Services/Products:
Service bureau; Call centre services/
systems

Member of:
FEDMA

HOME SHOPPING
Waversesteenweg 1676, b.28
Chaussée de Wavre 1676, b.28
Brussels
1160
Belgium
Tel: +32 2 675 26 30
Fax: +32 2 675 19 39
Email: info@homeshopping.be
Web: www.homeshopping.be
Hervé Thomas

Services/Products:
Electronic media; Internet services;
Direct response media

Member of:
BDMV

IN CONCRETO
Wijstraat 44
Lede
9340
Belgium
Tel: +32 53 80 34 05
Fax: +32 53 80 08 12
Email: inconcreto@tornado.be
Jo De Bruyn

Services/Products:
Training/recruitment; Training/
recruitment; Direct marketing agency

Member of:
BDMV

INFOTRADE
Stationsstraat 30
bus 2
Groot-Bijgaarden
1702
Belgium
Tel: +32 2 481 82 83
Fax: +32 2 481 82 00
Email: infotrade@ift.be
Web: www.ift.be
Bob Bervoets

Services/Products:
List services; Telemarketing agency

Member of:
BDMV

INNOVATIVE MARKETING PARTNERS
Rue François Dive 23
Sambreville
5060
Belgium
Tel: +32 800 96 771
Email: info@innovativemarketing.be
Dominique Pequet

Services/Products:
Telemarketing agency; Service bureau

Member of:
BDMV

INTER-MAILING
IZ Blauwe Steen
Satenrozen
Kontich
2550
Belgium
Tel: +32 3 450 88 88
Fax: +32 3 450 88 77
Peter De Vester

Services/Products:
Fulfilment and sampling house;
Database services; Mailing/Faxing
services

Member of:
BDMV

INTERMEDIAIR VUM
Schepen Alfons Gossetlaan 32
Groot-Bijgaarden
1702
Belgium
Tel: +32 2 467 49 11
Fax: +32 2 467 49 49
Email: intermediair@intermediair.be
Web: http://www.intermediair.be
Miranda Schoemans

Services/Products:
List services; Database services

Member of:
BDMV

JONGEREN & MEDIA/JEUNES & MéDIAS
De Lescluzestraat 83
Berchem
2600
Belgium
Tel: +32 3 281 48 27
Fax: +32 3 281 48 29
Email: freddy-degroux@online.be
Web: http://www.jem.be
Freddy Degroux

Services/Products:
Direct marketing agency; Direct
response media

Member of:
BDMV

JOTTRAND
Rue de Stalle 65
Brussels
1180
Belgium
Tel: +32 2 3701777
Fax: +32 2 3323042
Email: marie.jottrand@sopres.be
Marie Jottrand, Managing Director

Services/Products:
List services; Database services;
Service bureau

Member of:
FEDMA; DMA (US); BDMV

KAAT VRANCKEN
Vaesstraat 3
Bree
3960
Belgium
Tel: +32 89 47 36 57
Fax: +32 89 47 37 39
Email: kaat.vrancken@ping.be
Kaat Vrancken

Services/Products:
Copy adaptation

Member of:
BDMV

KARAMBA/ DRAFTWORLDWIDE
Artanstraat
Rue Artan 116
Brussels
1030
Belgium
Tel: +32 2 743 1414
Fax: +32 2 743 1415
Email: marc.frederix@karambo.be
Marc Frederix, General Manager

Services/Products:
Advertising Agency; Catalogue
producer; Consultancy services; Direct
marketing agency; Sales promotion
agency

E-Services:
E-Marketing consultant; Website
design

Member of:
National DMA; SPCA; EFSP; BMMA

KETELS DIRECT MARKETING NV
Kapelanielaan 1–5
Industriezone
Temse
9140
Belgium
Tel: +32 3 710 07 11
Fax: +32 3 710 08 06
Email: info@ketels.be
Web: www.ketels.be
Roland Ketels, Directeur Général

Services/Products:
List services; Database services;
Response analysis bureau; Service
bureau

Member of:
FEDMA; DMA (US); BDMV

KI DIRECT COMMUNICATION GROUP
Kazernestraat 80–82
Rue de la Caserne 80–82
Brussels
1000
Belgium
Tel: +32 2 501 27 11
Fax: +32 2 514 25 35
Liesbeth Box

Services/Products:
Telemarketing agency; Training/
recruitment; Direct marketing agency

Member of:
BDMV

KONCEPT DIRECT
Sint Alexiusstraat 1
Mechelen
2800
Belgium
Tel: +32 15 20 82 07
Fax: +32 15 20 07 38
Email: koncept@tornado.be
Karin Bourgeois

Services/Products:
Direct marketing agency

Member of:
BDMV

LA POSTE
Centre Monnaie
Muntcentrum/Centre Monnaie
Brussels
1000
Belgium
Tel: +32 2 2262111
Fax: +32 2 2262291
Frans Job, Administrateur Directeur

Services/Products:
List services; Fulfilment and sampling
house; Private delivery services;
Mailing/Faxing services

Member of:
FEDMA; DMA (US)

LA REDOUTE SA
4 rue de Menin
7730 Estaimpuis
Belgium
Tel: +32 56 85 12 11
Web: www.redoute.be
Valerie Meteyer, Director

Services/Products:
Mail order company

Member of:
National DMA

LUON
Molendreef 37
Overijse
3090
Belgium
Tel: +32 2 686 00 10
Fax: +32 2 686 00 19
Email: info@luon.be
Web: www.luon.com
Luc Robijns

Services/Products:
Direct marketing agency; Electronic
media; Internet services

Member of:
BDMV

M.I.G. 149
Tombulaan
Avenue Tombu 4
Brussels
1200
Belgium
Tel: +32 2 770 98 10
Fax: +32 2 772 61 82
Greta Dumont

Services/Products:
Database services; Mailing/Faxing
services

Member of:
BDMV

MAGNESIUM
Waversesteenweg/Chaussée de Wavre
1517
Brussels
1160
Belgium
Tel: +32 2 679 04 60
Fax: +32 2 679 04 75
Email: magnesium@skynet.be
Web: www.magnesium.be
Pierre Portevin

Services/Products:
Direct marketing agency; Electronic
media; Internet services

Member of:
BDMV

MAIL PARTNERS
Industrieterrein D
Dooren 97
Merchtem
1785
Belgium
Tel: +32 52 37 50 51
Fax: +32 52 37 49 35
Email: mailpartners@ping.be
Willy Vanderstraeten

Services/Products:
Fulfilment and sampling house;
Database services; Mailing/Faxing
services

Member of:
BDMV

MAIL RUNNER
Haachtsesteenweg 1211
Chaussée de Haecht 1211
Brussels
1130
Belgium
Tel: +32 2 215 03 70
Fax: +32 2 215 11 47
Patricia Acke

Services/Products:
Mailing/Faxing services

Member of:
BDMV

MAILING COMPANY
Aalstersesteenweg 264
Ninove
9400
Belgium
Tel: +32 2 582 84 92
Fax: +32 2 582 84 94
Edwin Vander Meersch

Services/Products:
Mailing/Faxing services

Member of:
BDMV

MAILING HOUSE
Boomsesteenweg 31
Schelle
2627
Belgium
Tel: +32 3 888 03 69
Fax: +32 3 844 46 06
C. Cluytmans

Services/Products:
Mail order company; Mailing/Faxing
services; Personalisation; Print service
Labelling/envelope services; List
services

Member of:
BDMV

MANAGEMENT CENTRE
   EUROPE
Rue de l'Aqueduc, 118
Brussels
B-1050
Belgium
Tel: +32 2 543 21 00
Fax: +32 2 543 24 00
Liliane Van Cauwenbergh, Head of
   Marketing & Communications

Services/Products:
Electronic media; Internet services

Member of:
BDMV

MANUFAST
Zelliksesteenweg 65
Chaussée de Zellik 65
Brussels
1082
Belgium
Tel: +32 2 464 26 11
Fax: +32 2 464 26 60
Email: manufast@euronet.be
Thierry Leclercq

Services/Products:
Fulfilment and sampling house;
Mailing/Faxing services

Member of:
BDMV

MARIE-PIERRE
   VANDERVELDE
Stuivenbergbaan 150
Mechelen
2800
Belgium
Tel: +32 15 41 85 40
Fax: +32 15 42 01 90
Email: marie.pierre@skynet.be
Marie-Pierre Vandervelde

Services/Products:
Copy adaptation

Member of:
BDMV

**MARIEN & GYBELS
   TELESERVICES NV**
Uitbreidingstraat 392
Antwerp
2600
Belgium
Tel: +32 3 285 48 48
Fax: +32 3 285 48 49
Email: marien.gybels@mgts.be
David Gybels, Managing Partner

Services/Products:
Database services; Telemarketing
agency; Market research agency

Member of:
FEDMA; BDMV

MARK VAN BOGAERT
Weverslaan 7
Lokeren
B-9160
Belgium
Tel: +32 9 348 5908
Fax: +32 9 349 2305
Email: mark.vanbogaert@skynet.be
Mark Van Bogaert, Freelance DM
   Copy-writer

Services/Products:
Consultancy services; Training/
recruitment; Copy adaptation; Direct
marketing agency; Translation services

MARKé
Molenaarsstraat 111
Gent
9000
Belgium
Tel: +32 9 225 58 99
Fax: +32 9 266 14 14
Email: marke@unicall.be
Gino Delmotte

Services/Products:
Direct marketing agency

Member of:
BDMV

MARKETING PLAN
Tijmlaan
avenue du Thym 13
Brussels
1080
Belgium
Tel: +32 2 465 87 50
Fax: +32 2 465 92 67
Jacques Hutsemekers

Services/Products:
Direct marketing agency

Member of:
BDMV

MARKETING POWER
18 Avenue Vandenriesschelaan
Brussels
1150
Belgium
Tel: +32 2 761 1900
Fax: +32 2 775 8955
Email: c.stockman@mprc.be
Catherine Stockman, Manager

Services/Products:
Direct marketing agency; Sales
promotion agency

Member of:
National DMA

**MARTINE CONSTANT &
   PARTNERS**
Avenue Emile Digneffe 38
Liège
4000
Belgium
Tel: +32 4 229 37 07
Fax: +32 4 229 37 08
Web: martineconstant.com
Martine Constant

Services/Products:
Telemarketing agency

Member of:
BDMV

MAXIMAIL
Kapelanielaan 1–5
Temse
9140
Belgium
Tel: +32 3 710 07 22
Fax: +32 3 710 08 06
Web: www.ketels.be
Filip Vekemans

Services/Products:
Mailing/Faxing services; Labelling/
envelope services; Print services;
Private delivery services

Member of:
BDMV

MCCANN DIRECT
Terhulpsesteenweg 122
Chaussée de la Hulpe 122
Brussels
1000
Belgium
Tel: +32 2 674 15 74
Fax: +32 2 672 29 30
Joëlle Vandeville

Services/Products:
Direct marketing agency

**MCLS-MANAGEMENT
   CONSULTING LISTBROKING
   SERVICES**
Henri Dunantlaan 13
Schoten
2900
Belgium
Tel: +32 3 658 38 83
Fax: +32 3 658 38 82
Email: mcls@pophost.eunet.be
Frans Hendrickx, General manager

Services/Products:
List services; Direct marketing agency

Member of:
FEDMA; DMA (US); BDMV

MEDDENS/GUTENBERG
Scheutlaan
Av. de Scheut 141–143
Brussels
1070
Belgium
Tel: +32 2 522 79 25
Fax: +32 2 520 19 60
Email: meddens.gutenberg@skynet.be
Martin Diesveld

Services/Products:
Print services

Member of:
BDMV

**MEDIA PARTNERS BELGIUM
   (ROTO SMEETS)**
Pagodenlaan
Avenue des Pagodes 1–3
b.4
Brussels
1020
Belgium
Tel: +32 2 245 06 70
Fax: +32 2 345 06 90
Email: mediapartners-
   belgium@rotonet.rsdb.nl
Sanja Chen

Services/Products:
Print services

Member of:
BDMV

MEERSMAN & DE MUL
Marialei 29
Antwerpen
2018
Belgium
Tel: +32 3 239 99 00
Fax: +32 3 230 04 44
Email: frank.de.mul@skynet.be
Erik Meersman

Services/Products:
Direct marketing agency

Member of:
BDMV

MERCURIUS
Neeroeterenstra. 41
Opoeteren-Maaseik
3680
Belgium
Tel: +32 891 864265
Fax: +32 891 861777
Email: mercurius@planetinternet.be
Web: www.mercuriundm
Cat'rina Vandersteegen

Services/Products:
Advertising Agency; Consultancy
services; Copy adaptation; Direct
marketing agency; Creation and
production handling

Member of:
National DMA; Chamber of
Commerce; Union of Independent
Enterpreneurs Industry

**MOORE RESPONSE
MARKETING**
Industrielaan 21
Erembodegem
9320
Belgium
Tel: +32 53 85 09 11
Fax: +32 53 85 09 00
Email:
    ludc.demiddele@email.moore.com
Luc de Middeleer, Sales Manager

Services/Products:
Lettershop; Service bureau;
Personalisation; Print services

Member of:
FEDMA; BDMV

MORAEL
De Burburestraat 6–8
Antwerpen
2000
Belgium
Tel: +32 3 216 30 03
Fax: +32 3 216 42 16
Email: hugo.morael@bbdo.be
Hugo Morael

Services/Products:
Direct marketing agency

Member of:
BDMV

MP LIST
Avenue Louise 327
Louizalaan
Brussels

B-1050
Belgium
Tel: +32 2 643 4949
Fax: +32 2 646 6459
Email: info@mediaprisme.be
Marina Desmyter, Commercial
    Director

Services/Products:
List services; Database services; Direct
marketing agency; Consultancy
services

E-Services:
Email list provider

Member of:
FEDMA; National DMA; ABMD

MULTIMEDIA
Kattenberg 19
Antwerpen
2140
Belgium
Tel: +32 3 235 09 02
Fax: +32 3 235 58 98
Email: welcome@mutimedia.be
Anne-Catherine De Meulder

Services/Products:
Direct marketing agency

Member of:
BDMV

MULTIROTAMAILNV
Industriepark de Vliet 18
Bornen
2880
Belgium
Tel: +32 3 890 19 11
Fax: +32 3 889 54 13
Email: alexj@joos.be
Freddy Mertens, General Manager

Services/Products:
Lettershop; Mailing/Faxing services;
Personalisation; Print services

Member of:
FEDMA; BDMV

**NECKERMANN BUSINESS
SERVICES**
NeBus
Winninglaan 3
Temse
9140
Belgium
Tel: +32 3 710 82 97
Fax: +32 3 711 04 30
Email: nebus.be@innet.be
F. Cornelis

Services/Products:
Lettershop; Fulfilment and sampling
house; Database services

Member of:
BDMV

**NEWS PHONE BELGIUM TELE-
MARKETING**
Koningsstraat
Rue Royale 163
Brussels
1210
Belgium
Tel: +32 2 227 63 88
Fax: +32 2 219 78 02
Email: newsphone@skynet.be
Alexis Oppeel

Services/Products:
Telemarketing agency

Member of:
BDMV

ODEON MARKETING BVBA
Meerkostraat 14
WAARDAMME
8020
Belgium
Tel: +32 50 281567
Fax: +32 50 281568
Email: odeon@pi.be
Web: www.communicbraut.com
Kurt Van de Weghe

Services/Products:
Card pack manufacturer; Catalogue
producer; Publisher

OGILVY ONE WORLDWIDE
Boulevard de l'Imperatrice 13
1000 Brussels
Belgium
Tel: +32 2 545 65 65
Fax: +32 2 545 65 99
Email: mail.us@ogilvyone.be
Web: www.ogilvyone.be
Jan Van Aken, President

Services/Products:
Call centre services/systems;
Consultancy services; Database
services; Direct marketing agency;
Interactive media; Telemarketing
agency

E-Services:
E-Marketing consultant; Website
design; Online/e-marketing agency

Member of:
FEDMA; National DMA

OGILVYONE WORLDWIDE
13 Boulevard de L'Impératrice
Brussels
1000
Belgium
Tel: +32 2 545 65 65
Fax: +32 2 545 65 99

Email: jan.vanaken@ogilvyone.be
Web: www.ogilvyone.com
Jan Van Aken, Managing Director

Services/Products:
Database services; Telemarketing
agency; Direct marketing agency;
Design/graphics/clip art supplier;
Service bureau

E-Services:
Website design

Member of:
FEDMA; BDMV

OMNI-LEVEL
Peperstraat 76H
Wetteren
9230
Belgium
Tel: +32 9 365 73 29
Fax: +32 9 369 94 40
Email: sky34734@skynet.be
Inge Van de Velde

Services/Products:
Fulfilment and sampling house;
Mailing/Faxing services

ONCLINX-VIéRIN
Koninklijke Prinsstraat 84
Rue du Prince Royal 84
Brussels
1050
Belgium
Tel: +32 2 5+55 11 70 01
Fax: +32 2 511 97 80
Email: info@onclinx-vierin.be
Web: www.onclinx-vierin.be
Marc Onclinx

Services/Products:
Direct marketing agency; Electronic
media; Internet services

Member of:
BDMV

ORDA-B
Leuvensesteenweg 384
Sint-Stevens-Woluwe
1932
Belgium
Tel: +32 2 714 96 00
Fax: +32 2 725 42 62
Email: williampenninckx@ordab.com
Web: coms@ordab.com
William Penninckx, Sales & Marketing
    Manager

Services/Products:
Lettershop; Database services

Member of:
BDMV

ORDA-M
Sneeuwbeslaan 20
Antwerpen
2610
Belgium
Tel: +32 3 829 75 00
Fax: +32 3 828 63 66
Email: sales@orda-m.nl
Kris Vanhaverbeke

Services/Products:
Database services; Software supplier

Member of:
BDMV

PAPER PLANES
Kartuizersstraat 19 b 16
Brussels
B-1000
Belgium
Tel: +32 2 512 6125
Fax: +32 2 512 8250
Email: paperplanes@skynet.be
Mark De Geest, Manager

Services/Products:
Copy adaptation; Consultancy
services; Food 'afairs': communication
about and events with food

PARATEL
Medialaan 1
Vilvoorde
1800
Belgium
Tel: +32 2 255 32 95
Fax: +32 2 253 32 95
Email: paratel@paratel.be
Ann Lanhove

Services/Products:
Telemarketing agency

Member of:
BDMV

PATRICK FIERENS (QUOTES)
Dokter Haekstraat 57
Dendermonde
9200
Belgium
Tel: +32 52 20 03 37
Fax: +32 52 22 58 35
Email: patrick.fierens@skynet.be
Patrick Fierens

Services/Products:
Creative agency

Member of:
BDMV

PAUL VAN DAMME
Wijngaard 11
Rotselaar
3110

Belgium
Tel: +32 16 44 85 96
Fax: +32 16 44 08 75
Email: paul.van.damme@skynet.be
Paul Van Damme

Services/Products:
Copy adaptation

Member of:
BDMV

PAUWELS DIRECT MAIL
    SERVICES
Parklaan 22
Turnhout
2300
Belgium
Tel: +32 14 42 07 43
Fax: +32 14 42 62 66
Email: direct.mail@ping.be
André Pauwels

Services/Products:
Fulfilment and sampling house;
Mailing/Faxing services

Member of:
BDMV

PB PAPIER
Riverside Business Park
Internationalelaan/Bd International 55,
b. 33
Brussels
1070
Belgium
Tel: +32 2 529 85 11
Fax: +32 2 520 26 65
Email: info@pbpapier.com
Web: www.pbpapier.com
Gonda Craeninckx

Services/Products:
Labelling/envelope services

Member of:
BDMV

PDG COPYWRITING
Leeuwenhof 41
Gent
9031
Belgium
Tel: +32 9 226 62 33
Fax: +32 9 227 82 11
Anne De Rouck

Services/Products:
Copy adaptation

Member of:
BDMV

PHIBO COPYWRITING
Graslei 7
Gent
9000

Belgium
Tel: +32 9 266 05 70
Fax: +32 9 266 05 74
Email: phibo@compuserve.com
Philip Bossuyt

Services/Products:
Copy adaptation

Member of:
BDMV

PHILIPSE
Lozenweg 9
Hamont-Achel
3930
Belgium
Tel: +32 +55 11 445 843
Fax: +32 11 448 540
Johanne Philipse, Director

Services/Products:
Telemarketing agency; Call centre
services/systems

Member of:
FEDMA

PIN POINT MARKETING
Stallestraat 65
Rue de Stalle 65
Brussels
1180
Belgium
Tel: +32 2 370 17 34
Fax: +32 2 376 87 15
Email: benny-salaets@sopres.be
Benny Salaets

Services/Products:
List services

Member of:
BDMV

PREPOST A DIVISION OF
BELGIAN MAILHOUSE
Brucargo Building 709
Zaventem
1931
Belgium
Tel: +32 2 752 32 32
Fax: +32 2 752 32 15
Email: michelc@belgianmailhouse.be
Michel Cuypers

Services/Products:
Lettershop; Fulfilment and sampling
house; Mailing/Faxing services

Member of:
BDMV

PRODUCTION+
Kardinaal Mercierstraat 35
Rue Cardinal Mercier 35
Brussels
1000

Belgium
Tel: +32 2 545 66 66
Fax: +32 2 545 66 70
Email: benot.dumortier@pplus.be
Bo Grell

Services/Products:
Lettershop

Member of:
BDMV

PROXIMITY BRUSSELS
Engerstraat 99
Kortenberg
3071
Belgium
Tel: +32 2 756 0956
Fax: +32 2 756 0999
Email: daniel.schots@dmc.be
Web: www.dmc.be

Services/Products:
Call centre services/systems;
Consultancy services; Database
services; Direct marketing agency;
Service bureau; Software supplier

E-Services:
Email software

PSI DIRECT RESPONSE
Entrada 134
EB Amsterdam, Nederland
1096
Belgium
Tel: +31 20 495 38 38
Fax: +31 20 600 34 96
Email: psiadam@worldonline.nl
P. Van de Vorst

Services/Products:
Mailing/Faxing services

Member of:
BDMV

PSS DIALOGUE
Kwadenplasstraat 12
Destelbergen
9070
Belgium
Tel: +32 9 228 18 66
Fax: +32 9 229 18 55
Email: pss.dialogue@planetinternet.be
Web: http://home.planetinternet.be/pss
Patrick Serck

Services/Products:
List services; Telemarketing agency

Member of:
BDMV

RADIKAL COMMUNICATIONS
Villain XIII-straat 24
Brussel
1000

Belgium
Tel: +32 2 648 58 66
Fax: +32 2 640 92 36
Email: info@radikal.be
Web: http://www.radikal.be
Peter Van Hoesen

Services/Products:
Electronic media; Internet services

Member of:
BDMV

RECLAMEBUREAU DU BOSCH
Wouter Haecklaan 16, b. 29
Deurne (Antwerpen)
2100
Belgium
Tel: +32 3 366 +55 11 55
Fax: +32 3 366 14 64
Email: jpdb@dubosch.be
Web: http://WWW.dubosch.be
Jean-Pierre Du Bosch

Services/Products:
Direct marketing agency

Member of:
BDMV

RECLAMEBUREAU HAENEN &
CO
Katwilgweg 7B
Antwerpen
2050
Belgium
Tel: +32 3 254 03 80
Fax: +32 3 354 03 20
Email: haenen@pophost.eunet.be
Marie-Jeanne Slechten

Services/Products:
Direct marketing agency

Member of:
BDMV

RITA VANGINDERTAEL
Ingendaallaan 3
Alsemberg
1652
Belgium
Tel: +32 2 380 56 47
Fax: +32 2 380 95 26
Email: rita-
   vangindertael@thelink.lexnet.be
Rita Vangindertael

Services/Products:
Copy adaptation

Member of:
BDMV

ROULARTA MEDIA GROUP
Research Park Zellik
De Haak
Zellik

1731
Belgium
Tel: +32 2 467 56 11
Fax: +32 2 467 57 57
Walter Verrijcken

Services/Products:
Print services

Member of:
BDMV

ROUTAGE BARBIER
Zone Industrielle Crealys
Isnes - Gembloux
B 5032
Belgium
Tel: +32 81 56 82 77
Fax: +32 81 55 9495
Email: routage.barbier@skynet.be
Web: www.routatebarbier.com
Philippe Demanet, Director

Services/Products:
Direct marketing agency; Fulfilment
and sampling house; Labelling/
envelope services; List services;
Mailing/Faxing services;
Personalisation

E-Services:
Email list provider

Member of:
National DMA; BDMV

SAMPLING CAMPAIGNS
Putterie 22
Brussels
1000
Belgium
Tel: +32 2 545 66 33
Fax: +32 2 545 66 32
Email: ann.petitjean@wpp.be
Corinne Soyeur

Services/Products:
Direct marketing agency

Member of:
BDMV

SBN CONSUT
Place de Plancenoit 6
Placenoit (Lasne)
1380
Belgium
Tel: +32 2 633 56 82
Fax: +32 2 633 56 92
Email: sbn@pophost.eunet.be
Nicolas Verwimp

Services/Products:
Lettershop; Database services

Member of:
BDMV

SCHOBER
DIREKTMARKETING
Paul Gilsonlaan 45–49
Ruisbroek
1601
Belgium
Tel: +32 2 334 94 80
Fax: +32 2 377 38 86
Marc Loermans

Services/Products:
List services; Lettershop

Member of:
BDMV

SCOOT
Romeinsesteenweg 468
Grimbergen
1853
Belgium
Tel: +32 2 263 65 65
Fax: +32 2 263 65 66
Email: valerie.baugnee@scoot.be
Web: www.scoot.be
Valerie Baugnee

Services/Products:
Telemarketing agency

Member of:
BDMV

SCRIPT
Haanstraat
Rue du Coq 29
Brussels
1180
Belgium
Tel: +32 2 332 39 74
Fax: +32 2 332 39 76
Email: script@skynet.be
Web: www.script.be
Jean-Paul Mathelot

Services/Products:
Training/recruitment; Training/
recruitment; Direct marketing agency;
Copy adaptation; Electronic media;
Internet services

Member of:
BDMV

SEBECO-MEDIAPHONE
Casinoplein 25
Gent
9000
Belgium
Tel: +32 9 223 32 40
Fax: +32 9 233 34 78
Email: sebeco@pophost.eunet.be
Ingrid Walry

Services/Products:
Database services; Telemarketing
agency

Member of:
BDMV

SEDIP
Rue Ernest Milcamps 26
La Louvière
7100
Belgium
Tel: +32 64 21 15 36
Fax: +32 64 26 22 08
Email: info@sedip.be
Jean Hecquet

Services/Products:
List services

Member of:
BDMV

SEE YOU SOON
Rogierlaan
Avenue Rogier 18
Brussels
1030
Belgium
Tel: +32 2 247 11 00
Fax: +32 2 242 07 05
Email: leonardj@dmbb.com
Web: http://www.sys.be
Chris Aertsen

Services/Products:
Direct marketing agency; Electronic
media; Internet services

Member of:
BDMV

SHORT LIST
Kasteellaan
Av. du Chateau 25
Brussels
1080
Belgium
Tel: +32 2 414 70 74
Fax: +32 2 411 45 95
Liliane Loos

Services/Products:
Media buying agency

Member of:
BDMV

SITEL BENELUX
Woluwelaan 158
Diegem
1831
Belgium
Tel: +32 2 713 95 11
Fax: +32 2 713 95 00
Email: info@benelyxsitel.com
Web: http://www.sitel.com
Annick Vanmeulder

Services/Products:
Fulfilment and sampling house;
Telemarketing agency

Member of:
BDMV

SKIM BVBA
Aalstersesteenweg 264
Ninove
9400
Belgium
Tel: +32 54 300111
Fax: +32 54 338816
Email: info@skim.be
Web: www.skim.be

Services/Products:
Database services; Fulfilment and
sampling house; Mailing/Faxing
services; Personalisation; Print services

SOPRES BELGIUM SA
rue de Stalle, 65
Brussels
1180
Belgium
Tel: +32 2 370 17 11
Fax: +32 2 332 10 70
Email: lds@sopres.be
Web: www.sopres.be
Laurent De Schouwer, Administrateur
    Directeur General

Services/Products:
List services; Database services;
Response analysis bureau; Service
bureau

Member of:
FEDMA; BDMV

SPECTRON
Kapelanielaan 1–5
Temse
9140
Belgium
Tel: +32 3 710 07 10
Fax: +32 3 710 07 14
Web: www.ketels.be
Ronny Van Mele

Services/Products:
List services

Member of:
BDMV

SPEOS BELGIUM
    (PROM'IMPRIM INFOPOST)
Bollinckxstraat
Rue Bollinckx 32
Brussels
1070
Belgium
Tel: +32 2 558 02 00
Fax: +32 2 520 70 37

Email: info@promimprim.be
Stephan Raymakers

Services/Products:
Fulfilment and sampling house;
Database services; Mailing/Faxing
services; Labelling/envelope services;
Print services

Member of:
BDMV

SPIRAL
Albertlaan
Av. Albert 114
Brussels
1190
Belgium
Tel: +32 2 343 6688
Fax: +32 2 343 5365
Email: spiral@spiral.be
Francis Spinoy

Services/Products:
Print services; Mail order company

E-Services:
Online/e-marketing agency

TARGET ONE
Nijverheidslaan 1
Diest
3290
Belgium
Tel: +32 13 35 52 03
Fax: +32 13 32 31 93
Dany Abeloos

Services/Products:
Database services; Software supplier

Member of:
BDMV

TARGET POWER GROUP
Rue d'Abhooz Telebase 2
Zoning Industriel des Hauts Sarts
Herstal
4040
Belgium
Tel: +32 4 256 9711
Fax: +32 4 248 2972
Email: nevin.mert@targetpower.be
Web: www.target-power-group.com
Nevin Mert, Project Manager

Services/Products:
Call centre services/systems; Database
services; Design/graphics/clip art
supplier; Direct marketing agency;
Fulfilment and sampling house;
Telemarketing agency; Website
creation; Multimedia (CD-Rom
creation)

E-Services:
Email list provider

Member of:
FEDMA; DMA (US)

TASK FORCE
Oude Molenstraat
Vieille Rue de Moulin 85c
Brussels
1180
Belgium
Tel: +32 2 375 72 30
Fax: +32 2 375 67 85
Email: robin.taskf.@skynet.be
Web: Skynet.
Robin de Ripainsel

Services/Products:
Direct marketing agency; Response
analysis bureau

Member of:
BDMV

TELE- TECHNIC
St. Rumoldusstraat 70
Grimbergen
1851
Belgium
Tel: +32 2 270 10 86
Fax: +32 2 270 23 29
Colette Geeraerts

Services/Products:
Telemarketing agency; Training/
recruitment

Member of:
BDMV

TELEPERFORMANCE EURO
    CALL CENTER
62, Rue de la Fusée
Brussels
1130
Belgium
Tel: +32 2 702 20 11
Fax: +32 2 702 21 21
Email:
    steph.hermans@teleperformance.be
Steph Hermans

Services/Products:
Telemarketing agency; Call centre
services/systems; Market research
agency

Member of:
FEDMA

THE HOUSE OF MARKETING
Zoutwerf 9
Mechelen
B-2800
Belgium
Tel: +32 15 450550
Fax: +32 15 450551
Email: nicole@ime.be
Nicole Berx, Partner

Services/Products:
Consultancy services; (Direct) marketing interim management

E-Services:
E-Marketing consultant; Online/e-marketing agency

Member of:
National DMA; National Marketing Association

THE RING RING COMPANY
Bergstraat
Rue de la Montagne 52
Brussels
1000
Belgium
Tel: +32 2 502 85 00
Fax: +32 2 502 76 07
Email: mortelmans@ringring.be
Walter Mortelmans

Services/Products:
Telemarketing agency

Member of:
BDMV

TO THE POINT CONCEPT & COPYWRITING
Violetlaan 5
Gierle
2275
Belgium
Tel: +32 14 55 28 19
Fax: +32 14 55 60 89
Email: point@skynet.be
An Verplancke

Services/Products:
Copy adaptation

Member of:
BDMV

TRENDS TOP 30,000
Brasschaatsteenweg 308
Kalmthout
2920
Belgium
Tel: +32 3 620 02 11
Fax: +32 3 620 03 61
Herman Van Hove

Services/Products:
List services

Member of:
BDMV

UCAN DIRECT
Tommeltlaan 65
Mortsel
2640
Belgium
Tel: +32 3 443 9870
Fax: +32 3 443 9877

Email: ucan.direct@skynet.be

Services/Products:
Advertising Agency; Direct marketing agency; DM copy

ULLI BROMBERG
Generaal De Gaullelaan 18
Avenue Général De Gaulle 18
Brussels
1050
Belgium
Tel: +32 2 640 55 13
Fax: +32 2 640 62 45
Email: ulli.bromberg@staynet.be
Ulli Bromberg

Services/Products:
Creative agency

Member of:
BDMV

UPS EUROPE
Avenue Ariane 5
Brussels
1200
Belgium
Tel: +32 2 776 98 34
Fax: +32 2 776 96 98
Rainer Diemann

Services/Products:
Private delivery services

Member of:
FEDMA

V-PRINT
Boulevard Industriel 95
Mouscron
7700
Belgium
Tel: +32 56 85 91 91
Fax: +32 56 85 91 92
Email: vprint@mail.ccim.be
Carl Looyens

Services/Products:
Print services

Member of:
BDMV

VAN DURME & PARTNERS
Ter Voortlaan 91
Edegem
2650
Belgium
Tel: +32 3 449 89 70
Fax: +32 3 449 15 18
Email: yves.van.durme@skynet.be
Yves Van Durme

Services/Products:
Direct marketing agency

Member of:
BDMV

VENTURE OPPORTUNITY COMPANY
Bredabaan, 397
Brasschaat
2930
Belgium
Tel: +32 3 651 35 20
Fax: +32 3 651 80 56
Email: psk@skynet.be
Pieter S.K. de Jong

Services/Products:
Direct marketing agency

Member of:
FEDMA

VESA DIRECT
Ottergemsesteenweg 703
Gent
9000
Belgium
Tel: +32 9 220 21 69
Fax: +32 9 220 10 37
Email: vesabel@village.uunet.be
Edwin Van der Straeten

Services/Products:
Print services

Member of:
BDMV

VNU BUSINESS PUBLICATIONS NV
Avenue du Houx 42
Brussels
1170
Belgium
Tel: +32 2 678 16 11
Fax: +32 2 660 36 00
Email: avd@vnubp.com
Web: www.vnubp.com
Antoine van Diem, Directeur

Services/Products:
List services

Member of:
FEDMA

VULCAN
Minckelerstraat 62
Leuven
3000
Belgium
Tel: +32 16 29 19 60
Fax: +32 16 29 19 60
Email: info@vulcan.be
Luk De Becker

Services/Products:
Direct marketing agency

Member of:
BDMV

**WEGENER DIRECT
    MARKETING BELGIUM**
Vandenbusschestraat 14–16
Brussels
1030
Belgium
Tel: +32 2 245 9595
Fax: +32 2 245 6834
Gerard van Hoeven, Managing
    Director

Services/Products:
List services

Member of:
DMA (US)

WILLEM COLEN
Templehof 46
Gent
B-9000
Belgium
Tel: +32 475 539118
Fax: +32 9 233 1391
Email: willem.colen@skynet.be
Willem Colen, Freelance Copywriter &
    Translator

Services/Products:
Copy adaptation; Translation services;
Copywriting (in Flemish or Dutch) for
direct marketing or advetising

Member of:
National DMA

WILLY BRAILLARD SA/NV
Avenue Joseph Jongen 51A
Brussels
1180
Belgium
Tel: +32 2 332 36 60
Fax: +32 2 332 19 70
Email: info@braillard.be
Web: www.braillard.be
Willy Braillard, Administrateur
    Délégué

Services/Products:
List services; Service bureau

Member of:
FEDMA; DMA (US); BDMV

**WUNDERMAN CATO JOHNSON
    BELGIUM SA**
Dieweg 3b
Brussels
1180
Belgium
Tel: +32 2 3756181
Fax: +32 2 3720309
Email: henrirysermans@wcj.com
Henry Rysermans, Managing Director

Services/Products:
Database services; Telemarketing
agency; Direct marketing agency; Sales
promotion agency

Member of:
FEDMA; BDMV

X-TENSION
Koningin Astridlaan 402
Kraainem
B-1950
Belgium
Tel: +32 2 731 1294
Fax: +32 2 731 1294
Email: jwouters@skynet.be
Web: www.x-tension.be
Jan Wouters

Services/Products:
Art-direction & design

**YELLOWSTONE TT MAR
    DISTRIBUTION**
Brucargo Bldg 734
Zaventem
1931
Belgium
Tel: +32 2 751 96 86
Fax: +32 2 751 79 06
Roxane Quenon, Office Manager

Services/Products:
Mailing/Faxing services; Print services;
Private delivery services; Plastic wrap
facilities

Member of:
FEDMA

YES, WE DO
Steenbeukstraat
Rue du Charme 34
Brussels
1190
Belgium
Tel: +32 2 343 42 69
Fax: +32 2 345 70 32
Email: michele-
    breart@thelink.lexnet.be
Michèle Bréart

Services/Products:
Copy adaptation

Member of:
BDMV

SERVICES/PRODUCT LISTING

(Direct) marketing interim management
The House of Marketing

Advertising Agency
DDB Group Belgium
Direxions
Dvn – De Vissher & Van Nevel
Karamba/DraftWorldwide
Mercurius
Ucan Direct

Art-direction & design
X-tension

Call centre services/systems
Callcenter Institute
Callmetrics
EUROCALL.net
Holiday Inns Of Belgium NV
Ogilvy One Worldwide
Philipse
Proximity Brussels
Target Power Group
Teleperformance Euro Call Center

Card pack manufacturer
Odeon Marketing BVBA

Catalogue producer
DDB Group Belgium
Delabie S.A.
Karamba/DraftWorldwide
Odeon Marketing BVBA

Consultancy services
2-Sigma
Direct Marketing Know-How Institu
Direct Partner International
Direxions
Dvn – De Vissher & Van Nevel
Effects
Karamba/DraftWorldwide
Mark Van Bogaert
Mercurius
MP List
Ogilvy One Worldwide
Paper Planes
Proximity Brussels
The House of Marketing

Copy adaptation
Copywise
Copywriting Wouters
Frank Anthoni
Good For You
Kaat Vrancken
Marie-Pierre Vandervelde
Mark Van Bogaert
Mercurius
Paper Planes
Paul Van Damme
PDG Copywriting
PHIBO Copywriting
Rita Vangindertael
Script
To the Point Concept & Copywritin

Willem Colen
Yes, we do

Copywriting (in Flemish or Dutch) for direct marketing or advetising
Willem Colen

Creation and production handling
Mercurius

Creative agency
Good For You
Patrick Fierens (Quotes)
Ulli Bromberg

DM copy
Ucan Direct

Database services
Bridge Marketing
CPP-Communicatie Pers Productie - Communication Presse Production
DataScope
Direxions
Euro DB SA
Experian Belgium
ExpertList
Fast Movers/Promo-Post
Fidelity Direct Marketing
Graphic Groups Sparks
Graydon Belgium, div.
Highway Productions
Inter-Mailing
Intermediair VUM
Jottrand
Ketels Direct Marketing NV
M.I.G. 149
Mail Partners
Marien & Gybels Teleservices NV
MP List
Neckermann Business Services
Ogilvy One Worldwide
Ogilvyone Worldwide
Orda-B
Orda-M
Proximity Brussels
SBN Consut
Sebeco-Mediaphone
Skim bvba
Sopres Belgium SA
SPEOS Belgium (Prom'Imprim Infopost)
Target One
Target Power Group
Wunderman Cato Johnson Belgium SA

Design/graphics/clip art supplier
Ogilvyone Worldwide
Target Power Group

Direct marketing agency
4ReAL
AB-Creations & Communications
ABC & D, Boomerang Collard & Detaeye, Direct Communication
Amazing Advertising
Artex
B & C
B.I.C.
BBDO/Direct
Bebop Direct Creactivities
Belgian DMA
Caribou Creative Business
Carlson Marketing Group
Communication Center
Consultants In Sports (CIS)
Copywise
CPP-Communicatie Pers Productie - Communication Presse Production
DDB Group Belgium
De Witte & Co
Denis Bodden Sa
Diabol'o
Direct Creations
Direct Marketing Atelier
Direxions
DSC - Direct Social Communications
Dvn – De Vissher & Van Nevel
Effects
Fast Communication Group
FCB
Feed Back
Fidelity Direct Marketing
Graphic Groups Sparks
Grey Direct
Harte-Hanks Response Management Europe
In Concreto
Jongeren & Media/Jeunes & Médias
Karamba/DraftWorldwide
KI Direct Communication Group
Koncept Direct
Luon
Magnesium
Mark Van Bogaert
Marké
Marketing Plan
Marketing Power
McCann Direct
Mcls-Management Consulting Listbroking Services
Meersman & De Mul
Mercurius
Morael
MP List
Multimedia
Ogilvy One Worldwide
Ogilvyone Worldwide
Onclinx-Viérin
Proximity Brussels
Reclamebureau Du Bosch
Reclamebureau Haenen & Co
Routage Barbier

Sampling Campaigns
Script
See You Soon
Target Power Group
Task Force
Ucan Direct
Van Durme & Partners
Venture Opportunity Company
Vulcan
Wunderman Cato Johnson Belgium SA

Direct response media
Home Shopping
Jongeren & Media/Jeunes & Médias

Electronic media
AB-Creations & Communications
Direxions
Fast Communication Group
Harte-Hanks Response Management Europe
Home Shopping
Luon
Magnesium
Management Centre Europe
Onclinx-Viérin
Radikal Communications
Script
See You Soon

Food 'afairs': communication about and events with food
Paper Planes

Fulfilment and sampling house
Denis Bodden Sa
DHU Communication
Fast Movers/Promo-Post
Fidelity Direct Marketing
Harte-Hanks Response Management Europe
Inter-Mailing
La Poste
Mail Partners
Manufast
Neckermann Business Services
Omni-Level
Pauwels Direct Mail Services
Prepost a division of Belgian Mailhouse
Routage Barbier
Sitel Benelux
Skim bvba
SPEOS Belgium (Prom'Imprim Infopost)
Target Power Group

Fully integrated communication agency
DDB Group Belgium

Interactive media
Direxions
Ogilvy One Worldwide

Internet services
AB-Creations & Communications
Fast Communication Group
Harte-Hanks Response Management
    Europe
Home Shopping
Luon
Magnesium
Management Centre Europe
Onclinx-Viérin
Radikal Communications
Script
See You Soon

Labelling/envelope services
Binpac
Bongs Enveltec
Drukkerij Strobbe
Elep
Envelbag
Mailing House
MaxiMail
PB Papier
Routage Barbier
SPEOS Belgium (Prom'Imprim
    Infopost)

Legal services
Association Gregoire

Lettershop
Belgian Mailhouse NV
Moore Response Marketing
MultirotamailNV
Neckermann Business Services
Orda-B
Prepost a division of Belgian Mailhouse
Production+
SBN Consut
Schober Direktmarketing

List services
Consultants In Sports (CIS)
DataScope
Denis Bodden Sa
Dun & Bradstreet
Euro DB SA
ExpertList
Family Service (NDPK/SNPME)
Fidelity Direct Marketing
Graydon Belgium, div.
Infotrade
Intermediair VUM
Jottrand
Ketels Direct Marketing NV
La Poste
Mailing House
Mcls-Management Consulting
    Listbroking Services

MP List
Pin Point Marketing
PSS Dialogue
Routage Barbier
Schober Direktmarketing
Sedip
Sopres Belgium SA
Spectron
Trends Top 30,000
Vnu Business Publications NV
Wegener Direct Marketing Belgium
Willy Braillard SA/NV

Mail order company
La Redoute SA
Mailing House
Spiral

Mailing/Faxing services
Belgian Mailhouse NV
Bruyneel
DistriMail
DMA
Fidelity Direct Marketing
Hageman Verpakkers België
Harte-Hanks Response Management
    Europe
Inter-Mailing
La Poste
M.I.G. 149
Mail Partners
Mail Runner
Mailing Company
Mailing House
Manufast
MaxiMail
MultirotamailNV
Omni-Level
Pauwels Direct Mail Services
Prepost a division of Belgian Mailhouse
PSI Direct Response
Routage Barbier
Skim bvba
SPEOS Belgium (Prom'Imprim
    Infopost)
Yellowstone Tt Mar Distribution

Market research agency
BBDO/Direct
Marien & Gybels Teleservices NV
Teleperformance Euro Call Center

Media buying agency
Bebop Direct Creactivities
DDB Group Belgium
Short List

Multimedia (CD-Rom creation)
Target Power Group

NGO promoting and supporting advertising self-regulation
EASA - European Advertising
    Standards Alliance

Personalisation
Belgian Mailhouse NV
Mailing House
Moore Response Marketing
MultirotamailNV
Routage Barbier
Skim bvba

Plastic wrap facilities
Yellowstone Tt Mar Distribution

Print services
Bruyneel
Crea
Delabie S.A.
Denis Bodden Sa
Direct Production
Drukkerij De Coker
Drukkerij Strobbe
Graphic Groups Sparks
Mailing House
MaxiMail
Meddens/Gutenberg
Media Partners Belgium (Roto
    Smeets)
Moore Response Marketing
MultirotamailNV
Roularta Media Group
Skim bvba
SPEOS Belgium (Prom'Imprim
    Infopost)
Spiral
V-Print
Vesa Direct
Yellowstone Tt Mar Distribution

Private delivery services
La Poste
MaxiMail
Ups Europe
Yellowstone Tt Mar Distribution

Publisher
Odeon Marketing BVBA

Response analysis bureau
DataScope
DHU Communication
Experian Belgium
ExpertList
Harte-Hanks Response Management
    Europe
Ketels Direct Marketing NV
Sopres Belgium SA
Task Force

Sales promotion agency
DDB Group Belgium
Dvn – De Vissher & Van Nevel
EUROCALL.net
Karamba/DraftWorldwide
Marketing Power
Wunderman Cato Johnson Belgium SA

Service bureau
Bebop Direct Creactivities
Denis Bodden Sa
Holiday Inns Of Belgium NV
Innovative Marketing Partners
Jottrand
Ketels Direct Marketing NV
Moore Response Marketing
Ogilvyone Worldwide
Proximity Brussels
Sopres Belgium SA
Willy Braillard SA/NV

Software supplier
Dacoteam
DataScope
Experian Belgium
Highway Productions
Orda-M
Proximity Brussels
Target One

Telemarketing agency
Bridge Marketing
Brucall
Callcenter Institute
Callmetrics
Communication Center
Diract
Direct Call

EUROCALL.net
Fillad
Harte-Hanks Response Management
  Europe
Infotrade
Innovative Marketing Partners
KI Direct Communication Group
Marien & Gybels Teleservices NV
Martine Constant & Partners
News Phone Belgium Tele-Marketing
Ogilvy One Worldwide
Ogilvyone Worldwide
Paratel
Philipse
PSS Dialogue
Scoot
Sebeco-Mediaphone
Sitel Benelux
Target Power Group
Tele- Technic
Teleperformance Euro Call Center
The Ring Ring Company
Wunderman Cato Johnson Belgium SA

Training/recruitment
Callcenter Institute
Direct Marketing Know-How Institute
Fillad
In Concreto
KI Direct Communication Group
Mark Van Bogaert
Script
Tele- Technic

Translation services
André Winandy Communication
Mark Van Bogaert
Willem Colen

Website creation
Target Power Group

E-SERVICES

E-Marketing consultant
2-Sigma
DDB Group Belgium
Effects
Karamba/DraftWorldwide
Ogilvy One Worldwide
The House of Marketing

Email list provider
MP List
Routage Barbier
Target Power Group

Email software
Proximity Brussels

Online/e-marketing agency
Direxions
Ogilvy One Worldwide
Spiral
The House of Marketing

Website design
Direxions
Effects
Karamba/DraftWorldwide
Ogilvy One Worldwide
Ogilvyone Worldwide

DENMARK

Population: 5.3million
Capital: Copenhagen
Language: Danish

GDP: $169 billion
GDP per capita: $32,250
Inflation: 2.2 per cent

Currency: Danish Krone (DKr) = 100 ore
Exchange rate: DKr6.91 : $1 (DKr7.43 : 1 euro)

Time: GMT +1 hour

OVERVIEW

Denmark is a small country in geographical terms, dwarfed in land area by its northern Scandinavian neighbours, and housing one of the smallest European populations. It has a robust and diverse economy, however, and the people of Denmark enjoy one of the highest standards of living in the world: GDP per capita is ranked fifth in the world, and in Europe is exceeded only by Switzerland and Luxembourg.

Denmark has a highly developed and efficient infrastructure, although direct marketing activity continues to hover in the middle of the European spectrum, with Danes receiving an average of 50 direct mailings per person in 1994. The market has grown in recent years, but its full potential must be limited by the legislative environment which forbids the sale of consumer address lists.

Post Denmark does however report a continuing high level of unaddressed mailings, totalling 1.3 billion items in 1994. This exceeds the volume of domestic letters by over 8 per cent, and is an advertising medium currently finding favour with large new groups of users from the retail sector.

LANGUAGE AND CULTURAL CONSIDERATIONS

When launching a DM campaign in Denmark, it is necessary to take local factors into consideration. It will always be an advantage to send one's message in Danish. English, however, is acceptable in certain areas, as a large proportion of the Danish population understands and speaks English.

For reasons of trust, it is always a good idea to have a local sender address for sales through mail order.

LEGISLATION AND CONSUMER PROTECTION

In terms of legislation, there are three major laws affecting the DM industry: the Register Law; the Marketing Law; the Door-to-Door Sales Law.

The Register Law specifies, among other things, what types of customer information may be kept in private databases. The Register Law forbids the sale of private addresses and in Denmark it is therefore only possible to sell company addresses. The Marketing Law includes limits on the uses of discount coupons.

Finally the Door-to-Door Sales Law legislates that it is only legal to contact private households directly via telemarketing for the purpose of selling newspapers, magazines and insurance.

THE DIRECT MARKETING ASSOCIATION

Name: Dansk Markedsførings Forbund
               (Danish Marketing Association/DMA)
Address: Store Strandstræde 21/-2th, DK-1255 Copenhagen K.
Tel: +45 33 11 8787
Fax: +45 33 11 9797
Director: Steen Læssøe
Contact: Ms Pia Tousig
Total staff: 6
Members: 6500

Facilities for overseas users of direct mail

The Danish Marketing Association (DMA) is a nationwide organization with approximately 6500 individual members. There are no corporate members.The DMA is an educational and social forum for all sectors of the marketing industry, and is not set up uniquely with the needs of direct marketers in mind.

The DMA is built around 15 committees with a board of approximately 10 people, representing the various interest groups in the industry (advertising, retail, market research, marketing management, sales, service management, industrial marketing, business to business, direct marketing etc). Central facilities are rudimentary – the DMA has no library, and no on-line information service. A regular newsletter is published, but catering as it does to a wide marketing audience, it is ulikely to provide the specialized information needed by direct marketers.

The DMA does not offer to help with legal advice, nor will it help prospective mailers to find venture partners in the local market. It does, however, provide the essential service of helping mailers to choose between a list of vetter and approved suppliers. For the most informed opinion on local suppliers, direct marketers should approach the board of the direct marketing club via the numbers given in this section. In its role as an educational forum, the asociation hosts a wide variety of industry seminars, meetings and conferences. Given that DMA membership is not open to foreign companies, however, these events will cater for the local Danish market, and may hold only limited value for overseas companies.

The DMA does not offer many of the services of a specialized direct marketing group, but it remains a highly efficient, friendly organization. Turnaround times on requests for information are hours, rather than weeks.

POSTAL SERVICES

Post Denmark is a state-owned, profit-making organization run on business principles. It offers a range of services useful to a direct marketer, including:

- *Direct Marketing Consultancy*: For business-to-business marketing, Post Denmark can offer access to their large address database, making it possible to buy both Danish and Scandinavian addresses for an exact target group. On the consumer market, they can distribute unaddressed printed matter, making it possible to come into contact with Denmark's five million private homes;

- *Fulfilment*: If you need letters printed, Post Denmark can both print and insert them in envelopes or plastic foil. Postage stamping is also part of the service. The Post Office is also a specialist in electronic mail;

- *Distribution of packages and freight*: Post Denmark can deliver packages of up to 50 kilos both nationally and internationally. In Scandinavia they also deliver freight of up to 750 kilos and offer a Consignment Service for companies that send large numbers of letters and packages to Scandinavia and Germany

For more information contact:

Post Denmark
Headquarters
Tietgensgade, 37
Dk - 1566 Copenhagen V
Denmark

Tel: +45 3375 4007
Fax: +45 3375 4007
Website: www.postdanmark.dk

PROVIDERS OF DM AND E-M SERVICES

AHEAD A/S
Kanonbadsvej 10
1433
Copenhagen K
Denmark
Tel: +45 32 64 82 00
Fax: +45 32 64 82 82
Email: tromholt@ahead.dk
Web: www.ahead.dk
Steen Tromholt, Managing Director

Services/Products:
Database services; Direct marketing
agency; Consultancy services; Design/
graphics/clip art supplier; Electronic
media

E-Services:
Website design

Member of:
FEDMA

AMMIRATI PURIS LINTAS
Kobmagergade 60
1150
Copenhagen K
Denmark
Tel: +45 33 18 71 00
Fax: +45 33 18 71 01

Services/Products:
Advertising Agency

BONNIER PUBLICATIONS A/S
Strandboulevarden 130
DK-2100
Copenhagen 0
Denmark
Tel: +45 39 29 55 00
Fax: +45 39 29 09 44
Tage Benner, Marketing Director

Services/Products:
Publisher

CALL CENTRE EUROPE A/S
Ellegaardvej 23a
6400
Sonderborg
Denmark
Tel: +45 74 18 18 18
Fax: +45 74 18 18 19
Christian Egenfeldt, Sales Manager

Services/Products:
Telemarketing agency

Member of:
DMA (US)

CAROE'S POSTORDRE
Engelsholmbej #33
8900
Randers
Denmark
Tel: +45 86 44 86 44
Fax: +45 86 44 86 00
Michael Caroe, President

Services/Products:
Advertising Agency; Direct marketing
agency

Member of:
DMA (US)

CHEFKONSULTENT
Bergsoe 4 Gruppen
Strandvejen 724
Klampenborg, 2930
Klampenborg
Denmark
Tel: +45 31 63 15 44
Fax: +45 31 63 14 22

Services/Products:
Advertising Agency

**DANISH MARKETING
ASSOCIATION**
Store Strandstræde 21
2th DK-1255
Copenhagen K
Denmark
Tel: +45 33 11 87 87
Fax: +45 33 11 97 97
Web: Sheen Losseoe
Director, Direct marketing association

**DANSK
ANNONCORFORFORENING**
Laederstraede 32–34
DK-1201
Copenhagen K
Denmark
Tel: +45 33 14 43 46
Fax: +45 33 14 05 03
Bent Vindelin Pedersen, Director

Member of:
Danish Advertising Association

**DANSK
POSTORDREFORENING**
Sundkrogskaj 14
DK-2100
Copenhagen
Denmark
Tel: +45 35 43 40 07
Fax: +45 31 23 70 42
Erik Ryge, Secretary General

Services/Products:
Media buying agency

**DUN & BRADSTREET
DANMARK A/S**
Egegaardsvej 39
2610
Rodovre
Denmark
Tel: +45 36 709 000
Fax: +45 36 704 505
Email: lauersen.hanne@dnb.com
Web: www.dbdanmark.dk
Hanne Lauersen, Cross Border
Manager

Services/Products:
List services; Database services;
Mailing/Faxing services; Direct
marketing agency

Member of:
FEDMA

FORBRUGER-KONTAKT A/S
11–13 Formervangen
2600
Glostrup
Denmark
Tel: +45 43 43 99 00
Fax: +45 43 43 90 22
Steen Andersen

Services/Products:
Fulfilment and sampling house;
Mailing/Faxing services; Response
analysis bureau; Private delivery
services

Member of:
FEDMA

**HOLCK-ANDERSEN & TYGE
SöRENSEN**
Nyhavn 6
1051
Copenhagen K
Denmark
Tel: +45 33 11 93 13
Fax: +45 33 32 08 48
Email: sha@adv-nyhavn.dk
Sören Holck-Andersen

Services/Products:
Legal services

Member of:
FEDMA

KLAUSEN & PARTNERS
Fredericiagade 13
DK-1310
Copenhagen
Denmark
Tel: +45 33 93 70 08
Fax: +45 33 93 92 99
Peter Svendsen, Managing Director

Services/Products:
Direct marketing agency

KRAKS FORLAG A/S
Virumgaardsvej 21
2830
Virum
Denmark
Tel: +45 45 95 65 00
Fax: +45 45 95 64 64
Email: krak@www.krak.dk
Web: www.krak.dk.b2b.dk
Carsten Engsig, Manager

Services/Products:
List services; Lettershop; Direct
marketing agency

Member of:
FEDMA

KTAS FORLAG A/S, BE
Rodovrevej 241
DK-2610
Rodovre
Denmark
Tel: +45 36 36 36 36
Fax: +45 36 36 76 71
Flemming Geel Weirsoe, Marketing
   Manager

Services/Products:
List services; Database services;
Mailing/Faxing services

MCCANN FOKUS
Oster Faelled Torv 17b
2100
Copenhagen
Denmark
Tel: +45 35 27 01 16
Fax: +45 35 27 01 05
Email: kenneth-petersen@mccann.dk
Kenneth Petersen, Account Director

Services/Products:
Advertising Agency; Direct marketing
agency

Member of:
FEDMA

OGILVY & MATHER DIRECT A/S
Martinsvej 7
Frederiksberg
Copenhagen, DK-1926
Copenhagen
Denmark
Tel: +45 35 28 88 88
Fax: +45 35 28 88 80
Karen Ostergaurd, Managing Director

Services/Products:
Direct marketing agency

Member of:
DMA (US)

**POST DENMARK SALES AND
   MARKETING**
Tietgensgade 37
Hovedkontoret
1566
Copenhagen V
Denmark
Tel: +45 33 75 44 75
Fax: +45 33 75 47 03
Soren-Michael Pihl, Manager, Letter
   Division

Services/Products:
Mailing/Faxing services

Member of:
FEDMA

**SAS DISTRIBUTION/ROYAL
   VIKING POST**
Amager Strandvej 400
DK-2770
Kastrup
Denmark
Tel: +45 32 32 37 89
Fax: +45 32 52 38 94
Per Sommer, Sales & Marketing
   Support

Services/Products:
Lettershop; Fulfilment and sampling
house; Mailing/Faxing services

SCANDIRECT A/S
Firskovvej 4
2800
Lyngby
Denmark
Tel: +45 45 93 22 66
Fax: +45 45 93 22 10
Email: scandirect@vipnet.dk
Peter Nyman, Managing Director

Services/Products:
Database services; Direct marketing
agency; Consultancy services;
Electronic media

E-Services:
Website design

Member of:
FEDMA; DMA (US)

**SDPS – SCANDINAVIAN
   DISTRIBUTION & POSTAL
   SERVICE**
Prags Boulevard 55a
2300
Copenhagens
Denmark
Tel: +45 77 32 70 20
Fax: +45 77 32 70 70
Email: chp@sdps.dk
Web: www.sdps.dk
Claus H. Pedersen, Business
   Development Manager

Services/Products:
Lettershop; Database services;
Mailing/Faxing services; Service
bureau; Print services

Member of:
FEDMA

SERVICES/PRODUCT LISTING

Advertising Agency
Ammirati Puris Lintas
Caroe's Postordre
Chefkonsultent
Mccann Fokus

Consultancy services
Ahead A/S
Scandirect A/S

Database services
Ahead A/S
Dun & Bradstreet Danmark A/S
KTAS Forlag A/S, BE
Scandirect A/S
Sdps – Scandinavian Distribution &
   Postal Service

**Design/graphics/clip art
   supplier**
Ahead A/S

Direct marketing agency
Ahead A/S
Caroe's Postordre
Dun & Bradstreet Danmark A/S
Klausen & Partners
Kraks Forlag A/S
Mccann Fokus
Ogilvy & Mather Direct A/S
Scandirect A/S

Electronic media
Ahead A/S
Scandirect A/S

Fulfilment and sampling house
Forbruger-Kontakt A/S
SAS Distribution/Royal Viking Post

Legal services
Holck-Andersen & Tyge Sörensen

Lettershop
Kraks Forlag A/S
SAS Distribution/Royal Viking Post
Sdps – Scandinavian Distribution &
   Postal Service

List services
Dun & Bradstreet Danmark A/S
Kraks Forlag A/S
KTAS Forlag A/S, BE

Mailing/Faxing services
Dun & Bradstreet Danmark A/S
Forbruger-Kontakt A/S
KTAS Forlag A/S, BE
Post Denmark Sales And Marketing
SAS Distribution/Royal Viking Post
Sdps – Scandinavian Distribution &
    Postal Service

Media buying agency
Dansk Postordreforening

Print services
Sdps – Scandinavian Distribution &
    Postal Service

Private delivery services
Forbruger-Kontakt A/S

Publisher
Bonnier Publications A/S

Response analysis bureau
Forbruger-Kontakt A/S

Service bureau
Sdps – Scandinavian Distribution &
    Postal Service

Telemarketing agency
Call Centre Europe A/S

E-SERVICES

Website design
Ahead A/S
Scandirect A/S

FINLAND

Population: 5.1 million
Capital: Helsinki
Languages: Finnish (94 per cent), Swedish (6 per cent)
GDP: $119 billion
GDP per capita: $23,230
Inflation: 0.9 per cent
Currency: Markka (FIM) = 100 penni
Exchange rate: FIM5.53 : $1 (FIM5.95 : 1 euro)
Time: GMT +2 hours

OVERVIEW

Finland is an advanced direct marketing country with all the infrastructures needed for top-level DM. The volume of addressed direct mail has grown considerably throughout the 1990s with 4 per cent growth in 1996–97. Direct mail advertising now accounts for approximately 30 per cent of total advertising and sales promotion expenditure in Finland.

The market still shows room for further growth. However, the nature of data protection legislation seriously limits the possibilities of targeting, and consumer protection is closely and efficiently controlled. This does not imply that the market cannot reach its full potential, but in order to avoid mistakes a potential mailer should research thoroughly and consider carrying out planning and implementation in Finland.

Media

Finns are heavy users of newspapers and magazines, which are sold on a subscription basis to both homes and offices. There are more than 100 daily newspapers, of which 12 are published in Swedish. *Helsingin Sanomat* has the widest distribution, reaching 23 per cent of all Finnish households.

Density per capita of mobile phones and telephone connections in office and domestic use is among the highest in Europe; Finnish households also have one of the highest levels of ownership of home computers in Europe. Finland is the leading European country in per capita use of the Internet.

Lists and databases

Official population and vehicle register data can be used in mailings to potential customers.

The civil register contains all basic information on Finnish citizens and foreigners living permanently in Finland; background information is available for profiling. The list is owned by The Population Register Centre, and sales enquiries can be directed to:

Tieto Corporation
PO Box 406
02101 ESPOO
Tel: +358 9 4571 Fax: +358 9 4573 756
website: www.tieto.com

The Vehicle Register can also be used as an address source, and contains data on all vehicles registered in Finland. It is owned by The Vehicle Registration Centre, and sales enquiries can be made to the address above. The register contains both owner and possessor data, and technical vehicle information, with various options for profiling.

There are in addition some 200 consumer mailing lists available, as well as the Acorn geodemographic system. Finnish data protection legislation stipulates that only consumers themselves can provide information for lifestyle databases; consumer targeting is therefore unlikely to grow much past its current level. As a result, companies tend to invest more in their own databases, and there is a lively market for list swapping.

Business lists are available, with standard segmentation criteria, although the quality of these lists can be disappointing.

LANGUAGE AND CULTURAL CONSIDERATIONS

With 94 per cent of the population speaking Finnish, this is the obvious language in which to conduct a DM campaign. However, with six per cent of the population speaking Swedish, and crossover with other Scandinavian languages, there is definitely room to consider a pan-Scandinavian campaign.

When invited to a Finnish home for the first time, it is usual to give flowers. Punctuality is important. Business meetings may sometimes be held in saunas.

LEGISLATION AND CONSUMER PROTECTION

Data protection is a sensitive issue in Finland, and full advice should be sought from the Data Protection Ombudsman (address at the end of this section).

The Finnish Direct Marketing Association (FDMA) holds a Robinson list, against which all databases must be run. In December 1998 this list contained 29,960 households (1.1 per cent of all Finnish households). In addition, unaddressed mailshots must not be delivered to households displaying a 'No advertising material' sticker; these are attached to about 2 per cent of mailboxes. The FDMA started a TeleRobinson service in 1994. In December 1998 the list contained 60,000 people (1.1 per cent of the population). Another code, *The Rules for Electronic Consumer Trade*, was drawn up to set a self-regulative code for the increasing use of electronic sales.

Direct Selling Industry Code of Conduct is a self-regulative code to be observed by all FDMA Direct Selling member companies. All above mentioned codes are available free of charge from the FDMA office.

Consumer protection legislation is strict and about 200 people are employed in controlling compliance. 1998 saw the implementation of the EU Data Protection Directive into Finnish legislation.

The FDMA has compiled a code of ethics called *The Rules of Fair Play*, covering all legislation regulating consumer and data protection. This is a 22-page document for companies approaching consumers, and can also be obtained from the FDMA free of charge.

For additional information, contact:

The Office of Data Protection Ombudsman
PO Box 315
FIN-00181 Helsinki
Tel: +358 9 18 251   Fax: +358 9 1825 7835
website: www.tietosuoja.fi

The Office of Consumer Protection Ombudsman
PO Box 306
FIN-00531 Helsinki
Tel: +358 9 77 261   Fax +358 9 7530 357

THE DIRECT MARKETING ASSOCIATION

Name:	Suomen Suoramarkkinointiliitto ry. (The Finnish Direct Marketing Association)
Address:	Lönnrotinkatu 11 A, FIN-00120 Helsinki
Tel:	+358 9 2287 7400
Fax:	+358 9 6121 039
Email:	sakke@ssml-fdma.fi
Website:	www.ssml-fdma.fi
Year founded:	1974
Chairman:	Mr. Timo Saini, Managing Director of Reader's Digest Nordic
Total staff:	4
Contact:	Mr. Sakari Virtanen, Managing Director, email: sakke@ssml-fdma.fi, direct phone: +358 9 2287 7401
Members:	236

DM and Ad agencies	33	Printers	17
List brokers	14	Telemarketing agencies	24
Mailing houses	22	DM consultants	13
Mail order companies	31	Database agencies	12

Others:

Non profit organizations	6	Banking and finance	16
Direct selling companies	24	Publishers	24

Facilities for overseas users of direct mail

Membership: overseas companies can join the association (annual fee ranging from EUR 535 to EUR 4.170, depending on company's DM turnover, and personnel; affiliation fee is always half of the annual fee) and they are required to abide by the association's Rules for Fair Play, which is a code of ethics. The Rules is essential reading for anyone considering advertising, sales or marketing activities in the country. Additional codes include: *Direct Selling Industry Code of Conduct* and *Rules for Electronic Consumer Trade*. All mentioned codes (printed in Finnish) can be obtained from the FDMA. In Finland there are authorities who keep track on companies' following legislation, therefore familiarization in these issues is essential.

Newsletter: the FDMA produces a newsletter four times a year and a yearbook is published annually in January. The yearbook includes articles for DM novices, as well as professional reports for advanced direct marketers. It also contains information on members' companies and lists of key persons and companies in the Finnish DM industry and the services they provide. The yearbook's circulation is 15,000 copies and it contains 230 pages. Both the newsletter and the yearbook are printed in Finnish.

Library: the FDMA library contains about 100 books and research reports on Finnish DM and some press cuttings from the current and previous year. The library is open to member companies, staff and students.

On-line information service: website www.ssml-fdma.fi provides basic information on DM and links to member companies. All member companies are entitled to ask for advice from the association's legal expert via e-mail.

Legal advice: the Rules for Fair Play contain extensive information regarding Consumer and Data protection. The FDMA has a legal expert, giving advice to member companies on marketing related legal issues. Non-members are guided to other legal advisers, specialized in marketing legislation.

Business liaison service: the FDMA will put potential marketers in touch with the full range of DM suppliers, and also help to find business partners for a shared enterprise. It also provides advice on the choice of research agencies, if required.

Other facilities: the FDMA provides training sessions and seminars for DM beginners and professinals alike, focusing on practical issues. It has also organised a two-day annual DM event. This has included an extensive exhibition, seminars and workshops. Services to consumers include Mailing Preference Service (began 1984), Telephone Preference Service (1994). All related information can be found in the FDMA website.

Finland is the only country in the world where direct selling companies are DM association's members. This is why the FDMA is a member of FEDSA (European) and WFDSA (Global). Mail order companies and e-traders are also FDMA members – that's why the association is a member of EMOTA (European). Since the FDMA member companies include DM users and service providers (ad agencies, internet advertising companies, telemarketers etc.), the FDMA is also a member of FEDMA (European), DMA and IFDMA (Global).

The Finnish DM Awards is a direct marketing competition, organized annually by the FDMA. The winners enter directly into FEDMA's Best of Europe semi-finals.

POSTAL SERVICES

In principle, Finnish postal services are open to competition but so far there is only one postal operator, the state-owned Post Finland, which offers all postal services for direct marketing and mail order.

These services include an addressed bulk mail service. To qualify for the bulk mail discount, the mailing should have at least 1000 items of standard weight, size and content. Further discounts depend on the total size of the mailing.

There is also a service for unaddressed bulk mail. Minimum size for a mailing of unaddressed bulk mail is 500 units. Delivery can be made within a calendar week, or on a specific day.

Reply services include:

- *Domestic reply paid service:* A reply paid item is a pre-printed postcard, coupon or envelope. It does not cost anything for your customer and, as the addressee, your company will pay the return postage only for the items sent back to you.

- *Nordic reply paid service:* A reply paid item to be used in Finland, Sweden, Norway, Denmark or Iceland.

- *International business reply service:* In addition to the Nordic countries, Finland Post Ltd has a contract on an IBRS with all UPU countries: Belgium, France, Germany, Greece, Ireland, Israel, Luxembourg, Monaco, the Netherlands, New Zealand, Portugal, Spain, the United Arab Emirates, the United Kingdom, the United States, Latvia, Croatia and Estonia.

- *Freepost service:* Free Response service means that you do not need to pre-print any reply envelopes or cards. The sender writes your address and your Freepost code on an envelope or postcard and sends it to you without postage. You as the addressee will pay the postage only for the replies sent to you. This is a domestic service only.

Finland Post Ltd
International Mail
PO Box 102
Fin-00011 Posti
Finland
Tel: +358 20 451 4990
Fax: +358 20 451 4994
Website: www.posti.fi

PROVIDERS OF DM AND E-M SERVICES

ACC-GROUP - ACTIVE CONTACTS & COMMUNICATION OY
Kanavaranta 7 D
Helsinki
160
Finland
Tel: +358 9 4133 3200
Fax: +358 9 4133 3222
Olli Sulander, Managing Director

Services/Products:
Telemarketing agency; Consultancy services

Member of:
FDMA

ADM-TELEMARKKINOINTI OY
Linnankatu 26 A
Turku
20100
Finland
Tel: +358 2 814 50900
Fax: +358 2 814 50940
Email: pasi.venho@
adm-telemarkkinointi.fi
Pasi Venho, Managing
Director

Services/Products:
Call centre services/systems;
Telemarketing agency

Member of:
FEDMA

ADSEK SUORA OY AB
PL 716
Tampere
33101
Finland
Tel: +358 3 2171211
Fax: +358 3 2171299
Antti Aro, Managing Director

Services/Products:
Advertising Agency; Direct marketing agency

Member of:
FDMA

ALVARI INTERNATIONAL OY (LTD)
Kylänevantie 6 A 5
Helsinki
320
Finland
Tel: +358 50 555 4442
Vuokko Alvari, Managing Director

Services/Products:
Consultancy services

Member of:
FDMA

AMMIRATI PURIS LINTAS OY
PL 115
Helsinki
161
Finland
Tel: +358 9 4761 9400
Fax: +358 9 4761 9429
Jukka Järvinen, Director

Services/Products:
Advertising Agency; Direct marketing agency

Member of:
DMA (US); FDMA

ANTTILA OY
PO Box 1060
Kesko
16
Finland
Tel: +358 1053 43
Fax: +358 1053 40661
Mr Esa Hannukainen,, Sales Director, Mail Order

Services/Products:
Mail order company

ARI AHOLA OY
Hirsikalliontie 7
Espoo
2710
Finland
Tel: +358 9 590306
Fax: +358 9 597525
Ari Ahola, Director

Services/Products:
Consultancy services

Member of:
FDMA

ASIANAJOTOIMISTO RISTO KURKI-SUONIO OY
Temppelikatu 4 A
Helsinki
100
Finland
Tel: +358 9 494500
Fax: +358 9 494447

Email: risto@kurkilaw.com
Risto Kurki-Suonio, Attorney At Law

Services/Products:
Legal services

Member of:
FDMA

ATELCON OY
Salomonkatu 17 A, 4 krs
Helsinki
100
Finland
Tel: +358 9 6154599
Fax: +358 9 61545699
Marja Hyvärinen, Managing Director

Services/Products:
Consultancy services

Member of:
FDMA

ATKO-MARKKINOINTI OY
Itätuulentie 2
Espoo
2100
Finland
Tel: +358 9 455 4040
Fax: +358 9 455 4043
Kaija Oinonen, Managing Director

Services/Products:
Telemarketing agency

Member of:
FDMA

ATKOS OY
PL 530
Vantaa
1511
Finland
Tel: +358 9 825811
Fax: +358 9 82581258
Jouko Kovero, Managing Director

Services/Products:
List services; Mailing/Faxing services; Private delivery services; Fulfilment and sampling house

Member of:
FDMA

BANZAI DIRECT MARKETING
Sörnäisten rantatie 27 A
Helsinki
500
Finland
Tel: +358 9 7002 9110
Fax: +358 9 7002 9119
Kari Ketola, Managing Director

Services/Products:
Advertising Agency; Direct marketing agency

Member of:
FDMA

BBDO HELSINKI OY / BBDO DIALOG

Pursimiehenkatu 7
Helsinki
150
Finland
Tel: +358 9 685 0140
Fax: +358 9 260 0577
Merja Salmi, Project Director

Services/Products:
Advertising Agency; Direct marketing agency

Member of:
FDMA

BONG SUOMI OY VANTAA

PL 7
Vantaa
1641
Finland
Tel: +358 9 329 6130
Fax: +358 9 329 61399
Tuomo Savolainen, Sales Manager

Services/Products:
Labelling/envelope services

Member of:
FDMA

CCN MARKNADS ANALYS OY

Aleksanterinkatu 21 H
Helsinki
100
Finland
Tel: +358 9 34870450
Fax: +358 9 34870455
Juhani Kiiskinen, Managing Director

Services/Products:
Consultancy services

Member of:
FDMA

CREATOR-GREY OY

Eerikinkatu 28
PL 147
Helsinki
180
Finland
Tel: +358 9 693021
Fax: +358 9 6930 415
Email: firstname.lastname@creator-grey.fi
Web: www.creator-grey.fi
Sara Suiven, Account Group Director

Services/Products:
Advertising Agency; Direct marketing agency

E-Services:
E-Marketing consultant; Website design; Email software; Online/e-marketing agency

Member of:
National DMA

DIRITTO RAPP COLLINS

Tehtaankatu 29A, 5 krs
Helsinki
150
Finland
Tel: +358 9 6869 920
Fax: +358 9 6869 9222
Virpi Kiviniemi, Account Manager

Services/Products:
Advertising Agency; Direct marketing agency

E-Services:
E-Marketing consultant

Member of:
FEDMA

DM ACES KY

Unioninkatu 45 B 36 a
Helsinki
170
Finland
Tel: +358 9 2600660
Fax: +358 9 2600661
Juha Penttinen, Managing Director

Services/Products:
Consultancy services

Member of:
FDMA

DM-TATE & CO OY

Eino Leinon katu 7 B 24
Helsinki
250
Finland
Tel: +358 9 4548145
Fax: +358 9 4548148
Taisto Hirvonen, Managing Director

Services/Products:
Consultancy services

Member of:
FDMA

DM-WAY OY

Mannerheimintie 15 B
Helsinki
260
Finland
Tel: +358 9 75128100
Fax: +358 9 75128128
Veikko Koskinen, Managing Director

Services/Products:
Advertising Agency; Direct marketing agency

Member of:
FDMA

DOUBLE CLICK D.A.R.T. ONLINE ADVERTISING AB

Kalevankatu 30
Helsinki
100
Finland
Tel: +358 9 685 9950
Fax: +358 9 685 99550
Salla Ainamo, Managing Director

Services/Products:
Electronic media

E-Services:
Website design

Member of:
FDMA

EDITA OY DIRECT

PL 410
EDITA
43
Finland
Tel: +358 9 56601
Fax: +358 9 5660695
Jari Mäkelä, Sales Director

Services/Products:
Print services

Member of:
FDMA

ELANDERS LITHOREX FINLAND OY

Miniatontie 6 A 2
Espoo
2360
Finland
Tel: +358 9 8022202
Fax: +358 9 8014561
Toni Ruokonen, Managing Director

Services/Products:
Print services

Member of:
FDMA

ELLOS OY

Tiilitetaankatu 7 PL 157
Kerava
4201
Finland
Tel: +358 47 661 206
Fax: +358 294 52 85
Email: antti.malkonen@ellos.fi
Antti Mälkönen,, Managing Director

Services/Products:
List services

Member of:
FEDMA

FINLAND POST LTD
Mannerheiminaukio 1
Helsinki
100
Finland
Tel: +358 204 51 5650
Fax: +358 204 51 4673
Email: antti.malkonen@ellos.fi
Markku Mäkitalo,, Director Media
Services

Services/Products:
Database services; Telemarketing
agency; Direct marketing agency; Mail
order company; Mailing/Faxing
services

Member of:
FEDMA

FINNET-LIITTO RY
PL 949
Helsinki
101
Finland
Tel: +358 9 228111
Fax: +358 9 605531
Riittamaija Ståhle, Communications
Manager

Member of:
FDMA

FINNMAIL OY
Tulppatie 16–18
Helsinki
880
Finland
Tel: +358 9 7591700
Fax: +358 9 7591622
John Lönnqvist, Managing Director

Services/Products:
Mailing/Faxing services; Print services

Member of:
FDMA

GREY DIRECT OY
Annankatu 27
Helsinki
100
Finland
Tel: +358 9 6945166
Fax: +358 9 6957424
Mirjami Mäkinen, Managing Director

Services/Products:
Advertising Agency; Database services;
Direct marketing agency

Member of:
DMA (US); FEDMA; FDMA

HANSAPOST OY
Toom Puistee 33 A
Tallin
EE-0011
Finland
Tel: +46 331 40000
Fax: +46 331 55122
Eevu Henriksson, Marketing Assistant

Services/Products:
Mailing/Faxing services; Private
delivery services; Lettershop

Member of:
FDMA

HANSAPRINT OY
PO Box 501
Turku
20101
Finland
Tel: +358 10 5422
Fax: +358 2 269 4403
Email: jukka.leino@hansaprint.fi
Jukka Leino, Vice President (Projects)

Services/Products:
Catalogue producer; Database
services; Personalisation; Print services;
Publisher; Labelling/envelope services

Member of:
National DMA

HEINONEN LAW OY
PO Box 671
Helsinki
101
Finland
Tel: +358 9 2530 0650
Fax: +358 9 6944 352
Marja Tommila, Attorney At Law

Services/Products:
Legal services

Member of:
FDMA

HELPRINT OY
PL 24
Mikkeli
50101
Finland
Tel: +358 9 6220640
Fax: +358 9 175360
Bertil Walli, Marketing Director

Services/Products:
Print services

Member of:
FDMA

HELSINGIN PUHELIN OYJ
PL 148
Helsinki
131
Finland
Tel: +358 9 6061
Fax: +358 9 626472
Ulla Killström, Marketing Director

Services/Products:
Telecommunications

Member of:
FDMA

HELSINKI MEDIA BLUE BOOK
PL 100
Helsinki Media
40
Finland
Tel: +358 9 1201
Fax: +358 9 1205 000
Email: bluebook@helsinkimedia.fi
Web: www.bluebook.fi
Jari Tarkiainen, Marketing Manager

Services/Products:
Database services; Publisher; List
services

E-Services:
Email list provider

Member of:
National DMA; European Association
of Database and Directory Publishers
(EADP); Scandinavian Association of
Database and Directory Publishers
(SADP)

HM & V RESEARCH OY
Westendintie 99 A
Espoo
2160
Finland
Tel: +358 9 4522211
Fax: +358 9 4523901
Matti Mäkelin, Managing Director

Services/Products:
Consultancy services

Member of:
FDMA

IBC EUROFORUM OY
Lönnrotinkatu 15 C 21
Helsinki
120
Finland
Tel: +358 9 6126 710
Fax: +358 9 6126 7110
Minna Stjernvall, Marketing Manager

Services/Products:
Training/recruitment; Training/
recruitment

Member of:
FDMA

ICMI OY
Salomonkatu 17B
Helsinki
100
Finland
Tel: +358 9 4520 740
Fax: +358 9 4520 7474
Kalevi Hellman, Managing Director

Services/Products:
Consultancy services

E-Services:
E-Marketing consultant

Member of:
National DMA

IIR FINLAND OY
Kasarmikatu 28
Helsinki
130
Finland
Tel: +358 9 6156 511
Fax: +358 9 6156 255
Katarina Petterson, Marketing Director

Services/Products:
Training/recruitment

Member of:
FDMA

IMPORT NUMERO 1 OY
PL1
Tampere
33341
Finland
Tel: +358 3 345 3366
Fax: +358 3 345 3399
Email: noproblem@nro1.com
Web: http://www.nro1.com
Heimo Lauhaluoma,, Managing
Director

Services/Products:
Direct marketing agency

INDATA OY
Itätuulenkuja 10
Espoo
2100
Finland
Tel: +358 9 613500
Fax: +358 9 61350625
Mikko Ranin, Managing Director

Services/Products:
Telemarketing agency

Member of:
FDMA

J. WALTER THOMPSON DIRECT OY
Bulevardi 42
Helsinki
120
Finland
Tel: +358 9 6188345
Fax: +358 9 61883499
Kari Björses, Managing Director

Services/Products:
Advertising Agency; Direct marketing agency

Member of:
FDMA

KIRJEKUORI OY
Liikkalankuja 6
Helsinki
00 950
Finland
Tel: +358 9 3434 250
Fax: +358 9 3434 2510
Email: myymtie@kirjekuori.fi
Web: www.kirjekuori.fi
Olli Kierikka, Export Manager

Services/Products:
Envelope producer and printer

Member of:
FDMA

KOHTISUORA OY
Pl 507
Espoo
2101
Finland
Tel: +358 9 613500
Fax: +358 9 61350625
Olli Saarinen, Managing Director

Services/Products:
Private delivery services

Member of:
FDMA

KY H.& R. AHTIAINEN
Pohjoisranta 2 E 10
Helsinki
170
Finland
Tel: +358 9 6213284
Fax: +358 9 6213285
Heikki Ahtiainen, Art Director

Services/Products:
Advertising Agency; Direct marketing agency

Member of:
FDMA

LEHTITILAAJAPALVELU RITVA ANTTILA OY
Hakakalliontie 10
Hyvinkää
5800
Finland
Tel: +358 19 457171
Fax: +358 19 45717250
Vesa Heino, Department Manager

Services/Products:
Mailing/Faxing services; Private delivery services; Lettershop

Member of:
FDMA

LIBRI-LOGISTIIKKA OY
Uudenmaankatu 15 C
Turku
20500
Finland
Tel: +358 9 2332404
Fax: +358 9 327824

Services/Products:
Telemarketing agency

Member of:
FDMA

LITOSET OY
Sahakatu 2
Vaasa
65100
Finland
Tel: +358 6 312 2155
Fax: +358 6 317 3310
Pauli Savela, Sales Manager

Services/Products:
Print services

Member of:
FDMA

LOMAKEVAIHTOEHTO OY
PL 24
Helsinki
381
Finland
Tel: +358 9 8534099
Fax: +358 9 846858
Olavi Lindholm, Managing Director

Services/Products:
Print services

Member of:
FDMA

MAILER OY
Valuraudankuja 1
Helsinki
700
Finland
Tel: +358 9 37511

Fax: +358 9 3751220
Matti Jantunen, Managing Director

Services/Products:
List services; Mailing/Faxing services

Member of:
FEDMA; FDMA

MAINOSKENTTä OY
Rongankatu 4 D
Tampere
33100
Finland
Tel: +358 3 2233444
Fax: +358 3 2133661
Risto Linna, Planning Director

Services/Products:
Advertising Agency; Direct marketing
agency

Member of:
FDMA

MAINOSTOIMISTO KONSEPTI OY
Aleksanterinkatu 15 A
Helsinki
100
Finland
Tel: +358 9 6226080
Fax: +358 9 62260810
Martti Viitamäki, Managing Director

Services/Products:
Advertising Agency; Direct marketing
agency

Member of:
FDMA

MAINOSTOIMISTO PRO DIRECT OY
Esterinportti 1 A
Helsinki
240
Finland
Tel: +358 9 8777055
Fax: +358 9 8777066
Kirsti Könönen, Managing Director

Services/Products:
Advertising Agency; Direct marketing
agency

Member of:
FDMA

MAINOSTOIMISTO RIENTOLA OY
Linnankatu 16
Turku
20100
Finland
Tel: +358 2 2735000
Fax: +358 2 2735001
Visa Nurmi, Managing Director

Services/Products:
Advertising Agency; Direct marketing
agency

Member of:
FDMA

MAINOSTOIMISTO SALAMA OY
Vapaudenkatu 8
Jyväskylä
40100
Finland
Tel: +358 14 4440 400
Fax: +358 14 4440 411
Email: kari.alander@mainoststo-salama.fi
Web: www.mainoststo-salama.fi
Kari Ålander, Managing Director

Services/Products:
Advertising Agency; Direct marketing
agency; Consultancy services; Market
research agency; Interactive media

E-Services:
Website design

Member of:
FEDMA; National DMA

MAINOSTOIMISTO SATUMAA OY
Itäinen Rantakatu 58
Turku
20810
Finland
Tel: +358 2 2743333
Fax: +358 2 2743344
Minna Koivurinta, Managing Director

Services/Products:
Advertising Agency; Direct marketing
agency

Member of:
FDMA

MAINOSTOIMISTO VPV EURO RSCG OY
PL 166
Helsinki
121
Finland
Tel: +358 9 61500400
Fax: +358 9 61500401
Markku Issakainen, Managing Director

Services/Products:
Advertising Agency; Direct marketing
agency

Member of:
FDMA

MAINOSTOIMISTOJEN LIITTO MTL (FINNISH ASS. OF ADVERTISING AGENCIES)
Helsinki
FIN-00100
Finland
Fax: +358 0 625 305
Web: www.mtl.fi

MEDIAPEX OY
Keilaranta 2
Espoo
2150
Finland
Tel: +358 9 75175700
Fax: +358 9 75175746

Services/Products:
Telemarketing agency

Member of:
FDMA

MICROMEDIA OY
PL164
Helsinki
811
Finland
Tel: +358 8000 5055
Fax: +358 9759 8234
Email: post@micromedia.fi
Web: www.micromedia.fi
Katri Heino, Sales Director

Services/Products:
Database services; Mailing/Faxing
services; Print services; Direct
marketing agency; List services;
Telemarketing agency

E-Services:
Email list provider

NNETS OY
Tapiolan keskustorni 11 krs
Espoo
2100
Finland
Tel: +358 9 4550520
Fax: +358 9 61650155
Ilkka Lahtinen, Managing Director

Services/Products:
Consultancy services

Member of:
FDMA

NORDIC PRINT MAIL OY (HKI)
PL 113
Helsinki
241
Finland
Tel: +358 20538800
Fax: +358 205 388504
Mira Iso-Markku, Customer Service
Manager

Services/Products:
Mailing/Faxing services; Print services;
Lettershop

Member of:
FDMA

NOVO GROUP OYJ
PL 38
Helsinki
381
Finland
Tel: +358 9 50671
Fax: +358 9 50672370
Tarja Virmala, Director

Services/Products:
Database services; Software supplier

Member of:
FDMA

OGILVY & MATHER OY
Mikonkatu 19 A
Helsinki
100
Finland
Tel: +358 9 5495711
Fax: +358 9 54957333
Anja Naarvala, Director

Services/Products:
Advertising Agency; Direct marketing
agency

Member of:
FEDMA; FDMA

OMD FINLAND OY
Kalevankatu 30
Helsinki
100
Finland
Tel: +358 9 693661
Fax: +358 9 6941005
Email: omd@omdfinland.fi
Web: www.omdfinland.fi
Päivi Aitkoski-Catani, Managing
Director

Services/Products:
Media buying agency

E-Services:
E-Marketing consultant; Online/e-
marketing agency

Member of:
National DMA; FDMA

OULU REPRO HELSINKI OY /
   PAINOMESTARIT
Tiilismäki 7
Espoo
2320
Finland
Tel: +358 9 6156500

Fax: +358 9 61565600
Matti Lindström, Managing Director

Services/Products:
Print services

Member of:
FDMA

OY LIIKEMAINONTA-MCCANN
   AB
Hietalahdenranta 13
Helsinki
180
Finland
Tel: +358 0 615551
Fax: +358 0 61555333
Mr Pekka Mäki,, Managing Director

Services/Products:
Advertising Agency; Direct marketing
agency; Sales promotion agency;
Electronic media; Internet services

E-Services:
Website design

PARTNERGROUP/CARDINAL
   INFORMATION SYSTEMS OY
Pursimiehenkatu 29–31 F
Helsinki
150
Finland
Tel: +358 9 6689770
Fax: +358 9 66897710
Christian Kvikant, Project Manager

Services/Products:
Database services; Software supplier

Member of:
FDMA

PASAMYYNTI OY
Koulurinteentie 4 C
Hollola
15870
Finland
Tel: +358 3 8820400
Fax: +358 3 8820410
Jari Salo, Sales Director

Services/Products:
Telemarketing agency

Member of:
FDMA

PHONEGATE OY
Linnankatu 6 D
Turku
20100
Finland
Tel: +358 2 282900
Fax: +358 2 2829020
Rhea Dahlström, Managing Director

Services/Products:
Telemarketing agency

Member of:
FDMA

PHS DIRECT OY
Tehtaankatu 1 A, 3 krs
Helsinki
140
Finland
Tel: +358 9 4133 5400
Fax: +358 9 4133 5611
Email: leena.vento@phsdirect.fi

Services/Products:
Advertising Agency

Member of:
National DMA

POSTITUSPOJAT OY
Myllypurontie 1
Helsinki
920
Finland
Tel: +358 9 3424230
Fax: +358 9 34242323
Olli Peltomäki, Managing Director

Services/Products:
Mailing/Faxing services; Lettershop

Member of:
FDMA

POSTLINK OY TAMPOST
PL 383
Tampere
33101
Finland
Tel: +358 3 31411100
Fax: +358 3 31411133
Kimmo Kuusi, Managing Director

Services/Products:
Mailing/Faxing services; Lettershop

Member of:
FDMA

POSTMEDIAT OY
Karhunkierros 5
Vantaa
1640
Finland
Tel: +358 9 8545310
Fax: +358 9 8521109
Yrjö Saharla, Managing Director

Services/Products:
Fulfilment and sampling house;
Mailing/Faxing services; Print services

Member of:
FDMA

PRIME ADVERTISING OY
Bulevardi 30 B
Helsinki
120
Finland
Tel: +358 9 6869050
Fax: +358 9 68690555
Pia Kärkkäinen, Managing Director

Services/Products:
Advertising Agency; Direct marketing agency

Member of:
FDMA

PROMAIL OY
Hyttimestarintie 6
Espoo
2780
Finland
Tel: +358 9 8190500
Fax: +358 9 812100
Yrjö Lindman, Managing Director

Services/Products:
Mailing/Faxing services

Member of:
FDMA

PUBLICIS-TÖRMä OY / DM TöRMä
Fredrikinkatu 48 A
Helsinki
100
Finland
Tel: +358 9 228561
Fax: +358 9 22856400
Arja Roininen, Planning Director

Services/Products:
Advertising Agency; Direct marketing agency

Member of:
FDMA

RIQ YHTIÖT OY
Ruoholahdenkatu 10 b 1
Helsinki
180
Finland
Tel: +358 9 348 35890
Fax: +358 9 348 35899
Riku Asikainen,, Managing Director

Services/Products:
Mail order company

Member of:
SSML

SARAJäRVI & HELLÉN OY
Tehtaankatu 29 A 8.krs.
Helsinki
150
Finland

Tel: +358 9 66893634
Fax: +358 9 6689616
Heikki Sarajärvi, Producer

Services/Products:
Electronic media

E-Services:
Website design

Member of:
FDMA

SCANDINAVIAN TELEMARKETING OY
Ludviginkatu 3–5 B
Helsinki
130
Finland
Tel: +358 9 2317 0700
Fax: +358 9 2317 0701
Email: riitta.laukkanen@
scandinaviantelemarketing.fi
Web:
www.scandinaviantelemarketing.fi
Riitta Laukkanen, Managing Director

Services/Products:
Telemarketing agency; Call centre services/systems; Database services; Mailing/Faxing services

Member of:
FDMA

SDM-MAILER OY AB
Sörnäisten rantatie 27 A
Helsinki
500
Finland
Tel: +358 9 701 7900
Fax: +358 9 701 7955
Kristina Lönnqvist, Managing Director

Services/Products:
Direct marketing agency

Member of:
FEDMA; FDMA

SEFEK OY
Ratavartijankatu 2 A
Helsinki
520
Finland
Tel: +358 9 4767 7550
Fax: +358 9 4767 7263
Anneli Tel:ama, Training Director

Services/Products:
Training/recruitment

Member of:
FDMA

SINORDIC AB
P.O. Box 397
Örebro

70147
Finland
Tel: +46 19 166004
Fax: +358 4 619166010
Staffan Jivemo,, Marketing & Sales

Services/Products:
Telemarketing agency

Member of:
FDMA

SISäSUOMI OY
PL 94
Jyväskylä
40101
Finland
Tel: +358 14 667600
Fax: +358 14 665649
Eero Kuusela,, Managing Director

Services/Products:
Print services

Member of:
FDMA

SONERA OY
PL 578
Sonera
51
Finland
Tel: +358 204011
Fax: +358 20402294
Esa Kanninen,, Product Marketing Director

Services/Products:
Telecommunications

Member of:
FDMA

SUOMEN NUMEROPALVELU OY
Ruoholahdenkatu 8
Helsinki
180
Finland
Tel: +358 9 6937741
Fax: +358 9 6948622
Kalevi Matikainen,, Managing Director

Services/Products:
Telephone number updating

Member of:
FDMA

SUOMEN OSOITEL:HDE OY
Köyhämäentie 12
Vantaa
1510
Finland
Tel: +358 9 82581208
Fax: +358 9 82581245
Pekka Suomi,, Project Director

Services/Products:
List services

Member of:
FDMA

**SUOMEN POSTI OY /
  MEDIAPALVELUT**
(Finland Post Ltd.) PL 7
Posti
11
Finland
Tel: +358 204511
Fax: +358 204514673
Timo Tarkkinen,, Marketing Manager

Services/Products:
Mailing/Faxing services

Member of:
FDMA

**SUOMEN SUORAMAINONTA
  OY**
Hankasuontie 3
Helsinki
390
Finland
Tel: +358 9 56156400
Fax: +358 9 56156444
Lasse Autio,, Managing Director

Services/Products:
Private delivery services

Member of:
FDMA

SUOMEN TELEPALVELU OY
Pihatörmä 1 A
Espoo
2240
Finland
Tel: +358 9 8558822
Fax: +358 9 8558833
Markku Kulmala,, Managing Director

Services/Products:
Telemarketing agency

Member of:
FDMA

SUORAKANAVA OY
Salomonkatu 17 A 2. krs
Helsinki
100
Finland
Tel: +358 9 61329200
Fax: +358 9 61329100
Mikko Saarela,, Managing Director

Services/Products:
Telemarketing agency

Member of:
FDMA

**SUORAMARKKINOINTI MEGA
  OY**
Luotsinmäen puistokatu 1
Pori
28100
Finland
Tel: +358 2 6412161
Fax: +358 2 6336284
Hannu Myöhänen,, Managing
Director

Services/Products:
Direct marketing agency

Member of:
FDMA

**SUORAMARKKINOINTI
  PENTTI PALÉN OY**
Urb. Alamar II, Casa 9
ESP
E-2978
Finland
Tel: +34 95 2523876
Fax: +34 95 2523876
Pentti Palén,, Managing Director

Services/Products:
Copy adaptation; Consultancy services

Member of:
FDMA

TAIVASSUORA OY
Unioninkatu 15
Helsinki
130
Finland
Tel: +358 9 666266
Fax: +358 9 666326
Seija Heikkilä,, Managing Director

Services/Products:
Advertising Agency; Direct marketing
agency

Member of:
FDMA

**TELEPERFORMANCE
  FINLAND OY**
Rautatienkatv 21B
PL 323
Tampere
33101
Finland
Tel: +358 3 411411
Fax: +358 3 411413 99
Email: crm@teleperformance.fi
Web: www.teleperformance.fi
Timo Juurakko, Managing Director

Services/Products:
Telemarketing agency; Call centre
services/systems; Consultancy services;
Mailing/Faxing services; Market
research agency; Multimedia contact

centre

E-Services:
Online/e-marketing agency

Member of:
National DMA

TIETO CORPORATION OYJ
Tietopalvelut
Suoramarkkinointiyksikkö PL 406
Espoo
2101
Finland
Tel: +358 9 4571
Fax: +358 9 4573756
Jarmo Hurttila,, Director

Services/Products:
List services; Fulfilment and sampling
house; Mailing/Faxing services;
Lettershop

Member of:
FDMA

TILASTOKESKUS
Tilastokeskus
22
Finland
Tel: +358 9 17341
Fax: +358 9 17342474
Petteri Baer,, Marketing Planner

Services/Products:
List services

Member of:
FDMA

**TURUN PUSSI- JA
  KIRJEKUORITEHDAS OY**
PL 169
Turku
20101
Finland
Tel: +358 2 271500
Fax: +358 2 388578
Mikko Mellanen,, Marketing Manager

Services/Products:
Labelling/envelope services

Member of:
FDMA

VIHERJUUREN SUORA OY
Urho Kekkosenkatu 4–6- A
Helsinki
100
Finland
Tel: +358 9 1255355
Fax: +358 9 12552242
Email: tarja.lento@viherjuuri.fi
Tarja Lento,, Managing Director

Services/Products:
Advertising Agency; Consultancy services; Direct marketing agency; Direct response TV services

E-Services:
Website design

Member of:
FEDMA; FDMA

VPV EURO RSGG
Fredrikinkatu 33A
Helsinki
121
Finland
Tel: +358 9 61 500 400
Fax: +358 9 61 500 401
Markku Issakainen,, General Manager

Services/Products:
Direct marketing agency

Member of:
DMA (US)

WUNDERMAN CATO JOHNSON
Munkkisaarenkatu 2
Helsinki
150
Finland
Tel: +358 9 6220350
Fax: +358 9 62203533
Leena Kuikka,, Director

Services/Products:
Advertising Agency; Direct marketing agency

Member of:
FDMA

SERVICES/PRODUCT LISTING

Advertising Agency
Adsek Suora Oy Ab
Ammirati Puris Lintas Oy
Banzai Direct Marketing
Bbdo Helsinki Oy / Bbdo Dialog
Creator-Grey Oy
Diritto Rapp Collins
Dm-Way Oy
Grey Direct Oy
J. Walter Thompson Direct Oy
Ky H.& R. Ahtiainen
Mainoskenttä Oy
Mainostoimisto Konsepti Oy
Mainostoimisto Pro Direct Oy
Mainostoimisto Rientola Oy
Mainostoimisto Salama Oy
Mainostoimisto Satumaa Oy
Mainostoimisto Vpv Euro Rscg Oy
Ogilvy & Mather Oy

Oy Liikemainonta-McCann AB
Phs Direct Oy
Prime Advertising Oy
Publicis-Törmä Oy / Dm Törmä
Taivassuora Oy
Viherjuuren Suora Oy
Wunderman Cato Johnson

Call centre services/systems
ADM-Telemarkkinointi Oy
Scandinavian Telemarketing Oy
Teleperformance Finland Oy

Catalogue producer
Hansaprint Oy

Consultancy services
ACC-Group - Active Contacts & Communication Oy
Alvari International Oy (Ltd)
Ari Ahola Oy
AtelCon Oy
CCN Marknads Analys Oy
Dm Aces Ky
Dm-Tate & Co Oy
HM & V Research Oy
ICMI Oy
Mainostoimisto Salama Oy
Nnets Oy
Suoramarkkinointi Pentti Palén Oy
Teleperformance Finland Oy
Viherjuuren Suora Oy

Copy adaptation
Suoramarkkinointi Pentti Palén Oy

Database services
Finland Post Ltd
Grey Direct Oy
Hansaprint Oy
Helsinki Media Blue Book
MicroMedia Oy
Novo Group Oyj
Partnergroup/Cardinal Information Systems Oy
Scandinavian Telemarketing Oy

Direct marketing agency
Adsek Suora Oy Ab
Ammirati Puris Lintas Oy
Banzai Direct Marketing
Bbdo Helsinki Oy / Bbdo Dialog
Creator-Grey Oy
Diritto Rapp Collins
Dm-Way Oy
Finland Post Ltd
Grey Direct Oy
Import Numero 1 Oy
J. Walter Thompson Direct Oy
Ky H.& R. Ahtiainen
Mainoskenttä Oy
Mainostoimisto Konsepti Oy
Mainostoimisto Pro Direct Oy

Mainostoimisto Rientola Oy
Mainostoimisto Salama Oy
Mainostoimisto Satumaa Oy
Mainostoimisto Vpv Euro Rscg Oy
MicroMedia Oy
Ogilvy & Mather Oy
Oy Liikemainonta-McCann AB
Prime Advertising Oy
Publicis-Törmä Oy / Dm Törmä
SDM-Mailer Oy Ab
Suoramarkkinointi Mega Oy
Taivassuora Oy
Viherjuuren Suora Oy
VPV Euro RSGG
Wunderman Cato Johnson

Direct response TV services
Viherjuuren Suora Oy

Electronic media
Double Click D.A.R.T. Online Advertising Ab
Oy Liikemainonta-McCann AB
Sarajärvi & Hellén Oy

Envelope producer and printer
Kirjekuori Oy

Fulfilment and sampling house
Atkos Oy
Postmediat Oy
Tieto Corporation Oyj

Interactive media
Mainostoimisto Salama Oy

Internet services
Oy Liikemainonta-McCann AB

Labelling/envelope services
Bong Suomi Oy Vantaa
Hansaprint Oy
Turun Pussi- Ja Kirjekuoritehdas Oy

Legal services
Asianajotoimisto Risto Kurki-Suonio Oy
Heinonen Law Oy

Lettershop
Hansapost Oy
Lehtitilaajapalvelu Ritva Anttila Oy
Nordic Print Mail Oy (Hki)
Postituspojat Oy
Postlink Oy Tampost
Tieto Corporation Oyj

List services
Atkos Oy
Ellos Oy
Helsinki Media Blue Book
Mailer Oy
MicroMedia Oy

110

Suomen Osoitel:hde Oy
Tieto Corporation Oyj
Tilastokeskus

Mail order company
Anttila Oy
Finland Post Ltd
RIQ Yhtiöt Oy

Mailing/Faxing services
Atkos Oy
Finland Post Ltd
Finnmail Oy
Hansapost Oy
Lehtitilaajapalvelu Ritva Anttila Oy
Mailer Oy
MicroMedia Oy
Nordic Print Mail Oy (Hki)
Postituspojat Oy
Postlink Oy Tampost
Postmediat Oy
Promail Oy
Scandinavian Telemarketing Oy
Suomen Posti Oy / Mediapalvelut
Teleperformance Finland Oy
Tieto Corporation Oyj

Market research agency
Mainostoimisto Salama Oy
Teleperformance Finland Oy

Media buying agency
OMD Finland Oy

Multimedia contact centre
Teleperformance Finland Oy

Personalisation
Hansaprint Oy

Print services
Edita Oy Direct
Elanders Lithorex Finland Oy
Finnmail Oy
Hansaprint Oy

Helprint Oy
Litoset Oy
Lomakevaihtoehto Oy
MicroMedia Oy
Nordic Print Mail Oy (Hki)
Oulu Repro Helsinki Oy /
    Painomestarit
Postmediat Oy
Sisäsuomi Oy

Private delivery services
Atkos Oy
Hansapost Oy
Kohtisuora Oy
Lehtitilaajapalvelu Ritva Anttila Oy
Suomen Suoramainonta Oy

Publisher
Hansaprint Oy
Helsinki Media Blue Book

Sales promotion agency
Oy Liikemainonta-McCann AB

Software supplier
Novo Group Oyj
Partnergroup/Cardinal Information
    Systems Oy

Telecommunications
Helsingin Puhelin Oyj
Sonera Oy

Telemarketing agency
ACC-Group - Active Contacts &
    Communication Oy
ADM-Telemarkkinointi Oy
Atko-Markkinointi Oy
Finland Post Ltd
Indata Oy
Libri-Logistiikka Oy
Mediapex Oy
MicroMedia Oy
Pasamyynti Oy
Phonegate Oy

Scandinavian Telemarketing Oy
SiNordic Ab
Suomen Telepalvelu Oy
Suorakanava Oy
Teleperformance Finland Oy

Telephone number updating
Suomen Numeropalvelu Oy

Training/recruitment
IBC Euroforum Oy
IIR Finland Oy
Sefek Oy

E-SERVICES

E-Marketing consultant
Creator-Grey Oy
Diritto Rapp Collins
ICMI Oy
OMD Finland Oy

Email list provider
Helsinki Media Blue Book
MicroMedia Oy

Email software
Creator-Grey Oy

Online/e-marketing agency
Creator-Grey Oy
OMD Finland Oy
Teleperformance Finland Oy

Website design
Creator-Grey Oy
Double Click D.A.R.T. Online
    Advertising Ab
Mainostoimisto Salama Oy
Oy Liikemainonta-McCann AB
Sarajärvi & Hellén Oy
Viherjuuren Suora Oy

FRANCE

Population: 58.5 million
Capital: Paris
Language: French

GDP: $1354 billion
GDP per capita: $23,100
Inflation: 1.1 per cent

Currency: Franc (FFr) = 100 centimes
Exchange rate: FFr6.10 : $1 (FFr6.56 : 1 euro)

Time: GMT +1 hour

OVERVIEW

France is widely held to have one of the most well developed and innovative direct marketing industries in Europe. Minitel, the French information and teleshopping system, is now installed in approximately 6.5 million homes, with both the network and response rates enjoying continued growth. PDMS figures show France to be among the most heavily mailed countries in Europe, receiving 63 items of addressed mail per capita in 1997.

Direct marketing media accounted for about a third of total advertising expenditure in 1996 (the latest available figures), broken down as follows:

Analysis of expenditure on direct marketing, 1996

Addressed mail	43%	Direct response press	4%
Unaddressed mail	39%	Direct response TV	6%
Catalogues	5%	Direct response radio	3%
In parcel advertising	1%		

(Statistics from the UFMD.)

Lists and databases

There is an extensive range of response lists available for rental. Costs per thousand are in the region of FFr 900, although compiled lists from telephone directory and car registration files are available at a third of the cost.

List quality is generally high, although there are restrictions on exporting magnetic tapes. Business lists are available for rental and swaps can be negotiated.

LANGUAGE AND CULTURAL CONSIDERATIONS

It is usual to shake hands on meeting or parting with personal acquaintances. Many people take their holidays in August, so it is best to avoid trying to make new business contacts in this month.

Business managers generally prefer to speak in their native language. Proper grammatical use of the French language is very important to the French. Translation can be expensive, but it is a worthwhile investment to have mailings thoroughly checked by a native speaker or professional translator.

LEGISLATION AND CONSUMER PROTECTION

France operates a Robinson list (Stop Publicité), managed by the UFMD. There are also two other lists managed by France Telecom, which compiles a register of all persons who do not want to be mailed by phone (Orange list), and by fax (Safran list).

In addition, the data protection legislation of 1978 is based on three basic principles:

1. All databases compiled must be declared to the Commission (see below for address).
2. Computerized and manual lists cannot be distributed except under the terms of the Act.
3. Individuals providing information for a list have the right to review the information on that list, on proof of identity.

For further details, contact:

Commission Nationale Informatique et Liberté (CNIL)
21 rue Saint-Guillaume
F-75007 Paris
Te;: +33 1 53 73 22 22   Fax: +33 1 53 73 22 00

THE DIRECT MARKETING ASSOCIATION

Name: Union Française du Marketing Direct (UFMD)
Address: 60 rue la Boétie, F-75008 Paris
Tel: +33 1 42 56 38 86
Fax: +33 1 45 63 91 95
Year founded: 1978
Total staff: 2
Contact: Bernard Siouffi (senior English-speaking staff member)

The French DMA has a complex structure, involving a main board (Union Francais du Marketing Direct) governing four semi-autonomous colleges:

- permanent/users of DM (mail order and home study);
- specialized suppliers;
- partners: (Post Office, Telecom);
- education: (formal DM education bodies and associations, Bureau de Vérification de la Publicité, Cercle du Marketing Direct).

The UFMD, as the main board, has only 16 members. In addition to coordinating the activities of the four colleges, the UFMD also acts as a clearing house for all enquiries, and will channel all contacts to the appropriate destination.

The most useful contact points for potential mailers are as follows:

Cercle du Marketing Direct (CMD)

President: Bernard Siouffi
Address: see UFMD
Members: 400

The CMD is an informal grouping of users and suppliers of DM. Membership is FFr 3500 per annum, which entitles members to join the CMD's bi-monthly meetings and to use library facilities. The meetings, held over lunch, are designed as an industry open day – a chance to exchange information and possibly meet new business partners. The library, with several thousand press cuttings, several hundred books and an on-line information service, is one of the most comprehensive DM databases in the world.

Syndicat des Entreprises de Vente par Correspondance et à Distance (SEVPCD)

President: Didier Lahache
Address: see UFMD
Website: www.sevpcd.com
Members: 220

A formal grouping of the first college, the SEVPCD is the lobbying and information arm of the massive French mail order industry. Prospective mail order companies looking at the country need go no further than the SEVPCD, whose newsletters, information bulletins and a library (see earlier) provide every possible analysis of the market. The depth of information is very impressive.

Association des Agences-Conseils en Communications (AACC)

Address: 40 boulevard Malesherbes, 75008 Paris, France
Tel: +33 1 47 42 13 42
Fax: +33 1 42 66 59 90
E-mail: info@aacc.fr
Website: www.aacc.fr
Year founded: 1972
President: Alain Cayzac
Total staff: 12
Members: 200
Contact: Jacques Bille/Philippe Legendre

The AACC is a trade association grouping over 200 French agencies working in the field of commercial communications, including advertising, direct marketing and sales promotion. All agencies must meet the selection requirements of the AACC and certify they abide by professional rules and laws. The AACC is ruled by an elected board and is managed by an elected staff. It has an online information service, and provides members with legal advice, library facilities and a newsletter. Membership, however, is not open to overseas companies.

Syndicat National de la Communication Directe (SNCD)

President: Jean Paul Vouhe
Address: 8 rue de Berry, 75008 Paris
Tel: +33 1 56 59 90 17
Members: 65

The SNCD can help prospective mailers who are looking for partners and suppliers. It publishes a very detailed brochure of members, specifying exactly what each agency, printer, handling house or list broker can offer. The brochure is free on request.

Syndicat du Marketing Telephonique (SMT)

Secretary General: Denise Bengidar
Address: 26 rue des Rigoles, F75020 Paris
Tel: +33 1 41 86 25 25

The SMT represents the country's telemarketing agencies and associated suppliers. The library (mentioned under the CMD) also contains a wealth of data on telemarketing, and the SMT will put any prospective telemarketer in touch with accredited agencies and suppliers.

POSTAL SERVICES

La Poste offers direct mailers a range of domestic and international services, known as Publiposte.

Domestic services include:

- *Postimpact:* designed for bulk addressed mailings. There are three products available:
    1) Postimpact Mécanisable (0–35g)
    2) Postimpact Standard Distribution (0–350g)
    3) Postimpact Libre (0–350g)
  The Postimpact range is for general or marketing correspondence which can be personalized.

- *Postcontact:* for the delivery of unaddressed mail to a defined area, using defined selection criteria: type of housing and income. The aim is to create or extend a customer file and to canvass a geographical area without an existing file.

- *Postcontact Targeted:* operated by Mediapost SA, a subsidiary of La Poste, this service offers more closely targeted delivery, using 11 selection criteria (housing, age, profession, etc). Its aims are to keep printing and distribution costs low and to increase the return on canvassing.

- *Postresponse:* business reply and parcel reply service. Its aims are to facilitate the reply to your offer, to reinforce its effectiveness, to measure its impact, and to allow your customers to return small parcels (films, etc) free of charge.

International services include:

- *International Addressed Mailing:* this offers two services, priority (first class) and economy (second class), with special rates available from 15kg and above, and tailor-made quotations for bulk mail.

- *International Unaddressed Mailing:* the aim of this service is to create a European address file.

- *International Business Reply Service:* this service enables foreign prospects to reply free of charge.

- *Chronopost International:* this is a courier service offering express deliveries to most countries in the world, on parcels up to 30kg.

La Poste produce a booklet called *La Poste: Your Direct Marketing Medium* which gives details of these services. Chronopost also produces a booklet called *Chronopost, partout à travers le monde*, which is only available in French.

For more information on all domestic and international services, contact:

La Poste
Direction du Courrier International
11 rue de Pré
F-75877 Paris Cedex 18
France
Tel: +33 1 44 72 22 06
Fax: +33 1 44 72 23 37
Website: www.laposte.fr

or

Chronopost
14 Bd des Frères Voisin
F-92795 Issy les Moulineaux
France
Tel: +33 1 46 48 2 08
Fax: +33 1 46 48 2 14

PROVIDERS OF DM AND E-M SERVICES

141 FRANCE – GMS
4, rue Sentou
Suresnes
92150
France
Tel: +33 1 41 38 93 50
Fax: +33 1 41 38 93 51
Email: 141@wanadoo.com
Claude Chabbiotte

Services/Products:
Database services; Telemarketing agency; Direct marketing agency; Consultancy services; Design/graphics/ clip art supplier; Software supplier; Electronic media

E-Services:
Website design

Member of:
AACC

ADDRESSING TECHNOLOGY
14 bis, rue du Ratrait
92150 Suresnes
France
Tel: +33 1 41 38 6500
Fax: +33 1 41 38 6501
Email: gclerquin@addressing.fr
Web: www.addressingtechnology.com
Gérard Clerquin, General Manager

Services/Products:
Mailing/Faxing services; Database services; Labelling/envelope services; Lettershop; List services; Call centre services/systems

E-Services:
Email list provider; Website design

Member of:
FEDMA; DMA (US); DDV; SNCD

ADRESS MEDIA
rue de Surene 7
Paris
75008
France
Tel: +33 1 53308040
Fax: +33 153308044
Frederic Sudres, Director

Services/Products:
List services; Direct marketing agency

Member of:
FEDMA

AID – ANALYSE INFORMATIQUE DES DONNEES
4 rue Henri Le Sidaner
Versailles
78000
France
Tel: +33 1 39 23 93 00
Fax: +33 1 39 23 93 01
Email: info@aid.fr
Olivier Coppet, President

Services/Products:
Database services; Service bureau

Member of:
FEDMA; DMA (US)

ALKEA CONSEIL
187 rue Legendre
Paris
75017
France
Tel: +33 1 42 26 31 92
Fax: +33 1 42 26 3192
Email: alkea.conseil@wanadoo.fr
Nathalie Rodary, Director

Services/Products:
Training/recruitment; Training/ recruitment; Mail order company; Market research agency

Member of:
FEDMA

ANDERSEN CONSULTING
55 Avenue George V
Paris
75008
France
Tel: +33 1 5323 5355
Fax: +33 1 5323 5323
Jean-Francois Nebel, Business Development Director

Services/Products:
Consultancy services

Member of:
DMA (US)

ASSOCIATION DES AGENCES-CONSEILS EN COMMUNICATION (AACC)
40 boulevard Malesherbes
Paris
75008
France
Tel: +33 1 4742 1342
Fax: +33 1 4266 5990
Email: info@aacc.fr
Web: www.aacc.fr
Philippe Legendre

Services/Products:
Advertising Agency; Direct marketing agency; Sales promotion agency

Member of:
FEDMA

AVERY DENNISON FRANCE S.A.
68, rue de Lille
Avelin
59710
France
Tel: +33 3 20620120
Fax: +33 3 20620151
Yseult Périlhou, Responsable Marketing Direct

Services/Products:
Labelling/envelope services; Personalisation

Member of:
FEDMA

AXIME DIRECT
La Vigne aux Loups
55, Route de Longjumeau
Chilly-Mazarin Cedex
91388
France
Tel: +33 1 69 10 63 63
Fax: +33 1 69 10 63 10
Pascal Bono, President

Services/Products:
Service bureau

Member of:
DMA (US)

BELLANGER FOUCAUCOURT & ASSOC.
14 Rue Pergelese
Paris
75116
France
Tel: +33 1 45 01 58 40
Jean De Foucaucourt, General Manager

Services/Products:
Advertising Agency; Direct marketing agency

Member of:
DMA (US)

BOTTIN ENTREPRISES - COFACE SRCL
31 rue Anatole
Levallois Perret
92685
France
Tel: +33 1 4748 7560
Fax: +33 1 4748 7550
Email: s-caudrelier@bottin.fr

Web: www.bottin.fr
Stephanie Caudrelier, International
  Account Executive

Services/Products:
Database services; List services;
Mailing/Faxing services; B to B
addresses

Member of:
FEDMA

CABINET ALAIN BENSOUSSAN
29 rue du Colonel Pierre Avia
Paris
75508
France
Tel: +33 1 41 33 35 35
Fax: +33 1 41 33 35 36
Brigitte Misse

Services/Products:
Legal services

Member of:
FEDMA

CEPAP
B.P. 14
L'Abbaye
La Couronne
16400
France
Tel: +33 5 45 24 36 00
Fax: +33 5 45 24 36 00
Denis Henault, Export Director

Services/Products:
Labelling/envelope services

Member of:
FEDMA

CIFEA-DMK
Zone Industrielle des Grives
B.P. 86
Rumilly Cedex
74153
France
Tel: +33 4 5001 5464
Fax: +33 4 5001 2548
Email: stouw@cifea-dmk.fr
Web: www.cifea-dmk.fr
Ms Sacha Touw, International Account
  Manager

Services/Products:
List services; Lettershop;
Personalisation; Print services

Member of:
FEDMA; National DMA

CLARITAS FRANCE
30 rue Victor Hugo
Levallois-Perret Cedex
92532
France

Tel: +33 1 41 06 93 30
Fax: +33 1 47 39 41 67
Email: info-fr@claritaseu.com
Hervé Pointillart

Services/Products:
List services; Database services;
Consultancy services; Response
analysis bureau

Member of:
AACC

COMMUNIDER
107, rue Anatole France
Levallois Perret
92300
France
Tel: +33 4 1 05 63 05
Fax: +33 41 05 63 00
Email: hkl@club-internet.fr
Web: www.communider.com

Services/Products:
Telemarketing agency; Direct
marketing agency; Consultancy
services; Electronic media

E-Services:
Website design

CONSODATA
105 rue Jules Guesde
Levallois Perret Cedex
92532
France
Tel: +33 1 41 27 20 60
Fax: +33 1 42 70 98 01
Marc Henon, Chairman

Services/Products:
List services; Database services

Member of:
FEDMA; DMA (US)

DIACOM
5/7 rue de L'Alma
Asnières
92600
France
Tel: +33 1 46 88 06 88
Fax: +33 1 46 88 06 99
Email: quina@diacom.imaginet.fr
Luis B. Quina, Managing Director

Services/Products:
Database services; Design/graphics/clip
art supplier; Response analysis bureau

E-Services:
Website design

Member of:
FEDMA; DMA (US)

DIALOGUES DIRECT
109 Boulevard Pereire
Paris
75017
France
Tel: +33 1 5679 1515
Fax: +33 1 5679 1510
Email: direct@dialogues.fr
Web: www.dialogues.fr
Mrs Christine Leblanc, General
  Manager

Services/Products:
Advertising Agency; Mail order
company; Personalisation; List
services; Private delivery services;
Database services

E-Services:
E-Marketing consultant; Website
design; Online/e-marketing agency

Member of:
FEDMA; DMA (US)

DIRECT ENTREPRISES
rue de la Republique 149–167
Z I des Vignes
Bobigny
93000
France
Tel: +33 1 41833124
Fax: +33 141833102
Email: franck.dreyer@wanadoo.fr
Franck Dreyer, Director

Services/Products:
List services; Mailing/Faxing services

Member of:
FEDMA

DIRECT ONE
3 rue Collange
Levallois-Perret
92100
France
Tel: +33 1 49 68 59 59
Fax: +33 1 49 68 59 55
Nick Heys, Co-President

Services/Products:
Advertising Agency; Direct marketing
agency

Member of:
DMA (US)

ECCLA
696, rue Yves Kermen
Boulogne Billancourt
92658
France
Tel: +33 1 55 20 92 00
Fax: +33 46 20 55 55
Email: agence.eccla@eccla.fr
Pierre Cohen-Tanugi

Services/Products:
Database services; Direct marketing agency; Consultancy services; Sales promotion agency; Electronic media

E-Services:
Website design

Member of:
AACC

EDM RELATIONSHIP MARKETING SARL
28/44 Rue des Arts
LILLE
59800
France
Tel: +33 3 2804 5240
Fax: +33 3 2804 5241
Email: info@edmgroup.fr
Web: www.edmgroup.fr
Karine Caby, Account Director

Services/Products:
Consultancy services; Direct marketing agency; List services; Direct mail production

E-Services:
Email list provider

Member of:
FEDMA; DMA (US); National DMA

ENOXA
30, Avenue Marceau
Paris
75008
France
Tel: +33 1 47230773
Fax: +33 1 47203414
Marcel Avargues, Consultant

Services/Products:
Consultancy services

Member of:
DMA (US)

ESC -ECOLE SUPERIEURE DE COMMERCE LILLE
Avenue Willy Brandt
Departement Marketing - Vente
Euralille
59777
France
Tel: +33 3 20215942
Fax: +33 320215959
Email: p.nicholson@esc-lille.fr
Patrick Nicholson

Services/Products:
Training/recruitment

Member of:
FEDMA

ETO
62 avenue Jean Lebas
Roubaix
59100
France
Tel: +33 3 20 69 17 17
Fax: +33 3 20 69 17 18
Yves Riquet, Directeur

Services/Products:
Database services; Mailing/Faxing services; Direct marketing agency; Service bureau; Mail order company

Member of:
FEDMA

EURO RSCG TELE ACTION
84 rue de Villiers
Levallois-Perret Cedex
92683
France
Tel: +33 1 41344425
Fax: +33 141344567
Corinne Julhiet Détroyat, Président

Services/Products:
Telemarketing agency

Member of:
FEDMA

EURODIRECT ILE DE FRANCE
rue de la Republique 149/167
BP 179
Bobigny Cedex
93003
France
Tel: +33 1 41833121
Fax: +33 141833102
Email: list.company@wanadoo.fr
Stephane Barthelemy, Directeur Dept Fich

Services/Products:
List services; Lettershop; Fulfilment and sampling house; Service bureau; Personalisation; Plastic wrap facilities

Member of:
FEDMA

EUROPROGRES
rue Forlen
Geispolsheim
67118
France
Tel: +33 3 88666400
Fax: +33 388678460
Email: i.westphal@wanadoo.fr
Web: www.eurodirectmarketing.com
Pierre Boeglin, President

Services/Products:
List services; Direct marketing agency; Mail order company

Member of:
FEDMA

GREY DIRECT/GREY PROMOTION
63 bis, rue de Sèvres
Boulogne Cedex
92514
France
Tel: +33 1 46 84 85 00
Fax: +33 1 46 84 85 50
Email: ceyrac@grey.fr
Philippe Ceyrac

Services/Products:
Advertising Agency; Direct marketing agency; Sales promotion agency

Member of:
AACC

GROUP/ ADRESS
51 rue de la Garenne
Sevres
92492
France
Tel: +33 1 4114 2800
Fax: +33 1 4114 2881
Email: gbirenbaum@groupadress.com
Web: www.groupadress.com
Guy Birenbaum, CEO

Services/Products:
Call centre services/systems; Database services; Fulfilment and sampling house; Telemarketing agency; Lettershop; Service bureau

E-Services:
Email list provider

Member of:
FEDMA; National DMA

GROUPE D
2, avenue Pasteur
Issy Les Moulineaux Cedex
92137
France
Tel: +33 1 41 09 17 00
Fax: +33 1 41 09 17 54
Email: agence@groupe-d.com
Web: www.groupe-d.com
Sylvain Forestier

Services/Products:
Database services; Telemarketing agency; Direct marketing agency; Response analysis bureau; Sales promotion agency; Direct response TV services

Member of:
AACC

INTERNATIONAL HERALD TRIBUNE
181 Avenue Charles de Gaulle
Neuilly Cedex
92521
France
Tel: +33 1 414393 60
Fax: +33 1 414392 16
Web: www.iht.com
Maria Kenned, Subscription
Marketing Manager

Services/Products:
List services

Member of:
FEDMA

ITL
13 rue du Canal
OBERSCHAEFFOLSHEIM
67203
France
Tel: +33 3 8877 4858
Fax: +33 3 8877 4855
Email: info@itl.fr
Web: www.itl.fr
Paul G. Adam, General Manager

Services/Products:
Database services; List services;
Translation services

E-Services:
Email list provider; E-Marketing
consultant; Website design

Member of:
FEDMA; DMA (US)

J. WALTER THOMPSON CONSUMER
35 Rue Baudin
Levallois Perret
92593
France
Tel: +33 1 41 05 81 47
Fax: +33 1 41 05 80 05
Debra Brown-Christie, Managing
Director

Services/Products:
Advertising Agency; Direct marketing
agency

Member of:
DMA (US)

LA POSTE COURRIER INTERNATIONAL
11, rue du Pré
Paris Cedex 18
75877
France
Tel: +33 1 44 722345
Fax: +33 1 44 722335

Email: francois.labat@wanadoo.fr
François Labat, Market Intelligence
Manager

Services/Products:
Private delivery services; Mailing/
Faxing services; Internet services

Member of:
FEDMA

LA POSTE INTERNATIONAL
11, rue du Pré
Paris Cedex 18
75877
France
Tel: +33 1 44 722318
Fax: +33 1 44 722337
Anne-Laurence Veyrine

Services/Products:
Mailing/Faxing services

Member of:
FEDMA; DMA (US)

LA POSTE MARKETING HEADQUARTERS
9 Bis rue Delerve
Montrouge
92120
France
Tel: +33 1 55 58 89 20
Fax: +33 1 55 58 89 30
Marc-Lionel Gatto, Direct Marketing
Manager

Services/Products:
Mailing/Faxing services

Member of:
FEDMA

LA REDOUTE S.A.
12 Square Henri Adjointe
Beagsone
Paris
75017
France
Tel: +33 1 42 27 32 88
Valerie Meteyer, Marketing
Department Director

Services/Products:
Advertising Agency; Direct marketing
agency

Member of:
DMA (US)

LIST-LINK INTERNATIONAL LTD
Les Bellegardes, Fillinges
Viuz-en-Sallaz
74250
France
Tel: +33 4 50 311 035

Fax: +33 4 50 311 038
Jacqueline Rowell, Managing Director

Services/Products:
List services; Software supplier;
Electronic media

E-Services:
Website design

Member of:
AACC

MANUEL-CONSEIL
3 Passage Turquetil
Cedex 08
Paris
75011
France
Tel: +33 55 25 25 65
Fax: +33 55 25 25 66
Bruno Manuel, President

Services/Products:
Consultancy services

Member of:
DMA (US)

MATRIXX MARKETING EUROPE SA
153, Avenue d'Italie
Paris
75013
France
Tel: +33 1 53606021
Fax: +33 153606064
Email: bdevogue@mattrixx.com
Bertrand de Vogüe

Services/Products:
Telemarketing agency; Market research
agency

Member of:
FEDMA; DMA (US)

MEDIAPOST
15 boulevard du Gen. de Gaulle
Montrouge Cedex
92126
France
Tel: +33 1 46 12 44 02
Fax: +33 1 40 84 01 16
Phillippe Thomas, Director, Direct
Mail

Services/Products:
Lettershop; Mailing/Faxing services

Member of:
DMA (US)

MEDIAVENTE
7 rue de Monceau
Paris
75008
France

Tel: +33 1 53 93 97 70
Fax: +33 1 42 89 43 80
Email: christian.renard@wanadoo.fr
Christian Renard, Président

Services/Products:
Advertising Agency; Database services;
Direct marketing agency; Response
analysis bureau; Mail order company

Member of:
FEDMA; DMA (US)

OGILVYONE WORLDWIDE LTD
44 Avenue George V
Paris
75008
France
Tel: +33 1 53233000
Fax: +33 153233128
Denis Bonnet

Services/Products:
Database services; Telemarketing
agency; Direct marketing agency;
Media buying agency

Member of:
FEDMA; AACC

PASSION DIRECTE
16 rue de l'Evangile
Paris
75018
France
Tel: +33 1 42 05 50 00
Fax: +33 1 42 05 43 44
Email: passiondirecte@calva.net
Web: www.srcommunication.com
Alain Boulet, Chairman and Managing
Director

Services/Products:
Direct marketing agency; Sales
promotion agency

Member of:
FEDMA; DMA (US); AACC

PLUME DIRECT
113 rue Victor Hugo
Levallois Perret
92300
France
Tel: +33 1 41 06 93 60
Fax: +33 1 41 06 93 61
Email: nhenriot@plume.imaginet.fr
Web: www.plumedirect.com
Nathalie Henriot, Chairman

Services/Products:
Telemarketing agency; Direct
marketing agency; Copy adaptation;
Design/graphics/clip art supplier; Sales
promotion agency; Electronic media

E-Services:
Website design

Member of:
FEDMA; AACC

PROCRéA CUSTOMER
103 Bis, rue Lauriston
Paris
75116
France
Tel: +33 1 53 65 78 00
Fax: +33 1 53 65 78 18
Email: gvillemot@procrea.fr
Mr Guillaume Villemot

Services/Products:
Advertising Agency; Consultancy
services; Database services; Direct
marketing agency; Telemarketing
agency

Member of:
AACC

R + B PARTNERS SOLUTIONS
8, rue Halevy
Paris, Cedex 09
75441
France
Tel: +33 1 44511430
Fax: +33 1 44511431
Bernard Gatinot, Chairman & CEO

Services/Products:
Consultancy services

Member of:
DMA (US)

REDOUTE FRANCE
57 Rue de Blanchemaille
Roubaix Cedex 2
59082
France
Tel: +33 3 20 69 60 00
Fax: +33 3 20 24 03 37
Valerie Meteyer, Marketing
Department Director

Services/Products:
Advertising Agency; Direct marketing
agency

Member of:
DMA (US)

REED EXPOSITIONS FRANCE
70 rue Rivay
Levallois Perret
92300
France
Tel: +33 14756 5230
Fax: +3314756 2412
Email:
emmanuel_armand@reedexpo.fr

Services/Products:
List services; Database services; Direct
marketing agency

E-Services:
Email list provider

Member of:
FEDMA

SHANTUNG
21 Rue du Faubourg St. Antoine
Paris
75011
France
Tel: +33 1 66 75 55 90
Fax: +33 1 66 75 55 89
Beatrice Royer

Services/Products:
Advertising Agency; Direct marketing
agency

Member of:
DMA (US)

**SOLAR COMMUNICATIONS,
INC. & DUALMEDIA.COM**
27, rue de la Villette
Lyon
69003
France
Tel: +33 4 7213 5324
Fax: +33 4 7213 5335
Email: jpouilly@compuserve.com
Web: www.LeaderOfThePack.com
www.SolarEUROPE.com
Julie Cassidy Pouilly, European
Marketing Manager

Services/Products:
Card pack manufacturer; Interactive
media; Print services; Online inquiry
and lead generation through web-based
advertising programmes; Printing and
demetalisation of metalised film

E-Services:
Online/e-marketing agency

Member of:
FEDMA; DMA (US); Association for
Interactive Media; Printing Industries
of America (PIA)

SOPRES FRANCE
BP 4
Lille Cedex 9
59861
France
Tel: +33 3 20612323
Fax: +33 320051839
Chantal Sellier, General Manager

Services/Products:
Database services; Response analysis
bureau; Service bureau

Member of:
FEDMA

TELEMEDIA
63 Avenue Marceau
Paris
75116
France
Tel: +33 1 53 23 11 37
Fax: +33 1 53 23 11 22
Pierre Guillermo, President

Services/Products:
Advertising Agency; Telemarketing
agency; Direct marketing agency; Sales
promotion agency; Direct response TV
services; Electronic media

E-Services:
Website design

Member of:
AACC

TELEPERFORMANCE
International Management
6–8, rue Firmin-Gillot
Paris Cedex 15
75737
France
Tel: +33 1 5576 4080
Fax: +33 1 5576 8686
Email: info@teleperformance.com
Web: www.teleperformance.com
Christophe Allard, COO and Member
of the Board

Services/Products:
Call centre services/systems;
Consultancy services; Interactive
media; Market research agency;
Software supplier; Telemarketing
agency

E-Services:
Email software

Member of:
FEDMA; DMA (US); National DMA

URSULA GRüBER
COMMUNICATION
INTERNATIONALE SA
83 rue St. Honore
Paris
75001
France
Tel: +33 1 42335761
Fax: +33 1 42214114
Email: ursula_gruber@msn.com
Web: 101531.304@compuserve.com
Ursula Grüber, President

Services/Products:
Direct marketing agency; Copy
adaptation

Member of:
FEDMA

VM DATA
7, Rue De Monceau
Paris
75008
France
Tel: +33 1 42–89–22–22
Fax: +33 1 42–89–43–80
Christian Renard, President

Services/Products:
Consultancy services

Member of:
DMA (US)

SERVICES/PRODUCT LISTING

Advertising Agency
Association des Agences-Conseils en
   Communication (AACC)
Bellanger Foucaucourt & Assoc.
Dialogues Direct
DIRECT ONE
Grey Direct/Grey Promotion
J. Walter Thompson Consumer
La Redoute S.A.
Mediavente
Procréa Customer
Redoute France
Shantung
Telemedia

B to B addresses
Bottin Entreprises - Coface SRCL

Call centre services/systems
Addressing Technology
GROUP/ adress
TELEPERFORMANCE

Card pack manufacturer
Solar Communications, Inc. &
   DualMedia.com

Consultancy services
141 France – GMS
Andersen Consulting
Claritas France
Communider
ECCLA
EDM Relationship Marketing SARL
ENOXA
Manuel-Conseil
Procréa Customer
R + B Partners Solutions
TELEPERFORMANCE
VM Data

Copy adaptation
Plume Direct

Ursula Grüber Communication
   Internationale Sa

Database services
141 France – GMS
Addressing Technology
Aid – Analyse Informatique Des
   Donnees
Bottin Entreprises - Coface SRCL
Claritas France
Consodata
Diacom
Dialogues Direct
ECCLA
Eto
GROUP/ adress
Groupe D
ITL
Mediavente
Ogilvyone Worldwide Ltd
Procréa Customer
Reed Expositions France
Sopres France

Design/graphics/clip art supplier
141 France – GMS
Diacom
Plume Direct

Direct mail production
EDM Relationship Marketing SARL

Direct marketing agency
141 France – GMS
Adress Media
Association des Agences-Conseils en
   Communication (AACC)
Bellanger Foucaucourt & Assoc.
Communider
DIRECT ONE
ECCLA
EDM Relationship Marketing SARL
Eto
Europrogres
Grey Direct/Grey Promotion
Groupe D
J. Walter Thompson Consumer
La Redoute S.A.
Mediavente
Ogilvyone Worldwide Ltd
Passion Directe
Plume Direct
Procréa Customer
Redoute France
Reed Expositions France
Shantung
Telemedia
Ursula Grüber Communication
   Internationale Sa

Direct response TV services
Groupe D
Telemedia

Electronic media
141 France – GMS
Communider
ECCLA
List-Link International Ltd
Plume Direct
Telemedia

Fulfilment and sampling house
Eurodirect Ile De France
GROUP/ adress

Interactive media
Solar Communications, Inc. &
   DualMedia.com
TELEPERFORMANCE

Internet services
La Poste Courrier International

Labelling/envelope services
Addressing Technology
Avery Dennison France S.A.
Cepap

Legal services
Cabinet Alain Bensoussan

Lettershop
Addressing Technology
CIFEA-DMK
Eurodirect Ile De France
GROUP/ adress
Mediapost

List services
Addressing Technology
Adress Media
Bottin Entreprises - Coface SRCL
CIFEA-DMK
Claritas France
Consodata
Dialogues Direct
Direct Entreprises
EDM Relationship Marketing SARL
Eurodirect Ile De France
Europrogres
International Herald Tribune
ITL
List-Link International Ltd
Reed Expositions France

Mail order company
Alkea Conseil
Dialogues Direct
Eto
Europrogres
Mediavente

Mailing/Faxing services
Addressing Technology
Bottin Entreprises - Coface SRCL
Direct Entreprises
Eto
La Poste Courrier International
La Poste International
La Poste Marketing Headquarters
Mediapost

Market research agency
Alkea Conseil
Matrixx Marketing Europe Sa
TELEPERFORMANCE

Media buying agency
Ogilvyone Worldwide Ltd

**Online inquiry and lead
generation through web-
based advertising
programmes**
Solar Communications, Inc. &
   DualMedia.com

Personalisation
Avery Dennison France S.A.
CIFEA-DMK
Dialogues Direct
Eurodirect Ile De France

Plastic wrap facilities
Eurodirect Ile De France

Print services
CIFEA-DMK
Solar Communications, Inc. &
   DualMedia.com

**Printing and demetalisation
of metalised film**
Solar Communications, Inc. &
   DualMedia.com

Private delivery services
Dialogues Direct
La Poste Courrier International

Response analysis bureau
Claritas France
Diacom
Groupe D
Mediavente
Sopres France

Sales promotion agency
Association des Agences-Conseils en
   Communication (AACC)
ECCLA
Grey Direct/Grey Promotion
Groupe D
Passion Directe
Plume Direct
Telemedia

Service bureau
Aid – Analyse Informatique Des
   Donnees
Axime Direct
Eto
Eurodirect Ile De France
GROUP/ adress
Sopres France

Software supplier
141 France – GMS
List-Link International Ltd
TELEPERFORMANCE

Telemarketing agency
141 France – GMS
Communider
Euro Rscg Tele Action
GROUP/ adress
Groupe D
Matrixx Marketing Europe Sa
Ogilvyone Worldwide Ltd
Plume Direct
Procréa Customer
Telemedia
TELEPERFORMANCE

Training/recruitment
Alkea Conseil
Esc -Ecole Superieure De Commerce
   Lille

Translation services
ITL

E-SERVICES

E-Marketing consultant
Dialogues Direct
ITL

Email list provider
Addressing Technology
EDM Relationship Marketing SARL
GROUP/ adress
ITL
Reed Expositions France

Email software
TELEPERFORMANCE

Online/e-marketing agency
Dialogues Direct
Solar Communications, Inc. &
   DualMedia.com

Website design
141 France – GMS
Addressing Technology
Communider
Diacom

Dialogues Direct
ECCLA

ITL
List-Link International Ltd

Plume Direct
Telemedia

GERMANY

Population: 82.1 million
Capital: Berlin
Language: German

GDP: $2183 billion
GDP per capita: $26,747
Inflation: 1.8 per cent

Currency: Deutsche Mark (DM) = 100 pfennig
Exchange rate: DM1.82 : $1 (DM1.96 : 1 euro)

Time: GMT +1 hour

OVERVIEW

With by far the largest population in Europe, and one of the biggest economies in the world (surpassed only by the US and Japan), Germany remains one of the most influential players on the European scene. Despite the huge cost of reunification, Germany still boasts one of the world's highest levels of purchasing power per capita and maintains high consumer spending.

While political union has been embraced, the full social and economic integration of the two Germanies proves a lengthier process; in marketing terms the regions should still be viewed as distinct markets, with markedly differing consumer profiles and infrastructures. Many companies view Germany as a stepping stone to the emerging Eastern European markets beyond.

Germany has a high total level of advertising expenditure, at nearly 1 per cent of GDP. Despite some of the most restrictive data protection laws in Europe, there is a booming DM industry, with high standards of technology and creativity. PDMS figures show Germany to account for some 30 per cent of total European direct mail volume. East Germany is developing rapidly, but can still be considered an emerging marketplace.

LANGUAGE AND CULTURAL CONSIDERATIONS

It is important to shake hands with hosts. It is no longer important to address people by their title except for academic titles, where the custom is to use the Herr/Frau Doktor and Herr/Frau Professor style.

LEGISLATION AND CONSUMER PROTECTION

The Robinson list, established by the DDV, is held by all computer bureaux and totals over 300,000 members. In addition, a label on private letterboxes indicating that the owner does not want to receive non-personalized DM advertising must be respected.

The current data protection legislation came into effect on 1 June 1991, and the Minister of the Interior is responsible for its implementation. The legislation covers only data relating to individuals – companies and institutions are not protected in the same way.

THE DIRECT MARKETING ASSOCIATION

Name:	Deutscher Direktmarketing Verband (DDV)
Address:	Hasengarten Strasse 14, D-65189 Wiesbaden
Tel:	+49 611 977930
Fax:	+49 611 9779399
Email:	info@ddv.de
Website:	www.ddv.de
Year founded:	1948
President:	Prof. Bernd Kracke
Total staff:	15
Members:	970

DM agencies	138	List brokers	25
Printers	68	Telemarketing agencies	192
Advertisers	205	Mail order companies	71
Mailing houses	44	DM consultants	34
Handling houses	49	Database agencies	56

Others: diverse service providers

Facilities for overseas users of direct mail

Membership: overseas companies can join the DDV. Details of membership on request. The organization works extremely hard to answer any enquiry which reaches them.

Newsletter: there is a newsletter every two weeks.

Library: there is a library which has technical literature with free access to members and non-members.

The movers database

Deutsche Post Adress GmbH is a joint venture between the Deutsche Post AG and Bertelsmann AG. Since its foundation in October 1994 Post Adress possesses the only up to date old/new file for updating addresses in Germany, and this grows daily by new entries.

Persons and companies who change their address on a permanent basis place a mail forwarding order with Deutsche Post AG and at the same time agree to the passing on of their data.

Over 75% of all people moving make use of this free service. The Deutsche Post AG immediately and exclusively provides the Deutsche Post Adress with this information.

This service was used by 6.3 million private persons and about 200,000 companies in the year 2000. Day by day over 20,000 new changes of addresses are entered.

After the registration of the new address and the entry of the effective date of the change of the address, each address is checked and corrected if necessary by Post Adress to ensure they are deliverable. This guarantees the high quality of the data.

For all companies using the postal service to stay in contact with their customers the large number of moves means to invest a lot of time and money to keep their files updated. In a worse case scenario they even risk losing their customers and prospects.

It is the aim of Deutsche Post Adress to assist you and avoid unnecessary costs!

The big mail-order businesses and financial services have already been convinced of the economic efficiency of this product.

The movers database of Deutsche Post Adress GmbH can be used in five different product variations: from subscription for large customers with millions of addresses right down to the extraction of a single address via the Internet.

On-line information service: www.ddv.de

Legal advice: the DDV offers a legal advice service for both members and non-members. This service is free for members.

Business liaison service: the DDV offers a roster of members including a full list of suppliers and agencies (100 pages of comprehensive data free of charge – postage paid on delivery).

Other facilities: the DDV produces a publication called *Direct Mail – the direct route to the customer.* It contains everything you need to know about addresses and publishing. Other services include membership services, publications, discounts, trade fair DIMA, professional training.

Other DM organizations: Bundesverband des Deutschen Versandhandels e.V., Johann Klotz Strasse 12, D-60528 Frankfurt; tel: +49 69 67 50 48; fax: +49 69 67 50 98. (A mail order trade organization).

POSTAL SERVICES

The Deutsche Post AG has a number of special products designed for the direct mailer, including:

- *Infopost (formerly Massendrucksache):* available both nationally and internationally, this is designed for multiple mailings where content is standardized, with the exception of the individual's details. Subject to a number of conditions, discounts are available;

- *Postwurfsendung:* delivery of standardized, unaddressed mailshots to households (max. weight 100g) or unaddressed letters to PO boxes (max. weight 500g);

- *International Business Reply Service:* available nationally and internationally to stimulate response. Discounts are dependent on quantity and whether or not mail has been presorted. The maximum discount is given for a quantity of over 4000, each with a weight of less than 20g.

For more information, contact:

Deutsche Post AG
Postfach 3000
53105 Bonn
Germany
Tel: +49 228 1822 4000
Fax: +49 228 1822 4009
Website: www.postag.de

The Deutsche Telekom Medien can provide reliable data for personalized mailings. This includes the cluster typology analysis and selection system (CAS), with over 27 million addresses available. CAS can segment by title, profession, number of telephones owned, creating a number of micro-residential grids. Forenames are also used as selection criteria. Names, like products, come in and out of fashion, and CAS offers 12 groupings by forename, targeting prospects by approximate age.

129

Contact:

Deutsche Telekom Medien GmbH
Postfach 16 02 11
D-60065 Frankfurt
Germany
Tel: +49 18 01 338363
Fax: +49 18 01 329338

The one address for European success

50 years of direct marketing experience for your successful start in Europe.

◆ 960 mio. consumer and 45 mio. businesses in our own European databases

◆ Unique in Europe: our BRANDNEW international catalogue with relevant information in international direct marketing

◆ comprehensive marketing information for each individual address

◆ full service range from country specific consultancy, international listbroking, dataprocessing and lettershop

◆ **ONE address for your European success!**

Interested? Just call and ask for our new international catalogue with counts, statistics and more useful information to 16 countries.

Call +49/7156/304-299

Schober International:
Amsterdam · Bratislava · Bruxelles
London · Madrid · Milano · New York
Paris · Praha · Stuttgart · Wien · Zürich

Schober Direktmarketing OHG
Max-Eyth-Straße 6–10
D-71254 Ditzingen/Stuttgart
Phone +49/7156/304-299 · Fax +49/7156/304-485
Internet: www.schober-international.com

INFORMATION GROUP

Information for Success

International Direct Marketing

The Schober Information Group – a successful full-service partner in international markets for more than 50 years – offers a comprehensive product and service portfolio for every aspect of international direct marketing: From proprietary business and consumer databases to international business and consumer lists; from list brokerage, list management, and market and customer analysis all the way to segmentation systems, marketing databases, and clusters. With eleven of our own companies in Europe and the USA as well as strategic alliance partners with worldwide reach, Schober is Europe's leading information provider and gives you access to every piece of data and information that's relevant to direct marketing campaigns. This customer-focused transfer of knowledge covers all direct marketing services from one easy source: From names all the way to mail-out. The newest highlight from Schober Information Group's broad spectrum of offers is the International Catalogue – a one-of-a-kind reference work with a wealth of information and details about 15 European countries and the USA.

E-Commerce

"Information for Success" – that's the motto by which the Schober Information Group innovatively opens new areas of business even in new markets: At *www.schober-international.com* you can access all the information in the Schober Catalogues; from Schober's home page, you can navigate to a wealth of supplemental information – for example, to country-specific data relevant to direct marketing activities. The Web site even includes business-to-business counts for Europe's most important countries and the USA – listed by NACE codes. Schober's business-to-business database on the Web, which counts as one of the databases with the greatest market coverage, offers a one-of-a-kind opportunity to define, to select, and to address specific target markets from more than five million German business names – all online.

Contact address:

Schober Direktmarketing OHG
Max-Eyth-Strasse 6–10
D-71254
Ditzingen/Stuttgart
GERMANY
Phone: ++49 / 7156 / 304–299
Fax: ++49 / 7156 / 304–485
e-Mail:
international@schober.de
Internet:
www.schober-international.com

PROVIDERS OF DM AND E-M SERVICES

141 DIALOG DIREKTMARKETING (GERMANY) GMBH
Hanauer Landstraße 287–289
Frankfurt
60314
Germany
Tel: +49 69 40572 265
Fax: +49 69 40572 359
Walther Kraft

Services/Products:
Direct marketing agency

Member of:
DDV

4SALE WERBEAGENTUR GMBH
Günsheimer Straße 1
Gustavsburg
65492
Germany
Tel: +49 6134 557 200
Fax: +49 6134 557 230
Email: info@4sale-gmbh.de
Matthias Schmidt

Services/Products:
Direct marketing agency

Member of:
DDV

A & L PARTNER DIREKTMARKETING GMBH
Hallerplatz 5
Hamburg
20146
Germany
Tel: +49 40 412071
Fax: +49 40 445282
Email: alpart@mail.hamburg.com
Web: http://www.a-l-partner.com
Anja Langenberger

Services/Products:
Direct marketing agency

Member of:
DDV

A S P I ARBEITSGEMEINSCHAFT FÜR SCHULPÄDAGOGISCHE INFORMATION GMBH
Konrad-Adenauer-Platz 6
Langenfeld
40764
Germany
Tel: +49 2173 9849 30
Fax: +49 2173 9849 48

Email: aspi-langenfeld@t-online.de
Web: http://www.aspi.de
Frank Steffes

Member of:
DDV

A.P.A. WERBEAGENTUR GMBH
Berliner Promenade 3
Saarbrücken
66111
Germany
Tel: +49 681 3905977
Fax: +49 681 374471
Karl Heinrich F. Wagner

Services/Products:
Direct marketing agency

Member of:
DDV

ABIS AG
Active Business Information Systems
Adalbertstraße 64
Frankfurt
60486
Germany
Tel: +49 69 792009 0
Fax: +49 69 792009 20
Email: abis@abis-ag.com
Web: www.abis-ag.com

Services/Products:
Direct marketing agency; Software supplier; Develop and distribute software for direct marketing

ABRESCH:DIRECT TEAM FÜR INTEGRIERTES DIALOGMARKETING GMBH
Elgendorfer Straße 55
Montabaur
56410
Germany
Tel: +49 2602 1601 00
Fax: +49 2602 1601 990
Lothar Birner

Services/Products:
Direct marketing agency

Member of:
DDV

ABS COMPUTER GMBH
Katernberger Str. 4
Wuppertal
42115
Germany
Tel: +49 202 37147 0
Fax: +49 20 2371 4749
Email: info@marketing-by-abs.com
Heino Müller

Services/Products:
Direct marketing agency

Member of:
DDV

ABT DRUCK GMBH
Bruchsaler Straße 5
Weinheim
69469
Germany
Tel: +49 6201 1890 0
Fax: +49 6201 1890 90
Email: info@abtdruck.de
Web: http://www.abtdruck.de
Irmgard Abt

Services/Products:
Print services

Member of:
DDV

ACKERLER TELEFONMARKETING
Bahnhofstr. 28
Hagen
58095
Germany
Tel: +49 2331 383383
Fax: +49 2331 383384
Hartmut Ackerler

Services/Products:
Telemarketing agency

Member of:
DDV

ACTON DIREKT-MARKETING GMBH
Kirschwiese 15
Kassel-Fuldatal
34233
Germany
Tel: +49 5607 93010
Fax: +49 5607 93011
Email: wgregg@acton.com
Web: http://www.acton.com
Werner Gregg

Services/Products:
Direct marketing agency

Member of:
DDV

AD-CON ADRESSEN-UND LETTERSHOPSERVICE GMBH
Florianweg 48
Frankfurt
60388
Germany
Tel: +49 6109 7342 60
Fax: +49 6109 7342 66
Thorsten Schmidt

Services/Products:
List services; Lettershop; Fulfilment and sampling house

Member of:
DDV

ADD-DIRECT MARKETING GMBH & CO. KG DATABASE ADDRESS DIRECT-SERVICE
Am Becketal 45
Bremen
28755
Germany
Tel: +49 421 663713
Fax: +49 421 663724
Kurt Pfeifenberger

Member of:
DDV

ADEO GESELLSCHAFT FÜR MARKETING UND TELEKOMMUNIKATIONSDI-ENSTE MBH
Kutterstraße 3
Wilhelmshaven
26386
Germany
Tel: +49 4421 967777
Fax: +49 4421 967796
Horst Kiel

Member of:
DDV

ADM ARBEITSGRUPPE FÜR DIREKTMARKETING GMBH
Hansastraße 15
München
80686
Germany
Tel: +49 89 578368 0
Fax: +49 89 578368 50
Email: adm_mue@compuserve.com
Rainer Tillich

Services/Products:
List services; Lettershop; Fulfilment and sampling house

Member of:
DDV

ADM-AGENTUR FÜR DIALOGMARKETING GMBH
Pettenkoferstraße 30
Mannheim
68169
Germany
Tel: +49 621 12752 0
Fax: +49 621 12752 74
Email:
  adm_mannheim@compuserve.com
Web: http://www.adm-mannheim.de
Thomas Steinle

Services/Products:
Telemarketing agency

Member of:
DDV

ADRESSEN + SERVICE GMBH
Wetterkreuz 11
Erlangen
91058
Germany
Tel: +49 9131 692 244
Fax: +49 9131 692 226
Email: as_tu@t-online.de
Web: http://www.Ullrich-direkt.com
Sylvana Turschner

Services/Products:
List services; Lettershop; Fulfilment and sampling house

Member of:
DDV

ADRESSMARKETING RUDOLF K. HÄRTEL GMBH
Sittarder Str. 23
Gangelt
52538
Germany
Tel: +49 2454 5032
Fax: +49 2454 5034
Rudolf K. Härtel

Services/Products:
List services; Lettershop; Fulfilment and sampling house

Member of:
DDV

ADTECH ADVERTISING SERVICE PROVIDING GMBH
Frankfurter Straße 135
Dreieich
63303
Germany
Tel: +49 6103 9307 0
Fax: +49 6103 9307 111
Email: info@adtech.de
Web: http://www.adtech.de
Michael Stusch

Services/Products:
Interactive media

Member of:
DDV

AFM GMBH AGENTUR FÜR FAX-UND TELEMARKETING
Möhnweg 13
Neufahrn
85375
Germany
Tel: +49 89 3610 9216
Fax: +49 89 3610 9217

Email: info@afmgmbh.de
Web: http://www.afmgmbh.de
Klaus Baumann

Services/Products:
Telemarketing agency

Member of:
DDV

AGENTUHR DIREKTMARKETINGGESEL-LSCHAFT MBH
Hohenzollernstraße 16
Pforzheim
75177
Germany
Tel: +49 7231 140060
Fax: +49 7231 140062
Mario Reuter

Services/Products:
Direct marketing agency

Member of:
DDV

AGENTUR FÜR KOMPAKTMARKETING GREMMER DIREKT GMBH
Herderstr. 82
Hilden
40721
Germany
Tel: +49 2103 4993 0
Fax: +49 2103 4993 606
Email: u.gremmer@t-online.de
Hartmut Dühr

Services/Products:
Direct marketing agency

Member of:
DDV

AGENTUR FÜR PUBLIKATION UND MEDIA (APM) HEINER GMBH
Auguststraße 1
Bonn
53229
Germany
Tel: +49 228 9732 0
Fax: +49 228 9732 140
Email: info@apm-heiner.de
Web: http://www.apm-heiner.de
Joern Heiner

Services/Products:
List services; Direct marketing agency; Media buying agency

Member of:
FEDMA; DDV

**AGENTUR FÜR TELEFON-
MARKETING URSULA
BELLENBAUM**
Friedhofstr. 31–35
Mülheim a.d.Ruhr
45478
Germany
Tel: +49 208 58864 0
Fax: +49 208 58864 20
Ursula Bellenbaum

Services/Products:
Telemarketing agency

Member of:
DDV

**AGENTUR FÜR
ZIELGRUPPENBERATUNG
GUDRUN SCHRÖDL**
Weiherweg 71c
Gröbenzell
82194
Germany
Tel: +49 8142 57693
Fax: +49 8142 57694
Email: stef.munich@t-online.de
Gudrun Schrödl

Services/Products:
List services; Lettershop; Fulfilment
and sampling house

Member of:
DDV

**AGENTUR LESSING
KREATIVES
DIREKTMARKETING GMBH**
Lessingstr. 6, Eingang Klüpfelstr. 6
Stuttgart
70193
Germany
Tel: +49 711 2269823
Fax: +49 711 2269820
Email: agenturlessing@t-online.de
Brigitte Lessing

Services/Products:
Direct marketing agency

Member of:
DDV

**AIS AXON INTERNET
SERVICES GMBH
VERMARKTER VON
DINO-ONLINE**
Hannoversche Straße 43–47
Göttingen
37075
Germany
Tel: +49 551 383700
Fax: +49 551 3837070
Email: kayser@dino-online.de
Web: http://www.dino-online-de
Holger Kayser

Services/Products:
Interactive media

Member of:
DDV

**AKTIV DIREKT MARKETING
GMBH**
Bruchsaler Straße 5
Weinheim
69469
Germany
Tel: +49 6201 189070
Fax: +49 6201 189079
Email: info@aktivdirekt.de
Web: www.aktivdirekt.de
Mr. Axel Rückert, Executive Director

Services/Products:
Consultancy services; Database
services; Direct marketing agency;
Lettershop; Personalisation; Print
services

Member of:
National DMA

**AKTIV
KOMMUNIKATIONSDIENST**
Eberhardstr. 12
Trier
54290
Germany
Tel: +49 651 9941588
Fax: +49 651 9941589
Email: asd@frosch.in-trier.de
Arnim Schmidt-Dominé

Services/Products:
Telemarketing agency

Member of:
DDV

ALL BY PHONE + NET
Wendenstraße 377
Hamburg
20537
Germany
Tel: +49 40 2541 44
Fax: +49 40 2541 4502
Email: info@allbyphone.de
Web: www.allbyphone.de
Felicitas Bohm, Call Centre Manager

Services/Products:
Call centre services/systems;
Telemarketing agency; Internet and e-
mail services

E-Services:
Email software

Member of:
National DMA

**ALLBECON
PERSONALDIENSTLEISTUN-
GEN MÜNCHEN GMBH**
Albert-Roßhaupter-Str. 65
München
81369
Germany
Tel: +49 89 596033
Fax: +49 89 553926
Herbert Spanger

Services/Products:
Direct marketing agency

Member of:
DDV

**ALMUC DIALOGMARKETING
GMBH & CO. KG**
Goethestraße 12
München
80336
Germany
Tel: +49 89 5438826
Fax: +49 89 5438828
Peter Felder

Services/Products:
Direct marketing agency

Member of:
DDV

**ALPHATEXT
DIREKTWERBUNG GMBH**
Bentelerstr. 33
Wadersloh
59329
Germany
Tel: +49 2523 1011
Fax: +49 2523 1509
Barbara Luebbert

Services/Products:
List services; Lettershop; Fulfilment
and sampling house

Member of:
DDV

**AMA ADRESS-UND
ZEITSCHRIFTENVERLAG
GMBH**
Postfach 11 53
Waghäusel
68743
Germany
Tel: +49 7254 9820
Fax: +49 7254 982222
Email: info@ama-adress.de
Web: http://www.ama-adress.de
Axel Hegel

Services/Products:
List services; Lettershop; Fulfilment
and sampling house

Member of:
DDV

AOL BERTELSMANN ONLINE GMBH & CO.KG
Stubbenhuk 3
Hamburg
20459
Germany
Tel: +49 40 36159 0
Fax: +49 40 36159 444
Email: thea_meuss@aol.com
Web: http://www.aol.com
Thea Meuss

Services/Products:
Interactive media

Member of:
DDV

AOS CONSULT GMBH
Weiherweg 4E
Groebenzell
D-82194
Germany
Tel: +49 8142 597624
Fax: +49 8142 597625
Email: info@AOS-consult.de
Web: www.AOS-consult.de
Albrecht O. Schweikert, President

Services/Products:
Consultancy services; Database
services; Response analysis bureau

Member of:
National DMA; DDV

ARNOLD, DEMMERER & PARTNER
Mittlerer Pfad 26
Stuttgart
70499
Germany
Tel: +49 711 8871 320
Fax: +49 711 8871 344
Email: deacon@arnold-demmerer.de
Helen Deacon, Director International

Services/Products:
List services; Service bureau; Database
services; Package inserts; Modelling,
regression; Merge-purge services

Member of:
National DMA

ARTS & WILES WERBEAGENTUR GMBH
August-Wessels-Straße 5
Augsburg
86154
Germany
Tel: +49 821 24163 01
Fax: +49 821 24163 63
René Kammermeier

Services/Products:
Direct marketing agency

Member of:
DDV

ARTWORK WERBE-UND KOMMUNIKATIONSAGENT-UR SVEN LORENZ
Wachhausstraße 13A
Karlsruhe
76227
Germany
Tel: +49 721 94412 0
Fax: +49 721 94412 40
Email: agentur@art-work.de
Web: http://www.art-work.de
Sven Lorenz

Services/Products:
Direct marketing agency

Member of:
DDV

ASCENA COMMUNICATION SERVICES GMBH
Willy-Brandt-Platz 1–3
Mannheim
68161
Germany
Tel: +49 621 166960
Fax: +49 621 16696399
Jochen Gross

Services/Products:
Telemarketing agency

Member of:
DDV

ASPECT COMMUNICATIONS GMBH
Frankfurter Strasse 233
Neu-Isenburg
63263
Germany
Tel: +49 6102 5677 350
Fax: +49 6102 5677 201
Email: fredrik.decker@aspect.com
Web: www.aspect.com/german
Fredrik Decker, Marketing Manager

Services/Products:
Call centre services/systems;
Consultancy services; Hardware
supplier; Software supplier

E-Services:
Email software

Member of:
DDV

ATKOS OY
Köyhämäentie 12
FIN -
Vantaa
1510
Germany
Tel: +358 9 825811
Fax: +358 9 82581258
Email: atkos@atkos.fi
Web: http://www.atkos.fi
Kari Penttinen

Services/Products:
Direct marketing agency

Member of:
DDV

ATM-TELEFONMARKETING GMBH
Eutiner Straße 5
Bad Segeberg
23795
Germany
Tel: +49 4551 8000 0
Fax: +49 4551 8000 60
Email: atm-telefonmarketing@t-online.de
Petra Hagemann

Services/Products:
Telemarketing agency

Member of:
DDV

ATOS TELESERVICES GMBH
Heinrich-Krumm-Straße 17
Offenbach
63073
Germany
Tel: +49 69 989550
Fax: +49 69 98955100
Pia Heitz

Services/Products:
Telemarketing agency

Member of:
DDV

ATRIKOM FULFILLMENT GESELLSCHAFT FÜR PROJEKT-DIENSTLEISTUN-GEN MBH
Nassaustr. 20
Hofheim-Wallau
65719
Germany
Tel: +49 6122 8005 0
Fax: +49 6122 800580
Email: kunden@atrikom-fulfillment
Web: http:\\\\atrikom-fulfillment.de
Uwe Nosbisch

Member of:
DDV

AUDIOFON GESELLSCHAFT FÜR PROFESSIONELLE TELEKOMMUNIKATION MBH
Lister Str. 18
Hannover
30163
Germany
Tel: +49 511 3989201
Fax: +49 511 3989111
Email: audiofon@aol.com
Web: Wolfgang Fuhrmann
Wolfgang Fuhrmann

Member of:
DDV

AUDIOSERVICE GMBH GESELLSCHAFT FÜR INFORMATIONSDIENSTE
Am Treptower Park 75
Berlin
12435
Germany
Tel: +49 30 534327
Fax: +49 30 53432929
Email: audioservice@blinx.de
Web: http://www.audioservice.blinx.de
Markus Broschk

Services/Products:
Telemarketing agency

Member of:
DDV

AXEL SPRINGER VERLAG AG DIE WELT/WELT AM SONNTAG
Axel-Springer-Platz 1
Hamburg
20350
Germany
Tel: +49 40 34724205
Fax: +49 40 34726039
Angela Roitzsch

Services/Products:
Telemarketing agency

Member of:
DDV

AZ BERTELSMANN DIRECT GMBH
Carl-Bertelsmann-Str. 161 S
Gütersloh
33311
Germany
Tel: +49 5241 80 5438
Fax: +49 5241 80 66962
Email: az@bertelsmann.de
Web: www.az.bertelsmann.de

Services/Products:
Database services; Direct marketing agency; Lettershop; List services; Service bureau; Telemarketing agency

E-Services:
Email list provider

Member of:
DMA (US); FEDMA; DDV

B & O GESELLSCHAFT FÜR DIALOG-MARKETING MBH
Maybachstraße 6A
Stuttgart
70469
Germany
Tel: +49 711 89027 0
Fax: +49 711 89027 50
Email: post@bo-dialog.de
Web: http://www.BO-Dialog.de
Eberhard F. Beuschel

Services/Products:
Direct marketing agency

Member of:
DDV

B PLUS B DIREKTMARKETING GMBH
Papenreye 18
Hamburg
22453
Germany
Tel: +49 40 554950 0
Fax: +49 40 580180
Wolfgang Christian Kielmann

Services/Products:
Direct marketing agency

Member of:
DDV

B U. W UNTERNEHMENSGRUPPE
Rheiner Landstrasse 195
Osnabrück
D-49078
Germany
Tel: +49 541 9462 180
Fax: +49 541 9462 121
Email: buw@buw.de
Web: www.buw.de

Services/Products:
Telemarketing agency; Call centre services/systems; Consultancy services; Database services; Direct marketing agency; Lettershop

E-Services:
Online/e-marketing agency

Member of:
National DMA

B&F BRÜGGEMANN & FREUNDE
Nordring 14
Borken
46325
Germany
Tel: +49 2861 928 0
Fax: +49 2861 928 111
Email: kontakt@bfbo.de
Web: www.bfbo.de
Ulrich Brüggemann, Managing Director

B. GÜRTLER MEDIADISTRIBUTION GMBH
Tegernseer Landstr. 161
München
81539
Germany
Tel: +49 89 62181 257
Fax: +49 89 62181 222
Email: info@guertler.de
Web: http://www.direct-shopping.de
Dirk Emmerichs

Services/Products:
List services; Lettershop; Fulfilment and sampling house

Member of:
DDV

B.A.S. DIRECT GMBH
Blütenstraße 15
München
80799
Germany
Tel: +49 89 27811 0
Fax: +49 89 27811 220
Email: mbeumers@bas.de
Monika Beumers

Services/Products:
Database services; Direct marketing agency; Design/graphics/clip art supplier; Call centre services/systems

E-Services:
Website design

Member of:
FEDMA; DDV

B.A.S. INTERACTIVE GMBH
Schellingstr. 35
München
80799
Germany
Tel: +49 89 286980 10
Fax: +49 89 2730303
Email: capreen@basinteractive.de
Web: http://www.bas.de
Claus Andreas Preen

Services/Products:
Interactive media

Member of:
DDV

B.A.S. TELEMEDIEN GMBH
Blütenstraße 15
München
80799
Germany
Tel: +49 89 27811 175
Fax: +49 89 24711 801
Email: hklocke@bas.de
Web: http://www.bas.de
Heike Klocke

Services/Products:
Telemarketing agency

Member of:
DDV

**B2 KOMMUNIKATION +
WERBUNG GMBH**
Muffendorfer Hauptstraße 37
Bonn
53177
Germany
Tel: +49 228 334424
Fax: +49 228 330013
Email: nb@b-2.de
Norbert A. Bleibtreu-Busquets

Services/Products:
Telemarketing agency

Member of:
DDV

BARRY BLAU & PARTNERS INC
Mailander Strasse 8, Suite 2800
Frankfurt
60598
Germany
Tel: +49 69 684096
Fax: +49 69 381053
Dennis Eastham, President

Services/Products:
Direct marketing agency

BAUCONTACT GMBH
Schnieringshof 10
Essen
45329
Germany
Tel: +49 201 83325 50
Fax: +49 201 83325 56
Heinz Sack

Services/Products:
Telemarketing agency

Member of:
DDV

**BAUER + KIRCH GMBH BKR
SOFTWARE**
Postfach 11 65
Röttgen

52157
Germany
Tel: +49 2471 3740
Fax: +49 2471 552
Email: a.kuenzer@bkr-software.de
Web: http://www.bkr-software.de
Alexander Künzer

Services/Products:
List services; Lettershop; Fulfilment
and sampling house

Member of:
DDV

BBDO INTERACTIVE GMBH
Gruenstr. 15
Düsseldorf
D-40212
Germany
Tel: +49 211 9308 300
Fax: +49 211 9308 5330
Email: cvd@bbdo-interactive.de
Web: www.bbdo-interactive.de

Services/Products:
Consultancy services; Database
services; Interactive media; Mailing/
Faxing services; Software supplier;
eCRM; eCommerce; eBusiness (BtoB,
BtoC)

E-Services:
E-Marketing consultant; Website
design; Email software; Online/e-
marketing agency

Member of:
National DMA

**BBE-UNTERNEHMENSBERAT-
UNG GMBH**
Gothaer Allee 2
Köln
50969
Germany
Tel: +49 221 93655 242
Fax: +49 221 93655 243
Email: hasj@bbeberatung.com
Web: www.bbeberatung.com
Anja Haß, Call Centre Manager

Services/Products:
Telemarketing agency; Call centre
services/systems; Consultancy services;
Market research agency; Training/
recruitment

Member of:
ESOMAR

**BDL BETRIEBSBERATUNGS-
UND
DATENVERARBEITUNGS
GMBH**
Am Holzweg 26
Kriftel/Ts.

65830
Germany
Tel: +49 6192 970 0
Fax: +49 6192 970199
Email: info@bdl.de
Web: http://www.bdl.de
Stephan Lissner

Services/Products:
List services; Lettershop; Fulfilment
and sampling house

Member of:
DDV

**BENNER & PARTNER
DIALOGMARKETING GMBH**
Münchner Str. 12
München-Unterföhring
85774
Germany
Tel: +49 89 957248 0
Fax: +49 89 957248 48
Email: info@benner-partner.de
Web: www.benner-partner.de
Ernst M. Benner, Chairman

Services/Products:
Advertising Agency; Consultancy
services; Direct marketing agency;
Interactive media; List services; Media
buying agency

E-Services:
E-Marketing consultant; Website
design; Online/e-marketing agency

Member of:
National DMA

**BERND HÖRTKORN
VERSANDSERVICE GMBH**
Industriestr. 14
Renningen
71272
Germany
Tel: +49 7159 17074
Fax: +49 7159 5927
Email: 0715917074–0001@t-online.de
Jörg Hörtkorn

Services/Products:
List services; Lettershop; Fulfilment
and sampling house

Member of:
DDV

**BEST WEB GESELLSCHAFT F.
INTERNET-MARKETING UND
ONLINE-DIENSTLEISTUNG-
EN MBH**
Marie-Curie-Str. 4–6
Elmshorn
25337
Germany
Tel: +49 4162 911025

Fax: +49 4162 911026
Email: c.eilmes@bestweb.de
Web: http://www.bestweb.de
Christian Eilmes

Member of:
DDV

BKD GMBH
Hubertusstraße 44
Recklinghausen
45657
Germany
Tel: +49 2361 9175 0
Fax: +49 2361 9175 233
Email: dialog@bkd.de
Web: www.bkd.de
Ulkrich Braukmann, Managing
  Director

Services/Products:
Call centre services/systems;
Consultancy services; Database
services; Direct marketing agency;
Fulfilment and sampling house;
Lettershop

E-Services:
Online/e-marketing agency

Member of:
National DMA; DDV

BKG BÜRO-KOMMUNIKATION UND GRAFIKDESIGN SERVICE GMBH
Barlachstr. 26
München
80804
Germany
Tel: +49 89 30616 530
Fax: +49 89 30616 627
Email: bkg.grimm@t-online.de
Manfred Häusler

Services/Products:
List services; Lettershop; Fulfilment
and sampling house

Member of:
DDV

BLUE MARS – GESELLSCHAFT FÜR DIGITALE KOMMUNIKATION MBH
Lersnerstr. 23
Frankfurt
60322
Germany
Tel: +49 69 95942400
Fax: +49 69 95942420
Email: office@bluemars.de
Web: http://www.bluemars.de
Tobias Kirchhofer

Services/Products:
Interactive media

Member of:
DDV

BLUE MOON MARKETING GMBH
Nestorstraße 36
Berlin
10709
Germany
Tel: +49 30 89672330
Fax: +49 30 89672380
Heike Zmrahl

Services/Products:
Direct marketing agency

Member of:
DDV

BLUELANE GESELLSCHAFT FÜR MARKETING UND KOMMUNIKATION MBH
Schwere-Reiter-Str. 35, Haus 41
München
80797
Germany
Tel: +49 89 30002005
Fax: +49 89 30002007
Email: ahudema@bluelane.de
Andreas Hudema

Services/Products:
Direct marketing agency

Member of:
DDV

BLUM & UFER WERBEAGENTUR GMBH
Darmstädter Landstr. 184
Frankfurt
60598
Germany
Tel: +49 69 968869 0
Fax: +49 69 968869 30
Rudolf Hammer

Services/Products:
Direct marketing agency

Member of:
DDV

BORGES & PARTNER GMBH
Manskestr. 55
Lehrte
31275
Germany
Tel: +49 5131 83300
Fax: +49 5132 833013
Götz von Bechtolsheim

Services/Products:
Direct marketing agency

Member of:
DDV

BOSCH TELECOM SERVICE CENTER GMBH
Lübecker Straße 13–14
Magdeburg
39124
Germany
Tel: +49 391 243 2001
Fax: +49 391 243 2431
Email: wessels@compuserve.com
Georg Wessels

Services/Products:
Telemarketing agency

Member of:
DDV

BOZELL DIRECT FRIENDS - UNIT INTERACTIVE-
Borsteler Chaussee 55
Hamburg
22453
Germany
Tel: +49 40 51432 152
Fax: +49 40 51432 100
Email: s.ruettinger@bozell-direct-
  friends.com
Web: http://www.bozell-direct-
  friends.com
Stefan Rüttinger

Services/Products:
Interactive media

Member of:
DDV

BR-VERSANDSERVICE DIREKTWERBUNG ANZEIGENVERMITTLUNG RÜTTGERS GMBH
Marconistr. 22
Köln
50769
Germany
Tel: +49 221 970014 0
Fax: +49 221 970014 40
Email: info@br-ruettgers.de
Web: http://www.br-ruettgers.de
Bernd Rüttgers

Member of:
DDV

BRIEFING GMBH LÖSUNGEN UND SERVICE FÜR DIREKTMARKETING
Obenhauptstr. 11
Hamburg
22335
Germany
Tel: +49 40 5006901
Fax: +49 40 50069100
Email: info@mail.briefing.de
Web: http://www.briefing.de
Ingo Jürgens

Services/Products:
List services; Lettershop; Fulfilment and sampling house

Member of:
DDV

BRÜGGEMANN & FREUNDE AGENTUR FÜR DIALOGMARKETING GMBH

Nordring 14
Borken
46325
Germany
Tel: +49 2861 928 0
Fax: +49 2861 928 211
Email: kontakt@b-und-f.de
Web: http://www.b-und-f.de
Ulrich Bruggeman

Services/Products:
Direct marketing agency

Member of:
DDV

BSD-WIRTSCHAFTSDIENSTE GMBH

Wandalenweg 24–26
Hamburg
20097
Germany
Tel: +49 40 23520300
Fax: +49 40 231768
Email: info@bsdhh.de
Web: http://www.bsdhh.de
Olaf Schmidt

Services/Products:
Telemarketing agency

Member of:
DDV

BT&T BUSINESS TALK & TRAINING TELEMARKETING & TRAINING RICHTER-ULRICH GBR

Gustav-Adolf-Str. 165
Berlin
13086
Germany
Tel: +49 30 42859977
Fax: +49 30 42859822
Cornelia Richter

Member of:
DDV

BTW TIME LINE GMBH

Maybachstr. 4
Rödermark-Ober-Roden
63322
Germany
Tel: +49 6074 8912 0
Fax: +49 6074 8912 12

Web: www.btw-timeline.de
Uta E. Pohl

Services/Products:
Telemarketing agency

Member of:
DDV

BÜRGEL WIRTSCHAFTSINFORMATI-ONEN GMBH & CO. KG

Gasstr. 18
Hamburg
22761
Germany
Tel: +49 40 89803 511
Fax: +49 40 89803 519
Meike Wrede

Services/Products:
List services; Lettershop; Fulfilment and sampling house

Member of:
DDV

BÜRO PROCHAZKA AGENTUR FÜR DIREKTMARKETING GMBH

Bernhardusstraße 6
Ettlingen
76275
Germany
Tel: +49 7243 30481
Fax: +49 7243 79645
Irmgard Martin

Services/Products:
Direct marketing agency

Member of:
DDV

BÜROMATIC DIREKTWERBUNG JOST DAMGAARD GMBH & CO. KG

Gruitener Str. 202
Wuppertal
42327
Germany
Tel: +49 202 273270
Fax: +49 202 2732727
Jost Damgaard

Services/Products:
List services; Lettershop; Fulfilment and sampling house

Member of:
DDV

BÜROTEL PROFICENTER FÜR VERTRIEBSOPTIMIERUNG GMBH

Harkortstr. 25–27
Dortmund
44225

Germany
Tel: +49 231 7939111
Fax: +49 231 772043
Email: info@bürotel.de
Renate Sitte

Services/Products:
Telemarketing agency

Member of:
DDV

C-FAKTORY, GESELLSCHAFT FÜR WERBUNG UND KOMMUNIKATION

Grabenstraße 3, Hof
Duisburg
47057
Germany
Tel: +49 203 99258 0
Fax: +49 203 99258 88
Email: welcome@faktory.com
Web: http://www.faktory.com
Andreas Ocklenburg

Services/Products:
Direct marketing agency

Member of:
DDV

C.C.P. VERLAG UND BUCHVERTRIEB

Hauptstraße 16–18
Langenburg
74595
Germany
Tel: +49 180 5255129
Fax: +49 7905 91095
Email: ccp@itgc.com
Web: http://www.itgc.com/ccp
Karin Kruse

Services/Products:
Telemarketing agency

Member of:
DDV

CALL & CARE AGENTUR FÜR KUNDEN-DIALOG UND MARKETING GMBH

Richardstraße 18
Hamburg
22081
Germany
Tel: +49 40 29876 100
Fax: +49 40 29876 127
Email: info@callandcare.com
Web: http://www.callandcare.com
Volker Rohweder

Services/Products:
Telemarketing agency

Member of:
DDV

CALL CENTER AUS-UND WEITERBILDUNG GGMBH
Leipziger Straße 214
Chemnitz
9114
Germany
Tel: +49 371 335950
Fax: +49 371 3389922
Email: ccakademie@aol.com
Web: http://www.cc-akademie.de
Kerstin Liebig

Services/Products:
Telemarketing agency

Member of:
DDV

CALL CENTER TELEMARKETING GMBH
Leipziger Straße 214
Chemnitz
9114
Germany
Tel: +49 371 33590
Fax: +49 371 3389922
Email: kontakt@cc-tele.de
Web: http://cc-tele.de
Bert Evenwel

Services/Products:
Telemarketing agency

Member of:
DDV

CALLISTO GERMANY.NET GMBH
Kennedyallee 89
Frankfurt
60596
Germany
Tel: +49 69 633989 0
Fax: +49 69 633989 90
Michaela Merz

Services/Products:
Interactive media

Member of:
DDV

CARAT DIRECT
Kreuzberger Ring 21
Wiesbaden
65205
Germany
Tel: +49 611 7399 0
Fax: +49 611 7399 458
Email: info@carat-direct.de
Web: www.hms-carat.de

Services/Products:
Advertising Agency; Call centre
services/systems; Database services;
Direct marketing agency; Media
buying agency; Dialogue marketing

Member of:
DDV

CARSTING GMBH
Motorstraße 56
München
80809
Germany
Tel: +49 89 35846 0
Fax: +49 89 35846 500

Services/Products:
Telemarketing agency

Member of:
DDV

CASSIOPEIA GMBH
Inselkammerstraße 4
Unterhaching
82008
Germany
Tel: +49 89 6129500
Fax: +49 89 612950 24
Email: pg@cassiopeia.de
Web: http://www.cassiopeia.de
Patrick Gruban

Services/Products:
Interactive media

Member of:
DDV

CFD, C. FABINGER AGENTUR FÜR DIREKTMARKETING
Heerstraße 85
Runkel
65594
Germany
Tel: +49 6431 97063
Fax: +49 6431 97086
Claudia Fabinger

Services/Products:
Direct marketing agency

Member of:
DDV

CLARITAS DEUTSCHLAND DATA + SERVICES GMBH
Martin-Behaim-Straße 12
Neu-Isenburg
63263
Germany
Tel: +49 6102 7363
Fax: +49 6102 736444
Email:
101565.2642@compuserve.com
Wolfhart H. Anders

Services/Products:
List services; Lettershop; Fulfilment
and sampling house; Database services;
Direct marketing agency

Member of:
DDV

COHEN NEW MEDIA BERATUNG
Feilitzschstr. 15
München
80802
Germany
Tel: +49 89 33040 350
Fax: +49 89 33+49 40 356
Email: info@cohen.de
Web: http://www.cohen.de
Andreas Cohen

Services/Products:
Interactive media

Member of:
DDV

COLOGNE:CALLCENTER GMBH
Subbelrather Straße 17
Köln
50823
Germany
Tel: +49 221 95171 0
Fax: +49 221 95171 290
Email: info@cologne-callcenter.de
Web: http://www.cologne-callcenter.de
Sabine Haas

Services/Products:
Telemarketing agency

Member of:
DDV

COMBERA GMBH
Schwanthalerstr. 2
München
80336
Germany
Tel: +49 89 55107 0
Fax: +49 89 55107220
Meik Bödeker

Services/Products:
Telemarketing agency

Member of:
DDV

COMPUTEL TELEFONSERVICE GMBH
Axel-Springer-Platz 1
Hamburg
20350
Germany
Tel: +49 40 34726241
Fax: +49 40 34726388
Wolfgang Bruhn

Services/Products:
Telemarketing agency

Member of:
DDV

CREAKOM DIRECT & TELEMARKETING GMBH
Creakom Call Center College
Personalvermittlung und Ausbildung
GmbH
Justus-von-Liebig-Str. 2
Erding
85435
Germany
Tel: +49 81 2295 880
Fax: +49 81 2295 8811
Email:
joseph.schoengruber@creakom.de
Web: www.creakom.de
Joseph F. Schöngruber

Services/Products:
Advertising Agency; Call centre
services/systems; Catalogue producer;
Consultancy services; Database
services; Design/graphics/clip art
supplier

E-Services:
Email list provider; E-Marketing
consultant; Website design; Email
software; Online/e-marketing agency

Member of:
DDV

CREATIV TEAM DIRECTMARKETING GMBH
Streiflingsweg 4
Niefern-Öschelbronn
75223
Germany
Tel: +49 7233 96060
Fax: +49 7233 960630
Email: creativteam@t-online.de
André Bernhard

Services/Products:
Direct marketing agency

Member of:
DDV

D & P FRANZ GMBH DIREKTMARKETING PRODUKTMARKETING
Gewerbering 12
Eresing
86922
Germany
Tel: +49 8193 9325 0
Fax: +49 8193 9325 20
Georg Franz

Services/Products:
Direct marketing agency

Member of:
DDV

D & S DIALOG MARKETING GMBH
Überseering 33
Hamburg
22297
Germany
Tel: +49 40 4114 382
Fax: +49 40 4114 384
Email: info@ds-dialog.com
Holger Schimming

Services/Products:
Telemarketing agency

Member of:
DDV

D&G DIREKT-MARKETING GERARDI GMBH & CO KG
Freiburger Strasse 7
Pforzheim
75179
Germany
Tel: +49 72 31 91 90 11
Fax: +49 72 31 91 90 15
Kurt Kuhn, Managing Director

Services/Products:
Lettershop; Direct marketing agency;
Print services

Member of:
FEDMA

D&G-SOFTWARE GMBH
Erlenweg 14
Karlsbad-Auerbach
76307
Germany
Tel: +49 7202 93930
Fax: +49 7202 939393
Email: dug-software@t-online.de
Web: http://www.dug-software.de
Claus D. Reinbacher

Services/Products:
List services; Lettershop; Fulfilment
and sampling house

Member of:
DDV

D.M. GROUP GESELLSCHAFT FÜR WERBUNG, VERKAUFSFÖRDERUNG UND DIREKT MARKETING MBH
Eschenheimer Anlage 1
Frankfurt
60316
Germany
Tel: +49 69 943383 0
Fax: +49 69 943383 33
Email: info@dm-group.com
Web: http://www.dm-group.com
Jürgen Gwosdz

Member of:
DDV

DATA INFORM JÜRGEN DICKOB
Freiherr-vom-Stein-Str. 80
Neuwied
56566
Germany
Tel: +49 2622 9421 0
Fax: +49 2622 9421 21
Email: datainform-dickob@t-online.de
Web: http://www. datainform-
dickob.de
Jürgen Dickob

Services/Products:
Telemarketing agency

Member of:
DDV

DATA SELECT GESELLSCHAFT FÜR MARKETING SERVICE MBH
Hugo-Junkers-Straße 5
Frankfurt
60386
Germany
Tel: +49 69 94139016
Fax: +49 69 94139017
Email: dataselect@t-online.de
Günther Kalbskopf

Services/Products:
List services; Lettershop; Fulfilment
and sampling house

Member of:
DDV

DATAFIN DIREKT MARKETING SERVICE AG
Ludwig-Erhard-Allee 3
Bonn
53175
Germany
Tel: +49 228 8882200
Fax: +49 228 8882203
Email: info@datafin.de
Web: http://www.datafin.de
Norbert Rollinger

Services/Products:
List services; Lettershop; Fulfilment
and sampling house

Member of:
DDV

DATEAM INTERMEDIA
Stuttgarter Straße 18–24
Frankfurt
60329
Germany
Tel: +49 69 2600 951
Fax: +49 69 2600 969

Email: info@dateam.de
Web: http://www.dateam.de
Kevin Brian Moore

Services/Products:
Interactive media

Member of:
DDV

DATEN-PARTNER GESELLSCHAFT FÜR ELEKTRONISCHE DATENVERABEITUNG MBH
Schlüterstraße 10
Erkrath
40699
Germany
Tel: +49 0211 9005 3
Fax: +49 211 9005500
Email: info@daten-partner.de
Web: http://www.daten-partner.de
Harry Surmund

Member of:
DDV

DATING GMBH
Am Holzweg 28–34
Kriftel
65830
Germany
Tel: +49 6192 97173 0
Thomas Wiegand, Office Manager

Services/Products:
List services; Lettershop; Fulfilment
and sampling house

Member of:
DDV

DCS DIREKTMARKETING & CARD SERVICE GMBH
Lierenfelder Straße 49
Düsseldorf
40231
Germany
Tel: +49 0211 9831 0
Fax: +49 211 9831 111
Wolfgang Neumes

Services/Products:
List services; Lettershop; Fulfilment
and sampling house

Member of:
DDV

DEBIS SYSTEMHAUS DIENSTLEISTUNGEN GMBH
Emanuel-Leutze-Str. 4
Düsseldorf
40547
Germany
Tel: +49 0211 5269 196
Fax: +49 211 5269 224

Email: pwegmann@debis.com
Petra Wegmann

Services/Products:
Interactive media

Member of:
DDV

DEFACTO MARKETING GMBH
Am Pestalozziring 1
Erlangen
91058
Germany
Tel: +49 9131 772 0
Fax: +49 9131 772188
Gerald Schreiber

Services/Products:
Telemarketing agency

Member of:
DDV

DETTERBECK, WIDER WERBUNG GMBH & CO. KG
Poststraße 18/Gerhof
Hamburg
20354
Germany
Tel: +49 40 351035 0
Fax: +49 40 351035 60
Andreas Detterbeck

Services/Products:
Direct marketing agency

Member of:
DDV

DEUTSCHE POST – INTERNATIONAL MAIL SERVICE
von-Humboldt Strasse 72
Bonn Center
Geilenkirchen
52511
Germany
Tel: +49 22818271300
Fax: +49 2281826910
Email: service@deutschepost.de
Web: www.deutschepost.de/
international/units/ims.html
Rainer Pliska, General Manager

Services/Products:
Mailing/Faxing services.

DEUTSCHE POST ADRESS GMBH
Westerbachstrasse 110
Frankfurt am Main
D-65936
Germany
Tel: +49 6990 9129 30
Fax: +49 6934 0516 62
Email:

parricia.Pfeiffer@postadresse.de
Web: www.postadress.de
Mr. Frédéric Cavro, International Sale
Director

Services/Products:
Database services; List services;
Market research agency; Relocation
database

E-Services:
E-Marketing consultant

Member of:
National DMA

DEUTSCHE POST AG – IMS
Bundeskanzlerplatz 2–10
1 Center Bonn
Bonn
53113
Germany
Tel: +49 245173350
Fax: +49 245173351
Donald E. Brooks, Managing Director
International Mail Services

Services/Products:
Mailing/Faxing services

DEUTSCHE POST AG - ZENTRALE-
Heinrich-von-Stephan-Straße 1
Bonn
53175
Germany
Tel: +49 228 180 55555
Fax: +49 228 180 25555
Email:
geschaeftskunden.service.brief@de-
utschepost.de
Web: www.deutschepost.de/
direktmarketing

Services/Products:
Consultancy services; Database
services; Direct marketing agency;
Lettershop; Mailing/Faxing services;
Print services

Member of:
FEDMA; DMA (US); National DMA

DEUTSCHE POST DIREKT GMBH
Heinrich-Konen-Str. 1
Bonn
53772
Germany
Tel: +49 228 4493161
Fax: +49 228 4493175
Web: www.postdirekt.de
Thomas Vogt

Services/Products:
List services; Lettershop; Fulfilment
and sampling house

Member of:
DDV

DEUTSCHE TELEKOM AG
In der Raste 18
Bonn
53129
Germany
Tel: +49 228 181 5176
Fax: +49 228 181 8998
Gunter Fritsche

Services/Products:
Telemarketing agency

Member of:
DDV

DEUTSCHE TELEKOM MEDIEN GMBH
Wiesenhüttenstr. 18
Frankfurt
60329
Germany
Tel: +49 69 2682 0
Fax: +49 69 26822201
Irene Sgalla

Services/Products:
List services; Database services; Call centre services/systems

Member of:
FEDMA; DDV

DFP TELEFONMARKETING GMBH
Amsinckstr. 71b/Poseidonhaus
Hamburg
20097
Germany
Tel: +49 40 23983000
Fax: +49 40 23983999
Email: info@dfp.de
Web: http://www.dfp.de
Christoph Dittler

Services/Products:
Telemarketing agency

Member of:
DDV

DIAL MARKETING GMBH
Grimm 14
Hamburg
20457
Germany
Tel: +49 40 30303900
Fax: +49 40 30303901
Email: info@dialmarketing.de
Web: http://www.dialmarketing.de
Claus-Michael Gerigk

Services/Products:
Telemarketing agency

Member of:
DDV

DIALOG FRANKFURT AGENTUR FÜR DIALOGMARKETING GMBH
Karlstraße 12
Frankfurt
60329
Germany
Tel: +49 69 27236 0
Fax: +49 69 27236 110
Email: dialog-frankfurt@t-online.de
Patrick Trapp

Services/Products:
Telemarketing agency

Member of:
DDV

DIALOG MARKETING D & M SERVICE-UND BERATUNGSGESELLSCHAFT MBH
Wilhelm-Stähle-Straße 13
Fellbach
70736
Germany
Tel: +49 711 51072 0
Fax: +49 711 51072 333
Email: dialogmarketing@t-online.de
Web: http://www.dialog-marketing.de
Peter Mosch

Member of:
DDV

DIALOG-KOMMUNIKATIONS + MARKETING GMBH
Kaiser-Friedrich-Ring 46
Düsseldorf
40545
Germany
Tel: +49 0211 5587800
Fax: +49 211 5587130
Email: dkm@dkm.com
Web: http://www.DKM.COM
Cornelia Jähn

Services/Products:
Telemarketing agency

Member of:
DDV

DIALOGHAUS GMBH
Am Falder 4
Management Center Schloss Elbroich
Düsseldorf
40589
Germany
Tel: +49 2117570756
Fax: +49 21192 42150
Email: info@dialoghaus.com
Web: www.dialoghaus.com
Carolyn Welge, International Direct Marketing Consultant

Services/Products:
List services; Database services; Direct marketing agency

Member of:
FEDMA

DIATEL DIREKT ASSEKURANZ-MARKETING GMBH
Reuterweg 47
Frankfurt
60323
Germany
Tel: +49 69 299299
Fax: +49 69 299290
Philipp J.N. Vogel

Services/Products:
Telemarketing agency

Member of:
DDV

DIE AGENTUR KAUSCHE UND PARTNER GMBH
Eppendorfer Landstr. 36
Hamburg
20249
Germany
Tel: +49 40 480607 0
Fax: +49 40 4800611
Email: sam@on-line.de
Thomas Kausche

Services/Products:
Direct marketing agency

Member of:
DDV

DIE ARGONAUTEN, AGENTUR FÜR MARKENDIALOG UND INTERAKTIVE KOMMUNIKATION GMBH
Osterwaldstraße 10/Haus C11
München
80805
Germany
Tel: +49 89 3681590
Fax: +49 89 36815959
Email: info@argonauten.de
Web: http://www.argonauten.de
Hansjörg Zimmermann

Member of:
DDV

DIETMAR ILTISBERGER GMBH
Großmannswiese 8
Runkel-Ennerich
65594

Germany
Tel: +49 6431 9915 0
Fax: +49 6431 9915 30
Mario Iltisberger

Services/Products:
List services; Lettershop; Fulfilment
and sampling house

Member of:
DDV

DIGITAL MEDIA CENTER
GMBH
Marienstraße 41
Stuttgart
70178
Germany
Tel: +49 711 601747 0
Fax: +49 711 601747 77
Email: info@dmc.de
Andreas Schwend

Services/Products:
Interactive media

Member of:
DDV

DIMA WERBE GMBH
Rüsselsheimer Str. 22
Frankfurt am Main
60326
Germany
Tel: +49 69 739939 0
Fax: +49 69 79939 10
Email: info@dima-online.de
Web: http://www.dima-online.de
Rebeka Serbec

Services/Products:
List services; Lettershop; Fulfilment
and sampling house

Member of:
DDV

DIRECT CENTER KNOLL
GMBH
Siebenlindenstraße 38
Rottenburg
72108
Germany
Tel: +49 7472 9875 0
Fax: +49 7472 9875 35
Email: dcknoll1@aol.com
Dominikus Knoll

Services/Products:
List services; Lettershop; Fulfilment
and sampling house

Member of:
DDV

DIRECT LINE MARKETING
UND KOMMUNIKATION
GMBH
Hammer Steindamm 3–7
Hamburg
D-22089
Germany
Tel: +49 40 27147 0
Fax: +49 40 27147 121
Email: info@directline.de
Web: www.directline.de
Matthias Malik, Manager

Services/Products:
Call centre services/systems; Mailing/
Faxing services; Market research
agency; Telemarketing agency;
Training/recruitment; E-commerce
support and e-mail response

E-Services:
E-Marketing consultant; Website
design; Online/e-marketing agency

Member of:
DDV

DIRECT. GESELLSCHAFT FÜR
DIREKTMARKETING MBH
Gotenstraße 12
Hamburg
20097
Germany
Tel: +49 40 237860 0
Fax: +49 40 237860 60
Frank Mittelstedt

Services/Products:
Direct marketing agency

Member of:
DDV

DIRECTA GESELLSCHAFT FÜR
WERBUNG, DIREKT-
MARKETING UND
VERKAUFSFÖRDERUNG
MBH
Harvestehuder Weg 88
Hamburg
20149
Germany
Tel: +49 40 414634 0
Fax: +49 40 414634 10
Karl-F. Lietz

Member of:
DDV

DIRECTEAM AGENTUR FÜR
DIREKTMARKETING GMBH
Julius-Moser-Str. 13
Pforzheim
75179
Germany
Tel: +49 7231 1688 0

Fax: +49 7231 1688 88
Wolfgang Hartmann

Services/Products:
Direct marketing agency

Member of:
DDV

DIRECTMEDIACOM
Hüttenstr. 31
Düsseldorf
40215
Germany
Tel: +49 0211 3807 490
Fax: +49 211 3807 555
Manuela Speckamp-Schmitt

Services/Products:
Direct marketing agency

Member of:
DDV

DIREKT-MARKETING
GERARDI GMBH & CO. KG
Freiburger Str. 7
Pforzheim
75179
Germany
Tel: +49 7231 9190 0
Fax: +49 7231 9190 90
Ernst Schmucker

Services/Products:
List services; Lettershop; Fulfilment
and sampling house

Member of:
DMA (US); DDV

DIREKT-WERBE-ATELIER
GMBH PLANUNG GESTAL-
TUNG DURCHFÜHRUNG
MARKTORIENTIERTER
WERBUNG
Am Zehnthof 189
Essen
45307
Germany
Tel: +49 201 59217 20
Fax: +49 201 59217 41
Birgit Stark

Member of:
DDV

DIREKTE DATA MARKETING
GMBH
Seyfferstraße 34
Stuttgart
70197
Germany
Tel: +49 711 612033 0
Fax: +49 711 612033 1959
Birgit Stark

Services/Products:
List services; Lettershop; Fulfilment and sampling house

Member of:
DDV

DIREKTMARKETING KURT W. WELZ GMBH
Siemensstr. 42
Korntal-Münchingen
70825
Germany
Tel: +49 7150 944 300
Fax: +49 7150 944 400
Email: dm.welz@t-online.de
Web: www.direktmarketing-welz.de
Kurt W. Welz

Services/Products:
List services; Lettershop; Fulfilment and sampling house

Member of:
DDV

DIREKTMARKETING SERVICE-CENTER GMBH & CO.
Mercedesstraße 2
Ditzingen
71254
Germany
Tel: +49 7156 304 370
Fax: +49 7156 304 379
Email: dsc-ditzingen@t-online.de
Ulrich Kahle

Services/Products:
List services; Lettershop; Fulfilment and sampling house

Member of:
DDV

DM-PLUS DIREKTMARKETING GMBH
Fürther Straße 27
Nürnberg
90429
Germany
Tel: +49 911 929934 0
Fax: +49 911 929934 59
Michael Stockmann

Services/Products:
List services; Lettershop; Fulfilment and sampling house

Member of:
DDV

DMC DATABASE MARKETING COMMUNICATION GMBH
An Fürthenrode 9–15
Geilenkirchen
52511
Germany

Tel: +49 2451 625 0
Fax: +49 2451 625 291
Web: www.csb.de
Peter Schimitzek

Services/Products:
Telemarketing agency

Member of:
DDV

DMC NORD DATABASE MARKETING COMMUNICATION GMBH
Flughafenallee 26
Bremen
28199
Germany
Tel: +49 421 5253 20
Fax: +49 421 5253 270
Theile Geber

Services/Products:
Telemarketing agency

Member of:
DDV

DMD DIREKT MARKETING DIENSTE BODO MANN GMBH
An der Güterhalle 2
Karlsdorf
76689
Germany
Tel: +49 7251 444 0
Fax: +49 7251 444 44
Bodo Mann

Services/Products:
List services; Lettershop; Fulfilment and sampling house

Member of:
DDV

DMI INSTITUT FÜR DIREKTMARKETING
Wolfratshausen
82501
Germany
Tel: +49 8171 4200 0
Fax: +49 8171 4200 42
Email: voegele@dmi.m.eunet.de
Web: http://www.voegele.de
Siegfried Vögele

Services/Products:
Interactive media

Member of:
DDV

DMT DIRECT MAIL TEAM SCHERER GMBH
Karlsruher Straße 71
Pforzheim
75179

Germany
Tel: +49 7231 145480
Fax: +49 7231 1454811
Heidemarie Scherer

Services/Products:
Direct marketing agency

Member of:
DDV

DOHMEN DISTRIBUTION
Robert-Bosch-Straße 21–23
Garching
München
D-85748
Germany
Tel: +49 89 32940 0
Fax: +49 89 32940 409
Email: info@dsdohmen.de
Web: www.dsdohmen.de
Kuno Neumeier, Director Sales and Marketing

Services/Products:
Call centre services/systems; Consultancy services; Fulfilment and sampling house; Mail order company; E-fulfilment (Europe wide); E-logistics (Europe wide)

Member of:
National DMA

DORFER DIALOG GMBH
Lersnerstr. 23
Frankfurt/M.
60322
Germany
Tel: +49 69 15052 0
Fax: +49 69 15052 199
Email: mdorfer@dorferdialog.de
Manfred Dorfer

Services/Products:
Direct marketing agency

Member of:
DDV

DPNY S. L.
C. / Francisco Rover 2B, bajos
E -
Palma de Mallorca
7003
Germany
Tel: +34 71 763040
Fax: +34 71 203707
Email: tomsen@dpny.com
Thomas Spengler

Services/Products:
Direct marketing agency

Member of:
DDV

**DR. SCHARM + PARTNER
GMBH I.G. MEDIZINISCHES
MARKETING**
Heinrich-Lilienfein-Weg 5
Karlsruhe
76229
Germany
Tel: +49 721 9463900
Fax: +49 721 9463901
Monika Scharm

Services/Products:
Telemarketing agency

Member of:
DDV

**DR. VON ARNIM
DIREKTMARKETING**
Haldenstieg 5a
Hamburg
22453
Germany
Tel: +49 40 557005 0
Fax: +49 40 557005 57
Email: dr._von_arnim@t-online.de
Dirk Steffke

Services/Products:
List services; Lettershop; Fulfilment
and sampling house

Member of:
DDV

**DREI-D DIREKTWERBUNG
GMBH & CO.KG**
Daimlerstr. 10
Elmshorn
25337
Germany
Tel: +49 4121 476 0
Fax: +49 4121 476 147
Email: 3d_direktwerbung@dreid.de
Web: http://www.DREID.DE
Nils Ulrich

Services/Products:
List services; Lettershop; Fulfilment
and sampling house

Member of:
DDV

**DTMS DEUTSCHE TELEFON-
UND MARKETING SERVICES
GMBH**
Isaac-Fulda-Allee 16
Mainz
55124
Germany
Tel: +49 6131 3289 120
Fax: +49 6131 3289 111
Email: info@dtms.de
Web: http://www.dtms.de
Cordula Mohr

Services/Products:
Telemarketing agency

Member of:
DDV

**DUN + BRADSTREET
DEUTSCHLAND GMBH**
Hahnstraße 31–35
Frankfurt
60528
Germany
Tel: +49 69 66092211
Fax: +49 69 66092215
Email: dbmail@dbgermany.com
Web: http://www.dbgermany.com
Gabriella Clauter-Schmitt

Services/Products:
List services; Lettershop; Fulfilment
and sampling house

Member of:
DDV

**DVS DATENVERARBEITUNGS-
UND DATENMANAGEMENT-
SERVICE GMBH**
Bergstraße 62
Angelbachtal
74918
Germany
Tel: +49 7265 9123 0
Fax: +49 7265 9123 99
Ernst Harbusch

Services/Products:
List services; Lettershop; Fulfilment
and sampling house

Member of:
DDV

**DVT
BÜRODIENSTLEISTUNGEN
GMBH**
Am Ziegelplatz 20
Schutterwald
77746
Germany
Tel: +49 781 95540
Fax: +49 781 955444
Email: dgl@dvt.de
Web: http://www.dvt.de
Michael Riemann

Services/Products:
Telemarketing agency

Member of:
DDV

**ECMC EUROPÄISCHES
ZENTRUM FÜR
MEDIENKOMPETENZ GMBH**
Bergstraße 8
Marl

45770
Germany
Tel: +49 2365 9404 40
Fax: +49 2365 9404 29
Email: cca.nrw@ecmc.de
Web: http://www.cca.nrw.de
Klaus Klenke

Services/Products:
Telemarketing agency

Member of:
DDV

**ECON-ALCA CONSULTING
GMBH**
Steigerweg 20
Gladbeck
45968
Germany
Tel: +49 2043 920892
Fax: +49 2043 920882
Hermann Roters

Services/Products:
List services; Lettershop; Fulfilment
and sampling house

Member of:
DDV

**EDS
INFORMATIONSTECHNOLO
GIE UND SERVICE
(DEUTSCHLAND) GMBH**
Eisenstraße 56
Rüsselsheim
65428
Germany
Tel: +49 6142 802539
Fax: +49 6142 802686
Web: www.eds.de oder eds.com
Henning Ahlert

Services/Products:
Telemarketing agency

Member of:
DDV

ENERGY WERBUNG GMBH
Diemershaldenstr. 23
Stuttgart
70184
Germany
Tel: +49 711 23952 0
Fax: +49 711 23952 18
Email: mhorlacher@tequila-energy.de
Web: http://www.energy-werbung.de
Michael Horlacher

Services/Products:
Direct marketing agency

Member of:
DDV

148

EPA DIRECT GESELLSCHAFT FÜR DIALOGMARKETING GMBH & CO.KG
Im Gewerbepark D 14
Regensburg
93059
Germany
Tel: +49 941 4634 0
Fax: +49 941 40364
Herbert Reinhard

Services/Products:
Direct marketing agency

Member of:
DMA (US); DDV

EPSILON DATA GMBH DATENBANKMARKETING – TELEMARKETING
Große Friedberger Str. 33–35
Frankfurt
60313
Germany
Tel: +49 69 2998970
Fax: +49 69 288726
Email: info@epsilon.de
Web: http://www.epsilon.de
Reiner Mirau

Services/Products:
Telemarketing agency

Member of:
DDV

ERICSSON GMBH UNTERNEHMENSBEREICH BUSINESS NETWORKS
Heerdter Landstraße 193
Düsseldorf
40549
Germany
Tel: +49 0211 5344 152
Fax: +49 211 5344 392
Thomas Gmeiner

Services/Products:
Telemarketing agency

Member of:
DDV

ERWIN BRAUN DIREKTWERBUNG
Postweg 7
Dellmensingen
89155
Germany
Tel: +49 7305 9661 0
Fax: +49 7305 9661 96
Erwin Braun

Services/Products:
List services; Lettershop; Fulfilment and sampling house

Member of:
DDV

ESD DIREKTMARKETING UND DATENVERARBEITUNG GMBH
Schwabener Weg 1
Kirchheim
85551
Germany
Tel: +49 89 904919 0
Fax: +49 89 9036495
Email:
101702.1450@compuserve.com
Web: http://www.esd-direct.com
Eva U. Scheiber

Services/Products:
Direct marketing agency

Member of:
DDV

ESKATOO - DIE AGENTUR FÜR INNOVATIVE KOMMUNIKATION GMBH
Münchener Straße 342
Nürnberg
90471
Germany
Tel: +49 911 81875 10
Fax: +49 911 81875 99
Email: spirit@eskatoo.de
Web: www.eskatoo.de
Guido Korff

Services/Products:
Advertising Agency; Call centre services/systems; Consultancy services; Database services; Design/graphics/clip art supplier; Direct marketing agency

E-Services:
Website design

Member of:
DMV

EURO-DIALOG-CALL CENTER GMBH
Arnold-Sommerfeld-Ring 2
Baesweiler
52449
Germany
Tel: +49 2401 801 100
Fax: +49 2401 801 101
Jürgen Burmester

Services/Products:
Telemarketing agency

Member of:
DDV

EUROPA-FACHPRESSE-VERLAG GMBH
Karlstraße 35–37
München
80333
Germany
Tel: +49 89 54852 261
Fax: +49 89 54852 109
Web: www.wuv.de
Volker Schmitt

Services/Products:
Interactive media

Member of:
DDV

EVOLO CALL & BUSINESSCENTER GMBH&CO.KG I.G.
Ziegetsdorfer Str. 50
Regensburg
93051
Germany
Tel: +49 941 9455766
Fax: +49 941 9455768
Jürgen Donhauser

Services/Products:
Telemarketing agency

Member of:
DDV

EYRETEL DEUTSCHLAND GMBH
Emmy-Noether-Str. 10
Karlsruhe
76131
Germany
Tel: +49 721 6105350
Fax: +49 721 6105355
Web: www.eyretel.com
Volker Marquardt

Services/Products:
Telemarketing agency

Member of:
DDV

FABER DIREKT, EGON FABER GMBH & CO. KG
Bunsenstraße 200
Kassel
34127
Germany
Tel: +49 561 9836666
Fax: +49 561 9836633
Egon Faber

Services/Products:
List services; Lettershop; Fulfilment and sampling house

Member of:
DDV

FAIßT CONSULTING
Waliser Straße 6/2
Ludwigsburg
71640
Germany
Tel: +49 7141 55323
Fax: +49 7141 55322
Email: gfaisst@aol.com
Gerhard Faißt

Services/Products:
Direct marketing agency

Member of:
DDV

FASTPHONE
   TELEMARKETING GMBH
Haldesdorfer Straße 55
Hamburg
22179
Germany
Tel: +49 40 6460460
Fax: +49 40 6424342
Email: fastphone-hh@t-online.de
Ralf Tiedemann

Services/Products:
Telemarketing agency

Member of:
DDV

FCB INTERNATIONAL
Beethoven Strasse 8–10
Frankfurt
60325
Germany
Tel: +49 69 97 554 343
Fax: +49 69 97 554 366
Email: mokeeffe@fcb.com
Margaret O'Keeffe, Director,
   Integrated Strategy and Business
   Development

Services/Products:
Advertising Agency; Database services;
Direct marketing agency; Media
buying agency; Sales promotion
agency; Electronic media

E-Services:
Website design

Member of:
FEDMA

FCB/WILKENS DIRECT
   AGENTUR F.
   DIREKTMARKETING GMBH
An der Alster 42
Hamburg
20099
Germany
Tel: +49 40 2881 1356
Fax: +49 40 28811277

Email: tkramer@wilkens-direct.com
Thomas A. Kramer

Services/Products:
Direct marketing agency

Member of:
DDV

FDS FULFILLMENT
   DIRECTMARKETING
   SERVICE GMBH
Wilhelmstr. 37
Bretten
75015
Germany
Tel: +49 7252 9377 0
Fax: +49 7252 87679
Email: fds-international@t-online.de
Siegfried W. Karbaum-Portisch

Services/Products:
List services; Lettershop; Fulfilment
and sampling house

Member of:
DMA (US); DDV

FELDT VISION'S
   COMMUNICATION GMBH
Gutenbergstraße 13
Eltville
65343
Germany
Tel: +49 6123 6780
Fax: +49 6123 678389
Email: info@feldt-visions.de
Web: http://www.feldt-visions.de
Rosemarie Feldt

Services/Products:
Direct marketing agency

Member of:
DDV

FH DIREKTMARKETING + EDV-
   DIENSTLEISTUNGEN OHG
Dieselstr. 28
Garching
85748
Germany
Tel: +49 89 326812 0
Fax: +49 89 326812 79
Email: fh-direktmarketing@t-online.de
Gerd F. Hollick

Services/Products:
List services; Lettershop; Fulfilment
and sampling house

Member of:
DDV

FISCH.MEIER.DIREKT AG
Webereistraße 56
CH -
Adliswil/Zürich

8134
Germany
Tel: +41 1711 7211
Fax: +41 1711 7272
Gilbert Fisch

Services/Products:
Direct marketing agency

Member of:
DDV

FISCHER & PARTNER
   DIREKTMARKETING GMBH
Immenhorstweg 86
Hamburg
22395
Germany
Tel: +49 40 604 8930
Fax: +49 40 604 6681
Email: fischerpartner@t-online.de
Web: www.direktmarketing-
   buchpartner.de
Heinz Fischer, Managing Director

Services/Products:
Consultancy services; List services;
Mail order company

Member of:
DMA (US); FEDMA; National DM

FOCUS ONLINE GMBH
Arabellastraße 23
München
81925
Germany
Tel: +49 89 92502788
Fax: +49 89 9250 2401
Email: mklaus@focus.de
Web: http://www.focus.de
Manfred Klaus

Services/Products:
Interactive media

Member of:
DDV

FRANK DATEN SERVICE
   SERVICELEISTUNGEN FÜR
   DAS DIREKTMARKETING
   GMBH
Schubertstr. 21
Ettlingen
76275
Germany
Tel: +49 7243 15983
Fax: +49 7243 15983
Dominik Frank, Frank

Member of:
DDV

FRB MARKETING PARTNER GMBH TELESERVICES

Peter-Sander-Straße 32
Mainz-Kastel
55252
Germany
Tel: +49 6134 714 0
Fax: +49 6134 714110
Uwe Fuchs

Services/Products:
Telemarketing agency

Member of:
DDV

FRIENDLY CALL

Von-Kühlmannstr. 25
Landsberg a. Lech
86899
Germany
Tel: +49 8191 942211
Fax: +49 8191 942212
Email: friendlycall@iname.com
Uwe Kornhaß

Services/Products:
Telemarketing agency

Member of:
DDV

FRITSCH HEINE RAPP COLLINS AGENTUR FÜR DIALOGMARKETING UND WERBUNG GMBH

Stadtdeich 5
Hamburg
20097
Germany
Tel: +49 40 339590
Fax: +49 40 33959100
Email: info@fhrc.de
Web: http://www.fhrc.de
Otfried A. Fritsch, s promotion agency;
Electronic media/internet services/
website design

Member of:
FEDMA; DDV

FRITSCHE WERBEAGENTUR GMBH

Weg beim Jäger 218
Hamburg
22335
Germany
Tel: +49 40 593969 0
Fax: +49 40 593969 99
Email: agentur@fritsche.de
Web: http://www.fritsche.de
Ulfried Fritsche

Services/Products:
Direct marketing agency

Member of:
DDV

FSW DIRECT GESELLSCHAFT FÜR DIRECTMARKETING MBH

Paul-Schallück-Str. 6
Köln
50939
Germany
Tel: +49 221 413078
Fax: +49 221 414130
Email: info@fsw.de
Web: http://www.fsw.de
Jürgen Fischer-Engert

Services/Products:
Direct marketing agency

Member of:
DDV

FUTURECOM GES.F.MKTG.-INFORMATIONSSYSTEME TELEMARKTG. UND DATA BASE TECHNOLOGIE MBH

Kleyerstr. 19
Frankfurt/Main
60326
Germany
Tel: +49 69 75027 02
Fax: +49 69 75027 124
Mathias Bauer, Bauer

Member of:
DDV

FUZZY! INFORMATIK GMBH

Eglosheimer Straße 40
Ludwigsburg
71636
Germany
Tel: +49 7141 44330
Fax: +49 7141 443322
Email: info@fuzzy-online.de
Web: http://www.fuzzy-online.de
Julia Marie Siech

Services/Products:
Interactive media

Member of:
DDV

G.K.K. FRANKFURT GMBH AGENTUR FÜR DIALOG-MARKETING

Theodor-Heuss-Allee 2
Frankfurt
60486
Germany
Tel: +49 69 754475
Fax: +49 69 754477
Harald Kling

Services/Products:
Telemarketing agency

Member of:
DDV

G/R/O GRUSCHKA RÜCKERT OTHER'S WERBEAGENTUR GMBH

Mollenbachstraße 37
Leonberg
71229
Germany
Tel: +49 7152 979260
Fax: +49 7152 9792611
Email: info@gro-werbeagentur.de
Web: www.gro-werbeagentur.de
Claus D. Gruschka, President

Services/Products:
Advertising Agency; Consultancy
services; Database services; Print
services; Direct marketing agency;
Interactive media; Event marketing

E-Services:
E-Marketing consultant; Website
design; Online/e-marketing agency

Member of:
National DMA; German
Communication Foundation

GALL, WEDEWARDT + PARTNER GMBH

Kaiserallee 119
Karlsruhe
76185
Germany
Tel: +49 721 594085
Fax: +49 721 594089
Ursula Wedewardt

Services/Products:
List services; Lettershop; Fulfilment
and sampling house

Member of:
DDV

GEBHARD MÜLLER GMBH

Fritz-Thiele-Straße 20
Bremen
28279
Germany
Tel: +49 421 83 85 10
Fax: +49 421 83 13 12
Gebhard Müller

Services/Products:
List services; Lettershop; Fulfilment
and sampling house

Member of:
DDV

GECCO WERBEAGENTUR GMBH

Sommerhuder Straße 12
Hamburg-Altona

22769
Germany
Tel: +49 40 431376 0
Fax: +49 40 431376 72
Email: letter@geccowerbe.de
Web: http://www.geccowerbe.de
Peter Klingenhäger

Services/Products:
Direct marketing agency

Member of:
DDV

**GEIS + PARTNER
    WERBEAGENTUR GMBH
    AGENTUR FÜR
    DIALOGMARKETING**
Schnieglingerstraße 53A
Nürnberg
90419
Germany
Tel: +49 911 333334
Fax: +49 911 333375
Email: info@geis-werbeagentur.de
Web: http:\\\\Geis-Werbeagentur.de
Herbert Lenzner

Member of:
DMA (US); DDV

**GENESIS, GESELLSCHAFT
    FÜR DATENGESTEUERTE
    KOMMUNIKATION MBH**
Düsseldorfer Str. 189
Mülheim a.d.Ruhr
45481
Germany
Tel: +49 208 99749 0
Fax: +49 208 99749 33
Email: moeltgen@genesis.de
Web: genesis.de
Christoph Möltgen

Member of:
DDV

**GFP GESELLSCHAFT FÜR
    PRODUKTINFORMATION
    MBH**
Weidestr. 122c
Hamburg
22083
Germany
Tel: +49 40 66961314
Fax: +49 40 66961322
Johann Peter Bösche

Services/Products:
List services; Lettershop; Fulfilment
and sampling house

Member of:
DDV

**GFS GESELLSCHAFT FÜR
    SOZIALMARKETING MBH**
Linzerstr. 21
Bad Honnef
53604
Germany
Tel: +49 2224 9182 50
Fax: +49 2224 9182 60
Email: gfs.de@t-online.de
Jürgen Grosse

Services/Products:
List services; Lettershop; Fulfilment
and sampling house

Member of:
DDV

GHP DIRECT MAIL GMBH
Kronacher Strasse 70
Bamberg
96052
Germany
Tel: +49 951 9426 410
Fax: +49 951 9426 397
Email: a.schricker@ghpdirectmail.de
Alexander Schricker, Sales Director

Services/Products:
Lettershop; Database services;
Labelling/envelope services; Service
bureau; Print services

Member of:
FEDMA

GIEL FRANKFURT GMBH
Hanauer Landstraße 126–128
Frankfurt
60314
Germany
Tel: +49 69 4070 0
Fax: +49 69 4070 2100
Email: info@giel-frankfurt.rhein-
    main.com
Web: http://www.giel.de
Bernd Schick

Services/Products:
Telemarketing agency

Member of:
DDV

**GLETTLER ANNEMARIE,
    DIREKTMARKETING**
Erich-Blum-Str. 64
Vaihingen/Enz
71665
Germany
Tel: +49 7042 92382
Fax: +49 7042 940745
Dietmar Glettler

Services/Products:
List services; Lettershop; Fulfilment
and sampling house

Member of:
DDV

**GLOCKAUER, HELLNER,
    PARTNER GMBH, AGENTUR
    FÜR INTEGRIERTES
    DIALOG-UND
    POS-MARKETING**
Admiralitätsstr. 56
Hamburg
20459
Germany
Tel: +49 40 37867601
Fax: +49 40 378676 66
Dirk Glockauer

Member of:
DDV

**GM DIREKT-MARKETING
    CENTER GMBH**
Postfach 50 05 40
Stuttgart
70335
Germany
Tel: +49 711 95324 0
Fax: +49 711 95324 49
Susanne Rasch

Services/Products:
List services; Lettershop; Fulfilment
and sampling house

Member of:
DDV

**GOTTLIEB LEHR
    DIREKTMARKETINGBERAT-
    UNG**
Albrecht-Dürer-Platz 4
Nürnberg
90403
Germany
Tel: +49 911 208837
Fax: +49 911 208837
Email: glehr@t-online.de
Gottlieb Lehr

Services/Products:
Direct marketing agency

Member of:
DDV

**GRAFFITI AGENTUR FÜR
    INNOVATIVE
    KOMMUNIKATION +
    WERBUNG GMBH & CO.KG**
Hofmannstraße 7
München
81379
Germany
Tel: +49 89 748228 0
Fax: +49 89 74822811
Web: www.graffiti.de
Holger Kalvelage

Member of:
DDV

GREY DIRECT
Hüttenstraße 5a
Düsseldorf
40215
Germany
Tel: +49 0211 3887 100
Fax: +49 211 3887 111
Jens Grunewald

Services/Products:
Direct marketing agency

Member of:
DDV

**GRUBE KOMMUNIKATION
GESELLSCHAFT FÜR
MARKETING UND NEUE
MEDIEN MBH**
Stargarder Straße 2B
Wedemark
30900
Germany
Tel: +49 5130 79390
Fax: +49 5130 793939
Email: gktamtam@aol.com
Web: http://www.tamtam.de
Reinhold W. Schmülling

Member of:
DDV

**GV KOMMUNIKATION AUF
PAPIER GMBH**
Hofener Weg 17
Remseck-Aldingen
71686
Germany
Tel: +49 7146 8963 0
Fax: +49 7146 8963 89
Email: gv@gv-online.de
Web: http://www.gv-online.de
Karl-Heinz Graf

Services/Products:
Direct marketing agency

Member of:
DDV

**GWV
VERLAGSGESELLSCHAFT
MBH REDAKTION CALL
CENTER PROFI**
Abraham-Lincoln-Str. 46
Wiesbaden
65189
Germany
Tel: +49 611 7878116
Fax: +49 611 7878421
Jan-Peter Kruse

Services/Products:
Telemarketing agency

Member of:
DDV

**HADASIK & KLEMENTZ
GESELLSCHAFT FÜR
MARKETING UND
KOMMUNIKATION MBH**
Deichstraße 19
Hamburg
20459
Germany
Tel: +49 40 3750 1676
Fax: +49 40 3750 1678
Email: nklementz@aol.com
Nikolai Klementz

Member of:
DDV

**HARVESTEHUDER
DATACONSULT GMBH**
Hudtwalcker Str. 11
Hamburg
22299
Germany
Tel: +49 40 4686 530
Fax: +49 40 4686 5454
Harald Gall

**HDM HULSINK DIRECT
MARKETING GMBH**
Neuenhauser Str. 95
Nordhorn
48527
Germany
Tel: +49 5921 833240
Fax: +49 5921 833250
Email: hdmgroup@t-online.de
Frank Dikken

Services/Products:
Telemarketing agency

Member of:
DDV

**HEINE, REITZEL UND
PARTNER GMBH & CO. KG
AGENTUR FÜR
DIREKTMARKETING UND
WERBUNG**
Am Hardtwald 7
Ettlingen
76275
Germany
Tel: +49 7243 5454 0
Fax: +49 7243 5454 54
Email: agentur@hrp-direkt.de
Web: http://www.hrp-direkt.de
Michael Heemann

Member of:
DDV

HEIRA GMBH
Robert-Bunsen-Straße 50
Gernsheim
64579
Germany
Tel: +49 6258 4072
Fax: +49 6258 3049
Klaus Heist

Services/Products:
List services; Lettershop; Fulfilment
and sampling house

Member of:
DDV

**HELLER & PARTNER
MARKETING SERVICES**
Possartstraße 14
München
81679
Germany
Tel: +49 89 45710 0
Fax: +49 89 474069
Email: hp@heller-partner.de
Web: http://www.heller-partner.de
Stephan Heller

Services/Products:
Direct marketing agency

Member of:
DDV

**HELLWEG UND BUYK,
PARTNER FÜR
DIREKTWERBUNG GMBH**
Thomas-Mann-Str. 44
Herzebrock
33442
Germany
Tel: +49 5245 2288
Fax: +49 5245 1696
Email: buyk@aol.com
Norbert Buyk

Services/Products:
List services; Lettershop; Fulfilment
and sampling house

Member of:
DDV

**HEUER & CO. VERLAGS-UND
WERBEVERSAND GMBH**
Stahltwiete 22
Hamburg
22761
Germany
Tel: +49 40 858696
Fax: +49 40 8505021
Liesa Heuer

Services/Products:
List services; Lettershop; Fulfilment
and sampling house

Member of:
DDV

**HM1 HEUSER, MAYER +
    PARTNER DIRECT
    MARKETING GMBH**
Bayerstr. 21
München
80335
Germany
Tel: +49 89 551860
Fax: +49 89 554194
Email: info@hm1.de
Web: http://www.hm1.de
Uwe Middeke

Services/Products:
Direct marketing agency; Electronic
media

E-Services:
Website design

Member of:
FEDMA; DDV

**HOTLINE TELEMARKETING
    OHG**
Breitestr. 5
Buchholz
21244
Germany
Tel: +49 4181 2887 0
Fax: +49 4181 2887 40
Email: hottele@aol.com
Web: http://www.hotline-tm.de
Marlies Steenweg

Services/Products:
Telemarketing agency

Member of:
DDV

**HSM DIREKT GESELLSCHAFT
    FÜR STRATEGISCHES
    DIREKTMARKETING MBH**
Pforzheimer Straße 15
Karlsruhe
76227
Germany
Tel: +49 721 407004
Fax: +49 721 495668
Email: hsmdirekt@compuserve.com
Web: Hans-Joachim Meyer
Hans-Joachim Meyer

Member of:
DDV

**HUMAN INFERENCE
    ADRESSENVERWALTUNGSS-
    OFTWARE GMBH**
Cockerillstraße 100
Stolberg
52222
Germany

Tel: +49 2402 125810
Fax: +49 2402 125805
Email: info@humaninference.com
Web: http://www.humanInference.com
Jörg Kleinbrahm

Services/Products:
List services; Lettershop; Fulfilment
and sampling house

Member of:
DDV

ICOM SOFTWARE RESEARCH
Feldstraße 41
Dortmund
44141
Germany
Tel: +49 231 554273
Fax: +49 231 554274
Email: info@icomsoftware.de
Thomas Zerwes

Services/Products:
Service bureau; Software supplier

Member of:
National DMA; DDV

IK TRANSCOM EUROPE GMBH
In der Steele 39 a
Düsseldorf
40599
Germany
Tel: +49 0211 74004708
Fax: +49 211 7405312
Email:
    tatjana.wilson@transcom.ikt.com
Dave Hayward

Services/Products:
Telemarketing agency

Member of:
DDV

IMA SOFTWARE GMBH
Lyoner Str. 15
Frankfurt/Main
60528
Germany
Tel: +49 69 66577 122
Fax: +49 69 66577 200
Email: anke.klauss@imaedge.com
Web: http://www.ima-inc.com
Anke Klauß

Services/Products:
Telemarketing agency

Member of:
DDV

IN + OUT TELESERVICE GMBH
Monschauer Straße 44
Mönchengladbach
41068
Germany

Tel: +49 180 2221888
Fax: +49 180 2221889
Email: postmaster@in-out.de
Web: http://www.IN-OUT.DE
Friedrich Mocker

Services/Products:
Telemarketing agency

Member of:
DDV

INA (GERMANY) GMBH
Haldenstieg 5
Hamburg
22453
Germany
Tel: +49 40 55707 07
Fax: +49 40 55707 100
Email: germany@ina-group.com
Web: http:\\\\ina-group.com
Marco Priewe

Services/Products:
Telemarketing agency

Member of:
DDV

**INDIREKT AGENTUR FÜR
    DIALOGMARKETING GMBH**
Schwanthalerstraße 182
München
80339
Germany
Tel: +49 89 68951262
Fax: +49 89 68951100
Beate Radermacher

Services/Products:
Direct marketing agency

Member of:
DDV

**INDUTEL
    TELEFONMARKETING H.
    KISO**
Erlenweg 18
Haan
42781
Germany
Tel: +49 2104 62105
Fax: +49 2104 61358
Helga Kiso

Services/Products:
Telemarketing agency

Member of:
DDV

INFOMEDIA SERVICE GMBH
Heltorferstraße 12
Düsseldorf
40472
Germany
Tel: +49 0211 4206 1406

Fax: +49 211 4206 1414
Email: mueller-
  mordhorst@infomedia.de
Web: infoMedia.de
Roland Waubert de Puiseau

Services/Products:
Telemarketing agency

Member of:
DDV

INFOX GMBH & CO. INFORMATIONSLOGISTIK KG

Gorch-Fock-Str. 2
Bonn
53229
Germany
Tel: +49 228 9750 100
Fax: +49 228 9750 111
Thomas Beer

Services/Products:
List services; Lettershop; Fulfilment
and sampling house

Member of:
DDV

INTERACTIVE MARKETING PARTNER GMBH

Planckstr. 13
Hamburg
22765
Germany
Tel: +49 40 37886 0
Fax: +49 40 37886 133
Email: headoffice@impartner.de
Web: http://www.impartner.de
Hendrik Dohmeyer

Services/Products:
Interactive media

Member of:
DDV

INTERACTIVE ONLINE SERVICES I.O.S. GMBH

Kedenburgstraße 44
Hamburg
22041
Germany
Tel: +49 40 6569900
Fax: +49 40 65699040
Email: info@interact.de
Web: http://www.interact.de
Rajiv Giri

Services/Products:
Interactive media

Member of:
DDV

INTERAD GMBH

Ludwigstr. 13
Augsburg
86152
Germany
Tel: +49 821 509040
Fax: +49 821 5090499
Email: info@interad.de
Web: http://www.interad.de
Michael Timinger

Services/Products:
Interactive media

Member of:
DDV

INTERSHOP COMMUNICATIONS GMBH

Amsinckstraße 57
Hamburg
20097
Germany
Tel: +49 40 237090
Fax: +49 40 23709112
Email: c. heinemann@intershop.de
Web: http://www.intershop.de
Christopher Heinemann

Services/Products:
Interactive media

Member of:
DDV

INTERTEL TELEFONSERVICE GMBH

Sperbersloherstr. 568
Wendelstein
90530
Germany
Tel: +49 9129 288100
Fax: +49 9122 288288
Email: fuenfgelt_meeder@t-online.de
H.-P. Fünfgelt

Services/Products:
Telemarketing agency

Member of:
DDV

INTERVIEW AG DIALOGMARKETING & RESEARCH

Plinganserstraße 13–15
München
81369
Germany
Tel: +49 89 746161 0
Fax: +49 89 746161 74
Email: info@interview-ag.de
Web: http://www.interview-ag.de
Stephan Primbs

Services/Products:
Telemarketing agency

Member of:
DDV

ISI MARKETING GMBH

Trimonte Park, Wasserstr. 219
Bochum
44799
Germany
Tel: +49 234 97630
Fax: +49 234 770210
Peter Steinbach

Services/Products:
Telemarketing agency

Member of:
DDV

ITEM GMBH ADVANCED PRESS & MAIL SERVICEWARE

Otterstadter Weg 1
Speyer
67346
Germany
Tel: +49 6232 6432 0
Fax: +49 6232 42044
Pascal Thull

Services/Products:
List services; Lettershop; Fulfilment
and sampling house

Member of:
DDV

IVANOV & IVANOV DIRECT MARKETING AGENCY

Maliy Cherkasskiy per. 1/3, Off. 409
Rus-
Moskau
103720
Germany
Tel: +49 7 095 7538223
Fax: +49 7 095 9288562
Email: ivanov@cea.ru
Thomas Baer

Services/Products:
Direct marketing agency

Member of:
DDV

J + P DIALOG MARKETING GMBH

Postfach 12 42
Ditzingen
71241
Germany
Tel: +49 7156 9392 0
Fax: +49 7156 9392 22
Michael Kraus

Services/Products:
List services; Lettershop; Fulfilment
and sampling house

Member of:
DDV

J&S DIALOG-MEDIEN GMBH
Bei den Mühren 91
Hamburg
20457
Germany
Tel: +49 40 369832 0
Fax: +49 40 36983236
Email: jagusch@jsdialog.de
Web: http://www.fischers-archiv.de + onetone.de
Johannes Jagusch

Services/Products:
Interactive media

Member of:
DDV

JÄGER + SCHMITTER DIALOG
Rolshover Str. 526
Köln
51105
Germany
Tel: +49 221 9839 0
Fax: +49 221 9839 390
Email: dialog@jsdialog-com
Bernd Schmitter

Services/Products:
Telemarketing agency

Member of:
DDV

JAHNS, RAPP COLLINS GMBH AGENTUR FÜR DIALOGMARKETING UND WERBUNG
Heerdter Sandberg 32
Düsseldorf
40549
Germany
Tel: +49 0211 55962 0
Fax: +49 211 55962 49
Email: info@jahns-rapp-collins.de
Web: http://www.jahns-rapp-collins.de
Rudolf Jahns

Member of:
DDV

JBBX MARKETING-UND WERBEAGENTUR GMBH
Bärenallee 33
Hamburg
22041
Germany
Tel: +49 40 659427 0
Fax: +49 40 659427 11
Günter Bauregger

Services/Products:
Direct marketing agency

Member of:
DDV

JM&K AGENTUR FÜR INTEGRIERTE KOMMUNIKATION GMBH
Parkstraße 91
Wiesbaden
65191
Germany
Tel: +49 611 562122
Fax: +49 611 562155
Email: jmundk@mac.com
Dr. Johannes Mißlbeck, CEO

Services/Products:
Advertising Agency; Consultancy services; Direct marketing agency; Interactive media

E-Services:
E-Marketing consultant; Online/e-marketing agency

Member of:
National DMA; DDV; Marketing-Club; Kommunikations-verbaud BDW

JOST TELEMARKETING GMBH
Hoenbergstraße 6
Limburg
65555
Germany
Tel: +49 6431 5010 0
Fax: +49 6431 5010 100
Email: jost@josttele.de
Web: http://www.josttele.de
Anne Jost

Services/Products:
Telemarketing agency

Member of:
DDV

JS VERSANDSERVICE UND DIREKTMARKETING GMBH
Rudolf-Diesel-Straße 4
Rödermark-Urberach
63322
Germany
Tel: +49 6074 841350
Fax: +49 6074 841333
Email: info@js-versand.de
Web: http:\\\\js-versand.de
Jürgen Scheer

Services/Products:
List services; Lettershop; Fulfilment and sampling house

Member of:
DDV

JUCKNIEß – DATENSERVICE GMBH
Goehtestr. 102
Essen
45130
Germany
Tel: +49 201 8775711
Fax: +49 201 791585
Johann Wimmer

Services/Products:
List services; Lettershop; Fulfilment and sampling house

Member of:
DDV

K & P MARKETING GMBH
Hohenzollernstraße 16
Pforzheim
75177
Germany
Tel: +49 7231 302990
Fax: +49 7231 302994
Email: info@kp-marketing.de
Web: http://www.kp-marketing.de
Harald Efthymiou

Services/Products:
Telemarketing agency

Member of:
DDV

K&R CONSULTING GMBH
Industriestr. 30–34
Eschborn
65760
Germany
Tel: +49 6196 9306351
Fax: +49 6196 9306355
Michael Roschanski

Services/Products:
Direct marketing agency

Member of:
DDV

K.M. + PARTNER GESELLSCHAFT FÜR MARKETING-KOMMUNIKAT-ION MBH
Bogenstraße 45a/b
Hamburg
20144
Germany
Tel: +49 40 4232550
Fax: +49 40 4206631
Email:
106411.2124@compuserve.com
Michael Kohl

Services/Products:
Telemarketing agency

Member of:
DDV

KARL TREBBAU GMBH ADRESSENVERLAG UND DIREKTWERBEUNTERNEH-MEN

Schönhauser Str. 21
Köln
50968
Germany
Tel: +49 221 37646 0
Fax: +49 221 3764634
Email: info@trebbau.de
Web: http://www.trebbau.de
Karl-P. Trebbau

Services/Products:
List services; Lettershop; Fulfilment and sampling house

Member of:
DDV

KARRASCH + PARTNER GMBH

Zum Quellenpark 29
Bad Soden
65812
Germany
Tel: +49 6196 65115 0
Fax: +49 6196 65115 11
Email: info@karrasch-partner.de
Web: http://www.Karrasch-Partner.de
Marcel Karrasch

Services/Products:
Direct marketing agency

Member of:
DDV

KAT MARKETING GMBH

Graeffstraße 5
Köln
50823
Germany
Tel: +49 221 5716 111
Fax: +49 221 5716 191
Email: info@kat-marketing.de
Web: http:\\\\kat-marketing.de
Helmut Becker

Services/Products:
Direct marketing agency

Member of:
DDV

KAUßEN PARTNERS WERBEAGENTUR FÜR VITAL DIALOG-KOMMUNIKATION GMBH

Goltsteinstr. 19
Düsseldorf
40211
Germany
Tel: +49 211 17356 14
Fax: +49 211 17356 40
Email: kaussen@online-club.de
Gerd Kaußen

Member of:
DDV

KIENOW & KEMPENER KG

Biebricher Allee 39
Wiesbaden
65187
Germany
Tel: +49 611 989800
Fax: +49 611 9898018
Email: kienow-kempener@t-online.de
Adolf Kempener

Services/Products:
Direct marketing agency

Member of:
DDV

KIOSK ONLINE-DIENSTE GMBH

Verdistr. 44
München
81247
Germany
Tel: +49 89 8912510
Fax: +49 89 89125125
Mirko Dudas

Services/Products:
Interactive media

Member of:
DDV

KIWI REPRO68 INTERAKTIVE MEDIEN GMBH

Alsterkrugchaussee 350
Hamburg
22297
Germany
Tel: +49 40 5130060
Fax: +49 40 5113332
Web: www.kiwi.de
Karl-Ludwig Freiherr von Wendt

Services/Products:
Interactive media

Member of:
DDV

KLOPOTEK & PARTNER GMBH

Schlüterstraße 39
Berlin
10629
Germany
Tel: +49 30 88453212
Fax: +49 30 88453264
Kolja Becker

Services/Products:
List services; Lettershop; Fulfilment and sampling house

Member of:
DDV

KLOSE & CO. WERBEAGENTUR GMBH

Zippelhaus 3
Hamburg
20457
Germany
Tel: +49 40 3254330
Fax: +49 40 32543399
Roland Klose

Services/Products:
Direct marketing agency

Member of:
DDV

KLUTH TELEMARKETING GMBH

Immermannstraße 59
Düsseldorf
40210
Germany
Tel: +49 211 1644 0
Fax: +49 211 1644 100
Email: info@KLUTH.de
Web: http://www.KLUTH.de
Herwig Kluth

Services/Products:
Telemarketing agency

Member of:
DDV

KNAUER + PARTNER MARKETING GMBH

Kanalstraße 7/1
Weingarten
76356
Germany
Tel: +49 7244 720 0
Fax: +49 7244 720 111
Peter Knauer

Services/Products:
Telemarketing agency

Member of:
DDV

KNAUER Y RUMP Y PARTNER WERBEAGENTUR GMBH

Schulterblatt 58
Hamburg
20357
Germany
Tel: +49 40 432003 0
Fax: +49 40 432003 23
Email: t.knauer@krp-hamburg.com
Web: www.krp-hamburg.com
Thomas Knauer

Services/Products:
Advertising Agency

E-Services:
Website design

Member of:
National DMA

KNOCHE TELEFONMARKETING
Brambuschweg 8B
Stuhr
28816
Germany
Tel: +49 421 892474
Fax: +49 421 801629
Andrea Knoche

Services/Products:
Telemarketing agency

Member of:
DDV

KOCHAN & PARTNER WERBUNG, DESIGN UND KOMMUNIKATION
Hirschgartenallee 25
München
80639
Germany
Tel: +49 89 1784978
Fax: +49 89 1781235
Email: kontakt@kochan.de
Web: http://www.kochan.de
Boris Kochan

Services/Products:
Direct marketing agency

Member of:
DDV

KOMDAT GESELLSCHAFT FÜR EXTERNES VERTRIEBSMANAGEMENT MBH
Südring 5
Wesel
46483
Germany
Tel: +49 281 33930 0
Fax: +49 281 33930 99
Matthias Hillenbach

Services/Products:
Telemarketing agency

Member of:
DDV

KONZEPT TELEMARKETING SERVICE GMBH
Elgendorfer Str. 55
Montabaur
56410
Germany
Tel: +49 2602 150 0
Fax: +49 2602 150 101
Email: konzept-telemarketing@t-online.de
Elke Kleinhammes

Services/Products:
Telemarketing agency

Member of:
DDV

KOOP DIREKTMARKETING GMBH & CO. KG
Zimmerstr. 9–11
Düsseldorf
40215
Germany
Tel: +49 0211 31084 0
Fax: +49 211 330537
Email: koop@vva.de
Web: http://www.vva.de/koop.htm
Johannes Palkus

Services/Products:
List services; Lettershop; Fulfilment and sampling house; Direct marketing agency

Member of:
FEDMA; DDV

KOOP INDIMA GES.F. INNOVATIVES DIREKTMARKETING MBH
Stuttgarter Straße 41
Pforzheim
75179
Germany
Tel: +49 7231 3963 0
Fax: +49 7231 3963 30
Email: indima2000.@aol.com
Peter Hiller

Services/Products:
List services; Lettershop; Fulfilment and sampling house; Response analysis bureau

Member of:
FEDMA; DDV

KÖSTER & VORHAUER GMBH
Malkastenstraße 17
Düsseldorf
40211
Germany
Tel: +49 211 176850
Fax: +49 211 1768555
Email: dialog@malkasten17.de
Web: http://www.malkasten17.de
Robert Köster

Services/Products:
Interactive media

Member of:
DDV

KPS INTERACTIVE MEDIA GMBH & CO.KG
Contrescarpe 46
Bremen

28195
Germany
Tel: +49 421 366602
Fax: +49 421 3666 290
Email: info@KPS.de
Web: http://www.KPS.de
Cornelia Einsiedel-Michaely

Services/Products:
Telemarketing agency

Member of:
DDV

KREDO DIREKWERBUNG GMBH
Hofener Weg 17
Remseck
71686
Germany
Tel: +49 7146 8962 0
Fax: +49 7146 8962 89
Karl-Heinz Graf

Services/Products:
List services; Lettershop; Fulfilment and sampling house

Member of:
DDV

KREUZER GMBH
Grenzstraße 1–3
Meckenheim
53340
Germany
Tel: +49 2225 959 0
Fax: +49 2225 959 199
Email: kreuzer@kreuzer.com
Web: http://www.kreuzer.com
Erwin Kreuzer

Services/Products:
Telemarketing agency

Member of:
DDV

KÜBLER TELEMARKETING GMBH & CO.KG
Chemiestr. 14 - 15
Lampertheim
68623
Germany
Tel: +49 6206 931 187
Fax: +49 6206 931 152
Peter F. Teupe

Services/Products:
Telemarketing agency

Member of:
DDV

KUVERTIER-SERVICE AUGUSTE STAAR GMBH
Albert-Schweitzer-Ring 19
Hamburg

22045
Germany
Tel: +49 40 6695293 94
Fax: +49 40 665658
Marlene Alfred

Services/Products:
List services; Lettershop; Fulfilment
and sampling house

Member of:
DDV

LAMMOTH MAILKONZEPT, WERBEAGENTUR FÜR DIREKTMARKETING/KOMM-UNIKATION
Rötelistr. 16/Dufourpark
CH -
St. Gallen
9000
Germany
Tel: +41 71 2776252
Fax: +41 71 2776444
Email: lammoth@access.ch
Friedhelm Lammoth, Lammoth

Member of:
DDV

LAMMOTH, NEUMARK & CO. ADRESSMARKETING GMBH
Im Katzentach 11
Ettlingen
76265
Germany
Tel: +49 7243 597080
Fax: +49 7243 597085
Email: lammothde@aol.com
Sylvio Neumark

Services/Products:
List services; Lettershop; Fulfilment
and sampling house

Member of:
DDV

LASERPRINT DRUCK-UND DIREKTWERBUNG GMBH
Hortensienweg 21
Stuttgart
70374
Germany
Tel: +49 711 95324 0
Fax: +49 711 95324 44
Dirk Schneider

Services/Products:
List services; Lettershop; Fulfilment
and sampling house

Member of:
DDV

LDZ LASERDRUCKZENTRUM GMBH
Luruper Chaussee 125
Hamburg
22761
Germany
Tel: +49 40 893076
Fax: +49 40 8901507
Kristian Kortha

Services/Products:
List services; Lettershop; Fulfilment
and sampling house

Member of:
DDV

LEGION TELEKOMMUNIKATION GMBH
Am Seestern 24
Düsseldorf
40547
Germany
Tel: +49 0211 52395 0
Fax: +49 211 52395 99
Email: ihde@legion.de
Rolf Ihde

Services/Products:
Telemarketing agency

Member of:
DDV

LEHR & BROSE ERSTE DIALOGAGENTUR GMBH & CO. KG
Gänsemarkt 35
Hamburg
20354
Germany
Tel: +49 40 357533 0
Fax: +49 40 35753333
Email: info@lbonline.de
Web: http://www.lbonline.de
Andreas Lehr

Services/Products:
List services; Telemarketing agency;
Direct marketing agency; Sales
promotion agency; Electronic media

E-Services:
Website design

Member of:
FEDMA; DDV

LETTERSHOP BRENDLER GMBH
Magdeburger Straße 6
Laatzen
30880
Germany
Tel: +49 5102 9359 0
Fax: +49 5102 9359 30

Email: lettershopbrendler@t-online.de
Carsten Brendler

Services/Products:
List services; Lettershop; Fulfilment
and sampling house

Member of:
DDV

LETTERSHOP SCHONARD GMBH & CO
Kelterstr. 69
Dettingen/Teck
73265
Germany
Tel: +49 7021 806 0
Fax: +49 7021 806 90
Email: lsgl@compuserve.com
Gerhard Erdkönig

Services/Products:
List services; Lettershop; Fulfilment
and sampling house; Database services;
Personalisation

Member of:
FEDMA; DDV

LICON LINDEN CONSULTING
Auguststr. 1
Bonn
53229
Germany
Tel: +49 228 9732 0
Fax: +49 228 9732 290
Email: mail@linden-consulting.de
Web: http://www.LINDEN-
CONSULTING.DE
Franz Linden

Services/Products:
Direct marketing agency

Member of:
DDV

LIFTA, LIFT UND ANTRIEB GMBH
Horbeller Straße 33
Köln
50858
Germany
Tel: +49 2234 504 171
Fax: +49 2234 504 500
Christian Fröhlich

Services/Products:
Telemarketing agency

Member of:
DDV

LINKENHEIL & FRIENDS TELEMARKETING GMBH
Am Sandfeld 15
Karlsruhe
76149

Germany
Tel: +49 721 9777 0
Fax: +49 721 9777 101
Email: kontakt@linkenheil-friends.de
Web: http://www.linkenheil-friends.de
Karl-Heinz Niedrist

Services/Products:
Telemarketing agency

Member of:
DDV

LITERATURAGENTUR PETRA + HEINZ RASZKOWSKI
Joseph-von-Fraunhofer-Str. 5
Alsdorf
52477
Germany
Tel: +49 2404 9464 0
Fax: +49 2404 9464 20
Email: welcome@
   literaturagentur.com
Web: http://www.literaturagentur.com
Heinz Raszkowski

Services/Products:
Direct marketing agency

Member of:
DDV

LOGO CALL GMBH
Beethovenstr. 65
Frankfurt
60325
Germany
Tel: +49 69 74222 200
Fax: +49 69 74222 111
Mario Levenhagen

Services/Products:
Telemarketing agency

Member of:
DDV

LPP CARLSON MARKETING GMBH AGENTUR FÜR INTEGRIERTE KOMMUNIKATION
Kreuzberger Ring 64
Wiesbaden
65205
Germany
Tel: +49 611 778470
Fax: +49 611 7784766
Dieter Plischka

Member of:
DDV

LUCENT TECHNOLOGIES BUSINESS COMMUNICATIONS SYSTEMS & MICROELECTRONIC GMBH
Darmstädter Landstraße 125
Frankfurt
60598
Germany
Tel: +49 69 96377 251
Fax: +49 69 96377 111
Web: www.lucent.de
Silke Eggert

Member of:
DDV

M + M MAIL + MORE DIREKTMARKETING GMBH
Alte Straße 57
Schwanstetten
90596
Germany
Tel: +49 9170 9490 0
Fax: +49 9170 9490 24
Kurt Stadlbauer

Services/Products:
Direct marketing agency

Member of:
DDV

M&H VERSANDHANDEL UND SERVICE GMBH & CO.
Reitschulstraße 7
A-
Lauterach
6923
Germany
Tel: +43 5574801 0
Fax: +43 5574801 6
Email: mh@mhdirekt.at
Web: http://www.mhdirekt.at
Monika Schindler-Greiter

Services/Products:
List services; Lettershop; Fulfilment and sampling house

Member of:
DDV

M&L COMMUNICATION MARKETING GMBH
Stresemannallee 61
Frankfurt/Main
60596
Germany
Tel: +49 69 9636700
Fax: +49 69 96367070
Email: jlozano.ml@t-online.de
Javier Lozano

Services/Products:
Telemarketing agency

Member of:
DDV

M&L MAUER MARKETING SERVICES GMBH
Stresemannallee 61
Frankfurt
60596
Germany
Tel: +49 69 963632 0
Fax: +49 69 6312098
Matthias Mauer

Services/Products:
Telemarketing agency

Member of:
DDV

M&V MÜNCHEN AGENTUR FÜR DIALOGMARKETING UND VERKAUFSFÖRDERUNG GMBH
Schatzbogen 43
München
81829
Germany
Tel: +49 89 420097 0
Fax: +49 89 420097 80
Email: muv_muc@compuserve.com
Herbert Schneider

Services/Products:
Database services; Electronic media

E-Services:
Website design

Member of:
FEDMA; DDV

M-S-B+K CONSULTING GMBH
Schottmüllerstraße 20a
Hamburg
20251
Germany
Tel: +49 40 480950
Fax: +49 40 48095200
Email: info@msbkcons.de
Dieter Reichert

Services/Products:
Direct marketing agency

Member of:
DDV

M-S-B+K STUTTGART WERBEAGENTUR FÜR DIRECT MARKETING GMBH
Rotebühlstr. 81
Stuttgart
70178
Germany
Tel: +49 711 61968 0
Fax: +49 711 6196819

Email: info@msbk.de
Web: http://www.msbk.de
Hans Widmann

Services/Products:
Direct marketing agency

Member of:
DDV

MA NETWORK
COMMUNICATION GMBH
Speckmannstraße 15
Hamburg
22391
Germany
Tel: +49 40 53696611
Fax: +49 40 53696610
Email: bernd.kracke@ma-network.de
Web: http://www.ma-network.de
Bernd Kracke

Services/Products:
Interactive media

Member of:
DDV

MAASSEN + PARTNER GMBH
Further Str. 102
Neuss
41462
Germany
Tel: +49 2131 200900
Fax: +49 2131 200901
Email: info@maassen.de
Web: http://www.maassen.de
Rainer Maassen

Services/Products:
Interactive media

Member of:
DDV

MADER UNTERNEHMENS
KOMMUNIKATION GMBH
Steinbeisstr. 4
Leonberg
71229
Germany
Tel: +49 7152 935 0
Fax: +49 7152 935 444
Email: mader-leonberg@t-online.de
Sandra Schwärzel

Services/Products:
Telemarketing agency

Member of:
DDV

MAIL BOX DIREKT-
MARKETING SERVICE
GMBH
Grumbkowstraße 46
Berlin
13156

Germany
Tel: +49 30 47611009
Fax: +49 30 47611019
Email: mb_direkt@t-online.de
Karen Hagenauer

Services/Products:
List services; Lettershop; Fulfilment
and sampling house

Member of:
DDV

MAIL COM
DIALOGMARKETING GMBH
Benzstraße 9
Puchheim
82178
Germany
Tel: +49 89 80079 0
Fax: +49 89 80079 100
Web: www.mailcom.de
Doris Oswald

Services/Products:
List services; Lettershop; Fulfilment
and sampling house

Member of:
DDV

MAIL*SELECT GMBH
Lange Reihe 2
Hamburg
D-20099
Germany
Tel: +49 40 357433 0
Fax: +49 40 357433 55
Email: info@mail-select.com
Mr. Detlev N. Heinrich, Managing
    Director

Services/Products:
List services; Consultancy services;
Database services; Service bureau;
Online marketing information services

Member of:
DMA (US); National DMA; DMA
(German); DMA (UK)

MAIL+ORDER G. BAUMANN
GMBH
Goldbergweg 26
Remseck
71686
Germany
Tel: +49 7146 89333 0
Fax: +49 7146 89333 15
Email: info@versacard.de
Günter Baumann

Services/Products:
Direct marketing agency

Member of:
DDV

MAILING GMBH
LAGERHALTG.U.DISTRIBUT-
ION V. WERBEMITTELN
Oberhauptstraße 11
Hamburg
22335
Germany
Tel: +49 40 5006902
Fax: +49 40 50069200
Email: aemus@mail.briefing.de
Web: http://www.briefing.de
Aribert Emus

Services/Products:
List services; Lettershop; Fulfilment
and sampling house

Member of:
DDV

MAILPOOL ADRESSEN-
MANAGEMENT GMBH
Birkenwaldstraße 200
Stuttgart
70191
Germany
Tel: +49 711 257 3050
Fax: +49 711 257 9240
Email: mailpool@wolffpartner.de
Volker Schöne, General Manager

Services/Products:
Card pack manufacturer; Database
services; Mailing/Faxing services;
Personalisation; Print services; List
services

E-Services:
Website design

Member of:
National DMA

MAR.CO.
MARKETING.COMMUNICAT-
ION. OLAF QUAST
Walddörferstraße 218 V.
Hamburg
22047
Germany
Tel: +49 40 6957454
Fax: +49 40 6933019
Olaf Quast

Services/Products:
List services; Lettershop; Fulfilment
and sampling house

Member of:
DDV

MARKETFORCE
GESELLSCHAFT FÜR
BUSINESS MARKETING MBH
Adickesalllee 63–65
Frankfurt
60322

Germany
Tel: +49 69 95930 0
Fax: +49 69 95930 333
Email: info@force-group.com
Web: http://www.force-group.com
Christoph von Gleichen

Services/Products:
Telemarketing agency; Direct
marketing agency; Call centre services/
systems; Market research agency

Member of:
FEDMA; DDV

**MD FACTORY MARKETING
DATENMANAGEMENT
GMBH**
Bayerstr. 21
München
80335
Germany
Tel: +49 89 545280
Fax: +49 89 5452810
Franz Hennemann

Services/Products:
Direct marketing agency

Member of:
DDV

**MDM MUNGENAST DIREKT
MARKETING GMBH**
Haussmannstr. 103B
Stuttgart
70188
Germany
Tel: +49 711 26867 0
Fax: +49 711 26867 27
Email: info@mdm-mungenast.de
Web: http://www.mdm-mungenast.de
Oliver Mungenast

Services/Products:
Direct marketing agency

Member of:
DDV

MEDIA DATA RENT GMBH
Lister Str. 18
Hannover
30163
Germany
Tel: +49 511 3989198
Fax: +49 511 3989111
Wolfgang Fuhrmann

Services/Products:
List services; Lettershop; Fulfilment
and sampling house

Member of:
DDV

**MEDIA PHON TV-
PRODUCTION GMBH**
Saarbrücker Str. 16
Schmelz
66839
Germany
Tel: +49 6887 90250
Fax: +49 6887 902514
Email: info@media-phon.de
Web: http://www.MEDIA-PHON.DE
Joachim Schorr

Services/Products:
Telemarketing agency

Member of:
DDV

**MEDIADIRECT MARKETING
GMBH**
Eschenstraße 64
Taufkirchen
82024
Germany
Tel: +49 89 666091 0
Fax: +49 89 666091 40
Email: g.jestaedt@mediadirect-
   marketing.de
Gerhard F. Jestädt

Services/Products:
List services; Lettershop; Fulfilment
and sampling house

Member of:
DDV

MEDIADRESS GMBH
Im Ermlisgrund 26
Waldbronn
76337
Germany
Tel: +49 7243 56850
Fax: +49 7243 568531
Email: mediadress@t-online.de
Herr Heinz-Dieter Kneiphoff

Services/Products:
Database services; Direct marketing
agency; List services

Member of:
National DMA

**MEDIAPHONE
TELEFONMARKETING
GMBH**
Sillenbucherstr. 23a
Stuttgart
70329
Germany
Tel: +49 711 4209202
Fax: +49 711 423915
Email: mediaphone@stb-citynet.de
Margit

Services/Products:
Interactive media

Member of:
DDV

**MEDIPLAN GESELLSCHAFT
FÜR DIALOGMARKETING IM
GESUNDHEITSWESEN MBH**
Hardt 9
Willich
47877
Germany
Tel: +49 2159 52040
Fax: +49 2159 1275
Klaus Keul

Member of:
DDV

MEILLER DIRECT GMBH
Gutenbergstraße 1–5
Schwandorf
92421
Germany
Tel: +49 9431 620–241
Fax: +49 9431 620–343
Email: info@meiller.de
Web: www.meiller.de
Armin Baier, Managing Director

Services/Products:
Catalogue producer; Fulfilment and
sampling house; Lettershop;
Personalisation; Print services

Member of:
DMA (US); FEDMA; National DMA

**MERCATO
DIALOGMARKETING GMBH**
Amsinckstraße 71b
Hamburg
20097
Germany
Tel: +49 40 239050
Fax: +49 40 239051
Mark Hustede

Services/Products:
Telemarketing agency

Member of:
DDV

**MERKUR DIREKTWERBEGES.
MBH & CO KG**
Kapellenstr. 44
Einbeck
37574
Germany
Tel: +49 5561 314 0
Fax: +49 5561 314 133
Email:
   merkur_einbeck@compuserve.com
Web: http://www.merkur-einbeck.de
Sighart Röpke

Services/Products:
List services; Lettershop; Fulfilment
and sampling house

Member of:
DDV

MEYER DIRECT
Krahenweg 3b
Hamburg
22459
Germany
Ute Maack, Office Manager

Services/Products:
Direct marketing agency

Member of:
DMA (US)

MINDMEDIA GMBH –
INSTITUT FÜR
MULTIMEDIALE
KOMMUNIKATION
Bismarckstraße 57
Stadtbergen
86391
Germany
Tel: +49 821 243010
Fax: +49 821 243013
Email: mindmedia@mindmedia.de
Web: http://www.mindmedia.de
Stefan Gottschling

Services/Products:
Interactive media

Member of:
DDV

MON MARKETING ONLINE
DIENSTE GMBH
Pretzfelder Str. 15
Nürnberg
90425
Germany
Tel: +49 911 38485 90
Fax: +49 911 38485 91
Email: makrauss@mon.de
Web: http:\\\\mon.de
Martin Krauß

Services/Products:
Interactive media

Member of:
DDV

MORE SALES AGENTUR GMBH
Schirmerstrasse 76
Düsseldorf
40211
Germany
Tel: +49 211 1781 0
Fax: +49 211 1781 400
Email: office@moresales.de
Web: www.moresales.de

Services/Products:
Advertising Agency; Consultancy
services; Copy adaptation; Design/
graphics/clip art supplier; Direct
marketing agency; Interactive media

E-Services:
E-Marketing consultant; Website
design; Online/e-marketing agency

Member of:
DDV

MORE! MARKETING GMBH
Brunsbütteler Damm 91 - 95
Berlin
13581
Germany
Tel: +49 30 351374 36
Fax: +49 30 35141 36
Christoff H. Wiethoff

Services/Products:
Direct marketing agency

Member of:
DDV

MPS MEDIA PHONE SERVICE
GMBH & CO. BETRIEBS-KG
Liesegangstr. 10
Düsseldorf
40211
Germany
Tel: +49 211 1745 0
Fax: +49 211 1745 11
Email: uschmidt@mediaphone.de
Web: http://www.mediaphone.de
Hans-Joachim Kruse

Services/Products:
Telemarketing agency

Member of:
DDV

MSBK,TEAM
DIALOGMARKETING GMBH
Dorotheenstraße 64
Hamburg
22301
Germany
Tel: +49 40 27852 0
Fax: +49 40 27852 110
Email: kontakt@msbk-team.de
Dieter Zorn

Services/Products:
Direct marketing agency; Sales
promotion agency

E-Services:
Website design

Member of:
FEDMA; DDV

MSU DIREKT –
GESELLSCHAFT FÜR
KUNDEN-AKQUISITION UND
-BINDUNG MBH
Tannenwaldallee 6
Bad Homburg v.d.H.
61348
Germany
Tel: +49 6172 963500
Fax: +49 6172 963501
Web: Jürgen C.F. Steimle
Jürgen C.F. Steimle

Member of:
DDV

MÜLLER ADRESS + NEUE
MEDIENGESELLSCHAFT
ULM MBH & CO. OHG
Pretzfelder Str. 15
Nürnberg
90425
Germany
Tel: +49 911 93471 10
Fax: +49 911 93471 13
Email: info@mueller-adress.de
Web: http://www.mueller-adress.de
Ute Degen

Services/Products:
Interactive media

Member of:
DDV

MULTIDATA SERVICE GMBH
Fössestraße 110
Hannover
30453
Germany
Tel: +49 511 9286106
Fax: +49 511 9286107
Elke Goosmann

Services/Products:
List services; Lettershop; Fulfilment
and sampling house

Member of:
DDV

MUNGENAST DIREKT
MARKETING GMBH
Haussmannstr. 103
Stuttgart
70188
Germany
Tel: +49 711 26 86 70
Fax: +49 711 26 86 727
Oliver Mungenast, President

Services/Products:
Database services; Telemarketing
agency; Direct marketing agency;
Market research agency

Member of:
FEDMA

MVS MANAGEMENT-UND VERSAND-SERVICE GMBH
Pforzheimer Str. 176
Ettlingen
76275
Germany
Tel: +49 7243 518 0
Fax: +49 7243 518100
Horst Sczepansky

Services/Products:
List services; Lettershop; Fulfilment
and sampling house; Database services;
Call centre services/systems

Member of:
FEDMA; DDV

N W S NEUBERT WERBESERVICE KG
Länderweg 7
Frankfurt/M.
60599
Germany
Tel: +49 69 619990
Fax: +49 69 61999211
Corinna Mickelthwate

Services/Products:
Direct marketing agency

Member of:
DDV

NETMEDIA GMBH
Schubertstraße 8
Saarbrücken
66111
Germany
Tel: +49 681 33880
Fax: +49 681 33893
Email: info@net-media.de
Web: http://www.net-media.de
Tim Miksa

Services/Products:
Interactive media

Member of:
DDV

NEUE MEDIENGESELLSCHAFT ULM MBH
Konrad-Celtis-Straße 77
München
81369
Germany
Tel: +49 89 74117 0
Fax: +49 89 74117 101
Web: www.nmg.de
Johann Miller

Services/Products:
Interactive media

Member of:
DDV

NEUSSER DRUCKEREI UND VERLAG GMBH
Moselstr. 14
Neuss
41464
Germany
Tel: +49 2131 404 148
Fax: +49 2131 404 283
Email: werner@kohn.net
Web: http://www.aladin.de od.
    www.ndv.de
Werner Kohn

Services/Products:
Interactive media

Member of:
DDV

NORDATA MARKETING-INFORMATIONS-SYSTEME GMBH
Steckelhörn 5
Hamburg
20457
Germany
Tel: +49 40 3786840
Fax: +49 40 37868430
Wolfgang Blass

Services/Products:
List services; Lettershop; Fulfilment
and sampling house

Member of:
DDV

O.TEL.O COMMUNICATIONS GMBH & CO.
Heerdter Lohweg 35
Düsseldorf
40549
Germany
Tel: +49 0211 5602 8163
Fax: +49 211 5602 8169
Email: heino.ophey@o-tel-o.de
Web: http://www.o-tel-o.de
Heino Ophey

Services/Products:
Telemarketing agency

Member of:
DDV

OBIMD INTERNATIONAL
Z.A. des Boutries - 9, rue des Cayennes
F-
Conflans Ste Honorine
78700
Germany
Tel: +33 01349006 78
Fax: +33 01349006 98
Gérard Didier Clerquin

Services/Products:
List services; Lettershop; Fulfilment
and sampling house

Member of:
DDV

OGILVYONE WORLDWIDE GMBH
Geleitsstr. 14
Frankfurt
60599
Germany
Tel: +49 69 60915 0
Fax: +49 69 618031
Web: www.ogilvyone.de
Rolf-Dieter Hölzel

Services/Products:
Database services; Telemarketing
agency; Direct marketing agency; Sales
promotion agency; Electronic media

E-Services:
Website design

Member of:
DMA (US); FEDMA; DDV

OK MARKETING ELISABETH KREUZIGER
Mauermattenstr. 7
Waldkirch
79183
Germany
Tel: +49 7681 47760
Fax: +49 7681 4776222
Elisabeth Kreuziger

Services/Products:
Telemarketing agency

Member of:
DDV

OMIKRON. SOFT + HARDWARE GMBH
Sponheimstraße 12
Pforzheim
75177
Germany
Tel: +49 7231 125970
Fax: +49 7231 1259725
Carsten Kraus

Services/Products:
List services; Lettershop; Fulfilment
and sampling house

Member of:
DDV

OPTIMAIL DIREKTWERBESERVICE GMBH

Postfach 10 36 27
Stuttgart
70031
Germany
Tel: +49 711 6602 606
Fax: +49 711 6602 485
Email: w.john@dasbeste.de
Wolfgang John

Services/Products:
List services; Lettershop; Fulfilment and sampling house

Member of:
DDV

PAN-ADRESS DIREKTMARKETING GESELLSCHAFT MBH

Semmelweisstr. 8
Planegg
82152
Germany
Tel: +49 89 85709 279
Fax: +49 89 85709 465
Email: pan-adress@t-online.de
Web: http://www.pan-adress.de
Emanuel Zehetbauer

Services/Products:
List services; Lettershop; Fulfilment and sampling house; Database services; Direct marketing agency

Member of:
DMA (US); FEDMA; DDV

PB DIREKT PRAUN, BINDER & PARTNER GMBH

Jahnstraße 4/1
Korntal-Münchingen
70825
Germany
Tel: +49 711 83632 10
Fax: +49 711 83632 36
Email: post@pbdirekt.de
Web: http://www.pbdirekt.de
Horst Praun

Services/Products:
List services; Lettershop; Fulfilment and sampling house

Member of:
DDV

PDC DIALOG MARKETING GMBH

Rossertstraße 9
Frankfurt
60323
Germany
Tel: +49 69 971222 0
Fax: +49 69 971222 40

Email: info-pdc@pdc-online.com
Web: http://www.PDC-ONLINE.COM
Manfred Opp

Services/Products:
Direct marketing agency

Member of:
DDV

PEPPERMIND NETWORK NEUE MEDIEN KOCHAN & PARTNER GMBH

Hirschgartenallee 25
München
80639
Germany
Tel: +49 89 1730130
Fax: +49 89 1781235
Email: kontakt@peppermind.de
Web: http://www.peppermind.de
Boris Kochan

Services/Products:
Interactive media

Member of:
DDV

PETER REINCKE DIREKT-MARKETING GMBH

Mühlstr. 98a
Aschaffenburg
63741
Germany
Tel: +49 6021 4024 0
Fax: +49 6021 402413
Email: kontakt@reincke.de
Web: http://www.reincke.de
Peter Reincke

Services/Products:
Direct marketing agency

Member of:
DDV

PETRA REIMANN BÜRO-U. DATENSERVICE GMBH

Tiedexer Tor 14
Einbeck
37574
Germany
Tel: +49 5561 9321 0
Fax: +49 5561 9321 16
Petra Reimann-Kirton

Services/Products:
List services; Lettershop; Fulfilment and sampling house

Member of:
DDV

PHARMA DIREKT GMBH

Fraunhoferstraße 18 a
Planegg

82152
Germany
Tel: +49 89 89520 200
Fax: +49 89 89520 102
Dieter Jung

Services/Products:
Direct marketing agency

Member of:
DDV

PHONECOM KOMMUNIKATIONSDIENSTE GMBH

Infanteriestr. 14
München
80797
Germany
Tel: +49 89 12566 0
Fax: +49 89 12566 116
Web: www.PhoneCom.de
Carola Schwarz

Services/Products:
Telemarketing agency

Member of:
DDV

PHONEPARTNER GMBH

Wilhelm-Leuschner-Straße 56
Dietzenbach
63128
Germany
Tel: +49 6074 8081
Fax: +49 6074 42833
Web: www.phonepartner.de
Dietmar Weixler

Services/Products:
Lettershop; Fulfilment and sampling house; Telemarketing agency; Training/recruitment; Call centre services/systems

Member of:
FEDMA; DDV

PL MARKETING GMBH

Moltkestraße 53
Karlsruhe
76133
Germany
Tel: +49 721 854487
Fax: +49 721 854454
Peter Lindner

Services/Products:
Direct marketing agency

Member of:
DDV

PMS – PHONE MEDIA SERVICE GMBH

Schadowstr. 74
Düsseldorf

40212
Germany
Tel: +49 0211 3559570
Fax: +49 211 355957 100
Email: kontakt@pms.de
Web: http://www.pms.de
Reinhard Kükel

Services/Products:
Telemarketing agency

Member of:
DDV

POINT INFORMATIONS SYSTEME GMBH
Karlsplatz 11
München
80335
Germany
Tel: +49 89 54866100
Fax: +49 89 54866486
Email: info@pointinfo.com
Web: http://www.pointinfo.com
Peter Zahnd

Services/Products:
Telemarketing agency

Member of:
DDV

POPNET GMBH & CO. KG
Bramfelder Straße 113
Hamburg
22305
Germany
Tel: +49 40 6116560
Fax: +49 40 61165699
Email: popnet@popnet.de
Web: http://www.popnet.de
Heike Jörn

Services/Products:
Interactive media

Member of:
DDV

PORTA MUNDI GMBH & CO. KG
Deutschherrnstraaae 15–19
Nürnberg
90429
Germany
Tel: +49 911 2723 0
Fax: +49 911 2723 222
Email: info@portamundi.de
Web: www.portamundi.de
Walter Firgau, Marketing Director

Services/Products:
Consultancy services; Interactive media; Internet agency

E-Services:
E-Marketing consultant; Website design; Online/e-marketing agency

PORTICA GMBH MARKETING SUPPORT
Von-Galen-Str- 35
Kempen
47906
Germany
Tel: +49 2152 9151 66
Fax: +49 2152 915 100
Email: portica@portica.de
Web: http://www.PORTICA.DE
Hans P Barthel

Services/Products:
List services; Lettershop; Fulfilment and sampling house

Member of:
DDV

POWER ADRESS ZIELGRUPPENMARKETING GMBH
Linzer Straße 21
Bad Honnef
53604
Germany
Tel: +49 2224 918273
Fax: +49 2224 918260
Email: gfs.de@-t-online.de
Jürgen Grosse

Services/Products:
List services; Lettershop; Fulfilment and sampling house

Member of:
DDV

PPWS WERBUNG GMBH
Städelstraße 19
Frankfurt
60596
Germany
Tel: +49 69 962151 0
Fax: +49 69 627408
Volker Lehmann

Services/Products:
Direct marketing agency

Member of:
DDV

PRINT DIRECT GMBH
Am Weistlesberg 4
Utting-Holzhausen
86919
Germany
Tel: +49 8806 9227 0
Fax: +49 8806 9227 20
Email: printdirect@t-online.de
Klaus Rügemer

Services/Products:
Direct marketing agency

Member of:
DDV

PRISMA DIREKT GES. FÜR INFORMATIONSVER-ARBEI-TUNG UND DIREKT MARKETING MBH
Siemensstraße 6
Bad Homburg
61352
Germany
Tel: +49 6172 670 239
Fax: +49 6172 670 288
Email: mk_prisma@csi.com u. ag_prisma@csi.com
Web: http://www.prisma-direkt.de
Jürgen Piram

Services/Products:
Response analysis bureau; Personalisation; Software supplier

Member of:
FEDMA; DDV

PRISMA UNTERNEHMENSBERATUNG FÜR TELEFONKOMMUNIKATION GMBH
Ferdinand-Porsche-Ring 17
Rodgau
63110
Germany
Tel: +49 6106 6910
Fax: +49 6106 16373
Web: www.prisma-gmbh.de
Harald Henn

Services/Products:
Telemarketing agency

Member of:
DDV

PRISMA WERBEAGENTUR GMBH
Theodor-Heuss-Str. 4
Bonn
53177
Germany
Tel: +49 228 352970
Fax: +49 228 359398
Sabine Nikodem

Services/Products:
Direct marketing agency

Member of:
DDV

PRO MARKETING
Carl Zeiss-Strasse 6
Offenburg
77656
Germany
Tel: +49 78155883
Fax: +49 781606541
Manuela Seebacher, Director

Services/Products:
List services

**PRO:TAGON
DIRECTMARKETING GMBH**
Friedrich-Ebert-Straße
Bergisch Gladbach
51429
Germany
Tel: +49 2204 842370
Fax: +49 2204 842389
Email: braunbach@pro-tagon.de
Ulrich Braunbach

Services/Products:
List services; Lettershop; Fulfilment
and sampling house

Member of:
DDV

**PROCONTACT –
DIREKTMARKETING GMBH**
Machtlfinger Straße 26
München
81379
Germany
Tel: +49 89 74832 0
Fax: +49 89 74832 199
Email: info@procontact.de
Web: http://www.procontact.de
Hans-Peter Jochheim

Services/Products:
Telemarketing agency

Member of:
DDV

**PRODATA DATENBANKEN UND
INFORMATIONSSYSTEME
GMBH**
Südendstraße 42
Karlsruhe
76135
Germany
Tel: +49 721 98171 0
Fax: +49 721 98171 300
Web: www.prodata-gmbh.com
Mario Modlich

Services/Products:
List services; Lettershop; Fulfilment
and sampling house

Member of:
DDV

**PROFI CALL BREMEN GMBH &
CO. KG**
Otto-Lilienthal-Straße 15
Bremen
28199
Germany
Tel: +49 421 5252 0
Fax: +49 421 5252 111
Email: info@proficall.de

Web: http://www.proficall.de
Jürgen Reineke

Services/Products:
Telemarketing agency

Member of:
DDV

**PROFITEL CALL CENTER
CONSULTING GMBH**
Luruper Chaussee 125
Hamburg
22761
Germany
Tel: +49 40 8979 2001
Fax: +49 40 8979 2099
Beate Middendorf

Services/Products:
Telemarketing agency

Member of:
DDV

**PROJEKT AGENTUR FLECK
GMBH**
Kleine Bahnstraße 10
Hamburg
22525
Germany
Tel: +49 40 8517060
Fax: +49 40 851706 10
Email: projekt-agentur-
fleck@msn.com
Stefan Pisters

Services/Products:
Direct marketing agency

Member of:
DDV

**PROMOTA DIRECT
MARKETING GMBH**
Bahndamm 9
Stockelsdorf
23617
Germany
Tel: +49 451 4904 127
Fax: +49 451 4904 128
Eva Hagen

Services/Products:
Telemarketing agency

Member of:
DDV

**PROMOTA MARKEN-SERVICE
VERWALTUNGS GMBH
BEREICH TELEFON-
SERVICE**
Herforder Str. 46
Bielefeld
33602
Germany
Tel: +49 521 5252 0

Fax: +49 521 5252 100
Erika Haack

Member of:
DDV

**PROWERB WERBE-UND
VERSANDSERVICE GMBH**
Huissenerstr. 7–9
Kleve
47533
Germany
Tel: +49 2821 7218 0
Fax: +49 2821 7218 25
Email: prowerb@aol.com
Hans Noy

Services/Products:
List services; Lettershop; Fulfilment
and sampling house

Member of:
DDV

**PS PACKEN UND SCHICKEN
GMBH**
Maudacher Straße 109
Ludwigshafen
67065
Germany
Tel: +49 621 570050
Fax: +49 621 5700525
Theophil Ling

Services/Products:
List services; Lettershop; Fulfilment
and sampling house

Member of:
DDV

**PUBLICA DATA-SERVICE
GMBH**
Steinerne Furt 72
Augsburg
86167
Germany
Tel: +49 821 70015 0
Fax: +49 821 70015 124
Helmut Nestler

Services/Products:
List services; Lettershop; Fulfilment
and sampling house

Member of:
DDV

PUBLICIS DIALOG
Große Elbstraße 39
Hamburg
22767
Germany
Tel: +49 40 3810701
Fax: +49 40 38107100
Web: www.publicisdialog.de
Peter Wendt

Services/Products:
Direct marketing agency; Market research agency; Sales promotion agency

Member of:
FEDMA; DDV

PULL RESPONSE-WERBE-GMBH
Laufertorgraben 2
Nürnberg
90489
Germany
Tel: +49 911 533345
Fax: +49 911 580940 0
Walter Reketat

Services/Products:
Direct marketing agency

Member of:
DDV

PVS PRESSEVERSAND SERVICE GMBH
Kanalstr. 15
Neckarsulm
74172
Germany
Tel: +49 7132 979 0
Fax: +49 7132 979 200
Horst Baumgartner

Services/Products:
List services; Lettershop; Fulfilment and sampling house

Member of:
DDV

QUELLE AG
Nuernberger Str. 91–95
PO Box 4000
Fuerth
90762
Germany
Tel: +49 911 14 23459
Fax: +49 911 14 24330
Email:
   unternehmens.kommunikation@qu-elle.de
Web: www.quelle.de
Erich R. Jeske, Director of the Unternehmenskommunikation

Services/Products:
Call centre services/systems; Catalogue producer; Database services; Mail order company

Member of:
National DMA

R & P WERBEAGENTUR MÜNCHEN GMBH
Rosenheimer Str. 145 E-F
München
81671
Germany
Tel: +49 89 49067 0
Fax: +49 89 49067 100
Email: info@rempenmuc.de
Web: http://rempenmuc.de
Zeljko Ratkovic

Services/Products:
Direct marketing agency

Member of:
DDV

R. M. SITTARZ HERO SERVICES GMBH
Mechtildisstraße 6
Aachen
52066
Germany
Tel: +49 241 607155
Fax: +49 241 607125
Email: info@hero-services.com
Web: http://dvd.de/hero
Helmut Sittarz

Services/Products:
List services; Lettershop; Fulfilment and sampling house

Member of:
DDV

RAAB KARCHER ELEKTRONIK GMBH
Lötscher Weg 66
Nettetal
41334
Germany
Tel: +49 2153 733195
Fax: +49 2153 733348
Email: bschulz@rke.de
Bernd Schulz

Services/Products:
Telemarketing agency

Member of:
DDV

RBC DIASYS CONSULTING AG
Felsenstraße 88
CH -
St. Gallen
9001
Germany
Tel: +41 71 2284525
Fax: +41 71 2284540
Email: diasys@bluewin.ch
Christian Huldi

Services/Products:
Direct marketing agency

Member of:
DDV

REAL CONSULTANTS GMBH
Siegfriedstr. 14–20
Worms
67547
Germany
Tel: +49 6241 4701
Fax: +49 6241 4272
Email: real-consultants@t-online.de
Web: http://home.t-online.de/home/
   Real-Consultants/
Klaus Herrmann

Services/Products:
Telemarketing agency

Member of:
DDV

REALDESIGN INTELLIGENT COMMUNICATION GMBH I.G.
Seckbacher Landstr. 12
Frankfurt/Main
60389
Germany
Tel: +49 69 4693044
Fax: +49 69 4693054
Email: info@realdesign.de
Web: http://www.realdesign.de
Martin Debus

Services/Products:
Direct marketing agency

Member of:
DDV

REMPEN & PARTNER WERBEAGENTUR GMBH
Kavalleriestr. 16
Düsseldorf
40213
Germany
Tel: +49 0211 83950
Fax: +49 211 8395111
Jan Blomenkamp

Services/Products:
Direct marketing agency

Member of:
DDV

RICHARD BOREK GMBH & CO KG
Theodor-Heuss-Str. 7
Braunschweig
38090
Germany
Tel: +49 531 205 01
Fax: +49 531 205 1543
Richard Borek

Member of:
DDV

**RIEK, DIRECT MARKETING
FAIRMARKTUNG GMBH &
CO. KG**
Am Seeberg 7
Bad Homburg
61352
Germany
Tel: +49 6172 488100
Fax: +49 6172 488102
Email: riek.direkt@t-online.de
Udo Riek

Services/Products:
Direct marketing agency

Member of:
DDV

**RITTER, WOLEK
WERBEAGENTUR GMBH**
Robert-Bosch-Strasse 11
Langen
D-63225
Germany
Tel: +49 6103 921797
Fax: +49 6103 26320
Email: mail@ritter-wolek.de
Web: www.ritter-wolek.de
Bernd Ritter, President

Services/Products:
Advertising Agency; Direct marketing
agency; Interactive media; Sales
promotion agency

E-Services:
Website design

Member of:
DDV

**RJ MARKETING-SERVICE
GMBH**
Keppentaler Weg 19
Wörrstadt
55286
Germany
Tel: +49 6732 94010
Fax: +49 6732 940194
Robert Janka

Services/Products:
List services; Lettershop; Fulfilment
and sampling house

Member of:
DDV

**RM BUCH UND MEDIEN
VERTRIEB GMBH**
Ringstraße 16–20
Rheda-Wiedenbrück
33378
Germany

Tel: +49 5242 914432
Fax: +49 5242 916962
Email: ralf.ehlers@bertelsmann.de
Ralf Ehlers

Services/Products:
Telemarketing agency

Member of:
DDV

**RÖSCH MARKETING –
AGENTUR FÜR MARKETING
UND KOMMUNIKATION IM
IT-MARKT GMBH**
Martinusstraße 36
Kaarst
41564
Germany
Tel: +49 2131 76750
Fax: +49 2131 767574
Lore P. Rösch

Member of:
DDV

**ROSENZWEIG & SCHWARZ
AGENTUR FÜR
DIALOGMARKETING GMBH**
Hofweg 61a
Hamburg
22085
Germany
Tel: +49 40 6694 090
Fax: +49 40 6694 0919
Email: info@rs-dialog.de
Web: www.RS-Dialog.de
Mike H. Rosenzweig

Services/Products:
Catalogue producer; Consultancy
services; Mailing/Faxing services;
Personalisation; Print services; Direct
marketing agency

E-Services:
E-Marketing consultant; Website
design; Online/e-marketing agency

Member of:
DDV

**RTV KARIN RUDOLF, DATEN-
TEXT-UND
INFORMATIONSVERARBEIT-
UNG**
Neuweg 16
Groß-Gerau
64521
Germany
Tel: +49 6152 1784 0
Fax: +49 6152 1784 17
Gerd Rudolf

Services/Products:
List services; Lettershop; Fulfilment
and sampling house

Member of:
DDV

**S & H COMMUNICATION GES.
FÜR WERBUNG UND
TELEMARKETING MBH**
Unterdorfstraße 9
Ubstadt-Weiher
76698
Germany
Tel: +49 7253 888 0
Fax: +49 7253 888 101
Email: info@sh-communication.de
Web: http://www.sh-communication.de
Monika Hagendorn

Services/Products:
Telemarketing agency

Member of:
DDV

**S DIREKT SPARKASSEN
SERVICE RHEINLAND GMBH**
Kuhlenwall 20
Duisburg
47051
Germany
Tel: +49 203 28600
Fax: +49 203 2860199
Carmen Reynders

Services/Products:
Telemarketing agency

Member of:
DDV

**S DIREKT-MARKETING GMBH
& CO.KG**
Grenzstraße 21
Halle
6112
Germany
Tel: +49 345 5698990
Fax: +49 345 5606233
Rainer Pohl

Services/Products:
Telemarketing agency

Member of:
DDV

S.B.W. WERBUNG GMBH
Hans-Böckler-Straße 20
Dinslaken
46539
Germany
Tel: +49 2064 412232
Fax: +49 2064 412250
Theodor Brakmann

Services/Products:
Direct marketing agency

Member of:
DDV

**SALE AGENTUR FÜR DIREKTE
    KOMMUNIKATION GMBH**
Kattrepelsbrücke 1
Hamburg
20095
Germany
Tel: +49 40 323326 0
Fax: +49 40 323326 36
Klaus Borgschulte

Services/Products:
Direct marketing agency

Member of:
DDV

SALES TEAM GMBH
Mainzer Str. 118
Darmstadt
64293
Germany
Tel: +49 6151 815311
Fax: +49 6151 815333
Joachim Henseler

Services/Products:
Call centre services/systems; Database
services; Personalisation; Direct
marketing agency; Fulfilment and
sampling house; Sales promotion
agency

Member of:
National DMA

**SALESCONCEPT
    TELESERVICES &
    DATABASE-MARKETING
    GMBH**
Frankenallee 26
Kelkheim
65779
Germany
Tel: +49 6195 9915 0
Fax: +49 6195 9915 22
Email: sales@salesconcept.de
Web: www.salesconcept.com
Christoph von Reichenbach, Managing
    Director/Co-owner

Services/Products:
Telemarketing agency; Advertising
Agency; Call centre services/systems;
Consultancy services; Database
services; Fulfilment and sampling
house; Operative marketing and sales
support especially for high tech
products and for all IT subjects

E-Services:
Email list provider; Email software;
Website design; Online/e-marketing
agency

Member of:
National DMA; DDV

SAZ DIALOG AGENTUR GMBH
Gutenbergstraße 3
Garbsen
30823
Germany
Tel: +49 5137 878 100
Fax: +49 5137 878 110
Email: dialog@saz.net
Web: http://www.saz.net/dialog
Manfred Hörnschemeyer

Services/Products:
List services; Lettershop; Fulfilment
and sampling house; Direct marketing
agency; Response analysis bureau

Member of:
FEDMA; DDV

SAZ LISTBROKING GMBH
Gutenbergstr. 3
Garbsen
30823
Germany
Tel: +49 5137 878553
Fax: +49 5137 878555
Email: flistbr@aol.com
Web: http://www.saz.net\\listbroking\\
Nicole Bittner

Services/Products:
List services; Lettershop; Fulfilment
and sampling house; Advertising
Agency

Member of:
FEDMA; DDV

**SBS MEDIASERVICE
    WERBEAGENTUR GMBH**
Metzer Straße 7
Saarlouis
66740
Germany
Tel: +49 6831 9413 0
Fax: +49 6831 9413 13
Michael Hahn

Services/Products:
Direct marketing agency

Member of:
DDV

**SCHAFFHAUSEN
    WERBEAGENTUR**
Daimlerstr. 17
Elmshorn
25337
Germany
Tel: +49 4121 4729 0
Fax: +49 4121 4729 47
Email: webmaster@schaffhausen.de
Web: http://www.schaffhausen.de
Martina Rausch

Services/Products:
Direct marketing agency

Member of:
DDV

**SCHERER TEAM & HAGEMANN
    AGENTUR FÜR
    TELEKOMMUNIKATIVES
    MARKETING**
Prinz-Georg-Straße 91
Düsseldorf
40479
Germany
Tel: +49 0211 94603 0
Fax: +49 211 94603 12
Web: Thomas Hagemann
Hagemann

Member of:
DDV

**SCHERER TEAM MRM GMBH &
    CO. KG**
Enzianstraße 2
Starnberg
82319
Germany
Tel: +49 8151 7707 0
Fax: +49 8151 16216
Email: info@schererteam.com
Web: http://www.schererteam.com
Michael Metzgen

Services/Products:
Database services; Direct marketing
agency; Response analysis bureau

Member of:
FEDMA; DDV

**SCHOBER D&G DIRECT
    MEDIA GMBH & CO.**
Max-Eyth-Straße 6–10
Ditzingen
71254
Germany
Tel: +49 7156 304318
Fax: +49 7156 304431
Email: kpraetzke@aol.com
Klaus-Peter Rätzke

Services/Products:
List services; Lettershop; Fulfilment
and sampling house

Member of:
FEDMA; DDV

**SCHOBER
    DIREKTMARKETING GMBH
    & CO.**
Max-Eyth-Str. 6–10
Ditzingen
71254
Germany
Tel: +49 7156 304 95

170

Fax: +49 156 304 431
Email: schober.info@t-online.de
Web: http://www.schober.de
Arnold Steinke

Services/Products:
List services; Lettershop; Fulfilment
and sampling house; Database services

Member of:
DMA (US); FEDMA; DDV

SCHOLZ VERSAND SERVICE INH. SIEGFRIED SCHOLZ
Sandforter Straße 143
Osnabrück
49086
Germany
Tel: +49 541 937020
Fax: +49 541 9370240
Email: svs.de@t-online.de
Siegfried Scholz

Services/Products:
List services; Lettershop; Fulfilment
and sampling house

Member of:
DDV

SCHWENK KORTUS & TEAM TRAININGSINSTITUT UND TELEFONMARKETING
Längerach 18
Sipplingen a. B.
78354
Germany
Tel: +49 7551 3001
Fax: +49 7551 3004
Web: Marielouise Schwenk-Kortus
Schwenk-Kortus

Member of:
DDV

SCITEX DIGITAL PRINTING
Auenstrasse 4
München
80469
Germany
Tel: +49 89 20241990
Fax: +49 89 20241993
Manfred Dreissinger

Services/Products:
Print services

Member of:
FEDMA

SEKA TEAM TELEFONMARKETING GMBH
Brauhausstr. 17–19
Hamburg
22041
Germany

Tel: +49 40 6523725
Fax: +49 40 680409
Email: info@seka-team.de
Volker Kauerauf

Services/Products:
Telemarketing agency

Member of:
DDV

SELLBYTEL CALL-& COMMUNICATION-CENTER GMBH
Postfach 48 45
Nürnberg
90026
Germany
Tel: +49 911 9339 0
Fax: +49 911 9339 1200
Email: info@sellbytel.de
Web: http://www.sellbytel.de
Michael Raum

Services/Products:
Telemarketing agency

Member of:
DDV

SERVICE GESELLSCHAFT FÜR VERKAUFSFÖRDERUNG VERTREILUNG VERSAND EDV POSTBEARBEITUNG MBH
Am Industriehof 7–9
Frankfurt
60487
Germany
Tel: +49 69 2477150
Fax: +49 69 700891
Gerd Milanowski

Member of:
DDV

SERVICE PARTNER AGENTUR FÜR DIREKTWERBUNG GMBH
Siemensstr. 25a
Bad Homburg
61352
Germany
Tel: +49 6172 92550
Fax: +49 6172 925555
Birgit Wiederhold

Services/Products:
List services; Lettershop; Fulfilment
and sampling house

Member of:
DDV

SHB INDIVIDUAL MARKETING & ADVERTISING STUTTGART GMBH
Rosenbergstraße 113
Stuttgart
70193
Germany
Tel: +49 711 993450
Fax: +49 711 9934555
Email: info@shb.de
Web: http://www.shb.de
Stephan H. Bausback

Services/Products:
Direct marketing agency

Member of:
DDV

SICHTIG DIREKTWERBUNG GMBH
Gießener Str. 19
Nürnberg
90427
Germany
Tel: +49 911 936690
Fax: +49 911 9366920
Email: edv@sichtig.de
Web: http://www.sichtig.de
Herbert Uttinger

Services/Products:
Telemarketing agency

Member of:
DDV

SIEGERT & DR. BREINLINGER – DM LAWYER
Fischerau 6
Freiburg
79098
Germany
Tel: +49 761 381 141
Fax: +49 761 281 029
Email: raesiegert-dr.breinlinger@t-
online.de
Michael Siegert

Services/Products:
Legal services

Member of:
FEDMA

SIPA UNTERNEHMER BERATUNG GMBH
Altneugasse 25
Saarbrücken
66117
Germany
Tel: +49 681 926220
Fax: +49 681 926221
Email: sipa@sipa.de
Web: http://www.sipa.de
Rainer H. Wagner

Services/Products:
Direct marketing agency

Member of:
DDV

SITEL GMBH
Europark A17
Krefeld
47807
Germany
Tel: +49 2151 385 0
Fax: +49 2151 385 4000
Web: www.sitel.com
Norbert Greifenberg

Services/Products:
Telemarketing agency

Member of:
DDV

SK-TELEKOMMUNIKATION IN KS-UNTERNEHMENSGRUP-PE
Stengelstraße 1
Saarbrücken
66117
Germany
Tel: +49 681   926070
Fax: +49 681 9260749
Gerlinde Schwarz

Services/Products:
Telemarketing agency

Member of:
DDV

SKRIPTURA DIENSTLEISTUNGEN SCHMALE & WOLF OHG
Karl-Wiechert-Allee 20
Hannover
30625
Germany
Tel: +49 511 54294 0
Fax: +49 511 54294 47
Email: skriptura@t-online.de
Dirk Wolf

Services/Products:
List services; Lettershop; Fulfilment and sampling house

Member of:
DDV

SLOGAN WERBEAGENTUR GMBH
Mühlwiesenstr. 32
Filderstadt
70794
Germany
Tel: +49 7158 93902 0
Fax: +49 7158 93902 77
Email: info@slogan.de

Web: http://slogan.de
Wolf Hirschmann

Services/Products:
Direct marketing agency

Member of:
DDV

SMILE & SELL TELESERVICES GMBH
Goethering 22–24
Osnabrück
49074
Germany
Tel: +49 541 3499 0
Fax: +49 541 3499 250
Email: quermann@smileandsell.de
Web: http:\\\\smileandsell.de
Burkhard Quermann

Services/Products:
Telemarketing agency; Call centre services/systems

Member of:
FEDMA; DDV

SMILE AND SELL TELESERVICES GMBH
Postfach 2443
Goethering 22–24
Osnabrück
49074
Germany
Tel: +49 54134990
Fax: +49 5413499250
Email: info@smileandsell.de
Burkhard Quermann, President

Services/Products:
Telemarketing agency; Service bureau; Call centre services/systems

Member of:
FEDMA

SMP – WERBESERVICE GMBH
Gewerbestraße 7
Irxleben/Magdeburg
39167
Germany
Tel: +49 39204 799 0
Fax: +49 39204 799 97
Email: smp@smp-werbeservice
Web: http://www.SMP-Werbeservice.de
Gerd Piechotzki

Services/Products:
List services; Lettershop; Fulfilment and sampling house

Member of:
DDV

SOBA GMBH UNTERNEHMENSBERATUNG
Linzer Straße 21
Bad Honnef
53604
Germany
Tel: +49 2224 918 376
Fax: +49 2224 918 374
Email: spbaub@soba.de
Web: http://www.SOBA.de
Arne Peper

Services/Products:
List services; Lettershop; Fulfilment and sampling house

Member of:
DDV

SOCIAL CONCEPT GMBH AGENTUR FÜR SOZIALMARKETING
Thieboldsgasse 150
Köln
50676
Germany
Tel: +49 221 921640 0
Fax: +49 221 921640 40
Franz Orth

Services/Products:
List services; Lettershop; Fulfilment and sampling house

Member of:
DDV

SONY INTERNATIONAL (EUROPE) GMBH
Hugo-Eckener-Straße 20
Köln
50829
Germany
Tel: +49 0211 5966328
Fax: +49 211 5966597
Gregor Erkel

Services/Products:
Interactive media

Member of:
DDV

SPECTRUM GMBH MARKETING SERVICES & CONSULTING
Lohweg 27
Neufahrn
85375
Germany
Tel: +49 8165 9551 0
Fax: +49 8165 9551 28
Email:
   100130.3456@compuserve.com
Web: http://www.ecdm/spectrum
Kerstin Plehwe

Services/Products:
Database services; Direct marketing agency; Software supplier; Response analysis bureau

Member of:
FEDMA; DDV

SPELLBOUND GESELLSCHAFT FÜR INNOVATIVES MARKETING MBH
Haferstraße 28
Melle
49324
Germany
Tel: +49 5422 9512 0
Fax: +49 5422 9512 22
Nihad Muracevic

Services/Products:
Telemarketing agency

Member of:
DDV

SPT MARKETING SERVICE GBR MBH
Raiffeisenstraße 19 + 19A
Filderstadt
70794
Germany
Tel: +49 711 77397 10
Fax: +49 711 7776756
Email: spt_gbr@t-online.de
Web: http://www.spt.de
Sigurd Skutnik

Services/Products:
List services; Lettershop; Fulfilment and sampling house

Member of:
DDV

SSM SYSTEM SERVICE MARKETING GMBH
Dudenstr. 37–43
Mannheim
68167
Germany
Tel: +49 621 33839 0
Fax: +49 621 3383970
Email:
106113.3631@compuserve.com
Frank M. Paul

Services/Products:
List services; Lettershop; Fulfilment and sampling house

Member of:
DDV

STAMMCOM MEDIA GMBH
Beethovenstraße 21
Düsseldorf

40233
Germany
Tel: +49 0211 681293
Fax: +49 211 966330
Elmar Stamm

Services/Products:
Telemarketing agency

Member of:
DDV

STEIGERWALD MARKETING GMBH
Waldschmidtstraße 90a
Passau
94034
Germany
Tel: +49 851 46676
Fax: +49 851 45885
Wolfgang F. Steigerwald

Services/Products:
List services; Lettershop; Fulfilment and sampling house

Member of:
DDV

STETTIN DIRECT MARKETING
Hugo-Eckener-Straße 18
Mainz
55122
Germany
Tel: +49 6131 968980
Fax: +49 6131 9689815
Thomas Stettin

Services/Products:
List services; Lettershop; Fulfilment and sampling house

Member of:
DDV

STOLLMANN GMBH
Esternaystr. 23D
Waldbronn
76337
Germany
Tel: +49 7243 572806
Fax: +49 7243 572808
Email: mail@stollmann-gmbh.de
Web: http://www.stollmann-gmbh.de
Friedel Stollmann

Services/Products:
Direct marketing agency

Member of:
DDV

SUCCESS MARKETING + KOMMUNIKATION HARRY RÖDER GMBH
Peutestraße 53c
Hamburg
20539

Germany
Tel: +49 40 780880
Fax: +49 40 78088222
Email: info@success-marketing.de
Web: http://www.SUCCESS-MARKETING.DE
Harry Röder

Services/Products:
Telemarketing agency

Member of:
DDV

SUPERCOM GMBH AUDIOTEX SYSTEME
Schadowstraße 74
Düsseldorf
40212
Germany
Tel: +49 0211 352020
Fax: +49 211 356838
Nina Zenz

Services/Products:
Telemarketing agency

Member of:
DDV

SWI SÜD-WEST-INFORMATION GMBH
Rheinstraße 105
Münster-Sarmsheim
D-55424
Germany
Tel: +49 6721 965 315
Fax: +49 6721 965 300
Email: info@sw-information.com
Web: www.sw-information.com
Rüdiger Harrer, Manager

Services/Products:
Direct marketing agency; List services

Member of:
DDV

SYKES TAS TELEMARKETING GES. F. KOMMUNIKATION & DIALOG MBH
Königsallee 178a
Bochum
44799
Germany
Tel: +49 234 97610
Fax: +49 234 9761100
Iris Gordelik

Services/Products:
Telemarketing agency

Member of:
DDV

SYMBOL MARKETING GMBH BERATUNG + SERVICE

Abraham-Lincoln-Str. 17
Wiesbaden
65189
Germany
Tel: +49 611 97754 0
Fax: +49 611 97754 77
Email: kontakt@symbol.de
Web: http://www.symbol.de
Thomas Böhm

Services/Products:
Direct marketing agency

Member of:
DDV

SYMPA TEL TELEMARKETING GMBH

Teichstraße 19
Pirmasens
66953
Germany
Tel: +49 6331 5330
Fax: +49 6331 533181
Email: vertrieb@sympatel.de
Web: http://www.SympaTel.de
Wolfgang Barth

Services/Products:
Telemarketing agency

Member of:
DDV

T & M GESELLSCHAFT FÜR TELEFONMARKETING MBH

Max-Högg-Str. 3
Friedberg
86316
Germany
Tel: +49 821 6000 0
Fax: +49 821 6000 300
Email: tm_telefonmarketing@t-online.de
Hannelore Picking

Services/Products:
Telemarketing agency

Member of:
DDV

T-PUNKT-MARKETING GMBH

Holsteinischer Kamp 12
Hamburg
22081
Germany
Tel: +49 40 291103
Fax: +49 40 2996623
Email: t-punkt@aol.com
Norbert Prien

Services/Products:
Telemarketing agency

Member of:
DDV

T.D.M. TELEFON-DIREKT-MARKETING GMBH

Käthe-Paulus-Straße 12
Sarstedt
31157
Germany
Tel: +49 5066 606 00
Fax: +49 5066 606 010
Email: info@tdm.de
Web: www.tdm.de

Services/Products:
Telemarketing agency; Training/recruitment; Call centre services/systems; Consultancy services; Database services; IT support

E-Services:
E-Marketing consultant; Email software

Member of:
FEDMA; National DMA

TALKLINE INFODIENSTE GMBH

Poppelsdorfer Allee 34
Bonn
53115
Germany
Tel: +49 228 969720
Fax: +49 228 9697220
Renatus Zilles

Services/Products:
Telemarketing agency

Member of:
DDV

TARNOW COMMUNICATIONS WERBEAGENTUR GMBH

Im Förstergrund 6a
Kelkheim/Ts.
65779
Germany
Tel: +49 6195 900116
Fax: +49 6195 900216
Klaus M. Tarnow

Services/Products:
Direct marketing agency

Member of:
DDV

TAS GMBH NORD

Windausstraße1
Hannover
30163
Germany
Tel: +49 511 676760
Fax: +49 511 676761
Michael Emmert

Services/Products:
Telemarketing agency

Member of:
DDV

TAS TELEMARKETING GES. FÜR KOMMUNIKATION UNI DIALOG MBH

Königsallee 178a
Bochum
44799
Germany
Tel: +49 234 97610
Fax: +49 234 9761100
Email: iris.gordelik@bo.de.sykes.com
Iris Gordelik

Services/Products:
Telemarketing agency; Call centre services/systems

Member of:
FEDMA; DDV

TAURUS WERBEAGENTUR GMBH

Am Heerbach 5
Waldaschaff
63857
Germany
Tel: +49 6095 950 145
Fax: +49 6095 950 149
Email: taurus_rz@altavista.net
Eckardt Bülten

Services/Products:
List services; Lettershop; Fulfilment and sampling house

Member of:
DDV

TC TELECONSULT DIPL.KFM. DR. HERIBERT STRATHMANN

Frangenheim-Straße 9
Köln
50931
Germany
Tel: +49 221 94075 0
Fax: +49 221 94075 50
Heriber Strathmann

Services/Products:
Telemarketing agency

Member of:
DDV

TEAM SEITZ GMBH

Moltkestr. 21
Karlsruhe
76133
Germany
Tel: +49 721 91201 0

Fax: +49 721 91201 10 20
Friedbert Seitz

Services/Products:
Direct marketing agency

Member of:
DDV

**TECHNODIRECT AGENTUR
FÜR DIALOG-MARKETING**
Albert-Nestler-Straße 7
Karlsruhe
76131
Germany
Tel: +49 721 6261340
Fax: +49 721 6261256

Services/Products:
Direct marketing agency

Member of:
DDV

TEL-INFORM GMBH
Ludwig-Jahn-Straße 15
Kleve
47533
Germany
Tel: +49 2821 7776 0
Fax: +49 2821 7776 99
Email: telinform@t-online.de
Heinz Sack

Services/Products:
Telemarketing agency

Member of:
DDV

TELE-INFO VERLAG GMBH
Carl-Zeiss-Str. 27
Garbsen
30827
Germany
Tel: +49 5131 94822
Fax: +49 5131 700015
Web: www.etv.de
Ralf A. Sood

Services/Products:
List services; Lettershop; Fulfilment
and sampling house

Member of:
DDV

TELE-SCOUT GMBH
Magazinstr. 15–16
Berlin
10179
Germany
Tel: +49 30 24301301
Fax: +49 30 24301303
Gunnar Zielaskowski

Services/Products:
Telemarketing agency

Member of:
DDV

**TELECASH
KOMMUNIKATIONSSERVICE
GMBH**
Raimundstraße 48 - 54
Frankfurt
60431
Germany
Tel: +49 69 95221 0
Fax: +49 69 95221 214
Email: reinhold.fiederer@telecash.de
Web: http://www.telecash.de
Reinhold Fiederer

Services/Products:
Interactive media

Member of:
DDV

**TELECONCEPT TELEFON
MARKETING GMBH**
Assmannweg 3
Essen
45141
Germany
Tel: +49 201 3206801
Fax: +49 201 3206840
Holger Braun

Services/Products:
Telemarketing agency

Member of:
DDV

**TELEFAIR TELEFON-DIALOG-
DIENSTLEISTUNGEN
ULRICH ZIMMER GMBH**
Züchnerstr. 6–8
Koblenz
56068
Germany
Tel: +49 261 80707 0
Fax: +49 261 80707 100
Email: telefair@telefair.de
Web: http://www.telefair.de
Ulrich Zimmer

Services/Products:
Telemarketing agency

Member of:
DDV

**TELEFFEKT GESELLSCHAFT
FÜR DIREKT-MARKETING
MBH**
Am Falder 4
Düsseldorf
40589
Germany
Tel: +49 0211 7570781
Fax: +49 211 9750052
Christiane Hannemann

Services/Products:
Telemarketing agency

Member of:
DDV

**TELEFIN DIREKT MARKETING
SERVICE AG**
Ludwig-Erhard-Allee 3
Bonn
53175
Germany
Tel: +49 228 888 1310
Fax: +49 228 888 1313
Email: klaus.vahle@telefin.de
Klaus Vahle

Services/Products:
Telemarketing agency

Member of:
DDV

**TELEFON-MARKETING UND
VERLAGSSERVICE TVM
GMBH**
Karl-Liebknecht-Straße 29
Berlin
10178
Germany
Tel: +49 30 23275123
Fax: +49 30 23275220
Marianne Laufenberg

Services/Products:
Telemarketing agency

Member of:
DDV

**TELEKONTAKT
DIREKTMARKETING GMBH**
Cäsarstraße 6–10
Köln
50968
Germany
Tel: +49 221 9347720
Fax: +49 221 93477216
Email: info@telekontakt.de
Web: http://www.telekontakt.de
Hans Jürgen Schröder

Services/Products:
Telemarketing agency

Member of:
DDV

**TELEMARKT –
BERATUNGSGES. FÜR
VERTRIEB UND
KOMMUNIKATION –
VERTRIEBSBERATUNG
GMBH**
Kaiserstraße 28
Reutlingen
72764

Germany
Tel: +49 7121 344 0
Fax: +49 7121 344 201
Email: telemarkt-reutlingen@t-online
Web: http://www.telemarkt-
    reutlingen.de
Udo D. Rogotzki

Member of:
DDV

**TELEMARKT CALL-CENTER
    GMBH & CO. KG**
Zinkmattenstraße 6a
Freiburg
79108
Germany
Tel: +49 761 5599 0
Fax: +49 761 5599 555
Email: info@telemarkt-call-center.com
Web: http://www.telemarkt-call-
    center.com
Reiner Maier

Services/Products:
Telemarketing agency

Member of:
DDV

**TELEMARKT TELEFONDIENST
    GMBH**
Kaiserstraße 28
Reutlingen
72764
Germany
Tel: +49 7121 344 0
Fax: +49 7121 344 201
Email: telemarkt-reutlingen@t-
    online.de
Web: http://www.telemarkt-
    reutlingen.de
Elvira Rogotzki

Services/Products:
Telemarketing agency

Member of:
DDV

**TELEPERFORMANCE
    DEUTSCHLAND**
Tassiloplatz 7
München
81541
Germany
Tel: +49 89 6886822
Fax: +49 89 6886833
Email: info@teleperfomance.de
Web: http://www.teleperformance.com
Jean-Pierre Cismaresco

Services/Products:
Telemarketing agency

Member of:
DDV

**TELEPUBLIC VERLAG GMBH &
    CO. MEDIEN KG**
Eichstr. 57
Hannover
30161
Germany
Tel: +49 511 3348400
Fax: +49 511 3348499
Email: info@teletalk.de
Web: http://www.teletalk.de
Lisa Mießen

Services/Products:
Telemarketing agency

Member of:
DDV

**TEMA GESELLSCHAFT FÜR
    MARKETING SERVICE MBH**
Werderstraße 23–25
Mannheim
68165
Germany
Tel: +49 621 42330
Fax: +49 621 423399
Email: tema-marketing.ma@t-
    online.de
Web: http://www.tema-marketing.de
Ute Will-Ellinghaus

Services/Products:
Telemarketing agency

Member of:
DDV

**TETEL PERSÖNLICHER
    TELEFONAUFTRAGSDIENST
    & FULLTIME INTERMEDIEN
    SERVICE GMBH**
Centroallee 271
Oberhausen
46047
Germany
Tel: +49 20 88203040
Fax: +49 20 8820 3050
Email: tetel@t-online.de
Rainer Schmitz

Member of:
DMA (US); DDV

THE SALES MACHINE GMBH
Kaiserwerther Strasse 135
Düsseldorf
D-40474
Germany
Tel: +49 211 96885 0
Fax: +49 221 96885 649
Email: info@thesalesmachine.de
Gerald Kremer, Ulrich Förster,
    Managing Director

THE SALES MACHINE GMBH
Gautinger Strasse 10
Starnberg
D-82319
Germany
Tel: +49 8151 2780
Fax: +49 8151 2782 50
Email: infosta@thesalesmachine.de
Dirk Gäbler, Oliver Neumann,
    Managing Director

Member of:
DMA (US); DDV

THIEKA GMBH
An der Gümpgesbrücke 22
Kaarst
41546
Germany
Tel: +49 2131 793900
Fax: +49 2131 7939039
Wilfried Felting

Services/Products:
List services; Lettershop; Fulfilment
and sampling house

Member of:
DDV

THOMA DIRECT MARKETING
Zimmersmühlenweg 79
Oberursel/Ts.
61440
Germany
Tel: +49 6171 97550
Fax: +49 6171 975525
Hans Thoma

Services/Products:
List services; Lettershop; Fulfilment
and sampling house

Member of:
DDV

THOMPSON CONNECT GMBH
Brook 1
Hamburg
20457
Germany
Tel: +49 40 374 8310
Fax: +49 40 374 83141
Email: tc@jut.com
Web: www.thompsonconnect.de
Helmut Kotschisch, Managing
    Director

Services/Products:
Advertising Agency; Consultancy
services; Direct marketing agency

E-Services:
Website design

TIEN VERSAND GMBH
Hollandstraße 7
Nordhorn
48522
Germany
Tel: +49 5921 871 287
Fax: +49 5921 871 805
Dieter Tien

Services/Products:
Telemarketing agency

Member of:
DDV

**TIP WERBEVERLAG
GMBH+CO.KG**
Postfach 3547
Heilbronn
74025
Germany
Tel: +49 7131 15403
Fax: +49 7131 15485 63
Heike Hellerich

Services/Products:
Private delivery services

Member of:
DDV

**TM 24 CALL CENTER
CONSULTING GMBH**
Frankfurter Str. 3 B/ARTmax
Braunschweig
38122
Germany
Tel: +49 531 88 54 40
Fax: +49 531 88 54 422

Services/Products:
Telemarketing agency

Member of:
DDV

TMS SONJA MÜLLER
Düsseldorfer Straße 10–14
Mannheim
68219
Germany
Tel: +49 621 80456
Fax: +49 621 8045950
Email: humburger@tms.mannheim-
netz.de
Sonja Müller

Services/Products:
Telemarketing agency

Member of:
DDV

**TMS TELEMARKETING
SERVICE STUTTGART GMBH**
Alexanderstr. 116
Stuttgart
70180

Germany
Tel: +49 711 64660
Fax: +49 711 6466 111
Email: antoniadou@tms-stuttgart.de
Web: www.TMS-stuttgart.de
Marina Antoniadou-Geiss, Managing
Director

Services/Products:
Call centre services/systems;
Consultancy services; Telemarketing
agency; Training/recruitment;
Telemarketing consulting

Member of:
National DMA

**TMT TELEFON-MARKETING-
TEAM**
Königsträßle 2
Stuttgart-Degerloch
70597
Germany
Tel: +49 711 97680 0
Fax: +49 711 97680 15
Birgit Weber

**TOBIEN UND RITTER
DIREKTMARKETING-SERVI-
CES GMBH**
Fechnerstraße 5
Berlin
10717
Germany
Tel: +49 30 8618013 14
Fax: +49 30 8619244
Ute Tobien

Services/Products:
Direct marketing agency

Member of:
DDV

TPD MEDIEN GMBH
Nymphenburger Straße 81
München
80636
Germany
Tel: +49 89 357593 10
Fax: +49 89 357593 59
Email: info@tpd.de
Web: www.tpd.de
Gerhard Brauer, Editor-in-Chief

Services/Products:
Advertising Agency; Consultancy
services; Design/graphics/clip art
supplier; Market research agency;
Publisher; Translation services;
Production of customer loyalty
magazines

Member of:
DDV

**TREBBAU LISTBROKING UND
DATENVERARBEITUNGS
GMBH**
Schönhauser Straße 21
Köln
50968
Germany
Tel: +49 221 3764641
Fax: +49 221 3764646
Email: liebetrau@trebbau.de
Web: http://www.trebbau.de
Peter Liebetrau

Services/Products:
List services; Lettershop; Fulfilment
and sampling house

Member of:
DDV

**TRENDCOMMERCE ST.
GALLEN GMBH**
Heiligkreuzstraße 2
CH-
St. Gallen
9008
Germany
Tel: +41 71 242 9060
Fax: +41 71 242 9061
Email: info@trendcommerce.ch
Web: www.trendcommerce.ch
Oliver P. Künzler or Filippo Zanchi,
Managing Directors

Services/Products:
Database services; Lettershop;
Fulfilment and sampling house;
Mailing/Faxing services;
Personalisation; Print services;
Personalised coloured digital print

Member of:
DDV; SDV

**TS-COMMUNICATIONSCENT-
RUM FÜR VERSENDER**
Pforzheimer Str. 128
Ettlingen
76275
Germany
Tel: +49 7243 5812100
Fax: +49 7243 5812170
Email: ts@walternet.de
Michael Martin

Services/Products:
Telemarketing agency

Member of:
DDV

**TU WAS! MARKETING DIREKT-
SERVICE SCHRÖDER**
Eisenstraße 99
Düsseldorf
40227
Germany

Tel: +49 0211 7881632
Fax: +49 211 7881432
Email: direktservice@online.de
Kathrin Schröder

Services/Products:
Telemarketing agency

Member of:
DDV

UNISERV GMBH
Stuttgarter Straße 20–22
Pforzheim
75179
Germany
Tel: +49 7231 936 0
Fax: +49 7231 936 250
Email: www.uniserv.de
Web: info@uniserv.de
Udo Fischer

Services/Products:
List services; Lettershop; Fulfilment
and sampling house; Database services;
Software supplier

Member of:
FEDMA; DDV

**UPDATE MARKETING SERVICE
DEUTSCHLAND GMBH**
Bleichstr. 1–3
Wiesbaden
65183
Germany
Tel: +49 611 18441 0
Fax: +49 611 18441 41
Uta Florstedt

Services/Products:
Direct marketing agency

Member of:
DDV

**URBAN SCIENCE
INTERNATIONAL GMBH**
Stresemann Allee 30
Frankfurt
60596
Germany
Tel: +49 69 975814 0
Fax: +49 69 975814 44

Services/Products:
Direct marketing agency

**UW SERVICE GESELLSCHAFT
FÜR DIREKTWERBUNG UND
MARKETINGBERATUNG
MBH**
Alter Deutzer Postweg 221
Köln
51107
Germany
Tel: +49 221 98696 0

Fax: +49 21 98696 20
Email: info@uw-service.de
Uschi Wiesehahn

Member of:
DDV

V-TEX GMBH
Wichmannstr. 4 Haus 10 Süd
Hamburg
22607
Germany
Tel: +49 40 89090400
Fax: +49 40 89090490
Axel Dunker

Services/Products:
Telemarketing agency

Member of:
DDV

**VERBAND DER VEREINE
CREDITREFORM E.V.**
Hellersbergstraße 12
Neuss
41460
Germany
Tel: +49 2131 109 119
Fax: +49 2131 109 309
Email:
    j.stenmans@verband.creditreform.d-
    e
Web: http://www.creditreform.de
Jan Stenmans

Services/Products:
List services; Lettershop; Fulfilment
and sampling house

Member of:
DDV

**VERLAG RECHT U. PRAXIS
GMBH/FACHINFORMATION
FÜR RECHTSBERATENDE
BERUFE**
Römerstraße 4
Kissing
86438
Germany
Tel: +49 8233 23660
Fax: +49 8233 23881
Email: hans-joachim_voit@vrp.de
Web: http://www.vrp.de
Hans-Joachim Voit

Member of:
DDV

**VERLAGSGRUPPE
HANDELSBLATT GMBH**
Kasernenstraße 67
Düsseldorf
40213
Germany
Tel: +49 0211 887 2305

Fax: +49 211 887 2340
Email: gwp.om@vhb.de
Web: http://www.gwp.de
Gabriele Reichard

Services/Products:
Interactive media

Member of:
DDV

**VETHERS, DENNINGER UND
PARTNER WERBEAGENTUR
FÜR DIREKTMARKETING
GMBH**
Echterdinger Str. 30
Stuttgart
70599
Germany
Tel: +49 711 45889 0
Fax: +49 711 4560290
Web: Roman Vethers
Vethers

Member of:
DDV

VIAFON GMBH
Hirtenstrasse 19
Berlin
10178
Germany
Tel: +49 30 2404 1420
Fax: +49 30 2404 1810
Email: viafon@viafon.de
Web: www.viafon.de

Services/Products:
Lettershop; Software supplier;
Telemarketing agency; Training/
recruitment

Member of:
DDV; ABCC

VIDI MEDIEN WEBSOLUTIONS
Concordiahütte
Bendorf/Rhein
56170
Germany
Tel: +49 2622 923405
Fax: +49 2622 923406
Web: www.fachbuchhandlung.de
Valenka M. Dorsch

Services/Products:
Interactive media

Member of:
DDV

VISION DIRECT
Hanauer Landstraße 175 - 179
Frankfurt
60314
Germany
Tel: +49 69 904366 0

Fax: +49 69 904366 66
Email: vision.direct@pop-
    frankfurt.com
Klaus Lemke

Services/Products:
Direct marketing agency

Member of:
DDV

VOGEL ADRESS
Max-Planck-Straße 7/9
Würzburg
D-97082
Germany
Tel: +49 931 418 2531
Fax: +49 931 418 2529
Email: jutta_weigand@vogel-adress.de
Web: www.vogel-adress.de
Jutta Weigand, Sales Manager

Services/Products:
Call centre services/systems; Database
services; Lettershop; List services;
Publisher

Member of:
Deutsher Direktmarketing Verband
e.V. (DDV)

VSP VERSAND-SERVICE PLATE DATA SERVICE GMBH + CO. OHG
Am Bahnhof 3
Plate
19086
Germany
Tel: 03861 5514 0
Fax: +49 3861 5514 55
Jens Krischkowski

Services/Products:
List services; Lettershop; Fulfilment
and sampling house

Member of:
DDV

W. SCHORSCH & CO.
Berlichingenstraße 14
Schwabach
91126
Germany
Tel: +49 9122 9367 22
Fax: +49 9122 9367 33
Email: Peter.Brueck@SchorschCo.de
Web: www.SchorschCo.de
Harald Fischer

Services/Products:
Card pack manufacturer; Mailing/
Faxing services; Personalisation; Print
services; Lettershop

Member of:
National DMA; DDV; German Direct
Marketing Federation

W.I.L.I.-MARKETING AG
Daimlerstr. 6
Alzenau
63755
Germany
Tel: +49 6023 954 0
Fax: +49 6023 954 200
Email: marketing@wili.de
Web: http:\\www.wili.de
Marion Daniel

Services/Products:
Telemarketing agency

Member of:
DDV

WAGNER DIREKTMARKETING GMBH
Schanzweg 8
Grossaitingen
86845
Germany
Tel: +49 8203 96060
Fax: +49 8203 960660
Wulf Dieter Wagner

Services/Products:
List services; Lettershop; Fulfilment
and sampling house

Member of:
DMA (US); DDV

WALSH INTERNATIONAL HOLDINGS GMBH
Carl-Zeiss-Ring 3
Ismaning
85737
Germany
Tel: +49 89 96108 0
Fax: +49 89 96108 102
Nicola Bräunling

Services/Products:
List services; Lettershop; Fulfilment
and sampling house

Member of:
DDV

WALTER TELEMARKETING & VERTRIEB GMBH & CO.
Pforzheimer Straße 128
Ettlingen
76263
Germany
Tel: +49 7243 55 1999
Fax: +49 7243 55 1905
Bernhard Maisenhälder

Services/Products:
Telemarketing agency

Member of:
DDV

WALTER TELEMEDIENSERVICE GMBH & CO.
Gutenbergstraße 2
Schutterwald
77746
Germany
Tel: +49 781 964 920
Fax: +49 781 964 9919
Email: info@wtms.de
Cord P. Schulz-Klingauf

Services/Products:
Telemarketing agency

Member of:
DDV

WAW DIALOGMARKETING GMBH
Albert-Schweitzer-Ring 22
Hamburg
22045
Germany
Tel: +49 40 669917 75
Fax: +49 40 669917 66
Email: info@waw.de
Web: http://www.waw.de
Jürgen Uthardt

Services/Products:
Direct marketing agency

Member of:
DDV

WELCOME WELLNET E.K.
Frankfurter Ring 243
München
80807
Germany
Tel: +49 89   32376 0
Fax: +49 89   32376 300
Email: office@welcome-wellnet.de
Web: http://www.welcome-wellnet.de
Eva-Imana Meier

Services/Products:
Telemarketing agency

Member of:
DDV

WELTER DIALOG GMBH WERBEAGENTUR FÜR EFFIZIENTES DIREKTMARKETING
Schockenriedstraße 17
Stuttgart
70565
Germany
Tel: +49 711 99018 30
Fax: +49 711 99018 40
Email: mail@welterdialog.de
Web: http://www.welterdialog.de
Frank A. Welter

Member of:
DDV

WERBETEAM JACOB DIREKTMARKETING GMBH
Berggate 57
Bochum
44809
Germany
Tel: +49 234 578235
Fax: +49 234 578397
Herbert Sundermann

Services/Products:
List services; Lettershop; Fulfilment
and sampling house

Member of:
DDV

WERBUNG IM NETZ GMBH
Konrad-Celtis-Str. 77
München
81369
Germany
Tel: +49 89 74117 600
Fax: +49 89 74117 630
Email: info@admaster.de
Web: http://www.admaster.de
Martina Dresler

Services/Products:
Interactive media

Member of:
DDV

WIEGMANN GMBH KUVERTIER-UND VERPACKUNGSSERVICE
Dingbreite 16
Petershagen
32469
Germany
Tel: +49 5702 820 0
Fax: +49 5702 820 140
Ortwin Wiegmann

Services/Products:
List services; Lettershop; Fulfilment
and sampling house

Member of:
DDV

WINTER DRUCKERZEUGNISSE GMBH
Hermann-Böcker-Str. 21
Neu-Esting/München
82140
Germany
Tel: +49 8142 303 0
Fax: +49 8142 303170
Email: business.account.winter@t-
online.de
Web: http://www.Winter-

Wertdruck.com
Thomas Winter

Services/Products:
Print services

Member of:
DDV

WJP WOLFGANG JOHANSEN & PARTNER GMBH
Am Tiergarten 26
Frankfurt
60316
Germany
Tel: +49 69 430885 0
Fax: +49 69 430885 99
Email: info@wjp-gmbh.com
Web: http://www.wjp-gmbh.com
Wolfgang Johansen

Services/Products:
Telemarketing agency

Member of:
DDV

WKW MÜNSTER, GESELLSCHAFT FÜR MARKETING UND KOMMUNIKATION MBH
Meinerts Brook 5
Emsdetten
48282
Germany
Tel: +49 2572 2010
Fax: +49 2572 20110
Email: info@wkw-muenster.de
Web: http://www.wkw-muenster.de
Walter Künnemann

Member of:
DDV

WOLFF & PARTNER GMBH
Birkenwaldstr. 200
Stuttgart
70191
Germany
Tel: +49 711 2573050
Fax: +49 711 2579240
Eike Wolff

Services/Products:
Direct marketing agency

Member of:
DDV

WOLFGANG MUNDT DIREKT GMBH
Hintere Straße 20
Leonberg
71229
Germany
Tel: +49 7152 9349 0
Fax: +49 7152 9349 23

Email: mundt-direkt@t-online.de
Wolfgang Mundt

Services/Products:
List services; Lettershop; Fulfilment
and sampling house

Member of:
DDV

WUNDERMAN CATO JOHNSON GMBH
Kleyerstraße 19
Frankfurt
60326
Germany
Tel: +49 69 75009208
Jan Steinbach, Office Manager

Services/Products:
Database services; Direct marketing
agency; Response analysis bureau;
Sales promotion agency

Member of:
FEDMA; DDV

WWL CONNECT ONLINE SERVICES GMBH
Südwestpark 60
Nürnberg
90449
Germany
Tel: +49 911 6886670
Fax: +49 911 68866711
Email: info@wwl.de
Web: http://wwl.de
Andreas Butz

Member of:
DDV

XEROX DIRECT GMBH
Carl-Schurz-Straße 2
Neuss
41460
Germany
Tel: +49 2131 706 1583
Fax: +49 2131 706 1589
Uwe Pflug

Services/Products:
Telemarketing agency

Member of:
DDV

XPEDITE SYSTEMS GMBH
Garmischer Straße 35
München
81377
Germany
Tel: +49 89 74308 0
Fax: +49 89 74308199
Tanja Funk

Services/Products:
Telemarketing agency

Member of:
DDV

ZIEGENHORN TOURISM DATABASE

PO Box 1645
17-er Str. 17
Germersheim
76726
Germany
Tel: +49 7274 2759
Fax: +49 7274 3631
Email: info@ziegenhorn.de
Web: www.ziegenhorn.de
Heinz Ziegenhorn, CEO

Services/Products:
Database services; List services

E-Services:
Email list provider

Member of:
DDV; German Direktmarketing
Association

SERVICES/PRODUCT LISTING

Advertising Agency
Benner & Partner Dialogmarketing
    GmbH
Carat Direct
CreaKom Direct & Telemarketing
    GmbH
eskatoo - Die Agentur für innovative
    Kommunikation GmbH
Fcb International
G/R/O Gruschka Rückert Other's
    Werbeagentur GmbH
JM&K Agentur für integrierte
    Kommunikation GmbH
Knauer y Rump y Partner
    Werbeagentur GmbH
MORE SALES Agentur GmbH
Ritter, Wolek Werbeagentur GmbH
SalesConcept Teleservices & Database-
    Marketing GmbH
SAZ Listbroking GmbH
Thompson Connect GmbH
TPD Medien GmbH

Call centre services/systems
all by phone + net
Aspect Communications GmbH
b u. w UNTERNEHMENSGRUPPE
b.a.s. direct GmbH
BBE-Unternehmensberatung GmbH
BKD GmbH
Carat Direct
CreaKom Direct & Telemarketing
    GmbH

Deutsche Telekom Medien GmbH
Direct Line Marketing und
    Kommunikation GmbH
Dohmen Distribution
eskatoo - Die Agentur für innovative
    Kommunikation GmbH
Marketforce Gesellschaft für Business
    Marketing mbH
MVS Management-und Versand-
    Service GmbH
PhonePartner GmbH
Quelle AG
Sales Team GmbH
SalesConcept Teleservices & Database-
    Marketing GmbH
Smile & Sell Teleservices GmbH
Smile And Sell Teleservices GmbH
T.D.M. Telefon-Direkt-Marketing
    GmbH
TAS Telemarketing Ges. für
    Kommunikation und Dialog mbH
TMS Telemarketing Service Stuttgart
    GmbH
Vogel Adress

Card pack manufacturer
mailpool Adressen-Management
    GmbH
W. Schorsch & Co.

Catalogue producer
CreaKom Direct & Telemarketing
    GmbH
Meiller Direct GmbH
Quelle AG
Rosenzweig & Schwarz Agentur für
    Dialogmarketing GmbH

Consultancy services
Aktiv Direkt Marketing GmbH
AOS Consult GmbH
Aspect Communications GmbH
b u. w UNTERNEHMENSGRUPPE
BBDO Interactive GmbH
BBE-Unternehmensberatung GmbH
Benner & Partner Dialogmarketing
    GmbH
BKD GmbH
CreaKom Direct & Telemarketing
    GmbH
Deutsche Post AG -Zentrale-
Dohmen Distribution
eskatoo - Die Agentur für innovative
    Kommunikation GmbH
Fischer & Partner Direktmarketing
    GmbH
G/R/O Gruschka Rückert Other's
    Werbeagentur GmbH
JM&K Agentur für integrierte
    Kommunikation GmbH
Mail*Select GmbH
MORE SALES Agentur GmbH
porta mundi GmbH & Co. KG

Rosenzweig & Schwarz Agentur für
    Dialogmarketing GmbH
SalesConcept Teleservices & Database-
    Marketing GmbH
T.D.M. Telefon-Direkt-Marketing
    GmbH
Thompson Connect GmbH
TMS Telemarketing Service Stuttgart
    GmbH
TPD Medien GmbH

Copy adaptation
MORE SALES Agentur GmbH

Database services
Aktiv Direkt Marketing GmbH
AOS Consult GmbH
Arnold, Demmerer & Partner
AZ Bertelsmann Direct GmbH
b u. w UNTERNEHMENSGRUPPE
b.a.s. direct GmbH
BBDO Interactive GmbH
BKD GmbH
Carat Direct
Claritas Deutschland Data + Services
    GmbH
CreaKom Direct & Telemarketing
    GmbH
Deutsche Post Adress GmbH
Deutsche Post AG -Zentrale-
Deutsche Telekom Medien GmbH
Dialoghaus GmbH
eskatoo - Die Agentur für innovative
    Kommunikation GmbH
Fcb International
G/R/O Gruschka Rückert Other's
    Werbeagentur GmbH
Ghp Direct Mail GmbH
Lettershop Schonard GmbH & Co
M&V München Agentur für
    Dialogmarketing und
    Verkaufsförderung GmbH
Mail*Select GmbH
mailpool Adressen-Management
    GmbH
Mediadress GmbH
Mungenast Direkt Marketing GmbH
MVS Management-und Versand-
    Service GmbH
OgilvyOne worldwide GmbH
pan-adress Direktmarketing
    Gesellschaft mbH
Quelle AG
Sales Team GmbH
SalesConcept Teleservices & Database-
    Marketing GmbH
Scherer Team MRM GmbH & Co.
    KG
Schober Direktmarketing GmbH &
    Co.
Spectrum GmbH Marketing Services
    & Consulting
T.D.M. Telefon-Direkt-Marketing

GmbH
Trendcommerce St. Gallen GmbH
Uniserv GmbH
Vogel Adress
Wunderman Cato Johnson GmbH
Ziegenhorn Tourism Database

Design/graphics/clip art supplier

b.a.s. direct GmbH
CreaKom Direct & Telemarketing GmbH
eskatoo - Die Agentur für innovative Kommunikation GmbH
MORE SALES Agentur GmbH
TPD Medien GmbH

Develop and distribute software for direct marketing

ABIS AG

Dialogue marketing

Carat Direct

Direct marketing agency

141 Dialog Direktmarketing (Germany) GmbH
4sale Werbeagentur GmbH
A & L Partner Direktmarketing GmbH
A.P.A. Werbeagentur GmbH
ABIS AG
Abresch:Direct Team für integriertes Dialogmarketing GmbH
ABS Computer GmbH
Acton Direkt-Marketing GmbH
AgentUhr direktmarketinggesellschaft mbH
Agentur für Kompaktmarketing Gremmer Direkt GmbH
Agentur für Publikation und Media (APM) Heiner GmbH
Agentur Lessing Kreatives Direktmarketing GmbH
Aktiv Direkt Marketing GmbH
Allbecon Personaldienstleistungen München GmbH
ALMUC Dialogmarketing GmbH & Co. KG
Arts & Wiles Werbeagentur GmbH
Artwork Werbe-und Kommunikationsagentur Sven Lorenz
Atkos Oy
AZ Bertelsmann Direct GmbH
B & O Gesellschaft für Dialog-Marketing mbH
b plus b Direktmarketing GmbH
b u. w UNTERNEHMENSGRUPPE
b.a.s. direct GmbH
Barry Blau & Partners Inc
Benner & Partner Dialogmarketing GmbH

BKD GmbH
blue moon marketing GmbH
bluelane Gesellschaft für Marketing und Kommunikation mbH
Blum & Ufer Werbeagentur GmbH
Borges & Partner GmbH
Brüggemann & Freunde Agentur für Dialogmarketing GmbH
Büro Prochazka Agentur für Direktmarketing GmbH
C-Faktory, Gesellschaft für Werbung und Kommunikation
Carat Direct
CFD, C. Fabinger Agentur für Direktmarketing
Claritas Deutschland Data + Services GmbH
creativ Team Directmarketing GmbH
D & P Franz GmbH Direktmarketing Produktmarketing
D&G Direkt-Marketing Gerardi Gmbh & Co Kg
Detterbeck, Wider Werbung GmbH & Co. KG
Deutsche Post AG -Zentrale-Dialoghaus GmbH
die Agentur Kausche und Partner GmbH
direct. Gesellschaft für Direktmarketing mbH
Directeam Agentur für Direktmarketing GmbH
DirectMediaCom
DMT Direct Mail Team Scherer GmbH
Dorfer Dialog GmbH
DPNY S. L.
Energy Werbung GmbH
EPA Direct Gesellschaft für Dialogmarketing GmbH & Co.KG
ESD Direktmarketing und Datenverarbeitung GmbH
eskatoo - Die Agentur für innovative Kommunikation GmbH
Faißt Consulting
Fcb International
FCB/Wilkens Direct Agentur f. Directmarketing GmbH
Feldt Vision's Communication GmbH
Fisch.Meier.Direkt AG
Fritsche Werbeagentur GmbH
FSW Direct Gesellschaft für Directmarketing mbH
G/R/O Gruschka Rückert Other's Werbeagentur GmbH
Gecco Werbeagentur GmbH
Gottlieb Lehr Direktmarketingberatung
Grey Direct
GV Kommunikation auf Papier GmbH
heller & partner Marketing Services
HM1 Heuser, Mayer + Partner Direct Marketing GmbH

inDIREKT Agentur für Dialogmarketing GmbH
Ivanov & Ivanov Direct Marketing Agency
JBBX Marketing-und Werbeagentur GmbH
JM&K Agentur für integrierte Kommunikation GmbH
K&R Consulting GmbH
Karrasch + Partner GmbH
KAT Marketing GmbH
Kienow & Kempener KG
Klose & Co. Werbeagentur GmbH
Kochan & Partner Werbung, Design und Kommunikation
KOOP Direktmarketing GmbH & C KG
Lehr & Brose Erste Dialogagentur GmbH & Co. KG
Licon Linden Consulting
Literaturagentur Petra + Heinz Raszkowski
M + M Mail + More Direktmarketir GmbH
M-S-B+K Consulting GmbH
M-S-B+K Stuttgart Werbeagentur fu Direct Marketing GmbH
mail+order G. Baumann GmbH
Marketforce Gesellschaft für Busines Marketing mbH
MD Factory Marketing Datenmanagement GmbH
MDM Mungenast Direkt Marketing GmbH
Mediadress GmbH
Meyer Direct
MORE SALES Agentur GmbH
more! Marketing GmbH
MSBK,Team DialogMarketing Gmb
Mungenast Direkt Marketing GmbH
n w s neubert werbeservice KG
OgilvyOne worldwide GmbH
pan-adress Direktmarketing Gesellschaft mbH
PDC Dialog Marketing GmbH
Peter Reincke Direkt-Marketing GmbH
Pharma Direkt GmbH
PL Marketing GmbH
PPWS Werbung GmbH
Print Direct GmbH
Prisma Werbeagentur GmbH
Projekt Agentur Fleck GmbH
Publicis Dialog
Pull Response-Werbe-GmbH
R & P Werbeagentur München Gmb
RBC DiaSys Consulting AG
realdesign intelligent communicatior gmbh i.G.
Rempen & Partner Werbeagentur GmbH
Riek, direct Marketing Fairmarktung GmbH & Co. KG

Ritter, Wolek Werbeagentur GmbH
Rosenzweig & Schwarz Agentur für
  Dialogmarketing GmbH
S.B.W. Werbung GmbH
Sale Agentur für direkte
  Kommunikation GmbH
Sales Team GmbH
SAZ Dialog Agentur GmbH
SBS Mediaservice Werbeagentur
  GmbH
Schaffhausen Werbeagentur
Scherer Team MRM GmbH & Co.
  KG
SHB Individual Marketing &
  Advertising Stuttgart GmbH
SIPA Unternehmer Beratung GmbH
Slogan Werbeagentur GmbH
Spectrum GmbH Marketing Services
  & Consulting
Stollmann GmbH
SWI Süd-West-Information GmbH
Symbol Marketing gmbH Beratung +
  Service
Tarnow Communications
  Werbeagentur GmbH
Team Seitz GmbH
TechnoDirect Agentur für Dialog-
  Marketing
Thompson Connect GmbH
Tobien und Ritter Direktmarketing-
  Services GmbH
UpDate Marketing Service
  Deutschland GmbH
Urban Science International GmbH
Vision Direct
WAW Dialogmarketing GmbH
Wolff & Partner GmbH
Wunderman Cato Johnson GmbH

E-commerce support and e-mail response
Direct Line Marketing und
  Kommunikation GmbH

E-fulfilment (Europe wide)
Dohmen Distribution

E-logistics (Europe wide)
Dohmen Distribution

Electronic media
Fcb International
Fritsch Heine Rapp Collins Agentur
  für Dialogmarketing und Werbung
  GmbH
HM1 Heuser, Mayer + Partner Direct
  Marketing GmbH
Lehr & Brose Erste Dialogagentur
  GmbH & Co. KG
M&V München Agentur für
  Dialogmarketing und
  Verkaufsförderung GmbH
OgilvyOne worldwide GmbH

Event marketing
G/R/O Gruschka Rückert Other's
  Werbeagentur GmbH

Fulfilment and sampling house
ad-con Adressen-und
  Lettershopservice GmbH
ADM Arbeitsgruppe für
  Direktmarketing GmbH
Adressen + Service GmbH
Adressmarketing Rudolf K. Härtel
  GmbH
Agentur für Zielgruppenberatung
  Gudrun Schrödl
alphatext Direktwerbung GmbH
AMA Adress-und Zeitschriftenverlag
  GmbH
B. Gürtler MediaDistribution GmbH
Bauer + Kirch GmbH BKR Software
BDL Betriebsberatungs-und
  Datenverarbeitungs GmbH
Bernd Hörtkorn Versandservice
  GmbH
BKD GmbH
BKG Büro-Kommunikation und
  Grafikdesign Service GmbH
Briefing GmbH Lösungen und Service
  für Direktmarketing
Bürgel Wirtschaftsinformationen
  GmbH & Co. KG
Büromatic Direktwerbung Jost
  Damgaard GmbH & Co. KG
Claritas Deutschland Data + Services
  GmbH
D&G-Software GmbH
Data Select Gesellschaft für Marketing
  Service mbH
Datafin Direkt Marketing Service AG
Dating GmbH
DCS Direktmarketing & Card Service
  GmbH
Deutsche Post Direkt GmbH
Dietmar Iltisberger GmbH
DIMA Werbe GmbH
Direct Center Knoll GmbH
Direkt-Marketing Gerardi GmbH &
  Co. KG
Direkte Data Marketing GmbH
Direktmarketing Kurt W. Welz GmbH
Direktmarketing Service-Center
  GmbH & Co.
dm-plus Direktmarketing GmbH
DMD Direkt Marketing Dienste Bodo
  Mann GmbH
Dohmen Distribution
dr. von arnim Direktmarketing
Drei-D Direktwerbung GmbH &
  Co.KG
Dun + Bradstreet Deutschland GmbH
DVS Datenverarbeitungs-und
  Datenmanagement-Service GmbH
econ-alca Consulting GmbH
Erwin Braun Direktwerbung

Faber Direkt, Egon Faber GmbH &
  Co. KG
FDS Fulfillment Directmarketing
  Service GmbH
fh direktmarketing + edv-
  dienstleistungen ohg
Gall, Wedewardt + Partner GmbH
Gebhard Müller GmbH
GFP Gesellschaft für
  Produktinformation mbH
GfS Gesellschaft für Sozialmarketing
  mbH
Glettler Annemarie, Direktmarketing
GM Direkt-Marketing Center GmbH
HeiRa GmbH
Hellweg und Buyk, Partner für
  Direktwerbung GmbH
Heuer & Co. Verlags-und
  Werbeversand GmbH
Human Inference
  Adressenverwaltungssoftware
  GmbH
Infox GmbH & Co.
  Informationslogistik KG
item GmbH advanced press & mail
  serviceware
J + P Dialog Marketing GmbH
JS Versandservice und Direktmarketing
  GmbH
Jucknieß – Datenservice GmbH
Karl Trebbau GmbH Adressenverlag
  und Direktwerbeunternehmen
Klopotek & Partner GmbH
KOOP Direktmarketing GmbH & Co.
  KG
KOOP indima Ges.f. innovatives
  Direktmarketing mbH
Kredo Direkwerbung GmbH
Kuvertier-Service Auguste Staar
  GmbH
Lammoth, Neumark & Co.
  ADRESSMARKETING GmbH
Laserprint Druck-und Direktwerbung
  GmbH
LDZ Laserdruckzentrum GmbH
Lettershop Brendler GmbH
Lettershop Schonard GmbH & Co
M&H Versandhandel und Service
  GmbH & Co.
Mail Box Direkt-Marketing Service
  GmbH
Mail Com Dialogmarketing GmbH
Mailing GmbH
  Lagerhaltg.u.Distribution v.
  Werbemitteln
Mar.Co. Marketing.Communication.
  Olaf Quast
Media Data Rent GmbH
MediaDirect Marketing GmbH
Meiller Direct GmbH
Merkur Direktwerbeges. mbH & Co
  KG
Multidata Service GmbH

MVS Management-und Versand-
Service GmbH
Nordata Marketing-Informations-
Systeme GmbH
OBIMD International
Omikron. Soft + Hardware GmbH
Optimail Direktwerbeservice GmbH
pan-adress Direktmarketing
Gesellschaft mbH
pb direkt Praun, Binder & Partner
GmbH
Petra Reimann Büro-u. Datenservice
GmbH
PhonePartner GmbH
Portica GmbH Marketing Support
Power Adress Zielgruppenmarketing
GmbH
pro:tagon directmarketing GmbH
Prodata Datenbanken und
Informationssysteme GmbH
prowerb Werbe-und Versandservice
GmbH
PS Packen und Schicken GmbH
Publica data-service gmbh
PVS Presseversand Service GmbH
R. M. Sittarz hero services GmbH
RJ Marketing-Service GmbH
RTV Karin Rudolf, Daten-Text-und
Informationsverarbeitung
Sales Team GmbH
SalesConcept Teleservices & Database-
Marketing GmbH
SAZ Dialog Agentur GmbH
SAZ Listbroking GmbH
Schober D&G Direct Media GmbH &
Co.
Schober Direktmarketing GmbH &
Co.
Scholz Versand Service Inh. Siegfried
Scholz
Service Partner Agentur für
Direktwerbung GmbH
Skriptura Dienstleistungen Schmale &
Wolf oHG
SMP – Werbeservice GmbH
SOBA GmbH Unternehmensberatung
social concept GmbH Agentur für
Sozialmarketing
SPT Marketing Service GbR mbH
SSM System Service Marketing
GmbH
Steigerwald Marketing GmbH
Stettin Direct Marketing
Taurus Werbeagentur GmbH
Tele-Info Verlag GmbH
Thieka GmbH
Thoma Direct Marketing
Trebbau Listbroking und
Datenverarbeitungs GmbH
Trendcommerce St. Gallen GmbH
Uniserv GmbH
Verband der Vereine Creditreform e.V.
VSP Versand-Service Plate Data

Service GmbH + Co. oHG
Wagner Direktmarketing GmbH
Walsh International Holdings GmbH
Werbeteam Jacob Direktmarketing
GmbH
Wiegmann GmbH Kuvertier-und
Verpackungsservice
Wolfgang Mundt Direkt GmbH

Hardware supplier
Aspect Communications GmbH

IT support
T.D.M. Telefon-Direkt-Marketing
GmbH

Interactive media
Adtech Advertising Service Providing
GmbH
AIS Axon Internet Services GmbH
Vermarkter von DINO-Online
AOL Bertelsmann Online GmbH &
Co.KG
b.a.s. interactive GmbH
BBDO Interactive GmbH
Benner & Partner Dialogmarketing
GmbH
Blue Mars – Gesellschaft für digitale
Kommunikation mbH
Bozell Direct Friends -Unit Interactive-
callisto germany.net GmbH
cassiopeia GmbH
Cohen New Media Beratung
dateam InterMedia
debis Systemhaus Dienstleistungen
GmbH
Digital Media Center GmbH
DMI Institut für Direktmarketing
Europa-Fachpresse-Verlag GmbH
Focus Online GmbH
Fuzzy! Informatik GmbH
G/R/O Gruschka Rückert Other's
Werbeagentur GmbH
Interactive Marketing Partner GmbH
Interactive Online Services I.O.S.
GmbH
INTERad GmbH
Intershop Communications GmbH
J&S Dialog-Medien GmbH
JM&K Agentur für integrierte
Kommunikation GmbH
Kiosk Online-Dienste GmbH
kiwi repro68 interaktive medien gmbh
Köster & Vorhauer GmbH
MA Network Communication GmbH
Maassen + Partner GmbH
MediaPhone Telefonmarketing GmbH
mindmedia gmbh – institut für
multimediale kommunikation
MON Marketing Online Dienste
GmbH
MORE SALES Agentur GmbH
Müller adress + Neue

Mediengesellschaft Ulm mbH & Co.
OHG
NetMedia GmbH
Neue Mediengesellschaft Ulm mbH
Neusser Druckerei und Verlag GmbH
peppermind Network Neue Medien
Kochan & Partner GmbH
PopNet GmbH & Co. KG
porta mundi GmbH & Co. KG
Ritter, Wolek Werbeagentur GmbH
Sony International (Europe) GmbH
TeleCash Kommunikationsservice
GmbH
Verlagsgruppe Handelsblatt GmbH
vidi medien Websolutions
werbung im netz gmbh

Internet agency
porta mundi GmbH & Co. KG

Internet and e-mail services
all by phone + net

Labelling/envelope services
Ghp Direct Mail GmbH

Legal services
Siegert & Dr. Breinlinger – Dm Lawyer

Lettershop
ad-con Adressen-und
Lettershopservice GmbH
ADM Arbeitsgruppe für
Direktmarketing GmbH
Adressen + Service GmbH
Adressmarketing Rudolf K. Härtel
GmbH
Agentur für Zielgruppenberatung
Gudrun Schrödl
Aktiv Direkt Marketing GmbH
alphatext Direktwerbung GmbH
AMA Adress-und Zeitschriftenverlag
GmbH
AZ Bertelsmann Direct GmbH
b u. w UNTERNEHMENSGRUPPE
B. Gürtler MediaDistribution GmbH
Bauer + Kirch GmbH BKR Software
BDL Betriebsberatungs-und
Datenverarbeitungs GmbH
Bernd Hörtkorn Versandservice
GmbH
BKD GmbH
BKG Büro-Kommunikation und
Grafikdesign Service GmbH
Briefing GmbH Lösungen und Service
für Direktmarketing
Bürgel Wirtschaftsinformationen
GmbH & Co. KG
Büromatic Direktwerbung Jost
Damgaard GmbH & Co. KG
Claritas Deutschland Data + Services
GmbH
D&G Direkt-Marketing Gerardi

Gmbh & Co Kg
D&G-Software GmbH
Data Select Gesellschaft für Marketing
    Service mbH
Datafin Direkt Marketing Service AG
Dating GmbH
DCS Direktmarketing & Card Service
    GmbH
Deutsche Post AG -Zentrale-
Deutsche Post Direkt GmbH
Dietmar Iltisberger GmbH
DIMA Werbe GmbH
Direct Center Knoll GmbH
Direkt-Marketing Gerardi GmbH &
    Co. KG
Direkte Data Marketing GmbH
Direktmarketing Kurt W. Welz GmbH
Direktmarketing Service-Center
    GmbH & Co.
dm-plus Direktmarketing GmbH
DMD Direkt Marketing Dienste Bodo
    Mann GmbH
dr. von arnim Direktmarketing
Drei-D Direktwerbung GmbH &
    Co.KG
Dun + Bradstreet Deutschland GmbH
DVS Datenverarbeitungs-und
    Datenmanagement-Service GmbH
econ-alca Consulting GmbH
Erwin Braun Direktwerbung
Faber Direkt, Egon Faber GmbH &
    Co. KG
FDS Fulfillment Directmarketing
    Service GmbH
fh direktmarketing + edv-
    dienstleistungen ohg
Gall, Wedewardt + Partner GmbH
Gebhard Müller GmbH
GFP Gesellschaft für
    Produktinformation mbH
GfS Gesellschaft für Sozialmarketing
    mbH
Ghp Direct Mail GmbH
Glettler Annemarie, Direktmarketing
GM Direkt-Marketing Center GmbH
HeiRa GmbH
Hellweg und Buyk, Partner für
    Direktwerbung GmbH
Heuer & Co. Verlags-und
    Werbeversand GmbH
Human Inference
    Adressenverwaltungssoftware
    GmbH
Infox GmbH & Co.
    Informationslogistik KG
item GmbH advanced press & mail
    serviceware
J + P Dialog Marketing GmbH
JS Versandservice und Direktmarketing
    GmbH
Jucknieß – Datenservice GmbH
Karl Trebbau GmbH Adressenverlag
    und Direktwerbeunternehmen

Klopotek & Partner GmbH
KOOP Direktmarketing GmbH & Co.
    KG
KOOP indima Ges.f. innovatives
    Direktmarketing mbH
Kredo Direkwerbung GmbH
Kuvertier-Service Auguste Staar
    GmbH
Lammoth, Neumark & Co.
    ADRESSMARKETING GmbH
Laserprint Druck-und Direktwerbung
    GmbH
LDZ Laserdruckzentrum GmbH
Lettershop Brendler GmbH
Lettershop Schonard GmbH & Co
M&H Versandhandel und Service
    GmbH & Co.
Mail Box Direkt-Marketing Service
    GmbH
Mail Com Dialogmarketing GmbH
Mailing GmbH
    Lagerhaltg.u.Distribution v.
    Werbemitteln
Mar.Co. Marketing.Communication.
    Olaf Quast
Media Data Rent GmbH
MediaDirect Marketing GmbH
Meiller Direct GmbH
Merkur Direktwerbeges. mbH & Co
    KG
Multidata Service GmbH
MVS Management-und Versand-
    Service GmbH
Nordata Marketing-Informations-
    Systeme GmbH
OBIMD International
Omikron. Soft + Hardware GmbH
Optimail Direktwerbeservice GmbH
pan-adress Direktmarketing
    Gesellschaft mbH
pb direkt Praun, Binder & Partner
    GmbH
Petra Reimann Büro-u. Datenservice
    GmbH
PhonePartner GmbH
Portica GmbH Marketing Support
Power Adress Zielgruppenmarketing
    GmbH
pro:tagon directmarketing GmbH
Prodata Datenbanken und
    Informationssysteme GmbH
prowerb Werbe-und Versandservice
    GmbH
PS Packen und Schicken GmbH
Publica data-service gmbh
PVS Presseversand Service GmbH
R. M. Sittarz hero services GmbH
RJ Marketing-Service GmbH
RTV Karin Rudolf, Daten-Text-und
    Informationsverarbeitung
SAZ Dialog Agentur GmbH
SAZ Listbroking GmbH
Schober D&G Direct Media GmbH &

Co.
Schober Direktmarketing GmbH &
    Co.
Scholz Versand Service Inh. Siegfried
    Scholz
Service Partner Agentur für
    Direktwerbung GmbH
Skriptura Dienstleistungen Schmale &
    Wolf oHG
SMP – Werbeservice GmbH
SOBA GmbH Unternehmensberatung
social concept GmbH Agentur für
    Sozialmarketing
SPT Marketing Service GbR mbH
SSM System Service Marketing
    GmbH
Steigerwald Marketing GmbH
Stettin Direct Marketing
Taurus Werbeagentur GmbH
Tele-Info Verlag GmbH
Thieka GmbH
Thoma Direct Marketing
Trebbau Listbroking und
    Datenverarbeitungs GmbH
Trendcommerce St. Gallen GmbH
Uniserv GmbH
Verband der Vereine Creditreform e.V.
Viafon GmbH
Vogel Adress
VSP Versand-Service Plate Data
    Service GmbH + Co. oHG
W. Schorsch & Co.
Wagner Direktmarketing GmbH
Walsh International Holdings GmbH
Werbeteam Jacob Direktmarketing
    GmbH
Wiegmann GmbH Kuvertier-und
    Verpackungsservice
Wolfgang Mundt Direkt GmbH

List services
ad-con Adressen-und
    Lettershopservice GmbH
ADM Arbeitsgruppe für
    Direktmarketing GmbH
Adressen + Service GmbH
Adressmarketing Rudolf K. Härtel
    GmbH
Agentur für Publikation und Media
    (APM) Heiner GmbH
Agentur für Zielgruppenberatung
    Gudrun Schrödl
alphatext Direktwerbung GmbH
AMA Adress-und Zeitschriftenverlag
    GmbH
Arnold, Demmerer & Partner
AZ Bertelsmann Direct GmbH
B. Gürtler MediaDistribution GmbH
Bauer + Kirch GmbH BKR Software
BDL Betriebsberatungs-und
    Datenverarbeitungs GmbH
Benner & Partner Dialogmarketing
    GmbH

Bernd Hörtkorn Versandservice GmbH
BKG Büro-Kommunikation und Grafikdesign Service GmbH
Briefing GmbH Lösungen und Service für Direktmarketing
Bürgel Wirtschaftsinformationen GmbH & Co. KG
Büromatic Direktwerbung Jost Damgaard GmbH & Co. KG
Claritas Deutschland Data + Services GmbH
D&G-Software GmbH
Data Select Gesellschaft für Marketing Service mbH
Datafin Direkt Marketing Service AG
Dating GmbH
DCS Direktmarketing & Card Service GmbH
Deutsche Post Adress GmbH
Deutsche Post Direkt GmbH
Deutsche Telekom Medien GmbH
Dialoghaus GmbH
Dietmar Iltisberger GmbH
DIMA Werbe GmbH
Direct Center Knoll GmbH
Direkt-Marketing Gerardi GmbH & Co. KG
Direkte Data Marketing GmbH
Direktmarketing Kurt W. Welz GmbH
Direktmarketing Service-Center GmbH & Co.
dm-plus Direktmarketing GmbH
DMD Direkt Marketing Dienste Bodo Mann GmbH
dr. von arnim Direktmarketing
Drei-D Direktwerbung GmbH & Co.KG
Dun + Bradstreet Deutschland GmbH
DVS Datenverarbeitungs-und Datenmanagement-Service GmbH
econ-alca Consulting GmbH
Erwin Braun Direktwerbung
Faber Direkt, Egon Faber GmbH & Co. KG
FDS Fulfillment Directmarketing Service GmbH
fh direktmarketing + edv-dienstleistungen ohg
Fischer & Partner Direktmarketing GmbH
Gall, Wedewardt + Partner GmbH
Gebhard Müller GmbH
GFP Gesellschaft für Produktinformation mbH
GfS Gesellschaft für Sozialmarketing mbH
Glettler Annemarie, Direktmarketing
GM Direkt-Marketing Center GmbH
HeiRa GmbH
Hellweg und Buyk, Partner für Direktwerbung GmbH
Heuer & Co. Verlags-und

Werbeversand GmbH
Human Inference Adressenverwaltungssoftware GmbH
Infox GmbH & Co. Informationslogistik KG
item GmbH advanced press & mail serviceware
J + P Dialog Marketing GmbH
JS Versandservice und Direktmarketing GmbH
Jucknieß – Datenservice GmbH
Karl Trebbau GmbH Adressenverlag und Direktwerbeunternehmen
Klopotek & Partner GmbH
KOOP Direktmarketing GmbH & Co. KG
KOOP indima Ges.f. innovatives Direktmarketing mbH
Kredo Direkwerbung GmbH
Kuvertier-Service Auguste Staar GmbH
Lammoth, Neumark & Co. ADRESSMARKETING GmbH
Laserprint Druck-und Direktwerbung GmbH
LDZ Laserdruckzentrum GmbH
Lehr & Brose Erste Dialogagentur GmbH & Co. KG
Lettershop Brendler GmbH
Lettershop Schonard GmbH & Co
M&H Versandhandel und Service GmbH & Co.
Mail Box Direkt-Marketing Service GmbH
Mail Com Dialogmarketing GmbH
Mail*Select GmbH
Mailing GmbH Lagerhaltg.u.Distribution v. Werbemitteln
mailpool Adressen-Management GmbH
Mar.Co. Marketing.Communication. Olaf Quast
Media Data Rent GmbH
MediaDirect Marketing GmbH
Mediadress GmbH
Merkur Direktwerbeges. mbH & Co KG
Multidata Service GmbH
MVS Management-und Versand-Service GmbH
Nordata Marketing-Informations-Systeme GmbH
OBIMD International
Omikron. Soft + Hardware GmbH
Optimail Direktwerbeservice GmbH
pan-adress Direktmarketing Gesellschaft mbH
pb direkt Praun, Binder & Partner GmbH
Petra Reimann Büro-u. Datenservice GmbH

Portica GmbH Marketing Support
Power Adress Zielgruppenmarketing GmbH
Pro Marketing
pro:tagon directmarketing GmbH
Prodata Datenbanken und Informationssysteme GmbH
prowerb Werbe-und Versandservice GmbH
PS Packen und Schicken GmbH
Publica data-service gmbh
PVS Presseversand Service GmbH
R. M. Sittarz hero services GmbH
RJ Marketing-Service GmbH
RTV Karin Rudolf, Daten-Text-und Informationsverarbeitung
SAZ Dialog Agentur GmbH
SAZ Listbroking GmbH
Schober D&G Direct Media GmbH & Co.
Schober Direktmarketing GmbH & Co.
Scholz Versand Service Inh. Siegfried Scholz
Service Partner Agentur für Direktwerbung GmbH
Skriptura Dienstleistungen Schmale & Wolf oHG
SMP – Werbeservice GmbH
SOBA GmbH Unternehmensberatung
social concept GmbH Agentur für Sozialmarketing
SPT Marketing Service GbR mbH
SSM System Service Marketing GmbH
Steigerwald Marketing GmbH
Stettin Direct Marketing
SWI Süd-West-Information GmbH
Taurus Werbeagentur GmbH
Tele-Info Verlag GmbH
Thieka GmbH
Thoma Direct Marketing
Trebbau Listbroking und Datenverarbeitungs GmbH
Uniserv GmbH
Verband der Vereine Creditreform e.V
Vogel Adress
VSP Versand-Service Plate Data Service GmbH + Co. oHG
Wagner Direktmarketing GmbH
Walsh International Holdings GmbH
Werbeteam Jacob Direktmarketing GmbH
Wiegmann GmbH Kuvertier-und Verpackungsservice
Wolfgang Mundt Direkt GmbH
Ziegenhorn Tourism Database

Mail order company
Dohmen Distribution
Fischer & Partner Direktmarketing GmbH
Quelle AG

Mailing/Faxing services
BBDO Interactive GmbH
Deutsche Post – International Mail
  Service
Deutsche Post Ag – Ims
Deutsche Post AG -Zentrale-
Direct Line Marketing und
  Kommunikation GmbH
mailpool Adressen-Management
  GmbH
Rosenzweig & Schwarz Agentur für
  Dialogmarketing GmbH
Trendcommerce St. Gallen GmbH
W. Schorsch & Co.

Market research agency
BBE-Unternehmensberatung GmbH
Deutsche Post Adress GmbH
Direct Line Marketing und
  Kommunikation GmbH
Marketforce Gesellschaft für Business
  Marketing mbH
Mungenast Direkt Marketing GmbH
Publicis Dialog
TPD Medien GmbH

Media buying agency
Agentur für Publikation und Media
  (APM) Heiner GmbH
Benner & Partner Dialogmarketing
  GmbH
Carat Direct
Fcb International

Merge-purge services
Arnold, Demmerer & Partner

Modelling, regression
Arnold, Demmerer & Partner

Online marketing information
  services
Mail*Select GmbH

Operative marketing and sales
  support especially for high
  tech products and for all IT
  subjects
SalesConcept Teleservices & Database-
  Marketing GmbH

Package inserts
Arnold, Demmerer & Partner

Personalisation
Aktiv Direkt Marketing GmbH
Lettershop Schonard GmbH & Co
mailpool Adressen-Management
  GmbH
Meiller Direct GmbH
Prisma Direkt Ges. für
  Informationsver-arbeitung und
  Direkt Marketing mbH

Rosenzweig & Schwarz Agentur für
  Dialogmarketing GmbH
Sales Team GmbH
Trendcommerce St. Gallen GmbH
W. Schorsch & Co.

Personalised coloured digital
  print
Trendcommerce St. Gallen GmbH

Print services
ABT Druck GmbH
Aktiv Direkt Marketing GmbH
D&G Direkt-Marketing Gerardi
  Gmbh & Co Kg
Deutsche Post AG -Zentrale-
G/R/O Gruschka Rückert Other's
  Werbeagentur GmbH
Ghp Direkt Mail GmbH
mailpool Adressen-Management
  GmbH
Meiller Direct GmbH
Rosenzweig & Schwarz Agentur für
  Dialogmarketing GmbH
Scitex Digital Printing
Trendcommerce St. Gallen GmbH
W. Schorsch & Co.
Winter Druckerzeugnisse GmbH

Private delivery services
Tip Werbeverlag GmbH+Co.KG

Production of customer loyalty
  magazines
TPD Medien GmbH

Publisher
TPD Medien GmbH
Vogel Adress

Relocation database
Deutsche Post Adress GmbH

Response analysis bureau
AOS Consult GmbH
KOOP indima Ges.f. innovatives
  Direktmarketing mbH
Prisma Direkt Ges. für
  Informationsver-arbeitung und
  Direkt Marketing mbH
SAZ Dialog Agentur GmbH
Scherer Team MRM GmbH & Co.
  KG
Spectrum GmbH Marketing Services
  & Consulting
Wunderman Cato Johnson GmbH

Sales promotion agency
Fcb International
Lehr & Brose Erste Dialogagentur
  GmbH & Co. KG
MSBK,Team DialogMarketing GmbH
OgilvyOne worldwide GmbH

Publicis Dialog
Ritter, Wolek Werbeagentur GmbH
Sales Team GmbH
Wunderman Cato Johnson GmbH

Service bureau
Arnold, Demmerer & Partner
AZ Bertelsmann Direct GmbH
Ghp Direct Mail GmbH
ICOM Software Research
Mail*Select GmbH
Smile And Sell Teleservices GmbH

Software supplier
ABIS AG
Aspect Communications GmbH
BBDO Interactive GmbH
ICOM Software Research
Prisma Direkt Ges. für
  Informationsver-arbeitung und
  Direkt Marketing mbH
Spectrum GmbH Marketing Services
  & Consulting
Uniserv GmbH
Viafon GmbH

Telemarketing agency
Ackerler Telefonmarketing
adm-agentur für dialogmarketing
  GmbH
AFM GmbH Agentur für Fax-und
  Telemarketing
Agentur für Telefon-Marketing Ursula
  Bellenbaum
aktiv Kommunikationsdienst
all by phone + net
Ascena Communication Services
  GmbH
ATM-Telefonmarketing GmbH
Atos Teleservices GmbH
AudioService GmbH Gesellschaft für
  Informationsdienste
Axel Springer Verlag AG die Welt/Welt
  Am Sonntag
AZ Bertelsmann Direct GmbH
b u. w UNTERNEHMENSGRUPPE
b.a.s. telemedien GmbH
B2 Kommunikation + Werbung
  GmbH
BauContact GmbH
BBE-Unternehmensberatung GmbH
Bosch Telecom Service Center GmbH
BSD-Wirtschaftsdienste GmbH
BTW Time Line GmbH
bürotel ProfiCenter für
  Vertriebsoptimierung GmbH
C.C.P. Verlag und Buchvertrieb
Call & Care Agentur für Kunden-
  Dialog und Marketing GmbH
Call Center Aus-und Weiterbildung
  gGmbH
Call Center Telemarketing GmbH
Carsting GmbH

cologne:callcenter gmbh
Combera GmbH
CompuTel Telefonservice GmbH
D & S Dialog Marketing GmbH
Data Inform Jürgen Dickob
defacto marketing GmbH
Deutsche Telekom AG
dfp Telefonmarketing GmbH
dial Marketing GmbH
Dialog Frankfurt Agentur für
 Dialogmarketing GmbH
Dialog-Kommunikations + Marketing
 GmbH
Diatel Direkt Assekuranz-Marketing
 GmbH
Direct Line Marketing und
 Kommunikation GmbH
DMC Database Marketing
 Communication GmbH
DMC Nord Database Marketing
 Communication GmbH
Dr. Scharm + Partner GmbH i.G.
 Medizinisches Marketing
dtms Deutsche Telefon-und Marketing
 Services GmbH
DVT Bürodienstleistungen GmbH
ecmc Europäisches Zentrum für
 Medienkompetenz GmbH
EDS Informationstechnologie und
 Service (Deutschland) GmbH
Epsilon Data GmbH
 Datenbankmarketing –
 Telemarketing
Ericsson GmbH Unternehmensbereich
 Business Networks
Euro-Dialog-Call Center GmbH
Evolo Call & Businesscenter
 GmbH&Co.KG i.G.
Eyretel Deutschland GmbH
fastphone telemarketing GmbH
FRB Marketing Partner GmbH
 Teleservices
Friendly Call
G.K.K. Frankfurt GmbH Agentur für
 Dialog-Marketing
Giel Frankfurt GmbH
GWV Verlagsgesellschaft mbH
 Redaktion Call Center Profi
HDM Hulsink Direct Marketing
 GmbH
Hotline Telemarketing oHG
IK Transcom Europe GmbH
IMA Software GmbH
IN + OUT Teleservice GmbH
INA (Germany) GmbH
Indutel Telefonmarketing H. Kiso
infoMedia Service GmbH
Intertel Telefonservice GmbH
InterView AG Dialogmarketing &
 Research
ISI Marketing GmbH
Jäger + Schmitter DiaLog
Jost Telemarketing GmbH

K & P Marketing GmbH
K.M. + Partner Gesellschaft für
 Marketing-Kommunikation mbH
Kluth Telemarketing GmbH
Knauer + Partner Marketing GmbH
Knoche Telefonmarketing
Komdat Gesellschaft für externes
 Vertriebsmanagement mbH
Konzept Telemarketing Service GmbH
KPS Interactive Media GmbH &
 Co.KG
Kreuzer GmbH
Kübler Telemarketing GmbH &
 Co.KG
Legion Telekommunikation GmbH
Lehr & Brose Erste Dialogagentur
 GmbH & Co. KG
Lifta, Lift und Antrieb GmbH
Linkenheil & Friends Telemarketing
 GmbH
Logo Call GmbH
M&L Communication Marketing
 GmbH
M&L Mauer Marketing Services
 GmbH
Mader Unternehmens Kommunikation
 GmbH
Marketforce Gesellschaft für Business
 Marketing mbH
Media Phon TV-Production GmbH
mercato dialogmarketing gmbh
MPS Media Phone Service GmbH &
 Co. Betriebs-KG
Mungenast Direkt Marketing GmbH
o.tel.o communications GmbH & Co.
OgilvyOne worldwide GmbH
OK Marketing Elisabeth Kreuziger
PhoneCom KommunikationsDienste
 GmbH
PhonePartner GmbH
PMS – Phone Media Service GmbH
Point Informations Systeme GmbH
Prisma Unternehmensberatung für
 Telefonkommunikation GmbH
ProContact – Direktmarketing GmbH
Profi Call Bremen GmbH & Co. KG
profiTel Call Center Consulting
 GmbH
promota direct marketing gmbh
Raab Karcher Elektronik GmbH
Real Consultants GmbH
RM Buch und Medien Vertrieb GmbH
S & H Communication Ges. für
 Werbung und Telemarketing mbH
S direkt Sparkassen Service Rheinland
 GmbH
S Direkt-Marketing GmbH & Co.KG
SalesConcept Teleservices & Database-
 Marketing GmbH
seka team Telefonmarketing GmbH
Sellbytel Call-& Communication-
 Center GmbH
Sichtig Direktwerbung GmbH

Sitel GmbH
SK-Telekommunikation in KS-
 Unternehmensgruppe
Smile & Sell Teleservices GmbH
Smile And Sell Teleservices GmbH
Spellbound Gesellschaft für
 innovatives Marketing mbH
StammCom Media GmbH
Success Marketing + Kommunikation
 Harry Röder GmbH
Supercom GmbH Audiotex Systeme
Sykes TAS Telemarketing Ges. f.
 Kommunikation & Dialog mbH
Sympa Tel Telemarketing GmbH
T & M Gesellschaft für
 Telefonmarketing mbH
T-Punkt-Marketing GmbH
T.D.M. Telefon-Direkt-Marketing
 GmbH
Talkline InfoDienste GmbH
TAS GmbH Nord
TAS Telemarketing Ges. für
 Kommunikation und Dialog mbH
tc teleconsult Dipl.Kfm. Dr. Heribert
 Strathmann
tel-inform GmbH
Tele-Scout GmbH
TeleConcept Telefon Marketing
 GmbH
Telefair Telefon-Dialog-
 Dienstleistungen Ulrich Zimmer
 GmbH
TelEffekt Gesellschaft für Direkt-
 Marketing mbH
Telefin Direkt Marketing Service AG
Telefon-Marketing und Verlagsservice
 TVM GmbH
Telekontakt Direktmarketing GmbH
Telemarkt Call-Center GmbH & Co.
 KG
Telemarkt Telefondienst GmbH
Teleperformance Deutschland
telepublic Verlag GmbH & Co. Medien
 KG
TEMA Gesellschaft für Marketing
 Service mbH
Tien Versand GmbH
TM 24 Call Center Consulting GmbH
TMS Sonja Müller
TMS Telemarketing Service Stuttgart
 GmbH
TS-CommunicationsCentrum für
 Versender
Tu Was! Marketing Direkt-Service
 Schröder
V-TEX GmbH
Viafon GmbH
W.I.L.I.-Marketing AG
Walter Telemarketing & Vertrieb
 GmbH & Co.
walter TeleMedienService GmbH &
 Co.
welcome wellnet e.k.

WJP Wolfgang Johansen & Partner
  GmbH
Xerox Direct GmbH
Xpedite Systems GmbH

Telemarketing consulting
TMS Telemarketing Service Stuttgart
  GmbH

Training/recruitment
BBE-Unternehmensberatung
  GmbH
Direct Line Marketing und
  Kommunikation GmbH
PhonePartner GmbH
T.D.M. Telefon-Direkt-Marketing
  GmbH
TMS Telemarketing Service Stuttgart
  GmbH
Viafon GmbH

Translation services
TPD Medien GmbH

eBusiness (BtoB, BtoC)
BBDO Interactive GmbH

eCRM
BBDO Interactive GmbH

eCommerce
BBDO Interactive GmbH

E-SERVICES

E-Marketing consultant
BBDO Interactive GmbH
Benner & Partner Dialogmarketing
  GmbH
CreaKom Direct & Telemarketing
  GmbH
Deutsche Post Adress GmbH

Direct Line Marketing und
  Kommunikation GmbH
G/R/O Gruschka Rückert Other's
  Werbeagentur GmbH
JM&K Agentur für integrierte
  Kommunikation GmbH
MORE SALES Agentur GmbH
porta mundi GmbH & Co. KG
Rosenzweig & Schwarz Agentur für
  Dialogmarketing GmbH
T.D.M. Telefon-Direkt-Marketing
  GmbH

Email list provider
AZ Bertelsmann Direct GmbH
CreaKom Direct & Telemarketing
  GmbH
SalesConcept Teleservices & Database-
  Marketing GmbH
Ziegenhorn Tourism Database

Email software
all by phone + net
Aspect Communications GmbH
BBDO Interactive GmbH
CreaKom Direct & Telemarketing
  GmbH
SalesConcept Teleservices & Database-
  Marketing GmbH
T.D.M. Telefon-Direkt-Marketing
  GmbH

Online/e-marketing agency
b u. w UNTERNEHMENSGRUPPE
BBDO Interactive GmbH
Benner & Partner Dialogmarketing
  GmbH
BKD GmbH
CreaKom Direct & Telemarketing
  GmbH
Direct Line Marketing und
  Kommunikation GmbH
G/R/O Gruschka Rückert Other's
  Werbeagentur GmbH

JM&K Agentur für integrierte
  Kommunikation GmbH
MORE SALES Agentur GmbH
porta mundi GmbH & Co. KG
Rosenzweig & Schwarz Agentur für
  Dialogmarketing GmbH
SalesConcept Teleservices & Database-
  Marketing GmbH

Website design
b.a.s. direct GmbH
BBDO Interactive GmbH
Benner & Partner Dialogmarketing
  GmbH
CreaKom Direct & Telemarketing
  GmbH
Direct Line Marketing und
  Kommunikation GmbH
eskatoo - Die Agentur für innovative
  Kommunikation GmbH
Fcb International
G/R/O Gruschka Rückert Other's
  Werbeagentur GmbH
HM1 Heuser, Mayer + Partner Direct
  Marketing GmbH
Knauer y Rump y Partner
  Werbeagentur GmbH
Lehr & Brose Erste Dialogagentur
  GmbH & Co. KG
M&V München Agentur für
  Dialogmarketing und
  Verkaufsförderung GmbH
mailpool Adressen-Management
  GmbH
MORE SALES Agentur GmbH
MSBK, Team DialogMarketing GmbH
OgilvyOne worldwide GmbH
porta mundi GmbH & Co. KG
Ritter, Wolek Werbeagentur GmbH
Rosenzweig & Schwarz Agentur für
  Dialogmarketing GmbH
SalesConcept Teleservices & Database-
  Marketing GmbH
Thompson Connect GmbH

GREECE

Population: 10.5 million
Capital: Athens
Language: Greek

GDP: $120 billion
GDP per capita: $11,440
Inflation: 5.5 per cent

Currency: Drachma (Dr) = 100 leptae
Exchange rate: Dr301.99 : $1 (Dr325.40 : 1 euro)

Time: GMT +2 hours

OVERVIEW

In the mid-1990s advertising expenditure represented 1.25 per cent of Greek gross domestic product – the highest percentage in Europe; and at +22.6 per cent the Greeks showed the highest European year-on-year growth of adspend per capita.

Despite this burgeoning of advertising activity, the market has generated little demand for direct marketing. Television advertising seems to have overwhelmed the market, accounting for over 65 per cent of total advertising expenditure – the highest percentage in Europe – while Direct Marketing accounts for only 11–15 per cent. The impression is that the industry is in its infancy. Consumers and businesses simply do not receive enough mailshots to have formed a relationship with the medium.

The fundamental factor behind the country's relative lack of DM presence is, perhaps, the Greek alphabet. Only a handful of Greek lists have been re-profiled into Roman characters – at an international level, this impedes the importation of much of the latest data processing technology.

As a result, Greece is marginalized as a candidate for inclusion in a pan-European campaign, while the domestic market offers only basic facilities. With direct marketing not well understood as a concept, there are few companies claiming to specialize in it. Some do exist, however, and the best route into the market may be via FEDMA's list of Greek member companies.

LANGUAGE AND CULTURAL CONSIDERATIONS

As mentioned above, the Greek alphabet is the main stumbling block to a DM campaign in Greek. Any campaign in Greek would need to be carried out through a Greek agent, and using a Greek printer and typesetter, which could well add considerably to the cost.

LEGISLATION AND CONSUMER PROTECTION

There is currently no Robinson list and no data protection legislation in Greece.

POSTAL SERVICES

The Hellenic Post will respond to written enquiries in English, and publishes a five-page guide to its postal rates and services (overseas companies are sent a version written in French).

Discounts are available if mail-outs are scheduled, pre-sorted and batched in advance. The rates also specify discounts for volumes of over 20 units, but there is little in the guide in the way of special services designed to stimulate the use of direct mail.

For more information, contact:

Postes Helléniques (ELTA)
Division of International Relations
GR-10188 Athens
Greece
Tel: +30 1 32 40080
Fax: +30 1 32 27916

International Service Enquiries:
Mr Georges Foumas
Head of Division of International Relations

DO YOU CARE WHOM TO TARGET ?

We provide you with integrated Direct Marketing services through innovative techniques and Marketing solutions.

We maximize your Return on Investment through high response rates, that increase the effectiveness of your communication.

But above all, we offer you our expertise in both strategy and execution of tailor made programs.

- Database Management
- List Brokerage
- Sampling Programs
- Loyalty Schemes
- Mail House
- Fulfilment

- Warehousing
- Postal Services
- Inbound/Outbound Telemarketing
- CRM
- Telephone Surveys
- Events and Special Programs

CARE
D I R E C T

14, GRAVIAS str. 172 35 DAFNI, ATHENS, GREECE, TEL.+301-97 65 773, FAX.+301-97 65 774
E-MAIL: care-dir@otenet.gr
WEBSITE: **www.caredirect.gr**

PROVIDERS OF DM AND E-M SERVICES

CARE DIRECT LTD
Gravias 14
Dafni
Athens
17235
Greece
Tel: +30 1 976 5773
Fax: +30 1 976 5774
Email: care-dir@otenet.gr
Web: www.caredirect.gr

Services/Products:
Call centre services/systems;
Database services; Direct marketing
agency; Fulfilment and sampling
house; Labelling/envelope services;
Lettershop

E-Services:
Website design

Member of:
FEDMA

COMPACT DISC CLUB
13 A Kapodistrou Street
Athens
152 37 Filothel
Greece
Tel: +30 1 68 11 111
Fax: +30 1 68 14 406
Email: cdclub@hol.gr
Harris Karaolides, Marketing Director

Services/Products:
List services; Telemarketing agency;
Catalogue producer

Member of:
FEDMA

IMPACT DIRECT
100 Alexandras Ave
Athens
11472
Greece
Tel: +30 1 6464167
Fax: +30 1 646 4167
Paul Gergos, General Manager

Services/Products:
Direct marketing agency; Media
buying agency

Member of:
FEDMA; DMA (US)

IMPIRIC/PAN MAIL
137 Chrysostomou Siyirnis
18346 Mashato
Greece
Tel: +301 4805 600
Fax: +301 4818 010

Email:
    touia_kontartatou@eu.impiric.com
Web: www.impiric.com
Panos Vatsis, General

Services/Products:
Database services; Direct marketing
agency; Interactive media; Lettershop;
Personalisation; Telemarketing agency

E-Services:
Website design; Online/e-marketing
agency

Member of:
FEDMA; DMA (US)

LEO BURNETT
371 Syngrou Avenue
Athens
17564
Greece
Tel: +30 1 941 2365
Fax: +30 1 943 0437
Paradodemas Alexandros, Marketing
    Department

Services/Products:
Advertising Agency; Direct marketing
agency

Member of:
DMA (US)

PLAISIO COMPUTERS SA
5 Favierou Str.
Athens
14452
Greece
Tel: +30 2 84 2268
Fax: +30 1 284 1362
George Gerardos, Managing Director

Services/Products:
Service bureau

Member of:
DMA (US)

**SERVICE 800 SA
    TELEPERFORMANCE
    GREECE**
Thisseos 330
Athens
17675
Greece
Tel: +30 1 93 03 373
Fax: +30 1 930 3383
John Tourcomanis, Managing Director

Services/Products:
Telemarketing agency

Member of:
DMA (US)

SERVICES/PRODUCT LISTING

Advertising Agency
Leo Burnett

Call centre services/systems
Care Direct Ltd

Catalogue producer
Compact Disc Club

Database services
Care Direct Ltd
IMPIRIC/Pan Mail

Direct marketing agency
Care Direct Ltd
Impact Direct
IMPIRIC/Pan Mail
Leo Burnett

Fulfilment and sampling house
Care Direct Ltd

Interactive media
IMPIRIC/Pan Mail

Labelling/envelope services
Care Direct Ltd

Lettershop
Care Direct Ltd
IMPIRIC/Pan Mail

List services
Compact Disc Club

Media buying agency
Impact Direct

Personalisation
IMPIRIC/Pan Mail

Service bureau
Plaisio Computers SA

Telemarketing agency
Compact Disc Club
IMPIRIC/Pan Mail
Service 800 SA Teleperformance
    Greece

E-SERVICES

Online/e-marketing agency
IMPIRIC/Pan Mail

Website design
Care Direct Ltd
IMPIRIC/Pan Mail

REPUBLIC OF
─────── IRELAND ───────

Population: 3.6 million
Capital: Dublin
Languages: English, Irish

GDP: $77 billion
GDP per capita: $21,083
Inflation: 2.1 per cent

Currency: Irish Pound or Punt (Ir£) = 100 pence
Exchange rate: IR£0.73 : $1 (IR£0.79 : 1 euro)

Time: GMT

OVERVIEW

With a population of 3.6 million, Ireland is one of the smaller markets in the EU. A population of 1.1 million households, however, will still yield potentially profitable sub-groups, as will Ireland's 110,000 businesses.

Direct mail currently accounts for nearly 20 per cent of Ireland's total media expenditure (10 per cent of the total advertising budget), with the volume of direct mailings per capita rising steadily over recent years to a current average of 20 items per capita. Direct response TV and related media are also well favoured by the availability of a high number of call centres.

Limited market size means that there are a smaller number of local specialist DM services available. However, the IDMA has done much to enhance the professionalism of all aspects of the DM industry in Ireland. The IDMA has introduced a primary Code of Practice for direct marketers, a Telemarketing Code, and Europe's first Code for List and Database Owners/Processors (Data Protection). Now with two full-time staff, IDMA is able to respond quickly to enquiries from prospective mailers.

List and databases

Fairly comprehensive selection criteria are available within both business and consumer lists, but the total number of lists is still very limited. About 20 consumer lists are commercially available at an average cost of IR£135 per 1000 names; a total of 60 business lists are available at a cost of some IR£175 per 1000 names. Undeliverables average at 2–2.5 per cent. Several geodemographic overlays are available.

LANGUAGE AND CULTURAL CONSIDERATIONS

Both English and Irish are spoken in the Republic of Ireland, so a DM campaign could be launched in either language. However, with English being more widely spoken and no Irish monoglots left, there is no need to embark on a campaign in Irish unless it is for reasons of goodwill.

LEGISLATION AND CONSUMER PROTECTION

All databases must be registered with the Data Protection Commission, stating how they will be used. Database owners/managers must supply details held on any individual, to that individual, if requested. There are, however, no laws restricting the export of data. A Mailing Preference Scheme administered by the IDMA was launched in April 1997, and a Telephone Preference Service was launched in April 1998.

THE DIRECT MARKETING ASSOCIATION

Name:	Irish Direct Marketing Association (IDMA)
Address:	Clipton House, Lwc Fitzwilliam St., Dublin 2
Tel:	+353 1 6613 808
Fax:	+353 1 6615 200
Year founded:	1988
Email::	info@idma.ie
Website::	www.idma.ie
CEO:	Michael Nolan
Total staff:	2
Total members:	350
Contact:	Michael Nalan, CEO

Facilities for overseas users of direct mail

Membership: membership of IDMA is open to overseas companies, and the standard membership fee is IR£399. Companies apply for membership and are approved by the Board. All applicant companies must agree to adhere to out Codes of Practice.

Whether you know your customers or not, at least you know who to use.

Publicity Post

Postaim

In Direct Marketing there are only two kinds of customers. Those you already know and those you want to know. With Direct Marketing services from An Post, you can talk to both. With **Postaim**, we will help you sort through all the commercially available lists in order for you to assemble the most accurate, detailed list of prospects possible. Then we make sure they get the message - right into their hands. **Publicity Post** will make you famous - in a street, a town or a county. Choose the area you wish to target and Publicity Post will get you into every home there.

For more information call direct on 353 1 705 7300 or visit www.anpost.ie

Newsletter: the IDMA produces a free monthly newsletter for members. *GoDirect*, the IDMA's official magazine, is also circulated on a regular basis. A directory of members and services is available.

On-line information service: the IDMA has an on-line information service: www.idma.ie195

Legal advice: the IDMA can provide free legal advice to members on the laws pertaining to data protection, sales promotion and consumer rights.

Business liaison service: the IDMA helps both members and non-members to find local venture partners, and helps them in the choice of local, accredited suppliers.

Other facilities: the IDMA holds quarterly meetings, as well as evening seminars and breakfast meetings and an annual national conference. It also runs an annual Awards for Excellence scheme sponsored by Telecom Eireann; the brochure provides a very useful overview of local creative work and campaign strategies. The IDMA offers a 400-page market research document priced at Ir£95.

POSTAL SERVICES

An Post, the postal service of the Republic of Ireland, offers a range of direct marketing by direct mail services, including the following:

Postaim

Postaim is the service for pre-approved, pre-sorted, addressed advertising or promotional mailings, posted from the Republic of Ireland to within the Republic and Northern Ireland. There are two Postaim services: Standard Postaim and Special Postage Prepaid Postaim Envelopes. Standard Postaim is for mailings of at least 2000 items. The mailer must overprint the envelopes with the appropriate licence details. Special Postage Prepaid Envelopes are for lower-volume mailings when the mailer does not wish to overprint envelopes. The minimum number of prepaid envelopes which can be purchased from An Post is 500. For conditions for Postaim, contact either An Post or the PDMS.

Publicity Post

An Post also offers an unaddressed delivery service called Publicity Post. This service allows advertisers to target either urban or rural households, or businesses.

Business response services

An Post offers both national and international business reply services and a national Freepost service.

Precision Marketing Information Ltd

Precision Marketing Information Ltd (PMI) offers a wide range of products and services to support the information needs of companies wishing to use direct mail to communicate with existing and potential Irish customers.

PMI has developed the Irish Customer Marketing Database (ICMD), the first ever Irish database with reference files and software capable of handling Irish names and addresses. The database is the source of PMI's data protection compliant products and services. PMI can be contacted on Tel: +353 1 676 6144.

Publisher's service

A special publisher's service exists, offering reduced rates for the posting of newspapers and periodicals by the publisher or printer.

Primary information services include the following leaflets and brochures published by *An Post: A Guide to Postaim; Your Guide to An Post Mail Services; Application Form for Business Reply and Freepost; Publicity Post; Mailmover – Speeding Your Mail into the 21st Century.* For more information contact:

An Post
General Post Office
O'Connell Street
Dublin 1
Ireland

Tel: +353 1 705 7085
Fax: +353 1 705 7447
Website: www.anpost.ie

PROVIDERS OF DM AND E-M SERVICES

ALUSET LTD.
Broombridge House
87 Lagan Road
Dublin Industrial Estate
Dublin
11
Republic of Ireland
Tel: +353 1 8307 533
Fax: +353 1 8600 563
Email: ddawson@aluset.ie
Mr. Diarmuid Dawson, Personalisation
  Sales Manager

Services/Products:
Fulfilment and sampling house;
Design/graphics/clip art supplier;
Personalisation; Print services; Direct
marketing agency

Member of:
IDMA

141 IRELAND
9 Upper Pembroke Street
Dublin
2
Republic of Ireland
Tel: +353 1 6760 560
Fax: +353 1 6625 065
Email: whelehan@141ireland.iol.ie
Mr. Peter Whelehan

Services/Products:
Sales promotion agency; Direct
marketing agency; Design/graphics/clip
art supplier; Campaign management

A.S.A. MARKETING GROUP
The Marketing Centre
Ballinlough Road
Cork
Republic of Ireland
Tel: +353 21 312677
Fax: +353 21 312938
Mr. Aodh Bourke, Managing Director

Services/Products:
Direct marketing agency; Database
services; Print services; Fulfilment and
sampling house; Campaign
management

A.S.A. MARKETING GROUP
Larchfield House
Dundrum Road
Dublin
14
Republic of Ireland
Tel: +353 1 298 3466
Fax: +353 1 295 1680
Email: sales@asamarketing.ie

Web: www.asamarketing.ie
Mr. Paul Miley, General Manager

Services/Products:
Consultancy services; Database
services; Personalisation; Direct
marketing agency; Lettershop;
Promotional products/corporate gifts

Member of:
IDMA

ABISCOM
3 Sandyford Office Park
Blackthorn Avenue
Dublin
18
Republic of Ireland
Tel: +353 1 2941 050
Fax: +353 1 2941 050
Email: peter@abiscom.ie
Mr. Peter Williams, Sales Director

Services/Products:
Mailing/Faxing services; Direct
marketing agency; Personalisation

ADAPTT CALL AND DATA MANAGEMENT
Hanover House
85–89 South Main Street
Cork
Republic of Ireland
Tel: +353 21 4802 500
Fax: +353 21 4802 569
Email: adaptt@adaptt.com
Web: www.adaptt.com
Mr. Gerald Fitzgerald

Services/Products:
Fulfilment and sampling house;
Telemarketing agency; Call centre
services/systems

Member of:
IDMA

ADC BAR CODE SYSTEMS
Unit 1 Sandyford Park
Sandyford Industrial Estate
Dublin
18
Republic of Ireland
Tel: +353 1 2076 777
Fax: +353 1 2076 766
Email: sales@adcbarcode.com
Web: www.adcbarcode.com
Mr. Alan O'Malley, Managing
  Director

Services/Products:
Database services

ADLER
PO Box 4498
Ballymount Industrial Estate
Ballymount Drive

Dublin
12
Republic of Ireland
Tel: +353 1 6611 711
Fax: +353 1 6611 722
Mr. Richard Carter

Services/Products:
Mail order company

ADVERTISING STANDARDS AUTHORITY FOR IRELAND (ASAI)
IPC House
35/39 Shelbourne Road
Dublin
4
Republic of Ireland
Tel: +353 1 6608 766
Fax: +353 1 6608 113
Email: info@asai.ie
Web: www.asai.ie
Mr. Eward McCumiskey

Services/Products:
Advertising Agency; Sales promotion
agency

AGRIPOST - FARMERS JOURNAL MAILING SERVICES
Irish Farm Centre
Bluebell
Dublin
12
Republic of Ireland
Tel: +353 1 4199 500
Fax: +353 1 4500 669
Email: rthompson@farmersjournal.ie
Ms. Ruth Thompson, Manager

Services/Products:
List services; Direct marketing agency;
Database services

Member of:
IDMA

AIG EUROPE (IRELAND) LIMITED
AIG House
Merrion Road
Dublin
4
Republic of Ireland
Tel: +353 1 2081 400
Fax: +353 1 2837 774
Email: martin.kennedy@aig.com
Web: www.aig.com
Mr. Martin Kennedy, Accident &
  Health Manager

Services/Products:
Direct marketing agency

AMARACH CONSULTING
28 Upper Fitzwilliam Street
Dublin
2
Republic of Ireland
Tel: +353 1 6619 147
Fax: +353 1 6610 312
Email: info@amarach.com
Web: www.amarach.com
Ms. Liz McKeever, Director

AME PROGRAM MANAGEMENT
5 Dundrum Business Park
Dundrum
Dublin
14
Republic of Ireland
Tel: +353 1 2079 700
Fax: +353 1 2079 701
Mr. Jim O'Reilly, Managing Director

Services/Products:
Fulfilment and sampling house;
Labelling/envelope services; Software
supplier; Call centre services/systems;
Direct marketing agency

Member of:
IDMA

AN POST
Regional Office
89–90 South Mall
Cork
Republic of Ireland
Tel: +353 1 275533
Fax: +353 1 272407
Mr. Matt Moran Key, Account
Manager

Services/Products:
Mailing/Faxing services; Direct
marketing agency

AN POST
General Post Office
O'Connell Street
Dublin
1
Republic of Ireland
Tel: +353 1 705 7000
Fax: +353 1 705 8105
Ms. Freda Burke

Services/Products:
Private delivery services; Mailing/
Faxing services; Direct marketing
agency

Member of:
FEDMA; IDMA

AOC MARKETING LIMITED
AOC House
5 Church Place
Fermoy
Co Cork
Republic of Ireland
Tel: +353 25 33011
Fax: +353 25 32870
Email: aocmktg@indigo.ie
Ms. Edel Fleming, Assistant Manager

Services/Products:
Fulfilment and sampling house;
Database services; Direct marketing
agency; Response analysis bureau

Member of:
IDMA

ARDMORE DIRECT
24 Upper Mount Street
Dublin
2
Republic of Ireland
Tel: +353 1 6610 997
Fax: +353 1 6767 756
Email: arddubl@iol.ie
Web: www.ardmore.co.uk
Ms. Sharon Dunlea, Business
Development Manager

Services/Products:
Personalisation; Mailing/Faxing
services; Database services; Response
analysis bureau; Fulfilment and
sampling house; List services

BILL MOSS & ASSOCIATES
The Powerhouse
Pigeon House Harbour
Dublin
4
Republic of Ireland
Tel: +353 1 6080 571
Fax: +353 1 6687 945
Email: bmoss@indigo.ie
Web: www.bill-moss.com
Ms. Geraldine Hatch, Office Manager

Services/Products:
List services; Mailing/Faxing services

Member of:
National DMA; UK DMA

BUSINESS & FINANCE BUSINESS INFORMATION
6 Merrion Row
Dublin
2
Republic of Ireland
Tel: +353 1 6618 625
Fax: +353 1 6762 343
Email: carmel.murray@
businessandfinance.ie

Web: www.businessandfinance.ie
Ms. Carmel Murray, Marketing
Information Manager

Services/Products:
List services; Database services

Member of:
IDMA

CANON IRELAND
Arena Road
Sandyford Industrial Estate
Dublin
18
Republic of Ireland
Tel: +353 1 2052 400
Fax: +353 1 2958 141
Email: canonirl@indigo.ie
Web: www.canon.ie
Ms. Olwyn Adams

Services/Products:
Hardware supplier; Software supplier

Member of:
National DMA

CLP & ASSOCIATES LTD
13 Clarinda Park North
Dun Laoghaire
Co Dublin
Republic of Ireland
Tel: +353 1 2846 921
Fax: +353 1 2846 923
Email: clp@indigo.ie
Mr. Peter Purcell

Services/Products:
Consultancy services; Loyalty systems

Member of:
IDMA

CONDUIT EUROPE
Conduit House
East Point Business Park
Fairview
Dublin
3
Republic of Ireland
Tel: +353 1 8190 000
Fax: +353 1 8190 050
Email: info@conduit.ie
Web: www.conduit.ie
Ms. Mary Ann Brem, Conduit
Software

Services/Products:
Telemarketing agency

Member of:
IDMA

CORE DIRECT MARKETING
Response House
Unit 3 M50 Business Park
Ballymount

Dublin
12
Republic of Ireland
Tel: +353 1 4092 700
Fax: +353 1 4092 701
Email: mkelly@coredm.ie
Mr. Mark Kelly, Business
  Development Manager

Services/Products:
Fulfilment and sampling house;
Database services; Mailing/Faxing
services; Print services; Direct
marketing agency; Print services

Member of:
IDMA

CREATIVE CONCEPTS
Henley
1 Ballintemple
Blackrock
Cork
Republic of Ireland
Tel: +353 21 294095
Fax: +353 21 294094
Email: info@creativeconcepts.ie
Ms. Terri O'Hara

Services/Products:
Advertising Agency; Direct marketing
agency; Sales promotion agency

Member of:
IDMA

CREATIVE RESOURCES
    LIMITED
The Mews
24 Lad Lane
Dublin
2
Republic of Ireland
Tel: +353 1 6614 077
Fax: +353 1 6614 209
Email: creatres@indigo.ie
Mr. Gerry Coleman

Services/Products:
Consultancy services; Design/graphics/
clip art supplier

Member of:
IDMA

CREATIVE SOLUTIONS
    LIMITED
10 Terminus Mills
Clonskeagh
Dublin
6
Republic of Ireland
Tel: +353 1 2838 118
Fax: +353 1 2600 306
Email: neary.g@solutions-group.ie
Geraldine Neary, Account Director

Services/Products:
Database services; Direct marketing
agency; Copy adaptation; Sales
promotion agency; Response analysis
bureau

Member of:
IDMA

DATACONVERSION DIRECT
    LTD
25/26 Westland Square
Dublin
2
Republic of Ireland
Tel: +353 1 6771 466
Fax: +353 1 6771 521
Email: answers@dataconversion.ie
Web: www.dataconversion.ie
Mr. Raymond J. O'Kelly, Managing
  Director

Services/Products:
List services; Database services;
Response analysis bureau; Print
services; Software supplier; Mailing/
Faxing services

Member of:
IDMA

DC KAVANAGH LIMITED
43 Dolphin's Barn Street
Dublin
8
Republic of Ireland
Tel: +353 1 4544 299
Fax: +353 1 4540 532
Email: info@dck.ie
Mr. Conor Kavanagh

Services/Products:
Fulfilment and sampling house;
Personalisation; Print services

Member of:
IDMA

DES O'MEARA & PARTNERS
23 Fitzwilliam Place
Dublin
2
Republic of Ireland
Tel: +353 1 6762 753
Fax: +353 1 6789 499
Mr. Des O'Meara, Chairman

Services/Products:
Advertising Agency; Direct marketing
agency

Member of:
IDMA

DIALOGUE MARKETING
    COMMUNICATIONS
37 Leeson Close
Dublin
2
Republic of Ireland
Tel: +353 1 662 2277
Fax: +353 1 662 2278
Email: administrator@dialogue-
  dublin.com
Web: www.dialogue-dublin.com
Mr. Michael Killeen, Managing
  Director

Services/Products:
Advertising Agency; Direct marketing
agency; Design/graphics/clip art
supplier; Media buying agency;
Consultancy services

Member of:
FEDMA; IDMA

DIMENSION
70 Upper Leeson Sreet
Dublin
2
Republic of Ireland
Tel: +353 1 667 3222
Fax: +353 1 667 3077
Email: niamh.moore@dimension.ie
Web: www.dimension.ie
Mr. Niamh Moore, Managing Director

Services/Products:
Advertising Agency; Consultancy
services; Design/graphics/clip art
supplier; Direct marketing agency;
Sales promotion agency; Recruitment
advertising

DIRECTION MARKETING
    CONSULTANTS
21 Windsor Place
Lower Pembroke Street
Dublin
2
Republic of Ireland
Tel: +353 1 676 5678
Fax: +353 1 676 5682
Email:
  messages@directionmarketing.ie
Tasmin Leavy, Office Manager

Services/Products:
Consultancy services; Sales promotion
agency; Database services; Direct
marketing agency

DMA (DIRECT MARKETING
    ASSOCIATES)
Burlington House
Waterloo Lane
Dublin
4

Republic of Ireland
Tel: +353 1 6671 144
Fax: +353 1 6602 204
Email: dma@dma.ie
Web: www.dma.ie
Mr. Mark Cassin, Managing Director

Services/Products:
Direct marketing agency; Consultancy services

Member of:
DMA (US); IDMA

DMT INTERNATIONAL
3 Buttermilk Walk
Galway
Republic of Ireland
Tel: +353 91 500100
Fax: +353 91 565936
Email: info@dmtintl.com
Web: www.dmtintl.com
Matthew McNamara, Joint Chief
    Executive

Services/Products:
Software supplier; Telemarketing agency; Consultancy services

Member of:
IDMA

DUN & BRADSTREET
455a Holbrook House
Holles Street
Dublin
2
Republic of Ireland
Tel: +353 1 6764 239
Fax: +353 1 6789 301
Email: dbireland@dnb.com
Web: www.dbireland.com
Ms. Beverly Cox, National Account
    Manager

Services/Products:
List services; Database services

Member of:
IDMA

EIGHTY TWENTY
2 Clanwilliam Court
Lower Mount Street
Dublin
2
Republic of Ireland
Tel: +353 1 6785 215
Fax: +353 1 6628 719
Email: create@iol.ie
Mr. Aidan Devlin

Services/Products:
Database services; Consultancy services

Member of:
IDMA

FLASHPAK LIMITED
Mail House, Unit F4 Eklad Close
Malahide Road Industrial Park
Malahide Road
Dublin
17
Republic of Ireland
Tel: +353 1 8486 106
Fax: +353 1 8487 891
Email: Flashpak@iol.ie
Mr. Ronan O'Sullivan, Managing
    Director

Services/Products:
Mailing/Faxing services; Labelling/
envelope services; Sales promotion
agency

Member of:
IDMA

GEMINI DIRECT MAIL
13/14 Herbert Street
Dublin
2
Republic of Ireland
Tel: +353 1 678 9755
Fax: +353 1 661 1896
Email: info@gemini.ie
Web: www.gemini.ie
Mr. Matthew Folan, Managing
    Director

Services/Products:
Mailing/Faxing services; Labelling/
envelope services; Direct marketing
agency; Service bureau; Catalogue
producer; Personalisation

Member of:
IDMA

GUS IRELAND LIMITED
1–2 Upper O'Connell Street
Dublin
1
Republic of Ireland
Tel: +353 1 872 6600
Fax: +353 1 874 5237
Ms. Carmel Gartland

Services/Products:
Mail order company

Member of:
IDMA

ICAN
32 Herbert Lane
Dublin
2
Republic of Ireland
Tel: +353 1 6627 257
Fax: +353 87 6765 292
Email: info@ican.ie

Web: www.ican.ie
Mr. Damian Ryan, Chief Executive
    Officer

Services/Products:
Advertising Agency; Electronic media

E-Services:
Website design

Member of:
IDMA

ICT EUROTEL LIMITED
Unit A1 East Point Business Park
Fairview
Dublin
3
Republic of Ireland
Tel: +353 1 8654 011
Fax: +353 1 8650 000
Email: dobyrne@ie.ictgroup.com
Web: www.ictgroup.com
Ms. Dorothy O'Byrne

Services/Products:
Telemarketing agency; E-commerce
support

Member of:
IDMA

IDS DIRECT MARKETING
3 Sandyford Office Park
Blackthorn Avenue
Dublin
18
Republic of Ireland
Tel: +353 1 2604 818
Fax: +353 1 2604 816
Email: sales@idsdirectmarketing.com
Web: www.idsdirectmarketing.com
Ms. Marie Reilly, Sales & Marketing
    Manager

Services/Products:
List services; Database services;
Telemarketing agency

Member of:
IDMA

INDOCOM
3050 Lake Drive
City West
Co Dublin
4
Republic of Ireland
Tel: +353 1 411 2020
Fax: +353 1 411 2022
Email: indocom@independent.ie
Ms. Norma Curran, Account
    Executive

Services/Products:
Fulfilment and sampling house;
Database services; Call centre services
systems; Telemarketing agency

Member of:
IDMA

IRELAND DIRECT COMMUNICATIONS LTD
4 Upper Fitzwilliam Street
Dublin
2
Republic of Ireland
Tel: +353 1 6614 808
Fax: +353 1 6616 893
Email: info@irdirect.org
Mr. Lorcan Lynch, Director

Services/Products:
Direct marketing agency; Database
services

Member of:
IDMA

IRISH INTERNATIONAL GROUP
17 Gilford Road
Sandymount
Dublin
4
Republic of Ireland
Tel: +353 1 260 2000
Fax: +353 1 260 2333
Email: gary@irish-international.ie
Mr. Gary Daly

Services/Products:
Direct marketing agency; Design/
graphics/clip art supplier

Member of:
IDMA

JAVLIN DIRECT LIMITED
Dawson House
Dawson Street
Dublin
2
Republic of Ireland
Tel: +353 1 6798 770
Fax: +353 1 6798 798
Email: kyla@javelin.ie
Ms. Kyla O'Kelly, Director

Services/Products:
Direct marketing agency

Member of:
IDMA

JWT COMMUNICATIONS
4 Inns Court
Winetavern Street
Dublin
8
Republic of Ireland
Tel: +353 1 6123 600
Fax: +353 1 6123 699
Email: phillip.carpenter@jwt.ie
Mr. Phillip Carpenter

Services/Products:
Telemarketing agency; Direct
marketing agency; Direct response TV
services

Member of:
IDMA

KILKENNY PEOPLE GROUP
34 High Street
Kilkenny
Co. Kilkenny
Republic of Ireland
Tel: +353 56 21015
Fax: +353 56 70080
Email: akeane@kilkennypeople.ie
Web: www.kilkennypeople.ie
Ms. Adriana Kerry Keane, Marketing
Director

Services/Products:
Print services; Publisher; Catalogue
producer

Member of:
IDMA

KOMPASS IRELAND
Kompass House
Parnell Court
1 Granby Row
Dublin
1
Republic of Ireland
Tel: +353 1 872 8800
Fax: +353 1 873 3711
Email: info@kompass.ie
Web: www.kompass.ie
Mr. Michael McGowan, Sales &
Marketing Manager

Services/Products:
List services; Database services;
Mailing/Faxing services; Publisher;
Telemarketing agency; Direct
marketing agency

Member of:
IDMA

LALOR INTERNATIONAL HOLDINGS LTD
4 Upper Fitzwilliam Street
Dublin
2
Republic of Ireland
Tel: +353 1 661 4488
Fax: +353 1 661 4330
Email: lalorint@iol.ie
Web: www.iol.ie/~lalorint
Mr. Francis G. Lalor, Chief Executive
Officer

Services/Products:
Advertising Agency; Database services;
Direct marketing agency; Copy
adaptation; Market research agency;

Consultancy services

Member of:
DMA (US); FEDMA; IDMA

MAIL MARKETING (DUBLIN) LTD
117/118 Bann Road
Dublin Industrial Estate
Glasnevin
Dublin
9
Republic of Ireland
Tel: +353 1 8680 577
Fax: +353 1 8680 594
Email: mailmktg@iol.ie
Web: www.factfinder.ie/mailmarketing
Mr. Richard Lindsay, Chairman

Services/Products:
Database services; Mailing/Faxing
services; Labelling/envelope services;
Personalisation; Print services;
Fulfilment and sampling house

Member of:
IDMA

MARKETING INSTITUTE OF IRELAND
South County Business Park
Leopardstown
Dublin
18
Republic of Ireland
Tel: +353 1 2952 355
Fax: +353 1 2952 453
Email: info@mii.ie
Web: www.mii.ie
Mr. John Casey, Chief Executive

Member of:
IDMA

MCCONNELL'S MARKETING
McConnell House
Charlemont Place
Dublin
2
Republic of Ireland
Tel: +353 1 4781 544
Fax: +353 1 4757 886
Email: jeff.chisnall@mcconnells.ie
Web: www.mcconnells.ie
Mr. Jeff Chisnall, Head of Relationship
Marketing

Services/Products:
Database services; Direct marketing
agency; Design/graphics/clip art
supplier

Member of:
IDMA

NATIONAL ENVELOPE COMPANY LIMITED
Unit 30 Stillorgan Industrial Estate
Stillorgan
Co Dublin
Republic of Ireland
Tel: +353 1 2956 277
Fax: +353 1 2957 559
Email: sales@nationalenvelope.ie
Mr. William Murphy, Manager

Services/Products:
Labelling/envelope services; Print
services

Member of:
IDMA

NATIONAL PEN LIMITED
Finnabair Industrial Park
Dundalk
Co Louth
Republic of Ireland
Tel: +353 42 9388 500
Fax: +353 42 9339 813
Email: pdonnell@pens.com
Web: www.pens.com
Mr. Peter Donnelly, Managing
  Director

Services/Products:
Personalisation; Manufacturer and
supplier of promotional and crporate
gifts

Member of:
FEDMA; IDMA; BAGDA; BPMA

OPTIMAS IRELAND
8 Priory Hall
Stillorgan
Co. Dublin
Republic of Ireland
Tel: +353 1 2784 445
Fax: +353 1 2784 446
Email: info@optimas-ireland.com
Web: www.optimas.group.com
Mr. Declan Mooney, Managing
  Director

Services/Products:
Consultancy services; Training/
recruitment; Direct marketing agency;
Call centre services/systems

Member of:
IDMA

PENTAGON
Catalyst House
14 Adelaide Street
Dun Laoghaire
Co. Dublin
Republic of Ireland
Tel: +353 1 2806 661
Fax: +353 1 2806 670

Email: pentagon@iol.ie
Ms. Deirdre Kelly, Client Service
  Director

Services/Products:
Direct marketing agency; Consultancy
services; Sales promotion agency

Member of:
DMA (US); IDMA

PERFORMANCE MARKETING LIMITED
29 Airways Industrial Park
Santry
Dublin
17
Republic of Ireland
Tel: +353 1 8060 500
Fax: +353 1 8621 482
Email: info@perform.ie
Web: www.perform.ie
Mr. Bill Egan, Director

Services/Products:
List services; Database services;
Mailing/Faxing services; Direct
marketing agency; Telemarketing
agency; Training/recruitment

Member of:
IDMA

PHONENET TELEMARKETING SERVICES
Unit 4
Sandyford Office Park
Sandyford Industrial Estate
Co. Dublin
Republic of Ireland
Tel: +353 1 2942 262
Fax: +353 1 2942 260
Email: karl@phonenet.ie
Web: www.phonenet.ie
Mr. Karl Llewellyn, Director

Services/Products:
Telemarketing agency; Market research
agency

Member of:
IDMA

PHONOVATION LIMITED
Phonovation House
8 Clarinda Park North
Dun Laoghaire
Co. Dublin
Republic of Ireland
Tel: +353 1 284 3011
Fax: +353 1 284 3223
Email: phono@indigo.ie
Web: www.phonovation.com
Mr. Paddy Woods, Managing Director

Services/Products:
Fulfilment and sampling house;
Interactive media; Call centre service
systems; Direct marketing agency;
Telemarketing agency; Sales promotio
agency

Member of:
National DMA

PHS IRELAND LIMITED
Response House
Unit 3 M50 Business Park
Ballymount
Dublin
12
Republic of Ireland
Tel: +353 1 4092 700
Fax: +353 1 4092 701
Email: info@responsegroup.ie
Web: www.responsegroup.ie
Mr. John Keane, Managing Director

Services/Products:
Lettershop; Fulfilment and sampling
house; Mailing/Faxing services; Sales
promotion agency; Database services

Member of:
IDMA

POSTGEM LIMITED
Alexandra House
Earlsfort Centre
Earlsfort Terrace
Dublin
2
Republic of Ireland
Tel: +353 1 6768 744
Fax: +353 1 6768 727
Email: info@postgem.ie
Web: www.postgem.ie
Ms. Therese Ni Dhuibhir

Services/Products:
Mailing/Faxing services; Electronic
media

E-Services:
Website design

Member of:
IDMA

PRECISION MARKETING INFORMATION LTD
c/o GPO
O'Connell Street
Dublin
1
Republic of Ireland
Tel: +353 1 6766 144
Fax: +353 1 6766 252
Email: info@pmi.ie
Web: www.pmi.ie
Ernie Parker, General Manager

Services/Products:
List services; Database services;
Response analysis bureau; Service
bureau

**ROBERT HAYES-MCCOY
COPYWRITERS LTD**
13 Lea Road
Sandymount
Dublin
4
Republic of Ireland
Tel: +353 1 2603 949
Fax: +353 1 2603 951
Email: copy@iol.ie
Mr. Robert Hayes-McCoy

Services/Products:
Training/recruitment; Copy
adaptation; Direct marketing agency

Member of:
IDMA

ROTHCO
21 Northumberland Road
Ballsbridge
Dublin
4
Republic of Ireland
Tel: +353 1 6673 053
Fax: +353 1 6673 191
Email: rothco@iol.ie
Mr. Patrick Hickey, Director

Services/Products:
Consultancy services

Member of:
IDMA

RTE
Donnybrook
Dublin
4
Republic of Ireland
Tel: +353 1 664 2003
Fax: +353 1 664 3097
Email: sales@rte.ie
Mr. Paul Mulligan

Services/Products:
Advertising Agency; Direct marketing
agency

Member of:
IDMA

SDL EXHIBITIONS LIMITED
18 Main Street
Rathfarnham
Dublin
14
Republic of Ireland
Tel: +353 1 4900 600
Fax: +353 1 4908 934
Email: sean@sdlexpo.com

Web: www.sdlexpo.com
Mr. Sean Lemass, Managing Director

Services/Products:
Telemarketing agency; Direct
marketing agency

Member of:
IDMA

SITEL TMS
Sitel House
8 Park West Business Park
Walkinstown
Nangor Road
Dublin
12
Republic of Ireland
Tel: +353 1 6300 300
Fax: +353 1 6300 333
Email: sitel@indigo.ie
Web: www.sitel.com
Mr. Nick Wheeler, Managing Director

Services/Products:
Telemarketing agency; Training/
recruitment; Consultancy services; List
services; Database services

Member of:
IDMA

SMURFIT WEB PRESS
Botanic Road
Glasnevin
Dublin
9
Republic of Ireland
Tel: +353 1 8303 511
Fax: +353 1 8303 706
Email: tamoroso@smurfitwebpress.ie
Mr. Tony Amoroso, Executive
    Director - Sales & Marketing

Services/Products:
Print services

Member of:
IDMA

**SUPERCLUB TARGET
    MARKETING (STM)**
PO Box 4444
Sutton Cross
Dublin
13
Republic of Ireland
Tel: +353 1 832 6300
Fax: +353 1 832 6544
Email: sam@superclub.ie
Web: www.superclub.ie
Ms. Lorraine Ryan, General Manager

Services/Products:
List services

Member of:
IDMA

TARGET MARKETING LIMITED
The Stockyard
20 Upper Sheriff Street
Dublin
1
Republic of Ireland
Tel: +353 1 8555 012/016
Fax: +353 1 8556 954
Email: target@target-marketing.ie
Web: www.target-marketing.ie
Ms. Geraldine Doherty, Creative
    Director

Services/Products:
Direct marketing agency; Consultancy
services; Copy adaptation

Member of:
IDMA

TELECONCEPTS
4 Upper Fitzwilliam Street
Dublin
2
Republic of Ireland
Tel: +353 1 6614 488
Fax: +353 1 6614 330
Email: craig@iol.ie
Web: www.iol.ie/~craig
Mr. Craig Matthews, Managing
    Director

Services/Products:
Telemarketing agency; Training/
recruitment; Call centre services/
systems

Member of:
IDMA

THE BLUE WATER AGENCY
6 Market Square
Dundalk
Co. Louth
Republic of Ireland
Tel: +353 42 9351 101
Fax: +353 42 9351 102
Email: watersblue@eircom.net
Ms. Florence Van Dijk

Services/Products:
Database services; Consultancy
services

Member of:
IDMA

THE HELME PARTNERSHIP
Clyde Lane
Ballsbridge
Dublin
4
Republic of Ireland
Tel: +353 1 660 5333
Fax: +353 1 660 5309
Email: lita@helme.ie
Ms. Lita Notte, Account Executive

Services/Products:
Advertising Agency; Direct marketing agency

Member of:
IDMA

TICO DIRECT
9 Georges Avenue
Blackrock
Co. Dublin
Republic of Ireland
Tel: +353 1 2833 244
Fax: +353 1 2833 248
Email: alex@tico-group.ie
jacq@tico-group.ie
Web: www.tico-group.ie
Mr. Alex Pigot, Managing Director

Services/Products:
Lettershop; Fulfilment and sampling house; Database services; Mailing/ Faxing services; Telemarketing agency; Electronic media

E-Services:
Website design

Member of:
IDMA

TRIMFOLD LIMITED
Duggan Industrial Estate
Athboy Road
Trim
Co. Meath
Republic of Ireland
Tel: +353 46 31497
Fax: +353 46 36049
Email: Envelopes@trimfold.com
Mr. Des Ryan, Sales Manager

Services/Products:
Labelling/envelope services; Print services

Member of:
IDMA

WATERMARQUE MARKETING COMMUNICATIONS LIMITED
The Malt Building
Fumbally Court
Fumbally Lane
Dublin
8
Republic of Ireland
Tel: +353 1 4538 722
Fax: +353 1 4540 171
Email: info@watermarque.ie
Web: www.watermarque.com
Louise Durning, Head of Direct Marketing

Services/Products:
Sales promotion agency; Direct marketing agency; Database services; Consultancy services; Response analysis bureau; Design/graphics/clip art supplier

Member of:
FEDMA; IDMA; IISPC

WEBSTER BURKE
57 Botanic Road
Glasnevin
Dublin
9
Republic of Ireland
Tel: +353 1 8308 520
Fax: +353 1 8308 383
Email: webster@indigo.ie
Ms. Katriona Breslin, Sales & Marketing

Services/Products:
Design/graphics/clip art supplier; Print services

Member of:
IDMA

WHELAN BANKS MG
120 Baggot Lane
Ballsbridge
Dublin
4
Republic of Ireland
Tel: +353 1 6689 977
Fax: +353 1 6689 947
Email: paul@whelanbanks.com
info@whelanbanks.com
Mr. Paul Banks, Managing Director

Services/Products:
Direct marketing agency; Sales promotion agency

Member of:
IDMA

WIGGINS TEAPE IRELAND (SALES) LTD
Gateway House
East Wall Road
Dublin
3
Republic of Ireland
Tel: +353 1 8742 455
Fax: +353 1 8364 323
Ms. Maura Quinn

Services/Products:
Labelling/envelope services

Member of:
IDMA

WINSTON
Brookfield Terrace
Carysfort Avenue
Blackrock
Co. Dublin
Republic of Ireland
Tel: +353 1 2834 875
Fax: +353 1 2836 970
Email: dmdept@winston.ie
Web: www.winston.ie
Ms. Louise Buggy, Marketing Mananger

Services/Products:
Design/graphics/clip art supplier; Personalisation; Print services; Direct marketing agency

Member of:
IDMA

SERVICES/PRODUCT LISTING

Advertising Agency
Advertising Standards Authority for Ireland (ASAI)
Creative Concepts
Des O'Meara & Partners
Dialogue Marketing Communication
Dimension
ICAN
Lalor International Holdings Ltd
RTE
The Helme Partnership

Call centre services/systems
Adaptt Call and Data Management
AME Program Management
IndoCom
optimAS Ireland
Phonovation Limited
Teleconcepts

Campaign management
141 Ireland
A.S.A. Marketing Group

Catalogue producer
Gemini Direct Mail
Kilkenny People Group

Consultancy services
A.S.A. Marketing Group
CLP & Associates Ltd
Creative Resources Limited
Dialogue Marketing Communication
Dimension
Direction Marketing Consultants
DMA (Direct Marketing Associates)
DMT International

Eighty Twenty
Lalor International Holdings Ltd
optimAS Ireland
Pentagon
Rothco
Sitel TMS
Target Marketing Limited
The Blue Water Agency
Watermarque Marketing
    Communications Limited

Copy adaptation
Creative Solutions Limited
Lalor International Holdings Ltd
Robert Hayes-McCoy Copywriters Ltd
Target Marketing Limited

Database services
A.S.A. Marketing Group
A.S.A. Marketing Group
ADC Bar Code Systems
Agripost - Farmers Journal Mailing
    Services
AOC Marketing Limited
Ardmore Direct
Business & Finance Business
    Information
Core Direct Marketing
Creative Solutions Limited
Dataconversion Direct Ltd
Direction Marketing Consultants
Dun & Bradstreet
Eighty Twenty
IDS Direct Marketing
IndoCom
Ireland Direct Communications Ltd
Kompass Ireland
Lalor International Holdings Ltd
Mail Marketing (Dublin) Ltd
McConnell's Marketing
Performance Marketing Limited
PHS Ireland Limited
Precision Marketing Information Ltd
Sitel TMS
The Blue Water Agency
TICo Direct
Watermarque Marketing
    Communications Limited

Design/graphics/clip art supplier
Aluset Ltd.
141 Ireland
Creative Resources Limited
Dialogue Marketing Communications
Dimension
Irish International Group
McConnell's Marketing
Watermarque Marketing
    Communications Limited
Webster Burke
Winston

Direct marketing agency
Aluset Ltd.
141 Ireland
A.S.A. Marketing Group
A.S.A. Marketing Group
ABISCOM
Agripost - Farmers Journal Mailing
    Services
AIG Europe (Ireland) Limited
AME Program Management
An Post
An Post
AOC Marketing Limited
Core Direct Marketing
Creative Concepts
Creative Solutions Limited
Des O'Meara & Partners
Dialogue Marketing Communications
Dimension
Direction Marketing Consultants
DMA (Direct Marketing Associates)
Gemini Direct Mail
Ireland Direct Communications Ltd
Irish International Group
Javlin Direct Limited
JWT Communications
Kompass Ireland
Lalor International Holdings Ltd
McConnell's Marketing
optimAS Ireland
Pentagon
Performance Marketing Limited
Phonovation Limited
Robert Hayes-McCoy Copywriters Ltd
RTE
SDL Exhibitions Limited
Target Marketing Limited
The Helme Partnership
Watermarque Marketing
    Communications Limited
Whelan Banks MG
Winston

Direct response TV services
JWT Communications

E-commerce support
ICT Eurotel Limited

Electronic media
ICAN
PostGEM Limited
TICo Direct

Fulfilment and sampling house
Aluset Ltd.
A.S.A. Marketing Group
Adaptt Call and Data Management
AME Program Management
AOC Marketing Limited
Ardmore Direct
Core Direct Marketing
DC Kavanagh Limited

IndoCom
Mail Marketing (Dublin) Ltd
Phonovation Limited
PHS Ireland Limited
TICo Direct

Hardware supplier
Canon Ireland

Interactive media
Phonovation Limited

Labelling/envelope services
AME Program Management
Flashpak Limited
Gemini Direct Mail
Mail Marketing (Dublin) Ltd
National Envelope Company Limited
Trimfold Limited
Wiggins Teape Ireland (Sales) Ltd

Lettershop
A.S.A. Marketing Group
PHS Ireland Limited
TICo Direct

List services
Agripost - Farmers Journal Mailing
    Services
Ardmore Direct
Bill Moss & Associates
Business & Finance Business
    Information
Dataconversion Direct Ltd
Dun & Bradstreet
IDS Direct Marketing
Kompass Ireland
Performance Marketing Limited
Precision Marketing Information Ltd
Sitel TMS
SuperClub Target Marketing (STM)

Loyalty systems
CLP & Associates Ltd

Mail order company
Adler
GUS Ireland Limited

Mailing/Faxing services
ABISCOM
An Post
An Post
Ardmore Direct
Bill Moss & Associates
Core Direct Marketing
Dataconversion Direct Ltd
Flashpak Limited
Gemini Direct Mail
Kompass Ireland
Mail Marketing (Dublin) Ltd
Performance Marketing Limited
PHS Ireland Limited

PostGEM Limited
TICo Direct

Manufacturer and supplier of promotional and crporate gifts
National Pen Limited

Market research agency
Lalor International Holdings Ltd
Phonenet Telemarketing Services

Media buying agency
Dialogue Marketing Communications

Personalisation
Aluset Ltd.
A.S.A. Marketing Group
ABISCOM
Ardmore Direct
DC Kavanagh Limited
Gemini Direct Mail
Mail Marketing (Dublin) Ltd
National Pen Limited
Winston

Print services
Aluset Ltd.
A.S.A. Marketing Group
Core Direct Marketing
Dataconversion Direct Ltd
DC Kavanagh Limited
Kilkenny People Group
Mail Marketing (Dublin) Ltd
National Envelope Company Limited
Smurfit Web Press
Trimfold Limited
Webster Burke
Winston

Private delivery services
An Post

Promotional products/corporate gifts
A.S.A. Marketing Group

Publisher
Kilkenny People Group
Kompass Ireland

Recruitment advertising
Dimension

Response analysis bureau
AOC Marketing Limited
Ardmore Direct
Creative Solutions Limited
Dataconversion Direct Ltd
Precision Marketing Information Ltd
Watermarque Marketing
    Communications Limited

Sales promotion agency
141 Ireland
Advertising Standards Authority for
    Ireland (ASAI)
Creative Concepts
Creative Solutions Limited
Dimension
Direction Marketing Consultants
Flashpak Limited
Pentagon
Phonovation Limited
PHS Ireland Limited
Watermarque Marketing
    Communications Limited
Whelan Banks MG

Service bureau
Gemini Direct Mail

Precision Marketing Information Ltd

Software supplier
AME Program Management
Canon Ireland
Dataconversion Direct Ltd
DMT International

Telemarketing agency
Adaptt Call and Data Management
Conduit Europe
DMT International
ICT Eurotel Limited
IDS Direct Marketing
IndoCom
JWT Communications
Kompass Ireland
Performance Marketing Limited
Phonenet Telemarketing Services
Phonovation Limited
SDL Exhibitions Limited
Sitel TMS
Teleconcepts
TICo Direct

Training/recruitment
optimAS Ireland
Performance Marketing Limited
Robert Hayes-McCoy Copywriters Ltd
Sitel TMS
Teleconcepts

E-SERVICES

Website design
ICAN
PostGEM Limited
TICo Direct

ITALY

Population: 58 million
Capital: Rome
Language: Italian

GDP: $1139 billion
GDP per capita: $19,834
Inflation: 2.0 per cent

Currency: Lira
Exchange rate: L1,800.34 : $1 (L1,936.99 : 1 euro)

Time: GMT +1 hour

OVERVIEW

From an agrarian base, Italy has evolved rapidly since the Second World War to become a strong and diversified economy. It has thriving manufacturing and engineering industries, a dynamic financial sector and a lively tourist industry. The Italian economy is now the third largest in Europe, behind only Germany and France.

A large percentage of Italy's advertising expenditure is taken up by television: 57.3 per cent in 1994. In previous years there were few statistics available to assess the extent of DM activity in this market, but it displayed characteristics typical of a young, underdeveloped market with potential for rapid growth. Direct Marketing now accounts for 24 per cent of the total advertising expenditure, and has a growth rate of 12 per cent.

The list market is expanding in Italy. A wide range of consumer response lists is available, with rental prices varying widely depending on type of list, quantity, support format, selection criteria and conditions of rental; and list quality is not always high. There are approximately 20 subscriber/controlled circulation lists available, with a limited market for swaps. These lists are updated annually.

Public domain lists are available from SEAT, the official distributor of lists from the telephone directory. Over 18 million names are available, with lists updated every two months. SEAT also distributes compiled business lists, derived from the yellow pages of the telephone directory. Lists can be selected by business sector, geographic area, number of telephone lines and registered status. Lists are updated every two months.

209

Rental prices range from L200 to L500 per address, depending on the list type, selection criteria, and quantity.

LANGUAGE AND CULTURAL CONSIDERATIONS

As the north/south divide is shrinking and becoming less of an obstacle to commerce, Italy is becoming an easier market to target as a whole.

LEGISLATION AND CONSUMER PROTECTION

The data protection law introduced in Italy in July 1997 (D.L 675/96) sets very restrictive conditions for the collection, treatment, communication and use of personal data. Among others: obligation of explicit consent of the data subject, adequate updating and security measures; filing with the Data Protection National Authority (Garante) and definition of the responsibilities of the various players in the process of list handling and management procedures. Only public domain lists (telephone directories, Yellow Pages, and trade directories, professional orders/association members' lists) are exempted from the obligation of obtaining the data subject's consent. Filing with the National Data Protection Authority is compulsory for all list holders, also for public domain lists used exclusively for direct marketing.

THE DIRECT MARKETING ASSOCIATION

Name:	Associazione Italiana del Marketing Interattivo(AIDiM)
Address:	Via della Moscova 38, 20121 Milan
Tel:	+39 02 2901 41 57
Fax:	+39 02 2901 31 72
Email:	aidim@tin.it
Website:	www.aidim.it
Year founded:	1984
Chairman/CEO:	Silvano Boroli (Chairman), Mirko Planta (CEO)
Total staff:	7
Members:	100
Contact:	Mr. Mirko Planta, CEO

DM agencies	15	Printers	11
List brokers	2	Telemarketing agencies	7
Advertisers	2	DM consultants	4
Mailing houses	3	Handling houses	1
Mail order companies	6	Database agencies	3
Associations	10	Banks and insurances	15
Other (TLC, DM users, etc)	21		

Facilities for overseas users of direct mail

Membership: overseas organizations can become members of the AIDIM. The annual fees are as follows:

1. Supporting members   Lir 40,000,000 + one-off fee of Lir 3,000,000
2. Regular members   Lir 15,000,000 + one-off fee of Lir 2,000,000
3. Affiliated members   Lir 4,000,000 + one-off fee of Lir 1,000,000

Newsletter: the AIDIM produces a weekly newsletter called *La Settimana AIDIM* which can be sent by fax or email.
Library: the AIDIM has a library of 250 books and 200 press cuttings.
On-line information service: the association has an on-line information service in Italian. The website address is: www.aidim.it
Legal advice: the association offers legal advice to both members and non-members on the first steps to understanding local legislation affecting DM.
Business liaison service: the AIDIM offers information on both accredited suppliers of DM services, and on business partners.
Other facilities: the AIDIM has a Minitel (videotext) information service available to its members. It also offers a mail preference service. Every month, the AIDIM holds industry meetings, which offer companies the opportunity to meet and discuss DM opportunities.

POSTAL SERVICES

The Italian Post Office is not the best equipped to provide information to enquiries from overseas. They do not, as yet, produce a single guide to their services but do offer a selection of simple fact sheets (some are more comprehensive than others).

The services highlighted via the fact sheets are:

- Postel - an electronic mail system with the flexibility for stamped printed delivery;
- EMS CAI Post - accelerated airmail delivery to 116 countries;
- Post insurance.

For more information contact:

Poste Italiane, S.p.A.
International Mail Department
Viale Europe, 190
00144 Rome
Italy
Tel: +39 06 5958 3691
Fax: +39 06 5942 663
Website: www.posteitaliane.it

PROVIDERS OF DM AND E-M SERVICES

ADDRESSVITT SRL
Via della Moia, 2
Arese Mi
20020
Italy
Tel: +39 02 934501
Fax: +39 02 934503 00
Email: info@addressvitt.it
Web: www.addressvitt.it
Raffaella Mioti, International Account
  Executive

Services/Products:
List services; Mailing/Faxing services;
Fulfilment and sampling house

Member of:
FEDMA; ANVED

AGENZIA FLASH
Via De Francesco 19
Oggiono (Co)
22048
Italy
Tel: +39 341 577 402
Fax: +39 341 576 318
Vittorio Spreafico

Services/Products:
Direct marketing agency

Member of:
AIDiM

ART'E' – SOC.INTERNAZ.DI ARTE E CULTURA SPA
Via Stalingrado 27/5
Bologna
40128
Italy
Tel: +39 51 4194 111 6311 524
Fax: +39 51 374 703
Marilena Ferrari

Services/Products:
Mail order company

Member of:
AIDiM

BLACK BOX ITALIA
Viale Delle Industrie 11
Vimodrone (Mi)-
20090
Italy
Tel: +39 2 2740 0280
Fax: +39 2 2740 0219
Giancarlo Mauri

Services/Products:
Telecommunications

Member of:
AIDiM

C.S. CENTRO SERVIZI DIRECT MARKETING
Via Eschilo 194
Rome
125
Italy
Tel: +39 6 50 91 32 54
Fax: +39 6 50 91 22 89
Email: f.scotti@flashnet.it
Franco Scotti, Managing Director

Services/Products:
Database services; Telemarketing
agency; Training/recruitment; Direct
marketing agency; Call centre services/
systems

Member of:
FEDMA

CASSINE DI PIETRA
Via La Fabbrica 1
S.Petro Mussolino (Vi)
36070
Italy
Tel: +39 444 488911
Fax: +39 444 687995
Valerio Briganti

Services/Products:
Mail order company

Member of:
AIDiM

CBM SAS
V.Le C.Lennormant 236–240
Roma
119
Italy
Tel: +39 6 5231 3011
Fax: +39 6 5231 3030
Massimo Cinti

Services/Products:
Telemarketing agency

Member of:
AIDiM

CBM SRL
Viale Piave 14
Roma
197
Italy
Tel: +39 6 4620191
Fax: +39 6 4826462
Giuseppe Ardizzone

Services/Products:
Direct marketing agency

Member of:
AIDiM

CEMIT DIRECT MEDIA SPA
Via Toscana 9
S. Mauro (Torino)
10099
Italy
Tel: +39 11 2227411
Fax: +39 11 2238701
Web: www.cemit.it
Gianluca Ferrauto

Services/Products:
Advertising Agency; Database services;
Direct marketing agency; Service
bureau; Response analysis bureau;
International Development and
Account Director

E-Services:
Email list provider; E-Marketing
consultant; Website design

Member of:
DMA (US); AIDiM

CENTRO DELLA COMUNICAZIONE INTERATTIVA
Via Turati 70
Cerro Maggiore (Milan)
20023
Italy
Tel: +39 331422031
Fax: +39 331517324
Email: info@cci.it
Web: www.cci.it
Ezio Arrigoni, Art Director and Owner

Services/Products:
Advertising Agency; Direct marketing
agency; Catalogue producer; Mail
order company; Sales promotion
agency; Electronic media

E-Services:
Website design

Member of:
FEDMA; AIDiM

CICRESPI SPA
Via Trieste 11
Liscate
20060
Italy
Tel: +39 2 95754259
Fax: +39 2 9587203
Giancarla Brontesi

Services/Products:
Service bureau

Member of:
AIDiM

CLARITAS ITALIA SRL
Via M. Gorki, 69
Cinisello B. Milano
20092

Italy
Tel: +39 26186181
Fax: +39 261861828
Email: info-it@claritaseu.com
Simona Gadda, Database Manager

Services/Products:
List services; Database services;
Consultancy services; Response
analysis bureau

Member of:
FEDMA; AIDiM

CODATO COMMUNICATION SRL

Via Miranese 420
Chirignago (Ve)
30030
Italy
Tel: +39 41 5440566
Fax: +39 41 917478
Massimo Codato

Services/Products:
Service bureau

Member of:
AIDiM

CONSODATA ITALIA SRL

Foro Buonaparte 16
Milano
20121
Italy
Tel: +39 2 724 091
Fax: +39 2 7240 9260
Sophie Heller

Services/Products:
Database services

Member of:
AIDiM

DIALOGO SRL

Via Buonarroti, 14
Milan
20145
Italy
Tel: +39 2 48 00 77 36
Fax: +39 2 48 16 74 7
Email: dialogo@micronet.it
Luigi Bacchiani, Managing Director

Services/Products:
Direct marketing agency

Member of:
FEDMA; DMA (US)

DIRECT POOL

Via Arenula 29
Roma
186
Italy
Tel: +39 6 6830 9076

Fax: +39 6 6816 2390
Guido Ferraguti

Services/Products:
Consultancy services

Member of:
AIDiM

DRAFTDIRECT WORLDWIDE SRL

Via Ariosto 23
Milano
20145
Italy
Tel: +39 2 4801 8011
Fax: +39 2 4801 9836
Francesca Sorge

Services/Products:
Direct marketing agency

Member of:
AIDiM

DUN & BRADSTREET KOSMOS SPA

Via Valtorta 48
Milano
20127
Italy
Tel: +39 2 2845 5746
Fax: +39 2 2845 5817
Alessandro Cederle

Services/Products:
List services

Member of:
AIDiM

EDITORIALE ALTRO CONSUMO SRL

Via Valassina 22
Milano
20159
Italy
Tel: +39 2 6689 01
Fax: +39 2 6689 0288
Crescenzo Passaro

Services/Products:
Publisher

Member of:
AIDiM

EDIZIONI ARCHIVIO SRL

Via Arch.E.Marcucci 17/17
Bibbiena (Ar)
52011
Italy
Tel: +39 575 5364 61
Fax: +39 575 5934 27
Marcus Deimann

Services/Products:
Publisher

Member of:
AIDiM

EISE INTERNATIONAL SPA

P.Le Giotto 5
Perugia
6100
Italy
Tel: +39 75 5822 1
Fax: +39 75 5822 506
Giuseppe Piria

Services/Products:
List services

Member of:
AIDiM

EPI SERVICE SRL

Via Maiocchi 8
Voghera (Pv)
27058
Italy
Tel: +39 383 343 233
Fax: +39 383 343 235
Mario Cesari

Services/Products:
Mailing/Faxing services

Member of:
AIDiM

EURONOVA SRL

Via Liberta' 2
Vigliano Biellese (Vc)
13069
Italy
Tel: +39 15 3595 1
Fax: +39 15 3595 218
Rosanna Lopez

Services/Products:
Mail order company

Member of:
AIDiM

GN COMTEXT SRL

Via Marina, 6
Milano
20121
Italy
Tel: +39 2 7733 81
Fax: +39 2 7733 8240
Giuseppe D'Onofrio

Services/Products:
Telecommunications

Member of:
AIDiM

GRAF 3 SPA

V.Le Romagna 18–20
Rozzano (Mi)
20089
Italy

Tel: +39 2 5751 1282
Fax: +39 2 8253 887
Sergio De Mio

Services/Products:
Design/graphics/clip art supplier;
Advertising Agency

Member of:
AIDiM

GRUPPO PIRAMIDE SRL
Via Manzoni 43
Milano
20121
Italy
Tel: +39 2 6888 305
Fax: +39 2 6080 186
Giannino Mazzoli

Services/Products:
Database services

Member of:
AIDiM

HERALD DIRECT
via Morazzo 12/1
Bologna
40132
Italy
Tel: +39 51 616 5911
Fax: +39 51 616 5941
Kim Berger Christensen, Creative
    Director

Services/Products:
Fulfilment and sampling house;
Database services; Direct marketing
agency; Response analysis bureau;
Service bureau

Member of:
FEDMA

IL SOLE 24 ORE SPA
Via P.Lomazzo 52
Milano
20154
Italy
Tel: +39 2 3022 2959
Fax: +39 2 3022 2440
Angelo Galli

Services/Products:
Publisher

Member of:
AIDiM

IMX ITALY SRL –
INTERNATIONAL MAIL
EXPRESS
Via G. di Vittorio 307/1
Sesto S. Giovanni - MI
20099
Italy
Tel: +39 2 2421398

Fax: +39 4 2 22476559
Geoffrey Barton, Director

Services/Products:
Lettershop; Fulfilment and sampling
house; Mailing/Faxing services; Direct
marketing agency; Private delivery
services

Member of:
FEDMA

INFOSTRADA SPA
Via Lorenteggio 257
Milano
20152
Italy
Tel: +39 2 413 311
Fax: +39 2 4836 6795
Riccardo Ruggiero

Services/Products:
Telecommunications

Member of:
AIDiM

INTERACTIVE
Via Nizza 59
Roma
198
Italy
Tel: +39 6 84462 448
Fax: +39 6 84462 255
Cristina Casacci

Services/Products:
Direct marketing agency

Member of:
AIDiM

INTERNATIONAL MASTER
PUBLISHER – IMP
Pal.Galileo Galilei 21/B C.Dir.Mi 3
City
Basiglio
20080
Italy
Tel: +39 2 90459 1
Fax: +39 2 90459 201
Maria Pia Gianellini

Services/Products:
Publisher

Member of:
AIDiM

ISTITUTO GEOGRAFICO DE
AGOSTINI SPA
Via G.Da Verrazzano 15
Novara
28100
Italy
Tel: +39 321 424 537
Fax: +39 321 424 293
Fulvio Morezzi

Services/Products:
Publisher

Member of:
AIDiM

LEADERFORM SRL
Via Molina 19/21
Sona (Vr)
37060
Italy
Tel: +39 45 6080 822
Fax: +39 45 6080 815
Carlo Andreoni

Services/Products:
Design/graphics/clip art supplier

Member of:
AIDiM

MARKAB SAS
Via G. Carducci 38
Milano
20123
Italy
Tel: +39 2 4800 8739
Fax: +39 2 4800 8753
Email: info@markab.it
Web: www.markab.it
Mario Massone, CEO

Services/Products:
Consultancy services

Member of:
CMMC

METRON DIRECT SRL
Via F. Massimo 95
Roma
192
Italy
Tel: +39 6 321 8218
Fax: +39 6 322 2207
Albino Della Camera

Services/Products:
Direct marketing agency

Member of:
AIDiM

MILANO LIST SERVICE SRL
P.zza Scolari 4
Milano
20151
Italy
Tel: +39 2 4091 8358
Fax: +39 2 4091 7227
Email: mlslist@iol.it
Marco Merlo

Services/Products:
List services; Consultancy services

Member of:
AIDiM

MORI ANTONIO
Piazza Don Mapelli 1
Sesto S.Giovanni
20099
Italy
Tel: +39 2 2622 1312
Fax: +39 2 2409 673
Antonio Mori

Services/Products:
Direct marketing agency

Member of:
AIDiM

MULTIDIRECT SRL
Via Ripamonti 272/1
Milano
20141
Italy
Tel: +39 2 539 8026
Fax: +39 2 537 833
Renato Mariano

Services/Products:
Service bureau

Member of:
AIDiM

N.C.H. ITALIA SPA
Via Grosio 10/8
Milano
20151
Italy
Tel: +39 2 3803 131
Fax: +39 2 3803 1399
Email: marbened@tin.it
Marina Bisio

Services/Products:
Fulfilment and sampling house

Member of:
AIDiM

ODM DIRECT
Ufficio 16H
Piazza Velasca, 5
Milan
20122
Italy
Tel: +39 2 86 45 01 44
Fax: +39 2 86 45 16 07
Email: odmmi@interbusiness.it
Web: www.odm.it
Aldo Scaiano, General Manager

Services/Products:
List services; Fulfilment and sampling
house; Database services; Mailing/
Faxing services; Telemarketing agency;
Direct response TV services

Member of:
FEDMA

ON LINE TELEMARKETING
Via Torri Bianche 9-Edificio Quercia
Vimercate (Mi)
20059
Italy
Tel: +39 6918 258
Fax: +39 39 6918 180
Email: online@interbusiness
Pio Micieli

Services/Products:
Telemarketing agency

Member of:
AIDiM

PAVIA E ANSALDO
Via dell' Annunciata 7
Milan
20121
Italy
Tel: +39 263381
Fax: +39 276013435
Email: pa_lawfirm@pavia-ansaldo.it
Gerolamo Pellican-, Lawyer

Services/Products:
Legal services

Member of:
FEDMA

PDM – POZZONI DIRECT MARKETING SRL
Viale Restelli 3/7
Milan
20124
Italy
Tel: +39 2 66 82 668
Fax: +39 2 66 88 511
Mina Dapri, Sales Director

Services/Products:
Fulfilment and sampling house;
Database services; Direct marketing
agency; Response analysis bureau;
Service bureau

Member of:
FEDMA; AIDiM

PUBBLIBABY SRL
Via E. Fermi 18
Cusago - MI
20090
Italy
Tel: +39 2 901 19700
Fax: +39 2 903 90464
Ermenegildo Livraghi, President

Services/Products:
Advertising Agency; Direct marketing
agency

Member of:
DMA (US)

R.C.D.-RIGOTTI CASATI DE MAS & ASS. SRL
Via Goldoni 1
Milano
20121
Italy
Tel: +39 2 7600 3986
Fax: +39 2 7600 4421
Italo De Mas

Services/Products:
Direct marketing agency

Member of:
AIDiM

R.C.S. LIBRI SPA
Via Mecenate 91
Milano
20138
Italy
Tel: +39 2 5095 1
Fax: +39 2 5095 2855
Laura Comini

Services/Products:
Publisher

Member of:
AIDiM

R.C.S. PERIODICI SPA
Via A. Rizzoli 2
Milano
20132
Italy
Tel: +39 2 2584 3004
Fax: +39 2 2584 4214
Attilio Lipparini

Services/Products:
Publisher

Member of:
AIDiM

R.S.O. SPA
Via Leopardi 1
Milano
20123
Italy
Tel: +39 2 72401 1
Fax: +39 2 72401 205
Gianluca Rosada

Member of:
AIDiM

RBS – RETAIL BUSINESS SERVICES SRL
Via Livenza 6
Roma
198
Italy
Tel: +39 6 8449 31
Fax: +39 6 8449 3400
Alessandro De Angelis

Services/Products:
Telemarketing agency

Member of:
AIDiM

RIBOTTI MAURIZIO
Via Juvara 23
Biella
13051
Italy
Tel: +39 15 849 4530 849 5512
Fax: +39 15 849 5587
Maurizio Ribotti

Services/Products:
Direct marketing agency

Member of:
AIDiM

**RIGOTTI, CASATI, DE MAS &
  ASSOCIATI**
Via Goldoni, 1
Milan
20129
Italy
Tel: +39 2 76003986
Fax: +39 2 76 00 42 21
Italo De Mas, Managing Director

Services/Products:
Advertising Agency; Direct marketing
agency

Member of:
DMA (US)

S. LORENZO SRL
Via Nazionale 373
Imperia
18100
Italy
Tel: +39 183 290 407
Fax: +39 183 293 546
Massimo Vezza

Services/Products:
Mail order company

Member of:
AIDiM

**SEAT DIRECT, DIVISIONE
  DELLA SEAT PAGINE GIALLE
  SPA**
S.S. Pontina Km 29.100
Pomezia, RM
40
Italy
Tel: +39 6 910 981
Fax: +39 6 910 98 607
Email: fiaschi.federico@seat.it
Web: www.seatdirect.com
Federico Fiaschi

Services/Products:
List services; Database services;
Mailing/Faxing services; Direct
marketing agency

Member of:
FEDMA; DMA (US); AIDiM

SEK SRL
Via T. Romagnola, 136
Pontedera (Pi)
56025
Italy
Tel: +39 587 298 111
Fax: +39 587 55 030
Gianluca Puccinelli

Services/Products:
Response analysis bureau; Market
research agency

Member of:
AIDiM

SELEDATI SRL
Via Dei Missaglia 97
Milano
20142
Italy
Tel: +39 2 8939 01
Fax: +39 2 8930 2900
Marco Dimitri

Services/Products:
Electronic media

E-Services:
Website design

Member of:
AIDiM

**SELEZIONE DAL READER'S
  DIGEST**
Via Alserio 10
Milano
20159
Italy
Tel: +39 2 6987 1
Fax: +39 2 6987 259 428
Charles Lobkowicz

Services/Products:
Publisher

Member of:
AIDiM

SEND ITALIA SPA
Via Bava 16
Torino
10124
Italy
Tel: +39 11 8819 1
Fax: +39 11 8819 302
Franco Defendini

Services/Products:
Mailing/Faxing services

Member of:
AIDiM

SITCAP SAS
Via S.Francesco Da Paola 18
Torino
10123
Italy
Tel: +39 11 810 6511
Fax: +39 11 810 6565
Raffaele Crispino

Services/Products:
Direct marketing agency

Member of:
AIDiM

STREAM
Via Salaria 1021
Roma
138
Italy
Tel: +39 6 8866 3318
Fax: +39 6 8866 3434
Raffaella Rasi

Services/Products:
Telecommunications

Member of:
AIDiM

STS ITALIANA
Via Giardini 474/M
Modena
41100
Italy
Tel: +39 59 343 707
Fax: +39 59 349 049
Email: direct@stsitaliana.it
Web: www.stsitaliana.it
Isabella Dapinguente

Services/Products:
Direct marketing agency; Advertising
Agency; Consultancy services

Member of:
AIDiM

STUDIO LENTATI
Via Conservatorio, 30
Milano
20122
Italy
Tel: +39 2 7600 3304
Fax: +39 2 7600 0719
Beatrice Lentati

Services/Products:
Direct marketing agency

Member of:
AIDiM

**SWISS POST INTERNATIONAL-
    ITALIA SRL**
Via G. Di Vittorio 8/10
Liscate (Mi)
20060
Italy
Tel: +39 2 9535 0241
Fax: +39 2 9500 0349
Giovanni Papagno

Services/Products:
Mailing/Faxing services

Member of:
AIDiM

**SYSMAN SYSTEM MANPOVER
    SRL**
S.S.Lago Di Viverone 27
Burolo (To)
10010
Italy
Tel: +39 125 614 211
Fax: +39 125 577 448
Carla Bertolino

Services/Products:
Software supplier

Member of:
AIDiM

TARGA SERVICE
Corso Settembrini 215
Torino
10135
Italy
Tel: +39 11 6841 777
Fax: +39 11 6841 091
Giorgio Maltinti

Services/Products:
List services

Member of:
AIDiM

TELECOM ITALIA
Viale Regina Giovanna 29
Milano
20129
Italy
Tel: +39 2 621 1
Fax: +39 2 6218 010
Gianni Bettazzoni

Services/Products:
Telecommunications

Member of:
AIDiM

TELECONTATTO SPA
Via Soperga 36
Milano
20127
Italy
Tel: +39 2 2611 1111

Fax: +39 2 2610 500
Alberto Zunino De Pignier

Services/Products:
Telemarketing agency

Member of:
AIDiM

TELEPROFESSIONAL SRL
Via Mentana 17
Monza (Mi)
20052
Italy
Tel: +39 2321 071
Fax: +39 39 836 110
Ferruccio Lusardi

Services/Products:
Telemarketing agency

Member of:
AIDiM

TELEWORK ITALIA SRL
Via Buzzi, 16
Mazzo Di Rho Mi
20017
Italy
Tel: +39 2 9390 4441
Fax: +39 2 9390 0632
Fabrizio Menozzi

Services/Products:
Telemarketing agency

Member of:
AIDiM

THE HERALD GROUP SRL
Via Morazzo 12/1
Bologna
40132
Italy
Tel: +39 51 616 5911
Fax: +39 51 616 5941
Alessandro Merlanti

Services/Products:
Direct marketing agency

Member of:
AIDiM

TOPS DIRECT MARKETING
Via Guelfo Civinini 20
Roma
141
Italy
Tel: +39 6 86 89 52 05
Fax: +39 6 86 80 18 73
Email: info@tops.it
Web: www.tops.it
· Paolo Luzi, Managing Director

Services/Products:
Call centre services/systems;
Consultancy services; Database
services; Direct marketing agency;
Fulfilment and sampling house;
Telemarketing agency

Member of:
FEDMA; DMA (US); ASSODIRECT

SERVICES/PRODUCT
LISTING

Advertising Agency
Cemit Direct Media Spa
Centro Della Comunicazione
    Interattiva
Graf 3 Spa
Pubblibaby Srl
Rigotti, Casati, De Mas & Associati
STS Italiana

Call centre services/systems
C.S. Centro Servizi Direct Marketing
Tops Direct Marketing

Catalogue producer
Centro Della Comunicazione
    Interattiva

Consultancy services
Claritas Italia Srl
Direct Pool
Markab Sas
Milano List Service Srl
STS Italiana
Tops Direct Marketing

Database services
C.S. Centro Servizi Direct Marketing
Cemit Direct Media Spa
Claritas Italia Srl
Consodata Italia Srl
Gruppo Piramide Srl
Herald Direct
ODM Direct
PDM – Pozzoni Direct Marketing Srl
Seat Direct, Divisione Della Seat
    Pagine Gialle Spa
Tops Direct Marketing

**Design/graphics/clip art
    supplier**
Graf 3 Spa
Leaderform Srl

Direct marketing agency
Agenzia Flash
C.S. Centro Servizi Direct Marketing
CBM Srl
Cemit Direct Media Spa

Centro Della Comunicazione
　　Interattiva
Dialogo Srl
Draftdirect Worldwide Srl
Herald Direct
IMX Italy Srl – International Mail
　　Express
Interactive
Metron Direct Srl
Mori Antonio
PDM – Pozzoni Direct Marketing Srl
Pubblibaby Srl
R.C.D.-Rigotti Casati De Mas & Ass.
　　Srl
Ribotti Maurizio
Rigotti, Casati, De Mas & Associati
Seat Direct, Divisione Della Seat
　　Pagine Gialle Spa
Sitcap Sas
STS Italiana
Studio Lentati
The Herald Group Srl
Tops Direct Marketing

Direct response TV services
ODM Direct

Electronic media
Centro Della Comunicazione
　　Interattiva
Seledati Srl

Fulfilment and sampling house
ADDRESSVITT srl
Herald Direct
IMX Italy Srl – International Mail
　　Express
N.C.H. Italia Spa
ODM Direct
PDM – Pozzoni Direct Marketing Srl
Tops Direct Marketing

**International Development
and Account Director**
Cemit Direct Media Spa

Legal services
Pavia E Ansaldo

Lettershop
IMX Italy Srl – International Mail
　　Express

List services
ADDRESSVITT srl
Claritas Italia Srl
Dun & Bradstreet Kosmos Spa
Eise International Spa
Milano List Service Srl
ODM Direct
Seat Direct, Divisione Della Seat
　　Pagine Gialle Spa
Targa Service

Mail order company
Art'E' – Soc.Internaz.Di Arte E
　　Cultura Spa
Cassine Di Pietra
Centro Della Comunicazione
　　Interattiva
Euronova Srl
S. Lorenzo Srl

Mailing/Faxing services
ADDRESSVITT srl
Epi Service Srl
IMX Italy Srl – International Mail
　　Express
ODM Direct
Seat Direct, Divisione Della Seat
　　Pagine Gialle Spa
Send Italia Spa
Swiss Post International-Italia Srl

Market research agency
Sek Srl

Private delivery services
IMX Italy Srl – International Mail
　　Express

Publisher
Editoriale Altro Consumo Srl
Edizioni Archivio Srl
Il Sole 24 Ore Spa
International Master Publisher – Imp
Istituto Geografico De Agostini Spa
R.C.S. Libri Spa
R.C.S. Periodici Spa
Selezione Dal Reader's Digest

Response analysis bureau
Cemit Direct Media Spa
Claritas Italia Srl
Herald Direct
PDM – Pozzoni Direct Marketing Srl
Sek Srl

Sales promotion agency
Centro Della Comunicazione
　　Interattiva

Service bureau
Cemit Direct Media Spa
Cicrespi Spa
Codato Communication Srl
Herald Direct
Multidirect Srl
PDM – Pozzoni Direct Marketing Srl

Software supplier
Sysman System Manpover Srl

Telecommunications
Black Box Italia
GN Comtext Srl
Infostrada Spa
Stream
Telecom Italia

Telemarketing agency
C.S. Centro Servizi Direct Marketing
CBM Sas
ODM Direct
On Line Telemarketing
RBS – Retail Business Services Srl
Telecontatto Spa
Teleprofessional Srl
Telework Italia Srl
Tops Direct Marketing

Training/recruitment
C.S. Centro Servizi Direct Marketing

E-SERVICES

E-Marketing consultant
Cemit Direct Media Spa

Email list provider
Cemit Direct Media Spa

Website design
Cemit Direct Media Spa
Centro Della Comunicazione
　　Interattiva
Seledati Srl

LUXEMBOURG

Population: 425,000
Capital: Luxembourg-Ville
Languages: Luxembourgish, French and German

GDP: $595.9 billion (1997)
GDP per capita: LFr 1,400,000 (1997)
Inflation: 1.0 per cent (1998)

Currency: Luxembourg Franc (LFr) = 100 centimes
Exchange rate: LFr37.51 : $1 (LFr40.36 : 1 euro)

Time: GMT +1 hour

OVERVIEW

Despite the small size of the market, there are a number of features which might make Luxembourg attractive to exporters. The country lies at the heart of Europe's Golden Triangle', the area bordered by London, Paris and Cologne that represents over 60 per cent of the total wealth and population of the EU. In addition, the population is multi-lingual, with both French and German spoken by the majority of the population. It is therefore a conveniently located market with relatively wealthy, polyglot consumers.

There is a local DM industry (with a range of specialized suppliers) but as a result of the multi-lingual nature of the market and its central position, many mailers tend to view Luxembourg as an extension of their French and German campaigns and prepare all the elements of the package outside the country. Lists for Luxembourg can be obtained via brokers in France, Germany and Belgium.

LANGUAGE AND CULTURAL CONSIDERATIONS

There are three languages spoken in Luxembourg: Luxembourgish, French and German. However, French and German are the primary business languages.

LEGISLATION AND CONSUMER PROTECTION

The data protection legislation of 1979 makes it illegal to buy and sell consumer lists, thus limiting the market to business lists.

THE DIRECT MARKETING ASSOCIATION

The local Federation of Marketing and Communication Professionals supplies DM data and figures.

Name: Fédération des Professionnels de la Communication asbl
Address: 7, rue Alcide de Gasperi, L-2981 Luxembourg
Tel: + 352 43 94 44
Fax: + 352 43 83 26
Email: chamcom.@cc.lu

POSTAL SERVICES

P & T Luxembourg (state-owned company) is the leading company for postal services in Luxembourg. Special conditions are offered for bulk mailings of all formats. Requests for information and technical assistance are handled quickly and efficiently.

Services offered:

- Bulk, discounted rates for addressed/unaddressed mail
- Periodical mailing rates
- International business reply services
- Postage paid by addressee
- PO Box addresses
- Registered post
- Express mail services (EMS)
- Business reply services (BRS)

For further information contact:

P & T Luxembourg
Division des Postes
Unite Commercial
L-2998 Luxembourg
Tel: + 352 4088 7671
Fax: + 352 4883 94
Email: Service_Commercial_DP@EPT.lu

Domestic/international service enquiries:
Mr. Jos Roeder, Chef d'Unite

PROVIDERS OF DM AND E-M SERVICES

FLEMING FUND MANAGEMENT (LUXEMBOURG) SA
European Bank & Business Centre
6, route de Treves
Senningerberg
L-2633
Luxembourg
Tel: +352 34 10 20 92
Fax: +352 34 10 21 12
Hans Heller, European Marketing Manager

Services/Products:
Electronic media

TRANSCOM EUROPE
45 rue des Scillas
Howald
2529
Luxembourg
Tel: +352 40 14 21000
Fax: +352 40 14 21500
Email:
   dider.gausset@transcom.ikt.com
Web: www.transcom-europe.com
Didier Gausset, Pan European Sales and Marketing Manager

Services/Products:
Telemarketing agency; Call centre services/systems

Member of:
FEDMA

SERVICES/PRODUCT LISTING

Call centre services/systems
Transcom Europe

Electronic media
Fleming Fund Management (Luxembourg) SA

Telemarketing agency
Transcom Europe

NETHERLANDS

Population: 15.8 million
Capital: Amsterdam
Language: Dutch

GDP: $318 billion
GDP per capita: $20,707
Inflation: 2.0 per cent

Currency: Guilder (G/fl) = 100 cents
Exchange rate: G2.05 : $1 (G2.20 : 1 euro)

Time: GMT +1 hour

OVERVIEW

The Netherlands is a well-developed industrial nation, with high levels of import/export activity; its trading activity on a per capita basis is exceeded in Europe only by Switzerland. Rotterdam is the largest port in the world, used by many international companies as their freight shipping gateway to Europe.

The Dutch are discerning consumers, with an eye for high-quality merchandise and competitive price. They are an educated nation, with over half the population speaking English – the highest percentage in continental Europe. Technology has been embraced in the home, with recent statistics showing that 44 per cent of Dutch households own a computer.

Direct marketing in the Netherlands is well developed. PDMS figures show that, after a low of 43 items in 1991, Dutch volumes of direct mail per capita have since risen steadily to a current level of 72 items – a dramatic increase to the third highest figure in Europe for 1994.

Direct Marketing in the Netherlands is well developed. In 1996, 2832 million ECU was spent on Direct Marketing, of which 60 per cent was accounted for by Direct Mail. PDMS figures show that in 1996 every Dutch person received an average of 82 pieces of addressed mail – one of the highest volumes per capita in Europe.

Lists and databases

The selection of lists available in the Netherlands is growing and there is a good range of specialized business-to-business and consumer lists available. The list quality is good and the number of undeliverables is low – varying between 1–3% for consumer lists and 2–5% for business lists. Various pan-European Lists are also available.

As well as some 300–400 consumer lists being available on the market, there are several suppliers of sophisticated targeting systems such as Omni-data, Claritas, Response Plus and Geo Market Profile, which combine geodemographic and lifestyle data. These lifestyle databases are compiled on the basis of self-completed questionnaires.

LANGUAGE AND CULTURAL CONSIDERATIONS

Dutch is spoken throughout the Netherlands and direct mailings should preferably be written in Dutch. Alternatively, English is also widely spoken – to a very high standard – thus it may be possible to include the Netherlands in an international marketing campaign conducted in English. The Dutch are known for being informal, tolerant and friendly, but they are also to the point. Quality and prices are the most important considerations to them.

LEGISLATION AND CONSUMER PROTECTION

The Dutch Robinson list, known as Antwoordnummer 666, is managed by the DMSA and holds 70,000 addresses. There is a telemarketing equivalent to the Robinson list – tel: 0800-0224666.

The DMSA has a code of conduct on data protection and direct market-ing. DMSA is also a member of the world convention of mailing preference services. It can provide stickers against door-to-door direct marketing deliveries. There is also a list for relatives of deceased persons who do not want to be contacted with the deceased person's name.

The Data Protection Act (July 1989) defines the circumstances in which data can be stored and sold. The government is currently debating the amendment of the Data Protection Act.

For further details, contact the DMSA.

THE DIRECT MARKETING ASSOCIATION

Name: Dutch Association for Direct Marketing, Distance Selling and Sales Promotion (DMSA)
Address: Weerdestein 96, 1083 GG Amsterdam
Tel: +31 20 642 95 95
Fax: +31 20 644 01 99
Year founded: The DMIN, NPOB and SPIN merged to form the DMSA on 1 January 1995
President: Theo Schellekens
Contact: Frits van Dorst or Herbert Haaij
Total staff: 15
Members: 580

Direct mail agencies	59	Telemarketing agencies	29
List brokers	14	Mail order companies	12
Handling house/Printers/DM consultants/Database agencies			29

Facilities for overseas users of direct mail

Membership: overseas companies can join the association.
Newsletter: the DMSA produces a quarterly, six-page, Dutch language newsletter.
Library: the DMSA has a library of over 300 books.
On-line information: an on-line information service is available to members.
Legal advice: the DMSA provides legal advice for both members and non-members on the first steps to understanding the market.
Business liaison service: the association produces three extremely high-quality guides to agencies and suppliers in the region: DM agencies; telemarketing agencies; lettershops and fulfilment houses. Free on request to both members and non-members. They also put potential venture partners in touch.
Other facilities: the DMSA also offers seminars and a series of lectures covering a range of topics.

POSTAL SERVICES

The PTT Post is one of the most innovative and dynamic postal services in the world. Being a subsidiary of TNT Post Group, which has local offices in 200 countries, it has the size, expertise and facilities to help you reach new customers and expand your operations across the world. The TNT Post Group is listed at the stock exchanges of Amsterdam, New York, London and Frankfurt. As a private company, the PTT Post is competitive, cost-effective and adds value by integrating complementary quality services along the way. Within PTT Post, PTT Post International is specialized in a range of distribution and value-added services for companies wishing to target foreign markets. It offers advice and services on the following aspects of International Direct Mail:

- *Addresses*: International Formats and Lists.
- *Database services*: such as data-entry, maintenance and enhancement.
- *Country specific issues* such as cultural characteristics and holidays, business customs, direct marketing infrastructure, buying habits, mailing tips, language and other issues to consider.
- *International Business Reply Service.*
- *Handling of document streams*: which includes data processing, printing, enveloping and other fulfilment services.
- *Transport and distribution*: including legal and postal requirements.
- *Response handling.*
- *Global Collect*: a service designed to make the collection of international payments more efficient and cost-effective, creating substantial financial and marketing benefits.
- *Bulk volume discounts*: subject to prescribed sorting and bundling, will qualify for discounts. Contractual discounts are available for large volume mailers.

For Dutch Domestic Direct Marketing Services, PTT Post International works closely together with another division of the PTT Post: PTT Post Mediaservice. They are innovative and rapidly growing from a mainly direct mail organization to an almost full service direct marketing organization. PTT Post Mediaservice is considered a major player within the Netherlands in the fields of direct communication strategy, databased marketing and top-quality distribution. Through a network of ten regional offices, workshops, a wide range of specialized personal advisors and ongoing extensive research, they service the Dutch domestic market, aiming at high quality direct communication between advertisers and their clients or prospects.

For further information on any of the above, contact:

PTT Post International
Neptunusstraat 2
2132 JB Hoofddorp
P.O. Box 1992
2130 GC Hoofddorp
The Netherlands

Tel: +31 23 567 5101
Fax: +31 23 562 5384
Email: ppi_lo@wxs.nl
Website: www.ptt-post.nl

PROVIDERS OF DM AND E-M SERVICES

24/7 MEDIA EUROPE
Herengracht 444
Amsterdam
1017BZ
Netherlands
Tel: +31 20 5247 812
Fax: +31 20 5247 850
Web: www.247europe.com

Services/Products:
Database services; Interactive media;
List services; Response analysis
bureau; Service bureau

E-Services:
Email list provider; E-Marketing
consultant; Online/e-marketing agency

Member of:
DMA (US); National DMA

ACCESS24 EUROPEAN TELEMARKETING
Overtoom 519–521
Amsterdam
1054 LH
Netherlands
Tel: +31 20 607 0888
Fax: +31 20 607 0991
Email: info@access24.nl
Web: www.emis.nl\\access24
Ruud Geensen, Business Unit
Manager

Services/Products:
Fulfilment and sampling house;
Telemarketing agency; Direct
marketing agency; Response analysis
bureau; Call centre services/systems

Member of:
FEDMA

ADVOCATENKANTOOR GEERLING
PO Box 19352
Amsterdam
NL-1000 GJ
Netherlands
Tel: +31 20 622 19 44
Fax: +31 20 626 05 57
G. J. Ribbink

ALBRACHT GROEP BV
P.O. Box 53
Montfoort
3417 ZH
Netherlands
Tel: +31 348 479 600
Fax: +31 348 470 129
Email: groep@albracht.com

Web: www.albracht.com
Frans Moraal

Services/Products:
Lettershop; Fulfilment and sampling
house; Service bureau; Personalisation;
Software supplier

Member of:
FEDMA

AMERICAN EXPRESS SERVICES EUROPE LTD
Amsteldijk 166
Amsterdam
NL-1079 LH
Netherlands
Tel: +31 20 504 84 03
Fax: +31 20 504 80 01
Sabine Riezebos, European
Telemarketing

Services/Products:
Catalogue producer; Mail order
company; Publisher

ANWB MEDIA
Wassenaarseweg 220
The Hague
2596 EC
Netherlands
Tel: +31 70 314 61 91
Fax: +31 70 324 25 09
Cees de Jong,
Hoofd Advertentie-Exploitatie

Services/Products:
Catalogue producer

Member of:
FEDMA

ARCHITECTS IN MARKETING INFORMATICS (AMI)
PO Box 75961
Amsterdam
1070 AZ
Netherlands
Tel: +31 20 3053 111
Fax: +31 20 3053 222
Email: info@amitimes.com
Web: www.amitimes.com

Services/Products:
Database services; Consultancy
services; Direct marketing agency; List
services; Personalisation; Training/
recruitment

E-Services:
E-Marketing consultant;
Online/e-marketing agency

Member of:
National DMA

ASPEN DIRECT BV
Gebouw Byzantium
Stadhouderskade 14C
Amsterdam
1054 ES
Netherlands
Tel: +31 20 683 5301
Fax: +31 20 685 3871
Paul van der Starre, Managing
Director

Services/Products:
Advertising Agency

Member of:
DMA (US)

AVERY DENNISON
P.O. Box 118
Hazerswoude
2394 ZG
Netherlands
Tel: +31 71 342 15 00
Fax: +31 71 342 15 94
Email: vanessa.goedkoop@
averydennison.com
Vanessa Goedkoop, Marketing
Manager

Services/Products:
Direct marketing agency; Market
research agency; Sales promotion
agency

Member of:
FEDMA

BRIDGE 'ADMP
PO Box 77777
Amsterdam
1070 MS
Netherlands
Tel: +31 20 5046800
Fax: +31 20 5046888
Email: jan.7b@bridge-admp.nl
Web: www.optionsteam.com
Jan Zevenbergen, Director

Services/Products:
Advertising Agency; Database services;
Telemarketing agency; Direct
marketing agency; Sales promotion
agency; Electronic media

E-Services:
Website design

Member of:
FEDMA

CCN GROUP NEDERLAND BV
Savannahweg 17
Utrecht
3542 AW
Netherlands
Tel: +31 30 241 7111

Fax: +31 30 241 7100
Peter Smit, Marketing Director

Services/Products:
Fulfilment and sampling house;
Database services; Consultancy
services; Response analysis bureau;
Service bureau

CHESS CONSULTING
PO Box 2355
Leiden
2301 CJ
Netherlands
Tel: +31 71 566 1280
Fax: +31 71 566 1279
Email: chessx@wxs.nl
Xavier Gregory Layre, Managing
    Director

Services/Products:
Database services; Direct marketing
agency; Response analysis bureau;
Sales promotion agency

Member of:
FEDMA

CLARITAS NEDERLAND
Hoge Rijndokl 201
Zoeterwoude
2382 AK
Netherlands
Tel: +31 71 581 1111
Fax: +31 71 581 1118
Email: info-nl@claritaseu.com
Andre van Remmerden, Managing
    Director

Services/Products:
List services; Database services;
Consultancy services; Response
analysis bureau

Member of:
FEDMA

COHEN & PARTNERS
Van IJsendijkstraat 154
Purmerend
1442 LC
Netherlands
Tel: +31 299 41 83 70
Fax: +31 299 41 80 70
Han Cohen, General Manager

Services/Products:
Direct marketing agency

Member of:
FEDMA

**CONTINENTAL MAIL
    PROCESSING BV**
Elementenstraat 9–11
Amsterdam
1014 AR

Netherlands
Tel: +31 20 581 1999
Fax: +31 20 581 1991
Th. Clarke, Director

Services/Products:
Direct marketing agency

Member of:
FEDMA

**CORDENA CALL
    MANAGEMENT**
PO Box 16037
Den Haag
2500 BA
Netherlands
Tel: +31 70 3051755
Fax: +31 70 3051756
Email: info@cordena.com
Web: www.cordena.com
Carien van der Laan

Services/Products:
Database services; Telemarketing
agency; Call centre services/systems

Member of:
FEDMA; DMA (US)

**CREATIVE DIRECT
    MARKETING
    INTERNATIONAL, LTD**
Jupiterstraat 1–3
Hoofddorp
2132 HC
Netherlands
Tel: +31 23 562 9444
Fax: +31 23 555 3197
Email: info@cdmi.nl
Web: www.cdr-cdmi.com
Mrs. J. Eesmann-Foster, Vice President
    European Operations

Services/Products:
Consultancy services; Direct marketing
agency; List services; Specialised in
fundraising for non-profit
organisations

Member of:
FEDMA; DMA (US); National DMA;
DDV

DATA COMPANY BV
Eerste Van Der Helststraat 8
Amsterdam
1072 NV
Netherlands
Tel: +31 20 5715 700
Fax: +31 20 5715 701
Email: info@data-company.nl
Marja Klomp, Managing Director

Services/Products:
Database services; Response analysis
bureau; Service bureau; Legal services

Member of:
FEDMA

DATUS/CAK B.V.
Postbus 2613
Ravenswade 94–96
Nieuwegein
3439 LD
Netherlands
Tel: +31 30 281 67 67
Fax: +31 30 289 11 02
Email: rarenhaarsman@datus.nl
Web: www.datus.nl
Paul Cornelisse, Director

Services/Products:
Lettershop; Fulfilment and sampling
house; Database services; Mailing/
Faxing services; Service bureau

Member of:
FEDMA

**DC – DIRECT
    COMMUNICATIONS VENK
    BV**
Hoogstraat 300
Eindhoven
5654 NH
Netherlands
Tel: +31 40 2524800
Fax: +31 40 2525919
Email: dc-nl@iaehv.nl
Web: www.red-key.de/dc
Saskia de Leeuw

Services/Products:
List services; Database services; Direct
marketing agency; Service bureau;
Mailing/Faxing services

Member of:
FEDMA

**DERKS. STAR. BUSMANN.
    HANOTIAU**
P.O. Box 74773
Amsterdam
1070 BT
Netherlands
Tel: +31 20 301 63 01
Fax: +31 20 301 6333
G.J. Ribbink

Services/Products:
Legal services

Member of:
FEDMA

DIRECT COMPANY
Stadhouderskade 79
PO Box 74705
1070 BS Amsterdam
Netherlands
Tel: +31 20 751 5580
Fax: +31 20 751 5581

Email: jenny.elissen@tbwa.nl
Web: www.direct-company.nl
Jenny Elissen, Strategy Director

Services/Products:
Interactive media; Consultancy
services; Copy adaptation; Database
services; Design/graphics/clip art
supplier; Call centre services/systems

E-Services:
E-Marketing consultant; Website
design; Email software; Online/
e-marketing agency

Member of:
DMA (US); FEDMA; National DMA;
VEA

DIRECT INSURANCE
PROJECTS BV
Postbus 9070
Amstelveen
1180 MB
Netherlands
Tel: +31 20 640 3561
Fax: +31 20 640 35 91
Bert De Lange, Director

Services/Products:
Direct marketing agency

Member of:
FEDMA

DIRECT MARKETING
NETWORK
Takkebijsters 19 a
Breda
4817 BL
Netherlands
Tel: +31 76 5733733
Fax: +31 76 5712412
Email: dmnbv@worldonline.nl
Geert-Jan Vintges, Marketing Director

Services/Products:
Telemarketing agency; Call centre
services/systems

Member of:
FEDMA

DIRECT MEDIA
INTERNATIONAL
Laapersveld 27A
Hilversum
1213 VB
Netherlands
Tel: +31 35 623 6237
Fax: +31 35 623 6179
Azwin Ressang, Managing Director

Services/Products:
List services; Direct marketing agency

DIRECTVIEW BV
Takkebijsters 3A
Breda
4817 LN
Netherlands
Tel: +31 76 571 99 99
Fax: +31 76 571 87 87
Email: btob@directview.nl
Gert J. Laurman, Director

Services/Products:
List services; Database services;
Telemarketing agency; Service bureau

Member of:
FEDMA

DMC INTERNATIONAL LTD
Jupiterstraat 1–3
Hoofddorp
2132 HC
Netherlands
Tel: +31 23 555 6555
Fax: +31 23 555 3185
Email: infofedma@dmc-int.com
Web: www.dmc-int.com
Jim Foster, Director, European
Operations

Services/Products:
List services; Database services; Direct
marketing agency

Member of:
FEDMA

DMI SERVICE NEDERLAND BV
Eikenderweg 88
Heerlen
6411 VM
Netherlands
Tel: +31 45 571 77 75
Fax: +31 45 574 37 74
Email: ibc6401@cuci.nl
Patricia Schmalschläger, Managing
Director

Services/Products:
List services; Fulfilment and sampling
house; Direct marketing agency;
Response analysis bureau; Mail order
company

Member of:
FEDMA

DMP DIRECT MARKETING
PRESS BV
Zoutverkopersstraat 7
Zwÿndrecht
3334 KJ
Netherlands
Tel: +31 786 102 355
Fax: +31 786 101 540
Jim Domingo, Managing Director

Services/Products:
Lettershop; Response analysis bureau;
Service bureau

DUN & BRADSTREET
BUSINESS MARKETING
SERVICES
Postbus 278
Rotterdam
3000 AG
Netherlands
Tel: +31 10 400 9430
Fax: +31 10 400 9262
Email: bmsnl@dbnederland.nl
Web: www.dunandbrad.co.uk
Agnes Lugtenberg, Corporate
Development Consultant

Services/Products:
List services; Database services; Direct
marketing agency

Member of:
FEDMA

DYNAMIC ZONE – LEO
BURNETT
Buitenveldertselaan 106
Amsterdam
1081 AB
Netherlands
Tel: +31 20 504 61 61
Fax: +31 20 504 61 51
E K Greven

Services/Products:
Advertising Agency; Database services
Direct marketing agency; Design/
graphics/clip art supplier; Media
buying agency; Electronic media

E-Services:
Website design

Member of:
FEDMA; DMSA

E&R MANAGEMENT BV
Seyditz Straat 1
Axel
4571 PR
Netherlands
Tel: +31 114 650 645
Fax: +31 11 4650 830
Eric Poelmann, Owner

Services/Products:
Consultancy services

Member of:
DMA (US)

EDM BROKING &
MANAGEMENT B.V.
Zijlweg 199
Haarlem
NL-2015 CK

Netherlands
Tel: +31 235 530 501
Fax: +31 235 530 505
Email: info@edm.nl
Web: www.edm.nl
Fanneke Verlind, International Account
  Manager

Services/Products:
List services; Merge/purge

E-Services:
Email list provider; E-Marketing
consultant

Member of:
FEDMA; DMA (US); National DMA

EDM RELATIONSHIP
MARKETING B.V.
Zijlweg 199
Haarlem
NL-2015 CK
Netherlands
Tel: +31 23 553 1090
Fax: +31 23 553 1091
Email: info@edm.nl
Web: www.edm.nl
Jan Evers, Director

Services/Products:
Consultancy services; Direct marketing
agency; Direct mail production

Member of:
FEDMA; DMA (US); National DMA

EIS INTERNATIONAL INC
Snipweg 3
Schiphol-Zuid
1118 DN
Netherlands
Tel: +31 20 316 1350
Fax: +31 20 316 1351
Web: www.eisi.com
Catharina Willemse-Nyberg

Services/Products:
Telemarketing agency; Hardware
supplier; Software supplier; Call centre
services/systems

Member of:
FEDMA

EURO MAIL IT SERVICES BV
Postbus 501
Coenecoop 210
Gouda
2800 AM
Netherlands
Tel: +31 182 645 645
Fax: +31 18 264 0424
E.N.M. Renckens, Account Manager

Services/Products:
Database services; Mailing/Faxing
services; Service bureau; Print services

Member of:
FEDMA

EVERS DIRECT MARKETING
Kruisweg 615
Hoofddorp
NL-2132 NB
Netherlands
Tel: +31 20 653 1063
Fax: +31 20 653 2940
G. Jan Evers, President

Services/Products:
List services; Direct marketing agency;
Mail order company

EXPERIAN NEDERLAND BV
Savannahweg 17
Utrecht
3542 AW
Netherlands
Tel: +31 30 241 71 11
Fax: +31 30 241 71 00
Email: utrecht@experian.nl
Web: www.experian.nl
Hans Gillis, Marketing Director

Services/Products:
Database services; Response analysis
bureau; Service bureau; Software
supplier; Call centre services/systems

Member of:
FEDMA

FCA! WERNER & MESSELINK
Noordhollandstraat 71
Amsterdam
1081 AS
Netherlands
Tel: +31 20 646 1525
Fax: +31 20 5171531
Email: b.werner@fcagroep.nl
Bea Werner, Managing Director

Services/Products:
Advertising Agency; Database services;
Direct marketing agency; Sales
promotion agency; Electronic media

E-Services:
Website design

Member of:
FEDMA

GRAYDON-MARKTSELECT
Hoge Hilweg 6
Amsterdam
NL-1101 CC
Netherlands
Tel: +31 20 56 79 768
Fax: +31 20 69 13 520
Jan Barnhoorn, Executive Vice
  President

Services/Products:
Telemarketing agency

HEMELS VAN DER HART
Postbus 3147
Utrecht
3502 GC
Netherlands
Tel: +31 30 2898888
Fax: +31 30 2829998
Email: mail@hvdh.nl
Web: http://www.hvdh.nl
Pieter Hemels, Managing Director

Services/Products:
Direct marketing agency; Advertising
Agency; Interactive media; Electronic
media

E-Services:
E-Marketing consultant; Online/e-
marketing agency

Member of:
FEDMA

HEMELS WEYERS VAN DER
HART BV
Weerwal 11
PO Box 282
Purmerend
NL-1440 AG
Netherlands
Tel: +31 299 422 052
Fax: +31 299 421 050
Pieter Hemels, Managing Director

Services/Products:
Advertising Agency; Direct marketing
agency; Media buying agency; Sales
promotion agency

HULSINK DIRECT MARKETING
PO Box 92
Almelo
NL-7600 AB
Netherlands
Tel: +31 546 543 430
Fax: +31 546 543 444
Susan Boyle, VP Marketing & Sales

Services/Products:
Telemarketing agency; Direct
marketing agency

Member of:
DMA (US)

IMPRESS BV
PO Box 303
Woerden
NL-3440 AH
Netherlands
Tel: +31 348 43 31 44
Fax: +31 348 43 29 98
J.M.A. Halkes, Managing Director

Services/Products:
Fulfilment and sampling house;
Labelling/envelope services; Service
bureau; Electronic media; Internet
services

E-Services:
Website design

Member of:
FEDMA; DMA (US); DMSA

INDIGO EUROPE
P.O. Box 1653
Maastricht
6201 BR
Netherlands
Tel: +31 43 356 56 56
Fax: +31 43 356 56 00
Web: www.indigonet.com
Harvey Nadin, Customer Business
  Development Manager, Europe

Services/Products:
Personalisation; Print services

Member of:
FEDMA

INTERDIRECT NETWORK
Amstelstein House
PO Box 55
Ouderkerk a/d Amstel
NL-1190 AB
Netherlands
Tel: +31 20 496 5465
Fax: +31 20 496 5231
Clive Payne, Secretariat Manager

Services/Products:
Copy adaptation

KERN, HABBEMA & YAP BV
De Boelelaan 859
Amsterdam
NL-1082 RW
Netherlands
Tel: +31 20 642 99 55
Fax: +31 20 642 32 61
Diederik Habbema, Managing
  Director

Services/Products:
Direct marketing agency; Sales
promotion agency

KPN TELECOM
  TELECOMMERCE
P.O. Box 30150
The Hague
2500 GD
Netherlands
Tel: +31 70 3438105
Fax: +31 70 3434459
Email: w.visscher@kpn.com
Willem Visscher

Services/Products:
Response analysis bureau; Service
bureau; Electronic media; Internet
services

E-Services:
Website design

Member of:
FEDMA

L & W DIRECT
  COMMUNICATIONS
Marsstraat 21–23
PO Box 432
Hoofddorp
NL-2130 AK
Netherlands
Tel: +31 235 633 744
Fax: +31 235 630 455
Ria Lamsma

Services/Products:
Advertising Agency; Database services;
Direct marketing agency; Mail order
company

LANS MARKETING BV
Westerkade 7
Rotterdam
NL-3016 CL
Netherlands
Tel: +31 10 436 16 26
Fax: +31 10 4362 125
Carl Lockefeer, Director

Services/Products:
Fulfilment and sampling house;
Database services; Direct marketing
agency; Response analysis bureau;
Software supplier

LIVINGSTONES STRATEGIC
  BUSINESS SYSTEMS
PO Box 3111
Hoofddorp
NL-2130 KL
Netherlands
Tel: +31 23 5687 400
Fax: +31 23 5636 948
Joyce du Pont, Manager - Customer
  Service

Services/Products:
Database services

LOYALTY PROF BV C/O
  COUNTDOWN BENELUX
Korte Muiderweg 2A - P.O. Box 5097
De Muiderpoort
Weesp
1380 GB
Netherlands
Tel: +31 294 43 14 55
Fax: +31 294 43 21 81
Email: info@countdown.nl

Web: www.countdown.nl
Piet Hein Dankelman, Director

Services/Products:
Personalisation; Card pack
manufacturer; Response analysis
bureau

Member of:
FEDMA

MAILFAST
Hoogoorddreef 62
Amsterdam Zuidoost
NL-1101 BE
Netherlands
Tel: +31 20 652 52 52
Fax: +31 20 652 53 14
Brian Hardie

Services/Products:
Private delivery services

MAILPOINT INTERNATIONAL
  BV
Dollard 30
1454 Av Watergang
Amsterdam
1000 BE
Netherlands
Tel: +31 20 436 1654
Fax: +31 20 436 3390
Ton Vermey, Maria Lopez Ballasiurus,
  Ronald Sivoeks, Senior Vice
  Presidents

Services/Products:
Lettershop

MARKE-TEL TELEMARKETING
  SERVICES BV
Groniwgensinger 81
Arnhem
6803 AB
Netherlands
Tel: +31 26 8808 808
Fax: +31 26 880882
Email: info@marketel.nl
Web: www.marketel.nl
Marcel Barink, President

Services/Products:
Telemarketing agency; Call centre
services/systems; Database services;
Mailing/Faxing services; Market
research agency

E-Services:
Website design

Member of:
FEDMA; National DMA

MARKETING SCIENCE
Weena 290
Rotterdam
3012 NJ

Netherlands
Tel: +31 10 2821 635
Fax: +31 10 2820583
Email: jbirken@marketingscience.com
Jos Birken, Managing Director

Services/Products:
Database services; Media buying
agency; Market research agency; Sales
promotion agency; Mailing/Faxing
services; Electronic media

E-Services:
Website design

Member of:
FEDMA

MCCANN DIRECT
Startbaan 8a
Amstelveen
1185 XR
Netherlands
Tel: +31 20 54 30 519
Fax: +31 20 54 30 515
Email: peter.rijcken@mccann.nl
Peter Rijcken

Services/Products:
Direct marketing agency

Member of:
FEDMA; DMSA

MEDIA DEVELOPMENT
SERVICES
Hoogstraat 8
Abcoude
1391 BS
Netherlands
Tel: +31 294 285 760
Fax: +31 294 285 419
Email: mds@wxs.nl
Jan Soede, Director

Services/Products:
List services

Member of:
FEDMA

MEDIA PARTNERSGROUP BV
P.O. Box 2215
Amstelveen
1180 EE
Netherlands
Tel: +31 20 547 3548
Fax: +31 20 547 3559
Dick Suèr, Managing Director

Services/Products:
Database services; Electronic media

E-Services:
Website design

Member of:
FEDMA

MICROWAREHOUS BV
Postbus 90281
Amsterdam
1006 BG
Netherlands
Tel: +31 20 355 1600
Fax: +31 20 355 1699

Services/Products:
Catalogue producer; Mail order
company

Member of:
DMSA

MSP ASSOCIATES
Oranje Nassaulaan 35
Amsterdam
1075 AJ
Netherlands
Tel: +31 20 679 3077
Fax: +31 20 679 2224
Email: info@mspa.nl
Web: www.mspa.nl
Wil G. Wurtz

Services/Products:
Database services; Direct marketing
agency

Member of:
FEDMA

NEDERLANDSE
POSTORDERBOND
Postbus 75959
Amsterdam
NL-1070 AZ
Netherlands
Tel: +31 20 517 1212
Fax: +31 20 517 1299

Member of:
FEDMA; DMSA

OGILIVYONE
COMMUNICATIONS
PO Box 846
Amsterdam
1000 AV
Netherlands
Tel: +31 20 521 65 65
Fax: +31 20 521 65 60
Herman de Haan, Managing Director

Services/Products:
Database services; Telemarketing
agency; Direct marketing agency;
Consultancy services; Electronic media

E-Services:
Website design

Member of:
DMA (US); DMSA

OMNIDATA VOF
Hogehilweg 17
Amsterdam
1100 DJ
Netherlands
Tel: +31 20 567 88 00
Fax: +31 20 567 88 99
Email: info@omnidata.nl
Web: www.omnidata.nl
B.G. ter Weele, Director

Services/Products:
List services; Database services; Direct
marketing agency; Service bureau;
Software supplier

Member of:
FEDMA

ORDA-B NEDERLAND BV
Pelmolenlaan 1
Woerden
NL-3447 GW
Netherlands
Tel: +31 348 435 500
Fax: +31 348 416 497
Ernst Blok, Account Manager

Services/Products:
Database services; Labelling/envelope
services; Response analysis bureau;
Service bureau

OTS GROUP
P.O. Box 192
Zaltbommel
5300 AD
Netherlands
Tel: +31 418577777
Fax: +31 418577788
Email: info@otsgroup.nl
Graham Rhind

Services/Products:
Database services; Telemarketing
agency; Direct marketing agency;
Service bureau

Member of:
FEDMA; DMA (US)

OUTPOST BV
Nicolaas Maesstraat 120
Amsterdam
1071 RH
Netherlands
Tel: +31 20 6764 966
Fax: +31 20 6735 611
Email: info@outpost.nl
Edwin De Jager

Services/Products:
List services; Database services; Direct
marketing agency; Response analysis
bureau

Member of:
FEDMA

PIETER VAN DEN BUSKEN BV ADVERTISING & DIRECT MARKETING

Burg. Stramanweg
Ouderkerke/Amstel
1190 AB
Netherlands
Tel: +31 20 496 46 51
Fax: +31 20 496 40 81
Email: busken@euronet.nl
Web: www.busken.nl
Pieter van den Busken, Managing
  Director

Services/Products:
Advertising Agency; Consultancy
services; Copy adaptation; Database
services; Design/graphics/clip art
supplier; Electronic media

E-Services:
Website design

Member of:
FEDMA; DMSA

PRECISION FULFILLMENT SERVICES BV

P.O. Box 1661
Maastricht
6201 BR
Netherlands
Tel: +31 464 370 789
Fax: +31 464 370 783
Susana Gorissen, General Manager

Services/Products:
Fulfilment and sampling house;
Telemarketing agency; Response
analysis bureau; Service bureau; Mail
order company

Member of:
FEDMA

PRESS GROUP

P.O. Box 303
Woerden
3440 AH
Netherlands
Tel: +31 348 43 31 44
Fax: +31 348 43 29 98
Email: info@impress.nl
Web: www.impress.nl
Koos Halkes, Director

Services/Products:
Fulfilment and sampling house;
Database services; Mailing/Faxing
services; Service bureau;
Personalisation

Member of:
FEDMA

PRISMA DIRECT

Postbox 7503
Leeuwarden
8903 JM
Netherlands
Tel: +31 58 2800 345
Fax: +31 58 2800 008
Email: info@prismadirect.com
Web: www.prismadirect.com
Marco van Damme, Manager

Services/Products:
Database services; Direct marketing
agency; Fulfilment and sampling
house; Lettershop; Mail order
company; Personalisation; Plastic
cards; International customer loyalty
programmes

E-Services:
E-Marketing consultant; Online/e-
marketing agency

Member of:
FEDMA

PROGRESSIVE IMPRESSIONS INTERNATIONAL

Kronehoefstraat 64
Eindhoven
5622 AC
Netherlands
Tel: +31 4029 72828
Fax: +31 4029 72823
Email: cmpalm@piieurope.nl
Carol-Mart Palm, Marketing & Sales
  Manager Europe

Services/Products:
Consultancy services; Database
services; Design/graphics/clip art
supplier; Direct marketing agency;
Personalisation; Print services

E-Services:
E-Marketing consultant; Website
design; Online/e-marketing agency

Member of:
FEDMA

PSI DIRECT RESPONSE BV

Entrada 134
Amsterdam
1096 EB
Netherlands
Tel: +31 20 495 38 38
Fax: +31 20 600 34 96
Email: psiadam@worldonline.nl
Jan Krol, Managing Director

Services/Products:
List services; Mailing/Faxing services;
Direct marketing agency; Copy
adaptation; Consultancy services

Member of:
FEDMA; DMSA

PTT POST INTERNATIONAL

P.O. Box 1992
Hoofddorp
2130 GC
Netherlands
Tel: +31 23 567 5989
Fax: +31 23 555 34 02
Email: ppi_lo@wxs.nl
Web: www.ptt-post.nl
Sales Departmemt

Services/Products:
Fulfilment and sampling house;
Mailing/Faxing services; Labelling/
envelope services; Service bureau;
Translation services

Member of:
FEDMA; DMSA

PTT TELECOM BV MARKETING

ARC A 528
Maanweg 174
The Hague
NL-2516 AB
Netherlands
Tel: +31 70 343 21 45
Fax: +31 70 343 94 06
Susan Boyle, Manager Applicatie
  Marketing

Services/Products:
Telemarketing agency

PUBLICIS GROUP

PO Box 75499
Amsterdam
1070 AL
Netherlands
Tel: +31 205712222
Diederik Habbema, Managing
  Director

Services/Products:
Direct marketing agency; Sales
promotion agency

Member of:
FEDMA

RAPP + COLLINS BV

Leestraat 12
Baarn
3743 EJ
Netherlands
Tel: +31 2154 24616
Fax: +31 2154 17058
D. Vink, Managing Director

Services/Products:
Advertising Agency

RDMS DIRECT MARKETING BV
P.O. Box 30249
Arnhem
6803 AE
Netherlands
Tel: +31 263 242 121
Fax: +31 263 242 124
Email: postbox@rdms.com
Web: www.rdms.com
Henk Wassenaar, Commercial Director

Services/Products:
List services; Database services;
Service bureau

Member of:
FEDMA

REMARK REINSURERS MARKETING BV
Bavinckstaete
Prof. J.H. Bavincklaan 5
Amstelveen
NL-1183 AT
Netherlands
Tel: +31 20 647 44 80
Fax: +31 20 643 65 28
Peter Boerrigter, Manager, Marketing
   Projects

Services/Products:
Direct marketing agency

RM SERVICE BV
Pallasweg 11
Leeuwarden
8938 AP
Netherlands
Tel: +31 582800345
Fax: +31 582800008
Email: rmsdm@rmsdm.com
Ed van Damme, Director

Services/Products:
Lettershop; Fulfilment and sampling
house; Database services; Mailing/
Faxing services; Personalisation

Member of:
FEDMA

ROTO SMEETS BV
PO Box 2215
Amstelveen
NL-1180 EE
Netherlands
Tel: +31 20 547 3548
Fax: +31 20 547 3559
Dick Suèr, Managing Director

Services/Products:
Consultancy services; Publisher;
Electronic media; Internet services

Member of:
DMSA

SATURN B.V. EUROPE
Zekeringstraat 43H
Amsterdam
1014 BV
Netherlands
Tel: +31 20 400 33 22
Fax: +31 20 686 28 55
Email: fverbaas@compuserve.com
Web: www.saturcorp.com
Frans B. Verbaas, Marketing & Sales
   Director, Europe

Services/Products:
Database services; Response analysis
bureau; Service bureau

Member of:
FEDMA

SCAN LASER BV
Postbus 257
Zaandam
1500 EG
Netherlands
Tel: +31 75 631 0030
Fax: +31 75 616 6108
Frank Tol, Managing Director

Services/Products:
Database services; Response analysis
bureau; Service bureau; Publisher;
Electronic media; Internet services

Member of:
DMSA

SCHOBER HFS DIRECT MARKETING BV
Rechtzaad 15
Roosendaal
4703 RC
Netherlands
Tel: +31 165 59 57 00
Fax: +31 165 55 79 17
Email: verkoop@schober.nl
Web: www.schober.nl
Flip van der Kooij, Director

Services/Products:
List services; Mailing/Faxing services

Member of:
FEDMA

SNT HOLDING BV
Blauw-Roodlaan 100
Zoetermeer
2718 SJ
Netherlands
Tel: +31 79 368 6970
Fax: +31 79 361 5958
Email: info@snt.nl
Web: www.snt.nl
Tobias Walraven, CEO

Services/Products:
Database services; Telemarketing
agency; Call centre services/systems

Member of:
FEDMA

STRATING ACTIVE MARKETING DIRECT
Emmaplein 8
Amsterdam
1075 AW
Netherlands
Tel: +31 20 6767 578
Fax: +31 02 0673 3257
Marty Bogers, Business Director

Services/Products:
Advertising Agency; List services;
Database services; Direct marketing
agency; Sales promotion agency

TELE DYNAMICS BV
Pritnerweg 10
Amersfort
3821 AD
Netherlands
Tel: +31 334536200
Fax: +31 334536299
Email: info@teledynamics.nl
Web: www.teledynamics.nl
Ruud van Oostveen, Director

Services/Products:
Telemarketing agency; Hardware
supplier; Software supplier; Call centre
services/systems

Member of:
FEDMA

TESSELAAR BV
Kennemerplein 2
Haarlem
2011 MJ
Netherlands
Tel: +31 23 542 1313
Fax: +31 23 542 1242
Email: info@tesselaar.nl
Web: www.tesselaar.nl
Lenhard Los, Marketing & Sales
   Manager

Services/Products:
Call centre services/systems

Member of:
FEDMA; National DMA; WGCC

TNT
PO Box 23269
Amsterdam
1100 DT
Netherlands
Tel: +31 20 5008000
Fax: +31 20 5009000
Email: richard.thomas@tntpost.com

Web: www.tnt.com
Richard Thomas

Services/Products:
International Mailing Services

TNT POST GROUP
Diemerhof 24a
Diemen
1112 XN
Netherlands
Tel: +31 20 3989672
Fax: +31 20 3989671
Pieter Mohr, Project Manager

Services/Products:
Mailing/Faxing services

Member of:
FEDMA

VAN WISSEN TELEMARKETING BV
Oranjesingel 2a
Nijmegen
6511 NS
Netherlands
Tel: +31 243 240 422
Fax: +31 243 236 247
Barbara H van Wissen, Director

Services/Products:
Telemarketing agency

Member of:
FEDMA

VDBJ/COMMUNICATIE GROEP BV
PO Box 215
Bloemendaal
2060 AE
Netherlands
Tel: +31 23 541 1701
Fax: +31 23 541 1801
JJW (Sak) van den Boom, General
   Manager

Services/Products:
Publisher

Member of:
FEDMA

VENTURE OPPORTUNITY COMPANY
Noord Crailoseweg 16
Huizen
NL-1272 RE
Netherlands
Tel: +31 35 691 34 05
Fax: +31 35 693 65 91
Pieter de Jong

Services/Products:
Direct marketing agency

VIERHAND BV
PO Box 1620
Haarlem
NL-2003 BR
Netherlands
Tel: +31 235 176 262
Fax: +31 235 316 699
Rv.d. Horst, Manager

Services/Products:
List services; Database services;
Mailing/Faxing services; Lettershop

E-Services:
Email list provider

Member of:
National DMA

WAGENAAR PROJEKTEN & PUBLICATIONS BV
Postbus 487
Bussum
1400 AL
Netherlands
Tel: +31 35 692 07 47
Fax: +31 35 692 07 67
Email: wage@euronet.nl
Ewald Wagenaar, Director

Services/Products:
Advertising Agency; Direct marketing
agency; Copy adaptation; Print
services

Member of:
FEDMA

WALSH NEDERLAND BV
Rooseveltweg 15
Almere
NL-1314 SJ
Netherlands
Tel: +31 36 538 5750
Fax: +31 36 538 5650
Jan Marc Gozeling, Manager
   Operations

Services/Products:
List services; Fulfilment and sampling
house; Mailing/Faxing services;
Response analysis bureau

WEGENER DIRECT MARKEING GROEP
Wattbaan 1
PO Box 2700
Nieuwegein
3430 GC
Netherlands
Tel: +31 30 600 2000
Fax: +31 30 600 2629
Gerad van Hoeven, Managing Director

Services/Products:
List services; Database services; Direct
marketing agency

Member of:
DMA (US)

WEHKAMP BV
Postbus 400
Zwolle
8000 AK
Netherlands
Tel: +31 38 973 457
Fax: +31 38 973 493
Th. JA Schellekens, Managing Director

Services/Products:
Lettershop

Member of:
DMA (US)

WUNDERMAN CATO JOHNSON
4th Floor
Frans Van Mierisstraat 92
Amsterdam
1071 RZ
Netherlands
Tel: +31 20 570 642
John Bingle, CEO (Worldwide)

Services/Products:
Advertising Agency; Direct marketing
agency

Member of:
DMA (US)

SERVICES/PRODUCT LISTING

Advertising Agency
Aspen Direct BV
Bridge 'ADMP
Dynamic Zone – Leo Burnett
FCA! Werner & Messelink
Hemels Van Der Hart
Hemels Weyers Van Der Hart BV
L & W Direct Communications
Pieter Van Den Busken BV Advertising
   & Direct Marketing
Rapp + Collins BV
Strating Active Marketing Direct
Wagenaar Projekten & Publications BV
Wunderman Cato Johnson

Call centre services/systems
Access24 European Telemarketing
Cordena Call Management
Direct Company
Direct Marketing Network
EIS International Inc
Experian Nederland BV
Marke-Tel Telemarketing Services BV
SNT Holding BV
Tele Dynamics BV
Tesselaar BV

Card pack manufacturer
Loyalty Prof BV C/O Countdown
  Benelux

Catalogue producer
American Express Services Europe Ltd
Anwb Media
MicroWarehous BV

Consultancy services
Architects in Marketing Informatics
  (AMI)
CCN Group Nederland BV
Claritas Nederland
Creative Direct Marketing
  International, Ltd
Direct Company
E&R Management BV
EDM Relationship Marketing b.v.
Ogilivyone Communications
Pieter Van Den Busken BV Advertising
  & Direct Marketing
Progressive Impressions International
Psi Direct Response BV
Roto Smeets BV

Copy adaptation
Direct Company
Interdirect Network
Pieter Van Den Busken BV Advertising
  & Direct Marketing
Psi Direct Response BV
Wagenaar Projekten & Publications BV

Database services
24/7 Media Europe
Architects in Marketing Informatics
  (AMI)
Bridge 'ADMP
CCN Group Nederland BV
Chess Consulting
Claritas Nederland
Cordena Call Management
Data Company BV
Datus/Cak B.V.
DC – Direct Communications Venk
  BV
Direct Company
Directview BV
DMC International Ltd
Dun & Bradstreet Business Marketing
  Services
Dynamic Zone – Leo Burnett
Euro Mail It Services BV
Experian Nederland BV
FCA! Werner & Messelink
L & W Direct Communications
Lans Marketing BV
Livingstones Strategic Business
  Systems
Marke-Tel Telemarketing Services BV
Marketing Science
Media Partnersgroup BV

MSP Associates
Ogilivyone Communications
Omnidata Vof
Orda-B Nederland BV
OTS Group
Outpost BV
Pieter Van Den Busken BV Advertising
  & Direct Marketing
Press Group
Prisma Direct
Progressive Impressions International
RDMS Direct Marketing BV
RM Service BV
Saturn B.V. Europe
Scan Laser BV
SNT Holding BV
Strating Active Marketing Direct
Vierhand BV
Wegener Direct Markeing Groep

Design/graphics/clip art supplier
Direct Company
Dynamic Zone – Leo Burnett
Pieter Van Den Busken BV Advertising
  & Direct Marketing
Progressive Impressions International

Direct mail production
EDM Relationship Marketing b.v.

Direct marketing agency
Access24 European Telemarketing
Architects in Marketing Informatics
  (AMI)
Avery Dennison
Bridge 'ADMP
Chess Consulting
Cohen & Partners
Continental Mail Processing BV
Creative Direct Marketing
  International, Ltd
DC – Direct Communications Venk
  BV
Direct Insurance Projects BV
Direct Media International
DMC International Ltd
DMI Service Nederland BV
Dun & Bradstreet Business Marketing
  Services
Dynamic Zone – Leo Burnett
EDM Relationship Marketing b.v.
Evers Direct Marketing
FCA! Werner & Messelink
Hemels Van Der Hart
Hemels Weyers Van Der Hart BV
Hulsink Direct Marketing
Kern, Habbema & Yap BV
L & W Direct Communications
Lans Marketing BV
Mccann Direct
MSP Associates
Ogilivyone Communications

Omnidata Vof
OTS Group
Outpost BV
Prisma Direct
Progressive Impressions International
Psi Direct Response BV
Publicis Group
Remark Reinsurers Marketing BV
Strating Active Marketing Direct
Venture Opportunity Company
Wagenaar Projekten & Publications BV
Wegener Direct Markeing Groep
Wunderman Cato Johnson

Electronic media
Bridge 'ADMP
Dynamic Zone – Leo Burnett
FCA! Werner & Messelink
Hemels Van Der Hart
Impress BV
KPN Telecom Telecommerce
Marketing Science
Media Partnersgroup BV
Ogilivyone Communications
Pieter Van Den Busken BV Advertising
  & Direct Marketing
Roto Smeets BV
Scan Laser BV

Fulfilment and sampling house
Access24 European Telemarketing
Albracht Groep BV
CCN Group Nederland BV
Datus/Cak B.V.
DMI Service Nederland BV
Impress BV
Lans Marketing BV
Precision Fulfillment Services BV
Press Group
Prisma Direct
Ptt Post International
RM Service BV
Walsh Nederland BV

Hardware supplier
EIS International Inc
Tele Dynamics BV

Interactive media
24/7 Media Europe
Direct Company
Hemels Van Der Hart

International Mailing Services
TNT

International customer loyalty programmes
Prisma Direct

Internet services
Impress BV
KPN Telecom Telecommerce

Roto Smeets BV
Scan Laser BV

Labelling/envelope services
Impress BV
Orda-B Nederland BV
Ptt Post International

Legal services
Data Company BV
Derks. Star. Busmann. Hanotiau

Lettershop
Albracht Groep BV
Datus/Cak B.V.
DMP Direct Marketing Press BV
Mailpoint International BV
Prisma Direct
RM Service BV
Vierhand BV
Wehkamp BV

List services
24/7 Media Europe
Architects in Marketing Informatics
  (AMI)
Claritas Nederland
Creative Direct Marketing
  International, Ltd
DC – Direct Communications Venk
  BV
Direct Media International
Directview BV
DMC International Ltd
DMI Service Nederland BV
Dun & Bradstreet Business Marketing
  Services
EDM Broking & Management b.v.
Evers Direct Marketing
Media Development Services
Omnidata Vof
Outpost BV
Psi Direct Response BV
RDMS Direct Marketing BV
Schober Hfs Direct Marketing BV
Strating Active Marketing Direct
Vierhand BV
Walsh Nederland BV
Wegener Direct Markeing Groep

Mail order company
American Express Services Europe Ltd
DMI Service Nederland BV
Evers Direct Marketing
L & W Direct Communications
MicroWarehous BV
Precision Fulfillment Services BV
Prisma Direct

Mailing/Faxing services
Datus/Cak B.V.
DC – Direct Communications Venk
  BV

Euro Mail It Services BV
Marke-Tel Telemarketing Services BV
Marketing Science
Press Group
Psi Direct Response BV
Ptt Post International
RM Service BV
Schober Hfs Direct Marketing BV
TNT Post Group
Vierhand BV
Walsh Nederland BV

Market research agency
Avery Dennison
Marke-Tel Telemarketing Services BV
Marketing Science

Media buying agency
Dynamic Zone – Leo Burnett
Hemels Weyers Van Der Hart BV
Marketing Science

Merge/purge
EDM Broking & Management b.v.

Personalisation
Albracht Groep BV
Architects in Marketing Informatics
  (AMI)
Indigo Europe
Loyalty Prof BV C/O Countdown
  Benelux
Press Group
Prisma Direct
Progressive Impressions International
RM Service BV

Plastic cards
Prisma Direct

Print services
Euro Mail It Services BV
Indigo Europe
Progressive Impressions International
Wagenaar Projekten & Publications BV

Private delivery services
Mailfast

Publisher
American Express Services Europe Ltd
Roto Smeets BV
Scan Laser BV
VDBJ/Communicatie Groep BV

Response analysis bureau
24/7 Media Europe
Access24 European Telemarketing
CCN Group Nederland BV
Chess Consulting
Claritas Nederland
Data Company BV

DMI Service Nederland BV
DMP Direct Marketing Press BV
Experian Nederland BV
KPN Telecom Telecommerce
Lans Marketing BV
Loyalty Prof BV C/O Countdown
  Benelux
Orda-B Nederland BV
Outpost BV
Precision Fulfillment Services BV
Saturn B.V. Europe
Scan Laser BV
Walsh Nederland BV

Sales promotion agency
Avery Dennison
Bridge 'ADMP
Chess Consulting
FCA! Werner & Messelink
Hemels Weyers Van Der Hart BV
Kern, Habbema & Yap BV
Marketing Science
Publicis Group
Strating Active Marketing Direct

Service bureau
24/7 Media Europe
Albracht Groep BV
CCN Group Nederland BV
Data Company BV
Datus/Cak B.V.
DC – Direct Communications Venk
  BV
Directview BV
DMP Direct Marketing Press BV
Euro Mail It Services BV
Experian Nederland BV
Impress BV
KPN Telecom Telecommerce
Omnidata Vof
Orda-B Nederland BV
OTS Group
Precision Fulfillment Services BV
Press Group
Ptt Post International
RDMS Direct Marketing BV
Saturn B.V. Europe
Scan Laser BV

Software supplier
Albracht Groep BV
EIS International Inc
Experian Nederland BV
Lans Marketing BV
Omnidata Vof
Tele Dynamics BV

Specialised in fundraising for non-profit organisations
Creative Direct Marketing
  International, Ltd

Telemarketing agency

Access24 European Telemarketing
Bridge 'ADMP
Cordena Call Management
Direct Marketing Network
Directview BV
EIS International Inc
Graydon-Marktselect
Hulsink Direct Marketing
Marke-Tel Telemarketing Services BV
Ogilivyone Communications
OTS Group
Precision Fulfillment Services BV
PTT Telecom BV Marketing
SNT Holding BV
Tele Dynamics BV
Van Wissen Telemarketing BV

Training/recruitment

Architects in Marketing Informatics
(AMI)

Translation services

Ptt Post International

E-SERVICES

E-Marketing consultant

24/7 Media Europe
Architects in Marketing Informatics
(AMI)
Direct Company
EDM Broking & Management b.v.
Hemels Van Der Hart
Prisma Direct
Progressive Impressions
International

Email list provider

24/7 Media Europe
EDM Broking & Management b.v.
Vierhand BV

Email software

Direct Company

Online/e-marketing agency

24/7 Media Europe

Architects in Marketing Informatics
(AMI)
Direct Company
Hemels Van Der Hart
Prisma Direct
Progressive Impressions International

Website design

Bridge 'ADMP
Direct Company
Dynamic Zone – Leo Burnett
FCA! Werner & Messelink
Impress BV
KPN Telecom Telecommerce
Marke-Tel Telemarketing Services
BV
Marketing Science
Media Partnersgroup BV
Ogilivyone Communications
Pieter Van Den Busken BV Advertisin
& Direct Marketing
Progressive Impressions
International

NORWAY

Population: 4.4 million
Capital: Oslo
Languages: Norwegian and Lappish

GDP: $151 billion
GDP per capita: $34,780
Inflation: 2.6 per cent

Currency: Norwegian Krone (NKr) = 100 ore
Exchange rate: NKr7.65 : $1 (NKr 8.22 : 1 euro)

Time: GMT +1 hour

OVERVIEW

Norway has one of the smallest European populations, yet one of the wealthiest. While small in absolute terms, the 1996 economy provided inhabitants with the fourth highest GDP per capita in the world. With recent economic constraints now largely overcome, Norway is set to deliver one of the highest growth rates in Europe.

A relative newcomer to direct marketing, Norway has developed a buoyant DM industry, representing 35 per cent of its total advertising budget. Direct mail in particular has shown a tremendous increase. With print advertising in magazines and newspapers in drastic decline since 1987, most marketers rely on direct marketing for a more accountable and measurable way of doing business.

The most active users of direct mailings domestically are publishers; photo finishers; cosmetics firms; charity organizations; insurance companies; and general mail order/cataloguers. Indicators show that overall attitudes to the medium are positive. Mail order customers are becoming increasingly loyal, and business-to-business mailers are finding the same loyalty developing. Add to this an efficient local post office and the gradual improvement of in-house databases, and you have a recipe for a very healthy market.

SET YOUR SIGHTS ON

SCANDINAVIA

24 million population . . . Most affluent consumers in Europe
World class infrastructure . . . World's most wired Internet Community
Gateway to Eastern Europe
And the Scandinavian Postal Companies' One Stop Solution...

THE SCANDINAVIAN OPPORTUNITY

Imagine a market with 24 million consumers with strong purchasing power. A market where the standard of living is the highest in the world and the individual has a large disposable income. A market where 60% of the consumers have access to a personal computer and where people use the Internet and cellular phones more than anywhere in the world. A market where customers are informed, up to date, always willing to try new things, and therefore often used as test market for new products.

That market consists of consumers with the best attitude towards Catalog and e-Commerce shopping in Europe. And your business can get established there quickly.

The climate in the region fluctuates quite a bit from north to south and distances can be far from one town to the next. As a result building a strong infrastructure has been a priority. Far distances has also made Scandinavia highly suited for Catalog and e-Commerce business. More than 60% of Scandinavians have made a mail order purchase at one time or another. This is the highest number in Europe! Further more Scandinavia will make an excellent base, should you decide to expand your business to the rest of Europe, including Russia.

YOU WILL ONLY NEED ONE PARTNER TO MAKE YOUR START-UP IN SCANDINAVIA FAST AND EASY.

One Stop Solution is a collaboration service between the Swedish, Danish, Finnish and Norwegian Postal Services. Four of the most reliable postal Services in the world. One Stop Solution provides you with one partner who gives you the opportunity to test the Scandinavian market with minimum risk involved. The process is fast.

Contact us now and we will handle the rest!

	Denmark	Finland	Norway	Sweden
	Jens Nielsen	Niina Juura	Kjersti Østlund	Linda Gustafssen
Tel:	+45 33 75 47 71	+358 20 451 54 17	+47 23 14 83 85	+46 8 781 79 33
Fax:	+45 33 75 47 03	+358 20 451 5363	+47 22 42 66 87	+46 8 781 44 74
e-mail:	jni@post.dk	niina.juura@posti.fi	kjersti.ostlund@posten.no	linda.gustafssen@posten.se

There are, however, a number of negatives to the Norwegian market. Total market size, at 1.8 million households, is obviously an issue. Postal rates are among the highest in Europe. C-post is the most economical of the postal services, but mailings must be addressed to postboxes, where they exist, rather than street addresses.

The Norwegian DM industry has learned to work with all of the above and the market continues to surge ahead. It is a small market, but potentially a highly loyal and profitable one for the assiduous international mailer.

Lists and databases

The quality of both business and consumer lists is good in Norway. Nixies (returned mail) represent only 1.5 to 2.5 per cent for the largest and leading business lists (approximately 220,000 companies). In order to maintain the high quality of the lists, the list buyer is compensated for the pieces of mail that are returned. This is a common technique for keeping lists up-to-date. Nixies for consumer lists vary from 2 to 10 per cent. Returns of less than 5 per cent is most common. If the return mail exceeds more than 5 per cent, a discount can be negotiated with the list broker. Consumer lists comprise a total of three million names, and there are about 100 different lists on the market. However, neither public nor government lists are available.

LANGUAGE AND CULTURAL CONSIDERATIONS

Although Norwegian is spoken by the vast majority of the population, the Lapp language, Finno-Ugric, is spoken in the more rural northern areas. Danish, Swedish and English are understood by most of the population. A direct marketing campaign would be best conducted in Norwegian.

LEGISLATION AND CONSUMER PROTECTION

The Norwegian Data Inspectorate was established in 1978. Data protection legislation was introduced in June of the same year and became valid in January 1980.

The following regulations apply:

- Permission to operate as a direct marketing service firm, such as a list broker or computer house, must be obtained from the Norwegian Data Inspectorate;
- All broking of lists must be reported to the Data Inspectorate;
- Transfer of lists abroad must be approved in advance by the Data Inspectorate;
- Source (name of list owner) must be printed on labels or promotional material;

- List owners are required by law to remove names upon request from persons who do not wish to receive promotional material. These names must not be rented to other companies;

- Companies are required to disclose personal information about consumers to those individuals who request it (does not apply to any type of medical records);

- Insurance and banking sectors are required to obtain permission from the Data Inspectorate when registering individuals' personal information; list rental selections can only be made in the following variables: sex, geography (city and city code), and age (date of birth).

Generally the registration of sensitive information is prohibited, so a special concession is necessary for lists with this sort of data.

THE DIRECT MARKETING ASSOCIATION

Name: Norwegian Direct Marketing Association (NORDMA)
Address: Box 117 Lilleaker, N-0216 Oslo
Tel: +47 22 51 08 90
Fax: +47 22 51 08 95
Year founded: 1989
Chairman: Espen Fodstad
Members: 120

NORDMA is a small association, with a range of facilities for its members and interested parties.

Meetings are held four times a year with guest speakers on pertinent topics; the meetings also provide a discussion and networking forum. A conference is held annually, typically for some 600 participants, and is followed by an awards ceremony for the industry.

NORDMA produces a guide and a directory of members.

POSTAL SERVICES

Norway Post offers the following services:

- *A-Post*: a high-priority service, delivered by air to most national destinations overnight.

- *B-Post*: designed for mailings of 20 or more letters, B-Post is delivered by surface transport, and may take three days to be delivered within the local area, or five days to more remote areas.

- *C-Post*: addressed C-Post is bulk mail with low postage rates, requiring a minimum of 500 items to qualify. Delivery, however, is 5 weekdays for local areas, or 5-9 weekdays for outlying areas.

- *'Kundepost'*: a service with postal rates lower than C-Post, for companies which regularly send advertising publications, newsletters or business publications. Special authorization is required; details from Norway Post, address below.

- *International bulk delivery service*: available for Nordic countries and Germany.

- *Unaddressed bulk mail*: all letters must be of the same weight, format and packaging.

- *International business reply service*: a no-cost-to-responder service, to stimulate consumer response.

Other services

Posten DM is a division of Norway Post BA. It is responsible for the development, production and sale of services for Direct marketing in Norway Post. In addition it is responsible for fulfilment services enhancing the value of distribution services. Services offered include:

Target-group selection

- *Address services*: can define target groups or geographic areas
- *Business addresses*: the database contains more than 200,000 postal addresses to companies, organizations, and public institutions.
- *Demographic selection*: for unaddressed mail distributed to pre-defined target groups.
- *Postal codes*: to help companies keep their customer, member, or subscriber data bases updated with correct postal code.

Printing and packaging

- *Addressed mail*: printing on envelopes, and printing of sales letters or reply cards; enveloping; plastic wrapping.
- *Unaddressed mail*: pre-handling; sorting; packaging; label print; enveloping; plastic wrapping.

Reply handling

Data from questionnaires, Direct Mail, application forms, reply forms etc. can be scanned, registered, interpreted, verified, and transferred to the customer's database.

Database management and campaign analysis

Services include storing lists, updating and selection. In addition there are facilities for campaign surveys and analysis by Norsk Gallup in co-operation with Norway Post, Posten DM.

For further information, please contact:

Posten DM
Verkseier Furulundsvei 10b
N-0645 Oslo

Tel: +47 23 14 87 00
Fax: +47 23 14 87 87
Email: posten.dm@posten.no

Customer Service: +47 810 00 710

or you can contact:
Norway Post International
PO Box 1181 Sentrum
N-0107 Oslo
Norway

Tel: +47 23 148 021
Fax: +47 22 426 687
Website: www.posten.no

PROVIDERS OF DM AND E-M SERVICES

AFTENPOSTEN
Postboks 1178 Sentrum
Oslo 1
N-0107
Norway
Tel: +47 22 86 30 00
Fax: +47 22 42 63 25
Email: aftenposten@aftenposten.no
Web: www.aftenposten.no
Bente Aasebo, Marketing Manager

Services/Products:
Publisher

Member of:
NORDMA

AKERSHUS REKLAME TEAM AS
Industriv. 29, pb. 209
Skedsmokorset
2020
Norway
Tel: +47 63 87 94 15
Fax: +47 63 87 97 86
Email: abruun@online.no
Arne Bruun, Marketing

Services/Products:
Mailing/Faxing services; Print services

ARA TRAINING AS
Ole Deviksv, 4
Oslo
666
Norway
Tel: +47 23 03 96 00
Fax: +47 23 03 96 01
Email: bs@ara.no
Web: www.ara.no
Bent Slyngstad

Services/Products:
Training/recruitment; Training/recruitment

DIREKTE MARKEDSFORING KOMPETANSE AS (DM KOMPETANSE AS)
Briskebyveien 48 (visitor address)
PO Box 2713 Solli
Oslo
204
Norway
Tel: +47 22 54 06 10
Fax: +47 22 54 06 11
Email: vivi.landaasodm-kompetanse.no
Vivi Landaas

Services/Products:
List services; Consultancy services; Design/graphics/clip art supplier; Media buying agency; Response analysis bureau

DM DISTRIBUSJON A/S
Industriv. 9
Grimstad
N-4895
Norway
Tel: +47 37 25 02 00
Fax: +47 37 04 43 84
Sven Berg, Marketing

Services/Products:
Advertising Agency; Lettershop; Lettershop

Member of:
DMA (US); NORDMA

DM HUSET
Postboks 1419 Vika
Oslo
115
Norway
Tel: +47 22476700
Fax: +47 22476995
Email: dmhu.et@dmhuset.no
Kristin Lien, International Project Manager

Services/Products:
List services; Fulfilment and sampling house; Database services; Direct marketing agency; Consultancy services

DMB&B CLARION
Postboks 405 Skoyen
Oslo
212
Norway
Tel: +47 22 125200
Fax: +47 22 12 52 83
Email: klara.opdahl@dmbb.no
Klara Opdahl, Account Director

Services/Products:
Mailing/Faxing services; Market research agency; Direct marketing agency; Sales promotion agency; Electronic media

E-Services:
Website design

Member of:
FEDMA; DMA (US); NORDMA

DUN & BRADSTREET NORGE AS
Okernv, 145, pb. 34
Okern
Oslo
508

Norway
Tel: +47 22 91 52 00
Fax: +47 22 91 53 03
Email: info@dbn.no
Web: www.dbn.no
Karin Friis

Services/Products:
List services

GENNARO AS
Storg, 2, pb 60
Jessheim
2051
Norway
Tel: +47 63 97 30 00
Fax: +47 63 97 34 34
Email:
    gennaro@ullensaker.mail.telia.com
Terje Sorlie

Services/Products:
Telemarketing agency; Call centre services/systems

GRANADA AS
Svinesundv. 336, pb 145
Halden
1751
Norway
Tel: +47 69 19 50 00
Fax: +47 69 19 50 04
Email: granada@granada.no
Kathrine Garder Andersen

Services/Products:
Fulfilment and sampling house

LEO BURNETT DIREKTE A/S
Drammensveien 130
Oslo
277
Norway
Tel: +47 22 92 69 00
Fax: +47 22 92 69 55
Ina Riklter-Svendsen, Account Director

Services/Products:
Advertising Agency; Direct marketing agency

Member of:
FEDMA; DMA (US); NORDMA

MEDIACOM DIALOG
PO Box 8904
Youngstorget
Oslo
28
Norway
Tel: +47 2291 1000
Fax: +47 2291 1010
Email: knut.westgaard@mediacom.no
Mr. Knut Westgaard

Services/Products:
Database services; Direct marketing agency; Consultancy services; Direct response TV services; Electronic media; Internet services

E-Services:
Website design

NATURPOST NORGE AS
PB 256 Alnabru
Oslo
614
Norway
Tel: +47 2230 4530
Fax: +47 2232 8410
Email: naturpost@naturpost
Ingrid DeLong Grimshei

Services/Products:
List services; Database services; Telemarketing agency; Software supplier; Catalogue producer; Mailing/Faxing services

NORWAY POST
Verkseier Furulunds Vei 10
Posten DM
Oslo
645
Norway
Tel: +47 23146147
Fax: +47 23148787
Email: posten.dm@posten.no
Web: www.posten.no
Bjorn Petter Kjolo, Managing Director

Services/Products:
Response analysis bureau; Mailing/Faxing services; Plastic wrap facilities

Member of:
FEDMA; NORDMA

NTK AS
P O Box 34
Gjerorum
N-2022
Norway
Tel: +47 63 93 5200
Fax: +47 63 93 52 55
Johannes Havia, Managing Director

Services/Products:
Telemarketing agency

OGILVYONE WORLDWIDE LTD
Sorkedalsveien 10 A
Oslo
369
Norway
Tel: +47 22 56 85 95
Fax: +47 22 46 10 35
Web: www.ogilvy.com
Sindre Baardson, Managing Director

Services/Products:
Database services; Telemarketing agency; Direct marketing agency; Media buying agency

Member of:
FEDMA; NORDMA

POST PAKKING AS
Nordkilen 6
POB 1418
Fredrikstad
N-1602
Norway
Tel: +47 693 51180
Fax: +47 693 51190
Email: firmapost@postpakking.no
Web: www.postpakking.no
Geir Sletbakk, Manager

Services/Products:
Lettershop; Database services; Labelling/envelope services; Direct marketing agency; Consultancy services

PUBLICIS DIRECT
Bygdoy Alle 4
Oslo
257
Norway
Tel: +47 22 12 48 00
Fax: +47 22 56 25 55
Email: morten@publicis.no
Web: www.publicis.no
Morten Svensen, Managing Director

Services/Products:
Database services; Direct marketing agency; Design/graphics/clip art supplier; Electronic media

E-Services:
Website design

Member of:
FEDMA; NORDMA

REAL DEAL DDB/RAPP COLLINS NORWAY
Majorstuen
P.O. Box 7084,Majorstuen
Oslo
306
Norway
Tel: +47 22 59 32 00
Fax: +47 22 59 32 39
Email: svarod@realdeal.no
Oystein Svarod, Creative Director

Services/Products:
Advertising Agency; Fulfilment and sampling house; Database services; Direct marketing agency; Copy adaptation; Electronic media

E-Services:
Website design

Member of:
FEDMA; NORDMA

SANDBERG A/S
P.O. Box 105, Kjelsås
Frysjaveien 40
Oslo
411
Norway
Tel: +47 22 58 68 00
Fax: +47 22 58 68 01
Email: bjarne.Solberg@sandberg.no
Web: www.sandberg.no
Bjarne Solberg, Managing Director

Services/Products:
List services; Lettershop; Mailing/Faxing services; Service bureau

Member of:
FEDMA; DMA (US); NORDMA

SELEKTIV A/S
P.O. 4333 Torshov
Oslo
402
Norway
Tel: +47 22 046500
Fax: +47 22 046501
Kristian Halvorsen, Managing Director

Services/Products:
List services; Fulfilment and sampling house; Telemarketing agency; Direct marketing agency; Service bureau

Member of:
FEDMA; DMA (US); NORDMA

STROEDE DATA AS
Trollásv, 2
Kolbotn
1411
Norway
Tel: +47 66 81 86 00
Fax: +47 66 81 86 01
Email: lars.larsson@stroede.se
Web: www.stroede.se
Lars Bertil Larsson, Marketing

Services/Products:
List services; Fulfilment and sampling house; Mailing/Faxing services; Response analysis bureau; Service bureau

TELENOR DIREKTE AS
Thomasdalen 7
Servicebox 477
Gjovik
2801
Norway
Tel: +47 6113 0100

Fax: +47 6117 6260
Trond Arne Aas, Managing Director

Services/Products:
Call centre services/systems; Database
services; Mailing/Faxing services; Print
services; Direct marketing agency;
Telemarketing agency

Member of:
National DMA

**TELEPERFORMANCE NORGE
AS**
Sam Eydes g. 40, pb 98
Notodden
3671
Norway
Tel: +47 35 01 29 00
Fax: +47 35 01 24 88
Email: tpn@teleperformance.no
Web: www.tprinternational.com
Arlld Reinersten

Services/Products:
Telemarketing agency; Market research
agency

VOX PROSJEKT AS
Dronningensg. 8 a
Oslo
152
Norway
Tel: +47 22 31 79 00
Fax: +47 22 31 79 00
Email: firmapost@vox.no
Vigdis Elise Hansen

Services/Products:
Direct marketing agency

SERVICES/PRODUCT LISTING

Advertising Agency
DM Distribusjon A/S
Leo Burnett Direkte A/S
Real Deal Ddb/Rapp Collins Norway

Call centre services/systems
Gennaro AS
Telenor Direkte AS

Catalogue producer
Naturpost Norge AS

Consultancy services
Direkte Markedsforing Kompetanse
    AS (DM Kompetanse AS)
DM Huset
MediaCom Dialog
Post Pakking AS

Copy adaptation
Real Deal Ddb/Rapp Collins Norway

Database services
DM Huset
MediaCom Dialog
Naturpost Norge AS
Ogilvyone Worldwide Ltd
Post Pakking AS
Publicis Direct
Real Deal Ddb/Rapp Collins Norway
Telenor Direkte AS

**Design/graphics/clip art
    supplier**
Direkte Markedsforing Kompetanse
    AS (DM Kompetanse AS)
Publicis Direct

Direct marketing agency
DM Huset
Dmb&B Clarion
Leo Burnett Direkte A/S
MediaCom Dialog
Ogilvyone Worldwide Ltd
Post Pakking AS
Publicis Direct
Real Deal Ddb/Rapp Collins Norway
Selektiv A/S
Telenor Direkte AS
Vox Prosjekt AS

Direct response TV services
MediaCom Dialog

Electronic media
Dmb&B Clarion
MediaCom Dialog
Publicis Direct
Real Deal Ddb/Rapp Collins Norway

Fulfilment and sampling house
DM Huset
Granada AS
Real Deal Ddb/Rapp Collins Norway
Selektiv A/S
Stroede Data AS

Internet services
MediaCom Dialog

Labelling/envelope services
Post Pakking AS

Lettershop
DM Distribusjon A/S
Post Pakking AS
Sandberg A/S

List services
Direkte Markedsforing Kompetanse
    AS (DM Kompetanse AS)
DM Huset

Dun & Bradstreet Norge AS
Naturpost Norge AS
Sandberg A/S
Selektiv A/S
Stroede Data AS

Mailing/Faxing services
Akershus Reklame Team AS
Dmb&B Clarion
Naturpost Norge AS
Norway Post
Sandberg A/S
Stroede Data AS
Telenor Direkte AS

Market research agency
Dmb&B Clarion
Teleperformance Norge AS

Media buying agency
Direkte Markedsforing Kompetanse
    AS (DM Kompetanse AS)
Ogilvyone Worldwide Ltd

Plastic wrap facilities
Norway Post

Print services
Akershus Reklame Team AS
Telenor Direkte AS

Publisher
Aftenposten

Response analysis bureau
Direkte Markedsforing Kompetanse
    AS (DM Kompetanse AS)
Norway Post
Stroede Data AS

Sales promotion agency
Dmb&B Clarion

Service bureau
Sandberg A/S
Selektiv A/S
Stroede Data AS

Software supplier
Naturpost Norge AS

Telemarketing agency
Gennaro AS
Naturpost Norge AS
NTK AS
Ogilvyone Worldwide Ltd
Selektiv A/S
Telenor Direkte AS
Teleperformance Norge AS

Training/recruitment
Ara Training AS

E-SERVICES

Website design
Dmb&B Clarion
MediaCom Dialog
Publicis Direct
Real Deal Ddb/Rapp Collins Norway

PORTUGAL

Population: 9.9 million
Capital: Lisbon
Language: Portuguese

GDP: $105 billion
GDP per capita: $10,600
Inflation: 2.3 per cent

Currency: Portuguese Escudo (Esc) = 100 centavos
Exchange rate: Esc186.48 : $1 (Esc200.46 : 1 euro)

Time: GMT +1 hour

OVERVIEW

Portugal is one of the smallest of the European economies. The country has gradually been moving away from a traditional economy to an increasingly industrialized and modernized country, and with a continuous economic growth. The consumer demand for goods and services is expected to rise as standards of living improve.

Potrtugal has only become an active DM nation within the last eight or nine years. There are indications, however, that Portugese advertisers are increasingly using direct mail, with PDMS figures showing a rise from 5 units of direct mail per capita in 1991 to 7 units in 1997.

The choice of local suppliers of DM services is limited, but international agencies are increasingly moving in on the market, and service companies will presumably develop to meet the growing need.

LANGUAGE AND CULTURAL CONSIDERATIONS

For business purposes, Portugese, English, Spanish and French are used.

LEGISLATION AND CONSUMER PROTECTION

There have been several recent changes in the Portugese DM market. An example of this is the Portugese law No. 67/98 concerning the protection of individuals against the unauthorized use of personal data. The Directive No. 95/46/CE, related to personal data protection, approved by the European Parliament and Council on 24th October 1995, has now been included in the Portugese Legislation.

THE DIRECT MARKETING ASSOCIATION

Name: Associacão Portuguesa de Marketing Directo (AMD)
Address: Estrada Nacional 117–1, No91, Valejas, P-2795
                 Linda-a-Velha
Tel: +351 1 436 6727
Fax: +351 1 436 7845
Year founded: 1987
President: Jorge d'Orey Pinheiro
Total staff: 2
Members: 22
Contact: João Novais de Paula

Direct mail agencies	4	Handling houses	3
List brokers	4	Others	11

Facilities for overseas users of direct mail

Membership: overseas companies can join the AMD – there are no minimum standards, but members accept the codes of ethics. The organization is still in the early years of its establishment.
Newsletter: the AMD publishes a newsletter.
Library: there is no library.
On-line information service: there is no on-line information service.
Legal advice: this service is available to members only.
Business liaison service: the AMD provides details of accredited suppliers and also helps members in finding local venture partners for a DM project.

POSTAL SERVICES

The CTT – Correios de Portugal institution is an anonymous society, in which the Portuguese government is the major partner. It is inserted on the communications sector and is regulated by an external entity, the ICP – Instituto de Communicaçães de Portugal.

Its main activities are correspondences, philately, orders and postal financial services. CTT – Correios de Portugal also works with urgent mail, logistics and electronic postal mail, through owned enterprises.

It has around 1000 post offices and 400 postal distribution centres in the territory. We can also say that the postal traffic reaches 6.6 million objects daily.

Through the Direct Marketing Department, it offers to the enterprises complete and integrated solutions, which allow the realization of all the communications process by mail.

Discounts are based on quantity, and are available by special arrangement. To use the Direct Mail service, you must ask in advance for an authorization at the post office that is going to accept the correspondence. The request is made on a suitable document supplied by the Post Office and its presentation must be accompanied by a sample of the mailing to be sent. If the mailing is to be paid on a contract basis you also have to present one more sample of the item with the request.

Direct mail correspondences are identified by the DM symbol. Its representation must be placed on the item's cover, on the upper right corner, in a rectangular area 74mm long and 40mm high.

Direct mail can be paid either: on a contract basis, payment being made when the contract is signed or charged on an invoice sent later by the Post Office; or through a franking machine.

Services offered:

- Bulk, discounted rates for addressed/unaddressed mail
- Express mail services (EMS)
- PO Box addresses
- Registered post
- Postage paid by addressee
- Courier services
- Postal insurance
- Email services
- Printing and packaging
- Post expedition
- Domestic and international reply services
- Update of list against postal database

For further information contact:

CTT-Correios de Portugal, S.A.
Direct Marketing Department
Praça D. Luis I, 30-3
1208–148 Lisbon
Portugal
Tel: +351 21 322 94 78
Fax: +351 21 322 99 36
Email: gmkdirecto@ctt.pt
Website: www.ctt.pt/correios/marketing

Domestic service enquiries:
Carla Cruz
Direct Marketing Department Manager

International service enquiries:
José Abrantes
International Post Manager

PROVIDERS OF DM AND E-M SERVICES

ARENA DIRECT MARKETING
R. Jorge Afonso
40–1 Esp
Lisbon, 1600
Portugal
Tel: +351 1 798 8321
Fax: +351 1 795 8322

Services/Products:
Advertising Agency

CARTESIUS/PDM
Urbanizacao Matinha, Rua 2
Edificio Verde, 1' Dt'
Lisbon
P-1900
Portugal
Tel: +351 1 868 19 29
Fax: +351 1 868 21 72
Email: cartesius@cartesius.pt
Web: www.cartesius.pt
Joan Paixao, Director General

Services/Products:
List services; Fulfilment and sampling
house; Database services; Mailing/
Faxing services; Direct marketing
agency

Member of:
FEDMA

CTT - CORREIOS DE PORTUGAL; GABINETE DE MARKETING DIRECTO
Praça D. Luis I, 30–3'
Lisbon
1208–148
Portugal
Tel: +351 21 322 9479
Fax: +351 21 322 9936
Email: gmkdirecto@ctt.pt
Web: www.ctt.pt
Carlo Cruz, Director of Direct
Marketing Department

Services/Products:
Consultancy services; Mailing/Faxing
services

DIRECTIMEDIA, MARKETING DIRECTO E PROMOÇOES, LDA
Estrad Nacional 117–1 91
Valejas
Carnaxide
2799–527
Portugal
Tel: +351 21 436 6732
Fax: +351 21 436 6726

Email: directimedia@mail.telefax.pt
Sofi Novais de Paula, Marketing
Director

Services/Products:
Fulfilment and sampling house;
Labelling/envelope services;
Lettershop; List services;
Personalisation

Member of:
FEDMA; National DMA

DMP - SERVICIOS MARKETING
Rua 28 de Janeiro 350
Villa Nova de Gai, 4400
Portugal
Tel: +351 2 370 4051
Fax: +351 2 370 4273

Services/Products:
Advertising Agency

DMP - SERVIÇOS DE MARKETING E PUBLICIDADA, LDA
Rua Guerra Junqueiro, 455
Porto
4150–389
Portugal
Tel: +351 2 2605 1970
Fax: +351 2 2606 8086
Email: dmp@dmp.pt
Web: www.dmp.pt
Miguel Sousa Utto, Manager

Services/Products:
Advertising Agency; Direct marketing
agency; Service bureau

E-Services:
Website design; Online/e-marketing
agency

Member of:
DMA (US); Do Porto

MCCANN DIRECT
R. Jose Da Costa Pedreira
Lote 12
Lisbon
P-1700
Portugal
Tel: +351 1 751 7500
Fax: +351 1 751 7505
Maria José Franco

Services/Products:
Database services; Direct marketing
agency; Copy adaptation

Member of:
FEDMA

PUBLICIS PROMODIRECT
Rua Concalves Zarco
14–2 Esq
Lisboa

1400
Portugal
Tel: +351 1 301 3261
Fax: +351 1 302 0581
Ana Beiro, CEO

Services/Products:
Advertising Agency

WUNDERMAN CATO JOHNSON
Rua Soares de Passos
No 10A
Lisbon
1300
Portugal
Tel: +351 1 361 0589/90
Fax: +351 1 364 67 90
Fiona Herdman-Smith, Managing
Director

Services/Products:
Advertising Agency; Database services;
Direct marketing agency; Media
buying agency; Response analysis
bureau

Member of:
FEDMA

SERVICES/PRODUCT LISTING

Advertising Agency
Arena Direct Marketing
DMP - Servicios Marketing
DMP - Serviços de Marketing e
Publicidada, Lda
Publicis Promodirect
Wunderman Cato Johnson

Consultancy services
CTT - Correios de Portugal; Gabinete
de Marketing Directo

Copy adaptation
MCCANN Direct

Database services
Cartesius/PDM
MCCANN Direct
Wunderman Cato Johnson

Direct marketing agency
Cartesius/PDM
DMP - Serviços de Marketing e
Publicidada, Lda
MCCANN Direct
Wunderman Cato Johnson

Fulfilment and sampling house
Cartesius/PDM

Directimedia, Marketing Directo e
  Promoçoes, LDA

Labelling/envelope services
Directimedia, Marketing Directo e
  Promoçoes, LDA

Lettershop
Directimedia, Marketing Directo e
  Promoçoes, LDA

List services
Cartesius/PDM
Directimedia, Marketing Directo e
  Promoçoes, LDA

Mailing/Faxing services
Cartesius/PDM
CTT - Correios de Portugal; Gabinete
  de Marketing Directo

Media buying agency
Wunderman Cato Johnson

Personalisation
Directimedia, Marketing Directo e
  Promoçoes, LDA

Response analysis bureau
Wunderman Cato Johnson

Service bureau
DMP - Serviços de Marketing e
  Publicidada, Lda

E-SERVICES

Online/e-marketing agency
DMP - Serviços de Marketing e
  Publicidada, Lda

Website design
DMP - Serviços de Marketing e
  Publicidada, Lda

SPAIN

Population: 39.5 million
Capital: Madrid
Languages: Spanish (Castilian), Catalan,
Gallego-Galician, Basque

GDP: $563 billion
GDP per capita: $14,200
Inflation: 2.0 per cent

Currency: Peseta (Pta) = 100 centimos
Exchange rate: Pta154.76 : $1 (Pta166.44 : 1 euro)

Time: GMT +1 hour

OVERVIEW

After enjoying several years of sustained economic growth during the late
1980s and early 1990s, Spain has been struggling in recent years with the
economic difficulties of recession. Unemployment remains stubbornly high,
but with lower interest rates now taking effect a pattern of continued growth
is expected to emerge.

Spain is a relative newcomer to direct marketing, but there has been
significant growth in the use of direct mail, telemarketing and direct response television, and the country looks well placed for catching up with its
northern European neighbours in developing a modern, dynamic DM
industry. Direct marketing accounts for 25 per cent of total advertising
expenditure.

LANGUAGE AND CULTURAL CONSIDERATIONS

Most Spaniards understand Castilian, but a third of the population speaks
one of the other three official tongues: Catalan (which became an EU
language in 1990), Gallego (Galician) or Basque. English and French are
also spoken to a degree.

LEGISLATION AND CONSUMER PROTECTION

Data protection legislation was finally approved in October 1992, and proceeds towards full implementation. A Consultative Council has been set up, on which Elena Gomez, Managing Director of FECEMD (the Spanish Direct Marketing Association), has been appointed to represent the interests of the private sector.

A Robinson list has also been in operation since January 1993, managed entirely by FECEMD. In addition to carrying a Robinson list of consumers who do not wish to receive direct mail, FECEMD also compile a 'preference list' of consumers who have asked to receive more offers by mail.

All members of FECEMD are required to use the Robinson list, at no cost; non-members may use the list on payment of an annual subscription. FECEMD has also developed a code of practice for the DM industry.

THE DIRECT MARKETING ASSOCIATION

Name: Federación de Comercio Electrónico y Marketing Directo (FECEMD)
Address: Avda. Diagonal 437.5°,1a, 08036 Barcelona
Tel: +34 93 240 40 70
Fax: +34 93 201 29 88
Year founded: 1977
President: Mario Valls
Total staff: 13
Members: 265
Contact: Elena Gomez del Pozuelo, Managing Director

Direct mail agencies	25	Direct marketing consultants	5
List brokers	20	Mail order companies	46
Printers	10	Database agencies	33
Telemarketing agencies	15	New technologies	38
Big consumers	95		

Facilities for overseas users of direct mail

Membership: overseas companies can join the FECEMD and each application is examined by the Admissions Committee. Virtually all of the FECEMD's services are open to members only. Annual fees stand at 275,000 pesetas.

Newsletter: the FECEMD publishes a monthly, 16-page round-up of news, seminars and offers. It is in Castilian.

Library: the FECEMD has a library of over 100 books and thousands of press cuttings.

On-line information service: this is part of the library service.

Legal advice: the FECEMD offers advice on first steps in understanding national legislation concerning DM.

Business liaison service: the FECEMD helps business partners to find venture partners for Spanish campaigns.

Other facilities: there are also quarterly industry meetings, attended by an average of 100 members, and an annual DM awards brochure.

The FECEMD also organizes conferences and other DM events.

POSTAL SERVICES

Correos and Telégrafos is a public operator providing postal, telegraph and financial services and is also the operator responsible for the Universal Postal Service Provided throughout Spain to all citizens at economical prices and on the basis of established quality criteria.

The company reaches 17 million addresses and 2 million companies every day through 64,515 employees and 10,386 customer service points in its postal network. The volume managed by Correos and Telégrafos during last year was 5,021 million items.

The Spanish Post Office provides private individuals and companies with a wide range of products from traditional letters and express parcel services to direct mail products. The customers can also access a wide range of information and services through its web page www.correos.es.

Services offered:

- Bulk, discounted rates for addressed mail
- Express mail services (EMS)
- Business reply services (BRS)
- International business reply services
- Postage paid by addressee
- PO Box addresses
- Courier services
- Registered post
- Postal insurance
- Email services
- Printing and packaging
- Hybrid mail

Services designed for the direct mailer include:

Direct Mail
A communication consisting solely of advertising, marketing, or publicity material and comprising and identical message, except for the addressee's name, address and identifying number. Must be sent to at least 500 addresses, to be conveyed and delivered to the address indicated by the sender on the item itself or on its wrapping. Bills, invoices, financial statements and other non-identical messages shall not be regarded as direct mail.

Products
Impresos Publicatarios:

Content:	Advertising, marketing or publicity information
Max. weight:	2kg (home deliver up to 500g)
Scope:	Domestic/cross-border

Pequeño Paquete:

Content:	Advertising, marketing or publicity information combined with promotional samples or presents
Max. weight:	500 (international up to 1–2kg, dependng on country)
Scope:	Domestic/cross-border

Publicorreo:
(Introduced in 1990, its tariffs and 30% cheaper than Impreso Publicatario tariffs and it is possible to obtain discounts.)

Content:	Advertising, marketing or publicity information
Max. weight:	500
Scope:	Domestic
Customers:	Direct mail companies, mail order companies, or customers with large annual quantities of this kind of mail (150,000 items per year). Correos and Telegrafos must previously authorize these companies (under contract).

Publicorreo Plus:
(Introduced in 1999.)

Content:	Advertising, marketing or publicity information
Max. weight:	500g
Scope:	Domestic
Customers:	Direct mail companies, mail order companies, or customers with large annual quantities of this kind of mail (150,000 its per year). Correos and Telegrafos must previously authorize these companies (under contract).

International Business Reply Service (IBRS or CCRI):
(Introduced in 1990, this service stimulats response.)

For further information contact:

The Public Corporation Correos and Telegrafos
Subdirección de Marketing
Vía Dublin, n.7
Campo de las Naciones
28070-Madrid
Spain
Tel: +34 91 596 3101
Fax: +34 91 596 3133
Email: monica.espinosa@correos.es
Website: www.correos.es

Domestic service enquiries:
Valentín Pedro García Martín
Department Manager of National Service

International service enquiries:
Miguel Angel Valiente
Department Manager of International Service
Tel: +34 91 596 3155
Fax: +34 91 596 3267

PROVIDERS OF DM AND E-M SERVICES

ACCENTURE (ANTES ANDERSEN CONSULTING)
Plaza Pablo Ruiz Picasso
s/n Torre Picasso, Pl. 31
28020 Madrid
Spain
Tel: +34 91 596 6000
Fax: +34 91 596 6695
Web: www.accenture.com
Alfonso González, Socio CRM

Services/Products:
Consultancy services; Database
services; Market research agency

E-Services:
E-Marketing consultant; Website
design

ACP ELOQUENCE
Balmes, 299, 5o, 2.su
08006 Barcelona
Spain
Tel: +34 93 200 39 33
Fax: +34 93 200 36 18
Eduardo Ramos

Services/Products:
Direct marketing agency

Member of:
FECEMD

B D MAIL
Camino de Hormigueras
175 Navea 12–13
28031 Madrid
Spain
Tel: +34 91 777 72 12
Fax: +34 91 778 67 76
Juan Salmeron Simon

Services/Products:
List services; Software supplier

Member of:
FECEMD

BATES DIRECT
Goys. 8
28001 Madrid
Spain
Tel: +34 91 577 18 48
Fax: +34 91 577 45 49
Pilar Garcia

Services/Products:
Direct marketing agency

Member of:
FECEMD

CANDI CLUB
Gran Via, 32–30
20813 Madrid
Spain
Tel: +34 91 396 4519
Fax: +34 91 396 5844
Pablo Alzugaray, President

Services/Products:
Advertising Agency; Direct marketing
agency

Member of:
DMA (US)

CANON ESPANA SA
Joaquin Costa, 41
28002 Madrid
Spain
Tel: +34 91 538 45 00
Fax: +34 91 532 02 27
Eduardo Gonzalez

Services/Products:
Sales promotion agency

Member of:
FECEMD

CDC CLUB EXPRESS SA
Via Dos Castillas
33, Edif, Atica 3
Madrid
28224 Pozuelo
Spain
Tel: +34 91 352 00 46
Fax: +34 91 351 25 10
Carlos del Romero

Services/Products:
Telemarketing agency

Member of:
FECEMD

CENTRO DE ASISTENCIA TELEFONICA SA
Albasanz, 75
28037 Madrid
Spain
Tel: +34 91 396 59 00
Fax: +34 91 396 57 23
Jose M. Torres

Services/Products:
Telemarketing agency; Software
supplier; Sales promotion agency

Member of:
FECEMD

CEPSA
Avenida del Partenon, 12
Campo de las Naciones
28042 Madrid
Spain
Tel: +34 91 337 6000

Fax: +34 91 337 7205
Pablo Alzugaray, President

Services/Products:
Advertising Agency; Direct marketing
agency

Member of:
DMA (US)

CLARITAS ESPANA
Edificio Alba
Rosa de Lima, IBIS
Madrid
28290 Las Matas
Spain
Tel: +34 91 630 7130
Fax: +34 91 630 1778
Email: claritas@flashnet.es
Ernst Verbeek, Managing Director

Services/Products:
List services; Database services;
Consultancy services; Response
analysis bureau

CLUB INTERNACIONAL DEL LIBRO SA DE PROMOCION Y EDICIONES
Avda. Manoteras No. 50
28050 Madrid
Spain
Tel: +34 91 302 6240
Fax: +34 91 302 5674
Miguel Reiris Alvarez

Services/Products:
Labelling/envelope services

Member of:
DMA (US)

CP COMMUNICACION (GRUPO CONTRAPUNTO)
c/Jerez, 3
28016 Madrid
Spain
Tel: +34 91 350 9207
Fax: +34 91 345 2852
Email: alzugaray.p@cpcom.bbdo.es
Pablo Alzugaray, Managing Director

Services/Products:
Advertising Agency; Database services;
Direct marketing agency; Service
bureau; Sales promotion agency;
Electronic media

E-Services:
Website design

Member of:
DMA (US); FEDMA

CRECENDO SL
Edit Euronova
Ronda Poniente, 6
Madrid

28760 Tres Cantos
Spain
Tel: +34 91 804 02 50
Fax: +34 91 803 10 30
Ernesto Gallud

Services/Products:
List services; Telemarketing agency;
Direct marketing agency

Member of:
FECEMD

DATA SEGMENTO SL
Alcala 89–4 Izqa
28009 Madrid
Spain
Tel: +34 91 575 7076
Fax: +34 91 575 8142
Web: www.datasegmento.com
D. Angel Gonzalez

Services/Products:
List services; Database services;
Response analysis bureau

DHL INTERNACIONAL ESPANA SA
Plaza Ruiz Picasso, s/n
Torre Picasso Pta. 21
28020 Madrid
Spain
Tel: +34 91 586 77 66
Fax: +34 91 586 77 60
Alvaro Martinez-Arroyo

Services/Products:
Private delivery services

Member of:
FECEMD

DIFUSIO TELEMARKETING GRUP SL
Comte d'Urgell, 240 7o A-D
08036 Barcelona
Spain
Tel: +34 93 439 59 00
Fax: +34 93 439 29 99
Albert Olle

Services/Products:
Telemarketing agency

Member of:
FECEMD

DIMENSION MARKETING DIRECTO SL
Po del Maestro Arbos, 19
Villa Cristemanal
Guipuzcoa
20013 San Sebastian
Spain
Tel: +34 943 32 02 10
Fax: +34 943 27 82 76
Guillermo Viglionte

Services/Products:
Direct marketing agency

Member of:
FECEMD

DRAFTWORLDWIDE
C/Almagro, 36
28010 Madrid
Spain
Tel: +34 91 310 4549
Fax: +34 91 310 4840
Howard Draft, Chairman & CEO

Services/Products:
Advertising Agency; Direct marketing
agency

Member of:
DMA (US)

DUN & BRADSTREET ESPANA, SA
Salvador de Madariaga, 1. 2
28027 Madrid
Spain
Tel: +34 91 377 91 00
Fax: +34 91 377 91 01
Email: attencioncliente-es@dnb.com
Web: www.dnb.com
Javier Perez

Services/Products:
Database services

Member of:
FECEMD

EIDOS DIRECT (EIDOS IMATGE SL)
General Ricardo Ortega. 29, 1.oB
Baleares
07706 Palma de Mallorca
Spain
Tel: +34 97 146 68 11
Fax: +34 97 146 69 50
Bartomeu Garcias

Services/Products:
List services; Direct marketing agency;
Sales promotion agency

Member of:
FECEMD

FECEMD
Avenida Diagonal 437, 5°, 1a
08036 Barcelona
Spain
Tel: +34 93 240 4070
Fax: +34 93 2403134
Email: lourdes@fecemd.es
Web: www.fecemd.es
Elena Gomez, Chief Executive

Member of:
FEDMA

GISCA
Avda. Josep Tarradellea, 147. 2o, 2a
08029 Barcelona
Spain
Tel: +34 93 419 12 07/09 13
Fax: +34 93 410 68 94
Guillermo Cisneros

Services/Products:
Sales promotion agency

Member of:
FECEMD

GLOBAL DIRECT SL
Via Augusta, 59. 8sa
08006 Barcelona
Spain
Tel: +34 93 415 01 96
Fax: +34 93 218 98 39
Josep Maria Salvat

Services/Products:
Direct marketing agency

Member of:
FECEMD

GRUPO UNIDO DE PROYECTOS Y OPERACIONES SA
Avda. de Llano Castellano, 13. 4o A
Madrid
28034
Spain
Tel: +34 91 3750 791
Fax: +34 91 3272 615
Email: dperez@eurogrupo.com
Web: www.eurogrupo.com
David Pérez

Services/Products:
Advertising Agency; Catalogue
producer; Consultancy services;
Market research agency;
Personalisation; Print services

E-Services:
E-Marketing consultant; Website
design

Member of:
FECEMD

GUPOST, SA PUBLICIDAD DIRECTA
Camino Illarra, 4
San Sebastian (Gipuzkoa)
Spain
Tel: +34 43 310350
Fax: +34 43 310356
Email: info@gupost.grupogureak.com
Web: www.gupost.com

Services/Products:
Database services; Labelling/envelope
services; Lettershop; List services;
Personalisation

Member of:
FECEMD; PD&BD

HIT XOP SA
Mariano Cubi, 122
08021 Barcelona
Spain
Tel: +34 93 200 01 02
Fax: +34 93 200 16 16
Agustin Bartolome

Services/Products:
Telemarketing agency

Member of:
FECEMD

IBERPHONE SA
Agustin de Foxa, 31
28036 Madrid
Spain
Tel: +34 91 334 92 33
Fax: +34 91 334 92 56
Tomas Muriana

Services/Products:
List services; Telemarketing agency;
Sales promotion agency

Member of:
FECEMD

IDE-MARKETING S.L
Consell de Cent, 341
Pral. 2a
Barcelona
8007
Spain
Tel: +34 93 215 1519
Fax: +34 93 215 3575
Email: ide@ide-marketing.com
Web: www.ide-marketing.com
Xavier Duran

Services/Products:
Direct marketing agency; Interactive
media; Sales promotion agency;
Telemarketing agency

E-Services:
Website design; E-Marketing
consultant; Online/e-marketing agency

IDEAS FIJAS SL
Clavileno, 22
28002 Madrid
Spain
Tel: +34 91 519 85 55
Fax: +34 91 519 65 54
Francisco Ramirez

Services/Products:
Direct marketing agency

Member of:
FECEMD

IMP (DIVISION BELOW THE LINE)
Lagaaca, 88 7o
28001 Madrid
Spain
Tel: +34 91 431 48 11
Fax: +34 91 431 57 09
Victor Conde

Services/Products:
Direct marketing agency

Member of:
FECEMD

INSTRUMENTS RAPP & COLLINS
Enrique Granados, 86–88, 2.a
08008 Barcelona
Spain
Tel: +34 93 415 55 54
Fax: +34 93 415 60 84
Eduard Casammitjana

Services/Products:
Direct marketing agency

Member of:
FECEMD

LEADER LINE
Almansa, 66
Madrid
28039
Spain
Tel: +34 91 537 6700
Fax: +34 91 537 7101
Email: informacion@grupoleader.com
Web: www.grupoleader.com

Services/Products:
Telemarketing agency

E-Services:
Email software; Online/e-marketing
agency

Member of:
FECEMD; AEMT

LEADER MIX
Almansa, 66
Madrid
28039
Spain
Tel: +34 91 537 6700
Fax: +34 91 537 5665
Email: informacion@grupoleader.com
Web: www.grupoleader.com

Services/Products:
Direct marketing agency

Member of:
FECEMD; AEMT

LETTER GRAPHIC SL
Monturiol 9
Barcelona
08912 Badalona
Spain
Tel: +34 93 480 24 34
Fax: +34 93 480 24 18
Antonio Motos Martinez

Services/Products:
List services

Member of:
FECEMD

LORENTE ESTRATEOLAS DE VENTA SA
Frederic Mompou, 5
Barcelona
08960 Sant Just Desvern
Spain
Tel: +34 93 499 97 17
Fax: +34 93 499 97 18
Josep Alet

Services/Products:
Direct marketing agency

Member of:
FECEMD

MAILHOUSE SL
C/ Gonzalez Davila 18 – 6o D
E-28031 Madrid
Spain
Tel: +34 1 380 30 00
Fax: +34 91 380 20 42
Antonio Ordonez, President and CEO

Services/Products:
Lettershop; Fulfilment and sampling
house; Mailing/Faxing services; Direct
marketing agency

Member of:
FECEMD

MAILHOUSE SL
Avda Asegra, esquina c/ Sierra Nevada
18210 Peligros (Granada)
Spain
Tel: +34 958 405596
Fax: +34 958 405612
Cecilio Marin

Services/Products:
Fulfilment and sampling house;
Mailing/Faxing services

Member of:
FEDMA; FECEMD

MAILING ANDALUCIA SL
Avda. Almirante Topete, s/n
41013 Sevilla
Spain
Tel: +34 95 423 70 40

Fax: +34 95 423 07 49
Francisco Sanchez Montilla

Services/Products:
List services

Member of:
FECEMD

MAILING SHOP SA
Julian Rabanedo, 3
28045 Madrid
Spain
Tel: +34 91 468 43 82
Fax: +34 91 468 49 86
Oscar Guarido

Services/Products:
List services

Member of:
FECEMD

**MCCANN DIRECT &
    PROMOTIONS**
Po de la Castellana 165
28046 Madrid
Spain
Tel: +34 1 570 58 09
Fax: +34 1 571 93 96
Juan Daniel Sever

Services/Products:
Database services; Direct marketing
agency; Sales promotion agency

Member of:
FECEMD

MECAPOST SA
Fresa, 7 Pol. Ind. La Hoya
Madrid
28700 San Sebastian de los Reyes
Spain
Tel: +34 91 654 59 00
Fax: +34 91 654 53 05
Jesus Platero de Santos

Services/Products:
List services

Member of:
FECEMD

MENCOR, SA
Ctra. Nacional II, Km. 592, Nave 8
Pol. Can Sunyer
Barcelona
08740 Sant Andrer de la Barca
Spain
Tel: +34 93 682 25 55
Fax: +34 93 682 09 45
Xavier Ribo Quintana

Services/Products:
List services; Lettershop; Fulfilment
and sampling house; Database services;
Direct marketing agency

Member of:
FECEMD

MEYDIS, SA
Sepulveda, 12 Pol. Ind. Alcobendas
Madrid
28100 Alcobendas
Spain
Tel: +34 91 661 90 00
Fax: +34 91 661 81 96
Benjamin Caro Picon

Services/Products:
List services; Direct marketing agency;
Software supplier

Member of:
FECEMD

MICRODATA SERVICIOS SL
Juan Esplandiu, 15. 5o
28007 Madrid
Spain
Tel: +34 91 504 53 02
Fax: +34 91 504 39 88
Lucio de Andres

Services/Products:
Sales promotion agency

Member of:
FECEMD

**MQM (MARKETING QUALITY
    MANAGEMENT)**
Avda. de Brasil, 17 10
28020 Madrid
Spain
Tel: +34 91 555 1018
Fax: +34 91 555 3058
Antonio Martin, Managing Director

Services/Products:
Sales promotion agency

Member of:
DMA (US)

MRM CANO & MARTINEZ
Av. Diagonal
463 Bis, 3.o. 1a
08036 Barcelona
Spain
Tel: +34 93 430 25 35
Fax: +34 93 419 69 83
Fernando Cano

Services/Products:
Direct marketing agency; Consultancy
services

Member of:
FECEMD

MRW (TOPWAY SL)
Casanova, 75
08011 Barcelona
Spain

Tel: +34 93 451 43 39
Fax: +34 93 451 49 88
Carlos Vallejo

Services/Products:
Private delivery services

Member of:
FECEMD

OGILVYONE WORLDWIDE LTD
Enrique Larreta 2
28036 Madrid
Spain
Tel: +34 91 567 3200
Fax: +34 915673201
Web: www.ogilvy.com
Oscar Prats, President

Services/Products:
Database services; Direct marketing
agency; Response analysis bureau;
Service bureau; Software supplier

Member of:
DMA (US); FEDMA

OGILVYONE WORLDWIDE LTD
Avda Tibidabo 32
08022 Barcelona
Spain
Tel: +34 93 417 36 92
Fax: +34 93 418 55 36
Josep Fàbregas, Managing Director

Services/Products:
Database services; Telemarketing
agency; Direct marketing agency;
Media buying agency

Member of:
DMA (US); FEDMA

**PDM MARKETING Y
    PUBLICIDAD DIRECTA SA**
Xaudaró 7
28034 Madrid
Spain
Tel: +34 91 729 13 90
Fax: +34 91 729 07 90
Email: pdmmadrid@pdm.es
Web: www.pdm.es
Fernando Silos, Consultant

Services/Products:
List services; Database services;
Mailing/Faxing services; Direct
marketing agency; Response analysis
bureau

Member of:
FEDMA

PICKING PACK ACE IGT, SL
Pol. Ind. Can Prat c/Bilbao, s/n
Barcelona
08100 Mollet del Valles
Spain

Tel: +34 93 570 95 35
Fax: +34 93 570 89 30
Justo Almendros

Services/Products:
Lettershop; Fulfilment and sampling house; Mailing/Faxing services; Private delivery services

Member of:
FECEMD

POWER LINE MARKETING TELEFONICO SL
Av. Europa 1
Parque Empresarial la Moraleja
Madrid
28100 Alcobendas
Spain
Tel: +34 91 861 30 00
Fax: +34 91 661 50 00
Eduardo Visus

Services/Products:
Telemarketing agency

Member of:
FECEMD

PRESENT SERVICE SAE
Goya, 15. 4o Izda
28001 Madrid
Spain
Tel: +34 91 431 38 01
Fax: +34 91 575 13 97
Jose Ma Sitjar Santalo

Services/Products:
List services

Member of:
FECEMD

PRICE WATERHOUSE JURIDICO Y FISCAL, S.L.
Avda Diagonal, 640 7°
08017 Barcelona
Spain
Tel: +34 93 253 27 00
Fax: +34 93 405 90 32
Luis Comas, Directeur du Service
    Juridique

Services/Products:
Database services; Sales promotion agency; Legal services

Member of:
FEDMA

PROMOFON SA
Mallorca, 606–608
8a planta
08026 Barcelona
Spain
Tel: +34 93 247 12 11
Fax: +34 93 232 30 50
Caoncepcion Figueras Vidaurre

Services/Products:
Telemarketing agency; Software supplier

Member of:
FECEMD

PUBLIENVIO SA
San Salvador, 16
Barcelona
08950 Esplugues de Llobregat
Spain
Tel: +34 93 371 27 54
Fax: +34 93 371 72 44
Michael Unkelbach

Services/Products:
List services; Telemarketing agency; Mailing/Faxing services

Member of:
FECEMD

PUBLIMAIL SA
Ctra. Bilbao-Galdacano, no18, Edf. Arzubi
Vizcaya
48004 Bilbao
Spain
Tel: +34 94 412 9422/412 9198
Fax: +34 94 412 9867
Email: publimail@publimail.es
Web: www.publimail.es
Jose Miguel Alonso

Services/Products:
Catalogue producer; Database services; Mailing/Faxing services; Personalisation; Print services; Labelling/envelope services; Direct marketing services

Member of:
FEDMA; FECEMD

PUBLIPOST PUBLICIDAD POSTAL SL
San Serapio Street 2
E-28016 Madrid
Spain
Tel: +34 1 500 24 00
Fax: +34 1 500 21 18
Jose Cabrera de la Fuente, General
    Manager

Services/Products:
Fulfilment and sampling house; Direct marketing agency; Response analysis bureau; Service bureau

Member of:
FECEMD

RESPONSE JPS
Nicaragua 14
28016 Madrid
Spain
Tel: +34 91 350 47 66
Fax: +91 345 98 68
Email: jpsresp@sendanet.es
Jean-Pierre Simon, Managing Director

Services/Products:
Database services; Direct marketing agency; Consultancy services; Direct response TV services; Electronic media; Internet services

E-Services:
Website design

Member of:
DMA (US); FECEMD

SCHOBER PDM IBERIA SA
Arequipa, 1
28043 Madrid
Spain
Tel: +34 91 822 2002
Fax: +34 91 822 2001
Klaus Schober, President

Services/Products:
Advertising Agency; Direct marketing agency

Member of:
DMA (US)

SEDAM SL
La Riera, 14
Barcelona
08301 Mataro
Spain
Tel: +34 93 790 85 32
Fax: +34 93 790 65 60
Jordi Espin

Services/Products:
Software supplier

Member of:
FECEMD

SERVICIOS DE TELEMARKETING SA
Avda. Meridiana, 358
08027 Barcelona
Spain
Tel: +34 93 291 10 13
Fax: +34 93 311 19 10
Emi Amigo

Services/Products:
Telemarketing agency

Member of:
FECEMD

SITEL IBERICA TELESERVICES SA
Floor 10
C/ de la Retama 7, Indocentro Building
28045 Madrid
Spain

Tel: +34 91 3797474
Fax: +34 91 3797575
Email: olga.fernandez@sitel.es
Web: www.sitel.com
Ramon Basagoiti Zavala

Services/Products:
Telemarketing agency; Call centre
services/systems

Member of:
FEDMA

**SOCIEDAD DE TELEVISION
CANAL PLUS SA**
Cran Via, 32 3o
28013 Madrid
Spain
Tel: +34 91 396 55 00
Fax: +34 91 398 58 44
Alexia Dodd

Services/Products:
Telemarketing agency

Member of:
FECEMD

SURESA CIT SA
Pol. Ind. Gran Via Sur. c/Industria,
16–20
Barcelona
08908 Hospitalet de Llobregat
Spain
Tel: +34 92 223 25 52
Fax: +34 93 223 06 65
Antonio Sanchez

Services/Products:
Private delivery services

Member of:
FECEMD

TELEACTION SA
Edificio Teleaction
Narciso Serra 14
28007 Madrid
Spain
Tel: +34 1 322 6500
Fax: +34 1 322 6522
Vincente Lopez, General Manager

Services/Products:
Database services; Telemarketing
agency; Sales promotion agency

Member of:
FECEMD

**TELEFONICA PUBLICIDAD E
INFORMACION SA**
Avda de Manoteras No 12
E-28050 Madrid
Spain
Tel: +34 1 339 60 41
Fax: +34 1 339 64 10
Margarita Sanchez, President

Services/Products:
List services; Direct marketing agency

Member of:
FECEMD

**TELEMARKETING GOLDEN
LINE**
4th Floor
C/. Entenza, 157
08029 Barcelona
Spain
Tel: +34 93 419 65 66
Fax: +34 9 3 321 93 42
Email: goldenl@sct.ictnet.es
Margarita Utrillas, General Manager

Services/Products:
Telemarketing agency; Call centre
services/systems

Member of:
FEDMA

**TELEMARKETING INTEGRAL
SL**
Garcia Martin, 2. 2o
Madrid
28224 Pozuelo
Spain
Tel: +34 91 352 87 78
Fax: +34 91 351 01 86
Julio Marti

Services/Products:
Telemarketing agency

Member of:
FECEMD

TNT EXPRESS WORLDWIDE
Torrea Quevedo, 1
Madrid
28820 Coslada
Spain
Tel: +34 91 660 59 00
Fax: +34 91 660 59 45
Hector Lumbreras

Services/Products:
Private delivery services

Member of:
FECEMD

**TOMPLA (GRUPO TOMPLA
SOBRE-EXPRESS SL)**
Carretera de Daganzo, Km. 3
28806 Alcala de Henares
Spain
Tel: +34 91 882 05 00
Fax: +34 91 882 65 52
Ana Patricia Rico

Services/Products:
Labelling/envelope services; Print
services

Member of:
FEDMA

UNAT DIRECT
Avda. de los Toreros, 3
28028 Madrid
Spain
Tel: +34 91 725 38 18
Fax: +34 91 725 88 50
Daniel Hernandez

Services/Products:
Telemarketing agency; Direct
marketing agency

Member of:
FECEMD

VALENVIO SL
Campos Crespo, 57 Bajos
46017 Valencia
Spain
Tel: +34 96 378 9352
Fax: +34 96 357 4106
Email: valencio@feemd.org

Services/Products:
Labelling/envelope services;
Lettershop; Mail order company;
Mailing/Faxing services;
Personalisation; Print services

VINUALES SA
Gran Via Carlos III, 98, 4o, 3a
08028 Barcelona
Spain
Tel: +34 93 409 53 60
Fax: +34 93 409 34 26
Email: Vinuales.sa@vinualessa.es
Web: www.vinualessa.es
Juan Vinuales

Services/Products:
Database services; Mailing/Faxing
services; Direct marketing agency;
Consultancy services

Member of:
FECEMD

VINOSELECCIO SA
Conde de la Cimera, 4 Bajos
28040 Madrid
Spain
Tel: +34 91 535 22 67
Fax: +34 91 553 07 37
Fernando Carmona

Services/Products:
Telemarketing agency

Member of:
FECEMD

WUNDERMAN CATO JOHNSON SA
Avda. de Burgos, 21
Complejo Triada Torre C. 11o
28036 Madrid
Spain
Tel: +34 91 302 08 58
Fax: +34 91 766 84 24
Santiago Alonso

Services/Products:
Telemarketing agency; Direct marketing agency

Member of:
FECEMD

ZEBRA COMMUNICACION SL
Joaquin Costa, 15
28002 Madrid
Spain
Tel: +34 91 561 30 03
Fax: +34 91 561 09 39
Gilles Vincent

Services/Products:
Direct marketing agency

Member of:
FECEMD

SERVICES/PRODUCT LISTING

Advertising Agency
Candi Club
Cepsa
CP Communicacion (Grupo Contrapunto)
Draftworldwide
Grupo Unido De Proyectos Y Operaciones SA
Schober PDM Iberia SA

Call centre services/systems
Sitel Iberica Teleservices SA
Telemarketing Golden Line

Catalogue producer
Grupo Unido De Proyectos Y Operaciones SA
Publimail SA

Consultancy services
Accenture (Antes Andersen Consulting)
Claritas Espana
Grupo Unido De Proyectos Y Operaciones SA
MRM Cano & Martinez
Response JPS
Vinuales SA

Database services
Accenture (Antes Andersen Consulting)
Claritas Espana
CP Communicacion (Grupo Contrapunto)
Data Segmento SL
Dun & Bradstreet Espana, SA
Gupost, SA Publicidad Directa
McCann Direct & Promotions
Mencor, SA
Ogilvyone Worldwide LTD
Ogilvyone Worldwide LTD
PDM Marketing y Publicidad Directa SA
Price Waterhouse Juridico y Fiscal, S.L.
Publimail SA
Response JPS
Teleaction SA
Vinuales SA

Direct marketing agency
ACP Eloquence
Bates Direct
Candi Club
Cepsa
CP Communicacion (Grupo Contrapunto)
Crecendo SL
Dimension Marketing Directo SL
Draftworldwide
Eidos Direct (Eidos Imatge SL)
Global Direct SL
ide-marketing S.L
Ideas Fijas SL
IMP (Division Below The Line)
Instruments Rapp & Collins
Leader Mix
Lorente Estrateolas De Venta SA
Mailhouse SL
McCann Direct & Promotions
Mencor, SA
Meydis, SA
MRM Cano & Martinez
Ogilvyone Worldwide LTD
Ogilvyone Worldwide LTD
PDM Marketing y Publicidad Directa SA
Publipost Publicidad Postal SL
Response JPS
Schober PDM Iberia SA
Telefonica Publicidad E Informacion SA
Unat Direct
Vinuales SA
Wunderman Cato Johnson SA
Zebra Communicacion SL

Direct marketing services
Publimail SA

Direct response TV services
Response JPS

Electronic media
CP Communicacion (Grupo Contrapunto)
Response JPS

Fulfilment and sampling house
Mailhouse SL
Mailhouse SL
Mencor, SA
Picking Pack Ace IGT, SL
Publipost Publicidad Postal SL

Interactive media
ide-marketing S.L

Internet services
Response JPS

Labelling/envelope services
Club Internacional del Libro SA de Promocion y Ediciones
Gupost, SA Publicidad Directa
Publimail SA
Tompla (Grupo Tompla Sobre-Express SL)
Valenvio SL

Legal services
Price Waterhouse Juridico y Fiscal, S.L.

Lettershop
Gupost, SA Publicidad Directa
Mailhouse SL
Mencor, SA
Picking Pack Ace IGT, SL
Valenvio SL

List services
B D Mail
Claritas Espana
Crecendo SL
Data Segmento SL
Eidos Direct (Eidos Imatge SL)
Gupost, SA Publicidad Directa
Iberphone SA
Letter Graphic SL
Mailing Andalucia SL
Mailing Shop SA
Mecapost SA
Mencor, SA
Meydis, SA
PDM Marketing y Publicidad Directa SA
Present Service SAE
Publienvio SA
Telefonica Publicidad E Informacion SA

Mail order company
Valenvio SL

Mailing/Faxing services
Mailhouse SL
Mailhouse SL
PDM Marketing y Publicidad Directa SA
Picking Pack Ace IGT, SL
Publienvio SA
Publimail SA
Valenvio SL
Vinuales SA

Market research agency
Accenture (Antes Andersen Consulting)
Grupo Unido De Proyectos Y Operaciones SA

Media buying agency
Ogilvyone Worldwide LTD

Personalisation
Grupo Unido De Proyectos Y Operaciones SA
Gupost, SA Publicidad Directa
Publimail SA
Valenvio SL

Print services
Grupo Unido De Proyectos Y Operaciones SA
Publimail SA
Tompla (Grupo Tompla Sobre-Express SL)
Valenvio SL

Private delivery services
DHL Internacional Espana SA
MRW (Topway SL)
Picking Pack Ace IGT, SL
Suresa CIT SA
TNT Express Worldwide

Response analysis bureau
Claritas Espana
Data Segmento SL
Ogilvyone Worldwide LTD
PDM Marketing y Publicidad Directa SA
Publipost Publicidad Postal SL

Sales promotion agency
Canon Espana SA
Centro De Asistencia Telefonica SA
CP Communicacion (Grupo Contrapunto)
Eidos Direct (Eidos Imatge SL)
GISCA
Iberphone SA
ide-marketing S.L
McCann Direct & Promotions
Microdata Servicios SL
MQM (Marketing Quality Management)
Price Waterhouse Juridico y Fiscal, S.L.
Teleaction SA

Service bureau
CP Communicacion (Grupo Contrapunto)
Ogilvyone Worldwide LTD
Publipost Publicidad Postal SL

Software supplier
B D Mail
Centro De Asistencia Telefonica SA
Meydis, SA
Ogilvyone Worldwide LTD
Promofon SA
Sedam SL

Telemarketing agency
CDC Club Express SA
Centro De Asistencia Telefonica SA
Crecendo SL
Difusio Telemarketing Grup SL
Hit Xop SA
Iberphone SA

ide-marketing S.L
Leader Line
Ogilvyone Worldwide LTD
Power Line Marketing Telefonico SL
Promofon SA
Publienvio SA
Servicios De Telemarketing SA
Sitel Iberica Teleservices SA
Sociedad De Television Canal Plus SA
Teleaction SA
Telemarketing Golden Line
Telemarketing Integral SL
Unat Direct
Vinoseleccio SA
Wunderman Cato Johnson SA

E-SERVICES

E-Marketing consultant
Accenture (Antes Andersen Consulting)
Grupo Unido De Proyectos Y Operaciones SA
ide-marketing S.L

Email software
Leader Line

Online/e-marketing agency
ide-marketing S.L
Leader Line

Website design
Accenture (Antes Andersen Consulting)
CP Communicacion (Grupo Contrapunto)
Grupo Unido De Proyectos Y Operaciones SA
ide-marketing S.L
Response JPS

SWEDEN

Population: 8.8 million
Capital: Stockholm
Languages: Swedish and, in the north, Finnish and Saami

GDP: $217 billion
GDP per capita: $24,443
Inflation: 0.9 per cent

Currency: Swedish Krona (SKr) = 100 öre
Exchange rate: SKr8.31 : $1 (SKr8.94 : 1 euro)

Time: GMT +1 hour

OVERVIEW

Sweden is the largest of the Scandinavian countries, in both area and population. The economy growth rate was 1.9 per cent in 1997, but unemployment is still high. Full membership of the EU was attained in January 1995.

Sweden has a sophisticated and extensive DM industry, with SWEDMA's annual awards brochure testifying to the high standards of creativity and strategic thinking. The Swedish market has a high penetration of mail per capita, at 385 items in 1997.

LANGUAGE AND CULTURAL CONSIDERATIONS

There are three languages in Sweden, Swedish, Finnish and Saami, although Swedish remains the principal language. English is widely spoken.

LEGISLATION AND CONSUMER PROTECTION

The Database Inspection Institution has developed strict rules on building and servicing databases, with the objective of protecting individual privacy. It is illegal to own a database of sales prospects without special permission. A mailing preference scheme has been introduced.

THE DIRECT MARKETING ASSOCIATION

Name:	Swedish Direct Marketing Association (SWEDMA)
Postal Address:	Box 14308, 104 40 Stockholm
Visiting Address:	Strandvägen 7B, Entrance 3, S-10440 Stockholm
Tel:	+46 8 661 39 10
Fax:	+46 8 660 0713
Email:	direkt@swedma.se
Website:	www.swedma.se
Year founded:	1968
Director/Chairman	Tom Ekelund (Managing Director), Kjell-Otto Nelson (Chairman)
Total staff:	4
Members:	90 plus 200 associate members
Contact:	Tom Ekelund

The members are distributors of services in direct marketing.

Facilities for users of direct marketing

Membership: overseas companies can join SWEDMA, but only as associate members. There are no minimum standards for association.

Newsletter: SWEDMA publishes a quarterly newsletter which is available in Swedish only.

On-line information service: there is an on-line information service at the SWEDMA website: www.swedma.se

Legal advice: free legal advice is available for members.

Business liaison service: SWEDMA will supply a full list of members, which can be used as a business contact list.

Other facilities: copies of the annual awards brochure are available.

POSTAL SERVICES

Posten Sverige offers special direct marketing rates for pre-sorted mail, and therefore further discounts are not usually available. Specialist DM services they provide include:

Nationwide mailing: minimum of 5,000 items
Regional mailing: minimum of 2,500 items
Local mailing: minimum of 1,000 items
International business reply service

A surcharge exists for bulky items.

Addressed bulk mailings are the most common form of letter traffic, with a delivery time of five to seven days, and are the cheapest way of sending addressed mail.

For more information, contact:

Posten Sverige AB
S-10500 Stockholm
Sweden
Tel: +46 8 781 1004
Fax: +46 8 219 611
Website: www.posten.se

In recent years independent postal operators have also come into existence. The largest of these is:

City Mail
Box 90108
S-12021 Stockholm
Sweden
Tel: +46 8 709 4300
Fax: +46 8 709 4343

PROVIDERS OF DM AND E-M SERVICES

59:AN REKLAM & MARKNADSFORLING AB
Box 103
510 40 Sandared
Sweden
Tel: +46 33 25 8010
Fax: +46 33 25 8558
Lars-Ake Andersson

Services/Products:
Advertising Agency; Direct marketing agency

Member of:
SWEDMA

ADDIT INFORMATION & RESEARCH AB
Stora Badhusgatan 20
411 21 Göteborg
Sweden
Tel: +46 31 13 46 00
Fax: +46 31 13 66 45

Services/Products:
Telemarketing agency

Member of:
SWEDMA

ADRESSKOMPANIET SEMA AB
Box 17555
181 91 Stockholm
Sweden
Tel: +46 8 616 7100
Fax: +46 8669 0000
Marcus Muller

Services/Products:
List services; Fulfilment and sampling house; Database services; Telemarketing agency

Member of:
SWEDMA

ADRESSKOMPANIET SYD AB
Norra Vallgatan 60
211 22 Malmö
Sweden
Tel: +46 40 35 01 50
Fax: +46 40 30 65 55
Anders Nilsson

Services/Products:
List services; Fulfilment and sampling house; Database services

Member of:
SWEDMA

ADRITEL, AB
Box 340
201 23 Malmö
Sweden
Tel: +46 40 18 34 34
Fax: +46 40 18 25 35

Services/Products:
Telemarketing agency

Member of:
SWEDMA

ADVOKATFIRMAN ENGSTROM & CO
Stortorget 29
211 34 Malmo
Sweden
Tel: +46 40 30 90 70
Fax: +46 40 30 90 80
Email: lelaw@swipnet.se
Web: www.advokat-engstrom.se
Lars Engstrom, Senior Partner

Services/Products:
Legal services

Member of:
FEDMA

ALMEN DIRECT
P.O. Box 7852
103 99 Stockholm
Sweden
Tel: +46 8 617 10 80
Fax: +46 8 653 65 25
Carl Andreasson, Managing Director

Services/Products:
Direct marketing agency

Member of:
FEDMA

AVANCERA MARKNADSUTVECKLING AB
Dalagatan 100
113 43 Stockholm
Sweden
Tel: +46 8 51 90 66 00
Fax: +46 851 90 66 09

Services/Products:
Telemarketing agency

Member of:
SWEDMA

BELL TELEMARKETING AB
Box 21162
100 31 Stockholm
Sweden
Tel: +46 8 33 22 50
Fax: +46 833 95 05

Services/Products:
Telemarketing agency

Member of:
SWEDMA

BITE TELEMARKETING AB
Box 6777
113 85 Stockholm
Sweden
Tel: +46 8 610 22 00
Fax: +46 8587 90 000
Email: info@bite.se
Web: www.bite.se

Services/Products:
Call centre services/systems; Consultancy services; Fulfilment and sampling house; Market research agency; Telemarketing agency

Member of:
SWEDMA

BLECHERT & BLECHERT AB
P.O. Box 84
444 21 Stenungsund
Sweden
Tel: +46 303 69950
Fax: +46 303 88471
Email: blechert@blechert.se
Web: www.blechert.se
Bo Blechert, Owner

Services/Products:
Advertising Agency; Database services Training/recruitment; Direct marketing agency; Direct response TV services; Electronic media; Internet services

Member of:
FEDMA; SWEDMA

BONGS FABRIKER AB
Box 516
S-29125 Kristianstad
Sweden
Tel: +46 44 20 70 00
Fax: 0044 20 70 90
Mats Molin, Marketing Director

Services/Products:
Labelling/envelope services

Member of:
SWEDMA

BRAND MANAGEMENT
PO Box 5519
11486 Stockholm
Sweden
Tel: +46 8 463 2400
Fax: +46 8 463 2439
Peter Westerstahl, Managing Director

Services/Products:
Advertising Agency; Direct marketing agency

Member of:
DMA (US)

CITYMAIL SWEDEN AB
Box 90108
120 21 Stockholm
Sweden
Tel: +46 8 709 43 00
Fax: +46 8645 00 40

Services/Products:
Private delivery services

Member of:
SWEDMA

CLARITAS SVERIGE
PO Box 2039
169 02 Solna
Sweden
Tel: +46 8 564 824 50
Fax: +46 8 627 99 90
Bo Malstrom, Project Manager

Services/Products:
Database services; Consultancy
services; Response analysis bureau

CONVERZION REKLAM & DM-BYRA AB
Kopenhamnsvagen 6D
217 43 Malmö
Sweden
Tel: +46 40 91 64 65
Fax: +46 40 26 15 70
Anders Akerberg

Services/Products:
Advertising Agency; Database services;
Direct marketing agency

Member of:
SWEDMA

DAD DIRECT AB
Box 337
261 23 Landskrona
Sweden
Tel: +46 418 45 05 00
Fax: +46 418 108 08

Services/Products:
List services; Fulfilment and sampling
house; Database services; Mailing/
Faxing services; Labelling/envelope
services

Member of:
SWEDMA

DIALOG MARKETING AB
Gardsvagen 7
171 52 Solna
Sweden
Tel: +46 8 735 5547
Fax: +46 8730 2807
Christer Holmberg

Services/Products:
Advertising Agency; Direct marketing
agency

Member of:
SWEDMA

DIALOG MARKETING AB
Angantyrvag 29B
18254 Djurshoim
Sweden
Tel: +46 8 755 0970
Fax: +46 8 755 0970
Email: info@dialogmarketing.se
Web: www.dialogmarketing.se
Chriter Holmberg

Services/Products:
Direct marketing agency; Consultancy
services

E-Services:
E-Marketing consultant

Member of:
Ledningskonsulterna

DIREKTMEDIA BJELKHOLM LAESTADIUS OLOFSSON AB
Lorensbergsgatan 8
411 36 Gothenburg
Sweden
Tel: +46 31 81 03 30
Fax: +46 31 81 21 05
Email: direktmedia@direktmedia.se
Peter Bjelkholm, Managing Director

Services/Products:
List services; Response analysis
bureau; Service bureau

Member of:
DMA (US); FEDMA; SWEDMA

DISTRO PACK AB
Box 973
191 29 Sollentuna
Sweden
Tel: +46 8 625 23 50
Fax: +46 896 3883
Max Gustafsson

Services/Products:
Fulfilment and sampling house;
Database services; Mailing/Faxing
services; Labelling/envelope services

Member of:
SWEDMA

DM CONSULTERNA OLSHED AB
Lilla Torg 1
211 34 Malmö
Sweden
Tel: +46 40 12 19 90
Fax: +46 40 12 47 46

Services/Products:
Database services; Direct marketing
agency; Response analysis bureau

Member of:
SWEDMA

DM KONSULT AB
Surbrunnsgatan 44
S-113 48 Stockholm
Sweden
Tel: +46 8 673 07 05
Fax: +46 8673 07 57
Staffan Elinder, Director

Services/Products:
Database services; Direct marketing
agency; Marketing consultant

Member of:
SWEDMA

DM-DEPAN I STOCKHOLM AB
Box 21017
100 31 Stockholm
Sweden
Tel: +46 8 736 1090
Fax: +46 832 8410
Olle Edsmar

Services/Products:
Advertising Agency; Database services;
Direct marketing agency

Member of:
SWEDMA

EXIT MARKETING AB
Box 175
582 02 Linkoping
Sweden
Tel: +46 13 31 16 70
Fax: +46 13 12 72 23

Services/Products:
Telemarketing agency

Member of:
SWEDMA

FAKE TELEMARKETING AB
Jarnvagsgatan 29
252 24 Helsingborg
Sweden
Tel: +46 42 12 56 40
Fax: +46 42 12 46 80

Services/Products:
Telemarketing agency

Member of:
SWEDMA

FLOCK MARKETING AB
Tappgatan 4
151 33 Sodertalje
Sweden
Tel: +46 8 550 114 00
Fax: +46 8550 114 22

Services/Products:
Telemarketing agency

271

Member of:
SWEDMA

FUNDRAISING-GRUPPEN AB
Nybrokajen 7
111 48 Stockholm
Sweden
Tel: +46 8 678 28 02
Fax: +46 8678 86 10

Services/Products:
Telemarketing agency; Training/
recruitment; Direct marketing agency;
Consultancy services

Member of:
SWEDMA

**GAVLE
MARKNADSKOMMUNIKA-
TION AB**
Stromsbrovagen 20
803 09 Gävle
Sweden
Tel: +46 26 10 10 95
Fax: +46 26 10 66 10

Services/Products:
Telemarketing agency

Member of:
SWEDMA

**GEDDEHOLM CALLCENTER
AB**
Stora Gatan 3
722 12 Vaästeras
Sweden
Tel: +46 21 477 00 00
Fax: +46 21 477 00 99

Services/Products:
Telemarketing agency

Member of:
SWEDMA

**GRAFISKA KOMPANIET DAFA
AB**
Box 17555
118 91 Stockholm
Sweden
Tel: +46 8 616 7130
Fax: +46 8668 0007
Marcus Muller

Services/Products:
Fulfilment and sampling house;
Mailing/Faxing services; Labelling/
envelope services

Member of:
SWEDMA

**GRAHAMS TELEMARKETING
AB**
Box 2058
191 02 Sollentuna

Sweden
Tel: +46 8 18 10 98
Fax: +46 818 10 97

Services/Products:
Telemarketing agency

Member of:
SWEDMA

**HEDIN & RICHTER
REKLABYRA**
Box 3026
400 10 Göteborg
Sweden
Tel: +46 31 10 0960
Fax: +46 31 13 1705
Carl-Magnus Hedin

Services/Products:
Advertising Agency; Database services;
Direct marketing agency

Member of:
SWEDMA

HERMELIN TELEMARKETING
601 86 Norrkoping
Sweden
Tel: +46 11 26 41 00
Fax: +46 11 26 41 04

Services/Products:
Telemarketing agency

Member of:
SWEDMA

ICA FöRLAGET AB
721 85 Västeras
Sweden
Tel: +46 21 19 4000
Fax: +46 21 19 4469

Services/Products:
Lettershop; Mailing/Faxing services;
Labelling/envelope services; Private
delivery services

Member of:
SWEDMA

INCO MARKETING AB
Drottninggatan 31, 3 tr.
411 14 Göteborg
Sweden
Tel: +46 31 13 18 10
Fax: +46 31 711 04 56

Services/Products:
Telemarketing agency

Member of:
SWEDMA

INTRA KOMMUNIKATION AB
Box 3015
750 03 Uppsala
Sweden

Tel: +46 18 56 30 00
Fax: +46 18 56 30 10

Services/Products:
Direct marketing agency; Print
services; Direct response TV services;
Electronic media

E-Services:
Website design

Member of:
SWEDMA

K&A MARKETING AB
Dobelnsgatan 58–60
113 52 Stockholm
Sweden
Tel: +46 8 519 151 00
Fax: +46 8519 151 25

Services/Products:
Telemarketing agency

Member of:
SWEDMA

LAKEMEDELSSTATISTIK AB
Box 17608
118 92 Stockholm
Sweden
Tel: +46 8 462 37 00
Fax: +46 8462 02 85

Services/Products:
Fulfilment and sampling house;
Database services; Response analysis
bureau

Member of:
SWEDMA

MAILBUS GRUPPEN AB
Box 4040
181 04 Lidingo
Sweden
Tel: +46 8 731 50 20
Fax: +46 8731 88 22

Services/Products:
Mailing/Faxing services

Member of:
SWEDMA

**MEGA-PHONE
TELEMARKETING AB**
Albanoliden 5
506 30 Borås
Sweden
Tel: +46 33 41 63 00
Fax: +46 33 14 11 33

Services/Products:
Telemarketing agency

MITCOM AB
434 82 Kungsbacka
Sweden

Tel: +46 300 50 500
Fax: +46 30 01 93 15

Services/Products:
List services; Fulfilment and sampling house; Database services; Labelling/envelope services; Response analysis bureau

Member of:
SWEDMA

MODERN MARKNADSFORING
Box 1018
262 21 Angelholm
Sweden
Tel: +46 431 15342
Fax: +46 431 15335
Roger Ludvigsson

Services/Products:
Advertising Agency; Direct marketing agency

Member of:
SWEDMA

NERELL DIRECT MARKETING KB
Kungsgatan 44
111 35 Stockholm
Sweden
Tel: +46 8 20 1003
Fax: +46 8723 0250
Dan Rasmussen

Services/Products:
Advertising Agency; Database services; Direct marketing agency; Electronic media; Internet services

Member of:
SWEDMA

NIMROD REKLAMBYRA AB
Box 12891
112 08 Stockholm
Sweden
Tel: +46 8 54 570 570
Fax: +46 8 653 37 35
Email: nimrod@nrb.se
Web: www.nrd.se
Eva Janson, Managing Director

Services/Products:
Direct marketing agency; Design/graphics/clip art supplier

E-Services:
Website design

Member of:
FEDMA

NT MEDIA PRINT AB
Tryckerigatan 7
571 82 Nässjö
Sweden

Tel: +46 380 796 60
Fax: +46 380 749 71

Services/Products:
Fulfilment and sampling house; Database services; Mailing/Faxing services; Print services

Member of:
SWEDMA

ODM
Orebro Direkt Mailing AB
Box 1607
701 16 Orebro
Sweden
Tel: +46 19 30 86 50
Fax: +46 19 30 86 55
Sven Luthman

Services/Products:
Mailing/Faxing services; Labelling/envelope services

Member of:
SWEDMA

OGILVYONE WORLDWIDE AB
Box 7500
103 92 Stockholm
Sweden
Tel: +46 8 10 02 45
Fax: +46 820 88 45

Services/Products:
Direct marketing agency; Consultancy services; Response analysis bureau

Member of:
SWEDMA

ON TIME LAGER AND DISTRIBUTION AB
Box 35
131 06 Nacka
Sweden
Tel: +46 8 718 38 70
Fax: +46 8718 29 90
Thomas Haglund

Services/Products:
Fulfilment and sampling house; Mailing/Faxing services; Labelling/envelope services

Member of:
SWEDMA

PAR ADRESSREGISTRET AB
Arstaangsvagen 31 J
117 90 Stockholm
Sweden
Tel: +46 8 775 36 00
Fax: +46 8 775 50 88
Email: tore.thallaug@par.se
Web: www.par.se
Tore Thallaug, MD

Services/Products:
List services; Direct marketing agency

Member of:
FEDMA; SWEDMA

PARAJETT
Box 63
261 22 Landskrona
Sweden
Tel: +46 418 54501
Fax: +46 418 54574
Email: tord.olsson@pop.landskrona.se
Tord Ohlsson, President

Services/Products:
List services; Database services; Labelling/envelope services; Response analysis bureau

Member of:
FEDMA; SWEDMA

PHILIP COHEN CONSULTANT AB
Stationsgatan 3
S-931 31 Skelleftea
Sweden
Tel: +46 910 776699
Fax: +46 910 777296
Email: philco@philipcohen.se
Philip Cohen, CEO

Services/Products:
Consultancy services; Legal services; Training/recruitment; Advice on international site location and on call centre self-regulatory measures internationally

Member of:
DMA (US); FEDMA; National DMA; American Teleservices Association; International Charter of Commerce

PHILIPSON KUNDPARTNER AB
Helmfeltsgaten 9B
254 40 Helsingborg
Sweden
Tel: +46 42 21 00 47
Fax: +46 42 21 00 73
Email: info@kundpartner.se
Web: www.kundpartner.se
Pia Philipsson

Services/Products:
Database services; Direct marketing agency; Telemarketing agency; Response analysis bureau; Education

Member of:
FEDMA

PROMATEL TELEMARKETING
Jarnvagsgatan 93
245 34 Staffanstorp
Sweden

Tel: +46 25 00 60
Fax: +46 25 68 16

Services/Products:
Telemarketing agency

Member of:
SWEDMA

**PTM PROFESSIONELL
    TELEMARKETING AB**
Box 71
780 64 Lima
Sweden
Tel: +46 280 321 75
Fax: +46 28 03 23 75

Services/Products:
Telemarketing agency

Member of:
SWEDMA

RALTON AB
P.O. Box 842
251 08 Helsingborg
Sweden
Tel: +46 424901700
Fax: +46 424901701
Email: post@ralton.se
Web: www.ralton.se
Kjell-Otto Nelson, President

Services/Products:
Database services; Mailing/Faxing
services; Direct marketing agency;
Service bureau; Call centre services/
systems

Member of:
DMA (US); FEDMA; SWEDMA

**REPLY DIRECT MARKETING
    AB**
Box 4040
181 04 Lidingo
Sweden
Tel: +46 8 731 50 10
Fax: +46 8731 94 50

Services/Products:
Direct marketing agency

Member of:
SWEDMA

ROXX MEDIA AB
Box 164
598 23 Vimmerby
Sweden
Tel: +46 492 15092
Fax: +46 492 15775
Micael Glennfalk

Services/Products:
Advertising Agency; Direct marketing
agency

Member of:
SWEDMA

**SCB, FORETAGSREGISTRET
    BASUN**
Foretagsregistret Basun
701 89 Orebro
Sweden
Tel: +46 19 17 6000
Fax: +46 19 17 6117
Urban Fredriksson

Services/Products:
Database services

Member of:
SWEDMA

SCRIBENDI AB
PO Box 26048
75026 Uppsala
Sweden
Tel: +46 18 55 16 27
Fax: +46 18 52 58 93
Leif Johannson, President

Services/Products:
Advertising Agency; Direct marketing
agency

Member of:
DMA (US)

**SDM – SCANDANAVIAN
    DATABASE MARKETING AB**
Box 14068
104 40 Stockholm
Sweden
Tel: +46 86637000
Fax: +46 86114210
Ted Jacobson, President

Services/Products:
Direct marketing agency

Member of:
FEDMA; SWEDMA

SDR ACTION PEOPLE AB
Box 49040
100 28 Stockholm
Sweden
Tel: +46 8 692 3800
Fax: +46 8651 1880
Email: jan.gustafsson@sdrgruppen.se
Web: www.sdrgruppen.se
Jan Gustafsson, Managing Director

Services/Products:
Fulfilment and sampling house; Action
marketing service

Member of:
FEDMA; National DMA

SDR GRUPPEN AB
Box 1524
751 45 Uppsala

Sweden
Tel: +46 18 17 21 00
Fax: +46 18 15 41 66

Services/Products:
List services; Fulfilment and sampling
house; Database services; Labelling/
envelope services; Direct marketing
agency; Private delivery services

Member of:
SWEDMA

SDR MAILING AB
Hantverkarvagen 22
136 44 Haninge
Sweden
Tel: +46 8 741 3360
Fax: +46 8745 4897
Email: mailing@sdrgruppen.se
Web: www.sdrgruppen.se
K. G. Engström

Services/Products:
Fulfilment and sampling house; Servic
bureau; Response analysis bureau;
Labelling/envelope services

Member of:
National DMA

**SDR SVENSK DIREKTREKLAM
    AB**
Box 1524
751 45 Uppsala
Sweden
Tel: +46 18 17 21 00
Fax: +46 18 15 41 66

Services/Products:
Database services; Response analysis
bureau; Private delivery services

Member of:
SWEDMA

SEMA GROUP INFODATA AB
P.O. Box 34101
100 26 Stockholm
Sweden
Tel: +46 8 738 50 00
Fax: +46 8 618 97 78
Per Forsberg, Managing Director

Services/Products:
List services; Fulfilment and sampling
house; Direct marketing agency; Print
services

Member of:
FEDMA; SWEDMA

**STI TELEMARKETING
    INSTITUT AB**
Kungsaangsvagen 20
753 23 Uppsala
Sweden

Tel: +46 18 10 36 96
Fax: +46 18 14 87 66

Services/Products:
Telemarketing agency

Member of:
SWEDMA

STROEDE DATA AB
Varla Industriomrode
S-434 82 Kungsbacka
Sweden
Tel: +46 300 505 00
Fax: +46 30 01 93 15
Goran Lofgren

Services/Products:
List services; Fulfilment and sampling
house; Mailing/Faxing services;
Response analysis bureau; Service
bureau

Member of:
SWEDMA

STROEDE PRINT MEDIA AB
PO Box 5344
402 27 Goteborg
Sweden
Tel: +46 31400450
Fax: +46 31403729
Email: britt.albertsson@stroede.se
Britt Albertsson

Services/Products:
List services; Direct marketing agency;
Market research agency

Member of:
DMA (US); FEDMA; SWEDMA

TELEMARKETINGHUSET AB
Hantverkargatan 33
803 23 Gävle
Sweden
Tel: +46 26 10 23 00
Fax: +46 26 10 65 65

Services/Products:
Telemarketing agency

Member of:
SWEDMA

**TELEPERFORMANCE SWEDEN
AB**
Box 47625
117 94 Stockholm
Sweden
Tel: +46 8 775 37 70
Fax: +46 8775 30 80

Services/Products:
Telemarketing agency

Member of:
SWEDMA

**TELIA INFOMEDIA
INTERACTICE AB**
Box 818
161 24 Bromma
Sweden
Tel: +46 8 634 1700
Fax: +46 8634 1710
Olle Elliott

Services/Products:
List services

Member of:
SWEDMA

**TELIA INFOMEDIA RESPONS
AB**
Box 822
161 24 Bromma
Sweden
Tel: +46 8 634 73 00
Fax: +46 8634 74 00

Services/Products:
List services; Fulfilment and sampling
house; Database services;
Telemarketing agency; Response
analysis bureau

Member of:
SWEDMA

**TELIA INFOMEDIA RESPONS
AB/CALLCENTERSERVICES**
Nipanomradet Box 309
881 27 Sollefteå
Sweden
Tel: +46 620 561 01
Fax: +46 620 560 02

Member of:
SWEDMA

TIMU POINTER AB
Box 516
701 50 Orebro
Sweden
Tel: +46 19 10 22 50
Fax: +46 19 10 22 88

Services/Products:
List services; Database services;
Response analysis bureau

Member of:
SWEDMA

UNIMEDIA DM AB
Halsovagen 40
254 42 Helsingborg
Sweden
Tel: +46 42 12 03 60
Fax: +46 42 14 10 99
Email: robert.yarbray@unimedia.se
Robert T Yarbray, Jr., International
Business Manager

Services/Products:
List services; Direct marketing agency;
Service bureau; Market research
agency

Member of:
DMA (US); FEDMA; SWEDMA

UNIMEDIA DM AB
Box 5422
402 29 Gothenburg
Sweden
Tel: +46 313357585
Fax: +46 31814122
Email: info@unimedia.se
Web: www.unimedia.se
Leif Einarsson, Chairman

Services/Products:
List services; Database services;
Mailing/Faxing services; Training/
recruitment; Direct marketing agency

Member of:
FEDMA; SWEDMA

**WUNDERMAN CATO JOHNSON
AB**
Box 7581
Jokobsbergsgatan 7
103 93 Stockholm
Sweden
Tel: +46 8 587 644 00
Fax: +46 8 587 644 01/02
Email: info@wcj.se
Leena Bergerus

Services/Products:
Advertising Agency; Fulfilment and
sampling house; Database services;
Direct marketing agency; Response
analysis bureau

Member of:
FEDMA

SERVICES/PRODUCT
LISTING

Action marketing service
SDR Action People AB

Advertising Agency
59:AN Reklam & Marknadsforling AB
Blechert & Blechert AB
Brand Management
Converzion Reklam & DM-Byra AB
Dialog Marketing AB
DM-Depan I Stockholm AB
Hedin & Richter Reklabyra
Modern Marknadsforing
Nerell Direct Marketing KB
Roxx Media AB

Scribendi AB
Wunderman Cato Johnson AB

Advice on international site location and on call centre self-regulatory measures internationally
Philip Cohen Consultant AB

Call centre services/systems
BITE Telemarketing AB
Ralton AB

Consultancy services
BITE Telemarketing AB
Claritas Sverige
Dialog Marketing AB
Fundraising-Gruppen AB
OgilvyOne Worldwide AB
Philip Cohen Consultant AB

Database services
Adresskompaniet Sema AB
Adresskompaniet Syd AB
Blechert & Blechert AB
Claritas Sverige
Converzion Reklam & DM-Byra AB
DAD Direct AB
Distro Pack AB
DM Consulterna Olshed AB
DM Konsult AB
DM-Depan I Stockholm AB
Hedin & Richter Reklabyra
Lakemedelsstatistik AB
MITCOM AB
Nerell Direct Marketing KB
NT Media Print AB
Parajett
Philipson Kundpartner AB
Ralton AB
SCB, Foretagsregistret Basun
SDR Gruppen AB
SDR Svensk Direktreklam AB
Telia InfoMedia Respons AB
Timu Pointer AB
Unimedia DM AB
Wunderman Cato Johnson AB

Design/graphics/clip art supplier
Nimrod ReklambyrA AB

Direct marketing agency
59:AN Reklam & Marknadsforling AB
Almen Direct
Blechert & Blechert AB
Brand Management
Converzion Reklam & DM-Byra AB
Dialog Marketing AB
Dialog Marketing AB
DM Consulterna Olshed AB
DM Konsult AB
DM-Depan I Stockholm AB

Fundraising-Gruppen AB
Hedin & Richter Reklabyra
Intra Kommunikation AB
Modern Marknadsforing
Nerell Direct Marketing KB
Nimrod ReklambyrA AB
OgilvyOne Worldwide AB
Par Adressregistret AB
Philipson Kundpartner AB
Ralton AB
Reply Direct Marketing AB
Roxx Media AB
Scribendi AB
SDM – Scandanavian Database
    Marketing AB
SDR Gruppen AB
Sema Group Infodata AB
Stroede Print Media AB
Unimedia DM AB
Unimedia DM AB
Wunderman Cato Johnson AB

Direct response TV services
Blechert & Blechert AB
Intra Kommunikation AB

Education
Philipson Kundpartner AB

Electronic media
Blechert & Blechert AB
Intra Kommunikation AB
Nerell Direct Marketing KB

Fulfilment and sampling house
Adresskompaniet Sema AB
Adresskompaniet Syd AB
BITE Telemarketing AB
DAD Direct AB
Distro Pack AB
Grafiska Kompaniet Dafa AB
Lakemedelsstatistik AB
MITCOM AB
NT Media Print AB
On Time Lager and Distribution AB
SDR Action People AB
SDR Gruppen AB
SDR Mailing AB
Sema Group Infodata AB
Stroede Data AB
Telia InfoMedia Respons AB
Wunderman Cato Johnson AB

Internet services
Blechert & Blechert AB
Nerell Direct Marketing KB

Labelling/envelope services
Bongs Fabriker AB
DAD Direct AB
Distro Pack AB
Grafiska Kompaniet Dafa AB
ICA Förlaget AB

MITCOM AB
ODM
On Time Lager and Distribution AB
Parajett
SDR Gruppen AB
SDR Mailing AB

Legal services
Advokatfirman EngstrOM & Co
Philip Cohen Consultant AB

Lettershop
ICA Förlaget AB

List services
Adresskompaniet Sema AB
Adresskompaniet Syd AB
DAD Direct AB
Direktmedia Bjelkholm Laestadius
    Olofsson AB
MITCOM AB
Par Adressregistret AB
Parajett
SDR Gruppen AB
Sema Group Infodata AB
Stroede Data AB
Stroede Print Media AB
Telia Infomedia Interactice AB
Telia InfoMedia Respons AB
Timu Pointer AB
Unimedia DM AB
Unimedia DM AB

Mailing/Faxing services
DAD Direct AB
Distro Pack AB
Grafiska Kompaniet Dafa AB
ICA Förlaget AB
Mailbus Gruppen AB
NT Media Print AB
ODM
On Time Lager and Distribution AB
Ralton AB
Stroede Data AB
Unimedia DM AB

Market research agency
BITE Telemarketing AB
Stroede Print Media AB
Unimedia DM AB

Marketing consultant
Dialog Marketing AB
DM Konsult AB

Print services
Intra Kommunikation AB
NT Media Print AB
Sema Group Infodata AB

Private delivery services
CityMail Sweden AB
ICA Förlaget AB

SDR Gruppen AB
SDR Svensk Direktreklam AB

Response analysis bureau
Claritas Sverige
Direktmedia Bjelkholm Laestadius
    Olofsson AB
DM Consulterna Olshed AB
Lakemedelsstatistik AB
MITCOM AB
OgilvyOne Worldwide AB
Parajett
Philipson Kundpartner AB
SDR Mailing AB
SDR Svensk Direktreklam AB
Stroede Data AB
Telia InfoMedia Respons AB
Timu Pointer AB
Wunderman Cato Johnson AB

Service bureau
Direktmedia Bjelkholm Laestadius
    Olofsson AB
Ralton AB

SDR Mailing AB
Stroede Data AB
Unimedia DM AB

Telemarketing agency
Addit Information & Research AB
Adresskompaniet Sema AB
Adritel, AB
Avancera Marknadsutveckling AB
BELL Telemarketing AB
BITE Telemarketing AB
Exit Marketing AB
Fake Telemarketing AB
Flock Marketing AB
Fundraising-Gruppen AB
Gavle Marknadskommunikation AB
Geddeholm CallCenter AB
Grahams Telemarketing AB
Hermelin Telemarketing
INCO Marketing AB
K&A Marketing AB
Mega-Phone Telemarketing AB
Philipson Kundpartner AB
Promatel Telemarketing

Ptm Professionell Telemarketing AB
STI Telemarketing Institut AB
TeleMarketingHuset AB
Teleperformance Sweden AB
Telia InfoMedia Respons AB

Training/recruitment
Blechert & Blechert AB
Fundraising-Gruppen AB
Philip Cohen Consultant AB
Unimedia DM AB

E-SERVICES

E-Marketing consultant
Dialog Marketing AB

Website design
Intra Kommunikation AB
Nimrod ReklambyrA AB

Increase your attraction for international customers.

Never mind the EU – anyone who wants to gain a foothold on international markets can now easily afford to reach for the stars. Benefit from the traditional Swiss quality of our Direct Marketing International services to attract potential customers.

We'll help you to advertise in a focused, efficient and cost-effective manner so that you reach any number of consumers and companies. And we'll help you to set up a new customer base or increase the response rate to your international mailings.

Read more about Direct Marketing International, a tailor-made service package from Swiss Post International, on the Internet:

www.swisspost.com

SWITZERLAND

Population: 7.1 million
Capital: Berne
Languages: German, French and Italian
GDP: $246 billion
GDP per capita: $34,700
Inflation: 0.5 per cent
Currency: Swiss Franc (SFr) = 100 centimes
Exchange rate: SFr1.50 : $1 (SFr1.61 : 1 euro)
Time: GMT +1 hour

OVERVIEW

Switzerland's political system ensures a remarkable degree of stability, with the Swiss Franc providing a benchmark as one of the world's most steady currencies. Tourism and service industries, and the financial sector in particular, play important roles in the Swiss economy, which supports the highest standards of living in the world. The economy has been through a period of recession, but moderate growth is now set to resume.

The Swiss DM market has consistently been the strongest in Europe, with volumes of direct mail per capita into three digits for several years. Switzerland received 108 units of direct mail per capita in 1998 and DM accounts for 41 per cent of total advertising expenditure. Near market saturation and the image of DM as 'junk mail' may have begun to undermine the market, and there is an increasingly vocal element of opposition to DM on environmental grounds. SVD statistics show that the industry is relying more extensively on a committed core of heavy shoppers.

With a relatively small universe and profusion of languages, Switzerland is not the simplest market to approach.

279

LANGUAGE AND CULTURAL CONSIDERATIONS

Switzerland is a multi-language country. Most Swiss are able to speak several languages, usually including English. The national languages are German (72 per cent) in the north, central and east, French (23 per cent) in the west, Italian (4 per cent) in the south and Romansch (1 per cent) in the south-east.

LEGISLATION AND CONSUMER PROTECTION

The SVD maintains a Robinson list, which allows consumers to have their names removed from mailing lists used by affiliated companies.

THE DIRECT MARKETING ASSOCIATION

Name: Schweizer Direktmarketing Verband Postfach (SDV)
Address: Postfach, CH-8708 Männedorf
Tel: +41 1 790 34 70
Fax: +41 1 790 34 71
Email: r.waldburger@sdv-swissdma.ch
Website: www.sdv-direktmarketing.ch
Year founded: 1971
President: Heinz Rohrer
Total staff: 2
Members: 135
Contact: Rudolf Waldburger

DM agencies	30	List brokers	34
Telemarketing agencies	12	Mailing houses	27
Mail Order companies	20	Printers	10
Database agencies	40		

Facilities for overseas users of direct mail

Membership: overseas companies are not elegible to join the organization.
On-line services: There is no library or on-line information service.
Business liaison service: the SVD provides full details of approved suppliers of DM services. It also helps its members in finding venture partners in the local market.

POSTAL SERVICES

Due Schweizeriche Post (state-owned) currently has 3500 post offices nationwide with 55,000 employees at your service. On average, they process some 600,000 parcels and 10 million letters a day. 1.0 million people in

Switzerland have a postal giro account. Our aim: to give nothing less than total satisfaction.

Die Schweizensche Post offers a wide range of services designed specifically for direct marketers.

National services

Addressed Mail

The structure of Swiss postal rates for addressed mail is based on two service speeds – Priority and Economy – and four different categories of letters: lettre, standard letter, midi letter, big letter and maxi letter.

- A-Priority: delivery is one working day after posting, including Saturdays.
- Economy: delivery is within 2–3 working days (Monday – Friday).
- Economy bulk: delivery is within 2–6 working days, depending on the selections made and the degree of pre-sorting by the sender. Bulk mail discounts apply for mailings of over 500 items.

Unaddressed Mail

- Items are delivered from Monday to Friday, within two days of their arrival at the delivery post office.
- Unaddressed mail can be delivered within chosen sectors of towns or cities, or by postbox.

Business reply items

- Die Schweizer is che Post Offcie requires these items to conform to certain design specifications. A priority or economy rate is offered; a minimum surcharge applies. In addition to normal postage, there is a reply charge per item and basic monthly charge.

- For further information and brochures in either French, German or Italian, contact:

Die Schweizerische Post
Letterpost
Prouct Management
Viktoriastrasse 21
CH-3030 Berne
Switzerland

Tel: +41 31 338 11 11
Fax: +41 31 338 21 26
Email: webmaster@post.ch
Website: www.post.ch

International services

Addressed Mail

There are two speed categories for international mail: priority and economy.

- Priority: airmail delivery within Europe of two to four days, and overseas of three to seven days.
- Economy: average times are between four and eight days for European countries, and between seven and twelve days for the rest of the world.
- Direct Mail: the Direct Mail Service enables you to send mail-shots and magazines on the terms applicable in the country of destination. Contact Swiss Post Center national (address below) for further details.

Unaddressed mail

Contracts exist with various European countries. Contact the Swiss Post International (address below) for further details.

Business reply cards

- Global Response: Switzerland participates in a worldwide IBRS service (card or envelope). Contact Swiss Post for further information.
- Local Response: Switzerland also has a locally operating business reply service, in which reply cards are collected in a PO box in the sender country. Details can be obtained from Swiss Post International
- Combi Response: this combines the postal design regulations for business items both for Switzerland and other countries on one reply card or
- Direct Response Card International: a single C5 card can be used for both the mailing and the reply, thus combining information and feedback.

Services Offered:

- Bulk, discounted rates for addressed/unaddressed mail
- Periodical mail rates
- Mailsort
- Express mail services (EMS)
- Business reply service (BRS)
- International business reply service
- Printing and packaging
- Postage paid by addresses
- PO Box addresses
- Courier services
- Registered post
- Postal insurance
- Address updating services
- Email services

For further information and brochures in either French, German or Italian, contact:

Die Schweizeriche Post
Swiss Post International
Back Office
Postbahnhof
Viktoriastrasse 21
CH-3030 Berne
Switzerland

Tel: +41 31 338 11 11
Fax: +41 31 338 69 24
Email: infopi@post.ch
Website: www.swisspost.com

PROVIDERS OF DM AND E-M SERVICES

A & D ARNOLD, DEMMERER & PARTNER AG
Bundesplatz 2
Postfach 4025
Zug
6304
Switzerland
Tel: +41 41/710 75 55
Fax: +41 41710 75 66
M Scherrer

Services/Products:
List services; Database services

Member of:
SVD

AARMAIL AG
Hinterburg 118
Merishausen
8232
Switzerland
Tel: +41 52/654 23 23
Fax: +41 52654 23 24
E Künzler

Services/Products:
Private delivery services

Member of:
SVD

ABEWA
Gätziberg
Postfach 26
Altstätten
9450
Switzerland
Tel: +41 71/755 62 24
Fax: +41 71/755 62 25
Email: beu@abewa.ch
Walter Beutler

Services/Products:
List services; Database services;
Service bureau; Response analysis
bureau

Member of:
SVD

ADAMOS AG
Räffelstrasse 25
Zürich
CH 8045
Switzerland
Tel: +41 1 454 7700
Fax: +41 1 454 7711
Robert Schmidli, Managing Director

Services/Products:
List services

ADIM AGENTUR FüR DIREKTMARKETING AG
Alte St. Wolfgangstrasse 5
Hünenberg
6331
Switzerland
Tel: +41 41 785 5599
Fax: +41 41 785 5577
Email: contact@adim.ch
Web: www.adim.ch

Services/Products:
Database services; Mailing/Faxing
services; Direct marketing agency;
Personalisation; Event

E-Services:
E-Marketing consultant; Website
design; Email software; Online/e-
marketing agency

Member of:
National DMA

ADZ AGENTUR FüR DIREKTWERBUNG AG
Birsigstrasse 79
Basel
4054
Switzerland
Tel: +41 61/281 03 05
Fax: +41 61281 03 07
Hans Bodenschatz

Services/Products:
Private delivery services

Member of:
SVD

AKTIV - DIALOGMARKETING GMBH
Gartenrainstrasse 3
Tann/Rüti
8632
Switzerland
Tel: +41 55/240 22 51
Fax: +41 55/240 22 61
Email: aktivdm@active.ch
Theodor Sulzer

Services/Products:
Direct marketing agency; Advertising
Agency

Member of:
SVD

ALEX SCHMID AG
Seestrasse 33
Postfach
Zollikon 2
8702
Switzerland
Tel: +41 1/396 44 00
Fax: +41 1/396 44 10

Email: info@alex-schmid.ch
Alex Schmid

Services/Products:
Direct marketing agency; Advertising
Agency

Member of:
SVD

ALEXANDER HEGELE DIRECT
Postfach 179
Schwendenhaustrasse 16
Zollikon
8702
Switzerland
Tel: +41 1 391 24 11
Fax: +41 1 391 27 12
Email: hegele@swissonline.ch
Alexander Hégelé, Managing Director

Services/Products:
List services; Media buying agency

Member of:
FEDMA; SVD

ANZEIGER AG
Rathausquai 10
Postfach
Luzern
6002
Switzerland
Tel: +41 41/51 66 66
Fax: +41 4151 67 55
Peter Wüthrich

Services/Products:
Private delivery services

Member of:
SVD

APZ ADRESSEN- UND PROPAGANDAZENTRALE SCHAFFHAUSEN AG
Buhlstrasse 15
Postfach
Schaffhausen
8200
Switzerland
Tel: +41 52/632 31 30
Fax: +41 52632 31 90
Lukas Gruninger jun.

Services/Products:
List services; Lettershop; Fulfilment
and sampling house; Database services;
Mailing/Faxing services; Private
delivery services

Member of:
SVD

ATAG ERNST & YOUNG MARKETING-SERVICES AG
Feldeggstrasse 2
Glattbrugg

8152
Switzerland
Tel: +41 1/809 81 11
Fax: +41 1 809 81 00
Frau Ruth Wagner

Services/Products:
List services; Database services;
Mailing/Faxing services; Service
bureau; Response analysis bureau

Member of:
SVD

ATELIER ETTLIN
Aeschstrasse 1
Forch
8127
Switzerland
Tel: +41 1/982 22 22
Fax: +41 1/982 22 23
Email: mail@atelieretttlin.ch
Gilles Ettlin

Services/Products:
Design/graphics/clip art supplier;
Consultancy services

Member of:
SVD

ATHENA AG FüR DATA-
ENGINEERING UND
CONSULTING
Bellerivestrasse 2
Zürich
8008
Switzerland
Tel: +41 1/389 63 63
Fax: +41 1/389 63 64
Email: pl@athena.ch
Patric Lüthi

Services/Products:
Database services; Service bureau;
Response analysis bureau

Member of:
SVD

AWZ ADRESSEN- UND
WERBEZENTRALE BERN
Sulgenrain 24
Postfach
Bern 23
3000
Switzerland
Tel: +41 31/371 64 24
Fax: +41 31/371 83 87
Email: awzinfo@awz-bern.ch
René Bill

Services/Products:
List services; Lettershop; Fulfilment
and sampling house; Database services;
Mailing/Faxing services; Private
delivery services

Member of:
SVD

AWZ ADRESSEN- UND
WERBEZENTRALE ST.
GALLEN
Davidstrasse 25
Postfach 746
St. Gallen
9001
Switzerland
Tel: +41 71/22 99 22
Fax: +41 7123 55 42
Martin Feurer

Services/Products:
List services; Database services; Private
delivery services

Member of:
SVD

AWZ ADRESSEN- UND
WERBEZENTRALE ZüRICH
Binzstrasse 39
Postfach
Zürich
8045
Switzerland
Tel: +41 1/456 58 58
Fax: +41 1 456 58 60
Rolf Stucki

Services/Products:
List services; Lettershop; Fulfilment
and sampling house; Database services;
Mailing/Faxing services; Private
delivery services

Member of:
SVD

B.A.S. AG DIGITAL
MARKETING SERVICE
PO Box
Aarau
CH-5001
Switzerland
Tel: +41 62 839 1111
Fax: +41 62 839 1100
Email: welcome@bas.ch
Web: www.bas.ch

Services/Products:
Consultancy services; Database
services; Direct marketing agency;
Fulfilment and sampling house;
Lettershop; Mailing/Faxing services

E-Services:
Email list provider; E-Marketing
consultant; Website design; Online/e-
marketing agency

Member of:
FEDMA; DMA (US); National DMA;
Swiss ict; Swiss Public Affairs Society
(SPAG)

BAUMER AG
Laubgasse 31
Frauenfeld 1
CH-8500
Switzerland
Tel: +41 52 723 42 42
Fax: +41 52 723 42 90
Max Jud

Services/Products:
Advertising Agency; Lettershop;
Fulfilment and sampling house;
Mailing/Faxing services; Labelling/
envelope services

Member of:
SVD

BDK MAILING GMBH
Rainstrasse 3
Unterägeri
6314
Switzerland
Tel: +41 79/340 52 90
Fax: +41 033142556015
B Elchlepp

Services/Products:
List services; Database services; Direct
marketing agency; Advertising Agency

Member of:
SVD

BEORDA DIREKTWERBUNG
AG
Kantonsstrasse 101
Triengen
6234
Switzerland
Tel: +41 41 935 4060
Fax: +41 41 935 4077
Email: mail@beorda.ch

Services/Products:
Database services; Labelling/envelope
services; Lettershop; Personalisation;
Response analysis bureau

Member of:
SVD; Schweizer Direktmarketing
Verband

BISCHOF DIRECT MARKETING
Albisriederstrasse 414
Zürich
8047
Switzerland
Tel: +41 1 491 6600
Fax: +41 1 491 6607
Email: bdm-zurich@access.ch

Web: www.mediaforum.ch/bdm-zurich
Urs Bischof

Services/Products:
Direct marketing agency; Consultancy
services

Member of:
National DMA

BLICKLE & PARTNER GMBH
Hardhofstrasse 15
Embrach
8424
Switzerland
Tel: +41 1/865 72 00
Fax: +41 1/865 72 10
Email: blickle@blickle.ch
Eugen Blickle

Services/Products:
List services; Database services;
Service bureau; Response analysis
bureau

Member of:
SVD

BOL INTERNATIONAL BERTELSMANN E-COMMERCE
Oberdorfstrasse 9
PO Box 2064
Baar 2
CH-6342
Switzerland
Tel: +41 41 767 71 11
Fax: +41 41 767 71 12
Urs Anderegg, Vice President
Marketing

Services/Products:
Electronic media

E-Services:
Website design

BONO CONSULTING
Katrinenhof 68
Postfach 44
Altendorf
8852
Switzerland
Tel: +41 55/420 21 20
Fax: +41 55410 71 91
Tarzis Bono

Services/Products:
Direct marketing agency; Advertising
Agency

Member of:
SVD

BORNAND + GAENG
Avenue des Alpes 68
Montreux
CH-1820

Switzerland
Tel: +41 21 963 6565
Fax: +41 21 963 7910
Xavier Pellaton

Services/Products:
Advertising Agency; Direct marketing
agency; List services

Member of:
National DMA

BUREAU D'ADRESSES ET DE PUBLICITé DIRECT
11, Vy d'Etra
Neuchâtel 9
2000
Switzerland
Tel: +41 32/753 51 60
Fax: +41 32753 63 76
Jacques Peter

Services/Products:
Lettershop; Fulfilment and sampling
house; Mailing/Faxing services; Print
services; Private delivery services

Member of:
SVD

BUREAU GENEVOIS D'ADRESSES ET DE PUBLICITé
Case postale 369
Meyrin
1217
Switzerland
Tel: +41 22/782 55 66
Fax: +41 22783 04 15
Francis Mayoraz

Services/Products:
List services; Lettershop; Fulfilment
and sampling house; Database services;
Mailing/Faxing services; Private
delivery services

Member of:
SVD

BUREAU VAUDOIS D'ADRESSES
93, Route Aloys Fauquez
Lausanne
1018
Switzerland
Tel: +41 21/646 11 36
Fax: +41 21648 42 15
Olivier Cherpillod

Services/Products:
List services; Lettershop; Fulfilment
and sampling house; Database services;
Mailing/Faxing services; Private
delivery services

Member of:
SVD

BWV BERATUNG FüR WIRTSCHAFT & VERWALTUNG AG
Bionstrasse 7
St. Gallen
9015
Switzerland
Tel: +41 71/313 27 27
Fax: +41 71313 27 28
Jakob Nef

Services/Products:
List services; Database services;
Service bureau; Response analysis
bureau

Member of:
SVD

CONZETT + WALTER AG
Rietbachstr. 7
Postfach
Schlieren
8952
Switzerland
Tel: +41 1/733 77 77
Fax: +41 1 730 93 27
Dölf Gubser

Services/Products:
Lettershop; Fulfilment and sampling
house; Mailing/Faxing services; Print
services

Member of:
SVD

CORDENA TELEFONDIENST GMBH
Bionstrasse 4
St. Gallen
9015
Switzerland
Tel: +41 71/313 60 10
Fax: +41 71313 60 50
Carmela Dolder

Member of:
SVD

CSM SA COMMUNICATION, STRATéGIE, MARKETING
9, route des Jeunes
Case postale 1335
Genève 26
1211
Switzerland
Tel: +41 22/343 04 41
Fax: +41 22/343 04 42
Email: csm@iprolink.ch
Claude Hertzschuch

Services/Products:
Mailing/Faxing services; Telemarketing
agency; Direct marketing agency;
Advertising Agency

Member of:
SVD

DCB DATA CENTER BRüTTISELLEN AG

Birkenstrasse 17
Brüttisellen
8306
Switzerland
Tel: +41 1/805 55 55
Fax: +41 1/805 55 45
Email: anita.goeggel@dcs.adi.ch
Anita Göggel

Services/Products:
List services; Lettershop; Database services; Mailing/Faxing services; Direct marketing agency; Response analysis bureau

Member of:
SVD

DCL DATA CENTER LUZERN AG

Sternmatt 6, Kriens
Postfach
Luzern
6002
Switzerland
Tel: +41 41/317 33 00
Fax: +41 41317 33 27
Peter Delfosse

Services/Products:
Lettershop; Fulfilment and sampling house; Database services; Mailing/Faxing services; Service bureau

Member of:
SVD

DIE SCHWEIZERISCHE POST SWISS POST INTERNATIONAL

Schanzenstrasse 5
International Mail Division
Bern
3030
Switzerland
Tel: +41 31 338 38 48
Fax: +41 31 338 21 26
Web: www.swisspost.com
Daniel Tresch, Product Manager DM International

Services/Products:
List services; Database services; Direct marketing agency; Service bureau; Private delivery services; Mailing/Faxing services

Member of:
FEDMA

DIRECT MAIL COMPANY

Delsbergerallee 78
Basel
4018
Switzerland
Tel: +41 61/331 87 87
Fax: +41 61331 28 91
Markus F Hof

Services/Products:
Lettershop; Fulfilment and sampling house; Mailing/Faxing services; Print services; Private delivery services

Member of:
SVD

DIRECT MAIL HOUSE AG

Bionstrasse 4
St. Gallen
9015
Switzerland
Tel: +41 71/311 88 12
Fax: +41 61311 88 14
Erich Zaugg

Services/Products:
List services; Lettershop; Fulfilment and sampling house; Database services; Mailing/Faxing services

Member of:
SVD

DIREKTWERBUNG AG

Gröblistrasse 18
Postfach 464
St. Gallen
9001
Switzerland
Tel: +41 71/28 41 11
Fax: +41 7128 22 91
Max Akermann

Services/Products:
Lettershop; Fulfilment and sampling house; Mailing/Faxing services; Print services; Private delivery services

Member of:
SVD

DISTRIBA

Schlüsselberg 4
Basel
4001
Switzerland
Tel: +41 61/261 61 61
Fax: +41 61261 67 86
Daniel Weick

Services/Products:
Private delivery services

Member of:
SVD

DISTRIFORCE AG

Industriestrasse 57
Glattbrugg
8152
Switzerland
Tel: +41 1/829 64 10
Fax: +41 1 829 64 89
Hans Arndt

Services/Products:
Private delivery services

Member of:
SVD

DM MICHELOTTI AG DIREKT MARKETING

Riedstrasse 1
Rotkreuz
6343
Switzerland
Tel: +41 41/798 19 40
Fax: +41 41/798 19 99
Email: michelotti@dmm.ch
Marcus Michelotti

Services/Products:
List services; Database services; Service bureau; Response analysis bureau

Member of:
SVD

DMC DRUCK & MAIL CENTER AG

Röschstrasse 18
St. Gallen
9006
Switzerland
Tel: +41 71/25 40 70
Fax: +41 7125 41 20
Heinz Rohrer

Services/Products:
Lettershop; Fulfilment and sampling house; Mailing/Faxing services; Print services

Member of:
SVD

DR. MARC RUTSCHMANN AG CORPORATE STRATEGIES AND MARKETING COMMUNICATIONS

Limmatquai 1
Bellevue-Haus
Zürich
CH 8001
Switzerland
Tel: +41 1 262 19 33
Fax: +41 1 262 14 17
Email: mrutschmann@swissonline.ch
Ms Alicia Umbricht

Services/Products:
Database services; Direct marketing agency; Consultancy services; Direct response TV services; Electronic media; Internet services

E-Services:
Website design

DRUCKSACHEN-VERTEIL-ORGANISATION GLARNERLAND
Schwanden
8762
Switzerland
Tel: +41 58/81 29 81
Fax: +41 5881 11 55
Walter Feldmann

Services/Products:
Private delivery services

Member of:
SVD

FEPE EUROPEAN ENVELOPE MANUFACTURER'S ASSOCIATION
PO Box 134
Zürich
8030
Switzerland
Tel: +41 1 266 9922
Fax: +41 1 266 9949
Email: info@fepe.de
Web: www.fepe.de

Services/Products:
Labelling/envelope services; Association of all European envelope manufacturers

Member of:
FEDMA; CITPA

FISCH.MEIER DIREKT AG
Webereistrasse 56
Adliswil
8134
Switzerland
Tel: +41 1 711 72 11
Fax: +41 1 711 72 72
Email: fischmeier@access.ch
Gilbert W. Fisch, Director

Services/Products:
Advertising Agency; Database services; Direct marketing agency; Sales promotion agency

Member of:
FEDMA; SVD

FOCUS-CONSEIL AG
Gartenstrasse 11
Zürich
CH-8039

Switzerland
Tel: +41 1 283 64 64
Fax: +41 1 283 64 65
Pierre-Etienne Pointet

Services/Products:
Advertising Agency; Database services; Direct marketing agency; Design/graphics/clip art supplier; Sales promotion agency

G & S DIRECT MARKETING CONSULTING
Auenstrasse 10
Dübendorf
8600
Switzerland
Tel: +41 1/802 60 40
Fax: +41 1 802 60 44
Willy Goor

Services/Products:
Direct marketing agency; Advertising Agency

Member of:
SVD

GAGGINI-BIZZOZERO SA
Casella Postale 174
Lugano
6903
Switzerland
Tel: +41 91/58 10 48
Fax: +41 9156 51 56
Sp. Arigoni

Services/Products:
Private delivery services

Member of:
SVD

H. GOESSLER AG
Binzstrasse 24
Postfach 169
Zürich
8045
Switzerland
Tel: +41 1/463 66 60
Fax: +41 1 463 68 78
Eric Goessler

Services/Products:
Lettershop; Fulfilment and sampling house; Mailing/Faxing services; Print services

Member of:
SVD

HSW-DIREKTMARKETING
Dorfstrasse 75
Embrach
8424
Switzerland
Tel: +41 1/865 71 77

Fax: +41 1 865 71 80
Walter Hasler

Services/Products:
List services; Database services

Member of:
SVD

IDEM S.A.
40 rue des Vollandes
1207 Geneva
Switzerland
Tel: +41 22 736 4636
Fax: +41 22 736 4643
Email: ms@idem.ch
Michael J.O. Sutherland

Services/Products:
Consultancy services; List services

Member of:
FEDMA

IMPULS DIRECT AG
Freihofstrasse 22
Postfach 1279
Küsnacht
8700
Switzerland
Tel: +41 1/913 32 32
Fax: +41 1/913 32 33
Email: direct@impuls.ch
Peter Raissig

Services/Products:
Direct marketing agency; Advertising Agency

Member of:
SVD

JAEGGI & WEIBEL AG
Buckhauserstrasse 24
Postfach
Zürich
8048
Switzerland
Tel: +41 1/405 63 00
Fax: +41 1/405 63 33
Email: jw.vertrieb@bluewin.ch
Orlando Pavano

Services/Products:
List services; Lettershop; Fulfilment and sampling house; Database services; Mailing/Faxing services; Response analysis bureau

Member of:
SVD

JPJ DIRECT MARKETING AG
Dorfstrasse 1
Postfach
Bonstetten
8906
Switzerland

Tel: +41 1/701 81 11
Fax: +41 1 701 81 12
Jean-Pierre Jamet

Services/Products:
List services; Database services;
Mailing/Faxing services

Member of:
SVD

KASPARIAN
30–32 Florissant Avenue
Renens 1
1020
Switzerland
Tel: +41 21 252 420
Edouard Kasparian, Director

Services/Products:
Lettershop; Mailing/Faxing services

Member of:
DMA (US)

KB:DATA/CONSULT AG
Haupstrasse 128
Niederteufen
9052
Switzerland
Tel: +41 71/330 01 51
Fax: +41 71333 22 73
Hans-Peter Künzler

Services/Products:
List services; Database services;
Service bureau; Response analysis
bureau

Member of:
SVD

KIK KONZEPTE IN
KOMMUNIKATION
Neuenhoferstrasse 101
Postfach
Baden
5401
Switzerland
Tel: +41 56/203 25 00
Fax: +41 56203 25 99
Anton Wagner

Services/Products:
Direct marketing agency; Advertising
Agency

Member of:
SVD

KüNZLER-BACHMANN DIRECT
MEDIA AG
Rorschacherstrasse 270
St. Gallen
9016
Switzerland
Tel: +41 71/282 32 82

Fax: +41 71282 32 83
Marc Wilmes

Services/Products:
List services; Database services;
Service bureau; Response analysis
bureau

Member of:
SVD

KüNZLER-BACHMANN
RECHENZENTRUM AG
Rorschacherstr. 270
Postfach
St. Gallen
9016
Switzerland
Tel: +41 71/282 32 32
Fax: +41 71/282 32 33
Email: m.wilmes@kueba.ch
Max Künzler

Services/Products:
List services; Lettershop; Fulfilment
and sampling house; Database services;
Mailing/Faxing services; Response
analysis bureau

Member of:
SVD

LAMMOTH MAILKONZEPT
WERBEAGENTUR FüR
DIREKTMARKETING/KOM-
MUNIKATION
Rötelistrasse 16
Dufourpark
St. Gallen
9000
Switzerland
Tel: +41 71/277 62 52
Fax: +41 71/277 64 44
Email: lammoth@access.ch
Friedhelm Lammoth

Services/Products:
Direct marketing agency; Advertising
Agency

Member of:
SVD

LDM DIRECT MARKETING
Mayenfelserstrasse 4
Postfach 1605
Prattein 1
4133
Switzerland
Tel: +41 61/821 43 33
Fax: +41 61821 96 86
Heidy Fasler

Services/Products:
List services; Lettershop; Fulfilment
and sampling house; Database services;
Mailing/Faxing services

Member of:
SVD

M&F DIRECTMARKETING AG
Postfach 211
Seestrasse 60A
Uster
8612
Switzerland
Tel: +41 1 940 71 10
Fax: +41 1 940 71 70
Email: mail@mf-direct.ch
Web: www.direct-marketing.ch
Thomas W Mahler, President

Services/Products:
List services; Database services; Direct
marketing agency; Response analysis
bureau

Member of:
DMA (US); FEDMA; SVD

MAC MARKETING
CONSULTING AG
Ebnetstrasse 3
Postfach 425
Adligenswil
6043
Switzerland
Tel: +41 41/370 93 70
Fax: +41 41/370 73 08
Email: mac.ag@bluewin.ch
Helmuth Slattner

Services/Products:
Database services; Service bureau;
Response analysis bureau

Member of:
SVD

MAGAZINE ZUM GLOBUS
Postfach 414
Lowenstrasse 37
Zürich
8021
Switzerland
Thomas Mahler, President

Services/Products:
Direct marketing agency; Consultancy
services

Member of:
DMA (US)

MAURER DATA
12, Chemin des Sapins
Aubonne
1170
Switzerland
Tel: +41 21 808 72 94
Fax: +41 21808 72 86

Services/Products:
Database services; Service bureau; Response analysis bureau

Member of:
SVD

MEDIA MAIL AG
Steinackerstrasse 23–25
Kloten
8302
Switzerland
Tel: +41 1/813 22 33
Fax: +41 1 813 10 48
Roland Oehy

Services/Products:
Lettershop; Fulfilment and sampling house; Mailing/Faxing services; Print services

Member of:
SVD

MESSAGERIES DU RHôNE ET BVA SION S.A.
Route des Ronquoz 86
case postale 555
Sion
1951
Switzerland
Tel: +41 27/29 76 66
Fax: +41 2729 76 74
Jeane-Marie Torrenté

Services/Products:
List services; Lettershop; Fulfilment and sampling house; Database services; Mailing/Faxing services; Private delivery services

Member of:
SVD

MS DIREKTMARKETING AG
Fürstenlandstrasse 35
St. Gallen
9001
Switzerland
Tel: +41 71/274 66 88
Fax: +41 71274 66 89
Peter Stössel

Services/Products:
Lettershop; Fulfilment and sampling house; Database services; Service bureau; Print services

Member of:
SVD

NPO MARKETING AG
Gemeindestrasse 26
Postfach
Zürich
8032
Switzerland

Tel: +41 1/252 86 00
Fax: +41 1 261 27 61
Jolanda Schmitter

Services/Products:
Direct marketing agency; Advertising Agency

Member of:
SVD

OGILVYONE WORLDWIDE LTD
Bergstrasse 50
Zürich
8032
Switzerland
Tel: +41 1 268 63 03
Fax: +41 1 252 08 56
Web: www.ogilvy.com
Guido Cometti, Managing Director

Services/Products:
Advertising Agency; Database services; Direct marketing agency; Media buying agency

Member of:
FEDMA; SVD

OPTIMAS AG FÜR MARKTBEARBEITUNG
Zürichstrasse 38
Brüttisellen
8306
Switzerland
Tel: +41 848–80 44 45
Fax: +41 848–80 44 46
Email: roger.meili@optimas-group.com
Roger Meili

Services/Products:
Mailing/Faxing services; Telemarketing agency

Member of:
SVD

OPTIMAS AG FÜR MARKTBEARBEITUNG
Zürichstraße 38
Brüttisellen
CH-8306
Switzerland
Tel: +41 848 804445
Fax: +41 848 804446
Email: info@optimas-group.com
Web: www.optimas-group.com

Services/Products:
Advertising Agency; Call centre services/systems; Consultancy services; Direct marketing agency; Telemarketing agency; Training/recruitment

E-Services:
E-Marketing consultant; Website design; Online/e-marketing agency

Member of:
National DMA; Call Center Network Switzerland CallNet.ch

PDC AG
Landstr. 115
Postfach
Wettingen 2
5430
Switzerland
Tel: +41 56/426 06 44
Fax: +41 56/426 39 20
Email: info-pdc@pdc-online.com
Manfred Opp

Services/Products:
Database services; Direct marketing agency; Service bureau; Response analysis bureau; Advertising Agency

Member of:
SVD

PHONE MARKETING BUSINESS SA
Place de la Riponne 1
Case postale 439
Lausanne 17
1000
Switzerland
Tel: +41 21/317 07 07
Fax: +41 21/317 07 08
Email: pmb@worldcom.ch
Philippe Grunder

Services/Products:
Mailing/Faxing services; Telemarketing agency

Member of:
SVD

PP & PARTNER MAILING HOUSE SA
Ch. de la Fauvette 10
Lausanne
1012
Switzerland
Tel: +41 21 653 13 20
Fax: +41 21 653 13 67
Email: pplausanne@ppmailing.ch
Web: www.axecom.com/ppmailing
Antoine Pernet, Director

Services/Products:
List services; Lettershop; Mailing/Faxing services; Service bureau; Personalisation

Member of:
FEDMA

PP & PARTNERS MAILING HOUSE SA
Ch. de la Fauvette 10
Lausanne
CH-1012
Switzerland
Tel: +41 21 653 13 20
Fax: +41 21 653 13 67
Antoine Pernet, Director

Services/Products:
List services; Lettershop; Mailing/Faxing services

PRESENT-SERVICE ULLRICH & CO
Chollerstrasse 3
Zug
6303
Switzerland
Tel: +41 41/740 01 40
Fax: +41 41741 35 28
André Bühler

Services/Products:
List services; Database services

Member of:
SVD

PUBLICIS WERBEAGENTUR AG, BSW
Theaterstrasse 8
Zürich
8001
Switzerland
Tel: +41 1/265 31 11
Fax: +41 1/262 57 80
Email: dir.marketing@publicis.ch
Alexandra Nelischer

Services/Products:
Direct marketing agency; Advertising Agency

Member of:
SVD

RBC GRUPPE
General-Wille-Strasse 144
Postfach
Meilen
CH-8706
Switzerland
Tel: +41 1 925 3636
Fax: +41 1 925 3646
Email: info@rbc-gruppe.ch
Web: www.rbc-gruppe.ch

Services/Products:
Call centre services/systems; Consultancy services; Database services; Fulfilment and sampling house; Interactive media; Lettershop; Consulting; Coaching in database marketing; CRM

E-Services:
E-Marketing consultant

Member of:
National DMA

REGOR AG
Heerenstegstrasse 1
Rorbas
8427
Switzerland
Tel: +41 1/865 55 15
Fax: +41 1 865 55 40
Leo Arnold

Services/Products:
Lettershop; Fulfilment and sampling house; Mailing/Faxing services; Print services

Member of:
SVD

RESPONSE MEDIA AG
Lättenstr. 39
Schlieren
8952
Switzerland
Tel: +41 1/730 53 48
Fax: +41 1 730 53 41
Alfred Biefer

Services/Products:
Direct marketing agency; Advertising Agency

Member of:
SVD

RINGIER PRINT ZOFINGEN AG RINCOMAIL
Brühlstrasse 5
Zofingen
4800
Switzerland
Tel: +41 62/746 35 37
Fax: +41 62/746 34 76
Email: arh@ringier.ch
Heinz Arnold

Services/Products:
List services; Lettershop; Fulfilment and sampling house; Database services; Mailing/Faxing services; Response analysis bureau

Member of:
SVD

ROHNER DIREKTMARKETING
Seestrasse 13
Zollikon
8702
Switzerland
Tel: +41 1/390 29 20
Fax: +41 1/390 29 19

Email: hrohner@csi.ch
Hans Rohner

Services/Products:
List services; Database services; Direct marketing agency; Service bureau; Response analysis bureau; Advertising Agency

Member of:
SVD

ROHRBACH & PARTNER
Seestrasse 247
Zürich
8038
Switzerland
Tel: +41 1/480 08 88
Fax: +41 1/480 08 89
Email: info@rohrbach.partner.ch
Franz Rohrbach

Services/Products:
Direct marketing agency; Advertising Agency

Member of:
SVD

SCHOBER DIREKTMARKETING AG
Bramenstrasse 5
Bachenbülach
8184
Switzerland
Tel: +41 1/860 58 10
Fax: +41 1/860 55 15
Email: schober-ch@swissonline.ch
Heinz Rehmann

Services/Products:
List services; Lettershop; Fulfilment and sampling house; Database services; Mailing/Faxing services; Response analysis bureau

Member of:
SVD

SEETAL SCHALLER AG
Wildischachen
Brugg
5201
Switzerland
Tel: +41 56/462 80 00
Fax: +41 56462 80 80
Christian Wipf

Services/Products:
Lettershop; Fulfilment and sampling house; Mailing/Faxing services; Print services

Member of:
SVD

SEILER RAPP COLLINS
Bühistrasse 2
Zollikerberg-Zürich
8125
Switzerland
Tel: +41 1/395 41 33
Fax: +41 1 391 31 81
Reinhold Alther

Services/Products:
Database services; Direct marketing agency; Service bureau; Response analysis bureau; Advertising Agency

Member of:
SVD

SYSMAR AG FüR SYSTEM-MARKETING
Alte Steinhauserstrasse 19
Cham
6330
Switzerland
Tel: +41 41/748 78 78
Fax: +41 41/748 79 79
Email: sysmar@bluewin.ch
Paul E. Dobler

Services/Products:
Mailing/Faxing services; Telemarketing agency

Member of:
SVD

TEL'N'SELL AG FüR TELEMARKETING
Leimgrubenweg 6
Basel
4053
Switzerland
Tel: +41 61/338 39 39
Fax: +41 61/338 39 40
Email: tns@teinsell.ch
Thomas Eicher

Services/Products:
Mailing/Faxing services; Telemarketing agency

Member of:
SVD

TELAG AKTIV TELEMARKETING
Winkelriedstrasse 37
Postfach
Luzern 4
6000
Switzerland
Tel: +41 41/210 04 44
Fax: +41 41/210 01 04
Email: andersenf@abd.ihagfm.ch
Christian Gut

Services/Products:
Mailing/Faxing services; Telemarketing agency

Member of:
SVD

TELEMARKETING PLUS
Gerliswilstrasse 42
Emmenbrücke
6020
Switzerland
Tel: +41 41/267 07 30
Fax: +41 41/267 07 39
Email: schmidiger@teleplus.ch
Hansruedi Schmidiger

Services/Products:
Mailing/Faxing services; Telemarketing agency

Member of:
SVD

TELEPERFORMANCE SCHWEIZ
Denkmalstrasse 2
Luzern
6006
Switzerland
Tel: +41 41/419 02 02
Fax: +41 41419 02 92
Peter Sigrist

Services/Products:
Mailing/Faxing services; Telemarketing agency

Member of:
SVD

TNT INTERNAITONAL MAIL (SWITZERLAND) AG
Amsleracherweg 8
Buchs
5033
Switzerland
Tel: +41 62837 0000
Fax: +41 62837 0100
Thomas Knecht, Director for Commercial and Strategic Development

Services/Products:
Mailing/Faxing services; Private delivery services; Crossborder mail distribution

Member of:
National DMA

TRENDCOMMERCE ST. GALLEN GMBH
Heiligkreuzstrasse 2
St. Gallen
9008
Switzerland
Tel: +41 71/242 66 88
Fax: +41 71/242 66 81
Email: trendcommerce@st.gallen.ch
Oliver P. Künzler

Services/Products:
List services; Lettershop; Fulfilment and sampling house; Database services; Mailing/Faxing services; Response analysis bureau

Member of:
SVD

TRIO – AGENCE CONSEIL EN MARKETING ET PUBLICITE SA
1, Rue Voltaire, Case postale 200
Lausanne 13
1000
Switzerland
Tel: +41 21 614 60 00
Fax: +41 21 614 60 19
Email: triosa@trio.ch
Hansjörg Lippuner, Managing Director

Services/Products:
Direct marketing agency; Design/graphics/clip art supplier; Media buying agency; Sales promotion agency; Advertising Agency; Electronic media

E-Services:
Website design

Member of:
FEDMA

TRIO-AGENCE CONSEIL EN MARKETING ET PUBLICITE SA
1, Rue Voltaire
Case postale 200
Lausanne 13
CH-1000
Switzerland
Tel: +41 21 614 6000
Fax: +41 21 614 6019
Email: triosa@trio.ch
Hansjörg Lippuner, Managing Director

Services/Products:
Advertising Agency; Direct marketing agency; Copy adaptation; Media buying agency

Member of:
FEDMA

W. B. O. DIALOG AG
Weberstrassse 21
Postfach
Zürich
8036
Switzerland
Tel: +41 1/291 08 30
Fax: +41 1 240 38 18
Guido Wietlisbach

Services/Products:
Direct marketing agency; Advertising
Agency

Member of:
SVD

WALTER SCHMID AG
Stettbacherhof
Auenstrasse 10
Dübendorf
8600
Switzerland
Tel: +41 1/802 60 00
Fax: +41 1 802 60 10
Werner Hemmi

Services/Products:
List services; Database services

Member of:
SVD

WIRZ BRUGGER LüTHI DIREKT AG
Aeschstr. 1
Forch
8127
Switzerland
Tel: +41 1/980 36 00
Fax: +41 1/980 36 10
Email: wbl@wirz-direkt.ch
Markus Lüthi

Services/Products:
Direct marketing agency; Advertising
Agency

Member of:
SVD

ZM ZIELGRUPPEN MARKETING AG
Dierauerstr. 14
St. Gallen
9000
Switzerland
Tel: +41 71/228 55 22
Fax: +41 71228 55 12
Helen Kamer

Services/Products:
List services; Database services

Member of:
SVD

SERVICES/PRODUCT LISTING

Advertising Agency
AKTIV - Dialogmarketing GmbH
Alex Schmid AG
Baumer AG
BDK Mailing GmbH
Bono

Consulting
RBC Gruppe
Bornand + Gaeng
CSM SA communication, stratégie, marketing
Fisch.Meier Direkt Ag
Focus-Conseil AG
G & S Direct Marketing

Consulting
RBC Gruppe
Impuls Direct AG
kik Konzepte in Kommunikation
Lammoth Mailkonzept Werbeagentur für Direktmarketing/ Kommunikation
NPO Marketing AG
Ogilvyone Worldwide Ltd
optimAS AG für Marktbearbeitung
PDC AG
Publicis Werbeagentur AG, BSW
Response Media AG
Rohner Direktmarketing
Rohrbach & Partner
Seiler Rapp Collins
Trio – Agence Conseil En Marketing Et Publicite Sa
Trio-Agence Conseil en Marketing et Publicite SA
W. B. O. Dialog AG
Wirz Brugger Lüthi Direkt AG

Association of all European envelope manufacturers
FEPE European Envelope Manufacturer's Association

CRM
RBC Gruppe

Call centre services/systems
optimAS AG für Marktbearbeitung
RBC Gruppe

Coaching in database marketing
RBC Gruppe

Consultancy services
Atelier Ettlin
b.a.s. AG Digital Marketing Service
Bischof Direct Marketing

Dr. Marc Rutschmann AG Corporate strategies and marketing communications
Idem S.A.
Magazine Zum Globus
optimAS AG für Marktbearbeitung
RBC Gruppe

Consulting
RBC Gruppe

Copy adaptation
Trio-Agence Conseil en Marketing et Publicite SA

Crossborder mail distribution
TNT Internaitonal Mail (Switzerland) AG

Database services
A & D Arnold, Demmerer & Partner AG
abewa
ADIM Agentur für Direktmarketing AG
APZ Adressen- und Propagandazentrale Schaffhausen AG
ATAG Ernst & Young Marketing-Services AG
Athena AG für Data-Engineering und Consulting
AWZ Adressen- und Werbezentrale Bern
AWZ Adressen- und Werbezentrale St. Gallen
AWZ Adressen- und Werbezentrale Zürich
b.a.s. AG Digital Marketing Service
BDK Mailing GmbH
Beorda Direktwerbung AG
Blickle & Partner GmbH
Bureau genevois d'adresses et de publicité
Bureau vaudois d'adresses
bwv Beratung für Wirtschaft & Verwaltung AG
DCB Data Center Brüttisellen AG
DCL Data Center Luzern AG
Die Schweizerische Post Swiss Post International
Direct Mail House AG
dm michelotti ag Direkt Marketing
Dr. Marc Rutschmann AG Corporate strategies and marketing communications
Fisch.Meier Direkt Ag
Focus-Conseil AG
HSW-Direktmarketing
Jaeggi & Weibel AG
JPJ Direct Marketing AG
KB:DATA/CONSULT AG
Künzler-Bachmann Direct Media AG

Künzler-Bachmann Rechenzentrum
AG
LDM Direct Marketing
M&F Directmarketing Ag
MAC Marketing Consulting AG
Maurer Data
Messageries du Rhône et BVA Sion
S.A.
MS Direktmarketing AG
Ogilvyone Worldwide Ltd
PDC AG
Present-Service Ullrich & Co
RBC Gruppe
Ringier Print Zofingen AG RincoMail
Rohner Direktmarketing
Schober Direktmarketing AG
Seiler Rapp Collins
Trendcommerce St. Gallen GmbH
Walter Schmid AG
ZM Zielgruppen Marketing AG

Design/graphics/clip art supplier
Atelier Ettlin
Focus-Conseil AG
Trio – Agence Conseil En Marketing
Et Publicite Sa

Direct marketing agency
ADIM Agentur für Direktmarketing
AG
AKTIV - Dialogmarketing GmbH
Alex Schmid AG
b.a.s. AG Digital Marketing Service
BDK Mailing GmbH
Bischof Direct Marketing
Bono Consulting
Bornand + Gaeng
CSM SA communication, stratégie,
marketing
DCB Data Center Brüttisellen AG
Die Schweizerische Post Swiss Post
International
Dr. Marc Rutschmann AG Corporate
strategies and marketing
communications
Fisch.Meier Direkt Ag
Focus-Conseil AG
G & S Direct Marketing Consulting
Impuls Direct AG
kik Konzepte in Kommunikation
Lammoth Mailkonzept Werbeagentur
für Direktmarketing/
Kommunikation
M&F Directmarketing Ag
Magazine Zum Globus
NPO Marketing AG
Ogilvyone Worldwide Ltd
optimAS AG für Marktbearbeitung
PDC AG
Publicis Werbeagentur AG, BSW
Response Media AG
Rohner Direktmarketing

Rohrbach & Partner
Seiler Rapp Collins
Trio – Agence Conseil En Marketing
Et Publicite Sa
Trio-Agence Conseil en Marketing et
Publicite SA
W. B. O. Dialog AG
Wirz Brugger Lüthi Direkt AG

Direct response TV services
Dr. Marc Rutschmann AG Corporate
strategies and marketing
communications

Electronic media
BOL International Bertelsmann E-
Commerce
Dr. Marc Rutschmann AG Corporate
strategies and marketing
communications
Trio – Agence Conseil En Marketing
Et Publicite Sa

Event
ADIM Agentur für Direktmarketing
AG

Fulfilment and sampling house
APZ Adressen- und
Propagandazentrale Schaffhausen
AG
AWZ Adressen- und Werbezentrale
Bern
AWZ Adressen- und Werbezentrale
Zürich
b.a.s. AG Digital Marketing Service
Baumer AG
Bureau d'Adresses et de Publicité
Direct
Bureau genevois d'adresses et de
publicité
Bureau vaudois d'adresses
Conzett + Walter AG
DCL Data Center Luzern AG
Direct Mail Company
Direct Mail House AG
Direktwerbung AG
DMC Druck & Mail Center AG
H. Goessler AG
Jaeggi & Weibel AG
Künzler-Bachmann Rechenzentrum
AG
LDM Direct Marketing
Media Mail AG
Messageries du Rhône et BVA Sion
S.A.
MS Direktmarketing AG
RBC Gruppe
Regor AG
Ringier Print Zofingen AG RincoMail
Schober Direktmarketing AG
Seetal Schaller AG
Trendcommerce St. Gallen GmbH

Interactive media
RBC Gruppe

Internet services
Dr. Marc Rutschmann AG Corporate
strategies and marketing
communications

Labelling/envelope services
Baumer AG
Beorda Direktwerbung AG
FEPE European Envelope
Manufacturer's Association

Lettershop
APZ Adressen- und
Propagandazentrale Schaffhausen
AG
AWZ Adressen- und Werbezentrale
Bern
AWZ Adressen- und Werbezentrale
Zürich
b.a.s. AG Digital Marketing Service
Baumer AG
Beorda Direktwerbung AG
Bureau d'Adresses et de Publicité
Direct
Bureau genevois d'adresses et de
publicité
Bureau vaudois d'adresses
Conzett + Walter AG
DCB Data Center Brüttisellen AG
DCL Data Center Luzern AG
Direct Mail Company
Direct Mail House AG
Direktwerbung AG
DMC Druck & Mail Center AG
H. Goessler AG
Jaeggi & Weibel AG
Kasparian
Künzler-Bachmann Rechenzentrum
AG
LDM Direct Marketing
Media Mail AG
Messageries du Rhône et BVA Sion
S.A.
MS Direktmarketing AG
Pp & Partner Mailing House Sa
PP & Partners Mailing House SA
RBC Gruppe
Regor AG
Ringier Print Zofingen AG
RincoMail
Schober Direktmarketing AG
Seetal Schaller AG
Trendcommerce St. Gallen GmbH

List services
A & D Arnold, Demmerer & Partner
AG
abewa
Adamos Ag
Alexander Hegele Direct

APZ Adressen- und
  Propagandazentrale Schaffhausen
  AG
ATAG Ernst & Young Marketing-
  Services AG
AWZ Adressen- und Werbezentrale
  Bern
AWZ Adressen- und Werbezentrale St.
  Gallen
AWZ Adressen- und Werbezentrale
  Zürich
BDK Mailing GmbH
Blickle & Partner GmbH
Bornand + Gaeng
Bureau genevois d'adresses et de
  publicité
Bureau vaudois d'adresses
bwv Beratung für Wirtschaft &
  Verwaltung AG
DCB Data Center Brüttisellen AG
Die Schweizerische Post Swiss Post
  International
Direct Mail House AG
dm michelotti ag Direkt Marketing
HSW-Direktmarketing
Idem S.A.
Jaeggi & Weibel AG
JPJ Direct Marketing AG
KB:DATA/CONSULT AG
Künzler-Bachmann Direct Media
  AG
Künzler-Bachmann Rechenzentrum
  AG
LDM Direct Marketing
M&F Directmarketing Ag
Messageries du Rhône et BVA Sion
  S.A.
Pp & Partner Mailing House Sa
PP & Partners Mailing House SA
Present-Service Ullrich & Co
Ringier Print Zofingen AG RincoMail
Rohner Direktmarketing
Schober Direktmarketing AG
Trendcommerce St. Gallen GmbH
Walter Schmid AG
ZM Zielgruppen Marketing AG

Mailing/Faxing services
ADIM Agentur für Direktmarketing
  AG
APZ Adressen- und
  Propagandazentrale Schaffhausen
  AG
ATAG Ernst & Young Marketing-
  Services AG
AWZ Adressen- und Werbezentrale
  Bern
AWZ Adressen- und Werbezentrale
  Zürich
b.a.s. AG Digital Marketing Service
Baumer AG
Bureau d'Adresses et de Publicité
  Direct

Bureau genevois d'adresses et de
  publicité
Bureau vaudois d'adresses
Conzett + Walter AG
CSM SA communication, stratégie,
  marketing
DCB Data Center Brüttisellen AG
DCL Data Center Luzern AG
Die Schweizerische Post Swiss Post
  International
Direct Mail Company
Direct Mail House AG
Direktwerbung AG
DMC Druck & Mail Center AG
H. Goessler AG
Jaeggi & Weibel AG
JPJ Direct Marketing AG
Kasparian
Künzler-Bachmann Rechenzentrum
  AG
LDM Direct Marketing
Media Mail AG
Messageries du Rhône et BVA Sion
  S.A.
optimAS AG für Marktbearbeitung
Phone Marketing Business SA
Pp & Partner Mailing House Sa
PP & Partners Mailing House SA
Regor AG
Ringier Print Zofingen AG RincoMail
Schober Direktmarketing AG
Seetal Schaller AG
Sysmar AG für System-Marketing
Tel'n'Sell AG für Telemarketing
TELAG AKTIV Telemarketing
Telemarketing Plus
Teleperformance Schweiz
TNT Internaitonal Mail (Switzerland)
  AG
Trendcommerce St. Gallen GmbH

Media buying agency
Alexander Hegele Direct
Ogilvyone Worldwide Ltd
Trio – Agence Conseil En Marketing
  Et Publicite Sa
Trio-Agence Conseil en Marketing et
  Publicite SA

Personalisation
ADIM Agentur für Direktmarketing
  AG
Beorda Direktwerbung AG
Pp & Partner Mailing House Sa

Print services
Bureau d'Adresses et de Publicité
  Direct
Conzett + Walter AG
Direct Mail Company
Direktwerbung AG
DMC Druck & Mail Center AG
H. Goessler AG

Media Mail AG
MS Direktmarketing AG
Regor AG
Seetal Schaller AG

Private delivery services
Aarmail AG
ADZ Agentur für Direktwerbung AG
Anzeiger AG
APZ Adressen- und
  Propagandazentrale Schaffhausen
  AG
AWZ Adressen- und Werbezentrale
  Bern
AWZ Adressen- und Werbezentrale St.
  Gallen
AWZ Adressen- und Werbezentrale
  Zürich
Bureau d'Adresses et de Publicité
  Direct
Bureau genevois d'adresses et de
  publicité
Bureau vaudois d'adresses
Die Schweizerische Post Swiss Post
  International
Direct Mail Company
Direktwerbung AG
Distriba
Distriforce AG
Drucksachen-Verteil-organisation
  Glarnerland
Gaggini-Bizzozero SA
Messageries du Rhône et BVA Sion
  S.A.
TNT Internaitonal Mail (Switzerland)
  AG

Response analysis bureau
abewa
ATAG Ernst & Young Marketing-
  Services AG
Athena AG für Data-Engineering und
  Consulting
Beorda Direktwerbung AG
Blickle & Partner GmbH
bwv Beratung für Wirtschaft &
  Verwaltung AG
DCB Data Center Brüttisellen AG
dm michelotti ag Direkt Marketing
Jaeggi & Weibel AG
KB:DATA/CONSULT AG
Künzler-Bachmann Direct Media AG
Künzler-Bachmann Rechenzentrum
  AG
M&F Directmarketing Ag
MAC Marketing Consulting AG
Maurer Data
PDC AG
Ringier Print Zofingen AG RincoMail
Rohner Direktmarketing
Schober Direktmarketing AG
Seiler Rapp Collins
Trendcommerce St. Gallen GmbH

Sales promotion agency
Fisch.Meier Direkt Ag
Focus-Conseil AG
Trio – Agence Conseil En Marketing
Et Publicite Sa

Service bureau
abewa
ATAG Ernst & Young Marketing-
Services AG
Athena AG für Data-Engineering und
Consulting
Blickle & Partner GmbH
bwv Beratung für Wirtschaft &
Verwaltung AG
DCL Data Center Luzern AG
Die Schweizerische Post Swiss Post
International
dm michelotti ag Direkt Marketing
KB:DATA/CONSULT AG
Künzler-Bachmann Direct Media
AG
MAC Marketing Consulting AG
Maurer Data
MS Direktmarketing AG
PDC AG
Pp & Partner Mailing House Sa
Rohner Direktmarketing

Seiler Rapp Collins

Telemarketing agency
CSM SA communication, stratégie,
marketing
optimAS AG für Marktbearbeitung
optimAS AG für Marktbearbeitung
Phone Marketing Business SA
Sysmar AG für System-Marketing
Tel'n'Sell AG für Telemarketing
TELAG AKTIV Telemarketing
Telemarketing Plus
Teleperformance Schweiz

Training/recruitment
optimAS AG für Marktbearbeitung

E-SERVICES

E-Marketing consultant
ADIM Agentur für Direktmarketing
AG
b.a.s. AG Digital Marketing Service
optimAS AG für Marktbearbeitung
RBC Gruppe

Email list provider
b.a.s. AG Digital Marketing Service

Email software
ADIM Agentur für Direktmarketing
AG

Online/e-marketing agency
ADIM Agentur für Direktmarketing
AG
b.a.s. AG Digital Marketing Service
optimAS AG für Marktbearbeitung

Website design
ADIM Agentur für Direktmarketing
AG
b.a.s. AG Digital Marketing Service
BOL International Bertelsmann E-
Commerce
Dr. Marc Rutschmann AG Corporate
strategies and marketing
communications
optimAS AG für Marktbearbeitung
Trio – Agence Conseil En Marketing
Et Publicite Sa

—UNITED KINGDOM—

Population: 57.5 million

Capital: London

Languages: English

GDP: $1092 billion

GDP per capita: $18,600

Inflation: 3.1 per cent

Currency: Pound Sterling (£) = 100 cents

Exchange rate: £0.62 : $1 (£0.66 : 1 euro)

Time: GMT

OVERVIEW

As one of the fastest growing media of the last ten years, direct marketing acts as a precise targeting tool with widespread availability. In the UK, more and more advertisers are turning to direct marketing techniques – direct mail; telemarketing; direct response TV, press and radio – as accountable media that can provide precise information on the effectiveness of a campaign. Statistics illustrate this growth in the market, with expenditure on direct mail increasing by an average of 12 per cent a year. Moreover, 67 per cent of companies predict that direct marketing will drive their marketing strategies in the future.

This increasing acceptance of direct marketing as a successful advertising medium comes not only from the marketers but also from the businesses and consumers they target. Statistics provided by the Direct Marketing Information Service show that 83 per cent of consumer direct mail is opened, with 68 per cent being opened and read. Business direct mail performs even better, with 84 per cent being opened. While by no means the most heavily mailed of the European nations, the UK has experienced one of the highest growth rates in recent years, suggesting a receptive market capable of sustained growth.

LANGUAGE AND CULTURAL CONSIDERATIONS

The majority of the population speak English, and this is certainly the most sensible language in which to conduct a DM campaign. However, if the

target audience of a campaign is a minor ethnic group, whose members are likely to speak a native language, it would be advisable to consult a specialist or translator.

LEGISLATION AND CONSUMER PROTECTION

In addition to the many laws which affect advertising and direct marketing, there are various self-regulatory codes of practice which are very well developed in the UK.

The Advertising Standards Authority (ASA) is the principal body supervising the British Code of Advertising and Sales Promotion, which applies to all non-broadcast advertising, including direct mail.

Radio and television commercials, including DRTV, are governed by statutory regulations under the control of the Independent Television Commission and the Radio Authority. All commercials have to be cleared by the Broadcast Advertising Clearance Centre (BACC).

The Direct Marketing Association's Code of Practice is adhered to by its 700+ corporate members.

Consumer protection measures include the Mailing Preference Service (MPS), the Telephone Preference Service (TPS), and the Fax Preference Service (FPS).

The Direct Mail Accreditation and Recognition Centre (DMARC) ensures that suppliers deal only with companies whose material abides by the British Codes of Advertising and Sales Promotion and the ICSTIS Code.

The UK direct mail industry has its own independent self-regulatory watchdog:

The Direct Mail Accreditation and Recognition Centre
5th Floor
Haymarket House
1 Oxendon Street
London
SW1Y 4EE

Tel 0171 766 4430
Fax 0171 371 0191
Email: dma@dma.org.uk
Website: www.dma.org.uk

Contact: Tessa Kelly (Manager)

DMARC can also provide information on rules governing standards of practice for list and database management (the List and Database Suppliers Group – LADS). Contact DMARC for any confidential ad hoc advice on the regulatory environment for the DM industry in the UK.

Lists and databases

Overall list availability in the UK is generally good. There are over 3000 lists, of which approximately 50 per cent are consumer, and 50 per cent business-to-business. The electoral roll is available for rental, with a variety of geodemographic and lifestyle overlays. Response lists and lists of buyers are also on the market, as are lists of magazine subscribers. There are several lifestyle databases in existence.

List accuracy and data quality are generally good. Most files are fully postcoded, and some lists carry guarantees of deliverability of up to 99 per cent. Compiled lists will carry higher nixie rates, but this is reflected in their price. Standard selections are offered on most consumer lists, and geodemographic or lifestyle profiling is common. The business-to-business list market is dominated by large publishing groups, who hold names of readers of controlled circulation magazines; these are highly selectable by company characteristic and job function.

List exchanges are common between publishers, seminar organizations, and charities. If these are arranged through a broker, a fee will be charged. Consumer lists rent at between \$100–170 per thousand names, with extra charges for selections and delivery. Net name discounts are possible for significant quantities. Business-to-business lists range between \$150–270 per thousand names; the cheaper lists are generally compiled.

Special permission from the list owner is required for telemarketing, re-usage, and the retention of data. All mailing pieces will be checked by the list owner/manager, and must conform with the industry codes of practice.

THE DIRECT MARKETING ASSOCIATION

Name:	Direct Marketing Association (UK) Ltd
Address:	Haymarket House, 1 Oxendon Street, London SW1Y 4EE
Tel:	+44 20 7321 2525
Fax:	+44 20 7321 0191
Email:	dma@dma.org.uk
Website:	www.dma.org.uk
Year founded:	1994
President	Colin Lloyd
Total staff:	51
Members:	850
Contact:	Lara Shannon, PR & Marketing Manager

Advertisers/Mail order companies	210	List brokers	60
DM Agencies	20	Mailing/handling house	130
DM Consultants	30	Printers	20
Database agencies	60	Telemarketing agencies	90
Field marketing companies	10	Door to door distributors	30

300

Facilities for overseas users of direct mail

Membership: the membership fee for suppliers is based on a % of their gross profit from direct marketing. For advertisers, it is a % of their direct marketing expenditure. This is subject to a minimum fee of £1100. Lower rates are available for sole traders and companies less than two years old. Overseas companies are eligible to join. Membership is subject to satisfactory references audited accounts and DMA Board approval.

The DMA was founded in 1992, an amalgamation of four previous associations which came together to create a single, unified voice for the direct marketing industry. The mission of the DMA is to represent the best interests of members by raising the stature of direct marketing and building the consumer's trust and confidence in the industry.

Members and non-members can enjoy the following services:

Newsletter: the DMA produces a regular newsletter, as well as a range of other publications and public service literature, designed to communicate the benefits of direct marketing.

Library: the DMA has an extensive library.

On-line information service: the DMA has a web site. It can be found at www.dma.org.uk

Legal advice: the DMA offers expert legal advice to members on all aspects of the law as it relates to direct marketing.

Business liaison service: the DMA holds a Direct Marketing Agency Register, which computer matches direct marketing agencies to client needs.

Other facilities: the DMA also offers: extensive lobbying in Brussels and Westminster to stem the tide of restrictive legislation on direct marketing; the use of the DMA symbol, a recognized sign of best practice in direct marketing; training and development through a programme of events, seminars, work-shops, training days and forums throughout the year; the DMA/Royal Mail Awards, the industry's premier awards; and qualitative and quantitative industry research.

POSTAL SERVICES

Whether mailing within the UK or internationally, Royal Mail, the letters business of the British Post Office, aims to compete head-on with all businesses in the sector. Constant product development and research demonstrate Royal Mail's commitment to customer service.

Services and discounts specially designed for direct mailers include the following:

Inland

Mailsort

Addressed mail can be sent either first or second class, with price determining speed of delivery.

Senders of large volumes of addressed mail can benefit from the Mailsort range of services. By sorting the mail before collection, mailers can qualify for discounts of up to 32 per cent, depending on the service chosen and the volume of mail. Mailsort consists of three delivery options:

Mailsort 1   Delivery next working day
Mailsort 2   Delivery within three working days
Mailsort 3   Delivery within seven working days.

Royal Mail will advise on all database and logistical requirements of Mailsort. For further information contact:

Mailsort General Helpline
Tel: +44 1865 780 400
Fax: +44 1865 780 214

Door to Door
Unaddressed mail can be distributed by Royal Mail Door to Door, by postcode sector. Contact: Door to Door, Streamline House, Sandy Lane West, Oxford, OX4 5ZZ; tel: +44 1865 780 400; fax: +44 1865 780 214.

Other services

Response Services
Response Services offer a range of simple, cost effective services to encourage and maximise customer responses to your advertising or direct mail activity.

Business Reply and Freepost are perhaps the most well known.

Business Reply is intended primarily for business-to-business and financial communications. However, it is widely and successfully used by companies in all market sectors to encourage response to direct mailings and magazine inserts. Business Reply cards or envelopes are pre-printed with a first or second class design.

As with Business Reply, the Freepost service can be used with first or second class pre-printed response cards or envelopes. Alternatively, the Freepost address can be used in press ads, on radio and/ or on TV, allowing prospects to respond using their own stationery. (Only second class is available when used in this way.)

Postage on both services is payable on all items sent back at the normal rate plus a small handling charge. Discounts are available on the number of Response Service licences and responses received per annum.

Pre-printed Business Reply and Freepost can be used with a unique Response Services Barcode. If you are a high volume mailer, barcoding will provide you with cost savings, improved efficiency and a more professional image.

Freepost NAME is the latest addition to the Response Services range. It encourages customers to respond to you by simply writing 'Freepost' followed by your company, product or campaign name. No other address details are required. It is simple and highly memorable, and is particularly suitable for broadcast media.

For further information on Response Services, please contact your local Royal Mail Sales Centre on 0345 950 950.

Admail

Admail is a redirection service for direct response advertisers. The service allows the advertiser to publish a central, prestigious address, and have mail rerouted to a second operating centre. The Admail service is available under contract for fixed periods of 30 to 365 days. The service can be combined with Freepost to encourage greater response. Items returned through the Freepost system are subject to the normal Response Services charges.

International

Royal Mail International (RMI) operates as a separate business unit, with its own marketing and operational departments to ensure the most efficient passage of international mail.

RMI offers the following services:

- **International Unsorted:** A service for large volume business mailings, the International Unsorted service provides a rapid international door-to-door service at attractive rates.

- **International Unsorted on Demand:** A service within the International Unsorted Service that provides cost savings of up to 30% for one-off postings with a value as low as £100.

- **International Sorted Service:** An efficient and cost effective service for multiple printed matter items abroad.

    Three service levels are offered with different levels of speed and cost:

    - **Priority:** Is the fastest and uses airmail and the most efficient distribution methods.

    - **Standard:** Available for countries outside Europe, the standard service combines value for money plus speed. Mail is flown to the destination country and distributed in the most effective manner.

    - **Economy:** Is the cheapest and uses surface mail methods such as train and boat.

- In addition there is the **M-Bag service:** If you are sending a number of items to the same address you can save money by using an M-Bag. The M-Bag service is available for any of the three International Sorted services.

- **International Direct Entry:** This service gives your mail a 'local' look and can lead to improved response rates for your direct mail campaigns.

- **International Response Services:** RMI offers two response services:
  International Business Reply and International Admail.

With the Business Reply Service, replies are sent directly back to the UK, while with the Admail Service replies carry an address in the country of destination where they are first collected and then sent back to the UK.

- **Swiftair:** Is a world-wide express Airmail service that places your mail on the first available flight to the country of destination.

- **Swiftpacks:** Pre-paid envelopes in four sizes for items up to 50g, 100g, 150g or 500g in weight

  Swiftair and Swiftpack items can be used in conjunction with both the International Registered and International Recorded services.

For all International enquiries, in the first instance contact:

Royal Mail's International Services
49 Featherstone Street
London EC17 8SY
United Kingdom
Tel: +44 20 7320 4030
Fax: +44 20 7320 4139
Website: www.royalmail.co.uk

PROVIDERS OF DM AND E-M SERVICES

:PED:
New Pudsey Court
101 Bradford Road
Leeds
LS28 6A7
United Kingdom
Tel: +44 1132 361 211
Fax: +44 1132 361 210
Email: info@pedmax.co.uk
Web: www.pedmax.co.uk
Gordon Pearson; Phil Crossland

Services/Products:
Direct marketing agency; Direct
response TV services

Member of:
DMA

100 PERCENT LTD
124 Great Portland Street
London
W1N 5PG
United Kingdom
Tel: +44 20 7631 3351
Fax: +44 7436 9233
Email: a100percent@btinternet.com
Michael Howe, Chief Executive

Services/Products:
Database services; Design/graphics/clip
art supplier; Direct marketing agency;
Lettershop; List services

Member of:
National DMA

ABLE-DIRECT CENTRE LTD
Mallard Close
Earls Barton
Northampton
NN6 0LS
United Kingdom
Tel: +44 1604 810781
Fax: +44 1604 811251
Phillip Dickenson, Marketing Director

Services/Products:
Mail order company

Member of:
DMA

ACXIOM LTD
Becket House
60–68 St Thomas Street
London
SE1 3QU
United Kingdom
Tel: +44 20 73787244
Fax: +44 1713787885
Rick Matthews, Marketing Manager

Services/Products:
List services; Fulfilment and sampling
house; Database services; Response
analysis bureau; Service bureau

Member of:
FEDMA

ACXIOM/DIRECT MEDIA
Collins House, 68/72 High St
Burnham
Bucks
SL1 7JT
United Kingdom
Tel: +44 628 604 030
Fax: +44 628 668 522
Charles Morgan, Pres. & Chairman of
the Board

Services/Products:
List services

Member of:
DMA (US)

ADLER
119/120 Buckingham Ave.
Slough
Berkshire
SL 4LZ
United Kingdom
Tel: +44 207 5355 9300
Fax: +44 207 5369 6217
Mr. Jim Adler

Services/Products:
Mail order company

ADS TELEMARKETING
49 Picadilly
Manchester
M1 2AP
United Kingdom
Tel: +44 161 236 1515
Fax: +44 161 236 8312
Howard Seaton, Managing Director

Services/Products:
Telemarketing agency

Member of:
DMA (US)

ADVANCED TELECOM SERVICES
Abbey House
74–76 St John's St
London
EC1M 4JB
United Kingdom
Tel: +44 20 7608 7777
Fax: +44 20 7608 7788
Email: bretd@advancedtele.com
Bret Dunlap

Services/Products:
Call centre services/systems

Member of:
DMA

ADVANSTAR MARKETING SERVICES
Advanstar House
Sealand Road
Chester
CH1 4RN
United Kingdom
Tel: +44 12+44 378 888
Fax: +44 12+44 383 356
Email: pduff@advanstar.com
Web: www.ams-europe.co.uk
Peter Duff, Marketing Director

Services/Products:
Advertising Agency; Card pack
manufacturer; Service bureau; Sales
promotion agency; List services; Direct
response TV services

Member of:
FEDMA

ADVANSTAR MARKETING SERVICES
Advanstar House
Park West
Sealand Road
Chester
CH1 4RN
United Kingdom
Tel: +44 12+44 393 452
Fax: +44 1244 383 356
Email: mwalsh@advanstar.com
Web: ams-europe.co.uk
Melissa Walsh

Services/Products:
List services; Fulfilment and sampling
house; Mailing/Faxing services;
Design/graphics/clip art supplier;
Publisher

Member of:
FEDMA; DMA (US)

ADVERTISING ASSOCIATION
Abford House
15 Wilton Road
London
SW1V 1NJ
United Kingdom
Tel: +44 20 7828 2771
Fax: +44 171 931 0376
Lionel Stanbrook

AEDP (AE DATA PROCESSING)
10 Bramley Gardens
Bognor Regis
W. Sussex
PO22 9SP
United Kingdom
Tel: +44 1243 823 275
Fax: +44 1243 842 706

Email: aedp@aedata.com
Web: www.aedata.com
Mr.A. Lewison-White

Services/Products:
List services; Direct marketing agency

Member of:
DMA

**ALLIED MARKETING
    SERVICES LTD**
Salisbury House
Milton Road
Wokingham
Berkshire
RG40 1DB
United Kingdom
Tel: +44 118 977 5050
Fax: +44 118 989 0025
Email: ams@alliedmarketing.co.uk
Web: www.alliedmarketing.co.uk
Geoff Bullock, Managing Director

Services/Products:
Copy adaptation; Database services;
Design/graphics/clip art supplier;
Direct marketing agency; Mailing/
Faxing services; Telemarketing agency

E-Services:
Website design; Email list provider

Member of:
National DMA

AMWAY UK LIMITED
Ambassador House
Queensway
Bletchley
Milton Keynes
MK2 2EH
United Kingdom
Tel: +44 1908 363000
Fax: +44 1908 363222
Web: www.amway.co.uk
Ms. Sharon Norman, Regional
    Manager, Corporate Affairs &
    Communications

**ANDERSON WEINRIB
    ASSOCIATES**
4 & 5 Filmer Studios
Filmer Road
London
SW6 7JF
United Kingdom
Tel: +44 20 7731 1399
Fax: +44 20 7384 1090
Email: enquiries@awa-direct.co.uk
Andrew Creed

Services/Products:
List services; Consultancy services;
Media buying agency

Member of:
DMA

**ANDREW BODDINGTON
    ASSOCIATES**
The Coach House
2c Woodborough Road
Putney
London
SW15 6PT
United Kingdom
Tel: +44 20 8788 6005
Fax: +44 8789 1656
Andrew Boddington

Services/Products:
Database services; Direct marketing
agency; Consultancy services

Member of:
DMA

APAC CUSTOMER SERVICES
Quality Court
28/3 Maritime Lane
Edinburgh
EH6 6RZ
United Kingdom
Tel: +44 131 624 8950
Fax: +44 131 624 8951
Email: ron.peerenboom@apacuk.com
Web: www.apacteleservices.com
Ron T. Peerenboom, Senior Vice
    President International

Services/Products:
Database services; Response analysis
bureau; Service bureau; Software
supplier; Call centre services/systems

Member of:
FEDMA

ASPEN AGENCY
Tower House
8–14 Southampton Street
Covent Garden
London
WC2E 7HB
United Kingdom
Tel: +44 20 78360055
Fax: +44 20 7906 9199
Email: rec@aspenagency.co.uk
Web: www.aspen-direct.co.uk
Stephen Butler, Managing Director

Services/Products:
Database services; Direct marketing
agency; Response analysis bureau;
Service bureau; Software supplier

Member of:
FEDMA

ASPEN AGENCY
Avon House
Kensington Village
Avonmore Road
London
W14 8TS
United Kingdom
Tel: +44 20 7906 2000
Fax: +44 20 7906 1999
Email: alawson@aspenplc.co.uk
Web: www.aspenplc.com
Alan Lawson

Services/Products:
Database services; Direct marketing
agency; Consultancy services;
Electronic media; Internet services

E-Services:
Website design

Member of:
DMA

**ASSOCIATION OF PUBLISHING
    AGENCIES (APA)**
Queens House
55–56 Lincolns Inn Fields
London
WC2A 3LJ
United Kingdom
Tel: +44 20 7404 4166
Fax: +44 20 7404 4167
Email: hilary@apa.co.uk
Web: www.apa.co.uk
Hilary Weaver, Director

Services/Products:
Interactive media; Publisher;
Information/advice on producing a
customer magazine/selecting a
publishing agency

E-Services:
Website design; Online/e-marketing
agency

Member of:
National DMA

**ATI - ADVANCED
    TECHNOLOGIES
    INTERNATIONAL LTD**
ATI House
The Ridgeway
Iver
Buckinghamshire
SL0 9JB
United Kingdom
Tel: +44 1753 631 121
Fax: +44 1753 631 106
Julia Forde, Marketing Manager

Services/Products:
Hardware supplier

BANKERS INSURANCE COMPANY LTD
St. John's Place
Easton Street
High Wycombe
Buckinghamshire
HP11 1NL
United Kingdom
Tel: +44 1494 603 600
Fax: +44 1494 603 629
Tom Anderson, Managing Director

Services/Products:
Telemarketing agency

BARRACLOUGH HALL WOOLSTON GRAY
Thames Wharf, Rainville Road
London
W6 9HT
United Kingdom
Tel: +44 20 7610 0007
Fax: +44 171 610 0111
Simon Hall, Chief Executive

Services/Products:
Advertising Agency; Direct Response
Agency

Member of:
DMA (US)

BBH UNLIMITED
60 Kingly Street
London
W1R 6DS
United Kingdom
Tel: +44 20 7453 4720
Fax: +44 20 7437 2956
Email: philippak@bbh-unlimited
Web: www.bbh.co.uk
Philippa K. Ibusin, Business
   Development Manager

Member of:
FEDMA; DMA (US)

BELLSIZE DATAMATIC LIMITED
Bournehall House
Bournehall Road
Bushey
WD2 3YG
United Kingdom
Tel: +44 20 8421 8123
Fax: +44 20 8421 8155
Email: ramesh@bellsize.co.uk
Ramesh Mehta

Services/Products:
Database services; Service bureau

Member of:
DMA

BH& P DIRECT MAIL LIMITED
Darby House
Redhill
Surrey
RH1 3DN
United Kingdom
Tel: +44 1737 645233
Fax: +44 1737 645566
Email:
   BHPDirectMailLtd@onyxnet.co.uk
Simon Gandy, Managing Director

Services/Products:
Database services; Mailing/Faxing
services; Personalisation; Fulfilment
and sampling house; Lettershop;
Direct Response Agency

Member of:
DMA (US)

BLAZE BUSINESS TO BUSINESS LTD
Oakley Hay
Corby
Northants
NN18 9AS
United Kingdom
Tel: +44 15367+44 515
Fax: +44 20 1536 744 115
Email: blazebzb@blaze.co.uk
Web: www.blaze.co.uk
Michael Ford, Client Services Director

Services/Products:
Advertising Agency; Database services;
Direct marketing agency; Design/
graphics/clip art supplier; Media
buying agency

E-Services:
Website design

Member of:
FEDMA

BLUE SHEEP LIMITED
Prospect House
Parabola Rd
Cheltenham
Gloucestershire
GL 50 3BY
United Kingdom
Tel: +44 1242 517 551
Fax: +44 1242 226 310
Email: johnw@bluesheep.com
Web: www.bluesheep.com
John Wright

Services/Products:
List services; Direct marketing agency;
Catalogue producer

Member of:
DMA

BMG (BOSTOCK MARKETING GROUP LIMITED)
7 Holt Court North
Heneage Street West
Birmingham
B7 4AX
United Kingdom
Tel: +44 121 333 6006
Fax: +44 121 333 6800
Email: bmg@bostock.co.uk
Web: www.bostock.co.uk
David Bostock

Services/Products:
Database services; Call centre services/
systems; Market research agency

Member of:
DMA

BRANN LTD
26 Soho Square
London
W1V 5FJ
United Kingdom
Tel: +44 20 78067005
Fax: +44 1718067025
John Shaw, Vice Chairman

Services/Products:
Database services; Direct marketing
agency; Call centre services/systems;
Electronic media; Internet services

E-Services:
Website design

Member of:
FEDMA

BRANN S. J. A.
15 Horseshoe Park
Pangbourne
Reading
Berkshire
RG8 7JW
United Kingdom
Tel: +44 118 984 5299
Fax: +44 118 984 5302

Services/Products:
Direct marketing agency

Member of:
DMA

BRITANNIA MUSIC CO. LTD
60/70 Roden Street
Ilford
Essex
1G1 2XX
United Kingdom
Tel: +44 20 8910 6011
Fax: +44 181 910 6104
Tony Kane, Managing Director

Services/Products:
List services; Mail order company

Member of:
FEDMA; DMA (US)

BROADPRINT LTD
Atlantic St.
Broadheath
Altrincham
WA14 5EB
United Kingdom
Tel: +44 161 928 7801
Fax: +44 161 928 66 57
William Cockcroft, Managing Director

Services/Products:
Lettershop; Database services;
Mailing/Faxing services; Service
bureau; Print services

Member of:
FEDMA

BROOKS & BENTLEY
Weald Court
101–103 Tonbridge Road
Hildenborough
Tonbridge
Kent
TN11 9HL
United Kingdom
Tel: +44 1732 835 801
Fax: +44 1732 834 136
Keith A. Yea, Manging Director

Services/Products:
Mail order company

Member of:
FEDMA

BRUNNINGS ADVERTISING & MARKETING
Carter Bench House
Clarence Road
Bollington
Cheshire
SK10 5JZ
United Kingdom
Tel: +44 1625 572 556
Fax: +44 1625 572 584
Lawrence Whittle, Director

Services/Products:
Advertising Agency; Direct Response
Agency

Member of:
DMA (US)

BUSINESS LISTS UK
4 Gillbent Road
Cheadle Hulme
Cheshire
SK8 6NB
United Kingdom
Tel: +44 161 488 4166
Fax: +44 161 488 4160

Email:
info@business-listsuk.demon.co.uk
Malcolm Rae

Services/Products:
List services; Lettershop; Fulfilment
and sampling house; Mailing/Faxing
services; Labelling/envelope services

Member of:
DMA

BUSINESS TO BUSINESS DIRECT LTD
Prospect House, Parabda Road
Cheltenham
GL50 1HN
United Kingdom
Tel: +44 1242 517551
Fax: +44 1242 226310
Ian Lovatt, Managing Director

Services/Products:
Advertising Agency; Direct Response
Agency

Member of:
DMA (US)

CAMBERTOWN LTD
Unit 21 Commercial Road
Goldthorpe Industrial Estate
Goldthorpe
Rotherham
S63 9BL
United Kingdom
Tel: +44 1709 898 989
Fax: +44 1709 897 787
Email: sales@cambertown.com
Web: http://www.cambertown.com
Steve Rudd

Services/Products:
Lettershop; Database services;
Mailing/Faxing services; Labelling/
envelope services; Direct marketing
agency

Member of:
DMA

CAMPAIGN DIRECT LTD
10 Bush Walk
Market Place
Wokingham
Berkshire
RG40 1AT
United Kingdom
Tel: +44 118 978 1542
Fax: +44 118 978 1544
Email: cdirect@pavilion.co.uk
Mark Waldron, Managing Director

Services/Products:
Advertising Agency; Database services;
Direct marketing agency; Response
analysis bureau

Member of:
FEDMA

CASE DIRECT LTD
Viking House
Prince William Road
Loughborough
Leics
LE11 5GA
United Kingdom
Tel: +44 1509 210776
Fax: +44 1509 210749

Services/Products:
Call centre services/systems; Service
bureau; Telemarketing agency

Member of:
National DMA

CENTROBE AND EDS COMPANY
3rd floor, Marlborough Street
Wigmore Place
Wigmore Lane
Luton
Beds
LU2 9EX
United Kingdom
Tel: +44 158 281 6404
Fax: +44 158 281 6494
Email: jenny.collins@europe.eds.com
Web: www.centrobe.com
Jenny Collins, Marketing Manager,
EMEA

Services/Products:
Fulfilment and sampling house;
Database services; Telemarketing
agency; Call centre services/systems

Member of:
FEDMA

CLARITAS EUROPE (EUROPEAN HEADQUARTERS)
Causeway House
The Causeway
Teddington
Middlesex
TW11 0JR
United Kingdom
Tel: +44 20 8213 5500
Fax: +44 20 8407 7144
Email: info@claritasgroup.com
John Moore, Executive Director

Services/Products:
List services; Database services;
Consultancy services; Response
analysis bureau

Member of:
FEDMA

CLARITAS UK (HQ)
Park House
Station Road
Teddington
Middlesex
TW11 9AD
United Kingdom
Tel: +44 20 8213 5500
Fax: +44 20 8213 5588
Email: info@claritasgroup.com
Dawn Orr, Sales Director

Services/Products:
List services; Database services;
Consultancy services; Response
analysis bureau

Member of:
FEDMA; DMA (US)

**CLAYDON HEELEY
   INTERNATIONAL**
The Glassmill
1 Battersea Bridge
London
SW11 3BZ
United Kingdom
Tel: +44 20 7924 3000
Fax: +44 171 924 3096

Services/Products:
Direct marketing agency

Member of:
DMA

**CLEAR COMMUNICATIONS
   LTD**
Pryn Court
The Millfields
Plymouth
Devon
PL1 3JB
United Kingdom
Tel: +44 175 266 4262
Fax: +44 175 225 4980
Email:
   info@clearcommunications.co.uk
Web: www.clearcommunications.co.uk
Julie Clare, Managing Director

Services/Products:
Advertising Agency; Consultancy
services; Media buying agency; Print
services; Design/graphics/clip art
supplier; Direct marketing agency

Member of:
National DMA

**CLOCKWORK
   COMMUNICATIONS
   (LONDON) LIMITED**
10 Barley Mow Passage
Chiswick
London
W4 4PH

United Kingdom
Tel: +44 20 8994 7850
Fax: +44 20 8987 0120
Email: enquiries@clockwork.co.uk
Web: www.clockwork.co.uk
Steve Dyer

Services/Products:
Advertising Agency; Direct marketing
agency; Media buying agency; Sales
promotion agency

Member of:
DMA

**COLUMBUS DIRECT MEDIA
   LTD**
Columbus House
28 Charles Square
London
N1 6HT
United Kingdom
Tel: +44 20 7608 6400
Fax: +44 20 7417 0702
Email: lists@columbusdm.com
Web: www.columbusdm.com
Nigel Smart, Sales Director

Services/Products:
List services; Insert management

Member of:
FEDMA; National DMA; DMARC

COMMUNICATOR
2–4 Boundary St
London
E2 7JE
United Kingdom
Tel: +44 20 7739 6633
Fax: +44 20 7739 6565
Email:
   rachel.kemp@communicator1.com
Rachel Kemp, Business Development
   Director

Services/Products:
Database services; Direct marketing
agency; Copy adaptation; Consultancy
services; Sales promotion agency;
Private delivery services; Direct
response TV services; Electronic
media; Internet services

E-Services:
Website design

Member of:
DMA

CONNECTIONS PLUS LTD
Kings Mill
Queen Street
Briercliffe
Burnley
BB10 2AD
United Kingdom

Tel: +44 1282 704 000
Fax: +44 1282 704 099
Email: mike@connections-
   plus.demon.co.uk
Mike Bingham

Services/Products:
Fulfilment and sampling house;
Telemarketing agency; Call centre
services/systems; Direct response TV
services

Member of:
DMA

CONSUMER SURVEYS LTD
57 Southwark Street
London
SE1 1RU
United Kingdom
Tel: +44 20 7403 6885
Fax: +44 20 7403 4536
Email: marketing@surveys.co.uk
Web: www.surveys.co.uk
Graham Bate

Services/Products:
List services

Member of:
National DMA

CONSUMERDATA LTD
The Gardener's Cottage
Careby
Stamford
Lincolnshire
PE9–4EB
United Kingdom
Tel: +44 1780 410 653
Fax: +44 1780 410 653
Email: fneagle@consumerdata.com.uk
Frederick Neagle, Managing Director

Services/Products:
List services; Database services;
Service bureau; Market research
agency

Member of:
FEDMA

**CONVERGYS CUSTOMER
   MANAGEMENT**
Baron House
Neville Street
Newcastle Upon Tyne
NE1 5EA
United Kingdom
Tel: +44 191 233 3000
Fax: +44 191 233 3001
Web: www.convergys.com
Ian Taylor, Business Development
   Director

Services/Products:
Telemarketing agency; Call centre
services/systems; Direct response TV
services

Member of:
DMA

CRAMM FRANCIS WOOLF
Consort House
46–8 Albert St
Fleet
Hants
GU13 9RL
United Kingdom
Tel: +44 1252 625 151
Fax: +44 1252 624 707
Email: paulw@cfw.co.uk
Paul Woolf

Services/Products:
Advertising Agency; Consultancy
services; Direct marketing agency

Member of:
DMA

CROWCASTLE LIMITED
Marlborough Road Aldbourne
Marlborough
Wiltshire
SN8 2HP
United Kingdom
Tel: +44 1672 542200
Fax: +44 1672 540831
Philip Mellor, Managing Director

Services/Products:
Fulfilment and sampling house

Member of:
DMA (US)

**DATA PROCESSING DIRECT
(DPD) LTD**
Broadway House, Broadway Industrial
Estate
King William Street
Salford
Manchester
United Kingdom
Tel: +44 161 876 7862
Fax: +44 161 876 7864
Email: sales@dpd-ltd.co.uk
Web: www.dpd.ltd.co.uk
Duncan Edwards

Services/Products:
Fulfilment and sampling house;
Database services; Mailing/Faxing
services; Labelling/envelope services

Member of:
DMA

DATA2 LIMITED
100 Easton Street
High Wycombe
Bucks
HP11 1LT
United Kingdom
Tel: +44 1494 442 900
Fax: +44 1494 452 900
Email: sales@data2.co.uk
Lisa Bentall

Services/Products:
List services; Telemarketing agency;
Response analysis bureau

Member of:
DMA

**DATAMEX COMPUTER
SERVICES LTD**
Domino House
Morris Close
Park Farm Ind Estate
Wellingborough
NN8 6XF
United Kingdom
Tel: +44 1933 402 300
Fax: +44 1933 402 377
Email: sales@datamex.co.uk
Web: www.datamex.co.uk
Mrs. Mona Curtis

Services/Products:
Lettershop; Fulfilment and sampling
house; Database services; Mailing/
Faxing services; Service bureau

Member of:
DMA

**DBMS - DAVID BRANNAN
MARKETING SERVICES LTD**
Barn Close
Langage Industrial Estate
Plympton
Plymouth
Devon
PL7 5HQ
United Kingdom
Tel: +44 1752 201492
Fax: +44 1752 201327
Email: dbms@dbmseuro.com
Web: www.dbmseuro.com
David Brannan, Managing Director

Services/Products:
Database services; Mailing/Faxing
services; Direct marketing agency;
Service bureau; Print services

Member of:
FEDMA

DBT LIMITED
West Farmhouse
Cams Hall Estate
Fareham

Hants
PO16 8UT
United Kingdom
Tel: +44 1329 282011
Fax: +44 1329 282031
Email: info@dbt.co.uk
Web: www.dbt.co.uk

Services/Products:
Consultancy services; Database
services; Direct marketing agency;
Data-driven websites

E-Services:
E-Marketing consultant; Website
design; Email software; Online/e-
marketing agency

Member of:
National DMA; Institute of Direct
Marketing; Chartered Institute of
Marketing

**DIRECT DATA
CAPTURE LIMITED**
72B Ormskirk Business Park
New Court Way
Ormskirk
Lancs
L39 2YT
Tel: +44 1695 570707
Fax: +44 1695 570722
Email: brett@ddcltd.co.uk
Web: www.datacapture.com

DDC is an offshore data conversio
company with 1,400 operators in 8
fully-owned Philippine bureaus. W
also have onshore scanning facilitie
in the UK and the USA and a
permanent lease line link between
all sites. It is possible to scan
documents onshore and transmit
the resulting images in 'real time' t
our offshore production facilities.
This process achieves considerabl
cost savings without the problems o
transmit times usually associated
with offshore capture. Additionall
valuable documents do not have t
leave your own location.
ONSHORE TURNAROUND AT
OFFSHORE PRICES!

**DIRECT GROUP
INTERNATIONAL**
10 A Rotterdam Road
Sutton Fields Industrial Estate
Kingston upon Hull
HU7 0XD
United Kingdom
Tel: +44 1482 820 229

Fax: +44 1482 820 796
Email: gen@directgroup.com
Laurence White, Mail Order Manager

Services/Products:
List services; Fulfilment and sampling
house; Catalogue producer; Mail order
company

Member of:
FEDMA; DMA (US)

**DIRECT MARKETING
  INTERNATIONAL**
Media House
Hallidays Yard
Radcliffe Road
Stamford
PE9 1ED
United Kingdom
Tel: +44 1780 765 960
Fax: +44 1780 765 904
Email: directmi@compuserve.com
Peter Peskett, Publisher

Services/Products:
Publisher; Advertising Agency; Copy
adaptation

Member of:
FEDMA; DMA (US)

DMS
Rodney House
Rodney Road
Cheltenham
Gloucestershire
GL50 1HX
United Kingdom
Tel: +44 1242 584 175
Fax: +44 1242 580 769
Email: dma@directmarketing.co.uk
Web: http://www.directmarketing.co.uk
Adrian Batt, Marketing Director

Services/Products:
Direct marketing agency; Consultancy
services

Member of:
FEDMA; DMA (US)

DMS
Rodney House
Rodney Road
Cheltenham
Gloustershire
GL54 5LX
United Kingdom
Tel: +44 1242 584175
Fax: +44 1242 580769
Email: dms@directmarketing.co.uk
Web: www.directmarketing.co.uk
Ashley Grainger, Business
  Development Director

Services/Products:
Consultancy services; Direct marketing
agency; Design/graphics/clip art
supplier; Copy adaptation

Member of:
FEDMA; National DMA

DOWERHILL LTD
Dowerhill House
74A Gateford Road
Worksop
Notts
S80 1TY
United Kingdom
Tel: +44 1909 472 441
Fax: +44 1909 500 171
Simon Evans

Services/Products:
Database services; Service bureau;
Software supplier; Call centre services/
systems

Member of:
DMA

DRAFTWORLDWIDE
Eastgate House
16/19 Eastcastle Street
London
W1N 7PA
United Kingdom
Tel: +44 20 7323 4586
Fax: +44 20 7734 0324
Chris Rose, Managing Director

Services/Products:
Advertising Agency; Consultancy
services; Database services; Direct
marketing agency; Sales promotion
agency

E-Services:
E-Marketing consultant; Website
design; Online/e-marketing agency

Member of:
National DMA

**DUDLEY JENKINS
LIST BROKING LTD**
**2A Southwark Bridge Office
  Village**
60 Thrale Street
London
SE1 9JG
United Kingdom
Tel: +44 20 7407 4753
Fax: +44 20 7407 6294
Email: broking@djlb.co.uk
**Veronica Over, Managing
  Director**

Services/Products:
**List services; Mailing/Faxing
services**

Member of:
FEDMA

**OTHER AREAS OF THE
BUSINESS**

The List Register
Contact: Brenden McNally,
Tel: 020 7871 9120,
Fax: 020 7871 9121,
Email: tlr@djlb.co.uk,
Web: www.listregister.co.uk

The Schools Register
Contact: Susmita Sakar,
Tel: 020 7871 9170,
Fax: 020 7871 9140,
Email: schools@djlb.co.uk,
**Web:
www.schoolsregister.co.uk**

A-Mail Academic
Contact: Duncan Copplestone,
Tel: 020 7871 9139,
Fax: 020 7871 9140,
Email: a-mail@djlb.co.uk,
Web: www.a-mail.co.uk

*Dudley Jenkins International
  List Broking*
Contact: Savinder Mattu,
Tel: 020 7871 9076,
Email: smattu@djlb.co.uk,
Web: www.dudleyjenkins.co.uk

List Management Division
Contact: Graham Halling,
Tel: 020 7871 9000,
Fax: 020 7871 9121,
Email: ghalling@djlb.co.uk,
Web: www.dudleyjenkins.co.uk

**DUN & BRADSTREET EUROPE
  LTD**
Holmers Farm Way
High Wycombe
Bucks
HP12 4UL
United Kingdom
Tel: +44 1494 42 3334
Fax: +44 1494 42 3827
Email: lloydr@dnb.com
Web: www.dbeuro.com
Richard Lloyd, Business Development
  Manager BMS Europe

Services/Products:
List services; Database services; Response analysis bureau

Member of:
FEDMA

DUN & BRADSTREET LTD
Holmers Farm Way
High Wycombe
HP12 4UL
United Kingdom
Tel: +44 990 422 299
Fax: +44 1494 423 100
Email: dbdirect@easynet.co.uk
Web: www.dunandbrad.co.uk

Services/Products:
List services; Database services; Software supplier

Member of:
FEDMA; DMA (US)

EC DIRECT LTD
Brooklyn House
22 The Green
West Drayton
Middlesex
UB7 7PQ
United Kingdom
Tel: +44 1895 422 300
Fax: +44 1895 431 252
Robert Taylor, Operations Director

Services/Products:
List services; Database services; Telemarketing agency; Direct marketing agency; Market research agency

Member of:
FEDMA

EDM BROKING AND MANAGEMENT
Grosvenor House
1 High Street
Edgware
HA8 7TA
United Kingdom
Tel: +44 20 8238 5959
Fax: +44 20 8238 5959
Email: broking@edmgroup.co.uk
Web: www.edmgroup.co.uk
Elizabeth Sayer, Account Director

Services/Products:
List services

E-Services:
Email list provider

Member of:
FEDMA; National DMA

EDUCATION DIRECT
Lakeside
Neptune Close
Rochester
Kent
ME2 4LT
United Kingdom
Tel: +44 1634 291122
Fax: +44 1634 720269
Email: info@education.co.uk
Web: www.education.co.uk
Mark Regnier, Sales Director

Services/Products:
Call centre services/systems; Database services; Fulfilment and sampling house; Lettershop; List services; Mailing/Faxing services

E-Services:
Website design

Member of:
DMA (UK); DMARC

EQUIFAX EUROPE LTD
Capital House
25 Chapel Street
London
NW1 5DS
United Kingdom
Tel: +44 20 7298 3112
Fax: +44 20 7723 3800
Email: tony.reynolds@equifax.com
Tony Reynolds

Services/Products:
Database services; Direct marketing agency; Service bureau

Member of:
FEDMA

EURO DM LTD
150 Regent Street
London
W1R 5FA
United Kingdom
Tel: +44 20 7432 0358
Fax: +44 20 7629 6020
Email: mbh@cais.net
Mary Beth Healy, Managing Director

Services/Products:
Database services; Mailing/Faxing services; Direct marketing agency; Service bureau; Print services

Member of:
FEDMA

EURO RSCG
109 Wardour Street
London
W1V 3TD
United Kingdom
Tel: +44 20 74781800

Fax: +44 20 7478 1801
Email: results@erd.co.uk
Tony Mackness, Managing Director

Services/Products:
Database services; Direct marketing agency; Sales promotion agency

Member of:
FEDMA

EURO RSCG DIRECT
109 Wardour Street
London
WIV 3TD
United Kingdom
Tel: +44 20 74781800
Fax: +44 20 74781801
Email: resuirs@erd.co.uk
Nick Pond

Services/Products:
Database services; Direct marketing agency; Mail order company; Mailing/ Faxing services

Member of:
FEDMA

EURO RSCG WNEK GOSPER
41 Charing Cross Road
London
WC2H OAR
United Kingdom
Tel: +44 20 7257 9892
Fax: +44 171 287 2469
Kim Escobar, Head, Interactive Client Svcs.

Services/Products:
Advertising Agency; Direct Response Agency

Member of:
DMA (US)

EUROPE DIRECT (UK) LTD.
45 Queens Avenue
Muswell Hill
London
N10 3PE
United Kingdom
Tel: +44 20 8374 9388
Fax: +44 181 374 9387
Dirk Foch, Partner

Services/Products:
Marketing consultant

Member of:
DMA (US)

EVANS HUNT SCOTT
7 Soho Square
London
W1V 6EH
United Kingdom
Tel: +44 20 7878 2600

Fax: +44 20 7878 2610
Email: jonI@evsco.oy
John Ingall, Managing Director

Services/Products:
Direct marketing agency

Member of:
FEDMA

EWA LTD
St. Mary's Green
Chelmsford
Essex
CM1 3TU
United Kingdom
Tel: +44 1245 492 828
Fax: +44 1245 492 514
Julie Saunders, Business Analyst

Services/Products:
Database services; Direct marketing
agency; Service bureau

Member of:
FEDMA

FCS LASER-MAIL
Holly Lane
Holly Park
Erdington
Birmingham
B24 9PB
United Kingdom
Tel: +44 121 306 4300
Fax: +44 121 350 4353
Email: fcslaser@compuserve.com
James Kirby; Mick Fay; Alison Walker

Services/Products:
Lettershop; Fulfilment and sampling
house; Mailing/Faxing services;
Labelling/envelope services; Service
bureau

Member of:
DMA

**FINANCIAL TELEMARKETING
    SERVICES LIMITED**
New Horizons
Studio Way
Borehamwood
Herts
WD6 5XX
United Kingdom
Tel: +44 20 8324 3300
Fax: +44 20 8236 0560
Email: tclaytor@fts-ltd.com
Web: www.fts-ltd.com
Tony Claytor

Services/Products:
Telemarketing agency; Call centre
services/systems

Member of:
DMA

FIRSTBASE
Challenge House
616 Mitcham Road
Croydon
Surrey
CR0 3AA
United Kingdom
Tel: +44 20 8664 2300
Fax: +44 20 8664 2301
Email: sales@firstbaseuk.com
Web: www.firstbaseuk.com
Greg Spafford

Services/Products:
List services; Database services;
Mailing/Faxing services; Direct
marketing agency; Market research
agency; Sales promotion agency

Member of:
National DMA

**GB INFORMATION
    MANAGEMENT**
Winster House
Herons Way
Chester Business Park
Chester
CH4 9GB
United Kingdom
Tel: +44 1244 657333
Fax: +44 1255 680808
Email: marketing@gb.co.uk
Web: www.gb.co.uk
David Green, Marketing Manager

Services/Products:
Database services

Member of:
National DMA; CSSA

GGT DIRECT ADVERTISING
82 Dean Street
London
WIV 6HA
United Kingdom
Tel: +44 20 7439 4282
Fax: +44 20 7434 2925
Email: martin@ggt.co.uk
Martin Wright, Marketing Director

Services/Products:
Database services; Direct marketing
agency; Response analysis bureau;
Print services; Market research agency

Member of:
FEDMA

GALEDIRECT
Tuition House
5–6 Francis Grove
London
SW19 4DT

United Kingdom
Tel: +44 20 8947 1011
Fax: +44 20 8947 1163
Email: info@GaleDirect.com
Web: www.GaleDirect.com
**Sally Baird, Stuart Guzinski,
    Richard Penny**

Services/Products:
List services

Member of:
FEDMA

GaleDirect provides direct
marketers with access to more than
1.2 million named contacts and over
300,000 international companies,
organisations, libraries and
associations. Our market-leading
lists currently include:
The Major Companies Database – you
won't find a more accurate list of the
largest and biggest spending companies
from around the globe.
The International Associations
Database – hard-to-find data on
associations and professional bodies
worldwide.
Ward's Database of US Companies –
target decision makers in the USA
using a wide range of selects.
The International Library List – the
accurate list of international libraries
with selections by library type, subject
area and region.
The International Research Centres
List – unrivalled access to government,
university, independent and
commercial R&D agencies in 125
countries worldwide.

GRANGE DIRECT LTD
16 The Pines
Broad Street
Guildford
Surrey
GU3 3BH
United Kingdom
Tel: +44 1483 538 468
Fax: +44 1483 303 533
Email: clientservices@
    grange-direct.co.uk
Jane Barrett; Stephanie Ruddle

Services/Products:
Lettershop; Database services;
Mailing/Faxing services; Labelling/
envelope services

Member of:
DMA

GREENLAND INTERACTIVE LTD
4 Greenland Place
London
NW1 0AP
United Kingdom
Tel: +44 20 7428 4444
Fax: +44 20 7428 4423
Email: bbrookes@greenland.co.uk
Web: www.greenland.co.uk
Beverley Brookes

Services/Products:
Mailing/Faxing services; Telemarketing
agency; Consultancy services; Service
bureau; Call centre services/systems;
Direct response TV services

Member of:
DMA

GREY DIRECT INTERNATIONAL
95 New Cavendish str
London
W1M 7FR
United Kingdom
Tel: +44 20 75261003
Fax: +44 20 75261148
Email: pboggsp@greydirectww.co.uk
Peter L. Boggs, President

Services/Products:
Database services; Direct marketing
agency; Sales promotion agency;
Electronic media

E-Services:
Website design

Member of:
FEDMA; DMA (US)

GWC GROUP LTD
The Communications Centre
Faraday Road
Dorcan
Swindon
Wiltshire
SN38 1GW
United Kingdom
Tel: +44 1793 451000
Fax: +44 1793 451010
Email: sales@gwc.co.uk

Services/Products:
Call centre services/systems; Database
services; Fulfilment and sampling
house; Lettershop; Personalisation;
Telemarketing agency

E-Services:
Online/e-marketing agency

Member of:
DMA (US); National DMA

HAMILTON HOUSE MAILINGS
Earlstrees Court
Earlstrees Road
Corby
Northants
NN17 4HH
United Kingdom
Tel: +44 1536 399 000
Fax: +44 1536 399 012
Email: hhmailing@aol.com
Stephen Mister

Services/Products:
List services; Database services;
Mailing/Faxing services; Labelling/
envelope services

Member of:
DMA

HARTE-HANKS
Euston House
24 Eversholt Street
London
NW1 1DQ
United Kingdom
Tel: +44 20 7529 8300
Fax: +44 20 7529 8401
Email: marketing.uk@hartehanks.com
Web: www.hartehanks.com

Services/Products:
Software supplier; Database services

Member of:
National DMA; CSSA

HLB LTD
1 Riverside
Manbre Road
London
W6 9GB
United Kingdom
Tel: +44 20 7243 8500
Fax: +44 20 7243 2363
Email: kelann@wwavrc.co.uk
Annette Kelley, Managing Director

Services/Products:
List services

Member of:
FEDMA

HLB LTD.
Compass House
Redan Place
London
W2 4SA
United Kingdom
Tel: +44 20 7243 8500
Fax: +44 171 243 2363
Annette Kelley, Managing Director

Services/Products:
List services

Member of:
DMA (US)

HOBS 4DM
Unit 4
Kingsthorne Park
Henson Way
Kettering
NN16 8HD
United Kingdom
Tel: +44 1536 416 426
Fax: +44 1536 416 002
Email: alanb@hobs.co.uk
Alan Beavis

Services/Products:
Lettershop; Fulfilment and sampling
house; Database services; Mailing/
Faxing services

Member of:
DMA

HUBBARD HIWAIZI MCCANN
131–151 Great Titchfield Street
London
W1P 8AE
United Kingdom
Tel: +44 20 7891 9100
Fax: +44 20 7891 9102
Email: d.mccann@hhm.co.uk
David McCann

Services/Products:
Database services; Direct marketing
agency; Consultancy services; Design/
graphics/clip art supplier; Electronic
media; Internet services

E-Services:
Website design

Member of:
DMA

IBC UK CONFERENCES LTD
Gilmoora House
57–61 Mortimer Street
London
W1N 8JX
United Kingdom
Tel: +44 20 7637 4383
Fax: +44 20 7631 3214
Email: wendy.chapman@ibc-uk.co.uk
Web: www.ibc-uk.com
Wendy Chapman, Director of
  Marketing

Services/Products:
List services

Member of:
FEDMA

ICD MARKETING SERVICES
Garden Floor
Bain House
16 Connaught Place
London
W2 2ES
United Kingdom
Tel: +44 20 7664 1000
Fax: +44 20 7664 1111
Email: nancy.dull@icd-
marketing.co.uk
Nancy Dull, Associate Director of
Marketing

Services/Products:
List services; Database services;
Market research agency

Member of:
FEDMA

ICLP (INTERNATIONAL CUSTOMER LOYALTY PROGRAMMES PLC)
International House
500 Purley Way
Croydon
CRO 4NZ
United Kingdom
Tel: +44 20 8667 1116
Fax: +44 20 8667 1713
Email: loyalty@iclpfulham.co.uk

Services/Products:
List services; Database services;
Telemarketing agency; Consultancy
services; Service bureau; Loyalty
systems

Member of:
DMA

ICLP (INTERNATIONAL CUSTOMER LOYALTY PROGRAMMES PLC)
5 Brighton Road
Croydon
Surrey
CR2 6EA
United Kingdom
Tel: +44 208 505 0050
Fax: +44 208 667 1713
Email: loyalty@iclpcroydon.co.uk
Web: www.iclployalty.com
Carolyn Hubert, Marketing Director

Services/Products:
Consultancy services; Database
services; Call centre services/systems;
Direct marketing agency; Labelling/
envelope services; Telemarketing
agency

E-Services:
Online/e-marketing agency

Member of:
FEDMA; DMA (US); National DMA;
FTMA

ICT GROUP INC
Aspect Gate
166 College Road
Harrow
Middlesex
HA1 1BH
United Kingdom
Tel: +44 20 8901 3100
Fax: +44 20 8901 3111
Email: hmalby@uk.ictgroup.com
Web: www.ictgroup.com
Helen Malby, Business Development
Manager

Services/Products:
Direct marketing agency;
Telemarketing agency

E-Services:
Online/e-marketing agency

Member of:
FEDMA; DMA (US); National DMA

ID DATA GROUP
Wansell Road
Weldon North
Corby
Northants
NN17 5LX
United Kingdom
Tel: +44 1536 207 000
Fax: +44 1536 208 534
Email: enquiry@id-data.demon.co.uk
Caroline Hillhouse

Services/Products:
List services; Fulfilment and sampling
house; Mailing/Faxing services; Direct
marketing agency; Consultancy
services; Private delivery services

Member of:
DMA

IDENTEX
Beech House
Betts Way
Crawley
West Sussex
RH10 2GW
United Kingdom
Tel: +44 1293 561666
Fax: +44 1293 561614
Email: info@identex.co.uk
Web: www.identex.co.uk
Angela Reagan, Sales & Marketing
Administrator

Services/Products:
Database services; Response analysis
bureau; Software supplier; Campaign
management; global data quality

management solutions; ecampaign
management

Member of:
FEDMA; National DMA; MPS;
DMARC

IDS
Commercial House
15 Merchants Quay
Newry
Co. Down
BT35 6AH
United Kingdom
Tel: +44 1693 254 700
Fax: +44 1693 254 701
Email: ids@iol.ie
Web: www.irishbusiness.ie
Ms. Marie Reilly, Sales & Marketing
Manager

Services/Products:
List services; Fulfilment and sampling
house; Database services; Labelling/
envelope services; Telemarketing
agency

Member of:
DMA

IINTERNATIONAL AIRLINE PASSENGERS ASSOCIATION
5 Brighton Road
Croydon
Surrey
CR2 6EA
United Kingdom
Tel: +44 20 82569013
Fax: +44 20 8681 0234
Email: info@iapa.co.uk
Web: www.iapa.co.uk
Ros Martin

Services/Products:
List services

Member of:
FEDMA

IMP LTD
123 Buckingham Palace Road
London
SW1W 9DZ
United Kingdom
Tel: +44 20 7931 8000
Fax: +44 20 7931 8800
Email: ian.millner@implondon.co.uk
Ian Millner

Services/Products:
Database services; Direct marketing
agency; Design/graphics/clip art
supplier; Sales promotion agency;
Electronic media

E-Services:
Website design

315

Member of:
FEDMA

IMT-HARROWBROOK LTD
T/A PaperDirect
Nuffield Road
Harrowbrook Industrial Estate
Hinckley
Leics
LE10 3DG
United Kingdom
Tel: +44 1455 622 417
Fax: +44 1455 622 438
Email: patrick@paperdirect.co.uk
Terri Scholefield

Services/Products:
Catalogue producer; Mail order
company

INTERFOCUS NETWORK LTD
4 Lancer Square
Kensington
London
W8 4ES
United Kingdom
Tel: +44 20 7376 9000
Fax: +44 20 7376 9090
Email: postmaster@interfocus.co.uk.
Vanessa Hogg, Business Development
Manager

Services/Products:
Direct marketing agency; Print
services; Sales promotion agency;
Advertising Agency

Member of:
FEDMA

INTERMAIL PLC
Horizon West
Canal View Road
Newbury
Berkshire
RG14 5XF
United Kingdom
Tel: +44 1635 565000
Fax: +44 1635 41678
Email: karen.weston@intermail.co.uk
Web: www.intermail.co.uk
Karen Weston, New Business Manager

Services/Products:
Call centre services/systems; Database
services; Fulfilment and sampling
house; Private delivery services;
Telemarketing agency; E-commerce

E-Services:
Website design

Member of:
FEDMA; DMA (US); National DMA;
DMARC; MPS

**INTERMARKETING
COMMUNICATIONS LTD**
3–5 Alma Road
Headingley
Leeds
LS6 2AH
United Kingdom
Tel: +44 113 275 3912
Fax: +44 113 275 3174
Email: attn@intermarketing.co.uk

Services/Products:
List services; Direct marketing agency;
Media buying agency; Catalogue
producer

Member of:
DMA

ISIS DIRECT LIMITED
Windrush Court
56a High Street
Witney
Oxfordshire
OX8 6HJ
United Kingdom
Tel: +44 1993 773 373
Fax: +44 1993 773 397
Michelle Follett-Holt

Services/Products:
List services; Database services; Direct
marketing agency; Consultancy
services; Media buying agency

Member of:
DMA

J. WALTER THOMPSON
40 Berkeley Square
London
W1X 6AD
United Kingdom
Tel: +44 20 7499 4040
Fax: +44 20 7493 8432
Email: david.hall@jwthompson.com
Web: www.jwtworld.com
David Hall

Services/Products:
Advertising Agency; Consultancy
services; Sales promotion agency;
Direct response TV services

Member of:
DMA

JENNIFER D. BAKER
73 Addison Gardens
West Kensington
London
W14 0DT
United Kingdom
Tel: +44 20 7602 0493
Fax: +44 20 7371 2960
Email: jdbmc@aol.com
Jennie Baker

Services/Products:
Database services; Consultancy
services; Response analysis bureau;
Market research agency

Member of:
DMA

**JOHN S. TURNER DIRECT
MARKETING**
Brunel Court
Burrel Road
St. Ives
Huntingdon
PE17 4LE
United Kingdom
Tel: +44 1480 461 999
Fax: +44 1480 461 991
Email: jstdm@compuserve.com
Wane Borg

Services/Products:
List services; Mailing/Faxing services;
Labelling/envelope services;
Telemarketing agency

Member of:
DMA

**JOHN YATES COPY
CONSULTANTS
(COPYWRITERS)**
8 Farm Way
Rustington
Littlehampton
West Sussex
BN16 2PR
United Kingdom
Tel: +44 1903 776 977
Fax: +44 1903 770 015
John Yates, Principal

Services/Products:
Copy adaptation; Consultancy
services; Design/graphics/clip art
supplier

Member of:
DMA

JOSHUA AGENCY PLC
Wells Point
79 Wells Street
London
WIP 3RE
United Kingdom
Tel: +44 20 7453 7900
Fax: +44 171 453 7999
Peter Thompson, Chairman

Services/Products:
Direct marketing agency

Member of:
FEDMA

JUDITH DONOVAN ASSOCIATES LTD
Phoenix House
Rushton Avenue
Bradford
West Yorkshire
BD3 7BH
United Kingdom
Tel: +44 127 465 6222
Fax: +44 127 465 6167
Judith Donovan, Chairman

Services/Products:
Direct marketing agency

Member of:
FEDMA; DMA (US)

KETTLE GREEN STUDIOS
Kettle Green Studio
Kettle Green Lane
Much Hadham
Herts
SG10 6AJ
United Kingdom
Tel: +44 1279 841 021
Fax: +44 1279 843 768
Email: wdo@easynet.co.uk
Wendy Dockley

Services/Products:
Fulfilment and sampling house;
Database services; Telemarketing
agency; Media buying agency; Call
centre services/systems

Member of:
DMA

KOGAN PAGE LTD
120 Pentonville Road
London
N1 9JN
United Kingdom
Tel: +44 20 7278 0433
Fax: +44 20 7837 6348
Email: kpinfo@kogan-page.co.uk
Web: www.kogan-page.co.uk
Andrew Young, Marketing Manager

Services/Products:
List services

Member of:
FEDMA

KPA BUSINESS LISTS LIMITED
Half Century House
Wesex Road
Bourne End
Bucks
SL8 5DD
United Kingdom
Tel: +44 1628 533300
Fax: +44 1628 533399
Email: david@kpa.co.uk
David Ellison, Account Director

Services/Products:
Database services; Direct marketing
agency; Lettershop; List services

E-Services:
Email list provider

Member of:
National DMA

LEO BURNETT EUROPE
Leo Burnett Building
Sloane Av. 60
London
SW3 3XE
United Kingdom
Tel: +44 20 75919100
Fax: +44 1715919126
Jeff Ferguss, CEO

Services/Products:
Direct marketing agency

Member of:
FEDMA

LGM MARKETING SERVICES LTD
1 Dorset Street
London
W1H 4BB
United Kingdom
Tel: +44 20 7935 6040
Fax: +44 20 7935 1571
Email: susie_vivian@lgminel.co.uk
Susie Vivian, Managing Director

Services/Products:
Database services; Direct marketing
agency; Sales promotion agency

Member of:
FEDMA

LIMBO LTD
24–27 Great Pulteney Street
London
W1R 3DB
United Kingdom
Tel: +44 20 74394404
Fax: +44 20 7437 2956
Email: philippak@limbo.co.uk
Philippa Kilburn, Business
    Development Manager

Services/Products:
Database services; Direct marketing
agency; Sales promotion agency

Member of:
FEDMA

LISTMASTER DATABASE MARKETING
3rd Floor
Royalmead
Railway Place
Bath

BA1 1SR
United Kingdom
Tel: +44 1225 484 300
Fax: +44 1225 484 301
Email:
    rogergrimshaw@listmaster.co.uk
Web: www.listmaster.co.uk
Roger Grimshaw, Managing Director

Services/Products:
Database services; Response analysis
bureau; Service bureau; Software
supplier

Member of:
FEDMA

LLOYD JAMES LIST BROKING SERVICES LTD
Stephen House
School Lane
Weeling
Kent
DA16 1LU
United Kingdom
Tel: +44 20 8301 6545
Fax: +44 20 8301 6549
Email: lloydjames@lloydjames.co.uk
Web: www.lloydJames.co.uk
James Lloyd, Managing Director

Services/Products:
List services; Database services;
Service bureau

Member of:
FEDMA

LM SOFTWARE LTD
Apak House
Badminton Court
Station Road
Bristol
BS37 5HZ
United Kingdom
Tel: +44 1454 871060
Fax: +44 1454 871199
Email: lmsoft@apakgroup.com
Web: www.lmsoft.co.uk
Mrs Helen Picard, General Manager

Services/Products:
Consultancy services; Database
services; Mailing/Faxing services;
Software supplier; Address
Management Services

Member of:
FEDMA; National DMA

LOYALTY MANAGEMENT INTERNATIONAL LTD
Meadowcroft House
Balcombe Road
Horley, Surrey
RH6 9EH
United Kingdom

Tel: +44 1293434000
Fax: +44 1293433701
Philip Beard, Marketing Director

Services/Products:
Sales promotion agency

Member of:
FEDMA

LUDLOW MARKETING
Stokesay, Old Manor Close
Whaddon
Ste 200
Milton Keynes
MK17 0LY
United Kingdom
Tel: +44 1908 501887
David McGirr, Vice President, Sales

Services/Products:
Lettershop; Mailing/Faxing services

Member of:
DMA (US)

MAGAZINE MAILING LTD
Units 6, 7, and 8, Haslemere Industrial
Estate
Sutton Road
Parkwood
Maidstone
ME15 9LQ
United Kingdom
Tel: +44 1622 673 173
Fax: +44 1622 687 986
Mike Holman

Services/Products:
Fulfilment and sampling house;
Mailing/Faxing services

Member of:
DMA

MAILCOM PLC
Snowdon Drive
Winterhill
Milton Keynes
Buckinghamshire
MK6 1HQ
United Kingdom
Tel: +44 1908 675666
Fax: +44 1908 668801
Email: info@malcolm.co.uk
Web: www.malcolm.co.uk
Suzanna Cooper, Senior Brand
  Manager

Services/Products:
Personalisation; Print services; Mailing/
Faxing services; Lettershop; Service
bureau

Member of:
National DMA; DMARC

MAILING AND PRINTING
   COMPANY LTD
Unit B5 Haslemere Industrial Estate
Pig Pig Lane
Bishops Stortford
Herts
CM23 3HG
United Kingdom
Tel: +44 1279 656800
Fax: +44 1279 655777
Email: sales@map-int.com
Web: www.map-int.com
Giles Bullock

Services/Products:
Lettershop; Personalisation; Print
services

Member of:
National DMA; DMARC; MCA;
MPS

MALVERN MAILING SERVICES
16/17 Lion Court
Daneshill East
Basingstoke
RG24 8QU
United Kingdom
Tel: +44 1256 471 122
Email: mmsmailing@compuserve.com
Len Morgan; Ivy Quinlan

Services/Products:
List services; Fulfilment and sampling
house; Mailing/Faxing services;
Labelling/envelope services

Member of:
DMA

MANIFESTO
Melbray Mews
158 Hurlingham Road
Fulham
London
SW6 3NG
United Kingdom
Tel: +44 20 7736 5355
Fax: +44 20 7384 1800
Email: joe-g@manifesto-uk.com
Joseph Garton

Services/Products:
Database services; Consultancy
services; Response analysis bureau;
Electronic media; Internet services

E-Services:
Website design

Member of:
DMA

MARDEV
Quadrant House
The Quandrant
Sutton, Surrey

SM2 5AS
United Kingdom
Tel: +44 20 8643 0955
Fax: +44 20 8652 4580
Email: nick.martin@rbi.co.uk
Web: www.mardevlists.com
Nick Martin, General Manager

Services/Products:
List services

Member of:
FEDMA; DMA (US)

MARKET LOCATION LTD
1 Warwick Street
Leamington Spa
Warwickshire
CV32 5LW
United Kingdom
Tel: +44 1926 450 388
Fax: +44 1926 430 590
Peter Flood

Services/Products:
List services; Database services;
Consultancy services

Member of:
DMA

MARKET PHONE LTD
Lady Bay House
Meadow Grove
Nottingham
NG2 3HF
United Kingdom
Tel: +44 115 956 8833
Fax: +44 115 956 8844
Email: solutions@marketphone.com
Web: www.marketphone.com
Patrick Hughes, Group Marketing
  Manager

Services/Products:
List services; Fulfilment and sampling
house; Database services; Direct
marketing agency; Market research
agency

Member of:
DMA

MARKETING AND MEDIA
   SOLUTIONS LTD
4–6 Peterborough Road
Harrow
Middlesex
HA1 2BQ
United Kingdom
Tel: +44 20 84269855
Fax: +44 20 8423 3589
Email: alan_mms@compuserve.com
Paul Cowan

Services/Products:
List services; Database services; Direct marketing agency; Media buying agency; Service bureau

Member of:
FEDMA

MARKETING AND MEDIA SOLUTIONS LTD
4–6 Peterborough Road
Harrow
Middlesex
HA1 2BQ
United Kingdom
Tel: +44 20 8426 9855
Fax: +44 20 8423 3589
Email: alan-mms@compuserve.com
Paul Cowan

Services/Products:
List services; Database services; Direct marketing agency; Consultancy services; Media buying agency

Member of:
FEDMA; DMA (US)

MCCANN-ERICKSON MANCHESTER LTD
Bonis Hall
Bonis Hall Lane
Prestbury
Cheshire
SK10 4EF
United Kingdom
Tel: +44 1625 822200
Fax: +44 1625 829567
Email: nick_backhouse@
   europe.mccann.com
Nick Backhouse, Executive Director, Direct Marketing

Services/Products:
Advertising Agency; Database services; Direct marketing agency; Media buying agency

E-Services:
Website design; Online/e-marketing agency

Member of:
National DMA

MESSENGER MARKETING SERVICES LIMITED
26 Highfield Drive
Portishead
Bristol
BS20 8JD
United Kingdom
Tel: +44 1275 8+44 901
Fax: +44 1275 815 906
Email:
   fms@messengermarketing.co.uk
Terry Edwards

Services/Products:
Advertising Agency; Consultancy services; Service bureau; List services

Member of:
DMA

METRO MAIL
2–3 Palmer Road
S.W. Industrial Estate
Peterlee
Co Durham
United Kingdom
Tel: +44 191 554 6262
Fax: +44 191 554 6299
Web: www.metromail.co.uk
Terry Jackson

Services/Products:
List services; Lettershop; Database services; Mailing/Faxing services

Member of:
DMA

MILLER STARR LTD
20 Kentish Town Road
Camden Town
London
NW1 9NX
United Kingdom
Tel: +44 20 7267 4488
Fax: +44 20 7284 4950
Email: adam.harris@millerstarr.co.uk
Web: www.millerstarr.com
Adam Harris

Services/Products:
Database services; Response analysis bureau; Service bureau; Software supplier

Member of:
FEDMA; DMA (US)

MMS MARKET MOVEMENTS
Tey House
Market Hill
Royston
Herts
SG8 9JN
United Kingdom
Tel: +44 1763 248 828
Fax: +44 1763 245 151
Email: sales@marketmovements.com
Sebastian Kindersley

Services/Products:
Consultancy services; Market research agency

Member of:
DMA

NCH MARKETING SERVICES LTD
Bangrave Road
Corby
Northants
NN17 1NN
United Kingdom
Tel: +44 1536 400 123
Fax: +44 1536 400 678
Email: gbnch931@ibmmail.com
Andy Wood

Services/Products:
Database services; Software supplier

Member of:
DMA (US)

NEWSTEL INFORMATION LTD
2nd Floor
Pentagon Centre
36 Washington St
Glasgow
G3 8AZ
United Kingdom
Tel: +44 8705 133 345
Fax: +44 8705 133 366
Email: newstel@newstel.com
Web: www.newstel.com
Sarah Hunt

Services/Products:
List services; Database services; Telemarketing agency; Call centre services/systems; Electronic media; Internet services

E-Services:
Website design

Member of:
DMA

OAG WORLDWIDE
Church Street
Dunstable
Bedfordshire
LU5 4HB
United Kingdom
Tel: +44 1582600111
Fax: +44 1582695049
Email: corporate@oag.co.uk
Sarah Perito, Direct Marketing Director

Services/Products:
List services

Member of:
FEDMA

OCCAM DIRECT MARKETING LTD
The Stables
Manor Farm
Chilcompton
Bath

BA3 4HP
United Kingdom
Tel: +44 1761 233 833
Fax: +44 1761 233 844
Email: mark@occam-dm.com
Mark Gilden

Services/Products:
List services; Database services;
Consultancy services; Media buying
agency; Response analysis bureau;
Private delivery services

Member of:
DMA

OGILVYONE WORLDWIDE
Porters Place
11–33 St. John Street
London
EC1M 4GB
United Kingdom
Tel: +44 20 7566 7000
Fax: +44 20 7566 5100
Email: nigelc@ogilvy.co.uk
Web: www.ogilvy.com
Mark Runacus

Services/Products:
Database services; Telemarketing
agency; Direct marketing agency;
Media buying agency

Member of:
FEDMA; DMA (US)

**OMEGA MARKETING
    SERVICES**
200 Milton Park
Abingdon
Oxon
OX14 4TB
United Kingdom
Tel: +44 1235 824 466
Fax: +44 1235 824 304
Email:
    response@omega-marketing.co.uk
Web: www.omega-marketing.co.uk
Mr. Paul Miller

Services/Products:
Fulfilment and sampling house;
Mailing/Faxing services; Telemarketing
agency; Call centre services/systems

Member of:
FEDMA; DMA (US)

**ONE TO ONE MAILING
    SERVICES LTD**
62 Valley Road
Plympton
Plymouth
PL7 1RF
United Kingdom
Tel: +44 1752 205 121

Fax: +44 1752 205 086
Andrew Grainger, Commercial
    Director

Services/Products:
List services; Lettershop; Mailing/
Faxing services; Labelling/envelope
services; Personalisation

Member of:
FEDMA

OUTSIDE THE BOX PLC
Escher House
116 Cardigan Road
Headingley
Leeds
LS6 3BJ
United Kingdom
Tel: +44 113 216 2820
Fax: +44 113 216 2828
Email: studio@outsidethebox.co.uk
Web: www.outsidethebox.co.uk
Mark Davies, Managing Director

Services/Products:
Direct marketing agency; Design/
graphics/clip art supplier; Media
buying agency; Market research
agency; Advertising Agency

E-Services:
Website design

Member of:
FEDMA

POLYGRAM
Britannia International
60–70 Roden Street
Illford
Essex
1G12XX
United Kingdom
Email: kaneto@uk.polygram.com
Web: www.britannia-music.co.uk
Tony Kane

Services/Products:
List services

Member of:
FEDMA

**POLYPRINT MAILING FILMS
    LTD**
Mackintosh Road
Rackheath Ind. Est.
Rackheath
Norwich
NR13 6LJ
United Kingdom
Tel: +44 1603 721 807
Fax: +44 1603 721 813
Email: jneville@polyprint.co.uk
J. Neville

Services/Products:
Mailing/Faxing services; Labelling/
envelope services

Member of:
DMA

**PORTLAND DIRECT
    MARKETING LTD**
38–40 Victoria Street
Felixstowe
Suffolk
IP11 7EW
United Kingdom
Tel: +44 1394 285 678
Fax: +44 1394 275 034
Email: info@portland-direct.com
Web: www.portland-direct.com
Karen Page

Services/Products:
List services; Fulfilment and sampling
house; Mailing/Faxing services; Direct
marketing agency

Member of:
DMA

PRIME RESPONSE
Goat Wharf
Brentford
TW8 0BA
United Kingdom
Tel: +44 20 8400 3000
Fax: +44 20 8400 3133
Email:
    marketing@prime-response.com
Web: www.prime-response.com
Ronny Nicholas

Services/Products:
Database services; Service bureau;
Software supplier

Member of:
DMA

**PRINTRONIC INTERNATIONAL
    PLC**
1 Endeavour Way
London
SW19 8UH
United Kingdom
Tel: +44 20 8946 7537
Fax: +44 20 8947 2740
Email: sales@printronic.co.uk
Web: www.printronic.co.uk
Peter Kempsey, Managing Director

Services/Products:
Database services; Mailing/Faxing
services; Response analysis bureau;
Service bureau; Personalisation

Member of:
FEDMA

PRINTWARE DIRECT LIMITED
Printware Court
Northumberland Road
Southsea
Hants
PO12 3JH
United Kingdom
Tel: +44 1705 825 055
Fax: +44 1705 827 909
Email: mail@printware.co.uk
Vanessa MacWhirter

Services/Products:
List services; Fulfilment and sampling
house; Mailing/Faxing services;
Labelling/envelope services;
Telemarketing agency

PRISM DATA MANAGEMENT LTD.
Columbia House
Southwood
Farnborough
Camberley
GU14 0GT
United Kingdom
Tel: +44 1252 556900
Fax: +44 1252 556911
Email: sales@prism-dm.co.uk
Web: www.prism-dm.co.uk
Stewart Morgan, Sales & Marketing
  Director

Services/Products:
Call centre services/systems; Database
services; Mail order company; Direct
marketing agency; Fulfilment and
sampling house; Interactive media;
Online web service fulfilment; TV
fulfilment

E-Services:
E-Marketing consultant; Online/
e-marketing agency

Member of:
DMA (US); National DMA; DMARC

PROMOTIONAL CAMPAIGNS GROUP
Forest Lodge
Westerham Road
Keston
Kent
BR2 6HE
United Kingdom
Tel: +44 1689 853 344
Fax: +44 1689 862 517
Email: hugh@pcg.uk.com
Hugh Taylor

Services/Products:
Direct marketing agency; Consultancy
services; Sales promotion agency

Member of:
DMA

PROSPECT MAILING SERVICES LTD
Crown Point Mills
Wyke
Bradford
BD12 9QD
United Kingdom
Tel: +44 1274 674790
Fax: +44 1274 605347
Email:
  enquiries@prospectmailing.co.uk
Web: www.prospectmailing.co.uk
Miles Berry, Managing Director

Services/Products:
Database services; Lettershop;
Personalisation

Member of:
National DMA

PUBLICIS DIALOG LIMITED
82 Baker Street
London
W1M 2AE
United Kingdom
Tel: +44 20 7935 7744
Fax: +44 171 830 3686
Fred Kuys, Chief Executive Officer

Services/Products:
Advertising Agency; Direct Response
Agency

Member of:
DMA (US)

PUBLICIS TECHNOLOGY
1–2 Down Place
Hammersmith
London
W6 9JH
United Kingdom
Tel: +44 20 82141000
Fax: +44 181 2141001
Gary Pepler, Managing Director

Services/Products:
Direct marketing agency; Media
buying agency; Advertising Agency

Member of:
FEDMA

QAS SYSTEMS LTD
7 Old Town
London
SW4 0JT
United Kingdom
Tel: +44 20 7498 7777
Fax: +44 20 7498 0303
Email: info@qas.com
Web: www.qas.com
Jenny Cain

Services/Products:
Database services; Software supplier

Member of:
FEDMA; DMA (US)

QBASE DATA SERVICES
St James Court
Wilderspool Causeway
Warrington
WA4 6PS
United Kingdom
Tel: +44 1925 644800
Fax: +44 1925 644801
Email: admin@qbaseww.com
Ian Johnstone, Partner

Services/Products:
List services; Database services;
Service bureau; Software supplier;
Electronic media

E-Services:
Website design

Member of:
FEDMA; DMA (US)

QUALITY REGISTRATION SERVICES LTD
PO Box 26228
London
W3 7GX
United Kingdom
Tel: +44 20 8749 3941
Fax: +44 20 8743 3133
Email: info@qrs.co.uk
Web: http://www.qrs.co.uk
D. Harington

Services/Products:
Lettershop; Mailing/Faxing services;
Exhibition and conference registration

Member of:
DMA

QUALITY REGISTRATION SERVICES LTD
The Hollybush
Whitbourne
Worcester
WR6 5RB
United Kingdom
Tel: +44 1886 821 885
Fax: +44 1886 821 445
Email: info@qrs.co.uk
Web: http://www.qrs.co.uk
D. Harington

Services/Products:
Lettershop; Mailing/Faxing services;
Exhibition and conference registration

Member of:
DMA

RAVENSWORTH DESIGN
6–8 Ravensworth Terrace
Newcastle Upon Tyne
NE4 6AU
United Kingdom
Tel: +44 191 222 1270
Fax: +44 191 222 1172
Email: pgecc@ravensworth.co.uk
Justine N. Brown

Services/Products:
Direct marketing agency; Consultancy
services; Design/graphics/clip art
supplier; Print services

Member of:
DMA

RED BOX ADVERTISING LTD
Midas One
Calleva Park
Aldermaston
Reading
RG7 8GA
United Kingdom
Tel: +44 118 981 9661
Fax: +44 118 981 9507
Email: info@redboxad.co.uk
Chris Bird

Services/Products:
Advertising Agency; Direct marketing
agency; Electronic media; Internet
services

E-Services:
Website design

Member of:
DMA

RED FISH LIMITED
55 Riding House Street
London
W1P 7PS
United Kingdom
Tel: +44 20 7467 8111
Fax: +44 20 7467 8112
Email: mail@redfish.co.uk
Web: http://www.redfish.co.uk
Richard Burton

Services/Products:
Advertising Agency; Direct marketing
agency; Sales promotion agency;
Incentive travel & motivation agency

Member of:
DMA

RED SQUARE
   COMMUNICATIONS
Riverside
Becketts Place
Lower Teddington Road
Hampton Wick
Surrey

KT1 4EQ
United Kingdom
Tel: +44 20 8977 3830
Fax: +44 20 8977 9987
Email: talk@redsquare.co.uk
Web: www.redsquare.co.uk
Mark Hancock, Managing Director

Services/Products:
Database services; Direct marketing
agency; Consultancy services; Design/
graphics/clip art supplier; Direct
response TV services; Electronic
media; Internet services

E-Services:
Website design

Member of:
DMA

REDOUTE UK
18 Canal Road
Bradford
West Yorkshire
BD 994XB
United Kingdom
Tel: +44 1274 729544
Fax: +44 1274 274843930
Valerie Meteyer, Marketing
   Department Director

Services/Products:
Advertising Agency; Direct Response
Agency

Member of:
DMA (US)

RESPONSE MARKETING LTD
York House
St Judes Road
Englefield Green
Surrey
TW20 0DH
United Kingdom
Tel: +44 1784 430 730
Fax: +44 1784 438 820
Email: responsemk.co.uk
Web: htp://www.responsemk.co.uk
Michael York Palmer

Services/Products:
List services; Database services;
Mailing/Faxing services; Direct
marketing agency; Copy adaptation

Member of:
DMA

RESULTS (EUROPE) LTD
Mountbarrow House
12 Elizabeth Street
Victoria
London
SW1W 9RB
United Kingdom

Tel: +44 20 7730 6655
Fax: +44 20 7730 6644
Email: sue.fennell@resultseurope.com
Web: www.resultseurope.com

Services/Products:
Database services; Consultancy
services; Response analysis bureau;
Recommendations on varying
investment by customer group and
campaign; overall marketing strategy

REYNOLDS PORTER
   CHAMBERLAIN
Chichester House
278–282 High Holborn
London
WC1V 7HA
United Kingdom
Tel: +44 20 7242 2877
Fax: +44 20 7242 1431
Email: rbn@rpc.co.uk
Web: www.rpc.co.uk
Ronald Norman

Services/Products:
Legal services

Member of:
FEDMA

RICHARDSON PAILIN &
   FALLOW LTD. (RP&F)
No. 5 Staithgate Lane
Bradford
West Yorkshire
B06 1YA
United Kingdom
Tel: +44 1274 421 606
Fax: +44 1274 421 605
Mark Richardson, Managing Director

Services/Products:
Advertising Agency; Direct Response
Agency

Member of:
DMA (US)

RMA INTERNATIONAL LTD
RMA House
Blackthorne Road
Colnbrook
Berkshire
SL3 0AH
United Kingdom
Tel: +44 1753 681 211
Fax: +44 1753 684 140
Email: rma@rma-int.co.uk
Web: rma-int.co.uk
Chris Tait

Services/Products:
List services; Lettershop; Fulfilment
and sampling house; Mailing/Faxing
services; Labelling/envelope services;
Private delivery services

Member of:
DMA

ROSEMARY STOCKDALE ASSOCIATES

50 Hants Crescent
London
SW1X 0NB
United Kingdom
Tel: +44 20 7591 3812
Fax: +44 20 7591 8833
Email: rstockda@sterling-marketing.ltd.uk
Rosemary Stockdale

Services/Products:
Consultancy services

Member of:
DMA

ROYAL MAIL IMPACT HOUSE

2 Edridge Road, Croydon CR9, IPJ
UK-
Croydon
CR9 IPJ
United Kingdom
Tel: +44 181 681 9410
Fax: +44 20 8681 9318
Roger Andriessen

Services/Products:
List services; Lettershop; Fulfilment and sampling house

Member of:
DDV

ROYAL MAIL INTERNATIONAL

49 Featherstone Street
London
EC1Y 8SY
United Kingdom
Tel: +44 20 7320 4495/4541
Fax: +44 20 7320 4173
Email: treina.smyth@royalmail.co.uk
Treina Smyth, Business Solutions Marketing Manager

Services/Products:
Mailing/Faxing services

Member of:
FEDMA

SAATCHI & SAATCHI

80 Charlotte Street
London
W1A 1AQ
United Kingdom
Tel: +44 20 76365060
Fax: +44 20 7637 8489
Email: fibi_duke@saatchi.co.uk
Fibi Duke, Account Director

Services/Products:
Database services; Direct marketing agency; Sales promotion agency; Advertising Agency; Electronic media

E-Services:
Website design

Member of:
FEDMA

SALESTRAC LTD

3 Manor Court
Dix's Field
Exeter
EX1 1ST
United Kingdom
Tel: +44 1392 429 429
Fax: +44 1392 431 025
Email: l.still@uk.cordena.com
Len Still, Managing Director

Services/Products:
Fulfilment and sampling house; Telemarketing agency; Service bureau; Call centre services/systems; Direct response TV services; Electronic media; Internet services

E-Services:
Website design

Member of:
DMA

SCIENCE INTERNATIONAL

Bateman House
82–88 Hills Rd
Cambridge
Cambridgeshire
CB2 1LQ
United Kingdom
Tel: +44 1223 326 500
Fax: +44 1223 326 501
Jane Pennington, Marketing Manager

Services/Products:
Consultancy services; Service bureau; Sales promotion agency; Publisher

SEFTON POLYTHENE LTD

Long Lane
Liver Industrial Estate
Liverpool
L9 7ES
United Kingdom
Tel: +44 151 521 7070
Fax: +44 151 525 2458
John Newman

Services/Products:
Labelling/envelope services

Member of:
DMA

SENIOR KING LTD

14/15 Carlisle Street
London
W1V 5RX
United Kingdom
Tel: +44 20 7734 5855
Fax: +44 20 7437 1908
Email: senior.king@dial.pipex.com
Grahame Senior, Chairman and Chief Executive

Services/Products:
Direct marketing agency; Media buying agency; Market research agency; Sales promotion agency; Advertising Agency

Member of:
FEDMA

SITEL CORPORATION

Sitel House
Timothy's Bridge Road
Stratford Upon Avon
Warwickshire
CV37 9HY
United Kingdom
Tel: +44 1789 299 622
Fax: +44 1789 416 593
Email: info@sitel.co.uk
Web: www.sitel.com
Peter Hall

Services/Products:
Telemarketing agency

Member of:
FEDMA; DMA (US)

SMARTFOCUS

1 Redcliff Street
Bristol
Gl10 3SF
United Kingdom
Tel: +44 117 943 5800
Fax: +44 117 927 7588
Emma Chablo, Marketing Director

Services/Products:
Marketing consultant

Member of:
DMA (US)

SMITH GARDNER & ASSOCIATES LTD

Grove House
Huntingdon Road
Fenstanton
Huntingdon
Cambridgeshire
PE18 9JG
United Kingdom
Tel: +44 1480 460 940
Fax: +44 1480 460 981
Email: acglover@compuserve.com

Web: www.smith-gardner.com
Tony C. Glover, Managing Director

Services/Products:
Direct marketing agency; Software
supplier; Mail order company; Internet
services

Member of:
FEDMA

SPACE CITY PRODUCTIONS
77 Blythe Road
London
W14 0HP
United Kingdom
Tel: +44 20 7371 4000
Fax: +44 20 7371 4001
Nicola Corrie

Services/Products:
Advertising Agency; Direct response
TV services

Member of:
DMA

**SPEARHEAD MARKETING
  AGENCY PLC**
The Limes
123 Mortlake High Street
London
SW14 8SN
United Kingdom
Tel: +44 20 8876 0011
Fax: +44 20 8876 0444
Email:
   steve@spearheadmarketing.co.uk
Web: www.spearheadmarketing.co.uk
Steve Ward, Chief Executive

Services/Products:
Database services; Direct marketing
agency; Consultancy services; Market
research agency; Sales promotion
agency; Advertising Agency

E-Services:
Website design; Email list provider;
E-Marketing consultant; Online/e-
marketing agency

Member of:
National DMA

SR COMMUNICATIONS PLC
64–65 Childers Street
SR House
London
SE8 1SR
United Kingdom
Tel: +44 20 8692 7575
Fax: +44 181 692 8057
D. Brock, Divisional Director

Services/Products:
Fulfilment and sampling house;
Mailing/Faxing services; Direct
marketing agency; Print services

Member of:
FEDMA

STERLING MARKETING LTD.
50 Hans Crescent
London
SW1X 0NB
United Kingdom
Tel: +44 20 7591 8800
Fax: +44 171 591 8833
Justin Metcalf, Managing Director

Services/Products:
Marketing consultant

Member of:
DMA (US)

**STEVENS-KNOX
  INTERNATIONAL**
Manfield House
1 Southampton Street
London
WC2R 0LR
United Kingdom
Tel: +44 20 7240 4670
Fax: +44 20 7240 4726
Email: jol.33@aol.com
Web: www.stevens-knox.com
Jora Milton-King; Liz Pickering

Services/Products:
List services

Member of:
DMA

STORMARK LIMITED
Stormark House
30a Horsefair
Banbury
Oxon
OX16 0AE
United Kingdom
Tel: +44 1295 268143
Fax: +44 1295 268149
Email: jilellis@stormark.ltd.uk
Web: www.stormark.ltd.uk
Jil Ellis, Managing Director

Services/Products:
Telemarketing agency

Member of:
National DMA

SUMMIT SERVICES
Rosebery Avenue
High Wycombe
Buckinghamshire
HP13 7YZ
United Kingdom

Tel: +44 1494 447 562
Fax: +44 1494 441 498
Email: summit@summit-services.co.uk
Web: www.summit-services.co.uk
Bob Street

Services/Products:
Lettershop; Fulfilment and sampling
house; Database services; Mailing/
Faxing services

Member of:
DMA

SUNLINE DIRECT MAIL LTD
Cotton Way
Loughborough
Leicestershire
LE11 5FJ
United Kingdom
Tel: +44 1509 263 434
Fax: +44 1509 264 225
Email: sales@sunlinedirect.co.uk
Nigel Maybury; Tony Whiteman

Services/Products:
Fulfilment and sampling house;
Mailing/Faxing services

Member of:
DMA

SUPERFAX LTD
2 Sinclair House
Hastings Street
London
WC1H 9PZ
United Kingdom
Tel: +44 20 7209 1109
Fax: +44 20 7916 8355
Email: superfax@london.abel.co.uk
Alan Morgan

Services/Products:
List services; Mailing/Faxing services;
Translation services

Member of:
DMA

SURVEY FORCE LTD
Algarve House
140 Borden Lane
Sittingbourne
ME9 8HW
United Kingdom
Tel: +44 179 542 3778
Fax: +44 179 542 3778
Keith Lainton, Director

Services/Products:
List services; Mailing/Faxing services;
Direct marketing agency; Market
research agency

SWETENHAMS
Northumberland House
15 Petersham Road
Richmond
Surrey
TW10 6TP
United Kingdom
Tel: +44 20 8939 1600
Fax: +44 20 8939 1699
Email: marka@alto-e.com
Web: www.swetenhams.co.uk
   www.alto-e.com

Services/Products:
List services; Database services;
Response analysis bureau; Service
bureau; Software supplier; Marketing
software

E-Services:
Email list provider; Online/e-marketing
agency

Member of:
FEDMA; National DMA

SYKES
Calder House
599 Calder Road
Edinburgh
EH11 4GA
United Kingdom
Tel: +44 131 458 6500
Fax: +44 131 458 6565
Web: www.sykes.com
Vicki Greenwood

Services/Products:
Database services; Telemarketing
agency; Service bureau; Call centre
services/systems; Translation services;
Direct response TV services

Member of:
FEDMA; DMA (US)

SYNERGY PARTNERSHIP LTD.
Calthorpe House
31 Belmont Road
Ilfracombe
N. Devon
EX34 8DR
United Kingdom
Tel: +44 271 866 112
Fax: +44 271 866 040
Jane Revell-Higgins, Chief Executive

Services/Products:
Marketing consultant

Member of:
DMA (US)

TARP EUROPE LTD
6, Spring Gardens
Citadel Place
Tinworth Street
London
SE11 5EH
United Kingdom
Tel: +44 20 7793 1866
Fax: +44 20 7793 1940
Email: tarp@dial.pipex.com
Mathieu Rossano, Director Satisfaction
   Measurement

Services/Products:
Direct marketing agency

Member of:
FEDMA

TELELINK LIMITED
11B Stubbington Green
Fareham
PO14 2JG
United Kingdom
Tel: +44 1329 331 331
Fax: +44 1329 330 034
Email: reception@telelink.co.uk
Web: www.telelink.co.uk
Lynne Grierson

Services/Products:
Fulfilment and sampling house;
Database services; Telemarketing
agency; Direct marketing agency; Call
centre services/systems; Electronic
media; Internet services

E-Services:
Website design

Member of:
DMA

TELETECH UK LTD
Access 24 House
Bancroft Road
Reigate
Surrey
RH2 7RP
United Kingdom
Tel: +44 1737 235 200
Fax: +44 1737 235 235
Email: mtb@teletecheuro.com
Michael Tarte-Booth, Vice President
   Europe

Services/Products:
Telemarketing agency; Call centre
services/systems

Member of:
FEDMA

TEQUILA PAYNE STRACEY
82 Charing Cross Road
London
WC2H 0BA
United Kingdom
Tel: +44 20 7490 7555
Fax: +44 171 490 8511
Peter Burton, Development Director

Services/Products:
Advertising Agency; Card pack
manufacturer; Direct marketing
agency; Response analysis bureau

Member of:
FEDMA; DMA (US)

TEQUILA PAYNE STRACEY
82, Charing Cross Road
London
WC2H 0BA
United Kingdom
Tel: +44 20 7557 6100
Fax: +44 20 7557 6111
Email: info@tequila-uk.com
Web: www.tequila-uk.com
Jane Asscher, Chief Operating Officer

Services/Products:
Database services; Direct marketing
agency; Copy adaptation; Sales
promotion agency; Advertising
Agency; Electronic media

E-Services:
Website design

Member of:
FEDMA

THA MARKETING LTD
The Old Chapel
186 Watling St East
Towcester
Northants
NN1Z 6DB
United Kingdom
Tel: +44 1327 359 025
Fax: +44 1327 359 985
Email: i.mcmillan@tha.co.uk
Web: http://www.tha.co.uk
Isabel McMillan

Services/Products:
Direct marketing agency; Consultancy
services

Member of:
DMA

THE CATALOG WORKSHOP
Parallel House
32 London Road
Guildford
Surrey
GU1 2AB
United Kingdom
Tel: +44 1483 450 740
Fax: +44 1483 452 650
Robert Grech, Principal

Services/Products:
Catalogue producer

Member of:
DMA (US)

THE CLOCKHOUSE PRESS LIMITED

Court 1, Bedfont Lakes
Challenge Road
Ashford
Middlesex
TW15 1AX
United Kingdom
Tel: +44 1784 264 300
Fax: +44 1784 264 364
Email: karen@clockhousepress.co.uk
Karen Horton

Services/Products:
Design/graphics/clip art supplier; Print services

Member of:
DMA

THE COMPACT GROUP LTD

Unit 4, Deacon Industrial Estate
Forstal Road
Aylesford
Maidstone
Kent
ME20 7SP
United Kingdom
Tel: +44 162 271 9365
Fax: +44 162 271 8831
Terry Gilbert, Group Managing
    Director

Services/Products:
Lettershop; Fulfilment and sampling house; Mailing/Faxing services; Labelling/envelope services; Print services; Direct marketing agency

Member of:
DMA

THE COMPUTING GROUP

Beech House, Betts Way
Crawley
W. Sussex
RH10 2GW
United Kingdom
Tel: +44 293 561 666
Fax: +44 293 561 890
Judi Gehlcken, Managing Director

Services/Products:
List services

Member of:
DMA (US)

THE DATABASE GROUP

Colston Centre
Colston Ave
Bristol
BS1 4UH
United Kingdom
Tel: +44 1179 291 571
D.L. O'Reilly, Chairman

Services/Products:
Database services

Member of:
DMA (US)

THE DAVIS COMPANY

4th Floor
Canberra House
315 Regent Street
London
W1R 7YB
United Kingdom
Tel: +44 20 7323 6696
Fax: +44 20 7323 6697
Email: jane@daviscompany.co.uk
Web: www.daviscompany.co.uk
Jane Alexander, Joint Managing
    Director

Services/Products:
Training/recruitment

Member of:
National DMA

THE DIRECT AGENCY

Victoria House
St. James Square
Cheltenham
Gloucestershire
GL50 3PR
United Kingdom
Tel: +44 1242 633 111
Fax: +44 1242 263 818
Email: heather-w@the
    directagency.co.uk
Mrs. Heather Westgate

Services/Products:
Advertising Agency; Consultancy services; Copy adaptation; Direct marketing agency; Direct response TV services; Creative services

Member of:
DMA

THE DRAYTON BIRD PARTNERSHIP

MCB House
133–137 Westbourne Grove
London
W11 2RS
United Kingdom
Tel: +44 20 7243 0196
Fax: +44 20 7229 0426
Email: dbp@draytonbird.com
Web: www.draytonbird.com
Peter Hardingham, Managing Director

Services/Products:
Direct marketing agency

Member of:
FEDMA; National DMA

THE INSTITUTE OF DIRECT MARKETING

No. 1 Park Road
Teddington
Middlesex
TW11 OAR
United Kingdom
Tel: +44 20 8977 5705
Fax: +44 181 943 2535
Derek Holder, Managing Director

Services/Products:
Training/recruitment; Training/recruitment; Direct marketing agency

Member of:
FEDMA

THE JAVELIN GROUP

18 Savile Row
London
W1X 1AE
United Kingdom
Tel: +44 20 7287 2323
Fax: +44 171 734 1690
Anthony Stockil, Managing Director

Services/Products:
Marketing consultant

Member of:
DMA (US)

THE KNOWLEDGE STORE

(part of the William Reed Group)
Broadfield Park
Crawley
West Sussex
RH11 9RT
United Kingdom
Tel: +44 1293 610400
Fax: +44 1293 610499
Email: knowledge.store@wrks.co.uk
Web: www.theknowledgestore.co.uk
David Craft, Managing Director

Services/Products:
Database services; Direct marketing agency; List services; Telemarketing agency

Member of:
National DMA; Institute of DM

THE LETTERSHOP GROUP

Whitehall Park
Whitehall Road
Leeds
LS12 5XX
United Kingdom
Tel: +44 113 231 1113
Fax: +44 113 231 1444
Email: enquiries@tlg.co.uk
Web: www.tlg.co.uk
Mr. James Hewlings, Regional Sales
    Director

Services/Products:
Lettershop; Direct marketing agency;
Personalisation; Print services

E-Services:
Website design

Member of:
National DMA

THE LIST REGISTER
2A Southwark Bridge Office Village
Thrale Street
London
SE1 9JG
United Kingdom
Tel: +44 20 7407 5987
Fax: +44 171 407 6294
Duncan Walton, Sales Manager

Services/Products:
List services

Member of:
FEDMA; DMA (US)

THE MAIL MARKETING GROUP
Springfield House
West Street
Bedminster
Bristol
BS3 3NX
United Kingdom
Tel: +44 117 966 6900
Fax: +44 117 963 6737
Email: ian.hughes@mmgroup.co.uk
Web: www.mailmktg.com
Ian Hughes, Sales and Marketing
   Director

Services/Products:
Lettershop; Telemarketing agency;
Print services; Direct marketing agency

Member of:
FEDMA

THE MARKETING ORGANISATION
Vantage Court
Tickford Street
Newport Pagnell
Bucks
MK16 9EZ
United Kingdom
Tel: +44 1908 214 700
Fax: +44 1908 214 777
Email: jsmith@tmo.co.uk
Web: www.tmo.co.uk
Jerry Smith

Services/Products:
Database services; Telemarketing
agency; Direct marketing agency;
Consultancy services; Design/graphics/

clip art supplier

Member of:
DMA

THE MARKETING PARTNERSHIP LTD
69 Hatton Garden
London
EC1N 8JT
United Kingdom
Tel: +44 20 7831 9190
Fax: +44 20 7831 1852
Email: tmpl@marketing-
   partnership.com
David Drakes

Services/Products:
Direct marketing agency; Consultancy
services; Design/graphics/clip art
supplier; Sales promotion agency

Member of:
DMA

THE MARKETING STORE WORLDWIDE
Prince of Wales House
Bluecoats
Hertford
Herts
SG14 1PB
United Kingdom
Tel: +44 1992 553 831
Fax: +44 1992 504 534
Email: mike.lapsley@tmsw.com
Web: www.tmsw.com
Mike Lapsley

Services/Products:
Advertising Agency; Consultancy
services; Direct marketing agency;
Sales promotion agency

E-Services:
Website design

Member of:
DMA

THE MCLEOD NEW BUSINESS MACHINE
37 Richmond Park Road
London
SW14 8JU
United Kingdom
Tel: +44 208 878 4144
Fax: +44 208 878 4144
Email: carmcleod@aol.com
Carina McLeod, Partner

Services/Products:
New business services for direct
marketing and e-marketing agencies

THE MERCHANTS GROUP
Southgate House
449–499 Midsummer Boulevard
Milton Keynes
Bucks
MK9 3BN
United Kingdom
Tel: +44 1908 232 323
Fax: +44 1908 242 444
Email: kathy.dipple@merchants.co.uk
Web: www.merchants.co.uk
Kathy Dipple, Head of Public
   Relations

Services/Products:
Database services; Direct marketing
agency; Design/graphics/clip art
supplier; Market research agency

E-Services:
Website design

Member of:
FEDMA

THE MERCHANTS GROUP
Southgate House
449–499 Midsummer Boulevard
Milton Keynes
Bucks
MK9 3BN
United Kingdom
Tel: +44 1908 232 323
Fax: +44 1908 242 444
Kim Wilkins, Marketing Services
   Manager

Services/Products:
Telemarketing agency; Direct
marketing agency; Direct response TV
services

Member of:
FEDMA; DMA (US)

THE OPS ROOM LTD
Twickenham House
159 Heath Road
Twickenham
Middlesex
TW1 4BJ
United Kingdom
Tel: +44 20 8410 8000
Fax: +44 20 8410 8001
Email: enquiries@opsroom.co.uk
Web: www.opsroom.co.uk
Stuart Macmillan Pratt, Managing
   Director

Services/Products:
Direct marketing agency; Database
services; Fulfilment and sampling
house; Telemarketing agency;
Lettershop; Mail order company;
Marketing services

Member of:
National DMA; Institute of Sales
Promotion (UK)

THE POLK COMPANY
Port House Square Rigger Row
Plantation Wharf, York Place
London
SW11 3TY
United Kingdom
Tel: +44 20 7738 0511
Stephen Polk, Chairman & CEO

Services/Products:
List services

Member of:
DMA (US)

THE RD CONSULTANCY
Castle House
20 Bear Lane
Farnham
GU9 7LF
United Kingdom
Tel: +44 1252 726 484
Fax: +44 1252 711 225
Richard Dorsett

Services/Products:
Consultancy services

Member of:
DMA (US)

THE RD CONSULTANCY
Castle House
20 Bear Lane
Farnham
Surrey
GU9 7LF
United Kingdom
Tel: +44 1252 726 484
Fax: +44 1252 733 906
Richard Dorsett, Consultant

Services/Products:
Marketing consultant

Member of:
DMA (US)

THINK DIRECT
7 Trowley Heights
Flamstead
St. Albans
Hertfordshire
AL3 8DE
United Kingdom
Tel: +44 1582 842121
Fax: +44 1582 842121
Email: shane.redding@btinternet.com
Web: www.thinkdirect.btinternet.co.uk
Shane Redding, Director

Services/Products:
Consultancy services

E-Services:
E-Marketing consultant

Member of:
FEDMA; National DMA

TOUCHDOWN DIRECT LTD
26 Ashford Road
Bearsted
Maidstone
ME14 4LP
United Kingdom
Tel: +44 1622 737 670
Fax: +44 1622 737 670
Email: touchdd@cwcom.net
Jim Sheehy, Director

Services/Products:
List services; Database services;
Consultancy services

TRANSMAIL LTD
Hurricane Way
Norwich
NR6 6EY
United Kingdom
Tel: +44 1603 404217
Fax: +44 1603 483944
Jackie Bell

Services/Products:
Manufacturer and supplier of
polythene mailing envelopes and
packaging

TULLO MARSHALL WARREN
81 King's Road
Chelsea
London
SW3 4NX
United Kingdom
Tel: +44 20 7349 4000
Fax: +44 20 7349 4001
Email: direct@tmw.co.uk
Web: www.tmw.co.uk
Richard Marshall

Services/Products:
Database services; Direct marketing
agency; Consultancy services; Direct
response TV services; Electronic
media; Internet services

Member of:
DMA

TWO TEN COMMUNICATIONS LTD
Thorp Arch Trading Estate
Wethorby
West Yorkshire
LS23 7EL
United Kingdom
Tel: +44 1937 840 210
Fax: +44 1937 845 381
Email: mss@twoten.press.net

Web: http://www.twoten.press.net
Mark Hepworth

Services/Products:
Lettershop; Fulfilment and sampling
house; Mailing/Faxing services;
Labelling/envelope services;
Telemarketing agency

Member of:
DMA

UK DATA GROUP LTD
Kensington House
2 Northcourt
Armstrong Road
Maidstone
Kent
ME15 6JZ
United Kingdom
Tel: +44 1622 765 765
Fax: +44 1622 663 242
Email: ukdata@khg.co.uk
Vic Godding

Services/Products:
List services; Fulfilment and sampling
house; Design/graphics/clip art
supplier; Call centre services/systems
Mail order company

Member of:
DMA

UNI-MARKETING LTD
1 The Courtyard, Swan Centre
Fishers Lane
Chiswick
London
W4 1RX
United Kingdom
Tel: +44 20 8995 1919
Fax: +44 20 8742 7245
Email: info@uni-
   marketing.demon.co.uk
Jonathan Burston, Sales Director

Services/Products:
Consultancy services; List services;
Subscription strategies

E-Services:
Email list provider

Member of:
FEDMA; National DMA

WADDIES PRINT GROUP
97 Slateford Road
Edinburgh
EH11 1QS
United Kingdom
Tel: +44 131 337 3301
Fax: +44 131 347 3200
Email: mail@waddies.co.uk
Web: http://www.waddies.co.uk
Colin McDonald

Services/Products:
Lettershop; Mailing/Faxing services;
Service bureau

Member of:
DMA

WADDINGTON CHORLEYS PFB LTD.
Manston Lane
Cross Gates
Leeds
LS15 8AH
United Kingdom
Tel: +44 113 225 5248
Fax: +44 113 225 5308
Alan Ridyard, Director

Services/Products:
Lettershop; Mailing/Faxing services

Member of:
DMA (US)

WATSON WARD ALBERT VARNDELL
31 St. Petersburgh Place
London
W2 41A
United Kingdom
Tel: +44 20 7727 3481
Fax: +44 171 727 0520
John Watson, Managing Director

Services/Products:
Advertising Agency; Direct Response
Agency

Member of:
DMA (US)

WAVELENGTH PROMOTIONAL SUPPORT SERVICES
Aventine Way
Glebe Farm Industrial Park
Rugby
Warks
CV21 1RH
United Kingdom
Tel: +44 1788 545 555
Fax: +44 1788 579 244; 570 251
Email:
   info@wavelength-handling.co.uk
Web: www.wavelength-handling.co.uk
Julian Kent

Services/Products:
Fulfilment and sampling house;
Database services; Mailing/Faxing
services; Labelling/envelope services;
Call centre services/systems

Member of:
DMA

WESTEX LIMITED
7 St Andrews Way
Devons Road
Bromley By Bow
London
E3 3PA
United Kingdom
Tel: +44 20 7510 0100
Fax: +44 20 7510 0195
Email: persa.maclean@westex.co.uk
Persa Maclean

Services/Products:
Fulfilment and sampling house;
Database services; Mailing/Faxing
services; Labelling/envelope services;
Call centre services/systems; Private
delivery services

Member of:
DMA

WESTON MARKETING LIMITED
3 Farmbrough Close
Stocklake
Aylesbury
HP20 1DD
United Kingdom
Tel: +44 1296 425 952
Fax: +44 1296 393 902
Email:
   westonmkting@compuserve.com
Dick Weston

Services/Products:
Lettershop; Fulfilment and sampling
house; Database services; Direct
marketing agency

Member of:
DMA

WILMINGTON DIRECT MARKETING
Wilmington House
Church Hill
Wilmington
Dartford
Kent
DA2 7EF
United Kingdom
Tel: +44 1322 277 788
Fax: +44 1322 276 474
Email: wgp@wilmington.co.uk
Ian Sexton

Services/Products:
List services; Publisher

Member of:
DMA

WORLD WRITERS
162–170 Wardour Street
London
W1V 3AT
United Kingdom
Tel: +44 20 7287 4877
Fax: +44 20 7287 6159
Email:
   postman@worldwriters.com
Web: www.worldwriters.com
Caroline Bamber, Head of Direct
   Marketing

Services/Products:
Advertising Agency; Direct marketing
agency; Copy adaptation; Advertising
Agency

Member of:
FEDMA

WORLDWIDE MEDIA GROUP LTD
Eton House
64 High Street
Burnham
Buckinghamshire
SL1 7JT
United Kingdom
Tel: +44 1628 604030
Fax: +44 1628 668522
Email:
   jackie.cooper@compuserve.com
Jason Cooper, Director

Services/Products:
List services; Database services

Member of:
FEDMA; DMA (US)

WORTH COMMUNICATIONS LTD
Lawrence Parade
Swan Street
Old Isleworth
TW7 6RJ
United Kingdom
Tel: +44 20 8568 2434
Fax: +44 20 8568 1976
Email: mcotton@worth-comms.com
Web: www.worthcomms.com
Malcolm Cotton, Managing Director

Services/Products:
Advertising Agency; Direct marketing
agency; Design/graphics/clip art
supplier; Media buying agency; Mail
order company; Advertising Agency;
Electronic media

E-Services:
Website design

Member of:
FEDMA

WUNDERMAN CATO JOHNSON UK
Modo House, Rosemount Avenue
West Byfleet Ferry
United Kingdom
Tel: +44 48371600
Rosamund Lyster, Manager, Resource Services

Services/Products:
Advertising Agency; Direct Response Agency

Member of:
DMA (US)

WWAV RAPP COLLINS MEDIA LTD
31 St. Petersburgh Place
London
W2 4LA
United Kingdom
Tel: +44 20 7727 34 81
Fax: +44 171 221 05 20
Lesley Mair, Managing Director

Services/Products:
Database services; Direct marketing agency; Response analysis bureau

Member of:
FEDMA

WWAV RAPP COLLINS MEDIA LTD
Compass House
22 Redan Pl
4th Fl
London
W2 4SA
United Kingdom
Tel: +44 20 7727 7700
Fax: +44 171 313 4355
G. Steven Dapper, Chairman & CEO

Services/Products:
Advertising Agency; Direct Response Agency

Member of:
DMA (US) .

WWAV RAPP COLLINS SCOTLAND
16 Melville Street
4th Fl
Edinburgh
EH3 7NS
United Kingdom
Tel: +44 131 220 1012
Fax: +44 131 220 1014
G. Steven Dapper, Chairman & CEO

Services/Products:
Advertising Agency; Direct Response Agency

Member of:
DMA (US)

WYVERN DIRECT RESPONSE
6 The Business Park
Ely
Cambridgeshire
CB7 4JW
United Kingdom
Tel: +44 1353 667 733
Fax: +44 1353 669 030
Email: wdresponse@aol.com
Web: www.wyvern.co.uk/wyvern
Hayley Tooke

Services/Products:
List services; Database services

Member of:
DMA

SERVICES/PRODUCT LISTING

Address Management Services
LM Software Ltd

Advertising Agency
Advanstar Marketing Services
Barraclough Hall Woolston Gray
Blaze Business to Business Ltd
Brunnings Advertising & Marketing
Business To Business Direct Ltd
Campaign Direct Ltd
Clear Communications Ltd
Clockwork Communications (London) Limited
Cramm Francis Woolf
Direct Marketing International
DraftWorldwide
Euro RSCG WNEK GOSPER
Interfocus Network Ltd
J. Walter Thompson
McCann-Erickson Manchester Ltd
Messenger Marketing Services Limited
Outside The Box Plc
Publicis Dialog Limited
Publicis Technology
Red Box Advertising Ltd
Red Fish Limited
Redoute UK
Richardson Pailin & Fallow Ltd. (RP&F)
Saatchi & Saatchi
Senior King Ltd
Space City Productions
Spearhead Marketing Agency plc
Tequila Payne Stracey
Tequila Payne Stracey
The Direct Agency
The Marketing Store Worldwide
Watson Ward Albert Varndell

World Writers
Worth Communications Ltd
Wunderman Cato Johnson UK
WWAV Rapp Collins Media Ltd
WWAV Rapp Collins Scotland

Call centre services/systems
Advanced Telecom Services
APAC Customer Services
BMG (Bostock Marketing Group Limited)
Brann Ltd
Case Direct Ltd
Centrobe And EDS Company
Connections Plus Ltd
Convergys Customer Management
Dowerhill Ltd
Education Direct
Financial Telemarketing Services Limited
Greenland Interactive Ltd
GWC Group Ltd
ICLP (International Customer Loyalt Programmes Plc)
Intermail PLC
Kettle Green Studios
Newstel Information Ltd
Omega Marketing Services
Prism Data Management Ltd.
Salestrac Ltd
Sykes
Telelink Limited
Teletech UK Ltd
UK Data Group Ltd
Wavelength Promotional Support Services
Westex Limited

Campaign management
Identex

Card pack manufacturer
Advanstar Marketing Services
Tequila Payne Stracey

Catalogue producer
Blue Sheep Limited
Direct Group International
IMT-Harrowbrook Ltd
Intermarketing Communications Ltd
The Catalog Workshop

Consultancy services
Anderson Weinrib Associates
Andrew Boddington Associates
Aspen Agency
Claritas Europe (European Headquarters)
Claritas UK (HQ)
Clear Communications Ltd
Communicator
Cramm Francis Woolf
DBT Limited

DMS
DMS
DraftWorldwide
Greenland Interactive Ltd
Hubbard Hiwaizi McCann
ICLP (International Customer Loyalty
 Programmes PLC)
ICLP (International Customer Loyalty
 Programmes Plc)
ID Data Group
Isis Direct Limited
J. Walter Thompson
Jennifer D. Baker
John Yates Copy Consultants
 (Copywriters)
LM Software Ltd
Manifesto
Market Location Ltd
Marketing and Media Solutions Ltd
Messenger Marketing Services Limited
MMS Market Movements
Occam Direct Marketing Ltd
Promotional Campaigns Group
Ravensworth Design
Red Square Communications
Results (Europe) Ltd
Rosemary Stockdale Associates
Science International
Spearhead Marketing Agency plc
THA Marketing Ltd
The Direct Agency
The Marketing Organisation
The Marketing Partnership Ltd
The Marketing Store Worldwide
The RD Consultancy
Think Direct
Touchdown Direct Ltd
Tullo Marshall Warren
Uni-Marketing Ltd

Copy adaptation
Allied Marketing Services Ltd
Communicator
Direct Marketing International
DMS
John Yates Copy Consultants
 (Copywriters)
Response Marketing Ltd
Tequila Payne Stracey
The Direct Agency
World Writers

Creative services
The Direct Agency

Data-driven websites
DBT Limited

Database services
100 Percent Ltd
Acxiom Ltd
Allied Marketing Services Ltd
Andrew Boddington Associates

APAC Customer Services
Aspen Agency
Aspen Agency
Bellsize Datamatic Limited
BH& P Direct Mail Limited
Blaze Business to Business Ltd
BMG (Bostock Marketing Group
 Limited)
Brann Ltd
Broadprint Ltd
Cambertown Ltd
Campaign Direct Ltd
Centrobe And EDS Company
Claritas Europe (European
 Headquarters)
Claritas UK (HQ)
Communicator
Consumerdata Ltd
Data Processing Direct (DPD)
 Ltd
Datamex Computer Services Ltd
DBMS - David Brannan Marketing
 Services Ltd
DBT Limited
Dowerhill Ltd
DraftWorldwide
Dun & Bradstreet Europe Ltd
Dun & Bradstreet Ltd
EC Direct Ltd
Education Direct
Equifax Europe Ltd
Euro DM Ltd
Euro RSCG
Euro RSCG Direct
EWA LTD
Firstbase
GB Information Management
GGT Direct Advertising
Grange Direct Ltd
Grey Direct International
GWC Group Ltd
Hamilton House Mailings
Harte-Hanks
Hobs 4DM
Hubbard Hiwaizi McCann
ICD Marketing Services
ICLP (International Customer Loyalty
 Programmes PLC)
ICLP (International Customer Loyalty
 Programmes Plc)
Identex
IDS
IMP LTD
Intermail PLC
Isis Direct Limited
Jennifer D. Baker
Kettle Green Studios
KPA Business Lists Limited
LGM Marketing Services Ltd
Limbo Ltd
Listmaster Database Marketing
Lloyd James List Broking Services Ltd
LM Software Ltd

Manifesto
Market Location Ltd
Market Phone Ltd
Marketing and Media Solutions Ltd
Marketing and Media Solutions Ltd
McCann-Erickson Manchester Ltd
Metro Mail
Miller Starr Ltd
NCH Marketing Services Ltd
Newstel Information Ltd
Occam Direct Marketing Ltd
Ogilvyone Worldwide
Prime Response
Printronic International Plc
Prism Data Management Ltd.
Prospect Mailing Services Ltd
QAS Systems Ltd
QBASE Data Services
Red Square Communications
Response Marketing Ltd
Results (Europe) Ltd
Saatchi & Saatchi
Spearhead Marketing Agency plc
Summit Services
Swetenhams
Sykes
Telelink Limited
Tequila Payne Stracey
The Database Group
The Knowledge Store
The Marketing Organisation
The Merchants Group
The OPS Room Ltd
Touchdown Direct Ltd
Tullo Marshall Warren
Wavelength Promotional Support
 Services
Westex Limited
Weston Marketing Limited
Worldwide Media Group Ltd
WWAV Rapp Collins Media Ltd
Wyvern Direct Response

Design/graphics/clip art
 supplier
100 Percent Ltd
Advanstar Marketing Services
Allied Marketing Services Ltd
Blaze Business to Business Ltd
Clear Communications Ltd
DMS
Hubbard Hiwaizi McCann
IMP LTD
John Yates Copy Consultants
 (Copywriters)
Outside The Box Plc
Ravensworth Design
Red Square Communications
The Clockhouse Press Limited
The Marketing Organisation
The Marketing Partnership Ltd
The Merchants Group
UK Data Group Ltd

Worth Communications Ltd

Direct Response Agency
Barraclough Hall Woolston Gray
BH& P Direct Mail Limited
Brunnings Advertising & Marketing
Business To Business Direct Ltd
Euro RSCG WNEK GOSPER
Publicis Dialog Limited
Redoute UK
Richardson Pailin & Fallow Ltd.
  (RP&F)
Watson Ward Albert Varndell
Wunderman Cato Johnson UK
WWAV Rapp Collins Media Ltd
WWAV Rapp Collins Scotland

Direct marketing agency
:ped:
100 Percent Ltd
AEDP (AE Data Processing)
Allied Marketing Services Ltd
Andrew Boddington Associates
Aspen Agency
Aspen Agency
Blaze Business to Business Ltd
Blue Sheep Limited
Brann Ltd
Brann S. J. A.
Cambertown Ltd
Campaign Direct Ltd
Claydon Heeley International
Clear Communications Ltd
Clockwork Communications (London)
  Limited
Communicator
Cramm Francis Woolf
DBMS - David Brannan Marketing
  Services Ltd
DBT Limited
DMS
DMS
DraftWorldwide
EC Direct Ltd
Equifax Europe Ltd
Euro DM Ltd
Euro RSCG
Euro RSCG Direct
Evans Hunt Scott
EWA LTD
Firstbase
GGT Direct Advertising
Grey Direct International
Hubbard Hiwaizi McCann
ICLP (International Customer Loyalty
  Programmes Plc)
ICT Group Inc
ID Data Group
IMP LTD
Interfocus Network Ltd
Intermarketing Communications Ltd
Isis Direct Limited
Joshua Agency Plc

Judith Donovan Associates Ltd
KPA Business Lists Limited
Leo Burnett Europe
LGM Marketing Services Ltd
Limbo Ltd
Market Phone Ltd
Marketing and Media Solutions Ltd
Marketing and Media Solutions Ltd
McCann-Erickson Manchester Ltd
Ogilvyone Worldwide
Outside The Box Plc
Portland Direct Marketing Ltd
Prism Data Management Ltd.
Promotional Campaigns Group
Publicis Technology
Ravensworth Design
Red Box Advertising Ltd
Red Fish Limited
Red Square Communications
Response Marketing Ltd
Saatchi & Saatchi
Senior King Ltd
Smith Gardner & Associates Ltd
Spearhead Marketing Agency plc
SR Communications Plc
Survey Force Ltd
Tarp Europe Ltd
Telelink Limited
Tequila Payne Stracey
Tequila Payne Stracey
THA Marketing Ltd
The Compact Group Ltd
The Direct Agency
The Drayton Bird Partnership
The Institute of Direct Marketing
The Knowledge Store

Lettershop
100 Percent Ltd
BH& P Direct Mail Limited
Broadprint Ltd
Business Lists UK
Cambertown Ltd
Datamex Computer Services Ltd
Education Direct
FCS Laser-Mail
Grange Direct Ltd
GWC Group Ltd
Hobs 4DM
KPA Business Lists Limited
Ludlow Marketing
Mailcom PLC
Mailing and Printing Company Ltd
Metro Mail
One to One Mailing Services Ltd
Prospect Mailing Services Ltd
Quality Registration Services Ltd
Quality Registration Services Ltd
RMA International Ltd
Royal Mail Impact House
Summit Services
The Compact Group Ltd
The Lettershop Group

The Mail Marketing Group
The OPS Room Ltd
Two Ten Communications Ltd
Waddies Print Group
Waddington Chorleys PFB Ltd.
Weston Marketing Limited
The Mail Marketing Group
The Marketing Organisation
The Marketing Partnership Ltd
The Marketing Store Worldwide
The Merchants Group
The Merchants Group
The OPS Room Ltd
Tullo Marshall Warren
Weston Marketing Limited
World Writers
Worth Communications Ltd
WWAV Rapp Collins Media Ltd

Direct response TV services
:ped:
Advanstar Marketing Services
Communicator
Connections Plus Ltd
Convergys Customer Management
Greenland Interactive Ltd
J. Walter Thompson
Red Square Communications
Salestrac Ltd
Space City Productions
Sykes
The Direct Agency
The Merchants Group
Tullo Marshall Warren

E-commerce
Intermail PLC

Electronic media
Aspen Agency
Brann Ltd
Communicator
Grey Direct International
Hubbard Hiwaizi McCann
IMP LTD
Manifesto
Newstel Information Ltd
QBASE Data Services
Red Box Advertising Ltd
Red Square Communications
Saatchi & Saatchi
Salestrac Ltd
Telelink Limited
Tequila Payne Stracey
Tullo Marshall Warren
Worth Communications Ltd

Exhibition and conference
  registration
Quality Registration Services Ltd
Quality Registration Services Ltd

Fulfilment and sampling house

Acxiom Ltd
Advanstar Marketing Services
BH& P Direct Mail Limited
Business Lists UK
Centrobe And EDS Company
Connections Plus Ltd
Crowcastle Limited
Data Processing Direct (DPD) Ltd
Datamex Computer Services Ltd
Direct Group International
Education Direct
FCS Laser-Mail
GWC Group Ltd
Hobs 4DM
ID Data Group
IDS
Intermail PLC
Kettle Green Studios
Magazine Mailing Ltd
Malvern Mailing Services
Market Phone Ltd
Omega Marketing Services
Portland Direct Marketing Ltd
Printware Direct Limited
Prism Data Management Ltd.
RMA International Ltd
Royal Mail Impact House
Salestrac Ltd
SR Communications Plc
Summit Services
Sunline Direct Mail Ltd
Telelink Limited
The Compact Group Ltd
The OPS Room Ltd
Two Ten Communications Ltd
UK Data Group Ltd
Wavelength Promotional Support
    Services
Westex Limited
Weston Marketing Limited

Hardware supplier

ATI - Advanced Technologies
    International Ltd

Incentive travel & motivation agency

Red Fish Limited

Information/advice on producing a customer magazine/selecting a publishing agency

Association of Publishing Agencies
    (APA)

Insert management

Columbus Direct Media Ltd

Interactive media

Association of Publishing Agencies

(APA)
Prism Data Management Ltd.

Internet services

Aspen Agency
Brann Ltd
Communicator
Hubbard Hiwaizi McCann
Manifesto
Newstel Information Ltd
Red Box Advertising Ltd
Red Square Communications
Salestrac Ltd
Smith Gardner & Associates Ltd
Telelink Limited
Tullo Marshall Warren

Labelling/envelope services

Business Lists UK
Cambertown Ltd
Data Processing Direct (DPD) Ltd
FCS Laser-Mail
Grange Direct Ltd
Hamilton House Mailings
ICLP (International Customer Loyalty
    Programmes Plc)
IDS
John S. Turner Direct Marketing
Malvern Mailing Services
One to One Mailing Services Ltd
Polyprint Mailing Films Ltd
Printware Direct Limited
RMA International Ltd
Sefton Polythene Ltd
The Compact Group Ltd
Two Ten Communications Ltd
Wavelength Promotional Support
    Services
Westex Limited

Legal services

Reynolds Porter Chamberlain

Lettershop

100 Percent Ltd
BH& P Direct Mail Limited
Broadprint Ltd
Business Lists UK
Cambertown Ltd
Datamex Computer Services Ltd
Education Direct
FCS Laser-Mail
Grange Direct Ltd
GWC Group Ltd
Hobs 4DM
KPA Business Lists Limited
Ludlow Marketing
Mailcom PLC
Mailing and Printing Company Ltd
Metro Mail
One to One Mailing Services Ltd
Prospect Mailing Services Ltd

Quality Registration Services Ltd
Quality Registration Services Ltd
RMA International Ltd
Royal Mail Impact House
Summit Services
The Compact Group Ltd
The Lettershop Group
The Mail Marketing Group
The OPS Room Ltd
Two Ten Communications Ltd
Waddies Print Group
Waddington Chorleys PFB Ltd.
Weston Marketing Limited

List services

100 Percent Ltd
Acxiom Ltd
Acxiom/Direct Media
Advanstar Marketing Services
Advanstar Marketing Services
AEDP (AE Data Processing)
Anderson Weinrib Associates
Blue Sheep Limited
Britannia Music Co. Ltd
Business Lists UK
Claritas Europe (European
    Headquarters)
Claritas UK (HQ)
Columbus Direct Media Ltd
Consumer Surveys Ltd
Consumerdata Ltd
Data2 Limited
Direct Group International
Dudley Jenkins List Broking Ltd
Dun & Bradstreet Europe Ltd
Dun & Bradstreet Ltd
EC Direct Ltd
EDM Broking and Management
Education Direct
Firstbase
Graham & Whiteside Ltd
Hamilton House Mailings
HLB LTD
HLB Ltd.
IBC UK Conferences Ltd
ICD Marketing Services
ICLP (International Customer Loyalty
    Programmes PLC)
ID Data Group
IDS
Iinternational Airline Passengers
    Association
Intermarketing Communications Ltd
Isis Direct Limited
John S. Turner Direct Marketing
Kogan Page Ltd
KPA Business Lists Limited
Lloyd James List Broking Services Ltd
Malvern Mailing Services
Mardev
Market Location Ltd
Market Phone Ltd
Marketing and Media Solutions Ltd

Marketing and Media Solutions Ltd
Messenger Marketing Services Limited
Metro Mail
Newstel Information Ltd
OAG Worldwide
Occam Direct Marketing Ltd
One to One Mailing Services Ltd
Polygram
Portland Direct Marketing Ltd
Printware Direct Limited
QBASE Data Services
Response Marketing Ltd
RMA International Ltd
Royal Mail Impact House
Stevens-Knox International
Superfax Ltd
Survey Force Ltd
Swetenhams
The Computing Group
The Knowledge Store
The List Register
The Polk Company
Touchdown Direct Ltd
UK Data Group Ltd
Uni-Marketing Ltd
Wilmington Direct Marketing
Worldwide Media Group Ltd
Wyvern Direct Response

Loyalty systems
ICLP (International Customer Loyalty
   Programmes PLC)

Mail order company
Able-Direct Centre Ltd
Adler
Britannia Music Co. Ltd
Brooks & Bentley
Direct Group International
Euro RSCG Direct
IMT-Harrowbrook Ltd
Prism Data Management Ltd.
Smith Gardner & Associates Ltd
The OPS Room Ltd
UK Data Group Ltd
Worth Communications Ltd

Mailing/Faxing services
Advanstar Marketing Services
Allied Marketing Services Ltd
BH& P Direct Mail Limited
Broadprint Ltd
Business Lists UK
Cambertown Ltd
Data Processing Direct (DPD) Ltd
Datamex Computer Services Ltd
DBMS - David Brannan Marketing
   Services Ltd
Dudley Jenkins List Broking Ltd
Education Direct
Euro DM Ltd
Euro RSCG Direct
FCS Laser-Mail

Firstbase
Grange Direct Ltd
Greenland Interactive Ltd
Hamilton House Mailings
Hobs 4DM
ID Data Group
John S. Turner Direct Marketing
LM Software Ltd
Ludlow Marketing
Magazine Mailing Ltd
Mailcom PLC
Malvern Mailing Services
Metro Mail
Omega Marketing Services
One to One Mailing Services Ltd
Polyprint Mailing Films Ltd
Portland Direct Marketing Ltd
Printronic International Plc
Printware Direct Limited
Quality Registration Services Ltd
Quality Registration Services Ltd
Response Marketing Ltd
RMA International Ltd
Royal Mail International
SR Communications Plc
Summit Services
Sunline Direct Mail Ltd
Superfax Ltd
Survey Force Ltd
The Compact Group Ltd
Two Ten Communications Ltd
Waddies Print Group
Waddington Chorleys PFB Ltd.
Wavelength Promotional Support
   Services
Westex Limited

Manufacturer and supplier of polythene mailing envelopes and packaging
Transmail Ltd

Market research agency
BMG (Bostock Marketing Group
   Limited)
Consumerdata Ltd
EC Direct Ltd
Firstbase
GGT Direct Advertising
ICD Marketing Services
Jennifer D. Baker
Market Phone Ltd
MMS Market Movements
Outside The Box Plc
Senior King Ltd
Spearhead Marketing Agency plc
Survey Force Ltd
The Merchants Group

Marketing consultant
DBT Limited
DraftWorldwide
Europe Direct (UK) Ltd.

Prism Data Management Ltd.
Smartfocus
Spearhead Marketing Agency plc
Sterling Marketing Ltd.
Synergy Partnership Ltd.
The Javelin Group
The RD Consultancy
Think Direct

Marketing services
The OPS Room Ltd

Marketing software
Swetenhams

Media buying agency
Anderson Weinrib Associates
Blaze Business to Business Ltd
Clear Communications Ltd
Clockwork Communications (London
   Limited
Intermarketing Communications Ltd
Isis Direct Limited
Kettle Green Studios
Marketing and Media Solutions Ltd
Marketing and Media Solutions Ltd
McCann-Erickson Manchester Ltd
Occam Direct Marketing Ltd
Ogilvyone Worldwide
Outside The Box Plc
Publicis Technology
Senior King Ltd
Worth Communications Ltd

New business services for direct marketing and e-marketing agencies
The McLeod New Business Machine

Online web service fulfilment
Prism Data Management Ltd.

Personalisation
BH& P Direct Mail Limited
GWC Group Ltd
Mailcom PLC
Mailing and Printing Company Ltd
One to One Mailing Services Ltd
Printronic International Plc
Prospect Mailing Services Ltd
The Lettershop Group

Print services
Broadprint Ltd
Clear Communications Ltd
DBMS - David Brannan Marketing
   Services Ltd
Euro DM Ltd
GGT Direct Advertising
Interfocus Network Ltd
Mailcom PLC
Mailing and Printing Company Ltd

Ravensworth Design
SR Communications Plc
The Clockhouse Press Limited
The Compact Group Ltd
The Lettershop Group
The Mail Marketing Group

Private delivery services
Communicator
ID Data Group
Intermail PLC
Occam Direct Marketing Ltd
RMA International Ltd
Westex Limited

Publisher
Advanstar Marketing Services
Association of Publishing Agencies
   (APA)
Direct Marketing International
Science International
Wilmington Direct Marketing

Recommendations on varying
investment by customer
group and campaign
Results (Europe) Ltd

Response analysis bureau
Acxiom Ltd
APAC Customer Services
Aspen Agency
Campaign Direct Ltd
Claritas Europe (European
   Headquarters)
Claritas UK (HQ)
Data2 Limited
Dun & Bradstreet Europe Ltd
GGT Direct Advertising
Identex
Jennifer D. Baker
Listmaster Database Marketing
Manifesto
Miller Starr Ltd
Occam Direct Marketing Ltd
Printronic International Plc
Results (Europe) Ltd
Swetenhams
Tequila Payne Stracey
WWAV Rapp Collins Media Ltd

Sales promotion agency
Advanstar Marketing Services
Clockwork Communications (London)
   Limited
Communicator
DraftWorldwide
Euro RSCG
Firstbase
Grey Direct International
IMP LTD
Interfocus Network Ltd

J. Walter Thompson
LGM Marketing Services Ltd
Limbo Ltd
Loyalty Management International Ltd
Promotional Campaigns Group
Red Fish Limited
Saatchi & Saatchi
Science International
Senior King Ltd
Spearhead Marketing Agency plc
Tequila Payne Stracey
The Marketing Partnership Ltd
The Marketing Store Worldwide

Service bureau
Acxiom Ltd
Advanstar Marketing Services
APAC Customer Services
Aspen Agency
Bellsize Datamatic Limited
Broadprint Ltd
Case Direct Ltd
Consumerdata Ltd
Datamex Computer Services Ltd
DBMS - David Brannan Marketing
   Services Ltd
Dowerhill Ltd
Equifax Europe Ltd
Euro DM Ltd
EWA LTD
FCS Laser-Mail
Greenland Interactive Ltd
ICLP (International Customer Loyalty
   Programmes PLC)
Listmaster Database Marketing
Lloyd James List Broking Services Ltd
Mailcom PLC
Marketing and Media Solutions Ltd
Messenger Marketing Services Limited
Miller Starr Ltd
Prime Response
Printronic International Plc
QBASE Data Services
Salestrac Ltd
Science International
Swetenhams
Sykes
Waddies Print Group

Software supplier
APAC Customer Services
Aspen Agency
Dowerhill Ltd
Dun & Bradstreet Ltd
Harte-Hanks
Identex
Listmaster Database Marketing
LM Software Ltd
Miller Starr Ltd
NCH Marketing Services Ltd
Prime Response
QAS Systems Ltd
QBASE Data Services

Smith Gardner & Associates Ltd
Swetenhams

Subscription strategies
Uni-Marketing Ltd

TV fulfilment
Prism Data Management Ltd.

Telemarketing agency
ADS Telemarketing
Allied Marketing Services Ltd
Bankers Insurance Company Ltd
Case Direct Ltd
Centrobe And EDS Company
Connections Plus Ltd
Convergys Customer Management
Data2 Limited
EC Direct Ltd
Financial Telemarketing Services
   Limited
Greenland Interactive Ltd
GWC Group Ltd
ICLP (International Customer Loyalty
   Programmes PLC)
ICLP (International Customer Loyalty
   Programmes Plc)
ICT Group Inc
IDS
Intermail PLC
John S. Turner Direct Marketing
Kettle Green Studios
Newstel Information Ltd
Ogilvyone Worldwide
Omega Marketing Services
Printware Direct Limited
Salestrac Ltd
Sitel Corporation
Stormark Limited
Sykes
Telelink Limited
Teletech UK Ltd
The Knowledge Store
The Mail Marketing Group
The Marketing Organisation
The Merchants Group
The OPS Room Ltd
Two Ten Communications Ltd

Training/recruitment
The Davis Company
The Institute of Direct Marketing

Translation services
Superfax Ltd
Sykes

ecampaign management
Identex

global data quality
management solutions
Identex

335

overall marketing strategy
Results (Europe) Ltd

E-SERVICES

E-Marketing consultant
DBT Limited
DraftWorldwide
Prism Data Management Ltd.
Spearhead Marketing Agency plc
Think Direct

Email list provider
Allied Marketing Services Ltd
EDM Broking and Management
KPA Business Lists Limited
Spearhead Marketing Agency plc
Swetenhams
Uni-Marketing Ltd

Email software
DBT Limited

Online/e-marketing agency
Association of Publishing Agencies
  (APA)
DBT Limited
DraftWorldwide
GWC Group Ltd
ICLP (International Customer Loyalty
  Programmes Plc)
ICT Group Inc
McCann-Erickson Manchester Ltd
Prism Data Management Ltd.
Spearhead Marketing Agency plc
Swetenhams

Website design
Allied Marketing Services Ltd
Aspen Agency
Association of Publishing Agencies
  (APA)
Blaze Business to Business
  Ltd
Brann Ltd
Communicator
DBT Limited
DraftWorldwide

Education Direct
Grey Direct International
Hubbard Hiwaizi McCann
IMP LTD
Intermail PLC
Manifesto
McCann-Erickson Manchester
  Ltd
Newstel Information Ltd
Outside The Box Plc
QBASE Data Services
Red Box Advertising Ltd
Red Square Communications
Saatchi & Saatchi
Salestrac Ltd
Spearhead Marketing Agency
  plc
Telelink Limited
Tequila Payne Stracey
The Lettershop Group
The Marketing Store Worldwide
The Merchants Group
Worth Communications Ltd

EASTERN EUROPE[*]

REGIONAL OVERVIEW

The consumer

Direct mail is such a recent phenomenon in Eastern Europe that consumer and business reaction to the medium is almost entirely positive. A direct mail shot is seen as something interesting and important, and the contents will be given the reader's full attention, the basic premise being that the more personalized the information, the more flattering, as it picks out the individual from the masses. The entire concept of consumer segmentation is generally new, and only now are differences clearly emerging. However, the situation is changing fast and Eastern Europe is catching up.

Fastest-growing markets

As a general rule, the boom markets in the area tend to have a concrete, practical appeal. The practical benefit may be to a family's health, or a company's access to capital, but the list of industry sectors below, already active in the region, demonstrates that the medium is finding most success in supplying goods and services with a practical application:

- detergents/personal products;
- banks/investment funds;
- private repair services (carpentry/electrical);
- retail stores (opening/special sales);
- private education firms (languages/computer management);
- consumer electronics (shavers/white goods/computers).

Local DM facilities

Currently, addressed direct mail to consumers is rarely used in any market, due to problems of deliverability and lack of data sources. Unaddressed communications tend to be used to a higher degree, although often through street or windscreen wiper methods, rather than through the mail system.

Addressed direct mail to businesses, albeit of a low standard, is common in the Czech Republic and Hungary; less so in Poland, where most new developments have concentrated on the consumer market.

*The following section benefits from extensive contributions from Ogilvy & Mather, who offer a network of offices throughout the region

Current use of mail order advertising is quite common in Poland, although the goods – and the advertising – are seen to be of poor quality. Advertising which solicits a response directly to the advertiser is more common, as people are hungry for information, and not yet burned-out by heavy usage.

Lead generation for business or financial sales forces is much rarer – primarily because of the low cost and poor staffing of sales forces, who end up having much less guidance as to who to follow up. Mail order tends to have a bad reputation – shoddy goods, impossible to return. In Russia, DM in all its forms, be it direct mail, telemarketing, or direct response TV, is not yet part of any advertiser's marketing strategy.

The reason for this is two-fold:

1) Given the still low-cost access to mass advertising, all DM techniques are still irrelevant. The immensity factors (demographically, geographically), which can in the long term lead to massive use of DM, act now as a deterrent. As far as any niche currently available in the market is concerned, it can be as small as a couple of million people and can be reached by regional or national TV, given the current incredibly low cost of reach.

2) The basic infrastructure so crucial to DM, such as telephone lines or the mail system, is in a poor state and would immediately stop any adventurous try.

In addition to this, one also has to take into consideration that, because of the legacy of Soviet 'occupation', there are still no names attached to letter boxes or telephone numbers. This means that whenever you write or telephone, you never know to whom you are writing or calling. Because of former communal apartments (which still exist in some districts of Moscow, St Petersburg and large cities), Russian addresses are usually made up of an apartment number, the name of the street and number in the street, the postal code and the city. Seldom is a name mentioned unless it is a business address. As we know, effective DM relies on personalized communication, which is not yet available in Russia, and it is doubtful if newly born Russian consumers are really looking for it.

DM in Russia is now limited to some business-to-business mail courier-delivered and some mail dropped in people's letter boxes, the main theme being real estate (sell, rent or repair your apartment).

A letter in one's mail box or on one's desk is still a major event, which can sometimes give way to a lot of questions and worries about who is writing and for what reason, before even opening the package.

Agencies

Most of the multinational DM agency networks now have an office in Germany or Austria with a good deal of expertise in DM in Eastern Europe, but agencies based in the region are far fewer. As regards the few local shops which have emerged, there is no evidence as to whether they have the resources or experience to mount effective campaigns.

Most above-the-line agencies in all markets offer some kind of direct marketing as an additional service – as part of a culture where agencies generally offer a wider range of services to their clients than in the West. Some of the agencies offer DM expertise as an integrated part of their activities.

Postal services

None of the local postal systems is geared to accept bulk mail shipments, or offer discounts for this service (except for Slovakia). However, it is usually possible to negotiate arrangements given time, and this would merely take some dealing with the state bureaucracy. Reliability is seen as good in Poland, and fair in Hungary and the Czech Republic. However, all countries warn against including valuable items – or producing work which looks valuable – and against inter-country mail as this is usually opened at the point of transit. Pre-paid business reply services and bulk discounts are not always available, although contract posting is possible.

List/fulfilment houses

In both the Czech Republic and Hungary there are companies who advertise as computer bureaux with experience of maintaining name and address databases. However, they are largely untested. List quality is questionable but higher than average responses compensate for this. Contemporary database software is widely available and programming skills are highly developed in both the Czech Republic and Hungary. Record types are standardized in a way almost identical to that in the USA (four-line addresses, five-digit zip code).

Privacy laws covering the storing of data on individuals/companies are generally vague. It seems to be an area which has not been legislated due to the lack of activity.

In Hungary, the Czech Republic and Poland there are commercial mailing houses in existence, with experience and equipment for enclosing of direct mail packages. Hungary also has laser printing facilities available.

Fulfilment houses exist in every market, but as a region there is little experience of using them and, therefore, it is difficult to evaluate their ability/reliability.

Business-to-business DM is used actively, and most active DM companies are now building their own lists in this sector, but creative standards are very poor.

Market research

Market research is fairly sophisticated through companies like GfK, AISA and newer competitors.

Telemarketing

Phone systems in the area are often rudimentary and unreliable. It will take several years and significant investment before the telemarketing industry can establish itself in Eastern Europe.

Most promising national market

The experience of most exporters shows the Czech Republic, Poland and Hungary to be the most promising markets for Western goods and services.

Legislation and consumer protection

Some legislation specific to direct marketing has been introduced, but it is vague.

Further information

Direct marketing associations are only beginning to emerge. The prospective exporter may be faced with a labour-intensive trawl of the various interested parties:

- advertising agencies (local offices and multinationals);
- postal services;
- Government Ministry of the Interior;
- local advertisers;
- local trade associations.

BULGARIA

Population: 8.3 million
Capital: Sofia
Languages: Bulgarian and Russian

GDP: $10.2 billion
GDP per capita: $1,223
Inflation: 191 per cent

Currency: Lev (BGL) = 100 stotinki
Exchange rate: BGL1,817.90 : $1

Time: GMT +2 hours

OVERVIEW

After the troubles of recent years, Bulgaria has now reached political
stability. The present government of the Union of the Democratic Forces
(UDF) took power in 1997 and introduced the Currency Board. These
events have contributed greatly to creating favourable conditions for reform.

The consumer

Direct marketing is still in its infancy and as such official statistics regarding
direct mail campaigns are not yet available. Due to the fact that it is a
relatively new concept, more than 85 per cent of recipients read the material
they receive.

Payment systems

With credit cards being non-existent, payments can be made by money
orders and deposits. There is now also a debit card system serving the
Bulgarian market.

Legislation and Consumer Protection

There are no data protection laws in Bulgaria.

341

Local DM facilities

Local direct marketing facilities are sparse, with companies generally organizing their own campaigns. Most of the international advertising agencies and some market research companies offer a degree of DM expertise. During the last two years a direct marketing association has been established in Bulgaria.

THE DIRECT MARKETING ASSOCIATION

Name: Institute for Bulgarian and World Direct Marketing (IBWDM)
Address: 12 Elin Vrah Str., Sofia 1407, Bulgaria
Tel: +359 2 962 4549
Fax: +359 2 962 4358
Website: www.come.to/ibwdm
Contact: Iliana Marinova, Head of International Cooperation Dept.

Facilities for overseas users of direct mail

Membership: overseas companies can join the IBWDM. A wide range of free services are offered to those companies willing to invest in the Bulgarian economy.

Newsletter: The IBWDM does not currently publish a newsletter.

Library: The IBWDM library contains over 70 books, specialised dictionaries and press cuttings.

On-line information service: the IBWDM have a website at www.come.to/ibwdm

Legal advice: Legal advice is offered by the IBWDM with regard to national legislation.

Business liaison service: The IBWDM is willing to help business partners and also has the opportunity to lobby in most state institutions for clients willing to invest in Bulgaria.

Other facilities: As well as offering consultations on leasing, factoring and franchising, the IBWDM works together with the National Palace of Culture to organize conferences, fairs, meetings, and bazaars. They also have state of the art printing facilities.

POSTAL SERVICES

The postal service in Bulgaria has markedly improved in recent years, and Bulgarian Posts now offers the following services:

- Express mail services to 75 destinations in Bulgaria and 84 destinations worldwide.
- Advertising postal services.

- City service post: a postal delivery service provided by large post offices.

Discounts are available when:

- more than 1000 standard letters, each with a maximum weight of 20g, are mailed simultaneously.
- more than 500 parcels are mailed simultaneously
- printed matter is delivered as a subscription.

Other services offered by Bulgarian Posts include the transport of items by container, and PO Box usage. For more information on any of the above services, contact:

Bulgarian Posts Ltd
1, Arso Pandurski Str., bl. 31
1700 Sofia
Bulgaria

Tel: +359 2 9800 089
Fax: +359 2 9877 657
Website: www.bgpost.bg

PROVIDERS OF DM AND E-M SERVICES

BALKAN BRITISH SOCIAL SURVEYS – GALLUP INTERNATIONAL
12 Gurko Str
Sofia
1000
Bulgaria
Tel: +359 2 884 800/818 772/805 554
Fax: +359 2 806 323

Services/Products:
Market research agency

FORCE DIRECT - DIRECT MARKETING AGENCY
4 Dondoukov Blvd
Entr. 4, Floor 1, Ap. 2
Sofia
1000
Bulgaria
Tel: +359 2 986 6377
Fax: +359 2 989 2205
Email: office@fd-bg.com
Web: www.fd-bg.com
Peter Dilovsky, General Manager

Services/Products:
Consultancy services; Database services; Mailing/Faxing services; Labelling/envelope services; Direct marketing agency

E-Services:
E-Marketing consultant; Online/e-marketing agency

Member of:
International Advertising Association

GFK BULGARIA – MARKET RESEARCH INSTITUTE
10 Tzar Osvoboditel Blvd
Sofia
1000
Bulgaria
Tel: +359 2 870 249/833 384
Fax: +359 2 98 01239

Services/Products:
Market research agency

INSTITUTE FOR BULGARIAN AND WORLD DIRECT MARKETING
12 Elin Vrah Str.
Sofia
1407
Bulgaria
Tel: +359 2 962 4549
Fax: +359 2 962 4358
Email: ibwdm@bgnet.bg
Mr. Hristo Obesnikov, Chairman

Services/Products:
Consultancy services; Database services; Direct marketing agency; Print services; Training/recruitment; Translation services

E-Services:
E-Marketing consultant; Website design

Member of:
FEDMA; Bulgarian Association of Alternative Tourism (BAAT)

KIMMS HD
8 Javorets Str
Sofia
1421
Bulgaria
Tel: +359 2 654 539
Email: kolarovi@ttm.bg

Services/Products:
Market research agency

SERVICES/PRODUCT LISTING

Consultancy services
Force Direct - Direct Marketing Agency
Institute for Bulgarian and World Direct Marketing

Database services
Force Direct - Direct Marketing Agency
Institute for Bulgarian and World Direct Marketing

Direct marketing agency
Force Direct - Direct Marketing Agency
Institute for Bulgarian and World Direct Marketing

Labelling/envelope services
Force Direct - Direct Marketing Agency

Mailing/Faxing services
Force Direct - Direct Marketing Agency

Market research agency
Balkan British Social Surveys – Gallup International
GFK Bulgaria – Market Research Institute
Kimms Hd

Print services
Institute for Bulgarian and World Direct Marketing

Training/recruitment
Institute for Bulgarian and World Direct Marketing

Translation services
Institute for Bulgarian and World Direct Marketing

E-SERVICES

E-Marketing consultant
Force Direct - Direct Marketing Agency
Institute for Bulgarian and World Direct Marketing

Online/e-marketing agency
Force Direct - Direct Marketing Agency

Website design
Institute for Bulgarian and World Direct Marketing

CZECH
REPUBLIC

Population: 10.3 million
Capital: Prague
Languages: Czech; some Russian and German

GDP: $52.4 billion
GDP per capita: $4,298
Inflation: 8.4 per cent

Currency: Koruna (Kc) = 100 heller
Exchange rate: Kc34.90 : $1

Time: GMT: +1 hour

OVERVIEW

The last few years have seen a remarkable transformation of the Czech Republic economy. Formerly one of the most orthodox of centrally planned economies, it is now seen to be one of the most deregulated and privatized of the former Communist satellites. Million of citizens have become shareholders through one of the most ambitious privatization programmes ever undertaken.

The strides taken in economic and social liberation make this market an attractive prospect. The economy has been prudently managed to achieve a GDP growth of 3.5 per cent in 1996. Inflation has been halved to below 10 per cent, while the Czech koruna has become one of the most stable currencies in Europe.

Direct marketing techniques are as yet not widely used in this market, but there are positive signals that the will to develop such expertise is there; once the medium has found a proper toe-hold, growth rates are likely to be high.

The main impediment to the development of direct marketing at present is the low quality of databases. The situation is improving, however, with

DM companies working particularly on personalizing business-to-business lists. There are several list brokers using advanced database technologies.

There are a range of suppliers of DFM services, including market research companies. Telemarketing is not yet established in the Czech Republic, with companies relying on above-the-line advertising activities. Some individual companies, however, such as DHL and Rank Xerox, have developed their own in-house telemarketing activities. There is a tremendous boom in the telecommunications industry at present, with large-scale modernization of the telephone network in progress. Again, given a little experience and user confidence, the medium is likely to expand rapidly.

THE DIRECT MARKETING ASSOCIATION

Name:	Asociace Direct Marketingu a Zasilkoveho Obchodu (ADMAZ)
Address:	Domazlicka 3, 130 00 Prague 3, Czech Republic
Tel:	+420 2 2019 8341
Fax:	+420 2 644 2940
Email:	info@admaz.cz
website:	www.admaz.cz
Year founded:	1997
President:	Petr Vána
Total staff:	1
Members:	25
Contact:	Petr Vána

Membership: overseas companies can join ADMAZ, but must be registered in the Czech Republic. The annual fee is approximately Kc20-80,000, and is dependent on turnover.

On-line information service: an on-line information service is available. The website address for ADMAZ is www.admaz.cz.

POSTAL SERVICES

Czech Post is a state enterprise offering a number of postal direct mail and other special services, in particular:

- Letter, parcel and money mailing;
- EMS – express delivery of documents and goods: inland mailing across the whole Czech Republic or international mailing into 80 countries worldwide;
- Express parcel mailing in the Czech republic - 'commercial parcel', including reply mail;
- Reply mail;
- Delivery of newspapers and magazines;

- Distribution of leaflets and other promotional materials;
- P.O. Boxes;
- Services to mailing houses: mail collection, addressing, packing;
- Packing, wrapping in foils and enveloping mail;
- Direct mail events: preparation of promotional materials, addressing, performance of event, evaluation of response;
- Databases: Postal Directory of Households, Business Database, Database of Postal Codes;
- Discount policy for contractual clients: technology and volume discounts, discounts for commercial printed matter, delivery of newspapers and magazines, commercial parcels.

For details about services and charges contact:

Ceská Posta
State Enterprise Headquarters
Olsanská 9
22599 Prague 3
Czech Republic

Tel: +420 2 691 9240
Fax: +420 2 671 96431
Website: www.cpost.cz

PROVIDERS OF DM AND E-M SERVICES

ADMA – ASOCIACIE DIRECT MARKETING OVYCH AGENTUR
Domazlicka 3
Prague 3
CS-130 00
Czech Republic
Tel: +42 2 61 21 60 30
Fax: +42 2 61 21 60 31
Dr Petr Vána, Director

Services/Products:
Media buying agency

DMMS CZ, INC
Zámek Dobrejovice
Prague-vychod
251 70
Czech Republic
Tel: +42 02 04 637 191
Fax: +42 02 04 637 137
Email: dmms@dmms.cz
Web: www.dmms.cz
Jaroslav Varina, Managing Director

Services/Products:
Database services; Mailing/Faxing services; Direct marketing agency; Service bureau; Sales promotion agency

Member of:
FEDMA

INFORM MAIL SRO
Herspická 6
Brno
CS-639 00
Czech Republic
Tel: +42 5 4316 9255
Fax: +42 5 4316 9314
Vladimír Sálovsky, Managing Director

Services/Products:
Database services; Card pack manufacturer; Direct marketing agency

SCHOBER DIREKTMARKETING
Domazlicka 3
Prague 3
CS-130 00
Czech Republic
Tel: +42 2 612 161 99
Fax: +42 2 612 160 31
Petr Vána, Director

Services/Products:
Lettershop; Fulfilment and sampling house; Direct marketing agency; Design/graphics/clip art supplier; Mail order company

WEGENER DIRECT MARKETING SRO
Cermakova 7
Prague
12000
Czech Republic
Tel: +42 02 2201 5251
Fax: +42 02 2423 6516
Email: wegener@terminal.cz
Heidi Stone, Director

Services/Products:
Database services; Telemarketing agency; Direct marketing agency; Service bureau; Call centre services/systems

Member of:
FEDMA

SERVICES/PRODUCT LISTING

Call centre services/systems
Wegener Direct Marketing SRO

Card pack manufacturer
Inform Mail SRO

Database services
DMMS CZ, Inc
Inform Mail SRO
Wegener Direct Marketing SRO

Design/graphics/clip art supplier
Schober Direktmarketing

Direct marketing agency
DMMS CZ, Inc
Inform Mail SRO
Schober Direktmarketing
Wegener Direct Marketing SRO

Fulfilment and sampling house
Schober Direktmarketing

Lettershop
Schober Direktmarketing

Mail order company
Schober Direktmarketing

Mailing/Faxing services
DMMS CZ, Inc

Media buying agency
ADMA – Asociacie Direct Marketing Ovych Agentur

Sales promotion agency
DMMS CZ, Inc

Service bureau
DMMS CZ, Inc
Wegener Direct Marketing SRO

Telemarketing agency
Wegener Direct Marketing SRO

HUNGARY

Population: 10.0 million
Capital: Budapest
Languages: Hungarian, Russian, German
GDP: $56 billion
GDP per capita: $5,700
Inflation: 18.3 per cent
Currency: Forint (Ft) =100 filler
Exchange rate: Ft232.45 : $1
Time: GMT +1 hour

OVERVIEW

Hungary is the most economically advanced of the Eastern European countries. An ever-increasing range of consumer goods and services is available, and many Western products are now sold. Hungary hopes to achieve full membership of the European Union in the near future.

Direct marketing is developing rapidly in Hungary. An increasing level of professionalism and sophistication is developing in the market, helped by DM expertise from abroad.

The consumer

Consumers are receptive to direct mail, though its reputation was somewhat dented in the early 1990s by a flood of poor quality 'junk mail'. An improved reputation is being restored with the appearance of international and national agencies and mail order companies such as Ogilvy & Mather, McCann Communications, Wunderman Cato Johnson, Dono, Quelle, Otto, etc.

Business-to-business direct marketing offers good opportunities in Hungary, although reliable lists of companies and names of managers are not

349

readily available; DM agencies tend to use telemarketing firms first to identify the right individuals by phone.

Unaddressed mailings are frequently used, but addressed mailings are increasingly coming to the fore, where suitable target group listings are available. Lead generation is becoming more frequent, where a salesforce exists to serve clients.

Local DM facilities

Local DM facilities are developing apace. Ever-more print shops are emerging in the Hungarian market, many providing a full service. Realizing the potential boom in the field, many are now acquiring professional laser printing technology.

The list market

Previously business lists could only be acquired from ministries and other state institutions. In the last two years, however, list brokers have started building their own business lists with named personnel, although this is proving to be a slow process. DM agencies too are building their own consumer lists from activity generated during campaigns.

Legislation

A new Data Protection Act was passed in January 1996. The Act is one of the toughest in Europe.

Telemarketing

Telemarketing facilities are improving rapidly. Four or five large, professional companies have emerged, providing efficient and reliable services. Some bigger businesses, in the insurance and banking sectors in particular, have developed their own telemarketing systems with which to both serve clients and undertake market research.

THE DIRECT MARKETING ASSOCIATION

The Hungarian Direct Marketing Association was established in 1995 with ten members, and now has 25 member companies.

Name: Direkt Marketing Egyesület
Address: 1025 Bp., Szèpvölgyi út 86/B
Tel: +36 1 325 8903/325 5220
Fax: +36 1 325 5344

POSTAL SERVICES

The Hungarian Post Office Ltd is a state-owned company with 42,000 employees. It offers several services for direct marketers, including:

- Inland and international distribution of mail and parcels; bulk mailing services
- Express services (express mailing, courier service, EMS)
- Distribution of newspapers and magazines for subscribers
- NDD (next day delivery) service
- Hybrid mail services (printing, personalization, enveloping, packing, inserting)
- Circulation of money for business purposes
- Quantity discounts for the biggest mailers.

1999 brings about the opening of the Direct Marketing Department. Those services offered include:

- Education of direct marketing for client representatives; providing consultations before campaigns
- Arrangement of DM campaigns from conception to follow-up activity.
- Offering, building and updating consumer databases
- Business reply service
- Special zip codes for the biggest clients
- Market research activities.

For further information please contact:

Hungarian Post Office Ltd.
Headquarters
Krisztina krt. 6–8
1540 Budapest
Republic of Hungary

Tel: +36 1 3744 206
Fax: +36 1 3744 208
Website: www.posta.hu

PROVIDERS OF DM AND E-M SERVICES

CID CÉG-INFO DIREKT MARKETING KFT
H-1139 Hungary
Petneházy u.21.
Budapest
1386
Hungary
Tel: +36 1 350 0479
Fax: +36 1 270 9066
Email: info@ceg-info.hu
Web: www.ceg-info.hu
Jozsef Szabo, Director

Services/Products:
List services; Database services; Direct marketing agency; List services; Response analysis bureau; Consultancy services

E-Services:
Email list provider; Online/e-marketing agency

Member of:
FEDMA; National DMA; Hungarian Advertising Association

DONO DIRECT MARKETING LTD
Ráday U.8
II/12
Budapest
1092
Hungary
Tel: +36 1 218 0542, 46
Fax: +36 1 217 5330
Lakatos Zsolt, Managing Director

Services/Products:
List services; Mailing/Faxing services; Direct marketing agency; Personalisation

WUNDERMAN CATO JOHNSON
Szilagyi Erzsebet Fasor 22/A
Budapest
1125
Hungary
Tel: +36 1 275 24 72
Fax: +36 1 275 24 89
Birgit Baier-Büsgen, General Manager

Services/Products:
Advertising Agency; Fulfilment and sampling house; Database services; Direct marketing agency; Response analysis bureau

Member of:
FEDMA

SERVICES/PRODUCT LISTING

Advertising Agency
Wunderman Cato Johnson

Consultancy services
CID Cég-Info DIREKT MARKETING Kft

Database services
CID Cég-Info DIREKT MARKETING Kft
Wunderman Cato Johnson

Direct marketing agency
CID Cég-Info DIREKT MARKETING Kft
Dono Direct Marketing Ltd
Wunderman Cato Johnson

Fulfilment and sampling house
Wunderman Cato Johnson

List services
CID Cég-Info DIREKT MARKETING Kft
Dono Direct Marketing Ltd

Mailing/Faxing services
Dono Direct Marketing Ltd

Personalisation
Dono Direct Marketing Ltd

Response analysis bureau
CID Cég-Info DIREKT MARKETING Kft
Wunderman Cato Johnson

E-SERVICES

Email list provider
CID Cég-Info DIREKT MARKETING Kft

Online/e-marketing agency
CID Cég-Info DIREKT MARKETING Kft

POLAND

Population: **38.6** million
Capital: Warsaw
Languages: Polish, Russian

GDP: **$125** billion
GDP per capita: **$3,230**
Inflation: **9.0** per cent

Currency: Zloty (Zl) = 100 groszy
Exchange rate: Zl 3.89 : $1

Time: GMT +1 hour

OVERVIEW

Direct marketing is still a very recent marketing tool in Poland. However, it is developing quickly, particularly in areas such as publishing, finance, insurance, and catalogue businesses. There are now approximately 50 companies with databases, and over 100,000 active customers.

The consumer

Polish consumers respond very positively to personalized mailings, with response rates ranging from 15–40 per cent on average. However, there is an increasing concern about data protection.

Local DM facilities

There are an increasing number of mailing houses offering mailing and packaging services: prices, together with the quality of the services, do vary. They also provide data inserting and database management services.

Mail order is still becoming popular, especially with the entry to the market of such companies as Quelle and Trois Suisse.

Business-to-business communication is very popular. Many sales departments of companies operating in the field have their own databases and they

353

are getting more and more professional. Additionally, listings companies manage and sell business databases.

Fulfilment houses, lettershops and database brokers are active in the market, and well developed in Poland. However, personalization services are still quite poor and in need of improvement.

Agencies

Network direct marketing agencies in the market include GGK Direct, Ogilvy and Mather, and McCann Communications. There are some local agencies; however, there is a general lack of widespread DM expertise, experience and know-how.

Market research

Although market research is quite sophisticated, no agencies specialize in direct marketing research. A number of agencies recently announced plans to organize departments specializing in researching below the line services in general.

Telemarketing

Despite the poor infrastructure in rural areas in particular, telephone services are used a lot, especially for party lines, horoscopes and different promotional competitions.

Telemarketing is mainly used by companies having their own telemarketing departments, which for them is an important tool, representing 40-50 per cent of total sales. Some local agencies providing telemarketing services are present on the market, offering services like telesales, teleresearch, and teleconsulting.

The National Post Office has recently introduced toll-free numbers and telemarketing is becoming increasingly popular. There are a growing number of specialized telemarketing agencies.

Payment systems

In the main, payment is made by Giro through the post office. Credit cards (Visa, Mastercard) have recently been introduced and approximately 1.5 million have been issued.

LEGISLATION AND CONSUMER PROTECTION

Poland's new Data Protection Act came into force in 1998. Under this law companies that compile and use databases are now obliged to seek permission before potential clients are contacted by direct mail or telephone.

THE DIRECT MARKETING ASSOCIATION

Name: Stowarzyszenie Marketingu Bezposredniego
Address: Ul. Lucka 2/4/6, 00-845 Warsaw
Tel: +48 22 654 68 33
Fax: +48 22 654 55 33
Email: info@smb.pl
Website: www.smb.pl
Year founded 1995
President: Tomasz Kostyra (tkostyra@smb.pl)
Total staff: 3
Members: 72
Contact: Monika Zarzycka, General Manager (mzarzycko@smb.pl)

DM agencies	20	Printers	2
Lst brokers	9	Telemarketing agencies	13
Advertisers	18	Handling houses	13
Mailing houses	18	Database agencies	7
Mail order companies	6		

Facilities for overseas users of direct mail

Membership: overseas companies are eligible to join the SMB on the condition that they have two recommendations from members. The fees are as follows:
Registration fee: 500 PLN
Quarter membership fee for companies: 900 PLN
1 year membership fee for people: 100 PLN
Newsletter: we have a free monthly newsletter.
Library: in our library we have two publications concerning personnel data protection.
On-line information service: log on to our website at www.smb.pl
Legal advice: we don't offer legal advice but we do recommend experienced lawyers.
Business liaison service: we have a mailing list.
Other facilities: all members can use our logo in their application to increase credibility.
There are discounts for seminars and advertising.

POSTAL SERVICES

The National Post Office, having noticed opportunities in creating new services and adapting to market requirements, is now much more flexible than in former years and has developed a marketing department which is responsible for establishing contacts with potential direct marketing clients.

For further information contact:

La Poste Polonaise
Marketing Department
Pl. Malachowskiego 2
00-940 Warsaw
Poland

Tel: +48 22 656 5373
Fax: +48 22 826 1907
Mr. Lech Jakubik

PROVIDERS OF DM AND E-M SERVICES

ABC DIRECT CONTACT
Pl. Sloneczny 4
Warszawa
Poland
Tel: +48 22 39 22 53/39 94 41
Krzysztof Brzeski

Services/Products:
Direct marketing agency

BAKKER POLSKA SP.
ul. Takowa, 14
Michatowice k/Warsawy
05–816
Poland
Tel: +48 22 723 9125
Fax: +48 22 723 8515
Email: bakker@it.com.pl
Jasja van der Veen, Business
    Development Manager

Services/Products:
Lettershop; Fulfilment and sampling
house; Mailing/Faxing services; Direct
marketing agency; Sales promotion
agency

Member of:
FEDMA; SMB

CEAC POLONIA
Opalinskiego 12a
Warszawa
Poland
Tel: +48 22 33 24 72
Fax: +48 22 33 84 33
Maria Tomaszek

Services/Products:
Direct marketing agency

CLARITAS POLSKA
ul. Dabrowskiego 64a
Warszawa
02–561
Poland
Tel: +48 22 845 6194
Fax: +48 22 845 4010
Email: info-pl@claritaseu.com
Krzysztof Kuwalek, Managing
    Director

Services/Products:
List services; Database services;
Consultancy services; Response
analysis bureau

EMITRADE LTD
ul. Rumiana 90
Warszawa
2956
Poland

Tel: +48 22 642 7442
Fax: +48 22 642 7441
Tomasz Kusinski

Services/Products:
Fulfilment and sampling house;
Telemarketing agency; Direct
marketing agency; Copy adaptation;
Media buying agency; Direct response
TV services

Member of:
SMB

HARING PROJECT SUPPORT LTD
ul. Pijarska 19/6
Cracow
31–015
Poland
Tel: +48 12 423 19 58
Fax: +48 12 423 19 41
Email: Haring@bci.krakow.pl
James Walters, Business Development
    Director

Services/Products:
List services; Database services; Direct
marketing agency; Service bureau;
Software supplier

Member of:
FEDMA

MARCOM
ul. Obręzna 11b
Warszawa
Poland
Tel: +48 22 42 53 33
Krzysztof Czupryna

Services/Products:
Direct marketing agency

NATIONAL POST OFFICE
Pl. Malachowskiego 2
Warszawa
Poland
Tel: +48 22 656 55 70
Fax: +48 22 26 19 07
Iwona Malkiewicz

Services/Products:
Lettershop; Database services;
Consultancy services; Private delivery
services; Mailing/Faxing services

NET KORPORACJA MARKETINGU
ul. Felinskiego 30
Warszawa
Poland
Tel: +48 22 39 88 48
Hanna Lozowska

Services/Products:
Direct marketing agency; Market
research agency; Sales promotion
agency; Private delivery services

OGILVY & MATHER DIRECT
ul. Marszalkowska 77/79
Warszawa
Poland
Tel: +48 22 622 80 00
Fax: +48 22 625 23 70
Piotr Badowski

Services/Products:
Direct marketing agency

POLISH MARKETING CENTER SP Z O O
25 Minska Street
Warsaw
03–808
Poland
Tel: +48 226771406
Fax: +48 226771409
Email: pcm@pcm.com.pl
Web: www.pcm.com.pl
Jan Zalecki, Managing Director

Services/Products:
Database services; Direct marketing
agency; Design/graphics/clip art
supplier; Print services; Market
research agency

E-Services:
Website design

Member of:
FEDMA

POLKOMTES SA
Al. Jerololimskie 81
Warszawa
02–001
Poland
Tel: +48 22 607 1320
Fax: +48 22 607 1340
Beata Hoffman, Telemarketing
    Manager

Services/Products:
Telemarketing agency

Member of:
DMA (US)

POLSKA TELEWIZJA KABLOWA (PTK)
ul. Pawinskiego 5A blok D
Warsaw
106
Poland
Tel: +48 22 60 89 841
Fax: +48 22 66 87 200
Email: sarah.harrison@ptk.com.pl
Sarah Harrison, Database
    Development Consultant

Services/Products:
List services

Member of:
FEDMA

TELESHOPPING POLSKA
Al. Krakowska 110/114
Warszawa
02–256
Poland
Tel: +48 22 868 30 10
Fax: +48 22 868 28 92
Email: teleshop@pol.pl
Jean Paul Hildebrandt, Managing
  Director

Services/Products:
Telemarketing agency; Call centre
services/systems; Catalogue producer

Member of:
FEDMA

SERVICES/PRODUCT LISTING

Call centre services/systems
Teleshopping Polska

Catalogue producer
Teleshopping Polska

Consultancy services
Claritas Polska
National Post Office

Copy adaptation
Emitrade Ltd

Database services
Claritas Polska
Haring Project Support Ltd
National Post Office
Polish Marketing Center Sp Z O O

Design/graphics/clip art supplier
Polish Marketing Center Sp Z O O

Direct marketing agency
ABC Direct Contact
Bakker Polska Sp.
Ceac Polonia
Emitrade Ltd
Haring Project Support Ltd
Marcom
Net Korporacja MarketingU
Ogilvy & Mather Direct
Polish Marketing Center Sp Z O O

Direct response TV services
Emitrade Ltd

Fulfilment and sampling house
Bakker Polska Sp.
Emitrade Ltd

Lettershop
Bakker Polska Sp.
National Post Office

List services
Claritas Polska
Haring Project Support Ltd
Polska Telewizja Kablowa (Ptk)

Mailing/Faxing services
Bakker Polska Sp.
National Post Office

Market research agency
Net Korporacja MarketingU
Polish Marketing Center Sp Z O O

Media buying agency
Emitrade Ltd

Print services
Polish Marketing Center Sp Z O O

Private delivery services
National Post Office
Net Korporacja MarketingU

Response analysis bureau
Claritas Polska

Sales promotion agency
Bakker Polska Sp.
Net Korporacja MarketingU

Service bureau
Haring Project Support Ltd

Software supplier
Haring Project Support Ltd

Telemarketing agency
Emitrade Ltd
Polkomtes Sa
Teleshopping Polska

E-SERVICES

Website design
Polish Marketing Center Sp Z O O

ROMANIA

Population: 22.7 million
Capital: Bucharest
Languages: Romanian, Hungarian (7%), German (1%)

GDP: US$64.7 billion
GDP per capita: US$1000
Inflation: 108 per cent

Currency: Romanian Leu (L)
Exchange rate: L14,955 : US$1

Time: GMT +2 hours

OVERVIEW

One of the largest and most populous countries in central and eastern Europe, Romania has only just begun to emerge and claim its place among the rapidly developing economies of the area. The 1989 revolution in Romania was the most dramatic regime change seen in Eastern Europe, bringing the country out of 40 years of communism. But it was not until 1996, that a democratically elected new coalition government was swept to power on a mandate of extensive reform.

Most multinationals entering the Romanian market, when considering advertising and promotion to support their products or services, will discover a well-established media range consisting of state and private local television, radio and print. Although the terrain is not well defined, effective, competent and cost-efficient media are now available and even measurable. Direct mail has increased enormously in recent years, but still only makes up 1% of total advertising budget, 70% being dominated by television.

LEGISLATION AND CONSUMER PROTECTION

There are no laws relating to the export of data, and no restrictions apply to list broking.

THE DIRECT MARKETING ASSOCIATION

There is no Direct Marketing Association in Romania at present.

POSTAL SERVICES

There are no discount schemes currently available.

For further information contact:

Regie Autonome Poste Roumaine
International Post Direction
Soseaua Givlesti 6–8
78251 Bucharest
Romania

Tel: +40 1 4003 115
Fax: +40 1 3113 213
Mme Silvia Badulescu

RUSSIA

Population: 149.9 million

Capital: Moscow

Language: Russian

GDP: $712.2 billion

GDP per capita: $4,820

Inflation: 14.6 per cent

Currency: Rouble = 100 kopeck

Exchange rate: Rb24.30 : $1

Time: GMT + 2 to + 12 hours (Moscow +2 hours; Vladivostock +10 hours)

OVERVIEW

The Russian Federation continues to struggle with the dual problems both of establishing a new political identity and implementing structural economic reform. Shaking off the yoke of the past has not been easy, and with accelerating rates of inflation and declining economic growth, coupled with continuing domestic conflict, the end is not yet in sight. The sheer size of the market, however, and its concessions to a free market economy, make it a source of potentially huge opportunity to the international marketer.

Direct marketing has only recently begun to emerge in the Russian Federation. Russia and CIS countries have had no practical experience in using direct marketing media; receiving advertising material by mail was unheard of in the former Soviet Union, given both the under-developed infrastructure and overriding ideological constraints.

Recent years, however, have seen significant initial strides being taken in establishing a DM community. The number of companies specializing in the field has grown considerably: there are now over 100 agencies providing DM services in Russia, 15 of which have evolved into full service DM agencies. The quality of the services they provide is high.

In particular the modern Russian Direct Marketing industry is characterized by:

- Step-by-step transfer to a wider variety of the used DM tools (from impersonal direct mail some years ago to personalized dialogue by means of direct mail, call-centers, Internet, TV-shops, personal meetings, direct response advertising, etc);
- DM consulting and development of DM campaigns concepts, long term multistage campaigns built-in to a general marketing strategy;
- Monitoring and forecasting DM campaigns' effectiveness;
- Creative approaches to DM package development;
- B-to-B and B-to-C databases market;
- Publications on different DM subjects (by Russian and Western authors);
- Active participation of Russian DM representatives in DM workshops, exhibitions and conferences;
- Russian DM agencies' membership in world and national professional associations and international networks.

In Russia the growth rate of DM is much higher than that of general advertising. There are several reasons for the active development of DM in Russia, the main ones being that the effectiveness of general advertising methods has reduced, innovative computer and telecommunications technology has spread and the public – unaccustomed to personalized mailings – are keen to read anything they receive and answer any questionnaires.

In June 1995, the five largest Russian DM companies ('Kniga-Service', POSTER Publicity, RAGI, DMS and 'Third Point') combined efforts to establish the Russian Direct Marketing Association (RDMA). List owners, trade associations and industrial organizations are expected to join the RDMA, as well as DM agencies themselves. The RDMA aims to promote industry standards, and to provide legal and market research support for domestic and international users of direct marketing. A number of initiatives have already been launched to promote understanding of the media and to acknowledge and resolve impediments to its development.

List brokerage is becoming established as a function in Russia. The main list owners recently gathered under the aegis of the RDMA to propose general standards of handling address information, and to promote cooperation with DM agencies. The appearance of new DM media such as telemarketing, direct response television and mail order catalogues all create exciting new opportunities for developing private list data, where previously no such possibilities existed.

In addition, the legal regulations relating to DM have improved with the development of the industy. In January 1995, the State Duma (parliament) of the Russian Federation adopted a law relating to information and information security. The law defines basic relationships between citizens and legal entities, with reference to the ownership, storage and usage of information. The law stipulates that the State will 'provide conditions for the development and protection of all forms of information resources ownership' as well as 'work out legislative norms and standards pertaining to the sphere of information processes...and information security'. While somewhat rudimentary, and largely yet to be implemented, the new law is a significant step forward and marks a basic acknowledgement of the issues surrounding active marketing to consumers.

The country has some way to go in furthering consumer confidence, and in securing improvements in its infrastructure; but with a vast population, for whom the concept of DM communications is still fresh, Russia holds significant opportunities for the the astute marketer to position for potentially dynamic growth.

THE DIRECT MARKETING ASSOCIATION

Name: Russian Direct Marketing Association (RDMA)
Address: 17b Butlerova St, Moscow 117342, Russia
Tel: +7 095 334 7971
Fax: +7 095 334 7971
Email: rdma@com2com.ru
Year founded: 1995
President: Sergei Novikov

POSTAL SERVICES

For information on the Russian postal services please contact:

Postal Services of the Federation of Russia
International Post Office
37, Varchavskogé Chaussée
113105 Moscow
Federation of Russia

Tel: +7 095 1144 584
Fax: +7 095 2302 719

PROVIDERS OF DM AND E-M SERVICES

ADVERTISING AGENCY RAGY
Bumazhny proezd, 14
Moscow
SU-101462
Russia
Tel: +7 095 250 38 51
Fax: +7 095 257 36 84
Alexey Mezentsev, President

Services/Products:
Advertising Agency; Direct marketing agency; Market research agency; Translation services

AGENCY RUSSIA DIRECT
PO Box 26
Moscow
113191
Russia
Tel: +7 095 232 26 96
Fax: +7 095 232 26 98
Mikhall Simonov, General Director

Services/Products:
Direct marketing agency

Member of:
FEDMA

INDEPENDENT DISTRIBUTORS
Ulitsa Vyborgskaya, 16
6th Floor
Moscow
SU-125212
Russia
Tel: +7 095 150 99 30
Fax: +7 095 232 176 1
Harro Van Graafeiland, General Manager

Services/Products:
Database services; Card pack manufacturer; Direct marketing agency; Response analysis bureau

IVANOV & IVANOV DIRECT
Office 409
Maliy Cheskassiy per. 1/3
Moscow
103720
Russia
Tel: +7 095 753 8223
Fax: +7 095 928 8562
Email: ivanova@cea.ru
Thomas Bär

Services/Products:
List services; Fulfilment and sampling house; Database services; Direct marketing agency; Response analysis bureau

Member of:
FEDMA

KNIGA-SERVICE
14/1 Krzhizhanovskogo St.
Moscow
117168
Russia
Tel: +7 095 124 3058
Fax: +7 095 129 0154
Email: bazhenov@akc.ru
Alexander Bazhenor

Services/Products:
Fulfilment and sampling house; Database services; Direct marketing agency; Consultancy services; Response analysis bureau

SERVICES/PRODUCT LISTING

Advertising Agency
Advertising Agency Ragy

Card pack manufacturer
Independent Distributors

Consultancy services
Kniga-Service

Database services
Independent Distributors
Ivanov & Ivanov Direct
Kniga-Service

Direct marketing agency
Advertising Agency Ragy
Agency Russia Direct
Independent Distributors
Ivanov & Ivanov Direct
Kniga-Service

Fulfilment and sampling house
Ivanov & Ivanov Direct
Kniga-Service

List services
Ivanov & Ivanov Direct

Market research agency
Advertising Agency Ragy

Response analysis bureau
Independent Distributors
Ivanov & Ivanov Direct
Kniga-Service

Translation services
Advertising Agency Ragy

— SLOVAK REPUBLIC —

Population: 5.3 million
Capital: Bratislava
Languages: Slovak, Hungarian

GDP: US$18 billion
GDP per capita: US$3,400
Inflation: 6.1 per cent

Currency: Koruna (Kc)
Exchange rate: Kc42.01 : US$1

Time: GMT +1 hour

LEGISLATION AND CONSUMER PROTECTION

The export of data is controlled by the Personal Data Protection Act No. 52/1998.

THE DIRECT MARKETING ASSOCIATION

Name: Asociacia Direct Marketingu (ADiMa)
Address: Galvaniho 10, 821 04 Bratislava, Slovak Republic
Tel: +421 7 506 336 93
Fax: +421 7 506 336 93
Email: adima@adima.sk
Website: www.adima.sk
Year founded: 1997
President: Ms. Jaroslava Dzugasova
Members: 6

DM agencies   6

Membership: overseas companies can join ADiMa. There is an annual fee of SK 48,000 and an entrance fee of SK 50,000. ADiMa is open for any new members – companies in branche directmarketing.

On-line service: ADiMa has an on-line service. The website address is www.adima.sk.

Other facilities: ADiMa arranges courses for marketing managers, and offers full service direct marketing.

POSTAL SERVICES

The Slovak Post is a state-owned company regulated by the Ministry of Transport, Posts and Telecommunications. It employs more than 18,000 personnel and operates 1624 post offices directed by four regional directorates. The Slovak Post provides porfolio of letter, parcel, financial and agency services and handles more than 500 million items in domestic letter traffic per year.

Services offered:

- Bulk, discounted rates for addressed/unaddressed mail
- Periodical mailing rates
- Express mail services (EMS)
- Business reply services (BRS)
- PO Box addresses
- Registered post
- Postage paid by addressee
- Mailsort
- Courier services
- Postal insurance
- Database services and direct campaign analysis
- Printing and packaging

For further information contact:

Marketing Department
The Slovak Post
Partizánska cesta 9
97599 Banská Bystrica
Slovak Republic

Tel: +421 88 411 5220
Fax: +421 88 4115 5208
Email: ustr@ustr.slposta.sk
Website: www.slposta.sk

Domestic service enquiries:
RNDr. Jaroslav Mauda
Product Marketing Department Manager
Tel: +421 88 411 5220

International service enquiries:
Ing. Ján Kollár
Director of International Department
Tel: +421 07 544 35100

PROVIDERS OF DM AND E-M SERVICES

DIRECT MARKETING, S.R.O.
Hviezdna 38
Bratislava
821 06
Slovak Republic
Tel: +421 7 4552 2915
Fax: +421 7 4552 2906
Email:
    directmarketing@directmarketing.sk
Web: www.directmarketing.sk
Mr Jan Faltys

Services/Products:
Direct marketing agency

Member of:
ADiMa

DMMS BRATISLAVA, S.R.O.
Galvaniho 10
Bratislava
821 04
Slovak Republic
Email: dmms@dmms.sk
Web: www.dmms.sk
Ms Jaroslava Dzugasova

Services/Products:
Direct marketing agency

Member of:
ADiMa

**HERMES DIRECT
    MARKETING, S.R.O.**
Odborárska 3
Bratislava 3
831 02
Slovak Republic
Tel: +421 7 4445 5012
Fax: +421 7 4445 5013
Email: hermesdm@isternet
Mr Karol Riedl

Services/Products:
Direct marketing agency

Member of:
ADiMa

KOLOS, S.R.O.
Pribisova 47
Bratislava
841 05
Slovak Republic
Tel: +421 7 6531 523
Fax: +421 7 6531 504
Email: kolos@kolos.sk
Web: www.kolos.sk
Mr Henrich Lauko

Services/Products:
Direct marketing agency

Member of:
ADiMa

**MADE IN. . . , FINANCIAL
    MANAGEMENT, S.R.O.**
Trnavská cesta 84
Bratislava
821 02
Slovak Republic
Tel: +421 7 5254745, 5254742
Email: marianm@madein.sk
Mr Marian Mráz

Services/Products:
Direct marketing agency

Member of:
ADiMa

**SCHOBER
    DIREKTMARKETING, S.R.O.**
Pribinova 25
Bratislava 111
810 11
Slovak Republic
Email: schober@gaston.sk
Ms Alzbeta Vojtusová

Services/Products:
Direct marketing agency

Member of:
ADiMa

SERVICES/PRODUCT LISTING

Direct marketing agency
Direct Marketing, s.r.o.
DMMS Bratislava, s.r.o.
Hermes Direct Marketing, s.r.o.
KOLOS, s.r.o.
Made In. . . , financial management,
    s.r.o.
Schober Direktmarketing, s.r.o.

SLOVENIA

Population: 2 million
Capital: Ljubljana
Languages: Slovene, Serbo-Croat

GDP: US$16 billion
GDP per capita: US$8110
Inflation: 9.1 per cent

Currency: Slovenian Tolar
Exchange rate: SLT179.66 : US$1

Time: GMT +1 hour

LANGUAGE AND CULTURAL CONSIDERATIONS

The vast majority of the population speak Slovene, and 7% speak Serbo-Croat. There is a remaining 2% of the population that speak other languages.

POSTAL SERVICES

For further information please contact:

Posta Slovenije, d.o.o.
SI-2500 Maribor
Slovenia

Tel: +386 62 449 2221
Fax: +386 62 449 2112
Email: info@posta.si
Website: www.posta.si
Mr. Marian Osvald, Head of International Affiars

PROVIDERS OF DM
AND E-M SERVICES

STUDIO MODERNA
Vilharjeva 29
Yubjana
1000
Slovenia
Tel: +386 61 173 3800
Fax: +386 61 173 3897
Email: maja.golob@stud-moderna.sl
Maja Golob, International Sales
    Director

Services/Products:
Advertising Agency; List services;
Fulfilment and sampling house; Direct
marketing agency; Media buying
agency

Member of:
FEDMA

SERVICES/PRODUCT
LISTING

Advertising Agency
Studio Moderna

Direct marketing agency
Studio Moderna

Fulfilment and sampling house
Studio Moderna

List services
Studio Moderna

Media buying agency
Studio Moderna

UKRAINE

Population: 50.85 million
Capital: Kiev
Languages: Ukrainian, Russian
GDP: US$51 billion
GDP per capita: US$720
Inflation: 15.9 per cent
Currency: Hryvnia
Exchange rate: Hr4.00 : US$1
Time: GMT +2 hours

LEGISLATION AND CONSUMER PROTECTION

There are no laws or restrictions with regard to either the export of data or list broking.

THE DIRECT MARKETING ASSOCIATION

There is currently no local direct marketing association.

POSTAL SERVICES

The postal system is very slow and not open to innovation. Discounts based on quantity are available.

For further information contact:

Ukrpochta
22 rue Khrestchatyk
252001 Kiev 1
Ukraine
Tel: +380 44 229 9232
Fax: +380 44 228 79 69
Mme. G. Ratnikova, Head of Postal Services

PROVIDERS OF DM
AND E-M SERVICES

DISTRIMEDIA KY1V LTD
Vul. Desiatynna 4/6
Room 22 + 23
C/o Sputnik Ukraine
Kyiv
252 025
Ukraine
Tel: +380 44 212 8353
Fax: +380 44 212 2450
Email: dmedia@webber.kiev.ua
Pieter Stroop, Director

Services/Products:
Lettershop; Database services;
Mailing/Faxing services;
Personalisation; Private delivery
services

Member of:
FEDMA

SERVICES/PRODUCT
LISTING

Database services
Distrimedia KY1V Ltd

Lettershop
Distrimedia KY1V Ltd

Mailing/Faxing services
Distrimedia KY1V Ltd

Personalisation
Distrimedia KY1V Ltd

Private delivery services
Distrimedia KY1V Ltd

CANADA

Population: 30.1 million

Capital: Ottawa

Languages: English and French

GDP: $633 billion

GDP per capita: $21,031

Inflation: 0.2 per cent

Currency: Canadian dollar (C$) = 100 cents

Exchange rate: C$1.45 : $1

Time: GMT –3 ½ to –8 hours

(Ottawa –5 hours; Vancouver –8 hours)

OVERVIEW

Highlights from the Canadian DMA's *Annual Fact Book 1997–98* show Canada to have a buoyant DM industry:

- revenue from direct marketing activities in 1996 conservatively estimated at $11.2 billion;
- the annual growth rate for direct marketing was estimated at 12 per cent for 1996;
- the outlook for 1997 was even brighter with sales derived from direct response marketing projected to rise a further 12.4 per cent to over $12 billion.

There has been increased use of a range of different direct response media. Direct response television has been growing, following beneficial regulatory changes in 1996. A majority of Canadian cataloguers are now using outbound telemarketing and interactive techniques to contact their customers. Usage of Internet marketing and electronic commerce is increasing rapidly as its viability proves to be extremely positive.

LANGUAGE AND CULTURAL CONSIDERATIONS

The 1991 census reported that English was the mother tongue of over 16 million Canadians. For the 6.5 million Canadians who indicated that French was their mother tongue, nine out of ten lived in the province of Quebec. According to the law, all advertising in this region must be in French, unless the customer has requested in writing that he or she wishes to receive it in English.

About 16 per cent of Canadians considered themselves bilingual in French and English, the majority living in Quebec.

LEGISLATION AND CONSUMER PROTECTION

The Canadian government has introduced legislation to protect personal information with respect to all commercial activity. The first reading of this legislation has already taken place, and the government plans to implement the law by the year 2000.

The Canadian Marketing Association requires all members to purge lists against its 200,000-name mail and telephone preference list. It has also established a relationship with the Canadian Funeral Association and implemented procedures to obtain the names of deceased consumers; the names are then incorporated into its purge lists. In addition, it has instituted a compulsory privacy code for members. The eight point privacy code and consumer protection principles govern industry members, with an emphasis on self-regulation.

THE DIRECT MARKETING ASSOCIATION

Name:	Canadian Marketing Association (CMA)*
Address:	1 Concorde Gate, Suite 607, Don Mills, Ontario, M3C 3N6
Tel:	+1 416 391 2362
Fax:	+1 416 441 4062
Website:	www.the-cma.org
Year founded:	1967
President:	John Gustavson (CEO)
Total staff:	20
Members:	750

DM agencies	60	DM consultants	65
Fulfilment houses	52	List brokers	31
Catalogue management	23	Mailing houses	68
Printers	40	Database marketers	139
Telemarketing agencies	44		

*Note: The Canadian Direct Marketing Association changed its name in 1999 to the Canadian Marketing Association (CMA). The Association will continue its current activities and programmes, but will broaden its scope to reflect the evolution and integration of marketing disciplines.

Facilities for overseas users of direct mail

Membership: overseas companies can join CMA, but must be approved by them. The membership fee works on a sliding scale, reflecting the applicant's level of involvement in DM. Annual fees range from $825 to $12,650. Members enjoy a very high standard of service.

Newsletter: the CMA issue a quarterly newsletter, featuring a round-up of industry news, as well as social and political issues affecting the market.

Library: the CMA has a library with approximately 250 books.

On-line information service: website address: www.cdma.org

Legal advice: the CMA does not offer legal advice.

Business liaison service: the CMA provides access to its files of accredited suppliers for both members and non-members.

Other facilities: the CMA publishes the *Canadian Direct Marketing Fact Book*. The Association provides both members and non-members with legislative lobbying in addition to numerous educational seminars and conferences.

POSTAL SERVICES

Canada Post Corporation, the crown corporation that runs Canada's postal service, is an active promoter of national and international direct marketing. Canada Post offers a host of direct marketing services including:

- **Addressed Admail:** which enables you to reach the right people with your advertising message. As the name implies, this product is mailed directly to a specific name and address. Typical items mailed include product information, catalogues, newsletters, announcements, renewal notices and offers of goods and services;

- **Unaddressed Admail:** which is simply advertising that is delivered by mail and without an address. Unaddressed admail can go to entire postal walks, it can go to every home in the city, or even the entire country. Items can vary from printed matter to product samples. Rates vary according to volume, method of delivery and use of standard or non-standard sizes;

- **Electronic Admail:** a computerized mail production and delivery service supported by a network of distributed print sites;

- **Business Reply Mail:** Postage paid business reply mail (BRM) provides prospects, customers or donors orders with a way to respond directly to any offer – because you are paying the postage for the BRM card or envelope, you will get a higher response rate and a better return on investment.

For further details contact:

Canada Post Corporation
2701 Riverside Drive, Suite No 176
Ottawa, ON K1A 0B1
Canada
Tel: +1 416 979 8822
Email: service@canadapost.ca
Website: www.canadapost.ca

PROVIDERS OF DM AND E-M SERVICES

1:1 INC.
130 Royal Crest Crt.
Markham
ON
L3R 0A1
Canada
Tel: +1 905 305 0498
Fax: +1 905 305 9195

Services/Products:
List services; Lettershop; Fulfilment and sampling house; Database services

Member of:
CMA

A&L MAILING SERVICES INC.
1040 Martin Grove Road
Unit #13
Etobicoke
ON
M9W 4W4
Canada
Tel: +1 416 247 2629
Fax: +1 416 247 9211
Laurie S.Gutmann, President and CEO

Services/Products:
Lettershop; Fulfilment and sampling house; Mailing/Faxing services

Member of:
CMA

A.M. STONE DIRECT MAIL SERVICES
PO Box 515
Peterborough
ON
K9J 6Z6
Canada
Tel: +1 705 944 5632
Fax: +1 705 944 5700
Mark Stone, Marketing Manager

Services/Products:
Lettershop; Mailing/Faxing services; Print services; Personalisation

Member of:
CMA

ACCESS CANADA
100 Armstrong Avenue
Georgetown
ON
L7G 5S4
Canada
Tel: +1 905 877 5163
Fax: +1 905 877 8262
John Duncan, President

Services/Products:
Lettershop; Fulfilment and sampling house; Private delivery services

Member of:
DMA (US); CMA

ACTUS MARKETING INC.
3914 Autumnwood Street
Gloucester
ON
K1T 1C1
Canada
Tel: +1 613 733 9488
Fax: +1 613 733 3191
Alain Doucet, Partner

Services/Products:
Fulfilment and sampling house; Telemarketing agency; Sales promotion agency

ADVANTAGE CALL CENTRE SOLUTIONS
160 Elgin St.
Floor 21
Ottawa
ON
K1G 3J4
Canada
Tel: +1 613 781 5103
Fax: +1 613 781 3661

Services/Products:
List services; Lettershop; Fulfilment and sampling house; Database services

Member of:
CMA

ALLIANCE CALL CENTRE SERVICES INC.
123 George St.
Suite 110
London
ON
N6A 3A1
Canada
, Office Manager

Services/Products:
Telemarketing agency

AMW DIRECT
1910 Younge Street
4th Floor
Toronto
ON
M4S 1Z5
Canada
Tel: +1 416 480 1967
Fax: +1 416 484 0726
David Foyle, Vice President

Services/Products:
Database services; Telemarketing agency; Direct marketing agency

AON DIRECT GROUP
Willowdale
2255 Sheppard Ave East
Suite E400
ON
M2J 4YI
Canada
Tel: +1 416 756 1573
Fax: +1 416 756 9290
Email: dsim@benoitborg.com
Katherine Chan, VP Business Development

Services/Products:
Database services; Response analysis bureau; Market research agency

Member of:
FEDMA

ARCAS GROUP INC.
#2–395 Park Street
Regina
SK
S4N 5B2
Canada
Tel: +1 306 721 0646
Fax: +1 306 721 0647

Services/Products:
Lettershop; Fulfilment services

Member of:
CMA

ARROW CANADIAN MAILING SERVICES
3780 Peter Street
Windsor
ON
N9C 4H2
Canada
Tel: +1 313 961 8334
Fax: +1 313 961 7849
Jeff Williams, Vice President

Services/Products:
Lettershop; Mailing/Faxing services

Member of:
DMA (US)

ASSERTIVE MARKETING SERVICES INC.
PO Box 108
#9 8671 Number 1 Road
Richmond
BC
V7C 1V2
Canada
Tel: +1 604 270 3400
Fax: +1 604 276 8561
Avy Zohar, President

Services/Products:
Telemarketing agency

Member of:
DMA (US)

AUTOMATED FULFILLMENT SYSTEMS
80 Van Kirk Drive
Brampton
ON
L7A 1B1
Canada
Tel: +1 905 840 4230
Fax: +1 905 840 4143
John Dickson, President

Services/Products:
Fulfilment and sampling house;
Telemarketing agency

Member of:
CMA

AVANT IMAGING & INFORMATION MANAGEMENT INC.
205 Industrial Parkway North
Aurora
ON
L4G 4C4
Canada
Tel: +1 905 841 6444
Fax: +1 905 841 2177

Services/Products:
Lettershop; Fulfilment sevices

Member of:
CMA

AXCIOM/DIRECT MEDIA
74A Hogarth Avenue
Toronto
ON
M4K 1K3
Canada
Tel: +1 416 406 4420
Fax: +1 416 406 4424
Charles Morgan, Pres. & Chairman of
  the Board

Services/Products:
List services

Member of:
DMA (US)

AXIS DATABASE MARKETING GROUP INC.
75 Horner Avenue
Unit 7
Etobicoke
ON
M8Z 4X5
Canada
Tel: +1 416 503 3210
Fax: +1 416 503 2729
Michael Booth, President

Services/Products:
Direct marketing agency

Member of:
CMA

B.J. HUNTER INFORMATION
600 Rene-Levesque West
Montreal
QC
H3B 1N4
Canada
Tel: +1 514 866 8588
Fax: +1 514 866 1717

Services/Products:
Lettershop; Fulfilment services

Member of:
CMA

BAKER-BLAIS MARKETING INC.
295 Hymus
Pointe Claire
Quebec
H9R 6A5
Canada
Tel: +1 514 693 9900
Fax: +1 514 693 9960
Email: donbaker@bakerblais.com
  info@bakerblais.com
Web: www.bakerblais.com
Don Baker, President

Services/Products:
Direct marketing agency

Member of:
DMA (US); CMA; SQMD

BASSETT DIRECT
450 Hood Road
Markham
ON
L3R 9Z3
Canada
Tel: +1 905 940 0824
Fax: +1 905 940 3440
Rich Bassett, President & CEO

Services/Products:
Lettershop; Print services;
Personalisation

Member of:
CMA

BBDO RESPONSE
2 Bloor Street West
29th Fl
Toronto
ON
M4W 3R6
Canada
Tel: +1 416 413 7497

Fax: +1 416 944 7886
Sarah Simpson, SVP & Managing
  Director

Services/Products:
Advertising Agency; Direct Response
Agency

Member of:
DMA (US)

BCP DIRECT
1200 Bay Street
Ste 1200
Toronto
ON
MR5 2A5
Canada
Tel: +1 416 975 0403
Fax: +1 416 975 0442
Andy Kardos, General Manager

Services/Products:
Advertising Agency; Direct Response
Agency

Member of:
DMA (US)

BDC DIRECT
PO Box 9060
Woodstock
NB
E7M 5C3
Canada
Tel: +1 506 328 8853
Fax: +1 506 328 4608
Lloyd Henderson, Vice President &
  General Manager

Services/Products:
Database services; Telemarketing
agency; Fulfilment and sampling hou

Member of:
CMA

BDP BUSINESS DATA SERVICES LIMITED
85 The East Mall
Toronto
ON
M8Z 5W4
Canada
Tel: +1 416 503 1800
Fax: +1 416 503 8899

Services/Products:
Lettershop; Fulfilment services

Member of:
CMA

BLAKELY EPTON & ASSOCIATES INC.
225 Industrial Parkway South
Unit B
PO Box 95

Aurora
ON
L4G 3H1
Canada
Tel: +1 905 727 6188
Fax: +1 905 727 1589
Leon Epton, Vice-President

Services/Products:
Direct marketing agency

BLITZ DIRECT
425 Grande-Allee Est
Quebec
QC
GIR 2S5
Canada
Tel: +1 418 647 6434
Fax: +1 418 647 3161
Danielle Perron, Director, Direct
Marketing

Services/Products:
Advertising Agency; Direct Response
Agency

Member of:
DMA (US)

BLITZ DIRECT
931 Yonge Street
Toronto
ON
M4W 2H2
Canada
Tel: +1 416 922 6434
Fax: +1 416 922 4809
Nancy Lee Jobin, Vice President,
General Manager

Services/Products:
Direct marketing agency; Sales
promotion agency

Member of:
CMA

BOSS COMMUNICATIONS
CORP.
490–10991 Shellbridge Way
Richmond
BC
V6X 3C6
Canada
Tel: +1 604 273 6836
Fax: +1 604 276 8561
Beverly Moss, Vice President

Services/Products:
Lettershop; Mailing/Faxing services

Member of:
DMA (US)

BRADFORD DIRECT
990 Roselawn Avenue
Toronto

ON
M6B 1C1
Canada
Tel: +1 416 789 7411
Fax: +1 416 785 7514
Rainer Fischer, President

Services/Products:
Lettershop; Direct marketing agency

Member of:
CMA

BRUCE MOORE RUSSELL–
DIRECT RESPONSE
466 Tremblay Road
Ottawa
ON
K1G 3R1
Canada
Tel: +1 613 749 7070
Fax: +1 613 749 6555
Wilf Brousseau, President

Services/Products:
Lettershop; Fulfilment and sampling
house; Direct marketing agency

Member of:
CMA

CALL RESPONSE
61 Advance Road
Toronto
ON
M8Z 2S6
Canada
Tel: +1 416 237 5555
Fax: +1 416 237 0863

Services/Products:
List services; Lettershop; Fulfilment
and sampling house; Database services

Member of:
CMA

CAMPBELL ABBOT LASER
MAIL
555 Eastern Avenue
Toronto
ON
M4M 1C8
Canada
Tel: +1 416 465 8844
Fax: +1 416 465 7456
Norman Moreau, President

Services/Products:
Lettershop; Print services; Fulfilment
and sampling house

Member of:
CMA

CANADA POST CORPORATION
Suite N0176
2701 Riverside Drive
Ottawa
ON
K1A OB1
Canada
Tel: +1 613 734 8932
Fax: +1 613 734 3378
Al Vlietstra, General Manager
Communication Business

Member of:
FEDMA

CANADIAN DIRECT MAILING
SYSTEMS/NORTH
AMERICAN PRINTING
680 E.C. Row
P.O. Box 1150
Windsor
ON
N9A 6P8
Canada
Tel: +1 519 966 1970
Fax: +1 519 966 6701

Services/Products:
List services; Lettershop; Fulfilment
and sampling house; Database services

Member of:
CMA

CANADIAN HEALTHCARE
ASSOCIATION
17 York Street
Ottawa
ON
K1N 9J6
Canada
Tel: +1 613 241 8005
Fax: +1 613 241 5055

Services/Products:
List services; Lettershop; Fulfilment
and sampling house; Database services

Member of:
CMA

CARLSON MARKETING GROUP
3300 Bloor Street West
Toronto
ON
M8X 2Y2
Canada
Tel: +1 416 236 8370
Fax: +1 416 233 3034
Thomas Lacki, Sr. Dir., Measurement/
Analysis

Services/Products:
Advertising Agency; Direct Response
Agency

Member of:
DMA (US)

**CARLSON MARKETING GROUP
CONSUMER & LOYALTY
MARKETING DIVISION 3300
BLOOR STREET**
West Centre Tower
15th Floor
Toronto
ON
M8X 2Y2
Canada
Canada
Tel: +1 416 233 3034
Web: Robert Clarkson
Vice President, General Manager,
    Direct marketing agency

CD DIRECT
200 Yorkland Blvd
Suite 710
Toronto
ON
M2J 5C1
Canada
Tel: +1 416 756 0734
Fax: +1 416 756 3403
Sharon Read, Manager

Services/Products:
Lettershop; Direct marketing agency;
Print services

**CENTRAL CANADA
TELEMANAGEMENT**
514–1661 Portage Ave
Winnipeg
MB
A3J 3T7
Canada
Tel: +1 204 982 3511
Fax: +1 204 982 3512
Robert Janzic, General Manager

Services/Products:
Mailing/Faxing services; Telemarketing
agency

**CHECKMATE MARKETING
LTD.**
2 Tarlton Road
Toronto
ON
M5P 2M4
Canada
Tel: +1 416 482 2010
Fax: +1 416 487 7998
John Yokom, President

Services/Products:
Marketing consultant

Member of:
DMA (US)

**CHIAT/DAY DIRECT
MARKETING, INC.**
10 Lower Spadina
Toronto
ON
M5V 2Z1
Canada
Tel: +1 416 260 6600
Velda Ruddock, Director, Intelligence

Services/Products:
Advertising Agency; Direct Response
Agency

Member of:
DMA (US)

CINRAM NEW MEDIA GROUP
5590 Finch Avenue East
Scarborough
ON
M1B 1T1
Canada
Tel: +1 416 332 9000
Fax: +1 416 298 4314

Services/Products:
List services; Lettershop; Fulfilment
and sampling house; Database services

Member of:
CMA

CLICK MEDIA INC.
12994 Keele Street
Unit 7
King City
ON
L7B 1H8
Canada
Tel: +1 905 833 3994
Fax: +1 905 8334 499
Robert Brunet, President

Services/Products:
Internet services

E-Services:
Website design

COHN & WELLS, LTD.
8 Price Street
Toronto
ON
M4W 1Z4
Canada
Tel: +1 416 961 7188
Fax: +1 416 961 3618
Elizabeth Ciccone, Vice President &
    Partner

Services/Products:
Advertising Agency; Direct Response
Agency

Member of:
DMA (US)

**COMMUNICATION & MAILING
SERVICE**
46 Alice St.
Brantford
ON
N3R 1Y2
Canada
Tel: +1 519 752 0198
Fax: +1 519 752 0599

Services/Products:
List services; Lettershop; Fulfilment
and sampling house; Database service

Member of:
CMA

**COMMUNICATIONS REAL
LAFORTE INC.**
1955 Robertine-Barry
Montreal
QC
H4N 3G0
Canada
Tel: +1 514 335 1523
Fax: +1 514 335 5981
Real Laforte, President

Services/Products:
List services

Member of:
CMA

CONTACT MARKETING INC.
608–1661 Portage Avenue
Winnipeg
MB
R3J 3T7
Canada
Tel: +1 204 982 3535
Fax: +1 204 982 3520
Bill Scurfield, Managing Partner

Services/Products:
List services; Fulfilment and sampling
house; Database services; Direct
marketing agency

Member of:
CMA

**CONTACTS TARGET
MARKETING INC.**
201–460 Nanaimo Street
Vancouver
BC
V5L 4W3
Canada
Tel: +1 604 253 1111
Fax: +1 604 253 3939
Robert Gibson, President

Services/Products:
List services; Direct marketing agency

CORNERSTONE
2200 Yonge St.
8th Floor
Toronto
ON
M4S 2C6
Canada
Tel: +1 416 932 9555
Fax: +1 416 932 9566

Services/Products:
List services; Lettershop; Fulfilment
and sampling house; Database services

Member of:
CMA

CORPORATE MAILING
  SERVICES
30 Royal Crest Court
Suite #10
Markham
ON
L3R 9W8
Canada
Tel: +1 905 513 8589
Fax: +1 905 513 1778

Services/Products:
List services; Lettershop; Fulfilment
and sampling house; Database services

Member of:
CMA

COVER-ALL DIRECT
  RESPONSE SYSTEMS LTD
80 Gough Road
Markham
ON
L3R 6E8
Canada
Tel: +1 905 940 1919
Fax: +1 905 940 2107
Eric Farncombe, Vice President, Sales

Services/Products:
Lettershop; Print services; Response
analysis bureau; Fulfilment and
sampling house

COVER-ALL DIRECT
  RESPONSE SYSTEMS LTD.
80 Gough Road
Markham
ON
L3R 6E8
Canada
Tel: +1 905 940 1919
Fax: +1 905 940 2107

Services/Products:
List services; Lettershop; Fulfilment
and sampling house; Database services

Member of:
CMA

CPC LOYALTY
  COMMUNICATIONS
2001 Sheppard Avenue East
Suite 800
Toronto
ON
M2J 4Z8
Canada
Tel: +1 416 494 9995
Fax: +1 416 494 2328
Kevin Bell, Vice President

Services/Products:
Direct marketing agency

Member of:
CMA

CW AGENCIES
2020 Yukon Street
Vancouver
BC
V5Y 3N8
Canada
Tel: +1 604 871 3400
Fax: +1 604 871 3426
Annette Syberg Olsen, VP, Media
  Services

Services/Products:
Advertising Agency; Direct Response
Agency

Member of:
DMA (US)

DATA FOCUS – DIVISION OF
  DATA BUSINESS FORMS
200 Ronson Drive
Suite 201
Etobicoke
ON
M9W 5Z9
Canada
Tel: +1 416 245 3987
Fax: +1 416 245 2959

Services/Products:
List services; Lettershop; Fulfilment
and sampling house; Database services

Member of:
CMA

DATA INSIGHT GROUP
92 Jarvis St
Toronto
ON
M5C 2H5
Canada
Tel: +1 416 862 2336x328
Fax: +1 416 862 0995

Services/Products:
List services; Lettershop; Fulfilment
and sampling house; Database services

Member of:
CMA

DE JONG ENTERPRISES INC.
P.O. Box 39
RR#3
Norwich
ON
N0J 1P0
Canada
Tel: +1 519 424 9007
Fax: +1 519 424 2399

Services/Products:
List services; Lettershop; Fulfilment
and sampling house; Database services

Member of:
CMA

DIMARK MARKETING
  SERVICES INC.
1146 Waverley Street
Unit 6
Winnipeg
MB
R3T 0PH
Canada
Tel: +1 204 987 1950
Fax: +1 204 783 9748
, Fulfilment and sampling house

DIRECT MEDIA CANADA INC.
74A Hogarth Avenue
Toronto
ON
M4K 1K3
Canada
Tel: +1 416 406 4420
Fax: +1 416 406 4424
Tony Gilroy, Managing Director

Services/Products:
List services

DIRECTWEST PUBLISHERS
#800–1900 Albert St.
Regina
SK
S4P 4K8
Canada
Tel: +1 306 777 0353
Fax: +1 306 352 6514

Services/Products:
List services; Lettershop; Fulfilment
and sampling house; Database services

Member of:
CMA

DKY INTEGRATED
  COMMUNICATIONS
440 rue St. Pierre
Montreal
QC

H2Y 2M5
Canada
Tel: +1 514 499 1133
Fax: +1 514 499 0907
Gary Yott, President

Services/Products:
Media buying agency; Advertising
Agency; Direct Response Agency

DMP DIRECT MARKETING PRODUCTS LTD.
P. O. Box 428
Oakville
ON
L6J 5A8
Canada
Tel: +1 905 844 1175
Fax: +1 905 844 2888
John Cundill, President

Services/Products:
Advertising Agency; Direct Response
Agency

Member of:
DMA (US)

DOCULINK INTERNATIONAL
880 Wellington
Suite 310
Ottawa
ON
K1R 6K7
Canada
Tel: +1 613 563 3210
Fax: +1 613 563 2546

Services/Products:
List services; Lettershop; Fulfilment
and sampling house; Database services

Member of:
CMA

DOLPHIN DIRECT PRINTING, MAILING & DATA SYSTEMS INC.
7 Labatt Avenue
Suite 102
Toronto
ON
M5A 1Z1
Canada
Tel: +1 416 365 7446
Fax: +1 416 365 1985

Services/Products:
List services; Lettershop; Fulfilment
and sampling house; Database services

Member of:
CMA

DUN & BRADSTREET CANADA LIMITED
5770 Hurontario Street
8th Floor
Mississauga
ON
L5R 3G5
Canada
Tel: +1 905 568 6000
Fax: +1 905 568 6197
, List broker/compiler

Member of:
CMA

ERA DIRECT LTD.
275 Renfrew Drive
Suite 208
Markham
ON
L3R 0C8
Canada
Tel: +1 905 474 5944
Fax: +1 905 474 5947

Services/Products:
List services; Lettershop; Fulfilment
and sampling house; Database services

Member of:
CMA

EXCLUSIVE COMMUNICATIONS LTD.
1881 Yonge Street
Suite 710
Toronto
ON
M4S 3C4
Canada
Tel: +1 416 486 3477
Fax: +1 416 486 3475
Email: info@exclusivecom.com
Web: www.exclusivecom.com
Peter Jennings, President

Services/Products:
Advertising Agency; Consultancy
services; Media buying agency;
Design/graphics/clip art supplier;
Direct marketing agency; Sales
promotion agency

E-Services:
E-Marketing consultant; Website
design; Online/e-marketing agency

EXTEND COMMUNICATIONS INC.
49 Charlotte Street
Brantford
ON
N3T 2W4
Canada
Tel: +1 519 759 6820

Fax: +1 519 754 1994
Scott Lyons, General Manager

Services/Products:
Fulfilment and sampling house;
Telemarketing agency

FCB DIRECT
245 Eglinton Ave. #300
Toronto
ON
M4P 3C2
Canada
Tel: +1 416 483 3624
Fax: +1 416 483 3606
Email: mjvinet@fcb.ca
Marie-Josée Vinet, Vice President and
Managing Director

Services/Products:
Advertising Agency

E-Services:
Online/e-marketing agency

Member of:
DMA (US); Canadian Marketing
Association (CMA)

FCB DIRECT CANADA
1250 Rene-Levesque West
Suite 3650
Montreal
QC
H3B 4W8
Canada
Tel: +1 514 938 4141
Fax: +1 514 938 2022
Mark Goodman, President

Services/Products:
Direct marketing agency

FIRST AVENUE
47 Jutland Rd
Etobicoke
ON
M8Z 2G6
Canada
Tel: +1 416 259 3600
Fax: +1 416 259 4730
James Higginson, President

Services/Products:
Advertising Agency; Direct Response
Agency

Member of:
DMA (US); CMA

FRONTIER DISTRIBUTING
P.O. Box 1051
1031 Helena Street
Fort Erie
ON
L2A 5N8
Canada

Tel: +1 905 871 3358
Fax: +1 905 871 9175

Services/Products:
List services; Lettershop; Fulfilment
and sampling house; Database services

Member of:
CMA

FSA INC.
132 Denison Street
Markham
ON
L3R 1B6
Canada
Tel: +1 905 415 9438
Fax: +1 905 415 8194

Services/Products:
List services; Lettershop; Fulfilment
and sampling house; Database services

Member of:
CMA

GETKO DIRECT RESPONSE
910–2345 Yonge Street
Toronto
ON
M4P 2E5
Canada
Tel: +1 416 322 8153
Fax: +1 416 322 8896
Jonathan Latsky, Managing Director

Services/Products:
List services

Member of:
DMA (US); CMA

GINGKO DIRECT LTD.
4950 Yonge Street
Suite 600
Toronto
ON
M2N 6K1
Canada
Tel: +1 416 221 2244
Fax: +1 416 221 8130
Irvin Lebovits, Co-Chairman

Services/Products:
Advertising Agency; Direct marketing
agency; Sales promotion agency

GLOBEL DIRECT MARKETING
1324 36th Street, N.E.
Calgary
AB
T2E 8S1
Canada
Tel: +1 403 531 6550
Fax: +1 403 273 2642
Sandi Gilbert, Vice President

Services/Products:
Lettershop; Mailing/Faxing services

Member of:
DMA (US); CMA

**GRANT'S MAILING SERVICES
INC.**
940 Matheson Boulevard East
Mississauga
ON
L4W 2R8
Canada
Tel: +1 905 624 9082
Fax: +1 905 624 0007
Michael Keyes, Vice President

Services/Products:
Mailing/Faxing services; Labelling/
envelope services

GREY DIRECT
1881 Yonge Street
2nd Floor
Toronto
ON
M4S 3C4
Canada
Tel: +1 416 486 0700
Fax: +1 416 486 7299

Services/Products:
List services; Lettershop; Fulfilment
and sampling house; Database services

Member of:
CMA

GROUP 1 SOFTWARE
2 Robert Speck Parkway
Suite 670
Mississauga
ON
L4Z 1H8
Canada
Tel: +1 905 272 5877
Fax: +1 905 272 1090

Services/Products:
List services; Lettershop; Fulfilment
and sampling house; Database services

Member of:
CMA

GROUPE RR INTERNATIONAL
2322 Sherbrooke E
Ste 1
Montreal
QC
H2K 1E5
Canada
Tel: +1 514 521 8148
Fax: +1 514 521 2097
Louis-Luc Roy, President

Services/Products:
Advertising Agency; Direct Response
Agency

Member of:
DMA (US)

GWE GROUP INC.
200–417 14th Street N.W.
Calgary
AB
T2N 2A1
Canada
Tel: +1 403 531 6157
Fax: +1 403 531 6133
Wendy Wenaas, Manager, Data
Services

Services/Products:
Telemarketing agency

Member of:
DMA (US)

HERBERT A WATTS LTD.
455 Horner Avenue
Toronto
ON
M8W 4W9
Canada
Tel: +1 416 252 7741
Fax: +1 416 252 0037
Email: rgauthier@wattsgroup.com
Web: www.wattsgroup.com
Rip Gauthier, Chairman

Services/Products:
Call centre services/systems; Database
services; Mailing/Faxing services;
Fulfilment and sampling house;
Labelling/envelope services; Lettershop

E-Services:
Email list provider; Website design

Member of:
National DMA; MASA

HONDERICH INVESTMENTS
8 Moorehill Drive
Toronto
ON
M4G 1A1
Canada
Tel: +1 416 425 6431
Fax: +1 416 425 9118

Services/Products:
List services; Lettershop; Fulfilment
and sampling house; Database services

Member of:
CMA

HSH GROUP OF COMPANIES
30 Greenfield Ave.
1810 Rodeo Walk
North York

ON
M2N 6N3
Canada
Fax: +1 416 229 03 73
Maryanne Tam-Po Fong

Services/Products:
Mailing/Faxing services; Telemarketing
agency; Design/graphics/clip art
supplier; Market research agency; Sales
promotion agency

E-Services:
Website design

Member of:
FEDMA

HUGHES RAPP COLLINS
2381 Bristol Circle
4th Fl
Oakville
ON
L6H 5S9
Canada
Tel: +1 905 829 2002
Fax: +1 905 8294346
G. Steven Dapper, Chairman & CEO

Services/Products:
Advertising Agency; Direct Response
Agency

Member of:
DMA (US)

I.C.S. LOGISTICS/ALLTOUR
245 Britannia Road East
Mississauga
ON
L4Z 2Y7
Canada
Tel: +1 905 890 3400
Fax: +1 905 890 4507

Services/Products:
List services; Lettershop; Fulfilment
and sampling house; Database services

Member of:
CMA

I.M.S. – INQUIRY
MANAGEMENT SYSTEMS
LTD.
1 Westside Drive
Unit 6
Etobicoke
ON
M9C 1B2
Canada
Tel: +1 416 620 1965
Fax: +1 416 620 9790

Services/Products:
List services; Lettershop; Fulfilment
and sampling house; Database services

Member of:
CMA

ICOM
41 Metropolitan Road
Toronto
ON
M1R 2T5
Canada
Tel: +1 416 297 7887
Fax: +1 416 297 7084
David Lefkowich, Gen. Mgr.,
    Canadian List Div.

Services/Products:
List services

Member of:
DMA (US); CMA

INDAS LIMITED
35 Riviera Drive
Unit 17
Markham
ON
L3R 8N4
Canada
Tel: +1 905 946 0400
Fax: +1 905 946 0410
Bill Kaluski, President & Owner

Services/Products:
Database services; Mailing/Faxing
services

Member of:
CMA

INFO CANADA
1290 Central Parkway West
Suite 104
Mississauga
ON
L5C 4R3
Canada
Tel: +1 905 306 9800
Fax: +1 905 306 9014
Email: canada@infousa.com
Web: www.infoCANADA.ca

Services/Products:
List services; Database services

Member of:
National DMA; CDMA

INFO CANADA
1290 Central Parkway West
Suite 104
Mississauga
ON
L5C 4R3
Canada
Tel: +1 905 306 9800
Fax: +1 905 306 7272

Services/Products:
List services; Lettershop; Fulfilment
and sampling house; Database servic

Member of:
CMA

INFODIRECT
325 Milner Avenue
10th Floor
Scarborough
ON
M1B 5S8
Canada
Tel: +1 416 412 5571
Fax: +1 416 412 5585
Hany Kirolos, General Manager

Services/Products:
List services

Member of:
CMA

INFOWORKS
50 Burnhamthorpe Rd. West
Suite 402
Mississauga
ON
L5B 3C2
Canada
Tel: +1 905 848 4636
Fax: +1 905 848 0008
Frances Prindiville, Vice President

Services/Products:
Database services

Member of:
DMA (US)

INTERACT DIRECT (LONDON
INC.
538 Adelaide Street North
London
ON
N6B 3J4
Canada
Tel: +1 519 439 6245
Fax: +1 519 439 9869
Jeffrey Bisset, President

Services/Products:
Lettershop; Mailing/Faxing services

Member of:
DMA (US); CMA

INTERACTIVE MARKETING
GROUP ULC
150 Eglinton Avenue East
Suite 401
Toronto
ON
M4P 1E8
Canada
Tel: +1 416 483 3797

Fax: +1 416 483 6869

Services/Products:
List services; Lettershop; Fulfilment
and sampling house; Database services

Member of:
CMA

INTERAD MEDIA DESIGN CORP.
1258A St. Clair Avenue West
Toronto
ON
M6E 1B9
Canada
Tel: +1 416 654 5121
Fax: +1 416 654 3747

Services/Products:
List services; Lettershop; Fulfilment
and sampling house; Database services

Member of:
CMA

J R DIRECT RESPONSE INTERNATIONAL
4703 51st Street
Suite 1
Delta
BC
CDN-V4K 2W1
Canada
Tel: +1 604 940 0277
Fax: +1 604 946 1419
Email: jim@jrdri.com
Web: www.jrdirect.com
Jim Ripplinger, President

Services/Products:
List services; Direct marketing agency;
Service bureau

Member of:
FEDMA; CMA

JONCAS POSTEXPERTS INC.
7875 route Transcanadienne
St-Laurent
QC
H4S 1L3
Canada
Tel: +1 514 333 7480
Fax: +1 514 332 6915

Services/Products:
List services; Lettershop; Fulfilment
and sampling house; Database services

Member of:
CMA

JONES DIRECT MARKETING SERVICES LTD.
130 McLevin Avenue
Scarborough
ON
M1B 3R6
Canada
Tel: +1 416 297 7311
Fax: +1 416 297 4703
Esme Hurst, Sales & Marketing
   Manager

Services/Products:
Lettershop; Mailing/Faxing services

Member of:
DMA (US); CMA

JSI DATA SYSTEMS LIMITED
14 Concourse Gate
Suite 100
Nepean
ON
K2E 7S6
Canada
Tel: +1 613 727 9353
Fax: +1 613 727 0372
Janet Black-Evans, Sales and
   Marketing Manager

Services/Products:
Service bureau

Member of:
CMA

KAIZEN MEDIA SERVICES INC.
400 St. Mary Avenue
Suite 500
Winnipeg
MB
R3C 4K5
Canada
Tel: +1 204 925 8526
Fax: +1 204 946 5435

Services/Products:
List services; Lettershop; Fulfilment
and sampling house; Database services

Member of:
CMA

KEY MAIL CANADA INC.
2756 Slough Street
Mississauga
ON
L4T 1G3
Canada
Tel: +1 905 677 1692
Fax: +1 905 677 8086
Richard Thornton, Managing Director

Services/Products:
Lettershop; Mailing/Faxing services

Member of:
DMA (US); CMA

KEYCONTACT
555 Admiral Drive
London
ON
N5V 4L6
Canada
Tel: +1 519 452 3000
Fax: +1 519 453 8652

Services/Products:
List services; Lettershop; Fulfilment
and sampling house; Database services

Member of:
CMA

KEYSTONE RESPONSE MANAGEMENT
2200 Yonge St
8th Floor
Toronto
ON
M4S 2C6
Canada
Tel: +1 416 932 1414
Fax: +1 416 932 3561

Services/Products:
List services; Lettershop; Fulfilment
and sampling house; Database services

Member of:
CMA

KNOWLEDGEBASE MARKETING INC.
90 Eglinton Avenue East
Suite 410
Toronto
ON
M4P 2Y3
Canada
Tel: +1 416 488 5320
Fax: +1 416 488 5229

Services/Products:
List services; Lettershop; Fulfilment
and sampling house; Database services

Member of:
CMA

KPMG NATIONAL CONSULTING
4120 Yonge Street
Toronto
ON
M2P 2B8
Canada
Tel: +1 416 228 7138
Fax: +1 416 228 7123
Robert Westrope, Principal

Services/Products:
Marketing consultant

Member of:
DMA (US)

KPN/INTERPOST NORTH AMERICA
1655 Inkster Boulevard
4th Fl
Winnipeg
MB
R2X 2W7
Canada
John Costanzo, President

Services/Products:
Private delivery services

Member of:
DMA (US)

KUBAS CONSULTANTS
2300 Yonge Street
Ste 2002
Toronto
ON
M4P 1E4
Canada
Tel: +1 416 487 7040
Fax: +1 416 487 0816
Leonard Kubas, President

Services/Products:
Market research agency

Member of:
DMA (US)

LAUNCH DIRECT
20 Plastics Avenue
Toronto
ON
M8Z 4B7
Canada
Tel: +1 416 201 3510
Fax: +1 416 259 0187

Services/Products:
List services; Lettershop; Fulfilment
and sampling house; Database services

Member of:
CMA

LEADER DIRECT MARKETING LTD
13071 Vanier Place
Suite 150
V6V 2VI Richmond
BC
Canada
Tel: +1 604 303 7667
Fax: +1 604 303 06 69
Dione Costanzo, President

Member of:
FEDMA

LIVINGSTON INTERNATIONAL INC.
405 The West Mall
Ste 300

Toronto
ON
M9C 5K7
Canada
Tel: +1 416 626 2800
Fax: +1 416 622 7721
Dean Wood, Marketing Manager

Services/Products:
Lettershop; Mailing/Faxing services

Member of:
DMA (US)

LOVELL & COMPANY CONSULTING
313 Runnymede Road
2nd Floor
Toronto
ON
M6S 2Y5
Canada
Tel: +1 416 763 7173
Fax: +1 416 763 2360

Services/Products:
List services; Lettershop; Fulfilment
and sampling house; Database services

Member of:
CMA

LOWE RMP DIRECT
22 St Clair Av E.
14th Floor
Toronto
ON
M4T 2S3
Canada
Tel: +1 416 260 4772
Fax: +1 416 975 8534
Email: coish@rochemacaulay.com
Peter Coish, V P General Manager

Services/Products:
Advertising Agency; Database services

Member of:
FEDMA

MACLAREN MCCANN DIRECT
10 Bay Street
Toronto
ON
M5J 2S3
Canada
Tel: +1 416 594 6000
Fax: +1 416 643 7020
Kay Ganser, EVP & General Manager

Services/Products:
Advertising Agency; Direct Response
Agency

Member of:
DMA (US)

MAIL-O-MATIC SERVICES
2720 South Ingleton Avenue
Burnaby
BC
V5C 5X4
Canada
Tel: +1 604 439 9668
Fax: +1 604 439 9609
Ken Frew, President

Services/Products:
List services; Mailing/Faxing services

Member of:
CMA

MAILING INNOVATIONS LIMITED
3397 American Drive
Unit #20
Mississauga
ON
L4V 1T8
Canada
Tel: +1 905 677 4441
Fax: +1 905 677 4480

Services/Products:
List services; Lettershop; Fulfilment
and sampling house; Database service

Member of:
CMA

MAILMARKETING CORPORATION
4075 Gordon Baker Road
Scarborough
ON
M1W 2P4
Canada
Tel: +1 416 490 8030
Fax: +1 416 490 8455

Services/Products:
List services; Lettershop; Fulfilment
and sampling house; Database service

Member of:
CMA

MC DIRECT
200 Consumers Road
Ste 240
Toronto
ON
M2K 4R4
Canada
Tel: +1 416 493 5401
Fax: +1 416 493 6846
John Besterd, President

Services/Products:
Advertising Agency; Direct Response
Agency

Member of:
DMA (US)

MEDIA EXPRESS
1134 St. Catherine Street W.
Ste 101
Montreal
QC
H3B 1H4
Canada
Tel: +1 800 563 6655
Fax: +1 514 876 8746
Claude Cohen, Chief Executive Officer

Services/Products:
Telemarketing agency

Member of:
DMA (US)

MEDIA SERVICE
CORPORATION
7800 Whipple Avenue NW
North Canton
OH
44720
Canada
Tel: +1 330 487 6866
Fax: +1 330 497 6838

Services/Products:
List services; Lettershop; Fulfilment
and sampling house; Database services

Member of:
CMA

MEDIA SYNERGY INC.
260 King Street East
Building C
Toronto
ON
M5A 1K3
Canada
Tel: +1 416 369 1100
Fax: +1 416 369 9037
Craig Rennick, VP, Sales

Services/Products:
List services

Member of:
DMA (US)

MEDIAIR DIRECT MAIL
SERVICES
45 Comstock Road
Scarborough
ON
M1L 2G6
Canada
Tel: +1 416 288 8800
Fax: +1 416 288 8881

Services/Products:
List services; Lettershop; Fulfilment
and sampling house; Database services

Member of:
CMA

MEDIAMIX MARKETING
GROUP INC.
1–1885 Meyerside Drive
Mississauga
ON
L5T 1G7
Canada
Tel: +1 905 795 0930
Fax: +1 905 795 0932
Brad Robinson, General Manager

Services/Products:
Lettershop; Mailing/Faxing services

Member of:
DMA (US); CMA

MICROMEDIA LIMITED
20 Victoria Street
Toronto
ON
M5C 2N8
Canada
Tel: +1 416 362 5211
Fax: +1 416 362 6161

Services/Products:
List services; Lettershop; Fulfilment
and sampling house; Database services

Member of:
CMA

MLS COMPUTER SERVICES
2200 Yonge Street
Suite 910
Toronto
ON
M4S 2C6
Canada
Tel: +1 416 480 1747
Fax: +1 416 480 1513
Dale Pye, General Manager

Services/Products:
Database services

Member of:
CMA

MOKRYNSKI & ASSOCIATES
INC.
401 Hackensack Ave
2nd Floor
Hackensack
NJ
7601
Canada
Tel: +1 201 488 5656
Fax: +1 201 488 2808

Services/Products:
List services; Lettershop; Fulfilment
and sampling house; Database services

Member of:
CMA

MOORE BUSINESS
COMMUNICATION SERVICE
350 Britannia Road East
Mississauga
ON
L4Z 2H1
Canada
Tel: +1 905 890 1534
Fax: +1 905 890 5282
Gord Angus, Marketing Manager

Services/Products:
List services; Database services; Print
services; Loyalty systems

Member of:
CMA

MULTIACTIVE DATA INC.
1066 West Hastings Street
3rd Floor
Vancouver
BC
V6E 3X1
Canada
Tel: +1 604 899 6400
Fax: +1 604 899 6499

Services/Products:
List services; Lettershop; Fulfilment
and sampling house; Database services

Member of:
CMA

MVC ASSOCIATES
INTERNATIONAL
36 Toronto Street
Ste 850
Toronto
ON
M5C 2C5
Canada
Tel: +1 416 489 1917
Fax: +1 416 489 2573
Mark Van Clieaf, Managing Director

Services/Products:
Marketing consultant

Member of:
DMA (US)

NCH PROMOTIONAL
SERVICES LTD.
160 McNabb Street
Markham
ON
L3R 4B8
Canada
Tel: +1 905 475 3449
Fax: +1 905 475 6244

Services/Products:
List services; Lettershop; Fulfilment
and sampling house; Database services

Member of:
CMA

OGILVYONE WORLDWIDE
33 Yonge Street
Toronto
ON
M5E 1X6
Canada
Tel: +1 416 363 9514
Fax: +1 416 363 7736

Services/Products:
Advertising Agency; Direct Response
Agency

Member of:
DMA (US)

OMEGA DIRECT RESPONSE INC.
5255 Yonge Street
North York
ON
M2N 6P4
Canada
Tel: +1 416 733 9911
Fax: +1 416 733 8202
Bharat Hansraj, President

Services/Products:
Advertising Agency; Direct Response
Agency

Member of:
DMA (US)

ONE TO ONE COMMUNICATIONS
1920 Yonge Street
Toronto
ON
M4S 3E4
Canada
Tel: +1 416 487 9393
Fax: +1 416 487 4668
Heather MacPherson, President

Services/Products:
Advertising Agency; Direct Response
Agency

Member of:
DMA (US)

OPTUS CORPORATION
66 Northline Road
Toronto
ON
M4B 3E5
Canada
Tel: +1 416 752 6941
Fax: +1 416 752 9437

Services/Products:
List services; Lettershop; Fulfilment
and sampling house; Database services

Member of:
CMA

PANCONTINENTAL EQUITY CORPORATION
700, 340–12 Avenue S.W.
Calgary
AB
T2R 1L5
Canada
Tel: +1 403 263 7337
Fax: +1 403 263 5791
Patricia Hardy, Vice President,
Marketing

Services/Products:
Marketing consultant

Member of:
DMA (US)

PARKS PRODUCTIONS LTD.
240 Cordova Road
Oshawa
ON
L1J 1K6
Canada
Tel: +1 905 436 1142
Fax: +1 905 436 8944

Services/Products:
List services; Lettershop; Fulfilment
and sampling house; Database services

Member of:
CMA

PHONETTIX INTELECOM LTD.
40 Dundas Street West
Ste 300
Toronto
ON
M5G 2C2
Canada
Tel: +1 416 340 2300
Fax: +1 416 340 2000
Dorothy Millman, President

Services/Products:
Telemarketing agency

Member of:
DMA (US); CMA

POSTAL PROMOTIONS LIMITED
1100 Birchmount Road
Scarborough
ON
M1K 5H9
Canada
Tel: +1 416 752 8100
Fax: +1 416 752 8239
Frank Mangialardi, VP, Sales &
Marketing

Services/Products:
Lettershop; Mailing/Faxing services

Member of:
DMA (US); CMA

POSTEHASTE SYSTEMS
6010 Tomken Road
Unit B
Mississauga
ON
L5T 1X8
Canada
Tel: +1 905 670 5300
Fax: +1 905 670 2396

Services/Products:
List services; Lettershop; Fulfilment
and sampling house; Database services

Member of:
CMA

PRAIRIE ADVERTISING
588–1st Avenue East
Regina
SK
S4N 5T6
Canada
Tel: +1 306 721 4330
Fax: +1 306 721 4626

Services/Products:
List services; Lettershop; Fulfilment
and sampling house; Database services

Member of:
CMA

PRIDE MARKETING GROUP
33 Crerar Avenue
Welland
ON
L3C 2Z2
Canada
Tel: +1 905 714 1500
Fax: +1 905 714 1555

Services/Products:
List services; Lettershop; Fulfilment
and sampling house; Database services

Member of:
CMA

PRISM DATA SERVICES LTD.
2–425 Horner Avenue
Etobicoke
ON
M8W 4W3
Canada
Tel: +1 416 255 5556
Fax: +1 416 255 1466
Ron Joiner, General Manager

Services/Products:
List services

Member of:
DMA (US)

PROJECT BY PROJECT
172 Manitoba Street
Toronto
ON
M8Y 1E3
Canada
Tel: +1 416 252 7062
Fax: +1 416 252 9580
Sandi Ruffo, President

Services/Products:
Advertising Agency; Direct Response
Agency

Member of:
DMA (US)

PROMO LASER INC.
9625 Ignace
Brossard
QC
J4Y 2P3
Canada
Tel: +1 450 444 5000
Fax: +1 450 444 1365

Services/Products:
List services; Lettershop; Fulfilment
and sampling house; Database services

Member of:
CMA

PROSPECTS UNLIMITED
330 Front Street West
Ste 1100
Toronto
ON
M5V 3B7
Canada
Tel: +1 416 581 1273
Fax: +1 416 581 0258
Nancy Sprague, President

Services/Products:
List services

Member of:
DMA (US); CMA

PUBLICIS DIALOG LIMITED
300 Leo-Pariseau
Montreal
QC
H2W 2N1
Canada
Tel: +1 514 285 1414
Fax: +1 514 285 2400
Fred Kuys, Chief Executive Officer

Services/Products:
Advertising Agency; Direct Response
Agency

Member of:
DMA (US)

QUANTUM FAX COMMUNICATIONS
500 Lawrence Ave. W.
Box 54112
Toronto
ON
M6A 3B7
Canada
Tel: +1 416 247 3491
Fax: +1 416 247 3483

Services/Products:
Mailing/Faxing services

Member of:
CMA

QUINN DATA SERVICES INC.
5610 Timberlea Blvd
Mississauga
ON
L4W 4M6
Canada
Tel: +1 905 206 1100
Fax: +1 905 206 1766
Norm Woods, Director of Sales &
Marketing

Services/Products:
Lettershop; Telemarketing agency;
Direct marketing agency

Member of:
CMA

RAPP COLLINS COMMUNICAIDE
50 Burnhamthorpe Road West
5th Fl
Mississauga
ON
L5B 3C2
Canada
Tel: +1 905 281 2424
Fax: +1 905 281 1304
G. Steven Dapper, Chairman & CEO

Services/Products:
Advertising Agency; Direct Response
Agency

Member of:
DMA (US); CMA

RESEARCH AND RESPONSE INTERNATIONAL INC.
P.O. Box 8660
Station A
36 Austin Street
St. John's
NF
A1B 3T7
Canada
Tel: +1 709 722 8500

Fax: +1 709 722 2228

Services/Products:
List services; Lettershop; Fulfilment
and sampling house; Database services

Member of:
CMA

RESPONSE SYSTEMS INTERNATIONAL (CANADA) LTD.
111 Richmond Street West
Ste 1100
Toronto
ON
M5H 2G4
Canada
Tel: +1 416 367 8276
Fax: +1 416 368 8631
Mel Gottlieb, Chairman

Services/Products:
Marketing consultant

Member of:
DMA (US)

ROSS ROY COMMUNICATIONS
1737 Walker Road
P.O. Box 2235
Windsor
ON
N8Y 4R8
Canada
Tel: +1 519 258 7584
Fax: +1 519 258 4242
Shel Green, VP & Service Line
Manager Dir.

Services/Products:
Advertising Agency; Direct Response
Agency

Member of:
DMA (US)

ROYAL ENVELOPE
111 Jacob Keffer Pkwy
Concord
ON
L4K 4V1
Canada
Tel: +1 905 879 0000
Fax: +1 905 879 0156
Peter Bowles, President

Services/Products:
Labelling/envelope services

S.I.R. MAIL ORDER
1385 Ellice Aveue
Winnipeg
MB
R3G 3N1
Canada
Tel: +1 204 788 4867

Fax: +1 204 786 8964
Email: sir@sirmailorder.ca
Web: www.sirmailorder.ca
Gerald Zak, Marketing Director

Services/Products:
Mail order and retail sports store

Member of:
National DMA; CMA

SMR MARKETING
201 Carlaw Avenue
Ste 200
Toronto
ON
M4M 2S3
Canada
Tel: +1 416 461 9271
Fax: +1 416 461 9201
Rich Richardson, President

Services/Products:
Lettershop; Mailing/Faxing services

Member of:
DMA (US)

SOUTHAM MAGAZINE GROUP LIMITED
1450 Don Mills Road
Don Mills
ON
M3B 2X7
Canada
Tel: +1 416 445 6641
Fax: +1 416 442 2261

Services/Products:
List services; Lettershop; Fulfilment
and sampling house; Database services

Member of:
CMA

STEPHEN THOMAS
2383 Queen Street East
Toronto
ON
M4E 1H5
Canada
Tel: +1 416 690 8801
Fax: +1 416 690 7256
Email: mail@stephenthomas.ca
Web: www.stephenthomas.ca

Services/Products:
Advertising Agency; Consultancy
services; Direct marketing agency; List
services; Not for profit direct response
fund raising specialist

E-Services:
E-Marketing consultant

Member of:
National DMA

STRAND COMMUNICATIONS
40 Castle Knock Road
Toronto
ON
M5N 2J4
Canada
Tel: +1 416 482 5125
Fax: +1 416 482 6313

Services/Products:
List services; Lettershop; Fulfilment
and sampling house; Database services

Member of:
CMA

STS SYSTEMS
2600 Trans-Canada
Pointe-Claire
PQ
H9A 3A8
Canada
Tel: +1 514 426 0822
Fax: +1 514 426 2556
Danielle Silverman, Mgr., Mktg. &
  Communications

Services/Products:
List services

Member of:
DMA (US)

SUPREMEX DIRECT
7355 Notre Dame East
Montreal
QC
H1N 3S7
Canada
Tel: +1 877 251 7355
Fax: +1 877 251 7356
Henri Gaumond, GM, U.S. Sales
  Development

Services/Products:
Labelling/envelope services

Member of:
DMA (US)

TAMARACK CREEK CORPORATE COMMUNICATIONS
19314 County Road ~24
Dunvegan
ON
K0C 1J0
Canada
Tel: +1 613 527 1201
Fax: +1 613 527 3164
Email: tamarack@tam-creek.ca
Web: www.tam-creek.ca

Services/Products:
Copy adaptation; Design/graphics/clip
art supplier; Direct marketing agency;
Lettershop; Sales Collateral; Design &

Production

E-Services:
Website design

Member of:
CMA

TDC DIRECT
1030 Lorimar Drive
Mississauga
ON
L5R 1R8
Canada
Tel: +1 905 564 6616
Fax: +1 905 564 6621

Services/Products:
List services; Lettershop; Fulfilment
and sampling house; Database services

Member of:
CMA

TELEPERFORMANCE CANADA
465 Bloor Street East
Box 46
Toronto
ON
M4W 3L4
Canada
Tel: +1 416 922 3519
Fax: +1 416 922 7830
Erifili Morfidis, President & Managing
  Director

Services/Products:
Database services; Telemarketing
agency

Member of:
CMA

TELEPHONE COMMUNICATORS CANADA LIMITED
The Market House
106 Front Street East
Suite 303
Toronto
ON
M5A 1E1
Canada
Tel: +1 416 367 5255
Fax: +1 416 367 5999

Services/Products:
Telemarketing agency

Member of:
CMA

TELUS MARKETING SERVICES
112–28 Street SE
2nd Fl
Calgary
AB
T2A 6J9

Canada
Tel: +1 403 207 2100
Fax: +1 403 207 2139
Chris Beadle, VP, Marketing & Sales

Services/Products:
Telemarketing agency

Member of:
DMA (US)

THE FANEUIL GROUP
363 Broadway
Winnipeg
MB
R3C 3N9
Canada
Tel: +1 204 987 1800
Fax: +1 204 987 1820
Daniel Mahoney, SVP, Marketing

Services/Products:
Telemarketing agency

Member of:
DMA (US); CMA

THE MINACS GROUP INC.
915 Sandy Beach Road
Pickering
ON
L1W 1Z5
Canada
Tel: +1 905 837 6000
Fax: +1 905 837 1873
Meda Mitchell, Director, Marketing &
  Sales

Services/Products:
Telemarketing agency

Member of:
DMA (US)

THE PENTE CORPORATION
250 The Esplanade
The Keep
Toronto
ON
M5A 1J2
Canada
Tel: +1 416 214 2014
Fax: +1 416 214 1202

Services/Products:
List services; Lettershop; Fulfilment
and sampling house; Database services

Member of:
CMA

**THE PROFESSIONAL
  COMPUTER GROUP INC.**
4075 Gordon Baker Road
Suite 101
Toronto
ON
M1W 2P4

Canada
Tel: +1 416 492 4366
Fax: +1 416 492 2427

Services/Products:
List services; Lettershop; Fulfilment
and sampling house; Database services

Member of:
CMA

**THE YORKVILLE PRINTING
  GROUP LIMITED**
8 Tidemore Avenue
Etobicoke
ON
M9W 5H4
Canada
Tel: +1 416 741 1900
Fax: +1 416 401 2222

Services/Products:
Print services

Member of:
CMA

**TRANSCONTINENTAL
  PRINTING INC.**
395 Lebeau Blvd
St. Laurent
QC
H4N 1S2
Canada
Tel: +1 514 337 8560
Fax: +1 514 339 2240

Services/Products:
Print services

Member of:
CMA

TROI MAILING SERVICES INC.
16–445 Midwest Road
Toronto
ON
M1P 4Y9
Canada
Tel: +1 416 757 5598
Fax: +1 416 757 4232
Email: troimail@troimail.com
Web: www.troimail.com
Kirk Barton, President

Services/Products:
Lettershop; Print services; Mailing/
Faxing services; Database services;
Fulfilment and sampling house;
Labelling/envelope services

**TRUE NORTH LIST
  MARKETING, LLC.**
755 Main Street
Building 2
Monroe
CT

6468
Canada
Tel: +1 203 459 4348
Fax: +1 203 459 4350

Services/Products:
List services; Lettershop; Fulfilment
and sampling house; Database services

Member of:
CMA

TYCHO & CLAY DESIGN
8626 Saffron Place
Burnaby
V5A 4H9
Canada
Tel: +1 604 609 3353
Fax: +1 604 421 4155
Brian Tycho, Partner

Services/Products:
Creative consultant

Member of:
DMA (US)

UPSHOT INTEGRATED INC.
174 West Beaver Creek Road
Richmond Hill
ON
L4B 1B4
Canada
Tel: +1 416 494 6245
Fax: +1 905 771 9349
Email: sales@yourmail.com
Web: www.yourmail.com

Services/Products:
Labelling/envelope services;
Lettershop; Service bureau; Database
services; Mailing/Faxing services;
Personalisation

E-Services:
Website design

Member of:
National DMA

VAL-PAK OF CANADA LIMITED
40 Wynford Drive
Suite 301
Don Mills
ON
M3C 1J5
Canada
Tel: +1 416 510 5001
Fax: +1 416 510 5002

Services/Products:
List services; Lettershop; Fulfilment
and sampling house; Database services

Member of:
CMA

VICKERS & BENSON
1920 Yonge Street
Toronto
ON
M4S 3E4
Canada
Tel: +1 416 487 6446
Fax: +1 416 487 4668
Heather MacPherson, President

Services/Products:
Advertising Agency; Direct Response
Agency

Member of:
DMA (US)

VISION QUEBEC
380 St. Antoine St. W.
Suite 7900
Montreal
QC
H2Y 3X7
Canada
Tel: +1 514 288 2666
Fax: +1 514 288 6800
Diane Jeannotte, Marketing Support

Services/Products:
Call centre services/systems; Training/
recruitment; Assistance in the areas of
real estate/technology/government
grant obtainment

Member of:
DMA

VISTA MAIL INTERNATIONAL INC.
390 Millen Road
Stoney Creek
ON
L8E 2P7
Canada
Tel: +1 905 662 4733
Fax: +1 905 662 3252
Lou Cafolla, General Manager

Services/Products:
Fulfilment and sampling house

Member of:
DMA (US)

VOXDATA
1000 Sherbrooke West
23rd Fl
Montreal
QC
H3A 1G4
Canada
Tel: +1 514 281 1920
Fax: +1 514 281 2036
France Couture, President

Services/Products:
Telemarketing agency

Member of:
DMA (US)

WATTS AJ MARKETING LTD.
115A Chambers Drive
Ajax
ON
L1Z 1E2
Canada
Tel: +1 905 619 2353
Fax: +1 905 619 2456

Services/Products:
List services; Lettershop; Fulfilment
and sampling house; Database services

Member of:
CMA

WATTS DIRECT MARKETING SERVICES LTD.
455 Horner Avenue
Toronto
ON
M8W 4W9
Canada
Tel: +1 416 252 7741
Fax: +1 416 252 0037
Email: abrodeur@wattsgroup.com
Web: www.wattsgroup.com
Alan Brodeur, President

Services/Products:
Database services; Personalisation;
Fulfilment and sampling house;
Lettershop; List services;
Telemarketing agency

E-Services:
Email list provider; Email software

Member of:
DMA (US); National DMA; MASA;
NAMMU

WESTERN SHORES DIRECT MARKETING GROUP
1200 West Pender Street
Suite 200
Vancouver
BC
V6E 2S9
Canada
Tel: +1 604 681 4911
Fax: +1 604 687 4990

Services/Products:
List services; Lettershop; Fulfilment
and sampling house; Database
services

Member of:
CMA

WOOD & ASSOCIATES DIRECT MARKETING SERVICES LTD
450 Tapscott Road
Unit 1
Scarborough
ON
M1B 5W1
Canada
Tel: +1 416 293 2511
Fax: +1 416 293 2594

Services/Products:
List services; Lettershop; Fulfilment
and sampling house; Database service

Member of:
CMA

WORLD WIDE MAILERS
2744 Edna Street
Windsor
ON
N8Y 1V2
Canada
Tel: +1 519 254 6245
Fax: +1 519 254 2608
Sandra Meredith, President

Services/Products:
Lettershop; Mailing/Faxing services

Member of:
DMA (US); CMA

WUNDERMAN CATO JOHNSON
60 Bloor Street West
Ste 700
Toronto
ON
M5J 2R9
Canada
Tel: +1 416 324 2066
Karen Manion, Office Manager

Services/Products:
Advertising Agency; Direct Response
Agency

Member of:
DMA (US)

XENTEL DM INCORPORATED
417–14th Street North West
Suite 200
Calgary
AB
T2N 2A1
Canada
Tel: +1 800 661 0178
Fax: +1 403 270 4398

Services/Products:
List services; Lettershop; Fulfilment
and sampling house; Database
services

Member of:
CMA

YOUNG DIRECT MARKETING LTD.
505 Cochrane Drive
Markham
ON
L3R 8E3
Canada
Tel: +1 905 470 9298
Fax: +1 905 470 6411

Services/Products:
List services; Lettershop; Fulfilment and sampling house; Database services

Member of:
CMA

SERVICES/PRODUCT LISTING

Advertising Agency
BBDO Response
BCP Direct
Blitz Direct
Carlson Marketing Group
Chiat/Day Direct Marketing, Inc.
Cohn & Wells, Ltd.
CW Agencies
DKY Integrated Communications
DMP Direct Marketing Products Ltd.
Exclusive Communications Ltd.
FCB Direct
First Avenue
Gingko Direct Ltd.
Groupe RR International
Hughes Rapp Collins
Lowe RMP Direct
MacLaren McCann Direct
MC Direct
OgilvyOne Worldwide
Omega Direct Response Inc.
One To One Communications
project by project
Publicis Dialog Limited
Rapp Collins Communicaide
Ross Roy Communications
Stephen Thomas
Vickers & Benson
Wunderman Cato Johnson

Assistance in the areas of real estate/technology/government grant obtainment
Vision Quebec

Call centre services/systems
Herbert A Watts Ltd.
Vision Quebec

Consultancy services
Exclusive Communications Ltd.
Stephen Thomas

Copy adaptation
Tamarack Creek Corporate Communications

Creative consultant
Tycho & Clay Design

Database services
1:1 Inc.
Advantage Call Centre Solutions
AMW Direct
AON Direct Group
BDC Direct
Call Response
Canadian Direct Mailing Systems/ North American Printing
Canadian Healthcare Association
Cinram New Media Group
Communication & Mailing Service
Contact Marketing Inc.
Cornerstone
Corporate Mailing Services
Cover-All Direct Response Systems Ltd.
Data Focus – Division Of Data Business Forms
Data Insight Group
De Jong Enterprises Inc.
DirectWest Publishers
DocuLink International
Dolphin Direct Printing, Mailing & Data Systems Inc.
Era Direct Ltd.
Frontier Distributing
FSA Inc.
Grey Direct
Group 1 Software
Herbert A Watts Ltd.
Honderich Investments
I.C.S. Logistics/Alltour
I.M.S. – Inquiry Management Systems Ltd.
Indas Limited
Info Canada
Info Canada
Infoworks
Interactive Marketing Group ULC
Interad Media Design Corp.
Joncas Postexperts Inc.
Kaizen Media Services Inc.
Keycontact
Keystone Response Management
KnowledgeBase Marketing Inc.
Launch Direct
Lovell & Company Consulting
Lowe RMP Direct
Mailing Innovations Limited
MailMarketing Corporation
Media Service Corporation

Mediair Direct Mail Services
Micromedia Limited
MLS Computer Services
Mokrynski & Associates Inc.
Moore Business Communication Service
Multiactive Data Inc.
NCH Promotional Services Ltd.
Optus Corporation
Parks Productions Ltd.
Postehaste Systems
Prairie Advertising
Pride Marketing Group
Promo Laser Inc.
Research And Response International Inc.
Southam Magazine Group Limited
Strand Communications
TDC Direct
Teleperformance Canada
The PENTE Corporation
The Professional Computer Group Inc.
Troi Mailing Services Inc.
True North List Marketing, Llc.
Upshot Integrated Inc.
Val-Pak Of Canada Limited
Watts AJ Marketing Ltd.
Watts Direct Marketing Services Ltd.
Western Shores Direct Marketing Group
Wood & Associates Direct Marketing Services Ltd.
Xentel DM Incorporated
Young Direct Marketing Ltd.

Design & Production
Tamarack Creek Corporate Communications

Design/graphics/clip art supplier
Exclusive Communications Ltd.
HSH Group Of Companies
Tamarack Creek Corporate Communications

Direct Response Agency
BBDO Response
BCP Direct
Blitz Direct
Carlson Marketing Group
Chiat/Day Direct Marketing, Inc.
Cohn & Wells, Ltd.
CW Agencies
DKY Integrated Communications
DMP Direct Marketing Products Ltd.
First Avenue
Groupe RR International
Hughes Rapp Collins
MacLaren McCann Direct
MC Direct
OgilvyOne Worldwide

Omega Direct Response Inc.
One To One Communications
project by project
Publicis Dialog Limited
Rapp Collins Communicaide
Ross Roy Communications
Vickers & Benson
Wunderman Cato Johnson

Direct marketing agency
AMW Direct
Axis Database Marketing Group Inc.
Baker-Blais Marketing Inc.
Blakely Epton & Associates Inc.
Blitz Direct
Bradford Direct
Bruce Moore Russell–Direct Response
Carlson Marketing Group Consumer
    & Loyalty Marketing Division 3300
    Bloor Street
CD Direct
Contact Marketing Inc.
Contacts Target Marketing Inc.
CPC Loyalty Communications
Exclusive Communications Ltd.
FCB Direct Canada
Gingko Direct Ltd.
J R Direct Response International
Quinn Data Services Inc.
Stephen Thomas
Tamarack Creek Corporate
    Communications

Fulfilment and sampling house
1:1 Inc.
A&L Mailing Services Inc.
Access Canada
Actus Marketing Inc.
Advantage Call Centre Solutions
Arcas Group Inc.
Automated Fulfillment Systems
Avant Imaging & Information
    Management Inc.
BDP Business Data Services Limited
BDC Direct
B.J. Hunter Information
Bruce Moore Russell–Direct Response
Call Response
Campbell Abbot Laser Mail
Canadian Direct Mailing Systems/
    North American Printing
Canadian Healthcare Association
Cinram New Media Group
Communication & Mailing Service
Contact Marketing Inc.
Cornerstone
Corporate Mailing Services
Cover-All Direct Response Systems
    Ltd
Cover-All Direct Response Systems
    Ltd.
Data Focus – Division Of Data
    Business Forms

Data Insight Group
De Jong Enterprises Inc.
Dimark Marketing Services Inc.
DirectWest Publishers
DocuLink International
Dolphin Direct Printing, Mailing &
    Data Systems Inc.
Era Direct Ltd.
Extend Communications Inc.
Frontier Distributing
FSA Inc.
Grey Direct
Group 1 Software
Herbert A Watts Ltd.
Honderich Investments
I.C.S. Logistics/Alltour
I.M.S. – Inquiry Management Systems
    Ltd.
Info Canada
Interactive Marketing Group ULC
Interad Media Design Corp.
Joncas Postexperts Inc.
Kaizen Media Services Inc.
Keycontact
Keystone Response Management
KnowledgeBase Marketing Inc.
Launch Direct
Lovell & Company Consulting
Mailing Innovations Limited
MailMarketing Corporation
Media Service Corporation
Mediair Direct Mail Services
Micromedia Limited
Mokrynski & Associates Inc.
Multiactive Data Inc.
NCH Promotional Services
    Ltd.
Optus Corporation
Parks Productions Ltd.
Postehaste Systems
Prairie Advertising
Pride Marketing Group
Promo Laser Inc.
Research And Response International
    Inc.
Southam Magazine Group Limited
Strand Communications
TDC Direct
The PENTE Corporation
The Professional Computer Group
    Inc.
Troi Mailing Services Inc.
True North List Marketing, Llc.
Val-Pak Of Canada Limited
Vista Mail International Inc.
Watts AJ Marketing Ltd.
Watts Direct Marketing Services Ltd.
Western Shores Direct Marketing
    Group
Wood & Associates Direct Marketing
    Services Ltd.
Xentel DM Incorporated
Young Direct Marketing Ltd.

Internet services
Click Media Inc.

Labelling/envelope services
Grant's Mailing Services Inc.
Herbert A Watts Ltd.
Royal Envelope
Supremex Direct
Troi Mailing Services Inc.
Upshot Integrated Inc.

Lettershop
1:1 Inc.
A&L Mailing Services Inc.
A.M. Stone Direct Mail Services
Access Canada
Advantage Call Centre Solutions
Arcas Group Inc.
Arrow Canadian Mailing Services
Avant Imaging & Information
    Management Inc.
B.J. Hunter Information
Bassett Direct
BDP Business Data Services Limited
Boss Communications Corp.
Bradford Direct
Bruce Moore Russell–Direct Response
Call Response
Campbell Abbot Laser Mail
Canadian Direct Mailing Systems/
    North American Printing
Canadian Healthcare Association
CD Direct
Cinram New Media Group
Communication & Mailing Service
Cornerstone
Corporate Mailing Services
Cover-All Direct Response Systems
    Ltd
Cover-All Direct Response Systems
    Ltd.
Data Focus – Division Of Data
    Business Forms
Data Insight Group
De Jong Enterprises Inc.
DirectWest Publishers
DocuLink International
Dolphin Direct Printing, Mailing &
    Data Systems Inc.
Era Direct Ltd.
Frontier Distributing
FSA Inc.
Globel Direct Marketing
Grey Direct
Group 1 Software
Herbert A Watts Ltd.
Honderich Investments
I.C.S. Logistics/Alltour
I.M.S. – Inquiry Management Systems
    Ltd.
Info Canada
Interact Direct (London) Inc.
Interactive Marketing Group ULC

Interad Media Design Corp.
Joncas Postexperts Inc.
Jones Direct Marketing Services Ltd.
Kaizen Media Services Inc.
Key Mail Canada Inc.
Keycontact
Keystone Response Management
KnowledgeBase Marketing Inc.
Launch Direct
Livingston International Inc.
Lovell & Company Consulting
Mailing Innovations Limited
MailMarketing Corporation
Media Service Corporation
Mediair Direct Mail Services
Mediamix Marketing Group Inc.
Micromedia Limited
Mokrynski & Associates Inc.
Multiactive Data Inc.
NCH Promotional Services Ltd.
Optus Corporation
Parks Productions Ltd.
Postal Promotions Limited
Postehaste Systems
Prairie Advertising
Pride Marketing Group
Promo Laser Inc.
Quinn Data Services Inc.
Research And Response International
    Inc.
SMR Marketing
Southam Magazine Group Limited
Strand Communications
Tamarack Creek Corporate
    Communications
TDC Direct
The PENTE Corporation
The Professional Computer Group
    Inc.
Troi Mailing Services Inc.
True North List Marketing, Llc.
Upshot Integrated Inc.
Val-Pak Of Canada Limited
Watts AJ Marketing Ltd.
Watts Direct Marketing Services Ltd.
Western Shores Direct Marketing
    Group
Wood & Associates Direct Marketing
    Services Ltd.
World Wide Mailers
Xentel DM Incorporated
Young Direct Marketing Ltd.

List services

1:1 Inc.
Advantage Call Centre Solutions
AXCIOM/Direct Media
Call Response
Canadian Direct Mailing Systems/
    North American Printing
Canadian Healthcare Association
Cinram New Media Group
Communication & Mailing Service

Communications Real Laforte Inc.
Contact Marketing Inc.
Contacts Target Marketing Inc.
Cornerstone
Corporate Mailing Services
Cover-All Direct Response Systems
    Ltd.
Data Focus – Division Of Data
    Business Forms
Data Insight Group
De Jong Enterprises Inc.
Direct Media Canada Inc.
DirectWest Publishers
DocuLink International
Dolphin Direct Printing, Mailing &
    Data Systems Inc.
Era Direct Ltd.
Frontier Distributing
FSA Inc.
GETKO Direct Response
Grey Direct
Group 1 Software
Honderich Investments
I.C.S. Logistics/Alltour
I.M.S. – Inquiry Management Systems
    Ltd.
ICOM
Info Canada
Info Canada
Infodirect
Interactive Marketing Group ULC
Interad Media Design Corp.
J R Direct Response International
Joncas Postexperts Inc.
Kaizen Media Services Inc.
Keycontact
Keystone Response Management
KnowledgeBase Marketing Inc.
Launch Direct
Lovell & Company Consulting
Mail-O-Matic Services
Mailing Innovations Limited
MailMarketing Corporation
Media Service Corporation
Media Synergy Inc.
Mediair Direct Mail Services
Micromedia Limited
Mokrynski & Associates Inc.
Moore Business Communication
    Service
Multiactive Data Inc.
NCH Promotional Services Ltd.
Optus Corporation
Parks Productions Ltd.
Postehaste Systems
Prairie Advertising
Pride Marketing Group
Prism Data Services Ltd.
Promo Laser Inc.
Prospects Unlimited
Research And Response International
    Inc.
Southam Magazine Group Limited

Stephen Thomas
Strand Communications
STS Systems
TDC Direct
The PENTE Corporation
The Professional Computer Group
    Inc.
True North List Marketing, Llc.
Val-Pak Of Canada Limited
Watts AJ Marketing Ltd.
Watts Direct Marketing Services Ltd.
Western Shores Direct Marketing
    Group
Wood & Associates Direct Marketing
    Services Ltd.
Xentel DM Incorporated
Young Direct Marketing Ltd.

Loyalty systems
Moore Business Communication
    Service

Mail order and retail sports store
S.I.R. Mail Order

Mailing/Faxing services
A&L Mailing Services Inc.
A.M. Stone Direct Mail Services
Arrow Canadian Mailing Services
Boss Communications Corp.
Central Canada Telemanagement
Globel Direct Marketing
Grant's Mailing Services Inc.
Herbert A Watts Ltd.
HSH Group Of Companies
Indas Limited
Interact Direct (London) Inc.
Jones Direct Marketing Services Ltd.
Key Mail Canada Inc.
Livingston International Inc.
Mail-O-Matic Services
Mediamix Marketing Group Inc.
Postal Promotions Limited
Quantum Fax Communications
SMR Marketing
Troi Mailing Services Inc.
Upshot Integrated Inc.
World Wide Mailers

Market research agency
AON Direct Group
HSH Group Of Companies
Kubas Consultants

Marketing consultant
Checkmate Marketing Ltd.
Exclusive Communications Ltd.
KPMG National Consulting
MVC Associates International
Pancontinental Equity Corporation

Response Systems International
(Canada) Ltd.
Stephen Thomas

Media buying agency
DKY Integrated Communications
Exclusive Communications Ltd.

**Not for profit direct response
fund raising specialist**
Stephen Thomas

Personalisation
A.M. Stone Direct Mail Services
Bassett Direct
Upshot Integrated Inc.
Watts Direct Marketing Services Ltd.

Print services
A.M. Stone Direct Mail Services
Bassett Direct
Campbell Abbot Laser Mail
CD Direct
Cover-All Direct Response Systems
Ltd
Moore Business Communication
Service
The Yorkville Printing Group Limited
Transcontinental Printing Inc.
Troi Mailing Services Inc.

Private delivery services
Access Canada
KPN/InterPost North America

Response analysis bureau
AON Direct Group

Cover-All Direct Response Systems
Ltd

Sales Collateral
Tamarack Creek Corporate
Communications

Sales promotion agency
Actus Marketing Inc.
Blitz Direct
Exclusive Communications Ltd.
Gingko Direct Ltd.
HSH Group Of Companies

Service bureau
J R Direct Response International
JSI Data Systems Limited
Upshot Integrated Inc.

Telemarketing agency
Actus Marketing Inc.
Alliance Call Centre Services Inc.
AMW Direct
Assertive Marketing Services Inc.
Automated Fulfillment Systems
BDC Direct
Central Canada Telemanagement
Extend Communications Inc.
GWE Group Inc.
HSH Group Of Companies
Media Express
Phonettix Intelecom Ltd.
Quinn Data Services Inc.
Teleperformance Canada
Telephone Communicators Canada
Limited
TELUS Marketing Services

The Faneuil Group
The Minacs Group Inc.
Voxdata
Watts Direct Marketing Services Ltd.

Training/recruitment
Vision Quebec

E-SERVICES

E-Marketing consultant
Exclusive Communications Ltd.
Stephen Thomas

Email list provider
Herbert A Watts Ltd.
Watts Direct Marketing Services Ltd.

Email software
Watts Direct Marketing Services Ltd.

Online/e-marketing agency
Exclusive Communications Ltd.
FCB Direct

Website design
Click Media Inc.
Exclusive Communications Ltd.
Herbert A Watts Ltd.
HSH Group Of Companies
Tamarack Creek Corporate
Communications
Upshot Integrated Inc.

UNITED STATES OF
AMERICA

Population: 269.4 million

Capital: Washington DC

Languages: English (although certain states, including Florida and California, have significant Spanish-speaking communities)

GDP: $7434 billion

GDP per capita: $27,590

Inflation: 2.3 per cent

Currency: US Dollar ($) = 100 cents

Exchange rate: £1 : $1.63

Time: GMT –5 hours to –11 hours
(New York, Washington DC –5 hours;
Los Angeles –8 hours)

OVERVIEW

The sheer size of the US market is one of the principal barriers to entry for most prospective direct mailers. Where do you start to look for a toehold in a market of nearly 270 million consumers? Having taken a decision, the marketer will immediately discover that the laws affecting direct marketing vary greatly from state to state. The US may be the world's largest homogeneous market, but local lifestyles, shopping habits and business practices change dramatically as you move across the continent.

Given these complicating factors, the US still offers the irresistible combination of a vast population of proven DM shoppers, and a highly sophisticated and cost-efficient DM supplier market.

It is not an arena for the faint-hearted. Test mailings in the US would represent a major campaign for many European markets. The potential, however, is breathtaking – as are, in many cases, the competition and the investment.

The US Direct Marketing Association's Statistical Fact Book 1998 is one of the most thorough analyses of the American DM market, and is essential reading for anyone considering a campaign in the US, or simply wanting to understand the dynamics of the world's most sophisticated DM market. It provides statistics on the size and range of the market, as well as an analysis of consumer attitudes towards direct marketing.

DMA statistics reveal that direct marketing sales in the United States exceeded $1.2 trillion (US) in 1997. Approximately $705 billion in direct marketing purchases were made by consumers and $554 billion were made by businesses.

LANGUAGE AND CULTURAL CONSIDERATIONS

Given the racial and social diversity of the American population, a DM campaign should usually be targeted at a specific group to be most effective. The language and cultural characteristics of the group should be taken into consideration; for example, a campaign aimed at the Hispanic population of Florida or California should be conducted in Spanish. This is where a local DM specialist or the US DMA should be able to advise.

LEGISLATION AND CONSUMER PROTECTION

The Direct Marketing Association's mailing preference service has been in operation since 1971, but pressure for legislation at both state and federal level is increasing, including a proposal to set up a Data Protection Board. So far the DMA's highly effective lobbying has kept restrictive measures at bay, but the Association urges all US marketers to adopt its own privacy guidelines, to subscribe to its mailing preference service, and create in-house suppression files.

THE DIRECT MARKETING ASSOCIATION

Name:	Direct Marketing Association Inc (DMA)
Address:	1120 Avenue of the Americas, New York, NY 10036-6700
Tel:	+1 212 768 7277
Fax:	+1 212 302 6714
Year founded:	1917
President:	H. Robert Weintzen
Senior member of staff:	Charles Prescott (Vice President, International Business Development and Government Affairs, ext 1552)
Total staff:	175
Members:	3900 in the USA and 500 overseas members in 53 other countries

398

Direct mail agencies	485	List brokers	166
Mailing houses	79	Printers	105
Direct mail consultants	268	Handling houses	49
Mail order companies	700	Telemarketing agencies	151

Facilities for overseas users of direct mail

Membership: overseas companies can join the DMA. There are no minimum standards set for membership, but companies will be evaluated according to their adherence to the DMA's ethical guidelines.

For members and non-members, the DMA sets the gold standard for service offered by any DM Association. Whatever the request – legal bulletins, market surveys or member lists – the DMA always produces impeccably researched and presented material.

Services open to members include:

Newsletter: the USDMA produces several newsletters, including:

- *DMA Insider* – members-only information from industry experts;
- *Washington Report* – a monthly legislative update (14 pages);
- *Bottom Line* – a quick read on trends, research and current events via e-mail.

Library: the USDMA library holds 700 books and some 36,000 articles.

On-line information service: the USDMA provides this service. There is a web site at http://www.the-dma.org

Other facilities:

- DMA conference calendar: a guide to the many specialist conferences and seminars sponsored by the DMA.
- Publications catalogue: a very detailed guide to over 60 specialist direct marketing titles.
- Members' Directory – subdivided by service sector, very thorough.
- Resource guides: specialist guides to DM techniques (postal rate strategies, business-to-business strategies). Some of the best practical guides ever produced on the medium.
- Some of the above services are available to non-members for a fee.

DIRECT MARKETING ASSOCIATION

NEW YORK – The Direct Marketing Association (The DMA) is the largest trade association in the world for businesses interested in interactive and database marketing. There are more than 5,000 member companies from the United States and 53 other nations from Europe, Asia, Africa, North and South America.

Founded in 1917, its members include direct marketers from every business segment as well as the non-profit and electronic marketing sectors. Included are catalogers, Internet retailers and service providers, financial services providers, book and magazine publishers, book and music clubs, retail stores, industrial manufacturers, telecommunications companies, and a host of other vertical segments including the service industries that support them. According to a DMA-commissioned study conducted by The WEFA Group, direct marketing sales in the United States exceeded $1.7 trillion in 2000. Approximately US$937 billion in direct marketing purchases were made by consumers in the U.S. and US$793 billion were made by U.S. businesses.

The DMA sponsors numerous conferences with delegates in attendance from over 50 countries including the DMA Annual Conference & Exhibition, Annual Catalog Conference & Exhibition, National Business Sales & Marketing Summit, National Center for Database Marketing, Global Direct Marketing Weekend, net.marketing conference & exhibition, Non-Profit Conference, Telephone Marketing Conference and Worldwide Business-to-Business Marketing Forum among others.

Through its Professional Development and Training Department, the DMA also annually conducts nearly 225 business training seminars in direct marketing basics, catalog essentials, fulfillment & customer service, insurance direct marketing, marketing to the mature marketplace and telephone training & coaching for consumer marketers. Furthermore, DMA teaches a business-to-business series which includes everything from basics and catalog creative critique to sales lead management and telesales management, among others.

As direct marketing has captured an ever increasing share of expenditures around the world, the DMA has developed the goal of helping members to enter new markets profitably, by developing programs and resources and by identifying and eliminating or, at least, mitigating the barriers. A new country by country profile in all major direct marketing markets around the world will give demographic and infrastructure information to enable a marketer to make an early decision about investigating that market.

The DMA's Library and Resource Center includes periodicals, direct mail samples, catalogs, video cassettes and samples of successful and award-winning marketing campaign portfolios. DirectLINK, the DMA's online database, provides an up-to-date electronic information resource with over 35,000 records available to DMA members 52 weeks a year.

The DMA Bookstore carries the most important book selections, directories, and research reports in the field. The DMA publishes a quarterly magazine, *The DMA Insider;* bi-weekly e-newsletter (*The DMA Bottom Line*) and more than 600 web pages of information at its continually updated website (*www.the-dma.org*).

The DMA International Department takes leadership in advancing the interests of the industry before the International Chamber of Commerce, the Organization for Economic Co-operation and Development, the European Commission, and, in concert with our Washington office, before the U.S. Congress and Executive agencies. In addition to answering specific questions of members on international business and markets, the Department prepares programs and conferences of specific interest to those members engaged in multinational aspects of direct marketing. Through its Itinerary Service, the Department also arranges meetings and company visits for non-U.S. members with executives and personnel from US member companies in any chosen field (i.e, lettershops, catalogs, agencies, etc.) This provides advantages for overseas executives who want to learn US techniques and operations or who may be investigating entry into the US marketplace.

The DMA publishes numerous consumer pamphlets that assist in the process of buying directly by mail, telephone or computer, including: *The Great Catalog Guide; Opening the Door to Opportunity: A Simple Guide to Understanding How Direct Marketers Use Information; Make Knowledge Your Partner in Mail or Telephone Order Shopping; Sweepstakes Advertising: A Consumer's Guide; and Shopping by Phone - A One-Stop Guide to Consumer Protection.*

The DMA sponsors four important consumer programs. The DMA's Mail Preference Service (MPS), established in 1971, enables people to reduce the volume of advertising mail they receive at home by having their names removed from many national mailing lists, including commercial and non-profit solicitations. The Telephone Preference Service (TPS), launched in 1985, offers consumers the same kind of name removal program for national telephone solicitation lists. In 2000, the DMA launched an email preference service (eMPS). The Mail Order Action Line (MOAL), also established in 1971, helps consumers who have unresolved problems with mail order transactions.

The DMA sponsors an extensive ethics program. The DMA Committee on Ethical Business Practice, a peer review committee, measures mailings and offerings against DMA-established ethics guidelines. The DMA Ethics Policy Committee analyzes consumer concerns about current marketing practices as new issues arise. It then translates the responses to these concerns into recommended operational guidelines, which it disseminates through its guidelines booklets: *DMA Guidelines for Ethical Business Practice, DMA Guidelines for Personal Information Protection, DMA Guidelines for Mailing List Practices, DMA Guidelines for Acceptance of Print Mail Order Advertising, DMA Guidelines for Acceptance of Direct Response Broadcast Advertising, DMA Guidelines for Marketing by Telephone and Online Privacy Principles and Guidance.*

DMA sponsors a yearly Global Symposium in which DMA leaders from around the world collaborate to advance and adhere to a set of self-regulatory principles that will help, collectively, to ensure continued direct marketing success internationally. Many DMAs from around the globe have signed a global convention of Mailing Preference Services, where each association agrees to exchange the Mail Preference Service lists of the respective nations. This enables marketers in other countries to conduct mail marketing campaigns into a foreign country, and remove the names of those consumers who have asked not to receive mail advertising offers in their homes. The group of participating DMAs have also agreed to establish self-regulatory principles of best practices for online marketing.

POSTAL SERVICES

The United States Postal Service (USPS) is a very active partner in the DM industry and provides assistance to those interested in tapping this large and potentially lucrative market. Today, the USPS delivers 180 billion pieces of mail a year to 123 million different homes and businesses in America. Advertising mail (or direct mail) makes up a significant portion of that total, including more than 65 billion pieces of third class and 11 billion pieces sent via first class mail.

In 1993, marketers spent well over US$25 billion on advertising through the mail, making it the fastest growing advertising medium in the country.

Direct mail advertising is well accepted in the United States. Studies have shown that a full 72 per cent of all mail received is considered useful or interesting by recipients. In addition, a large and dynamic direct marketing infrastructure exists to help companies profitably utilize the medium.

A variety of postal products and discount programmes are available to enable mailers to use the USPS more efficiently and effectively. Postage rates within the United States are among the lowest in the developed world. Mailers can reduce their costs even further by taking advantage of work-sharing discounts offered for presorting and/or drop-shipping mail to designated locations.

Services offered by USPS include:

- **PAVE (Presort Accuracy Verification and Evaluation):** programme which will test accuracy of presort software.
- **CASS (Coding Accuracy Support System):** improves accuracy of address information on automation mail
- **Automation:** mail processing system which works using barcodes, so that mail can be sorted extremely quickly. Using this service, and following USPS guidelines, means mailing discounts are quite substantial.
- **List correction services:** there are several of these available that will check and update mailing lists. Incorrect addresses can be identified and corrected, and new addresses of existing customers inputted.
- **Post-mail services including DM campaign analysis:** USPS can track the responses of your mailing as well as the handling enquiries. Results are measured to work out the success of your campaign. From this you can improve your mailing list, and increase the success of future campaigns.

USPS can also provide help when planning a DM campaign. Lists and links to professional organisations are available, as is a copy of the FTC mail order regulations, which includes rules and guidelines for advertising in the mail.

Mailers who claim presort or automation rates for First Class Mail must demonstrate that they have updated the addresses in their mailing lists within 180 days or 6 months prior to the mailing date. The four USPS-approved updating methods include:

- Address Change Service (ACS)
- National Change of Address (NCOA)
- FASTforward^{SM}
- Ancillary Service Endorsements that indicate the mailer's preference for a mailpiece's disposition.

For more information concerning USPS services, contact:

United States Postal Service
475 L'Enfant Plaza SW Room 5300
Washington DC 20260-2410
United States of America
Tel: +1 202 268 6531
Fax: +1 202 268 5211
Website: www.new.usps.com

PROVIDERS OF DM AND E-M SERVICES

21ST CENTURY MARKETING
1750 New Highway
Farmingdale
NY
11735
USA
Tel: +1 516 293 8550
Fax: +1 516 293 8974
David Schwartz, President

Services/Products:
List services

Member of:
DMA

360 GROUP
700 Fifth Avenue
San Rafael
CA
94901–3203
USA
Tel: +1 415 485 5478
Fax: +1 415 485 0939
Ted Shuel, President

Services/Products:
Advertising Agency; Direct Response
Agency

Member of:
DMA

800 DIRECT
8130 Remmet
Canoga Park
CA
91304
USA
Tel: 818 713 1092
Fax: +1 818 226 3691
Charles Ciarlo, President

Services/Products:
Telemarketing agency

Member of:
DMA

800 SUPPORT
18277 S.W. Boones Ferry Road
Ste 210
Portland
OR
97224–7600
USA
Tel: +1 503 684 2826
Fax: +1 503 639 3946
Randy Warren, President & CEO

Services/Products:
Telemarketing agency

Member of:
DMA

95 INFO
25 Deerwood West
Irvine
CA
92604
USA
Tel: +1 714 559 9361
Fax: +1 714 559 9361
David Yuan, President

Services/Products:
Telemarketing agency

Member of:
DMA

A. CALDWELL LIST COMPANY, INC.
4350 Georgetown Square
Ste 701
Atlanta
GA
30338–6219
USA
Tel: +1 800 241 7425
Fax: +1 770 458 4245
Joseph Lachnicht, President

Services/Products:
List services

Member of:
DMA

A. EICOFF & COMPANY
401 North Michigan Avenue
Chicago
IL
60611
USA
Tel: +1 312 527 7100
Fax: +1 312 527 7192
Carla Hendra, President, New York

Services/Products:
Advertising Agency; Direct Response
Agency

Member of:
DMA

A. H. DIRECT MARKETING, INC.
3936 Central Avenue
St Petersburg
FL
33711
USA
Tel: 813 327 5229
Fax: +1 813 327 5411
Anthony Hallock, President

Services/Products:
List services

Member of:
DMA

AB STUDIOS, INC.
807 Third Avenue South
Nashville
TN
37210
USA
Tel: +1 615 256 3393
Fax: +1 615 256 3464
Richard Arnemann, President

Services/Products:
Design/graphics/clip art supplier;
Consultancy services

Member of:
DMA

AB&C GROUP INC.
8400 Westpark Drive
Ste 100
McLean
VA
22101–3522
USA
Tel: +1 703 827 8377
Fax: +1 703 827 8385
David Himes, Executive Vice President

Services/Products:
Fulfilment and sampling house

Member of:
DMA

ABERDEEN MARKETING GROUP, INC.
2030 Powers Ferry Road
Ste 120
Atlanta
GA
30339
USA
Tel: +1 77 0 644 1850
Fax: +1 770 644 1865
Emery Ellinger, Chief Executive
Officer

Services/Products:
Advertising Agency; Direct Response
Agency

Member of:
DMA

ACACIA TELESERVICES INTERNATIONAL
270 Oakway Center
Eugene
OR
97401
USA
Tel: +1 541 484 5544
Fax: +1 541 465 9406
Larry Miller, General Manager

Services/Products:
Telemarketing agency

Member of:
DMA

ACCESS DIRECT SYSTEMS, INC.
91 Executive Boulevard
Farmingdale
NY
11735–4713
USA
Tel: +1 516 420 0770
Fax: +1 516 420 1647
Lori Messina, Executive Vice President

Services/Products:
Lettershop; Mailing/Faxing services

Member of:
DMA

ACCESS DIRECT TELEMARKETING
2738 Edgewood Road, S.W.
Ste 466
Cedar Rapids
IA
52404
USA
Tel: +1 319 390 8900
Fax: +1 319 390 8901
Tom Cardella, President

Services/Products:
Telemarketing agency

Member of:
DMA

ACI TELECENTRICS
3100 West Lake Street
Ste 300
Minneapolis
MN
55416–4510
USA
Tel: +1 612 928 4700
Fax: +1 612 928 4701
Gary Cohen, President

Services/Products:
Telemarketing agency

Member of:
DMA

ACORN INFORMATION SERVICES, INC.
4 Corporate Drive
Ste 288
Shelton
CT
06484–6241
USA
Tel: +1 203 319 7520

Fax: +1 203 319 7530
Venka t Sharma, Chief Executive
   Officer

Services/Products:
Advertising Agency; Direct Response
Agency

Member of:
DMA

ACP INTERACTIVE, LLC
150 Spear Street
Ste 700
San Francisco
CA
94105
USA
Tel: +1 415 357 5100
Fax: +1 415 357 5110
Camille Wehner, President

Services/Products:
Telemarketing agency

Member of:
DMA

ACS INC.
1807 Michael Faraday Court
Reston
VA
20190
USA
Tel: +1 703 742 9798
Fax: +1 703 742 3774
Ben Spaisman, President

Services/Products:
List services

Member of:
DMA

ACS/TRADEONE MARKETING
3 Maplewood Drive
Danbury
CT
06811–4200
USA
Tel: +1 203 792 7794
Shirley Sorrells, Sr. Dir., Incentives
   Division

Services/Products:
Advertising Agency; Direct Response
Agency

Member of:
DMA

ACT ONE MAILING LIST SERVICES, INC.
165 Pleasant Street, Ste 19
Village Plz 1
Marblehead
MA
01945–2308

USA
Tel: +1 781 639 1919
Fax: +1 781 639 2733
Email: actlist@ma.ultranet.com
Web: www.actonelists.com
Steven Cushinsky, President & CEO

Services/Products:
List services

E-Services:
Email list provider

Member of:
DMA (US)

ACTION MARKETING RESEARCH, INC.
314 Clifton Avenue
Ste 206
Minneapolis
MN
55403
USA
Tel: +1 612 879 9212
Fax: +1 612 879 9265
Jan Kihm, Senior Consultant

Services/Products:
Market research agency

Member of:
DMA

ACTON, INTERNATIONAL
4900 Highway 77 North
P.O. Box 5059
Lincoln
NE
68505–0059
USA
Tel: +1 402 466 8400
Fax: +1 402 466 9074
Jonathan Lambert, Chairman

Services/Products:
List services

Member of:
DMA

ACXIOM
P. O. Box 2000
Conway
AR
72033–2000
USA
Tel: +1 501 336 1000
Fax: +1 501 336 3913
Charles Morgan,
   Pres. & Chairman of the Board

Services/Products:
List services

Member of:
DMA

AD PLACEMENT SERVICES
8 Ridgedale Avenue
Cedar Knolls
NJ
7927
USA
Tel: 973 984 6700
Fax: +1 973 984 6757
Joe Pellegrino, Vice Preseident

Services/Products:
Advertising Agency; Direct Response
Agency

Member of:
DMA

AD TAPE & LABEL
N140 9504 Fountain Boulevard
Menomonee Falls
WI
53052
USA
Tel: +1 414 255 6150
Fax: +1 414 255 4301
Kris Collins, Director, Sales &
    Marketing

Services/Products:
List services

Member of:
DMA

ADDRESSING SERVICES
  COMPANY, INC.
88 Long Hill Street
East Hartford
CT
06108–1458
USA
Tel: 860 290 6655
Fax: +1 860 290 6661
Frank Failla, President

Services/Products:
Lettershop; Mailing/Faxing services

Member of:
DMA

ADISTRA
101 Union Street
Plymouth
MI
48170
USA
Tel: +1 313 425 2600
Fax: +1 313 416 5624
Michael Barga, VP & General Manager

Services/Products:
Lettershop; Mailing/Faxing services

Member of:
DMA

ADLER, BOSCHETTO,
  PEEBLES & PARTNERS
919 Third Avenue
New York
NY
10022–3902
USA
Tel: +1 212 684 5220
Fax: +1 212 684 0469
Beth Lipset, Account Management

Services/Products:
Advertising Agency; Direct Response
Agency

Member of:
DMA

ADMARK GROUP
318 Ponce De Leon Avenue
San Juan
PR
901
USA
Tel: +1 787 721 5050
Fax: +1 787 725 6067
Adolfo Soto, President & CEO

Services/Products:
Advertising Agency; Direct Response
Agency

Member of:
DMA

ADMERASIA
14 East 33rd Street
New York
NY
10016
USA
Tel: +1 212 686 3333
Fax: +1 212 686 8998
Alex Nakhapetian, Director, Direct
  Mail

Services/Products:
Advertising Agency; Direct Response
Agency

Member of:
DMA

ADMIRAL PACKAGING
10 Admiral Street
Providence
RI
2908
USA
Tel: +1 401 274 0320
Fax: +1 401 331 1910
Ann Pare, Sales Manager

Services/Products:
Labelling/envelope services

Member of:
DMA

ADREA RUBIN MARKETING,
  INC.
Adrea Rubin Management, Inc.
441 Lexington Avenue
9th Fl
New York
NY
10017
USA
Tel: +1 212 983 0020
Fax: +1 212 983 1057
Adrea Rubin, CEO

Services/Products:
List services

Member of:
DMA

ADRESAFE, INC.
3997 S Industrial
Las Vegas
NV
89103
USA
Tel: +1 702 796 2925
Fax: +1 702 796 2924
Jan Schollmeier, American Division
  Rep.

Services/Products:
List services

Member of:
DMA

ADRIAN MILLER DIRECT
  MARKETING
Telesales & Customer Service
  Consultants
43 Park Avenue
Port Washington
NY
11050
USA
Tel: +1 516 767 9288
Fax: +1 516 767 0702
Adrian Miller, President

Services/Products:
Marketing consultant

Member of:
DMA

ADSOUTH, INC.
1220 Compass Pointe Crossing
Alpharetta
GA
30005–8858
USA
Tel: +1 770 346 8600
Fax: +1 770 346 8601
Joe Marino, President

Services/Products:
Advertising Agency; Direct Response
Agency

Member of:
DMA

**ADVANCED COMPILATIONS
INC. (ACI)**
59 Wharf Street
Salem
MA
1970
USA
Tel: 978 7+44 5255
Fax: +1 978 744 1205
Charles Lundrigan, President

Services/Products:
List services

Member of:
DMA

ADVANCED DATA-COMM, INC.
700 Locust Street
Ste 300
Dubuque
IA
52001–6804
USA
Tel: +1 800 582 9501
Fax: +1 319 582 2003
Michael Budde, President & CEO

Services/Products:
Telemarketing agency

Member of:
DMA

**ADVANCED INTERACTIVE
MARKETING, INC.**
288 Walnut Street
Newton
MA
02460–1947
USA
Tel: +1 617 558 1131
Fax: +1 617 558 1141
Andrew Russo, Executive Vice
President

Services/Products:
Database services

Member of:
DMA

**ADVANCED RESPONSE
SYSTEMS**
7165 Boone Avenue North
Ste 150
Brooklyn Park
MN
55428–1512
USA

Tel: +1 612 533 5055
Fax: +1 612 533 9631
Wayne Reinking, President

Services/Products:
Lettershop; Mailing/Faxing services

Member of:
DMA

**ADVANCED TECHNOLOGY
MARKETING**
6053 W. Century Boulevard
P.O. Box 45028
Los Angeles
CA
90045–0028
USA
Tel: +1 310 342 2229
Fax: +1 310 337 0434
Mary Adams, President

Services/Products:
List services

Member of:
DMA (US); FEDMA

**ADVANCED TELEMARKETING
CORP.**
7880 Bent Branch Drive
Irving
TX
75063
USA
Tel: 972 830 1800
Fax: +1 972 830 1844
Edward Blank, Vice Chairman

Services/Products:
Telemarketing agency

Member of:
DMA

ADVANTAGE LINE
2218 4th Avenue West
Williston
ND
58801
USA
Tel: +1 701 774 4000
Fax: +1 701 774 2901
Mark Hardy, President

Services/Products:
Telemarketing agency

Member of:
DMA

**ADVANTAGE PLUS
MARKETING GROUP**
23181 Verdugo Drive
Ste 104-A
Laguna Hills
CA
92653

USA
Tel: +1 714 461 5800
Fax: +1 714 583 1700
Barry Lieberman, President

Services/Products:
Advertising Agency; Direct Response
Agency

Member of:
DMA

**ADVERTISING DISTRIBUTORS
OF AMERICA, INC.**
230 Adams Avenue
Hauppauge
NY
11788
USA
Tel: +1 516 231 5700
Fax: +1 516 434 1063
Dominick Iannaccone, President &
CEO

Services/Products:
Lettershop; Mailing/Faxing services

Member of:
DMA

**AEGIS COMMUNICATIONS
GROUP, INC.**
71 West 23rd Street
New York
NY
10010
USA
Tel: +1 212 807 3285
Fax: +1 212 807 3201
Edward Blank, Vice Chairman

Services/Products:
Telemarketing agency

Member of:
DMA

AFFINA CORPORATION
100 West Big Beaver Road
Ste 300
Troy
MI
48084
USA
Tel: +1 248 526 1200
Fax: +1 248 526 1250
Mark Entenman, Senior Vice President

Services/Products:
Market research agency

Member of:
DMA

AGA
Two Park Avenue
4th Fl
New York

NY
10016
USA
Tel: +1 212 726 7000
Fax: +1 212 726 7002
John Mathewson, President & CEO

Services/Products:
Advertising Agency; Direct Response
Agency

Member of:
DMA

AGE WAVE HOUSE SERVICES
2000 Powell Street
11th Fl
Emeryville
CA
94608–1804
USA
Tel: +1 510 601 7500
Fax: +1 510 601 6150
Bill Burkart, President

Services/Products:
Marketing consultant

Member of:
DMA

AGGRESSIVE LIST MANAGEMENT, INC.
18–5 East Dundee Road
Ste 300
Barrington
IL
60010
USA
Tel: +1 847 304 4030
Fax: +1 847 304 4032
Email: alminc1@aol.com
Kenneth Bieschke, President

Services/Products:
List services

Member of:
DMA (US)

AIM MARKETING
525 North D Street
P.O. Box 129
Fremont
NE
68025
USA
Tel: +1 402 721 2077
Fax: +1 402 721 9171
Nancy Johnson, Director, Sales &
Marketing

Services/Products:
Fulfilment and sampling house

Member of:
DMA

ALAMO DIRECT
280 Oser Avenue
Hauppauge
NY
11788–3610
USA
Tel: +1 516 231 7900
Fax: +1 516 231 7999
Walter Sosnowski, Senior Account
Executive

Services/Products:
Fulfilment and sampling house

Member of:
DMA

ALAN DREY COMPANIES
333 North Michigan Avenue
Chicago
IL
60601
USA
Tel: +1 312 346 7453
Fax: +1 312 346 5834
Alan Drey, Chairman & CEO

Services/Products:
List services

Member of:
DMA

ALANIZ AND SONS, INC.
501 North Iris Street
P.O. Box 799
Mount Pleasant
IA
52641
USA
Tel: +1 319 385 7259
Fax: +1 319 385 2825
Joseph Alaniz, President

Services/Products:
Lettershop; Mailing/Faxing services

Member of:
DMA (US); FEDMA

ALCOTT & ROUTON, INC.
One Burton Hills Boulevard
Ste 110
Nashville
TN
37215–6197
USA
Tel: +1 615 665 9991
Fax: +1 615 665 1646
Edmund Routon, Chairman & CEO

Services/Products:
Advertising Agency; Direct Response
Agency

Member of:
DMA

ALDATA
7000 West 151st Street
Apple Valley
MN
55124
USA
Tel: +1 952 432 6900
Fax: +1 952 432 7064
Email: mharris@aldata.com
Web: www.aldata.com
H. Michael Harris, President & CEO

Services/Products:
Consultancy services; Database
services; Mailing/Faxing services; Print
services; Fulfilment and sampling
house; Labelling/envelope services

E-Services:
Email list provider

Member of:
DMA (US)

ALEX SHESHENOFF MANAGEMENT SERVICES, INC.
98 San Jacinto Boulevard
Austin
TX
78701
USA
Tel: +1 512 472 4000
Fax: +1 512 479 8189
Pat Garland, Director, Database
Marketing

Services/Products:
Marketing consultant

Member of:
DMA

ALEXANDER & COMPANY, LLC
178 Water Street
Stonington
CT
06378–1209
USA
Tel: 860 535 9160
Fax: +1 860 535 9161
James Alexander, Direct Mail Catalog
Consultant

Services/Products:
Catalogue producer

Member of:
DMA

ALL CITY CALL CENTER
620 North Barstow Street
Waukesha
WI
53186
USA
Tel: +1 414 542 9899

Fax: +1 414 542 2120
John Ditrich, Branch Manager

Services/Products:
Telemarketing agency

Member of:
DMA

ALLEN & GERRITSEN
85 School Street
Watertown
MA
2172
USA
Tel: +1 617 926 4005
Fax: +1 617 926 0133
Andrew Graff, Vice President,
Marketing

Services/Products:
Advertising Agency; Direct Response
Agency

Member of:
DMA

ALLEN ENVELOPE CORP.
1001 Cassatt Road
P.O. Box 521
Berwyn
PA
19312
USA
Tel: +1 610 296 0500
Fax: +1 610 640 2819
John Jordan, President & CEO

Services/Products:
Labelling/envelope services

Member of:
DMA

ALLMEDIA INC.
17060 Dallas Parkway
Ste 105
Dallas
TX
75248–1905
USA
Tel: +1 972 818 4060
Fax: +1 972 818 4061
Email: scaufield@allmediainc.com
Web: www.allmediainc.com
Laura McClendon, President

E-services:
Email list provider

Services/Products:
Consultancy services; List services;
Media buying agency

Member of:
DMA

ALLSTATE INTERNATIONAL
3100 Sanders Road, Suite K5D
Northbrook
IL
60062
USA
Tel: +1 847 402 4611
Fax: +1 847 326 0262
Arlene G Johnson, Assistant Vice
President Direct Marketing

Services/Products:
Advertising Agency; Direct Response
Agency

Member of:
FEDMA

ALMSKOG + FRYDMAN COMMUNICATIONS
P. O. Box 20969
Columbus Circle Station
New York
NY
10023
USA
Tel: +1 212 316 6169
Fax: +1 212 866 6574
Isaac Frydman, Principal

Services/Products:
Marketing consultant

Member of:
DMA

ALPHA MARKETING & CONSULTING
800 Summer Street
Ste 315
Stamford
CT
06901–1723
USA
Tel: +1 203 359 2420
Fax: +1 203 325 4443
Email: glginsburg@snet.net
Web:
  www.internationallists.com
Gerry Ginsburg, President

Services/Products:
List services; Consultancy
services; Direct marketing
agency

E-Services:
Email list provider; Email
software

Member of:
DMA (US)

ALTERNATE POSTAL
Delivery, Inc.
500 East Remington Road
Ste 104
Schaumburg
IL
60173
USA
Tel: +1 847 490 6000
James Bernstein, Group Dir.,
Distribution Mktg.

Services/Products:
Private delivery services

Member of:
DMA

ALTERNATIVE DIRECT MEDIA, INC.
6017 Pine Ridge Road
Naples
FL
34119–3956
USA
Tel: +1 941 352 3240
Fax: +1 941 342 3241
Peter Argyros, President

Services/Products:
Marketing consultant

Member of:
DMA

ALTERNATIVE MARKETING SOLUTIONS (AMS, INC.)
16 Industrial Boulevard
Ste 210
Paoli
PA
19301
USA
Tel: +1 610 407 9841
Fax: +1 610 407 9844
Mike Guntick, President

Services/Products:
Advertising Agency; Direct Response
Agency

Member of:
DMA

AMBASSADOR ENVELOPE
6705 Keaton Corporate Parkway
St. Charles
MO
63304–8680
USA
Tel: +1 314 477 1300
Fax: +1 314 477 7648
Mark Levine

Services/Products:
Labelling/envelope services

Member of:
DMA

AMBROSI
1100 West Washington
Chicago
IL
60607
USA
Tel: +1 312 666 9200
Fax: +1 312 666 8660
Email: info@ambrosi.com
Web: www.ambrosi.com
Johanna Haukl, Marketing Manager

Services/Products:
Advertising Agency; Catalogue
producer; Design/graphics/clip art
supplier; Direct marketing agency;
Photography (for print and online use)

Member of:
DMA (US); Retail Advertising &
Marketing Association (RAMA)

AMERICALIST
div. of Haines & Company
8050 Freedom Avenue, N.W.
North Canton
OH
44720
USA
Tel: +1 800 321 0448
Charles Grandjean, General Manager

Services/Products:
List services

Member of:
DMA

AMERICALL CORPORATION
550 Diehl Road
Naperville
IL
60563
USA
Tel: +1 630 955 9100
Fax: +1 630 955 9955
Susan Best, Vice President, Sales

Services/Products:
Telemarketing agency

Member of:
DMA

AMERICAN BUSINESS
  INFORMATION INC.
100 Plaza Drive
Secaucus
NJ
7094
USA
Tel: +1 201 902 0900
Fax: +1 201 864 0855
Vin Gupta, Chairman & CEO

Services/Products:
List services

Member of:
DMA

AMERICAN COMPUTER
  GROUP
1950 East Watkins
Ste 160
Phoenix
AZ
85034
USA
Tel: +1 602 382 2500
Fax: +1 602 252 3720
Thomas Castellanos, Chief Operations
  Officer

E-Services:
Website design

Member of:
DMA

AMERICAN DATA
  CONSULTANTS
a division of Polk
1010 Washington Boulevard
Stamford
CT
6901
USA
Tel: +1 203 358 9909
Fax: +1 203 358 9882
Stephen Polk, Chairman & CEO

Services/Products:
List services

Member of:
DMA

AMERICAN DIRECT
  MARKETING
1065 Bristol Road
Mountainside
NJ
7092
USA
Tel: 908 232 3800
Fax: +1 908 232 9398
Anthony Catalano, CFO, Direct Mail
  Business Unit

Services/Products:
Lettershop; Mailing/Faxing services

Member of:
DMA

AMERICAN DIRECT
  MARKETING RESOURCES,
  INC.
400 Chesterfield Center
Ste 500
Chesterfield

MO
63017–4800
USA
Tel: +1 314 532 7703
Fax: +1 314 532 2427
Ed Smith, President

Services/Products:
Advertising Agency; Direct Response
Agency

Member of:
DMA

AMERICAN LEADS CO.
P. O. Box 1425
Benicia
CA
94510
USA
Tel: +1 707 747 6334
Fax: +1 707 747 5323
Richard Bottom, Vice President

Services/Products:
List services

Member of:
DMA

AMERICAN LIST COUNSEL,
  INC.
88 Orchard Road
(CN 5219)
Princeton
NJ
8543
USA
Tel: +1 908 874 4300
Fax: +1 908 874 4433
Web: www.amlist.com
Donn Rappaport, Chairman & CEO

Services/Products:
Database services; Direct marketing
agency; Interactive media; List services

E-Services:
Email list provider

Member of:
DMA (US)

AMERICAN MAIL SYSTEMS
  INC.
211-A Progress Drive
Montgomeryville
PA
18936
USA
Tel: +1 215 699 7551
Fax: +1 215 699 0872
Deborah Grace, General Manager

Services/Products:
List services

Member of:
DMA

AMERICAN MAIL UNION
420 Lexington Avenue
Ste 502
New York
NY
10170
USA
Tel: +1 212 682 3777
Fax: +1 212 370 5181
Ajit Dey, Director, Operation

Services/Products:
Lettershop; Mailing/Faxing services

Member of:
DMA

AMERICAN MAILERS
Illinois, Inc.
820 Frontenac Road
Naperville
IL
60563–1743
USA
Tel: +1 630 579 8800
Shane Randall, President

Services/Products:
Lettershop; Mailing/Faxing services

Member of:
DMA

**AMERICAN MARKETING &
   COMMUNICATION CORP.**
1688 East Gude Drive
Ste 301/303
Rockville
MD
20850
USA
Tel: +1 301 738 5787
Fax: +1 301 762 5887
Lisa Boyle, President

Services/Products:
Marketing consultant

Member of:
DMA

**AMERICAN MONEY
   MANAGEMENT**
5053 Fieldwood Drive
Houston
TX
77056
USA
Tel: +1 713 965 0300
Fax: +1 713 965 0373
Richard Alford, President

Services/Products:
Marketing consultant

Member of:
DMA

**AMERICAN PROFESSIONAL
   LISTS**
567 Split Rock Road
Syosset
NY
11791
USA
Tel: +1 516 922 2926
Fax: +1 516 624 3461
Anthony Gaito, President

Services/Products:
List services

Member of:
DMA

AMERICAN PROMARK
3135 Heartleaf Place
Ste 400
Winter Park
FL
32792
USA
Burton Bines, President

Services/Products:
Telemarketing agency

Member of:
DMA

**AMERICAN STUDENT LIST
   COMPANY, INC.**
330 Old Country Road
Mineola
NY
11501
USA
Tel: +1 516 248 6100
Fax: +1 516 248 6364
Martin Lerner, President

Services/Products:
List services

Member of:
DMA

AMERICAN TARGET DATA
55 Cragmere Road
Suffern
NY
10901
USA
Tel: 914 369 3696
Fax: +1 914 368 0018
Scott Shedler, President

Services/Products:
Advertising Agency; Direct Response
Agency

Member of:
DMA

AMERICAN TELECOM, INC.
110 Gibraltar Road
Ste 202
Horsham
PA
19044
USA
Tel: +1 215 957 2410
Fax: +1 215 957 6763
John Quinn, President

Services/Products:
Telemarketing agency

Member of:
DMA

AMERICAN TELNET
Stone Mill Office Park
722 Yorklyn Rd
Hockessin
DE
19707
USA
Tel: +1 302 234 6700
Fax: +1 302 234 6741
John Crouthamel, President

Services/Products:
Telemarketing agency

Member of:
DMA

**AMERICOMM DIRECT
   MARKETING, INC.**
1825 Blue Hills Circle, N.E.
Roanoke
VA
24012
USA
Tel: +1 540 853 8082
Fax: +1 540 853 8172
Anthony Catalano, CFO, Direct Mail
   Business Unit

Services/Products:
Lettershop; Mailing/Faxing services

Member of:
DMA

**AMICHETTI, LEWIS AND
   ASSOCIATES, INC.**
300 North Pottstown Pike
Ste 120
Exton
PA
19341
USA
Tel: +1 610 594 7400
Fax: +1 610 594 7460
Dennis Amichetti, President

Services/Products:
Advertising Agency; Direct Response
Agency

Member of:
DMA

AMMIRATI PURIS LINTAS
One Dag Hammarskjold Plaza
New York
NY
10017
USA
Tel: +1 212 605 8000
Fax: +1 212 605 4713
Robert Solomon, President, Direct
    Marketing

Services/Products:
Advertising Agency; Direct Response
Agency

Member of:
DMA

AMS RESPONSE
16105 Gundry Avenue
Paramount
CA
90723
USA
Tel: +1 562 634 6484
Fax: +1 562 531 3721
Rob Grainger, Vice President, Finance

Services/Products:
Advertising Agency; Direct Response
Agency

Member of:
DMA

ANALYTIC SOLUTIONS
59 Old Lowell Road
Westford
MA
1886
USA
Tel: 978 692 0559
Robert Blumstein, Principal

Services/Products:
Market research agency

Member of:
DMA

ANCHOR COMPUTER, INC.
1900 New Highway
Farmingdale
NY
11735
USA
Tel: +1 516 293 6100
Fax: +1 516 293 0891
Len Schenker, President

Services/Products:
List services

Member of:
DMA

ANDERSEN CONSULTING
600 West Fulton Street
Chicago
IL
60661
USA
Tel: +1 312 507 0600
Fax: +1 312 507 9730
Douglas Withington

Services/Products:
Marketing consultant

Member of:
DMA

ANGELES MARKETING GROUP
315 Arden Avenue, Suite 24
Glendale
CA
91203 -1148
USA
Tel: +1 818 543 5942
Fax: +1 818 543 5944
Email: paul.rottler@amgweb.com
Web: www.amgweb.com
Paul Rottler, President

Services/Products:
Advertising Agency; Catalogue
producer; Design/graphics/clip art
supplier; Interactive media; Market
research agency; Sales promotion
agency; Direct Response Agency

E-Services:
Email list provider; E-Marketing
consultant; Website design; Online/
e-marketing agency

Member of:
DMA (US)

ANTARES ITI
1140 Motor Parkway
Hauppauge
NY
11788
USA
Tel: +1 516 234 5700
Fax: +1 516 234 5472
Steve Hertz, VP, Sales & Marketing

Services/Products:
List services

Member of:
DMA

**AOL BERTELSMANN ONLINE
    EUROPE**
18–21 Cavaye Place
London
SW10 9PG
USA
Tel: +1 32 2 2305984

Fax: +1 32 2 2303754
Simon Hampton, Director European
    Public Affairs

Services/Products:
Internet services

Member of:
FEDMA

APAC TELESERVICES
P. O. Box 3300
Cedar Rapids
IA
52406–3300
USA
Tel: +1 800 270 2722
Fax: +1 319 399 2420
Jim Nikrant, SVP & GM, Sales
    Solutions

Services/Products:
Telemarketing agency

Member of:
DMA

APERIO, INC.
288 Walnut Street
Newtonville
MA
2160
USA
Tel: +1 617 928 1114
Fax: +1 617 928 3388
Michael Caccavale, President

Services/Products:
Marketing consultant

Member of:
DMA

**APPLIED COMPUTER
    CONCEPTS**
120 Brighton Road
Clifton
NJ
7012
USA
Tel: +1 201 778 5588
Bill Rella, President

Services/Products:
List services

Member of:
DMA

**APPLIED INFORMATION
    GROUP**
100 Market Street
Kenilworth
NJ
7033
USA
Tel: 908 241 7007

Fax: +1 908 241 7088
Mitchell Rubin, President

Services/Products:
List services

Member of:
DMA

APPLIED INTERACTIVE MEDIA, LLC
49 West 27th Street
4th Fl
New York
NY
10001–6936
USA
Tel: +1 212 532 7300
Fax: +1 212 532 8771
John Gatti, CFO

Services/Products:
Advertising Agency; Direct Response Agency

Member of:
DMA

ARCHER/MALMO DIRECT
65 Union Avenue
Memphis
TN
38103–5127
USA
Tel: 901 523 2000
Fax: +1 901 524 5578
Mary Caywood, VP & General Manager

Services/Products:
Advertising Agency; Direct Response Agency

Member of:
DMA

ARMY TIMES PUBLISHING COMPANY
6883 Commercial Drive
Springfield
VA
22159
USA
Tel: +1 703 750 8971
Ruth Baker, Director, Database Marketing

Services/Products:
Telemarketing agency

Member of:
DMA

ARNOLD DIRECT
101 Huntington Avenue
23rd Fl
Boston
MA

2199
USA
Tel: +1 617 587 8000
Fax: +1 617 587 8587
Shari Williams, President

Services/Products:
Advertising Agency; Direct Response Agency

Member of:
DMA

AROCOM DIRECT
The Renaissance
1350 Euclid Ave
Cleveland
OH
44115
USA
Tel: +1 216 696 9660
Fax: +1 216 479 2439
Steve Zweig, President

Services/Products:
Advertising Agency; Direct Response Agency

Member of:
DMA

ASATSU/BBDO
1285 Avenue of the Americas
New York
NY
10019
USA
Tel: +1 212 459 6115
Fax: +1 212 459 5643
Shinichi Morita, Senior Group Account Director

Services/Products:
Advertising Agency; Direct Response Agency

Member of:
DMA

ASI
2866 Michener Drive
Lancaster
PA
17601–1902
USA
Tel: +1 717 291 6653
Tara Marullo, Marketing Director

E-Services:
Website design

Member of:
DMA

ASI DIRECT MARKETING
102 East Moreno
Colorado Spgs
CO

80903
USA
Tel: +1 719 633 2833
Fax: +1 719 635 3017
Joseph Alaniz, President

Services/Products:
Lettershop; Mailing/Faxing services

Member of:
DMA

ASK TELEMARKETING
600 South Court Street
Ste 104
Montgomery
AL
36104
USA
Tel: +1 334 270 2755
Fax: +1 334 270 2755
Rick Burley, President

Services/Products:
Telemarketing agency

Member of:
DMA

ATLANTES CORPORATION
90 Madison
Denver
CO
80206–5414
USA
Tel: +1 303 394 9077
Fax: +1 303 394 2902
E. Thomas Detmer, President

Services/Products:
List services

Member of:
DMA

ATLANTIC ENVELOPE COMPANY
1420 Peachtree Street, N.E.
Atlanta
GA
30309
USA
Tel: +1 404 853 6755
Fax: +1 404 853 6799
Randy Zook, President

Services/Products:
Labelling/envelope services

Member of:
DMA

ATLANTIC LIST COMPANY, INC.
2425 Wilson Boulevard
Ste 500
Arlington
VA

22201–3385
USA
Tel: +1 703 528 7482
Fax: +1 703 528 7492
Dodee Black, President & COO

Services/Products:
List services

Member of:
DMA

ATLAS MARKETING
Logsal 3513
8424 NW 56th St
Miami
FL
33166
USA
Tel: 817 545 8304
Fax: +1 817 545 2920
Salvador Arce, Commercial Manager

Services/Products:
Telemarketing agency

Member of:
DMA

ATLUX CORPORATION
c/o NIAC
1211 Avenue of the Americas
New York
NY
10036
USA
Tel: +1 212 704 6690
Fax: +1 212 704 6961
Toru (Tom) Suzuki, President

Services/Products:
List services

Member of:
DMA

AUDIENCE IDENTIFICATION INC.
1982 Ohio Street
Lisle
IL
60532
USA
Tel: +1 630 435 0460
Fax: +1 630 435 0470
Ronald Marsh, President

Services/Products:
Database services

Member of:
DMA

AURORA MARKETING MANAGEMENT, INC.
66 Witherspoon Street
Ste 600
Princeton

NJ
8542
USA
Tel: 908 904 1125
Fax: +1 908 359 1108
Doreen Blanc, President

Services/Products:
Telemarketing agency

Member of:
DMA

AUSTIN KNIGHT INC.
352 Park Avenue S
12th Fl
New York
NY
10010–1709
USA
Tel: +1 212 695 5055
Fax: +1 212 695 5164
John Meagle, VP, Enrollment Marketing

Services/Products:
Advertising Agency; Direct Response Agency

Member of:
DMA

AUTOMATED CALL PROCESSING (ACP)
757 Third Avenue
Ste 700
New York
NY
10017
USA
Tel: +1 212 326 4606
Camille Wehner, President

Services/Products:
Telemarketing agency

Member of:
DMA

AUTOMATED RESOURCES GROUP, INC.
21 Philips Parkway
Montvale
NJ
7645
USA
Tel: +1 201 391 1500
Fax: +1 201 391 8357
Thomas Amoriello, President

Services/Products:
List services

Member of:
DMA

AYER DEARE & PARTNERS
149 Fifth Avenue
New York
NY
10010
USA
Tel: +1 212 388 1313
Fax: +1 212 388 1314
Trissie Rost, Co - President

Services/Products:
Advertising Agency; Direct Response Agency

Member of:
DMA

AZ MARKETING SERVICES, INC.
31 River Road
Cos Cob
CT
6807
USA
Tel: +1 203 629 8088
Fax: +1 203 661 1068
Alice Zea, Chairman of Board & CEO

Services/Products:
List services

Member of:
DMA (US); FEDMA

B & K LIST SERVICES, INC.
425 East Sixth Street
Conway
AR
72032
USA
Tel: +1 501 336 1410
Fax: +1 501 336 2972
Lee Anne Kline, President & Owner

Services/Products:
List services

Member of:
DMA

B & W PRESS
401 East Main Street
Georgetown
MA
01833–2513
USA
Tel: +1 508 352 6100
Fax: +1 508 352 5955
Paul Beegan, President

Services/Products:
Labelling/envelope services

Member of:
DMA

B.W.R.
650 Commodore Sloat Drive
Los Angeles
CA
90048
USA
Tel: +1 213 938 4163
Fax: +1 213 938 4163
Thierry Mutin, President

Services/Products:
Advertising Agency; Direct Response
Agency

Member of:
DMA

BAIGLOBAL INC.
580 White Plains Road
Tarrytown
NY
10591
USA
Tel: 914 332 5300
Fax: +1 914 631 8300
Kate Permut, Vice President,
    Marketing

Services/Products:
Market research agency

Member of:
DMA

**BAKER ADVERTISING &
    MAILING**
3923 West Sixth Street
Los Angeles
CA
90020
USA
Tel: +1 213 385 2939
Fax: +1 213 385 9234
Joan Ragusa, Manager

Services/Products:
List services

Member of:
DMA

BANNER DIRECT
Rockefeller Center
630 Fifth Avenue
Suite 2109
New York
NY
10111
USA
Tel: +1 212 218 7522
Fax: +1 212 218 7527
Email: bdirect@bannerdirect.com
Web: www.bannerdirect.com
Christine Fontana, President

Services/Products:
Direct marketing agency

E-Services:
E-Marketing consultant; Website
design

Member of:
DMA (US)

**BARBER CONSULTING
    SERVICES**
126 Ocean Boulevard
Atlantic Highlands
NJ
7716
USA
Tel: +1 732 708 1011
Fax: +1 732 708 0940
Kathryn Barber, Partner

Services/Products:
Telemarketing agency

Member of:
DMA

**BARKLEY EVERGREEN &
    PARTNERS, INC.**
423 West 8th Street
Kansas City
MO
64105–1408
USA
Tel: 816 842 1500
Fax: +1 816 842 6494
Susan Hipp, VP, Direct & Database
    Mktg.

Services/Products:
Advertising Agency; Direct Response
Agency

Member of:
DMA

**BARRACLOUGH HALL
    WOOLSTON GRAY**
1285 Avenue of Americas 5th fl
New York
NY
10019
USA
Tel: +1 212 459 5289
Simon Hall, Chief Executive

Services/Products:
Advertising Agency; Direct Response
Agency

Member of:
DMA

**BARRY BLAU & PARTNERS,
    INC.**
241 Danbury Road
Ste 2800
Wilton
CT
06897–4046

USA
Tel: +1 203 834 6900
Fax: +1 203 834 7000
Dennis astham, President

Services/Products:
Advertising Agency; Direct Response
Agency

Member of:
DMA (US); FEDMA

BBDO
1285 Avenue of the Americas
New York
NY
10019
USA
Tel: +1 212 459 5000
Fax: +1 212 459 6645
Cynthia Dale, Vice President,
    Interactive

Services/Products:
Advertising Agency; Direct Response
Agency

Member of:
DMA

BBDO RESPONSE
400 West 43rd Street
Ste 27C
29th Fl
New York
NY
10036
USA
Tel: +1 212 594 3997
Sarah Simpson, SVP & Managing
    Director

Services/Products:
Advertising Agency; Direct Response
Agency

Member of:
DMA

**BEACH DIRECT MARKETING
    RESOURCES, INC.**
18331 Pines Boulevard
Ste 229
Pembroke Pines
FL
33029
USA
Tel: 954 437 1460
Fax: +1 954 441 2739
Donald McCormick, President

Services/Products:
Telemarketing agency

Member of:
DMA

BEACON GROUP, INC.
8320 Bellona Avenue
Windsor Court
Ste 250
Baltimore
MD
21204
USA
Tel: +1 410 583 1203
Fax: +1 410 583 1506
Paul Wingate, President & CEO

Services/Products:
Advertising Agency; Direct Response
Agency

Member of:
DMA

BEECHTREE ASSOC., INC.
P. O. Box 15461
Winston-Salem
NC
27113
USA
Tel: +1 336 659 3345
Fax: +1 336 659 0760
Jay Foliano, President

Services/Products:
Marketing consultant

Member of:
DMA

BEL-AIRE ASSOCIATES
730 Fifth Avenue
New York
NY
10019
USA
Tel: +1 212 245 5700
Fax: +1 212 245 5705
Gregory Chislovsky, President

Services/Products:
Advertising Agency; Direct Response
Agency

Member of:
DMA

**BENEFIT SERVICES OF
   AMERICA, INC.**
101 Wymore Road
Ste 400
Altamonte Spgs
FL
32714
USA
Tel: +1 407 772 0300
Fax: +1 407 772 0133
Burton Bines, President

Services/Products:
Telemarketing agency

Member of:
DMA

BENNETT KUHN VARNER, INC.
2964 Peachtree Road
Ste 700
Atlanta
GA
30305
USA
Tel: +1 404 233 0332
Fax: +1 404 233 0302
Brent Kuhn, President

Services/Products:
Advertising Agency; Direct Response
Agency

Member of:
DMA

**BERENSON, ISHAM &
   PARTNERS, INC.**
31 Milk Street
Boston
MA
2109
USA
Tel: +1 617 423 1120
Fax: +1 617 423 4597
Paul Berenson, Chairman & CEO

Services/Products:
Advertising Agency; Direct Response
Agency

Member of:
DMA

BERNHEIMER ASSOCIATES
Ten Laurel Avenue
Wellesley
MA
02181–7523
USA
Tel: +1 617 237 8910
Fax: +1 781 237 7887
Walter Bernheimer, President

Services/Products:
Marketing consultant

Member of:
DMA

BERNICE BUSH COMPANY
3 Corporate Park
Ste 200
Irvine
CA
92606–5111
USA
Tel: 949 752 4210
Fax: +1 949 752 4220
Barbara Spaulding, President

Services/Products:
List services

Member of:
DMA

**BERT O'MALLEY DIRECT
   MARKETING CONSULTING**
7465 81st Place, S.E.
Mercer Island
WA
98040
USA
Tel: +1 206 275 0202
Fax: +1 206 275 0203
Bert O'Malley

Services/Products:
Marketing consultant

Member of:
DMA

BEST MAILING LISTS, INC.
888 South Craycroft Road
Ste 109
Tucson
AZ
85711
USA
Tel: +1 520 745 0200
Fax: +1 520 745 3800
Karen Kirsch, President & CEO

Services/Products:
List services

Member of:
DMA

**BETA RESEARCH
   CORPORATION**
6400 Jericho Turnpike
Syosset
NY
11791
USA
Tel: +1 516 935 3800
Fax: +1 516 935 4092
Manny Mallo, President

Services/Products:
Market research agency

Member of:
DMA

BETHESDA LIST CENTER, INC.
7508 Wisconsin Avenue
Ste 300
Bethesda
MD
20814–3500
USA
Tel: +1 301 986 1455
Fax: +1 301 907 4870
David James, President

Services/Products:
List services

Member of:
DMA

BI PERFORMANCE SERVICES
7630 Bush Lake Road
Minneapolis
MN
55439
USA
Tel: +1 612 8+44 4359
Fax: +1 612 844 4038
Donna Wald, Marketing Director

Services/Products:
Advertising Agency; Direct Response
Agency

Member of:
DMA

BIGGS/GILMORE
COMMUNICATIONS
100 West Michigan
Ste 300
Kalamazoo
MI
49007
USA
Tel: +1 616 349 7711
Fax: +1 616 349 3051
Phil Long, President

Services/Products:
Advertising Agency; Direct Response
Agency

Member of:
DMA

BIRKHOLM DIRECT
150 North Santa Anita Avenue
Ste 460
Arcadia
CA
91006–3121
USA
Tel: +1 626 445 4712
Fax: +1 626 445 5062
MikeBirkholm, President

Services/Products:
Advertising Agency; Direct Response
Agency

Member of:
DMA

BLAGMAN MEDIA
INTERNATIONAL
1901 Avenue of the Stars
Los Angeles
CA
90067
USA

Tel: +1 310 788 5444
Fax: +1 310 788 5440
Carla Hendra, President, New York

Services/Products:
Advertising Agency; Direct Response
Agency

Member of:
DMA

BLAIN, OLSEN, WHITE, GURR
ADVERTISING
375 West 200 South
Ste 300
Salt Lake City
UT
84101
USA
Tel: 801 539 1818
Fax: +1 801 539 8484
Eric Weight, Managing Director

Services/Products:
Advertising Agency; Direct Response
Agency

Member of:
DMA

BLANK & ASSOCIATES
4802 North Broadway Street
2nd Fl
Chicago
IL
60640–3622
USA
Tel: +1 778 878 7600
Fax: +1 778 878 1392
Email: sblank@bandanet.com
Web: www.bandanet.com
Steven Blank, President

Services/Products:
Advertising Agency; Catalogue
producer; Consultancy services; Direct
marketing agency; Interactive media;
Market research agency

BLAU MARKETING
TECHNOLOGIES
875 North Michigan Avenue
Ste 2800
Chicago
IL
60611
USA
Tel: +1 312 397 3200
Fax: +1 312 397 3208
Dennis Eastham, President

Services/Products:
Advertising Agency; Direct Response
Agency

Member of:
DMA

BLITZ RESEARCH, INC.
1524 South 16th Street
Ste 400
Wilmington
NC
28401
USA
Tel: 910 343 1520
Fax: +1 910 343 0562
Michael Harms, President

Services/Products:
Telemarketing agency

Member of:
DMA

BLUE DOLPHIN
COMMUNICATIONS
83 Boston Post Road
Sudbury
MA
1776
USA
Tel: +1 617 443 8214
Fax: +1 508 443 9728
Donald Nicholas, President

Services/Products:
Advertising Agency; Direct Response
Agency

Member of:
DMA

BLUM & COMPANY
81 Clinton Street
Fairfield
CT
06430–690
USA
Tel: +1 203 255 4813
Fax: +1 203 255 3936
Sandra Blum, President

Services/Products:
Marketing consultant

Member of:
DMA

BLUMENFIELD MARKETING,
INC.
20 Academy Street
Norwalk
CT
06850–4032
USA
Tel: +1 203 854 6737
Fax: +1 203 854 9365
Email: barry@bmigroup.com
Web: www.bmigroup.com
Barry Blumenfield, CEO & Chairman
of the Board

Services/Products:
Fulfilment and sampling house

Member of:
DMA (US)

BOB CASTLE & ASSOCIATES
530 East 72nd Street
New York
NY
10021
USA
Tel: +1 212 585 1670
Fax: +1 212 517 6214
Robert Castle, President

Services/Products:
Marketing consultant

Member of:
DMA

**BOWERS ENVELOPE
COMPANY**
5331 North Tacoma Avenue
Indianapolis
IN
46220
USA
Tel: +1 317 253 4321
Fax: +1 317 254 2239
Thomas Cristelli, President & CEO

Services/Products:
Labelling/envelope services

Member of:
DMA

BOZELL DIRECT
40 West 23rd Street
New York
NY
10010
USA
Tel: +1 212 727 5717
Fax: +1 212 727 5019
Beverly Beaudoin, Managing Partner

Services/Products:
Advertising Agency; Direct Response
Agency

Member of:
DMA

BRAINARD ASSOCIATES
1802 West MLK, Jr. Parkway
Ste 206
Durham
NC
27707
USA
Tel: 919 489 1501
Fax: +1 919 489 1427
Carol Brainard, President

Services/Products:
Database services

Member of:
DMA

**BRANDYWINE CONSULTING
GROUP**
1398 Morstein Road
Ste 4
West Chester
PA
19380–5848
USA
Tel: +1 610 696 1905
Fax: +1 610 429 1954
Benjamin Ventresca, President

Services/Products:
Marketing consultant

Member of:
DMA

**BRAREN & CONSTANTINO
PARTNERS**
58 Paret Lane
Hartsdale
NY
10530
USA
Tel: 914 946 0321
Fax: +1 914 946 2840
Warren Braren, Partner

Services/Products:
Marketing consultant

Member of:
DMA

BRAUN TECHNOLOGY GROUP
30 West Monroe
Ste 300
Chicago
IL
60603
USA
Tel: +1 312 630 5711
Fax: +1 312 630 5799
Marilyn Maurer, Business
Development

Services/Products:
List services

Member of:
DMA

**BRIGAR COMPUTER
SERVICES**
5 Sand Creek Road
Albany
NY
12205
USA
Tel: +1 518 438 8050
Fax: +1 518 438 0542
Christopher Addington, VP, Finance

Services/Products:
List services

Member of:
DMA

BRIGHTON AGENCY
25 North Brentwood
Clayton
MO
63105–3709
USA
Tel: +1 314 725 8025
Fax: +1 314 725 8001
Donna Cooper, Director, Direct
Marketing

Services/Products:
Advertising Agency; Direct Response
Agency

Member of:
DMA

BROKERS WORLDWIDE, INC.
701 Ashland Avenue
Ashland Center III
Folcroft
PA
19032
USA
Tel: +1 610 461 3661
Fax: +1 610 461 4239
Gary Shunk, Senior Vice President

Services/Products:
Lettershop; Mailing/Faxing services

Member of:
DMA

**BRONNER SLOSBERG
HUMPHREY**
The Prudential Tower
800 Boylston Street
Boston
MA
2199
USA
Tel: +1 617 867 1000
Fax: +1 617 867 1111
Michael Bronner, CEO

Services/Products:
Advertising Agency; Direct Response
Agency

Member of:
DMA

BROWN RADMAN WOLPER
1860 Blake Street
Ste 640
Denver
CO
80202
USA

Tel: +1 303 298 8470
Fax: +1 303 298 8570
Deborah Radman, CEO

Services/Products:
Sales promotion agency

Member of:
DMA

BRUCE W. EBERLE & ASSOCIATES, INC.
1420 Spring Hill Road
Ste 490
McLean
VA
22102
USA
Tel: +1 703 821 1550
Fax: +1 703 821 0920
Bruce Eberle, Chairman, Board of Directors

Services/Products:
Advertising Agency; Direct Response Agency

Member of:
DMA

BUDGET MARKETING, INC.
1171 Seventh Street
Des Moines
IA
50314
USA
Tel: +1 515 243 7000
Fax: +1 515 243 7721
Steve Winkelman

Services/Products:
Telemarketing agency

Member of:
DMA

BULLSEYE DATABASE MARKETING, INC.
601 South Boulder Avenue
12th Fl
Tulsa
OK
74119–1312
USA
Tel: 918 587 1731
Fax: +1 918 587 0450
Kenyon Blunt, President

Services/Products:
Advertising Agency; Direct Response Agency

Member of:
DMA

BURNETT DIRECT, INC.
31700 West Thirteen Mile Road
Ste 101

Farmington Hls
MI
48334–2170
USA
Tel: +1 248 932 7100
Fax: +1 248 932 7107
Mark Burnett, President

Services/Products:
List services

Member of:
DMA

BURRELL/DFA ADVERTISING INC.
20 North Michigan Avenue
Chicago
IL
60602
USA
Tel: +1 312 443 8576
Fax: +1 312 443 0974
Ed Forti

Services/Products:
Advertising Agency; Direct Response Agency

Member of:
DMA

BUSINESS ADVERTISING SPECIALTIES CORP.
9351 De Soto Avenue
Chatsworth
CA
91311–4948
USA
Tel: 818 998 3300
Fax: +1 818 998 2635
Mark Schwartz, President

Services/Products:
Advertising Agency; Direct Response Agency

Member of:
DMA

BUSINESS DEVELOPMENT SOLUTIONS, INC.
133 Gaither Drive
Suite P
Mount Laural
NJ
8054
USA
Tel: +1 609 787 1500
Fax: +1 609 787 1510
Robert Bloom, President

Services/Products:
Database services

Member of:
DMA

BUSINESS DIRECT MARKETING ASSOCIATES, INC.
4545 Quail Point Way N.E.
Hoschton
GA
30548–1649
USA
Tel: +1 77 0 945 6003
Fax: +1 770 945 0643
Joe Staffieri, President & CEO

Services/Products:
Advertising Agency; Direct Response Agency

Member of:
DMA

BUSINESS RESPONSE, INC.
1100 Corporate Square Drive
2nd Fl
St. Louis
MO
63132
USA
Tel: +1 800 920 6565
Fax: +1 314 213 7878
Jan Devine, SVP, Marketing

Services/Products:
Telemarketing agency

Member of:
DMA

BUSINESS TRANSACTIONS EXPRESS
1010 West St. German
Ste 100
St. Cloud
NJ
55317
USA
Tel: +1 320 253 7722
Carl Tomasello, Director, Marketing

Services/Products:
List services

Member of:
DMA

BWC GROUP
305 Madison Avenue
New York
NY
10165
USA
Tel: +1 212 308 8888
Fax: +1 212 867 2592
Ric h Fontana, President

Services/Products:
Advertising Agency; Direct Response Agency

Member of:
DMA

**BYRNE ADVERTISING COPY/
   CONSULTANCY**
122 North Marguerita
Alhambra
CA
91801
USA
Tel: 818 284 5838
Fax: +1 818 284 5838
Jim Cerasani, President

Services/Products:
Advertising Agency; Direct Response
Agency

Member of:
DMA

C-E COMMUNICATIONS
30400 Van Dyke Avenue
Warren
MI
48093
USA
Tel: 810 574 3400
Fax: +1 810 575 9925
Louis Schultz, President & CEO

Services/Products:
Advertising Agency; Direct Response
Agency

Member of:
DMA

C.D.C. LISTS
1475 West Cypress Creek Road
Ste 204
Ft. Lauderdale
FL
33309
USA
Tel: +1 800 248 7973
Fax: +1 954 757 8770
Robert Bercik, President

Services/Products:
List services

Member of:
DMA

CADMUS
2750 White Hall Park Drive
Ste 1000
Charlotte
NC
28273
USA
Tel: +1 800 991 7225
Fax: +1 704 583 6780
Dennis Duffy, President

Services/Products:
Advertising Agency; Direct Response
Agency

Member of:
DMA

CAHNERS BUSINESS LISTS
1350 East Touhy Avenue
Des Plaines
IL
60018
USA
Tel: +1 800 323 4958
Fax: +1 847 390 2779
Rick Kasper, VP & General Manager

Services/Products:
List services

Member of:
DMA

CALL CENTER MARKETING
1365 East 10600 South
Sandy
UT
84092
USA
Tel: 801 523 0660
Fax: +1 801 523 6111
Robert Caldwell, Senior Vice President

Services/Products:
Telemarketing agency

Member of:
DMA

CALL INTERACTIVE
2301 North 117th Avenue
Omaha
NE
68164
USA
Tel: +1 402 498 4000
Fax: +1 402 498 7900
Clifton Critchlow, Sales VP, Direct
   Response

Services/Products:
Telemarketing agency

Member of:
DMA

CALLOWAY HOUSE, INC.
451 Richardson Drive
Lancaster
PA
17603
USA
Tel: +1 717 299 5703
Fax: +1 717 299 6754
John Ternovan, President

Services/Products:
Lettershop; Mailing/Faxing services

Member of:
DMA

CAM LOGISTICS
2187 New London Turnpike
South Glastonbury
CT
6073
USA
Tel: +1 800 506 7475
Fax: +1 800 659 1420
Howard Goldman, Vice President,
   Sales

Services/Products:
Lettershop; Mailing/Faxing services

Member of:
DMA

CAMPBELL ASSOCIATES
185 Martling Avenue
Tarrytown
NY
10591
USA
Tel: 914 332 1177
Arnold Thiesfeldt

Services/Products:
Marketing consultant

Member of:
DMA

CAMPBELL MITHUN DIRECT
222 South Ninth Street
Minneapolis
MN
55402
USA
Tel: +1 612 347 1827
Fax: +1 612 347 1848
Email: michelle_arntza@
   cambell-mithun.com
Michelle Arntzen, VP, Director

Services/Products:
Advertising Agency; Direct marketing
agency

E-Services:
E-Marketing consultant; Online/
e-marketing agency

Member of:
DMA (US); National DMA

CAMPBELL RESEARCH
218 West Carmen Lane
Ste 110
Santa Maria
CA
93454
USA
Tel: +1 805 922 0880

421

Fax: +1 805 922 3909
Dirk Rinker, Vice President

Services/Products:
Market research agency

Member of:
DMA (US)

CANADIAN DIRECT MAILING
1700 West Fort Street
Detroit
MI
48216
USA
Tel: +1 800 759 1300
Fax: +1 519 971 2712
Susan Olde, President

Services/Products:
Lettershop; Mailing/Faxing services

Member of:
DMA

**CAPELL'S CIRCULATION
REPORT, INC.**
60 East 42nd Street
Ste 3810
New York
NY
10165–0006
USA
Tel: +1 212 697 5753
Fax: +1 212 949 7294
Harry Chevan, Senior Vice President

Services/Products:
Marketing consultant

Member of:
DMA

CAPITAL MARKETING, INC.
231 South Bemiston
Ste 1210
Clayton
MO
63105
USA
Tel: +1 314 726 1800
Fax: +1 314 726 2624
Harold Sarner, President

Services/Products:
Marketing consultant

Member of:
DMA

CARDINAL MARKETING INC.
3340 North West 53rd Street
Ft. Lauderdale
FL
33309
USA
Tel: 954 735 1900
Anthony Catalano, CFO, Direct Mail

Business Unit
Services/Products:
Lettershop; Mailing/Faxing services

Member of:
DMA

**CARL BLOOM ASSOCIATES,
INC.**
232 Madison Avenue
New York
NY
10016
USA
Tel: +1 212 679 6900
Fax: +1 212 679 6913
Carl Bloom, President

Services/Products:
Advertising Agency; Direct Response
Agency

Member of:
DMA

CARLSON MARKETING GROUP
P. O. Box 59159
Minneapolis
MN
55459–8332
USA
Tel: +1 612 540 5400
Fax: +1 612 449 1840
Thomas Lacki, Sr. Dir., Measurement/
Analysis

Services/Products:
Advertising Agency; Direct Response
Agency

Member of:
DMA

CARMICHAEL LYNCH
800 Hennepin Avenue
Minneapolis
MN
55403
USA
Tel: +1 612 334 6168
Fax: +1 612 334 6171
Diane Jordan, Director

Services/Products:
Advertising Agency; Direct Response
Agency

Member of:
DMA

CARNEY DIRECT MARKETING
15530 B Rockfield Boulevard
Ste C
Irvine
CA
92618
USA

Tel: +1 714 581 5100
Fax: +1 714 581 4564
Peter Carney, President

Services/Products:
List services

Member of:
DMA

CAROL ENTERS LIST CO., INC.
(CELCO)
9663 C Main Street
Fairfax
VA
22032–3739
USA
Tel: +1 703 425 0052
Fax: +1 703 425 0056
Barbara Sims Cheever, VP, Sales

Services/Products:
List services

Member of:
DMA

CARTWHEEL, INC.
1415 West 22nd Street
Ste 310
Oak Brook
IL
60523
USA
Tel: +1 630 571 8861
Fax: +1 630 571 8860
Martin Johnson, President

Services/Products:
Marketing consultant

Member of:
DMA

CAS, INC.
10303 Crown Point Avenue
Omaha
NE
68134–1061
USA
Tel: +1 402 964 9998
Fax: +1 402 963 2100
Kent Stormberg, President

Services/Products:
List services

Member of:
DMA

CASTEL
14 Summer Street
Malden
MA
2148
USA
Tel: +1 781 324 0140

Fax: +1 781 324 0277
Robert McDermott, Director, Sales &
    Marketing

Services/Products:
List services

Member of:
DMA

CATALOGS BY DESIGN
500 North Gulph Road
King of Prussia
PA
19406
USA
Tel: +1 610 337 2343
Fax: +1 610 768 9511
Christine Carrington, President

Services/Products:
Catalogue producer

Member of:
DMA

CATALYST DIRECT INC.
110 Marina Drive
Rochester
NY
14626
USA
Tel: +1 716 453 8300
Fax: +1 716 453 8301
Michael Osborn, Managing Director

Services/Products:
Advertising Agency; Direct Response
Agency

Member of:
DMA

**CATALYST DIRECT
    MARKETING**
169 Ramapo Valley Road
Oakland
NJ
7436
USA
Tel: +1 201 405 1414
Fax: +1 201 405 1544
Fred Litzky, President

Services/Products:
List services

Member of:
DMA

CATHEDRAL CORPORATION
P. O. Box 290
488 Route 295
Chatham
NY
12037–0290
USA
Tel: +1 518 392 3333

Fax: +1 518 392 9334
Marianne Wilcox Gaige, President

Services/Products:
List services

Member of:
DMA

**CCMR ADVERTISING &
    MARKETING
    COMMUNICATIONS**
260 Fair Street
Kingston
NY
12401–3852
USA
Tel: 914 331 4620
Fax: +1 914 331 3026
Frank Rocco, Managing Partner

Services/Products:
Advertising Agency; Direct Response
Agency

Member of:
DMA

**CELEBRATE
    COMMUNICATIONS L.L.C.**
4300 44th Avenue
Moline
IL
61265
USA
Tel: +1 309 797 4274
Fax: +1 309 797 6470
Scott Anderson, General Manager

Services/Products:
Telemarketing agency

Member of:
DMA

**CENTER FOR SIMPLIFIED
    STRATEGIC PLANNING, INC.**
P. O. Box 3324
Vero Beach
FL
32964–3324
USA
Tel: +1 561 231 3636
Fax: +1 561 231 1099
Charles Bradford, Chairman

Services/Products:
Database services

Member of:
DMA

CENTROBE, INC.
10 South 5th Street
Minneapolis
MN
55402
USA

Tel: +1 612 359 3700
Fax: +1 612 359 9395
Mark Lacek, President, The Lacek
    Group

Services/Products:
Fulfilment and sampling house

Member of:
DMA

**CENTURY DIRECT
    MARKETING, INC.**
10960 Wilshire Boulevard
Ste 1000
Los Angeles
CA
90024–3713
USA
Tel: 805 957 0050
Fax: +1 805 957 9130
Lisa Sultan, Director, Public Relations

Services/Products:
Telemarketing agency

Member of:
DMA

**CERES INTEGRATED
    SOLUTIONS**
3725 National Drive
Ste 213
Raleigh
NC
27612
USA
Tel: 919 785 0575
Fax: +1 919 785 0735
Judy Bayer, VP, Analytic Solutions

Services/Products:
Marketing consultant

Member of:
DMA

CFM DIRECT
1801 South Meyers Road
Ste 900
Oakbrook Ter
IL
60181
USA
Tel: +1 630 916 6020
Fax: +1 630 916 6030
Claude Grizzard, Principal

Services/Products:
List services

Member of:
DMA

CHD DIRECT
426 Marietta Street
Atlanta
GA

30313
USA
Tel: +1 404 892 4500
Fax: +1 404 681 1550
Asa Johnson, Vice President

Services/Products:
Marketing consultant

Member of:
DMA

CHIAT/DAY/MOJO INC. ADVERTISING
340 Main Street
Venice
CA
90291
USA
Tel: +1 213 314 5819
Fax: +1 213 396 1773
Vela Ruddock, Director, Intelligence

Services/Products:
Advertising Agency; Direct Response Agency

Member of:
DMA

CHILCUTT DIRECT MARKETING
9301 Cedar Lake Avenue
Oklahoma City
OK
73113–7803
USA
Tel: +1 405 478 7245
Fax: +1 405 478 2984
Matt Chilcutt, President

Services/Products:
List services

Member of:
DMA

CHINNICI DIRECT INC.
49 West 27th Street
New York
NY
10001
USA
Tel: +1 212 685 0564
Fax: +1 212 685 0592
Michael Chinnici, President & CEO

Services/Products:
Advertising Agency; Direct Response Agency

Member of:
DMA

CHIROPRACTIC ELITE ORGANIZATION, INC.
2064 Prospector Avenue
Ste 103

Park City
UT
84060–7321
USA
Tel: 801 647 5937
Fax: +1 801 647 5927
Lawton Howell, Chairman of the Board

Services/Products:
Advertising Agency; Direct Response Agency

Member of:
DMA

CHOICEPOINT
1000 Alderman Drive
MD 70T
Alpharetta
GA
30005
USA
Tel: +1 77 0 752 5720
Fax: +1 770 752 5929
Thomas Whitfield, Director, Marketing Services

Services/Products:
Marketing consultant

Member of:
DMA

CIMETRY INC.
Two Clock Tower Place
Ste 600
Maynard
MA
1754
USA
Tel: 978 461 2444
Fax: +1 978 461 0109
Dan Cerutti, Chief Executive Officer

E-Services:
Website design

Member of:
DMA

CIMINO DIRECT, INC.
720 Yorklyn Road, Ste 1
Stone Mill Offices
Hockessin
DE
19707–1407
USA
Tel: +1 302 235 0841
Fax: +1 302 235 0845
John Cimino, President

Services/Products:
Advertising Agency; Direct Response Agency

Member of:
DMA

CIRCULATION SPECIALISTS, INC.
49 Richmondville Avenue
Westport
CT
6880
USA
Tel: +1 203 454 0344
Fax: +1 203 454 8871
Stuart Jordan, Executive Vice President

Services/Products:
Marketing consultant

Member of:
DMA

CITATION TELESERVICES, INC.
2424 South 130th Circle
Omaha
NE
68144–2596
USA
Tel: +1 402 691 6384
Fax: +1 402 330 8688
Libby Irvine, Marketing Manager

Services/Products:
Telemarketing agency

Member of:
DMA

CITIPOST
500 West 37th Street
New York
NY
10018
USA
Tel: +1 212 328 1444
Fax: +1 212 328 1445
Gary Schultz, Managing Director

Services/Products:
Private delivery services

Member of:
DMA

CKS PARTNERS
1341 Connecticut Avenue, N.W.
Washington
DC
20036
USA
Tel: +1 202 822 6200
Fax: +1 202 822 9645
Leslie Jump, VP, Strategic Planning

Services/Products:
Advertising Agency; Direct Response Agency

Member of:
DMA

CLARITAS
1525 Wilson Boulevard
Ste 1000
Arlington
VA
22209
USA
Tel: +1 703 812 2700
Fax: +1 703 812 2701
Eddie Pickle, Executive Vice President

Services/Products:
Market research agency

Member of:
DMA

CLARK.MACKAIN
156 Fifth Avenue
Ste 230
New York
NY
10010–7002
USA
Tel: +1 212 367 7890
Fax: +1 212 367 7898
David Clark, Partner

Services/Products:
List services

Member of:
DMA

CM PARTNERS, INC.
5550 Meadowbrook Drive
Rolling Meadows
IL
60008
USA
Tel: 847 593 3232
Fax: +1 847 593 8744
Kenneth Ralston, Chairman & CEO

Services/Products:
Advertising Agency; Direct Response
Agency

Member of:
DMA

CMC
2251 - 42nd Avenue
San Francisco
CA
94116–1522
USA
Tel: +1 415 566 4358
Fax: +1 415 566 4265
Catherine Connolly

Services/Products:
Marketing consultant

Member of:
DMA

CMC
8001 Centerview Parkway
Ste 400
Cordova
TN
38018
USA
Tel: 901 751 4800
Fax: +1 901 751 4805
Teresa Hartsaw, President

Services/Products:
Telemarketing agency

Member of:
DMA

CMC MARKETING SERVICES
65 Lincoln Road
Wellesley
MA
2181
USA
Tel: +1 617 237 4596
Fax: +1 617 235 6640
Cynthia Connelly, Principal

Services/Products:
Marketing consultant

Member of:
DMA

CME LIBRARY
222 South Ninth Street
Minneapolis
MN
55402
USA
Michelle Arntzen, VP, Director, CME
  Direct

Services/Products:
Advertising Agency; Direct Response
Agency

Member of:
DMA

CMF&Z DIRECT MARKETING
  GROUP
600 East Court
P.O. Box 4807
4th Fl
Des Moines
IA
50306
USA
Tel: +1 515 246 3500
John Bingle, CEO, Worldwide

Services/Products:
Advertising Agency; Direct Response
Agency

Member of:
DMA

CMF&Z/Y&R
4211 Signal Ridge Road, N.E.
P.O. Box 2879
4th Fl
Cedar Rapids
IA
52406–2879
USA
Tel: +1 319 395 6500
Fax: +1 319 395 6595
John Bingle, CEO, Worldwide

Services/Products:
Advertising Agency; Direct Response
Agency

Member of:
DMA

CMG DIRECT CORPORATION
187 Ballardvale Street
Ste B-110
Wilmington
MA
01887–7000
USA
Tel: 978 657 7000
Fax: +1 978 657 5062
Edward Mullen, President

Services/Products:
List services

Member of:
DMA

CMS, INC.
300 Second Street, N.W.
St. Paul
MN
55112
USA
Tel: +1 651 636 6265
Fax: +1 651 636 0879
Steven Neseth, SVP, Sales & Marketing

Services/Products:
List services

Member of:
DMA

COLANGELO MARKETING
50 Washington Street
8th Fl
South Norwalk
CT
6854
USA
Tel: +1 203 857 0064
Fax: +1 203 857 3467
Steve Bachler, Dir., Relationship
  Marketing

Services/Products:
Advertising Agency; Direct Response
Agency

Member of:
DMA

COLE & WEBER
115 N.W. First Avenue
Ste 400
Portland
OR
97209
USA
Tel: +1 503 226 2821
Fax: +1 503 226 6059
Dee Ann McCay, Group Director

Services/Products:
Advertising Agency; Direct Response
Agency

Member of:
DMA

**COLEMAN HOYT
CONSULTANTS**
Saddlebow Farm
R.F.D. 2 Box 764
Woodstock
VT
05091–9403
USA
Tel: 802 672 3634
Fax: +1 802 672 5116
Coleman Hoyt, Principal

Services/Products:
Marketing consultant

Member of:
DMA

**COLFAX ENVELOPE
CORPORATION**
951 Commerce Court
Buffalo Grove
IL
60089
USA
Tel: 847 215 1122
Fax: +1 847 215 1145
Charles Patten, Chairman & President

Services/Products:
Labelling/envelope services

Member of:
DMA

COLLINGER & ASSOCIATES
7 North Brentwood Boulevard
Ste 214
St. Louis
MO
63105
USA
Tel: +1 314 727 7488
Fax: +1 314 727 0299
W. Collinger, President

Services/Products:
Marketing consultant

Member of:
DMA

**COLUMBIA CONSULTING
GROUP**
20 South Charles Street
Baltimore
MD
21201
USA
Tel: +1 410 385 2525
Fax: +1 410 385 0044
Cory Holmes, Director, Research

Services/Products:
Marketing consultant

Member of:
DMA

**COLUMBIAN DIRECT
MARKETING**
Division of Columbian Advertising
201 East Ohio Street
Chicago
IL
60611–3234
USA
Tel: +1 312 943 7600
Fax: +1 312 943 6148
Bernard Miller, President

Services/Products:
Advertising Agency; Direct Response
Agency

Member of:
DMA

**COMMERCIAL ENVELOPE
MANUFACTURERS, INC.**
900 Grand Boulevard
Deer Park
NY
11729
USA
Tel: +1 516 242 2500
Fax: +1 516 242 6122
Mindy Kristel, Vice President

Services/Products:
Labelling/envelope services

Member of:
DMA

COMMON HEALTH DIRECT
30 Lanidex Plaza West
Parsippany
NJ
07054–2792
USA
Tel: 973 884 2200

Fax: +1 973 560 3800
Jennifer Cerulli, Manager, Precision
Marketing

Services/Products:
Database services

Member of:
DMA

**COMMUNICATION CONCEPTS
INC.**
1044 Pulinski Road
Ivyland
PA
18974–1571
USA
Tel: +1 215 672 6900
Fax: +1 215 957 4366
Mitchell Goldklank, SVP, Sales &
Marketing

Services/Products:
List services

Member of:
DMA

**COMMUNICATION SERVICE
CENTERS**
777 South State Road 7
Margate
FL
33068
USA
Tel: 954 537 8000
Fax: +1 954 969 2407
Wendy Shooster-Leucht, Senior Vice
President

Services/Products:
Telemarketing agency

Member of:
DMA

**COMMUNICATION SERVICES
GROUP**
6390–1 East Thomas Road
Ste 210
Scottsdale
AZ
85251
USA
Tel: +1 602 606 0180
Fax: +1 602 606 0189
Randy Warren, President & CEO

Services/Products:
Telemarketing agency

Member of:
DMA

COMMUNICATIONS PLUS, INC.
102 Madison Avenue
8th Fl
New York

NY
10016–7417
USA
Tel: +1 212 686 9570
Fax: +1 212 686 9687
Chris Bodden, President

Services/Products:
Advertising Agency; Direct Response
Agency

Member of:
DMA

COMMUNICATIONS TWO GROUP, INC.
220 East 42nd Street
Ste 3105
New York
NY
10017
USA
Tel: +1 212 808 4950
Fax: +1 212 808 4952
Louis Bilka, President

Services/Products:
List services

Member of:
DMA

COMMUNICOMP
6950 Cypress Road
Ste 209
Fort Lauderdale
FL
33317
USA
Tel: 954 581 0665
Fax: +1 954 581 1490
Carol Nelson, President

Services/Products:
Advertising Agency; Direct Response
Agency

Member of:
DMA

COMPILERS DIRECT
5106 N.W. 87th Terrace
Coral Springs
FL
33067–1968
USA
Tel: 954 3+44 0553
Vin Gupta, Chairman & CEO

Services/Products:
List services

Member of:
DMA

COMPUTER STRATEGY COORDINATORS, INC.
1100 Woodfield Road
Ste 320
Schaumburg
IL
60173–5123
USA
Tel: 847 +1 330 1313
Fax: +1 847 330 9155
Michael Brostoff, President

Services/Products:
List services

Member of:
DMA

CONRAD DIRECT, INC.
List Management Division
300 Knickerbocker Road
Cresskill
NJ
7626
USA
Tel: +1 201 567 3200
Fax: +1 201 567 1530
Jerry Gould, President

Services/Products:
List services

Member of:
DMA

CONSOLIDATED MARKET RESPONSE
700 West Lincoln
Ste 200
Charleston
IL
61920
USA
Tel: +1 217 348 7050
Fax: +1 217 345 1634
Paul Bunting, Vice President &
   General Mgr.

Services/Products:
Telemarketing agency

Member of:
DMA

CONSORTIA
233 South 13th Street
Ste 1200
Lincoln
NE
68508–2000
USA
Tel: +1 402 464 3600
Fax: +1 402 434 0299
Laurie Kobza, Account Director

Services/Products:
Market research agency

Member of:
DMA

CONSUMER HEALTHWORKS/ RAPP
Collins
16 West 22nd Street
4th Fl
New York
NY
10010
USA
Tel: +1 212 822 6603
G. Steven Dapper, Chairman & CEO

Services/Products:
Advertising Agency; Direct Response
Agency

Member of:
DMA

CONTINENTAL ENVELOPE CORP.
1700 Averill Road
Geneva
IL
60134
USA
Tel: +1 800 621 8155
Fax: +1 630 262 1450
Fred Margulies, Vice President

Services/Products:
Labelling/envelope services

Member of:
DMA

CORNWELL DATA SERVICES, INC.
352 Evelyn Street
Paramus
NJ
7652
USA
Tel: +1 201 261 1050
Fax: +1 201 261 7569
Peter Cornwell, President

Services/Products:
List services

Member of:
DMA

CORPORATE CALLING CENTER
500 Griswold Street
GB31
Detroit
MI
48226
USA
Tel: +1 313 256 6400

Fax: +1 313 256 6428
Gregory Tomaszewski, Operations
   Manager

Services/Products:
Telemarketing agency

Member of:
DMA

**CORRY DIRECT MARKETING,
   LLC**
109 Limekiln Road
Ridgefield
CT
6877
USA
Tel: +1 203 438 1478
Fax: +1 203 431 0217
Thomas Corry, Managing Member

Services/Products:
Marketing consultant

Member of:
DMA

COSGROVE ASSOCIATES
747 Third Avenue
16th Fl
New York
NY
10017
USA
Tel: +1 212 888 7202
Fax: +1 212 888 7201
Christina Smith, VP & Managing
   Director

Services/Products:
Advertising Agency; Direct Response
Agency

Member of:
DMA

COUNTRY MARKETING LTD.
176 East Main Street
Ilion
NY
13357
USA
Tel: +1 315 895 7737
Fax: +1 315 895 7392
Joseph Russo, Vice President

Services/Products:
List services

Member of:
DMA

COX COMMUNICATIONS, INC.
CableRep Advertising
2381 Morse Avenue
Irvine
CA
92714

USA
Tel: 949 660 0500
Fax: +1 949 660 0547
Jane D'Alessandro, Target Media
   Account Developer

Services/Products:
Advertising Agency; Direct Response
Agency

Member of:
DMA

CPC ASSOCIATES
33 Rock Hill Road
Bala Cynwyd
PA
19004
USA
Tel: +1 215 667 1780
Fax: +1 215 667 5650
David Lewis, President & CEO

Services/Products:
List services

Member of:
DMA

CPS DIRECT, INC.
20 Cabot Road
Woburn
MA
01801–1004
USA
Tel: +1 781 935 5007
Fax: +1 781 933 5716
John Bell, President

Services/Products:
Advertising Agency; Direct Response
Agency

Member of:
DMA

CPU, INC.
7 Holland Street
Irvine
CA
92618–2506
USA
Tel: +1 800 345 0145
Fax: +1 949 457 9694
Doug Engebrethson, VP, Sales &
   Marketing

Services/Products:
List services; Specialist packaging

Member of:
DMA

CRAMER-KRASSELT
225 North Michigan Avenue
24th Fl
Chicago
IL

60601
USA
Tel: +1 312 616 9600
Fax: +1 312 938 3157
Peter Krivkovich, President

Services/Products:
Advertising Agency; Direct Response
Agency

Member of:
DMA

CRANE PRODUCTION
2121 Watterson Trail
Louisville
KY
40299
USA
Tel: +1 502 261 9060
Fax: +1 502 261 9070
John Martin, President

Services/Products:
Sales promotion agency

Member of:
DMA

**CRANFORD JOHNSON
   ROBINSON WOODS, INC.**
150 Fayetteville Street Mall
Ste 2720
Raleigh
NC
27601
USA
Tel: 919 821 7303
Fax: +1 919 821 0036
Barbara Perkins, Vice President

Services/Products:
Advertising Agency; Direct Respons
Agency

Member of:
DMA

**CRAVER, MATHEWS, SMITH &
   CO.**
300 North Washington Street
Falls Church
VA
22046
USA
Tel: +1 703 237 0600
Fax: +1 703 237 0622
Rosemary Amatetti, President & CE

Services/Products:
Database services

Member of:
DMA

CRAWFORD COMMUNICATIONS GROUP
6C Culnen Drive
Somerville
NJ
08876–5400
USA
Tel: +1 800 935 5224
Fax: +1 908 722 8569
Jack Smeader, Vice President

Services/Products:
Fulfilment and sampling house

Member of:
DMA

CREATIVE AUTOMATION COMPANY
220 Fencl Lane
Hillside
IL
60162–2098
USA
Tel: +1 708 449 2800
Fax: +1 708 449 3282
John Fournier, President

Services/Products:
List services

Member of:
DMA

CREATIVE CONCEPT COORDINATORS INC
3100 Boardwalk 3008/1
Atlantic City
NJ
8401
USA
Tel: +1 609 348 5659
Fax: +1 609 344 0738
E G Axel, President & Chief Operating Officer

Services/Products:
Mail order company

Member of:
FEDMA

CREATIVE MAILINGS, INC.
1211 East Artesia Boulevard
Carson
CA
90746–1603
USA
Tel: +1 310 637 7100
Fax: +1 310 637 7747
Gayle Clark, Executive Vice President

Services/Products:
Lettershop; Mailing/Faxing services

Member of:
DMA

CREATIVE MARKETING
3 Meehan Lane
Ste D
Rockville Centre
NY
11570
USA
Tel: +1 516 594 1875
Fax: +1 516 536 1801
Alicia James, Consultant

Services/Products:
Marketing consultant

Member of:
DMA

CREATIVE STRATEGY, INC.
4550 Montgomery Avenue
Ste 649 N
Bethesda
MD
20814–3304
USA
Tel: +1 301 718 4550
Fax: +1 301 718 8828
Sally Roffman, President

Services/Products:
Advertising Agency; Direct Response Agency

Member of:
DMA

CREATIVES STRATEGIES & SOLUTIONS
853 Seventh Avenue
Ste 11-C
New York
NY
10019
USA
Tel: +1 212 541 4886
Fax: +1 212 977 9589
David Christenson, Consultant

Services/Products:
Design/graphics/clip art supplier; Consultancy services

Member of:
DMA

CREDENTIALS SERVICES INTERNATIONAL, INC.
333 City Boulevard West
Orange
CA
92668
USA
Tel: +1 714 704 6528
Fax: +1 714 704 6499
Gerry Keehan, EVP, Marketing

Services/Products:
Marketing consultant

Member of:
DMA

CRK COMPUTER SERVICES
16250 Northland Drive
Ste 012
Southfield
MI
48075
USA
Tel: +1 248 569 3050
Fax: +1 248 569 5259
Dan Neagoe, Vice President

Services/Products:
List services

Member of:
DMA

CROSS COUNTRY COMPUTER CORP.
75 Corporate Drive
Hauppauge
NY
11788–2021
USA
Tel: +1 516 231 4200
Fax: +1 516 231 9248
Richard Berger, Founder

Services/Products:
List services

Member of:
DMA

CROSS WORLD NETWORK, INC.
828 South Broadway
Tarrytown
NY
10591
USA
Tel: 914 591 6700
Fax: +1 914 591 2041
Richard Cross, President

Services/Products:
Marketing consultant

Member of:
DMA

CROSS WORLD NETWORK, INC.
828 S. Broadway
Tarrytown
NJ
10591
USA
Tel: +1 914 631 9100
Email: rcross@crossworldnetwork.com
Richard Cross, President

Services/Products:
Consultancy services; Publisher;
Website content management

E-Services:
Website design; E-Marketing
consultant

Member of:
DMA (US)

CRYOVAC
16201 Commerce Way
Cerritos
CA
90703–2324
USA
Tel: +1 800 631 9127
Fax: +1 562 404 7866
Larry Colando, Marketing Manager

Services/Products:
List services; Specialist packaging

Member of:
DMA

CSC WESTON GROUP
10 Westport Road
P. O. Box 590
Wilton
CT
06897–0590
USA
Tel: +1 203 761 7549
Fax: +1 203 762 9955
Aileen Cahill, Principal

Services/Products:
Marketing consultant

Member of:
DMA

CTC DISTRIBUTION DIRECT
6300 Shingle Creek Parkway
Ste 600
Minneapolis
MN
55430–2124
USA
Tel: +1 612 560 6000
Fax: +1 612 560 1580
John Clark, Chairman & CEO

Services/Products:
Private delivery services

Member of:
DMA

CTC TELESERVICES, INC.
2021 Midwest Road
Ste 205
Oak Brook
IL
60523
USA

Tel: +1 630 953 2826
Fax: +1 630 953 6186
Guy Scarpelli, President

Services/Products:
Telemarketing agency

Member of:
DMA

CULPEPER LISTS, INC.
10160 S.W. Nimbus Avenue
Ste F/1A
Portland
OR
97223
USA
Tel: +1 503 620 9072
Fax: +1 503 624 3671
Thelma Clark, Account Manager

Services/Products:
List services

Member of:
DMA

**CULTURAL ACCESS
WORLDWIDE**
2200 Clarendon Boulevard
Ste 1109
Arlington
VA
22201
USA
Tel: +1 703 528 7000
Fax: +1 703 812 9561
Christopher Purdy, Vice President,
Marketing

Services/Products:
Telemarketing agency

Member of:
DMA

CUNNINGHAM DIRECT, INC.
333 Jericho Turnpike
Ste 101
Jericho
NY
11753
USA
Tel: +1 516 935 4142
Fax: +1 516 935 4156
Kathleen Cunningham, President

Services/Products:
Advertising Agency; Direct Response
Agency

Member of:
DMA

**CUSTOM COMPUTER
SOFTWARE**
Services Inc.

980 Broadway
Ste 150
Thornwood
NY
10594–1139
USA
Tel: 914 747 9303
Kevin Martyn, President

Services/Products:
List services

Member of:
DMA

CUSTOM LIST SERVICES
14440 Cherry Lane Court
Ste 219
Laurel
MD
20707
USA
Tel: +1 301 497 1858
Fax: +1 301 497 1687
Cori Reider, List Services Manager

Services/Products:
List services

Member of:
DMA

**CUSTOMER DEVELOPMENT
CORP.**
8600 North Industrial Road
Peoria
IL
61615–1513
USA
Tel: +1 309 689 1000
Fax: +1 309 692 0011
Timothy Prunk, Chief Operating
Officer

Services/Products:
Advertising Agency; Direct Response
Agency

Member of:
DMA

**CUSTOMER INSIGHT
COMPANY**
5670 Greenwood Plaza Boulevard
Englewood
CO
80111–2405
USA
Tel: +1 303 790 7002
Fax: +1 303 792 9302
Connell Saltzman, Chief Finacial
Officer

Services/Products:
List services

Member of:
DMA

**CYBER M@RKETING
    SERVICES**
908 Warren Parkway
Teaneck
NJ
7666
USA
Tel: +1 201 862 0186
Fax: +1 201 837 3132
Sheri Greenhaus, Principal

E-Services:
Website design

Member of:
DMA

CYRK, INC.
3 Pond Road
Gloucester
MA
01930–1834
USA
Tel: 978 283 5800
Fax: +1 978 281 8062
Deborah Chertok, VP & Dir., Mktg.
    Operations

Services/Products:
Sales promotion agency

Member of:
DMA

D R PROSE
1724 Clarkson
Ste 143
St. Louis
MO
63017–4976
USA
Tel: +1 314 519 9219
Fax: +1 314 519 0944
Thomas Przybylski, Principal

Services/Products:
Marketing consultant

Member of:
DMA

D-J ASSOCIATES
75 Danbury Road
P.O. Box 2048
Ridgefield
CT
6877
USA
Tel: +1 203 431 8777
Fax: +1 203 431 3302
Kathy Duggan-Josephs, President

Services/Products:
List services

Member of:
DMA

D. A. LEWIS ASSOCIATES
3805 Old Easton Road
Doylestown
PA
18901
USA
Tel: +1 215 340 6800
Fax: +1 215 340 6855
David Lewis, President & CEO

Services/Products:
List services

Member of:
DMA

D. B. MARKETING INC.
234 Kennedy Drive
Horseheads
NY
14845
USA
Tel: +1 607 796 2445
Fax: +1 607 796 0655
Darcy Bevelacqua, President

Services/Products:
Database services

Member of:
DMA

D. L. BLAIR INC.
1051 Franklin Avenue
Garden City
NY
11530–2907
USA
Howard Draft, Chairman & CEO

Services/Products:
Advertising Agency; Direct Response
Agency

Member of:
DMA

D.M. ASSOCIATES
392 Amy Court
Glen Allyn
TX
60137
USA
Tel: +1 281 565 4867
Fax: +1 281 565 4876
Deone Matichak, Sole Proprietor

Services/Products:
Advertising Agency; Direct Response
Agency

Member of:
DMA

D/A/P ASSOCIATES
100 Cummings Center
Ste 400
Beverly

MA
01915–8102
USA
Tel: 978 524 8555
Fax: +1 978 524 8585
Dorothy Pike, President

Services/Products:
Advertising Agency; Direct Response
Agency

Member of:
DMA

DAISYTEK
500 North Central Expressway
Plano
TX
75074
USA
Tel: +1 214 881 4700
Fax: +1 214 881 7111
Jeff Chick, VP, Sales & Marketing

Services/Products:
Fulfilment and sampling house

Member of:
DMA

DAKOTAH DIRECT, INC.
214 North Wall Street
Spokane
WA
99201
USA
Tel: +1 509 624 2401
Fax: +1 509 624 1505
Connie Browning, Dir., Corporate
    Development

Services/Products:
Telemarketing agency

Member of:
DMA

DALY COMMUNICATIONS
4515 Willard Avenue
Ste S-1903
Chevy Chase
MD
20815–3622
USA
Tel: +1 301 656 2510
Fax: +1 301 656 8069
John Jay Daly, President, APR Fellow
    PRSA

Services/Products:
Marketing consultant

Member of:
DMA

DALY DIRECT MARKETING
8911 Bradley Boulevard
Potomac

MD
20854
USA
Tel: +1 301 365 3201
Fax: +1 301 365 7517
M. Virginia Daly, President

Services/Products:
Design/graphics/clip art supplier;
Consultancy services

Member of:
DMA

DANIEL GONZALEZ & ASSOCIATES

370 Lexington Avenue
Ste 1607
New York
NY
10017
USA
Tel: +1 212 682 0333
Fax: +1 212 682 9833
Email: gonzalezda@aol.com
Daniel Gonzalez, President

Services/Products:
Consultancy services; Copy
adaptation; Translation services;
Creative copy and concept

Member of:
DMA (US)

DATA BASE OF NORTH FLORIDA, INC.

4031-B N.W. 43rd Street
Gainesville
FL
32606–4563
USA
Tel: +1 352 694 8103
Fax: +1 352 694 3505
Carl Roepe, President

Services/Products:
List services

Member of:
DMA

DATA DECISIONS CORPORATION

225 North Federal Highway
Ste 210
Pompano Beach
FL
33062
USA
Tel: 954 781 0989
Fax: +1 954 781 5156
Randy Warren, President & CEO

Services/Products:
Telemarketing agency

Member of:
DMA

DATA HEALTH

100 Avenue of the Americas
New York
NY
10013
USA
Tel: +1 212 966 0077
Fax: +1 212 925 0178
Frank Hone, General Manager

Services/Products:
Advertising Agency; Direct Response
Agency

Member of:
DMA

DATA MAVEN

400 West 58th Street
New York
NY
10019–1117
USA
Tel: +1 212 765 4551
Fax: +1 212 246 1136
Robert Burns, Chief Engineer

Services/Products:
Marketing consultant

Member of:
DMA

DATA SERVICES INC

1800 Diagonal Road, Suite 600
Alexandria
VA
22314
USA
Tel: +1 703 684 4409
Fax: +1 703 548 8959
Gerald F Messer, President/CEO

Services/Products:
List services

Member of:
FEDMA

DATA SERVICES, INC.

31516 Winterplace Parkway
Salisbury
MD
21804
USA
Tel: +1 410 546 2206
Fax: +1 410 546 2274
Joseph Ollinger, Chairman

Services/Products:
List services

Member of:
DMA

DATA TECHNOLOGY RESOURCES,INC.

45 Mercedes Way
Edgewood
NY
11717–8349
USA
Tel: +1 516 667 5800
Fax: +1 516 667 4682
Daniel Tamilio, Senior Vice President

Services/Products:
List services

Member of:
DMA

DATA WAREHOUSE CORPORATION

2691 E. Oakland Park Blvd.
4th Fl
Ft. Lauderdale
FL
33306
USA
Tel: 888 707 7600
Fax: +1 954 781 1836
Ben Waldshan, President

Services/Products:
List services

Member of:
DMA

DATA-MAIL, INC.

240 Hartford Avenue
Newington
CT
6111
USA
Tel: 860 666 0399
Fax: +1 860 665 1226
Andrew Mandell, President

Services/Products:
Lettershop; Mailing/Faxing services

Member of:
DMA

DATABASE AMERICA COMPANIES

100 Paragon Drive
Montvale
NJ
07645–0416
USA
Tel: +1 201 476 2300
Fax: +1 201 476 2405
Vin Gupta, Chairman & CEO

Services/Products:
List services

Member of:
DMA

DATABASE MANAGEMENT
304 Park Avenue South
6th Fl
New York
NY
10010
USA
Tel: +1 212 388 8800
Fax: +1 212 388 8890
Ralph Stevens, President

Services/Products:
List services

Member of:
DMA

DATABASE MARKETING ASSOCIATES, INC.
25555 Windy Walk Drive
Unit 2
Scottsdale
AZ
85255
USA
Tel: +1 602 473 5775
Fax: +1 602 473 5777
John Coe, President

Services/Products:
Database services

Member of:
DMA

DATABASE MARKETING CONCEPTS INC.
30 Floyd Run
Bohemia
NY
11716
USA
Tel: +1 516 218 0389
Fax: +1 516 218 0395
William Korn, President

Services/Products:
List services

Member of:
DMA

DATABASE MARKETING SOLUTIONS
802 Seal Pointe Drive
Redwood Shores
CA
94065
USA
Tel: +1 650 592 8909
Fax: +1 800 452 3705
Rebecca Bell Ellis, President

Services/Products:
Marketing consultant

Member of:
DMA

DATABASE MARKETING STRATEGIES
216 Lafayette Road
Ste 204
North Hampton
NH
3862
USA
Tel: +1 603 964 6011
Fax: +1 603 964 5606
Andrew Goldstein, President

Services/Products:
Database services

Member of:
DMA

DATABASE NETWORK
169 Ramapo Valley Road
Oakland
NJ
7436
USA
Tel: +1 201 651 9015
Fred Litzky, President

Services/Products:
List services

Member of:
DMA

DATABASE PRODUCTION SERVICES
430 Eisenhower North
Lombard
IL
60148
USA
Tel: +1 630 495 5478
Fax: +1 630 495 5578
Andy Pappas, Executive Vice President

Services/Products:
List services

Member of:
DMA

DATAMANN, INC.
P. O. Box 501
Wilder
VT
5088
USA
Tel: +1 800 451 4263
Fax: +1 802 296 3623
John Mann, President

Services/Products:
List services

Member of:
DMA

DATAMARK SYSTEMS, INC.
488 East Winchester Street
Salt Lake City
UT
84107
USA
Tel: 801 268 1001
Fax: +1 801 268 2292
Fred Lederman, President & CEO

Services/Products:
Lettershop; Mailing/Faxing services

Member of:
DMA

DATAPROSE INC.
765 Arroyo
Los Alto
CA
94024
USA
Tel: 805 255 5006
William Murray, Vice President

Services/Products:
Database services

Member of:
DMA

DATAQUICK LIST SERVICES
577 Airport Boulevard
Ste 650
Burlingame
CA
94010–2023
USA
Tel: +1 800 945 5478
Fax: +1 415 548 0240
R. David Lewis, SVP/Director, List Services

Services/Products:
List services

Member of:
DMA

DATATIEMPO
7500 N.W. Street
Ste 519
Miami
FL
33122
USA
Tel: 954 438 8551
Libardo Salcedo, General Manager

Services/Products:
Database services

Member of:
DMA

DAVID GANZ MARKETING, INC.
566 Westchester Avenue
Rye Brook
NY
10573–2817
USA
Tel: 914 937 1680
Fax: +1 914 937 1968
David Ganz, President

Services/Products:
Market research agency

Member of:
DMA

DAVID HENEBERRY ASSOCIATES
1705 Bradford Drive
Danbury
CT
6811
USA
Tel: +1 203 778 0692
David Heneberry, President

Services/Products:
Marketing consultant

Member of:
DMA

DAVID SHEPARD ASSOCIATES, INC.
2 Micole Court
Dix Hills
NY
11746
USA
Tel: +1 516 271 5567
Fax: +1 516 271 5589
David Shepard, President

Services/Products:
Marketing consultant

Member of:
DMA

DAYSTAR DATA GROUP, INC.
105 West Central Road
Schaumburg
IL
60195–1945
USA
Tel: 847 +1 202 0100
Fax: +1 847 202 0107
Jim Calhoun, President

Services/Products:
List services

Member of:
DMA

DCI MARKETING
2727 West Good Hope Road
Milwaukee
WI
53209
USA
Tel: +1 414 228 7000
Fax: +1 414 228 4399
Lynn Imus, SVP & Managing Director

Services/Products:
Advertising Agency; Direct Response Agency

Member of:
DMA

DDB NEEDHAM DIRECT
437 Madison Avenue
New York
NY
10022
USA
Tel: +1 212 415 3134
Danny Snyder, SVP & Executive Creative Dir.

Services/Products:
Advertising Agency; Direct Response Agency

Member of:
DMA

DDB NEEDHAM WORLDWIDE
200 East Randolph Drive
Ste 280
Chicago
IL
60601–6414
USA
Tel: +1 312 552 6000
Fax: +1 312 552 2370
Lori Bihun, VP, Direct Marketing

Services/Products:
Advertising Agency; Direct Response Agency

Member of:
DMA

DEAVER-DANOWITZ
12 East 86th Street
Ste 605
New York
NY
10028
USA
Tel: +1 212 570 0991
Fax: +1 212 570 0991
Jeffrey Danowitz, Principal

Services/Products:
Marketing consultant

Member of:
DMA

DEBROUX MARKETING, INC.
555 South Industrial Drive
Hartland
WI
53029–2338
USA
Tel: +1 414 367 3933
Fax: +1 414 367 5352
Daniel DeBroux, Chief Executive Officer

Services/Products:
List services

Member of:
DMA

DEC INTERNATIONAL INC.
5775 Peachtree Dunwoody Road
Atlanta
GA
30342
USA
Tel: +1 404 256 1123
Fax: +1 404 705 9929
Anthony Catalano, CFO, Direct Mail Business Unit

Services/Products:
Lettershop; Mailing/Faxing services

Member of:
DMA

DEES COMMUNICATIONS, INC./FULLER FUND RAISING CO.
2540 East Fifth Street
P.O. Box 931
Montgomery
AL
36107
USA
Tel: +1 334 263 4436
Fax: +1 334 263 4437
Allen Dees, President

Services/Products:
Advertising Agency; Direct Response Agency

Member of:
DMA

DEPENDABLE LISTS, INC.
1450 East American Lane
Ste 1545
Schaumburg
IL
60173
USA
Tel: 847 995 1234
Fax: +1 847 995 0358
Carl Bender, Chairman & CEO

Services/Products:
List services

Member of:
DMA

DESIGN VECTORS, INC.
725 Greenwich Street
4th Fl
San Francisco
CA
94133
USA
Tel: +1 415 391 0399
Fax: +1 415 391 0454
Anthony Williams, President & Owner

Services/Products:
Database services

Member of:
DMA

**DEUTSCHE POST GLOBAL
 MAIL**
22560 Glenn Drive
Ste 105
Sterling
VA
20164–4400
USA
Tel: +1 800 545 8794
Fax: +1 703 450 7638
Web: www.globalmail.com
Katherine Renaud, Director, Business
 Development

Services/Products:
Consultancy services; Database
services; Mailing/Faxing services;
Lettershop; Private delivery services;
International mailing service

Member of:
FEDMA; DMA (US)

**DEUTSCHE POST GLOBAL
 MAIL**
22560 Glenn Drive
Suite 105
Sterling
VA 20164
USA
Katherine Renaud, Director of
 Business Development, USA

Services/Products:
Consultancy services; Labelling/
envelope services; Lettershop; List
services; Mailing/Faxing services;
Private delivery services; International
postal mailing services

Member of:
FEDMA; DMA (US)

DEVON DIRECT
200 Berwyn Park
Berwyn
PA

19312–1178
USA
Tel: +1 610 644 0333
Fax: +1 610 651 2627
Ronald Greene, CEO & President

Services/Products:
Advertising Agency; Direct Response
Agency

Member of:
DMA

DEVRIES DIRECT MARKETING
Assistance
4 Chapel Road
North Hampton
NH
3862
USA
Tel: +1 603 964 9867
Wes DeVries, President

Services/Products:
Marketing consultant

Member of:
DMA

DFA ADVERTISING INC.
sub. of Burrell Comm. Corp.
432 Park Avenue South
New York
NY
10016
USA
Tel: +1 212 252 1501
Fax: +1 212 252 1913
Ed Forti

Services/Products:
Advertising Agency; Direct Response
Agency

Member of:
DMA

**DIALAMERICA MARKETING
 INC.**
960 Macarthur Boulevard
Mahwah
NJ
7495
USA
Tel: +1 201 327 0200
Robert Fischer, SVP, Finance

Services/Products:
Telemarketing agency

Member of:
DMA

DIALOG SOFTWARE
708 Third Avenue
New York
NY
10017

USA
Tel: +1 212 697 2690
Fax: +1 212 697 2129
Peter Tobeason, President

Services/Products:
List services

Member of:
DMA

DIALOGOS, INC.
12 Farnsworth Street
6th Fl
Boston
MA
02210–1224
USA
Tel: +1 617 357 4722
Fax: +1 617 357 4727
Vernon Tirey, President

Services/Products:
Marketing consultant

Member of:
DMA

DIALOGUE MARKETING
26899 Northwestern Highway
Ste 421
Southfield
MI
48034
USA
Tel: 810 827 4700
Fax: +1 810 357 4583
Roberta Black, President & CEO

Services/Products:
Telemarketing agency

Member of:
DMA

**DIAMOND LIST MARKETING
 COMPANY**
6715 Little River Turnpike
Ste 207
Annandale
VA
22003–3546
USA
Tel: +1 703 750 9649
Fax: +1 703 914 1499
Steven LeBlanc, President

Services/Products:
List services

Member of:
DMA

DICKINSON DIRECT
120 Campanelli Drive
Braintree
MA
2184

USA
Tel: +1 781 849 3700
Fax: +1 781 843 1338
Randy Burge, VP, Creative Services

Services/Products:
Advertising Agency; Direct Response
Agency

Member of:
DMA

DIEBOLD INCORPORATED
3792 Boettler Oaks Drive, Suite A
Uniontown
Ohio
44685–7769
USA
Tel: +1 330 899 2500
Fax: +1 330 899 2553
Email: supplies@diebold.com
Web: www.diebold.com/dm
Pamela G Barron, Director of Direct
   Marketing

Services/Products:
Call centre services/systems; Catalogue
producer; Direct marketing agency

Member of:
DMA (US)

DIEDRE MOIRE
   CORPORATION, INC.
510 Horizon Center
Robbinsville
NJ
8691
USA
Tel: +1 609 584 9000
Fax: +1 609 584 9575
Stephen Reuning, President

Services/Products:
List services

Member of:
DMA

DIGISOFT COMPUTERS, INC.
369 Lexington Avenue
New York
NY
10017
USA
Tel: +1 212 687 1810
Fax: +1 212 687 1781
Andrew Davidson, Marketing
   Coordinator

Services/Products:
Telemarketing agency

Member of:
DMA

DIGITAL IMPACT
1730 South Ampalett Boulevard
Ste 217
San Mateo
CA
94402
USA
Tel: +1 650 286 7300
Fax: +1 650 286 7310
William Park, President

E-Services:
Website design

Member of:
DMA

DIGITAL MARKETING
   SERVICES, INC.
2413 Cypress Drive
Lewisville
TX
75067–6523
USA
Tel: +1 214 459 1159
Fax: +1 214 459 1170
Dennis Gonier, President

Services/Products:
Market research agency

Member of:
DMA

DIMAC DIRECT
One Corporate Woods Drive
Bridgeton
MO
63044–3838
USA
Tel: +1 314 344 8000
Fax: +1 314 344 8099
Anthony Catalano, CFO, Direct Mail
   Business Unit

Services/Products:
Lettershop; Mailing/Faxing services

Member of:
DMA

DIMARK MARKETING
2050 Cabot Boulevard West
Langhorne
PA
19047–1895
USA
Tel: +1 800 543 2212
Fax: +1 215 750 7418
John Harrison, President

Services/Products:
Advertising Agency; Direct Response
Agency

Member of:
DMA

DIMASSIMO
20 Cooper Square
6th Fl
New York
NY
10003
USA
Tel: +1 212 253 7500
Fax: +1 212 228 8810
Mark DiMassimo, President &
   Creative Director

Services/Products:
Advertising Agency; Direct Response
Agency

Member of:
DMA

DIRECT ACCESS MARKETING
   SERVICES, INC.
33 Queens Street
Syosset
NY
11791–3007
USA
Tel: +1 516 364 2777
Fax: +1 516 364 0644
Thomas Saracco, President

Services/Products:
List services

Member of:
DMA

DIRECT AD-VANTAGE, INC.
223 West Erie
Ste 5EC
Chicago
IL
60610
USA
Tel: +1 312 440 0999
Fax: +1 312 440 9349
Dan Grisko, President

Services/Products:
Advertising Agency; Direct Response
Agency

Member of:
DMA

DIRECT COMM
8 Morgan Avenue
Norwalk
CT
6851
USA
Tel: +1 203 831 8000
Fax: +1 203 831 8004
Gay Tucker, Database Analyst

Services/Products:
Marketing consultant

Member of:
DMA

DIRECT DATA CAPTURE LTD.
755 New York Ave.
Suite 307
Huntington
NY
11743
USA
Tel: +1 631 547 5500
Fax: +1 631 547 6800
Email: jan@datacapture.com
Web: www.datacapture.com
Jan Trevalyan, President

DIRECT DEUTSCH
215 Park Avenue South
New York
NY
10003
USA
Tel: +1 212 995 7500
Fax: +1 212 777 1178
Adrienne Perkov, VP & Account
   Director

Services/Products:
Advertising Agency; Direct Response
Agency

Member of:
DMA

DIRECT EFFECT
1201 Camino del Mar
Ste 214
Del Mar
CA
92014
USA
Tel: +1 619 792 9259
Fax: +1 619 792 9946
Bernard Ryan, President

Services/Products:
List services

Member of:
DMA

DIRECT IMPACT
3911 Capital of Texas Highway
Ste A-101
Austin
TX
78759
USA
Tel: +1 512 231 8544
Fax: +1 512 231 8524
Janet Rubio, President

Services/Products:
Advertising Agency; Direct Response
Agency

Member of:
DMA

DIRECT IMPACT, INC.
8420 Delmar Boulevard
Ste LL6
St. Louis
MO
63124–2170
USA
Tel: +1 314 567 0024
Fax: +1 314 567 1497
Susan Christensen, Managing Partner

Services/Products:
Advertising Agency; Direct Response
Agency

Member of:
DMA

DIRECT INTERNATIONAL, INC.
1501 Third Avenue
New York
NY
10028–2101
USA
Tel: +1 212 861 4188
Fax: +1 212 986 3757
Alfred Goodloe, President

Services/Products:
Marketing consultant

Member of:
DMA

DIRECT LANGUAGE COMMUNICATIONS, INC.
301 Mission Street
Ste 350
San Francisco
CA
94105
USA
Tel: +1 415 546 6885
Fax: +1 415 495 4926
Amy Gard, VP, Strategic Planning

Services/Products:
Advertising Agency; Direct Response
Agency

Member of:
DMA

DIRECT MAIL DYNAMICS, INC.
3301 W 5th Street
Oxnard
CA
93030
USA
Tel: 805 383 9518

Fax: +1 805 382 9428
Gerry Waite, President

Services/Products:
List services

Member of:
DMA

DIRECT MAIL OF MAINE
P. O. Box 10
Scarborough
ME
04070–0010
USA
Tel: +1 207 883 6930
Fax: +1 207 883 2160
Theresa McCann, Vice President,
   Marketing

Services/Products:
Fulfilment and sampling house

Member of:
DMA

DIRECT MAIL TRACKERS
(Division of List Technology Systems
   Group)
74D Southaven Avenue
Medford
NY
11763
USA
Tel: +1 631 207 0380
Fax: +1 631 207 0383
Email: khaining@aol.com
Web: www.ltsg.com
Kevin Haining, Director

Services/Products:
List services

E-Services:
Email list provider

Member of:
DMA (US)

DIRECT MARKETERS ON CALL
45 Christopher Street
New York
NY
10014
USA
Tel: +1 212 691 1942
Fax: +1 212 924 1331
Heather Frayne, President

Services/Products:
Consultancy services

E-Services:
E-Marketing consultant

437

Member of:
DMA (US); Direct Marketing Club of
New York; New York New Media
Association; Woman in Direct
Marketing

**DIRECT MARKETING
ASSISTANCE, INC.**
80 Sea Road
P.O. Box 60
Rye Beach
NH
3871
USA
Tel: +1 603 964 6156
Fax: +1 603 964 1427
Wes DeVries, President

Services/Products:
Marketing consultant

Member of:
DMA

**DIRECT MARKETING
ASSOCIATES, INC.**
4545 Annapolis Road
Baltimore
MD
21227
USA
Tel: +1 410 636 6660
Fax: +1 410 636 2638
Kenneth Boone, President

Services/Products:
Lettershop; Mailing/Faxing services

Member of:
DMA

**DIRECT MARKETING DATA
CORP.**
60 East 42nd Street
Ste 3810
New York
NY
10165
USA
Tel: +1 212 697 5751
Harry Chevan, Senior Vice President

Services/Products:
Marketing consultant

Member of:
DMA

**DIRECT MARKETING
EXPERTS**
699 Hampshire Road
Ste 100
Westlake Village
CA
91361
USA
Tel: 805 379 0822

Fax: +1 805 379 0622
Spencer Schmerling, Founder

Services/Products:
List services

Member of:
DMA

**DIRECT MARKETING
MANAGEMENT**
8100 Three Chopt Road
Ste 104
Richmond
VA
23229–4833
USA
Tel: 804 285 3128
Fax: +1 804 285 7838
Joan Lassiter, President

Services/Products:
Marketing consultant

Member of:
DMA

**DIRECT MARKETING
PARTNERS**
55 East Front Street
M15
Bridgeport
PA
19405
USA
Tel: +1 610 279 9930
Fax: +1 610 279 9935
Galen Denton, President

Services/Products:
List services

Member of:
DMA

**DIRECT MARKETING
RESEARCH ASSOCIATES**
4151 Middlefield Road
Ste 200
Palo Alto
CA
94303
USA
Tel: +1 650 856 9988
Fax: +1 650 856 9192
Michael Green, President

Services/Products:
Market research agency

Member of:
DMA

**DIRECT MARKETING
RESOUCE GROUP, INC.**
23113 North 89th Place
Scottsdale
AR

85255
USA
Tel: +1 480 513 4956
Fax: +1 480 473 1481
Email: devomeg@aol.com
George Hunter, President

Services/Products:
Database services; Consultancy
services; Response analysis bureau

Member of:
DMA (US)

**DIRECT MARKETING
RESOURCES GROUP, INC.**
305 Madison Avenue
Ste 1166
New York
NY
10165–1001
USA
Tel: +1 212 679 1881
Fax: +1 212 679 2552
Vince Dema, President, CEO

Services/Products:
Marketing consultant

Member of:
DMA

**DIRECT MARKETING
RESOURCES, INC.**
301 Duck Road
Grandview
MO
64030
USA
Tel: 816 767 9700
Fax: +1 816 767 0770
Larry Medlin, President

Services/Products:
List services

Member of:
DMA

**DIRECT MARKETING
SERVICES**
3 Ridley Court
Glen Ridge
NJ
7028
USA
Tel: 973 259 9115
Fax: +1 973 259 9105
Mel Lundy-Day, Owner

Services/Products:
Marketing consultant

Member of:
DMA

DIRECT MARKETING SERVICES INTERNATIONAL

13723 Butterfly Lane
Houston
TX
77079–7031
USA
Tel: +1 713 463 6999
Fax: +1 713 463 7737
Email: dmsi@gateway.net
Robert Overton, President

Services/Products:
Consultancy services; Marketing consultant

Member of:
DMA (US); FEDMA

DIRECT MARKETING SERVICES, INC.

6390 East Thomas Road
Ste 300
Scottsdale
AZ
85251
USA
Tel: +1 602 994 9900
Fax: +1 602 994 9919
Dorothy Millman, President

Services/Products:
Telemarketing agency

Member of:
DMA

DIRECT MARKETING TECHNOLOGY

955 American Lane
Schaumburg
IL
60173–4998
USA
Tel: 847 517 5600
Fax: +1 847 517 5189
Gwenn Kyzer, Vice President

Services/Products:
List services

Member of:
DMA

DIRECT OPTIONS

9292 Cincinnati Columbus Road
Cincinnati
OH
45241
USA
Tel: +1 513 779 7335
Fax: +1 513 779 7706
Jan Moore, President

Services/Products:
Advertising Agency; Direct Response Agency

DIRECT PARTNERS

902 Colorado Avenue
Santa Monica
CA
90401
USA
Tel: +1 310 393 6222
Fax: +1 310 395 1499
Skip Reed, Partner

Services/Products:
Advertising Agency; Direct Response Agency

Member of:
DMA

DIRECT RESOURCES INTERNATIONAL INTERACTIVE

591 Broadway
New York
NY
10012
USA
Tel: +1 212 226 0060
Fax: +1 212 226 0974
Andrew C ohen, President & CEO

Services/Products:
Advertising Agency; Direct Response Agency

Member of:
DMA

DIRECT RESPONSE ENHANCEMENTS

12772 East Sunnyside Drive
Scottsdale
AZ
85259
USA
Tel: +1 602 451 7384
Fax: +1 602 661 8460
Gail Eberlein, President

Services/Products:
Marketing consultant

Member of:
DMA

DIRECT RESULTS GROUP, INC.

266 Summer Street
Boston
MA
2210
USA
Tel: +1 617 250 5000
Fax: +1 617 250 5001
James Hackett, President

Services/Products:
Advertising Agency; Direct Response Agency

Member of:
DMA

DIRECT SUCCESS COMMUNICATIONS

308 Lynne Place
Ste 100
Chester Springs
PA
19425
USA
Tel: +1 610 321 0321
Fax: +1 610 321 0322
Stephanie Schmidt, Principal

Services/Products:
Advertising Agency; Direct Response Agency

Member of:
DMA

DIRECTCOM, INC.

3 Garret Mountain Plaza
West Paterson
NJ
7424
USA
Tel: 973 523 2500
Fax: +1 973 523 6646
Nicholas Robinson, Chief Executive Officer

Services/Products:
Database services

Member of:
DMA

DIRECTECH, INC.

450 Bedford Street
Lexington
MA
2420
USA
Tel: +1 781 861 9797
Fax: +1 781 861 1904
Barry Silverstein, President

Services/Products:
Advertising Agency; Direct Response Agency

Member of:
DMA

DIRECTIVES/TARGETED MARKETING AND COMMUNICATIONS

246 High Street
Milford
CT
6460

USA
Tel: +1 203 783 1+1 203
Fax: +1 203 783 1203
Carolyn Gould, President

Services/Products:
Marketing consultant

Member of:
DMA

DIRECTORY DISTRIBUTING ASSOCIATES INC.
P. O. Box 116
Somerville
MA
02143–0116
USA
Tel: +1 617 623 1685
Fax: +1 617 623 2136
Stan Sivori, Vice President

Services/Products:
Private delivery services

Member of:
DMA

DIRKX DIRECT INTERNATIONAL
One Vista Loma
Ste 101
Rancho Mirage
CA
92270–2959
USA
Tel: +1 760 321 4312
Fax: +1 760 321 8130
Gerard Dirkx, Consultant

Services/Products:
Marketing consultant

Member of:
DMA

DISPATCH CONSUMER SERVICES
7801 North Central Drive
P.O. Box 262
Lewis Center
OH
43035–0262
USA
Tel: +1 740 548 2100
Fax: +1 740 548 9738
Stephen Zonars, VP, Sales & Marketing

Services/Products:
Private delivery services

Member of:
DMA

DIVERSIFIED DIRECT
1301 Burton Street
Fullerton
CA

92831–5212
USA
Tel: +1 714 776 4520
Fax: +1 714 776 2590
Email: sales@diversified-direct.com
Web: www.diversified-direct.com
Peter Friedrich, General Manager

Services/Products:
Personalisation; Print services;
Fulfilment and sampling house;
Labelling/envelope services;
Lettershop; List services

Member of:
DMA (US); MASA

DKP & ASSOCIATES, INC.
8340 North Lincoln Avenue
Ste 100
Skokie
IL
60077–2462
USA
Tel: 847 933 9808
Fax: +1 847 933 9821
Deborah Pearlman, Consultant

Services/Products:
Telemarketing agency

Member of:
DMA

DM GROUP
8903 Presidential Parkway
Ste 201
Upper Marlboro
MD
20772
USA
Tel: +1 301 420 5695
Fax: +1 301 420 5616
Clifford Stewart, Vice President

Services/Products:
Lettershop; Mailing/Faxing services

Member of:
DMA

DM GROUP
251 West Garfield Rd. #220
Aurora
OH
44202
USA
Tel: +1 330 995 0864
Fax: +1 330 995 6259
Robert Hicks, President

Services/Products:
Advertising Agency; Direct Response
Agency

Member of:
DMA

DM NEWS/DM NEWS INTERNATIONAL
100 Avenue of the Americas, 6th Floor
New York
NY
10013
USA
Tel: +1 212 925 7300
Fax: +1 212 925 8752
Email: adrian @dmnews.com
Web: www.dmnews.com
Adrian Courtenay, President

Services/Products:
Publisher

Member of:
FEDMA; DMA (US)

DMDA, INC.
2410 Gateway Drive
Irving
TX
75063–2727
USA
Tel: +1 214 466 9600
Fax: +1 214 466 0433
Ronda Evans, Director, Corporate
Marketing

Services/Products:
Database services

Member of:
DMA

DMG LISTS LTD.
1981 Marcus Avenue
Ste 214
Lake Success
NY
11042–1038
USA
Tel: +1 516 775 3400
Fax: +1 516 775 7900
Fred Bruno, President & CEO

Services/Products:
List services

Member of:
DMA

DMRS GROUP, INC.
304 Park Avenue South
11th Floor
New York
NY
10010
USA
Tel: +1 212 590 2340
Fax: +1 212 590 2341
Email: bgrossman@dmrsgroup.com
Web: www.dmrsgroup.com
Bernice Grossman, President

Services/Products:
Database services; Call centre services/ systems; Consultancy services

E-Services:
E-Marketing consultant

Member of:
DMA (US); National DMA; WDRG; NYDM Club

DMS
P. O. Box 2995
Guaynabo
PR
00970–2995
USA
Tel: +1 787 792 7005
Fax: +1 787 792 6755
Kenneth Sewell, President

Services/Products:
List services

Member of:
DMA

DMS DIRECT MARKETING SERVICES, INC.
6390–4 East Thomas
Ste 210
Scottsdale
AZ
85251
USA
Tel: +1 602 606 0000
Fax: +1 602 606 0197
Randy Warren, President & CEO

Services/Products:
Telemarketing agency

Member of:
DMA

DMTG, INC.
350 7th Avenue
Ste 702
New York
NY
10001
USA
Tel: +1 212 924 6774
Fax: +1 212 924 5327
Jane Moritz, President

Services/Products:
Advertising Agency; Direct Response Agency

Member of:
DMA

DMW WORLDWIDE
1325 Morris Drive
Chesterbrook Village
Wayne
PA

19087
USA
Tel: +1 610 407 0407
Fax: +1 610 407 0410
Thomas McClure, Chairman & CEO

Services/Products:
Advertising Agency; Direct Response Agency

Member of:
DMA

DMW WORLDWIDE
45 Braintree Hill Office Park
Braintree
MA
02184–8723
USA
Tel: +1 617 356 3200
Fax: +1 617 356 3299
Anthony Catalano, CFO, Direct Mail Business Unit

Services/Products:
Lettershop; Mailing/Faxing services

Member of:
DMA

DODD SMITH DANN, INC.
125 E. Sir Francis Drake Blvd.
Larkspur
CA
94939
USA
Tel: +1 415 461 6202
Fax: +1 415 461 7953
Rosemary Amatetti, President & CEO

Services/Products:
Database services

Member of:
DMA

DONER DIRECT
400 East Pratt Street
Baltimore
MD
21202
USA
Tel: +1 410 347 1600
Fax: +1 410 385 9316
Judy Carpenito, Group Account Director

Services/Products:
Advertising Agency; Direct Response Agency

Member of:
DMA

DORAN & FORGACS, INC.
1306 Barkway Lane
West Chester
PA

19380
USA
Tel: +1 610 344 0570
Fax: +1 610 344 7203
Barbara Doran, President

Services/Products:
Marketing consultant

Member of:
DMA

DOROTHY KERR & ASSOCIATES
1509 East Standish Place
Milwaukee
WI
53217–1960
USA
Tel: +1 414 228 0335
Fax: +1 414 228 0337
Dorothy Kerr, President

Services/Products:
Marketing consultant

Member of:
DMA

DOT-COM DIRECT
1035 South Semoran Boulevard
Ste 1012
Winter Park
FL
32677
USA
Tel: +1 407 677 6531
Fax: +1 407 677 8768
Email: info@Dot-ComDIRECT
Web: www.Dot-ComDIRECT.com
Michael Dambro, President

Services/Products:
Advertising Agency; Consultancy services; Direct marketing agency; Interactive media; List services

E-Services:
E-Marketing consultant; Online/ e-marketing agency

Member of:
American Advertising Federation; Association of Internet Professionals

DOUBLE ENVELOPE CORPORATION
Convertagraphics Division
7702 Plantation Road, N.W.
P.O. Box 7000
Roanoke
VA
24019–7000
USA
Tel: +1 540 362 3311

Fax: +1 540 366 8401
Anthony Catalano, CFO, Direct Mail
   Business Unit

Services/Products:
Lettershop; Mailing/Faxing services

Member of:
DMA

**DOUBLE ENVELOPE
   CORPORATION**
P. O. Box 15550
Ft Lauderdale
FL
33318–5550
USA
Tel: 954 583 3595
Anthony Catalano, CFO, Direct Mail
   Business Unit

Services/Products:
Lettershop; Mailing/Faxing services

Member of:
DMA

**DOUGLAS NEWTON &
   ASSOCIATES**
344 South Avenue
New Canaan
CT
06840–6312
USA
Tel: +1 203 801 4347
Fax: +1 203 972 3081
Douglas Newton, President

Services/Products:
Marketing consultant

Member of:
DMA

DRAFTWORLDWIDE
633 North St. Clair Street
Chicago
IL
60611–3211
USA
Tel: +1 312 944 3500
Fax: +1 312 944 3566
Howard Draft, Chairman & CEO

Services/Products:
Advertising Agency; Direct Response
Agency

Member of:
DMA

**DRAKE BUSINESS SERVICES,
   INC.**
460 Park Avenue South
11th Fl
New York
NY
10016

USA
Tel: +1 212 679 4777
Fax: +1 212 679 7227
Rhonda Knehans Drake, President

Services/Products:
Marketing consultant

Member of:
DMA

**DRAKE BUSINESS SERVICES,
   INC.**
3 Depot Plaza
11th Fl
Bedford Hills
NY
10507
USA
Tel: 914 2+44 1866
Fax: +1 914 244 1856
Rhonda Knehans Drake, President

Services/Products:
Marketing consultant

Member of:
DMA

DRESDEN DIRECT, INC.
1200 High Ridge Road
Stamford
CT
6905
USA
Tel: +1 203 329 3030
Fax: +1 203 322 6107
Phillip Dresden, President

Services/Products:
List services

Member of:
DMA

DROP SHIP EXPRESS
2725 Wayzata Boulevard West
Long Lake
MN
55356–0847
USA
Tel: +1 612 473 8606
Fax: +1 612 476 7488
Roy Ferber, President

Services/Products:
Private delivery services

Member of:
DMA

**DUFFEY, PETROSKY &
   COMPANY**
29425 Northwestern Highway
Ste 300
Southfield
MI
48034

USA
Tel: +1 248 204 6200
Fax: +1 248 204 6201
William Patterson, Dir., Relationship
   Marketing

Services/Products:
Advertising Agency; Direct Response
Agency

Member of:
DMA

DUGAN VALVA CONTESS
10 Park Avenue
Morristown
NJ
07960–4709
USA
Tel: +1 201 539 8880
Fax: +1 201 984 2320
Joseph Poggi, SVP & Account Director

Services/Products:
Sales promotion agency

Member of:
DMA

DUNCAN/SHANNON
1010 B Street
San Rafael
CA
94901
USA
Tel: +1 415 485 6066
Robert Duncan, President

Services/Products:
Advertising Agency; Direct Response
Agency

Member of:
DMA

**DUNHILL INTERNATIONAL
   LIST COMPANY, INC.**
1951 N.W. 19th Street
Boca Raton
FL
33431–7344
USA
Tel: +1 561 347 0200
Fax: +1 561 347 0400
Robert Dunhill, President

Services/Products:
List services

Member of:
DMA

**DW STEVENSON &
   ASSOCIATES**
9638 North 27th Place
Phoenix
AZ
85028–4725

USA
Tel: +1 602 494 7441
Fax: +1 602 494 7481
Dudley Stevenson, CEO

Services/Products:
Marketing consultant

Member of:
DMA

DYDACOMP DEVELOPMENT CORP.
150 River Road
Ste N1
Montville
NJ
7045
USA
Tel: 973 335 0961
Fax: +1 973 335 1123
Dave Kopp, President

Services/Products:
List services

Member of:
DMA

DYNAMARK, INC.
4295 Lexington Avenue North
St. Paul
MN
55126–6164
USA
Tel: +1 651 482 8593
Fax: +1 651 486 9688
Judy German, Director, Marketing

Services/Products:
List services

Member of:
DMA

DYNAMIC INFORMATION SYSTEMS CORPORATION (DISC)
5733 Central Avenue
Boulder
CO
80301
USA
Tel: +1 303 444 4000
Fax: +1 303 444 7460
Michael Lin, Director, Marketing

Services/Products:
Database services

Member of:
DMA

E-DIALOG INC.
1646 Massachusetts Avenue
Lexington
MA
2420

USA
Tel: +1 781 863 8117
Fax: +1 781 863 8117
William Herp, President

E-Services:
Website design

Member of:
DMA

EAGLE DIRECT
5105 East 41st Avenue
Denver
CO
80216
USA
Tel: +1 303 320 5411
Fax: +1 303 393 6584
Howard Harris, President

Services/Products:
Advertising Agency; Direct Response Agency

Member of:
DMA

EAGLE PUBLSHING
One Massachusetts Avenue, N.W.
Ste 207
Washington
DC
USA
Tel: +1 202 216 0600
Fax: +1 202 216 0614
Steven LeBlanc, President

Services/Products:
List services

Member of:
DMA

ECLASS DIRECT
625 Miramontes Street
Ste 206
Half Moon Bay
CA
94019
USA
Tel: +1 650 712 6700
Fax: +1 650 712 6719
Thomas Klenke, President

Services/Products:
Advertising Agency; Direct Response Agency

Member of:
DMA

ECOCENTERS/TMSI
31225 Bainbridge Road
Solon
OH
44139–6400
USA

Tel: +1 440 498 4900
Fax: +1 440 498 4920
Rob Meister, Senior Consultant

Services/Products:
List services

Member of:
DMA

ED BURNETT CONSULTANTS, INC.
A Database America Company
100 Paragon Drive
Montavale
NJ
07645–0416
USA
Tel: +1 201 476 2300
Fax: +1 201 476 2405
Vin Gupta, Chairman & CEO

Services/Products:
List services

Member of:
DMA

EDELMAN PUBLIC RELATIONS
Worldwide
200 East Randolph Drive
Chicago
IL
60601
USA
Tel: +1 312 240 3000
Fax: +1 312 240 2900
Clifton Critchlow, Sales VP, Direct Response

Services/Products:
Telemarketing agency

Member of:
DMA

EDIRECT, INC.
4680 Blue Lake Drive
Ste 200
Boca Raton
FL
33431
USA
Tel: +1 561 999 4650
Fax: +1 561 999 4699
Steve Hardigree, President & CEO

E-Services:
Website design

Member of:
DMA

EDITH ROMAN ASSOCIATES, INC
Blue Hill Plaza, 16th Fl
P.O. Box 1556
Pearl River

NY
10965–3104
USA
Tel: +1 800223 2194
Fax: +1 914 620 9035
John Ganis, Director, List
  Management

Services/Products:
List services

Member of:
DMA

EDITORIAL PERFIL
200 East 58th Street
New York
NY
10022
USA
Tel: +1 212 888 6453
Carlos Andalo

Services/Products:
Advertising Agency; Direct Response
Agency

Member of:
DMA

EDMARO'S, INC.
301 Wilcrest Drive
Ste 3305
Houston
TX
77042
USA
Tel: +1 713 784 4606
Fax: +1 713 784 4651
W. O'Shields, Director

Services/Products:
List services

Member of:
DMA

**EDUCATIONAL LIST
  SERVICES, INC**
7229 Olde Salem Circle
Hanover Park
IL
60103
USA
Tel: +1 630 213 2128
Fax: +1 630 830 3840
Jeffrey Quinn, VP & General Manager

Services/Products:
List services

Member of:
DMA

EDWARD RAST AND COMPANY
235 Montgomery Street
Ste 901
San Francisco

CA
94104–3002
USA
Tel: +1 415 986 1710
Fax: +1 415 986 1711
Edward Rast, Managing Director

Services/Products:
Marketing consultant

Member of:
DMA

EISNER & ASSOCIATES INC.
12 West Madison Street
Baltimore
MD
21201
USA
Tel: +1 410 685 3390
Fax: +1 410 685 0387
Cory Farrugia, VP, Direct Marketing

Services/Products:
Advertising Agency; Direct Response
Agency

Member of:
DMA

ELEANOR L. STARK CO., INC.
515 Madison Avenue
Ste 2300
New York
NY
10022
USA
Tel: +1 212 838 1935
Fax: +1 212 751 2024
Email: elstarkco@aol.com
Eleanor Stark, President

Services/Products:
List services; List management

Member of:
DMA (US)

ELEPHANT & CHUMLEY, LLC
2540 Mass Avenue, N.W.
Washington
DC
20008
USA
Tel: +1 202 797 0570
Fax: +1 202 588 5830
Susannah Smith

Services/Products:
Marketing consultant

Member of:
DMA

**ELIZABETH TAYLOR
  MARKETING SERVICES**
1430 Park Circle
Tampa

FL
33604
USA
Tel: 813 237 8497
Fax: +1 813 239 2175
Elizabeth Taylor, President

Services/Products:
Marketing consultant

Member of:
DMA

EMAGINET, INC.
6903 Rockledge Drive
Ste 1200
Bethesda
MD
20817
USA
Tel: +1 301 564 6700
Fax: +1 301 564 6250
Michelle Tennant, Marketing
  Coordinator

E-Services:
Website design

Member of:
DMA

EMAIL CHANNEL, INC.
751 Park of Commerce Drive
Ste 124
Boca Raton
FL
33487
USA
Tel: +1 561 226 3624
Fax: +1 561 226 3636
John Lawlor, President

E-Services:
Website design

Member of:
DMA

EMERGINGMEDIA, INC.
123 Townsend Street
Ste 550
San Francisco
CA
94107
USA
Tel: +1 415 977 1616
Fax: +1 415 977 1620
Laura Faucett, President

Services/Products:
Advertising Agency; Direct Response
Agency

Member of:
DMA

**EMMERLING POST
ADVERTISING, INC.**
415 Madison Avenue
New York
NY
10017–1163
USA
Tel: +1 212 753 4700
Fax: +1 212 753 4996
Peter Post, President

Services/Products:
Advertising Agency; Direct Response
Agency

Member of:
DMA

ENPACK DIGITAL MEDIA
3553 South Main Street
Salt Lake City
UT
84115
USA
Tel: 801 266 2280
Fax: +1 801 266 2576
Fernando Delgado, President

Services/Products:
Market research agency

Member of:
DMA

ENTELECHY SYSTEMS, INC.
2727 Paces Ferry Road
One Paces West
14th Fl
Atlanta
GA
30339
USA
Tel: +1 770 240 7400
Fax: +1 770 240 7474
Jack Jessen, President

Services/Products:
Telemarketing agency

Member of:
DMA

**ENTERON CREATIVE
SERVICES**
557 West Polk Street
Chicago
IL
60607
USA
Tel: +1 312 347 0175
Fax: +1 312 347 4563
Ted Leeper, President

Services/Products:
Design/graphics/clip art supplier;
Consultancy services

Member of:
DMA

EPSILON
50 Cambridge Street
Burlington
MA
1803
USA
Tel: +1 781 273 0250
Fax: +1 781 229 6005
Ronda Evans, Director, Corporate
Marketing

Services/Products:
Database services

Member of:
DMA

ERA
1255 New York Avenue, NW, Suite
1200
Washington
DC
20005
USA
Tel: +1 202 289 6462
Fax: +1 202 962 83006
Elissa Matulis-Myers, President and
CEO

Services/Products:
Advertising Agency; Direct Response
Agency

Member of:
FEDMA

ERIC MOWER & ASSOCIATES
350 Linden Oaks Drive
Rochester
NY
14625
USA
Tel: +1 716 385 2000
Fax: +1 716 385 2003
Kathleen Tighe Gaye, Partner, DM
Services

Services/Products:
Advertising Agency; Direct Response
Agency

Member of:
DMA

ERLANDSON ASSOCIATES
8456 Hunt Valley Drive
Vienna
VA
22182
USA
Tel: +1 703 827 7545
Fax: +1 703 827 7546
Barbara Erlandson, President

Services/Products:
Marketing consultant

Member of:
DMA

**ERNAN ROMAN DIRECT
MARKETING CORPORATION**
3 Melrose Lane
Douglas Manor
NY
11363
USA
Tel: +1 718 225 4151
Fax: +1 718 225 4889
Ernan Roman, President

Services/Products:
Marketing consultant

Member of:
DMA

ERS DIRECT MARKETING
A division of ERS MEDIA
SERVICES, INC.
24009 Ventura Boulevard
Ste 230
Calabasas
CA
91302–1418
USA
Tel: 818 591 7600
Fax: +1 818 591 7659
Eilee Rhudy-Sonheim, President &
CEO

Services/Products:
Advertising Agency; Direct Response
Agency

Member of:
DMA

ESTEE LIST SERVICES, INC.
270 North Avenue
Ste 805
New Rochelle
NY
10801
USA
Tel: 914 235 7080
Fax: +1 914 235 6518
Sara Tarascio, Chief Executive Officer

Services/Products:
List services

Member of:
DMA

ETHNIC TECHNOLOGIES, LLC
600 Huyler Street
S Hackensack
NJ
7606
USA

Tel: +1 201 440 8900
Fax: +1 201 440 2168
Ginger Nelson, Executive Vice
  President

Services/Products:
List services

Member of:
DMA

EURO RSCG
350 Hudson Street
New York
NY
10014
USA
Tel: +1 212 886 +1 2032
Fax: +1 212 886 2016
Danie Morel, CEO, Marketing
  Services

Services/Products:
Advertising Agency; Direct Response
Agency

Member of:
DMA

EXCALIBUR ENTERPRISES, INC.
P. O. Box 7372
Winston-Salem
NC
27109–7372
USA
Tel: +1 336 744 5000
Fax: +1 336 767 8257
Jackson Wilson, President

Services/Products:
Lettershop; Mailing/Faxing services

Member of:
DMA

EXCELL CUSTOMER CARE
2175 West 14th Street
Tempe
AZ
85281
USA
Tel: +1 602 808 1511
Fax: +1 602 929 0812
Jon Delnegro, EVP & General
  Manager

Services/Products:
Telemarketing agency

Member of:
DMA

EXECUTIVE CALL CENTERS
714 Union Street
Manchester
NH
3104

USA
Tel: +1 800 888 3188
Fax: +1 603 644 8086
Michael Holzberg

Services/Products:
Telemarketing agency

Member of:
DMA

EXECUTIVE MARKETING SERVICES, INC.
Park Lake Center
184 Shuman Blvd
Ste 300
Naperville
IL
60563–1258
USA
Tel: +1 800 367 7311
Fax: +1 630 355 3090
Debra Arana, Director, Marketing

Services/Products:
Telemarketing agency

Member of:
DMA

EXODUS COMMUNICATIONS
2650 San Tomas Expressway
Santa Clara
CA
95051
USA
Tel: +1 408 302 8855
Fax: +1 408 346 2207
Barbara Lymberis, Marketing
  Specialist

Services/Products:
List services

Member of:
DMA

EXPERIAN
701 Experian Parkway
Allen
TX
75013–3715
USA
Tel: 972 390 5000
Fax: +1 972 390 5100
Gwenn Kyzer, Vice President

Services/Products:
List services

Member of:
DMA

EXPRESS MESSENGER INT'L
2280 Terminal Road
Roseville
MN
55113

USA
Tel: +1 612 628 3201
Fax: +1 612 628 3235
Dawn Stasney, Market Development
  Manager

Services/Products:
Lettershop; Mailing/Faxing services

Member of:
DMA

FABRIK COMMUNICATIONS
100 Bush Street
Ste 1300
San Francisco
CA
94104
USA
Tel: +1 415 439 6643
Fax: +1 415 986 4427
Dana Loof, Director, Events

Services/Products:
List services

Member of:
DMA

FAIRFIELD MARKETING GROUP, INC.
830 Sport Hill Road
Easton
CT
06612–1250
USA
Tel: +1 203 261 5585
Fax: +1 203 261 0884
Ed Washchilla, President

Services/Products:
List services

Member of:
DMA

FALA DIRECT MARKETING, INC.
70 Marcus Drive
Melville
NY
11747–4278
USA
Tel: +1 516 694 1919
Fax: +1 516 694 5414
Robert Jurick, Chairman

Services/Products:
Lettershop; Mailing/Faxing services

Member of:
DMA

FALLON MCELLIGOTT
901 Marquette Avenue
Minneapolis
MN
55402

USA
Tel: +1 612 321 2345
Fax: +1 612 321 2346
Steph Olsen, Manager, Information
    Unit

Services/Products:
Advertising Agency; Direct Response
Agency

Member of:
DMA

FARRAR & FARRAR
200 Park Ave South
Ste 1603
New York
NY
10003
USA
Tel: +1 212 475 6749
Fax: +1 212 475 6827
Carol Estrich, President

Services/Products:
Advertising Agency; Direct Response
Agency

Member of:
DMA

FASANO & ASSOCIATES
3599 Cahuenga Boulevard, West
4th Fl
Los Angeles
CA
90068
USA
Tel: +1 323 874 4400
Fax: +1 323 874 0230
Patricia Fasano, President

Services/Products:
List services

Member of:
DMA

FBC TELEMARKETING
513 Main Street
Wayne
NE
68787
USA
Tel: +1 402 375 5911
Fax: +1 402 375 5999
Shelley Schuttler, Operations Officer

Services/Products:
Telemarketing agency

Member of:
DMA

FCB (FOOTE, CONE & BELDING) LATIN AMERICA
1401 Brickell Avenue
Ste 1100

Miami
FL
33131
USA
Tel: +1 305 373 8855
Fax: +1 305 373 0306
Web: www.fcb.com
Natalia Insignares, Regional Co-
    ordinator

Services/Products:
Advertising Agency

FCB DIRECT CHICAGO
101 East Erie Street
Chicago
IL
60611–2897
USA
Tel: +1 312 425 5000
Fax: +1 312 425 6321
Jim Cerasani, President

Services/Products:
Advertising Agency; Direct Response
Agency

Member of:
DMA

FCB PUERTO RICO
1510 Roosevelt Avenue
Corner San Patricio
Ste 1100
Caparra
PR
968
USA
Tel: +1 787 793 3500
Fax: +1 787 783 6795
William Clark, Senior Vice President

Services/Products:
Advertising Agency; Direct Response
Agency

Member of:
DMA

FEDERAL DIRECT
95 Main Avenue
Clifton
NJ
07014–1707
USA
Tel: 973 667 9800
Fax: +1 973 667 0228
Mark DeLuccia, VP, Sales & Marketing

Services/Products:
Lettershop; Mailing/Faxing services

Member of:
DMA

FEDERAL ENVELOPE COMPANY
608 Country Club Drive
Bensenville
IL
60106–1303
USA
Tel: +1 630 595 2000
Fax: +1 630 595 1212
Lee Shaw, General Manager

Services/Products:
Labelling/envelope services

Member of:
DMA

FEDERAL UNION, INC.
900 North Federal Highway
Ste 260
Boca Raton
FL
33432
USA
Tel: +1 561 367 1113
Fax: +1 561 392 7999
John Fischer, President

Services/Products:
List services

Member of:
DMA

FIDELIS CONSULTING
123 Hardenburgh Avenue
Demarest
NJ
7627
USA
Tel: +1 201 784 8683
Fax: +1 201 784 8639
Jean Tenuto, Partner

Services/Products:
Marketing consultant

Member of:
DMA

FIND/SVP, INC.
625 Avenue of the Americas
2nd Fl
New York
NY
10011
USA
Tel: +1 212 645 4500
Fax: +1 212 645 7681
Jay Crane, Senior Consultant

Services/Products:
Market research agency

Member of:
DMA

FINE LIGHT INC.
100 Fountain Square
Bloomington
IN
47404
USA
Tel: 812 339 6700
Fax: +1 812 339 6743
Jeannene Manning, Director, Business
    Development

Services/Products:
Advertising Agency; Direct Response
Agency

Member of:
DMA

**FINERTY & WOLFE
    ADVERTISING, INC.**
2418 North Burling Street
Chicago
IL
60614
USA
Tel: +1 77 3 348 3918
Fax: +1 773 348 5873
Judith Finerty, President

Services/Products:
Advertising Agency; Direct Response
Agency

Member of:
DMA

FIRST DATA SOLUTIONS
717 Park Street
Naperville
IL
60563
USA
Tel: +1 630 637 1000
Fax: +1 630 637 6445
William Bak, President

Services/Products:
List services

Member of:
DMA

FIRST MARKETING COMPANY
3300 Gateway Drive
Pompano Beach
FL
33069
USA
Tel: 954 979 0700
Fax: +1 954 971 4707
Email: marketing@first-marketing.com
Web: www.first-marketing.com
Terry Pitman, Vice President

Services/Products:
Market research agency;
Personalisation; Publisher; Direct
marketing agency

E-Services:
E-Marketing consultant; Website
design; Online/e-marketing agency

Member of:
DMA (US); National DMA

FIRST MEDIA GROUP
6900 Yumuri Street
2nd Fl
Coral Gables
FL
33146
USA
Tel: +1 305 661 4969
Fax: +1 305 661 4907
Margaret Daly, President

Services/Products:
Marketing consultant

Member of:
DMA

**FLETCHER AND WILDER
    COMMUNICATIONS**
50 Jaffrey Road
Peterborough
NH
3458
USA
Tel: +1 603 924 6383
Fax: +1 603 924 6562
Marilyn Fletcher, President

Member of:
DMA

FLYNN, SABATINO & DAY
9049 Springboro Pike
Miamisburg
OH
45342
USA
Tel: 937 859 0599
Fax: +1 937 859 4081
Lea Ann Stevenson, Director, Client
    Services

Member of:
DMA

FMG MARKETING, INC.
12667 Alcosta Boulevard
Ste 355
San Ramon
CA
94583
USA
Tel: 925 866 8895
Fax: +1 925 866 8918
Joe Freiberg, Owner

Services/Products:
Advertising Agency; Direct Response
Agency

Member of:
DMA

FOCALPOINT
2323 Horsepen Road
Ste 502
Herndon
VA
20171
USA
Tel: +1 703 713 0003
Fax: +1 703 713 0849
Alice Gray Dasek, Director, Research

Services/Products:
Marketing consultant

Member of:
DMA

FOCUS DIRECT
9707 Broadway
P.O. Box 17568
San Antonio
TX
78217–0568
USA
Tel: +1 210 805 9185
Fax: +1 210 804 1071
Fred Lederman, President & CEO

Services/Products:
Lettershop; Mailing/Faxing services

Member of:
DMA

FOCUS USA
2 University Plaza
Ste 500
Hackensack
NJ
07601–6222
USA
Tel: +1 201 489 2525
Fax: +1 201 489 4499
Chicca D'Agostino, President

Services/Products:
List services

Member of:
DMA

FOCUS: PRODUCTIVITY, INC
635 Danbury Road
Ridgefield
CT
06877–2700
USA
Tel: +1 203 431 9999
Fax: +1 203 431 7708
Pamela Tournier, Principal

Services/Products:
Marketing consultant

Member of:
DMA

FOGARTY KLEIN & PARTNERS
7155 Old Katy Road
Houston
TX
77024
USA
Tel: +1 713 867 3197
Fax: +1 713 869 6560
Randy Crimmins, Partner

Services/Products:
Advertising Agency; Direct Response
Agency

Member of:
DMA

FOOTE, CONE & BELDING
150 East 42nd Street
New York
NY
10153
USA
Tel: +1 212 885 3590
Fax: +1 212 885 3484
Jim Cerasani, President

Services/Products:
Advertising Agency; Direct Response
Agency

Member of:
DMA

FORECAST DIRECT
MARKETING GROUP
37 Terminal Way
Pittsburgh
PA
15219
USA
Tel: +1 412 481 4233
Fax: +1 412 481 0872
Donna Aiello, Vice President

Services/Products:
Advertising Agency; Direct Response
Agency

Member of:
DMA

FOREIGN OBJECTS
11232 Leo Lane
Dallas
TX
75229
USA
Tel: 888 916 0603
Fax: +1 800 704 1114
Robert Williams, President

Services/Products:
Advertising Agency; Direct Response
Agency

Member of:
DMA

FORRESTER RESEARCH, INC.
1033 Massachuetts Avenue
Cambridge
MA
2138
USA
Tel: +1 617 497 7090
Fax: +1 617 868 0577
Bill Bass, Senior Analyst, Media &
Tech.

Services/Products:
Market research agency

Member of:
DMA

FORT WORTH STAR
TELEGRAM
400 West 7th Street
Fort Worth
TX
76102
USA
Tel: 817 390 7558
Fax: +1 817 390 7250
Gary Kromev, Director, Research &
DBM

Services/Products:
Database services

Member of:
DMA

FOSDICK FULFILLMENT
CORPORATION
10 Alexander Drive
Wallingford
CT
6492
USA
Tel: +1 203 269 0211
Fax: +1 203 269 5307
Steven Konstantino, VP, Sales &
Marketing

Services/Products:
Fulfilment and sampling house

Member of:
DMA

FOXHALL CORPORATION
6849 Old Dominion Drive
Ste 320
McLean
VA
22101
USA

Tel: +1 703 749 3102
Fax: +1 703 749 0962
C. Hughey, President

Services/Products:
Marketing consultant

Member of:
DMA

FPS MARKETING
COMMUNICATIONS
57 Plains Road
3rd Fl
Milford
CT
6460
USA
Tel: +1 203 783 1940
Fax: +1 203 783 1950
Thomas Cabeen, President

Services/Products:
Advertising Agency; Direct Response
Agency

Member of:
DMA

FRANK MAYER & ASSOCIATES,
INC.
1975 Wisconsin Avenue
Grafton
WI
53024
USA
Tel: +1 414 377 4700
Fax: +1 414 377 3449
David Zoerb, Senior Vice President

Services/Products:
Sales promotion agency

Member of:
DMA

FRANK W. CAWOOD &
ASSOCIATES, INC.
103 Clover Green
Peachtree City
GA
30269
USA
Tel: +1 77 0 487 6307
Fax: +1 770 631 4357
Frank Cawood, President

Services/Products:
Advertising Agency; Direct Response
Agency

Member of:
DMA

FRANKEL
111 East Wacker Drive
Chicago
IL

60601–4884
USA
Tel: +1 312 552 3650
Fax: +1 312 552 5404
Donna Bonnell Tracy, VP, Frankel
  Direct

Services/Products:
Sales promotion agency

Member of:
DMA

FRED SINGER D.M.
700 White Plains Road
Ste 209
Scarsdale
NY
10583
USA
Tel: 914 472 7100
Fax: +1 914 472 9022
Sandra Roscoe, Vice President,
  Management

Services/Products:
List services

Member of:
DMA

FRED WOOLF LIST CO., INC.
110 Corporate Park Drive
White Plains
NY
10604–3800
USA
Tel: 914 694 4466
Fax: +1 914 694 1710
Sheila Woolf, Senior Vice President

Services/Products:
List services

Member of:
DMA

FREQUENCY MARKETING, INC.
6101 Meijer Drive
Milford
OH
45150
USA
Tel: +1 513 248 2882
Fax: +1 513 248 2672
Richard Barlow, President

Services/Products:
Advertising Agency; Direct Response
Agency

Member of:
DMA

FRONTERA DEVELOPMENT CORPORATION
22 Melrose Lane
Lincolnshire
IL
60069–3134
USA
Tel: +1 800 332 4225
Fax: +1 847 374 1828
Steven Levin, President

Services/Products:
Marketing consultant

Member of:
DMA

FULFILLMENT CORPORATION OF AMERICA
205 West Center Street
Marion
OH
43302–3707
USA
Tel: +1 614 383 5231
Fax: +1 614 382 0409
Patty Bridgeman, Manager, Marketing

Services/Products:
Fulfilment and sampling house

Member of:
DMA

FURGIUELE & COMPANY, INC.
276 Read Avenue
Crestwood
NY
10707
USA
Fax: +1 914 779 6447
Joseph M.Furgiuele, President

Services/Products:
Marketing consultant

Member of:
DMA

FUTURECALL TELEMARKETING
1749 North Academy Boulevard
Colorado Spgs
CO
80909–2721
USA
Tel: 888 Future 1
Fax: +1 719 591 0133
Sid Scott, Vice President, Marketing

Services/Products:
Telemarketing agency

Member of:
DMA

G.A. WRIGHT, INC.
P. O. Box 7176
Denver
CO
80207–0176
USA
Tel: +1 303 333 4453
Fax: +1 303 393 5320
Gary Wright, President

Services/Products:
Fulfilment and sampling house

Member of:
DMA

GAGE LETTERSHOP/ PERSONALIZATION SERVICES
401 13th Avenue North
P.O. Box 707
Howard Lake
MN
55349
USA
Tel: +1 320 543 3737
Fax: +1 320 543 3228
Michael Barga, VP & General Manager

Services/Products:
Lettershop; Mailing/Faxing services

Member of:
DMA

GAITSKILL & ASSOCIATES
3082 Clair Road
Ste B
Lexington
KY
40502
USA
Tel: +1 606 269 9239
Fax: +1 606 335 6199
Russ Gaitskill, President

Services/Products:
Marketing consultant

Member of:
DMA

GANNETT TELEMARKETING, INC.
6883 Commercial Drive
Springfield
VA
22159
USA
Tel: +1 703 750 8730
Fax: +1 703 750 8737
Paul Link, Vice President

Services/Products:
Telemarketing agency

Member of:
DMA

GARTNER GROUP
56 Top Gallant Road
P.O. Box 10212
Stamford
CT
6904
USA
Tel: +1 203 316 6915
Fax: +1 203 316 6143
Barbara Herbster, Director, Events
Marketing

Services/Products:
Market research agency

Member of:
DMA

GAZETTE DIRECT MARKETING SERVICES
621 4th Avenue, S.E.
Cedar Rapids
IA
52401–1904
USA
Tel: +1 319 399 5999
Fax: +1 319 399 5998
Timothy Gustin, Dir., Planning &
Development

Services/Products:
Marketing consultant

Member of:
DMA

GC SERVICES
1 World Trade Center
New York
NY
10048
USA
Fax: +1 973 938 8938
Jeff Shiovitz, Director, Marketing
Operations

Services/Products:
Telemarketing agency

Member of:
DMA

GDT
a division of Polk
11 Lafayette Street
Lebanon
NH
3766
USA
Tel: +1 603 643 0330
Stephen Polk, Chairman & CEO

Services/Products:
List services

Member of:
DMA

GEORGE MANN ASSOCIATES
569 Abbington Drive
P.O. Box 930
Hightstown
NJ
8520
USA
Tel: +1 609 443 1330
Fax: +1 609 443 0397
Sara Rohrer, Vice President

Services/Products:
List services

Member of:
DMA

GEORGIA K. FRIEDMAN, INC.
196 East 75th Street
New York
NY
10021
USA
Tel: +1 212 744 5915
Georgia Friedman, President

Services/Products:
Marketing consultant

Member of:
DMA

GERALD SIEGEL & ASSOCIATES, INC.
506 North Clark Street
Chicago
IL
60610
USA
Tel: +1 312 661 1818
Fax: +1 312 661 0588
Gerald Siegel, President

Services/Products:
Advertising Agency; Direct Response
Agency

Member of:
DMA

GERMAN MARKETING SERVICES
206 West 15th Street
New York
NY
10011–6501
USA
Tel: +1 212 727 8572
Fax: +1 212 206 1904
Heide Stuebel, President

Services/Products:
Marketing consultant

Member of:
DMA

GIANFAGNA MARKETING & COMMUNICATIONS, INC.
30400 Detroit Road
Ste 402
Cleveland
OH
44145–1855
USA
Tel: +1 440 808 4700
Fax: +1 440 808 4707
Jean Gianfagna, President

Services/Products:
Advertising Agency; Direct Response
Agency

Member of:
DMA

GIBRALTER MARKETING LIMITED
P. O. Box 338
Jacksonville
NC
28540
USA
Tel: 910 455 3004
Fax: +1 910 455 3042
Yvonne Guy, Director, Marketing

Services/Products:
List services

Member of:
DMA (US); FEDMA

GIBSON DIRECT, INC.
204 Plantation
Coppell
TX
75019
USA
Tel: +1 472 462 7580
Fax: +1 47 23 04 92 02
Steve Gibson, President

Services/Products:
Marketing consultant

Member of:
DMA

GILBERT WHITNEY & JOHNS
110 South Jefferson Road
Whippany
NJ
7981
USA
Tel: 973 386 1776
Fax: +1 973 386 0589
Ann Wallace, VP, Direct Marketing
Group

Services/Products:
Advertising Agency; Direct Response
Agency

Member of:
DMA

GILLESPIE
P. O. Box 3333
Princeton
NJ
8543
USA
Tel: +1 609 895 0200
Fax: +1 609 895 0222
Marcy Samet, Mng. Ptnr., Dir. Client
Svcs.

Services/Products:
Advertising Agency; Direct Response
Agency

Member of:
DMA

GLENN SNYDER &
  ASSOCIATES
474 Osceola Avenue
Jacksonville Bch
FL
32250
USA
Tel: 904 246 6223
Fax: +1 904 246 6229
Glenn Snyder, Owner

Services/Products:
Telemarketing agency

Member of:
DMA

GLOBAL CARD
  TECHNOLOGIES, INC.
8 Thomas
Ste 100
Irvine
CA
92618
USA
Tel: 949 595 8290
Fax: +1 949 595 8287
Michele Massey, Chief Executive
Officer

Services/Products:
Lettershop; Mailing/Faxing services

Member of:
DMA

GLOBAL DM SOLUTIONS
416 Main St
Boonton
NJ 07005 1702
USA
Tel: +1 973 402 2205
Fax: +1 973 402 2305
Email:
  sdonovan@globaldmsolutions.com

Web: www.globaldmsolutions.com

Services/Products:
Direct marketing agency

Member of:
DMA (US)

GLOBAL LOGISTIC SERVICES
6903 Rockledge Drive
Ste 510
Bethesda
MD
20817
USA
Tel: +1 301 896 0500
Fax: +1 301 896 0760
Michael Tallent, President

Services/Products:
Fulfilment and sampling house

Member of:
DMA

GLOBAL-Z INTERNATIONAL
508 Main St.
Boonton
NJ
07005–1716
USA
Tel: 973 402 1456
Fax: +1 973 402 9010
Sheila Donovan, VP., Sales & New
  Business Dev.

Services/Products:
List services

Member of:
DMA (US); FEDMA

GLS TELESERVICES
2000 Market Street
Ste 1408
Philadelphia
PA
19103
USA
Tel: +1 800 232 1100
Fax: +1 215 988 0188
Ross Housley, President & CEO

Services/Products:
Telemarketing agency

Member of:
DMA

GOOD ADVERTISING
5050 Poplar Avenue
19th Fl
Memphis
TN
38157
USA
Tel: 901 761 0741

Fax: +1 901 682 2568
Maury Eikner, Director, Media
  Services

Services/Products:
Advertising Agency; Direct Response
Agency

Member of:
DMA

GORDON PUBLICATIONS, INC.
301 Gibraltar Drive
P.O. Box 650
Morris Plains
NJ
07950–0650
USA
Tel: +1 201 292 5100
Rick Kasper, VP & General Manager

Services/Products:
List services

Member of:
DMA

GORDON W. GROSSMAN, INC.
606 Douglas Road
Chappaqua
NY
10514
USA
Fax: +1 914 238 1635
Gordon Grossman, President

Services/Products:
Marketing consultant

Member of:
DMA

GRAHAM GREGORY BOZELL,
  INC.
40 West 23rd Street
New York
NY
10010–5201
USA
Tel: +1 212 727 5000
Beverly Beaudoin, Managing Partner

Services/Products:
Advertising Agency; Direct Response
Agency

Member of:
DMA

GRAMERCY GROUP
235 Park Avenue South
11th Fl
New York
NY
10003
USA
Tel: +1 212 460 9300

Fax: +1 212 460 9475
Pamela Meirowitz, VP, Account
  Services

Services/Products:
Advertising Agency; Direct Response
Agency

Member of:
DMA

GRAPEVINE MARKETING, INC.
1353 Newport Street
Mundelein
IL
60060
USA
Tel: 847 918 0350
Fax: +1 847 918 0389
Mitchell Kreger, President

Services/Products:
Advertising Agency; Direct Response
Agency

Member of:
DMA

GRAPHIC ARTS & PRODUCTION
2040 Jay-Mar Road
Ste 2
Plover
WI
54467
USA
Tel: +1 715341 6180
Fax: +1 715 341 7971
Sarah Straub, President

Services/Products:
Advertising Agency; Direct Response
Agency

Member of:
DMA

GRAPHIC ARTS CENTER
2000 N.W. Wilson Street
Portland
OR
97209
USA
Tel: +1 503 224 7777
Fax: +1 503 222 0735
Gerald Mahoney, Chairman & CEO,
  Mail Well, Inc

Services/Products:
Labelling/envelope services

Member of:
DMA

GRAPHIC INNOVATIONS
65 Kingsland Avenue
Clifton
NJ

7014
USA
Tel: +1 201 614 1090
Fax: +1 201 614 8896
Anthony Catalano, CFO, Direct Mail
  Business Unit

Services/Products:
Lettershop; Mailing/Faxing services

Member of:
DMA

GRAPHOGRAPHY, LTD.
215 Lexington Avenue
11th Fl
New York
NY
10016
USA
Tel: +1 212 213 0900
Fax: +1 212 683 1506
Jerry Freundlich, President

Services/Products:
List services

Member of:
DMA

GRAY & GRAHAM MARKETING GROUP
136 Main Street
Westport
CT
06880–3304
USA
Tel: +1 203 227 3900
Fax: +1 203 227 3593
Jeffrey Gray, Chairman

Services/Products:
Advertising Agency; Direct Response
Agency

Member of:
DMA

GREATLISTS.COM
8130 Boone Boulevard, Suite 310
Vienna
VA
22182
USA
Tel: +1 703 821 8130
Fax: +1 703 821 8243
Email: info@GreatLists.com
Web: www.GreatLists.com
Philip Dismukes, President

Services/Products:
List services

E-Services:
Email list provider

Member of:
FEDMA

GREENBERG CONSULTING
390 Heritage Hills
Somers
NY
10589
USA
Tel: +1 914 669 8080
Fax: +1 914 669 8888
Email: mgreenb@attglobal.net
Martin Greenberg, President

Services/Products:
Advertising Agency; Consultancy
services; Copy adaptation; Direct
marketing agency

Member of:
DMA (US); National DMA

GREY DIRECT
875 Third Avenue
New York
NY
10022
USA
Tel: +1 212 303 2300
Fax: +1 212 303 2333
George Wiedemann, Chairman &
  CEO, Grey DM Group

Services/Products:
Advertising Agency; Direct Response
Agency

Member of:
DMA

GRIZZARD
1480 Colorado Blvd
Ste 900
Atlanta
GA
30303
USA
Tel: +1 323 254 6147
Fax: +1 323 254 7359
Email: phil.stolberg@grizzard.com
Web: www.grizzard.com
Phil Stolberg, Senior Vice President

Services/Products:
Database services; Direct marketing
agency; Lettershop; Market research
agency

E-Services:
E-Marketing consultant; Website
design; Online/e-marketing agency

Member of:
DMA (US)

GROUP 1 SOFTWARE, INC.
4200 Parliament Place
Ste 600
Lanham
MD

20706–1844
USA
Tel: +1 301 731 2300
Fax: +1 301 731 0360
Ronald Friedman, President

Services/Products:
List services

Member of:
DMA

GROUP M MARKETING, INC.
3355 Bee Cave Road
Ste 202
Austin
TX
78746
USA
Tel: +1 512 328 4442
Fax: +1 512 328 4464
Michael Kimble, President

Services/Products:
Advertising Agency; Direct Response
Agency

Member of:
DMA

GRUEN + SELLS LTD.
875 North Michigan Avenue
Chicago
IL
60611–1803
USA
Tel: +1 312 280 5432
Fax: +1 312 280 0785
Mark Gruen, VP & General Manager

Services/Products:
Advertising Agency; Direct Response
Agency

Member of:
DMA

GRUND & ASSOCIATES
73 Hawthorn Place
Briarcliff Mnr
NY
10510–2226
USA
Tel: 914 941 0928
Fax: +1 914 762 3568
Victor Grund, President

Services/Products:
Marketing consultant

Member of:
DMA

GRUPPO, LEVEY & CAPELL, INC.
60 East 42nd Street
Ste 3810
New York

NY
10165–0006
USA
Tel: +1 212 697 5753
Fax: +1 212 949 7294
Harry Chevan, Senior Vice President

Services/Products:
Marketing consultant

Member of:
DMA

GSP GROUP, INC.
1343 Boswall Drive
Ste 200
Worthington
OH
43085
USA
Tel: +1 614 885 7502
Fax: +1 614 885 1165
Sharon Kissner, Managing Director

Services/Products:
Database services

Member of:
DMA

GTE, THE FOCUS AGENCY
919 Garland Road
Dallas
TX
75218
USA
Johanna Grilli, Senior Vice President

Services/Products:
Advertising Agency; Direct Response
Agency

Member of:
DMA

HAMILTON TELECOMMUNICATIONS
1006 Twelfth Street
Aurora
NE
68818–2003
USA
Tel: +1 800 972 3237
Fax: +1 402 694 4433
Sondra Short, National Sales Director

Services/Products:
Telemarketing agency

Member of:
DMA

HANN & DEPALMER
28 Engelhard Drive
Cranbury
NJ
8512
USA

Tel: +1 609 655 4646
Fax: +1 609 655 0782
Landis Hann, Executive Vice President

Services/Products:
Fulfilment and sampling house

Member of:
DMA

HARBOR ASSOCIATES
2 Greenwich Plaza
Greenwich
CT
6830
USA
Tel: +1 203 622 1345
Fax: +1 203 622 7607
Sheila James, President

Services/Products:
Marketing consultant

Member of:
DMA

HARRIS MARKETING, INC.
The Glendale Building
Ste 427
Indianapolis
IN
46220
USA
Tel: +1 317 251 9729
Fax: +1 317 251 9733
Janet Harris, President

Services/Products:
List services

Member of:
DMA

HARRISON FULFILLMENT SERVICES
2515 East 43rd Street
Chattanooga
TN
37407
USA
Tel: +1 423 867 8221
Fax: +1 423 867 8523
Joe Dresnok, President & COO

Services/Products:
Fulfilment and sampling house

Member of:
DMA

HARTE-HANKS DIRECT MARKETING
260 Madison Avenue
21st Fl
New York
NY
10016
USA

Tel: +1 212 889 5000
Fax: +1 212 481 6232
Richard Hochhauser, President &
  CEO

Services/Products:
List services

Member of:
DMA

**HARTFORD DIRECT
  MARKETING**
60 Pigeon Hill Road Ext.
Windsor
CT
06095–2122
USA
Tel: 860 688 1212
Fax: +1 860 688 2242
Francis Barkyoumb, President

Services/Products:
Lettershop; Mailing/Faxing services

Member of:
DMA

HARTMANN ASSOCIATES
8210 South Street
Lincoln
NE
68506
USA
Tel: +1 402 483 6849
Fax: +1 402 483 7380
Ken Hartmann, President

Services/Products:
Database services

Member of:
DMA

**HARVEY ASSOCIATES-DIRECT
  MARKETING SOLUTIONS**
63 Hoover Drive
Cresskill
NJ
7626
USA
Tel: +1 201 816 1780
Fax: +1 201 816 1781
Harvey Feldman, President

Services/Products:
Marketing consultant

Member of:
DMA

HAUSER LIST SERVICES, NMIS
3 Commercial Street
Hicksville
NY
11801
USA
Tel: +1 516 735 1680

Fax: +1 516 735 1797
Barry Hauser, President

Services/Products:
Marketing consultant

Member of:
DMA

**HAYNES & PARTNERS
  COMMUNICATION, INC.**
5561 West 74th Street
Indianapolis
IN
46268–4184
USA
Tel: +1 317 328 4650
Fax: +1 317 328 4646
David Skripsky, President

Services/Products:
Advertising Agency; Direct Response
Agency

Member of:
DMA

HB&G/ACSC
1480 Colorado Boulevard
Los Angeles
CA
90041
USA
Tel: +1 213 254 6147
Fax: +1 213 254 2370
Phil Stolberg, Senior Vice President

Services/Products:
Advertising Agency; Direct Response
Agency

Member of:
DMA

HEALTH COMMUNICATIONS
Richard Simmons & Friends
Three Park Avenue
New York
NY
10016
USA
Tel: +1 212 683 4774
Fax: +1 212 683 0260
Manny Mallo, President

Services/Products:
Market research agency

Member of:
DMA

HEENEHAN & ASSOCIATES
44 Merrimac Street
Newburyport
MA
1950
USA
Tel: +1 508 465 3500

Fax: +1 508 465 6340
William Heenehan, President

Services/Products:
Database services

Member of:
DMA

HEINRICH MARKETING, INC.
1350 Independence Street
Denver
CO
80215–4629
USA
Tel: +1 303 233 8660
Fax: +1 303 233 4564
George Heinrich, President

Services/Products:
Advertising Agency; Direct Response
Agency

Member of:
DMA

**HEMISPHERE MARKETING
  INC.**
601 Montgomery Street
Ste 770
San Francisco
CA
94111
USA
Tel: +1 415 956 6100
Fax: +1 415 956 6180
Meg Gamble, Business Development
  Director

Services/Products:
Advertising Agency; Direct Response
Agency

Member of:
DMA

HEMMINGS IV DIRECT
427 South Marengo Avenue
Cottage 7
Pasadena
CA
91101
USA
Tel: +1 626 796 7188
Fax: +1 626 796 9436
Robert Hemmings, President

Services/Products:
Advertising Agency; Direct Response
Agency

Member of:
DMA

**HEMMINGS, BIRKHOLM &
  GRIZZARD**
1480 Colorado Boulevard
Los Angeles

CA
90041
USA
Tel: +1 213 254 6147
Fax: +1 213 254 8479
Phil Stolberg, Senior Vice President

Services/Products:
Advertising Agency; Direct Response
Agency

Member of:
DMA

HENRY M. GREENE & ASSOC., INC.
28457 North Ballard Drive
Ste A1
Lake Forest
IL
60045–4545
USA
Tel: +1 800 356 1300
Fax: +1 847 816 0576
Henry Greene, President

Services/Products:
Telemarketing agency

Member of:
DMA

HERBERT KRUG & ASSOCIATES INC.
500 Davis Center
Ste 1010
Evanston
IL
60201–4691
USA
Tel: 847 864 0550
Fax: +1 847 864 0575
E. Herbert Krug, President

Services/Products:
Marketing consultant

Member of:
DMA

HERITAGE MARKETING CORPORATION
113 Post Road East
Westpost
CT
6880
USA
Tel: +1 203 454 3311
Fax: +1 203 453 3033
Peter Olaynack, Chief Financial Officer

Services/Products:
Market research agency

Member of:
DMA

HERRING/NEWMAN
388 Imperial Way
12th Fl
Daly City
CA
94015–2540
USA
Susan Goodman, EVP, Mktg. &
Business Dev.

Services/Products:
Marketing consultant

Member of:
DMA

HERSHEY COMMUNICATIONS NY, INC.
257 Park Avenue South
New York
NY
10010
USA
Tel: +1 212 477 9100
Fax: +1 212 505 8421
Ed Hershey

Services/Products:
Advertising Agency; Direct Response
Agency

Member of:
DMA

HILL HOLLIDAY
200 Clarendon Street
Boston
MA
2116
USA
Tel: +1 617 437 1600
Fax: +1 617 572 3534
Donald White, Executive Vice
President

Services/Products:
Advertising Agency; Direct Response
Agency

Member of:
DMA

HIPPO DIRECT
34472 Summerset Drive
Solon
OH
44139
USA
Tel: +1 440 519 0730
Fax: +1 440 519 0727
Greg Branstetter, President

Services/Products:
List services

Member of:
DMA

HISPANAGENCIA
2 North Lake Avenue
Ste 600
Pasadena
CA
91101
USA
Tel: 818 449 6100
Fax: +1 818 449 6190
Constance Snapp DeBord, SVP &
Dir., Strategic Mktg.

Services/Products:
Advertising Agency; Direct Response
Agency

Member of:
DMA

HMS DIRECT
One Columbus
10 W Broad St
Ste 5
Columbus
OH
45215
USA
Tel: +1 614 221 7667
Fax: +1 614 222 5076
Jeff Coopersmith, President

Services/Products:
Telemarketing agency

Member of:
DMA

HOFFMAN YORK
330 East Kilbourn Avenue
Milwaukee
WI
53202–6636
USA
Tel: +1 414 225 9534
Fax: +1 414 289 0177
Troy Peterson, VP, Dir., Marketing
Services

Services/Products:
Advertising Agency; Direct Response
Agency

Member of:
DMA

HOLLAND MARK MARTIN EDMUND
312 Stuart Street
Boston
MA
2116
USA
Tel: +1 617 960 3500
Fax: +1 617 960 3535
William Davis, Chief Executive Office

Services/Products:
Advertising Agency; Direct Response
Agency

Member of:
DMA

HOLLDON
TELEMANAGEMENT GROUP
8428 Kings Trail Drive
Cordova
TN
38018
USA
Tel: 901 754 9309
Fax: +1 901 754 7503
Donald Swogger, Senior Consultant

Services/Products:
Telemarketing agency

Member of:
DMA

HOWARD, MERRELL &
PARTNERS,INC
8521 Six Forks Road
Raleigh
NC
27615
USA
Tel: 919 848 2400
Fax: +1 919 676 1035
Deirdre O'Boyle, Manager, Database
   Marketing

Services/Products:
Advertising Agency; Direct Response
Agency

Member of:
DMA

HUBER HOGE AND SONS
ADVERTISING, INC.
19 North Columbia Street
Port Jefferson Sta
NY
11776
USA
Tel: +1 516 473 7308
Fax: +1 516 473 7398
Cecil Hoge, President

Services/Products:
Advertising Agency; Direct Response
Agency

Member of:
DMA

HUDSON STREET PARTNERS
375 Hudson Street
New York
NY
10014
USA

Tel: +1 212 463 3939
Fax: +1 212 463 3960
Myrna Gardner, President

Services/Products:
Advertising Agency; Direct Response
Agency

Member of:
DMA

HUGO DUNHILL MAILING
LISTS, INC.
30 East 33rd Street
12th Fl
New York
NY
10016–5337
USA
Tel: +1 212 213 9300
Fax: +1 212 213 0840
Adam Dunhill, President

Services/Products:
List services

Member of:
DMA

HUNT MARKETING GROUP
900 Broadacres Building
1601 2nd Ave, Ste 900
Seattle
WA
98101
USA
Tel: +1 206 728 6245
Fax: +1 206 728 0139
Brian Hunt, President

Services/Products:
Advertising Agency; Direct Response
Agency

Member of:
DMA

HUNTER BUSINESS DIRECT
INC.
4650 N. Port Washington Road
Milwaukee
WI
53212–0970
USA
Tel: +1 414 332 8050
Fax: +1 414 332 7377
Victor Hunter, President

Services/Products:
Marketing consultant

Member of:
DMA

HUNTSINGER & JEFFER, INC.
809 Brook Hill Circle
Richmond
VA

23227
USA
Tel: 804 266 2499
Fax: +1 804 266 8563
Paul Braeckmans, President

Services/Products:
Advertising Agency; Direct Response
Agency

Member of:
DMA

HUSKY ENVELOPE
PRODUCTS, INC.
P. O. Box 523
Walled Lake
MI
48390
USA
Tel: 810 624 7070
Fax: +1 810 624 5990
Peter Macres, VP, National Sales

Services/Products:
Labelling/envelope services

Member of:
DMA

HYAID GROUP
6 Commercial Street
Hicksville
NY
11801
USA
Tel: +1 516 433 3800
Fax: +1 516 822 8028
Richard Levinson, President

Services/Products:
List services

Member of:
DMA

I MARKET INC
460 Totten Pond Road, 7th Floor
Waltham
MA
02451–1908
USA
Tel: +1 781 672 9200
Fax: +1 781 672 9290
Web: www.imarketinc.com
   www.zapdata.com
Greg F. Den Herder, Manager
   International Business Development

Services/Products:
List services; Direct marketing agency;
Labelling/envelope services; Service
bureau; Software supplier

E-Services:
Online/e-marketing agency

Member of:
FEDMA; DMA (US)

I. C. SYSTEM, INC.
P. O. Box 64226
444 E Highway 96
St. Paul
MN
55164–0226
USA
Tel: +1 800 245 8875
Fax: +1 651 481 6363
Dieter Pape, Senior Vice President

Services/Products:
List services

Member of:
DMA

IBIS COMMUNICATIONS, INC.
201 22nd Avenue North
Ste C
Nashville
TN
37203–0804
USA
Tel: +1 615 242 1981
Fax: +1 615 242 2045
Maryanne Howland, President

Services/Products:
Advertising Agency; Direct Response
Agency

Member of:
DMA

ICOM
2611 Lighthouse Lane
Parlin
NJ
8859
USA
Tel: +1 732 721 4259
Fax: +1 732 721 4289
David Lefkowich, Gen. Mgr.,
    Canadian List Div.

Services/Products:
List services

Member of:
DMA

**ICON DIGITAL
    PHOTOGRAPHY**
49 West 27th Street
New York
NY
10001
USA
Tel: +1 212 685 1191
Fax: +1 212 681 0592
Michael Chinnici, President & CEO

Services/Products:
Advertising Agency; Direct Response
Agency

Member of:
DMA

ICT GROUP, INC.
800 Town Center Drive
Langhorne
PA
19047–1748
USA
Tel: +1 215 757 0200
Fax: +1 215 757 7877
John Brennan, CEO, ICT Group

Services/Products:
Market research agency

Member of:
DMA (US); FEDMA

**IDELMAN TELEMARKETING,
    INC.**
43–585 Monterey Avenue
Palm Desert
CA
92260
USA
Tel: +1 619 563 0270
Fax: +1 619 340 0883
John Calk, VP, Marketing & Business
    Dev.

Services/Products:
Telemarketing agency

Member of:
DMA

**IDRC (INTERNATIONAL DATA
    RESPONSE CORPORATION)**
P. O. Box 7130
6041 La Flecha
Ste 350
Rancho Santa Fe
CA
92067
USA
Tel: +1 619 759 3300
Fax: +1 619 759 3350
Dawn Wahler, Marketing Manager

Services/Products:
Telemarketing agency

Member of:
DMA

IMAGINE DIRECT
552 Main Street
Williamstown
MA
1267
USA
Tel: +1 413 458 1803

Fax: +1 413 458 1804
Richard Elliott, President

Services/Products:
Advertising Agency; Direct Response
Agency

Member of:
DMA

IMARK CORP
1040 First Avenue, Suite 337
New York
NY
10022
USA
Tel: +1 212 758 3735
Fax: +1 212 688 8849
Collette Richardson, President

Services/Products:
Media buying agency

Member of:
FEDMA

IMC DIRECT
81 South Hotel Street
Ste 315
Honolulu
HI
96813
USA
Tel: 808 545 1680
Fax: +1 808 528 4293
Victor Fujita, Owner

Services/Products:
Advertising Agency; Direct Response
Agency

Member of:
DMA

**IMPACT CONSULTING
    INTERNATIONAL**
415 Ninth Street
Ste 41
Brooklyn
NY
11215–4155
USA
Tel: +1 718 788 3139
Fax: +1 718 788 2916
Stuart Cowan, Managing Director

Services/Products:
Marketing consultant

Member of:
DMA

INAME, INC.
11 Broadway
Ste 660
New York
NY
10004

USA
Tel: +1 212 425 4200
Fax: +1 212 425 3487
Brad Shapiro, Director, Direct
   Marketing

E-Services:
Website design

Member of:
DMA

INCEPT CORPORATION
4150 Belden Village
Canton
OH
44718
USA
Tel: +1 330 649 8000
Jeff White, President

Services/Products:
Telemarketing agency

Member of:
DMA

INDIANA DESIGN CONSORTIUM, INC.
416 Main Street
P.O. Box 180
Lafayette
IN
47902
USA
Tel: +1 765 423 5469
Fax: +1 765 423 4440
Richard Hines, Dir., Marketing
   Communications

Services/Products:
Advertising Agency; Direct Response
Agency

Member of:
DMA

INDUSTRY WEEK
1100 Superior Avenue
Cleveland
OH
44114
USA
Tel: +1 216 696 7000
Ilene Schwartz, Director

Services/Products:
List services

Member of:
DMA

INFINITE MEDIA
48 Richbell Road
White Plains
NY
10605–4621
USA

Tel: 914 949 1547
Fax: +1 914 949 1605
Steven Sheck, President

Services/Products:
List services

Member of:
DMA

INFO USA
1020 Cambridge Square
Alpharetta
GA
30004
USA
Tel: +1 77 0 667 1818
Fax: +1 770 667 9576
Vin Gupta, Chairman & CEO

Services/Products:
List services

Member of:
DMA

INFOBASE
441 Lexington Avenue
New York
NY
10017
USA
Tel: +1 212 983 0154
Fax: +1 212 599 3247
Charles Morgan, Pres. & Chairman of
   the Board

Services/Products:
List services

Member of:
DMA

INFOCISION MANAGEMENT CORPORATION
325 Springside Drive
Akron
OH
44333
USA
Tel: +1 330 668 1400
Fax: +1 330 668 3055
Alisa Getzinger, VP, Direct Response
   Marketing

Services/Products:
Telemarketing agency

Member of:
DMA

INFOCORE, INC.
626 Silas Deane Hwy.
2nd Floor
Wethersfield
CT
6109
USA

Tel: +1 860 563 6360
Fax: +1 860 563 6265
Email: dsacks@infocoreinc.com
Web: www.infocoreinc.com
Douglas Sacks, Senior Vice-President

Services/Products:
Consultancy services; Market research
agency; List services

E-Services:
Email list provider

Member of:
DMA (US)

INFORMATION RESOURCES, INC.
150 North Clinton Street
Chicago
IL
60661–1416
USA
Tel: +1 312 474 8760
Fax: +1 312 474 8465
William Montbriand, VP, Panel
   Management

Services/Products:
Market research agency

Member of:
DMA

INFOSPAN INC.
Executive Suites
3740 N Josey Ln
Ste 210
Carrollton
TX
75007
USA
Tel: 972 395 2222
Fax: +1 972 395 2230
Edward Pitts, President

Services/Products:
List services

Member of:
DMA

INFOWORKS
8410 West Bryn Mawr
4th Fl
Chicago
IL
60631
USA
Tel: +1 77 3 693 4970
Fax: +1 773 693 4988
G.Steven Dapper, Chairman & CEO

Services/Products:
Advertising Agency; Direct Response
Agency

Member of:
DMA

INGALLS ONE TO ONE MARKETING
One Design Center Place
Boston
MA
2210
USA
Tel: +1 617 295 7000
Fax: +1 617 295 7514
Diana Scott, SVP, Managing Director

Services/Products:
Advertising Agency; Direct Response Agency

Member of:
DMA

INNOTRAC CORPORATION
1828 Meca Way
Norcross
GA
30093
USA
Tel: +1 77 0 717 2000
Fax: +1 770 717 2111
David Ellin, Vice President

Services/Products:
Fulfilment and sampling house

Member of:
DMA

INSIGHT ENTERPRISES INC
6820 South Harl Ave.
Tempe
AZ
85283
USA
Tel: +1 602 902 1000
Fax: +1 602 760 8086
Peter W Tewksbury, Vice President
  Financial Services

Services/Products:
Mail order company

Member of:
FEDMA

INSIGHT OUT OF CHAOS
305 East 46th Street
9th Fl
New York
NY
10017
USA
Tel: +1 212 935 0044
Fax: +1 212 935 0523
Spencer Hapoienu, President

Services/Products:
Database services

Member of:
DMA

INSITE MARKETING
100 Washington Street
South Norwalk
CT
6854
USA
Tel: +1 203 855 9108
Fax: +1 203 855 9164
Susan Reavis, Principal

Services/Products:
Marketing consultant

Member of:
DMA

INSURANCE PROCESSING CENTER, INC.
741 North Milwaukee Street
Milwaukee
WI
53202
USA
Tel: +1 414 278 0827
Fax: +1 414 278 7460
Stephen Dearholt, Partner

Services/Products:
Design/graphics/clip art supplier;
Consultancy services

Member of:
DMA

INTECK INFORMATION INC.
370 17th Street
Denver
CO
80202
USA
Tel: +1 303 357 3000
Fax: +1 303 405 8420
Tim O'Crowley, Chief Executive
  Officer

Services/Products:
Telemarketing agency

Member of:
DMA

INTEGRATED MANAGEMENT SERVICES
61 Wilton Road
Westport
CT
6880
USA
Tel: +1 203 221 1732
Fax: +1 203 221 7261
Robin Bellagamba, Market Research
  Director

Services/Products:
Marketing consultant

Member of:
DMA

INTEGRATED MARKETING, INC.
P. O. Box 556
Round Hill
VA
20142–0556
USA
Tel: +1 540 338 6048
Fax: +1 540 338 2172
Staci Fromwiller, President

Services/Products:
Advertising Agency; Direct Response
Agency

Member of:
DMA

INTELITEC
152 Taylor Street
Granby
MA
01033–9526
USA
Tel: +1 413 467 7420
Fax: +1 413 467 9476
Email: joef@intelitec.com
Web: www.intelitec.com
Joseph Furnia, President

Services/Products:
Consultancy services; Database
services; List services; Response
analysis bureau; Service bureau;
Software supplier

E-Services:
Email list provider; E-Marketing
consultant

Member of:
DMA (US); FEDMA; National DM

INTELLIGENT MARKETING SYSTEMS, INC. (IQ)
7601 France Avenue South
Ste 350
Edina
MN
55435
USA
Tel: +1 612 897 7300
Fax: +1 612 820 8041
Janet Finken, CEO

Services/Products:
Database services

Member of:
DMA

INTELLIQUEST INFORMATION GROUP
380 Interstate North Parkway
Ste 310
Atlanta
GA
30339
USA
Tel: +1 770 612 8008
Fax: +1 770 612 9008
Diane Stuckey, VP, Strategic
   Marketing

Services/Products:
List services

Member of:
DMA

INTELLISELL CORPORATION
129 North Corporation
Ste 350
Villa Park
IL
60181
USA
Tel: +1 708 782 1979
Fax: +1 708 782 1980
Dawn Wahler, Marketing Manager

Services/Products:
Telemarketing agency

Member of:
DMA

INTELOGISTICS
3305 Corporate Avenue
Weston
FL
33331
USA
Tel: 954 453 5710
Fax: +1 954 453 5799
John Crouthamel, President

Services/Products:
Telemarketing agency

Member of:
DMA

INTERACTIVE MARKETING GROUP, INC.
50 Commerce Drive
Allendale
NJ
7401
USA
Tel: +1 201 327 0974
Fax: +1 201 327 3596
Matthew Staudt, President & CEO

Services/Products:
Advertising Agency; Direct Response
Agency

Member of:
DMA

INTERACTIVE RESOURCES, INC.
PO Box 19137
Boulder
CO
80308 2137
USA
Tel: +1 800 203 8745
Fax: +1 800 203 8745
Email: rjsharette@inter-res.com
Web: www.inter-res.com
Roland J. Sharette, President

Services/Products:
Advertising Agency; Consultancy
services; Interactive media;
Personalisation

E-Services:
E-Marketing consultant; Online/
e-marketing agency

Member of:
DMA (US); GLIMA, AIM

INTERACTIVE RESPONSE TECHNOLOGIES INC.
4500 North State Road Seven
Ste 200
Ft. Lauderdale
FL
33319
USA
Tel: 954 484 4973
Fax: +1 954 484 0818
Paul Kavanaugh, Director, Operations

Services/Products:
Telemarketing agency

Member of:
DMA

INTERACTIVE TELESERVICES CORPORATION
21 East State Street
18th Fl
Columbus
OH
43215
USA
Tel: +1 614 280 1600
Fax: +1 614 280 1610
Andy Jacobs, Chief Executive Officer

Services/Products:
Telemarketing agency

Member of:
DMA

INTERMAIL DIRECT INC
16135 New Ave. Suite #12
Chicago

IL
60439
USA
Tel: +1 630 243 1144
Fax: +1 630 243 8250
Charles Cerniglia, President

Services/Products:
Fulfilment and sampling house

Member of:
FEDMA

INTERNATIONAL BILLING SERVICES
5220 Robert J. Mathews Parkway
El Dorado Hills
CA
95762–5712
USA
Tel: 916 939 4656
Fax: +1 916 939 4691
Tom Roberts, Vice President,
   Marketing

Services/Products:
List services

Member of:
DMA

INTERNATIONAL CUSTOMER LOYALTY PROGRAMMES (ICLP)
P. O. Box 700907
Dallas
TX
75370–0907
USA
Tel: +1 214 713 8033
Fax: +1 214 233 5348
Terry Evans, President - The Americas

Services/Products:
Marketing consultant

Member of:
DMA

INTERNATIONAL DATA
6633 North Mesa
Ste 601
El Paso
TX
79912
USA
Tel: 915 581 6237
Fax: +1 915 584 7990
Linn Cornick, VP, Promotion Services

Services/Products:
List services

Member of:
DMA

**INTERNATIONAL DIRECT
  MARKETING
  CONSULTANTS, INC.**
3419 Westminster
Lock Box 209
Dallas
TX
75205
USA
Tel: +1 214 443 9494
Fax: +1 214 443 9512
Lee William McNutt, President

Services/Products:
Marketing consultant

Member of:
DMA (US); FEDMA

INTERNATIONAL
  DIRECT RESPONSE,
  INC.
**1125 Lancaster Avenue
Berwyn
PA
19312–1243
USA
Tel: +1 610 993 0500
Fax: +1 610 993 9938
Email: mike@idronline.com
Web: www.idronline.com
Michael Guyer, Vice President
  & Director of Marketing**

Services/Products:
**List services; Consultancy
services; Copy adaptation;
Media buying agency; Direct
marketing agency; Product
sampling**

E-Services:
Email list provider

Member of:
**DMA (US); Association of
Interactive Media (AIM);
Promotion Marketing
Association (PMA);
Philadelphia Direct Marketing
Association (PDMA)**

**INTERNATIONAL MARKETING
  SOLUTIONS, INC.**
1999 Broadway
Ste 1900
Denver
CO
80202
USA

Tel: +1 303 672 1952
Fax: +1 303 377 3752
Elizabeth Weimer, International Acct.
  Manager

Services/Products:
Marketing consultant

Member of:
DMA (US); FEDMA

**INTERNATIONAL POSTAL
  CONSULTANTS, INC.**
7483 Candlewood Road
Hanover
MD
21076–3142
USA
Tel: +1 410 604 3010
Fax: +1 410 498 1223
Christopher Taylor, Regional Vice
  President

Services/Products:
Lettershop; Mailing/Faxing services

Member of:
DMA

**INTERNATIONAL RESOURCE
  MANAGEMENT CO.**
P. O. Box 200516
Arlington
TX
76006–0516
USA
Tel: 817 861 9191
Fax: +1 817 277 0868
James Johnson, Director

Services/Products:
Marketing consultant

Member of:
DMA

**INTERNET CATALOG
  SERVICES**
291 Jefferson Avenue
New London
CT
6320
USA
Tel: 860 442 7535
Fax: +1 860 447 0630
Michael Brown

Services/Products:
Catalogue producer

Member of:
DMA

INTERPOST NORTH AMERICA
471–06 176 Street
4th Fl
Jamaica
NY

11434
USA
Tel: +1 718 995 5511
Fax: +1 718 995 5519
John Costanzo, President

Services/Products:
Private delivery services

Member of:
DMA

INTERVAL INTERNATIONAL
6262 Sunset Drive
PH 1
Miami
FL
33143
USA
Tel: +1 305 666 1861
Fax: +1 305 662 7895
Patrica Rasekhi, AVP, Membership
  Marketing

Services/Products:
Advertising Agency; Direct Respons
Agency

Member of:
DMA

IQI, INC.
1645 North Vine Street
Los Angeles
CA
90028
USA
Tel: +1 800 840 4243
Fax: +1 213 856 9733
Edward Blank, Vice Chairman

Services/Products:
Telemarketing agency

Member of:
DMA

IRA THOMAS ASSOCIATES
5121 Mahoning Avenue
Youngstown
OH
44515–1847
USA
Tel: +1 330 793 3000
Fax: +1 330 793 7469
Mark Bachmann, Executive Vice
  President

Services/Products:
Advertising Agency; Direct Respons
Agency

Member of:
DMA

IRMA S. MANN, STRATEGIC MARKETING, INC.
360 Newbury Street
Boston
MA
2115
USA
Tel: +1 617 353 1822
Fax: +1 617 266 1890
Linzee Brown, Mgr., Direct Response Mktg.

Services/Products:
Advertising Agency; Direct Response Agency

Member of:
DMA

IRRESISTIBLE INK INC.
126 North 3rd Street
Ste 412
Minneapolis
MN
55401–1633
USA
Tel: +1 800 543 8396
Fax: +1 612 339 3788
Jon Petters, Chief Executive Officer

Services/Products:
Lettershop; Mailing/Faxing services

Member of:
DMA

ISG/AVNE SYSTEMS
1595 Bathgate Avenue
Bronx
NY
10457–8102
USA
Tel: +1 718 716 7600
Fax: +1 718 583 8640
Daniel Solomon, President

Services/Products:
List services; Specialist packaging

Member of:
DMA

ISPI (INTERNET SERVICE PROVIDERS INTERNATIONAL)
237 South 70th Street
Ste 220
Lincoln
NE
68510–2457
USA
Tel: +1 402 441 3295
Fax: +1 402 483 5418
David Hahn, President

E-Services:
Website design

Member of:
DMA

ITAGROUP
4800 Westown Parkway
Ste 300
West Des Moines
IA
50266
USA
Tel: +1 515 224 3400
Fax: +1 515 221 8344
Email: hkroner@itagroup.com
Web: www.itagroup.com
Heidi Kroner, E-Marketing Business Development

Services/Products:
Database services; Print services; Interactive media; Sales promotion agency; Consultancy services

E-Services:
E-Marketing consultant

Member of:
DMA (US)

ITI MARKETING SERVICES, INC.
Idelman Telemarketing
902 North 91st Plaza
Omaha
NE
68114
USA
Tel: +1 402 393 8000
Fax: +1 402 393 3454
John Calk, VP, Marketing & Business Dev.

Services/Products:
Telemarketing agency

Member of:
DMA

IVIE & ASSOCIATES, INC.
2322 East Kimberly Road
Ste 150E
Davenport
IA
52807
USA
Tel: +1 319 355 9755
Fax: +1 319 355 9518
Robert Epping, Director, Communications

Services/Products:
Advertising Agency; Direct Response Agency

Member of:
DMA

J. F. GLASER INCORPORATED
999 Main Street
Ste 103
Glen Ellyn
IL
60137
USA
Tel: +1 630 469 2075
Fax: +1 630 790 5244
Joseph Glaser, President

Services/Products:
List services

Member of:
DMA

J. FELVEY & ASSOCIATES, INC.
1910 Byrd Avenue
Ste 203
Richmond
VA
23230
USA
Tel: 804 288 9440
Fax: +1 804 288 9824
John Felvey, President

Services/Products:
Marketing consultant

Member of:
DMA

J. SCHMID & ASSOC. INC.
9000 West 64th Terrace
Shawnee Mission
KS
66202
USA
Tel: +1 913 385 0220
Fax: +1 913 385 0221
Email: jacks@jschmid.com
Web: www.jschmid.com
Jack Schmid, President

Services/Products:
Advertising Agency; Catalogue producer; Consultancy services; Database services; Media buying agency; Print services; Catalogue design

E-Services:
E-Marketing consultant

Member of:
DMA (US)

J. WALTER THOMPSON DIRECT
466 Lexington Avenue
New York
NY
10017–3140
USA
Tel: +1 212 210 7070

Fax: +1 212 210 7770
Debra Brown-Christie, Managing
  Director

Services/Products:
Advertising Agency; Direct Response
Agency

Member of:
DMA

J.G. COMMUNICATIONS
Three Park Avenue
New York
NY
10016
USA
Tel: +1 212 683 4774
Fax: +1 212 683 0260
Manny Mallo, President

Services/Products:
Market research agency

Member of:
DMA

**JACK LEONARD COMPANY
  INC.**
795 Bramblewood Drive
Loveland
OH
45140
USA
Tel: +1 513 583 9610
Fax: +1 513 583 9610
Jack Leonard, President

Services/Products:
Marketing consultant

Member of:
DMA

JACOBS & CLEVENGER, INC.
401 North Wabash Avenue
Ste 620
Chicago
IL
60611
USA
Tel: +1 312 894 3000
Fax: +1 312 645 9825
Ron Jacobs, President

Services/Products:
Advertising Agency; Direct Response
Agency

Member of:
DMA

JAMES A. REIMAN, P.C.
1291 Asbury Avenue
Winnetka
IL
60093
USA

Tel: 847 784 8100
Fax: +1 847 784 8108
James Reiman, Principal

Services/Products:
Marketing consultant

Member of:
DMA

JAMI MARKETING SERVICES
1 Blue Hill Plaza
P.O. Box 1662
Pearl River
NY
10965
USA
Tel: 914 620 0700
Fax: +1 914 620 1885
Fran Golub, VP & Dir., List
  Management

Services/Products:
List services

Member of:
DMA

**JC PENNY DIRECT
  MARKETING SERVICES**
2700 West Plano Parkway
Plano
TX
75075–8200
USA
Tel: 972 881 6462
Fax: +1 972 881 4023
Ed Suiter, Executive Vice President-
  Marketing and New Business
  Development FEDMA

Services/Products:
Advertising Agency; Direct Response
Agency

**JDM - JETSON DIRECT MAIL
  SERVICES, INC.**
2 Penn Plaza
New York
NY
10121–1999
USA
Tel: +1 212 629 4500
Fax: +1 212 760 2635
Vincent Carosella, President

Services/Products:
List services

Member of:
DMA

JDR MARKETING INC.
2875 Union Road
Buffalo
NY
14227

USA
Tel: +1 800 318 8626
Fax: +1 716 686 0224
Neil Hertzman, Chief Operating
  Officer

Services/Products:
Telemarketing agency

Member of:
DMA

**JEFFERY ADVERTISING
  AGENCY**
P. O. Box 15378
Colorado Spgs
CO
80935
USA
Tel: +1 719 591 9043
Fax: +1 719 597 5845
Tamara Ward, List & Media Broker

Services/Products:
Advertising Agency; Direct Response
Agency

Member of:
DMA

JF DIRECT MARKETING, INC.
73 Croton Avenue
Ste 106
Ossining
NY
10562
USA
Tel: 914 762 8633
Fax: +1 914 762 9247
John Ferrini, President

Services/Products:
List services

Member of:
DMA

JLM HOLDING, INC.
1716 Corporate Landing Parkway
Virginia Beach
VA
23454
USA
Tel: +1 757 430 3999
Fax: +1 757 430 1947
Bill Brunke, VP, Finance & Sales

Services/Products:
Telemarketing agency

Member of:
DMA

JOAN GREENFIELD CREATIVE
111 Perkins Street
Ste 043
Boston
MA

2130
USA
Tel: +1 617 983 2055
Fax: +1 617 983 2056
Joan Greenfield, Creative & Mktg.
  Consultant

Services/Products:
Design/graphics/clip art supplier;
Consultancy services

Member of:
DMA

JOAN THROCKMORTON, INC.
Box 452
Pound Ridge
NY
10576
USA
Tel: 914 764 4036
Fax: +1 914 764 4139
Joan Throckmorton, President

Services/Products:
Design/graphics/clip art supplier;
Consultancy services

Member of:
DMA

JOHN CONDON & ASSOCIATES
38 Angus Lane
Greenwich
CT
6831
USA
Tel: +1 203 869 7006
Fax: +1 203 622 1488
John Condon, President

Services/Products:
Marketing consultant

Member of:
DMA

JOHN CUMMINGS & PARTNERS
6 Blair Road
Armonk
NY
10504–2522
USA
Tel: 914 273 4691
John Cummings, President

Services/Products:
Marketing consultant

Member of:
DMA

JOHNSON & QUIN, INC.
7460 North Lehigh Avenue
Niles
IL
60714–4099
USA

Tel: 847 588 4800
Fax: +1 847 647 6949
David Henkel, President & Chairman

Services/Products:
List services

Member of:
DMA

**JORDAN, MCGRATH, CASE &
  TAYLOR/DIRECT**
110 Fifth Avenue
New York
NY
10011
USA
Tel: +1 212 463 1000
David Willis, President & Creative
  Director

Services/Products:
Advertising Agency; Direct Response
Agency

Member of:
DMA

JUST PARTNERS
1710 East Franklin Street
Ste 150
Richmond
VA
23223
USA
Tel: 804 225 0100
Fax: +1 804 225 0369
Melinda Daniels, Partner

Services/Products:
Advertising Agency; Direct Response
Agency

Member of:
DMA

JWP GROUP
P. O. Box 3139
New York
NY
10163–3139
USA
Tel: +1 212 664 8085
Fax: +1 212 664 0296
James Prendergast, President

Services/Products:
Advertising Agency; Direct Response
Agency

Member of:
DMA

**JWT SPECIALIZED
  COMMUNICATIONS**
500 N.E. Spanish River Blvd.
Ste 201
Boca Raton

FL
33431–4517
USA
Tel: +1 561 368 5003
Fax: +1 561 368 5133
Kathy Woods, Direct Mail Manager

Services/Products:
Advertising Agency; Direct Response
Agency

Member of:
DMA

**KABLE FULFILLMENT
  SERVICES**
Kable Square
315 E Hitt St
Mount Morris
IL
61054
USA
Tel: 815 734 5296
Fax: +1 815 734 5228
Patty Bridgeman, Manager, Marketing

Services/Products:
Fulfilment and sampling house

Member of:
DMA

KANG & LEE ADVERTISING
315 Fifth Avenue
New York
NY
10016
USA
Tel: +1 212 889 4509
Fax: +1 212 889 2924
Cynthia Park, VP, Group Account

Services/Products:
Advertising Agency; Direct Response
Agency

Member of:
DMA

KANNON CONSULTING, INC.
208 South La Salle Street
Ste 1240
Chicago
IL
60604
USA
Tel: +1 312 346 2244
Fax: +1 312 346 3665
Sarah Merz, Partner

Services/Products:
Marketing consultant

Member of:
DMA

KARL ANALYTICAL SERVICES
One American Lane
Greenwich
CT
6831
USA
Tel: +1 203 552 0252
Fax: +1 203 552 6763
Sheldon Zaslansky, President

Services/Products:
List services

Member of:
DMA

KARLIN/PIMSLER, INC.
205 Lexington Avenue
New York
NY
10016
USA
Tel: +1 212 252 5835
Fax: +1 212 252 5816
Malcolm Karlin, President & CEO

Services/Products:
Advertising Agency; Direct Response
Agency

Member of:
DMA

KCI COMMUNICATIONS, INC.
1101 King Street
Ste 300
Alexandria
VA
22314–2944
USA
Tel: +1 703 548 2400
Fax: +1 703 683 6974
Cherice Calhoun, Director, List
    Services

Services/Products:
List services

Member of:
DMA

**KENT MARKETING GROUP,
    INC.**
1880 Willamette Falls Drive
Suite 200
West Linn
OR
97068
USA
Tel: +1 503 722 9080
Fax: +1 503 722 1481
Email:
    dkent@kentmarketinggroup.com
Web: www.kentmarketinggroup.com
Donald D. Kent, President

Services/Products:
Consultancy services; Market research
agency; Direct marketing agency; Sales
promotion agency

E-Services:
E-Marketing consultant

Member of:
DMA (US)

KERN DIRECT
20300 Ventura Boulevard
Ste 240
Woodland Hills
CA
91364
USA
Tel: 818 +1 703 8775
Fax: +1 818 703 8458
Russell Kern, President

Services/Products:
Advertising Agency; Direct Response
Agency

Member of:
DMA

KETCHUM COMMUNICATIONS
1050 Battery Street
San Francisco
CA
94111
USA
Tel: +1 415 984 2242
Fax: +1 415 984 6110
Web: www.ketchum.com
, Director

Services/Products:
Advertising Agency; Direct Response
Agency

Member of:
DMA

KILLION DIRECT
3112 Prestonwood Drive
Plano
TX
75093
USA
Tel: 972 307 2355
Fax: +1 972 307 5224
James Killion, President

Services/Products:
Marketing consultant

Member of:
DMA

KING TELESERVICES
40 Cragwood Road
S Plainfield
NJ
07080–2406

USA
Tel: +1 800 817 5468
Fax: +1 908 769 8+1 900
Arleen Stefan, Vice President

Services/Products:
Telemarketing agency

Member of:
DMA

**KIRSHENBAUM BOND &
    PARTNERS**
145 Avenue of the Americas
New York
NY
10013
USA
Tel: +1 212 633 0080
Fax: +1 212 727 9390
Lisa Zakarin, VP & Dir., Response
    Marketing

Services/Products:
Advertising Agency; Direct Response
Agency

Member of:
DMA

KLASEK LETTER CO., INC.
2850 South Jefferson Avenue
St. Louis
MO
63118–1599
USA
Tel: +1 314 664 0023
Fax: +1 314 664 9457
Charles Klasek, President

Services/Products:
Lettershop; Mailing/Faxing services

Member of:
DMA

KLEMTNER ADVERTISING
375 Hudson Street
New York
NY
10014
USA
Tel: +1 212 463 3400
Fax: +1 212 463 3541
Rebecca Sroge, Dir, Direct &
    Interactive Mktg

Services/Products:
Advertising Agency; Direct Response
Agency

Member of:
DMA

**KNIGHT STRATEGIC
    CONSULTING**
30 Michael Lane
Stoughton

MA
2072
USA
Tel: +1 617 364 2426
Fax: +1 617 364 2426
John Knight, Founder

Services/Products:
Database services

Member of:
DMA

**KNOWLEDGE BASE
    MARKETING**
5884 Point West Drive
Houston
TX
77036–2612
USA
Tel: +1 713 995 2200
Fax: +1 713 995 2307
Henry Ponder, President

Services/Products:
List services

Member of:
DMA

**KNOWLEDGEBASE
    MARKETING, INC.**
208 West Franklin Street
Chapel Hill
NC
27516
USA
Tel: 919 933 1118
Fax: +1 919 969 5210
Timothy Toben, Chief Executive
    Officer

Services/Products:
Database services

Member of:
DMA

**KOBS STRATEGIC
    CONSULTING**
205 North Michigan Avenue
39th Floor
Chicago
IL
60601
USA
Tel: +1 312 819 2300
Fax: +1 312 819 2323
Email: kgp@kgp.com
Jim Kobs, Chairman

Services/Products:
Consultancy services

E-Services:
E-Marketing consultant

Member of:
National DMA

KOVEL KRESSER & PARTNERS
308 Washington Blvd.
Venice
CA
90292
USA
Tel: +1 310 577 4300
Fax: +1 310 577 4400
Michael Oddi, VP & Dir., Integrated
    Advtg.

Services/Products:
Advertising Agency; Direct Response
Agency

Member of:
DMA

KOWAL ASSOCIATES, INC.
75 Federal Street
8th Fl
Boston
MA
02110–1904
USA
Tel: +1 617 521 9000
Fax: +1 617 521 9010
Jay Williamson, Vice President

Services/Products:
Telemarketing agency

Member of:
DMA

KRAUS ENTERPRISES
209 Highland Terrace
Pittsburgh
PA
15215
USA
Tel: +1 412 782 2632
Fax: +1 412 782 4632
Kathleen Kraus, Consultant,
    Advertising/Mktg.

Services/Products:
Marketing consultant

Member of:
DMA

KROLL DIRECT MARKETING
Media Management Group
666 Plainsboro Road
Ste 540
Plainsboro
NJ
8536
USA
Tel: +1 609 275 2900
Fax: +1 609 275 6606
Leland Kroll, President

Services/Products:
List services

Member of:
DMA

KROLL DIRECT MARKETING
666 Plainsboro Road
Ste 540
Plainsboro
NY
8536
USA
Tel: +1 609 275 2900
Fax: +1 609 275 6606
Leland Kroll, President

Services/Products:
List services

Member of:
DMA

KROLL DIRECT MARKETING
Compiled Solutions
666 Plainsboro Road
Ste 540
Plainsboro
NJ
8536
USA
Tel: +1 609 275 6452
Fax: +1 609 275 6606
Leland Kroll, President

Services/Products:
List services

Member of:
DMA

**KUHN & WITTENBORN
    ADVERTISING**
2405 Grand Boulevard
Kansas City
MO
64108
USA
Tel: 816 471 7888
Fax: +1 816 471 7530
Margaret Horan, Sr. Direct Marketing
    Strat

Services/Products:
Advertising Agency; Direct Response
Agency

Member of:
DMA

KURANT DIRECT INC.
372 Central Park West
Ste 1-B
New York
NY
10025–8202
USA

Tel: +1 212 866 0770
Fax: +1 212 866 0806
Gloria Kurant, President

Services/Products:
Telemarketing agency

Member of:
DMA

L & E MERIDIAN
7400 Fullerton Road
Ste 110
Springfied
VA
22153
USA
Tel: +1 703 913 0300
Fax: +1 703 913 7050
Sylvia Pearson, President

Services/Products:
List services

Member of:
DMA

L.I.S.T. INCORPORATED
320 Northern Boulevard
Great Neck
NY
11021
USA
Tel: +1 516 482 2345
Fax: +1 516 487 7721
Email: info@l-i-s-t.com
Web: www.listincorporated.com
Glenn Freedman, President

Services/Products:
List services; List broker/list manager

E-Services:
Email list provider

Member of:
DMA (US)

L.I.S.T.S. INC.
8789 San Jose Boulevard
Ste 104
Jacksonville
FL
32217–4281
USA
Tel: 904 733 6106
Fax: +1 904 730 7540
Gerry Galbreath, General Manager

Services/Products:
List services

Member of:
DMA

**LA AGENCIA DE ORCI &
ASOCIADOS**
11620 Wilshire Boulevard
Ste 600
Los Angeles
CA
90025
USA
Tel: +1 310 444 7300
Fax: +1 310 478 3587
Email: mgarcia@laagencia.com
Web: www.laagencia.com
Rose Roeder, New Business
Coordinator

Services/Products:
Advertising Agency; Media buying
agency; Specialises in the US Hispanic
market

E-Services:
E-Marketing consultant; Website
design

Member of:
DMA (US); AHAA; NHCCI; NAA;
AEF; AAF

LA&ATINO
1571 Calle Alda Urb. Caribe
Rio Piedras
PR
927
USA
Tel: +1 787 250 0006
Fax: +1 787 282 7747
Rafael Arteaga, Administration

Services/Products:
Advertising Agency; Direct Response
Agency

Member of:
DMA

LABEL ART
One Riverside Way
P.O. Box 660
Wilton
NH
03086–0660
USA
Tel: +1 800 258 1050
Anthony Catalano, CFO, Direct Mail
Business Unit

Services/Products:
Lettershop; Mailing/Faxing services

Member of:
DMA

**LABURNUM MARKETING
PARTNERS, INC.**
250 West 57th Street
Ste 416
New York

NY
10107
USA
Tel: +1 212 265 4193
Fax: +1 212 265 4202
Mary Beth Colucci, President

Services/Products:
Marketing consultant

Member of:
DMA

LACROSSE TRIBUNE
401 North Third Street
LaCrosse
WI
54601
USA
Tel: +1 608 782 9710
Timothy Keane, President

Services/Products:
Marketing consultant

Member of:
DMA

LAGNIAPPE MARKETING
447 Leath Avenue
Cincinnati
OH
45238
USA
Tel: +1 513 244 6487
Fax: +1 513 244 6187
Larry Kavanagh, President

Services/Products:
Database services

Member of:
DMA

LAREAU & ASSOCIATES
140 West End Avenue
New York
NY
10023
USA
Tel: +1 212 877 6533
Fax: +1 212 712 0304
Marybeth Lareau, Copywriter &
Consultant

Services/Products:
Advertising Agency; Direct Response
Agency

Member of:
DMA

**LAWRENCE BUTNER
ADVERTISING, INC.**
228 East 45th Street
New York
NY
10017

USA
Tel: +1 212 338 5000
Fax: +1 212 682 4866
Lawrence Butner, President

Services/Products:
Advertising Agency; Direct Response
Agency

Member of:
DMA

LAZARUS MARKETING INC.
3530 Oceanside Road
Oceanside
NY
11572–5829
USA
Tel: +1 516 678 5107
Fax: +1 516 766 3160
Warren Lazarus, President

Services/Products:
Lettershop; Mailing/Faxing services

Member of:
DMA

LCG LATINO
230 West 41st Street
17th Fl
New York
NY
10036–7207
USA
Tel: +1 212 730 7230
Fax: +1 212 730 7450
Shelly Lipton, President

Services/Products:
Advertising Agency; Direct Response
Agency

Member of:
DMA

**LCS DIRECT MAIL
   ADVERTISING & PRINTING**
3590 North West 54th Street
Ste 6
Ft. Lauderdale
FL
33309
USA
Tel: 954 733 8105
Fax: +1 954 733 8108
James McCartney, President

Services/Products:
Advertising Agency; Direct Response
Agency

Member of:
DMA

LCS INDUSTRIES, INC.
120 Brighton Road
Clifton

NJ
07012–1694
USA
Tel: 973 778 5588
Fax: +1 973 778 6001
Bill Rella, President

Services/Products:
List services

Member of:
DMA

LEC LTD.
311 West Superior
Chicago
IL
60610–3537
USA
Tel: +1 312 787 8800
Fax: +1 312 787 8902
Beth Pope, Account Executive

Services/Products:
Design/graphics/clip art supplier;
Consultancy services

Member of:
DMA

LEDGEMERE HISPANIC LISTS
216 Chesley Lane
6th Fl
Chapel Hill
NC
27514
USA
Tel: 919 929 0919
Fax: +1 919 929 9589
Ralph Stevens, President

Services/Products:
List services

Member of:
DMA

LEE HILL, INC.
445 East Illinois Street
Chicago
IL
60611
USA
Tel: +1 312 245 8921
Fax: +1 312 245 8908
Martin Reilly, VP & General Manager

Services/Products:
Sales promotion agency

Member of:
DMA

LEN SACKS ASSOCIATES INC.
116 Ox Yoke Drive
Wethersfield
CT
6109

USA
Tel: 860 563 6360
Fax: +1 860 563 6265
Douglas Sacks, President

Services/Products:
Marketing consultant

Member of:
DMA

LENSER & ASSOCIATES, INC.
1346 Fourth Street
Ste 206
San Rafael
CA
94901
USA
Tel: +1 415 485 4335
Fax: +1 415 485 1967
John Lenser, Cat. & Dir. Resp.
   Consultant

Services/Products:
Marketing consultant

Member of:
DMA

LEO BURNETT U.S.A.
35 West Wacker Drive
Chicago
IL
60601
USA
Tel: +1 312 220 5959
Fax: +1 312 220 6576
Tim Classey, EVP, Managing Director

Services/Products:
Advertising Agency; Direct Response
Agency

Member of:
DMA (US); FEDMA

LETT DIRECT, INC.
12933 Brighton Court
Carmel
IN
46032–9275
USA
Tel: +1 317 844 8228
Fax: +1 317 844 1770
Stephen Lett, President

Services/Products:
Marketing consultant

Member of:
DMA

**LEVENSON PUBLIC
   RELATIONS**
600 North Pearl
Ste 910
Dallas
TX

75201
USA
Tel: +1 214 880 0200
Fax: +1 214 880 0601
Stan Levenson, CEO

Services/Products:
Advertising Agency; Direct Response
Agency

Member of:
DMA

LEVEY MARKETING SERVICES
161 West 61st Street
#4C
New York
NY
10023
USA
Tel: +1 212 262 0035
Fax: +1 212 399 0033
Marilyn Levey, Owner

Services/Products:
Marketing consultant

Member of:
DMA

LEWIS ADVERTISING, INC.
P. O. Drawer L
1050 Country Club Rd
Rocky Mount
NC
27802–4012
USA
Tel: +1 252 443 5131
Fax: +1 252 443 9340
Donald Williams, President

Services/Products:
Advertising Agency; Direct Response
Agency

Member of:
DMA

**LEWIS ADVERTISING/
BIRMINGHAM**
2 Chase Corporate Drive
Ste 200
Birmingham
AL
35244
USA
Tel: +1 205 733 0024
Fax: +1 205 733 1079
Val Holman, Director, Database
Marketing

Services/Products:
Advertising Agency; Direct Response
Agency

Member of:
DMA

**LEWIS DESIGN/BARRY LEWIS
PHOTOGRAPHY, INC.**
2401 South Ervay
Ste 203
Dallas
TX
75215
USA
Tel: +1 214 421 5665
Fax: +1 214 421 2007
Elizabeth Lewis, Art Director

Services/Products:
Design/graphics/clip art supplier;
Consultancy services

Member of:
DMA

LIBERTY ENVELOPE INC.
298 Midland Avenue
Saddle Brook
NJ
07663–6318
USA
Tel: 973 546 5600
Fax: +1 973 546 4721
Lee Guarderas, President

Services/Products:
Labelling/envelope services

Member of:
DMA

LIEBER & ASSOCIATES
3740 North Lake Shore Drive
Ste 15B-2
Chicago
IL
60613–4202
USA
Tel: +1 77 3 325 9400
Fax: +1 773 325 0621
Mitchell Lieber, President

Services/Products:
Telemarketing agency

Member of:
DMA

**LIEBER, LEVETT, KOENIG,
FARESE, BABCOCK, INC.**
299 West Houston Street
New York
NY
10014–3660
USA
Tel: +1 212 206 5800
Fax: +1 212 206 5801
Harry Koenig, COO

Services/Products:
Advertising Agency; Direct Response
Agency

Member of:
DMA

LIFE PLUS INTERNATIONAL
268 West Main Street
Batesville
AK
72501
USA
Tel: 870 698 2311
Fax: +1 870 698 3422
Kimberly Rudick, Executive Assistant

E-Services:
Website design

Member of:
DMA

**LIFESTYLE CHANGE
COMMUNICATIONS, INC.**
1700 Water Place
Ste 150
Atlanta
GA
30339
USA
Tel: +1 77 0 984 1100
Fax: +1 770 984 8111
Robert Perlstein, President

Services/Products:
List services

Member of:
DMA

**LIGGETT-STASHOWER
DIRECT**
1228 Euclid Avenue
Cleveland
OH
44115
USA
Tel: +1 216 348 8500
Fax: +1 216 622 0429
Sylvia Morrison, General Manager/
SVP

Services/Products:
Advertising Agency; Direct Response
Agency

Member of:
DMA

LIGHTHOUSE LIST CO.
6499 Powerline Road
Ste 206
Ft Lauderdale
FL
33309
USA
Tel: 954 489 3008
Fax: +1 954 489 3040
Mark Traverso, Dir., List Management
Svcs.

Services/Products:
List services

Member of:
DMA

LINDA GOODMAN ASSOC.
2 Farmstead Lane
Avon
CT
6001
USA
Tel: 860 677 7167
Fax: +1 860 677 5972
Linda Goodman, Retail Marketing
  Consultant

Services/Products:
Marketing consultant

Member of:
DMA

LINK MARKETING
5005 Kingsley Drive
Cincinnati
OH
45227–1114
USA
Tel: +1 513 527 3000
Fax: +1 513 527 3015
William Carroll, President

Services/Products:
Fulfilment and sampling house

Member of:
DMA

LINK TO SUCCESS, INC.
17113 Minnetonka Boulevard
Ste 110
Minnetonka
MN
55345
USA
Tel: +1 612 945 0712
Fax: +1 612 945 0715
James Daughton, Owner & President

Services/Products:
Marketing consultant

Member of:
DMA

LISSEN AUDIO COMPANY
11337 S.W. 112 Circle Lane, N.
Miami
FL
33176
USA
Tel: +1 305 971 9820
Fax: +1 305 227 0575
Alex Aguirre, President

Services/Products:
Advertising Agency; Direct Response
Agency

Member of:
DMA

LIST ADVISOR, INC.
500 BI County Boulevard
Ste 125
Farmingdale
NY
11735–3931
USA
Tel: +1 516 777 2900
Fax: +1 516 777 3050
Thomas Frenz, President

Services/Products:
List services

Member of:
DMA

LIST COUNSELLORS
3 South Main Street
P.O. Box 546
Allentown
NJ
8501
USA
Tel: +1 609 259 0600
Fax: +1 609 259 7753
Richard Reinhart, President

Services/Products:
List services

Member of:
DMA

**LIST PROCESS COMPANY,
  INC./LIST PROCESS
  MANAGEMENT, INC.**
420 East 79th Street
Ste 1C
New York
NY
10021
USA
Tel: +1 212 517 8550
Fax: +1 212 517 9728
Paulette Kranjac, President

Services/Products:
List services

Member of:
DMA

LIST SERVICES CORPORATION
6 Trowbridge Drive
P.O. Box 516
Bethel
CT
06801–0516
USA

Tel: +1 203 743 2600
Fax: +1 203 778 4299
Malcolm McCluskey, President

Services/Products:
List services

Member of:
DMA (US); FEDMA

LIST STRATEGIES, INC.
565 Fifth Avenue
8th Fl
New York
NY
10017
USA
Tel: +1 212 767 1000
Fax: +1 212 541 4408
Joel Cooper, President

Services/Products:
List services

Member of:
DMA

**LIST TECHNOLOGY SYSTEMS
  GROUP, INC.**
1001 Avenue of the Americas
New York
NY
10018
USA
Tel: +1 212 719 3850
Fax: +1 212 719 1878
Email: ttaylor@ltsg.com
Web: www.ltsg.com
Thomas Taylor, President

Services/Products:
List services

E-Services:
Email list provider

Member of:
DMA (US)

LKH&S
142 East Ontario Street
Chicago
IL
60611
USA
Tel: +1 312 629 5547
Fax: +1 312 629 5540
Stanton Lewin, Director, Client
  Services

Services/Products:
Advertising Agency; Direct Response
Agency

Member of:
DMA

LOCUS DIRECT MARKETING GROUP, INC.
275 South Memorial Drive
San Bernardino
CA
92408
USA
Tel: 909 382 2422
Fax: +1 909 382 2152
Brian Murphy, Executive Vice
   President

Services/Products:
Fulfilment and sampling house

Member of:
DMA

LONG HAYMES CARR
140 Charlois Boulevard
P.O. Box 5627
Winston-Salem
NC
27103
USA
Tel: +1 336 765 3630
Fax: +1 336 659 8913
Brandt Conner, Director, Relationship
   Mktg.

Services/Products:
Advertising Agency; Direct Response
Agency

Member of:
DMA

LOOKING GLASS INC.
1624 Market Street
Ste 311
Denver
CO
80202
USA
Tel: +1 303 893 8600
Fax: +1 303 893 8611
Jock Bickert, Chief Executive Officer

Services/Products:
Database services

Member of:
DMA

LORD SULLIVAN YODER
250 Old Wilson Bridge Road
Columbus
OH
43085–0800
USA
Tel: +1 614 846 8500
Fax: +1 614 846 2679
Charlene Boyer, VP & Dir.,
   Relationship Mktg.

Services/Products:
Advertising Agency; Direct Response
Agency

Member of:
DMA

LOREN G. SMITH & ASSOCIATES
140 Bishop Lane
P.O. Box 871
Madison
CT
6443
USA
Tel: +1 203 245 4130
Fax: +1 203 245 4179
Loren Smith, President

Services/Products:
Marketing consultant

Member of:
DMA

LORTZ DIRECT MARKETING INC.
13936 Gold Circle
Omaha
NE
68144
USA
Tel: +1 402 334 9446
Fax: +1 402 334 9622
Gary Lortz, Cheif Executive Officer

Services/Products:
Advertising Agency; Direct Response
Agency

Member of:
DMA

LOVE ENVELOPES, INC.
10733 East Ute
Tulsa
OK
74116
USA
Tel: 918 936 3535
Fax: +1 918 832 9978
Michael Love, President

Services/Products:
Labelling/envelope services

Member of:
DMA

LOWE DIRECT
2300 Greenlawn Boulevard
Austin
TX
78664
USA
Tel: +1 512 728 8166

Fax: +1 512 728 4439
Neil Fox, President & CEO

Services/Products:
Advertising Agency; Direct Response
Agency

Member of:
DMA

LOWE FOX PAVLIKA
1114 Avenue of the Americas
New York
NY
10036–7703
USA
Tel: +1 212 403 7700
Fax: +1 212 403 7702
Neil Fox, President & CEO

Services/Products:
Advertising Agency; Direct Response
Agency

Member of:
DMA

M&I CAPITAL MARKETS GROUP
644 Science Drive
Ste 301
Madison
WI
53711
USA
Tel: +1 608 232 9444
Fax: +1 608 232 9411
Rodney Schwegel, National Accounts
   Manager

Services/Products:
Telemarketing agency

Member of:
DMA

M. JOSEPH DUNN & ASSOCIATES
6 Marblehead Drive
Nashua
NH
03063–7012
USA
Tel: +1 603 882 6953
Fax: +1 603 882 6953
M. Joseph Dunn, Consultant

Services/Products:
Marketing consultant

Member of:
DMA

M.I.T. SPECIALIST
4535 West Sahara Avenue
Ste 105
Las Vegas
NV

89102
USA
Tel: +1 702 380 8040
Fax: +1 702 383 8313
Gary Yue, Chief Financial Officer

Services/Products:
Marketing consultant

Member of:
DMA

M/S DATABASE MARKETING, LLC.

10866 Wilshire Boulevard
Ste 370
Los Angeles
CA
90024–4311
USA
Tel: +1 310 208 2024
Fax: +1 310 208 5681
Robert McKim, CEO

Services/Products:
Database services

Member of:
DMA

MACKAY ENVELOPE CORPORATION

2100 Elm Street, S.E.
Minneapolis
MN
55414
USA
Tel: +1 800 622 5299
Fax: +1 612 331 8229
Scott Johnson, VP, Sales & Marketing

Services/Products:
Labelling/envelope services

Member of:
DMA

MACROMARK, INC.

1841 Broadway
Ste 24
New York
NY
10023
USA
Tel: +1 212 397 6600
Fax: +1 212 397 3987
Howard Linzer, President

Services/Products:
List services

Member of:
DMA

MAGNETIX GROUP DIRECTIONS

770 West Bay Street
Winter Gardens

FL
34787
USA
Tel: +1 407 656 4494
Fax: +1 407 656 4825
Ron Panepinto, Senior Vice President

Services/Products:
Lettershop; Mailing/Faxing services

Member of:
DMA

MAIER MARKETING SYNERGY

181 Cheshire Lane
Minneapolis
MN
55441
USA
Tel: +1 612 404 5800
Fax: +1 612 404 5848
Matt Maier, President

Services/Products:
Marketing consultant

Member of:
DMA

MAIL MARKETING, INCORPORATED

171 Terrace Street
Haworth
NJ
7641
USA
Tel: +1 201 387 1010
Fax: +1 201 387 2976
Hal Roberson, President

Services/Products:
List services

Member of:
DMA

MAIL-WELL, INC. CORPORATE OFFICE

23 Inverness Way East
Englewood
CO
80112
USA
Tel: +1 303 790 8023
Fax: +1 303 397 7400
Gerald Mahoney, Chairman & CEO,
    Mail Well, Inc

Services/Products:
Personalisation; Print services;
Labelling/envelope services

Member of:
DMA (US)

MAILCOM PLC

11 Seneca Drive
Hampton Bays

NY
11946
USA
Tel: +1 516 728 0884
Neil Shotton, Marketing Manager

Services/Products:
Advertising Agency; Direct Response
Agency

Member of:
DMA

MAILFAST

8701 Bellanca Avenue
Ste 400
Los Angeles
CA
90045
USA
Tel: +1 310 410 1419
Fax: +1 310 410 0218
Ingrid Werner, Marketing Director

Services/Products:
Private delivery services

Member of:
DMA

MAILING CONCEPT, INC.

1533 Bay Point Drive
Virginia Beach
VA
23454
USA
Tel: +1 757 481 6917
Fax: +1 757 481 6918
Ray Ellis, President

Services/Products:
Advertising Agency; Direct Response
Agency

Member of:
DMA

MAILING SERVICES OF PITTSBURG, INC.

155 Commerce Drive
Freedom
PA
15042–9201
USA
Tel: +1 724 774 3244
Fax: +1 724 774 6996
Richard Bushee

Services/Products:
Lettershop; Mailing/Faxing services

Member of:
DMA

MAILMEN INC.

317 Madison Avenue
Ste 1518
New York

NY
10017–5375
USA
Tel: +1 212 986 4862
Fax: +1 212 949 8268
Lee Epstein, Chairman

Services/Products:
Lettershop; Mailing/Faxing services

Member of:
DMA

MAKE IT SO, INC.
2471 Flores Street
San Mateo
CA
94403
USA
Tel: +1 650 524 2000
Fax: +1 650 524 2020
Jerry Sandoval, President

Services/Products:
Advertising Agency; Direct Response
Agency

Member of:
DMA

MAL DUNN ASSOCIATES, INC.
Two Hardscrabble Road
Croton Falls
NY
10519–9999
USA
Tel: 914 277 5558
Fax: +1 914 277 3127
Stephen Dunn, President

Services/Products:
List services

Member of:
DMA

MALCHOW ADAMS & HUSSEY
1400 I Street, N.W.
Ste 650
Washington
DC
20005–2205
USA
Tel: +1 202 682 2500
Fax: +1 202 682 1500
Hal Malchow, Chairman

Services/Products:
Marketing consultant

Member of:
DMA

**MALCOLM DECKER
ASSOCIATES INC.**
36 Rockwood Lane
Greenwich
CT
6830
USA
Tel: +1 203 661 1693
Fax: +1 203 661 6254
Email: malbdecker@aol.com
Malcolm Decker, President

Services/Products:
Advertising Agency; Consultancy
services; Copy adaptation;
Personalisation; Print services

E-Services:
E-Marketing consultant; Online/e-
marketing agency

Member of:
DMA (US); DMIX (NY)

MANEX
48001 Fremont Boulevard
Fremont
CA
94002
USA
Tel: +1 510 249 1480
Fax: +1 510 249 1499
Justin Whitten, Events & Leads
Coordinator

Services/Products:
Marketing consultant

Member of:
DMA

**MANNING MEDIA
INTERNATIONAL**
3309 Westfield
Plano
TX
75093
USA
Tel: 972 473 2163
Fax: +1 972 473 7449
Mike Manning, President

Services/Products:
List services

Member of:
DMA

MANUS DIRECT
1130 Rainier Avenue, South
P.O. Box 440406
Seattle
WA
98114
USA
Tel: +1 206 325 2200

Fax: +1 206 325 1893
Larry Granston, President

Services/Products:
Advertising Agency; Direct Response
Agency

Member of:
DMA

MANUS DIRECT MARKETING
1130 Rainier Avenue, South
P.O. Box 440406
Seattle
WA
98114
USA
Tel: +1 206 325 2200
Fax: +1 206 325 1893
Larry Granston, President

Services/Products:
Advertising Agency; Direct Response
Agency

Member of:
DMA

MARCOM
7771 West Oakland Park Blvd.
Ste 210
Sunrise
FL
33351
USA
Tel: 954 747 6566
Fax: +1 954 741 1329
Randy Warren, President & CEO

Services/Products:
Telemarketing agency

Member of:
DMA

MARCOM, INC.
1413 Farington Drive
Plano
TX
75075–2721
USA
Tel: 972 509 4867
Fax: +1 972 423 1550
Linda Johns, President

Services/Products:
Database services

Member of:
DMA

MARDEN-KANE, INC.
36 Maple Place
Manhasset
NY
11030–1427
USA
Tel: +1 516 365 3999

Fax: +1 516 365 5250
Paul Goldman, Executive Vice
    President

Services/Products:
Sales promotion agency

Member of:
DMA

MARDEV
475 Park Avenue South
2nd Fl
New York
NY
10016–6901
USA
Tel: +1 800 545 8517
Fax: +1 212 545 6901
Karie Burt, Sales Director

Services/Products:
List services

Member of:
DMA

MARIS, WEST & BAKER
18 Northtown Drive
P.O. Box 12426
Jackson
MS
39236–2426
USA
Tel: +1 601 362 6306
Fax: +1 601 981 1902
Kenneth Sandridge, President

Services/Products:
Advertising Agency; Direct Response
Agency

Member of:
DMA

MARITZ PERFORMANCE
IMPROVEMENT COMPANY
1315 North Highway Drive
Fenton
MO
63099
USA
Tel: +1 314 827 4000
Fax: +1 314 827 3223
Karen McDonough, Dir., Direct
    Marketing Service

Services/Products:
Advertising Agency; Direct Response
Agency

Member of:
DMA

MARKE
COMMUNICATIONS,
INC.
39 Broadway 3FL
New York
NY
10016
USA
Tel: +1 212 684 5600
Fax: +1 212 213 0785
Email:
    arosenberg@marke.com
Web: www.marke.com
Allen Rosenberg, Executive
    Vice President

Services/Products:
Advertising Agency; Catalogue
producer; Consultancy
services; Print services; Direct
marketing agency; Sales
promotion agency

E-Services:
E-Marketing consultant;
Website design; Online/e-
marketing agency

Member of:
DMA (US); NEDMA; RFA;
Catalog Council

MARKET PLACE PRIUT
600 Grant Street
4800 USX Twr
Pittsburgh
PA
15219
USA
Tel: +1 412 395 7700
Fax: +1 412 395 7701
Michael Monsour, President

Services/Products:
Advertising Agency; Direct Response
Agency

Member of:
DMA

MARKET RESPONSE
INTERNATIONAL
Harbor View Lane
P.O. Box 387
North Chatham
MA
02650–0387
USA
Tel: +1 508 945 4010
Fax: +1 508 945 4011
Richard Miller, Managing Partner

Services/Products:
Marketing consultant

Member of:
DMA (US); FEDMA

MARKET U.S.A. INC.
2200 East Devon Avenue
Ste 200
Des Plaines
IL
60018
USA
Tel: 847 803 1900
Fax: +1 847 803 1825
S. Okner, President

Services/Products:
Telemarketing agency

Member of:
DMA

MARKETING ALTERNATIVES,
INC.
3721 Ventura Drive
Ste 180
Arlington Hts
IL
60004
USA
Tel: 847 253 1410
Fax: +1 847 253 2232
Gary Stanko, President

Services/Products:
Advertising Agency; Direct Response
Agency

Member of:
DMA

MARKETING ASSOCIATES/
USA, INC.
Tampa International Airport
Tampa
FL
33607
USA
Tel: 813 875 7799
Fax: +1 813 877 1490
Gene Smith, Executive Vice President

Services/Products:
Sales promotion agency

Member of:
DMA

MARKETING
COMMUNICATION
SYSTEMS, INC.
1044 Pulinski Road
Ivyland
PA
18974
USA

Tel: +1 215 675 2000
Fax: +1 215 957 4370
William Korn, President

Services/Products:
List services

Member of:
DMA

MARKETING CORPORATION OF AMERICA
285 Riverside Avenue
Westport
CT
6880
USA
Tel: +1 203 222 1000
Fax: +1 203 222 6540
Martin Reilly, VP & General Manager

Services/Products:
Sales promotion agency

Member of:
DMA

MARKETING DATA, INC.
145 West 28th Street
New York
NY
10001
USA
Tel: +1 212 714 2333
Fax: +1 212 290 0254
Derek Schoettle, Sales Manager

Services/Products:
List services

Member of:
DMA

MARKETING ECONOMICS, INC.
1636 North Wells Street
Ste 3112
Chicago
IL
60614
USA
Tel: +1 312 642 2188
Fax: +1 312 642 3091
F. Cody Heiderer, President

Services/Products:
List services

Member of:
DMA

MARKETING INFORMATION & TECHNOLOGY
100 Cummings Park
Woburn
MA
1801
USA

Tel: +1 781 937 3311
Fax: +1 781 937 3355
James Alvarez, President

Services/Products:
Marketing consultant

Member of:
DMA

MARKETING MANAGEMENT INTERNATIONAL
1500 S.W. 130th Street
Seattle
WA
98146
USA
Tel: +1 206 246 7660
Fax: +1 206 246 7696
Mike Gilbert, President

Services/Products:
Marketing consultant

Member of:
DMA

MARKETING MODELS
132 Lincoln Street
3rd Fl
Boston
MA
2111
USA
Tel: +1 617 423 1780
Fax: +1 617 423 1995
Robert Dufault, President

Services/Products:
Market research agency

Member of:
DMA

MARKETING RESOURCES OF NEW YORK, INC.
3385 Orchard Park Road
Orchard Park
NY
14127–1695
USA
Tel: +1 716 675 5300
Fax: +1 716 675 5325
Gary Guyton, President

Services/Products:
Advertising Agency; Direct Response Agency

Member of:
DMA

MARKETING RESULTS ASSOCIATES, INC.
634 Lost Pine Way
Absecon
NJ
8201

USA
Tel: +1 609 748 8880
Fax: +1 609 652 8330
Patrice Gianni, President

Services/Products:
Marketing consultant

Member of:
DMA

MARKETING SOFTWARE COMPANY
6200 Canoga Avenue
Ste 102
Woodland Hills
CA
91367
USA
Tel: 818 346 1600
Fax: +1 818 712 0122
David Merzanis, President

Services/Products:
List services

Member of:
DMA

MARKETING SYNERGY INC.
4701 Auvergne Ave
Ste 201
Lisle
IL
60532
USA
Tel: +1 630 663 0070
Fax: +1 630 663 0072
Randy Hlavac, President

Services/Products:
Market research agency

Member of:
DMA

MARKETING/MEDIA DYNAMICS, INC.
607 Main Avenue
Norwalk
CT
06851–1058
USA
Tel: +1 203 750 0295
Fax: +1 203 750 0294
David Jedele, Executive Vice President

Services/Products:
Market research agency

Member of:
DMA

MARKETIQ, INC.
740 River Road
Ste 210
Fair Haven
NJ

7704
USA
Tel: +1 732 933 9800
Fax: +1 732 933 4604
Marcia Waite, Vice President,
  Marketing

Services/Products:
Market research agency

Member of:
DMA

MARKETONE
141 East Trinity Place
Decatur
GA
30030
USA
Tel: +1 404 377 0001
Fax: +1 404 378 1196
Email:
  mark.ogletree@marketoneinc.com
Web: www.marketoneinc.com
Mark Ogletree, VP Business
  Development

Services/Products:
Consultancy services; Database
services; Personalisation; Direct
marketing agency; Interactive media;
Sales promotion agency

MARKETRAC, INC.
131 Executive Drive
New Hyde Park
NY
11040
USA
Tel: +1 516 365 4330
Fax: +1 516 365 5789
Louise Donnelly, President

Services/Products:
Marketing consultant

Member of:
DMA

MARKETRY, INC.
1601 114th Avenue, N.E.
Ste 130
Bellevue
WA
98004–6904
USA
Tel: +1 425 451 1262
Fax: +1 425 451 1941
Norman Swent, President

Services/Products:
List services

Member of:
DMA

MARKETTOUCH
11660 Alpharetta Highway
Ste 455
Roswell
GA
30076
USA
Tel: +1 77 0 754 9066
Fax: +1 770 754 9067
James Dekle, President

Services/Products:
List services

Member of:
DMA ·

MARKETWORKS, INC.
7358 Fairway Lane
Parker
CO
80134–5900
USA
Tel: +1 303 805 4060
Fax: +1 303 805 4066
Linda Bortis, President

Services/Products:
Database services

Member of:
DMA

MARKITECTURE SYSTEMS GROUP
71 East Avenue
Ste B
Norwalk
CT
06851–4903
USA
Robert Shulman, Chief Marketing
  Officer

Services/Products:
Marketing consultant

Member of:
DMA

MARQUARDT & ROCHE/ MEDITZ & HACKETT
999 Summer Street
Stamford
CT
6905
USA
Tel: +1 203 327 0890
Fax: +1 203 353 8487
Howard Meditz, President

Services/Products:
Advertising Agency; Direct Response
Agency

Member of:
DMA

MARTIN DIRECT
One Shockoe Plaza
Richmond
VA
23219–4132
USA
Tel: 804 698 8000
Fax: +1 804 698 +1 8001
Barbara Thornhill, EVP & CAO

Services/Products:
Advertising Agency; Direct Response
Agency

Member of:
DMA

MARY CULNAN CONSULTANT
3711 39th Street N.W.
Ste B188
Washington
DC
20016
USA
Tel: +1 202 687 3802
Mary Culnan, Principal

Services/Products:
Marketing consultant

Member of:
DMA

MARY ELIZABETH GRANGER & ASSOCIATES, INC.
110 West Road
Ste 235
Baltimore
MD
21204
USA
Tel: +1 410 842 1170
Fax: +1 410 842 1185
Bonnie Granger, President

Services/Products:
List services

Member of:
DMA ·

MASADA GROUP TECHNOLOGIES CORPORATION
23 Hubbard Road
Wilton
CT
6897
USA
Tel: +1 203 762 2300
Fax: +1 203 762 7200
Robert Brody, President

Services/Products:
List services

Member of:
DMA

MASON & GELLER DIRECT, LLC
261 Madison Avenue
18th fl
New York
NY
10016
USA
Tel: +1 212 697 4477
Fax: +1 212 697 2919
Lois Geller, President

Services/Products:
Advertising Agency; Direct Response Agency

Member of:
DMA

MATCHLOGIC, INC.
10333 Church Ranch Boulevard
‘
Westminister
CO
80021
USA
Tel: +1 303 222 2000
Fax: +1 303 222 2001
Kelly Meeter, MarCom Manager

Services/Products:
Advertising Agency; Direct Response Agency

Member of:
DMA

MATRIXX MARKETING INC.
One Matrixx Plaza
Ogden
UT
84405
USA
Tel: 801 329 6213
Fax: +1 801 629 6272
Clifton Critchlow, Sales VP, Direct Response

Services/Products:
Telemarketing agency

Member of:
DMA

MATT BROWN & ASSOCIATES, INC.
2769 Orchard Run Road
Dayton
OH
45449
USA
Tel: 937 434 3949
Fax: +1 937 434 6272
Matt Brown, President

Services/Products:
List services

Member of:
DMA

MATTHIAS TELEMARKETING MANAGEMENT, INC.
P. O. Box 540411
Omaha
NE
68154
USA
Tel: +1 402 334 2690
Fax: +1 402 333 4998
Dennis Matthias, President

Services/Products:
Telemarketing agency

Member of:
DMA

MAVERICK MARKETING GROUP, INC.
100 Oceangate
Ste 1200
Long Beach
CA
90802
USA
Tel: +1 562 628 5577
Fax: +1 562 628 5578
Michael Irwin, President & CEO

Services/Products:
Advertising Agency; Direct Response Agency

Member of:
DMA

MAXIMARKETING
333 East 30th Street
New York
NY
10016
USA
Tel: +1 212 779 1575
Fax: +1 212 779 1856
Richard Cross, President

Services/Products:
Marketing consultant

Member of:
DMA

MAXWELL SROGE COMPANY, INC.
522 Forest Avenue
Evanston
IL
60202–3005
USA
Tel: +1 847 866 1890
Fax: +1 847 866 1899
Email: msroge@catalog-news.com
Web: www.catalog-news.com
Maxwell Sroge, President

Services/Products:
Advertising Agency; Catalogue producer; Consultancy services; Database services; Direct marketing agency

E-Services:
E-Marketing consultant; Website design

Member of:
DMA (US)

MAY & SPEH ENERGY MARKET CONNECT
1501 Opus Place
Downers Grove
IL
60515
USA
Tel: +1 630 719 0566
Fax: +1 630 971 4866
Cindy Randazzo, VP, Marketing

Services/Products:
List services

Member of:
DMA

MAY DEVELOPMENT SERVICES
200 Pemberwick Road
Greenwich
CT
6830
USA
Tel: +1 203 532 2546
Charles Morgan, Pres. & Chairman of the Board

Services/Products:
List services

Member of:
DMA

MAYNE ASSOCIATES, INC.
3527 Mt. Diablo Blvd.
P.O. Box 48
Ste 323
Lafayette
CA
94549
USA
Tel: 925 284 8500
Fax: +1 925 284 8502
Clifton Mayne, President

Services/Products:
Design/graphics/clip art supplier; Consultancy services

Member of:
DMA

MBS/MULTIMODE, INC.
570 South Research Place
Central Islip
NY
11722–4415
USA
Tel: +1 516 851 5000
Fax: +1 516 851 1338
Stanley Braunstein, President

Services/Products:
List services

Member of:
DMA

MC DIRECT
12625 Stowe Drive
Poway
CA
92064–6805
USA
Tel: +1 619 679 3584
Fax: +1 619 679 3593
RayEll is, President

Services/Products:
Advertising Agency; Direct Response
Agency

Member of:
DMA

**MCCANN RELATIONSHIP
   MARKETING**
750 Third Avenue
New York
NY
10017
USA
Tel: +1 212 286 0460
Fax: +1 212 984 8993
Pamela Maphis Larrick, EVP &
   Managing Director, N.A.

Services/Products:
Advertising Agency; Direct Response
Agency

Member of:
DMA

**MCCARTHY MEDIA GROUP,
   INC.**
819 South Wabash Avenue
Ste 505
Chicago
IL
60605
USA
Tel: +1 312 431 1080
Fax: +1 312 431 1083
Michael McCarthy, President

Services/Products:
List services

Member of:
DMA

MCI/EVS
220 Jackson Street
Ste 700
San Francisco
CA
94111
USA
Tel: +1 415 989 2200
Camille Wehner, President

Services/Products:
Telemarketing agency

Member of:
DMA

MCINTYRE DIRECT
102 North Hayden Bay Drive
Portland
OR
97217–7956
USA
Tel: +1 503 735 9515
Fax: +1 503 286 7622
Susan McIntyre, President

Services/Products:
Marketing consultant

Member of:
DMA

MCRB SERVICE BUREAU, INC.
9171 Oso Avenue
Chatsworth
CA
91311–6049
USA
Tel: 818 407 4300
Fax: +1 818 407 0248
Stephen Allen, Executive Vice
   President

Services/Products:
Fulfilment and sampling house

Member of:
DMA

MEDIA MARKETPLACE, INC.
P. O. Box 500
140 Terry Dr
Ste 103
Newtown
PA
18940–0500
USA
Tel: +1 215 968 5020
Fax: +1 215 968 9410
Thomas Kellogg, President & Co-
   Chairman

Services/Products:
List services

MEDIA MART
1750 Old Meadow Road
Ste 300
McLean
VA
22102–4318
USA
Tel: +1 703 905 8000
Fax: +1 703 905 8097
Cherice Calhoun, Director, List
   Services

Services/Products:
List services

Member of:
DMA

MEDINA ASSOCIATES
12 Hilltop Road
Wallingford
PA
19086
USA
Tel: +1 610 565 8836
Fax: +1 610 565 8184
Email: KurtMedina@aol.com
Kurt Medina, President

Services/Products:
Consultancy services; 50+ mature
market specialised marketing
consultancy; custom seminars

E-Services:
E-Marketing consultant

Member of:
DMA (US); Philadelphia Direct
Marketing Association; Business
Forum on Aging; Mature Market
Resource Centre

MEMBERSHIP CARDS ONLY
8000 Towers Crescent Drive
Ste 1350
Vienna
VA
22182
USA
Tel: +1 800 772 2737
Fax: +1 703 573 5417
Richard Faust, President

Services/Products:
Advertising Agency; Direct Response
Agency

Member of:
DMA

MERCATA
110 110th Avenue N.E.
Ste 390

Bellevue
WA
98004–5840
USA
Tel: +1 425 462 7242
Fax: +1 425 637 5886
Richard Halbert, Director, Business
  Development

E-Services:
Website design

Member of:
DMA

MERCATUS, INC.
4092 Pebble Beach Drive
Longmont
CO
80503
USA
Tel: +1 303 786 7944
Mark Harjes, Vice President

Services/Products:
Database services

Member of:
DMA

MERCURY MEDIA
2670 South White Road
Ste 261
San Jose
CA
95148
USA
Tel: +1 408 223 6671
Fax: +1 408 223 6673
Vincent J. McCastle, President

Services/Products:
Marketing consultant

Member of:
DMA

MERGE PURGE CORP.
Division of HYAID GROUP
7 Commercial Street
Hicksville
NY
11801
USA
Tel: +1 516 433 3015
Fax: +1 516 433 6760
Richard Levinson, President

Services/Products:
List services

Member of:
DMA

MERIDIAN ADVERTISING
4805 G Street
Ste 500
Omaha

NE
68117
USA
Tel: +1 402 33 1369
Fax: +1 402 733 7270
Jeff Jacobs, Vice President

Services/Products:
Advertising Agency; Direct Response
Agency

Member of:
DMA

MERKAFON
3191 Coral Way
Miami
FL
33145
USA
Tel: +1 305 529 2860
Gerardo Estevane V., Marketing
  Director

Services/Products:
Telemarketing agency

Member of:
DMA

**MERKLE DIRECT MARKETING
  INC.**
8400 Corporate Drive
Lanham
MD
20785
USA
Tel: +1 301 459 9700
Fax: +1 301 459 8431
David Williams, President & CEO

Services/Products:
List services

Member of:
DMA

METRO DIRECT
333 Seventh Avenue
Ste 103
New York
NY
10001–5004
USA
Tel: +1 212 594 7688
Fax: +1 212 465 8877
Thomas Kellogg, President & Co-
  Chairman

Services/Products:
List services

Member of:
DMA

METROMAIL/EXPERIAN
200 Madison Avenue
New York

NY
10016–3903
USA
Tel: +1 212 532 2299
Fax: +1 212 390 5100
Gwenn Kyzer, Vice President

Services/Products:
List services

Member of:
DMA

**MEYER ASSOCIATES
  TELEMARKETING**
14 Seventh Avenue North
St. Cloud
MN
56303
USA
Tel: +1 320 259 4000
Fax: +1 320 259 4064
Thomas Caprio, President

Services/Products:
Telemarketing agency

Member of:
DMA

**MFP&W PROMOTIONS AND
  DIRECT**
P. O. Box 11868
San Juan
PR
922
USA
Tel: +1 787 781 1616
Fax: +1 787 793 5355
Edgar Hernandez, VP & General
  Manager

Services/Products:
Sales promotion agency

Member of:
DMA

MGI LISTS
209 Madison Street
Ste 300
Alexandria
VA
22314–1764
USA
Tel: +1 800 899 4420
Fax: +1 703 549 6057
Lynne Robie, Senior Account
  Executive

Services/Products:
List services

Member of:
DMA

MGT. ASSOCIATES
11111 Santa Monica Boulevard
Ste 620
Los Angeles
CA
90025
USA
Tel: +1 310 473 7550
Fax: +1 310 473 1616
Marjorie Webb, President

Services/Products:
List services

Member of:
DMA

**MICHAEL EDWARDS DIRECT,
INC.**
875 North Michigan Avenue
Ste 2710
Chicago
IL
60611
USA
Tel: +1 312 944 0606
Fax: +1 312 944 5533
Michael McNicholas, President

Services/Products:
Advertising Agency; Direct Response
Agency

Member of:
DMA

**MICHAEL I. GRANT &
ASSOCIATES, INC.**
115 Carthage Road
Scarsdale
NY
10583–7201
USA
Tel: 914 722 4177
Fax: +1 914 722 4179
Michael Grant, Mktg. & Database
Consultant

Services/Products:
Marketing consultant

Member of:
DMA

MICHIGAN MESSAGE CENTER
341 West Lovell
Kalamazoo
MI
49007
USA
Tel: +1 616 382 2800
Fax: +1 616 382 3000
Peter DeHaan, President

Services/Products:
Telemarketing agency

Member of:
DMA

**MICROAGE SERVICE
SOLUTIONS**
2400 South MicroAge Way
Tempe
AZ
85281
USA
Tel: +1 602 804 2000
Fax: +1 602 366 2820
Dan Ater, Group Vice President

Services/Products:
Telemarketing agency

Member of:
DMA

MID-AMERICA MAILERS, INC.
430 Russell Street
P.O. Box 646
Hammond
IN
46320–0646
USA
Tel: +1 219 933 0137
Fax: +1 219 933 3525
Donald Harle, President

Services/Products:
Lettershop; Mailing/Faxing services

Member of:
DMA

MIDAMERICA LISTS INC.
315 Third Avenue, S.E.
Skyway Ste 200
Cedar Rapids
IA
52401–1506
USA
Tel: +1 800 747 5900
Fax: +1 319 365 3666
Robert Campbell, President & Owner

Services/Products:
List services

Member of:
DMA

MIDCO COMMUNICATIONS
410 South Phillips Avenue
Sioux Falls
SD
57104
USA
Tel: +1 800 888 1300
Fax: +1 605 339 4419
Pat Johnson, Marketing Director

Services/Products:
Telemarketing agency

Member of:
DMA

MIDLAND MARKETING
11457 Olde Cabin Road
Ste 300
St. Louis
MO
63141
USA
Tel: +1 314 993 1888
Fax: +1 314 993 2349
Gary Gerchen, President

Services/Products:
List services

Member of:
DMA

**MIDWEST DIRECT
MARKETING, INC.**
501 North Webster
Spring Hill
KS
66083
USA
Tel: 913 686 2220
Fax: +1 913 686 2320
R. Scott Robbins, President

Services/Products:
List services

Member of:
DMA

MIGLINO ASSOCIATES
210 Hamilton Street
Harrisburg
PA
17102
USA
Tel: +1 717 234 7448
Fax: +1 717 234 6229
Thomas Miglino, Owner

Services/Products:
Marketing consultant

Member of:
DMA

MILICI VALENTI NG PACK
999 Bishop Street
Honolulu
HI
96813
USA
Tel: 808 536 0881
Fax: +1 808 529 6208
Kristy Bertsch, Manager, Direct
Marketing

Services/Products:
Advertising Agency; Direct Response
Agency

481

Member of:
DMA

MILLARD GROUP, INC.
10 Vose Farm Road
Peterborough
NH
03458–0890
USA
Tel: +1 603 924 9262
Fax: +1 603 924 7810
Benjamin Perez, President

Services/Products:
List services

Member of:
DMA

MILLENNIUM TELESERVICES
900 Route 9 North
Plaza 9, 6th Fl
Woodbridge
NJ
7095
USA
Tel: 888 252 5689
Fax: +1 800 474 5045
Eric Greenberg, President

Services/Products:
Telemarketing agency

Member of:
DMA

**MILLER MEESTER
  ADVERTISING**
17 North Washington Avenue
Minneapolis
MN
55401
USA
Tel: +1 612 337 6600
Fax: +1 612 337 9100
James Stimson, VP, Direct Marketing

Services/Products:
Advertising Agency; Direct Response
Agency

Member of:
DMA

**MILLER/HUBER
  RELATIONSHIP MARKETING**
470 Carolina Street
San Francisco
CA
94107
USA
Tel: +1 415 487 2000
Fax: +1 415 487 2010
Floyd Miller, President

Services/Products:
Advertising Agency; Direct Response
Agency

Member of:
DMA

MILLERNIA DIRECT, INC.
One Louis Allan Drive
Danbury
CT
6811
USA
Tel: +1 203 778 8011
Fax: +1 203 790 7025
Marybeth Vandergrift, Partner & EVP

Services/Products:
Advertising Agency; Direct Response
Agency

Member of:
DMA

**MILLSTAR ELECTRONIC
  PUBLISHING GROUP**
1170 Wheeler Way
Langhorne
PA
19047
USA
Tel: +1 215 752 2900
Fax: +1 215 752 9454
Tara Marullo, Marketing Director

E-Services:
Website design

Member of:
DMA

MITCHELL & RESNIKOFF
8003 Old York Road
Elkins Park
PA
19027
USA
Tel: +1 215 635 1000
Fax: +1 215 635 6542
Ronald Resnikoff, President

Services/Products:
Advertising Agency; Direct Response
Agency

Member of:
DMA

MITCHELL MADISON GROUP
520 Madison Avenue
12th Fl
New York
NY
10022
USA
Tel: +1 212 372 9000

Fax: +1 212 372 9006
Mary Caputi, Manager, Information
  Services

Services/Products:
Marketing consultant

Member of:
DMA

MLS COMPUTER SERVICES
711 Directors Drive
Arlington
TX
76011–5103
USA
Tel: 817 640 7007
Fax: +1 817 633 8008
Rick Yater, VP, U.S. Sales & Marketing

Services/Products:
List services

Member of:
DMA (US); FEDMA

MMI - SOUTHERN BRANCH
1408 Country Ridge Place
Orlando
FL
32835
USA
Tel: +1 407 578 9686
Fax: +1 407 290 5421
Nora Brophy, Vice President,
  Marketing

Services/Products:
List services

Member of:
DMA

MMS, INC.
185 Hansen Court
Ste 110
Wood Dale
IL
60191–1146
USA
Tel: +1 630 350 1717
Fax: +1 630 350 1896
Richard Elliott, President

Services/Products:
List services

Member of:
DMA

MODEM MEDIA.POPPE TYSON
228 Saugatuck Avenue
Westport
CT
06880–6425
USA
Tel: +1 203 341 5200

482

Fax: +1 203 341 5260
Jonathan Ewert, Vice President,
  Marketing

Services/Products:
Advertising Agency; Direct Response
Agency

Member of:
DMA

**MOKRYNSKI & ASSOCIATES
  INC.**
401 Hackensack Avenue
2nd Fl
Hackensack
NJ
7601
USA
Tel: +1 201 488 5656
Fax: +1 201 488 9225
Melina Shiner, Account Executive

Services/Products:
List services

Member of:
DMA

MORAN DIRECT, INC.
2299 White Street
Houston
TX
77007
USA
Tel: +1 713 880 3725
Fax: +1 713 869 0125
Ron Moran, President

Services/Products:
Marketing consultant

Member of:
DMA

MSF CORPORATION
P. O. Box 600
5025 S Packard Ave
Cudany
WI
53110–0600
USA
Tel: +1 414 483 5025
Fax: +1 414 483 5618
Greg Guerard, Vice President

Services/Products:
Fulfilment and sampling house

Member of:
DMA

MSGI
333 Seventh Avenue
Ste 103
New York
NY
10001–5004

USA
Tel: +1 212 594 7688
Fax: +1 212 465 8877
Thomas Kellogg, President &
  Co-Chairman

Services/Products:
List services

Member of:
DMA

MSI LIST MARKETING
625 North Michigan Avenue
Ste 1920
Chicago
IL
60611
USA
Tel: +1 312 642 1620
Fax: +1 312 642 0679
Jeffrey Sutton, President

Services/Products:
List services

Member of:
DMA

MULDOON & BAER, INC.
158 Shore Lane
Sugarloaf Key
FL
33042
USA
Tel: +1 305 744 9779
Fax: +1 305 744 9939
Katie Muldoon, President

Services/Products:
Marketing consultant

Member of:
DMA

**MULTICULTURAL MARKETING
  RESOURCES, INC.**
332 Bleecker Street
Ste G41
New York
NY
10014
USA
Tel: +1 212 242 3351
Fax: +1 212 691 5969
Lisa Skriloff, President

Services/Products:
Marketing consultant

Member of:
DMA

MURPHY MARKETING
1120 Arizona Avenue
Ste B
Santa Monica
CA

90401–2055
USA
Tel: +1 310 395 9722
Fax: +1 310 395 8286
Maureen Murphy, Owner

Services/Products:
Marketing consultant

Member of:
DMA

MUSIC MARKETING NETWORK
West Coast
13323 Washington Boulevard
Los Angeles
CA
90066
USA
Tel: +1 310 448 4400
Fax: +1 310 448 4404
Kym Bamford, Dir., Corporate
  Communications

Services/Products:
Advertising Agency; Direct Response
Agency

Member of:
DMA

MUSIC MARKETING NETWORK
The Galleria 2 Bridge Avenue
Red Bank
NJ
7701
USA
Tel: +1 732 219 9327
Fax: +1 732 219 0172
Kym Bamford, Dir., Corporate
  Communications

Services/Products:
Advertising Agency; Direct Response
Agency

Member of:
DMA

MVI MARKETING LTD.
470 South Beverly Drive
Beverly Hills
CA
90212
USA
Tel: +1 310 284 6070
Fax: +1 310 284 8319
M. Hurwitz, Chief Executive Officer

Services/Products:
Marketing consultant

Member of:
DMA

MYERS EQUITY EXPRESS
2160 Lundy Avenue
Ste 128

San Jose
CA
95131–1868
USA
Tel: +1 408 453 7390
Fax: +1 408 453 7391
Warren Myers, Chief Executive Officer

Services/Products:
Marketing consultant

Member of:
DMA

MYSTIC TRANSPORT SERVICES
2187 New London Turnpike
South Glastonbury
CT
6073
USA
Tel: +1 800 969 1566
Fax: +1 860 659 1420
Howard Goldman, Vice President, Sales

Services/Products:
Lettershop; Mailing/Faxing services

Member of:
DMA

NAME-FINDERS LISTS, INC.
160 Sansome Street
Ste 400
San Francisco
CA
94104
USA
Tel: +1 415 955 8585
Fax: +1 415 955 8580
Rosalie Bulach, President

Services/Products:
List services

Member of:
DMA

NAMES & ADDRESSES, INC.
160 East Marguardt Drive
Wheeling
IL
60090–6428
USA
Tel: +1 708 465 1500
Fax: +1 708 465 1521
Philip Staples, President

Services/Products:
List services

Member of:
DMA

NAMES IN THE NEWS CALIFORNIA, INC.
One Bush Street
Ste 300
San Francisco
CA
94104
USA
Tel: +1 415 989 3350
Fax: +1 415 433 7796
Susan Anstrand, CEO & President

Services/Products:
List services

Member of:
DMA

NATIONAL ANALYSTS, INC.
1700 Market Street
Ste 1700
Philadelphia
PA
19103–3992
USA
Tel: +1 215 496 6800
Fax: +1 215 496 6801
Beth Rothschild, Vice President

Services/Products:
Marketing consultant

Member of:
DMA

NATIONAL BUSINESS SEMINARS
7 Barharbor Court
P.O. Box 7221
Algonquin
IL
60102–7221
USA
Tel: +1 800 669 8763
Fax: +1 847 669 8920
Jeff Pears, President

Services/Products:
Marketing consultant

Member of:
DMA

NATIONAL COMPUTER PRINT
5200 East Lake Boulevard
Birmingham
AL
35217
USA
Tel: +1 205 849 5200
Fax: +1 205 849 6605
Victor Gilmore, Vice President

Services/Products:
Lettershop; Mailing/Faxing services

Member of:
DMA

NATIONAL DIRECT CORPORATION
2570 West International Spdwy.
Daytona Beach
FL
32114
USA
Tel: 904 258 8111
Fax: +1 904 238 6059
Bowman Lackey, CEO

Services/Products:
Advertising Agency; Direct Response Agency

Member of:
DMA

NATIONAL FULFILLMENT SERVICE
100 Pine Avenue
Holmes
PA
19043
USA
Tel: +1 610 532 4700
Fax: +1 610 586 3232
Thomas Krueger, Vice President

Services/Products:
Fulfilment and sampling house

Member of:
DMA

NATIONAL LIST PROTECTION
System, Inc.
116 New Montgomery Street
Ste 3810
San Francisco
CA
94105
USA
Harry Chevan, Senior Vice President

Services/Products:
Marketing consultant

Member of:
DMA

NATIONAL TELE-COMMUNICATIONS
150 Commerce Road
Cedar Grove
NJ
17009
USA
Tel: 973 857 4200
Fax: +1 973 571 4327
Anthony Provenzano, Dir., National Outsource Sales

Services/Products:
Marketing consultant

Member of:
DMA

NATIONSMAIL
1245 Knoxville Street
San Diego
CA
92110–3718
USA
Tel: +1 619 276 2600
Fax: +1 619 276 2626
Redd Gardner, Marketing

Services/Products:
Lettershop; Mailing/Faxing services

Member of:
DMA

NAVIGATION TECHNOLOGIES
740 East Arques Avenue
Sunnyvale
CA
94086–3833
USA
Tel: +1 408 737 3200
Fax: +1 408 736 3734
Suneel Kelkar, Director, Distribution

Services/Products:
List services

Member of:
DMA

NC DIRECT MARKETING
1304 Broad Street
P.O. Box 2478
Durham
NC
27715–2478
USA
Tel: 919 286 0100
Fax: +1 919 286 5058
Charles Lasitter, President

Services/Products:
List services

Member of:
DMA

NCI DIRECT
41 Madison Avenue
29th Fl
New York
NY
10010
USA
Tel: +1 212 686 8555
Fax: +1 212 686 8573
Linda Connelly, President & COO

Services/Products:
Advertising Agency; Direct Response
Agency

Member of:
DMA

NCRI LIST MANAGEMENT
429 Sylvan Avenue
Englewood Clfs
NJ
7632
USA
Tel: +1 201 569 7272
Fax: +1 201 569 5552
Michael Young, President

Services/Products:
List services

Member of:
DMA

NEIL RANSICK MARKETING
212 Teresita Boulevard
San Francisco
CA
94127–1729
USA
Tel: +1 415 664 6728
Fax: +1 415 664 4107
Neil Ransick, Principal

Services/Products:
Marketing consultant

Member of:
DMA

NETCREATIONS, INC.
47 Joralemon Street
Brooklyn
NY
11201
USA
Tel: +1 718 522 1531
Fax: +1 212 625 1387
Rosalind Resnick, President

Services/Products:
Marketing consultant

Member of:
DMA

NETMARQUEE INC.
687 Highland Avenue
Needham
MA
2194
USA
Tel: +1 781 433 5890
Fax: +1 781 449 2128
Jack MacSwan, Director, Client
    Services

E-Services:
Website design

Member of:
DMA

**NETSCAPE
    COMMUNICATIONS**
Membership Marketing Division

501 East Middlefield Road
MS MV-053
Mountain View
CA
94043–4042
USA
Tel: +1 650 937 4408
Fax: +1 650 428 2098
Jane Smith, Group Mgr., Netcenter
    Mktg.

E-Services:
Website design

Member of:
DMA

NETWORK ASSOCIATES
3965 Freedom Circle
Ste 400
Santa Clara
CA
95054
USA
Rosalie Bulach, President

Services/Products:
List services

Member of:
DMA

NETWORKDIRECT, INC.
2300 Computer Avenue
Bldg G
Willow Grove
PA
19090
USA
Tel: +1 215 942 7797
Fax: +1 215 396 1191
Steve Emory, President

Services/Products:
Advertising Agency; Direct Response
Agency

Member of:
DMA

**NEW RESIDENT MARKETING
    CORPORATION, INC.**
33 Rock Hill Road
Bala Cynwyd
PA
19004
USA
Tel: +1 215 667 1780
Fax: +1 215 667 5650
David Lewis, President & CEO

Services/Products:
List services

Member of:
DMA

NISSHO IWAI AMERICAN CORP.
1211 Avenue of the Americas
New York
NY
10036
USA
Tel: +1 212 704 6699
Fax: +1 212 704 6961
Toru (Tom) Suzuki, President

Services/Products:
List services

Member of:
DMA

NKH&W INC.
600 Broadway
Kansas City
MO
64105
USA
Tel: 816 842 8881
Fax: +1 816 842 6340
Janet Schwing, VP & Director,
    Database Mktg.

Services/Products:
Advertising Agency; Direct Response
Agency

Member of:
DMA

NORDIS MARKETING & MAILING
1501 South University Drive
Plantation
FL
33324
USA
Tel: 954 475 8471
Fax: +1 954 475 8248
Ron Selinger, President

Services/Products:
Advertising Agency; Direct Response
Agency

Member of:
DMA

NORTH AMERICAN COMMUNICATIONS
20 Maple Avenue
Armonk
NY
10504
USA
Tel: 914 273 8620
Fax: +1 914 273 3135
Robert Paltrow, President

Services/Products:
Advertising Agency; Direct Response
Agency

Member of:
DMA

NORTH CASTLE DIRECT
300 First Stamford Place
Stamford
CT
6902
USA
Tel: +1 203 358 2166
Fax: +1 203 323 1806
David Cramoy, President

Services/Products:
Advertising Agency; Direct Response
Agency

Member of:
DMA

NORTH SHORE AGENCY, INC.
117 Cuttermill Road
Great Neck
NY
11021
USA
Tel: +1 516 466 9300
Fax: +1 516 466 9391
Jerry Goodman, President

Services/Products:
Lettershop; Mailing/Faxing services

Member of:
DMA

NORTHBROOK SERVICES
1600 South Wolf Road
Wheeling
IL
60090
USA
Tel: 847 402 7461
Fax: +1 847 459 1450
Tony McGhee, Project Manager

Services/Products:
Lettershop; Mailing/Faxing services

Member of:
DMA

NORTHLICH STOLLEY LAWARRE
151 West Fourth Street
Cincinnati
OH
45202
USA
Tel: +1 513 421 8840
Fax: +1 513 287 1868
Christopher McConaughey, VP &
    Dir., Direct Marketing

Services/Products:
Advertising Agency; Direct Response
Agency

Member of:
DMA

NRL DIRECT
100 Union Avenue
Cresskill
NJ
7626
USA
Tel: +1 201 568 0707
Fax: +1 201 568 9893
Stephen Bogner, President

Services/Products:
List services

Member of:
DMA

NS & G DIRECT MARKETING
2817 Millwood Avenue
P.O. Box 5267
Columbia
SC
29250
USA
Tel: 803 779 1869
Fax: +1 803 252 2016
Kathryn Carson, General Manager

Services/Products:
Advertising Agency; Direct Response
Agency

Member of:
DMA

NTS MARKETING, INC.
3550 Young Place
Lynchburg
VA
24501
USA
Tel: 804 947 0000
Fax: +1 804 856 6FAX
Charles Judd, CEO

Services/Products:
Telemarketing agency

Member of:
DMA

NYKAMP CONSULTING GROUP (NCG)
2500 South Highland
Ste 110
Lombard
IL
60148
USA
Tel: +1 630 424 0500
Fax: +1 630 424 0530
Melinda Nykamp, President

Services/Products:
Database services

Member of:
DMA

O'CONNELL MEIER
1727 King Street
3rd Fl
Alexandria
VA
22314–2720
USA
Tel: +1 703 739 2266
Fax: +1 703 739 0478
Rich Meier, President

Services/Products:
Advertising Agency; Direct Response
Agency

Member of:
DMA

**O'CONNOR KENNEY
PARTNERS, INC.**
2670 Union Extended
Ste 606
Memphis
TN
38112
USA
Tel: 901 458 2529
Fax: +1 901 458 1086
Denise Hussein, Direct Marketing
Manager

Services/Products:
Advertising Agency; Direct Response
Agency

Member of:
DMA

OBIMD INTERNATIONAL
4450 Arapahoe Avenue
Boulder
CO
80303
USA
Tel: +1 303 494 0628
Fax: +1 303 494 8529
Gerard Clerquin, Manager

Services/Products:
Database services

Member of:
DMA

OBSERVATORY GROUP, INC.
700 Walnut Street
Ste 450
Cincinnati
OH
45202–2015
USA
Tel: +1 513 621 0300
Fax: +1 513 621 5344
Dawn Hornback, President & CEO

Services/Products:
Marketing consultant

Member of:
DMA

OCS AMERICA
49–27 31st Street
Long Island City
NY
11101
USA
Tel: +1 718 784 6080
Fax: +1 718 433 1881
Sho Torii, General Manager

Services/Products:
Private delivery services

Member of:
DMA

OETTING & COMPANY, INC.
1995 Broadway, Ste 402
Ansonia Station, Box 1702
New York
NY
10023
USA
Tel: +1 212 580 5470
Fax: +1 212 873 3844
Rudy Oetting, Senior Partner

Services/Products:
Telemarketing agency

Member of:
DMA

OGILVYONE WORLDWIDE
309 West 49th Street
New York
NY
10019–7399
USA
Tel: +1 212 237 6000
Fax: +1 212 237 5123
Carla Hendra, President, New York

Services/Products:
Advertising Agency; Direct Response
Agency

Member of:
DMA

OHIO VENTURES, INC.
6500 Fiesta Drive
Columbus
OH
43235
USA
Tel: +1 614 343 4006
Fax: +1 614 340 4011
Stanford Apseloff, President

Services/Products:
List services

Member of:
DMA

**OLWEN INTERNATIONAL
DIRECT MAIL, INC.**
100 East Pratt Street
Ste 1520
Baltimore
MD
21202
USA
Tel: +1 410 576 9181
Fax: +1 410 576 0211
Wesley Brook, VP, Marketing & Sales,
U.S.

Services/Products:
List services

Member of:
DMA (US); FEDMA

OMNI GRAPHIC INC.
6920 South Holly Circle
Ste 170
Englewood
CO
80112–6216
USA
Tel: +1 303 741 6671
Fax: +1 303 741 6612
Thomas Caccia, Owner

Services/Products:
Design/graphics/clip art supplier;
Consultancy services

Member of:
DMA

**ONLINE DEVELOPMENT
CORPORATION**
99 Moody Street
Waltham
MA
2453
USA
Tel: 888 ODC TEAM
Fax: +1 781 647 7623
William Bender, President

E-Services:
Website design

Member of:
DMA

OPTION ONE
60 South 6th Street
Ste 2800
Minneapolis
MN
55402–4444
USA
Tel: +1 612 340 0800
Fax: +1 612 342 9700
Christopher Rahill, VP & Account

Group Supervisor

Services/Products:
Advertising Agency; Direct Response
Agency

Member of:
DMA

ORINOCO INCORPATED
420 East 51st Street
Ste A
New York
NY
10022
USA
Tel: +1 212 688 8922
Fax: +1 212 223 0893
Vesna Besarabic, Managing Director

Services/Products:
Marketing consultant

Member of:
DMA

ORION MARKETING
12000 Network Boulevard
San Antonio
TX
78249
USA
Tel: +1 210 694 4114
Fax: +1 210 690 9215
Deanna Desmet, Vice President,
  Marketing

Services/Products:
Telemarketing agency

Member of:
DMA

ORSATTI & PARTNERS LLC
7 Faneuil Hall Maketplace
Boston
MA
2109
USA
Tel: +1 617 570 9110
Fax: +1 617 570 9111
Lou Orsatti, Chief Executive Officer

Services/Products:
Advertising Agency; Direct Response
Agency

Member of:
DMA

OUR TRIBE MARKETING
70A Greenwich Avenue
Box 380
New York
NY
10011
USA
Tel: +1 212 462 0036

Fax: +1 212 462 0039
Charles Conard, President

Services/Products:
Marketing consultant

Member of:
DMA

OVATION MARKETING, INC.
201 Main Street
6th Fl
La Crosse
WI
54601
USA
Tel: +1 608 785 2460
Fax: +1 608 785 2496
Ralph Heath, President

Services/Products:
Advertising Agency; Direct Response
Agency

Member of:
DMA

**P.J. MCNERNEY AND
  ASSOCIATES**
652 Main Street
Cincinnati
OH
45202–2509
USA
Tel: +1 513 241 9951
Fax: +1 513 651 2638
Patrick McNerney, President

Services/Products:
Fulfilment and sampling house

Member of:
DMA

PACER ASSOCIATES
5165 Ramblewood Court
Solon
OH
44139–6015
USA
Tel: +1 440 349 1970
Fax: +1 440 340 0187
Andrew Birol, President

Services/Products:
Marketing consultant

Member of:
DMA

**PACIFIC EAST RESEARCH
  CORPORATION**
603 Cherry Street, Ste 10
P.O. Box 432
Sumas
WA
98295
USA

Tel: +1 800 665 8400
Fax: +1 604 504 7370
Allan Dawes, President

Services/Products:
List services

Member of:
DMA

PALM COAST DATA INC.
A DIMAC Marketing Company
11 Commerce Boulevard
Palm Coast
FL
32164
USA
Tel: 904 445 4662
Fax: +1 904 445 2728
Anthony Catalano, CFO, Direct Mai
  Business Unit

Services/Products:
Lettershop; Mailing/Faxing services

Member of:
DMA

PAMET RIVER PARTNERS, IN
360 Newbury Street
Boston
MA
02155–2737
USA
Tel: +1 617 267 5700
Fax: +1 617 536 0886
Margaret Coughlin, President & CE

Services/Products:
Advertising Agency; Direct Respons
Agency

Member of:
DMA

PARADIGM DIRECT
A division of PARADIGM Direct
  Marketing Inc.
400 Perimeter Center Ter., NE
Atlanta
GA
30346–1227
USA
Tel: +1 77 0 698 8444
Fax: +1 770 933 3207
Jan Slaton, Vice President, List
  Brokerage

Services/Products:
List services

Member of:
DMA

PARADIGM DIRECT, INC.
2 Executive Drive
Fort Lee
NJ

7024
USA
Tel: +1 201 461 5665
Fax: +1 201 461 1963
Marc Byron, Chairman & CEO

Services/Products:
Marketing consultant

Member of:
DMA

PARADYSZ MATERA & COMPANY
215 Park Avenue South
Ste 1401
New York
NY
10003–1603
USA
Tel: +1 212 387 0300
Fax: +1 212 387 7647
Chris Paradysz, Managing Partner

Services/Products:
List services

Member of:
DMA

PARAGON DIRECT MARKETING, LLC
75 Fleetwood Drive
Ste 200
Rockaway
NJ
7866
USA
Tel: 973 989 8300
Fax: +1 973 989 8118
Eric Silverman, President

Services/Products:
List services

Member of:
DMA

PARAGON DIRECT, INC.
8350 North Steven Road
Milwaukee
WI
53223–3355
USA
Tel: +1 414 362 1111
Fax: +1 414 362 1110
Terry Schacht, President

Services/Products:
List services

Member of:
DMA

PARAGON SOLUTIONS
P. O. Box 2156
119 B Springhill Dr
Goose Creek

SC
29445–2156
USA
Tel: 803 572 9897
Fax: +1 803 553 5355
Darren Dather, Director, Sales & Marketing

Services/Products:
Telemarketing agency

Member of:
DMA

PARTNERS & SHEVACK DIRECT
1211 Avenue of the Americas
New York
NY
10036
USA
Tel: +1 212 596 0200
Fax: +1 212 354 2103
James Battin, Managing Director

Services/Products:
Advertising Agency; Direct Response Agency

Member of:
DMA

PAT FRIESEN & COMPANY
9636 Meadow Lane
Leawood
KS
66206
USA
Tel: 913 341 1211
Fax: +1 913 341 4343
Patricia Friesen, President

Services/Products:
Design/graphics/clip art supplier;
Consultancy services

Member of:
DMA

PATHFINDER BUSINESS GROWTH CONSULTANTS, LLC.
6321 Norway Road
Dallas
TX
75230
USA
Tel: +1 214 987 9003
Fax: +1 214 987 9577
Kim Burnside, Owner

Services/Products:
Marketing consultant

Member of:
DMA

PATHWAY MARKETING INC.
77 West Washington Street
Ste 1507
Chicago
IL
60602–2901
USA
Tel: +1 312 201 8039
Fax: +1 312 201 8579
Karen Feil, President

Services/Products:
List services

Member of:
DMA

PATRICIA DOWD, INC.
5001 Oceanaire
Oxnard
CA
93035
USA
Tel: 805 985 8243
Fax: +1 805 985 5013
Patricia Dowd, President

Services/Products:
Marketing consultant

Member of:
DMA

PAUL ZOELLNER INTERNATIONAL CONSULTING SERVICES.
12728 Lakestone Drive
Midlothian
VA
23113
USA
Tel: +1 804 897 6930
Fax: +1 804 897 6930
Email: Pzoellner@aol.com
Paul Zoellner, President

Services/Products:
Copy adaptation; Direct marketing agency; Translation services

Member of:
DMA (US); DMA of Washington;
National Society of Fund Raising Executives

PBG MARKETING, INC.
5 Airport Road
Lakewood
NJ
8701
USA
Tel: +1 732 364 1900
Fax: +1 732 364 3716
Kenneth Varga, President

Services/Products:
Marketing consultant

Member of:
DMA

PCS LIST & INFORMATION
Technologies
39 Cross Street
Ste 301–307
Peabody
MA
01960–1628
USA
Tel: +1 800 532 LIST
Fax: +1 508 532 9181
James Healy, President & Founder

Services/Products:
List services

Member of:
DMA

PDM TECHNOLOGIES L.L.C.
1305 Wertland Street
Ste B-9
Charlottesville
VA
22903
USA
Tel: 804 971 7994
Fax: +1 804 1 923 3252
Eric Powders, General Partner

Services/Products:
List services

Member of:
DMA

PDS
393 Jericho Turnpike
Mineola
NY
11501
USA
Tel: +1 516 877 7770
Fax: +1 516 742 1760
Andrew Lehrfeld, Vice President

Services/Products:
Lettershop; Mailing/Faxing services

Member of:
DMA

PEACHTREE DATA, INC.
1959 Parker Court
Suite G
Stone Mountain
GA
30087
USA
Tel: +1 404 934 2972
Fax: +1 404 925 4489
Bill Gentry, Vice President

Services/Products:
List services

Member of:
DMA

PEGG NADLER ASSOCIATES, INC.
7302 Greentree Road
Bethesda
MD
20817
USA
Tel: +1 301 767 1168
Fax: +1 301 767 1169
Pegg Nadler, President

Services/Products:
Database services

Member of:
DMA

PENTON LISTS
Penton Publishing
1100 Superior Avenue
Cleveland
OH
44114
USA
Tel: +1 216 696 7000
Fax: +1 216 696 6662
Ilene Schwartz, Director

Services/Products:
List services

Member of:
DMA

PEOPLESUPPORT
1575 Westwood Boulevard
Los Angeles
CA
90024
USA
Tel: +1 310 914 5999
Fax: +1 310 914 5998
Sarah Stealey, Business Development Manager

E-Services:
Website design

Member of:
DMA

PERFORMANCE DATA
4606 Tipton Lane
Alexandria
VA
22310
USA
Tel: +1 703 924 0565
Fax: +1 703 924 0546
Jay Frank, Senior Vice President

Services/Products:
List services

Member of:
DMA

PERIODICAL PUBLISHERS' SERVICE BUREAU, INC.
1 North Superior St
Sandusky
Ohio
44870
USA
Tel: +1 419 626 0623
Fax: +1 419 621 4383
Email: sporterfield@hearst.com
Web: www.ppsb.com
Scott Porterfield, Sales & Marketing Manager

Services/Products:
Call centre services/systems; Direct marketing agency; Fulfilment and sampling house; Response analysis bureau; Telemarketing agency

Member of:
DMA

PERSIMMON IT, INC.
4813 Emperor Boulevard
Ste 130
Durham
NC
27703
USA
Tel: 919 941 9339
Fax: +1 919 941 9378
Barbara Barry, Marketing Services Manager

Services/Products:
List services

Member of:
DMA

PERSON TO PERSON MARKETING
82 Newark Pompton Turnpike
Riverdale
NJ
7457
USA
Tel: +1 201 835 8112
Fax: +1 201 835 5463
Steven Alario, President

Services/Products:
Telemarketing agency

Member of:
DMA

PETER A. MAYER ADVERTISING INC.
324 Camp Street
New Orleans
LA
70130

USA
Tel: +1 504 581 7191
Fax: +1 504 581 3009
Mark Mayer, President

Services/Products:
Advertising Agency; Direct Response
Agency

Member of:
DMA

PHILADELPHIA INTERNATIONAL MARKETING INC.
1100 East Hector Street
Ste 320
Conshohocken
PA
19428
USA
Tel: +1 610 940 9890
Fax: +1 610 940 9891
John Nissim, President

Services/Products:
Advertising Agency; Direct Response
Agency

Member of:
DMA

PHILLIPS DIRECT MARKETING GROUP
6619 North Scottsdale Road
Scottsdale
AZ
85250
USA
Tel: +1 602 596 3944
Fax: +1 602 596 3963
Tina Phillips, President

Services/Products:
Advertising Agency; Direct Response
Agency

Member of:
DMA

PHOENIX DATA PROCESSING, INC.
645 Blackhawk Drive
Westmont
IL
60559–1115
USA
Tel: +1 630 654 4400
Fax: +1 630 654 4470
Email: mstuermer@
  phoenixdataprocessing.com
Web: www.phoenixdataprocessing.com
Michael Stuermer, Account Executive

Services/Products:
Service bureau

Member of:
DMA (US)

PHOENIX GROUP, INC.
34115 West Twelve Mile Road
Ste 200
Farmington Hls
MI
48331–5638
USA
Tel: 810 553 8355
Fax: +1 810 488 3696
Ed Dorrington, EVP, Marketing &
  Sales

Services/Products:
Marketing consultant

Member of:
DMA

PHOENIX MARKETING GROUP LTD.
57 Danbury Road
Wilton
CT
6897
USA
Tel: +1 203 762 8665
Fax: +1 203 762 8285
Bruce Seide, Chairman

Services/Products:
Marketing consultant

Member of:
DMA

PHONE FOR SUCCESS
181 Hudson Street
Ste 3C
New York
NY
11743
USA
Tel: +1 212 431 6700
Fax: +1 212 941 9382
Joel Linchitz, President

Services/Products:
Marketing consultant

Member of:
DMA

PHONE INTERACTICE COMMUNICATIONS
600 South Dixie Highway
Boca Raton
FL
33432
USA
Tel: +1 561 391 9686
Fax: +1 561 391 4147
Phillip Kemp, President

Services/Products:
Telemarketing agency

Member of:
DMA

PLANET U
333 Bryant Street
Ste 330
San Francisco
CA
94107
USA
Tel: +1 415 979 0600
Fax: +1 415 979 0660
Andrea Post, Marketing Coordinator

E-Services:
Website design

Member of:
DMA

PMH CARAMANNING INC.
34705 West 12 Mile Road
Ste 200
Farmington Hills
MI
48331
USA
Tel: +1 248 488 5300
Fax: +1 248 488 5363
Nick Poulos, President

Services/Products:
Database services

Member of:
DMA

PMM MARKETING INC.
999 Eighteenth Street
Ste 2420
Denver
CO
80202
USA
Tel: +1 303 295 3070
Fax: +1 303 295 1166
Bruce Gache, President

Services/Products:
List services

Member of:
DMA

POLK/VERITY MULTI-DIMENSIONAL INTELLIGENCE
1621 18th Street
Denver
CO
80202–1294
USA
Tel: +1 303 298 5257

Fax: +1 303 298 5683
Stephen Polk, Chairman & CEO

Services/Products:
List services

Member of:
DMA

POLKVERITY
790 The City Drive South
Ste 200
Orange
CA
92868
USA
Tel: +1 714 591 1800
Fax: +1 714 703 9951
Brenda Siragusa, Manager, Database
 Marketing

Services/Products:
Market research agency

Member of:
DMA

POLY-FLEX CORP.
445 North State Road
P.O. Box 2250
Briarcliff Mnr
NY
10510
USA
Tel: +1 800 592 0500
Fax: +1 914 762 2378
Barry Neustein, President

Services/Products:
Labelling/envelope services

Member of:
DMA

POLY-TECH INDUSTRIES, INC.
P. O. Box 309
Ridgewood
NJ
7450
USA
Tel: +1 201 445 4300
Fax: +1 201 445 5093
Walter Engel, President

Services/Products:
Marketing consultant

Member of:
DMA

**POST COMMUNICATIONS,
 INC.**
1550 Bryant Street
6th Fl
San Francisco
CA
94103
USA

Tel: +1 415 431 3000
Fax: +1 415 431 3007
Claire Dean, Dir., Mkgt. &
 Communications

E-Services:
Website design

Member of:
DMA

POWELL DIRECT
48 Hillandale Road
Westport
CT
6880
USA
Tel: +1 203 266 7338
Fax: +1 203 226 7884
Valerie Powell, Owner

Services/Products:
Advertising Agency; Direct Response
Agency

Member of:
DMA

**PRECISION ANALYTICAL
 SERVICES**
4889 Clearwater Circle
Savage
MN
55378
USA
Tel: +1 612 440 6615
Fax: +1 612 440 6619
Roxanne Best, President

Services/Products:
Database services

Member of:
DMA

**PRECISION MARKETING
 CONSULTING**
c/o Direct Mktg. Technology
955 American Lane
Schaumberg
IL
60173
USA
Tel: 847 517 5821
Gwenn Kyzer, Vice President

Services/Products:
List services

Member of:
DMA

**PRECISION RESPONSE
 CORPORATION**
1505 Northwest 167th Street
Miami
FL
33169

USA
Tel: +1 305 626 4600
Fax: +1 305 626 4650
David Epstein, President

Services/Products:
Telemarketing agency

Member of:
DMA

PRESENTATION PACKAGING
870 Louisiana Avenue South
Minneapolis
MN
55426–1614
USA
Tel: +1 612 540 9600
Fax: +1 612 540 9522
Carol Sylvester, General Manager

Services/Products:
List services; Specialist packaging

Member of:
DMA

PRESTIGE MAILING LISTS IN
1539 Sawtelle Boulevard
Ste 1
Los Angeles
CA
90025–3263
USA
Tel: +1 310 473 7116
Fax: +1 310 477 3217
Deborah Hile-Saenz, President,
 Brokerage Division

Services/Products:
List services

Member of:
DMA

**PRICE/MCNABB FOCUSED
 COMMUNICATIONS**
2800 Nations Bank Corp Center
100 N Tryon St
Charlotte
NC
28202
USA
Tel: +1 704 375 0123
Fax: +1 704 375 0222
Norm Cosand, Director, Database
 Marketing

Services/Products:
Advertising Agency; Direct Respons
Agency

Member of:
DMA

PRIME ACCESS INC.
18 West 27th Street
New York

NY
10001
USA
Tel: +1 212 696 5000
Fax: +1 212 696 5075
C.Howard Buford, President

Services/Products:
Advertising Agency; Direct Response
Agency

Member of:
DMA

PRIME DIRECT, INC.
1780 Wehrle Drive
Williamsville
NY
14221
USA
Tel: +1 716 631 2601
Fax: +1 716 634 8617
Louis Volpini, President

Services/Products:
Advertising Agency; Direct Response
Agency

Member of:
DMA

PRIME RESPONSE INC.
1099 18th Street
Ste 500
Denver
CO
80202
USA
Tel: +1 303 382 4380
Fax: +1 303 296 7726
Stephanie Franks, Dir., Marketing
    Communications

Services/Products:
List services

Member of:
DMA

PRIMENET MARKETING SERVICES
2250 Pilot Knob Road
St. Paul
MN
55120–1127
USA
Tel: +1 651 405 4000
Fax: +1 651 405 4100
Mark Keefe, President

Services/Products:
List services

Member of:
DMA

PRIORITY DATA SYSTEMS, INC.
5035 South 110th Street
P.O. Box 45011
Omaha
NE
68145
USA
Tel: +1 800 228 9410
Fax: +1 402 592 5052
Marcie Flynn, President

Services/Products:
List services

Member of:
DMA

PRIORITY FULFILLMENT SERVICES
500 North Central Expressway
Plano
TX
75074
USA
Tel: 972 881 4700
Email: psinfo@pfsweb.com
Jeff Chick, VP, Sales & Marketing

Services/Products:
Fulfilment and sampling house

Member of:
DMA

PRISM MARKETING
P. O. Box 478
Schaller
IA
51053
USA
Tel: +1 712 275 4211
Fax: +1 712 275 4121
Jerry Schoemann, Sales Manager

Services/Products:
Telemarketing agency

Member of:
DMA

PRIZEPOINT ENTERTAINMENT CORP.
240 West 35th Street
18th Fl
New York
NY
10001
USA
Tel: +1 212 714 9500
Fax: +1 212 244 5295
Christopher Hassett, President

E-Services:
Website design

Member of:
DMA

PROBE COMMUNICATIONS INTERNATIONAL, INC.
250 West 57th Street
Ste 1632
New York
NY
10016–5010
USA
Tel: +1 212 489 0470
Fax: +1 212 489 0471
Email:
    info@probecommunications.com
Web: www.probecommunications.com
Arthur Heydendael, President

Services/Products:
Print services; Copy adaptation; Direct
marketing agency; List services; Media
buying agency; Translation services;
Direct Response Agency

E-Services:
E-Marketing consultant; Website
design

Member of:
DMA (US)

PRODUCERS AMERICA, INC.
10638 Burt Circle
Omaha
NE
68114
USA
Tel: +1 402 431 1618
Fax: +1 402 431 4228
Gregory Vacek, President

Services/Products:
Telemarketing agency

Member of:
DMA

PROFESSIONAL MARKETING ASSOCIATES, INC.
903 South Hohokam Drive
Tempe
AZ
85281
USA
Tel: +1 602 829 0131
Fax: +1 602 829 9202
Lou Hagen, President

Services/Products:
Fulfilment and sampling house

Member of:
DMA

PROFILE AMERICA LIST INC.
429 Sylvan Avenue
Englwood Clfs
NJ
7632
USA

Tel: +1 201 569 7272
Fax: +1 201 569 5552
Michael Young, President

Services/Products:
List services

Member of:
DMA

**PROFIT BOOSTERS
COPYWRITING**
251 West Garfield
2nd Fl
Aurora
OH
44202
USA
Tel: +1 330 995 0480
Fax: +1 330 995 0592
Email: prboosters@aol.com
Web: profitbooterscopy.com
Mike Pavlish, Owner

Services/Products:
Copywriting

E-Services:
Website design

Member of:
DMA (US)

PROFITABLE MARKETING
P. O. Box 2200
Conway
NH
03818–2200
USA
Tel: +1 603 356 8743
Fax: +1 603 356 8743
Cynthia Johnson, President

Services/Products:
Marketing consultant

Member of:
DMA

**PROFITEC BUSINESS
SERVICES, INC.**
26A Barnes Park North
Wallingford
CT
6492
USA
Tel: +1 800 352 2003
Fax: +1 203 949 0097
Marie Marcarelli, President

Services/Products:
Telemarketing agency

Member of:
DMA

**PROGRAMMERS INVESTMENT
CORP.**
125 Armstrong Road
Des Plaines
IL
60018
USA
Tel: 847 299 2300
Fax: +1 847 299 8286
Gary Scherer, CEO

Services/Products:
Fulfilment and sampling house

Member of:
DMA

PROMARK ONE
14040 North Cave Creek Road
Ste 350
Phoenix
AZ
85022
USA
Tel: +1 800 933 0233
Fax: +1 602 493 8506
Dawn Wahler, Marketing Manager

Services/Products:
Telemarketing agency

Member of:
DMA

**PROMARK ONE, AN IDRC
COMPANY**
7272 East Indian School Road
Ste 350
Scottsdale
AZ
85251
USA
Tel: +1 602 941 6200
Fax: +1 602 941 2380
Dawn Wahler, Marketing Manager

Services/Products:
Telemarketing agency

Member of:
DMA

PRONTO CONNECTIONS, INC.
820 North Orleans
Ste 300
Chicago
IL
60610
USA
Tel: +1 312 649 3600
Fax: +1 312 649 3627
Michele Ringwood, VP, Sales &
Marketing

Services/Products:
Telemarketing agency

Member of:
DMA

**PROXY COMMUNICATIONS,
INC.**
2700 Flora Street
Ste 200
Dallas
TX
75201–2519
USA
Tel: +1 214 220 2700
Fax: +1 214 220 2707
Gail Thoma Patterson, President

Services/Products:
Telemarketing agency

Member of:
DMA

PSI TELEMARKETING
2945 West Peterson Avenue
Chicago
IL
60659
USA
Tel: +1 77 3 878 0800
Fax: +1 773 878 4219
Phillip Immergluck, President

Services/Products:
Telemarketing agency

Member of:
DMA

PTC
105 Madison Avenue
New York
NY
10016
USA
Tel: +1 212 532 1900
Fax: +1 212 521 5262
Cathy Tweedy, Principal

Services/Products:
Advertising Agency; Direct Response
Agency

Member of:
DMA

PTM COMMUNICATIONS
352 Seventh Avenue
New York
NY
10001
USA
Tel: +1 212 643 5458
Fax: +1 212 643 5486
Gail Stone, President

Services/Products:
Telemarketing agency

Member of:
DMA

PTM INC.
1650 Farnam Street
Omaha
NE
68102
USA
Tel: +1 402 341 2525
Fax: +1 402 390 0870
John Calk, VP, Marketing & Business
    Dev.

Services/Products:
Telemarketing agency

Member of:
DMA

**PUBLIC INTEREST
    COMMUNICATIONS, INC.**
7700 Leesburg Pike
Ste 301
Falls Church
VA
22043–2615
USA
Tel: +1 703 847 8300
Fax: +1 703 734 9620
David Andelman, President

Services/Products:
Telemarketing agency

Member of:
DMA

PUBLICIS
110 Social Hall Avenue
Salt Lake City
UT
84111
USA
Tel: 801 364 7452
Fax: +1 801 364 7484
Wendy Jackson, President, Direct
    Marketing

Services/Products:
Advertising Agency; Direct Response
Agency

Member of:
DMA

PUROLATOR
8410 West Bryn Mawr Avenue
Ste 400
Chicago
IL
60631
USA
Tel: +1 77 3 380 1331
Fax: +1 773 380 1268
Conal Finnegan, Regional Sales
    Manager

Services/Products:
Private delivery services

Member of:
DMA

PUTNAM DIRECT MARKETING
Group, Ltd.
777 Peekskill Hollow Road
Putnam Valley
NY
10579
USA
Tel: 914 526 6170
Patrick Kenny, President

Services/Products:
Marketing consultant

Member of:
DMA

Q.E.D. MARKETING INC.
75 Corporate Drive
Hauppauge
NY
11788
USA
Tel: +1 516 231 3607
Fax: +1 516 231 9248
Peter Muzzy, President

Services/Products:
List services

Member of:
DMA

Q5 LIST MARKETING
156 Fifth Avenue
Ste 1219
New York
NY
10010
USA
Tel: +1 212 367 7577
Fax: +1 212 367 7909
Christine Simunovich, President

Services/Products:
List services

Member of:
DMA

QLM MARKETING
6501 East Claire
Scottsdale
AZ
85254–2631
USA
Tel: +1 602 348 2592
Fax: +1 602 951 0944
Ann Toca, SVP & Account Director

Services/Products:
Sales promotion agency

Member of:
DMA

QUAD/DATA SERVICES
555 South 108th Street
West Allis
WIS
53214
USA
Tel: +1 414 443 33967
Fax: +1 414 266 8392
Jean Staven, Director

Services/Products:
Lettershop; Mailing/Faxing services

Member of:
FEDMA

QUALITY STRATEGIES
7850 North Belt Line Road
Irving
TX
75063
USA
Tel: 972 506 3431
Fax: +1 972 506 3612
Jack Wolf, President

Services/Products:
Advertising Agency; Direct Response
Agency

Member of:
DMA

**QUALITY TELEMARKETING
    INC.**
13434 A Street
Omaha
NE
68144–3657
USA
Tel: +1 402 697 1661
Fax: +1 402 697 1611
Mike Albers, President

Services/Products:
Telemarketing agency

Member of:
DMA

QUIKPAK, INC.
P. O. Box 5685
Lafayette
IN
47903
USA
Tel: +1 800 447 7791
Fax: +1 765 448 1948
Ed Farrer, Chief Executive Officer

Services/Products:
Fulfilment and sampling house

Member of:
DMA

QUINN FABLE ADVERTISING INC.
250 West 57th Street
25th fl
New York
NY
10107
USA
Tel: +1 212 974 8700
Fax: +1 212 974 0554
Kathleen Fable, President

Services/Products:
Advertising Agency; Direct Response
Agency

Member of:
DMA

R.C. DIRECT, INC.
200 South Water Street
Milwaukee
WI
53204
USA
Tel: +1 414 271 3313
Fax: +1 414 271 4244
Jill Cohen, President

Services/Products:
List services

Member of:
DMA

RAAB ASSOCIATES
345 Millwood Road
Chappaqua
NY
10514
USA
Tel: +1 914 241 2117
Fax: +1 914 241 0050
Email: info@raabassociates.com
Web: www.raabassociates.com
David M. Raab, Partner

Services/Products:
Consultancy services; Marketing and
e-marketing software evaluation

Member of:
DMA (US)

RACINE JOURNAL TIMES
212 Fourth Street
Racine
WI
53403
USA
Tel: +1 414 634 3322
Timothy Keane, President

Services/Products:
Marketing consultant

Member of:
DMA

RAD MARKETING & RADIOBASE
167 Crary-On-The-Park
Mount Vernon
NY
10550
USA
Tel: 914 668 3563
Fax: +1 914 668 4247
Bob Dadarria, President

Services/Products:
Database services

Member of:
DMA

RAINMAKER SYSTEMS, INC.
1800 Greenhills Road
Ste 201
Scotts Valley
CA
95066
USA
Tel: 831 461 5038
Fax: +1 831 461 4750
Michael Silton, President & CEO

Services/Products:
Telemarketing agency

Member of:
DMA

RAPP COLLINS WORLDWIDE
11 Madison Avenue
4th Fl
New York
NY
10010
USA
Tel: +1 212 590 7400
Fax: +1 212 686 7047
G. Steven Dapper, Chairman & CEO

Services/Products:
Advertising Agency; Direct Response
Agency

Member of:
DMA

RAY SLYPER ASSOCIATES
420 East 72nd Street
Ste 2L
New York
NY
10021
USA
Tel: +1 212 439 0710
Fax: +1 212 439 0739
Ray Slyper, President

Services/Products:
Marketing consultant

Member of:
DMA

RDM GROUP, INC.
3010 Old Ranch Parkway
Ste 400
Seal Beach
CA
90740
USA
Tel: +1 562 430 9080
Fax: +1 562 430 7998
Santo Polito, Vice President, Marketing

Services/Products:
Advertising Agency; Direct Response
Agency

Member of:
DMA

RDW GROUP
89 Ship Street
Providence
RI
2903
USA
Tel: +1 401 521 2700
Fax: +1 401 521 0014
Jay Conway, Vice President

Services/Products:
Advertising Agency; Direct Response
Agency

Member of:
DMA

REES ASSOCIATES, INC.
P. O. Box 831
Des Moines
IA
50304
USA
Tel: +1 515 243 2127
Fax: +1 515 243 1026
Stephen Lundstrom, President

Services/Products:
Lettershop; Mailing/Faxing services

Member of:
DMA

REESE BROTHERS, INC.
925 Penn Avenue
Pittsburgh
PA
15222–3883
USA
Tel: +1 800 365 3500
Fax: +1 412 261 9730
Barry Reese, President

Services/Products:
Telemarketing agency

Member of:
DMA

RELATIONSHIP MARKETING, INC.
11122 Aurora Avenue
Des Moines
IA
50322
USA
Tel: +1 515 276 6900
Fax: +1 515 276 6200
James Lewis, President

Services/Products:
Advertising Agency; Direct Response
Agency

Member of:
DMA

RESEARCH & RESPONSE INTERNATIONAL
250 West 57th Street
Ste 1112
New York
NY
10107
USA
Tel: +1 212 489 8610
Fax: +1 212 262 3474
George Collins, President

Services/Products:
List services

Member of:
DMA

RESODIRECT
19 Gregory Drive
S Burlington
VT
5403
USA
Tel: +1 800 862 8900
Fax: +1 802 865 2308
Email: schubart@ResoDirect.com
Web: www.ResoDirect.com
William Schubart, Chairman & CEO

Services/Products:
Call centre services/systems; Fulfilment
and sampling house; Interactive media;
E-commerce Customer Service &
Fulfilment

Member of:
DMA (US)

RESOURCE & DEVELOPMENT GROUP, INC.
8416 Melrose Drive
Lenexa
KS
66214–1646
USA
Tel: 913 888 6222

Fax: +1 913 495 9822
Jennifer Mayes, Vice President, Direct
Mktg.

Services/Products:
Advertising Agency; Direct Response
Agency

Member of:
DMA

RESOURCE MARKETING, INC.
515 North Park Street
Columbus
OH
43215
USA
Tel: +1 614 621 2888
Fax: +1 614 621 2837
Leslie Viragh, Director

Services/Products:
Advertising Agency; Direct Response
Agency

Member of:
DMA

RESPONSE ADVERTISING
22 Harrison Avenue
Ste 301
Highland Park
NJ
08904–1848
USA
Tel: +1 732 246 4186
Fax: +1 732 846 9856
Email: danbreau@netzero.net
Dan Breau, President

Services/Products:
Advertising Agency; Consultancy
services; Copy adaptation; Direct
marketing agency; Strategic and
creative development for direct
marketing campaigns - consumer,
business-to-business, industrial

Member of:
DMA (US); New York Direct
Marketing Club; Women's Direct
Marketing International

RESPONSE ASSOCIATES
680 8th Street
Ste 260
San Francisco
CA
94103
USA
Tel: +1 415 861 0451
Fax: +1 415 621 4126
Paul Pedrazas, President

Services/Products:
Advertising Agency; Direct Response
Agency

Member of:
DMA

RESPONSE MARKETING GROUP, ASIA PACIFIC
4490 Cox Road
Glen Allen
VA
23060
USA
Tel: 804 968 7300
Fax: +1 804 968 7351
Max Coats, Mgr., Database Marketing
Svcs.

Services/Products:
Advertising Agency; Direct Response
Agency

Member of:
DMA

RESPONSE MEDIA PRODUCTS, INC.
2323 Perimeter Park Drive
Ste 200
Atlanta
GA
30341
USA
Tel: +1 77 0 451 5478
Fax: +1 770 451 4929
Betty Abion, Chief Executive Officer

Services/Products:
List services

Member of:
DMA

RETAIL RESOURCES
Database Marketing LLC
1099 Wall Street West
Lyndhurst
NJ
7071
USA
Tel: +1 201 460 1300
Fax: +1 201 460 0144
Richard Spigai, President

Services/Products:
Database services

Member of:
DMA

RETAIL TARGET MARKETING SYSTEMS, INC.
N16 W23250 Stone Ridge Drive
Waukesha
WI
53188
USA
Tel: +1 414 650 8228
Fax: +1 414 650 8270
Timothy Keane, President

Services/Products:
Marketing consultant

Member of:
DMA

REX MEDIA DESIGN
216 Westminster Avenue
Venice
CA
90291–3306
USA
Tel: +1 310 396 +1 2034
Fax: +1 310 396 9569
Art Rex, Owner

Services/Products:
Catalogue producer

Member of:
DMA

RHEA & KAISER ADVERTISING
400 East Diehl Road
Ste 500
Naperville
IL
60563
USA
Tel: +1 708 505 1100
Fax: +1 708 505 1109
David Grinnell, VP, Direct Marketing

Services/Products:
Advertising Agency; Direct Response
Agency

Member of:
DMA

**RHINA INTERNATIONAL
DIRECT, INC.**
300 Merrick Road
Ste 206
Lynbrook
NY
11563
USA
Tel: +1 516 593 8787
Fax: +1 516 593 4705
Jan Stumacher, President

Services/Products:
Advertising Agency; Direct Response
Agency

Member of:
DMA

RICHARD A. PETERS &
Associates, Inc.
P. O. Box 18560
Rochester
NY
14618
USA

Tel: +1 716 232 8799
Richard Peters, President

Services/Products:
Marketing consultant

Member of:
DMA

**RICHARD SAUNDERS
INTERNATIONAL**
3851 Edwards Road
Cincinnati
OH
45244
USA
Tel: +1 513 271 9911
Fax: +1 513 271 9966
Douglas Hall, President

Services/Products:
Marketing consultant

Member of:
DMA

RICKARD LIST MARKETING
500 Bi-County Boulevard
Farmingdale
NY
11735
USA
Tel: +1 516 249 8710
Fax: +1 516 249 9655
Mark Rickard, Vice President

Services/Products:
List services

Member of:
DMA

RIGHT COAST MARKETING
26 Walnut Street
Narragansett
RI
2884
USA
Tel: +1 401 782 3514
Fax: +1 401 782 6551
Christine Anderson, President

Services/Products:
Marketing consultant

Member of:
DMA

RIGHT SIDE UP, INC.
15071 Keswick Street
Van Nuys
CA
91405
USA
Tel: 818 785 0101
Fax: +1 818 785 0464
Jay Catlin, VP, Sales & Marketing

Services/Products:
Fulfilment and sampling house

Member of:
DMA

**RJ PODELL CATALOG
SERVICES**
3065 Copp Road
Niles
MI
49120
USA
Tel: +1 616 687 8390
Fax: +1 616 687 8322
Rebecca Podell, President

Services/Products:
Marketing consultant

Member of:
DMA

RK HISPANICA DIRECT
45 East 30th Street
9th fl
New York
NY
10016
USA
Tel: +1 212 447 0210
Fax: +1 212 447 0214
Fernando Rola, President

Services/Products:
Advertising Agency; Direct Response
Agency

Member of:
DMA

RMH TELESERVICES
40 Morris Avenue
Bryn Mawr
PA
19010
USA
Tel: +1 800 367 5733
Fax: +1 610 520 5356
MarySue Lucci, President

Services/Products:
Telemarketing agency

Member of:
DMA

RMI DIRECT MARKETING, INC
42 Old Ridgebury Road
Danbury
CT
06810–5100
USA
Tel: +1 203 798 0448
Fax: +1 203 778 6130
Martin Stein, President

Services/Products:
List services

Member of:
DMA

RMS DIRECT, LLC
1205 Daviswood Drive
Suite 1000
McLean
VA
22102–2221
USA
Tel: +1 703 893 8181
Fax: +1 703 893 8835
Email: jremondi@rms-direct.com
Judith Remondi, President

Services/Products:
Consultancy services; Database
services; Direct marketing agency;
Business-to-Business Marketing

E-Services:
E-Marketing consultant

Member of:
DMA (US); DMAW; BMA; DMIX

RMX
P. O. Box 20684
Reno
NV
89515–0684
USA
Tel: +1 702 352 8600
Fax: +1 702 352 8636
Shannon Palacios, Spec., Corporate
Sales & Mktg.

Services/Products:
Private delivery services

Member of:
DMA

ROBERT E. SHALLER
Advertising
8074 Aberdeen Drive
#102
Boynton Beach
FL
33437
USA
Robert Shaller, President

Services/Products:
Advertising Agency; Direct Response
Agency

Member of:
DMA

**ROBERT FRANCIS STUDIOS,
INC.**
P. O. Box 295
Hanover
MA

2339
USA
Tel: +1 781 829 0012
Fax: +1 781 829 0801
John Upton, Vice President

Services/Products:
Advertising Agency; Direct Response
Agency

Member of:
DMA

**ROBERTS COMMUNICATIONS
INC.**
64 Commercial Street
Rochester
NY
14614–1010
USA
Tel: +1 716 325 6000
Fax: +1 716 325 6001
Email: sremy@robertscomm.com
Web: www.robertscomm.com
Sue Remy, Vice President,
Relationship Marketing

Services/Products:
Advertising Agency; Direct marketing
agency; Design/graphics/clip art
supplier; Sales promotion agency;
Interactive media

Member of:
DMA (US); UNYDMA (Local DMA
chapter); AAAA; PSA; AMA
(American Marketing Association)

**ROCKINGHAM✱JUTKINS✱MAR-
KETING, INC.**
Rockingham Ranch
Roll
AZ
85347–7066
USA
Tel: +1 520 785 9400
Fax: +1 520 785 9356
Email: Ray@RayJutkins.com
Web: www.RayJutkins.com
Ray Jutkins

Services/Products:
Consultancy services; Copy
adaptation; Direct marketing agency;
Training/recruitment

Member of:
DMA (US); Arizona DMA; National
Speakers Association

RON PERRELLA DRS
29632 Seriana
Laguna Niguel
CA
92677–7967
USA
Tel: +1 714 495 7661

Fax: +1 714 495 7660
Ronald Perrella, President

Services/Products:
Marketing consultant

Member of:
DMA

**RON WEBER & ASSOCIATES,
INC.**
185 Plains Road
Milford
CT
6460
USA
Tel: +1 203 799 0000
Fax: +1 203 882 9998
Jared Weber, VP, Inbd. Telesvcs./Client
Svc

Services/Products:
Marketing consultant

Member of:
DMA

ROSALIE S. LEVINE CREATIVE
470 West End Avenue
New York
NY
10024–4933
USA
Tel: +1 212 873 0639
Fax: +1 212 873 0639
Rosalie Sacks Levine, Direct
Marketing Copywriter

Services/Products:
Design/graphics/clip art supplier;
Consultancy services

Member of:
DMA

ROSEN/BROWN DIRECT, INC.
338 N.W. Fifth Avenue
Portland
OR
97209–3814
USA
Tel: +1 503 224 9811
Fax: +1 503 224 9761
Richard Rosen, President

Services/Products:
Advertising Agency; Direct Response
Agency

Member of:
DMA

ROSENFIELD & ASSOCIATES
7676 Hazard Center Drive
San Diego
CA
92108
USA

Tel: +1 619 497 2568
Fax: +1 619 296 1534
Karl Dentino, President

Services/Products:
Advertising Agency; Direct Response
Agency

Member of:
DMA

ROSENFIELD/DENTINO, INC.
239 Washington Street
Jersey City
NJ
7302
USA
Tel: +1 201 332 1219
Fax: +1 201 332 4262
Karl Dentino, President

Services/Products:
Advertising Agency; Direct Response
Agency

Member of:
DMA

ROSKA DIRECT
211 B Progress Drive
Montgomeryville
PA
18936
USA
Tel: +1 215 699 9200
Fax: +1 215 699 9240
Jon Roska, Chief Executive Officer

Services/Products:
Advertising Agency; Direct Response
Agency

Member of:
DMA

ROSS ROY COMMUNICATIONS
100 Bloomfield Hills Parkway
Bloomfield Hls
MI
48304
USA
Tel: 810 433 6000
Fax: +1 810 433 6330
Shel Green, VP & Service Line
Manager Dir.

Services/Products:
Advertising Agency; Direct Response
Agency

Member of:
DMA

ROYAL ENVELOPE COMPANY
4414 South Peroria
Chicago
IL
60609–2521

USA
Tel: +1 77 3 376 1212
Fax: +1 773 376 3011
Mike Pusatera, Sales Manager

Services/Products:
Labelling/envelope services

Member of:
DMA

ROYAL ENVELOPE COMPANY
6516 West 74th Street
Bedford Park
IL
60638
USA
Tel: +1 312 594 1888
Mike Pusatera, Sales Manager

Services/Products:
Labelling/envelope services

Member of:
DMA

ROYAL MAIL US INC.
152 Madison Avenue
Ste 200
New York
NY
10016
USA
Tel: +1 212 725 5460
Fax: +1 212 725 4968
David McGirr, Vice President, Sales

Services/Products:
Lettershop; Mailing/Faxing services

Member of:
DMA

RP ASSOCIATES
454 South Anderson Road
Ste BTC552
Rock Hill
SC
29730
USA
Tel: 803 329 0900
Fax: +1 803 329 0958
Eric Burns, Vice President

Services/Products:
List services

Member of:
DMA

RPS
1000 RPS Drive
Coraopolis
PA
15108
USA
Tel: +1 412 269 1000

Fax: +1 412 747 4295
Mark Cyphers

Services/Products:
Private delivery services

Member of:
DMA

RTC DIRECT
1055 Thomas Jefferson St., NW
Washington
DC
20007
USA
Tel: +1 202 625 2111
Fax: +1 202 338 0266
Becky Chidester, Managing Director

Services/Products:
Advertising Agency; Direct Response
Agency

Member of:
DMA

RUBIN RESPONSE SERVICES, INC.
1111 Plaza Drive
8th Fl
Schaumburg
IL
60173
USA
Tel: 847 619 9800
Fax: +1 847 619 0150
William Rubin, President

Services/Products:
List services

Member of:
DMA

RUSS REID COMPANY
2 North Lake Avenue
Ste 600
Pasadena
CA
91101–1868
USA
Tel: +1 626 449 6100
Fax: +1 626 449 6190
Constance Snapp DeBord, SVP &
Dir., Strategic Mktg.

Services/Products:
Advertising Agency; Direct Response
Agency

Member of:
DMA

RYAN PARTNERSHIP
Ryan Direct
55 Post Road West
Westport
CT

6880
USA
Tel: +1 203 226 3136
Fax: +1 203 227 3715
Dawn DeMague, Administrative
  Assistant

Services/Products:
Advertising Agency; Direct Response
Agency

Member of:
DMA

S. CONNELLY & CO., INC.
5168 County Road 33
Buffalo
MN
55313
USA
Tel: +1 612 682 6270
Fax: +1 612 682 6466
Stephen Connelly, President

Services/Products:
Advertising Agency; Direct Response
Agency

Member of:
DMA

S. R. HOEFT DIRECT, INC.
132 East Monroe Avenue
St. Louis
MO
63122–6125
USA
Tel: +1 314 821 1135
Fax: +1 314 821 7511
Steven Hoeft, President

Services/Products:
Advertising Agency; Direct Response
Agency

Member of:
DMA

**S.E.S. MARKETING
  ASSOCIATES**
123 East 75th Street
New York
NY
10021
USA
Tel: +1 212 517 5734
Fax: +1 212 737 8685
Susan Shankman, President

Services/Products:
Marketing consultant

Member of:
DMA

**SAATCHI & SAATCHI
  BUSINESS
  COMMUNICATION**
60 Corporate Woods
Rochester
NY
14623
USA
Tel: +1 716 272 6100
Fax: +1 716 272 6344
Daniel Boone, VP, Director of Direct
  Mktg.

Services/Products:
Advertising Agency; Direct Response
Agency

Member of:
DMA

SADER & ASSOCIATES, INC.
277 Clinton Avenue
Dobbs Ferry
NY
10522–3003
USA
Archie Sader, President

Services/Products:
Advertising Agency; Direct Response
Agency

Member of:
DMA

SAFANI DIRECT INC.
520 Madison Avenue
25th Fl
New York
NY
10022
USA
Tel: +1 212 758 9494
Fax: +1 212 758 9499
Lily Safani, President

Services/Products:
Advertising Agency; Direct Response
Agency

Member of:
DMA

SAGARDIA & CALDERON
B-12 Quintas de Parkville
Guaynabo
PR
969
USA
Tel: +1 787 720 2601
Fax: +1 787 789 0614
Maria Calderon Sagardia, Partner

Services/Products:
Advertising Agency; Direct Response
Agency

Member of:
DMA

SALES BUILDING SYSTEMS
9325 Progress Parkway
Mentor
OH
44060
USA
Tel: +1 216 639 9100
Fax: +1 216 639 9190
Jamie Bertone, Vice President,
  Marketing

Services/Products:
Advertising Agency; Direct Response
Agency

Member of:
DMA

SALZMANN GAY ASSOCIATES
275 Commerce Drive
Ste 236
Fort Washington
PA
19034
USA
Tel: +1 215 654 0285
Marth Gay, President

Services/Products:
Marketing consultant

Member of:
DMA

**SANNA MATTSON MACLEOD,
  INC.**
811 West Jericho Turnpike
Smithtown
NY
11787
USA
Tel: +1 516 265 5160
Fax: +1 516 265 5185
Email: cmacleod@smmadagency.com
Web: www.smmadagency.com
Charles MacLeod, Executive Vice
  President

Services/Products:
Advertising Agency; Direct marketing
agency; Market research agency;
Media buying agency; Print services;
Training/recruitment

E-Services:
E-Marketing consultant; Website
design

Member of:
DMA (US); AAAA; LIAC; MMA

SARGEANT HOUSE
1433 Johnny's Way
P.O. Box 299
Westtown
PA
19395
USA
Tel: +1 610 399 1983
Fax: +1 610 399 8953
Richard Hodgson, President

Services/Products:
Marketing consultant

Member of:
DMA

SAS GLOBAL DIRECT INC
540 Brickell Key Drive
Ste 1007
Miami
FL
33131
USA
Tel: +1 305 377 8182
Fax: +1 305 377 9405
Sheryl Stopka, President

Services/Products:
Marketing consultant

Member of:
DMA

SATURN CORPORATION
4701 Lydell Road
Cheverly
MD
20781
USA
Tel: +1 301 772 7000
Fax: +1 301 386 4538
Fielding Yost, President

Services/Products:
List services

Member of:
DMA

**SAUGATUCK MARKETING
   GROUP**
P. O. Box 191
Green's Farms
CT
6436
USA
Tel: +1 203 454 7018
Fax: +1 203 221 0849
Thomas, Sr. Dir., Measurement/
   Analysis

Services/Products:
Advertising Agency; Direct Response
Agency

Member of:
DMA

SAVESMART
501 Ellis Street
Mount View
CA
94043–2205
USA
Tel: +1 650 919 0800
Fax: +1 650 919 0808
Bob, Director, National Sales

Services/Products:
Advertising Agency; Direct Response
Agency

Member of:
DMA

SBDP CORPORATION
4208 Airport Road
Cincinnati
OH
45226
USA
Tel: +1 513 871 7019
Fax: +1 513 871 7019
William Fryer, President

Services/Products:
List services

Member of:
DMA

**SCANDINAVIAN
   DISTRIBUTION & POSTAL
   SERVICE, INC. (SDPS)**
570 Bercik Street
Ste 3015
Elizabeth
NJ
7201
USA
Tel: 908 289 0703
Fax: +1 908 289 0705
John Cucciniello, President

Services/Products:
Lettershop; Mailing/Faxing services

Member of:
DMA

**SCHOBER DIRECT
   MARKETING**
87 North Broadway
White Plains
NY
10603
USA
Tel: 914 683 6586
Fax: +1 914 683 6587
Klaus, President

Services/Products:
Advertising Agency; Direct Response
Agency

Member of:
DMA

SCHUS & COMPANY
5804 Marbury Road
Bethesda
MD
20817–6042
USA
Tel: +1 301 320 2177
Fax: +1 301 320 3042
Stephanie Schus, Consultant

Services/Products:
Marketing consultant

Member of:
DMA

**SCHWARTZ RAHMAN
   CANDELARIA**
1805 North Vine Street
Los Angeles
CA
90028
USA
Tel: +1 323 465 3160
Fax: +1 323 465 5653
Dianna Garrett, Senior Account
   Supervisor

Services/Products:
Advertising Agency; Direct Respons
Agency

Member of:
DMA

SEALED AIR CORPORATION
301 Mayhill Street
Saddle Brook
NJ
07663–5303
USA
Tel: +1 201 712 7000
Fax: +1 201 712 7070
Kathleen Owczarski, Mgr., Marketir
   Communications

Services/Products:
Protective packaging materials and
systems

Member of:
DMA (US)

**SEGMENT DATA
   MANAGEMENT, INC.**
3435 Wilshire Boulevard
Los Angeles
CA
90010
USA
Tel: +1 213 389 2900
Fax: +1 213 389 9973
Cynthia Park, VP, Group Account

Services/Products:
Advertising Agency; Direct Response
Agency

Member of:
DMA

**SEKLEMIAN/NEWELL
  INTERNATIONAL
  MARKETING CONSULTANTS**
27 Antigua Court
Coronado
CA
92118
USA
Tel: +1 619 423 2050
Fax: +1 619 435 1155
Email: frednote@aol.com
Web: www.loyalty.vg
Frederick Newell, CEO

Services/Products:
Database services; Consultancy
services; Customer relationship
marketing; wireless e-commerce

Member of:
DMA

**SELECT INFORMATION
  EXCHANGE**
244 West 54th Street
New York
NY
10019
USA
Tel: +1 212 247 7123
Fax: +1 212 247 7326
George Wein, Owner

Services/Products:
Advertising Agency; Direct Response
Agency

Member of:
DMA

**SELLTEL INC. NATIONAL
  PROTECTION SERVICE**
393 Mantoloking Road
Brick
NJ
08723–5773
USA
Tel: 908 920 8700
Fax: +1 908 367 9225
David Gartenberg, President

Services/Products:
Telemarketing agency

Member of:
DMA

**SENIOR CITIZENS UNLIMITED,
  INC.**
200 Business Park Drive
Ste 310
Armonk
NY
10504–1719
USA
Tel: 914 273 6672
Fax: +1 914 273 6617
William Dunhill, President

Services/Products:
List services

Member of:
DMA

SENSE OF DESIGN INC.
5800 Baker Road
Ste 200
Minnetonka
MN
55345
USA
Tel: +1 612 935 8827
Fax: +1 612 935 8726
Lynda Dahlheimer, President, Sales &
  Marketing

Services/Products:
Advertising Agency; Direct Response
Agency

Member of:
DMA

SEROKA & ASSOCIATES
Chancellory Park One
450 N Sunnyslope Rd
Brookfield
WI
53005
USA
Tel: +1 414 784 5010
Fax: +1 414 784 3725
Patrick Seroka, President

Services/Products:
Advertising Agency; Direct Response
Agency

Member of:
DMA

**SERVICE ASSOCIATES OF
  AMERICA**
6001 Savoy Drive
Ste 100
Houston
TX
77036–3322
USA
Tel: +1 713 778 5100
Fax: +1 713 778 5140
D. Austin, President

Services/Products:
Advertising Agency; Direct Response
Agency

Member of:
DMA

SHAIN COLAVITO
Pensabene, Inc.
11 Madison Avenue
12th Fl
New York
NY
10010–3629
USA
Tel: +1 212 590 7777
Michael Colavito, Executive Vice
  President

Services/Products:
Advertising Agency; Direct Response
Agency

Member of:
DMA

SHASHO JONES DIRECT
130 Fifth Avenue
9th Fl
New York
NY
10011
USA
Tel: +1 212 929 2300
Fax: +1 212 929 5630
Glenda Shasho Jones, President &
  CEO

Services/Products:
Catalogue producer

Member of:
DMA

SHAVER DIRECT, INC.
9 Commonwealth Avenue
Boston
MA
02116–2106
USA
Tel: +1 617 266 8628
Fax: +1 617 266 8632
Dick Shaver, President

Services/Products:
Advertising Agency; Direct Response
Agency

Member of:
DMA

SHESHENOFF INFORMATION
Services
505 Barton Springs Road
Austin
TX
78704

USA
Tel: +1 512 472 2244
Pat Garland, Director, Database
   Marketing

Services/Products:
Marketing consultant

Member of:
DMA

**SHUGART MATSON
   MARKETING**
3160 Crow Canyon Road
Ste 400
San Ramon
CA
94583
USA
Tel: +1 510 855 3700
Fax: +1 510 855 3710
Kim Shugart, Executive Vice President

Services/Products:
Advertising Agency; Direct Response
Agency

Member of:
DMA

SIBONEY/FCB
101 Park Avenue
New York
NY
10178
USA
Tel: +1 212 499 0910
Jim Cerasani, President

Services/Products:
Advertising Agency; Direct Response
Agency

Member of:
DMA

SIGMA MARKETING GROUP
1850 South Winton Road
Rochester
NY
14618–3992
USA
Tel: +1 716 473 7300
Fax: +1 716 473 0332
David Stirling, President

Services/Products:
Advertising Agency; Direct Response
Agency

Member of:
DMA

SITEL CORPORATION
13215 Birch Street
Omaha
NE
68164

USA
Tel: +1 402 963 2691
Fax: +1 402 963 2699
Phillip Clough, President

Services/Products:
Telemarketing agency

Member of:
DMA

**SK&A INFORMATION
   SERVICES, INC.**
2601 Main Street
Ste 650
Irvine
CA
92614
USA
Tel: +1 714 476 2051
Fax: +1 714 476 2168
Al Cosentino, President & COO

Services/Products:
List services

Member of:
DMA

SKY ALLAND MARKETING
6740 Alexander Bell Drive
Columbia
MD
21046
USA
Tel: +1 410 312 1515
Fax: +1 410 312 4970
Richard Hebert, Chief Executive
   Officer

Services/Products:
Telemarketing agency

Member of:
DMA

SKYTELLER, L.L.C.
6200 South Quebec Street
Ste 350
Englewood
CO
80111
USA
Tel: +1 303 967 6238
Fax: +1 303 967 8812
Daniel Dudley, SVP & GM,
   Information Services

Services/Products:
Market research agency

Member of:
DMA (US); FEDMA

**SMARTBASE/ACXIOM DIRECT
   MEDIA**
200 Pemberwick Road
Greenwich

CT
6830
USA
Tel: +1 203 532 1000
Fax: +1 203 532 1654
Charles Morgan, Pres. & Chairman of
   the Board

Services/Products:
List services

Member of:
DMA (US); FEDMA

SMITH HARRISON DIRECT
6056 S. Fashion Square Drive
Ste 210
Murray
UT
84107
USA
Tel: 801 539 1300
Peter Harrison, President & CCO

Services/Products:
Advertising Agency; Direct Response
Agency

Member of:
DMA

**SMITH-BROWNING DIRECT,
   INC.**
1606 Beach Trail
Indian Rks Bch
FL
33785
USA
Tel: 813 596 3325
Fax: +1 813 596 0464
Timothy Smith, Co-Owner

Services/Products:
Marketing consultant

Member of:
DMA

SPARKS MARKETING
2360 N.W. 38th Street
Boca Raton
FL
33431
USA
Tel: +1 561 218 9133
Fax: +1 561 218 9144
Joan Sparks, President

Services/Products:
Database services

Member of:
DMA

**SPAULDER & ASSOCIATES,
   INC.**
4304 Fannin Drive
Irving

TX
75038–6233
USA
Tel: 972 570 0835
Fax: +1 972 570 0918
Peter Spaulder, President

Services/Products:
Marketing consultant

Member of:
DMA

SPECIAL EXPEDITIONS
720 Fifth Avenue
Ste B
New York
NY
10019–4107
USA
Tel: +1 212 527 2725
Fax: +1 212 527 2706
Robert Shulman, Chief Marketing
    Officer

Services/Products:
Marketing consultant

Member of:
DMA

SPECIALIST
4879 Ronson Court
San Diego
CA
92111
USA
Tel: +1 619 268 9540
Fax: +1 619 268 0141
Bill Rella, President

Services/Products:
List services

Member of:
DMA

SPECTRA-CONSUMER
   MARKETING GROUP
8300 Boone Boulevard
Ste 1000
Vienna
VA
22182
USA
Tel: +1 703 883 8900
Fax: +1 703 883 8910
Blair Zucker, Vice President

Services/Products:
Market research agency

Member of:
DMA

SPERBER DIRECT INC.
250 West 57st Street
Ste 1801

New York
NY
10107
USA
Tel: +1 212 459 0403
Fax: +1 212 459 0249
Beth Sperber, Vice President

Services/Products:
Advertising Agency; Direct Response
Agency

Member of:
DMA

SPRINGHOUSE CORPORATION
1111 Bethlehem Pike
P.O. Box 908
Spring House
PA
19477–0908
USA
Tel: +1 215 646 8700
Fax: +1 215 646 4399
Thomas Hennessy, Database Services
    Manager

Services/Products:
List services

Member of:
DMA

SPYGLASS CONSULTING
   ASSOCIATES
7045 Spyglass Court
Westerville
OH
43082
USA
Tel: +1 614 898 1939
Fax: +1 614 899 1829
Kim Hansen, President

Services/Products:
Marketing consultant

Member of:
DMA

STANTON DIRECT
   MARKETING, INC.
1009 West Water Street
Elmira
NY
14905–2003
USA
Tel: +1 607 734 1665
Fax: +1 607 734 3708
Aloysius Stanton, President

Services/Products:
Marketing consultant

Member of:
DMA

STAR DMRA/EMA
33 Carriglea Drive
Ste 200
Riverside
CT
6878
USA
Tel: +1 203 637 5410
Fax: +1 203 698 1584
Michael Green, President

Services/Products:
Market research agency

Member of:
DMA

STARK HOLDING LTD.
201 East 16th Street
New York
NY
10003
USA
Tel: +1 212 677 9111
Fax: +1 212 677 9593
Karen Stark, President

Services/Products:
Advertising Agency; Direct Response
Agency

Member of:
DMA

STATEWIDE DATA SERVICES
7 North Baylen Street
Pensacola
FL
32501
USA
Tel: 904 433 0710
Fax: +1 904 434 6836
Timothy Falzone, President

Services/Products:
List services

Member of:
DMA

STATLISTICS, INC.
11 Lake Avenue, Extension
Danbury
CT
6811
USA
Tel: +1 203 778 8700
Fax: +1 203 778 4839
Donna Buckner, Executive Vice
    President

Services/Products:
List services

Member of:
DMA

STEALTH MARKETING/GAGE MARKETING GROUP
13520 Inverness Road
Minnetonka
MN
55305
USA
Tel: +1 320 939 0086
Fax: +1 320 939 1057
Michael Barga, VP & General Manager

Services/Products:
Lettershop; Mailing/Faxing services

Member of:
DMA

STEPHEN L. GELLER, INC.
Greenwich Office Park
Bldg 2
Greenwich
CT
06831–5115
USA
Tel: +1 203 622 6669
Fax: +1 203 622 8885
Sue Geller, President

Services/Products:
Advertising Agency; Direct Response Agency

Member of:
DMA

STEPHEN WINCHELL & ASSOCIATES
2425 Wilson Boulevard
Ste 500
Arlington
VA
22201–3326
USA
Tel: +1 703 276 9032
Fax: +1 703 528 7492
Dodee Black, President & COO

Services/Products:
List services

Member of:
DMA

STEPHENS DIRECT
417 East Stroop Road
Dayton
OH
45429
USA
Tel: +1 513 299 4993
Fax: +1 513 299 9355
Phillip Stephens, President

Services/Products:
Advertising Agency; Direct Response Agency

Member of:
DMA

STEVENS-KNOX LIST MANAGEMENT
304 Park Avenue South
6th Fl
New York
NY
10010
USA
Tel: +1 212 388 8800
Fax: +1 212 388 8890
Ralph Stevens, President

Services/Products:
List services

Member of:
DMA

STRAND MARKETING
55 New Montgomery
Ste 601
San Francisco
CA
94105
USA
Tel: +1 415 777 5070
Fax: +1 415 777 5340
Michelle Strand, Owner & Consultant

Services/Products:
Marketing consultant

Member of:
DMA

STRATEGIC DECISION SERVICES
May & Speh
11 Piedmont Center
Atlanta
GA
30305
USA
Tel: +1 404 869 2054
Fax: +1 404 266 0528
Cindy Randazzo, VP, Marketing

Services/Products:
List services

Member of:
DMA

STRATEGIC INSIGHT
201 Bolinas Court
Chapel Hill
NC
27514–8344
USA
Tel: 919 969 9218
Fax: +1 919 969 9163
Cynthia Wheaton, President

Services/Products:
Database services

Member of:
DMA

STRATEGIC INSIGHTS, INC.
1325 13th Street, N.W.
Ste 47
Washington
DC
20005
USA
Tel: +1 202 387 2646
Fax: +1 202 387 2647
John McCracken, Managing Partner

Services/Products:
Marketing consultant

Member of:
DMA

STRATEGIC PARTNERS GROUP, INC.
1320 Old Chain Bridge Road
Ste 420
McLean
VA
22101
USA
Tel: +1 703 883 0100
Fax: +1 703 893 6790
John Mullin, Account Supervisor

Services/Products:
Advertising Agency; Direct Response Agency

Member of:
DMA

STRATEGIC TELECOMMUNICATIONS
2610 University Avenue West
Ste 500
St. Paul
MN
55114
USA
Tel: +1 612 649 0404
Fax: +1 612 649 0424
Jeff Larson, Vice President

Services/Products:
Telemarketing agency

Member of:
DMA

STRATEGY OUTFITTERS
33705 North 64th Street
Scottsdale
AZ 85262
USA
Tel: +1 480 595 9139
Fax: +1 480 595 0890

Email: jeff@strategyoutfitters.com
Web: www.strategyoutfitters.com
Jeff Walters, President

Services/Products:
Consultancy services; Market research agency

E-Services:
E-Marketing consultant

Member of:
FEDMA

STRUBCO, INC
Old Chelsea Station
P.O. Box 1274
New York
NY
10113–0920
USA
Tel: +1 212 242 1900
Fax: +1 212 242 1963
Sean Strub, President

Services/Products:
List services

Member of:
DMA

STS SYSTEMS LTD.
780 Third Avenue
New York
NY
10017
USA
Tel: +1 212 755 0130
Danielle Silverman, Mgr., Mktg. & Communications

Services/Products:
List services

Member of:
DMA

STURNER & KLEIN
11900 Parklawn Drive
Rockville
MD
20852
USA
Tel: +1 301 881 2720
Fax: +1 301 881 3745
Jerold Sturner, President

Services/Products:
Telemarketing agency

Member of:
DMA

SUISSA MILLER ADVERTISING
11601 Wilshire Boulevard
16th Fl
Los Angeles
CA

90025–1770
USA
Tel: +1 310 392 9666
Fax: +1 310 396 8370
Marna Bullard, Account Director

Services/Products:
Advertising Agency; Direct Response Agency

Member of:
DMA

SULLIVAN ADVERTISING, INC.
602 Main Street
Ste 500
Cincinnati
OH
45202
USA
Tel: +1 513 684 0600
Fax: +1 513 684 0333
Thomas Link, Vice President

Services/Products:
Advertising Agency; Direct Response Agency

Member of:
DMA

SUPPORT SERVICES CORP.
11922 Fairway Lakes Drive
Ste 1
Fort Myers
FL
33913–8337
USA
Tel: 941 768 2858
Fax: +1 941 768 1912
Steve Ward, President

Services/Products:
List services

Member of:
DMA

SUTTON & ASSOCIATES, INC.
7355 Garden Court
River Forest
IL
60305–2213
USA
Tel: +1 708 771 0400
Fax: +1 708 771 0436
John Sutton, President

Services/Products:
Marketing consultant

Member of:
DMA

SWAN PACKAGING FULFILLMENT
415 Hamburg Turnpike
Wayne

NJ
7470
USA
Tel: 973 790 0990
Fax: +1 973 790 0216
Timothy Werkley, VP, Sales & Marketing

Services/Products:
Fulfilment and sampling house

Member of:
DMA

SWANSON COMMUNICATIONS
109 Broadway
Ste 300
Fargo
ND
58102
USA
Tel: +1 701 235 4620
Fax: +1 701 235 9762
Kim Reierson-Kelsh, Vice President

Services/Products:
Advertising Agency; Direct Response Agency

Member of:
DMA

SYNAPSE GROUP
4514 Travis Street
Ste 220
Dallas
TX
75205–4135
USA
Tel: +1 214 599 2929
Fax: +1 214 599 9087
BenjaminMcLemore, President & CEO

Services/Products:
Marketing consultant

Member of:
DMA

SYNAPSE INFUSION GROUP
4188 Oak Place Drive
Atrium Level
Westlake Village
CA
91362
USA
Tel: 805 494 6693
Fax: +1 805 494 9535
Stan Fridstein, President

Services/Products:
List services

Member of:
DMA

SYNERCOMM
80 Wheeler Avenue
Pleasantville
NY
10570
USA
Tel: 914 747 1580
Fax: +1 914 747 1541
Elie Aslan, President

Services/Products:
Marketing consultant

Member of:
DMA

T C I M SERVICES
1334 E. Chandler Blvd.
#5-C14
Ste 403
Phoenix
AZ
85048
USA
Tel: +1 602 460 1565
Fax: +1 602 460 2890
Linda Drake, Chief Executive Officer

Services/Products:
Telemarketing agency

Member of:
DMA

TABS DIRECT
1002 Texas Parkway
Ste 900
Stafford
TX
77477
USA
Tel: +1 281 499 0417
Fax: +1 281 499 6144
Claude Grizzard, Principal

Services/Products:
List services

Member of:
DMA

TAILWIND
107 John Street
Southport
CT
6490
USA
Tel: +1 203 254 9765
Fax: +1 203 637 0602
Brad Fisher, President

Services/Products:
Market research agency

Member of:
DMA

TANEN ADVERTISING
57 Wilton Road
Westport
CT
6880
USA
Tel: +1 203 454 4111
Fax: +1 203 454 4114
Ilene Cohn Tanen, President

Services/Products:
Advertising Agency; Direct Response
Agency

Member of:
DMA

TARGET DATA MANAGEMENT
1030 Massachusetts Avenue
Cambridge
MA
2138
USA
Tel: +1 617 876 2275
Fax: +1 617 354 0895
Lee Gartley, Vice President

Services/Products:
Database services

Member of:
DMA

TARGETBASE MARKETING
7850 North BeltLine Road
Irving
TX
75063
USA
Tel: +1 214 506 3400
Fax: +1 214 506 3898
Jack Wolf, President

Services/Products:
Advertising Agency; Direct Response
Agency

Member of:
DMA

TARGETCOM, INC.
401 East Illinois Street
Ste 333
Chicago
IL
60611–4395
USA
Tel: +1 312 822 1100
Fax: +1 312 822 9628
Jay Miller, President

Services/Products:
Advertising Agency; Direct Response
Agency

Member of:
DMA

TARGETRENDS ASSOCIATES
38 Laurel Hill Road
Ridgefield
CT
6877
USA
Tel: +1 203 544 8997
Fax: +1 203 544 8397
Paul Hall, President

Services/Products:
Marketing consultant

Member of:
DMA

TATUM TOOMEY & WHICKER
1820 Eastchester
High Point
NC
27265
USA
Tel: 910 889 3009
Fax: +1 910 889 3006
Roger Tatum, Partner

Services/Products:
Advertising Agency; Direct Response
Agency

Member of:
DMA

TAURUS DIRECT MARKETING
861 Lafayette Road, #6
P.O. Box 1620
Hampton
NH
3842
USA
Tel: +1 603 926 4477
Fax: +1 603 926 1728
Tracy Emerick, Director

Services/Products:
Advertising Agency; Direct Response
Agency

Member of:
DMA

TBWA CHIAT/DAY
340 Main Street
Venice
CA
90291
USA
Tel: +1 310 314 5000
Fax: +1 310 396 1273
Velda Ruddock, Director, Intelligence

Services/Products:
Advertising Agency; Direct Response
Agency

Member of:
DMA

TCI DIRECT
10911 Riverside Drive
Toluca Lake
CA
91602
USA
Tel: 818 752 1800
Fax: +1 818 752 1808
James Thulin, President

Services/Products:
List services

Member of:
DMA

TEAM ONE ADVERTISING
1960 East Grand Avenue
El Segundo
CA
90245
USA
Tel: +1 310 615 2000
Fax: +1 310 322 3819
Michael Hughes, Dir., Relationship
Marketing

Services/Products:
Advertising Agency; Direct Response
Agency

Member of:
DMA

TEAM SERVICES
1047 Ardmore Avenue
Itasca
IL
60143
USA
Tel: +1 630 775 1500
Fax: +1 630 775 1570
Thomas Patrevito, Vice President

Services/Products:
Lettershop; Mailing/Faxing services

Member of:
DMA

TEAMNASH, INC.
275 Madison Avenue
Ste 1905
New York
NY
10016
USA
Tel: +1 212 376 NASH
Fax: +1 212 376 6277
Edward Nash, President & CEO

Services/Products:
Advertising Agency; Direct Response
Agency

Member of:
DMA

**TECHNICAL LIST
COMPUTING, INC.**
221 East First Street
Ste A
Ferdinand
IN
47532–0027
USA
Tel: 812 367 2545
Fax: +1 812 367 2546
Richard Wilson, Chief Executive
Officer

Services/Products:
List services

Member of:
DMA

**TECHNION COMMUNICATION
CORPORATION**
190 N.E. 199th Street
Ste 201
Miami
FL
33179
USA
Tel: +1 305 770 1994
Fax: +1 305 770 3433
Sandy Papunen, President

Services/Products:
Database services

Member of:
DMA

TEL-A-SELL MARKETING INC.
8240 Clara Avenue
Cincinnati
OH
45242
USA
Tel: +1 513 728 2600
Fax: +1 513 728 2603
Edd O'Connor, Executive Vice
President

Services/Products:
Telemarketing agency

Member of:
DMA

TELE RESOURCES INC.
69 North 28th Street
Superior
WI
54880
USA
Tel: +1 715 395 2740
Fax: +1 715 395 2750
Jack Keenan, President & CEO

Services/Products:
Telemarketing agency

Member of:
DMA

TELECHECK/FIRST DATA
5251 Westheimer
Huston
TX
77056
USA
Tel: +1 713 331 7909
Fax: +1 713 331 7186
William Bak, President

Services/Products:
List services

Member of:
DMA

**TELEDEVELOPMENT
SERVICES, INC.**
4615 West Streetboro Road
Ste 102
Richfield
OH
44286
USA
Tel: +1 330 659 4441
Fax: +1 330 659 4442
Web: www.teledevelopment.com
Jon Kaplan, President

Services/Products:
Consultancy services; Training/
recruitment; Executive search - call
centre

Member of:
DMA (US); FEDMA; ICSA; ATA;
ASTD

TELEMARKETING CONCEPTS
2013 Crompond Road
Yorktown Heights
NY
10598
USA
Tel: 914 245 0701
Fax: +1 914 245 0655
Richard Penn, Chief Executive Officer

Services/Products:
Telemarketing agency

Member of:
DMA

TELEMASTERS INC.
1252 East 7th Street
Brooklyn
NY
11230
USA
Tel: +1 718 951 3312
Fax: +1 718 677 7872
Daniel Soloff, President

Services/Products:
Telemarketing agency

Member of:
DMA

TELEMATCH
6883 Commercial Drive
Springfield
VA
22159
USA
Tel: +1 800 523 7346
Fax: +1 703 658 8301
Ruth Baker, Director, Database
  Marketing

Services/Products:
Telemarketing agency

Member of:
DMA

TELEQUEST
1250 East Copeland Road
Ste 850
Arlington
TX
76011
USA
Tel: 817 460 5700
Fax: +1 817 258 6505
Gordon McKenna, Chairman

Services/Products:
Telemarketing agency

Member of:
DMA

TELESERVICE RESOURCES
4201 Cambridge Road
Fort Worth
TX
76155
USA
Tel: +1 800 325 2580
Fax: +1 817 354 8144
Artie White, Legal Regulatory
  Compliance

Services/Products:
Telemarketing agency

Member of:
DMA (US); FEDMA

TELESERVICES PARTNERS
197 Yulupa Circle
Ste 14
Santa Rosa
CA
95405
USA
Tel: +1 707 527 6729
Fax: +1 707 527 6729
Brent Welch, President

Services/Products:
Marketing consultant

Member of:
DMA

**TELESPECTRUM
  WORLDWIDE, INC.**
443 South Gulph Road
King of Prussia
PA
19406
USA
Tel: +1 610 878 7400
Fax: +1 610 878 7480
Chris Gongol, SVP, Business
  Development

Services/Products:
Telemarketing agency

Member of:
DMA

TELETECH
1700 Lincoln Street
Ste 1400
Denver
CO
80203–4514
USA
Tel: +1 303 894 4000
Fax: +1 303 813 4610
Jean Wagner, Director, Marketing

Services/Products:
Telemarketing agency

Member of:
DMA

TELSERV
421 S.W. 6the Avenue
Ste 1100
Portland
OR
97204–1614
USA
Tel: +1 503 274 8240
Fax: +1 503 274 8234
Marc Alexander, President & CEO

Services/Products:
Telemarketing agency

Member of:
DMA

TEMERLIN MCCLAIN DIRECT
201 East Carpenter Freeway
Irving
TX
75062
USA
Tel: 972 556 1100
Fax: +1 972 830 1391
Beverly Beaudoin, Managing Partner

Services/Products:
Advertising Agency; Direct Response
Agency

Member of:
DMA

**TENSION ENVELOPE
  CORPORATION**
819 East 19th Street
Kansas City
MO
64108–1498
USA
Tel: 816 471 3800
Fax: +1 816 283 1498
Dan Imler, Dir., Advtg. &
  Communications

Services/Products:
Labelling/envelope services

Member of:
DMA

TERADYNE
30801 Agoura Road
Bldg 1
Agoura Hills
CA
91301–4324
USA
Tel: 818 991 2900
Fax: +1 818 735 5623
Andrea Hart, Marketing Comms.
  Specialist

Services/Products:
List services

Member of:
DMA

**TESSERA ENTERPRISE
  SYSTEMS**
Seven Audubon Road
Wakefield
MA
1880
USA
Tel: +1 781 246 9024
Fax: +1 781 246 1958
Nicole Correnti, Manager, Marketing

Services/Products:
Fulfilment and sampling house

Member of:
DMA

TEXAS DIRECT, INC.
5600 Stratum Drive
Fort Worth
TX
76137
USA
Tel: +1 800 937 4226

Fax: +1 817 232 5006
John Barber, Sales Manager

Services/Products:
List services

Member of:
DMA

THE ASSOCIATES
Harte-Hanks
257 East 200 South
21st Fl
Salt Lake City
UT
84111
USA
Richard Hochhauser, President &
   CEO

Services/Products:
List services

Member of:
DMA

THE BARROWS GROUP
7777 Bonhomme Avenue
Ste 1400
St. Louis
MO
63105
USA
Tel: +1 314 854 1342
Fax: +1 314 854 1343
Kathy Warnick, President

Services/Products:
Advertising Agency; Direct Response
Agency

Member of:
DMA

THE BOSTON GROUP
29 Commonwealth Avenue
7th Fl
Boston
MA
2116
USA
Tel: +1 617 536 1666
Fax: +1 617 536 7292
Mary Lou Pritchett, Managing Partner

Services/Products:
Advertising Agency; Direct Response
Agency

Member of:
DMA

THE BRAVO GROUP
230 Park Avenue South
4th Fl
New York
NY
10003

USA
Tel: +1 212 768 5176
Fax: +1 212 598 5457
John Bingle, CEO, Worldwide

Services/Products:
Advertising Agency; Direct Response
Agency

Member of:
DMA

**THE BROADMOORE GROUP,
   LTD**
69115 Ramon Road
Ste 1386
Cathedral City
CA
92234
USA
Tel: +1 760 324 3072
Fax: +1 760 321 5314
Jean-Claude Koven, President

Services/Products:
Mail order company; List services

THE CALLAHAN GROUP, L.L.C.
5600 North River Road
Suite 800
Rosemont
IL
60018
USA
Tel: +1 847 292 4433
Fax: +1 847 202 4404
Email: callahangrp@aol.com
Web: www.callahangroup.com
John J. Flieder, President & COO

Services/Products:
Consultancy services; Managing
change; Human resources; Executive
recruitment

E-Services:
E-Marketing consultant

Member of:
DMA (US); Chicago Association of
Direct Marketing

THE CATALOG CONNECTION
900 Chelmsford Street
Twr 2, 7th Fl
Lowell
MA
01851–8207
USA
Tel: 978 551 5626
Fax: +1 978 551 5020
Joan Burden Litle, Creative Merch.
   Consultant

Services/Products:
Design/graphics/clip art supplier;
Consultancy services

Member of:
DMA

THE CHAPMAN AGENCY
675 Avenue Of The Americas
3rd & 4th Fl
New York
NY
10010–1591
USA
Tel: +1 212 614 3880
Fax: +1 212 614 3888
Janet Coombs, CEO & Chairman

Services/Products:
Advertising Agency; Direct Response
Agency

Member of:
DMA

THE CHARLTON GROUP INC.
644 Science Drive
Ste 301
Madison
WI
53711
USA
Tel: +1 608 273 5555
Fax: +1 608 273 5561
Rodney Schwegel, National Accounts
   Manager

Services/Products:
Telemarketing agency

Member of:
DMA

THE COASTAL GROUP
149 5th Avenue
4th Fl
New York
NY
10010
USA
Tel: +1 212 505 6000
Fax: +1 212 505 6997
David Weiss, President

Services/Products:
Advertising Agency; Direct Response
Agency

Member of:
DMA

THE CODE CORPORATION
37 King Street
Charleston
SC
29401
USA
Tel: 803 722 9830
Fax: +1 803 722 9840
T.B.Pickens, President

Services/Products:
Advertising Agency; Direct Response
Agency

Member of:
DMA

THE CONNECTION-INBOUND
Telemarketing
11351 Rupp Drive
Ste 300
Burnsville
MN
55337
USA
Tel: +1 800 883 5777
Fax: +1 612 948 5498
Gary Cohen, President

Services/Products:
Telemarketing agency

Member of:
DMA

THE COOLIDGE COMPANY, INC.
25 West 43rd Street
New York
NY
10036
USA
Tel: +1 212 997 2424
Fax: +1 212 302 7695
Richard Steeg, President

Services/Products:
List services

Member of:
DMA

THE CORPORATE COMMUNICATIONS GROUP
26 Parsippany Road
Whippany
NJ
7981
USA
Tel: 973 386 1444
Fax: +1 973 386 0735
James Pinkin, President

Services/Products:
Fulfilment and sampling house

Member of:
DMA

THE CREDIT INDEX
100 Stierli Court
Ste 100
Mt. Arlington
NJ
07856–1312
USA
Tel: +1 201 770 4007

Fax: +1 201 770 4006
Carl Tomasello, Director, Marketing

Services/Products:
List services

Member of:
DMA

THE CUSTOMER CONNECTION, INC.
621 South Andreasen Drive
Ste B
Escondido
CA
92029–1904
USA
Tel: +1 619 489 8339
Fax: +1 619 489 1075
Judd Goldfeder, President

Services/Products:
List services

Member of:
DMA

THE DATA BASE, INC.
1710 Highway 35
Oakhurst
NJ
7755
USA
Tel: +1 732 531 2212
Fax: +1 732 531 4640
Donald Nissim, Chief Executive
  Officer

Services/Products:
List services

Member of:
DMA

THE DELAY GROUP
4121 East Via Del Cuculin
Tucson
AZ
85718–3320
USA
Tel: +1 520 615 8235
Fax: +1 520 615 8297
Robert DeLay, President

Services/Products:
Marketing consultant

Member of:
DMA

THE DEVELOPMENT CENTER, INC.
601 Walnut Street
Ste 210
Philadelphia
PA
19106–3378
USA

Tel: +1 215 238 7300
Fax: +1 215 238 7310
Randy Warren, President & CEO

Services/Products:
Telemarketing agency

Member of:
DMA

THE DIRECT MARKETING SPECIALISTS, INC.
900 North Franklin
Chicago
IL
60610
USA
Tel: +1 312 266 7906
Fax: +1 312 266 9230
Randi Wine, President

Services/Products:
Advertising Agency; Direct Response
Agency

Member of:
DMA

THE DIRECT NETWORK
2 Hudson Place
8th Floor
Hoboken
NJ
7030
USA
Email:
  pmarshall@thedirectnetwork.com
Web: www.thedirectnetwork.com
Peter Marshall, President & Creative
  Director

Services/Products:
Advertising Agency; Design/graphics
clip art supplier; Direct marketing
agency; Commercial film production
company

Member of:
DMA (US); National DMA

THE DISPATCH PRINTING COMPANY
34 South Third Street
Columbus
OH
43215
USA
Tel: +1 614 461 5000
Fax: +1 614 461 7551
Stephen Zonars, VP, Sales & Marketir

Services/Products:
Private delivery services

Member of:
DMA

THE DOMAIN GROUP
720 Olive Way
Ste 1700
Seattle
WA
98101–1816
USA
Tel: +1 206 682 3035
Fax: +1 206 621 0139
Jeff Nickel, Dir., Strategic Plng. &
  Mktg.

Services/Products:
Advertising Agency; Direct Response
Agency

Member of:
DMA

THE E-TAILING GROUP, INC.
308 West Erie Street
Ste 710
Chicago
IL
60610
USA
Tel: +1 312 255 9590
Fax: +1 312 255 9591
Lauren Freedman, President

Services/Products:
Consultancy services

E-Services:
E-Marketing consultant

Member of:
DMA (US); National DMA; NRF;
NAWBO; SNOPORG

THE EXPRESS GROUP
1981 Dallavo Drive
Walled Lake
MI
48390
USA
Tel: +1 248 669 4060
Fax: +1 248 669 3090
Lisa Miller, Sales Manager

Services/Products:
Fulfilment and sampling house

Member of:
DMA

THE FALA GROUP
70 Marcus Drive
Melville
NY
11747–4278
USA
Tel: +1 516 391 0214
Fax: +1 516 694 7493
Robert Jurick, Chairman

Services/Products:
Lettershop; Mailing/Faxing services

Member of:
DMA

THE FANEUIL GROUP
2 Faneuil Hall South
Boston
MA
02109–1605
USA
Tel: +1 617 742 4888
Fax: +1 617 742 3666
Daniel Mahoney, SVP, Marketing

Services/Products:
Telemarketing agency

Member of:
DMA

THE FINAL PRODUCT
10306 Eaton Place
Ste 180
Fairfax
VA
22030
USA
Tel: +1 703 691 8300
Fax: +1 703 691 8390
Kim Roman, President

Services/Products:
Advertising Agency; Direct Response
Agency

Member of:
DMA

THE FMP DIRECT MARKETING GROUP
1019 West Park Avenue
Libertyville
IL
60048
USA
Tel: 847 816 1919
Fax: +1 847 816 1969
Michael Wilmet, Chief Executive
  Officer

Services/Products:
List services

Member of:
DMA

THE FOCUS AGENCY
200 Crescent Court
Dallas
TX
75201
USA
Tel: +1 214 855 2900
Fax: +1 214 999 2715
Johanna Grilli, Senior Vice President

Services/Products:
Advertising Agency; Direct Response
Agency

Member of:
DMA

THE GALLUP ORGANIZATION
300 South 68th Street Place
Ste 311
Lincoln
NE
68510
USA
Tel: +1 800 288 8593
Fax: +1 402 485 6393
Jock Bickert, Chief Executive Officer

Services/Products:
Database services

Member of:
DMA

THE GAZETTE COMPANY
200 Second Avenue S.E.
Cedar Rapids
IA
52401–1945
USA
Tel: +1 319 365 5597
Fax: +1 319 365 5694
Timothy Gustin, Dir., Planning &
  Development

Services/Products:
Marketing consultant

Member of:
DMA

THE GNAMES ADVANTAGE, LLC
3250 Skyway Circle
Irving
TX
75038
USA
Tel: 972 550 1140
Fax: +1 972 550 1053
Holly Hammond, Principal

Services/Products:
List services

Member of:
DMA

THE GRAHAM GROUP
2014 West Pinhook
Ste 210
Lafayette
LA
70508
USA
Tel: +1 318 232 8214

Fax: +1 318 235 3787
Jeffrey Wright, Direct Response
  Manager

Services/Products:
Advertising Agency; Direct Response
Agency

Member of:
DMA

THE HACKER GROUP, LTD.
855–106th Avenue, N.E.
Ste 100
Bellevue
WA
98004–4309
USA
Tel: +1 425 454 8556
Fax: +1 425 455 5694
Robert Hacker, President

Services/Products:
Advertising Agency; Direct Response
Agency

Member of:
DMA

THE HAUSER GROUP
3 Commercial Street
Hicksville
NY
11801
USA
Tel: +1 516 935 8603
Fax: +1 516 935 2495
Barry Hauser, President

Services/Products:
Marketing consultant

Member of:
DMA

THE HEISLER GROUP, INC.
3174 Toulouse Circle
Thousand Oaks
CA
91362
USA
Tel: 805 492 5820
Fax: +1 805 492 5860
Jerold Heisler, President

Services/Products:
Marketing consultant

Member of:
DMA

THE HIBBERT GROUP
400 Pennington Avenue
P.O. Box 8116
Trenton
NJ
08650–0116
USA

Tel: +1 609 394 7500
Fax: +1 609 392 1237
Paul Zukowski, VP, Account
  Management

Services/Products:
Fulfilment and sampling house

Member of:
DMA

THE HORAH GROUP
49 West 37th Street
13th Fl
New York
NY
10018
USA
Tel: +1 212 921 4521
Fax: +1 212 921 4831
Richard Goldsmith, President

Services/Products:
Advertising Agency; Direct Response
Agency

Member of:
DMA

THE INFORMATION REFINERY, INC.
200 Route 17
Ste 5
Mahwah
NJ
07430–1267
USA
Tel: +1 201 529 2600
Fax: +1 201 529 4030
Gordon Clotworthy, President

Services/Products:
List services

Member of:
DMA

THE JACKSON CONSULTING GROUP, INC.
P.O. Box 246
Middletown
DE
19709
USA
Tel: +1 302 378 0218
Fax: +1 302 378 0219
Email: donjackson@jcg-ltd.com
Web: www.jcg-ltd.com
Donald Jackson, Chairman

Services/Products:
Consultancy services

E-Services:
E-Marketing consultant

Member of:
DMA (US); National DMA; DDMA

THE KAPLAN AGENCY
1200 High Ridge Road
Stamford
CT
06905–1202
USA
Tel: +1 203 968 8800
Fax: +1 203 968 8871
Thomas Kaplan, President

Services/Products:
List services

Member of:
DMA

THE LAKE GROUP
411 Theodore Fremd Avenue
Rye
NY
10580
USA
Tel: 914 925 2400
Fax: +1 914 925 2499
Walter Lake, Chairman & CEO

Services/Products:
Marketing consultant

Member of:
DMA

THE LELAND COMPANY
1801 West Leland Avenue
Chicago
IL
60640–4595
USA
Tel: +1 77 3 561 4005
Fax: +1 773 561 4099
Paulette Gaudet, Manager, List Mktg
  & Sales

Services/Products:
List services

Member of:
DMA

THE LIST CONNECTION INC.
540 West Boston Post Road
Mamaroneck
NY
10543
USA
Tel: 914 381 2010
Fax: +1 914 381 2163
Elaine Canter, President

Services/Products:
List services

Member of:
DMA

THE LIST SOURCE, INC.
1415 Route 70 East
Ste 100

Cherry Hill
NJ
8034
USA
Tel: +1 609 795 3344
Fax: +1 609 795 9498
Allan Bilofsky, President

Services/Products:
List services

Member of:
DMA

THE LISTWORKS CORPORATION
One Campus Drive
Pleasantville
NY
10570–1602
USA
Tel: 914 769 7100
Fax: +1 914 769 3804
Robert Givone, President

Services/Products:
List services

Member of:
DMA

THE LOOP COMPANY INC.
c/o North Castle Partners
300 Stamford Place
Stamford
CT
6902
USA
Tel: +1 203 358 2132
Fax: +1 203 353 8699
Jean Wheaton Shaw, Director

Services/Products:
Market research agency

Member of:
DMA

THE M/A/R/C GROUP
7850 North Belt Line Road
Irving
TX
75063
USA
Jack Wolf, President

Services/Products:
Advertising Agency; Direct Response
Agency

Member of:
DMA

THE MARCOM CONSULTING GROUP
44 Rockaway Avenue
San Francisco
CA

94127–1030
USA
Tel: +1 415 661 4000
Fax: +1 415 759 1995
Thomas Downing, Consultant

Services/Products:
Marketing consultant

Member of:
DMA

THE MARKETING PLACE
A Direct Marketing Product Services
Group
12455 Branford Street
Ste 24
Arleta
CA
91331–3429
USA
Tel: 818 834 8500
Fax: +1 818 834 8511
Howard Oberstein, President

Services/Products:
Advertising Agency; Direct Response
Agency

Member of:
DMA

THE MARTIN AGENCY
One Shockoe Plaza
Richmond
VA
23219–4132
USA
Tel: 804 698 8957
Fax: +1 804 698 8201
Barbara Thornhill, EVP & CAO

Services/Products:
Advertising Agency; Direct Response
Agency

Member of:
DMA

THE MCNICHOLS GROUP, INC.
51 Sherwood Terrace
Ste L
Lake Bluff
IL
60044–2232
USA
Tel: 847 295 0300
Fax: +1 847 295 0334
John McNichols, President

Services/Products:
List services

Member of:
DMA

THE MONSTER BOARD
5 Clock Tower Place
Ste 500
Maynard
MA
1754
USA
Tel: 978 461 8000
Fax: +1 978 461 8100
Victoria L'Homme, Direct Mail
Manager

E-Services:
Website design

Member of:
DMA

THE NPD GROUP, INC.
900 West Shore Road
Port Washington
NY
11050–0402
USA
Tel: +1 516 625 0700
Fax: +1 516 625 2233
Richard Catrone, Dir., Panel
Department

Services/Products:
Market research agency

Member of:
DMA

THE PARABLE GROUP, INC.
815 Fiero Lane
San Luis Obispo
CA
93401–2202
USA
Tel: 805 543 2644
Fax: +1 805 543 2136
Jim Seybert, Vice President

Services/Products:
Advertising Agency; Direct Response
Agency

Member of:
DMA

THE PHELPS GROUP
901 Wilshire Boulevard
Santa Monica
CA
90401
USA
Tel: +1 310 752 4400
Fax: +1 310 752 4444
Scott Cohan, Direct Specialists

Services/Products:
Advertising Agency; Direct Response
Agency

Member of:
DMA

THE PINNACLE GROUP
1925 Vaughn Road
Ste 200
Kennesaw
GA
30144
USA
Tel: +1 770 422 8300
Fax: +1 770 422 2211
Barry Green, President

Services/Products:
Marketing consultant

Member of:
DMA

THE POLK COMPANY
26955 Northwestern Highway
Southfield
MI
48034–8455
USA
Tel: +1 248 728 7000
Fax: +1 248 728 6945
Stephen Polk, Chairman & CEO

Services/Products:
List services

Member of:
DMA

THE POWER LINE
1 Expressway Plaza
Ste 222
Roslyn Heights
NY
11577
USA
Tel: +1 516 625 1222
Fax: +1 516 625 1660
Peg Kuman, President

Services/Products:
Telemarketing agency

Member of:
DMA

THE PRODUCT LINE, INC.
2370 South Trenton Way
Denver
CO
80231–3844
USA
Tel: +1 303 671 8000
Fax: +1 303 696 7300
Richard Sims, President

Services/Products:
Telemarketing agency

Member of:
DMA

THE RIVER NORTH GROUP, INC.
432 North Clark Street
Ste 302
Chicago
IL
60610
USA
Tel: +1 312 595 9260
Fax: +1 312 595 9265
Steven Levin, VP, Business
   Development

Services/Products:
Marketing consultant

Member of:
DMA

THE SCHMIDT GROUP
International, Inc.
1535 Harvest Lane
Manasquan
NJ
8736
USA
Tel: +1 732 223 7109
Fax: +1 732 223 7931
Email: catalogprofit@the-schmidt-
   group.com
Web: www.the-schmidt-group.com

Services/Products:
Consultancy services; Catalogue
consultant

Member of:
DMA (US); Catalog Council

THE SERVICES GROUP
820 North Orleans Street
Chicago
IL
60610
USA
Tel: +1 312 944 5094
Fax: +1 312 944 6819
John Tosarello, President

Services/Products:
Marketing consultant

Member of:
DMA

THE SPECIALISTS, LTD.
1200 Harbor Boulevard
Weehawken
NJ
7087
USA
Tel: +1 201 865 5800
Fax: +1 201 867 2450
Bill Rella, President

Services/Products:
List services

Member of:
DMA

THE STAR GROUP
Cherry Tree Corporate Center
Rte 38
Cherry Hill
NJ
8002
USA
Tel: +1 609 488 5500
Fax: +1 609 488 1180
Angela DiBartolo, Managing Partner

Services/Products:
Advertising Agency; Direct Response
Agency

Member of:
DMA

THE TELEMARKETING COMPANY
7900 North Milwaukee Avenue
Ste 234
Niles
IL
60714
USA
Tel: +1 800 777 6348
Fax: +1 847 635 8738
Mary Shanley, President

Services/Products:
Telemarketing agency

Member of:
DMA

THE VERDI GROUP, INC.
400 Andrews Street
Rochester
NY
14604
USA
Tel: +1 716 325 6304
Fax: +1 716 325 5571
Robert Green, President

Services/Products:
Marketing consultant

Member of:
DMA

THE ZIMMERMANN AGENCY INC.
4A Roads End
Brookville
NY
11545–3102
USA
Tel: +1 516 626 5555
Fax: +1 516 626 5567
Caroline Zimmermann, Pres. & Chief
   Creative Officer

Services/Products:
Advertising Agency; Direct Response
Agency

Member of:
DMA

THINK NEW IDEAS, INC.
45 West 36th Street
12th Fl
New York
NY
10018
USA
Tel: +1 212 629 6800
Fax: +1 212 629 6850
Susan Goodman, EVP, Mktg. &
  Business Dev.

Services/Products:
Marketing consultant

Member of:
DMA

THOMAS & PERKINS
1451 Larimer Square
Ste 300
Denver
CO
80202
USA
Tel: +1 303 573 4911
Fax: +1 303 573 6472
Lora Petcoff, VP, Direct Marketing

Services/Products:
Advertising Agency; Direct Response
Agency

Member of:
DMA

THOMPSON & PRICE
50 Peabody Place
3rd Fl
Memphis
TN
38103
USA
Tel: 901 527 8000
Fax: +1 901 527 3697
M.S.Price, President

Services/Products:
Advertising Agency; Direct Response
Agency

Member of:
DMA

THORN ASSOCIATES
121 Bouton Road
South Salem
NY
10590
USA

Tel: 914 763 8756
Fax: +1 914 763 8756
Christine Thorn, President

Services/Products:
Telemarketing agency

Member of:
DMA

TICKETMASTER DIRECT
555 West 57th Street
New York
NY
10019
USA
Tel: +1 212 713 6000
Fax: +1 212 713 6366
John Ruscin, President & COO

Services/Products:
Telemarketing agency

Member of:
DMA

TIDS, INC.
500 Post Road East
Westport
CT
6880
USA
Tel: +1 203 226 2300
Fax: +1 203 226 5292
Ian Bass, President & CEO

Services/Products:
List services

Member of:
DMA

TIERNEY & PARTNERS
200 South Broad Street
Philadelphia
PA
19102
USA
Tel: +1 215 790 4100
Fax: +1 215 790 4363
Diane Rodwell, SVP & Management
  Director

Services/Products:
Advertising Agency; Direct Response
Agency

Member of:
DMA

**TIMBERLINE TECHNOLOGY
  GROUP LLC**
21641 N.W. Dairy Creek Road
Mountaindale
OR
97113
USA
Tel: +1 503 647 5627

Fax: +1 503 647 9958
Douglas Spink, Partner, Strategy

Services/Products:
Database services

Member of:
DMA

**TIMES DIRECT MARKETING,
  INC.**
501 Folson Street
Ste 400
San Francisco
CA
94105–3111
USA
Tel: +1 415 247 2880
Fax: +1 415 247 2884
Chris Peterson, Director

Services/Products:
List services

Member of:
DMA

TJS PRINTNET
20 Boone Street
Yonkers
NY
10704
USA
Tel: 914 968 2455
Fax: +1 914 476 6195
Theresa Smith, President

Services/Products:
Marketing consultant

Member of:
DMA

TLP DIRECT
100 Crescent Court
Dallas
TX
75201
USA
Tel: +1 214 855 2424
Fax: +1 214 855 2425
Danny Snyder, SVP & Executive
  Creative Dir.

Services/Products:
Advertising Agency; Direct Response
Agency

Member of:
DMA

TMA INC.
1907 Dunbarton Drive
Ste D
Jackson
MS
39216
USA

Tel: +1 601 713 2020
Fax: +1 601 713 2022
Todd Sandridge, Vice President

Services/Products:
Advertising Agency; Direct Response Agency

Member of:
DMA

TMP WORLDWIDE
600 International Drive
Mount Olive
NJ
7828
USA
Tel: +1 973 347 9400
Fax: +1 973 347 8773
Email: dcollins@tmpwdirect.com
Web: www.tmpwdirect.com
Daniel Collins, VP, Sales & Marketing

Services/Products:
Call centre services/systems; Database services; Fulfilment and sampling house; Lettershop; Response analysis bureau; Service bureau

E-Services:
Online/e-marketing agency

Member of:
DMA (US); SOCAP; HMCC

TNT
200 Garden City Plaza
4th Fl
Garden City
NY
11530
USA
Tel: +1 516 535 5800
Fax: +1 516 535 5880
John Costanzo, President

Services/Products:
Private delivery services

Member of:
DMA

TNT MAILFAST/INTERPOST
200 Garden City Plaza
Ste 400
Garden City
NY
11530–3301
USA
Tel: +1 516 535 1000
Ingrid Werner, Marketing Director

Services/Products:
Private delivery services

Member of:
DMA

TODD TRAVEL PROMOTIONS
22 Research Way
East Setauket
NY
11733
USA
Tel: +1 516 689 2980
Fax: +1 516 689 2988
Douglas Todd, President

Services/Products:
Advertising Agency; Direct Response Agency

Member of:
DMA

TOLLIVER, INC.
123 East 54th Street
Ste 5E
New York
NY
10022
USA
Tel: +1 212 758 7344
Fax: +1 212 750 8617
Suzanne Taliaferro, President

Services/Products:
Design/graphics/clip art supplier; Consultancy services

Member of:
DMA

TOMARKIN/GREENAWALT, INC.
24 Lewis Avenue
Hartsdale
NY
10530
USA
Tel: 914 683 8833
Fax: +1 914 288 9072
Peggy Greenawalt, President & Creative Director

Services/Products:
Design/graphics/clip art supplier; Consultancy services

Member of:
DMA

TONY MURRAY & ASSOCIATES
9663C Main Street
Fairfax
VA
22032
USA
Tel: +1 703 425 5356
Fax: +1 703 425 4537
Anthony Murray, President

Services/Products:
List services

Member of:
DMA

TOTAL FULFILLMENT SERVICE LLC/TFS LIMITED
25 Ford Road
Westport
CT
6880
USA
Tel: +1 203 454 9552
Fax: +1 203 454 8827
Robert Mandel, Director

Services/Products:
Fulfilment and sampling house

Member of:
DMA

TOTAL RESPONSE INC.
5804 Churchman By-Pass
Indianapolis
IN
46203–6109
USA
Tel: +1 317 781 4600
Fax: +1 317 781 4609
George Steinbrenner, VP & Group Director

Services/Products:
Fulfilment and sampling house

Member of:
DMA

TOTAL TACTIX INC.
9306 Amsden Way
Eden Praire
MN
55347
USA
Mark Keefe, President

Services/Products:
List services

Member of:
DMA

TOUCHSTAR MEDIA
2230 Corporate Circle
Ste 220
Henderson
NV
89014
USA
Tel: +1 800 459 8858
Fax: +1 702 990 9000
Steven Lebow, Chief Executive Officer

Services/Products:
Design/graphics/clip art supplier; Consultancy services

Member of:
DMA

TPC
174 Middlesex Turnpike
Burlington
MA
01803–4467
USA
Tel: +1 781 270 5100
Fax: +1 781 221 0738
William Davis, Chief Executive Officer

Services/Products:
Advertising Agency; Direct Response
Agency

Member of:
DMA

TRACY-LOCKE ADVERTISING
216 16th Street Mall
Denver
CO
80202
USA
Tel: +1 303 892 4500
Danny Snyder, SVP & Executive
   Creative Dir.

Services/Products:
Advertising Agency; Direct Response
Agency

Member of:
DMA

TRANS UNION CORPORATION
555 West Adams Street
Chicago
IL
60661
USA
Tel: +1 312 466 7815
Fax: +1 312 466 7991
Jay Frank, Senior Vice President

Services/Products:
List services

Member of:
DMA

TRANSCOM
11611 North Meridian Street
Ste 800
Carmel
IN
46032
USA
Tel: +1 317 571 3600
Fax: +1 317 571 3685
Tim Searcy, VP, Sales & Marketing

Services/Products:
Telemarketing agency

Member of:
DMA

TRANSITIONS OPTICAL, INC.
9251 Belcher Road
P.O. Box 700
Pinellas Park
FL
33780–0700
USA
Tel: 813 545 0400
Fax: +1 813 545 7151
N. Lillian Golgano, Database
   Marketing Coordinator

Services/Products:
List services

Member of:
DMA

TRANSKRIT CORPORATION
1825 Blue Hill Circle, N.E.
Roanoke
VA
24012–8607
USA
Tel: +1 540 853 8000
Anthony Catalano, CFO, Direct Mail
   Business Unit

Services/Products:
Lettershop; Mailing/Faxing services

Member of:
DMA

TRANSLATIONS UNLIMITED
67–35 Yellowstone Boulevard
Apt 3S
Forest Hills
NY
11375–2669
USA
Tel: +1 718 575 1047
Fax: +1 718 575 8157
Marina Karmalsky, Director & Owner

Services/Products:
Design/graphics/clip art supplier;
Consultancy services

Member of:
DMA

TRANSO ENVELOPE COMPANY
1900 North Austin Avenue
Chicago
IL
60639–5001
USA
Tel: +1 77 3 385 9200
Fax: +1 773 804 3294
Robert Blanke, President & CEO

Services/Products:
Labelling/envelope services

Member of:
DMA

TRASE MILLER
17 West 642 Butterfield Road
Oakbrook Terrance
IL
60181
USA
Tel: +1 630 629 4172
Fax: +1 630 629 4456
James Quinn, VP, Sales & Marketing

Services/Products:
Telemarketing agency

Member of:
DMA

TRI-STATE ENVELOPE CORP.
20th & Market Streets
Ashland
PA
17921
USA
Tel: +1 717 875 0433
Fax: +1 717 875 0125
Joel Orgler, President

Services/Products:
Labelling/envelope services

Member of:
DMA

TRIAD, INC.
14 E. Sir Francis Drake Blvd
Suite B
Larkspur
CA
94939–1702
USA
Tel: +1 781 821 2800
Fax: +1 781 821 2866
Web: www.triadinc.com
Fred Barson, COOO

Services/Products:
Advertising Agency; Consultancy
services; Design/graphics/clip art
supplier; Interactive media

E-Services:
E-Marketing consultant; Website
design

Member of:
DMA (US)

TRIAD, INC.
14 E. Sir Francis Drake Blvd.
Ste B
Larkspur
CA
94939–1702
USA
Tel: +1 415 925 3300
Fax: +1 415 925 3330
Michael Hinshaw, President

Services/Products:
Advertising Agency; Direct Response
Agency

Member of:
DMA

**TRIANGLE MARKETING
SERVICES, INC.**
80 8th Avenue Suite 305
Ste 305
New York
NY
10011
USA
Tel: +1 212 242 4040
Fax: +1 212 242 1344
John Knoebel, President

Services/Products:
List services

Member of:
DMA

TRIPAR INTERNATIONAL, INC.
20 Presidential Drive
Roselle
IL
60172–3913
USA
Tel: +1 630 980 5100
Fax: +1 630 980 9417
Marta Duffy, Vice President,
Operations

Services/Products:
Fulfilment and sampling house

Member of:
DMA

**TRIPLEX DIRECT MARKETING
CORP.**
20 Leveroni Court
P.O. Box 1800
Novato
CA
94949–1800
USA
Tel: +1 415 382 7000
Fax: +1 415 382 7161
Sheila Martin, President

Services/Products:
List services

Member of:
DMA

TRUE NORTH ADVERTISING
441 Lexington Avenue
New York
NY
10017
USA
Tel: +1 212 557 4202

Fax: +1 212 557 4204
Steve Fuchs, Exec. Dir., Account
Services

Services/Products:
Advertising Agency; Direct Response
Agency

Member of:
DMA

**TSP - TELESERVICES
PARTNERS**
14707 California Street
Ste 14
Omaha
NE
68154
USA
Tel: +1 402 445 4100
Fax: +1 402 445 9186
Brent Welch, President

Services/Products:
Marketing consultant

Member of:
DMA

**TYLIE JONES & ASSOCIATES
INC.**
3519 West Pacific Avenue
Burbank
CA
91505
USA
Tel: 818 955 7600
Fax: +1 818 955 8542
Tylie Jones, President

Services/Products:
Fulfilment and sampling house

Member of:
DMA

U. S. MONITOR
86 Maple Avenue
New City
NY
10956–5036
USA
Tel: 914 634 1331
Fax: +1 914 634 9618
Martin Sass, Vice President

Services/Products:
Lettershop; Mailing/Faxing services

Member of:
DMA

U.S. DIRECT
P. O. Box 2043
Coppell
TX
75019
USA

Tel: 972 462 8818
Fax: +1 972 304 4575
Mark Shriver, President

Services/Products:
Marketing consultant

Member of:
DMA

U.S.A. DIRECT, INC.
2901 Blackbridge Road
York
PA
17402
USA
Tel: +1 717 852 1000
Fax: +1 717 852 1030
Richard Osborne, Chief Executive
Officer

Services/Products:
Lettershop; Mailing/Faxing services

Member of:
DMA

UNI-MAIL LIST CORPORATION
352 Park Avenue South
New York
NY
10010–1709
USA
Tel: +1 212 679 7000
Fax: +1 212 679 7590
Michael Bryant, President

Services/Products:
List services

Member of:
DMA

**UNIBASE DIRECT/DATA
SERVICES DIRECT**
3 Century Drive
3rd Fl
Parsippany
NJ
07054–4610
USA
Tel: 973 285 1700
Fax: +1 973 285 9246
Russell Thomas, Director, Sales &
Marketing

Services/Products:
Telemarketing agency

Member of:
DMA

**UNITED AMERICA
ADVERTISING**
1018 West Cherry Avenue
Ste 300
Enid
OK

73703
USA
Tel: 972 991 3370
Fax: +1 972 991 2724
Tim Morgan, President

Services/Products:
Telemarketing agency

Member of:
DMA

UNITED MARKETING GROUP INC.
1280 Iroquois Drive
Ste 206
Naperville
IL
60563
USA
Tel: +1 630 961 1300
Fax: +1 630 961 1495
William Hoaglund, President

Services/Products:
List services

Member of:
DMA

UNITED STATES POSTAL SERVICE
475 L'Enfant Plaza, 370 IBU
Washington
DC
20260–6500
USA
Tel: +1 202 268 2274
Fax: +1 202 314 7193
John C Manzolillo, Manager, Overseas
   Business Development

Services/Products:
Mailing/Faxing services

Member of:
FEDMA

UNITED TELEMARKETING CORP.
United Tele-Solutions
121 Hampton Avenue
Kingstree
SC
29556
USA
Tel: 803 354 7711
Fax: +1 803 354 9202
Nancy Forte, Director, Sales &
   Marketing

Services/Products:
Telemarketing agency

Member of:
DMA

UNITEL CORPORATION
8300 Greensboro Drive
Ste 600
McLean
VA
22102
USA
Tel: +1 800 425 0000
Fax: +1 703 917 1556
S. Tien Wong, Chief Executive Officer

Services/Products:
Telemarketing agency

Member of:
DMA

UPSHOT
P. O. Box 390460
Mt. View
CA
94039
USA
Tel: +1 650 426 2200
Fax: +1 650 965 1996
Lissa Menge, Web Marketing Manager

E-Services:
Website design

Member of:
DMA

URBAN SCIENCE APPLICATIONS, INC.
200 Renaissance Center
19th Fl
Detroit
MI
48243
USA
Tel: +1 313 259 9900
Fax: +1 313 259 1362
Mitchell Phillips, Senior Manager

Services/Products:
Marketing consultant

Member of:
DMA

USCS/IBS
5220 Robert J. Mathews Parkway
El Dorado Hill
CA
95762–5712
USA
Tel: 916 939 4609
Fax: +1 916 939 4561
Tom Roberts, Vice President,
   Marketing

Services/Products:
List services

Member of:
DMA

USPS/NY METRO AREA SALES OFFICE
142–02 20th Avenue
Flushing
NY
11351–0001
USA
Tel: +1 718 321 5845
Fax: +1 718 463 8391
Vito Fortuna, National Account
   Manager

Services/Products:
Private delivery services

Member of:
DMA

USY CONSULTING
710 Cathy Lane
Mount Prospect
IL
60056
USA
Tel: 847 259 6140
Fax: +1 847 259 6180
Reizo Yoshida, President

Services/Products:
Marketing consultant

Member of:
DMA

VALERIE DAVIS & ASSOCIATES
500 North Commerical Street
Manchester
NH
3101
USA
Tel: +1 603 624 9220
Fax: +1 603 624 9229
Valerie Davis, President

Services/Products:
List services

Member of:
DMA

VANGUARD CELLULAR SYSTEMS
2002 Pisgah Church Road
Ste 300
Greensboro
NC
27455
USA
Tel: 910 282 3690
Fax: +1 910 545 2265
Mark Long, Director, Marketing
   Services

Services/Products:
Telemarketing agency

Member of:
DMA

VARIED ASSOCIATES
One Poetry Plaza
Owings Mills
MD
21117
USA
Tel: +1 410 356 1122
Fax: +1 410 356 8990
Howard Friedman, President

Services/Products:
Advertising Agency; Direct Response
Agency

Member of:
DMA

VENTURA ASSOCIATES, INC.
1040 Avenue of the Americas
20th Fl
New York
NY
10018
USA
Tel: +1 212 302 8277
Fax: +1 212 +1 302 2587
Marla Altberg, SVP, Marketing

Services/Products:
Sales promotion agency

Member of:
DMA

**VENTURE COMMUNICATIONS
INTERNATIONAL, INC.**
60 Madison Avenue
3rd Fl
New York
NY
10010
USA
Tel: +1 212 684 4800
Fax: +1 212 545 1680
Bette Anne Keane, Vice President

Services/Products:
List services

Member of:
DMA

**VERSATILE CARD
TECHNOLOGY, INC (VCT)**
5200 Thatcher Road
Downers Grove
IL
60515
USA
Tel: +1 630 852 5600
Fax: +1 630 852 5817
Email: cathy@versacard.com
Web: www.versacard.com
Cathy Klebokski, Marketing Manager

Services/Products:
Print services

Member of:
FEDMA; DMA (US)

VERTICAL MARKETING, INC.
2323 South Troy Street
Ste 3–108
Aurora
CO
80014
USA
Tel: +1 303 755 4800
Harold Bingaman, President

Services/Products:
Telemarketing agency

Member of:
DMA

VESTCOM MID-ATLANTIC
P. O. Box 5000
Dover
NJ
07802–5000
USA
Tel: 973 328 2800
Fax: +1 973 361 3121
Gary Marcello, Chairman of the Board

Services/Products:
Lettershop; Mailing/Faxing services

Member of:
DMA

**VIDAL, REYNARDUS, MOYA,
INC.**
228 East 45th Street
11th Fl
New York
NY
10017
USA
Tel: +1 212 867 5185
Fax: +1 212 661 7650
Federico Mejer

Services/Products:
Advertising Agency; Direct Response
Agency

Member of:
DMA

**VISION INTEGRATED
MARKETING**
501 Second Street
Ste 707
San Francisco
CA
94107
USA
Tel: +1 415 974 1700
Fax: +1 415 974 1701
Brock Greene, Director, Client
    Services

Services/Products:
Advertising Agency; Direct Response
Agency

Member of:
DMA

VISION MARKETING INC.
429 Sylvan Avenue
Englwood Clfs
NJ
7632
USA
Tel: +1 201 816 1560
Fax: +1 201 816 1610
Michael Young, President

Services/Products:
List services

Member of:
DMA

**VOLT DIRECT MARKETING,
    LTD.**
One Sentry Parkway
Blue Bell
PA
19422
USA
Tel: +1 610 825 7720
Fax: +1 610 941 6874
Sal Caimano, Vice President

Services/Products:
Telemarketing agency

Member of:
DMA

**W-R MARKETING RESOURCES
    INC.**
7810 Millicent Circle
Shreveport
LA
71105–5608
USA
Tel: +1 318 798 3039
Fax: +1 318 798 8105
Richard Wadsack, Partner

Services/Products:
Marketing consultant

Member of:
DMA

W. B. DONER DIRECT
25900 North Western Highway
Southfield
MI
48075
USA
Tel: +1 313 354 9700
Judy Carpenito, Group Account
    Director

Services/Products:
Advertising Agency; Direct Response
Agency

Member of:
DMA

W.I. MAIL MARKETING
470 Main Street
Ste 317
Ridgefield
CT
6877
USA
Tel: +1 203 438 6822
Fax: +1 203 438 7756
William Iller, President

Services/Products:
List services

Member of:
DMA

W.J. TOTTEN & ASSOCIATES,
  LLC
6 High Fields Drive
Danbury
CT
6811
USA
Tel: +1 203 798 9924
William Totten, President

Services/Products:
Marketing consultant

Member of:
DMA

W3DM
2800 Hoover Road
Ste 2
Stevens Point
WI
54481
USA
Tel: +1 715 341 4554
Sarah Straub, President

Services/Products:
Advertising Agency; Direct Response
Agency

Member of:
DMA

WALT KLEIN & ASSOCIATES,
  INC.
725 Highland Oaks Drive
Ste 200
Winston-Salem
NC
27103
USA
Tel: +1 336 659 6800

Fax: +1 336 659 6802
Walt Klein, Chief Executive Oficer

Services/Products:
Advertising Agency; Direct Response
Agency

Member of:
DMA

WALTER KARL, INC.
One American Lane
Greenwich
CT
6831
USA
Tel: +1 203 552 6700
Fax: +1 203 552 6799
Sheldon Zaslansky, President

Services/Products:
List services

Member of:
DMA

WALTER LATHAM
1400 West 16th Street
Ste 300
Oak Brook
IL
60523
USA
Tel: +1 630 573 8787
Fax: +1 630 573 0210
Robert Soljacich, President & CEO

Services/Products:
Advertising Agency; Direct Response
Agency

Member of:
DMA

WARM THOUGHT
  COMMUNICATION, INC.
300 Harmon Meadow Boulevard
Secaucus
NJ
7094
USA
Tel: +1 201 330 9276
Fax: +1 201 223 1555
Richard Goldberg, President

Services/Products:
Advertising Agency; Direct Response
Agency

Member of:
DMA

WARRANTECH DIRECT INC.
150 West Park Way
Ste 200
Euless
TX
76040–4152

USA
Tel: 817 354 4440
Fax: +1 817 354 6940
Randall San Antonio, President &
  General Manager

Services/Products:
Telemarketing agency

Member of:
DMA

WATSON COMMUNICATION
3 Market Square
Portsmouth
NH
03801–4063
USA
Tel: +1 603 430 7999
Fax: +1 603 430 9211
Pamela Watson, President

Services/Products:
Advertising Agency; Direct Response
Agency

Member of:
DMA

WATSON/MAIL
  COMMUNICATIONS, INC.
2401 Revere Beach Parkway
Everett
MA
2149
USA
Tel: +1 617 389 5350
Fax: +1 617 389 0237
Bob Clarkson, Vice President

Services/Products:
List services

Member of:
DMA

WEB DIRECT MARKETING
401 South Milwaukee Avenue
Wheeling
IL
60090
USA
Tel: 847 459 0800
Fax: +1 847 459 7378
Vernon Carson, President

Services/Products:
Marketing consultant

Member of:
DMA

WEBPRIME
1167 Route 52
Fishkill
NY
12524–1616
USA

Tel: 914 896 2787
Fax: +1 914 896 2789
Dwight Lodge, President & CEO

Member of:
DMA

WEBTREND DIRECT
1811 Riverview Drive
San Bernardino
CA
92408
USA
Tel: 909 799 5435
Fax: +1 909 799 5449
Robert Pollard, President

Services/Products:
Lettershop; Mailing/Faxing services

Member of:
DMA

**WESLEY R. WEBER &
ASSOCIATES, INC.**
901 Messner Road
Chester Springs
PA
19425
USA
Tel: +1 610 827 7202
Fax: +1 610 827 7249
Email: wesweber@aol.com
Wesley Weber, Principal

Services/Products:
Consultancy services

E-Services:
E-Marketing consultant

Member of:
DMA (US)

**WEST COAST MAILING &
DISTRIBUTION**
12251 Iavellie Way
Poway
CA
92064
USA
Tel: +1 619 492 1123
Fax: +1 619 492 1277
Parvin Saleni, President

Services/Products:
Lettershop; Mailing/Faxing services

Member of:
DMA

WEST INDIES & GREY
P. O. Box 366518
San Juan
PR
00936–6518
USA
Tel: 809 723 1000

Fax: +1 809 723 4536
George Wiedemann, Chairman &
CEO, Grey DM Group

Services/Products:
Advertising Agency; Direct Response
Agency

Member of:
DMA

**WEST INTERACTIVE
CORPORATION**
11808 Miracle Hills Avenue
Omaha
NE
68154
USA
Tel: +1 800 841 9000
Fax: +1 402 963 1603
Deanna Desmet, Vice President,
Marketing

Services/Products:
Telemarketing agency

Member of:
DMA

**WESTERN UNION FINANCIAL
SERVICES INC.**
6200 South Quebec Street
Ste 310AD
Englewood
CO
80111
USA
Tel: +1 303 488 8000
Fax: +1 303 889 6099
Christopher Avery, Director, Domestic
Marketing

Services/Products:
Lettershop; Mailing/Faxing services

Member of:
DMA

**WESTVACO ENVELOPE
DIVISION**
2001 Roosevelt Avenue
Springfield
MA
01104–9691
USA
Tel: +1 413 736 7211
Fax: +1 413 787 9625
Richard Smith, VP & Division
Manager

Services/Products:
Labelling/envelope services

Member of:
DMA (US); FEDMA

WHAT A CONCEPT!
1522 San Ignacio Avenue
Coral Gables
FL
33146
USA
Tel: +1 305 663 1083
Fax: +1 305 665 0306
Karen Pfeffer, President

Services/Products:
Advertising Agency; Direct Response
Agency

Member of:
DMA

WHITE SPACE, INC.
1250 North Dearborn
Ste 22-E
Chicago
IL
60610
USA
Tel: +1 312 951 2940
Fax: +1 312 944 4192
Jennifer MacLean, President

Services/Products:
Database services

Member of:
DMA

**WICKERSHAM HUNT
SCHWANTNER**
420 Boylston Street
Boston
MA
2116
USA
Tel: +1 617 424 0300
Fax: +1 617 424 0399
Lysle Wickersham, Chairman & CCO

Services/Products:
Advertising Agency; Direct Response
Agency

Member of:
DMA

WILCOX & ASSOCIATES
420 Lexington Avenue
New York
NY
10170
USA
Tel: +1 212 551 2944
Fax: +1 212 551 2901
Thomas McClure, Chairman & CEO

Services/Products:
Advertising Agency; Direct Response
Agency

Member of:
DMA

WILLIAMS WORLDWIDE
3130 Wilshire Boulevard
Santa Monica
CA
90403
USA
Tel: +1 310 828 8600
Fax: +1 310 828 8684
Gerald Bagg, SVP, Acct. Management
& Mktg.

Services/Products:
Advertising Agency; Direct Response
Agency

Member of:
DMA

WILLIAMSON CONSULTING, INC.
25 Farrar Road
Lincoln
MA
1773
USA
Tel: +1 781 259 0091
Fax: +1 781 259 3447
Jim Williamson, President

Services/Products:
Marketing consultant

Member of:
DMA

WILSON & ELLIS CONSULTING
500 Debra Drive, N.E.
Marietta
GA
30066
USA
Tel: +1 770 421 9403
Fax: +1 770 421 0297
Debra Ellis, Principal

Services/Products:
Marketing consultant

Member of:
DMA

WM. STROH, INC.
568–570 54th Street
West New York
NJ
7093
USA
Tel: +1 201 864 4800
Fax: +1 201 864 2956
William Stroh, President

Services/Products:
List services

Member of:
DMA

WOL DIRECT
925 Oak Street
Scranton
PA
18515
USA
Tel: +1 717 347 1625
Fax: +1 717 343 8172
David Beach, President

Services/Products:
Advertising Agency; Direct Response
Agency

Member of:
DMA

WOLF GROUP DIRECT
40 Fountain Plaza
Buffalo
NY
14202
USA
Tel: +1 716 853 1200
Fax: +1 716 853 1214
Janet Stanek, Vice President &
Manager

Services/Products:
Advertising Agency; Direct Response
Agency

Member of:
DMA

WONG WONG BOYACK
100 California
9th Floor
San Francisco
CA
94111
USA
Tel: +1 415 394 6636
Fax: +1 415 394 6633
Email: pwong@wongwong.com
Web: www.wongwongboyack.com
Penelope Wong, President & CEO

Services/Products:
Advertising Agency; Consultancy
services; Copy adaptation; Design/
graphics/clip art supplier; Direct
marketing agency; Asian advertising
and direct marketing

E-Services:
Online/e-marketing agency

Member of:
DMA

WORCESTER ENVELOPE COMPANY
P. O. Box 406
Auburn
MA
01501–0406

USA
Tel: +1 800 343 1398
Fax: +1 508 832 3796
James Dufresne, Sales Manager

Services/Products:
Labelling/envelope services

Member of:
DMA

WORDS AT WORK
126 North Third Street
Ste 309
Minneapolis
MN
55401–1675
USA
Tel: +1 612 334 5960
Fax: +1 612 334 3170
Laurie Kumerow, Sr. Writer &
Account Executive

Services/Products:
Marketing consultant

Member of:
DMA

WORLD ACCESS SERVICE CORPORATION
420 Lexington Avenue
Ste 1422
New York
NY
10170
USA
Tel: +1 212 499 9200
Fax: +1 212 499 9211
W. Gregory Kerwick, Senior Vice
President

Services/Products:
Telemarketing agency

Member of:
DMA

WORLD INNOVATORS, INC.
72 Park Street
New Canaan
CT
6840
USA
Tel: +1 203 966 0374
Fax: +1 203 966 0926
Email:
apeterson@WorldInnovators.com
Web: www.WorldInnovators.com
Anne M. Peterson, President

Services/Products:
Database services; Lettershop; List
services

E-Services:
Email list provider

Member of:
DMA (US); FEDMA; International
List Council

**WORLD MARKETING
 INTEGRATED SOLUTIONS
 INC.**
7420 Country Line Road
Ste 8
Burr Ridge
IL
60521
USA
Tel: +1 630 734 9900
Fax: +1 630 734 9942
Cyndi Greenglass, President

Services/Products:
Database services

Member of:
DMA

WORLDATA, INC.
3000 North Military Trail
Boca Raton
FL
33431–6375
USA
Tel: +1 561 393 8200
Fax: +1 561 368 8345
Roy Schwedelson, CEO

Services/Products:
List services

Member of:
DMA

**WORLDNOW ONLINE
 NETWORK**
488 East Winchester Street
Salt Lake City
UT
84107–7950
USA
Tel: 801 268 2202
Fax: +1 801 268 2292
Fred Lederman, President & CEO

Services/Products:
Lettershop; Mailing/Faxing services

Member of:
DMA

WORLDWIDE 1 ON 1
100 Bloomfield Hills Parkway
Bloomfield Hls
MI
48304
USA
Tel: +1 313 433 6000
Shel Green, VP & Service Line
 Manager Dir.

Services/Products:
Advertising Agency; Direct Response
Agency

Member of:
DMA

**WORLDWIDE TELCOM
 PARTNERS**
241 Danbury Road
Ste 2800
Wilton
CT
6897
USA
Tel: +1 203 834 6900
Dennis Eastham, President

Services/Products:
Advertising Agency; Direct Response
Agency

Member of:
DMA

WOW! MARKETING, INC.
P. O. Box 25520
Ste 201
Colorado Spgs
CO
80936
USA
Tel: +1 719 265 1000
Fax: +1 719 265 1001
Henry Tippie, President

Services/Products:
Marketing consultant

Member of:
DMA

WUNDERMAN CATO JOHNSON
675 Avenue of the Americas
4th Fl
New York
NY
10010–5104
USA
Tel: +1 212 941 3000
Fax: +1 212 627 8521
John Bingle, CEO, Worldwide

Services/Products:
Advertising Agency; Direct Response
Agency

Member of:
DMA

**WUNDERMAN, SADH &
 ASSOCIATES LLC**
350 Theodore Fremd Avenue
Ste 300
Rye
NY
10580

USA
Tel: 914 925 3414
Fax: +1 914 925 3434
Lynn Wunderman, President

Services/Products:
Marketing consultant

Member of:
DMA

WWAV RAPP COLLINS GROUF
251 Park Street
4th Fl
Montclair
NJ
7043
USA
Tel: 973 746 1497
Fax: +1 973 744 3290
G. Steven Dapper, Chairman & CE(

Services/Products:
Advertising Agency; Direct Response
Agency

Member of:
DMA

**WYER CREATIVE
 COMMUNICATIONS**
One Vantage Way
Ste E-100
Nashville
TN
37228–1515
USA
Tel: +1 615 242 9800
Fax: +1 615 242 7711
Steven Wyer, President

Services/Products:
Telemarketing agency

Member of:
DMA

WYSE DIRECT
25 Prospect Avenue West
Cleveland
OH
44115
USA
Tel: +1 216 696 2427
Fax: +1 216 736 4440
David Schiever, President

Services/Products:
Advertising Agency; Direct Response
Agency

Member of:
DMA

YANKELOVICH PARTNERS
101 Merritt 7 Corporate Park
Norwalk
CT

6851
USA
Tel: +1 203 846 0100
Fax: +1 203 845 8200
Maribeth Becker, Associate Director

Services/Products:
Market research agency

Member of:
DMA

YATES ADVERTISING
188 The Embarcadero
Ste 470
San Francisco
CA
94105
USA
Tel: +1 415 356 9000
Fax: +1 415 356 9010
Susan Yates, President

Services/Products:
Advertising Agency; Direct Response
Agency

Member of:
DMA

YECK BROTHERS GROUP
2222 Arbor Boulevard
Dayton
OH
45439
USA
Tel: 937 294 4000
Fax: +1 937 294 6985
John Yeck, Partner

Services/Products:
Advertising Agency; Direct Response
Agency

Member of:
DMA

YOUNG & RUBICAM
285 Madison Avenue
4th Fl
New York
NY
10016
USA
Tel: +1 212 210 5033
Fax: +1 212 490 9073
John Bingle, CEO, Worldwide

Services/Products:
Advertising Agency; Direct Response
Agency

Member of:
DMA

YOUNG AMERICA CORP.
1400 Madison Avenue E.
Mankato

MN
58002
USA
Tel: +1 507 386 4891
Fax: +1 507 388 4893
Charles Weil, President & CEO

Services/Products:
Fulfilment and sampling house

Member of:
DMA

**YOUNG AMERICA
CORPORATION**
717 Faxon Road
Young America
MN
55397–9481
USA
Tel: +1 612 467 1100
Fax: +1 612 467 3895
Charles Weil, President & CEO

Services/Products:
Fulfilment and sampling house

Member of:
DMA

ZELLER & LETICA, INC.
15 East 26th Street
(CN 5219)
New York
NY
10010
USA
Tel: +1 212 685 7512
Donn Rappaport, Chairman & CEO

Services/Products:
List services

Member of:
DMA

**ZIMMERMAN, LAURENT &
RICHARDSON**
303 Keo Way
Ste 100
Des Moines
IA
50309–1799
USA
Tel: +1 515 2+44 4456
Fax: +1 515 244 5749
Louie Laurent, President, Client
Services

Services/Products:
Advertising Agency; Direct Response
Agency

Member of:
DMA

ZIP SORT INC.
277 North 12th Avenue
Minneapolis
MN
55401–1021
USA
Tel: +1 612 341 2633
Fax: +1 612 341 0337
Tom Murray, Vice President

Services/Products:
Fulfilment and sampling house

Member of:
DMA

ZOETICS, INC.
599 Broadway
10th Fl
New York
NY
10012
USA
Tel: +1 212 941 8344
Fax: +1 212 941 8348
Joel Tucciarone, President

Services/Products:
Marketing consultant

Member of:
DMA

ZUBI ADVERTISING
3300 Ponce de Leon
Ponce de Leon
FL
33134
USA
Tel: +1 305 448 9824
Fax: +1 305 443 1573
Aida Pacheco, Account Executive

Services/Products:
Advertising Agency; Direct Response
Agency

Member of:
DMA

SERVICES/PRODUCT
LISTING

**50+ mature market specialised
marketing consultancy**
Medina Associates

Advertising Agency
360 Group
A. Eicoff & Company
Aberdeen Marketing Group, Inc.
Acorn Information Services, Inc.
ACS/TradeOne Marketing
Ad Placement Services

Adler, Boschetto, Peebles & Partners
Admark Group
Admerasia
AdSouth, Inc.
Advantage Plus Marketing Group
AGA
Alcott & Routon, Inc.
Allen & Gerritsen
Allstate International
Alternative Marketing Solutions (Ams, Inc.)
Ambrosi
American Direct Marketing Resources, Inc.
American Target Data
Amichetti, Lewis and Associates, Inc.
Ammirati Puris Lintas
AMS Response
Angeles Marketing Group
Applied Interactive Media, LLC
Archer/Malmo Direct
Arnold Direct
Arocom Direct
ASATSU/BBDO
Austin Knight Inc.
Ayer Deare & Partners
B.W.R.
Barkley Evergreen & Partners, Inc.
Barraclough Hall Woolston Gray
Barry Blau & Partners, Inc.
BBDO
BBDO Response
Beacon Group, Inc.
Bel-Aire Associates
Bennett Kuhn Varner, Inc.
Berenson, Isham & Partners, Inc.
BI Performance Services
Biggs/Gilmore Communications
Birkholm Direct
Blagman Media International
Blain, Olsen, White, Gurr Advertising
Blank & Associates
Blau Marketing Technologies
Blue Dolphin Communications
Bozell Direct
Brighton Agency
Bronner Slosberg Humphrey
Bruce W. Eberle & Associates, Inc.
Bullseye Database Marketing, Inc.
Burrell/DFA Advertising Inc.
Business Advertising Specialties Corp.
Business Direct Marketing Associates, Inc.
BWC Group
Byrne Advertising Copy/Consultancy
C-E Communications
Cadmus
Campbell Mithun Direct
Carl Bloom Associates, Inc.
Carlson Marketing Group
Carmichael Lynch
Catalyst Direct Inc.
CCMR Advertising & Marketing

Communications
Chiat/Day/Mojo Inc. Advertising
Chinnici Direct Inc.
Chiropractic Elite Organization, Inc.
Cimino Direct, Inc.
CKS Partners
CM Partners, Inc.
CME Library
CMF&Z Direct Marketing Group
CMF&Z/Y&R
Colangelo Marketing
Cole & Weber
Columbian Direct Marketing
Communications Plus, Inc.
Communicomp
Consumer Healthworks/Rapp
Cosgrove Associates
Cox Communications, Inc.
CPS Direct, Inc.
Cramer-Krasselt
Cranford Johnson Robinson Woods, Inc.
Creative Strategy, Inc.
Cunningham Direct, Inc.
Customer Development Corp.
D. L. Blair Inc.
D.M. Associates
d/a/p associates
Data Health
DCI Marketing
DDB NEEDHAM DIRECT
DDB Needham Worldwide
Dees Communications, Inc./Fuller Fund Raising Co.
Devon Direct
DFA Advertising Inc.
Dickinson Direct
DiMark Marketing
DiMassimo
Direct Ad-Vantage, Inc.
Direct Deutsch
Direct Impact
Direct Impact, Inc.
Direct Language Communications, Inc.
Direct Options
Direct Partners
Direct Resources International Interactive
Direct Results Group, Inc.
DIRECT SUCCESS Communications
Directech, Inc.
DM Group
DMTG, Inc.
DMW Worldwide
Doner Direct
Dot-Com DIRECT
DraftWorldwide
Duffey, Petrosky & Company
Duncan/Shannon
EAGLE DIRECT
eClass Direct
Editorial Perfil

Eisner & Associates Inc.
eMergingMedia, Inc.
Emmerling Post Advertising, Inc.
ERA
Eric Mower & Associates
ERS DIRECT MARKETING
EURO RSCG
Fallon McElligott
Farrar & Farrar
FCB (Foote, Cone & Belding) Latin America
FCB Direct Chicago
FCB Puerto Rico
Fine Light Inc.
Finerty & Wolfe Advertising, Inc.
FMG Marketing, Inc.
Fogarty Klein & Partners
Foote, Cone & Belding
Forecast Direct Marketing Group
Foreign Objects
FPS Marketing Communications
Frank W. Cawood & Associates, Inc.
Frequency Marketing, Inc.
Gerald Siegel & Associates, Inc.
Gianfagna Marketing & Communications, Inc.
Gilbert Whitney & Johns
Gillespie
Good Advertising
Graham Gregory Bozell, Inc.
Gramercy Group
Grapevine Marketing, Inc.
Graphic Arts & Production
Gray & Graham Marketing Group
Greenberg Consulting
Grey Direct
Group M Marketing, Inc.
Gruen + Sells Ltd.
GTE, The Focus Agency
Haynes & Partners Communication, Inc.
HB&G/ACSC
Heinrich Marketing, Inc.
Hemisphere Marketing Inc.
Hemmings IV Direct
Hemmings, Birkholm & Grizzard
Hershey Communications NY, Inc.
Hill Holliday
HispanAgencia
Hoffman York
Holland Mark Martin Edmund
Howard, Merrell & Partners,Inc
Huber Hoge and Sons Advertising, Inc.
Hudson Street Partners
Hunt Marketing Group
Huntsinger & Jeffer, Inc.
IBIS Communications, Inc.
ICON Digital Photography
Imagine Direct
IMC Direct
Indiana Design Consortium, Inc.
InfoWorks

528

Ingalls One To One Marketing
Integrated Marketing, Inc.
Interactive Marketing Group, Inc.
Interactive Resources, Inc.
Interval International
Ira Thomas Associates
Irma S. Mann, Strategic Marketing, Inc.
Ivie & Associates, Inc.
J. Schmid & Assoc. Inc.
J. Walter Thompson Direct
Jacobs & Clevenger, Inc.
JC Penny Direct Marketing Services
Jeffery Advertising Agency
Jordan, McGrath, Case & Taylor/ Direct
Just Partners
JWP Group
JWT Specialized Communications
Kang & Lee Advertising
Karlin/Pimsler, Inc.
Kern Direct
Ketchum Communications
Kirshenbaum Bond & Partners
Klemtner Advertising
Kovel Kresser & Partners
Kuhn & Wittenborn Advertising
La Agencia de Orci & Asociados
LA&ATINO
Lareau & Associates
Lawrence Butner Advertising, Inc.
LCG Latino
LCS Direct Mail Advertising & Printing
Leo Burnett U.S.A.
Levenson Public Relations
Lewis Advertising, Inc.
Lewis Advertising/Birmingham
Lieber, Levett, Koenig, Farese, Babcock, Inc.
Liggett-Stashower Direct
Lissen Audio Company
LKH&S
Long Haymes Carr
Lord Sullivan Yoder
Lortz Direct Marketing Inc.
Lowe Direct
Lowe Fox Pavlika
Mailcom plc
Mailing Concept, Inc.
Make It So, Inc.
Malcolm Decker Associates Inc.
Manus Direct
Manus Direct Marketing
Maris, West & Baker
Maritz Performance Improvement Company
Marke Communications, Inc.
Market Place Priut
Marketing Alternatives, Inc.
Marketing Resources of New York, Inc.
Marquardt & Roche/Meditz & Hackett
Martin Direct

Mason & Geller Direct, LLC
MatchLogic, Inc.
Maverick Marketing Group, Inc.
Maxwell Sroge Company, Inc.
MC Direct
McCann Relationship Marketing
Membership Cards Only
Meridian Advertising
Michael Edwards Direct, Inc.
Milici Valenti Ng Pack
Miller Meester Advertising
Miller/Huber Relationship Marketing
Millernia Direct, Inc.
Mitchell & Resnikoff
Modem Media.Poppe Tyson
Music Marketing Network
Music Marketing Network
National Direct Corporation
NCI Direct
NETWORKDIRECT, INC.
NKH&W Inc.
Nordis Marketing & Mailing
North American Communications
North Castle Direct
Northlich Stolley LaWarre
NS & G Direct Marketing
O'Connell Meier
O'Connor Kenney Partners, Inc.
OgilvyOne Worldwide
OPTION ONE
Orsatti & Partners LLC
Ovation Marketing, Inc.
Pamet River Partners, Inc.
Partners & Shevack Direct
Peter A. Mayer Advertising Inc.
Philadelphia International Marketing Inc.
Phillips Direct Marketing Group
Powell Direct
Price/McNabb Focused Communications
Prime Access Inc.
Prime Direct, Inc.
PTC
Publicis
Quality Strategies
Quinn Fable Advertising Inc.
Rapp Collins Worldwide
RDM Group, Inc.
RDW Group
Relationship Marketing, Inc.
Resource & Development Group, Inc.
Resource Marketing, Inc.
Response Advertising
Response Associates
Response Marketing Group, Asia Pacific
Rhea & Kaiser Advertising
Rhina International Direct, Inc.
RK Hispanica Direct
Robert E. Shaller
Robert Francis Studios, Inc.
Roberts Communications Inc.

Rosen/Brown Direct, Inc.
Rosenfield & Associates
Rosenfield/Dentino, Inc.
Roska Direct
Ross Roy Communications
RTC Direct
Russ Reid Company
Ryan Partnership
S. Connelly & Co., Inc.
S. R. Hoeft Direct, Inc.
Saatchi & Saatchi Business Communication
Sader & Associates, Inc.
Safani Direct Inc.
Sagardia & Calderon
Sales Building Systems
Sanna Mattson MacLeod, Inc.
Saugatuck Marketing Group
SaveSmart
Schober Direct Marketing
Schwartz Rahman Candelaria
Segment Data Management, Inc.
Select Information Exchange
Sense of Design Inc.
Seroka & Associates
Service Associates of America
Shain Colavito
Shaver Direct, Inc.
Shugart Matson Marketing
Siboney/FCB
Sigma Marketing Group
Smith Harrison Direct
Sperber Direct Inc.
Stark Holding Ltd.
Stephen L. Geller, Inc.
Stephens Direct
Strategic Partners Group, Inc.
Suissa Miller Advertising
Sullivan Advertising, Inc.
Swanson Communications
Tanen Advertising
Targetbase Marketing
TargetCom, Inc.
Tatum Toomey & Whicker
Taurus Direct Marketing
TBWA Chiat/Day
Team One Advertising
TeamNash, Inc.
Temerlin McClain Direct
The Barrows Group
The Boston Group
The Bravo Group
The Chapman Agency
The Coastal Group
The Code Corporation
The Direct Marketing Specialists, Inc.
The Direct Network
The Domain Group
The Final Product
The Focus Agency
The Graham Group
The Hacker Group, Ltd.
The Horah Group

The M/A/R/C Group
THE MARKETing PLACE
The Martin Agency
The Parable Group, Inc.
The Phelps Group
The STAR Group
The Zimmermann Agency Inc.
Thomas & Perkins
Thompson & Price
Tierney & Partners
TLP DIRECT
TMA Inc.
Todd Travel Promotions
TPC
Tracy-Locke Advertising
Triad, Inc.
Triad, Inc.
True North Advertising
Varied Associates
Vidal, Reynardus, Moya, Inc.
Vision Integrated Marketing
W. B. Doner Direct
W3DM
Walt Klein & Associates, Inc.
Walter Latham
Warm Thought Communication, Inc.
Watson Communication
West Indies & Grey
What a Concept!
Wickersham Hunt Schwantner
Wilcox & Associates
Williams Worldwide
WOL Direct
Wolf Group Direct
Wong Wong Boyack
Worldwide 1 on 1
WorldWide Telcom Partners
Wunderman Cato Johnson
WWAV Rapp Collins Group
Wyse Direct
Yates Advertising
Yeck Brothers Group
Young & Rubicam
Zimmerman, Laurent & Richardson
Zubi Advertising

Asian advertising and direct marketing
Wong Wong Boyack

Business-to-Business Marketing
RMS Direct, LLC

Call centre services/systems
Diebold Incorporated
DMRS Group, Inc.
Periodical Publishers' Service Bureau, Inc.
ResoDirect
TMP Worldwide

Catalogue consultant
The Schmidt Group

Catalogue design
J. Schmid & Assoc. Inc.

Catalogue producer
Alexander & Company, LLC
Ambrosi
Angeles Marketing Group
Blank & Associates
Catalogs By Design
Diebold Incorporated
Internet Catalog Services
J. Schmid & Assoc. Inc.
Marke Communications, Inc.
Maxwell Sroge Company, Inc.
Rex Media Design
Shasho Jones Direct

Commercial film production company
The Direct Network

Consultancy services
AB Studios, Inc.
Aldata
Alpha Marketing & Consulting
Blank & Associates
Creatives Strategies & Solutions
Cross World Network, Inc.
Daly Direct Marketing
Daniel Gonzalez & Associates
Deutsche Post Global Mail
Deutsche Post Global Mail
Direct Marketers On Call
Direct Marketing Resouce Group, Inc.
Direct Marketing Services International
DMRS Group, Inc.
Dot-Com DIRECT
Enteron Creative Services
Greenberg Consulting
INFOCORE, INC.
Insurance Processing Center, Inc.
Intelitec
Interactive Resources, Inc.
International Direct Response, Inc.
ITAGroup
J. Schmid & Assoc. Inc.
Joan Greenfield Creative
Joan Throckmorton, Inc.
KENT MARKETING GROUP, INC.
Kobs Strategic Consulting
LEC Ltd.
Lewis Design/Barry Lewis Photography, Inc.
Malcolm Decker Associates Inc.
Marke Communications, Inc.
MarketOne
Maxwell Sroge Company, Inc.
Mayne Associates, Inc.
Medina Associates

Omni Graphic Inc.
Pat Friesen & Company
Raab Associates
Response Advertising
RMS Direct, LLC
ROCKINGHAM★JUTKINS★ marketing, Inc.
Rosalie S. Levine Creative
Seklemian/Newell International Marketing Consultants
Strategy Outfitters
TeleDevelopment Services, Inc.
The Callahan Group, L.L.C.
The Catalog Connection
The E-Tailing Group, Inc.
The Jackson Consulting Group, Inc.
The Schmidt Group
Tolliver, Inc.
Tomarkin/Greenawalt, Inc.
TouchStar Media
Translations Unlimited
Triad, Inc.
Wesley R. Weber & Associates, Inc.
Wong Wong Boyack

Copy adaptation
Daniel Gonzalez & Associates
Greenberg Consulting
International Direct Response, Inc.
Malcolm Decker Associates Inc.
Paul Zoellner International Consulting Services.
Probe Communications International, Inc.
Response Advertising
ROCKINGHAM★JUTKINS★marketing, Inc.
Wong Wong Boyack

Copywriting
Profit Boosters Copywriting

Creative copy and concept
Daniel Gonzalez & Associates

Customer relationship marketing
Seklemian/Newell International Marketing Consultants

Database services
Advanced Interactive Marketing, Inc.
Aldata
American List Counsel, Inc.
Audience Identification Inc.
Brainard Associates
Business Development Solutions, Inc.
Center for Simplified Strategic Planning, Inc.
Common Health Direct
Craver, Mathews, Smith & Co.
D. B. Marketing Inc.
Database Marketing Associates, Inc.

Database Marketing Strategies
DataProse Inc.
Datatiempo
Design Vectors, Inc.
Deutsche Post Global Mail
Direct Marketing Resouce Group, Inc.
DirectCom, Inc.
DMDA, Inc.
DMRS Group, Inc.
Dodd Smith Dann, Inc.
Dynamic Information Systems
    Corporation (DISC)
Epsilon
Fort Worth Star Telegram
Grizzard
GSP Group, Inc.
Hartmann Associates
Heenehan & Associates
Insight Out of Chaos
Intelitec
INTELLIGENT MARKETING
    SYSTEMS, INC. (IQ)
ITAGroup
J. Schmid & Assoc. Inc.
Knight Strategic Consulting
KnowledgeBase Marketing, Inc.
Lagniappe Marketing
Looking Glass Inc.
M/S Database Marketing, LLC.
MarCom, Inc.
MarketOne
MarketWorks, Inc.
Maxwell Sroge Company, Inc.
Mercatus
Nykamp Consulting Group (NCG)
OBIMD International
Pegg Nadler Associates, Inc.
pmh caramanning Inc.
Precision Analytical Services
RAD Marketing & RadioBase
Retail Resources
RMS Direct, LLC
Seklemian/Newell International
    Marketing Consultants
Sparks Marketing
Strategic Insight
Target Data Management
Technion Communication
    Corporation
The Gallup Organization
Timberline Technology Group LLC
TMP Worldwide
White Space, Inc.
World Innovators, Inc.
World Marketing Integrated Solutions
    Inc.

Design/graphics/clip art
    supplier
AB Studios, Inc.
Ambrosi
Angeles Marketing Group
Creatives Strategies & Solutions

Daly Direct Marketing
Enteron Creative Services
Insurance Processing Center, Inc.
Joan Greenfield Creative
Joan Throckmorton, Inc.
LEC Ltd.
Lewis Design/Barry Lewis
    Photography, Inc.
Mayne Associates, Inc.
Omni Graphic Inc.
Pat Friesen & Company
Roberts Communications Inc.
Rosalie S. Levine Creative
The Catalog Connection
The Direct Network
Tolliver, Inc.
Tomarkin/Greenawalt, Inc.
TouchStar Media
Translations Unlimited
Triad, Inc.
Wong Wong Boyack

Direct Response Agency
360 Group
A. Eicoff & Company
Aberdeen Marketing Group, Inc.
Acorn Information Services, Inc.
ACS/TradeOne Marketing
Ad Placement Services
Adler, Boschetto, Peebles & Partners
Admark Group
Admerasia
AdSouth, Inc.
Advantage Plus Marketing Group
AGA
Alcott & Routon, Inc.
Allen & Gerritsen
Allstate International
Alternative Marketing Solutions (Ams,
    Inc.)
American Direct Marketing Resources,
    Inc.
American Target Data
Amichetti, Lewis and Associates, Inc.
Ammirati Puris Lintas
AMS Response
Angeles Marketing Group
Applied Interactive Media, LLC
Archer/Malmo Direct
Arnold Direct
Arocom Direct
ASATSU/BBDO
Austin Knight Inc.
Ayer Deare & Partners
B.W.R.
Barkley Evergreen & Partners, Inc.
Barraclough Hall Woolston Gray
Barry Blau & Partners, Inc.
BBDO
BBDO Response
Beacon Group, Inc.
Bel-Aire Associates
Bennett Kuhn Varner, Inc.

Berenson, Isham & Partners, Inc.
BI Performance Services
Biggs/Gilmore Communications
Birkholm Direct
Blagman Media International
Blain, Olsen, White, Gurr Advertising
Blau Marketing Technologies
Blue Dolphin Communications
Bozell Direct
Brighton Agency
Bronner Slosberg Humphrey
Bruce W. Eberle & Associates, Inc.
Bullseye Database Marketing, Inc.
Burrell/DFA Advertising Inc.
Business Advertising Specialties Corp.
Business Direct Marketing Associates,
    Inc.
BWC Group
Byrne Advertising Copy/Consultancy
C-E Communications
Cadmus
Carl Bloom Associates, Inc.
Carlson Marketing Group
Carmichael Lynch
Catalyst Direct Inc.
CCMR Advertising & Marketing
    Communications
Chiat/Day/Mojo Inc. Advertising
Chinnici Direct Inc.
Chiropractic Elite Organization, Inc.
Cimino Direct, Inc.
CKS Partners
CM Partners, Inc.
CME Library
CMF&Z Direct Marketing Group
CMF&Z/Y&R
Colangelo Marketing
Cole & Weber
Columbian Direct Marketing
Communications Plus, Inc.
Communicomp
Consumer Healthworks/Rapp
Cosgrove Associates
Cox Communications, Inc.
CPS Direct, Inc.
Cramer-Krasselt
Cranford Johnson Robinson Woods,
    Inc.
Creative Strategy, Inc.
Cunningham Direct, Inc.
Customer Development Corp.
D. L. Blair Inc.
D.M. Associates
d/a/p associates
Data Health
DCI Marketing
DDB NEEDHAM DIRECT
DDB Needham Worldwide
Dees Communications, Inc./Fuller
    Fund Raising Co.
Devon Direct
DFA Advertising Inc.
Dickinson Direct

531

DiMark Marketing
DiMassimo
Direct Ad-Vantage, Inc.
Direct Deutsch
Direct Impact
Direct Impact, Inc.
Direct Language Communications,
Inc.
Direct Options
Direct Partners
Direct Resources International
Interactive
Direct Results Group, Inc.
DIRECT SUCCESS Communications
Directech, Inc.
DM Group
DMTG, Inc.
DMW Worldwide
Doner Direct
DraftWorldwide
Duffey, Petrosky & Company
Duncan/Shannon
EAGLE DIRECT
eClass Direct
Editorial Perfil
Eisner & Associates Inc.
eMergingMedia, Inc.
Emmerling Post Advertising, Inc.
ERA
Eric Mower & Associates
ERS DIRECT MARKETING
EURO RSCG
Fallon McElligott
Farrar & Farrar
FCB Direct Chicago
FCB Puerto Rico
Fine Light Inc.
Finerty & Wolfe Advertising, Inc.
FMG Marketing, Inc.
Fogarty Klein & Partners
Foote, Cone & Belding
Forecast Direct Marketing Group
Foreign Objects
FPS Marketing Communications
Frank W. Cawood & Associates, Inc.
Frequency Marketing, Inc.
Gerald Siegel & Associates, Inc.
Gianfagna Marketing &
Communications, Inc.
Gilbert Whitney & Johns
Gillespie
Good Advertising
Graham Gregory Bozell, Inc.
Gramercy Group
Grapevine Marketing, Inc.
Graphic Arts & Production
Gray & Graham Marketing Group
Grey Direct
Group M Marketing, Inc.
Gruen + Sells Ltd.
GTE, The Focus Agency
Haynes & Partners Communication,
Inc.

HB&G/ACSC
Heinrich Marketing, Inc.
Hemisphere Marketing Inc.
Hemmings IV Direct
Hemmings, Birkholm & Grizzard
Hershey Communications NY, Inc.
Hill Holliday
HispanAgencia
Hoffman York
Holland Mark Martin Edmund
Howard, Merrell & Partners,Inc
Huber Hoge and Sons Advertising,
Inc.
Hudson Street Partners
Hunt Marketing Group
Huntsinger & Jeffer, Inc.
IBIS Communications, Inc.
ICON Digital Photography
Imagine Direct
IMC Direct
Indiana Design Consortium, Inc.
InfoWorks
Ingalls One To One Marketing
Integrated Marketing, Inc.
Interactive Marketing Group, Inc.
Interval International
Ira Thomas Associates
Irma S. Mann, Strategic Marketing,
Inc.
Ivie & Associates, Inc.
J. Walter Thompson Direct
Jacobs & Clevenger, Inc.
JC Penny Direct Marketing Services
Jeffery Advertising Agency
Jordan, McGrath, Case & Taylor/
Direct
Just Partners
JWP Group
JWT Specialized Communications
Kang & Lee Advertising
Karlin/Pimsler, Inc.
Kern Direct
Ketchum Communications
Kirshenbaum Bond & Partners
Klemtner Advertising
Kovel Kresser & Partners
Kuhn & Wittenborn Advertising
LA&ATINO
Lareau & Associates
Lawrence Butner Advertising, Inc.
LCG Latino
LCS Direct Mail Advertising &
Printing
Leo Burnett U.S.A.
Levenson Public Relations
Lewis Advertising, Inc.
Lewis Advertising/Birmingham
Lieber, Levett, Koenig, Farese,
Babcock, Inc.
Liggett-Stashower Direct
Lissen Audio Company
LKH&S
Long Haymes Carr

Lord Sullivan Yoder
Lortz Direct Marketing Inc.
Lowe Direct
Lowe Fox Pavlika
Mailcom plc
Mailing Concept, Inc.
Make It So, Inc.
Manus Direct
Manus Direct Marketing
Maris, West & Baker
Maritz Performance Improvement
Company
Market Place Priut
Marketing Alternatives, Inc.
Marketing Resources of New York, In
Marquardt & Roche/Meditz & Hacke
Martin Direct
Mason & Geller Direct, LLC
MatchLogic, Inc.
Maverick Marketing Group, Inc.
MC Direct
McCann Relationship Marketing
Membership Cards Only
Meridian Advertising
Michael Edwards Direct, Inc.
Milici Valenti Ng Pack
Miller Meester Advertising
Miller/Huber Relationship Marketing
Millernia Direct, Inc.
Mitchell & Resnikoff
Modem Media.Poppe Tyson
Music Marketing Network
Music Marketing Network
National Direct Corporation
NCI Direct
NETWORKDIRECT, INC.
NKH&W Inc.
Nordis Marketing & Mailing
North American Communications
North Castle Direct
Northlich Stolley LaWarre
NS & G Direct Marketing
O'Connell Meier
O'Connor Kenney Partners, Inc.
OgilvyOne Worldwide
OPTION ONE
Orsatti & Partners LLC
Ovation Marketing, Inc.
Pamet River Partners, Inc.
Partners & Shevack Direct
Peter A. Mayer Advertising Inc.
Philadelphia International Marketing
Inc.
Phillips Direct Marketing Group
Powell Direct
Price/McNabb Focused
Communications
Prime Access Inc.
Prime Direct, Inc.
Probe Communications Internationa
Inc.
PTC
Publicis

Quality Strategies
Quinn Fable Advertising Inc.
Rapp Collins Worldwide
RDM Group, Inc.
RDW Group
Relationship Marketing, Inc.
Resource & Development Group, Inc.
Resource Marketing, Inc.
Response Associates
Response Marketing Group, Asia
　　Pacific
Rhea & Kaiser Advertising
Rhina International Direct, Inc.
RK Hispanica Direct
Robert E. Shaller
Robert Francis Studios, Inc.
Rosen/Brown Direct, Inc.
Rosenfield & Associates
Rosenfield/Dentino, Inc.
Roska Direct
Ross Roy Communications
RTC Direct
Russ Reid Company
Ryan Partnership
S. Connelly & Co., Inc.
S. R. Hoeft Direct, Inc.
Saatchi & Saatchi Business
　　Communication
Sader & Associates, Inc.
Safani Direct Inc.
Sagardia & Calderon
Sales Building Systems
Saugatuck Marketing Group
SaveSmart
Schober Direct Marketing
Schwartz Rahman Candelaria
Segment Data Management, Inc.
Select Information Exchange
Sense of Design Inc.
Seroka & Associates
Service Associates of America
Shain Colavito
Shaver Direct, Inc.
Shugart Matson Marketing
Siboney/FCB
Sigma Marketing Group
Smith Harrison Direct
Sperber Direct Inc.
Stark Holding Ltd.
Stephen L. Geller, Inc.
Stephens Direct
Strategic Partners Group, Inc.
Suissa Miller Advertising
Sullivan Advertising, Inc.
Swanson Communications
Tanen Advertising
Targetbase Marketing
TargetCom, Inc.
Tatum Toomey & Whicker
Taurus Direct Marketing
TBWA Chiat/Day
Team One Advertising
TeamNash, Inc.

Temerlin McClain Direct
The Barrows Group
The Boston Group
The Bravo Group
The Chapman Agency
The Coastal Group
The Code Corporation
The Direct Marketing Specialists, Inc.
The Domain Group
The Final Product
The Focus Agency
The Graham Group
The Hacker Group, Ltd.
The Horah Group
The M/A/R/C Group
THE MARKETing PLACE
The Martin Agency
The Parable Group, Inc.
The Phelps Group
The STAR Group
The Zimmermann Agency Inc.
Thomas & Perkins
Thompson & Price
Tierney & Partners
TLP DIRECT
TMA Inc.
Todd Travel Promotions
TPC
Tracy-Locke Advertising
Triad, Inc.
True North Advertising
Varied Associates
Vidal, Reynardus, Moya, Inc.
Vision Integrated Marketing
W. B. Doner Direct
W3DM
Walt Klein & Associates, Inc.
Walter Latham
Warm Thought Communication, Inc.
Watson Communication
West Indies & Grey
What a Concept!
Wickersham Hunt Schwantner
Wilcox & Associates
Williams Worldwide
WOL Direct
Wolf Group Direct
Worldwide 1 on 1
WorldWide Telcom Partners
Wunderman Cato Johnson
WWAV Rapp Collins Group
Wyse Direct
Yates Advertising
Yeck Brothers Group
Young & Rubicam
Zimmerman, Laurent & Richardson
Zubi Advertising

Direct marketing agency
Alpha Marketing & Consulting
Ambrosi
American List Counsel, Inc.
Banner Direct

Blank & Associates
Campbell Mithun Direct
Diebold Incorporated
Dot-Com DIRECT
First Marketing Company
Global DM Solutions
Greenberg Consulting
Grizzard
I Market Inc
International Direct Response, Inc.
KENT MARKETING GROUP, INC.
Marke Communications, Inc.
MarketOne
Maxwell Sroge Company, Inc.
Paul Zoellner International Consulting
　　Services.
Periodical Publishers' Service Bureau,
　　Inc.
Probe Communications International,
　　Inc.
Response Advertising
RMS Direct, LLC
Roberts Communications Inc.
ROCKINGHAM★JUTKINS★marketi-
　　ng, Inc.
Sanna Mattson MacLeod, Inc.
The Direct Network
Wong Wong Boyack

E-commerce Customer Service & Fulfilment
ResoDirect

Executive recruitment
The Callahan Group, L.L.C.

Executive search - call centre
TeleDevelopment Services, Inc.

Fulfilment and sampling house
AB&C Group Inc.
AIM Marketing
Alamo Direct
Aldata
Blumenfield Marketing, Inc.
Centrobe, Inc.
Crawford Communications Group
DaisyTek
Direct Mail of Maine
Diversified Direct
Fosdick Fulfillment Corporation
Fulfillment Corporation of America
G.A. Wright, Inc.
Global Logistic Services
Hann & DePalmer
Harrison Fulfillment Services
Innotrac Corporation
Intermail Direct Inc
Kable Fulfillment Services
Link Marketing
Locus Direct Marketing Group, Inc.
MCRB Service Bureau, Inc.
MSF Corporation

National Fulfillment Service
P.J. McNerney and Associates
Periodical Publishers' Service Bureau, Inc.
Priority Fulfillment Services
Professional Marketing Associates, Inc.
Programmers Investment Corp.
Quikpak, Inc.
ResoDirect
Right Side Up, Inc.
Swan Packaging Fulfillment
Tessera Enterprise Systems
The Corporate Communications Group
The Express Group
The Hibbert Group
TMP Worldwide
Total Fulfillment Service LLC/TFS Limited
Total Response Inc.
Tripar International, Inc.
Tylie Jones & Associates Inc.
Young America Corp.
Young America Corporation
Zip Sort Inc.

Human resources
The Callahan Group, L.L.C.

Interactive media
American List Counsel, Inc.
Angeles Marketing Group
Blank & Associates
Dot-Com DIRECT
Interactive Resources, Inc.
ITAGroup
MarketOne
ResoDirect
Roberts Communications Inc.
Triad, Inc.

International mailing service
Deutsche Post Global Mail

International postal mailing services
Deutsche Post Global Mail

Internet services
AOL Bertelsmann Online Europe

Labelling/envelope services
Admiral Packaging
Aldata
Allen Envelope Corp.
Ambassador Envelope
Atlantic Envelope Company
B & W Press
Bowers Envelope Company
Colfax Envelope Corporation
Commercial Envelope Manufacturers, Inc.
Continental Envelope Corp.

Deutsche Post Global Mail
Diversified Direct
Federal Envelope Company
Graphic Arts Center
Husky Envelope Products, Inc.
I Market Inc
Liberty Envelope Inc.
Love Envelopes, Inc.
Mackay Envelope Corporation
Mail-Well, Inc. Corporate Office
Poly-Flex Corp.
Royal Envelope Company
Royal Envelope Company
Tension Envelope Corporation
Transo Envelope Company
Tri-State Envelope Corp.
Westvaco Envelope Division
Worcester Envelope Company

Lettershop
Access Direct Systems, Inc.
Addressing Services Company, Inc.
Adistra
Advanced Response Systems
Advertising Distributors of America, Inc.
Alaniz and Sons, Inc.
American Direct Marketing
American Mail Union
American Mailers
AmeriComm Direct Marketing, Inc.
ASI Direct Marketing
Brokers Worldwide, Inc.
Calloway House, Inc.
CAM Logistics
Canadian Direct Mailing
Cardinal Marketing Inc.
Creative Mailings, Inc.
Data-Mail, Inc.
DataMark Systems, Inc.
DEC International Inc.
Deutsche Post Global Mail
Deutsche Post Global Mail
DIMAC DIRECT
Direct Marketing Associates, Inc.
Diversified Direct
DM Group
DMW Worldwide
Double Envelope Corporation
Double Envelope Corporation
Excalibur Enterprises, Inc.
Express Messenger Int'l
FALA Direct Marketing, Inc.
Federal Direct
FOCUS DIRECT
Gage Lettershop/Personalization Services
Global Card Technologies, Inc.
Graphic Innovations
Grizzard
Hartford Direct Marketing
International Postal Consultants, Inc.
Irresistible Ink Inc.

Klasek Letter Co., Inc.
Label Art
Lazarus Marketing Inc.
Magnetix Group Directions
Mailing Services of Pittsburg, Inc.
MAILMEN Inc.
Mid-America Mailers, Inc.
Mystic Transport Services
National Computer Print
NationsMail
North Shore Agency, Inc.
Northbrook Services
Palm Coast Data Inc.
PDS
Quad/Data Services
Rees Associates, Inc.
Royal Mail US Inc.
Scandinavian Distribution & Postal Service, Inc. (SDPS)
Stealth Marketing/Gage Marketing Group
Team Services
The FALA Group
TMP Worldwide
Transkrit Corporation
U. S. Monitor
U.S.A. Direct, Inc.
Vestcom Mid-Atlantic
Webtrend Direct
West Coast Mailing & Distribution
Western Union Financial Services Inc
World Innovators, Inc.
Worldnow Online Network

List broker/list manager
L.I.S.T. INCORPORATED

List management
Eleanor L. Stark Co., Inc.

List services
21st Century Marketing
A. Caldwell List Company, Inc.
A. H. Direct Marketing, Inc.
ACS Inc.
ACT ONE Mailing List Services, Inc
ACTON, International
ACXIOM
AD Tape & Label
Adrea Rubin Marketing, Inc.
ADRESAFE, Inc.
Advanced Compilations Inc. (ACI)
Advanced Technology Marketing
Aggressive List Management, Inc.
Alan Drey Companies
AllMedia Inc.
Alpha Marketing & Consulting
Americalist
American Business Information Inc.
American Data Consultants
American Leads Co.
American List Counsel, Inc.
American Mail Systems Inc.

American Professional Lists
American Student List Company, Inc.
Anchor Computer, Inc.
Antares ITI
Applied Computer Concepts
Applied Information Group
Atlantes Corporation
Atlantic List Company, Inc.
Atlux Corporation
Automated Resources Group, Inc.
AZ Marketing Services, Inc.
B & K List Services, Inc.
Baker Advertising & Mailing
Bernice Bush Company
BEST MAILING LISTS, INC.
Bethesda List Center, Inc.
Braun Technology Group
Brigar Computer Services
Burnett Direct, Inc.
Business Transactions Express
C.D.C. Lists
Cahners Business Lists
Carney Direct Marketing
Carol Enters List Co., Inc.
CAS, Inc.
Castel
Catalyst Direct Marketing
Cathedral Corporation
CFM Direct
Chilcutt Direct Marketing
Clark.Mackain
CMG Direct Corporation
CMS, Inc.
Communication Concepts, Inc.
Communications Two Group, Inc.
Compilers Direct
Computer Strategy Coordinators, Inc.
Conrad Direct, Inc.
Cornwell Data Services, Inc.
Country Marketing Ltd.
CPC Associates
CPU, Inc.
Creative Automation Company
CRK Computer Services
Cross Country Computer Corp.
CRYOVAC
Culpeper Lists, Inc.
Custom Computer Software
Custom List Services
Customer Insight Company
D-J Associates
D. A. Lewis Associates
Data Base of North Florida, Inc.
Data Services Inc
Data Services, Inc.
Data Technology Resources,Inc.
Data Warehouse Corporation
Database America Companies
Database Management
Database Marketing Concepts Inc.
Database Network
Database Production Services
Datamann, Inc.

DataQuick List Services
Daystar Data Group, Inc.
DeBroux Marketing, Inc.
Dependable Lists, Inc.
Deutsche Post Global Mail
Dialog Software
Diamond List Marketing Company
Diedre Moire Corporation, Inc.
Direct Access Marketing Services, Inc.
Direct Effect
Direct Mail Dynamics, Inc.
Direct Mail Trackers
Direct Marketing Experts
Direct Marketing Partners
Direct Marketing Resources, Inc.
Direct Marketing Technology
Diversified Direct
DMG Lists Ltd.
DMS
Dot-Com DIRECT
Dresden Direct, Inc.
Dunhill International List Company,
   Inc.
Dydacomp Development Corp.
DynaMark, Inc.
Eagle Publshing
Ecocenters/TMSI
Ed Burnett Consultants, Inc.
Edith Roman Associates, Inc
Edmaro's, Inc.
Educational List Services, Inc
Eleanor L. Stark Co., Inc.
Estee List Services, Inc.
Ethnic Technologies, LLC
Exodus Communications
Experian
Fabrik Communications
Fairfield Marketing Group, Inc.
Fasano & Associates
Federal Union, Inc.
First Data Solutions
Focus USA
Fred Singer D.M.
Fred Woolf List Co., Inc.
GDT
George Mann Associates
Gibralter Marketing Limited
Global-Z International
Gordon Publications, Inc.
Graphography, Ltd.
GreatLists.com
Group 1 Software, Inc.
HARRIS Marketing, Inc.
Harte-Hanks Direct Marketing
Hippo Direct
Hugo Dunhill Mailing Lists, Inc.
HYAID GROUP
I Market Inc
I. C. System, Inc.
ICOM
Industry Week
Infinite Media
Info USA

InfoBase
INFOCORE, INC.
InfoSpan Inc.
Intelitec
IntelliQuest Information Group
International Billing Services
International Data
International Direct Response, Inc.
ISG/Avne Systems
J. F. Glaser Incorporated
JAMI Marketing Services
JDM - Jetson Direct Mail Services, Inc.
JF Direct Marketing, Inc.
Johnson & Quin, Inc.
Karl Analytical Services
KCI Communications, Inc.
Knowledge Base Marketing
Kroll Direct Marketing
Kroll Direct Marketing
Kroll Direct Marketing
L & E Meridian
L.I.S.T. INCORPORATED
L.I.S.T.S. Inc.
LCS Industries, Inc.
Ledgemere Hispanic Lists
Lifestyle Change Communications,
   Inc.
Lighthouse List Co.
List Advisor, Inc.
List Counsellors
List Process Company, Inc./List
   Process Management, Inc.
List Services Corporation
List Strategies, Inc.
List Technology Systems Group, Inc.
Macromark, Inc.
Mail Marketing, Incorporated
Mal Dunn Associates, Inc.
Manning Media International
Mardev
Marketing Communication Systems,
   Inc.
Marketing Data, Inc.
Marketing Economics, Inc.
Marketing Software Company
Marketry, Inc.
MarketTouch
Mary Elizabeth Granger & Associates,
   Inc.
Masada Group Technologies
   Corporation
Matt Brown & Associates, Inc.
May & Speh Energy Market
   Connect
May Development Services
MBS/Multimode, Inc.
McCarthy Media Group, Inc.
Media Marketplace, Inc.
Media Mart
Merge Purge Corp.
Merkle Direct Marketing Inc.
Metro Direct
Metromail/Experian

MGI Lists
MGT. Associates
MidAmerica Lists Inc.
Midland Marketing
Midwest Direct Marketing, Inc.
Millard Group, Inc.
MLS Computer Services
MMI - Southern Branch
MMS, Inc.
Mokrynski & Associates Inc.
MSGI
MSI List Marketing
Name-Finders Lists, Inc.
Names & Addresses, Inc.
Names In The News California, Inc.
Navigation Technologies
NC Direct Marketing
NCRI List Management
Network Associates
New Resident Marketing Corporation, Inc.
Nissho Iwai American Corp.
NRL Direct
Ohio Ventures, Inc.
Olwen International Direct Mail, Inc.
Pacific East Research Corporation
PARADIGM Direct
Paradysz Matera & Company
Paragon Direct Marketing, LLC
Paragon Direct, Inc.
Pathway Marketing Inc.
PCS List & Information
PDM Technologies L.L.C.
Peachtree Data, Inc.
Penton Lists
Performance Data
Persimmon IT, Inc.
PMM Marketing Inc.
Polk/Verity Multi-Dimensional Intelligence
Precision Marketing Consulting
Presentation Packaging
Prestige Mailing Lists Inc.
Prime Response Inc.
PrimeNet Marketing Services
Priority Data Systems, Inc.
Probe Communications International, Inc.
PROFILE AMERICA LIST INC.
Q.E.D. Marketing Inc.
Q5 List Marketing
R.C. Direct, Inc.
Research & Response International
Response Media Products, Inc.
Rickard List Marketing
RMI Direct Marketing, Inc.
RP Associates
Rubin Response Services, Inc.
Saturn Corporation
SBDP Corporation
Senior Citizens Unlimited, Inc.
SK&A Information Services, Inc.
Smartbase/ACXIOM Direct Media

SpeciaList
Springhouse Corporation
Statewide Data Services
Statlistics, Inc.
Stephen Winchell & Associates
Stevens-Knox List Management
Strategic Decision Services
Strubco, Inc
STS Systems Ltd.
Support Services Corp.
Synapse Infusion Group
TABS Direct
TCI Direct
Technical List Computing, Inc.
Telecheck/First Data
TERADYNE
Texas Direct, Inc.
The Associates
The Broadmoore Group, LTD
The Coolidge Company, Inc.
The Credit Index
The Customer Connection, Inc.
The Data Base, Inc.
The FMP Direct Marketing Group
The Gnames Advantage, LLC
The Information Refinery, Inc.
The Kaplan Agency
The Leland Company
The List Connection Inc.
The List Source, Inc.
The Listworks Corporation
The McNichols Group, Inc.
The Polk Company
The SpeciaLists, Ltd.
TIDS, Inc.
Times Direct Marketing, Inc.
Tony Murray & Associates
Total Tactix Inc.
Trans Union Corporation
Transitions Optical, Inc.
Triangle Marketing Services, Inc.
Triplex Direct Marketing Corp.
Uni-Mail List Corporation
United Marketing Group Inc.
USCS/IBS
Valerie Davis & Associates
Venture Communications International, Inc.
Vision Marketing Inc.
W.I. Mail Marketing
Walter Karl, Inc.
Watson/Mail Communications, Inc.
Wm. Stroh, Inc.
World Innovators, Inc.
Worldata, Inc.
Zeller & Letica, Inc.

Mail order company

Creative Concept Coordinators Inc
Insight Enterprises Inc
The Broadmoore Group, LTD

Mailing/Faxing services

Access Direct Systems, Inc.
Addressing Services Company, Inc.
Adistra
Advanced Response Systems
Advertising Distributors of America, Inc.
Alaniz and Sons, Inc.
Aldata
American Direct Marketing
American Mail Union
American Mailers
AmeriComm Direct Marketing, Inc.
ASI Direct Marketing
Brokers Worldwide, Inc.
Calloway House, Inc.
CAM Logistics
Canadian Direct Mailing
Cardinal Marketing Inc.
Creative Mailings, Inc.
Data-Mail, Inc.
DataMark Systems, Inc.
DEC International Inc.
Deutsche Post Global Mail
Deutsche Post Global Mail
DIMAC DIRECT
Direct Marketing Associates, Inc.
DM Group
DMW Worldwide
Double Envelope Corporation
Double Envelope Corporation
Excalibur Enterprises, Inc.
Express Messenger Int'l
FALA Direct Marketing, Inc.
Federal Direct
FOCUS DIRECT
Gage Lettershop/Personalization Services
Global Card Technologies, Inc.
Graphic Innovations
Hartford Direct Marketing
International Postal Consultants, Inc.
Irresistible Ink Inc.
Klasek Letter Co., Inc.
Label Art
Lazarus Marketing Inc.
Magnetix Group Directions
Mailing Services of Pittsburg, Inc.
MAILMEN Inc.
Mid-America Mailers, Inc.
Mystic Transport Services
National Computer Print
NationsMail
North Shore Agency, Inc.
Northbrook Services
Palm Coast Data Inc.
PDS
Quad/Data Services
Rees Associates, Inc.
Royal Mail US Inc.
Scandinavian Distribution & Postal Service, Inc. (SDPS)

Stealth Marketing/Gage Marketing Group
Team Services
The FALA Group
Transkrit Corporation
U. S. Monitor
U.S.A. Direct, Inc.
United States Postal Service
Vestcom Mid-Atlantic
Webtrend Direct
West Coast Mailing & Distribution
Western Union Financial Services Inc.
Worldnow Online Network

Managing change
The Callahan Group, L.L.C.

Market research agency
Action Marketing Research, Inc.
AFFINA Corporation
Analytic Solutions
Angeles Marketing Group
BAIGlobal Inc.
Beta Research Corporation
Blank & Associates
Campbell Research
Claritas
Consortia
David Ganz Marketing, Inc.
Digital Marketing Services, Inc.
Direct Marketing Research Associates
EnPack Digital Media
FIND/SVP, Inc.
First Marketing Company
Forrester Research, Inc.
Gartner Group
Grizzard
Health Communications
Heritage Marketing Corporation
ICT Group, Inc.
INFOCORE, INC.
Information Resources, Inc.
J.G. Communications
KENT MARKETING GROUP, INC.
Marketing Models
Marketing Synergy Inc.
Marketing/Media Dynamics, Inc.
MarketIQ, Inc.
PolkVerity
Sanna Mattson MacLeod, Inc.
SkyTeller, L.L.C.
Spectra-Consumer Marketing Group
Star DMRA/EMA
Strategy Outfitters
Tailwind
The Loop Company Inc.
The NPD Group, Inc.
Yankelovich Partners

Marketing and e-marketing software evaluation
Raab Associates

Marketing consultant
Adrian Miller Direct Marketing
Age Wave House Services
Alex Sheshenoff Management Services, Inc.
Almskog + Frydman Communications
Alternative Direct Media, Inc.
American Marketing & Communication Corp.
American Money Management
Andersen Consulting
Angeles Marketing Group
Aperio, Inc.
Banner Direct
Beechtree Assoc., Inc.
Bernheimer Associates
Bert O'Malley Direct Marketing Consulting
Blum & Company
Bob Castle & Associates
Brandywine Consulting Group
Braren & Constantino Partners
Campbell Associates
Campbell Mithun Direct
Capell's Circulation Report, Inc.
Capital Marketing, Inc.
Cartwheel, Inc.
CERES Integrated Solutions
CHD Direct
ChoicePoint
Circulation Specialists, Inc.
CMC
CMC Marketing Services
Coleman Hoyt Consultants
Collinger & Associates
Columbia Consulting Group
Corry Direct Marketing, LLC
Creative Marketing
Credentials Services International, Inc.
Cross World Network, Inc.
Cross World Network, Inc.
CSC Weston Group
D R Prose
Daly Communications
Data Maven
Database Marketing Solutions
David Heneberry Associates
David Shepard Associates, Inc.
Deaver-Danowitz
Devries Direct Marketing
DiaLogos, Inc.
Direct Comm
Direct International, Inc.
Direct Marketers On Call
Direct Marketing Assistance, Inc.
Direct Marketing Data Corp.
Direct Marketing Management
Direct Marketing Resources Group, Inc.
Direct Marketing Services
Direct Marketing Services International
Direct Response Enhancements

Directives/Targeted Marketing and Communications
Dirkx Direct International
DMRS Group, Inc.
Doran & Forgacs, Inc.
Dorothy Kerr & Associates
Dot-Com DIRECT
Douglas Newton & Associates
Drake Business Services, Inc.
Drake Business Services, Inc.
DW Stevenson & Associates
Edward Rast and Company
Elephant & Chumley, LLC
Elizabeth Taylor Marketing Services
Erlandson Associates
Ernan Roman Direct Marketing Corporation
Fidelis Consulting
First Marketing Company
First Media Group
Focalpoint
Focus: Productivity, Inc.
Foxhall Corporation
Frontera Development Corporation
Furgiuele & Company, Inc.
Gaitskill & Associates
Gazette Direct Marketing Services
Georgia K. Friedman, Inc.
German Marketing Services
Gibson Direct, Inc.
Gordon W. Grossman, Inc.
Grizzard
Grund & Associates
Gruppo, Levey & Capell, Inc.
Harbor Associates
Harvey Associates-Direct Marketing Solutions
Hauser List Services, NMIS
Herbert Krug & Associates Inc.
Herring/Newman
Hunter Business Direct Inc.
Impact Consulting International
Insite Marketing
Integrated Management Services
Intelitec
Interactive Resources, Inc.
International Customer Loyalty Programmes (ICLP)
International Direct Marketing Consultants, Inc.
International Marketing Solutions, Inc.
International Resource Management Co.
ITAGroup
J. Felvey & Associates, Inc.
J. Schmid & Assoc. Inc.
Jack Leonard Company Inc.
James A. Reiman, P.C.
John Condon & Associates
John Cummings & Partners
Kannon Consulting, Inc.
KENT MARKETING GROUP, INC.
Killion Direct

Kobs Strategic Consulting
Kraus Enterprises
La Agencia de Orci & Asociados
Laburnum Marketing Partners, Inc.
LaCrosse Tribune
Len Sacks Associates Inc.
Lenser & Associates, Inc.
Lett Direct, Inc.
Levey Marketing Services
Linda Goodman Assoc.
Link to Success, Inc.
Loren G. Smith & Associates
M. Joseph Dunn & Associates
M.I.T. Specialist
Maier Marketing Synergy
Malchow Adams & Hussey
Malcolm Decker Associates Inc.
Manex
Marke Communications, Inc.
Market Response International
Marketing Information & Technology
Marketing Management International
Marketing Results Associates, Inc.
Marketrac, Inc.
Markitecture Systems Group
Mary Culnan Consultant
MaxiMarketing
Maxwell Sroge Company, Inc.
McIntyre Direct
Medina Associates
Mercury Media
Michael I. Grant & Associates, Inc.
Miglino Associates
Mitchell Madison Group
Moran Direct, Inc.
Muldoon & Baer, Inc.
Multicultural Marketing Resources,
 Inc.
Murphy Marketing
MVI Marketing Ltd.
Myers Equity Express
National Analysts, Inc.
National Business Seminars
National List Protection
National Tele-Communications
Neil Ransick Marketing
NetCreations, Inc.
Observatory Group, Inc.
Orinoco Incorpated
Our Tribe Marketing
Pacer Associates
Paradigm Direct, Inc.
Pathfinder Business Growth
 Consultants, LLC.
Patricia Dowd, Inc.
PBG Marketing, Inc.
Phoenix Group, Inc.
Phoenix Marketing Group Ltd.
Phone for Success
Poly-Tech Industries, Inc.
Probe Communications International,
 Inc.
Profitable Marketing

Putnam Direct Marketing
Racine Journal Times
Ray Slyper Associates
Retail Target Marketing Systems,
 Inc.
Richard A. Peters &
Richard Saunders International
Right Coast Marketing
RJ Podell Catalog Services
RMS Direct, LLC
Ron Perrella DRS
Ron Weber & Associates, Inc.
S.E.S. Marketing Associates
Salzmann Gay Associates
Sanna Mattson MacLeod, Inc.
Sargeant House
SAS Global Direct Inc
Schus & Company
Sheshenoff Information
Smith-Browning Direct, Inc.
SPAULDER & Associates, Inc.
Special Expeditions
Spyglass Consulting Associates
Stanton Direct Marketing, Inc.
Strand Marketing
Strategic Insights, Inc.
Strategy Outfitters
Sutton & Associates, Inc.
Synapse Group
SynerComm
TargeTrends Associates
TeleServices Partners
The Callahan Group, L.L.C.
The DeLay Group
The E-Tailing Group, Inc.
The Gazette Company
The Hauser Group
The Heisler Group, Inc.
The Jackson Consulting Group, Inc.
The Lake Group
The Marcom Consulting Group
The Pinnacle Group
The River North Group, Inc.
The Services Group
The Verdi Group, Inc.
THINK New Ideas, Inc.
TJS PrintNet
Triad, Inc.
TSP - TeleServices Partners
U.S. Direct
Urban Science Applications, Inc.
USY Consulting
W-R Marketing Resources Inc.
W.J. Totten & Associates, LLc
Web Direct Marketing
Wesley R. Weber & Associates, Inc.
Williamson Consulting, Inc.
Wilson & Ellis Consulting
Words At Work
WOW! Marketing, Inc.
Wunderman, Sadh & Associates
 LLC
Zoetics, Inc.

Media buying agency
Imark Corp
International Direct Response, Inc.
J. Schmid & Assoc. Inc.
La Agencia de Orci & Asociados
Probe Communications International,
 Inc.
Sanna Mattson MacLeod, Inc.

Personalisation
Diversified Direct
First Marketing Company
Interactive Resources, Inc.
Mail-Well, Inc. Corporate Office
Malcolm Decker Associates Inc.
MarketOne

Photography (for print and online use)
Ambrosi

Print services
Aldata
Diversified Direct
ITAGroup
J. Schmid & Assoc. Inc.
Mail-Well, Inc. Corporate Office
Malcolm Decker Associates Inc.
Marke Communications, Inc.
Probe Communications International,
 Inc.
Sanna Mattson MacLeod, Inc.
Versatile Card Technology, Inc (VCT)

Private delivery services
Alternate Postal
Citipost
CTC Distribution Direct
Deutsche Post Global Mail
Deutsche Post Global Mail
Directory Distributing Associates Inc.
Dispatch Consumer Services
Drop Ship Express
InterPost North America
Mailfast
OCS America
Purolator
RMX
RPS
The Dispatch Printing Company
TNT
TNT Mailfast/Interpost
USPS/NY Metro Area Sales Office

Product sampling
International Direct Response, Inc.

Protective packaging materials and systems
Sealed Air Corporation

Publisher
Cross World Network, Inc.

DM News/DM News International
First Marketing Company

Response analysis bureau
Direct Marketing Resouce Group, Inc.
Intelitec
Periodical Publishers' Service Bureau, Inc.
TMP Worldwide

Sales promotion agency
Angeles Marketing Group
Brown Radman Wolper
Crane Production
CYRK, Inc.
Dugan Valva Contess
Frank Mayer & Associates, Inc.
Frankel
ITAGroup
KENT MARKETING GROUP, INC.
Lee Hill, Inc.
Marden-Kane, Inc.
Marke Communications, Inc.
Marketing Associates/USA, Inc.
Marketing Corporation of America
MarketOne
MFP&W Promotions and Direct
QLM Marketing
Roberts Communications Inc.
Ventura Associates, Inc.

Service bureau
I Market Inc
Intelitec
Phoenix Data Processing, Inc.
TMP Worldwide

Software supplier
I Market Inc
Intelitec

Specialises in the US Hispanic market
La Agencia de Orci & Asociados

Specialist packaging
CPU, Inc.
CRYOVAC
ISG/Avne Systems
Presentation Packaging

Strategic and creative development for direct marketing campaigns – consumer, business-to-business, industrial
Response Advertising

Telemarketing agency
800 Direct
800 Support
95 Info

Acacia Teleservices International
Access Direct Telemarketing
ACI Telecentrics
ACP Interactive, LLC
Advanced Data-Comm, Inc.
Advanced Telemarketing Corp.
Advantage Line
Aegis Communications Group, Inc.
All City Call Center
AmeriCall Corporation
American ProMark
American Telecom, Inc.
American TelNet
APAC TeleServices
Army Times Publishing Company
ASK Telemarketing
Atlas Marketing
Aurora Marketing Management, Inc.
Automated Call Processing (ACP)
Barber Consulting Services
Beach Direct Marketing Resources, Inc.
Benefit Services of America, Inc.
Blitz Research, Inc.
Budget Marketing, Inc.
Business Response, Inc.
Call Center Marketing
Call Interactive
Celebrate Communications L.L.C.
Century Direct Marketing, Inc.
Citation TeleServices, Inc.
CMC
Communication Service Centers
Communication Services Group
Consolidated Market Response
Corporate Calling Center
CTC Teleservices, Inc.
Cultural Access Worldwide
Dakotah Direct, Inc.
Data Decisions Corporation
DialAmerica Marketing Inc.
Dialogue Marketing
Digisoft Computers, Inc.
Direct Marketing Services, Inc.
DKP & Associates, Inc.
DMS Direct Marketing Services, Inc.
Edelman Public Relations
Entelechy Systems, Inc.
Excell Customer Care
Executive Call Centers
Executive Marketing Services, Inc.
FBC Telemarketing
FutureCall Telemarketing
Gannett TeleMarketing, Inc.
GC Services
Glenn Snyder & Associates
GLS Teleservices
Hamilton Telecommunications
Henry M. Greene & Assoc., Inc.
HMS Direct
Holldon Telemanagement Group
Idelman Telemarketing, Inc.

IDRC (International Data Response Corporation)
Incept Corporation
InfoCision Management Corporation
Inteck Information Inc.
IntelliSell Corporation
Intelogistics
Interactive Response Technologies Inc.
Interactive Teleservices Corporation
IQI, Inc.
ITI Marketing Services, Inc.
JDR Marketing Inc.
JLM Holding, Inc.
King TeleServices
Kowal Associates, Inc.
Kurant Direct Inc.
Lieber & Associates
M&I Capital Markets Group
MarCom
Market U.S.A. Inc.
MATRIXX Marketing Inc.
Matthias Telemarketing Management, Inc.
MCI/EVS
Merkafon
Meyer Associates Telemarketing
Michigan Message Center
MicroAge Service Solutions
Midco Communications
Millennium Teleservices
NTS Marketing, Inc.
Oetting & Company, Inc.
Orion Marketing
Paragon Solutions
Periodical Publishers' Service Bureau, Inc.
Person To Person Marketing
Phone Interactice Communications
Precision Response Corporation
Prism Marketing
Producers America, Inc.
Profitec Business Services, Inc.
ProMark One
ProMark One, An IDRC Company
Pronto Connections, Inc.
Proxy Communications, Inc.
PSI Telemarketing
PTM Communications
PTM Inc.
Public Interest Communications, Inc.
Quality Telemarketing Inc.
Rainmaker Systems, Inc.
Reese Brothers, Inc.
RMH Teleservices
Selltel Inc. National Protection Service
SITEL Corporation
Sky Alland Marketing
Strategic Telecommunications
Sturner & Klein
T C I M Services
TEL-A-SELL Marketing Inc.
Tele Resources Inc.

Telemarketing Concepts
TeleMasters Inc.
Telematch
TeleQuest
TeleService Resources
TeleSpectrum Worldwide, Inc.
TeleTech
TelServ
The Charlton Group Inc.
The Connection-Inbound
The Development Center, Inc.
The Faneuil Group
The Power Line
The Product Line, Inc.
The Telemarketing Company
Thorn Associates
TicketMaster Direct
Transcom
Trase Miller
Unibase Direct/Data Services Direct
United America Advertising
United Telemarketing Corp.
Unitel Corporation
Vanguard Cellular Systems
Vertical Marketing, Inc.
Volt Direct Marketing, Ltd.
Warrantech Direct Inc.
West Interactive Corporation
World Access Service Corporation
Wyer Creative Communications

Training/recruitment
ROCKINGHAM*JUTKINS*
  marketing, Inc.
Sanna Mattson MacLeod, Inc.
TeleDevelopment Services, Inc.

Translation services
Daniel Gonzalez & Associates
Paul Zoellner International Consulting
  Services.
Probe Communications International,
  Inc.

Website content management
Cross World Network, Inc.

custom seminars
Medina Associates

wireless e-commerce
Seklemian/Newell International
  Marketing Consultants

E-SERVICES

E-Marketing consultant
Angeles Marketing Group
Banner Direct
Campbell Mithun Direct
Cross World Network, Inc.
Direct Marketers On Call
DMRS Group, Inc.
Dot-Com DIRECT
First Marketing Company
Grizzard
Intelitec
Interactive Resources, Inc.
ITAGroup
J. Schmid & Assoc. Inc.
KENT MARKETING GROUP, INC.
Kobs Strategic Consulting
La Agencia de Orci & Asociados
Malcolm Decker Associates Inc.
Marke Communications, Inc.
Maxwell Sroge Company, Inc.
Medina Associates
Probe Communications International,
  Inc.
RMS Direct, LLC
Sanna Mattson MacLeod, Inc.
Strategy Outfitters
The Callahan Group, L.L.C.
The E-Tailing Group, Inc.
The Jackson Consulting Group, Inc.
Triad, Inc.
Wesley R. Weber & Associates, Inc.

Email list provider
ACT ONE Mailing List Services, Inc.
Aldata
Alpha Marketing & Consulting
American List Counsel, Inc.
Angeles Marketing Group
Direct Mail Trackers
GreatLists.com
INFOCORE, INC.
Intelitec
International Direct Response, Inc.
L.I.S.T. INCORPORATED
List Technology Systems Group, Inc.
World Innovators, Inc.

Email software
Alpha Marketing & Consulting

Online/e-marketing agency
Angeles Marketing Group
Campbell Mithun Direct
Dot-Com DIRECT
First Marketing Company
Grizzard
I Market Inc
Interactive Resources, Inc.
Malcolm Decker Associates Inc.
Marke Communications, Inc.
TMP Worldwide
Wong Wong Boyack

Website design
American Computer Group
Angeles Marketing Group
ASI
Banner Direct
Cimetry Inc.
Cross World Network, Inc.
Cyber M@rketing Services
Digital Impact
E-Dialog Inc.
edirect, Inc.
Emaginet, Inc.
Email Channel, Inc.
First Marketing Company
Grizzard
iName, Inc.
ispi (Internet Service Providers
  International)
La Agencia de Orci & Asociados
Life Plus International
Marke Communications, Inc.
Maxwell Sroge Company, Inc.
Mercata
Millstar Electronic Publishing
  Group
NetMarquee Inc.
Netscape Communications
Online Development Corporation
PeopleSupport
Planet U
Post Communications, Inc.
PrizePoint Entertainment Corp.
Probe Communications International,
  Inc.
Profit Boosters Copywriting
Sanna Mattson MacLeod, Inc.
The Monster Board
Triad, Inc.
UpShot

540

LATIN AMERICA

REGIONAL OVERVIEW

The major change in the political economy of the continent in recent years has been the passage of the North American Free Trade Agreement (NAFTA).

The direct effect of NAFTA is a phased reduction of tariff barriers between the United States, Canada and Mexico. But the psychological impact of the treaty on all countries north and south of the Rio Grande far exceeds the immediate economic gains to exporters.

Many US companies are realizing for the first time the immense potential of Mexico, and, by extension, the rest of Latin America. They see it as a region of increasing wealth and stability where they have a head start over competitors from Japan and the European Union. Even the Spanish language does not daunt them; after all, publishers and cataloguers are already producing material in Spanish for the Hispanic communities in New York, California, Texas and Florida.

Within Mexico, businesses are looking forward to the challenge of improving quality and service to meet American demands. Lower tariffs will mean that with the low cost of labour that they already enjoy, their goods will be very price competitive in the United States. Consumers can expect more and more US retailers to open up in Mexico – Neiman Marcus and Costco are already there – and local services will benefit from new American-owned manufacturing plants. However, 1995 saw Mexico struggling with a severe financial crisis, the effects of which may prove to have serious implications for the economic stability and investor confidence across the continent.

The rest of Latin America is anticipating the extension of NAFTA and the creation of the Americas Free Trade Agreement (AFTA). Brazil, Argentina, Uruguay and Paraguay have formed Mercosur (Mercosul in Portugese), the Common Market of the South. This has combined GNP of US$800 billion and contains 200 million potential consumers (potential as Brazil's 150 million include about only 30 million as economically significant consumers). Chile became an associate member of Mercosur in 1996 and Bolivia in 1997, and the Andean Pact countries (Bolivia, Colombia, Ecuador, Venezuela and Peru) are negotiating.

Significant progress has also been made to combat the region's 'hyperinflation'. In 1996, Argentina and Chile had inflation rates in single figures, whilst Brazil's and Peru's rates were only just above 10 per cent.

Without question, the two nations with the most impressive economic credentials are Argentina and Chile. In both countries old-style Latin inflation is now definitely something of the past, and Chile in particular has enjoyed remarkable growth in recent years. By the standards of its own recent past Brazil is also doing better, and its enormous population gives plenty of scope for future development provided it can be properly controlled.

DIRECT MARKETING IN LATIN AMERICA

In the last few years American direct marketers, led by, but not confined to, publishers, have made a concerted effort to open up Latin America. This has resulted in a substantial improvement in the direct marketing infrastructure but all mailers should bear in mind the following:

Lists

The staple lists, especially for English language mailers, remain the subscriber files for *Time*, *Newsweek*, *Business Week* and others. There are good compiled business-to-business lists in Mexico – although none with a truly comprehensive SIC system – and some coverage in Chile, Brazil, Argentina, Venezuela and Colombia. For the rest there is nothing.

Good consumer mail order lists outside Mexico are hard to find, and list broking and management companies are still to emerge.

Lettershop and mailing

If you are mailing into Latin America as part of a larger international campaign you would be well advised to mail from your own country. Consider local mailings only if you want to create a local image or for ease of fulfilment. Another factor is that some list owners will only send lists to approved lettershops. Postal services are good in Brazil, improving in Mexico, and adequate in Argentina and Chile.

Notes

Major Latin American countries are detailed in this section. However, the following is a list of service providers and postal administrations in some of the smaller countries in Central and Latin America.

CHILE

PROVIDERS OF DM AND E-M SERVICES

AMD CHILE
Av. Del Parque 4980, Of. 231
Ciudad Impresarial, Huechuraba,
Santiago
Chile
Tel: +56 2 738 4455
Fax: +56 2 738 4422
Sergio A Pinada

Services/Products:
Direct marketing association

CTC MARKETING E INFORMACIAN SA
Paso Hondo 035, Santiago
Chile
Tel: +56 2 735 4000
Fax: +56 2 735 4290
Philipe Tomic

Services/Products:
Telemarketing agency

J WALTER THOMPSON DIRECT CHILE
Ricardo Lyon 1262, Santiago
Chile
Tel: +56 2 251 3303
Fax: +56 2 204 3625
Abraham Yudelevich, Manager

Services/Products:
Advertising agency

LOYALTY MARKETING
Huelen 75 4to Piso, Santiago
Chile
Tel: +56 2 235 4996
Fax: +56 2 236 1259

Services/Products:
Advertising agency

NEXCOM MARKETING DIRECTO
Paso Hondo 035
Providencia, Santiago
Chile
Tel: +56 2 735 4000
Fax: +56 2 735 4290
Leonardo Nualart Gho, Gerente
Comercial

WUNDERMAN CATO JOHNSON
Roger de Floor 2995, 4th Floor,
Santiago
Chile
Tel: +56 2 231 6961
Fax: +56 2 232 7652

Services/Products:
Advertising agency; Direct marketing
agency

SERVICES/PRODUCT LISTING

Advertising agency
J Walter Thompson Direct Chile
Loyalty Marketing
Wunderman Cato Johnson

Direct marketing agency
Wunderman Cato Johnson

Direct marketing association
AMD Chile

Telemarketing agency
CTC Marketing E Informacian SA

Association
DMA (USA)
CTC Marketing E Informacian SA
Wunderman Cato Johnson

COSTA RICA

PROVIDERS OF DM AND E-M SERVICES

CORREOS DE COSTA RICA
Centro Postal Zapote
Correao Interno
San José
Costa Rica
Tel: +506 233 94 01
Fax: +506 233 94 11
Luis Mora Vargas, Commercial
Manager

Services/Products:
Postal Administration

RAPP COLLINS CENTRAL AMERICA
Apartado Postal 12700-1000
San José
Costa Rica
Tel: +506 257 6390
Fax: +506 257 6325
Alun Munoz Mora, General Director

Services/Products:
Database marketing consultant

SERVICES/PRODUCT LISTING

Database marketing consultant
Rapp Collins Central America

Postal Administration
Correos De Costa Rica

Association
DMA (USA)
Rapp Collins Central America

ECUADOR

PROVIDERS OF DM AND E-M SERVICES

DIRECTO NINOS S.A.
9 de Octubre 2009 y Los Rios
Edif. El Marques, Rm 201
09-01-7544
Guayaquil
Ecuador
Tel: +593 4 450 930
Fax: +593 4 450 769
Raul Patino, President

Services/Products:
Lettershop; Mailing house

EMPRESSA NACIONAL DE CORREOS
Av. Eloy Alfaro 354 y 9 de Octubre
Quito
Ecuador
Tel: +593 2 554 067
Fax: +593 2 561 961
Walter Reyes Silva, Commercial
Director

Services/Products:
Postal administration

SERVICES/PRODUCT LISTING

Lettershop
Directo Ninos S.A.

Mailing House
Directo Ninos S.A.

Postal administration
Empressa Nacional De Correos

Association
DMA (USA)
Directo Ninos S.A.

EL SALVADOR
PROVIDERS OF DM AND E-M SERVICES

TV OFFER
Avenida y Colonia Las Mercedes
Calle Los Duraznos #1
El Salvador
Tel: +503 298 6088
Fax: +503 223 1515
Email: presidente@grupotvoffer.com
Web: www.grupotvoffer.com
Luis Armando Salaverria, CEO,
President

Services/Products:
Call centre services/systems;
Telemarketing agency; Direct
Response TV

Member of:
DMA (US); Electronic Retailing
Association (ERA)

GUATEMALA
PROVIDERS OF DM AND E-M SERVICES

CEMACO
PO Box 149
7a, Avenida 2–34 Zona 4
Guatemala City
Guatemala
Tel: +502 2 314018
Fax: +502 2 314631

Services/Products:
Advertising agency

URUGUAY
PROVIDERS OF DM AND E-M SERVICES

LINEA DIRECTA
25 de Mayo 467
Montevideo
Uruguay
Tel: +598 2 965 350
Fax: +598 2 965 351

Services/Products:
Advertising agency; Telemarketing
agency

ARGENTINA

Population: 35.2 million
Capital: Buenos Aires
Language: Spanish
GDP: $295 billion
GDP per capita: $8380
Inflation: 0.5 per cent
Currency: Peso (P) = 100 centavos
Exchange rate: P1 : $1
Time: GMT –3 hours

Argentina has enjoyed several years of steady economic growth, with a positive GDP growth of 5.3% in 1996 and 8.1% in the first quarter of 1997. Inflation, now down to 0.5%, is one of the lowest rates in the world.

Argentina's telecommunications network has recently undergone a revolution. The privatization of the state-run Entel led to a great improvement in line installations, and Argentinians were able to get a telephone in less than four months. There are still long waiting lists, however, and connection costs and call charges are relatively high, giving a less than favourable environment for telemarketing. The automated telephone system runs throughout the country, but local systems tend to be overloaded.

Direct marketing is still a small, unregulated industry. Hampered by very basic postal services and a lack of comprehensive, clean lists, the DM industry has the potential to take off, but needs an improvement in the communications infrastructure before it can do so.

LEGISLATION AND CONSUMER PROTECTION

There is no data protection legislation, although this is currently under consideration in Parliament.

THE DIRECT MARKETING ASSOCIATION

Name: Asoción de Marketing Directo de Argentina (AMDA)
Address: Tucumán 1455, piso 5 "F", C.P. 105, Buenos Aires
Tel/Fax: +54 11 4373 3030
E-mail: gerencia@amda.org.ar
Year founded: 1987
President: Salvador Filiba
Total staff: 4
Members: 200
Contact: José Maria Guitart, Manager

Facilities for overseas users of direct mail

Membership: overseas companies can join in the organization. Annual fees vary up to US$3000 for the largest companies.
Newsletter: the AMDA publishes a newsletter in Spanish 5 to 6 times a year.
There is no library or on-line information service and the AMDA does not offer legal advice.
Other facilities: the AMDA organizes exhibitions, conferences and seminars.

POSTAL SERVICES

For further information please contact:

Correo Argentino S.A.
Sarmiento 151, 7 piso, Oficinia 738 C
1000 Buenos Aires
Argentina

Tel: +54 11 4311 5030
Fax: +54 11 4311 3111
Website: www.correoargentino.com.ar

PROVIDERS OF DM AND E-M SERVICES

ACTION LINE DE ARGENTINA S.A.
Arriberos 2841
Buenos Aires
Argentina
Tel: +54 1 784 0043
Fax: +54 1 784 0043

Services/Products:
Telemarketing agency

Member of:
AMDA

CALANDRELLI & ASOCIADOS
San Martín 662 - piso 2 - B
Bueno Aires
Argentina
Tel: +54 1 312 8124
Fax: +54 1 311 2395

Member of:
AMDA

CLIENTING GROUP
Larrea 1007 - 8 Piso
Buenos Aires
1117
Argentina
Tel: +54 1 821 3900
Fax: +54 1 821 3900
Fernando Peydro, President

Services/Products:
List services; Telemarketing agency;
Direct marketing agency

Member of:
DMA (US); AMDA

DI PAOLA & ASOCIADOS/ THOMPSON CONNECT
Uruguay 1025, 9 Piso
Buenos Aires
1016
Argentina
Tel: +54 11 4816 0848
Fax: +54 11 4816 0849
Email: dipaola@dipaola.com.ar
Alejandro di Paola, Director

Services/Products:
Advertising Agency; Mail order
company; Telemarketing agency;
Direct marketing agency; Database
services; Interactive media

E-Services:
Online/e-marketing agency

Member of:
DMA (US); National DMA

EDITORIAL PERFIL
Chacabuco 271
Buenos Aires
1069
Argentina
Tel: +54 1 341 9052
Fax: +54 13 41 9053
Carlos Andalo

Services/Products:
Advertising Agency; List services;
Telemarketing agency; Direct
marketing agency

Member of:
DMA (US)

FELIX & FELIX CO.
A.Alsina 1433
3rd Floor
Bueno Aires
Argentina
Tel: +54 11 4381 1585
Fax: +54 11 4382 3317
Email: pablof@felix.com.ar
Web: www.felix.com.ar
Pablo Fabian Felix, Vice President

Services/Products:
Database services; Direct marketing
agency; List services; Personalisation

E-Services:
Email list provider

Member of:
AMDIA

FULL SALE TELEPERFORMANCE
Av.L.N.Alem 896 - 2 piso
Bueno Aires
Argentina
Tel: +54 1 317 2600
Fax: +54 1 317 2601

Services/Products:
Telemarketing agency; Direct
marketing agency

Member of:
AMDA

GRUPO BRAIN S.R.L.
V.de Obligado 2264 - piso 1 D
Bueno Aires
Argentina
Tel: +54 1 785 3992
Fax: +54 1 785 3992

Services/Products:
Telemarketing agency

Member of:
AMDA

GRUPO PYD
Reconquista 1011
Piso 4
Buenos Aires
Argentina
Tel: +54 11 4315 6543
Fax: +54 11 4315 5747
Email: pyd@pyd.com
Web: www.grupopyd.com
Marcos Fernandez Gorgolas, President

Services/Products:
Call centre services/systems;
Consultancy services; Direct marketing
agency; Market research agency;
Telemarketing agency; Training/
recruitment; Database analysis

E-Services:
E-Marketing consultant; Email
software

Member of:
AMDIA

I4S - IDEAS FOR SALE
Castex 3365, 7th
Buenos Aires
Argentina
Tel: +54 1 801 2031
Fax: +54 1 807 2116
Adalberto Rossi, Creative Director

Services/Products:
Advertising Agency; Direct marketing
agency

Member of:
DMA (US)

INES RUSQUELLAS/RR.PP. - TELEMARKETING
Pte.Quintana 440 - Piso 5 B
Bueno Aires
Argentina
Tel: +54 1 804 6803

Services/Products:
Telemarketing agency

Member of:
AMDA

LAUTREC DIRECTA
Av.Alicia M.de Justo 240 - piso 1
Bueno Aires
Argentina
Tel: +54 1 314 5050
Fax: +54 1 314 4105

Services/Products:
Telemarketing agency; Direct
marketing agency

Member of:
AMDA

MAILCO S.A.
Paraguay 523, Piso 4
Buenos Aires
1057
Argentina
Tel: +54 11 4312 3636
Fax: +54 11 4313 0847
Email: bvrtovec@mailcogroup.com
Web: www.mailcogroup.com
Bogdan Vrtovec, President

Services/Products:
List services; Database services; Direct
marketing agency

E-Services:
Email list provider; E-Marketing
consultant; Website design; Email
software; Online/e-marketing agency

Member of:
DMA (US); AMDIA

MARTIN & MEYER DIRECT S.A.
Avda.del Libertador 4980 - piso 1 -A
Bueno Aires
Argentina
Tel: +54 1 772 3405
Fax: +54 1 772 3405

Services/Products:
Telemarketing agency

Member of:
AMDA

**MCCANN RELATIONSHIP
MARKETING ARGENTINA**
Suipacha 268
8 Piso
Buenos Aires
1008
Argentina
Tel: +54 11 4329 9500
Fax: +54 11 4329 9501
Email: mrm-
argentina@mccann.com.ar
Web: www.mrmworldwide.com
Salvador Filiba, President, CEO

Services/Products:
Call centre services/systems;
Consultancy services; Database
services; Direct marketing agency;
Personalisation; Telemarketing agency;
Customer relationship centre

E-Services:
E-Marketing consultant; Website
design; Online/e-marketing agency

Member of:
DMA (US); National DMA

MEGA SALE S.A.
Av. Santa Fe 900
8th Fl
Buenos Aires

1059
Argentina
Tel: +54 1 313 3777
Fax: +54 1 315 1819
Carlos Alfredo Pithod, President

Services/Products:
Advertising Agency; Direct marketing
agency

Member of:
DMA (US)

MEYER & MEYER DIRECT S.A.
Av. Libertador 4980 Piso 1 A
Capital Federal
Buenos Aires
1426
Argentina
Tel: +54 1 772 3405
Fax: +54 1 775 4303
Martin Meyer, President

Services/Products:
Direct marketing agency; Consultancy
services

Member of:
DMA (US); AMDA

**MULTI VOICE MARKETING
DIRECTO**
Ituzaingo 270, piso 13
Cordoba, CB
5000
Argentina
Tel: +54 51 21 9000
Fax: +54 51 24 6603
Humberto Sahade, Chief Executive
Officer

Services/Products:
Advertising Agency; Direct marketing
agency

Member of:
DMA (US)

OGILVY ONE WORLDWIDE
Suipacha 568
Bueno Aires
Argentina
Tel: +54 1 394 3002
Fax: +54 1 325 4851

Services/Products:
Direct marketing agency

Member of:
AMDA

PROMOPHONE S.A.
México 441 - piso 1 B
Bueno Aires
Argentina
Tel: +54 1 343 7788
Fax: +54 1 343 8343

Services/Products:
Telemarketing agency

Member of:
AMDA

RAPP COLLINS ARGENTINA
Marcelo T. de Alvear 405
Buenos Aires
1058
Argentina
Tel: +54 1 315 9119
Fax: +54 1 315 9449
Gustavo Paris, President

Services/Products:
Advertising Agency

Member of:
DMA (US)

WUNDERMAN CATO JOHNSON
Demaría 4412
Bueno Aires
Argentina
Tel: +54 1 777 8500
Fax: +54 1 777 4919

Services/Products:
Direct marketing agency

Member of:
AMDA

SERVICES/PRODUCT
LISTING

Advertising Agency
Di Paola & Asociados/Thompson
Connect
Editorial Perfil
I4S - Ideas for Sale
Mega Sale S.A.
Multi Voice Marketing Directo
Rapp Collins Argentina

Call centre services/systems
Grupo PYD
McCann Relationship Marketing
Argentina

Consultancy services
Grupo PYD
McCann Relationship Marketing
Argentina
Meyer & Meyer Direct S.A.

Customer relationship centre
McCann Relationship Marketing
Argentina

Database analysis
Grupo PYD

Database services
Di Paola & Asociados/Thompson
   Connect
Felix & Felix Co.
Mailco S.A.
McCann Relationship Marketing
   Argentina

Direct marketing agency
Clienting Group
Di Paola & Asociados/Thompson
   Connect
Editorial Perfil
Felix & Felix Co.
Full Sale Teleperformance
Grupo PYD
I4S - Ideas for Sale
Lautrec Directa
Mailco S.A.
McCann Relationship Marketing
   Argentina
Mega Sale S.A.
Meyer & Meyer Direct S.A.
Multi Voice Marketing Directo
Ogilvy One Worldwide
Wunderman Cato Johnson

Interactive media
Di Paola & Asociados/Thompson
   Connect

List services
Clienting Group

Editorial Perfil
Felix & Felix Co.
Mailco S.A.

Mail order company
Di Paola & Asociados/Thompson
   Connect

Market research agency
Grupo PYD

Personalisation
Felix & Felix Co.
McCann Relationship Marketing
   Argentina

Telemarketing agency
Action Line De Argentina S.A.
Clienting Group
Di Paola & Asociados/Thompson
   Connect
Editorial Perfil
Full Sale Teleperformance
Grupo Brain S.R.L.
Grupo PYD
Ines Rusquellas/Rr.Pp. - Telemarketing
Lautrec Directa
Martin & Meyer Direct S.A.
McCann Relationship Marketing
   Argentina
Promophone S.A.

Training/recruitment
Grupo PYD

E-SERVICES

E-Marketing consultant
Grupo PYD
Mailco S.A.
McCann Relationship Marketing
   Argentina

Email list provider
Felix & Felix Co.
Mailco S.A.

Email software
Grupo PYD
Mailco S.A.

Online/e-marketing agency
Di Paola & Asociados/Thompson
   Connect
Mailco S.A.
McCann Relationship Marketing
   Argentina

Website design
Mailco S.A.
McCann Relationship Marketing
   Argentina

BRAZIL

Population: 161.8 million
Capital: Brasília
Language: Portuguese

GDP: $710 billion
GDP per capita: $4410
Inflation: 6.9 per cent

Currency: Real (R) = 100 centavos
Exchange rate: R1.65 : $1

Time: GMT –3 hours

OVERVIEW

Brazil has the fifth largest population in the world, and its economy represents nearly half the output of the whole of Latin America. However, it is a country that has yet to realize its full potential. Political failings and economic difficulties persist, but hyperinflation has now been controlled, with inflation falling to less than 10% in mid-1996, a level not seen for three decades.

This vast market of some 161 million inhabitants is steadily becoming more attractive as a destination for exports, as import licences are abolished and tariffs lowered in a continuing programme of trade liberalization. High-income groups exist in large numbers, and there is a broad industrial and services sector. Local publishers, cataloguers and financial services companies are all active.

Direct marketing activity in the area is relatively high, and techniques are more sophisticated than in other Latin American countries. The average number of pieces received per month is around 8.3.

Major operators in direct marketing are banks, credit card companies, publishers, book clubs, insurance, computers and general merchandise catalogues. Telemarketing activities are expanding also rapidly in Brazil.

Lists and databases

Local lists are available for rental, and universes are estimated by the ABEMD to be ten million consumers and two million businesses. A well-established publishing industry with over 700 magazines and 1300 newspaper titles pushes ever more lists onto the market. Lists are usually held by the owners, and some will insist on handling lettershopping themselves. Most, however, will allow you to mail when the lettershop is selected by them. Rental prices will vary between US$45 and US$150 per thousand.

With regard to the media, there are around 250 daily newspapers with a combined circulation of under five million. Due to distribution difficulties in such a large country, there are no national daily newspapers. However, numerous regional papers are published. The main newspapers are *Folha de São Paulo* (560,000), *O Globo* (350,000) and *O Estedo de São Paulo* (348,000).

LANGUAGE AND CULTURAL CONSIDERATIONS

Portuguese is the principal language of Brazil. Most Brazilian direct marketing professionals, however, are able to receive and send letters in English. Language does cause problems for international mailers, because while leading executives can be expected to read English, Brazil cannot be included in the Spanish language mailings sent to the rest of Latin America.

LEGISLATION AND CONSUMER PROTECTION

Brazil has had a direct marketing Self Regulatory Code since 1976, under the auspices of ABEMD. The association has also had a List Committee since 1989, to approve and validate all lists. In Brazil, consumers have the right to ask for the source of their name on any given list or database, thus allowing them to control the use of their name to a certain extent. On a government level, Consumer Defense Code Law was approved by the Congress in October 1991.

THE DIRECT MARKETING ASSOCIATION

Name: Associação Brasiliera de Marketing Direto (ABEMD)
Address: Av Paulista, 1471 cj 1301, BR-01311 São Paulo - SP
Tel: +55 11 288 2144
Fax: +55 11 284 8618
Email: abemd@abemd.com.br
Website: www.abemd.com.br
Year founded: 1979
President: Nelson Reis
Total staff: 20

551

Members: 850 companies, with 1680 executives associated to ABEMD
Contact: Felice Preziosi, Executive Director

Direct mail agencies	71	List brokers	79
Mailing houses	32	Printers	23
Telemarketing agencies	72	Direct mail consultants	78
Handling houses	44	Mail order companies	173
Database agencies	48		

Facilities for overseas users of direct mail

Membership: overseas companies are now able to join the ABEMD, and should fax the association for further information.

Newsletter: the ABEMD's newsletter (the only specialist DM publication in Brazil) is normally only circulated to members.

Library: the ABEMD library, which holds over 1000 press cuttings, is available only to members.

On-line information service: yes, but this service is not available to non-members

Legal advice: the association will provide first steps for legal advice for both members and non-members.

Business liaison service: the association will help all prospective mailers in their choice of supplier, whether they are members or not.

POSTAL SERVICES

There is an excellent postal system in Brazil, probably the best in Latin America.

The Brazilian national postal service, ECT (Empresa Brasiliera de Correios e Telégrafos) has several useful services for the direct marketer.

Commercial order: for the transportation of goods, particularly those of industrial markets and dealers. This service guarantees delivery within a specified amount of time, and specified price according to total weight and delivery distance.

Post paid: a simple way of sending large quantities of printed matter, both nationally and internationally. This service uses either stamps or the mechanical franking system.

Guaranteed delivery: if printed matter cannot be delivered to the intended recipient it will be returned to the sender.

Reply card: used for ordering products, requesting commercial or industrial information, or information regarding statistical data and research, this card can be put inside newspapers and magazines. Taxa Paga allows the sender to use an ordinary envelope to order goods, catalogues, commmercial information etc. There are specified limits regarding the size of cards for this service. The weight and dimensions must not exceed the following:

International reply card	max weight 50g
	minimum size 90mm × 140mm
	max size 114mm × 229mm
Conventional reply card	minimum size 90mm 140mm, 114mm 162mm (envelope format)
	max size 300mm × 400mm, 114mm × 229mm (envelope format)

Order reply envelopes: are used to send bulky/bigger items like undeveloped films, reports or product samples. Maximum weight for this service is 250g.

Unaddressed mail: this service is more economical and efficient for reaching potential clients. Promotional pieces can be distributed in a specified area. The weight limit for this service is 20g.

Postal telemarketing: for more information call (011) 159.

Express mail service (EMS) and Sedex Internacional: for more information contact:

Empresa Brasileira de Correios e Telégrafos (ECT)
Department international d'exploitation et marché postal
SBN - Quadra 1 - Bloco A, 4°Andar
70002-900 Brasília - DF Brèsil
Tel: +55 61 4262100
Fax: +55 61 4262114
Website: www.correios.com.br/ (this website is in Portuguese)

PROVIDERS OF DM AND E-M SERVICES

22 DIRECT MARKETING
R Lituania 798
Santo Andre
SP
9280261
Brazil
Tel: +55 11 4151717
Fax: +55 11 4151717
Luiz Carlos Ribeiro De Assis

Services/Products:
List services; Database services;
Labelling/envelope services; Direct
marketing agency; Consultancy
services

Member of:
ABEMD

3D CALL FREE TELEMARKETING
Av Brg Luis Antonio 2466 CJ 71
Sao Paulo
SP
1402000
Brazil
Tel: +55 11 2891105
Fax: +55 11 2891440
Jose Jorge Abdo Agame Neto

Services/Products:
Telemarketing agency

Member of:
ABEMD

3D COMUNICACAO
Av. Antonio J. De M. Andrade, 278
Sao Paulo
SP
4507000
Brazil
Tel: +55 11 8878051
Fax: +55 11 8878051
Eduardo Zanoni Strauch

Services/Products:
Advertising Agency

Member of:
ABEMD

A&C MARKETING E EVENTOS LTDA
R Pot Colombina 417
Sao Paulo
SP
5593010
Brazil
Tel: +55 11 8680484
Fax: +55 11 8680484
Carmen Murnikas Hamada

Services/Products:
List services; Mailing/Faxing services;
Training/recruitment

Member of:
ABEMD

A+ FCVA PROPAGANDA
R Furnas 239
Sao Paulo
SP
4562050
Brazil
Tel: +55 11 55058088
Fax: +55 11 55066885
Angelina Hodas Taddeo Do Val

Services/Products:
Advertising Agency

Member of:
ABEMD

A2 PUBLICIDADE E PROMOCOES LT
R Francisco Leitao 339 1 And CJ 11
Sao Paulo
SP
5414020
Brazil
Tel: +55 11 8538298
Fax: +55 11 30610872
Antonio Carlos Espilotro

Services/Products:
Advertising Agency; Consultancy
services; Direct marketing agency;
Hardware supplier; Software supplier

E-Services:
Website design

Member of:
ABEMD

ABRIL – ENTREGA DIRETA
Av Octaviano Alves De Lima 4400 7
And
Sao Paulo
SP
2909900
Brazil
Tel: +55 11 39901900
Fax: +55 11 39901834
Antonio Cesar Godoy Da Silva

Services/Products:
Mailing/Faxing services; Fulfilment
and sampling house

Member of:
ABEMD

ABRIL COLECOES
Av Pres Vargas 3131 16 A Sl 1601
Rio De Janeiro
RJ
20210030
Brazil
Tel: +55 21 5153500
Fax: +55 21 5153551
Andrea Portante

Services/Products:
Publisher

Member of:
ABEMD

ABRIL S/A
Av. Das Nacoes Unidas, 7221 – 10
And
Sao Paulo
SP
5477000
Brazil
Tel: +55 11 30376140
Fax: +55 11 30376106
William Pereira

Services/Products:
Publisher

Member of:
ABEMD

ACCESS TLMKT SERVICOS LTDA
R Augusta 2945 6 And CJ 61
Sao Paulo
SP
1413100
Brazil
Tel: +55 11 30619275
Fax: +55 11 30619274
Clovis Martins Chaves

Services/Products:
Telemarketing agency; Training/
recruitment; Consultancy services

Member of:
ABEMD

ACESSO DIRETO CONSULTORES
R Volunt Da Patria 89 6 A CJ 604
Rio De Janeiro
RJ
22270000
Brazil
Tel: +55 21 5355226
Fax: +55 21 5355226
Email: acdireto@uninet.com.br
Jeffrey Hanson Costa, Director

Services/Products:
Consultancy services; Direct marketing
agency; Telemarketing agency; Internet
services

E-Services:
E-Marketing consultant

Member of:
ABEMD; ABT

ACF CELESTINO BOURROUL
Av Celestino Bourroul 450
Sao Paulo
SP
2710000
Brazil
Tel: +55 11 2661787
Fax: +55 11 2661787
Andrea Pereira Mateo

Services/Products:
Labelling/envelope services; Mailing/
Faxing services

Member of:
ABEMD

ACF HEITOR PENTEADO
R Heitor Penteado 1240
Sao Paulo
SP
5438100
Brazil
Tel: +55 11 8646942
Fax: +55 11 38629773
Ignacio Alberto G Santin

Services/Products:
Mailing/Faxing services

Member of:
ABEMD

ACTION LINE
Av Paulista 1009 12 And
Sao Paulo
SP
1311000
Brazil
Tel: +55 11 50872700
Fax: +55 11 50872701
Simone Giudice

Services/Products:
Telemarketing agency

Member of:
ABEMD

**AD CENTRAL TEC GRAF
   LASER LTDA**
R Mto Chiaffarelli 45
Sao Paulo
SP
1432030
Brazil
Tel: +55 11 8877782
Fax: +55 11 8877782
Derek George Hamburger

Services/Products:
List services; Design/graphics/clip art
supplier; Personalisation

Member of:
ABEMD

**AD/MKD COML LTDA ART
   DIRETA**
Al Afonso Schimidt 818
Sao Paulo
SP
2450001
Brazil
Tel: +55 11 69502799
Fax: +55 11 69594526
Fabio Bom Angelo

Services/Products:
List services; Direct marketing agency;
Consultancy services

Member of:
ABEMD

**ADDRESS S. APOIO MALA D.
   LTDA**
Av Jose Cesar De Oliveira 175
Sao Paulo
SP
5317000
Brazil
Tel: +55 11 8326925
Fax: +55 11 8325822
Ricardo Gomes

Services/Products:
Labelling/envelope services

Member of:
ABEMD

**ADIRON CONSULTORES S/C
   LTDA**
R Lisboa 1208 CJ 71
Sao Paulo
SP
5413001
Brazil
Tel: +55 11 2828069
Fabio Adiron Ribeiro

Services/Products:
Database services; Consultancy
services

Member of:
ABEMD

**ADVB ASSOC. DIRI. VEND.
   BRASIL**
R Rolandia 138
Londrina
PR
86060310
Brazil
Tel: +55 43 3286010
Fax: +55 43 3285656
Jose Roberto Lourenco Mattos

Services/Products:
Advertising Agency; Consultancy
services; Labelling/envelope services;
Telemarketing agency; Publisher

Member of:
ABEMD

**AGROVERPA INFORMACAOS
   EM AGRIBUSINESS**
R Rego Freitas 454 10 And
Sao Paulo
SP
1220010
Brazil
Tel: +55 11 3822 1888
Fax: +55 11 3822 1888
Email: agroverpa@agroverpa.com.br
Web: www.agroverpa.com.br
Monica Caetano Navarro

Services/Products:
Database services; List services

Member of:
ABEMD

**ALBRA COMUNICACAO
   INTEGRADA LT**
Av. Brig. F. Lima, 1912–7 Andar SL 7
G
Sao Paulo
SP
1451907
Brazil
Tel: +55 11 8136393
Fax: +55 11 8136393
Humberto G. Branco

Services/Products:
Telemarketing agency; Direct
marketing agency; Internet services

Member of:
ABEMD

**ALPHA GRAPHICS –
   IBIRAPUERA**
Av Ibirapuera 3407
Sao Paulo
SP
4029200
Brazil
Tel: +55 11 5363253
Fax: +55 11 2411478
Jurg Muller

Services/Products:
Design/graphics/clip art supplier;
Personalisation

Member of:
ABEMD

ALPHA TELECOM
R Oscar Freire 1936
Sao Paulo
SP
5409011
Brazil
Tel: +55 11 30610074

Fax: +55 11 30610074
Ricardo Franco De Carvalho

Services/Products:
Telemarketing agency; Hardware
supplier; Software supplier

Member of:
ABEMD

ALVO PROMOÇOES E MALA DIRETA LTDA
Rua Margarida 298
Barra Funda
Sao Paulo
SP
01154–030
Brazil
Tel: +55 11 3824 9290
Fax: +55 11 3824 9292
Email:
alvomd@alvomaladirecta.com.br
Web: www.alvomaladirecta.com.br
Paulo B. Rezende, Commercial
Director

Services/Products:
List services

Member of:
ABEMD

ALWAYS PROP. PUBLIC. S/C LTDA
Rua Ribeiro De Barros, 132
Sao Paulo
SP
5027020
Brazil
Tel: +55 11 38650374
Fax: +55 11 38623881
Rodrigo Martins Seckler

Services/Products:
Advertising Agency

Member of:
ABEMD

AM3 TELEMARKETING S/C LTDA
Rua Cunha Gago, 394
Pinheiros
Sao Paulo
SP
05421–001
Brazil
Tel: +55 11 3819 7766
Fax: +55 11 3819 7766
Email: am3@am3tmk.com.br
Web: www.am3tmk.com.br
Ana Maria Moreira Monteiro,
Executive Director

Services/Products:
Consultancy services; Training/
recruitment; Call centre services/
systems

Member of:
DMA

AMDEXCOMERCIAL E INDUSTRIAL LTDA
Av. Professor Frederico Herman
Junior, 296
Alto de Pinheiros
Sao Paulo
SP
05459–010
Brazil
Tel: +55 11 3819 5170
Fax: +55 11 3031 5271
Email: amdex@amdex.com.br
Marcelo de Oliveira Lima Filho,
Commercial Director

Services/Products:
Hardware supplier

Member of:
ABEMD

AML MKT DE RELACIONAMENTO
R Rocha 167 CJ 132 E 133
Sao Paulo
SP
1330000
Brazil
Tel: +55 11 2530653
Fax: +55 11 2886270
Ana Maria Alves Leandro

Services/Products:
Database services; Telemarketing
agency; Training/recruitment; Copy
adaptation

Member of:
ABEMD

AOM GESTAO DE EMPRESAS E SOFTWARE S/C LTDA
R Baru, 41
Sao Paulo
SP
04639–030
Brazil
Tel: +55 11 5548 8022
Fax: +55 11 5523 0258
Email: chu@aom.com.br
Web: www.aom.com.br
Chu Shao Yong, Director

Services/Products:
Consultancy services; Interactive
media; Market research agency;
Personalisation; Service bureau;
Software supplier

E-Services:
Email list provider; E-Marketing
consultant; Website design

Member of:
ABEMD (Brazil)

ARANDA EDIT. TEC. E CULT. LTDA
Al. Olga, 315
Sao Paulo
SP
1155900
Brazil
Tel: +55 11 8264511
Fax: +55 11 36669585
Silvio Paulo Da Silva

Services/Products:
Publisher

Member of:
ABEMD

ARGUMENTO TLMKT COM E SERVS LT
R Do Imp D Pedro Ii 307 Sl 803 8 Ar
Recife
PE
50010240
Brazil
Tel: +55 81 4242166
Fax: +55 81 4244425
Silvia Sales Moury Fernandes

Services/Products:
Telemarketing agency; Private deliver
services

Member of:
ABEMD

ASSOC COMERCIAL DE SAO PAULO
R Boa Vista 51 4 And
Sao Paulo
SP
1014911
Brazil
Tel: +55 11 2443691
Fax: +55 11 2394113
Alencar Burti

Services/Products:
Publisher

Member of:
ABEMD

ASSOCIACAO ALUMNI
R Brasiliense 65
Sao Paulo
SP
4729110
Brazil
Tel: +55 11 5233655

Fax: +5511 5233655
Maria Filomena A Jorge

Services/Products:
Training/recruitment; Copy adaptation

Member of:
ABEMD

ATB COMUNICAÇOES SC LTDA
Rua Helena, 170 CJ 22
Conj. 21/22
Vila Olimpia
Sao Paulo
SP
04552–050
Brazil
Tel: +55 11 3846 4173
Fax: +55 11 3846 4173
Email:
   contacto@atbcomunicacoes.com.br
Web: www.atbcomunicacoes.com.br
Airton Bovo, Director

Services/Products:
Advertising Agency; Catalogue
producer; Design/graphics/clip art
supplier; Direct marketing agency

Member of:
ABEMD

**AUTTEL SERVICOS E TLMKT.
   LTDA**
Av Brg L Antonio 2050 15 A CJ 151
Sao Paulo
SP
1318002
Brazil
Tel: +55 11 31713200
Fax: +55 11 31713377
Oscar Teixeira Soares

Services/Products:
Telemarketing agency; Training/
recruitment; Consultancy services

Member of:
DMA (US); ABEMD

**BAMBERG AGNELO COM
   INTEGRADA L**
R Funchal 538 19 And
Sao Paulo
SP
4551060
Brazil
Tel: +55 11 8664192
Fax: +55 11 8226242
Judith Lea Adler

Services/Products:
Advertising Agency

Member of:
ABEMD

**BASE 4 COMUNICACAO
   INTEGRADA**
R Jacarezinho 305
Curitiba
PR
80710150
Brazil
Tel: +55 41 3392239
Fax: +55 41 3392239
Cintia Carla Takada

Services/Products:
Advertising Agency; Direct marketing
agency

Member of:
ABEMD

**BASE COMUNICACAO
   INTEGRADA**
R Gomes De Carvalho 1329
Sao Paulo
SP
4547005
Brazil
Tel: +55 11 8225777
Fax: +55 11 8225777
Donizeti Da Silva Leite

Services/Products:
Advertising Agency

Member of:
ABEMD

BASILE COMUNICACAO LTDA
Rua Cardoso De Almeida, 1005 – Casa
2
Sao Paulo
SP
5013001
Brazil
Tel: +55 11 2630955
Fax: +55 11 38656970
Luiz Antonio Basile Martins

Services/Products:
Copy adaptation; Design/graphics/clip
art supplier

Member of:
ABEMD

BE INTERACTIVE
R Ataulfo De Paiva 341 503
Rio De Janeiro
RJ
22440030
Brazil
Tel: +55 21 5292101
Fax: +55 21 5292101
Marcos Luis Barbato

Services/Products:
Hardware supplier; Software supplier;
Internet services

E-Services:
Website design

Member of:
ABEMD

BLACK BOX
Av Guido Caloi 1935 Bl B Terrio
Sao Paulo
SP
5802140
Brazil
Tel: +55 11 55154043
Fax: +55 11 55154002
Andrea De Morais Ferreira

Services/Products:
Hardware supplier

Member of:
ABEMD

BRAND MEMBER
Rua Alves Guimaraes, 205
Sao Paulo
SP
5410000
Brazil
Tel: +55 11 30689614
Fax: +55 11 30689614
Jayme Sillos Rosas Junior

Services/Products:
List services; Fulfilment and sampling
house; Database services;
Telemarketing agency; Consultancy
services

Member of:
ABEMD

**BRETZKE CONSULT. & ASSOC.
   LTDA**
Av Brg F Lima 1620 3 And Sl 304
Sao Paulo
SP
1451001
Brazil
Tel: +55 11 8157345
Fax: +55 11 8157345
Mirian Bretzke

Services/Products:
Telemarketing agency; Direct
marketing agency; Consultancy
services

Member of:
ABEMD

BUSSOLA BRASIL
Av Prof Luis Freire 700 Sl 114
Recife
PE
50740540
Brazil
Tel: +55 81 4534471

Fax: +55 81 4532133
Fernando Jose De Aguiar Sodre

Services/Products:
List services; Database services;
Hardware supplier

Member of:
ABEMD

C C CHEQUE CARD
R 7 De Abril 230 10 And
Sao Paulo
SP
1044000
Brazil
Tel: +55 11 2554585
Fax: +55 11 2557300
Douglas Paulo Andreghetti

Services/Products:
Telemarketing agency

Member of:
ABEMD

CAMELIER MKT & RESULTADOS
R Dos Brazoes 78 CJ 131
Sao Paulo
SP
4603030
Brazil
Tel: +55 11 5308953
Fax: +55 11 5439367
Sandra Camelier

Services/Products:
Consultancy services

Member of:
ABEMD

CAMELIER PROP INTELECTUAL
Al Dos Guainumbis 571
Sao Paulo
SP
4067001
Brazil
Tel: +55 11 50718438
Fax: +55 11 50717124
Alberto Luis C Da Silva

Services/Products:
Legal services

Member of:
ABEMD

CAPITAL SERVICES BRASIL LTDA
Rua Leopoldo, 351
Rio De Janeiro
RJ
20541170
Brazil
Tel: +55 21 5704600

Fax: +55 21 5709774
Luis Antonio Feio De Almeida

Services/Products:
Mailing/Faxing services; Labelling/
envelope services

Member of:
ABEMD

CAPT DIRECT MARKETING
Av. das Nacoes Unidas 10.989
6th Fl - Room 62, Vila Olimpia
Sao Paulo
SP
04578–000
Brazil
Tel: +55 11 829–7773
Fax: +55 11 829–9664
Maria Ines Moraes, Partner/Director

Services/Products:
Telemarketing agency

Member of:
DMA (US)

CASA MARKETING & COMUN. LTDA
Rua Baronesa De Bela Vista, 122
Sao Paulo
SP
4612000
Brazil
Tel: +55 11 2419900
Fax: +55 11 2412988
Celso Rocha Grecco

Services/Products:
Fulfilment and sampling house;
Labelling/envelope services; Direct
marketing agency; Consultancy
services

Member of:
ABEMD

CASE, SALGADO & ASSOCIADOS
Rua Eng. Antonio Jovino, 220 – CJ 22
Sao Paulo
SP
5727220
Brazil
Tel: +55 11 37793000
Fax: +55 11 37793000
Victor Sydow Salgado Filho

Services/Products:
Telemarketing agency

Member of:
ABEMD

CAT-CENTRO DE APERFEIÇOAMENTO EM TELEMARKETING
R. Minas Gerais, 58
Sao Paulo
SP
01244–010
Brazil
Tel: +55 11 2583 444
Fax: +55 11 2312 093
Email: cat@uol.com.br
Silvio Pires De Paula, Director

Services/Products:
Call centre services/systems; Direct
marketing agency; Market research
agency; Training/recruitment

Member of:
National DMA; ABEMD; ABT

CBC ASSES. GRAFICA S/C LTDA ME
Rua Persio De Azevedo, 3
Sao Paulo
SP
3633010
Brazil
Tel: +55 11 61913444
Fax: +55 11 61913433
Marcio Bassan Gomes De Sa

Services/Products:
Advertising Agency; Direct marketin
agency; Design/graphics/clip art
supplier

Member of:
ABEMD

CEDAT
R Maria Jose Da Conceicao 350
Sao Paulo
SP
5730170
Brazil
Tel: +55 11 8468608
Fax: +55 11 8468608
Amir Rodrigues Lobo

Services/Products:
Advertising Agency; List services

Member of:
ABEMD

CELMARTH LTDA.
Av. Rui Barbosa, 121
Carapicuiba
SP
6328330
Brazil
Tel: +55 11 4295066
Fax: +55 11 4295066
Nelson Ascencao De Mello

Services/Products:
Mailing/Faxing services; Fulfilment
and sampling house

Member of:
ABEMD

CELTEC CENTRO EDUC. L. TECNOL.
Av. Epitacio Pessoa, 874
Rio De Janeiro
RJ
22471000
Brazil
Tel: +55 21 5110774
Fax: +55 21 2596714
Mauricio Raposo

Services/Products:
Database services; Hardware supplier;
Software supplier

Member of:
ABEMD

CENTRAL 24 HORAS
R Voluntarios Da Patria 89 7 And
Rio De Janeiro
RJ
22270000
Brazil
Tel: +55 21 5373236
Fax: +55 21 5373751
Marcia Pollard

Services/Products:
Telemarketing agency; Training/
recruitment

Member of:
ABEMD

CENTRUM PROPAGANDA
Pc Monteiro Lobato 36
Sao Paulo
SP
5506030
Brazil
Tel: +55 11 8166637
Fax: +55 11 8159079
Lourival Do Valle Giuliano

Services/Products:
Advertising Agency; Consultancy
services; Direct marketing agency

Member of:
ABEMD

CERTUS PREST DE SERV S/C LTDA
R Oscar Freire 715 CJ 84
Sao Paulo
SP
1426001
Brazil
Tel: +55 11 30611965

Fax: +55 11 30611965
Diva Ione Silva Da Silveira

Services/Products:
Consultancy services

Member of:
ABEMD

CIA. VIDEO
R Pascoal Vita 412
Sao Paulo
SP
5445000
Brazil
Tel: +55 11 8153169
Fax: +55 11 8153567
Julio Luzio De Oliveira

Services/Products:
List services

Member of:
ABEMD

CIRCULO DO LIVRO
Av Jaguare 1643
Sao Paulo
SP
5346000
Brazil
Tel: +55 11 37662337
Fax: +55 11 37662366
Shozi Ikeda

Services/Products:
Design/graphics/clip art supplier;
Publisher

Member of:
ABEMD

CKAPT MARKETING DIRETO
Av. Nacoes Unidas, 10989 – 6And.
CJ62
Sao Paulo
SP
4578000
Brazil
Tel: +55 11 8297773
Fax: +55 11 8299664
Maria Ines Paula Leite Moraes

Services/Products:
List services; Fulfilment and sampling
house; Telemarketing agency;
Training/recruitment; Consultancy
services

Member of:
ABEMD

CKAPT TELEPERFORMANCE
Rua Florencio de Abreu, 623
Sao Paulo
SP
01029–001
Brazil

Tel: +55 11 3328 3377
Fax: +55 11 3328 3565
Email: ckapt@teleperformance.com.br
Web: www.teleperformance.com.br
Maria Evés Morau, Executive Director

Services/Products:
Call centre services/systems; Software
supplier

Member of:
DMA (US); ABT; ABEMD

CKL TELECOMUNICACOES S/A
Av Brg Luis Antonio 580 3 And
Sao Paulo
SP
1318000
Brazil
Tel: +55 11 2427699
Fax: +55 11 2325282
Claudio Marcelo Schmidt Rehder

Services/Products:
Telemarketing agency; Training/
recruitment

Member of:
ABEMD

CMC COMUNICACAO
R Augusto Mielke 120
Jaragua Do Sul
SC
89256030
Brazil
Tel: +55 47 3711177
Fax: +55 47 3711177
Christiane Hufenussler

Services/Products:
Advertising Agency

Member of:
ABEMD

COAD C ORIENT AT DESENV PROF L
R Souza Barros 90
Rio De Janeiro
RJ
20961150
Brazil
Tel: +55 21 5015122
Fax: +55 21 2015849
Carlos Alberto Ferreira Reis

Services/Products:
Consultancy services; Publisher

Member of:
ABEMD

COBRAM-CIA. BRAS. MKT S/C LTDA
Rua Moras, 92
Sao Paulo
SP

5434020
Brazil
Tel: +55 11 8150977
Fax: +55 11 8150064
Moyses A. Simantob

Services/Products:
Consultancy services

Member of:
ABEMD

COMPAN COMUNICAÇAO
Rua Helena 170
2 Andar
Sao Paulo
SP
04552–050
Brazil
Tel: +55 11 3845 7953
Fax: +55 11 3845 3689
Email: compan@compan.com.br
Web: www.compan.com.br
Fernando Compan, Director/President

Services/Products:
Advertising Agency; Catalogue
producer; Consultancy services; Direct
marketing agency; Print services;
Telemarketing agency

E-Services:
Website design

Member of:
National DMA; ABAP; CENP

COMPUGRAF SERVICOS S/C LTDA.
Rua Augusta, 1638 – 1 And
Sao Paulo
SP
1304001
Brazil
Tel: +55 11 2434550
Fax: +55 11 2434556
Salete Campeao Estevam

Services/Products:
Telemarketing agency

Member of:
ABEMD

COMPULASER GRAF. EDITORA LTDA
Av Lasar Segal 564
Sao Paulo
SP
2543010
Brazil
Tel: +55 11 39811919
Fax: +55 11 39811919
Renato De Oliveira

Services/Products:
Design/graphics/clip art supplier;
Publisher

Member of:
ABEMD

CONTACTO MARKETING & INTERNET SERVICE
Rua Gaspar Lourenço 61
Sao Paulo
SP
04107–000
Brazil
Tel: +55 11 5084 8111
Fax: +55 11 5539 7474
Email: nelson@contactonet.com.br
Web: www.contactonet.com.br
Nelson Hid Salvatore, Marketing
Director

Services/Products:
Database services; Direct marketing
agency; Labelling/envelope services;
List services; Service bureau; Internet
services

E-Services:
Email list provider; Website design

Member of:
ABEMD; AMCHAM

CONVIVIUM EVENTOS & PROMOCOES
Rua Groenlandia, 257
Sao Paulo
SP
1434000
Brazil
Tel: +55 11 8851294
Fax: +55 11 8851294
Mauricio Abdalla

Services/Products:
List services; Telemarketing agency

Member of:
ABEMD

COOPERDATA C. T. P. P. DADOS
Av Agua Fria 190
Sao Paulo
SP
2332000
Brazil
Tel: +55 11 69500671
Fax: +55 11 69500671
Carlos Fuser

Services/Products:
Database services; Telemarketing
agency; Training/recruitment

Member of:
ABEMD

COPYRIGHT CRIACAO E SERV. MKT
Av. 9 De Julho, 5345 – 3 Andar CJ 31
Sao Paulo
SP
1407010
Brazil
Tel: +55 11 8814972
Fax: +55 11 8522607
Deyse Mercedes Dias Leite

Services/Products:
Direct marketing agency

Member of:
ABEMD

CPM COMUNIC PROC MEC AUTOMACAO
Av Brg Faria Lima 1188 10 And
Sao Paulo
SP
1452000
Brazil
Tel: +55 11 8701944
Fax: +55 11 8701944
Diogo B Morales

Services/Products:
Telemarketing agency; Consultancy
services

Member of:
ABEMD

CREDICARD S/A ADM CART CREDITO
Av Henrique Schaumann 270 12 And
Sao Paulo
SP
5413010
Brazil
Tel: +55 11 30679533
Fax: +55 11 30679191
David Lederman

Services/Products:
List services

Member of:
ABEMD

CRIATIVA CONS. EM MKD LTDA
R Cnso Lafaiate 2005
Belo Horizonte
MG
31035560
Brazil
Tel: +55 31 4816818
Fax: +55 31 4829679
Ivagner Ferreira Jr

Services/Products:
List services; Telemarketing agency;
Training/recruitment; Consultancy
services

Member of:
ABEMD

CSU TELESYSTEM
Av Brg Faria Lima 1306 9 And
Sao Paulo
SP
1451914
Brazil
Tel: +55 11 8679922
Fax: +55 11 2101976
Jose Antonio C Carvalho

Services/Products:
Telemarketing agency; Training/
recruitment

Member of:
ABEMD

D&T TREIN. E DESENV. S/C LTDA
Rua Douro, 40
Sao Paulo
SP
4303180
Brazil
Tel: +55 11 2764116
Fax: +55 11 5789144
Marcelo Rivani

Services/Products:
Fulfilment and sampling house;
Database services; Labelling/envelope
services; Copy adaptation;
Personalisation

Member of:
ABEMD

DATALINK MKT COM INTERNACIONAL
Av. Paulista, 1159 – 14 Andar CJ 1414
Sao Paulo
SP
1311200
Brazil
Tel: +55 11 2533422
Fax: +55 11 2880461
Eli Marcio Roberto De Carvalho
    Ribeiro

Services/Products:
List services; Telemarketing agency;
Consultancy services; Hardware
supplier; Software supplier; Internet
services

Member of:
ABEMD

DATALISTAS S/A
Av Das Nacoes Unidas 7221 20 And
Sao Paulo
SP
5425902
Brazil

Tel: +55 11 30375919
Fax: +55 11 30375580
Paulo Fernando B Vasconcelos

Services/Products:
List services; Database services

Member of:
DMA (US); ABEMD

DATAMIDIA MKT RELACIONAMENTO
Av Paulista 460 11 And
Sao Paulo
SP
1310000
Brazil
Tel: +55 11 2534177
Fax: +55 11 2536298
Aurelio Lopes Jr

Services/Products:
List services; Fulfilment and sampling
house; Labelling/envelope services;
Copy adaptation; Consultancy services

Member of:
ABEMD

DATASEARCH TECN. B. DADOS LTDA
R Florida 1758 4 And
Sao Paulo
SP
4565001
Brazil
Tel: +55 11 55055742
Fax: +55 11 55073021
Antonio Carlos Q Carletto

Services/Products:
List services; Consultancy services

Member of:
ABEMD

DATAWISE MKT ANL DATA MINING
Av. Pres. Vargas, 435 – SL 1705
Rio De Janeiro
RJ
20071003
Brazil
Tel: +55 21 5078023
Fax: +5521 5078023
Mauro Jose Negrao

Services/Products:
Consultancy services; Market research
agency

Member of:
ABEMD

DBM MARKETING DIRETO LTDA
Al Prudente De Morais 133
Curitiba

PR
80430220
Brazil
Tel: +55 41 3358589
Fax: +55 41 3358589
Jorge Daniel

Services/Products:
List services; Labelling/envelope
services; Telemarketing agency; Direct
marketing agency; Copy adaptation

Member of:
ABEMD

DDM/INTRAL – ASSOCIATES
Rio Grande, 130
Caxias do Sul
95098–750
Brazil
Tel: +55 54 226–1188
Fax: +55 54 226–1281
Marcus D'Arrigo

Services/Products:
Consultancy services

Member of:
DMA (US)

DE MILLUS VENDAS POSTAIS LTDA
Av Lobo Jr 1672
Rio De Janeiro
RJ
21023900
Brazil
Tel: +55 21 5608122
Fax: +55 21 5608122
Marcel Gottlieb

Services/Products:
List services

Member of:
ABEMD

DHLONGHI MARKETING DIRETO
R Amaro Romeu Ramalho 100
Londrina
PR
86027450
Brazil
Tel: +55 43 3252866
Fax: +55 43 3252866
Darcio Helio Longhi

Services/Products:
Mailing/Faxing services; Labelling/
envelope services

Member of:
ABEMD

DIA DESIGN LTDA.
R. Augusta1939
11 Andar
Jardim Paulista
Sao Paulo
SP
01413–000
Brazil
Tel: +55 11 3061 3221
Fax: +55 11 3068 9750
Email: diadsp@diadesign.com.br
Web: www.diadesign.com.br
Gilberto Strunck, Director

Services/Products:
Direct marketing agency; Sales
promotion agency; Telemarketing
agency

Member of:
National DMA

DIAGNOSE CONSULTORIA
Rua Mexico, 119 – SL 2104
Rio De Janeiro
RJ
20031145
Brazil
Tel: +55 21 2219730
Fax: +55 21 2219730
Romualdo Ayres Costa

Services/Products:
Consultancy services; Software
supplier

Member of:
ABEMD

DIRECT CENTER MKD
R Pedro Americo 96 Ap 64
Santos
SP
11075400
Brazil
Tel: +55 13 9324485
Fax: +55 13 2213077
Daniel Oscar Mac Adden

Services/Products:
Telemarketing agency; Direct
marketing agency; Consultancy
services

Member of:
ABEMD

DIRECT LINK LTDA
Av. Anchieta 335-cj.72
Campinas
SP
13015–101
Brazil
Tel: +55 19 3236 8886
Fax: +55 19 3236 8886
Email: falecom@dlmarketing.com.br

Web: www.dlmarketing.com.br
Eduardo Faddul, Commercial Director

Services/Products:
Call centre services/systems;
Consultancy services; Database
services; Service bureau

DIRECT MARKETING LTDA
Rua Marjorie Prado, 269
Sao Paulo
SP
4663080
Brazil
Tel: +55 11 5243900
Fax: +55 11 5243900
Alexandre De Lima Pucci

Services/Products:
List services; Telemarketing agency;
Consultancy services

Member of:
ABEMD

DIRECT SHOPPING
Al. Rio Negro, 1105 – 8 Andar CJ 81
Barueri
SP
6454913
Brazil
Tel: +55 11 72956588
Fax: +55 11 72951732
Jose Burlamaqui De A. Neto

Services/Products:
Fulfilment and sampling house; Direct
response TV services

Member of:
ABEMD

DIRECTOTAL-BBN
Rua Luis Loelho,223
2 Andar
Brazil
Tel: +55 11 214 5055
Fax: +55 11 256 6727
Email: roberto@diretotal-bbn.com.br
Web: www.diretotal.com.br
Roberto E. Martinez, Director

Services/Products:
Advertising Agency; Direct marketing
agency; Database services;
Personalisation; Publisher; Sales
promotion agency; Loyalty
programmes; Marketing

E-Services:
Online/e-marketing agency

Member of:
ABEMD

DIRETO DA CASA-MKD LTDA
R Sta Cristina 17
Rio De Janeiro

RJ
20241250
Brazil
Tel: +55 21 2249447
Fax: +55 21 2422006
Noel De Simone Jr

Services/Products:
Direct marketing agency; Consultancy
services

Member of:
DMA (US); ABEMD

**DIRETOTAL BBN
PROPAGANDA**
R Luis Coleho 223 2 And
Sao Paulo
SP
1309001
Brazil
Tel: +55 11 2843334
Fax: +55 11 2843334
Solange Capozzi

Services/Products:
Advertising Agency; Direct marketing
agency; Hardware supplier; Software
supplier

E-Services:
Website design

Member of:
ABEMD

**DIRETOTAL TELEMIDIA
TLMKT S/C**
Av Luiz C Berrini 1461 1 And
Sao Paulo
SP
4571011
Brazil
Tel: +55 11 55068643
Fax: +55 11 55060312
Moracy Das Dores

Services/Products:
List services; Database services;
Telemarketing agency; Training/
recruitment; Hardware supplier

Member of:
ABEMD

**DIST PAULISTA PRODS SERV
LTDA**
Av 26 De Marco 205 Sl 7
Barueri
SP
6401050
Brazil
Tel: +55 11 2778005
Fax: +55 11 2778644
Fernando Saenz

Services/Products:
Advertising Agency; Telemarketing
agency

Member of:
ABEMD

DM COMPANY
Av Cidade Jardim 377 8 And
Sao Paulo
SP
1453000
Brazil
Tel: +55 11 30642406
Fax: +55 11 8538331
Wilmar Jose Munhos

Services/Products:
List services; Database services;
Consultancy services; Hardware
supplier; Software supplier

Member of:
DMA (US); ABEMD

DMS/DUN & BRADSTREET
Av. Eng. Luis C. Berrini,1700–7A CJ
72
Sao Paulo
SP
4571000
Brazil
Tel: +55 11 55057050
Fax: +55 11 55067109
James Arnold Finger

Services/Products:
List services; Consultancy services

Member of:
ABEMD

DRAFT WORLDWIDE LTDA
Av Alm Barroso 139 10 And Sl 1001
Rio De Janeiro
RJ
20031005
Brazil
Tel: +55 21 5441812
Fax: +55 21 5323191
Luiz R Pio Borges Da Cunha

Services/Products:
Advertising Agency; Consultancy
services; Direct marketing agency

Member of:
DMA (US); ABEMD

DTS SOFTWARE BRASIL LTDA
R Domingos De Moraes 1293
Sao Paulo
SP
4009003
Brazil
Tel: +55 11 5496599

Fax: +55 11 5707605
Jonathan Castellano

Services/Products:
Hardware supplier; Software supplier

Member of:
ABEMD

DYNAMIC REP ASSES EMPR LTDA
R Do Acre 28 Sl 901 E 902
Rio De Janeiro
RJ
20081000
Brazil
Tel: +55 21 2633542
Fax: +55 21 2633542
Jose Geraldo Caamano Gonzalez

Services/Products:
Advertising Agency; Consultancy
services; Mailing/Faxing services;
Labelling/envelope services

Member of:
ABEMD

E.B.F. EDITORA LTDA
Rod Fernao Dias Km 40
Sao Paulo
SP
12940000
Brazil
Tel: +55 11 4844789
Fax: +55 11 4844789
Eduardo Berzin Filho

Services/Products:
Publisher

Member of:
ABEMD

EBID EDIT PAGINAS AMARELAS LT
Av Da Liberdade 956
Sao Paulo
SP
1502001
Brazil
Tel: +55 11 2786622
Fax: +55 11 2786622
Pedro Renato Eckersdorff

Services/Products:
Mailing/Faxing services; Labelling/
envelope services

Member of:
ABEMD

EDICOES ADUANEIRAS LTDA
R Da Consolacao 77
Sao Paulo
SP
1301000
Brazil

Tel: +55 11 31203030
Fax: +55 11 31595044
Nelson Domingos Colete

Services/Products:
Personalisation; Publisher; Internet
services

Member of:
ABEMD

EDIOURO PUBLICACOES S/A
Rua Nova Jerusalem, 345
Rio De Janeiro
RJ
21042230
Brazil
Tel: +55 21 5606122
Fax: +55 21 2606143
Jorge Rodrigues Carneiro

Services/Products:
Publisher

Member of:
ABEMD

EDIT ATLAS
R Cnso Nebias 1384
Sao Paulo
SP
1203904
Brazil
Tel: +55 11 2219144
Fax: +55 11 2207830
Epson Andrade De Carvalho

Services/Products:
Publisher

Member of:
ABEMD

EDIT GLOBO S/A
Av. Jaguare, 1485 – 6 And
Sao Paulo
SP
5346902
Brazil
Tel: +55 11 37677200
Fax: +55 11 37663139
Fernando Alberto Da Costa

Services/Products:
Publisher

Member of:
ABEMD

EDIT GRAFICOS BURTI LTDA
R Do Oratorio 718
Sao Paulo
SP
3116010
Brazil
Tel: +55 11 60996383
Fax: +55 11 60996423
Leonardo De Lima Forte

Services/Products:
Design/graphics/clip art supplier;
Personalisation

Member of:
ABEMD

EDIT MODERNA LTDA
R Pe Adelino 758
Sao Paulo
SP
3303904
Brazil
Tel: +55 11 60901471
Fax: +55 11 60901474
Daniel Garcia

Services/Products:
Publisher

Member of:
ABEMD

EDIT NOVA CULTURAL LTDA
Rua Paes Leme, 524 – 10 And
Sao Paulo
SP
5424010
Brazil
Tel: +55 11 8165667
Fax: +55 11 8703220
Wanise Carla De Oliveira

Services/Products:
Publisher

Member of:
ABEMD

EDIT O DIA S/A
Rua Riachuelo, 359 – 5 And
Rio De Janeiro
RJ
20235900
Brazil
Tel: +55 21 2228045
Fax: +55 21 5071449
Sebastiao Goncalves

Services/Products:
Publisher

Member of:
ABEMD

EDIT PINI LTDA
R Anhaia 964
Sao Paulo
SP
1130900
Brazil
Tel: +55 11 2248811
Fax: +55 11 2240314
Ricardo Bertagnon

Services/Products:
Publisher

Member of:
ABEMD

EDIT SCIPIONE LTDA
R Br Do Iguape 110
Sao Paulo
SP
1507900
Brazil
Tel: +55 11 33463000
Fax: +55 11 2784062
Mauricio Fernandes Dias

Services/Products:
Publisher

Member of:
ABEMD

EDIT SIMBOLO LTDA
Rua S. Carlos Do Pinhal, 60 – 4 And
Sao Paulo
SP
1333000
Brazil
Tel: +55 11 2842255
Fax: +55 11 2890979
Regina Bucco

Services/Products:
Publisher

Member of:
ABEMD

EDIT. ATHENEU LTDA
R Bambina 74 A B
Rio De Janeiro
RJ
22251050
Brazil
Tel: +55 21 5391295
Fax: +55 21 5381284
Alexandre Massa Rzezinski

Services/Products:
Publisher

Member of:
ABEMD

EDIT. BATISTA REGULAR
R Kansas 770
Sao Paulo
SP
4558002
Brazil
Tel: +55 11 5304232
Fax: +55 11 5336843
Joel Amaral Da Silva

Services/Products:
Publisher

Member of:
ABEMD

EDITORA BANAS LTDA.
Rua Nelson Gama Oliveira, 825
Sao Paulo
SP
05734–150
Brazil
Tel: +55 11 3746 1908
Fax: +55 11 3746 1901
Email: grbanas@banas.com.br
Web: www.banas.com.br
Geraldo Roberto Banas

Services/Products:
List services; Publisher

Member of:
IDBM; ABEMD

EDITORA CARAS S.A.
Av. Eng. Luis Carlos Berrine, 1253 - 11
Andar
Sao Paulo
SP
04571–011
Brazil
Tel: +55 11 5508 2000
Fax: +55 11 5505 2814
Email: marcil@caras.com.br
Web: www.caras.com.br
Marciliano Silva Junior, Marketing
   Director

Services/Products:
Publisher; List services

Member of:
National DMA

EDITORA MEIO & MENSAGEM
R Jose M Lisboa 88 Blb 1 And
Sao Paulo
SP
1423000
Brazil
Tel: +55 11 8859700
Fax: +55 11 8899616
Roberto Tancredi

Services/Products:
Publisher

Member of:
ABEMD

**EDITORA MELHORAMENTOS
   LTDA**
Rua Tito 479
Lapa
Sao Paulo
SP
5051000
Brazil
Tel: +55 11 38740902
Fax: +55 11 38740855
Email:
   mktedit@melhoramentos.com.br

Web: www.melhoramentos.com.br
Fabricio Saldanha, Marketing

Services/Products:
Publisher

Member of:
ANL; CBL

EDITORA QUANTUM LTDA
Rua Milena Da Costa, 101
Bairro Pilarzinho
PR
82100450
Brazil
Tel: +55 41 338 4454
Fax: +55 41 338 3321
Email: atendimento@editoraquantum.
com.br
Web: www.editoraquantum.com.br
Claudia Pruner, Direct Marketing
Manager

Services/Products:
Direct marketing agency; List services;
Database services

E-Services:
Website design; Email software

Member of:
National DMA; ABEMD

EDITORA RECORD
R Argentina 171
Rio De Janeiro
RJ
20921380
Brazil
Tel: +55 21 5852000
Fax: +55 21 5804911
Roberto B Cordeiro E Silva

Services/Products:
List services; Labelling/envelope
services; Publisher

Member of:
ABEMD

EDITORA VERBO LTDA
R Da Figueira 215
Sao Paulo
SP
3003000
Brazil
Tel: +55 11 2278277
Fax: +55 11 2278277
Abilio Augusto Rodrigues Da Silva

Services/Products:
Publisher

Member of:
ABEMD

EDITORA VIDA LTDA
R Julio De Castilho 280
Sao Paulo
SP
3059000
Brazil
Tel: +55 11 60966833
Fax: +55 11 60966833
Eude Martins Da Silva

Services/Products:
Publisher

Member of:
ABEMD

EDITORA VOZES LTDA
R Fr Luiz 100
Petropolis
RJ
25685020
Brazil
Tel: +55 24 2375112
Fax: +55 24 2310226
Ildefonso Luiz De Oliveira

Services/Products:
Publisher

Member of:
ABEMD

EMPR JR DE ALUNOS DO ITA
Av Dr Nelson D'Avila Sn Cta Ita S
2207
S J Dos Campos
SP
12228900
Brazil
Tel: +55 12 3473010
Fax: +55 12 3473010
Senun Brasileiro Nunes

Services/Products:
Market research agency

Member of:
ABEMD

ENC BRIT DO BRASIL PUBL LTDA
R Rego Freitas 192 5 And
Sao Paulo
SP
1220907
Brazil
Tel: +55 11 2501928
Fax: +55 11 2501854
Pedro Sergio Venturine Martinez

Services/Products:
Publisher

Member of:
ABEMD

ENGENHO PROPAGANDA S/C LTDA
Av Higienopolis 2110
Londrina
PR
86015010
Brazil
Tel: +55 43 32323325
Fax: +55 43 3247868
Valduir Pagani

Services/Products:
Advertising Agency; Consultancy
services; Direct marketing agency; List
services; Telemarketing agency

Member of:
ABEMD

ESCRITORIO DE IDEIAS – MKTD
Rua Viuva Lacerda, 233
Rio De Janeiro
RJ
22261050
Brazil
Tel: +55 21 5374663
Fax: +55 21 2861589
Victor Murtinho

Services/Products:
Direct marketing agency

Member of:
ABEMD

EXCEL GRAPHIC EDIT ELETR E COM
R Correia Dias 282 CJ 13 14
Sao Paulo
SP
4104001
Brazil
Tel: +55 11 5737515
Fax: +55 11 5736693
Helinton Procopio De Alvarenga

Services/Products:
Design/graphics/clip art supplier

Member of:
ABEMD

EXERCERE COMUNIC E MARKETING
Av Do Contorno 6777 Sl 710
Belo Horizonte
MG
30110110
Brazil
Tel: +55 31 2973829
Fax: +55 31 2973851
Patricia De Oliveira Abreu

Services/Products:
Direct marketing agency; Copy
adaptation; Consultancy services;
Design/graphics/clip art supplier

Member of:
ABEMD

EXODUS ASSES. EDITORIAL LTDA
Av. Dr. Luis Arrobas Martins, 344
Sao Paulo
SP
4781000
Brazil
Tel: +55 11 2468100
Fax: +55 11 2473755
Renato Soares Fleischner

Services/Products:
Publisher

Member of:
ABEMD

EXPRESS MALA DIRETA SC LTDA
R Prof Jose Soares De Mello 117
Sao Paulo
SP
2882100
Brazil
Tel: +55 11 8507594
Fax: +55 11 8507594
Sebastiao Avanzi Filho

Services/Products:
Labelling/envelope services

Member of:
ABEMD

FÁBRICA
Av. Nove de Julho, 5617–14 Andar
Sao Paulo
SP
01407–200
Brazil
Tel: +55 11 3079 3933
Fax: +55 11 3079 3933
Email: fabrica@fabricad.com.br
Web: www.fabricad.com.br
Marisa Furtado, Luiz Buono

Services/Products:
Advertising Agency; Direct marketing
agency

E-Services:
Website design; Email software

Member of:
DMA (US); ABEMD

FALCAO CONSULTORIA LTDA
R Bartolomeu Gusmao 53
Recife
PE

50610190
Brazil
Tel: +55 81 2276234
Fax: +55 81 4450801
Eduardo Souza Falcao

Services/Products:
Consultancy services

Member of:
ABEMD

FAST HAND IND. E COMERCIO LTDA
R Basilio Da Cunha 206
Sao Paulo
SP
1544000
Brazil
Tel: +55 11 5751889
Fax: +55 11 5707317
Nelson Cohen

Services/Products:
Mailing/Faxing services; Labelling/
envelope services; Personalisation

Member of:
ABEMD

FAX EXPRESS – PUBLISYS
R Rego Freitas 454 10 And CJ 101
Sao Paulo
SP
1220010
Brazil
Tel: +55 11 2554066
Fax: +55 11 31592544
Regina Lucia Sundfeld Navarro

Services/Products:
Mailing/Faxing services

Member of:
ABEMD

FICHBEIN COMUN. INTEGRADA LTDA
Rua 24 De Outubro, 1681 – Sala 503
Porto Alegre
RS
90510003
Brazil
Tel: +55 51 3326022
Fax: +55 51 3326458
Gladys Cotliarenko Fichbein

Services/Products:
List services; Fulfilment and sampling
house; Labelling/envelope services;
Telemarketing agency; Training/
recruitment

Member of:
ABEMD

FINGERPRINT GRAFICA LTDA.
Al. Amazonas, 388
Barueri
SP
6454070
Brazil
Tel: +55 11 72950573
Fax: +55 11 4211121
Roberto Dimitrov

Services/Products:
Design/graphics/clip art supplier;
Service bureau; Personalisation

Member of:
ABEMD

FIRST DIRECT PROPAGANDA LTDA
Al Gabriel Monterio Da Silva 263
Sao Paulo
SP
1441000
Brazil
Tel: +55 11 8835544
Fax: +55 11 30688581
Patrick Barzel

Services/Products:
Advertising Agency; Fulfilment and
sampling house; Telemarketing agency;
Direct marketing agency

E-Services:
Website design

Member of:
ABEMD

FIRST LINE ASSES. E. S/C LTDA
Rua Dona Veridiana, 203 – CJ 4 Andar
Sao Paulo
SP
1238010
Brazil
Tel: +55 11 2215000
Fax: +55 11 2213262
Ailton Alves Pereira

Services/Products:
Consultancy services

Member of:
ABEMD

FLEXO COMMUNICAO DIRIGIDA LTDA
Rua Ernesto Alves, 1887
Conj. 201/202
Centro
RS
95020–360 Caxias do Sul
Brazil
Tel: +55 51 7112509
Fax: +55 11 7112423
Email: flexo_flexocd.com.br

Web: www.ondecaxias.com.br
Marcus Antonio D'Arrigo, Director

Services/Products:
Call centre services/systems;
Consultancy services; Database
services; Direct marketing agency;
Labelling/envelope services; List
services

Member of:
DMA (US)

FOLHA DE S. PAULO
Al Br De Limeira 425 10 And
Sao Paulo
SP
1202900
Brazil
Tel: +55 11 2243664
Fax: +55 11 2243296
Sebastiao Barbosa De Oliveira Filho

Services/Products:
List services; Publisher; Private
delivery services

Member of:
ABEMD

FORMA EDITORA LTDA
R Vieira De Moraes 1545
Sao Paulo
SP
4617015
Brazil
Tel: +55 11 5314400
Fax: +55 11 5314400
Email: forma@freeshop.com.br
Web: www.freeshop.com.br
Auli Prado De Vitto, Commercial
  Director

Services/Products:
Catalogue producer

Member of:
ABEMD

FORUM BRAS. DIRIG. EMPR.
  LTDA
Rua Tacito De Almeida, 123
Sao Paulo
SP
1251010
Brazil
Tel: +55 11 38729399
Fax: +55 11 38622289
Denis Mello

Services/Products:
Consultancy services

Member of:
ABEMD

FULFILLMENT
Av Paulista 171 6 And
Sao Paulo
SP
1311000
Brazil
Tel: +55 11 2849777
Fax: +55 11 2515164
Jorge Sukarie Neto

Services/Products:
List services; Fulfilment and sampling
house; Labelling/envelope services;
Telemarketing agency; Consultancy
services

Member of:
ABEMD

G & V MARKETING E DESENV.
  LTDA
Sep Sul, 714/914-Bl.E SL 28 Ed.
Talento
Brasilia
DF
70390145
Brazil
Tel: +55 61 2456411
Fax: +55 61 3466131
Mara Do Valle Abrahao

Services/Products:
Telemarketing agency; Training/
recruitment; Consultancy services

Member of:
ABEMD

G I IMPORT COML – GRUPO
  IMAGEM
Av. Brig. Faria Lima, 1912 – 15 Andar
Sao Paulo
SP
1451907
Brazil
Tel: +55 11 8703557
Fax: +55 11 8148507
David Gurevich

Services/Products:
Advertising Agency; List services;
Fulfilment and sampling house; Direct
response TV services

Member of:
ABEMD

G&K SOLUTION MKT DIRETO
Av Paulista 1106 16 And
Sao Paulo
SP
1310914
Brazil
Tel: +55 11 2532820
Fax: +55 11 2532837
Efraim Kapulski

Services/Products:
Advertising Agency; Consultancy
services; Direct marketing agency; List
services; Telemarketing agency

Member of:
ABEMD

GAZETA MERCANTIL S/A
R. Eng Francisco Pitta Brito, 125 4
Andar
Santo Amaro
Sao Paulo
SP
04753 080
Brazil
Tel: +55 11 5547 3605
Fax: +55 11 5547 3663
Email:
  awolffen@gazetamercantil.com.br
Andrèa Wolffenbüttel, Director of
  Information

E-Services:
Email list provider

Member of:
ABEMD

GIOVANNI, FCB
R Renato Paes De Barros 114 5 And
Sao Paulo
SP
4530001
Brazil
Tel: +55 11 8289400
Fax: +55 11 8298424
Sergio Pina

Services/Products:
Direct marketing agency

Member of:
ABEMD

GLOBALSYS PROJ TECNOL EM
  INFOR
R Gomes De Carvalho 1356 11 A CJ
112
Sao Paulo
SP
4547005
Brazil
Tel: +55 11 8208499
Fax: +55 11 8290068
Carlos Estevao M Rovigatti

Services/Products:
Hardware supplier; Software supplier

Member of:
ABEMD

GRAFICA BANDEIRANTES
R Prof Rubiao Meira 50
S B Do Campo
SP

9890430
Brazil
Tel: +55 11 7598400
Fax: +55 11 7598787
Mario Cesar M De Camargo

Services/Products:
Design/graphics/clip art supplier

Member of:
ABEMD

GRAFICA COCHRANE BRASIL
Av Brg Faria Lima 1800 2 And
Sao Paulo
SP
1451001
Brazil
Tel: +55 11 8700033
Fax: +55 11 8704482
Alexander Hamilton

Services/Products:
Design/graphics/clip art supplier

Member of:
ABEMD

**GRAFICA MORGAN
    INTERNACIONAL**
Al. Ribeirao Preto, 130 – CJ 42 4
Andar
Sao Paulo
SP
1331000
Brazil
Tel: +55 11 2884223
Fax: +55 11 2874451
Luis Maritan

Services/Products:
Design/graphics/clip art supplier

Member of:
ABEMD

GROTTERA.COM
R Butanta 518 6 And
Sao Paulo
SP
5424000
Brazil
Tel: +55 11 30380500
Fax: +55 11 8161872
Email: beia@grottera.com.br
Beatriz Messi C De Carvalho

Services/Products:
Advertising Agency

Member of:
ABEMD

GRUPO IMARES
R Catao 732
Sao Paulo
SP
5049000

Brazil
Tel: +55 11 38730777
Fax: +55 11 2624100
Carla T Kamoi V De Moraes

Services/Products:
Hardware supplier; Software supplier

Member of:
ABEMD

GRUPO SIMA
Rua Augusta, 101
Sao Paulo
SP
1305000
Brazil
Tel: +55 11 2311822
Fax: +55 11 2311822
Marta Romero Fernandes

Services/Products:
List services

Member of:
ABEMD

**HANDLING STATION C. S.
    MANUS.**
Rua Embiara, 21
Sao Paulo
SP
4374080
Brazil
Tel: +55 11 55639414
Fax: +55 11 55627946
Luciano Pires Da Costa

Services/Products:
List services; Fulfilment and sampling
house; Mailing/Faxing services;
Labelling/envelope services; Service
bureau

Member of:
ABEMD

**HARTE-HANKS DO BRASIL
    CONSULTORIA E SERVIÇOS
    LTDA.**
Av. Das Nacoés Unidas 13.797 Bl 3 19
Andar
Sao Paulo
SP
04794–000
Brazil
Tel: +55 11 5506 7488
Fax: +55 11 5506 4965
Web: www.harte-hanks.com.br
Silvio Ramos, General Manager, Latin
    America

Services/Products:
Consultancy services; Database
services; Software supplier

E-Services:
E-Marketing consultant; Email
software

Member of:
National DMA; IDBM

HERMES S/A
R S Luis Gonzaga 601
Rio De Janeiro
RJ
20910061
Brazil
Tel: +55 21 5855122
Fax: +55 21 5855122
Gustavo Mauroy

Services/Products:
Catalogue producer; Direct response
TV services

Member of:
ABEMD

**HUMAN RESOURCES
    SYSTEMS CONSUL**
Av S Gabriel 555 CJ 207
Sao Paulo
SP
1435001
Brazil
Tel: +55 11 8533011
Fax: +55 11 8533011
Jeronimo Jose Pilon

Services/Products:
Hardware supplier; Software supplier

Member of:
ABEMD

**HURRY MARKETING DIRETO
    LTDA**
Av. Pres. Wilson, 164 – 4 Andar
Rio De Janeiro
RJ
20030020
Brazil
Tel: +55 21 5332595
Fax: +55 21 5332046
Elias Dos Santos Monteiro

Services/Products:
Advertising Agency; Telemarketing
agency; Direct marketing agency

Member of:
ABEMD

**IBITIRAMA FORMULARIOS
    LTDA**
Rua Dr. Joao B. De Lacerda, 693
Sao Paulo
SP
3177901
Brazil
Tel: +55 11 6082133

Fax: +5511 2913686
Antonio Leopoldo Curi

Services/Products:
Design/graphics/clip art supplier;
Personalisation

Member of:
ABEMD

IBM BRASIL IND MAQ SERV LTDA
R Tutoia 1157 6 And
Sao Paulo
SP
4007900
Brazil
Tel: +55 11 30503451
Fax: +55 11 30505156
Mauro Galvani D'Angelo

Services/Products:
Hardware supplier; Software supplier;
Internet services

Member of:
ABEMD

IDEIA VISUAL
Al Santos 212
Sao Paulo
SP
1418000
Brazil
Tel: +55 11 2531812
Fax: +55 11 2851054
Jun Yokoyama

Services/Products:
Advertising Agency

Member of:
ABEMD

IMPACTO TELEMARKETING
Rua Coari, 177/195
Sao Paulo
SP
5022030
Brazil
Tel: +55 11 36761010
Fax: +55 11 36761010
Marco Antonio P. Silva

Services/Products:
Telemarketing agency

Member of:
ABEMD

IMPERADOR MANUSEIO SERV. LTDA
R Grama Da Praia 136
Sao Paulo
SP
8230780
Brazil
Tel: +55 11 61411988

Fax: +55 11 61411988
Valter Ribeiro

Services/Products:
Labelling/envelope services

Member of:
ABEMD

IN BRASIL INCENTIVOS E EDIT LT
R Sebastiao Velho 57
Sao Paulo
SP
5418040
Brazil
Tel: +55 11 30649011
Fax: +55 11 8817107
Leonardo Kehdi Jr

Services/Products:
Direct marketing agency

Member of:
ABEMD

INCENTIVE HOUSE
R Bela Cintra 1149 5 And
Sao Paulo
SP
1415001
Brazil
Tel: +55 11 30664458
Fax: +55 11 30646747
Anete Schonenberg Bekin

Services/Products:
Direct marketing agency

Member of:
ABEMD

INFRA DISTRIBUICAO
Av Dr Luis Arrobas Martins 289
Sao Paulo
SP
4781000
Brazil
Tel: +55 11 5249551
Fax: +55 11 5249551
Edivaldo Dias De Oliveira

Services/Products:
Mailing/Faxing services; Labelling/
envelope services

Member of:
ABEMD

INNOVA DO BRASIL LTDA
R Carlo Carra 66
Sao Paulo
SP
4367000
Brazil
Tel: +55 11 55638021
Fax: +55 11 55626131
Donald Anthony P E Whyte

Services/Products:
List services; Fulfilment and sampling
house; Labelling/envelope services;
Telemarketing agency; Direct
marketing agency

Member of:
ABEMD

INSTITUTO MONITOR S/C LTDA
R Dos Timbiras 263
Sao Paulo
SP
1208010
Brazil
Tel: +55 11 2207422
Fax: +55 11 2207422
Elaine Cristina P Guarisi

Services/Products:
Labelling/envelope services; Training/
recruitment; Design/graphics/clip art
supplier; Personalisation

Member of:
ABEMD

INTERACT RESP DIRETA TLMKT
Av Brg Faria Lima 1811 15 And
Sao Paulo
SP
1451001
Brazil
Tel: +55 11 8160016
Fax: +55 11 8160016
Maria Luiza Vasques Piccioli

Services/Products:
List services; Telemarketing agency;
Direct marketing agency; Consultancy
services

Member of:
ABEMD

INTERCOURIERS FK COURIER
Rua Hugo D'Antola, 46
Sao Paulo
SP
5038090
Brazil
Tel: +55 11 8613383
Fax: +55 11 8610567
Carlos Alberto G Filgueiras

Services/Products:
Private delivery services

Member of:
ABEMD

INTERLINE SERVS TLMKT LTDA
R Cel Xavier De Toledo 87 Sl 805
Sao Paulo

SP
1048000
Brazil
Tel: +55 11 2310088
Fax: +55 11 2310088
Antonio Carlos Freitas Veiga

Services/Products:
Telemarketing agency; Training/
recruitment

Member of:
ABEMD

IT MARKETING S/C LTDA
R Sampaio Viana 277 10 And
Sao Paulo
SP
4004000
Brazil
Tel: +55 11 8853554
Fax: +55 11 8856291
Marcelo Vidigal M De Barros

Services/Products:
Direct marketing agency

Member of:
ABEMD

J. COCCO ASSOCIADOS
Rua Fiandeiras, 962
Sao Paulo
SP
04545–006
Brazil
Tel: +55 11 3848 9966
Fax: +55 11 3848 0049
Email: jcocco@jcocco.com.br
Web: www.jcocco.com.br
José Estevao Cocco, President

Services/Products:
Advertising Agency; Consultancy
services; Direct marketing agency;
Media buying agency; Telemarketing
agency

E-Services:
Online/e-marketing agency

Member of:
ABEMD

JAF SERV. CORRES. MALA DIRETA
Al. Rainha Santa, 258
Sao Paulo
SP
3425060
Brazil
Tel: +55 11 69416481
Fax: +55 11 61930291
Jose Antonio Fernandes

Services/Products:
Fulfilment and sampling house;
Database services; Labelling/envelope
services

Member of:
ABEMD

JJPCC ASS OPER MKT DIRETO LTDA
Av Moaci 1716
Sao Paulo
SP
4083004
Brazil
Tel: +55 11 5354795
Fax: +55 11 5437038
Jocil R De C Menezes

Services/Products:
Fulfilment and sampling house;
Database services; Design/graphics/clip
art supplier; Service bureau;
Personalisation

Member of:
ABEMD

JOAO MARCELO MARKETING DIRETO
R Horacio Lafe 90 Ap 802
Sao Paulo
SP
4538080
Brazil
Tel: +55 11 8201418
Fax: +55 11 8201418
Joao Marcelo Rozario Da Silva

Services/Products:
Direct marketing agency; Copy
adaptation; Consultancy services

Member of:
ABEMD

KAVALLET COMUNICACOES
R Luis Goes 2109
Sao Paulo
SP
4043400
Brazil
Tel: +55 11 55895079
Fax: +55 11 55895079
Roberto Conrado

Services/Products:
Advertising Agency; Direct marketing
agency

Member of:
ABEMD

LE PERA MARKETING SOLUTION S/C LTDA
R Marechal Deodoro, 458
Santa Paula

Sao Caetano Do Sul
SP
09541–300
Brazil
Tel: +55 11 4227 3909
Fax: +55 11 4227 3105
Email: mkt@lepera.com.br
Web: www.lepera.com.br
Marcos Le Pera, Director

Services/Products:
Advertising Agency; Direct marketing
agency

E-Services:
Email list provider

Member of:
ABEMD

LEO BURNETT PUBLICIDADE LTDA
Av Nacoes Unidas 12995 15 And
Sao Paulo
SP
4578000
Brazil
Tel: +55 11 55050456
Fax: +55 11 55051855
Carlos Martins Neto

Services/Products:
Advertising Agency; Direct marketing
agency

Member of:
ABEMD

LEO T DESIGNER S/C LTDA
Rua Joaquim Tavora, 288
Sao Paulo
SP
4015010
Brazil
Tel: +55 11 5752811
Fax: +55 11 5710440
Leo Nobuyuki Takayasu

Services/Products:
Design/graphics/clip art supplier

Member of:
ABEMD

LETTERSHOP (GRUPO CATHO)
Al Joaquim E De Lima 19 Sobreloja
Sao Paulo
SP
1403900
Brazil
Tel: +55 11 31770895
Fax: +55 11 2843600
Walter Persson Hildebrandi

Services/Products:
List services; Fulfilment and sampling house; Database services; Direct marketing agency; Copy adaptation

Member of:
ABEMD

LISTEL LISTAS TELEFONICAS SA
R Florida 1738 12 And
Sao Paulo
SP
4565001
Brazil
Tel: +55 11 55081661
Fax: +55 11 55081748
Gladston Pereira

Services/Products:
Publisher

Member of:
ABEMD

LITTERA MUNDI EDITORA
Al Dos Pamaris 171
Sao Paulo
SP
4086020
Brazil
Tel: +55 11 5437299
Fax: +55 11 55615306
Gustavo R A Laranja

Services/Products:
Publisher

Member of:
ABEMD

LIVRARIA LTR LTDA
Rua Jaguaribe, 571
Sao Paulo
SP
1224001
Brazil
Tel: +55 11 36664691
Fax: +55 11 38240491
Aluizio Xavier Fialho

Services/Products:
Publisher

Member of:
ABEMD

LIVRARIA NOBEL S.A.
Rua Da Balsa, 559
Freguesia Do O
Sao Paulo
SP
02910–000
Brazil
Tel: +55 11 3933 2811
Fax: +55 11 3931 3988
Email: ednobel@livrarianobel.com.br

Web: www.livrarianobel.com.br
Ary Kuflik Benclowicz, Director

Services/Products:
Mail order company; Publisher

E-Services:
E-Marketing consultant; Website design

Member of:
Câmara Brasileira Do Livro;
Associaçao Brasileira De Direitos
Reprográficos; Sindicato Nacional Dos
Editores De Livro

LOGISTECH
Rua Doutor Rafael Correa, 33
Sao Paulo
SP
5043050
Brazil
Tel: +55 11 2639594
Fax: +55 11 8647093
Joao F De Oliveira Neto

Services/Products:
Mailing/Faxing services; Labelling/
envelope services; Consultancy
services; Private delivery services

Member of:
ABEMD

LUART COMUNICAÇO
Rua Sete de Setembro, 48 gr. 1008
Centro
RJ
20050–000
Brazil
Tel: +55 21 509 2084
Fax: +55 21 509 5216
Email: luart@olimpo.com.br
Luciana Aguiar, Proprietor

Services/Products:
Advertising Agency; Design/graphics/
clip art supplier; Direct marketing
agency; Interactive media; Homepage

Member of:
ABEMD

M&R MKT DE RELACIONAMENTO
Av. Bem Te Vi, 362 – CJ 102 B
Sao Paulo
SP
4524030
Brazil
Tel: +55 11 5315040
Fax: +55 11 5352768
Marcelo Rodrigues Jorge

Services/Products:
List services; Telemarketing agency;
Direct marketing agency; Copy
adaptation; Consultancy services

Member of:
DMA (US); ABEMD

MACROLOG TELEINFORMATICA LTDA
R Con Eugenio Leite 623 2 And
Sao Paulo
SP
5414011
Brazil
Tel: +55 11 30613168
Fax: +55 11 30613168
Izidro Pedro Santos C Filho

Services/Products:
Telemarketing agency; Consultancy
services; Hardware supplier; Software
supplier

Member of:
ABEMD

MAIL STORES
Rua Januario Cardoso, 15
Sao Paulo
SP
4507070
Brazil
Tel: +55 11 8859277
Fax: +55 11 8853970
Marcos Gouvea De Souza

Services/Products:
Catalogue producer; Direct response
TV services

Member of:
ABEMD

MAILING EXPRESS MKD E TLMKT
Av. Gov. Pedro Toledo, 1271
Campinas
SP
13070151
Brazil
Tel: +55 19 2421981
Fax: +55 19 2421981
Carlos Magno Trotta

Services/Products:
List services; Fulfilment and sampling
house; Database services; Labelling/
envelope services; Telemarketing
agency

Member of:
ABEMD

MAKRON BOOKS LTDA.
Rua Tabapua 1348
Itaim Bibi
Sao Paulo
SP
04533–004
Brazil
Tel: +55 11 3849 1518

Fax: +55 11 3849 4970
Email: milton@makron.com.br
Web: www.makron.com.br
Milton Mira De Assumpçao Filho,
    President

Services/Products:
Publisher

Member of:
ABEMD

MANPOWER-ETICA REC HUM SERV LT
R Jupi 215
Sao Paulo
SP
4755050
Brazil
Tel: +55 11 56419400
Fax: +55 11 5243830
Edison Belini

Services/Products:
Training/recruitment; Training/
recruitment

Member of:
ABEMD

MANTEL MARKETING LTDA
R Goeth 6
Rio De Janeiro
RJ
22281020
Brazil
Tel: +55 21 5373371
Fax: +55 21 5378535
Marcos Wettreich

Services/Products:
Consultancy services; Publisher

E-Services:
Website design

Member of:
ABEMD

MAPA PESQUISA E MKT DIRETO
Av Othon G D'Eca 900 Torre 1 Sl 402
Florianopolis
SC
88015240
Brazil
Tel: +55 48 2247700
Fax: +55 48 2247296
Jose Nazareno Vieira

Services/Products:
Telemarketing agency; Consultancy
services; Market research agency

Member of:
ABEMD

MARADEI NETO COMUNIC DIR SC LT
Rua Franca Pinto, 275 – 3 Andar
Sao Paulo
SP
4016031
Brazil
Tel: +55 11 5700341
Fax: +55 11 5700341
Jose Maradei Neto

Services/Products:
List services; Database services; Direct
marketing agency; Consultancy
services

Member of:
ABEMD

MARKETING MIX LTDA
Av Alexandre Ferreira 420 Ap 102
Rio De Janeiro
RJ
22470220
Brazil
Tel: +55 21 5278265
Fax: +55 21 5278265
Luiz Fernando Morau

Services/Products:
Consultancy services

Member of:
ABEMD

MARTINS & GUARNIERI COMUNIC LTDA
Rua Bartira, 885
Perdizes
Sao Paulo
SP
05009–000
Brazil
Tel: +55 11 3672 8996
Fax: +55 11 3672 8996
Email: martinsguarnieri@csf.com.br
Ana Luisa Martins, Proprietor

Services/Products:
Direct marketing agency

Member of:
ABEMD

MASTER DIRECT
Av. 7 De Setembro, 4476–9 Andar SL
902
Curitiba
PR
80250210
Brazil
Tel: +55 41 3425080
Fax: +55 41 3446519
Gustavo Luiz Biselli

Services/Products:
Direct marketing agency

Member of:
ABEMD

MASTHER
R Jose De Brito De Freitas 846
Sao Paulo
SP
2552000
Brazil
Tel: +55 11 8560746
Fax: +55 11 8578295
Sidney Gustavo Cavalcante Braoio

Services/Products:
Consultancy services

Member of:
ABEMD

MAXI-ACAO
R Tome De Souza 120
Sao Paulo
SP
5079000
Brazil
Tel: +55 11 8354512
Fax: +55 11 8354512
Jose Carlos V Rodrigues

Services/Products:
Telemarketing agency; Training/
recruitment; Consultancy services

Member of:
ABEMD

MAXIMAILING SERV. DE MKT LTDA
Av. Copacabana, 574
Barueri
SP
6465310
Brazil
Tel: +55 11 72952244
Fax: +55 11 4215500
Francisco Jose A. Pereira

Services/Products:
List services

Member of:
DMA (US); ABEMD

MCCANN ERICKSON BRASIL
R Vsc De Ouro Preto 5 12 And
Rio De Janeiro
RJ
22250180
Brazil
Tel: +55 21 5532400
Fax: +55 21 5544975
George Teichlolz

Services/Products:
Advertising Agency

Member of:
ABEMD

MD MKT DIRETO ASSOC. S/C LTDA
R Arizona 965
Sao Paulo
SP
4567003
Brazil
Tel: +55 11 55065321
Fax: +55 11 55065320
Ivelise Cristine Salgado

Services/Products:
Fulfilment and sampling house;
Labelling/envelope services; Training/
recruitment; Direct marketing agency;
Consultancy services

E-Services:
Website design

Member of:
ABEMD

MEDIALAB LTDA.
Rua Goethe, 6
Rio De Janeiro
RJ
22281020
Brazil
Tel: +55 21 5355952
Fax: +55 21 5355992
Bruno Fiorentini Junior

Services/Products:
Direct marketing agency

E-Services:
Website design

Member of:
ABEMD

MEDSI EDIT MEDICA CIENTIF LTDA
Rua Visconde De Cairu, 165
Rio De Janeiro
RJ
20270050
Brazil
Tel: +55 21 5694342
Fax: +55 21 2646392
Helber Alves De Oliveira

Services/Products:
Publisher

Member of:
ABEMD

MERIT COMUNICACOES LTDA
R Silvia 110 1 And
Sao Paulo
SP
1331010
Brazil
Tel: +55 11 2886255
Fax: +55 11 2889664
Andre Luis Goncalves

Services/Products:
Direct marketing agency

Member of:
ABEMD

METRO MD
Al Santos 466 1 And
Sao Paulo
SP
1418000
Brazil
Tel: +55 11 31755255
Fax: +55 11 31755257
Rubens Stephan Jr

Services/Products:
List services; Database services;
Telemarketing agency; Direct
marketing agency; Consultancy
services

Member of:
DMA (US); ABEMD

MICROCAP INFORMATICA LTDA
R Gomes Freire 517
Sao Paulo
SP
5075010
Brazil
Tel: +55 11 8377111
Fax: +55 11 8377195
Antonio Carlos Da Silva

Services/Products:
Internet services

E-Services:
Website design

Member of:
ABEMD

MICROMATIC CONS. E TREINAMENTO
Av Prestes Maia 1500 Sl 8
Osasco
SP
6040008
Brazil
Tel: +55 11 72052612
Fax: +55 11 72052612
Francisco Jose Estevam

Services/Products:
Hardware supplier

Member of:
ABEMD

MISSION EDICOES E EVENTOS LTDA
Al Santos 880 7 And
Sao Paulo
SP
1418100
Brazil
Tel: +55 11 31706943
Fax: +55 11 31706904
Elisabete Leite Nogueira

Services/Products:
List services; Training/recruitment;
Consultancy services

Member of:
ABEMD

MITSUCON TECNOLOGIA S/A
R Manuel Da Nobrega 1280 Ter
Sao Paulo
SP
4001004
Brazil
Tel: +55 11 5746244
Fax: +55 11 30515688
Ernesto Hiroshe Sunago

Services/Products:
Hardware supplier; Software supplier

Member of:
ABEMD

MKTEC DATABASE MARKETING
Av. Nilo Pecanha, 50 – SL 1413
Rio De Janeiro
RJ
20044900
Brazil
Tel: +55 21 2832002
Fax: +55 21 2832096
Flavio Geraldo Nogueira

Services/Products:
Consultancy services; Hardware
supplier; Software supplier

Member of:
ABEMD

MOORE FORMULARIOS LTDA
Via Anhanguera, – Km 17,3
Osasco
SP
6278240
Brazil
Tel: +55 11 72013483
Fax: +55 11 72013086
Luiz Felipe Vieira Fernandes

Services/Products:
Labelling/envelope services; Design/
graphics/clip art supplier;
Personalisation

Member of:
ABEMD

MOTIVARE PROMOCOES E EVENTOS L
R Hungria 888 CJ 21
Sao Paulo

SP
1455000
Brazil
Tel: +55 11 8165322
Fax: +55 11 8165322
Alain Soly Levi

Services/Products:
Advertising Agency; Consultancy
services; Design/graphics/clip art
supplier; Direct marketing agency

E-Services:
Website design

Member of:
ABEMD

MSI MKT SERVS INFORM COML LTDA
R Vieira De Moraes 420 7 And CJ 75
Sao Paulo
SP
4617000
Brazil
Tel: +55 11 5317849
Fax: +55 11 5317849
Email: contato@msi.com.br
Web: www.msi.com.br
Janine Avancini

Services/Products:
Database services; Labelling/envelope
services; Market research agency; List
services

Member of:
ABEMD

MULTI MARKETING LTDA
Av. Gal. Atalida Leonel, 93
10 Andar
Sao Paulo
SP
02033–000
Brazil
Tel: +55 11 6221 3466
Fax: +55 11 6221 4154
Email: multimarketing@uol.com.br
Web: www.uol.com.br/multimarketing
Névio Noronna, President

Services/Products:
Database services; Direct marketing
agency; Lettershop; List services;
Telemarketing agency; Mailing/Faxing
services

E-Services:
Email list provider; Online/e-marketing
agency

Member of:
ABEMD

MULTI MKT PUBL & MALA DIRETA
Av Gen A Leonel 93 10 And CJ 108
Sao Paulo
SP
2033000
Brazil
Tel: +55 11 62213466
Fax: +55 11 62214154
Nevio De Noronha Filho

Services/Products:
Advertising Agency; List services;
Direct marketing agency; Service
bureau

Member of:
ABEMD

MULTIPLA MARKETING DIRETO
Rua Barcelona 123-CJ 101
Santa Lucia
Belo Horizonte
MG
30360–260
Brazil
Tel: +55 31 3296 2270
Fax: +55 31 3296 8934
Email: multipla@gold.com.br
Web: www.multiplamarketing.com.br
Tarcisio Masson Barbosa, President

Services/Products:
Card pack manufacturer; Direct
marketing agency; Database services;
List services; Software supplier;
Consultancy services

Member of:
ABEMD

MURCE & AZEVEDO MKD P. PROPAG.
Av Mal Floriano 19 Grupo 1502
Rio De Janeiro
RJ
20080003
Brazil
Tel: +55 21 2031355
Fax: +55 21 2031355
Ricardo Murce Magalhaes

Services/Products:
Direct marketing agency

Member of:
ABEMD

NERYVALLE AS CONS FUND RAISING
Rua Dona Maria Paula, 123–2 A. CJ
21/22
Sao Paulo
SP
1319001
Brazil

Tel: +55 11 31075387
Fax: +55 11 31063949
Luiz Alberto Caldas Do Valle

Services/Products:
Telemarketing agency; Training/
recruitment; Consultancy services

Member of:
ABEMD

NEW WORK STATION TMKT LTDA
Rua Iperoig, 580
Sao Paulo
SP
5016000
Brazil
Tel: +55 11 36761110
Fax: +55 11 36761400
Gilson Feix

Services/Products:
Telemarketing agency; Training/
recruitment

Member of:
ABEMD

OGILVY INTERACTIVE BRASIL
Rua Medieros de Albuquerque 60
Sao Paulo
05436–060
Brazil
Tel: +55 11 814–7311

Services/Products:
Advertising Agency; Direct marketing
agency

Member of:
DMA (US)

OGILVY ONE
Av Nacoes Unidas 5777
Sao Paulo
SP
5465070
Brazil
Tel: +55 11 30309000
Fax: +55 11 8161033
Betinha Jote

Services/Products:
Direct marketing agency

Member of:
DMA (US); ABEMD

OLF CONSULTORES ASSOCIADOS
Rua Angustura, 210 – Bl A CJ 1
Belo Horizonte
MG
30220290
Brazil
Tel: +55 31 2273433

Fax: +55 31 2273758
Oto Lopes De Figueiredo

Services/Products:
Training/recruitment; Training/
recruitment; Copy adaptation;
Consultancy services

Member of:
ABEMD

OPEN CHANNEL
TELEMARKETING
Lg Do Machado 54 S 1107
Rio De Janeiro
RJ
22221020
Brazil
Tel: +55 21 5578392
Fax: +55 21 5578392
Rafael Sampaio

Services/Products:
Telemarketing agency; Training/
recruitment; Consultancy services

Member of:
ABEMD

OUTSOURCE INFORMATICA
LTDA
R Funchal 513 4 And
Sao Paulo
SP
4551060
Brazil
Tel: +55 11 8203676
Fax: +55 11 8204938
Marcelo Amorim

Services/Products:
List services; Database services;
Telemarketing agency; Consultancy
services

Member of:
ABEMD

PAGINA VIVA MKT
RELACIONAMENTO
Rua Dr. Virgilio De C. Pinto, 519
Sao Paulo
SP
5415030
Brazil
Tel: +55 11 30390800
Fax: +55 11 30390830
Luiz Claudio Rezende Correa

Services/Products:
Fulfilment and sampling house;
Labelling/envelope services;
Telemarketing agency; Consultancy
services; Design/graphics/clip art
supplier

Member of:
ABEMD

PALAVRA EXPRESSA S/C LTDA
Av. Rio Branco, 45 – CJ 601 E 602
Rio De Janeiro
RJ
20090003
Brazil
Tel: +55 21 2633677
Fax: +55 21 2633677
Lilia Paranhos Langhi

Services/Products:
List services; Fulfilment and sampling
house; Database services; Labelling/
envelope services; Copy adaptation

Member of:
ABEMD

PAVANEX ARTE FINAL S/C
LTDA
R Arthur Corradi 165
Sao Bernardo Campo
SP
9725240
Brazil
Tel: +55 11 43304912
Fax: +55 11 4486865
Marisa De F E Miranda

Services/Products:
Fulfilment and sampling house;
Database services; Labelling/envelope
services

Member of:
ABEMD

PCS DO BRASIL LTDA
Av. Joao Carlos Da S Borges, 693
Sao Paulo
SP
4726001
Brazil
Tel: +55 11 5481388
Fax: +55 11 5481388
Marlene Gracia De Oliveira

Services/Products:
Telemarketing agency

Member of:
ABEMD

PERFECT MALA DIRETA
Rua Rishin Matsuda, 484
Sao Paulo
SP
4371000
Brazil
Tel: +55 11 55653838
Fax: +55 11 55653838
Cesar Assai

Services/Products:
Fulfilment and sampling house;
Labelling/envelope services

Member of:
ABEMD

PERFIL TECNOLOG
Av. Jurubatuba, 178
Sao Paulo
SP
4583100
Brazil
Tel: +55 11 55073320
Fax: +55 11 55052900
Wanderley Schmidt Campos

Services/Products:
Consultancy services; Hardware
supplier; Software supplier

Member of:
ABEMD

PHOENIX TECNOL DE
COMUNICACAO
R Colibri 144
Sao Paulo
SP
4521030
Brazil
Tel: +55 11 5753090
Fax: +55 11 5753090
Renata Rotondo

Services/Products:
Hardware supplier; Software supplier

Member of:
ABEMD

PLANO EDITORIAL LTDA
Av Paulista 1159 10 And CJ 1017
Sao Paulo
SP
1311921
Brazil
Tel: +55 11 31781030
Fax: +55 11 31781001
Marcio Luiz Valente

Services/Products:
Publisher

Member of:
ABEMD

PLURAL EDITORA E GRAFICA
LTDA.
Av. Marcos Penteado de Ulhôa
Rodrigues 700
Tamboré
Santana de Parnaiba
SP
6500000
Brazil
Tel: +55 11 3351 6222
Fax: +55 11 3351 6122
Email: pluralco@uol.com.br
Alfredo G. Santos, Commercial
Director

Services/Products:
Print services

PLUS 4 COMUNICACAO
Av. Dr. Cardoso De Mello, 1855 – 3
Andar
Sao Paulo
SP
4548005
Brazil
Tel: +55 11 8220212
Fax: +55 11 8219976
Maria Egia Chamma

Services/Products:
Advertising Agency

Member of:
ABEMD

PLUSOFT INFORMÁTICA
Rua Michigan, 79
Sao Paulo
SP
04566–000
Brazil
Tel: +55 11 5317 822
Fax: +55 11 5317 822
Email: plusoft@plusoft.com.br
Web: www.plusoft.com.br
Anna Zappa, Marketing

Services/Products:
Interactive media; Software supplier;
Telemarketing agency; Consulting

E-Services:
Email software

Member of:
ABEMD; ABT

PMD MALA DIRETA LTDA
Av Paulo De Frontim 698
Rio De Janeiro
RJ
20261243
Brazil
Tel: +55 21 2737642
Fax: +55 21 2737675
Waldemar De Almeida Filho

Services/Products:
List services; Database services;
Labelling/envelope services; Copy
adaptation

Member of:
ABEMD

PMK MKD & CONSULTORIA LTDA
Al. Dos Guainumbis, 1105
Sao Paulo
SP
4067002
Brazil

Tel: +55 11 5363601
Fax: +55 11 5363601
Odair Cerdeira Gutirres

Services/Products:
Direct marketing agency; Copy
adaptation; Consultancy services

Member of:
ABEMD

PRATIKE MKT E ASSES. S/C LTDA
Av. Alcantara Machado, 80 – 8 Andar
Sao Paulo
SP
3102900
Brazil
Tel: +55 11 2780222
Fax: +55 11 2780222
David Orsi

Services/Products:
Telemarketing agency; Direct
marketing agency; Consultancy
services; Design/graphics/clip art
supplier

Member of:
ABEMD

PRINT TECHNOLOGY SERVICOS LTDA
Rua Do Senado, 50/52
Rio De Janeiro
RJ
20231000
Brazil
Tel: +55 21 2248545
Fax: +55 21 2324997
Arlindo Dos Santos Filho

Services/Products:
Labelling/envelope services; Design/
graphics/clip art supplier;
Personalisation

Member of:
ABEMD

PROACAO COMUNIC. & MARKETING
Av. Julio De Castilhos, 545 – SL 22
Caxias Do Sul
RS
95010003
Brazil
Tel: +55 54 2284622
Fax: +55 54 2281956
Norberto Casca Giongo

Services/Products:
Advertising Agency

Member of:
ABEMD

PROBUS IND COM DE PAPEIS LTDA
Av. Dr. Rudge Ramos, 1070
S B Do Campo
SP
9736300
Brazil
Tel: +55 11 4577711
Fax: +55 11 4579255
Cesar Jose Cinato

Services/Products:
Design/graphics/clip art supplier

Member of:
ABEMD

PROCENGE PROC DADOS ENG SIST L
Estr. Do Arraial, 3108
Recife
PE
52051380
Brazil
Tel: +55 81 4412877
Fax: +55 81 2682877
Othederaldo Araujo Da Silva Junior

Services/Products:
Database services; Hardware supplier;
Software supplier

Member of:
ABEMD

PRODEMARK
R Guimaraes Peixoto 52
Recife
PE
52051200
Brazil
Tel: +55 81 2682238
Fax: +55 81 2682238
Jose Eduardo A De Aragao Melo

Services/Products:
List services; Labelling/envelope
services; Consultancy services

Member of:
ABEMD

PROJETO DESIGN
Rua General Jardim, 633 – 3 Andar
Sao Paulo
SP
1223904
Brazil
Tel: +55 11 2599688
Fax: +55 11 2599688
Arlindo Mungioli

Services/Products:
Publisher

Member of:
ABEMD

PUBLICENTER PUBLICIDADE
Av. Ana Costa, 255 – CJ 32
Santos
SP
11060070
Brazil
Tel: +55 13 2226292
Fax: +55 13 2341777
Admilson Vieira Da Silva

Services/Products:
Advertising Agency

E-Services:
Website design

Member of:
ABEMD

PUBLINET BRAZILNET ED. C. LTDA
Rua Pires De Oliveira, 1365
Sao Paulo
SP
4716011
Brazil
Tel: +55 11 51823411
Fax: +55 11 51815682
Humberto Bertoni

Services/Products:
Internet services

Member of:
ABEMD

PUTERMAN PUBLIC. E CONS. LTDA
Rua Feliciano Maia, 216
Sao Paulo
SP
4503070
Brazil
Tel: +55 11 8840702
Fax: +55 11 8850738
Paulo Marcos Puterman

Services/Products:
Internet services

E-Services:
Website design

Member of:
ABEMD

QG COMUNICACAO
R Geraldo Flausino Gomes 78 4 And
CJ 43
Sao Paulo
SP
4575060
Brazil
Tel: +55 11 55051116
Fax: +55 11 55051116
Jane De Freitas Misseno

Services/Products:
Direct marketing agency

Member of:
ABEMD

QUALYHUMANA S/C LTDA
Rua Paula Carvalho, 1054
Descalvado
SP
13690000
Brazil
Tel: +55 19 5831953
Fax: +55 19 5832052
Luiz Oliveira Rios

Services/Products:
Consultancy services

Member of:
ABEMD

QUANTICA COMUNIC E MARKETING
R Jaguaribe 122
Sao Paulo
SP
1224000
Brazil
Tel: +55 11 2229300
Fax: +55 11 2221655
Ana Luiza Feres

Services/Products:
List services; Database services;
Telemarketing agency; Training/
recruitment; Direct marketing agency;
Internet services

E-Services:
Website design

Member of:
ABEMD

QUATRO/A TLMKT & CENTRAIS ATEN
Praca Da Republica, 295 – 10 And
Sao Paulo
SP
1045001
Brazil
Tel: +55 11 31175310
Fax: +55 11 31175511
Alexandre Accioly Rocha

Services/Products:
Telemarketing agency; Training/
recruitment

Member of:
DMA (US); ABEMD

QUATTOR MARKETING E INFORMATIC
R Sergio Tomas 482 486 2 And
Sao Paulo
SP

1131010
Brazil
Tel: +55 11 33612959
Fax: +55 11 33612959
Vania Amorim Cafe

Services/Products:
List services; Fulfilment and sampling
house; Database services;
Telemarketing agency; Personalisation

Member of:
ABEMD

RA NET MARKETING E INFORMATICA
Av Lacerda Franco 998
Sao Paulo
SP
1536000
Brazil
Tel: +55 11 2799035
Fax: +55 11 2799035
Adenilson Medeiros Teixeira

E-Services:
Website design

Member of:
ABEMD

RAPP COLLINS WORLDWIDE
Av Cidade Jardim 377 7 And
Sao Paulo
SP
1453000
Brazil
Tel: +55 11 30681300
Fax: +55 11 8531913
Abaete De Azevedo

Services/Products:
List services; Direct marketing agency;
Consultancy services

Member of:
DMA (US); ABEMD

RBC TELEMARKETING
Av. Isaac Povoas, 1331–11 Andar SL
113
Cuiaba
MT
78045640
Brazil
Tel: +55 65 6235796
Fax: +55 65 6235796
Mauro Noronha Romani

Services/Products:
Telemarketing agency; Service bureau

Member of:
ABEMD

READER'S DIGEST BRASIL LTDA
Av Pres Vargas 3131 Sl 1301
Rio De Janeiro
RJ
20210030
Brazil
Tel: +55 21 5036800
Fax: +55 21 5036888
Jaime G Guarita

Services/Products:
Publisher

Member of:
ABEMD

RED LINE TELESERVICES
Rua Baffin, 32 A 60 – 7 Andar
Sao Bernardo Campo
SP
9750620
Brazil
Tel: +55 11 4587699
Fax: +55 11 43322013
Jose Luiz Esteves U. Sanches

Services/Products:
Telemarketing agency

Member of:
ABEMD

RESOLVE ! GLOBAL MARKETING
R Airosa Galvao 120
Sao Paulo
SP
5002070
Brazil
Tel: +55 11 38732900
Fax: +55 11 38732900
Jimmy Cygler

Services/Products:
Advertising Agency; List services;
Database services; Labelling/envelope
services; Telemarketing agency

Member of:
ABEMD

RESPOSTA PESQUISA E MKD LTDA
Rua Texas, 658
Sao Paulo
SP
4557000
Brazil
Tel: +55 11 5438680
Fax: +55 11 5355074
Silvio Lefevre

Services/Products:
Consultancy services; Market research
agency

Member of:
ABEMD

REVISTA AMERICAECONOMIA
Rua Joaquim Floriano, 488 – Sobreloja
Sao Paulo
SP
4534002
Brazil
Tel: +55 11 8289770
Fax: +55 11 8289770
Valter Richetti

Services/Products:
Publisher

Member of:
ABEMD

REVISTA FAMILIA CRISTA
Rua Domingos De Morais, 678
Sao Paulo
SP
4010100
Brazil
Tel: +55 11 5499777
Fax: +55 11 5499772
Luiz Carlos Patricio

Services/Products:
Publisher

Member of:
ABEMD

RICARDO BOTELHO COMUNICACAO
Av. Brig. Faria Lima, 1234 -
conj. 81
Sao Paulo
01451–001
Brazil
Tel: +55 11 815–2177
Fax: +55 11 815–2177
Ricardo Jorge Botelho, Director

Services/Products:
Consultancy services

Member of:
DMA (US)

RK SERV & CONSULTORIA
Rua Das Palmeiras, 795 – SL 805
Vitoria
ES
29047550
Brazil
Tel: +55 27 2352170
Fax: +55 27 2352170
Denise Rocha Lemos

Services/Products:
Telemarketing agency

Member of:
ABEMD

RSVP
Pc Monteiro Lobato 36
Sao Paulo
SP
5506030
Brazil
Tel: +55 11 8166559
Fax: +55 11 8144147
Henrique Jose Alves Mello

Services/Products:
Advertising Agency; Telemarketing
agency; Direct marketing agency

Member of:
DMA (US); ABEMD

S&A MARKETING DIRETO E EDIT
Rua Campo Grande, 443
Sao Paulo
SP
5302051
Brazil
Tel: +55 11 36413211
Fax: +55 11 8327831
Roberto Stanic

Services/Products:
Consultancy services

Member of:
ABEMD

S/A O ESTADO DE S. PAULO
Av Eng Caetano Alvares 55 1 And
Sao Paulo
SP
2598900
Brazil
Tel: +55 11 8562677
Fax: +55 11 8562335
Carlos Alberto Romano

Services/Products:
Publisher

Member of:
ABEMD

SABEMI
R Tucuma 243 10 And
Sao Paulo
SP
1455010
Brazil
Tel: +55 11 2125526
Fax: +55 11 2127077
Moacyr Jarbas Artusi

Services/Products:
Consultancy services

Member of:
ABEMD

SALEM COMUNICACAO E MKD

Rua Geraldo Flauzino Gomes, 85 – 7
Andar
Sao Paulo
SP
4575060
Brazil
Tel: +55 11 55053001
Fax: +55 11 55051261
Marcio Salem

Services/Products:
Direct marketing agency

Member of:
DMA (US); ABEMD

SD&W LTDA

Rua Joao De Lacerda Soares, 316
Sao Paulo
SP
4707010
Brazil
Tel: +55 11 55615666
Fax: +55 11 5352345
Sueli Daffre Carvalho

Services/Products:
List services; Database services;
Hardware supplier; Software supplier

Member of:
ABEMD

SEMADI SERV. ENV. MALA D. LTDA

Av. Jose Maria Alkimin, 614 – Subsolo
Sao Paulo
SP
5366000
Brazil
Tel: +55 11 8193863
Fax: +55 11 8692139
Carlos Roberto Borduqui

Services/Products:
Labelling/envelope services

Member of:
ABEMD

SERCOMTEL

R Prof Joao Candido 555
Londrina
PR
86010000
Brazil
Tel: +55 43 1051619
Fax: +55 43 1051600
Adriano Boscheiro Do Espirito Santo

Services/Products:
Internet services

Member of:
ABEMD

SETIMIO MALA DIRETA COM. LTDA

Rua Alto Alegre, 288
Osasco
SP
6223070
Brazil
Tel: +55 11 70861445
Fax: +55 11 70861445
Carlos Roberto Setimio

Services/Products:
Labelling/envelope services

Member of:
ABEMD

SHOP LINE INTERNATIONAL LTDA

R Jose Cabalero 65 8 And
Santo Andre
SP
9040210
Brazil
Tel: +55 11 49946522
Fax: +55 11 49946522
Keller Dotto

Services/Products:
Fulfilment and sampling house;
Telemarketing agency

Member of:
ABEMD

SHOP TIME

Av Emb Abelardo Bueno 477
Rio De Janeiro
RJ
22775040
Brazil
Tel: +55 21 4211188
Fax: +55 21 4212059
Carlos Andre Laurentis

Services/Products:
Catalogue producer; Direct response
TV services

Member of:
ABEMD

SIGMA DESIGN

R Gen Osorio 119
Sao Joao Boa Vista
SP
13870000
Brazil
Tel: +55 19 6222836
Fax: +55 19 6222836
Ana Maria De Souza Sales

Services/Products:
Design/graphics/clip art supplier

Member of:
ABEMD

SINTESE

R Mipibu 116
Sao Paulo
SP
5049030
Brazil
Tel: +55 11 8642111
Fax: +55 11 36760550
Roberto Monteiro Pinto

Services/Products:
Database services; Service bureau;
Personalisation

Member of:
ABEMD

SKILL COMPUTER SERVICES LTDA

Rua Geraldo Flausino Gomes, 85 – 2
Andar
Sao Paulo
SP
4575060
Brazil
Tel: +55 11 55050122
Fax: +55 11 55050457
Douglas Navajas

Services/Products:
Hardware supplier; Software supplier

Member of:
ABEMD

SMART CLUB DO BRASIL LTDA

Al Madeira 53 CJ 31
Barueri
SP
6454010
Brazil
Tel: +55 11 72910003
Fax: +55 11 72910003
Tais De Moraes Cavalheiro

Services/Products:
Loyalty systems

Member of:
ABEMD

SOBRAL MARKETING DIRETO

Al. Ribeiro Da Silva, 772
Sao Paulo
SP
1217010
Brazil
Tel: +55 11 8267122
Fax: +55 11 8266449
Andre De Seixas Sobral

Services/Products:
Telemarketing agency

Member of:
DMA (US); ABEMD

SOCIEDADE BIBLICA DO BRASIL
Av Ceci 706
Barueri
SP
6460120
Brazil
Tel: +55 11 72959590
Fax: +55 11 72959591
Paulo Evangelista

Services/Products:
Publisher

Member of:
ABEMD

SOFTMARKETING MARKETING DIRETO
Av. Sete De Setembro, 4995
Curitiba
PR
80–240–000
Brazil
Tel: +55 41 340 8000
Fax: +55 41 340 8002
Email: onez@softmarketing.com.br
Web: www.softmarketing.com.br
Onez Mário Da Silva, Superintendent
  Director

Services/Products:
Call centre services/systems; Database
services; Direct marketing agency;
Market research agency

Member of:
National DMA; ABEMD; ABT

SOMA PUBLICIDADE LTDA
Av Julio De Castilho 1401 6 A Sl 1401
Caxias Do Sul
RS
95010003
Brazil
Tel: +55 54 2211920
Fax: +55 54 2237412
Osvaldo Ferreira

Services/Products:
Advertising Agency

Member of:
ABEMD

SOUZA ARANHA MKT & DIRETO
Rua Abilio Soares, 233 – 5 Andar
Sao Paulo
SP
4005000
Brazil
Tel: +55 11 8898799
Fax: +55 11 8850785
Eduardo Souza Aranha

Services/Products:
List services; Direct marketing agency;
Copy adaptation

Member of:
ABEMD

SPCOM – COMERCIO E PROM. LTDA
Av. Paulista, 688 – 2 Andar
Sao Paulo
SP
1310909
Brazil
Tel: +55 11 2432700
Fax: +55 11 2432701
Alexandra F. Periscinoto

Services/Products:
Telemarketing agency; Training/
recruitment; Service bureau;
Personalisation

Member of:
ABEMD

SPEED CARGO
Av Pedro Ii 374
Sao Cristovao
RJ
20941070
Brazil
Tel: +55 21 2530025
Fax: +55 21 2530025
Jose Augusto Saraiva

Services/Products:
Private delivery services

Member of:
ABEMD

SPEED CARGO ENCOMEND EXPRESSAS
Rua Jorge Duprat Figueiredo, 304
Sao Paulo
SP
4361000
Brazil
Tel: +55 11 55628790
Fax: +55 11 56774980
Cicero Costard Neto

Services/Products:
Mailing/Faxing services; Labelling/
envelope services

Member of:
ABEMD

SPEED MAIL MALA DIR. S/C LTDA
Rua Brigadeiro Galvao, 726
Sao Paulo
SP
1151000
Brazil

Tel: +55 11 36666466
Fax: +55 11 36666466
Paulo Sergio Rodrigues Gouveia

Services/Products:
Labelling/envelope services

Member of:
ABEMD

STABEL GREY DIRECT
Av Dr Cardoso De Melo 1855 5 A C
52
Sao Paulo
SP
4548005
Brazil
Tel: +55 11 8229822
Fax: +55 11 8226234
Jose Carlos Stabel

Services/Products:
Advertising Agency

Member of:
ABEMD

STT TELECOM LTDA
Al. Rio Negro, 433 – Pr Ii Nivel 3
Sao Paulo
SP
6454904
Brazil
Tel: +55 11 72665156
Fax: +55 11 72665157
Mauro Navarro Maiuri

Services/Products:
Hardware supplier; Software supplier

Member of:
ABEMD

SUMMUS EDITORIAL LTDA
Rua Cardoso De Almeida, 1287
Sao Paulo
SP
5013001
Brazil
Tel: +55 11 38723322
Fax: +55 11 38727476
Raul Wassermann

Services/Products:
Publisher

Member of:
ABEMD

SUN MARKETING DIRETO LTDA
Av Brg Faria Lima 1478 15 And
Sao Paulo
SP
1451913
Brazil
Tel: +55 11 2128499

Fax: +55 11 2128499
Flavio Da Costa Salles

Services/Products:
Direct marketing agency

Member of:
ABEMD

SURVEY DO BRASIL INF. LTDA
Rua Augusta, 1371 – CJ 113
Sao Paulo
SP
1305100
Brazil
Tel: +55 11 2888281
Fax: +55 11 2884353
Cristina Panella

Services/Products:
Consultancy services; Market research agency

Member of:
ABEMD

SVD SIST DE VENDA DIRETA LTDA
Rua Pref. Olimpio De Melo, 1485
Rio De Janeiro
RJ
20930001
Brazil
Tel: +55 21 5695394
Fax: +55 21 5695900
Paulo Geraldo F Cavalcanti

Services/Products:
Fulfilment and sampling house;
Labelling/envelope services;
Consultancy services

Member of:
ABEMD

TALENT COMUNICACAO SA
Rua Campos Bicudo #98
6th Fl
Sao Paulo
SA
04536 010
Brazil
Tel: +55 11 30671915
Fax: +55 11 282–4074
Eduardo Lorenzi, Strategic Planning
  Assistant

Services/Products:
Advertising Agency; Direct marketing agency

Member of:
DMA (US)

TECNET TELEINFORMATICA LTDA
Av. Imperatriz Leopoldina, 1496
Sao Paulo

SP
5305002
Brazil
Tel: +55 11 8321125
Fax: +55 11 8321126
Renato Fogagnoli Jr

Services/Products:
Hardware supplier; Software supplier

Member of:
ABEMD

TELE EVENTOS MKT DIRETO LTDA
R Cdor Eduardo Saccab 244
Sao Paulo
SP
4601071
Brazil
Tel: +55 11 55612522
Fax: +55 11 55612522
Luis Fernando Bordin Herlinger

Services/Products:
List services; Telemarketing agency;
Direct marketing agency; Service
bureau; Personalisation

Member of:
ABEMD

TELEMAKER LTDA
Avenida Angelica 1851/162
Sao Paulo
SP
01227–200
Brazil
Tel: +55 11 3663 0290
Fax: +55 11 3663 0275
Email: telemaker@originet.com.br
Pedro John Meinrath, Director

Services/Products:
Publisher; Consultancy services; Legal
services; Software supplier; Private
consulting services

Member of:
ABEMD

TELEMATIC SERVS DE TLMKT SC LT
R Borges Lagoa 564 CJ 83 84
Sao Paulo
SP
4038020
Brazil
Tel: +55 11 50854901
Fax: +55 11 5737026
Alice Mikie Ninomiya

Services/Products:
Telemarketing agency

Member of:
ABEMD

TELEPERFORMANCE BRASIL
Rua Professor Ernest Marcus, 36
Sao Paulo
SP
1246080
Brazil
Tel: +55 11 2597001
Fax: +55 11 2597711
Arsenio Martins Filho

Services/Products:
Telemarketing agency

Member of:
ABEMD

TK1 TELEMARKETING
Rua Antonina Junqueira, 216–4 A. SL 42
S Joao B Vista
SP
13870000
Brazil
Tel: +55 19 6331961
Fax: +55 19 6331998
Vera Antakly Adib Perez

Services/Products:
Telemarketing agency

Member of:
ABEMD

TMKT-MRM SERVIÇOS DE MARKETING LTDA
Rua Joao Moura, 650
Pinheiros
Sao Paulo
SP
05412–001
Brazil
Tel: +55 11 3065 5102
Fax: +55 11 3065 5105
Email: jau@tmkt-mrm.com.br
Web: www.tmkt-mrm.com.br
Alexandre Jau, CEO

Services/Products:
Call centre services/systems

Member of:
ABEMD; FEBAMDI

TOTALITY COMUNICACAO LTDA
Av Moema 170 CJ 61
Sao Paulo
SP
4077020
Brazil
Tel: +55 11 5395994
Fax: +55 11 5395994
Marcelo Sibille Cabral

Services/Products:
Advertising Agency

Member of:
ABEMD

**TRANSFOLHA TRANSP E
    DISTRIB LT**
Al Tocantins 755
Barueri
SP
6455020
Brazil
Tel: +55 11 72997201
Fax: +55 11 72997262
Clovis Toniolli

Services/Products:
Fulfilment and sampling house; Private
delivery services

Member of:
ABEMD

**TRD MARKETING DIRETO
    LTDA**
Av. Portugal, 1068
Sao Paulo
SP
4559002
Brazil
Tel: +55 11 55611714
Fax: +55 11 55611714
Greicy Correa

Services/Products:
Direct marketing agency

Member of:
ABEMD

**TRD MARKETING DIRETO
    LTDA**
Av. Portugal, 1068
Sao Paulo
SP
4559002
Brazil
Tel: +55 11 55611714
Fax: +55 11 55611714
Greicy Correa

Services/Products:
List services; Fulfilment and sampling
house; Database services; Labelling/
envelope services; Telemarketing
agency

Member of:
ABEMD

**TRILHA SIST DE COMUNIC
    LTDA**
Av Tancredo Neves 1186 Sl 902 1001
Salvador
BA
41820020
Brazil
Tel: +55 71 3529300

Fax: +55 71 3529399
Jorge Jose Santos Freire

Services/Products:
Telemarketing agency; Training/
recruitment

Member of:
ABEMD

TUGARE PUBLICIDADE
Rua Luigi Galvani, 70 – CJ 51
Sao Paulo
SP
4575020
Brazil
Tel: +55 11 55053112
Fax: +55 11 55072061
Nelson Doy Junior

Services/Products:
Advertising Agency

Member of:
ABEMD

**UPGRADE COMUNICACAO
    TOTAL LTDA**
R Prof M De Ornellas 303 1 And
Sao Paulo
SP
4719040
Brazil
Tel: +55 11 56413300
Fax: +55 11 56413300
Paulo Fernando Chueiri Gabriel

Services/Products:
Advertising Agency

Member of:
ABEMD

USS TELEMARKETING
Rua Campo Verde, 61 – 9 Andar
Sao Paulo
SP
1456010
Brazil
Tel: +55 11 8163231
Fax: +55 11 2100110
Ricardo Pereira Biserra

Services/Products:
Telemarketing agency

Member of:
ABEMD

VANTIVE DO BRASIL
R Verbo Divino 1400 6 And
Sao Paulo
SP
4719002
Brazil
Tel: +55 11 51887649
Fax: +55 11 51887667
Irani Ugarelli

Services/Products:
Publisher

Member of:
ABEMD

VENDE PUBLICIDADE
R Arlindo Nogueira 500 C 2 Piso
Teresina
PI
64000290
Brazil
Tel: +55 86 2210225
Fax: +55 86 2210235
Candido Gomes Neto

Services/Products:
Advertising Agency

Member of:
ABEMD

**VETTOR PROPAGANDA S/C
    LTDA**
Rua dos Piratinins 434
Sao Paulo
SP
04065–050
Brazil
Tel: +55 11 5584 0307
Fax: +55 11 5584 0307
Email: ad@vettor.com.br
Web: www.vettor.com.br
Milton Tortella, Director of Creation
    and Operations

Services/Products:
Advertising Agency; Direct marketing
agency; Media buying agency

Member of:
ABEMD

**VIA DIRECTA MANUSEIO E
    DISTRIB**
Av Eng Caetano Alvares 1613 S L
Sao Paulo
SP
2546000
Brazil
Tel: +55 11 2650116
Fax: +55 11 2656070
Eduardo Netto De Araujo

Services/Products:
Fulfilment and sampling house;
Labelling/envelope services

Member of:
ABEMD

VICOM
Pr De Botafogo 440 3 And
Rio De Janeiro
RJ
22250040
Brazil

Tel: +55 21 5366109
Fax: +55 21 5366182
Artur Levinstein

Services/Products:
Mailing/Faxing services

Member of:
ABEMD

VOX ASSES EM
   COMUNICACAO
R Itapicuru 613 8 And CJ 84
Sao Paulo
SP
5006000
Brazil
Tel: +55 11 8646449
Fax: +55 11 8647732
Angela Sardelli

Services/Products:
Telemarketing agency; Training/
recruitment

Member of:
ABEMD

VOZ PESQUISA E
   TELEMARKETING
Av. Dr. Cardoso De Melo, 1855 – CJ
92
Sao Paulo
SP
4508005
Brazil
Tel: +55 11 30440200
Fax: +55 11 30440201
Fernando J. Lacerda C. De Araujo

Services/Products:
Advertising Agency; Telemarketing
agency; Market research agency

Member of:
ABEMD

WCJ WUNDERMAN CATO
   JOHNSON
R Jundiai 50 4 And
Sao Paulo
SP
4001140
Brazil
Tel: +55 11 8851029
Fax: +55 11 8849425
Eduardo Bicudo

Services/Products:
Advertising Agency; Direct marketing
agency; Copy adaptation

Member of:
ABEMD

WORKING CONS. ASSES. COM.
   LTDA
Rua Do Rocio, 199 – 5 Andar CJ 52
Sao Paulo
SP
4552000
Brazil
Tel: +55 11 8291919
Fax: +55 11 8205480
Ana Maria Mesquita

Services/Products:
Direct marketing agency

Member of:
ABEMD

Y DE LOGON COMUNIC
   DIRIGIDA
Av Pres Wilson 164 12 And
Rio De Janeiro
RJ
20030020
Brazil
Tel: +55 21 5325473
Fax: +55 21 5320532
Carlos Alecrim

Services/Products:
Consultancy services

Member of:
ABEMD

ZERO HORA EDIT
   JORNALISTICA SA
R Silveiro 1111
Porto Alegre
RS
90850000
Brazil
Tel: +55 51 2187059
Fax: +55 51 2187555
Evandro Morais Maia

Services/Products:
List services; Publisher

Member of:
ABEMD

ZEST MARKETING DIRETO
Rua Euclides Da Cunha, 610
Batel
Curitiba
PR
80–730–60
Brazil
Tel: +55 41 340 4555
Fax: +55 41 340 4566
Email: zest@zest.com.br
Web: www.zest.com.br
Patricia, Marketing Assistant

Services/Products:
Direct marketing agency

Member of:
FEDMA; DMA (US); National DMA;
ABEMD

SERVICES/PRODUCT
LISTING

Advertising Agency
3D Comunicacao
A+ FCVA Propaganda
A2 Publicidade E Promocoes Lt
Advb Assoc. Diri. Vend. Brasil
Always Prop. Public. S/C Ltda
ATB Comunicaçoes Sc Ltda
Bamberg Agnelo Com Integrada L
Base 4 Comunicacao Integrada
Base Comunicacao Integrada
CBC Asses. Grafica S/C Ltda Me
Cedat
Centrum Propaganda
CMC Comunicacao
Compan Comunicaçao
Directotal-BBN
Diretotal Bbn Propaganda
Dist Paulista Prods Serv Ltda
Draft Worldwide Ltda
Dynamic Rep Asses Empr Ltda
Engenho Propaganda S/C Ltda
Fábrica
First Direct Propaganda Ltda
G I Import Coml – Grupo Imagem
G&K Solution Mkt Direto
Grottera.com
Hurry Marketing Direto Ltda
Ideia Visual
J. Cocco Associados
Kavallet Comunicacoes
Le Pera Marketing Solution S/C Ltda
Leo Burnett Publicidade Ltda
Luart Comunicaço
Mccann Erickson Brasil
Motivare Promocoes E Eventos L
Multi Mkt Publ & Mala Direta
Ogilvy Interactive Brasil
Plus 4 Comunicacao
Proacao Comunic. & Marketing
Publicenter Publicidade
Resolve ! Global Marketing
RSVP
Soma Publicidade Ltda
Stabel Grey Direct
Talent Comunicacao SA
Totality Comunicacao Ltda
Tugare Publicidade
Upgrade Comunicacao Total Ltda
Vende Publicidade
Vettor Propaganda S/C Ltda
Voz Pesquisa E Telemarketing
WCJ Wunderman Cato Johnson

Call centre services/systems
AM3 Telemarketing S/C Ltda
Cat-Centro de Aperfeiçoamento em
  Telemarketing
Ckapt Teleperformance
Direct Link Ltda
Flexo Communicao Dirigida Ltda
Softmarketing Marketing Direto
TMKT-MRM Serviços De Marketing
  Ltda

Card pack manufacturer
Multipla Marketing Direto

Catalogue producer
ATB Comunicaçoes Sc Ltda
Compan Comunicaçao
Forma Editora Ltda
Hermes S/A
Mail Stores
Shop Time

Consultancy services
22 Direct Marketing
A2 Publicidade E Promocoes Lt
Access Tlmkt Servicos Ltda
Acesso Direto Consultores
AD/MKD Coml Ltda Art Direta
Adiron Consultores S/C Ltda
Advb Assoc. Diri. Vend. Brasil
AM3 Telemarketing S/C Ltda
Aom Gestao De Empresas E Software
  S/C Ltda
Auttel Servicos E Tlmkt. Ltda
Brand Member
Bretzke Consult. & Assoc. Ltda
Camelier Mkt & Resultados
Casa Marketing & Comun. Ltda
Centrum Propaganda
Certus Prest De Serv S/C Ltda
Ckapt Marketing Direto
Coad C Orient At Desenv Prof L
Cobram-Cia. Bras. Mkt S/C Ltda
Compan Comunicaçao
CPM Comunic Proc Mec Automacao
Criativa Cons. Em Mkd Ltda
Datalink Mkt Com Internacional
Datamidia Mkt Relacionamento
Datasearch Tecn. B. Dados Ltda
Datawise Mkt Anl Data Mining
DDM/Intral – Associates
Diagnose Consultoria
Direct Center Mkd
Direct Link Ltda
Direct Marketing Ltda
Direto Da Casa-Mkd Ltda
DM Company
DMS/Dun & Bradstreet
Draft Worldwide Ltda
Dynamic Rep Asses Empr Ltda
Engenho Propaganda S/C Ltda
Exercere Comunic E Marketing
Falcao Consultoria Ltda

First Line Asses. E. S/C Ltda
Flexo Communicao Dirigida Ltda
Forum Bras. Dirig. Empr. Ltda
Fulfillment
G & V Marketing E Desenv. Ltda
G&K Solution Mkt Direto
Harte-Hanks Do Brasil Consultoria E
  Serviços Ltda.
Interact Resp Direta Tlmkt
J. Cocco Associados
Joao Marcelo Marketing Direto
Logistech
M&R Mkt De Relacionamento
Macrolog Teleinformatica Ltda
Mantel Marketing Ltda
Mapa Pesquisa E Mkt Direto
Maradei Neto Comunic Dir Sc Lt
Marketing Mix Ltda
Masther
Maxi-Acao
Md Mkt Direto Assoc. S/C Ltda
Metro Md
Mission Edicoes E Eventos Ltda
Mktec Database Marketing
Motivare Promocoes E Eventos L
Multipla Marketing Direto
Neryvalle As Cons Fund Raising
Olf Consultores Associados
Open Channel Telemarketing
Outsource Informatica Ltda
Pagina Viva Mkt Relacionamento
Perfil Tecnolog
Pmk Mkd & Consultoria Ltda
Pratike Mkt E Asses. S/C Ltda
Prodemark
Qualyhumana S/C Ltda
Rapp Collins Worldwide
Resposta Pesquisa E Mkd Ltda
Ricardo Botelho Comunicacao
S&A Marketing Direto E Edit
Sabemi
Survey Do Brasil Inf. Ltda
Svd Sist De Venda Direta Ltda
Telemaker Ltda
Y De Logon Comunic Dirigida

Consulting
Plusoft Informática

Copy adaptation
AML Mkt De Relacionamento
Associacao Alumni
Basile Comunicacao Ltda
D&T Trein. E Desenv. S/C Ltda
Datamidia Mkt Relacionamento
DBM Marketing Direto Ltda
Exercere Comunic E Marketing
Joao Marcelo Marketing Direto
Lettershop (Grupo Catho)
M&R Mkt De Relacionamento
Olf Consultores Associados
Palavra Expressa S/C Ltda
Pmd Mala Direta Ltda

Pmk Mkd & Consultoria Ltda
Souza Aranha Mkt & Direto
WCJ Wunderman Cato Johnson

Database services
22 Direct Marketing
Adiron Consultores S/C Ltda
Agroverpa Informacaos Em
  Agribusiness
AML Mkt De Relacionamento
Brand Member
Bussola Brasil
Celtec Centro Educ. L. Tecnol.
Contacto Marketing & Internet Servic
Cooperdata C. T. P. P. Dados
D&T Trein. E Desenv. S/C Ltda
Datalistas S/A
Direct Link Ltda
Directotal-BBN
Diretotal Telemidia Tlmkt S/C
DM Company
Editora Quantum Ltda
Flexo Communicao Dirigida Ltda
Harte-Hanks Do Brasil Consultoria F
  Serviços Ltda.
Jaf Serv. Corres. Mala Direta
Jjpcc Ass Oper Mkt Direto Ltda
Lettershop (Grupo Catho)
Mailing Express Mkd E Tlmkt
Maradei Neto Comunic Dir Sc Lt
Metro Md
Msi Mkt Servs Inform Coml Ltda
Multi Marketing Ltda
Multipla Marketing Direto
Outsource Informatica Ltda
Palavra Expressa S/C Ltda
Pavanex Arte Final S/C Ltda
Pmd Mala Direta Ltda
Procenge Proc Dados Eng Sist L
Quantica Comunic E Marketing
Quattor Marketing E Informatic
Resolve ! Global Marketing
Sd&W Ltda
Sintese
Softmarketing Marketing Direto
TRD Marketing Direto Ltda

Design/graphics/clip art supplier
AD Central Tec Graf Laser Ltda
Alpha Graphics – Ibirapuera
ATB Comunicaçoes Sc Ltda
Basile Comunicacao Ltda
CBC Asses. Grafica S/C Ltda Me
Circulo Do Livro
Compulaser Graf. Editora Ltda
Edit Graficos Burti Ltda
Excel Graphic Edit Eletr E Com
Exercere Comunic E Marketing
Fingerprint Grafica Ltda.
Grafica Bandeirantes
Grafica Cochrane Brasil
Grafica Morgan Internacional

Ibitirama Formularios Ltda
Instituto Monitor S/C Ltda
Jjpcc Ass Oper Mkt Direto Ltda
Leo T Designer S/C Ltda
Luart Comunicaço
Moore Formularios Ltda
Motivare Promocoes E Eventos L
Pagina Viva Mkt Relacionamento
Pratike Mkt E Asses. S/C Ltda
Print Technology Servicos Ltda
Probus Ind Com De Papeis Ltda
Sigma Design

Direct marketing agency
22 Direct Marketing
A2 Publicidade E Promocoes Lt
Acesso Direto Consultores
AD/MKD Coml Ltda Art Direta
Albra Comunicacao Integrada Lt
ATB Comunicaçoes Sc Ltda
Base 4 Comunicacao Integrada
Bretzke Consult. & Assoc. Ltda
Casa Marketing & Comun. Ltda
Cat-Centro de Aperfeiçoamento em
   Telemarketing
CBC Asses. Grafica S/C Ltda Me
Centrum Propaganda
Compan Comunicaçao
Contacto Marketing & Internet Service
Copyright Criacao E Serv. Mkt
DBM Marketing Direto Ltda
Dia Design Ltda.
Direct Center Mkd
Directotal-BBN
Direto Da Casa-Mkd Ltda
Diretotal Bbn Propaganda
Draft Worldwide Ltda
Editora Quantum Ltda
Engenho Propaganda S/C Ltda
Éscritorio De Ideias – Mktd
Exercere Comunic E Marketing
Fábrica
First Direct Propaganda Ltda
Flexo Communicao Dirigida Ltda
G&K Solution Mkt Direto
Giovanni, Fcb
Hurry Marketing Direto Ltda
In Brasil Incentivos E Edit Lt
Incentive House
Innova Do Brasil Ltda
Interact Resp Direta Tlmkt
IT Marketing S/C Ltda
J. Cocco Associados
Joao Marcelo Marketing Direto
Kavallet Comunicacoes
Le Pera Marketing Solution S/C Ltda
Leo Burnett Publicidade Ltda
Lettershop (Grupo Catho)
Luart Comunicaço
M&R Mkt De Relacionamento
Maradei Neto Comunic Dir Sc Lt
Martins & Guarnieri Comunic Ltda
Master Direct

Md Mkt Direto Assoc. S/C Ltda
Medialab Ltda.
Merit Comunicacoes Ltda
Metro Md
Motivare Promocoes E Eventos L
Multi Marketing Ltda
Multi Mkt Publ & Mala Direta
Multipla Marketing Direto
Murce & Azevedo Mkd P. Propag.
Ogilvy Interactive Brasil
Ogilvy One
Pmk Mkd & Consultoria Ltda
Pratike Mkt E Asses. S/C Ltda
Qg Comunicacao
Quantica Comunic E Marketing
Rapp Collins Worldwide
RSVP
Salem Comunicacao E Mkd
Softmarketing Marketing Direto
Souza Aranha Mkt & Direto
Sun Marketing Direto Ltda
Talent Comunicacao SA
Tele Eventos Mkt Direto Ltda
TRD Marketing Direto Ltda
Vettor Propaganda S/C Ltda
WCJ Wunderman Cato Johnson
Working Cons. Asses. Com. Ltda
Zest Marketing Direto

Direct response TV services
Direct Shopping
G I Import Coml – Grupo Imagem
Hermes S/A
Mail Stores
Shop Time

Fulfilment and sampling house
Abril – Entrega Direta
Brand Member
Casa Marketing & Comun. Ltda
Celmarth Ltda.
Ckapt Marketing Direto
D&T Trein. E Desenv. S/C Ltda
Datamidia Mkt Relacionamento
Direct Shopping
Fichbein Comun. Integrada Ltda
First Direct Propaganda Ltda
Fulfillment
G I Import Coml – Grupo Imagem
Handling Station C. S. Manus.
Innova Do Brasil Ltda
Jaf Serv. Corres. Mala Direta
Jjpcc Ass Oper Mkt Direto Ltda
Lettershop (Grupo Catho)
Mailing Express Mkd E Tlmkt
Md Mkt Direto Assoc. S/C Ltda
Pagina Viva Mkt Relacionamento
Palavra Expressa S/C Ltda
Pavanex Arte Final S/C Ltda
Perfect Mala Direta
Quattor Marketing E Informatic
Shop Line International Ltda
Svd Sist De Venda Direta Ltda

Transfolha Transp E Distrib Lt
TRD Marketing Direto Ltda
Via Directa Manuseio E Distrib

Hardware supplier
A2 Publicidade E Promocoes Lt
Alpha Telecom
AmdexComercial e Industrial Ltda
Be Interactive
Black Box
Bussola Brasil
Celtec Centro Educ. L. Tecnol.
Datalink Mkt Com Internacional
Diretotal Bbn Propaganda
Diretotal Telemidia Tlmkt S/C
DM Company
DTS Software Brasil Ltda
Globalsys Proj Tecnol Em Infor
Grupo Imares
Human Resources Systems Consul
IBM Brasil Ind Maq Serv Ltda
Macrolog Teleinformatica Ltda
Micromatic Cons. E Treinamento
Mitsucon Tecnologia S/A
Mktec Database Marketing
Perfil Tecnolog
Phoenix Tecnol De Comunicacao
Procenge Proc Dados Eng Sist L
Sd&W Ltda
Skill Computer Services Ltda
Stt Telecom Ltda
Tecnet Teleinformatica Ltda

Homepage
Luart Comunicaço

Interactive media
Aom Gestao De Empresas E Software
   S/C Ltda
Luart Comunicaço
Plusoft Informática

Internet services
Acesso Direto Consultores
Albra Comunicacao Integrada Lt
Be Interactive
Contacto Marketing & Internet Service
Datalink Mkt Com Internacional
Edicoes Aduaneiras Ltda
IBM Brasil Ind Maq Serv Ltda
Microcap Informatica Ltda
Publinet Brazilnet Ed. C. Ltda
Puterman Public. E Cons. Ltda
Quantica Comunic E Marketing
Sercomtel

Labelling/envelope services
22 Direct Marketing
ACF Celestino Bourroul
Address S. Apoio Mala D. Ltda
Advb Assoc. Diri. Vend. Brasil
Capital Services Brasil Ltda
Casa Marketing & Comun. Ltda

Contacto Marketing & Internet Service
D&T Trein. E Desenv. S/C Ltda
Datamidia Mkt Relacionamento
DBM Marketing Direto Ltda
Dhlonghi Marketing Direto
Dynamic Rep Asses Empr Ltda
Ebid Edit Paginas Amarelas Lt
Editora Record
Express Mala Direta Sc Ltda
Fast Hand Ind. E Comercio Ltda
Fichbein Comun. Integrada Ltda
Flexo Communicao Dirigida Ltda
Fulfillment
Handling Station C. S. Manus.
Imperador Manuseio Serv. Ltda
Infra Distribuicao
Innova Do Brasil Ltda
Instituto Monitor S/C Ltda
Jaf Serv. Corres. Mala Direta
Logistech
Mailing Express Mkd E Tlmkt
Md Mkt Direto Assoc. S/C Ltda
Moore Formularios Ltda
Msi Mkt Servs Inform Coml Ltda
Pagina Viva Mkt Relacionamento
Palavra Expressa S/C Ltda
Pavanex Arte Final S/C Ltda
Perfect Mala Direta
Pmd Mala Direta Ltda
Print Technology Servicos Ltda
Prodemark
Resolve ! Global Marketing
Semadi Serv. Env. Mala D. Ltda
Setimio Mala Direta Com. Ltda
Speed Cargo Encomend Expressas
Speed Mail Mala Dir. S/C Ltda
Svd Sist De Venda Direta Ltda
TRD Marketing Direto Ltda
Via Directa Manuseio E Distrib

Legal services
Camelier Prop Intelectual
Telemaker Ltda

Lettershop
Multi Marketing Ltda

List services
22 Direct Marketing
A&C Marketing E Eventos Ltda
AD Central Tec Graf Laser Ltda
AD/MKD Coml Ltda Art Direta
Agroverpa Informacaos Em
  Agribusiness
Alvo Promoçoes E Mala Direta Ltda
Brand Member
Bussola Brasil
Cedat
Cia. Video
Ckapt Marketing Direto
Contacto Marketing & Internet Service
Convivium Eventos & Promocoes
Credicard S/A Adm Cart Credito

Criativa Cons. Em Mkd Ltda
Datalink Mkt Com Internacional
Datalistas S/A
Datamidia Mkt Relacionamento
Datasearch Tecn. B. Dados Ltda
DBM Marketing Direto Ltda
De Millus Vendas Postais Ltda
Direct Marketing Ltda
Diretotal Telemidia Tlmkt S/C
DM Company
DMS/Dun & Bradstreet
Editora Banas Ltda.
Editora Caras S.A.
Editora Quantum Ltda
Editora Record
Engenho Propaganda S/C Ltda
Fichbein Comun. Integrada Ltda
Flexo Communicao Dirigida Ltda
Folha De S. Paulo
Fulfillment
G I Import Coml – Grupo Imagem
G&K Solution Mkt Direto
Grupo Sima
Handling Station C. S. Manus.
Innova Do Brasil Ltda
Interact Resp Direta Tlmkt
Lettershop (Grupo Catho)
M&R Mkt De Relacionamento
Mailing Express Mkd E Tlmkt
Maradei Neto Comunic Dir Sc Lt
Maximailing Serv. De Mkt Ltda
Metro Md
Mission Edicoes E Eventos Ltda
Msi Mkt Servs Inform Coml Ltda
Multi Marketing Ltda
Multi Mkt Publ & Mala Direta
Multipla Marketing Direto
Outsource Informatica Ltda
Palavra Expressa S/C Ltda
Pmd Mala Direta Ltda
Prodemark
Quantica Comunic E Marketing
Quattor Marketing E Informatic
Rapp Collins Worldwide
Resolve ! Global Marketing
Sd&W Ltda
Souza Aranha Mkt & Direto
Tele Eventos Mkt Direto Ltda
TRD Marketing Direto Ltda
Zero Hora Edit Jornalistica SA

Loyalty programmes
Directotal-BBN

Loyalty systems
Smart Club Do Brasil Ltda

Mail order company
Livraria Nobel S.A.

Mailing/Faxing services
A&C Marketing E Eventos Ltda
Abril – Entrega Direta

ACF Celestino Bourroul
ACF Heitor Penteado
Capital Services Brasil Ltda
Celmarth Ltda.
Dhlonghi Marketing Direto
Dynamic Rep Asses Empr Ltda
Ebid Edit Paginas Amarelas Lt
Fast Hand Ind. E Comercio Ltda
Fax Express – Publisys
Handling Station C. S. Manus.
Infra Distribuicao
Logistech
Multi Marketing Ltda
Speed Cargo Encomend Expressas
Vicom

Market research agency
Aom Gestao De Empresas E Softwa
  S/C Ltda
Cat-Centro de Aperfeiçoamento em
  Telemarketing
Datawise Mkt Anl Data Mining
Empr Jr De Alunos Do Ita
Mapa Pesquisa E Mkt Direto
Msi Mkt Servs Inform Coml Ltda
Resposta Pesquisa E Mkd Ltda
Softmarketing Marketing Direto
Survey Do Brasil Inf. Ltda
Voz Pesquisa E Telemarketing

Marketing
Acesso Direto Consultores
Aom Gestao De Empresas E Softwa
  S/C Ltda
Contacto Marketing & Internet Servi
Directotal-BBN
Editora Caras S.A.
Editora Melhoramentos Ltda
Editora Quantum Ltda
Harte-Hanks Do Brasil Consultoria
  Serviços Ltda.
Livraria Nobel S.A.
Plusoft Informática
Zest Marketing Direto

Media buying agency
J. Cocco Associados
Vettor Propaganda S/C Ltda

Personalisation
AD Central Tec Graf Laser Ltda
Alpha Graphics – Ibirapuera
Aom Gestao De Empresas E Softwa
  S/C Ltda
D&T Trein. E Desenv. S/C Ltda
Directotal-BBN
Edicoes Aduaneiras Ltda
Edit Graficos Burti Ltda
Fast Hand Ind. E Comercio Ltda
Fingerprint Grafica Ltda.
Ibitirama Formularios Ltda
Instituto Monitor S/C Ltda
Jjpcc Ass Oper Mkt Direto Ltda

Moore Formularios Ltda
Print Technology Servicos Ltda
Quattor Marketing E Informatic
Sintese
Spcom – Comercio E Prom. Ltda
Tele Eventos Mkt Direto Ltda

Print services
Compan Comunicaçao
Plural Editora e Grafica Ltda.

Private consulting services
Telemaker Ltda

Private delivery services
Argumento Tlmkt Com E Servs Lt
Folha De S. Paulo
Intercouriers Fk Courier
Logistech
Speed Cargo
Transfolha Transp E Distrib Lt

Publisher
Abril Colecoes
Abril S/A
Advb Assoc. Diri. Vend. Brasil
Aranda Edit. Tec. E Cult. Ltda
Assoc Comercial De Sao Paulo
Circulo Do Livro
Coad C Orient At Desenv Prof L
Compulaser Graf. Editora Ltda
Directotal-BBN
E.B.F. Editora Ltda
Edicoes Aduaneiras Ltda
Ediouro Publicacoes S/A
Edit Atlas
Edit Globo S/A
Edit Moderna Ltda
Edit Nova Cultural Ltda
Edit O Dia S/A
Edit Pini Ltda
Edit Scipione Ltda
Edit Simbolo Ltda
Edit. Atheneu Ltda
Edit. Batista Regular
Editora Banas Ltda.
Editora Caras S.A.
Editora Meio & Mensagem
Editora Melhoramentos Ltda
Editora Record
Editora Verbo Ltda
Editora Vida Ltda
Editora Vozes Ltda
Enc Brit Do Brasil Publ Ltda
Exodus Asses. Editorial Ltda
Folha De S. Paulo
Listel Listas Telefonicas SA
Littera Mundi Editora
Livraria Ltr Ltda
Livraria Nobel S.A.
Makron Books Ltda.
Mantel Marketing Ltda
Medsi Edit Medica Cientif Ltda

Plano Editorial Ltda
Projeto Design
Reader'S Digest Brasil Ltda
Revista Americaeconomia
Revista Familia Crista
S/A O Estado De S. Paulo
Sociedade Biblica Do Brasil
Summus Editorial Ltda
Telemaker Ltda
Vantive Do Brasil
Zero Hora Edit Jornalistica SA

Sales promotion agency
Dia Design Ltda.
Directotal-BBN

Service bureau
Aom Gestao De Empresas E Software
   S/C Ltda
Contacto Marketing & Internet Service
Direct Link Ltda
Fingerprint Grafica Ltda.
Handling Station C. S. Manus.
Jjpcc Ass Oper Mkt Direto Ltda
Multi Mkt Publ & Mala Direta
Rbc Telemarketing
Sintese
Spcom – Comercio E Prom. Ltda
Tele Eventos Mkt Direto Ltda

Software supplier
A2 Publicidade E Promocoes Lt
Alpha Telecom
Aom Gestao De Empresas E Software
   S/C Ltda
Be Interactive
Celtec Centro Educ. L. Tecnol.
Ckapt Teleperformance
Datalink Mkt Com Internacional
Diagnose Consultoria
Diretotal Bbn Propaganda
DM Company
DTS Software Brasil Ltda
Globalsys Proj Tecnol Em Infor
Grupo Imares
Harte-Hanks Do Brasil Consultoria E
   Serviços Ltda.
Human Resources Systems Consul
IBM Brasil Ind Maq Serv Ltda
Macrolog Teleinformatica Ltda
Mitsucon Tecnologia S/A
Mktec Database Marketing
Multipla Marketing Direto
Perfil Tecnolog
Phoenix Tecnol De Comunicacao
Plusoft Informática
Procenge Proc Dados Eng Sist L
Sd&W Ltda
Skill Computer Services Ltda
Stt Telecom Ltda
Tecnet Teleinformatica Ltda
Telemaker Ltda

Telemarketing agency
3D Call Free Telemarketing
Access Tlmkt Servicos Ltda
Acesso Direto Consultores
Action Line
Advb Assoc. Diri. Vend. Brasil
Albra Comunicacao Integrada Lt
Alpha Telecom
AML Mkt De Relacionamento
Argumento Tlmkt Com E Servs Lt
Auttel Servicos E Tlmkt. Ltda
Brand Member
Bretzke Consult. & Assoc. Ltda
C C Cheque Card
Capt Direct Marketing
Case, Salgado & Associados
Central 24 Horas
Ckapt Marketing Direto
CKL Telecomunicacoes S/A
Compan Comunicaçao
Compugraf Servicos S/C Ltda.
Convivium Eventos & Promocoes
Cooperdata C. T. P. P. Dados
CPM Comunic Proc Mec Automacao
Criativa Cons. Em Mkd Ltda
CSU Telesystem
Datalink Mkt Com Internacional
DBM Marketing Direto Ltda
Dia Design Ltda.
Direct Center Mkd
Direct Marketing Ltda
Diretotal Telemidia Tlmkt S/C
Dist Paulista Prods Serv Ltda
Engenho Propaganda S/C Ltda
Fichbein Comun. Integrada Ltda
First Direct Propaganda Ltda
Fulfillment
G & V Marketing E Desenv. Ltda
G&K Solution Mkt Direto
Hurry Marketing Direto Ltda
Impacto Telemarketing
Innova Do Brasil Ltda
Interact Resp Direta Tlmkt
Interline Servs Tlmkt Ltda
J. Cocco Associados
M&R Mkt De Relacionamento
Macrolog Teleinformatica Ltda
Mailing Express Mkd E Tlmkt
Mapa Pesquisa E Mkt Direto
Maxi-Acao
Metro Md
Multi Marketing Ltda
Neryvalle As Cons Fund Raising
New Work Station Tmkt Ltda
Open Channel Telemarketing
Outsource Informatica Ltda
Pagina Viva Mkt Relacionamento
Pcs Do Brasil Ltda
Plusoft Informática
Pratike Mkt E Asses. S/C Ltda
Quantica Comunic E Marketing
Quatro/A Tlmkt & Centrais Aten
Quattor Marketing E Informatic

Rbc Telemarketing
Red Line Teleservices
Resolve ! Global Marketing
Rk Serv & Consultoria
RSVP
Shop Line International Ltda
Sobral Marketing Direto
Spcom – Comercio E Prom. Ltda
Tele Eventos Mkt Direto Ltda
Telematic Servs De Tlmkt Sc Lt
Teleperformance Brasil
TK1 Telemarketing
TRD Marketing Direto Ltda
Trilha Sist De Comunic Ltda
Uss Telemarketing
Vox Asses Em Comunicacao
Voz Pesquisa E Telemarketing

Training/recruitment
A&C Marketing E Eventos Ltda
Access Tlmkt Servicos Ltda
AM3 Telemarketing S/C Ltda
AML Mkt De Relacionamento
Associacao Alumni
Auttel Servicos E Tlmkt. Ltda
Cat-Centro de Aperfeiçoamento em
   Telemarketing
Central 24 Horas
Ckapt Marketing Direto
CKL Telecomunicacoes S/A
Cooperdata C. T. P. P. Dados
Criativa Cons. Em Mkd Ltda
CSU Telesystem
Diretotal Telemidia Tlmkt S/C
Fichbein Comun. Integrada Ltda
G & V Marketing E Desenv. Ltda

Instituto Monitor S/C Ltda
Interline Servs Tlmkt Ltda
Manpower-Etica Rec Hum Serv Lt
Maxi-Acao
Md Mkt Direto Assoc. S/C Ltda
Mission Edicoes E Eventos Ltda
Neryvalle As Cons Fund Raising
New Work Station Tmkt Ltda
Olf Consultores Associados
Open Channel Telemarketing
Quantica Comunic E Marketing
Quatro/A Tlmkt & Centrais Aten
Spcom – Comercio E Prom. Ltda
Trilha Sist De Comunic Ltda
Vox Asses Em Comunicacao

E-SERVICES

E-Marketing consultant
Acesso Direto Consultores
Aom Gestao De Empresas E Software
   S/C Ltda
Harte-Hanks Do Brasil Consultoria E
   Serviços Ltda.
Livraria Nobel S.A.

Email list provider
Aom Gestao De Empresas E Software
   S/C Ltda
Contacto Marketing & Internet Service
Gazeta Mercantil S/A
Le Pera Marketing Solution S/C Ltda
Multi Marketing Ltda

Email software
Editora Quantum Ltda
Fábrica
Harte-Hanks Do Brasil Consultoria ▌
   Serviços Ltda.
Plusoft Informática

Online/e-marketing agency
Directotal-BBN
J. Cocco Associados
Multi Marketing Ltda

Website design
A2 Publicidade E Promocoes Lt
Aom Gestao De Empresas E Softwa▌
   S/C Ltda
Be Interactive
Compan Comunicaçao
Contacto Marketing & Internet
   Service
Diretotal Bbn Propaganda
Editora Quantum Ltda
Fábrica
First Direct Propaganda Ltda
Livraria Nobel S.A.
Mantel Marketing Ltda
Md Mkt Direto Assoc. S/C Ltda
Medialab Ltda.
Microcap Informatica Ltda
Motivare Promocoes E Eventos L
Publicenter Publicidade
Puterman Public. E Cons. Ltda
Quantica Comunic E Marketing
Ra Net Marketing E Informatica

COLOMBIA

Population: 37.3 million (1996)
Capital: Santa Fe de Bogotá
Language: Spanish

GDP: $80 billion
GDP per capita: $2140
Inflation: 18.5 per cent

Currency: Colombian Peso (Col P) = 100 centavos
Exchange rate: Col P1,630.50 : $1

Time: GMT −5 hours

Colombia is one of the Latin American economies to have enjoyed sustained growth over recent years, although tight monetary policies in response to rising inflation and unemployment slowed this to only 3 per cent in 1996. The country is fortunate in having plentiful natural resources, coupled with a well-diversified economic base. The medium-term outlook is positive, with continuing higher coffee prices and an impending boom in oil and gas exports as new fields come onstream.

There is one significant aspect of Colombian economic and political life which is not easily represented statistically: namely, the illegal drugs trade. Production and trafficking generate ample funds for corruption, and those involved are ruthless in achieving their aims. The government continues to make strenuous efforts to combat the trade, but it remains a source of tension between the Colombian and US authorities, and necessarily has a damaging effect on wider international relations.

Postal services are basic in Colombia. Telecommunications, however, are fairly well developed compared with other Latin American countries. Advertising spend is 2.1 per cent of GDP.

589

DIRECT MARKETING ASSOCIATION

Name: Asociacion Colombiana de Mecadeo Directo
Address: Calle 35, No. 6-40, Santa Fe de Bogota
Tel: +57 1 288 2688
Fax: +57 1 323 0007
E-mail: telemerc@latino.net.co
Contact: Frederico Pelaez

POSTAL SERVICES

Administracíon Postal Nacional
(Helio José Orduz Pico, Marketing Manager)
Edificio Murillo Toro Calle 12
Carreras 7a y 8a, Piso 6°, Oficina 607
Santa Fe de Bogota
Colombia

Tel:+571 341 5534
Fax: +57 1 283 3345

PROVIDERS OF DM AND E-M SERVICES

CARVAJAL SA
Calle 29 No. 6A-40
Cali
Columbia
Tel: +57 2 3 667 5011
Fax: +57 2 660 1833

Services/Products:
List services; Lettershop;
Telemarketing agency; Publisher;
Electronic media; Internet services

**COMPUTEC SA,
   INFORMATION**
Carrera 7 No. 76–35 P10y 11
Bogota
Columbia
Tel: +57 1 640 5868
Fax: +57 1 640 5867
Jorge Plazas Arevalo, Data Clientes
   Manager

Services/Products:
Service bureau

Member of:
DMA (US)

DATASET MARKETING GROUP
Carrera 19 #88–31
Bogota
Columbia
Tel: +57 1 236 2714
Fax: +57 1 218 0207
Alberto Castro, Managing Director

Services/Products:
Advertising Agency; Direct marketing
agency; Design/graphics/clip art
supplier; Media buying agency; Mail
order company

INTERPROJECT
Cra. 12 #119–78
Bogota DC
Columbia
Tel: +57 1 619 7585
Fax: +57 1 619 8387
Email: arturo@tvmarketing.com
Web: www.tvmarketing.com
Arturo Angel, Director

Services/Products:
Advertising Agency; Call centre
services/systems; Mail order company;
Direct marketing agency; Direct
response TV

Member of:
DMA (US); ERA

LISTA SA
Calle 94A No 11A-27P3
Bogota
Columbia
Tel: +57 1 622 0440
Fax: +57 1 622 0429
Gabriel Villaveces, President

Services/Products:
List services

Member of:
DMA (US)

LISTAS SA
Carrera 11A No 94–76 P3
Bogota
Columbia
Tel: +57 1 616 2070
Fax: +57 1 616 1914
Juan Patino, Executive Vice President

Services/Products:
List services; Lettershop;
Telemarketing agency

MERCALEGIS
Carrera 13 No 26–45
Oficina 502
Bogota
Columbia
Tel: +57 1 341 2946
Fax: +57 1 341 7450
Juan Carlos Pinilla, Second Manager

Services/Products:
Advertising Agency

OP DIRECT
Avenida Caracas 31–93
2nd Fl
Bogota DC
Columbia
Tel: +57 1 288 0899
Fax: +57 1 285 5508
Daniel Hernandez

Services/Products:
Lettershop; Mailing/Faxing services

Member of:
DMA (US)

**PUBLICACIONES PERIODICAS
   LTDA**
Ave. Jimenez No 6–77 Piso 3
Bogota
Columbia
Tel: +57 1 281 3165
Fax: +57 1 286 9594

Services/Products:
Advertising Agency; List services;
Telemarketing agency

RAPP COLLINS COLOMBIA
Carrera 19 #88–31
Bogota

Columbia
Tel: +57 1 610 2977
Fax: +57 1 530 0033
Julian Penalosa, President

Services/Products:
Consultancy services

Member of:
DMA (US)

**TELEFACIL PANAMERICANA
   DE MARKETING**
Carrera 44 No 22A-05
Bogota
Columbia
Tel: +57 1 268 7856
Fax: +57 1 335 0586

Services/Products:
Advertising Agency

SERVICES/PRODUCT LISTING

Advertising Agency
Dataset Marketing Group
Interproject
Mercalegis
Publicaciones Periodicas Ltda
Telefacil Panamericana de Marketing

Call centre services/systems
Interproject

Consultancy services
Rapp Collins Colombia

**Design/graphics/clip art
   supplier**
Dataset Marketing Group

Direct marketing agency
Dataset Marketing Group
Interproject

Direct response TV
Interproject

Electronic media
Carvajal SA

Internet services
Carvajal SA

Lettershop
Carvajal SA
Listas SA
OP Direct

List services
Carvajal SA

Lista SA
Listas SA
Publicaciones Periodicas Ltda

Mail order company
Dataset Marketing Group
Interproject

Mailing/Faxing services
OP Direct

Media buying agency
Dataset Marketing Group

Publisher
Carvajal SA

Service bureau
Computec SA, Information

Telemarketing agency
Carvajal SA
Listas SA
Publicaciones Periodicas Ltda

MEXICO

Population: 94.9 million
Capital: Mexico City
Language: Spanish

GDP: $342 billion
GDP per capita: $3690
Inflation: 20.6 per cent

Currency: Nuevo Peso (PS) = 100 centavos
Exchange rate: PS9.25 : $1

Time: GMT –6 hours

OVERVIEW

Mexico suffered from a deep recession in 1995 but has since had steady growth, mainly due to strong export performance. Annual population growth is 2.1 per cent and it is estimated that it will exceed 100 million by the year 2000, with 1 million Mexicans joining the labour force every year. Advertising spend is 1.2 per cent of GDP. Total advertising spend in 1995 was US$4.6 billion.

Great strides have been taken in the last few years to improve the DM infrastructure in Mexico. Foreign mailers, applying sophisticated techniques adapted to local language, culture and shopping patterns, have achieved excellent results. Business-to-business campaigns are generally more sophisticated, and better understood, than consumer mailings.

There is a wide choice of printers to suit most levels of volume, budget and quality. At the top of the market, standards are high. Local paper stocks vary wildly in terms of colour, weight and translucency, but imports are now becoming available, in a limited range of sizes.

In 1991, Mexico privatized its telephone company, Telmex, which has become a great success on the stock market. Indeed, Mexico's whole telecommunications industry has undergone something of a revolution,

593

growing 40 per cent annually during recent years. This revolution involves a necessary update of the telecommunications system, including the replacement of the old telephone lines with new optical-fibre lines. This update will give Mexican companies a real chance to use new telecommunications technology; however, the telephone charges which accompany it have come under fire. A particular cause for complaint is the heavy tax on all international calls: it can cost Mexicans seven times more to call the US than it costs the US partner to call Mexico – a definite consideration for telemarketing.

Lists and databases

Business-to-business – the largest database is the Direcciones list, which is accurate and up-to-date if lacking in full SIC segmentation. Other business list owners include: Mega Marketing; Expansion; Dun and Bradstreet; Key Market; Rodriguez Rivas y Asociados; Mercadotecnia Internacional; IIR; Tecnografix; Alpi Publicidad; Ibcon; Enlace Telefonico.

Consumer – there are no list brokers in Mexico so it is necessary to search hard for responsive consumer names. Most companies entering the market try to approach banks and credit card companies and directory publishers directly.

LANGUAGE AND CULTURAL CONSIDERATIONS

Spanish is spoken universally in Mexico, so it should always be the language of any campaign.

LEGISLATION AND CONSUMER PROTECTION

Local legislation has not turned its attention to DM – yet. However, the Mexican DMA has started the long process of setting up a code of ethics as a self-regulatory guide, to prevent the worst excesses.

THE DIRECT MARKETING ASSOCIATION

Name: Association Mexicana de Mercadotecnia Directa AC (AMMD)
Address: Montecito 38, Piso 23, Suite 14, Col. Napoles,
World Trade Centre
Mexico City DF 03810
Tel: +52 5 488 3163
Fax: +52 5 488 3165
Email: ammd@wtcmex.com.mx
Year founded: 1991

President: Manuel Avila
Total staff: 7 (includes board members)
Members: 70
Contact: Virgilio Torres

Direct mail agencies	10	List brokers	12
Mailing houses	5	Printers	5
Telemarketing agencies	7	Direct mail consultants	5
Handling houses	3	Mail order companies	10
Database agencies	13		

Facilities for overseas users of direct mail

Membership: overseas companies can join the AMMD; there are no formal standards for membership, but candidates should have a presence in the Mexican DM market, or a genuine intention to create one. Annual fees have yet to be fixed.

Newsletter: the AMMD does produce a newsletter.

Library: the Mexican DMA does have a sizeable library.

On-line information service: the association also has an on-line information service.

Legal advice: the AMMD offers advice on the first steps to understanding the market from a legal point of view.

Business liaison service: the AMMD offers details of local business suppliers and helps overseas companies to find local venture partners. It also offers a consultancy service of fee-based research into direct marketing subjects.

POSTAL SERVICES

Most agree that the Mexican Postal Service, Sepomex, has improved greatly over the last few years. In 1992 a full zip code-based bulk sorting system was established, and Sepomex claims a 24–48 hour delivery in urban areas and 48-72 hours in the rest of the country.

Any direct marketer with a minimum of 500 pieces of mail may obtain a commercial licence from Sepomex. The bulk rate may be as low as M$0.21 for a 20 gram piece. The full first class rate is M$0.39.

For further information please contact:

Servicio Postal Mexicano (SEPOMEX) (CORREOS)
Tel: +525 722 9500 ext. 20001
Fax: +525 709 9184

PROVIDERS OF DM AND E-M SERVICES

ASOCIACION MEXICANA DE TELEMARKETING
Homero No. 229–6 Piso
Col. Polanco
MX
Mexico DF
11570
Mexico
Tel: +52 5 313 705

Services/Products:
Media buying agency

DIRECCIONES, S.A.
Apartado Postal 17–591
Mecico D.F.
11411
Mexico
Tel: +52 5 527–0398
Fax: +52 5 399–0558
Cornelio Bos, General Director

Services/Products:
List services; Lettershop; Database
services; Mailing/Faxing services

Member of:
DMA (US); AMMD

ENTELSA
Nayarit 22
Colonia Roma
Mexico DF
6700
Mexico
Tel: +52 5 564 2056
Fax: +52 5 264 5594
Email: entelsa@entelsa.com.my
Web: www.entelsa.com

Services/Products:
Database services; Personalisation;
Direct marketing agency; Lettershop;
List services; Telemarketing agency

E-Services:
Email list providers; E-Marketing
consultant; Website design

Member of:
AMMD (Mexico)

GRUPO ACCOR
Lago Rodolfo 29
Colonia Granada
Mexico DF
11520
Mexico
Tel: +52 5 255 4260
Fax: +52 5 203 8851

Services/Products:
Sales promotion agency

INFOMAC DIRECT SA DE CV
Augusto Comte #26
Col. Anzures
Mexico DF
11590
Mexico
Tel: +52 5 250 0603
Fax: +52 5 250 0659
Eugenio Lopez, Sales Manager

Services/Products:
List services; Database services

J WALTER THOMPSON DIRECT
Ejercito Nacional 519
Col Granada
Mexico DF
11520
Mexico
Tel: +52 9 729 4089
Fax: +52 9 729 4048

Services/Products:
Advertising Agency

LEO BURNETT - MEXICO CITY
Bosque de Duraznos 65–8P
Bosque de Las Lomas
Mexico, D.F.
11700
Mexico
Tel: +52 5 596–6188
Tim Classey, EVP, Managing Director

Services/Products:
Advertising Agency; Direct marketing
agency

Member of:
DMA (US)

LETTER SHOP S.A. DE C.V.
Destajistas No.3
Fracc. Industrial Xhala
Cuautitlan Izcalli
54714
Mexico
Tel: +52 5 872–3935
Fax: +52 5 872 3849
Carlos Viniegra Dow, General
  Manager

Services/Products:
Lettershop; Mailing/Faxing services

Member of:
DMA (US)

MATTE-RAMSDELL & ASOCIADOS
Thiers 125, Col. Anzores
D.F. Mexico
11590
Mexico
Tel: +52 5 250–4122
Fax: +52 5 250–7957
Elizabeth Ramsdell, Director

Services/Products:
Advertising Agency; Direct marketing
agency

Member of:
DMA (US)

MEGA DIRECT, S.A. DE C.V.
Romulo O'Farril No. 262
Colonia Olivar de los Padres
Mexico City
1780
Mexico
Tel: +52 5 681–7746
Fax: +52 5 681–8239
Email: mdirect@infoabc.com
Web: www.megadirect.com
Eduardo Achach I., Director General

Services/Products:
Call centre services/systems; Databas
services; Mail order company; Mailin
Faxing services; Personalisation; Prin
services

E-Services:
Email list provider

Member of:
DMA (US); FEDMA; National DM
American Chamber of Commerce

MEGA MARKETING
Romulo O'Farril No 262
Colonia Olivar de los Padres
Deleg Alvaro Obregon
1780
Mexico
Tel: +52 5 681 7746
Fax: +52 5 681 8239
Eduardo Achach, President

Services/Products:
List services; Lettershop;
Telemarketing agency; Service burea

MENSAJES TELEFONICAS SA DE CV
Jaime Balmes 11
Torre B 201-B
Pulanso
Mexico DF
11510
Mexico
Tel: +52 5 281 4966
Fax: +52 5 281 4145

Services/Products:
Telemarketing agency

MERKAFON DE MEXICO, S.A DE C.V.
Ave. Cuauhtemoc 400 Sur
Col. Centro
Monterrey, N.L.
64000
Mexico

Tel: +52 8 150 00 00
Fax: +52 8 150 01 01
Gerardo Estevane V., Marketing
   Director

Services/Products:
Telemarketing agency

Member of:
DMA (US)

MERKAFON DE MEXICO, SA DE CV
Ave Roble 300 Mezzanine
Col Valle del Campestre
Garza Garcia, NL
66265
Mexico
Tel: +52 8 335 0202
Fax: +52 8 335 6993

Services/Products:
Telemarketing agency

RODRIGUEZ RIVAS Y ASOCIADO SC
Avenida Lomas Verde 450
Despacho 105
Lomas Verde, CP
53120
Mexico
Tel: +52 5 393 7046
Fax: +52 5 393 9866
Roberto Rodriguez R, President

Services/Products:
List services; Market research agency

SEGURIDAD TECNOLOGICO Y COMERCIAL SA DE C.VO
Viaducto Miguel Aleman # 239–101
MX-06760
Mexico DT
Mexico
Tel: +52 5 584 1821
Fax: +52 5 264 1335
Jorge Pedroza, General Manager

Services/Products:
Database services; Direct marketing
agency; Media buying agency; Mail
order company; Sales promotion
agency

SERVICIOS DE DISTRIBUCION ALPHA
Destajistas No. 3
Fracc. Industrial Xhala
Cuautitlan Izcalli
54714
Mexico
Tel: +52 5 360–0040
Fax: +52 5 872 3849
Carlos Viniegra Dow, General
   Manager

Services/Products:
Lettershop; Mailing/Faxing services

Member of:
DMA (US)

STC DIRECT
Viaducto Miguel Alemán 239 1 y 3
Col. Roma Sur
CP 06760
Mexico DF
Mexico
Tel: +52 5 584 1821
Fax: +52 5 264 1335
Email: stc@spin.com.mx
Jorge Pedroza Ms

Services/Products:
Database services; Direct marketing
agency; Consultancy services; Direct
response TV services; Electronic
media; Internet services

E-Services:
Website design

Member of:
AMMD

TECNOGRAFIX, SA DE CV
Porfirio Diaz No 156
Col. del Valle
Mexico, DF CP
3100
Mexico
Tel: +52 5 575 3733
Fax: +52 5 575 3842

Services/Products:
Fulfilment and sampling house

TELECONTACTO
Parque de los Remedios No. 6
Col. El Parque Naucalpan
MS 302
Edo. de Mexico C.P.
53390
Mexico
Tel: +52 5 358–1272
Fax: +52 5 358–3110
Ing. Hector Jaramillo V.

Services/Products:
Telemarketing agency

Member of:
DMA (US)

TELESERVICE
Av. Julian Adame No. 175
Col. Granjas Navidad
Cuajimalpa
DF
5210
Mexico
Tel: +52 5813 8855
Fax: +52 5813 8970

Email: teleservice@telnorm.com.mx
Web: www.telnorm.com.mx
Manuel Laborde, Director General

Services/Products:
Call centre services/systems;
Consultancy services; Database
services; Personalisation; Mailing/
Faxing services; Market research
agency; Web enabled call centre

Member of:
DMA

UNO A UNO S.A. DE C.V.
Rodolfo gaona 86E
Col. Lomas de Sotelo
Mexico D.F.
11200
Mexico
Tel: +52 5 283–5030
Fax: +52 5 283 5016
Rene Ybara, Director General

Services/Products:
Fulfilment and sampling house

Member of:
DMA (US)

SERVICES/PRODUCT LISTING

Advertising Agency
J Walter Thompson Direct
Leo Burnett - Mexico City
Matte-Ramsdell & Asociados

Call centre services/systems
Mega Direct, S.A. de C.V.
Teleservice

Consultancy services
STC Direct
Teleservice

Database services
Direcciones, S.A.
Entelsa
Infomac Direct SA DE CV
Mega Direct, S.A. de C.V.
Seguridad Tecnologico Y Comercial
   SA DE C.VO
STC Direct
Teleservice

Direct marketing agency
Entelsa
Leo Burnett - Mexico City
Matte-Ramsdell & Asociados
Seguridad Tecnologico Y Comercial
   SA DE C.VO
STC Direct

597

Direct response TV services
STC Direct

Electronic media
STC Direct

Fulfilment and sampling house
Tecnografix, SA DE CV
Uno a Uno S.A. de C.V.

Internet services
STC Direct

Lettershop
Direcciones, S.A.
Entelsa
Letter Shop S.A. de C.V.
Mega Marketing
Servicios De Distribucion Alpha

List services
Direcciones, S.A.
Entelsa
Infomac Direct SA DE CV
Mega Marketing
Rodriguez Rivas Y Asociado SC

Mail order company
Mega Direct, S.A. de C.V.
Seguridad Tecnologico Y Comercial
   SA DE C.VO

Mailing/Faxing services
Direcciones, S.A.
Letter Shop S.A. de C.V.
Mega Direct, S.A. de C.V.
Servicios De Distribucion Alpha
Teleservice

Market research agency
Rodriguez Rivas Y Asociado SC
Teleservice

Media buying agency
Asociacion Mexicana de Telemarketing
Seguridad Tecnologico Y Comercial
   SA DE C.VO

Personalisation
Entelsa
Mega Direct, S.A. de C.V.
Teleservice

Print services
Mega Direct, S.A. de C.V.

Sales promotion agency
Grupo Accor
Seguridad Tecnologico Y Comercial
   SA DE C.VO

Service bureau
Mega Marketing

Telemarketing agency
Entelsa
Mega Marketing
Mensajes Telefonicas SA DE CV
Merkafon de Mexico, S.A. De C.V.
Merkafon De Mexico, SA DE CV
TeleContacto

Web enabled call centre
Teleservice

E-SERVICES

E-Marketing consultant
Entelsa

Email list provider
Entelsa
Mega Direct, S.A. de C.V.

Website design
Entelsa
STC Direct

PANAMA

Population: 2.68 million
Capital: Panama City
Language: Spanish

GDP: $63.79 billion (1993)
GDP per capita: $2700
Inflation: 0.7 per cent (1996)

Currency: Balboa (B) = 100 centesimos
Exchange rate: B1 : $1 (Fixed)

Time: GMT –5 hours

Throughout the 1980s Panama experienced extreme political and economic difficulties, with political unease inevitably reflected in economic downturn. The last years of the Noriega regime saw a rapid decline in GDP. The democratic election of a new president, however, heralded a new era of recovery, with economic growth averaging a little over 7 per cent in the years 1990–93. The new president, elected in May 1999, will preside over an important period in Panama's history, overseeing the handover, at the end of the year, of the Panama Canal and its surrounding territory, which has been under American control since Panama won its independence from Colombia in 1903. This fifty-mile stretch of water handles an average of 35 ships a day and will provide Panama with a significant rise in income.

The economy is characterized by a dominant service sector, representing some 80 per cent of GDP. Transportation provides about half Panama's export revenues, with the Panama Canal currently accounting for 10 per cent of GDP. The Colon Free Zone is a re-exporting and warehousing centre for Central and South America with an annual turnover of $3.5 billion in 1991, accounting for about 5 per cent of GDP.

About half the population is urban, concentrated in the capital of Panama City and the large towns of Colon and David. Annual population growth is 1.9 per cent. Telecommunications are improving, as are media expenditure and penetration. Direct marketing is still very much in its infancy, but possibilities exist for imaginative marketers. Impact and laser printing facilities are available at competitive prices, and international list brokerage services exist, with average list prices ranging from $150-300.

Mailing out of Panama can offer savings to a direct marketer. Postcards, for example, can be mailed for as little as two cents each, since mail is paid by weight, not by unit; the country can also offer duty-free warehousing of inventory, prior to mailing anywhere in the world.

PROVIDERS OF DM SERVICES

Orlando Calvo, President
International Direct Marketing Services
PO Box 55-0625
Panama City
Panama

Tel: +507 269 2343   Fax: +507 269 2419

POSTAL SERVICES

All mail must be addressed Republic of Panama or RP.

For more information contact:

Correos Nationales de Panamá
Edif. Don Bosco
Frente a la Basilica Menor Don Bosco
3° Piso
Apdo. 3421 Zona 4
Republic of Panama

Tel: +507 225 2830/2831
Fax: +507 225 2671

PERU

Population: 24.4 million
Capital: Lima
Languages: Spanish (Quechua and Aymara also spoken)

GDP: $59 billion
GDP per capita: $2420
Inflation: 11.8 per cent (1996)

Currency: Nuevo Sol (NS) = 100 centimos
Exchange rate: NS3.33 : $1

Time: GMT −5 hours

Peru has achieved a degree of economic growth in recent years, with a reduction in the rate of inflation. Since 1991 the government has been engaged in an extensive programme of privatization of state-owned monopolies. This has been highly successful, and generated a substantial level of foreign investment.

Any benefits from liberalization, however, have been felt only by the middle and upper classes, the smallest sectors of the population. Peru remains a country of profound inequalities. Income distribution is extremely unequal, with the poorest 20 per cent of the population receiving less than 5 per cent of national income; the country is still largely composed of peasant farmers and underemployed shanty town dwellers.

Peru is in a state of transition. The acquisition of controlling stakes in the national telecommunication companies by TISA, the Spanish Telefonica Nacional, has already brought about rapid improvements in the telephone network, and further improvements in the communications infrastructure are inevitable in time. In spite of new sorting machinery, the postal service can still be erratic and many businesses prefer to use private courier services.

A direct marketing association was established in 1997 and an on-line information service and business liaison service are both currently under construction.

LEGISLATION AND CONSUMER PROTECTION

There are currently no data protection laws in Peru.

THE DIRECT MARKETING ASSOCIATION

Name: Asociacion de Marketing Directo del Peru (AMDP)
Address: Las Camelias 180, Lima 27 Peru
Tel: 51 1 222 5995
Fax: 51 1 221 9012
Year founded: 1997
President: Miguel Cantella
Total staff: 6
Members: 20
Contact: Miguel Cantella – President
                    Claudio Gutiérrez – Vice President

Facilities for overseas users of direct mail

Membership: overseas companies can join the Peruvian direct marketing association. The facilities are fairly limited, as the association has only very recently been established.
Newsletter: there is no newsletter.
Library: there is no library service at present.
On-line information service: this is currently under construction
Business liaison service: this is also currently under construction.

POSTAL SERVICES

For more information on postal services and rates contact:

Correo Central del Peru
170 Conde de Superunda
Lima 1
Peru

Tel: +51 1 428 7931/427 8876
Fax: +51 427 8391/427 9517
Email: postal@aerpost.com.pe

PROVIDERS OF DM AND E-M SERVICES

CALL CENTER
Camino Real 111 piso 6
Lima
27
Peru
Tel: +51 1 215 5000
Fax: +51 1 215 5000
Jorge Corchuello

Services/Products:
Telemarketing agency

Member of:
AMDP

CONTACTO MARKETING TELEFóNICO
Av. 2 de Mayo 416
Lima
27
Peru
Tel: +51 10221 6072/221 4820
Maria Rosalva Aguilar

Services/Products:
Telemarketing agency

Member of:
AMDP

FCB PUBLICIDAD/MAYO
Av. Jose Larco 1199
Ste 1100
Lima
18
Peru
Tel: +51 011 5112416500
Fax: +51 1 151 1445
William Clark, President

Services/Products:
Advertising Agency; Direct marketing agency

Member of:
DMA (US)

GREY DIRECT – PERU
Las Camelias 891
San Isidro
Lima
27
Peru
Tel: +51 14 409 889
Fax: +51 14 413 118
Mariajose Franco, General Manager

Services/Products:
Advertising Agency; Direct marketing agency

Member of:
DMA (US)

HAND RAISING
Las Camelias 180
Lima
27
Peru
Tel: +51 1 421 9997
Fax: +51 1 221 9012
Claudio Gutiérrez Ramos

Services/Products:
List services; Direct marketing agency; Consultancy services; Design/graphics/ clip art supplier; Electronic media; Internet services

E-Services:
Website design

Member of:
DMA (US); AMDP

MASTER LINK
Av. República de Panamá 3505–2 piso
Lima
27
Peru
Tel: +51 1 222 2122
Fax: +51 1 222 2947
Mely Miyoshi

Services/Products:
Telemarketing agency

Member of:
AMDP

MOSAIC
Av. Benavides 2150
Lima
18
Peru
Tel: +51 1 446 1871
Fax: +51 1 444 8709

Services/Products:
Telemarketing agency; Direct marketing agency; Micromarketing

Member of:
AMDP

PARK ADVERTISING & DIRECT
Avenida Larco 1199
Ste 1100
Miraflores
Lima
18
Peru
Tel: +51 14 449 577
Fax: +51 14 241 6500
William Clark, President

Services/Products:
Advertising Agency; Direct marketing agency

Member of:
DMA (US)

SEGMENTA
Santa Luisa 155–501
Lima
27
Peru
Tel: +51 1 442 6374/422 9691
Fax: +51 1 442 6374
Alberto Alvarado

Services/Products:
Consultancy services; Market research agency

Member of:
AMDP

TELEFóNICA MARKETING DIRECTO
Peru
Tel: +51 1 427 1077/0 800 1 7777
Fax: +51 1 427 1112
Javier Carmona

Services/Products:
Telemarketing agency

Member of:
AMDP

VíA DIRECTA
Av. Reducto 1290
Lima
18
Peru
Tel: +51 1 444 3133
Fax: +51 1 241 7112
Ignacio Garnica

Services/Products:
List services; Mailing/Faxing services; Telemarketing agency; Direct marketing agency

Member of:
AMDP

SERVICES/PRODUCT LISTING

Advertising Agency
FCB Publicidad/Mayo
Grey Direct – Peru
Park Advertising & Direct

Consultancy services
hand raising
Segmenta

Design/graphics/clip art supplier
hand raising

Direct marketing agency
FCB Publicidad/Mayo
Grey Direct – Peru

hand raising
Mosaic
Park Advertising & Direct
Vía Directa

Electronic media
hand raising

Internet services
hand raising

List services
hand raising

Vía Directa

Mailing/Faxing services
Vía Directa

Market research agency
Segmenta

Micromarketing
Mosaic

Telemarketing agency
Call Center

Contacto Marketing Telefónico
Master Link
Mosaic
Telefónica Marketing Directo
Vía Directa

E-SERVICES

Website design
hand raising

VENEZUELA

Population: 22.3 million
Capital: Caracas
Language: Spanish

GDP: $67 billion
GDP per capita: $3020
Inflation: 50 per cent

Currency: Bolivar (Bs) = 100 centimos
Exchange rate: B594.00 : $1

Time: GMT −4 hours

OVERVIEW

Direct marketing has made a start in Venezuela only in the last ten years or so. Local lists are limited, but a strong publishing industry with over 150 magazines and 75 newspaper titles should ensure that more emerge onto the market in time. Rental prices are between US$150 and US$350 per thousand. Lists are held by the owner and, as with other Latin American markets, release can be a problem.

There is a limited choice of local suppliers, though print quality is adequate. It should be noted, however, that the postal service has recently shown significant deterioration, and this should be carefully assessed before embarking on a campaign.

LANGUAGE AND CULTURAL CONSIDERATIONS

Any DM campaign should be conducted in Spanish.

LEGISLATION AND CONSUMER PROTECTION

No formal legislation addressing direct mail currently exists.

THE DIRECT MARKETING ASSOCIATION

Name: Asociación Venezolana de Mercadeo Directo (AVMD)
Address: 2da transversal Los Castaños Qta. Mi Campurusa,
Los Choros, Caracas 1071
Tel: +582 239 5532
Fax: +582 239 3343
Email: powermarketing@cantv.net
Year founded: 1991
President: Eduardo Alvarez Coello
Total staff: 12
Members: 46 companies
Contact: Orlando Lopez

DM agencies	8	Telemarketing agencies	5
DM consultants	9	List brokers	2
Advertisers	10	Mailing houses	1
Printers	3	Mail order companies	3
Database agencies	10		

Facilities for overseas users of direct mail

Membership: overseas companies are eligible to join the AVMD, with annual fees at US$600.
Newsletter: monthly, US$60 for a one year subscription.
Other facilities: we are very strong in DM education for our members. We hold at least 6 seminars every year, and 10 to 12 workshops.

POSTAL SERVICES

Delivery problems do exist. PO boxes can be used in an attempt to circumvent this. Venezuelan addresses are extremely long, and great care must be taken to ensure that the entire address is captured.

The postal service will send full postal rates free on request to prospective mailers. The information is printed in Spanish.

Contact:

Instituto Postal Telegrafico de Venezuelal
Av. Jose Angel Lamas – San Martin
Caracas
Venezuela

Tel: +58 2 462 4122
Fax: +58 2 451 4379 (ext.247)
Website: www.ipostel.gov.ve

PROVIDERS OF DM AND E-M SERVICES

BELOW THE LINE COMMUNICACIONES - LATIN AMERICA
Ofic. 3
Ed. Guarani
Av. Rio Janeiro
Las Mercedes
Caracas
MI 1060
Venezuela
Tel: +1 273 1 3981
Fax: +1 2731 0558
Email: below@sa.omnes.net
Web: www,dimacorp.com/below
Ricardo Morales, President

Services/Products:
Copy adaptation; Direct marketing agency; Private delivery services; Sales promotion agency; Telemarketing agency; Event Marketing agency

E-Services:
Email list provider; Online/e-marketing agency

Member of:
National DMA

FCB PUBLICIDAD
Apartado 62430
Ste 1100
Chacao, Caracas
1060
Venezuela
Tel: +58 2 951 0222
Fax: 2 951 0785
William Clark, Senior Vice President

Services/Products:
Advertising Agency; Direct marketing agency

Member of:
DMA (US)

KOBS & DRAFT MERCADEO DIRECTO
Torre Aco. Ave Principal Las Marcedes, Piso 6
Caracas
Venezuela
Tel: +58 2 92 2411
Fax: 2 993 0022
Howard Draft, Chairman & CEO

Services/Products:
Advertising Agency; Direct marketing agency

Member of:
DMA (US)

LINEA DIRECTA FISCHER GREY
Oficentro Los Ruices, Piso 1
Ave. Diego Cisneros
Caracas
1071
Venezuela
Tel: +58 2 2398033
Fax: 2 239 5861
William Esteves, General Manager

Services/Products:
Advertising Agency; Telemarketing agency; Direct marketing agency; Sales promotion agency; Electronic media

Member of:
DMA (US); AVMD

SERVICES/PRODUCT LISTING

Advertising Agency
FCB Publicidad
Kobs & Draft Mercadeo Directo
Linea Directa Fischer Grey

Copy adaptation
Below The Line Communicaciones - Latin America

Direct marketing agency
Below The Line Communicaciones - Latin America
FCB Publicidad
Kobs & Draft Mercadeo Directo
Linea Directa Fischer Grey

Electronic media
Linea Directa Fischer Grey

Event Marketing agency
Below The Line Communicaciones - Latin America

Private delivery services
Below The Line Communicaciones - Latin America

Sales promotion agency
Below The Line Communicaciones - Latin America
Linea Directa Fischer Grey

Telemarketing agency
Below The Line Communicaciones - Latin America
Linea Directa Fischer Grey

E-SERVICES

Email list provider
Below The Line Communicaciones - Latin America

Online/e-marketing agency
Below The Line Communicaciones - Latin America

ASIA

REGIONAL OVERVIEW

The Asian crisis, which began in 1997 and has dominated the last couple of years, finally looks to be on its way out, with strong stock market rises in the region since the beginning of 1999.

DIRECT AND DATABASE MARKETING CAPABILITIES IN ASIA/PACIFIC

Introduction

This article has been written by Paul O'Donnell, Ogilvy & Mather Direct Asia/Pacific and Paul Davies, Ogilvy & Mather Dataconsult Asia/Pacific for clients coming into Asia/Pacific from the Western world, and aims to explain the sophistication of direct/database marketing in the region. Asia offers many opportunities to the thoughtful direct marketer. Response rates are high; databases of affluent consumers can be built at a discount; new media opportunities are constantly presenting themselves; and supplier choice is widening every day.

However, Asia has still not achieved Western levels of sophistication in direct marketing, and a decision to enter the market needs to be carefully thought through, and even more judiciously executed. The information below is aimed at helping marketers to take that first step.

Regional Overview

There has been so much written in numerous travel and 'how to do business' books about the diversity of cultures, attitudes and peoples in Asia/Pacific that to repeat it here would be superfluous. The only point to state is that what has been written is largely true, and the diversity applies as much to the application of marketing and communication techniques (including direct marketing and database marketing) as anything else. Almost every country seems to have its idiosyncrasies and slightly different ways of doing things which should be understood when considering direct/database marketing in this region.

Having said this, it is possible to group certain countries as to their sophistication in the application of database marketing techniques and the associated capabilities. These levels of 'sophistication' are obviously closely associated with the 'state' of direct marketing and can be identified as follows:

- *Sophisticated* – Direct marketing is well established; a wide range of support services are available including computer bureaux. Clients with their respective agency are using direct marketing in a strategic way (for example, in customer loyalty programmes) rather than as a tactical promotional device. Certainly a wide spectrum of computer bureaux are available, providing similar services to those in Europe and the USA.
- *Intermediate* – Although direct marketing may have been established for a number of years, the use is primarily tactical (advertising in the post). Support services are at a relatively basic level or the applications of the 'tools of the trade' have yet to be applied by clients/agencies in their entirety. The surrounding infrastructure will not be either able or conducive to supporting large-volume direct mail.
- *Emerging* – Direct marketing is in its start-up phase, with the first DM agencies established in the last two to three years. The agencies have a limited choice of suppliers (usually just one or two) to support them.
- *Rudimentary* – No internationally recognized direct marketing agencies are present in the marketplace, and support services are non-existent. In some of these countries advertising agencies have yet to be developed or are supported purely by a representative office.

The countries can be grouped as follows:

Sophisticated	Intermediate	Emerging	Rudimentary
Australia	Hong Kong	India	Burma
New Zealand	Malaysia	Korea	Cambodia
Japan	Singapore	Philippines	China
	Thailand		India sub-region
	Taiwan		Indonesia
			Vietnam

For the countries that have been omitted, the status is unknown but assumed to be rudimentary.

Computer Bureaux in Asia/Pacific

The bureau capabilities can be broken down into two groups.

Australasia and Japan

A healthy supplier base of bureaux exists in both countries. However, the services they provide appear significantly to lag behind the USA and Europe. In Australia, certain capabilities exist in the area of address enhancement, post coding and personalization but not to the level of sophistication of Europe. Both markets may lack the development of packaged software for licensing to a third party.

All other countries

The situation differs markedly outside the above-mentioned countries. Only Malaysia offers a full bureau service and in general no computer bureaux exist. Primarily (there are some notable exceptions) the suppliers in these markets are data capture or fulfilment houses offering other services to provide a 'one-stop shop'.

As far as we are aware, no packaged software at any level of sophistication is available, and address enhancement and post coding are only available using manual methods. Effective personalization can only be done by asking individuals to specify the way they would like to be addressed at the time you capture the name and address.

It should be noted that there is a distinct lack of marketing expertise in the region generally and in direct marketing especially. Therefore people with IT experience in the marketing field are very rare. In terms of general IT skills, people resources are available but are also in high demand.

Customer Loyalty Programmes

A number of loyalty programmes are in force in Asia (mainly 'points get prizes' type of programmes) and they are primarily run for airlines, hotels, banks/credit card companies; a number of telecommunications suppliers are also starting to look at this area. A large number of these are by US companies. The majority tend to be in-house solutions.

Ogilvy & Mather (O & M) is the leading direct marketing agency across Asia/Pacific with 14 offices in 10 countries or territories. Its business stretches from Japan and Korea in the north, to Australia and New Zealand in the south. Dataconsult is the specialist marketing information and database management arm of O & M. O & M also offers telemarketing and interactive content development services across the region.

CHINA

Population: 1,232.1 million
Capital: Beijing
Language: Mandarin is the official spoken language

GDP: $906 billion
GDP per capita: $750
Inflation: 2.8 per cent

Currency: Yuan = 100 fen
Exchange rate: Yuan 8.28 : $1

Time: GMT +8 hours

OVERVIEW

With a vast population of over 1.2 billion, China represents the world's largest marketplace. Recent liberalization of the economy has created an astonishing economic growth rate, averaging over 9 per cent per annum since 1985; the population is increasingly finding itself with the resources to purchase everything from basic consumer goods to the most expensive luxury items.

Direct marketing was also introduced into China in the early 1990s. The number of direct marketing companies used to total around 160. However, the number was reduced to 48 by April 1996 as a result of government efforts to curb illegal practices, such as the sales of smuggled products or fake/inferior products, tax evasions, exaggeration of production function, etc, all of which have become problems of public attention. At the same time, a stringent approval process has been introduced to regulate direct marketing in China. In other words, special approval will have to be obtained from the industrial and commercial administration authorities. Multilayer direct marketing will undergo even more stringent approval procedures. Avon and Amway are the two leading direct market organisations active in China. While the infrastructure and the DM service sector are as yet rudimentary, the potential for growth is enormous. Consumers are fairly receptive to DM and are responsive to promotions. Free gift with purchase is popular.

611

To meet with success in any direct marketing venture in China, particular attention should be paid to:

- effective delivery of goods to consumers;
- remittances from customers within China (few have credit cards);
- conversion of payments into hard currency, preferably the US dollar;
- payment of customs duty and taxes for imported goods.

Suppliers and database availability

There are few DM suppliers available in China at present. Some data capture houses exist, but these tend to do a lot of work for Hong Kong based firms because of the cost savings. Agencies in China concentrate mainly on above-the-line advertising and an increasing number of promotional activities, with most DM activities at present being initiated by Hong Kong based agencies. Telemarketing is not available, and few consumers have fixed-line phones.

There are currently limited opportunities for list rental. Only directories are available, and 99 per cent of these represent compiled databases. The Post Office holds the addresses of most individuals and businesses in the country, and it is possible to mail to this list even though it does not carry individual names. Moves are under way to obtain details of magazine subscribers' listings as well as other national databases, with the agreement and endorsement of the relevant government departments.

LANGUAGE AND CULTURAL CONSIDERATIONS

China has only one form of written language in simplified mode, which differs from the script used in Taiwan and Hong Kong by having far fewer strokes. Mandarin is the only official spoken language, which, in theory at least, is accepted in all parts of China. More importantly, Mandarin is the language used for teaching in all educational institutions. Although people from different provinces might use a different dialect, most should understand Mandarin.

In all dealings with the Chinese people it is worth remembering a few cultural dos and don'ts, such as: do adopt a formal and respectful tone; don't hurry decision making; don't deliver late; avoid politics and pornography; and finally, never give clocks as gifts - they symbolize death.

LEGISLATION AND CONSUMER PROTECTION

There are no data protection or confidentiality laws in effect in China, but it is recommended that data users be careful when trading with data which might be construed as sensitive. Partnerships with district governmental bodies are advised, to avoid problems.

POSTAL SERVICES

The speed and efficiency of postal deliveries are variable according to location. For local mail, postal services can be described as satisfactory. Normal delivery takes two to five days within the same province and five to ten days to other provinces. The postage rate is probably the cheapest in the world in the context of territory covered.

Discounts are not offered for bulk inland mail and it is accepted only in some larger post offices. Payment of postage fee can be negotiated on monthly credit terms.

Postal requirements: the post code of the receiver must be provided at the top left-hand corner of every letter. Postal sorting machines are available in some larger provinces. Written postal regulations are not readily available.

Express mail service is recommended for documents as well as parcels of commercial value. It provides for pick-up and delivery to office addresses, and the service is represented in most major Chinese cities and networked with most international cities.

Services offered:

- Database services and direct marketing campaign analysis
- Printing and packaging
- Bulk, discounted rates for addressed/unaddressed mail
- Express mail service (EMS)
- Business reply services (BRS)
- International business reply services
- Free post
- PO Box addresses
- Courier services
- Registered post
- Postal insurance
- Addres updating service
- Email services

For further information contact:

China Post
8 Jia, Bei Li Shi Road
Xicheng District
100808 Beijing
China

Tel: +8610 6831 5484
Fax: +8610 6831 5560

HONG KONG

> *Population*: 6.6 million
> *Capital*: Victoria
> *Languages*: Cantonese and English
>
> *GDP*: $171 billion
> *GDP per capita*: $26,350
> *Inflation*: 5.7 per cent (1996)
>
> *Currency*: Hong Kong dollar (HK$) = 100 cents
> *Exchange rate*: HK$7.75 : $1
>
> *Time*: GMT +8 hours

OVERVIEW

Hong Kong's population of about 6.6 million is predominantly Chinese (97 per cent) with a small percentage of other groups, including an expatriate community of about 100,000. Uncertainty still lingers after the Chinese takeover in 1997, and the tendency has been to localize the market.

Hong Kong is one of the most economically developed as well as marketing-driven markets (outside Japan and Australasia). Even so, Hong Kong's direct marketing industry did not begin until about 10 years ago. Today there is a local Direct Marketing Association, and eight international direct marketing agencies have a presence there.

Hong Kong was widely held to be one of the most difficult DM markets in the world, since consumers are spoilt with duty-free goods and well-stocked department stores.

However, consumers are accustomed to receiving direct mail and actually receive quite a high proportion compared to the rest of Asia. Financial offers consistently perform quite well, and it is now only mail order direct marketing that proves to be a difficult market.

In recent years a number of mail order companies have successfully established operations with a view to using Hong Kong as a stepping stone into China. DRTV and infomercials were launched in 1993 and strong growth has been demonstrated in ad spend.

Direct marketing is still relatively tactical in use rather than strategic, and is driven predominantly by 'Western' multinational companies.

Suppliers

Hong Kong has various service organizations which offer support such as telemarketing, data capture, database management, fufilment (hand and machine based), fax on demand and interactive voice response. The sophistication and applications they use, however, are generally on a low level (estimated at five to ten years behind the US and UK). It may take three to five years to 'catch up', depending on various criteria such as market conditions, continued stability, growth levels, etc. English visualization is now common.

There are no postal or zip codes in Hong Kong, and no fixed address structure, which makes address management and deduplication difficult. No bureaux offer address enhancement and deduplication facilities as a computerized batch process, though it can be done manually in some bureaux. Data security in Hong Kong is not guaranteed, and suppliers must be investigated thoroughly. The use of seed names (preferably distributed throughout the database) is essential.

Personalization processes are possible, but face an immediate difficulty: a typical Chinese name can be written in about eight different ways. In addition, most Chinese use an English forename. Personalization is possible to achieve, however, if data are captured into separate title, forename and surname fields. It is also possible to laser print both sets of characters on the same page.

LANGUAGE AND CULTURAL CONSIDERATIONS

The language of 97 per cent of the population is Cantonese, with English as the second official language. Literacy is very high in Hong Kong. Mandarin (Putonghua) will become increasingly important now that Hong Kong is part of mainland China. It is usual to use both English and Chinese in printed material. Characters should be traditional.

Hong Kong has fewer cultural traps these days. Avoidance of certain shades of blue and the number four is recommended as they both signify death. The colour red is good, as is the number eight. Otherwise, exercise good taste.

LEGISLATION AND CONSUMER PROTECTION

The use of data for DM purposes now has to comply with the Hong Kong Privacy Ordnance. This means that when data are collected the subjects must be informed of whether the provision of that data is voluntary or obligatory, and the consequences of their failing to provide it. They must also be explicitly told for which purposes the data will be used, and to whom it may be transmitted. Once an individual has decided whether or not to provide the information, the decision may not be changed.

However, the Ordnance maintains that personal data should be accurate, kept up-to-date, and held no longer than necessary. Subjects have the right to confirm whether their personal data are held, and must be given the opportunity to correct any false information. Charges for correcting information may not be excessive. In order to update addresses, the Post Office change-of-address data should be used. Personal data should also be secure from unauthorized access.

THE DIRECT MARKETING ASSOCIATION

Name: Hong Kong Direct Mail and Marketing Association (HKDMA)
Address: C1 & C2, 13th Floor, United Centre, 95 Queensway, Hongkong
Tel: +852 2880 3690
Fax: +852 2880 3691
Year founded: 1980
President: Godfrey Rooke
Total staff: 2
Members: 90
Contact: Vikki Chow, Administrator

Direct mail agencies	14	Publishers	8
List brokers	4	Financial services	13
Mail order companies	5	Other	46

Facilities for overseas users of direct mail

Membership: overseas companies can join the HKDMA, and there are no minimum requirements for membership. Annual fees are HK$5000.

Newsletter: the HKDMA has a quarterly newsletter, and sends regular e-mails.

Library: the library offers a basic reference service.

On-line information service: there is no on-line information service but a website is under construction.

Legal advice: while the HKDMA does not offer legal or consulting services, the organization will respond promptly and efficiently to any enquiry on the market.

Business liaison service: the HKDMA will put members or non-members in touch with approved local suppliers.

Other facilities: the HKDMA provides a regular forum for meetings.

POSTAL SERVICES

The Hongkong Post is generally regarded as a very efficient and customer focused organization. It has developed many value added services to support the direct mail industry. These include Freepost Service, Business Reply Service, International Business Reply Service, Bulk Air Mail Service, Hong-kong Post Circular Service and Hongkong e-Post Service. Hongkong Post also offers discounts for bulk mailings and pre-sorted mail as an incentive for direct mail.

Freepost Service supports a wide range of media promotions including TV, radio, print and mail. It is designed for local mail items. With the Freepost Service, customers can respond to promotions by simply quoting the Freepost number on their replies without the need to pay for postage. No pre-printed reply envelope is required, which gives more flexibility and convenience. Even when a reply envelope is needed, there are no restrictions on the format and design. There is no minimum quantity set for Freepost items. Charges are only based on the number of replies received and can be settled on a monthly basis. There are two types of Freepost Service, the 'Standard Freepost' and the 'Freepost Name'. Charges per Freepost item are HK$0.60 in addition to the normal postage.

The **Business Reply Service** and the **International Business Reply Service** are response gathering mechanisms allowing both local and over-seas customers to respond to promotions by returning the reply item without having to pay for postages. Charges for every Business Reply item are HK$0.50 in addition to the normal postage; whereas an International Business Reply item are HK$6.00, inclusive of postage and handling fee.

The **Bulk Air Mail Service** has all along been a service enjoyed by thousands of Hong Kong companies who appreciate the benefits of low-cost and reliable service for all their overseas mail. The main features of the service are:

- Economical, with significant reduction in postage
- Convenient, with single rate for both printed papers and letters
- Flexible, as the minimum posting requirement is 20kg
- Simple payment method of either Postage Prepaid or Permit Mail
- Extensive posting network with 16 offices and extended operating hours.

Hongkong Post also offers the **Hongkong Post Circular Service** for delivery of unaddressed mail to every letterbox in Hong Kong. This service takes full advantage of Hongkong Post's network and facilities to get promotional messages across at very competitive rates. Eliminating the need to separately address the circulars will save time and money to prepare the lists and address labels. Premiums and samples can be included in the circulars, which makes the service a more effective promotional means. Special volume discount is also given to one-time posting for quantities of, or above, 200,000 items.

Hongkong e-Post is an advanced postal solution which handles the entire process of printing, enveloping, posting and distributing mail. This service is suitable for small to medium-sized businesses wanting to print and send personalized direct mail as well as statements and invoices on a regular basis. The Hongkong e-Post centres are secured by an access control system to ensure confidential business and personal information are highly protected. Savings can be achieved by economizing on bulk operations so that customers do not need to invest in extra capital equipment and manpower to do the job themselves.

Hongkong Post offers discounts to bulk mailings of more than 3,000 items per lodgement. Items in each lodgement of bulk mail need to be identical in size, shape and weight. Items in each bulk mail lodgement can be paid by various methods including franking machines, postage prepaid and permit mail. Items of different categories have to be clearly segregated at the time of posting. Apart from bulk mailings, Hongkong Post also offers discounts to pre-sorted mail. The amount of discount depends on the level of pre-sorting.

For more information on postal services offered by Hongkong Post, please contact the following:

Hong Kong Post
Hong Kong Post Headquarters
2 Connaught Place
Central
Hong Kong

Telephone Enquiry Hotline : +852 2921 2222
Fax: +852 2868 0094
Email: hkpo@hkpo.gcn.gov.hk
Web: www.hongkongpost.com

PROVIDERS OF DM AND E-M SERVICES

FOOTPRINTS DIRECT MARKETING (HK) LTD
5/F Flat G
Hop Hing Industrial Road
704 Castle Peak Road
Kowloon
Hong Kong
Tel: +852 2785 2528
Fax: +852 2785 2258
Email: michelle@footprints.com.hk
Amanda Chan/Michelle Chan, Client
  Service Manager

Services/Products:
Database services; Mailing/Faxing
services; Personalisation; Print services;
Labelling/envelope services; Lettershop

E-Services:
Website design

Member of:
HKDMA

GODFREY ROOKE & ASSOCIATES
6/F Shun Ho Tower
24–34 Ice House St.
Central
Hong Kong
Tel: +852 2850 5829
Fax: +852 2581 0227
Email: rookecon@netvigator.com

Services/Products:
Consultancy services

Member of:
National DMA

ICLP
Suite 1211–1214
12/F Cityplaza One
1111 Kings Road
Tai Koo Shing
Hong Kong
Tel: +852 2803 8100
Fax: +852 2803 8101
Email: loyalty@iclp.com.hk
Web: www.iclployalty.com
Kevin Boland

Services/Products:
Call centre services/systems;
Consultancy services; Database
services; Direct marketing agency;
Interactive media; Telemarketing
agency

E-Services:
E-Marketing consultant; Website
design; Email software; Online/e-
marketing agency

Member of:
DMA (US); National DMA

LEO BURNETT LTD
6/Floor Citiplaza 3
14 Taikoo Wan Road
Hong Kong
Tel: +852 2884 6401
Fax: +852 2539 0716
Email: Mark-
  Blears@hk.leoburnett.com
Web: www.leoburnett.com
Mark Blears, General Manager

Services/Products:
Advertising Agency; Copy adaptation;
Direct marketing agency; Media
buying agency

E-Services:
E-Marketing consultant; Website
design; Online/e-marketing agency

Member of:
National DMA; HKDMA

LS DIRECT FAR EAST LTD
Unit 6–6, 3th Floor, Fanling Industrial
Centre
21 On Kui Street
On Lok Tsuen
Fanling NT
Hong Kong
Tel: +852 2669 6911
Fax: +852 2677 5620
Email:
  customerservice@lsdirect.com.hk
Web: www.lsdirect.com.hk
Thomas Friedsan, Managing Director

Services/Products:
Mailing/Faxing services;
Personalisation; Direct marketing
agency; Labelling/envelope services;
Lettershop; List services

E-Services:
Email list provider; Email software;
Online/e-marketing agency

Member of:
National DMA

MAILING LISTS (ASIA) LTD
6/F, Sea Bird House
22–28 Wyndham Street
Central
Hong Kong
Tel: +852 2526 1208
Fax: +852 2524 9177
Email: mla@mlaltd.com
Luhdee Garcia

Services/Products:
List services; List brokerage/
management

E-Services:
Email list provider

Member of:
FEDMA; DMA (US); HKDMA

RAPP COLLINS WORLDWIDE
18/F Centre Point
181 Gloucester Road
Wan Chai
Hong Kong
Tel: +852 2838 6322
Fax: +852 2519 8803
Email: sean.cooper@rcw.com.hk
Web: www.rappcollins.com
Sean Cooper, Managing Director

Services/Products:
Advertising Agency; Consultancy
services; Database services; Direct
marketing agency

E-Services:
E-Marketing consultant; Website
design; Online/e-marketing agency

Member of:
HKDMA; IAA

800 TELESERVICES
Rm 2106–2108 Park-In Commercial
Centre
56 Dundas Street
Mong Kok
Kowloon
Hong Kong
Tel: +852 2111 8363
Fax: +852 2111 8383
Alex Wong

Services/Products:
Telemarketing agency

Member of:
HKDMA

ADCOM BBDO DIRECT
35/F Dorset House
Taikoo Place
979 King's Road
Quarry Bay
Hong Kong
Tel: +852 2820 1874
Fax: +852 2877 2167
Debbie Pong

Services/Products:
Direct marketing agency

Member of:
HKDMA

ADPOST HONG KONG LTD
Rm 1703 Stanhope House
738 Kings Road
North Point
Hong Kong
Tel: +852 2590 9688
Fax: +852 2597 5160
Thomson Lee

Services/Products:
Lettershop; Fulfilment and sampling
house

Member of:
HKDMA

**AMERICAN EXPRESS
    INTERNATIONAL INC**
21/F Somerset House
Taikoo Place
979 King's Road
Hong Kong
Christine Hai

Services/Products:
Card pack manufacturer; Card pack
manufacturer

Member of:
HKDMA

ASIA RESPONSE
6F, Sea Bird House
28 Wyndham Street
HK-Central
Hong Kong
Tel: +852 2526 1208
Fax: +852 2524 9177
Soli Gae, Media Director

Services/Products:
Direct marketing agency; Media
buying agency

Member of:
HKDMA

DATATRADE LTD
5/F Hollywood Centre
233 Hollywood Road
Central
Hong Kong
Tel: +852 2544 1377
Fax: +852 2546 8056
Monica Chan

Services/Products:
List services; Lettershop; Fulfilment
and sampling house; Direct marketing
agency

Member of:
DMA (US); HKDMA

**DIRECT MARKETING OF ASIA
    ADVERTISING SERVICE CO**
1811 Eastern Harbour Centre
28 Hoi Chak St
Quarry Bay
Hong Kong
Tel: +852 2880 5918
Fax: +852 2597 4325
Kathleen Tong, Mailing List Rentals

Services/Products:
Telemarketing agency; Direct
marketing agency

Member of:
HKDMA

DRAFTDIRECT WORLDWIDE
703–5 Siu On Centre
188 Lockhart Road
Wanchai
Hong Kong
Tel: +852 2531 8828
Fax: +852 2824 4386
Ana Lee

Services/Products:
List services; Direct marketing agency

Member of:
HKDMA

DUN & BRADSTREET
17/F Warwick House West
Tai Koo Place
979 Kings Road
Quarry Bay
Hong Kong
Tel: +852 2516 1222
Fax: +852 2562 6053
Joanna Wong

Services/Products:
List services

Member of:
HKDMA

**EURO RSCG BALL
    PARTNERSHIP**
21st Floor Devon House
Quarry Bay
Hong Kong
Tel: +852 2590 1892
Fax: +852 2516 5411
Michelle Vertop

Services/Products:
Advertising Agency

Member of:
HKDMA

FCB DIRECT ASIA-PACIFIC
2/F Harbour Centre
25 Harbour Road
Wanchai
Hong Kong

Tel: +852 2884 7608
Fax: +852 2824 2986
Richard McCandless

Services/Products:
Advertising Agency; Direct marketing
agency

Member of:
HKDMA

GREY DIRECT
19/F Devon House
Taikoo Place
919 Kings Road
Hong Kong
Tel: +852 2510 6614
Fax: +852 2510 8517
Candy Wan

Services/Products:
Direct marketing agency

Member of:
HKDMA

**INTERNATIONAL
    COLLECTIONS LTD**
26/Floor Wing On House
71 Des Voeux Road Central
Hong Kong
Tel: +852 2845 8330
Fax: +852 2845 9110
Josephine Cheung

Services/Products:
Direct marketing agency

Member of:
HKDMA

**J WALTER THOMPSON DIRECT
    HONG KONG**
5/F, Shui on Centre
6–8 Harbour Road
Wanchai
Hong Kong
Tel: +852 2584 4794
Fax: +852 2824 1807
Iren Cheh, General Manager

Services/Products:
Advertising Agency

Member of:
HKDMA

**LAWSONS MARKETING
    SERVICES**
Suite 1604 Eastern Harbour Centre
28 Hoi Chak Street
Quarry Bay
Hong Kong
Tel: +852 2880 5366
Fax: +852 2565 0080
Barry Chan

Services/Products:
Lettershop; Fulfilment and sampling house

Member of:
HKDMA

MCCANN-ERICKSON (HK) LTD
1/F Sunning Plaza
10 Hysan Avenue
Causeway Bay
Hong Kong
Tel: +852 2808 7727
Fax: +852 2881 6215
Henrik Monefeldt

Services/Products:
Advertising Agency

Member of:
HKDMA

MOTIV8
30 Harbour Road
Wanchai
Hong Kong
Chris Fjelddahl

Services/Products:
Sales promotion agency

Member of:
HKDMA

OGILVYONE WORLDWIDE
7/Floor Mount Parker House
Taikoo Shing
Hong Kong
Tel: +852 2884 8196
Fax: +852 2535 9472
Tal Adams

Services/Products:
Advertising Agency

Member of:
HKDMA

PACIFIC SOFTWARE RESOURCES LTD
11/F Well On Commercial Building
20 Wellington Street
Central
Hong Kong
Tel: +852 2869 9357
Fax: +852 2869 9347
Ian Wallace

Services/Products:
Database services

Member of:
HKDMA

PJ ASSOCIATES
10/F China United Plaza
1008 Tai Nan West Street
Cheung Sha Wan
Kowloon

Hong Kong
Tel: +852 2312 1065
Fax: +852 2369 2087
Judy Wong

Services/Products:
List services; Direct marketing agency

Member of:
HKDMA

SA DIRECT LTD
Rm 306 Westlands Centre
20 Westlands Rd
Quarry Bay
Hong Kong
Tel: +852 2411 4621
Fax: +852 2414 3032
Email: dlynn@saphk.com
Web: www.sadirect.com.hk
Daniel Lynn, Director

Services/Products:
Call centre services/systems; Catalogue producer; Consultancy services; Copy adaptation; Database services; Mailing/Faxing services

E-Services:
Website design

Member of:
HKDMA

STRATEGIC SOLUTIONS
1203–1204 Lyndhurst Tower
1 Lyndhurst terrace
Central
Hong Kong
Tel: +852 2521 6424
Fax: +852 2524 5040
Ian Brown

Services/Products:
Advertising Agency; Direct marketing agency

Member of:
HKDMA

TELEDIRECT (OGILVYONE)
15/F Eastern Commercial Centre
83 Nam On Street
Shau Kei Wan
Hong Kong
Tel: +852 2884 8250
Fax: +852 2884 1381
David Cowell

Services/Products:
Telemarketing agency

Member of:
HKDMA

TIMES ONLINE ASIA LTD
13/F United Centre
95 Queensway
Hong Kong
Tel: +852 2811 9111
Fax: +852 2811 9121
Email: info@tolasia.com
Web: www.tolasia.com
Kerry Powell

Services/Products:
Consultancy services; Database services; Direct marketing agency; Fulfilment and sampling house; List services; Telemarketing agency

E-Services:
Email list provider; E-Marketing consultant; Online/e-marketing agency

Member of:
DMA (US); National DMA; HKDMA

TIMES-TELEPERFORMANCE
2/F Zorastrian Building
101 Leighton Road
Causeway Bay
Hong Kong
Winnie Li

Services/Products:
Telemarketing agency

Member of:
HKDMA

WUNDERMAN CATA JOHNSON
33/F AIA Tower
183 Electric Road
North Point
Hong Kong
Tel: +852 2884 6660
Fax: +852 2567 5701
Chris Marsh

Services/Products:
Direct marketing agency

Member of:
DMA (US); HKDMA

SERVICES/PRODUCT LISTING

Advertising Agency
Leo Burnett Ltd
Rapp Collins Worldwide
Euro RSCG Ball Partnership
FCB Direct Asia-Pacific
J Walter Thompson Direct Hong Kong
McCann-Erickson (HK) Ltd
OgilvyOne Worldwide
Strategic Solutions

Call centre services/systems
ICLP
SA Direct Ltd

Card pack manufacturer
American Express International Inc

Catalogue producer
SA Direct Ltd

Consultancy services
Godfrey Rooke & Associates
ICLP
Rapp Collins Worldwide
SA Direct Ltd
Times Online Asia Ltd

Copy adaptation
Leo Burnett Ltd
SA Direct Ltd

Database services
Footprints Direct Marketing (HK) Ltd
ICLP
Rapp Collins Worldwide
Pacific Software Resources Ltd
SA Direct Ltd
Times Online Asia Ltd

Direct marketing agency
ICLP
Leo Burnett Ltd
LS Direct Far East Ltd
Rapp Collins Worldwide
Adcom BBDO Direct
Asia Response
Datatrade Ltd
Direct Marketing of Asia Advertising
    Service Co
Draftdirect Worldwide
FCB Direct Asia-Pacific
Grey Direct
International Collections Ltd
PJ Associates
Strategic Solutions
Times Online Asia Ltd
Wunderman Cata Johnson

Fulfilment and sampling house
Adpost Hong Kong Ltd
Datatrade Ltd
Lawsons Marketing Services
Times Online Asia Ltd

Interactive media
ICLP

Labelling/envelope services
Footprints Direct Marketing (HK) Ltd
LS Direct Far East Ltd

Lettershop
Footprints Direct Marketing (HK) Ltd
LS Direct Far East Ltd
Adpost Hong Kong Ltd
Datatrade Ltd
Lawsons Marketing Services

List brokerage/management
Mailing Lists (Asia) Ltd

List services
LS Direct Far East Ltd
Mailing Lists (Asia) Ltd
Datatrade Ltd
Draftdirect Worldwide
Dun & Bradstreet
PJ Associates
Times Online Asia Ltd

Mailing/Faxing services
Footprints Direct Marketing (HK) Ltd
LS Direct Far East Ltd
SA Direct Ltd

Media buying agency
Leo Burnett Ltd
Asia Response

Personalisation
Footprints Direct Marketing (HK) Ltd
LS Direct Far East Ltd

Print services
Footprints Direct Marketing (HK) Ltd

Sales promotion agency
Motiv8

Telemarketing agency
ICLP
800 Teleservices
Direct Marketing of Asia Advertising
    Service Co
Teledirect (OgilvyOne)
Times Online Asia Ltd
Times-Teleperformance

E-SERVICES

E-Marketing consultant
ICLP
Leo Burnett Ltd
Rapp Collins Worldwide
Times Online Asia Ltd

Email list provider
LS Direct Far East Ltd
Mailing Lists (Asia) Ltd
Times Online Asia Ltd

Email software
ICLP
LS Direct Far East Ltd

Online/e-marketing agency
ICLP
Leo Burnett Ltd
LS Direct Far East Ltd
Rapp Collins Worldwide
Times Online Asia Ltd

Website design
Footprints Direct Marketing (HK) Ltd
ICLP
Leo Burnett Ltd
Rapp Collins Worldwide
SA Direct Ltd

INDIA

Population: I billion
Capital: New Delhi
Languages: Hindi, English, as well as 13 dialects

GDP: $ 300 billion
GDP per capita: $ 400
Inflation: 8 per cent

Currency: Indian Rupee (Rs.)
Exchange rate: Rs. 42.72 : US $ I

Time: GMT +5.30 hours

OVERVIEW

India has the world's second largest population of approximately 1 billion. This huge market attracts the world's top companies to establish offices there. New Delhi is the commercial hub of northern India and the financial centre is in Mumbai on the West coast. Industries are geographically well-distributed.

Databases

List owners are increasingly willing to research customized lists from their existing databases. Tailormade research is also available and per inquiry deals can also be negotiated. Census/voter records are allowed to be used, as are telephone directories and Auto club lists.

Some Responsive Lists	Size	Cost in $ / K
Top executives of the largest companies (sales over US$25 million)	750	300
Board level executives (sales over US$10 million)	30,000	200
Professionals (lawyers, doctors, accountants, etc)	200,000	200
Wealthy Indians (at residential address)	50,000	200
Companies with sales of over US$1 million (industry-wide selection possible)	200,000	100

Telemarketing is available, but not popular because of poor telephone infrastructure. Firms like Video-on-Wheels are providing rural distribution for high priced consumables and for urban product distribution and fulfilment firms like First Flight Cargo are developing.

Direct Response TV is growing, and will continue to grow in 1999. Asian Sky Shop is using infomercials to target sales of $8 million. HOME TV, SONY TV and YES TV are expected to start carrying DR-TV spots.

Import regulations

The importation of many consumer goods is restricted. The average customs duty has been reduced to 42 per cent. Specific import duties can be provided on request.

LANGUAGE AND CULTURAL CONSIDERATIONS

Indian culture is diverse, with 12 major languages, 12 separate castes and 6 major religions.

Although many languages are spoken, the common language is English. While not being able to speak it fluently, most literate Indians can comprehend written English. Bilingual mail shots are therefore not necessary.

The market is fragmented. Consumers can be segmented on the basis of language, state, caste, religion or geography. Each criterion would merit a different strategy to maximize impact. However, for the first-time marketer, the income yardstick is a fairly safe bet:

- Wealthy Indian families have an income of over $40,000 per annum. They number 10 million people and are very conducive to international offers.

- The upper middle-class Indian family earns between $8,000 and $40,000. This 100 million-strong category can afford the latest gadgetry, but in contrast to the above category, are comfortable purchasing premium Indian brands.
- Lower middle-class Indians (with income between US$3,500 and US$8000) have strong aspirations. They invest in education, and setting up small businesses for their children. Numbering 500 million, they prefer products at an affordable price.

LEGISLATION AND CONSUMER PROTECTION

Direct marketing specific laws are non-existent on the statute book. This is no surprise given the relative infancy of the industry. However, the mail piece should conform to the regulations related to the service it is offering (for instance, certain professions are not allowed to advertise their services so would not be permitted). Self-regulation by the DMA India is of a guidance nature only. The concepts of privacy have not been tested in law courts and there are no restrictions on the use or transfer of data. Many catalogue companies voluntarily offer a money-back guarantee. A Mailing Preference Service is unlikely to be introduced in the foreseeable future, although an opt-in list would probably be a great success as it is considered a status symbol to be inundated with direct marketing offers.

DIRECT MARKETING ASSOCIATION

Name: Direct Marketing Association India (DMAI)
Address: Bedeshwar, Gujarat, 361002 India
Tel: +91 288 559135
Fax: +91 288 555311
E-mail: dmai@bigfoot.com
Contact: Mr G Nagalingappa, Secretary
Members: There are about 300 active members. There are two categories of membership, national and international.

POSTAL SERVICES

The State-run monopoly service has the advantage of low prices, but the problem lies in the reliability of delivery. Normal transit time is four to five days. The standard rate is 2 rupees per 20 grams.
Other mailing options available are:

- for an extra charge of 20 rupees, mailpieces are 'speed delivered'. There is a 'second class' mailing option for printed mail pieces. Periodicals can use a special low rate by registering themselves as a

625

newspaper. A business reply envelope licence can be obtained (costing 2 rupees per response plus postage);

- registered mail pieces take a couple of days longer to be delivered but are 100 per cent reliable. Extra charges are 12 rupees per piece;
- discounts of up to 5 per cent are available for bulk mailing (over 10,000 pieces);
- the Indian associates of the international courier companies (eg DHL Federal Express, UPS) provide reliable third-day delivery. A handful of quality local Indian firms provide cost-efficient service. A typical 200 gram package would cost about Rs.75 to deliver.

For further information contact:

Department of Posts

General Manager, Business Development Directorate
Dak Bhavan
Parliament Street
New Delhi 110001
India

Tel: +91 11 371 7695
Fax: +91 11 371 7695
Website: www.indiapost.org

PROVIDERS OF DM AND E-M SERVICES

BUSINESS LISTS
Digvijay Plot, P.B.No. 5026
Saurashtra
361 005
India
Tel: +91 288 559118
Fax: +91 288 551920
Email: businesslists@usa.net
Mr. R Debta

Services/Products:
List services

Member of:
DMAI

DATAMATION CONSULTANTS PVT. LTD.
361 Patparganj Industrial Area
New Delhi
110 092
India
Tel: +91 11 2167 230
Fax: +91 11 224 3087
Email: csharma@giasdlo1.vsnl.net.in
Web: www.datamationindia.com
Chetan Sharma, Executive Director

Services/Products:
Consultancy services; Database services; Mail order company; Market research agency; Personalisation; Print services

E-Services:
Email list provider; E-Marketing consultant; Website design; Email software; Online/e-marketing agency

Member of:
DMA (US)

GO DIRECT MAILING & MARKETING PVT. LTD
109, Udyog Mandir No.1
Bhagoji Kheer Marg
Mahim
Mumbai
400 016
India
Tel: +91 22 444 8566
Fax: +91 22 636 1221
Email: godir@vsnl.com
Mr Firoz F Havewala, Director

Services/Products:
Database services; Direct marketing agency; Fulfilment and sampling house; Labelling/envelope services; Lettershop; List services

E-Services:
Email list provider

Member of:
National DMA

INFO MARKETER INT'L
Krishn Kunj
Jamnagar
361 002
India
Tel: +91 288 554231
Fax: +91288 552637
Email: info.marketer@usa.net
N Singh, Manager

Services/Products:
Consultancy services; Media buying agency; Market research agency

Member of:
DMAI

IRIS SOFTWARE PVT LTD
B-1/43 Havz Khas
New Delhi
110016
India
Tel: +91 11 685 5441
Fax: +91 11 685 4525
Anil Apte

Services/Products:
Service bureau

Member of:
DMA (US)

M/S OTTO BURLINGTON'S MAIL ORDER PVT. LTD
A-90-Sector-2
Noida
UP 201 301
India
Tel: +91 118 4545506
Fax: +91 118 4546381
Email: ottoburl@delz.vsnl.net.in
Web: www.ottoburlington.com
MrNakul Kapur, Managing Director

Services/Products:
Mail order company

Member of:
DMAI

MAIL MARKETING
+91288 550943
India
Tel: +91 288 550943
Fax: +91 288 554072
Email: mailmarketing@usa.net
Mr S Hegde

Services/Products:
Lettershop; Print services

Member of:
DMAI

MARKETLINKS DIRECT
Express Towers
13th Fl
Nariman Point
Bombay
400 021
India
Tel: +91 22 2021577
Fax: +91 22 2043135
Rata Jalan

Services/Products:
Advertising Agency; Direct marketing agency

Member of:
DMA (US)

OGILVYONE WORLDWIDE
Rathname's Complex, 14th Fl
No1 Kasturba Road
Bangalore
560001
India
Tel: +91 812 221 5800
Fax: +91 812 221 9268
R Balachandran, Chairman

Services/Products:
Advertising Agency; Consultancy services; Direct marketing agency; List services; Telemarketing agency; Direct response TV services

E-Services:
Website design

Member of:
DMA (US)

RESULT MCCANN
B-149, Greater Kailash -1
New Delhi
110 048
India
Fax: +91 11628 1034
Mr Rajat Sethi, Senior Vice-President & General Manager

Services/Products:
Direct marketing agency

Member of:
DMAI

S M KUMAR & CO
PO Box 3004, Patel Colony P.O.
Saurashtra
361008
India
Tel: +91 288 550943
Fax: +91 288 554072
Email: smkumar@bigfoot.com
S Mala, Chief Executive

Services/Products:
Mailing/Faxing services; Labelling/
envelope services; Telemarketing
agency; Direct marketing agency;
Market research agency

Member of:
DMAI

SELECT DIRECT MARKETING COMMUNICATION P.LTD
Lalit Kunj Annexe
28 Dadabhai Road
Vile Parle (W)
Mumbai
400 056
India
Tel: +91 22 671 1599/0995
Fax: +91 22 671 8991
Email: sdirect@bom3.vsnl.net.in
Mr Ramesh Iyengar, Managing
    Director

Services/Products:
Direct marketing agency

Member of:
DMAI

SHANTI
95a, Mittal Tower
Nariman Point
Bombay
400021
India
Tel: +91 22 202 1767/79
Fax: +91 202 6397
GM Kinger, President

Services/Products:
Catalogue producer; Mail order
company; Sales promotion agency

SISTA SAATCHI & SAATCHI DIRECT
Asha Building
31 Church Street
Bangalore
5600001
India
Fax: +91 805591833
Email: malavika@blr.vsnl.net.in
Ms Malavika R Harita, General
    Manager

Services/Products:
Direct marketing agency

Member of:
DMAI

VIDEO ON WHEELS
Scindia Villa, Ring Road
Sarojini Nagar
New Delhi
110 023
India

Fax: +91 11 611 0014
Ms Sadhana Bharadwaj, Director

Services/Products:
Direct marketing agency

Member of:
DMAI

VISIONARY MARKETING
95/1 Ballygunj Place
Calcutta
India
Tel: +91 33 476 3978
Email: visionary.ask@gncal.globalnet.
    ems.vsnl.net.in
Mr L Sridhar, CEO

Services/Products:
Direct marketing agency

Member of:
DMAI

SERVICES/PRODUCT LISTING

Advertising Agency
Marketlinks Direct
OgilvyOne Worldwide

Catalogue producer
Shanti

Consultancy services
Datamation Consultants Pvt. Ltd.
Info Marketer Int'l
OgilvyOne Worldwide

Database services
Datamation Consultants Pvt. Ltd.
Go Direct Mailing & Marketing Pvt.
    Ltd

Direct marketing agency
Go Direct Mailing & Marketing Pvt.
    Ltd
Marketlinks Direct
OgilvyOne Worldwide
Result Mccann
S M Kumar & Co
Select Direct Marketing
    Communication P.Ltd
Sista Saatchi & Saatchi Direct
Video On Wheels
Visionary Marketing

Direct response TV services
OgilvyOne Worldwide

Fulfilment and sampling house
Go Direct Mailing & Marketing Pvt.
    Ltd

Labelling/envelope services
Go Direct Mailing & Marketing Pvt.
    Ltd
S M Kumar & Co

Lettershop
Go Direct Mailing & Marketing Pvt.
    Ltd
Mail Marketing

List services
Business Lists
Go Direct Mailing & Marketing Pvt.
    Ltd
OgilvyOne Worldwide

Mail order company
Datamation Consultants Pvt. Ltd.
M/S Otto Burlington's Mail Order Pv
    Ltd
Shanti

Mailing/Faxing services
S M Kumar & Co

Market research agency
Datamation Consultants Pvt. Ltd.
Info Marketer Int'l
S M Kumar & Co

Media buying agency
Info Marketer Int'l

Personalisation
Datamation Consultants Pvt. Ltd.

Print services
Datamation Consultants Pvt. Ltd.
Mail Marketing

Sales promotion agency
Shanti

Service bureau
Iris Software Pvt Ltd

Telemarketing agency
OgilvyOne Worldwide
S M Kumar & Co

E-SERVICES

E-Marketing consultant
Datamation Consultants Pvt. Ltd.

Email list provider
Datamation Consultants Pvt. Ltd.
Go Direct Mailing & Marketing Pvt
    Ltd

Email software

Datamation Consultants Pvt. Ltd.

Online/e-marketing agency

Datamation Consultants Pvt. Ltd.

Website design

Datamation Consultants Pvt. Ltd.
OgilvyOne Worldwide

INDONESIA

Population: 200.5 million
Capital: Jakarta
Languages: Bahasa Indonesian and English

GDP: $213 billion
GDP per capita: $1,080
Inflation: 6.6 per cent

Currency: Rupiah (Rp) = 100 sen
Exchange rate: Rp7,650 : $1

Time: GMT +7 to +8 hours

OVERVIEW

Indonesia has the fourth largest population in the world, and there is growing affluence especially at the upper socioeconomic levels.

Direct marketing in Indonesia is very new. Consumers welcome mailings, particularly when communications are personalized, as the novelty value is still high. However, the industry is very immature, with most companies preferring to spend on advertising. DM is tactical, with one-off mailings common, though DM has proven successful in the FMCG field and for sampling and research purposes.

Suppliers

There are as yet very few suppliers available and most functions are performed in house. Outside fulfilment is available and done by hand, but data security is a problem. List security is not guaranteed, and suppliers must be investigated thoroughly. The use of seed names (preferably distributed throughout the database) is essential.

Personalization is available through a few list brokers, but is uncommon, There are no suppliers that offer address enhancement and deduplication facilities.

LANGUAGE AND CULTURAL CONSIDERATIONS

The spoken language is mainly Bahasa Indonesian (roman-based character set), but English is used in business as well. Mailings will sometimes be bilingual in Bahasa and English, but databases typically hold name and address information in Bahasa only.

LEGISLATION AND CONSUMER PROTECTION

Since DM is relatively new, the government has not paid much attention to the discipline. Instead advertising regulations are followed. None of the regulations addresses privacy issues.

POSTAL SERVICES

The post office has made considerable strides in efficiency and reliability in recent years. Private courier companies are also an option, and are cheaper than the post for large items. There is a postal code but no fixed address structure, which will therefore make address management and deduplication difficult.

For further information contact:

PT Pos Indonesia

International Relations Department
Jl. Cilaki no. 73
Bandung 40115
Indonesia
Tel: +62 22 439 685/432 702   Fax: +62 22 420 7900

PROVIDERS OF DM AND E-M SERVICES

NEXUS PLUS
c/o Survey Research Indonesia
Wisma Bank Dharmala, 14f
Jln. Jen Surdinam kav 28
Jakarta
12190
Indonesia
Tel: +62 21 724 6141
Fax: +62 21 724 6141
David Sparkes

Services/Products:
Advertising Agency; Direct marketing
agency

Member of:
DMA (US)

SERVICES/PRODUCT LISTING

Advertising Agency
Nexus Plus

Direct marketing agency
Nexus Plus

JAPAN

Population: 124.9 million
Capital: Tokyo
Language: Japanese

GDP: $3927 billion
GDP per capita: $31,451
Inflation: 0.7 per cent

Currency: Yen (Y)
Exchange rate: Y120.98 : $1

Time: GMT +9 hours

OVERVIEW

Direct marketing in Japan has established a firm footing within the overall distribution industry through years of stable sales growth within an economy that has seen conspicuous changes in consumer shopping behaviour and rapid advances and diversification in information media. The industry has firm foundations, with the first direct marketing catalogue being produced in Japan over 90 years ago for a department store. Japanese consumers are now more open to mail order buying than ever before, with a number of foreign catalogues present in the market.

Recent economic problems in Japan have seen the first annual decrease in DM sales since records began, with 1997 sales down from 2.3 trillion yen in 1996 to 2.2 trillion yen. Nevertheless, Japan remains the Asian leader and the direct marketing business has become an indispensable feature of Japanese life.

A survey by the Japan Direct Mail Association showed that 62 per cent of respondents read most or all of the DM they received, and an additional 35 per cent read pieces if they looked interesting. Close to 43 per cent felt DM was useful to them and 37 per cent were happy to receive it. Free gift with purchase and discounts/price-offs are favoured.

Broadcast facsimile marketing is now taking shape, and it is found to be effective especially in business-to-business marketing. In addition, 30 per cent of catalogue orders are placed via fax, therefore databases of consumers with fax numbers are being developed. Fax on demand is also becoming popular and should be taken into consideration.

The infrastructure needed to support high-level direct marketing operations has improved dramatically in recent years. Japan has a good base of various service organizations which offer support such as telemarketing, data capture, database management, fulfilment (hand and machine based) and fax on demand.

There are four international direct marketing agencies represented in Japan and four major industry organizations, including Japan Direct Marketing Association, Japan Direct Mail Association, Japan Telemarketing Association, and the American Chamber of Commerce in Japan (DM committee).

Lists and databases

Only 50 per cent of the country's 2000 lists have been computerized, and standard formats have not been established. Over 80 per cent of lists on the open market are compiled, rather than response lists. Prices, however, are high, averaging US$200–300 per thousand. Price does not always guarantee quality: since lists are cleaned only once a year, 3 per cent undeliverability is common. Census overlays and value-added demographics are not available. Swaps are possible, but still rather uncommon.

Among mailing lists that are available for direct rental, the following are most often used:

Fuji DM Fan	Females	4,000,000+
Teikoku Databank	Company heads	900,000+
	High taxpayers	170,000+
Nikkei Business Publications	Subscribers	500,000+
Diamond-sha	Corporate managers	240,000+
Japan Directory	Internationalists	20,000+
Kennedy International	Expatriates	12,000+

Specialized lists of doctors, dentists, female professionals, university professors, trade show attenders and many other categories are also available, and local brokers can sometimes come up with exotic segmentations such as vegetarians, owners of pinball parlours, etc. On the other hand, lists of credit card holders, department store shoppers and mail order buyers exist in abundance, but they are not openly rented and can be accessed only through negotiation with the list owners.

Telemarketing

Telemarketing in Japan has been rapidly gaining in popularity. The Japan Telemarketing Association counts more than 200 members presently, and facilities for both inbound and outbound calling have become quite sophisticated, led by Bell System 24, NTT Telemarketing, Telemarketing Japan, Dai-ichi Ad Systems, and a number of other major service bureaux. Japan's version of toll-free dialling (the 0121 prefix) is now better known and accepted by Japanese consumers, and fax on demand, pay for call and voice response technologies are being utilized with some success.

However, outbound programmes aimed at consumers are still not widely practised and, given their low acceptance level, are probably best avoided.

Direct response TV sales are also increasing in popularity and currently account for nearly 8 per cent of the DM market.

LANGUAGE AND CULTURAL CONSIDERATIONS

In this booming DM market, however, there are a number of special factors which differentiate it from the norm, and which might prove an unsurmountable barrier to an exporter without guidance from local sources. The first of these is the language barrier. Japanese names are written in *kanji* (Chinese characters; an educated person should know 3,000 characters). Until the 1980s, computers could only handle *kana* (a total of 100 phonetic characters used for Japanese and foreign words). Relatively few lists were computerized, and even when they were, duplication of *Kanji/kana* lists remained almost impossible. This, plus the non-standardized addressing system, has slowed the DM industry down.

Until only a few years ago, it would have been unthinkable to mail English-language sales materials to this Japanese-speaking market, but recently a number of international cataloguers have been meeting with success in sending their unedited domestic editions to Japan, with only order forms and instructions translated into Japanese. Among these are LL Bean and Hanna Anderson from the USA and Freeman's from the UK. This trend seems to reflect not only a growing confidence in English language ability among Japanese consumers, but also a willingness to spend time with catalogues that offer true value.

Creative work in this market can seem baffling to an eye trained to judge Western media. Print ads appear to be either obscurely empty, or cluttered beyond comprehension. The very mention of competitors, superlatives or prices is considered taboo. Creative work, therefore, is best prepared locally. Regarding copy, straight translations from original English to Japanese can work, but original Japanese usually works better. Above all, it's important not to judge Japanese copy by its English translation: wordiness, inverted logic and an absence of any personalization are all common in everyday Japanese.

LEGISLATION AND CONSUMER PROTECTION

Although there are few national laws, JADMA has set up a Mail Preference Service System for consumers who do not wish to receive direct mail from member companies. Mailing information on such consumers is therefore deleted from member companies' lists. It also sets guidelines for personal data protection

JADMA established a Code of Ethics in February, 1984. Companies must meet stringent membership standards to be JADMA members, observe the Code of Ethics as set out in the Door-to-door Sales Law and by JADMA, and base their business firmly on a principle of trust.

THE DIRECT MARKETING ASSOCIATION

Name: Japan Direct Marketing Association (JADMA)
Address: 32, Mori Bldg, 3-4-30 Shibakoen, Minato-Ku,
                Tokyo 105-0011
Tel: +81 33 434 4700
Fax: +81 33 434 4518
E-mail: jadma@JADMA.org
Website: www.JADMA.org
Year founded: 1984
President: Hiroyasu Ishikawa
Total staff: 4
Members: 530 (288 full members)

Direct mail agencies	30	List brokers	11
Mailing houses	43	Printers	18
Telemarketing agencies	4	Publishing companies	19
Direct mail consultants	7	Handling houses	11
Mail order companies	27	Database agencies	5
Creative shops	16		

Contact: Yuichi Katsura, International Committee, Dentsu Wunderman Direct.

Facilities for overseas users of direct mail

Membership: overseas companies can join the JADMA. Minimum standards for membership are the same for Japanese and overseas companies, and both need the approval of the executive board to join. There are three categories of membership: Full, Associate and Supporting. Fees for full membership vary, depending on sales turnover, and there is an additional one-off joining fee for all categories.
Newsletter: JADMA publish a monthly newsletter, *JADMA News*, and other bulletins (Japanese language).
Library: there is currently no library.
On-line information service: JADMA now has a website at www.JADMA.org
Legal advice: JADMA offers help with the first steps in understanding local direct marketing legislation. This service is open to non-members.
Business liaison service: JADMA also offers help in finding local venture

partners and local accredited suppliers. Twice yearly seminars, attended by 70-80 members.

Other facilities: the association produces frequent surveys of the direct marketing industry in Japan, which are extremely useful and informative. It also hosts an annual postal forum, attended by 30,000 participants.

The JADMA states that while services are open to non-members, members will be given preferential service.

POSTAL SERVICES

The Postal Service is a state-run, not-for-profit business whose operations are funded entirely by revenues received from customers for the purchase of stamps, postcards, and other items.

The Ministry of Posts and Telecommunications has four classes of mail, as follows:

- 1st class: correspondence and sealed matter. Standard sizes up to 25 and 50g only. Non-standard up to 4kg.
- 2nd class: postcards.
- 3rd class: unsealed approved periodicals.
- 4th class: unsealed. Discount service for correspondence courses, publications in braille, and academic publications.

Bulk discounts on domestic parcels are available as follows:

No of packages:	10-49	50-99	100-299	300-499	Over 500
Discount (%)	20	23	25	28	30

Bulk discounts for pre-sorted DM are available as follows:

Quantity ('000s)	2	3	5	7.5	10	15	20	30	50	75	100
Discount (%)	15	18	21	22	24	25	26	27	28	29	30

Approval for bulk discounts must be obtained in advance, and the appropriate bulk rate indicia must be printed on outer envelopes.

Services offered:

- Bulk, discounted rates for addressed mail
- Periodical mailing rates
- Express mail services (EMS)
- Business reply services (BRS)
- International business reply services
- Postage paid by addressee
- PO Box addresses
- Registered post
- Postal insurance
- Email services
- Printing and packaging

For further information, contact:

The Postal Bureau, International Affairs Division
Ministry of Posts and Telecommunications
1-3-2 Kasumigaseki
Chiyoda-ku
Tokyo 100-9798
Japan

Tel: +81 3 3504 4394
Fax: +81 3 3593 9124
Website: www.postal.mpt.go.jp

PROVIDERS OF DM AND E-M SERVICES

ACCESS TSUSHIN CO., LTD.
Homat Bldg.
6–2 Gobancho
Chiyoda-ku
Tokyo
102
Japan
Tel: +81 3 3221 9251

Services/Products:
Direct marketing agency

Member of:
JADMA

ACE SERVICE, INC.
439–1 Sugatacho
Kanagawa-ku
Yokohama
221
Japan
Tel: +81 45 471 7371

Services/Products:
Private delivery services

Member of:
JADMA

ACTON FUJIMORI K.K.
2F, YKB Mike Garden
1-5-4 Shinjuku
Shinjuku-ku
Tokyo
160
Japan
Tel: +81 3 3351 9221

Services/Products:
Direct marketing agency

Member of:
JADMA

AD: DAISEN CO., LTD.
1-1-60 Tsuneyoshi
Konohana-ku
Osaka
554
Japan
Tel: +81 6 460 2212

Services/Products:
Mailing/Faxing services; Telemarketing agency

Member of:
JADMA

ADDRESS TSUSHO CO., LTD.
3–6-3 Rinkaicho
Edogawa-ku
Tokyo

134
Japan
Tel: +81 3 3877 3111

Services/Products:
Mailing/Faxing services

Member of:
JADMA

ADMS INC.
Ebisu Garden Place Tower 12F
4–20–3 Ebisu
Shibuya-ku
Tokyo
150
Japan
Tel: +81 3 5424 1610

Services/Products:
Direct marketing agency

Member of:
JADMA

AIDMA PROMOTION CO., LTD.
12F LC Tsurumai
4-8-3 Chiyoda
Naka-ku
Nagoya
460
Japan
Tel: +81 52 332 6031

Services/Products:
Direct marketing agency

Member of:
JADMA

AIM CREATE CO., LTD.
1–15–2 Hyakunincho
Shinjuku-ku
Tokyo
169
Japan
Tel: +81 3 3371 0101

Services/Products:
Advertising Agency

Member of:
JADMA

ALL TAKASIMAYA AGENCY CO., LTD.
6F, Takashimaya Bekkan
5-1-5 Nanba
Chuo-ku
Osaka
542
Japan
Tel: +81 6 631 9819

Services/Products:
Advertising Agency

Member of:
JADMA

APOLLO ADVERTISING CO. LTD.
Parashio 2 Building 7F
100 Minamiekimae-cho
Himeji-shi, Hyogo
670
Japan
Tel: +81 792 88 2195
Fax: +81 792 88 7039
Massaki Touji, President

Services/Products:
List services

Member of:
JDAMA

ARTEC CO., LTD.
2–44–6-2F Sangenjaya
Setagayaku Tokyo
Japan
Tel: +81 3 3421 4586
Fax: +81 3 3421 5318
Yoshisuke Sato, President & CEO

Services/Products:
Consultancy services

Member of:
DMA (US)

ASAHI ADVERTISING INC.
3-2-16 Kyobashi
Chuo-ku
Tokyo
104
Japan
Tel: +81 3 3272 6763

Services/Products:
Advertising Agency

Member of:
JADMA

ASATSU INC.
16–12, Ginza 7 Chrome
Chuo-ku, Tokyo
104
Japan
Tel: +81 3 3547 2504
Fax: +81 3 3547 2587
Shinichi Morita, Senior Group Account Director

Services/Products:
Advertising Agency

Member of:
DMA (US)

ATLUX CORPORATION
8–8, Akasaka 6-chome
Minato-ku
Tokyo
107
Japan
Tel: +81 3 3589 1470

Fax: +81 3 3589 1338
Toru (Tom) Suzuki, President

Services/Products:
Service bureau

Member of:
DMA (US)

BELL HEART, INC.
4–20–20, Minami-Aoyama
Minato-ku
Tokyo
107–0062
Japan
Tel: +81 3 5474 9900
Fax: +81 3 5474 9909
Sadao Tokuteru, President

Services/Products:
Telemarketing agency

Member of:
DMA (US)

BELLSYSTEM 24 INC
Minami-Ikebukuro 2 Chome
Tokyu Building East-3 2–16–8
Tokyo
171–0022
Japan
Tel: +81 3 3590 0024
Fax: +81 3 3590 4610
Sonoyama Yukio, President & CEO

Services/Products:
Telemarketing agency; Call centre
services/systems; Market research
agency; Sales promotion agency

Member of:
FEDMA; JADMA

BENESSE CORPORATION
Tama City
1–34 Ochiai
Tokyo
206–8686
Japan
Tel: +81 423564151
Fax: +81 423567302
Kazuko Takaichi, Deputy General
Manager

Member of:
FEDMA

BUNGEISHUNJU LTD.
3–23 Kioicho
Chiyoda-ku
Tokyo
102
Japan
Tel: +81 3 3265 1211

Services/Products:
Publisher

Member of:
JADMA

C&F-VAN CO., LTD.
2F, ShinSI Bldg.
6–20–2 Shinbashi
Minato-ku
Tokyo
105
Japan
Tel: +81 3 5403 7788

Services/Products:
Direct marketing agency

Member of:
JADMA

COSMO COMMUNICATIONS INC.
Aoyama Tower Building
2–24–15 Minami-Aoyama
Minato-ku, Tokyo
107
Japan
Tel: +81 3 3405 8146
Fax: +81 3 3405 8874
Ryoji Nakayama, Chief Planner

Services/Products:
Direct marketing agency; Sales
promotion agency

Member of:
DMA (US)

DAI NIPPON PRINTING CO., LTD.
1–1–1 Ichigaya-Kagacho
Shinjuku-ku
Tokyo
162–8001
Japan
Tel: +81 3 3266 2111
Fax: +81 3 5225 8239
Email: info@mail.dnp.co.jp
Web: www.dnp.co.jp
Rey Saida, Press and Public Relations
Assistant Manager

Services/Products:
Catalogue producer; Database
services; Design/graphics/clip art
supplier; Direct marketing agency;
Personalisation; Print services

E-Services:
E-Marketing consultant; Website
design; Online/e-marketing agency

DAI-ICHI TSUSHIN-SHA CO., LTD.
7F, New Edobashi Bldg.
1–7-2 Nihonbashi Honcho
Chuo-ku
Tokyo
104

Japan
Tel: +81 3 3242 4101

Services/Products:
Advertising Agency

Member of:
JADMA

DAIICHI ADO SYSTEM CO., LTD.
2–13 Kanda Tsukasa-cho
Chiyoda-ku
Tokyo
101
Japan
Tel: +81 3 5280 1100

Services/Products:
Telemarketing agency

Member of:
JADMA

DAIKAN BUSINESS SERVICE
2–11–9 Oyamadai
Setagaya-ku
Tokyo
154
Japan
Tel: +81 3 3703 3768

Services/Products:
Lettershop; Private delivery services

Member of:
JADMA

DAIKO ADVERTISING INC.
2–4-1 Shibakoen
Minato-ku
Tokyo
105
Japan
Tel: +81 3 3437 8111

Services/Products:
Advertising Agency

Member of:
JADMA

DAIPAC CO., LTD
2–22–16 Akabane Minami
Kita-ku
Tokyo
115
Japan
Tel: +81 3 3903 8603

Services/Products:
Mailing/Faxing services; Service
bureau

Member of:
JADMA

DDI CORPORATION (DDI)
8 Ichibancho
Chiyoda-ku
Tokyo
102
Japan
Tel: +81 3 3222 0077

Services/Products:
Telecommunications

Member of:
JADMA

DENTSU INC.
1–11 Tsukiji, Chuo-ku
Chuo-ku, Tokyo
104
Japan
Tel: +81 3 5551 5505
Fax: +81 3 5565 7639
Masaru Ariga, Senior Marketing
Planner

Services/Products:
Advertising Agency; Market research
agency; Sales promotion agency

Member of:
JDAMA

DENTSU WUNDERMAN CATO JOHNSON
3 F, Dentsu-Kosan Bldg No. 3
2–16–7, Ginza, Chuo-ku
Tokyo
104
Japan
Tel: +81 3 5551 8200
Fax: +81 3 5551 8281
Keiji Matsushima, President

Services/Products:
Advertising Agency

Member of:
JDAMA

DIK RELATIONASHIP-MARKETING CO., LTD.
Toranomon Ohtori Bldg. 7F-8F
1–4-3 Toranomon
Minato-Ku
Tokyo
105
Japan
Tel: +81 3 3580 2345
Fax: +81 3 3592 0709
Email: contact@drc-net.co.jp
Web: www.drc-net.co.jp
Makoto Itoh, Senior Managing
Director & COO

Services/Products:
Consultancy services; Direct marketing
agency; Interactive media; Response
analysis bureau

E-Services:
Online/e-marketing agency

Member of:
DMA (US)

DIRECT MARKETING GROUP. INC.
3F, Yoshida Bldg.
3–11–10 Toyo Koto-ku
Tokyo
135
Japan
Tel: +81 3 3647 6710

Services/Products:
Consultancy services

Member of:
JADMA

DIRECT MARKETING JAPAN, INC.
2–11–2-501, Nakano
Nakano-ku
Tokyo
164
Japan
Tel: +81 3 33 83 93 21
Fax: +81 3 33 83 93 40
Akira Oka, President

Services/Products:
List services; Database services; Direct
marketing agency; Consultancy
services

Member of:
JDAMA

DM BRAIN COMPANY LTD.
#309 New Plaza Bldg
2–21 Taiyuji-cho, Kita-ku
Osaka
530
Japan
Tel: +81 6 361 0353
Fax: +81 6 361 2773
Teruhiko Gato, President

Services/Products:
List services; Lettershop

Member of:
DMA (US)

DM KOKOKUSHA K.K.
2–15–20 Kitasuna
Koto-ku
Tokyo
136–0073
Japan
Tel: +81 3 3699 8558

Services/Products:
Mailing/Faxing services; Private
delivery services

Member of:
JADMA

DMS INC.
DMS Bldg., 1–11 Kanda Ogawacho
Chiyoda-ku
Tokyo
101
Japan
Tel: +81 3 3293 2961

Services/Products:
Direct marketing agency

Member of:
JADMA

EIGHT PRINTING CO., LTD.
5–3-2 Koishikawa
Bunkyo-ku
Tokyo
112
Japan
Tel: +81 3 3814 8131

Services/Products:
Print services

Member of:
JADMA

ENDEAVOR
1–9-15 Tagawa Yodogawa-ku
Osaka
532–0027
Japan
Tel: +81 6 838 2477
Fax: +81 6 838 2478
Scott Filipski

Services/Products:
Lettershop; Mailing/Faxing services

Member of:
DMA (US)

FOOT WORK DELIVERY
935 Izumicho
Tachikawa-shi
Tokyo
190
Japan
Tel: +81 425 27 1711

Services/Products:
Private delivery services

Member of:
JADMA

FOR LADY CO., LTD.
8F, Fukayama Bldg.
2–12–12 Ginza
Chuo-ku
Tokyo
104
Japan
Tel: +81 3 3545 0461

Services/Products:
Direct marketing agency

Member of:
JADMA

FUJI SEIHAN PRINTING CO., LTD.
2–4-33 Nishi-miyahara
Yodogawa-ku
Osaka
532
Japan
Tel: +81 6 394 1181

Services/Products:
Print services

Member of:
JADMA

FUJISANKEI ADVERTISING WORK CO., LTD.
Rakucho Bldg.
2–2-1 Yurakucho
Chiyoda-ku
Tokyo
100
Japan
Tel: +81 3 3573 7411

Services/Products:
Advertising Agency

Member of:
JADMA

GENESIS CORPORATION
2–15-5 Nihonbashi Hamacho
4F, Nihonbashi OST Bldg.
Chuo-Ku
Tokyo
103–0007
Japan
Tel: +81 3 5641 1741
Fax: +81 3 5641 1747
Email: negishi@genesisnet.co.jp
Ryosaku L. Negishi, President

Services/Products:
List services; Database services;
Mailing/Faxing services; Service
bureau; Sales promotion agency

Member of:
FEDMA; DMA (US); JADMA

GOEISHA
3–13–12 Nishihara
Shibuya-ku
Tokyo
151
Japan
Tel: +81 3 5453 8691

Services/Products:
Advertising Agency

Member of:
JADMA

GRANDE MARCHE, INC.
7F, TBS Akasaka Media Bldg.
5–3-6 Akasaka
Minato-ku
Tokyo
107
Japan
Tel: +81 3 3505 8686

Services/Products:
Direct response TV services

Member of:
JADMA

GREY DAIKO ADVERTISING INC.
3–30, Motoasahu 2-chome
Minato-ku
Tokyo
156
Japan
Tel: +81 3 5423 1723
Fax: +81 3 5423 1753
Atsuko Morimoto, Vice President

Services/Products:
Advertising Agency; Direct marketing
agency

Member of:
DMA (US)

HAKUHODO, INC.
Granpark Tower, 3–4-1 Shibaura
Minato-ku
Tokyo
108–8088
Japan
Tel: +81 3 5446 6431
Fax: +81 3 5446 6439
Email: fukuda@hakuhodo.co.jp
Yoshitaka Fukuda, Manager,
Interactive Marketing

Services/Products:
Advertising Agency; Direct marketing
agency; Interactive media

E-Services:
E-Marketing consultant; Website
design; Online/e-marketing agency

Member of:
DMA (US)

I & S CO.
1–5-3 Nihonbashi Muromachi
Chuo-ku
Tokyo
103
Japan
Tel: +81 3 3246 8585

Services/Products:
Advertising Agency

Member of:
JADMA

IMPRESS INC.
Seidai Bldg.
2–3-6 Hongo
Bunkyo-ku
Tokyo
113
Japan
Tel: +81 3 3815 8991

Services/Products:
Direct marketing agency

Member of:
JADMA

IMURA ENVELOPE CO., LTD.
2–1-13 Honcho
Chuo-ku
Osaka
540
Japan
Tel: +81 6 910 2511

Services/Products:
Mailing/Faxing services

Member of:
JADMA

ING INC.
400 Miyanaga Shinmachi
Matsuto-shi
Ishikawa
924–0018
Japan
Tel: +81 76 276 0821

Services/Products:
Print services; Creative agency

Member of:
JADMA

INTER SECT
1–32–8, Kita-Otsuka
Toshima-ku
Tokyo
170
Japan
Tel: +81 3 3915 2949
Fax: +81 3 3915 2944
Kazumichi Takada, Director

Services/Products:
Consultancy services

Member of:
DMA (US)

INTER VISION, INC.
Shibuya TOD Bldg.
1–21–14 Dogenzaka
Shibuya-ku

Tokyo
150
Japan
Tel: +81 3 5458 3333

Services/Products:
Advertising Agency

Member of:
JADMA

INTERNATIONAL DIRECT MARKETING INSTITUTE (IDMI)

1–20–2 Nishi-Shinjuku, Shinjuku-ku
c/o TELEMARKETING JAPAN - 5F
Hourai Bldg.
Tokyo
160
Japan
Tel: +81 3 5321 0800
Fax: +81 3 5321 0814
Tatsuya Kishi, Director International
Division

Services/Products:
Fulfilment and sampling house;
Database services; Telemarketing
agency; Direct marketing agency

Member of:
FEDMA; DMA (US)

ISI CORPORATION

5F 3–2–1 Kojimachi
Chiyoda-ku, Tokyo
102
Japan
Tel: +81 3 52 76 14 49
Fax: +81 3 52 76 14 59
Motonori Sato, President

Services/Products:
Advertising Agency

Member of:
DMA (US)

ITOCHU TECHNO-SCIENCE CORPORATION

1–11–5 Fujimi Chiyoda-ku
Tokyo
102
Japan
Tel: +81 3 5226 1850

Services/Products:
Telemarketing agency

Member of:
JADMA

JAPAN DIRECT MAIL ASSOCIATION

A-H-1 Bldg. 4F
9–14 Azabudai 1 chome
Minato-ku
Tokyo

106–0041
Japan
Tel: +81 3 3584 3447
Fax: +81 3 3584 3909
Email: jdmajun@aol.com
Narito Murakami, Senior Managing
Director

JAPAN TELECOM CO., LTD.

4–7–1 Hacchobori
Chuo-ku
Tokyo
104
Japan
Tel: +81 3 5540 8000

Services/Products:
Telecommunications

Member of:
JADMA

JOHOKU SENKOH

12–29 Hiroshiba-cho
Suita-shi
Osaka
564
Japan
Tel: +81 6 386 7541

Services/Products:
Advertising Agency

Member of:
JADMA

KEIHIN CO., LTD., THE

3–4–20 Kaigan
Minato-ku
Tokyo
108
Japan
Tel: +81 3 3456 7801

Services/Products:
Private delivery services

Member of:
JADMA

KEIHIN DISTRIBUTION CO., LTD.

3–1 Chiwakacho
Kanagawa-ku
Yokohama
221
Japan
Tel: +81 45 441 2951

Services/Products:
Private delivery services

Member of:
JADMA

KOBAYASHI KIROKUSHI CO., LTD.

115 Kita takane
Ogakiecho
Kariya-shi
Aichi
448
Japan
Tel: +81 566 26 5310

Services/Products:
Database services; Print services

Member of:
JADMA

KOBUNSHA PUBLISHERS, LTD.

1–16–6 Otowa
Bunkyo-ku
Tokyo
112
Japan
Tel: +81 3 5395 8188

Services/Products:
Publisher

Member of:
JADMA

KODANSHA

2–12–21 Otawa
Bunkyo-ku
Tokyo
112
Japan
Tel: +81 3 5395 3641

Services/Products:
Publisher

Member of:
JADMA

KOSHINSHA

Pashiko Bldg.
6–15–8 Honkomagome
Bunkyo-ku
Tokyo
113
Japan
Tel: +81 3 3944 1761

Services/Products:
Advertising Agency

Member of:
JADMA

KOTOBUKIDO KAMISEIHIN CO., LTD.

60–4 Yayoicho
Itabashi-ku
Tokyo
173
Japan
Tel: +81 3 3974 7111

Services/Products:
Mailing/Faxing services; Print services

Member of:
JADMA

KOYO 21
4F, Fuji Bldg.
2–10–9 Hongo
Bunkyo-ku
Tokyo
113
Japan
Tel: +81 3 5800 0621

Services/Products:
Service bureau

Member of:
JADMA

KYOBASHI AGENCY CO., LTD.
5-4-4 Sotokanda
Chiyoda-ku
Tokyo
101
Japan
Tel: +81 3 3836 2441

Services/Products:
Advertising Agency

Member of:
JADMA

KYODO PRINTING CO., LTD.
4–14–12 Koishikawa
Bunkyo-ku
Tokyo
112
Japan
Tel: +81 3 3817 2212

Services/Products:
Print services

Member of:
JADMA

LANDSCAPE CO., INC.
15F, Tokyo Opera City Tower
3–20–2 Nishi-shinjuku, Shinjuku-ku
Tokyo
163–14
Japan
Tel: +81 3 5388 7000
Fax: +81 3 5388 7300
Takanori Michikoshi, Sales &
Marketing

Services/Products:
List services

Member of:
JDAMA

MAGAZINE HOUSE, LTD.
3–13–10 Ginza
Chuo-ku

Tokyo
140–03
Japan
Tel: +81 3 3545 7111

Services/Products:
Publisher

Member of:
JADMA

MAIL
3–7-1 Kusayanagi
Yamato-shi
Kanagawa
242
Japan
Tel: +81 462 60 1800

Services/Products:
Mailing/Faxing services

Member of:
JADMA

**MCCANN RELATIONSHIP
MARKETING**
Shin-Aoyama Bldg., 21E
1–1-1 Minami-Aoyama
Minato-ku
Tokyo
107–8679
Japan
Tel: +81 3 3746 8642
Fax: +81 3 3746 8649
David L. Dallaire, General Manager

Services/Products:
Advertising Agency; Call centre
services/systems; Consultancy services;
Database services; Direct marketing
agency; CRM implementation

E-Services:
Website design; E-Marketing
consultant; Online/e-marketing agency

Member of:
DMA (US); National DMA

MEITETSU AGENCY
6F, Shirakawa Dai3 Bldg.
4–8-10 Naeki
Nakamura-ku
Nagoya
450
Japan
Tel: +81 52 582 4565

Services/Products:
Advertising Agency

Member of:
JADMA

**MEITETSU TRANSPORT CO.,
LTD.**
2–12–8 Aoi
Higashi-ku
Nagoya
461
Japan
Tel: +81 52 935 2240

Services/Products:
Private delivery services

Member of:
JADMA

**MITSUMURA PRINTING CO.,
LTD.**
1–15–9 Osaki
Shinagawa-ku
Tokyo
141
Japan
Tel: +81 3 3492 1181

Services/Products:
Print services

Member of:
JADMA

**MIURA PRINTING
CORPORATION**
2–3-9 Chitose
Sumida-ku
Tokyo
130
Japan
Tel: +81 3 3632 1111

Services/Products:
Print services

Member of:
JADMA

MOBA CO. LTD.
Wien Aoyama Bldg. #337
2–2-15 Mianmi-Aoyama
Minato-ku, Tokyo
Japan
Tel: +81 3 34706401
Fax: +81 3 34791216
Niwa Kazuo, President

Services/Products:
Advertising Agency

Member of:
DMA (US)

MOSHI MOSHI HOTLINE, INC.
Telecommunication Bldg.
2–6-5 Yoyogi
Shibuya-ku
Tokyo
151
Japan
Tel: +81 3 5351 7200

Services/Products:
Telemarketing agency

Member of:
JADMA

**MUTOW INFORMATION
CENTER CO., LTD.**
685 Wadacho
Hamamatsu-shi
Shizuoka
435
Japan
Tel: +81 53 460 6611

Services/Products:
Fulfilment and sampling house

Member of:
JADMA

NANBOKUSHA INC.
25F, Sunshine 60
3–1–1 Higashi-ikebukuro
Toshima-ku
Tokyo
170–6025
Japan
Tel: +81 3 5391 2918

Services/Products:
Advertising Agency

Member of:
JADMA

NIHON UNISIS, LTD.
1–1–1 Toyosu
Koto-ku
Tokyo
135
Japan
Tel: +81 3 5546 4111

Services/Products:
Software supplier

Member of:
JADMA

**NIKKEI BUSINESS
PUBLICATIONS, INC**
Chiyoda-ku
2–7–6 Hirakawacho
Tokyo
102–8622
Japan
Tel: +81 3 52 10 88 81/80 58
Fax: +81 3 52 10 80 62
Email: ishikura@nikkeibp.co.jp
Web: www.nikkeibp.com
Masanari Ishikura, Deputy Group
Manager

Services/Products:
List services; Market research agency

Member of:
FEDMA

**NIKKEI OSAKA PR
ADVERTISING CO., LTD.**
9F, Amashin Tenmabashi Bldg.
1–26 Kyomachi, Tenmabashi
Chuo-ku
Osaka
54
Japan
Tel: +81 6 947 0530

Services/Products:
Advertising Agency

Member of:
JADMA

NIPPON EXPRESS CO., LTD.
3–12–9 Sotokanda
Chiyoda-ku
Tokyo
101
Japan
Tel: +81 3 3253 1111

Services/Products:
Private delivery services

Member of:
JADMA

NIPPON INTAS INC.
2–5–5 Shintomi
Chuo-ku
Tokyo
104
Japan
Tel: +81 3 3553 1661

Services/Products:
Sales promotion agency

Member of:
JADMA

**NIPPON PRINT AND GRAPHICS
INC.**
Fuji TV Dai 2 Bekkan
1–16 Sumiyoshi-cho
Shinjuku-ku
Tokyo
162
Japan
Tel: +81 3 3358 8100

Services/Products:
Print services

Member of:
JADMA

**NIPPON TELEGRAPH AND
TELEPHONE CORPORATION**
NTT Shinjuku Honsha Bldg.
3–19–2 Nishi-Shinjuku
Shinjuku-ku

Tokyo
163–19
Japan
Tel: +81 3 5359 5178

Services/Products:
Telecommunications

Member of:
JADMA

NISHITAMA UNSO CO., LTD.
1–3–28 Showamachi
Akishima-shi
Tokyo
196
Japan
Tel: +81 425 46 6111

Services/Products:
Private delivery services

Member of:
JADMA

NISSHA PRINTING CO., LTD.
3 Mibu Hanaimachi
Nakagyo-ku
Kyoto
604
Japan
Tel: +81 75 811 8111

Services/Products:
Print services

Member of:
JADMA

NTT TELEMARKETING INC.
2–8–6 Nishishinbashi Minatoku
Tokyo
105
Japan
Tel: +81 3 55320200
Fax: +81 3 52320203
Masao Iseki, President & CEO

Services/Products:
Telemarketing agency

Member of:
JDAMA

NTT TELEMATE
11F, Nishiki Chuo Bldg.
3–5–27 Nishiki
Naka-ku
Nagoya
460
Japan
Tel: +81 52 961 7100

Services/Products:
Telemarketing agency

Member of:
JADMA

NTT TELEPHONE ASSIST CORPORATION
NTT Toyosaki Bldg.
3–17–21 Toyosaki
Kita-ku
Osaka
531
Japan
Tel: +81 6 377 0291

Services/Products:
Telemarketing agency

Member of:
JADMA

OCT CO., LTD.
4F, Koei Bldg. Shinkan
6-3-7 Nishitenma
Kita-ku
Osaka
530
Japan
Tel: +81 6 362 6841

Services/Products:
Direct response TV services

Member of:
JADMA

OHTE ADVERTISING, INC.
2–2–1 Yurakucho
Chiyoda-ku
Tokyo
100
Japan
Tel: +81 3573 1311

Services/Products:
Advertising Agency

Member of:
JADMA

ORICOM CO., LTD.
Roppongi 25 Mori Bldg.
1-4-30 Roppongi
Minato-ku
Tokyo
106
Japan
Tel: +81 3 3224 6052

Services/Products:
Advertising Agency

Member of:
JADMA

PROTON INC.
313, Toranomon Garden
3–10–4 Toranomon
Minato-ku
Tokyo
105
Japan
Tel: +81 3 3578 1002

Services/Products:
Consultancy services

Member of:
JADMA

PSY, INC.
1–6–1 Jingumae
Shibuya
Tokyo
150
Japan
Tel: +81 3 34 70 32 50
Fax: +81 3 34 03 25 30
Yuzo Shinjo, Managing Director

Services/Products:
Creative consultant

Member of:
DMA (US)

S.P.K.
3F, Forum Bldg.
3–6–4 Jingumae
Shibuya-ku
Tokyo
150
Japan
Tel: +81 3 5411 1711

Services/Products:
Direct marketing agency

Member of:
JADMA

SAGAWA EXPRESS
68 Kamitoba-tsunodamachi
Minami-ku
Kyoto
601
Japan
Tel: +81 75 691 6500

Services/Products:
Private delivery services

Member of:
JADMA

SANEI KOUKOKU-SHA
1–12–17 Iidabashi
Chiyoda-ku
Tokyo
102
Japan
Tel: +81 3 3264 7821

Services/Products:
Advertising Agency

Member of:
JADMA

SANKEI ADVERTISING AGENCY
2–5-1 Umeda
Kita-ku
Osaka
530
Japan
Tel: +81 6 341 7351

Services/Products:
Advertising Agency

Member of:
JADMA

SANKO AD CO., LTD.
4–6-3 Tenjin
Chuo-ku
Fukuoka
810
Japan
Tel: +81 92 771 8521

Services/Products:
Advertising Agency

Member of:
JADMA

SANKOSHA ADVERTISING AGENCY, LTD.
3–13–1 Ginza
Chuo-ku
Tokyo
104
Japan
Tel: +81 3 3544 7916

Services/Products:
Advertising Agency

Member of:
JADMA

SANPOST
3–10–2 Akasaka
Minato-ku
Tokyo
107
Japan
Tel: +81 3 3586 2701

Services/Products:
Sales promotion agency

Member of:
JADMA

SCITEX DIGITAL PRINTING INC.
4F, Kanda TKM Bldg.
15 Kanda-Konyamachi
Chiyoda-ku
Tokyo
101
Japan
Tel: +81 3 3256 2613

Services/Products:
Print services

Member of:
JADMA

SCOPE INC.
9 Tsukijicho
Shinjuku-ku
Tokyo
162
Japan
Tel: +81 3 3269 5593

Services/Products:
Advertising Agency

Member of:
JADMA

SHINCHOSHA
71 Yaraicho
Shinjuku-ku
Tokyo
162
Japan
Tel: +81 3 3266 5220

Services/Products:
Publisher

Member of:
JADMA

SHIZAWA PRINTING CO.
2-8-15 Chuo-cho
Meguro-ku
Tokyo
152
Japan
Tel: +81 3 3715 5569

Services/Products:
Advertising Agency; Print services

Member of:
JADMA

SHOGAKUKAN INC.
2-3-1 Hitotsubashi
Chiyoda-ku
Tokyo
101
Japan
Tel: +81 3 3230 5370

Services/Products:
Publisher

Member of:
JADMA

SHOPPING CHANNEL
1-2-1 Otemachi
Chiyoda-ku
Tokyo
100
Japan
Tel: +81 3 3285 7799

Services/Products:
Direct response TV services

Member of:
JADMA

SHUEISHA INC.
2-5-10 Hitotsubashi
Chiyoda-ku
Tokyo
101
Japan
Tel: +81 3 3230 6200

Services/Products:
Publisher

Member of:
JADMA

SIP COMPANY, LTD.
Jingumae-Green Bldg. 4F
Jingumae, Shibuya-ku 2-26-8
Tokyo
105
Japan
Tel: +81 3 3408 3090
Fax: +81 3 3408 3402
Junichiro Uchikawa, President

Services/Products:
Advertising Agency; Direct marketing
agency

Member of:
DMA (US)

SKD CORPORATION
Sogo Kojimachi Dai2 Bldg.
1-6 Kojimachi
Chiyoda-ku
Tokyo
102
Japan
Tel: +81 3 3263 4727

Services/Products:
Service bureau

Member of:
JADMA

SOWA TRADING CO., LTD.
6F Tekken Bldg.
8-1-30 Isogamidori
Chuo-ku
Kobe
651-0086
Japan
Tel: +81 78 271 3585

Services/Products:
Internet services

Member of:
JADMA

**SUEHIRO PRINTING
CORPORATION**
2F, Shinotsuka Plaza
5-9-2 Otsuka
Bunkyo-ku
Tokyo
112

Japan
Tel: +81 3 5395 0771

Services/Products:
Print services

Member of:
JADMA

**SUMITOMO CREDIT SERVICE
CO., LTD., THE**
5-2-10 Shinbashi
Minato-ku
Tokyo
105
Japan
Tel: +81 3 5470 7295

Services/Products:
Direct marketing agency

Member of:
JADMA

**SYMPHONY GOOD STAFF CO.,
LTD.**
2-8-8 Chiyoda-machi
Maebashi-shi
Gunma
3710022
Japan
Tel: +81 272 31 5116
Fax: +81 272 32 5111
Ichiro Niwayama, President

Services/Products:
Database services

Member of:
DMA (US)

SYNFORM CO., LTD.
10-1 Takayanagi-Higashicho
Okayama-shi
Okayama
700
Japan
Tel: +81 86 253 7423

Services/Products:
Service bureau

Member of:
JADMA

TAG PRO PRINTING
San-ai Bldg. 306
2-14-9 Takanawa
Minato-ku
Tokyo
108
Japan
Tel: +81 3 3280 2618

Services/Products:
Print services

Member of:
JADMA

647

TELEMARKETING JAPAN INC.
Hourai Bldg. 1–20–2 Nishi-Shinjuku
Sinjuku-ku
Tokyo
160–0023
Japan
Tel: +81 3 5321 0801
Fax: +81 3 5321 0807
Susanna Nakamura, Corporate
Planning

Services/Products:
Fulfilment and sampling house;
Database services; Telemarketing
agency; Direct marketing agency; Call
centre services/systems

Member of:
DMA (US)

**TNT EXPRESS WORLDWIDE
(JAPAN) LTD**
Tamachi Kyoda Bldg.
4-3-4 Shibaura
Minato-ku
Tokyo
108
Japan
Tel: +81 3 5445 1302

Services/Products:
Private delivery services

Member of:
JADMA

TOFAC CO., LTD.
2F, 7-4-2 Minami-aoyama
Minato-ku
Tokyo
107
Japan
Tel: +81 3 3400 7518

Services/Products:
Fulfilment and sampling house

Member of:
JADMA

TOKYO TSUUSHO
4–26–20 Sakuragaoka
Setagaya-ku
Tokyo
156
Japan
Tel: +81 3 3427 6551

Services/Products:
Mailing/Faxing services

Member of:
JADMA

TOKYU AGENCY
4-8-18 Akasaka
Minato-ku
Tokyo

107
Japan
Tel: +81 3 3404 5321

Services/Products:
Advertising Agency

Member of:
JADMA

TOPPAN PRINTING CO. LTD.
5–1, Taito 1-chome
Taito-ku
Tokyo
110
Japan
Tel: +81 3 38 35 59 58
Fax: +81 3 56 88 31 15
Hiroshi Yamamoto

Services/Products:
Print services; Catalogue producer

Member of:
JDAMA

**TOYOSHIGYO PRINTING CO.,
LTD.**
1–3 Ashihara
Naniwa-ku
Osaka
556
Japan
Tel: +81 6 567 2111

Services/Products:
Print services

Member of:
JADMA

TRANSCOM DIRECT
San Oaks II 5F
2–5-25 Toyosaki
Kita-ku
Osaka
531
Japan
Tel: +81 6 377 0096
Fax: +81 6 377 0098

Services/Products:
List services; Copy adaptation;
Consultancy services; Translation
services; Electronic media; Internet
services

USY CONSULTING, INC.
710 Cathy Lane
Mount Prospect
IL 60056
Japan
Tel: +81 8 472 596140

Services/Products:
Consultancy services

Member of:
JADMA

WITAN ACTEN
78–6, Minami-Enoki-cho
Shinjuku-ku
Tokyo
162
Japan
Tel: +81 3 32350081
Kazuko Rudy, President

Services/Products:
Creative consultant

Member of:
DMA (US)

**YAMATO TRANSPORT CO.,
LTD.**
2–16–10 Ginza
Chuo-ku
Tokyo
104
Japan
Tel: +81 3 3541 3411

Services/Products:
Private delivery services

Member of:
JADMA

YARAKASUKAN
2–6-6 Kawaramachi
Chuo-ku
Osaka
541
Japan
Tel: +81 6 201 2131

Services/Products:
Database services; Software supplier

Member of:
JADMA

YOMIKO ADVERTISING INC.
1–8-14 Ginza
Chuo-ku
Tokyo
104
Japan
Tel: +81 3 3567 8111

Services/Products:
Advertising Agency

Member of:
JADMA

**YOMIURI INFORMATION
SERVICE**
Hitotsubashi Bldg.
2–6-3 Hitotsubashi
Chiyoda-ku
Tokyo
101

Japan
Tel: +81 3 5276 4010

Services/Products:
Advertising Agency

Member of:
JADMA

SERVICES/PRODUCT LISTING

Advertising Agency
Aim Create Co., Ltd.
All Takasimaya Agency Co., Ltd.
Asahi Advertising Inc.
ASATSU Inc.
DAI-ICHI Tsushin-Sha Co., Ltd.
Daiko Advertising Inc.
Dentsu Inc.
Dentsu Wunderman Cato Johnson
Fujisankei Advertising Work Co., Ltd.
Goeisha
Grey Daiko Advertising Inc.
Hakuhodo, Inc.
I & S Co.
Inter Vision, Inc.
ISI Corporation
Johoku Senkoh
Koshinsha
Kyobashi Agency Co., Ltd.
McCann Relationship Marketing
Meitetsu Agency
MOBA Co. Ltd.
Nanbokusha Inc.
Nikkei Osaka PR Advertising Co., Ltd.
OHTE Advertising, Inc.
Oricom Co., Ltd.
Sanei Koukoku-Sha
Sankei Advertising Agency
Sanko Ad Co., Ltd.
Sankosha Advertising Agency, Ltd.
Scope Inc.
Shizawa Printing Co.
SIP Company, Ltd.
Tokyu Agency
Yomiko Advertising Inc.
Yomiuri Information Service

CRM implementation
McCann Relationship Marketing

Call centre services/systems
Bellsystem 24 Inc
McCann Relationship Marketing
Telemarketing Japan Inc.

Catalogue producer
Dai Nippon Printing Co., Ltd.
Toppan Printing Co. Ltd.

Consultancy services
ARTEC Co., Ltd.
DIK Relationaship-Marketing Co.,
    Ltd.
Direct Marketing Group. Inc.
Direct Marketing Japan, Inc.
INTER SECT
McCann Relationship Marketing
Proton Inc.
Transcom Direct
USY Consulting, Inc.

Copy adaptation
Transcom Direct

Creative agency
Ing Inc.

Creative consultant
PSY, Inc.
Witan Acten

Database services
Dai Nippon Printing Co., Ltd.
Direct Marketing Japan, Inc.
Genesis Corporation
International Direct Marketing
    Institute (IDMI)
Kobayashi Kirokushi Co., Ltd.
McCann Relationship Marketing
Symphony Good Staff Co., Ltd.
Telemarketing Japan Inc.
Yarakasukan

Design/graphics/clip art supplier
Dai Nippon Printing Co., Ltd.

Direct marketing agency
Access Tsushin Co., Ltd.
Acton Fujimori K.K.
ADMS Inc.
AIDMA Promotion Co., Ltd.
C&F-Van Co., Ltd.
Cosmo Communications Inc.
Dai Nippon Printing Co., Ltd.
DIK Relationaship-Marketing Co.,
    Ltd.
Direct Marketing Japan, Inc.
DMS Inc.
For Lady Co., Ltd.
Grey Daiko Advertising Inc.
Hakuhodo, Inc.
Impress Inc.
International Direct Marketing
    Institute (IDMI)
McCann Relationship Marketing
S.P.K.
SIP Company, Ltd.
Sumitomo Credit Service Co., Ltd.,
    The
Telemarketing Japan Inc.

Direct response TV services
Grande Marche, Inc.
Oct Co., Ltd.
Shopping Channel

Electronic media
Transcom Direct

Fulfilment and sampling house
International Direct Marketing
    Institute (IDMI)
Mutow Information Center Co., Ltd.
Telemarketing Japan Inc.
Tofac Co., Ltd.

Interactive media
DIK Relationaship-Marketing Co.,
    Ltd.
Hakuhodo, Inc.

Internet services
Sowa Trading Co., Ltd.
Transcom Direct

Lettershop
Daikan Business Service
DM Brain Company Ltd.
Endeavor

List services
Apollo Advertising Co. Ltd.
Direct Marketing Japan, Inc.
DM Brain Company Ltd.
Genesis Corporation
Landscape Co., Inc.
Nikkei Business Publications, Inc
Transcom Direct

Mailing/Faxing services
AD: Daisen Co., Ltd.
Address Tsusho Co., Ltd.
Daipac Co., Ltd
DM Kokokusha K.K.
Endeavor
Genesis Corporation
Imura Envelope Co., Ltd.
Kotobukido Kamiseihin Co., Ltd.
Mail
Tokyo Tsuusho

Market research agency
Bellsystem 24 Inc
Dentsu Inc.
Nikkei Business Publications, Inc

Personalisation
Dai Nippon Printing Co., Ltd.

Print services
Dai Nippon Printing Co., Ltd.
Eight Printing Co., Ltd.
Fuji Seihan Printing Co., Ltd.
Ing Inc.

Kobayashi Kirokushi Co., Ltd.
Kotobukido Kamiseihin Co., Ltd.
Kyodo Printing Co., Ltd.
Mitsumura Printing Co., Ltd.
Miura Printing Corporation
Nippon Print and Graphics Inc.
Nissha Printing Co., Ltd.
Scitex Digital Printing Inc.
Shizawa Printing Co.
Suehiro Printing Corporation
Tag Pro Printing
Toppan Printing Co. Ltd.
Toyoshigyo Printing Co., Ltd.

Private delivery services
Ace Service, Inc.
Daikan Business Service
DM Kokokusha K.K.
Foot Work Delivery
Keihin Co., Ltd., The
Keihin Distribution Co., Ltd.
Meitetsu Transport Co., Ltd.
Nippon Express Co., Ltd.
Nishitama Unso Co., Ltd.
Sagawa Express
TNT Express Worldwide (Japan) Ltd
Yamato Transport Co., Ltd.

Publisher
Bungeishunju Ltd.
Kobunsha Publishers, Ltd.
Kodansha
Magazine House, Ltd.
Shinchosha
Shogakukan Inc.

Shueisha Inc.

Response analysis bureau
DIK Relationaship-Marketing Co., Ltd.

Sales promotion agency
Bellsystem 24 Inc
Cosmo Communications Inc.
Dentsu Inc.
Genesis Corporation
Nippon Intas Inc.
Sanpost

Service bureau
Atlux Corporation
Daipac Co., Ltd
Genesis Corporation
Koyo 21
SKD Corporation
Synform Co., Ltd.

Software supplier
Nihon Unisis, Ltd.
Yarakasukan

Telecommunications
DDI Corporation (DDI)
Japan Telecom Co., Ltd.
Nippon Telegraph and Telephone Corporation

Telemarketing agency
AD: Daisen Co., Ltd.
Bell Heart, Inc.

Bellsystem 24 Inc
DAIICHI ADO System Co., Ltd.
International Direct Marketing Institute (IDMI)
Itochu Techno-Science Corporation
Moshi Moshi Hotline, Inc.
NTT Telemarketing Inc.
NTT Telemate
NTT Telephone Assist Corporation
Telemarketing Japan Inc.

Translation services
Transcom Direct

E-SERVICES

E-Marketing consultant
Dai Nippon Printing Co., Ltd.
Hakuhodo, Inc.
McCann Relationship Marketing

Online/e-marketing agency
Dai Nippon Printing Co., Ltd.
DIK Relationaship-Marketing Co., Ltd.
Hakuhodo, Inc.
McCann Relationship Marketing

Website design
Dai Nippon Printing Co., Ltd.
Hakuhodo, Inc.
McCann Relationship Marketing

650

MALAYSIA

Population: 20.6 million
Capital: Kuala Lumpur
Languages: Malay, English and Mandarin

GDP: $90 billion
GDP per capita: $4,360
Inflation: 2.7 per cent

Currency: Malaysian dollar/Ringgit (M$) = 100 sen
Exchange rate: M$3.80 : $1

Time: GMT +8 hour

OVERVIEW

Local direct marketing is becoming increasingly developed in Malaysia to a high level of sophistication, with large consumer and business databases which can be accessed. The market was pioneered by regional publications and financial institutions, often operating out of Singapore. Today, multinationals, regional and local companies all participate in direct marketing.

More multimedia strategies are now employed as the market continues to mature and marketers make increasing use of the telephone and audio-visual media. Marketers are also starting to focus more on strategic relationship marketing, and are making use of proprietary databases. Five international agencies are represented, as well as three local agencies, along with an official Direct Marketing Association of Malaysia.

Malaysia is a culturally diverse country. The main groups include Malay, Chinese and Indian. The majority of people are Muslims. The diversity within each group is wide. For example, a Chinese person could be Cantonese or Hokkien; Buddhist, Taoist or Christian; rural or urban, etc.

Consumers are generally receptive to DM, and respond particularly well to quality communications. 'Junk mail' is a problem, especially in the business sector, as certain marketers continue to produce poorly targeted and executed programmes.

651

Popular response mechanisms include business reply envelopes, fax reply and toll-free telephone numbers, therefore telecommunication capabilities will be an important consideration.

Suppliers

Sophisticated DM support services are not widely available. There are a small number of list brokers, telemarketers, data capture, lettershops (manual and automated) and fulfilment houses. Expertise in building and managing customer databases is very limited, though there are now several companies (Efficient LDP, Star Solutions, OlgilvyOne and Grey Direct, for example) that can offer a sophisticated service in terms of database management and list broking.

Data security is not the problem it used to be, as most list owners have instituted tight controls, including selective seeding and control of letter-shopping. Contractual security agreements are used with lettershops.

Addressing is difficult due to the number of cultural and language differences. For example, an Indian name may contain over 25 characters, and a Chinese name can be formatted in eight different ways. Addresses can be troublesome, although the post office is trying to promote a standard format and post codes are fairly established. Achievers and royalty will often be titled, and the full title must be respected in addressing them.

Personalization is available in roman characters only, but is complicated due to the number of cultural identities. If data are captured into separate title, forename and surname fields and the respondent's race is recorded, personalization can be successful.

LANGUAGE AND CULTURAL CONSIDERATIONS

Malay, English and Chinese are all used, but conveniently all names are in roman characters.

Lotteries and sweepstakes are forbidden and Muslim restrictions are in place against alcohol, bare flesh, etc. There is a strong local Consumer Association which acts as a watchdog.

LEGISLATION AND CONSUMER PROTECTION

The Direct Sales Act for organizations involved in mail order requires a licence, inspection of the goods at local urban centres, and a ten-day cooling-off period. Privacy issues are not specifically addressed, although data protection has been identified by the authorities as requiring legislation and this is due to be tabled during 1999.

THE DIRECT MARKETING ASSOCIATION

Name: The Direct Marketing Association of Malaysia (DMAM)
Address: No. 7–1B, Jalan Pandan Indha 4/34
                Pandan Indha
                55100 Kuala Lumpur
Tel: +60 3 494 8119
Fax: +60 3 494 8117
E-mail: dmam@tm.net.my
Year founded: 1997
President: Mr Sia Chon Ming
Total staff: 9 (Excom Members)
Members: 22
Contact: Adrine Lee

Facilities for overseas users of direct mail

Membership: overseas companies can join the DMAM as an associate member but must be approved by the committee. Annual fees are RM500.
Newsletter: DMAM is about to produce a bi-monthly newsletter in English covering news, seminar information, offers and DMAM activities.
Library: a library service is pending.
On-line information service: an on-line information service is being planned.
Legal advice: DMAM do not currently offer legal advice.
Business liaison service: this service does exist.

POSTAL SERVICES

The post office is becoming more responsive to the needs of direct marketers, and offers the following services:

- Freepost – similar to Business Reply Services but standard printed envelopes are not required.

- Admail – a targeted house drop service.

- Data Post – total service provider from printing, packaging to posting.

- Bulk mail pick-up service.

- Postage by telephone.

Discounts of up to 13 per cent are available on pre-sorted bulk mail. For more information contact:

653

Pos Malaysia Limited
Post Office Headquarters
Dayabumi Complex
Kuala Lumpur
Malaysia

Tel: +60 3274 5216/275 6511
Fax: +60 3 294 8369
Website: www.pos.com.my

PROVIDERS OF DM AND E-M SERVICES

141 MALAYSIA SDN BHD
11th Flr Pernas International
Jalan Sultan Ismail
Kuala Lumpur
50250
Malaysia
Tel: +60 3 2163 7677
Fax: +60 3 245 2718
Email: one41my@tm.net.my
Bob Houldsworth, Managing Director

Services/Products:
Advertising Agency; Direct marketing
agency; Database services; Lettershop;
Sales promotion agency

Member of:
DMA (US)

AUDIOTEL SDN BHD
Block B 2nd Floor
Glomac Business Centre
10 Jalan SS6/1, Kelana Jaya
Petaling Jaya
47301
Malaysia
Tel: +60 3–7046699
Fax: +60 3–7047799
Email: audiote@ibm.net
Ms Lynda Goh

Services/Products:
Telemarketing agency; Call centre
services/systems

Member of:
DMAM

DRTV (M) SDN BHD
No. 28 Jalan 6/91
Taman Shamelin Perkasa
Batu 31/2 Cheras
KL
56100
Malaysia
Tel: +60 3–9813888
Fax: +60 3–9812888
Email: trh@drtv.com.my
Web: www.drtv.com.my
Lee Geok Chai

Services/Products:
Direct response TV services

Member of:
DMAM

EFFICIENT LETTERSHOP & DATAPRINT S/B
No 49, Jln Petaling Utama 3
Taman Petaling Utama
7th Mile Off Jalan

Kelang Lama
46000 PJ
Malaysia
Tel: +60 3–7912555
Fax: +60 3–7916846
Email: ylsoon@pc.jaring.my
Web: http://www.visualad.com.sg//
efficient
Soon Yoke Leng

Services/Products:
Mailing/Faxing services

Member of:
DMAM

EPIC OMNILINK INTEGRATED SDN BHD
20A Jalan SS25/35 Taman Mayang
Petaling Jaya
47301
Malaysia
Tel: +60 3 704 3966
Fax: +60 3 704 3977
Michael B. Tan, Managing Director

Services/Products:
Fulfilment and sampling house;
Database services; Direct marketing
agency; Consultancy services; Design/
graphics/clip art supplier

Member of:
DMA (US)

FOOTE CONE & BELDING SDN BHD
22nd Floor, Menara MPPJ
PO Box 102
Jalan Tengah
Petaling Jaya
46710
Malaysia
Tel: +60 3–7573622
Fax: +60 3–7574080
Email: fcb@fcbmal.com.my
Robert Burr Maureen

Services/Products:
Advertising Agency; Direct marketing
agency

Member of:
DMAM

GRAPHIC PRESS GROUP SDN BHD
Lot 6486 Jalan Medan 3
Taman Medan
Mukim Petaling
Petaling Jaya
46000
Malaysia
Tel: +60 3–7939988
Fax: +60 3 7953622
Mr. Steven Yong

Services/Products:
Print services

Member of:
DMAM

GREY DIRECT
C17: 37th Floor
Empire Tower
Jalan Tun Razak
Kuala Lumpur
50400
Malaysia
Tel: +60 3–2626868 Ext: 196
Fax: +60 3–2626363
Email: greykl@tm.net.my
Rod Strother

Services/Products:
Direct marketing agency

Member of:
DMAM

INTERPOST MALAYSIA SDN BHD
1 Jalan Wahawan 5
Kawasan Perindustrian
Setapak
Kuala Lumpur
53200
Malaysia
Tel: +60 3–4223282
Fax: +60 3–4221282
Email: interpos@tm.net.my
R. L. Murthy

Services/Products:
Lettershop; Fulfilment and sampling
house; Mailing/Faxing services

Member of:
DMAM

JWT DIALOG
Menara Multi Purpose
Capital Sq., 8 Jln Munshi
Sclango
50100
Malaysia
Tel: +60 3 2940 139
Fax: +60 3 294 6404
Debra Brown-Christie, Managing
Director

Services/Products:
Advertising Agency; Direct marketing
agency

Member of:
DMA (US)

MOG (MALAYSIA) SDN BHD
69–2
Jln Bangkung
Off Jln Maarof
Kuala Lumpur

59000
Malaysia
Tel: +60 3–2544306
Fax: +60 3–2543875
Email: sewling@mogm.nasionet.net
Web: mogm@po.jaring.my
Anthony Yeo

Services/Products:
Direct response home shopping

Member of:
DMAM

OGILVYONE WORLDWIDE
5th Floor Wisma MCIS
Jalan Barat
Petaling Jaya
46200
Malaysia
Tel: +60 3–4615752
Fax: +60 3–7556431
Email: simon.si@ogilvy.com
Mr. Steven Palos

Services/Products:
Consultancy services

Member of:
DMAM

PERCETAKAN OSACAR SDN BHD
Lot 37659, No. 4/37A
Tmn Bukit Maluri
Industrial Area, Kepong
KL
52100
Malaysia
Tel: +60 6361474
Fax: +60 6341899
Email: osacar@tm.net.my
Eric K. H. Soong

Services/Products:
Print services

Member of:
DMAM

POS LOGISTICS-FULSERVE SDN BHD
427669-U, 4 Jalan Jurunilai
U1/20 Section U1
Hicom Glenmarie Industrial Park
Shah Alam
40150
Malaysia
Tel: +60 3–5191915/6/7
Fax: +60 3 5191920
Rashikin Abd Rashid

Services/Products:
Fulfilment and sampling house

Member of:
DMAM

POS MALAYSIA BHD
Tkt 1, Khidmat Pelangan
Dayabumi Complex
Kuala Lumpur
50670
Malaysia
Tel: +60 2734141(DL);
2741122(GL); 2756671
Fax: +60 2732254
Paul Danker

Services/Products:
Mailing/Faxing services

Member of:
DMAM

STAR SOLUTIONS SDN BHD
F202, Phileo Damansara 1
9, Jln 16/11
Petaling Jaya
46350
Malaysia
Tel: +60 3–4610202
Fax: +60 3–4610201
Email: kucing@ibm.net
Ms Liza Ramli

Services/Products:
Database services

Member of:
DMAM

TIME MAGAZINE SERVICES SDN BHD
Suite 11.01 11/F
MCB Plaza
Cangkat Raja Chulan
Kuala Lumpur
50200
Malaysia
Tel: +60 3–2017119
Fax: +60 3–2017062
Email: christine_chong@time-inc.com
Ms Christine Chong

Services/Products:
Publisher

Member of:
DMAM

UNITOUCH SDN BHD (SMARTSHOP)
No. 30 Jalan Liku
Bangsar
Kuala Lumpur
59100
Malaysia
Tel: +60 3–2844003
Fax: +60 3–2845004
Email: aasb@tv3.com.my
Web: www.TV3.com.my/Ambang
   Anika
Mohd Razin MD Mokhtar

Services/Products:
Direct response TV services

Member of:
DMAM

SERVICES/PRODUCT LISTING

Advertising Agency
141 Malaysia SDN BHD
Foote Cone & Belding Sdn Bhd
JWT Dialog

Call centre services/systems
Audiotel Sdn Bhd

Consultancy services
Epic Omnilink Integrated SDN BHD
Ogilvyone Worldwide

Database services
141 Malaysia SDN BHD
Epic Omnilink Integrated SDN BHD
Star Solutions Sdn Bhd

Design/graphics/clip art supplier
Epic Omnilink Integrated SDN BHD

Direct marketing agency
141 Malaysia SDN BHD
Epic Omnilink Integrated SDN BHD
Foote Cone & Belding Sdn Bhd
Grey Direct
JWT Dialog

Direct response TV services
DRTV (M) Sdn Bhd
Unitouch Sdn Bhd (Smartshop)

Direct response home shopping
MOG (Malaysia) Sdn Bhd

Fulfilment and sampling house
Epic Omnilink Integrated SDN BHD
Interpost Malaysia Sdn Bhd
Pos Logistics-Fulserve Sdn Bhd

Lettershop
141 Malaysia SDN BHD
Interpost Malaysia Sdn Bhd

Mailing/Faxing services
Efficient Lettershop & Dataprint S/B
Interpost Malaysia Sdn Bhd
Pos Malaysia Bhd

Print services
Graphic Press Group Sdn Bhd
Percetakan Osacar Sdn Bhd

Publisher
Time Magazine Services Sdn Bhd

Sales promotion agency
141 Malaysia SDN BHD

Telemarketing agency
Audiotel Sdn Bhd

PHILIPPINES

Population: 69.3 million
Capital: Manila
Languages: Tagalog is the national language. There are many dialects, but English is spoken by most of the population.
GDP: $83 billion
GDP per capita: $1160
Inflation: 5.1 per cent
Currency: Philippine peso (P) = 100 centavos
Exchange rate: P37.55 : $1
Time: GMT +8 hours

OVERVIEW

Since this is a large English language speaking market, prospects are good for direct marketing. Filipinos on regional and international lists respond well to offers from offshore since there is a lot of wealth at the top of the social strata in the Philippines. They do not mind paying duties when they are applied to merchandise ordered from overseas. Many wealthy Filipinos have undertaken postgraduate studies in the USA and elsewhere and are interested in products from overseas.

In Manila, Basic FCB, McCann and Ogilvy & Mather have established DM divisions. There is a lot of support for Subic Bay as an alternative to Hong Kong and Singapore, since the cost of doing business in the Philippines (including salaries, office rental, private accommodation and so on) is one-quarter that of Hong Kong.

Lists and databases

Local list availability is good and there are clean consumer, business, frequent traveller and credit cardholder lists which are based on responder rather than compiled files – and they work. Be careful whom you lettershop with – though this service is often performed by listowners. Locally, credit card companies are willing to deal on solo mailings. They accept monthly payment offers and pay you up-front for the full amount ordered.

LANGUAGE AND CULTURAL CONSIDERATIONS

The large proportion of the population who speak English respond well to direct marketing and, without the problem of a language barrier, a campaign can be launched with relative ease. Apart from the language issue, cultural considerations remain much the same as in the rest of South East Asia.

LEGISLATION AND CONSUMER PROTECTION

There are some local government controls covering premiums and discounts offered by companies engaged in direct selling, and print media advertising has to have the prior approval of an Advertising Board. Data protection is currently not an issue in the Philippines.

THE DIRECT MARKETING ASSOCIATION

Name: Direct Marketing Association of the Philippines
Address: A/Z Building 723, Sgp. Bumabay Street, Mandaluyong 1550
Tel: +63 2 533 7075
Fax: +63 2 533 2399
E-mail: azdmi@mnl.sequel.net
Contact: Mr. Pio Borges da Cunha

POSTAL SERVICES

A major downside to the Philippines is the postal service, and many DM companies prefer to deliver by courier in this market. As in Thailand, all DM is charged at first class rates. Tests have frequently been made between courier mail and overseas airmail, with flashes on the outer envelope (using the same mailing list). Overseas mail beats local mail by a very significant margin.

Post is slow and fulfilment is also gradual, using either the local system or courier delivery. Better delivery and improved response has been experienced by companies mailing into the Philippines with air-mail flashes on their outer envelope from offshore.

For further information contact:

Philippine Postal Corporation
Liwasang Bonifacio
1000 Manila
Philippines
Tel: +63 2 527 0043
Fax: +63 2 527 0082

PROVIDERS OF DM AND E-M SERVICES

MAILING LISTS (ASIA) LTD.
Suite 801 Alabang Business Tower
1216 Acacia Ave.
Madrigal Business Park
Ayala Alabang
Muntinlupa City
1780
Philippines
Tel: +63 2 809 2873
Fax: +63 2 807 1550
Email: listmgt@skyinet.net
Toti Ramos, List Manager

Services/Products:
List services

E-Services:
Email list provider

Member of:
FEDMA; DMA (US); Hong Kong
Direct Marketing Association

BCD-PINPOINT DIRECT MARKETING INC.
Room 406, Raman Condominium
1130 Pasong Tamo
Makati
Metro Manila
Philippines
Tel: +63 2 812 4403
Fax: +63 2 813 4427
Dicki Soriano, President

Services/Products:
Advertising Agency; List services

HARRISON COMMUNICATIONS (MCCANN RELATIONSHIP MARKETING)
3rd Floor, Dolma Building
107C Palancia Street
Legaspi Village
Makati City
1229
Philippines
Tel: +63 2 814 0409
Fax: +63 2 813 5957
Dino Laurena, General Manager

Services/Products:
Advertising Agency; Direct marketing agency

Member of:
DMA (US)

OLGILVYONE WORLDWIDE
14/F Solidbank Building
777 Passeo de Roxas
Makati City
1200
Philippines
Tel: +63 2 892 7021
Fax: +63 2 892 3791

Services/Products:
Advertising Agency; Direct marketing agency

Member of:
DMA (US)

QUARTERMASTER INTERNATIONAL, INC.
6/F Maripola Building
109 Perea St
Makati
1200
Philippines
Tel: +63 2 810 3003
Fax: +63 2 815 3970
Jose Gerardo B Castro, President & C.E.O.

Services/Products:
List services; Fulfilment and sampling house; Telemarketing agency; Catalogue producer; Mail order company

SERVICES/PRODUCT LISTING

Advertising Agency
BCD-Pinpoint Direct Marketing Inc.
Harrison Communications (McCann Relationship Marketing)
Olgilvyone Worldwide

Catalogue producer
Quartermaster International, Inc.

Direct marketing agency
Harrison Communications (McCann Relationship Marketing)
Olgilvyone Worldwide

Fulfilment and sampling hous
Quartermaster International, Inc.

List services
Mailing Lists (Asia) Ltd.
BCD-Pinpoint Direct Marketing Inc.
Quartermaster International, Inc.

Mail order company
Quartermaster International, Inc.

Telemarketing agency
Quartermaster International, Inc.

E-SERVICES

Email list provider
Mailing Lists (Asia) Ltd.

SINGAPORE

Population: 3.4 million
Capital: Singapore City
Languages: Mandarin
– but English understood by 91 per cent of the population
GDP: $93 billion
GDP per capita: $27,480
Inflation: 2.0 per cent
Currency: Singapore dollar (S$) = 100 cents
Exchange rate: S$1.7 : $1
Time: GMT +8 hours

OVERVIEW

The DM industry in Singapore saw significant growth in activity, serving not only Singapore but increasingly the Region with enhanced creativity, professionalism and productivity until the recent regional recession. Because of its location, effective services and stable political climate, a number of international agencies have moved their Asian base to Singapore in recent years.

The Singapore Government, recognising the importance of the DM industry, is actively encouraging its growth, education and professionalism, including tax breaks and other incentives for companies here to use DM or locate into Singapore. Its desire is to see Singapore become a 'hub' for the region. In this, the Singapore Trade Development Board and its regional offices are playing an active part.

Overall Singapore is considered a very easy market to work in, and is known for its efficiency and discipline. The general level of sophistication, however, is surprisingly low. There are relatively small numbers of list brokers, telemarketers, data capture bureaux, lettershops (manual and automated) and fulfilment houses. Some response-driven lists are available, but the quality of compiled lists is disappointing.

Merge/purge facilities are available but they are not sophisticated. In addition, distrust among list owners makes electronic deduplication difficult.

There are now several international DM agencies in operation, as well as the Direct Marketing Association of Singapore. The DMAS has grown considerably in recent years and has developed a number of initiatives to assist its members and the DM industry, both in Singapore and the region.

DMAS has worked ceaselessly with the TDB and other Government departments for the welfare and growth of DM in Singapore; the tax breaks and other concessions were a result of this. DMAS initiated and conducted the first ever preliminary study of the Singapore DM Industry, the 'Melcher Report' released in July 1998, leading to a full scale survey currently being undertaken to understand consumer and agency attitudes and usage, in addition to hard facts, i.e. hours staff are employed on DM, DM campaign revenues etc.

LANGUAGE AND CULTURAL CONSIDERATIONS

The official language is Mandarin, but 91 per cent of the population understand English. The choice of language will depend on the target audience: if a campaign is aimed at professionals and expatriates then it should be conducted in English. Fortunately, names in both English and Chinese are in roman characters, therefore the database need only hold this character set.

LEGISLATION AND CONSUMER PROTECTION

No specific regulations exist except for financial and medical products. Offers and promotional materials must be approved by their respective regulatory authorities. In addition, sweepstakes rules and regulations need to be submitted to the police for approval (Gaming Act). For the foreseeable future, issues of privacy and data protection are not likely to be addressed by the authorities, but the Direct Marketing Association has been in the forefront of making the Industry aware of the need for consumer protection and, working with DMA Inc [USA] and FEDMA [Europe], introduced a Mail Preference Scheme, whereby the public may 'opt out' of receiving DM mail from DMAS member companies. A similar scheme for telephone marketing is currently being developed and will be launched at DMAsia99.

THE DIRECT MARKETING ASSOCIATION

Name: Direct Marketing Association of Singapore (DMAS)
Address: 37 Jalan Pemimpin, Union Industrial Building, Blk B, #03-04, Singapore 577177
Tel: +65 353 6867
Fax: +65 356 9091
E-mail: dmasin@mbox2.singnet.com.sg
Website: http://web.singnet.com.sq/~dmasin

Year founded: 1983
President: B S Retnam
Members: 100
Contact: Nigel Boatman

Direct mail agencies	10	Direct mail consultants	5
List brokers	15	Handling houses	10
Mailing houses	5	Mail order companies	20
Printers	25	Database agencies	1
Telemarketing agencies	6	Publishers	4

Facilities for overseas users of direct mail

Membership: overseas companies can join the DMAS. There are no minimum requirements for entrance; DMAS charges a S$200 one-off fee, plus an annual subscription of S$240.
Newsletter: the DMAS produces a regular newsletter.
Library: the DMAS has library facilities.
On-line information service: there is no on-line information service.
Legal advice: the DMAS does not offer legal advice, nor does it undertake fee-based research.
Business liaison service: the DMAS provides details of accredited local suppliers, and also helps in finding local venture partners.
Other facilities:

- *DMAsia*: The Conference and Exhibition were established in 1996 to provide a venue for the regional DM industry. Initially focusing on Singapore it will, in 1999, be developed as a totally regional exhibition (see website: www.dmasia.com.sg). In 1998, 2,000 people attended the exhibition and 200 delegates the Conference, from 15 nations.

- *Publications*: DMAS is producing the first *List Directory*, to be launched at DMAsia99. Of great value to all Marketers the Directory will contain all lists available in Singapore, not only for the city, but for the Region. *The Direct Marketeer* – published quarterly by the Association. Conference & Exhibition: DMAsia99 – July 12–14 1999, Raffles City, Singapore.

- *Development*: Through the Members Activity Committee, DMAS endeavours to make aware to its members new developments, new technologies and other relevant activities, and to enhance the industry in all aspects.

- *Education*: Whilst DM has been included in a number of Marketing courses, the coverage is mostly cursory. Therefore last year DMAS established a 'Certificate of Direct Marketing'. Following the success of this, four courses are being run in 1999, and later in the year DMAS will be announcing a Diploma course with a leading and well-established International DM Institute in conjunction with EDB, the Singapore Economic Development Board.

POSTAL SERVICES

Recently privatised, the post office is user friendly and one of the most efficient in the world. Bulk mail and pre-sorted discounts are available as well as the following services:

Business reply service: charges are only made for replies received. For this service call +65 240 0650.

Datasource: this new consumer database can be rented for direct mail purposes. It includes lifestyle information (eg. shopping and banking habits and preferences) and is available as either a pre-selected or customised database. Other database services are also available. For more information call +65 240 0529.

Unaddressed maildrop service: with this service potential audiences can be targeted geographically, with a maximum saving of 60% on normal postage rates. Material can be delivered to all business and residential addresses in Singapore.

For the postage of printed papers there is a weight limit of 500g, and delivery should take 1–2 days. The delivery of bulk post is estimated at 2–3 days, with the minimum and maximum weights being 5kg and 30kg respectively. The postage of bulk mailings is only accepted at Bulk Mailing Counter, Mail & Processing Centre, 10 Eunos Road 8, Singapore Post Centre, Singapore 408600.

For further information please contact:

Singapore Post Private Ltd
10 Eunos Road 8
Singapore Post Centre
Singapore 408600

Tel: +65 845 6400
Fax: +65 841 1836
Website: www.singpost.com.sg

PROVIDERS OF DM AND E-M SERVICES

AMPEX DIRECT MEDIA PTE LTD
190 Middle Road
#17–07 Fortune Centre
Singapore
188979
Singapore
Singapore
Tel: +65 337 3626
Jacob Sim, Business Development Manager

Services/Products:
List services; Mailing/Faxing services; Telemarketing agency; Service bureau

AVANTE-GARDE SHOPPING PRIVATE LTD
89 Short Street #10–09
Golden Wall Centre
Singapore
SG-0718
Singapore
Singapore
Tel: +65 339 2966
Cheng Chua Eio, Managing Director

Services/Products:
Catalogue producer; Mail order company

CAXTON SERVICES CO PTE LTD
29 Tamplines Street 92
Caxton Building
Singapore
SG-528879
Singapore
Singapore
Tel: +65 784 29 93
Marcus Liew, Group Marketing Director

Services/Products:
Lettershop; Fulfilment and sampling house; Mailing/Faxing services; Mail order company

INTERPOST ASIA PTE LTD
29 Tampines Street 92
Caxton Building
Singapore
528879
Singapore
Singapore
Tel: +65 782 3183
B S Retnam, Vice President, Asia Pacific

Services/Products:
Lettershop; Fulfilment and sampling house; Mailing/Faxing services; Service bureau; Private delivery services

JWT DIRECT SINGAPORE
5 Temasek Boulevard #04–05
Suntec City Tower
Singapore
38985
Singapore
Singapore
Tel: +65 339 1942
Debra Brown-Christie, Managing Director

Services/Products:
Advertising Agency

Member of:
DMA (US)

MMS CONSULTANCY (ASIA) PL
30 Robinson Road #03–02A
Robinson Tower
Singapore
48546
Singapore
Singapore
Tel: +65 223 2022
Email: mmsasia@cyberway.com.sg
Nelson Wong, Branch Manager

Services/Products:
List services; Telemarketing agency; Direct marketing agency; Mail order company

Member of:
DMA (US); FEDMA

MOG INTERNATIONAL
6 Harper Road #02–00
Diamond Industries Building
Singapore
369673
Singapore
Singapore
Tel: +65 744 9961
Email: btian@singnet.com.sg
Bernard Tian, Regional Director

Services/Products:
Direct marketing agency

Member of:
FEDMA

OGILVYONE WORLDWIDE
1 Maritime Square #11–09
World Trade Ctr
Singapore
409
Singapore
Singapore
Tel: +65 273 8011

Services/Products:
Advertising agency

OH'S INTERNATIONAL DIRECT MAIL PTE LTD
1002 Aljunied Avenue 5
#04–15
Singapore
1438
Singapore
Singapore
Tel: +65 748 9039
William Oh, Managing Director

Services/Products:
List services; Lettershop; Fulfilment and sampling house

SINGAPORE EXHIBITION SERVICES PTE LTD
2 Handy Road
#15–09 Cathay Building
Singapore
229233
Singapore
Singapore
Tel: +65 338 5651
Jean Khoo, Public Relations Manager

TV IMAGE SINGAPORE
215 Intrepid Warehouse Complex
#02–00 Ubi Ave 4
Singapore
408809
Singapore
Singapore
Tel: +65 749 3175

Services/Products:
Telemarketing agency; Fulfilment and sampling house

SERVICES/PRODUCT LISTING

Advertising Agency
OgilvyOne Worldwide
JWT Direct Singapore

Catalogue producer
Avante-Garde Shopping Private Ltd

Direct marketing agency
MMS Consultancy (Asia) PL
MOG International

Fulfilment and sampling house
Caxton Services Co PTE Ltd
Interpost Asia PTE Ltd
OH'S International Direct Mail PTE Ltd
TV Image Singapore

Lettershop
Caxton Services Co PTE Ltd
Interpost Asia PTE Ltd
OH'S International Direct Mail PTE
Ltd

List services
Ampex Direct Media PTE Ltd
MMS Consultancy (Asia) PL
OH'S International Direct Mail PTE
Ltd

Mail order company
Avante-Garde Shopping Private
Ltd
Caxton Services Co PTE Ltd
MMS Consultancy (Asia) PL

Mailing/Faxing services
Ampex Direct Media PTE Ltd
Caxton Services Co PTE Ltd
Interpost Asia PTE Ltd

Private delivery services
Interpost Asia PTE Ltd

Service bureau
Ampex Direct Media PTE Ltd
Interpost Asia PTE Ltd

Telemarketing agency
Ampex Direct Media PTE Ltd
MMS Consultancy (Asia) PL
TV Image Singapore

SOUTH KOREA

Population: 45.3 million
Capital: Seoul
Language: Korean

GDP: $483 billion
GDP per capita: $10,660
Inflation: 4.4 per cent

Currency: Won (W) = 100 chon
Exchange rate: W1,198 : $1

Time: GMT +9 hours

OVERVIEW

Direct marketing is relatively new in Korea, but consumers are fairly receptive to it. Phone, fax and mail are used interchangeably for response mechanisms to direct mailings. Telecommunications capabilities will therefore be important considerations when building the database. Free gift with purchase is popular.

A peculiarity that has been observed in the Korean market is that six to eight large business conglomerates are operating, and it is difficult to do business with firms outside the group that you are in. For example, if client XYZ's distributor is part of group 'A', it would be most likely only to do business with other suppliers and businesses from group 'A', therefore the selection of suppliers is limited. Fortunately, this does not permeate into consumer buying habits.

There are not many reliable suppliers, and many have been in trouble with the government as of late because of list stealing. Due to problems with data security, many firms undertake activities in-house. Suppliers of data capture, fulfilment (manual only), and telemarketing (although not popular) are available, but are unsophisticated. Personalization is possible using Korean characters.

There is no direct marketing association yet in Korea.

LANGUAGE AND CULTURAL CONSIDERATIONS

The spoken and written language is Korean.

LEGISLATION AND CONSUMER PROTECTION

There are no data protection or confidentiality laws in effect at present.

POSTAL SERVICES

The post office offers an excellent service and discount on bulk mail. No local or international business reply mail service is available.
For further information contact:

Bureau of Posts
International Postal Division
Ministry of Information and Communication
100 Sejongro
Chongro-Ku
Seoul
Tel: +82 2 750 2231
Fax: +82 2 750 2239

PROVIDERS OF DM AND E-M SERVICES

CHEIL COMMUNICATIONS
13F Kukje Building
111 Da-dong
Chung-gu
Seoul
South Korea
Tel: +82 2 317 8385
Fax: +82 2 317 8389
Hyung Gon Kim, Researcher

Services/Products:
Advertising Agency; Direct marketing agency

Member of:
DMA (US)

INFOR NET
6th Floor, Kyoro Anarm Bldg
104–6 Anarm-dong 5-ga
Sungbuk-ku
Seoul
South Korea
Tel: +82 2 923 4844
Fax: +82 2 923 4846
Dr J Min

Services/Products:
Direct marketing agency

JAENEUNG EDUCATION COMPANY LTD
92–19 Shinsul Dong
Dongdaemoon-ku
Seoul
South Korea
Tel: +82 2 923 1132
Fax: +82 2 924 9140

Services/Products:
Fulfilment and sampling house

ORICOM, INC
105–7, Nonhyun-dong
Kangnam-ku
Seoul
South Korea
Tel: +82 2 510 4118
Fax: +82 2 516 3631

Services/Products:
Advertising Agency

SERVICES/PRODUCT LISTING

Advertising Agency
Cheil Communications
Oricom, Inc

Direct marketing agency
Cheil Communications
Infor Net

Fulfilment and sampling house
Jaeneung Education Company Ltd

TAIWAN

Population: 21.8 million
Capital: Taipei
Language: Mandarin

GDP: US$284.7 billion
GDP per capita: US$13,198
Inflation: 0.9 per cent

Currency: New Taiwan dollar (NT$)
Exchange rate: NT$32.72 : US$1

Time: GMT +8 hours

OVERVIEW

Direct marketing in Taiwan, though still far from mature, has been growing fast in recent years. Most companies pursuing DM tend to be multinational, although local companies have started venturing into direct marketing. The approach used is still quite tactical rather than strategic.

Factors that could impede DM growth include consumers' desire to inspect a product before buying and their view of shopping as an important social and leisure activity.

TV shopping has enjoyed increasing acceptance recently. Lengthy infomercials, though considered not very tasteful by some audiences, have been rather successful in achieving sales due to their vivid product demonstration. Popular items on the TV shopping channel include household appliances, facial care and cosmetics, appetite-control medicine, weight-loss programmes, etc.

To do business in Taiwan, foreign mail-order firms must be prepared to offer:

- Chinese language product catalogues, brochures and order forms;
- Chinese language customer service;
- convenient credit or payment terms; and
- reasonable shipping and handling costs.

670

LANGUAGE AND CULTURAL CONSIDERATIONS

Mandarin Chinese (traditional characters) is the spoken and written language. A database should therefore be in Chinese (except that roman numerals may be used for postal code, street number, etc).

The communal nature of the Chinese is perceived to be a cultural impediment to DM growth; for example, personal relationships in business are very important, and people expect to do business face to face. Personalization is, therefore, likely to play a key role in the successful development of direct marketing.

LEGISLATION AND CONSUMER PROTECTION

All DM business activities must follow the regulation of the Fair Trade Law, the Consumer Protection Law and the Computer-Processed Personal Data Protection Law.

THE DIRECT MARKETING ASSOCIATION

Name: Taiwan Direct Marketing Association (TDMA)
Address: 3F, #2, Min Sheng E. Rd., Sec. 5, Taipei 105, Taiwan
Tel: +886 2 2746 1510
Fax: +886 2 2762 8187
Year founded: 1994
Chairperson: Mr Simon Huang
Members: 58

POSTAL SERVICES

The Post Office level of efficiency and quality is fair. Domestic mails can be delivered within one to three days, if they are pre-sorted by ZIP codes. However, due to increasing direct mail volume, privately owned postal services (Home Delivery Agent) are often used.

Taiwanese addresses consist of one address line (about 50 characters long) and have a postal code of three or five digits, which will have an implication on the database system.

English language addresses are translated into Mandarin by the Post Office since they would otherwise not be understood by postal workers and hence not delivered.

Local postal rates of printed matters (in US$) in 1998:

	Regular	Express	Registered
Under 50g	$0.1073	$0.3219	$0.5365
51–100g	$0.2146	$0.4292	$0.6438
101–250g	$0.3066	$0.5212	$0.7357
251–500g	$0.6131	$0.8277	$1.0423

PROVIDERS OF DM AND E-M SERVICES

ASIAN LIFESTYLE DATABASE CO., LTD
6F, #149, Sec. 2
Min Sheng E. Rd
Taipei
Taiwan
Tel: +886 2 2501 4248
Fax: +886 2 2501 4348

Services/Products:
Direct marketing agency

Member of:
TDMA

BACON CULTURAL ENTERPRISE CO., LTD
12F-A, 177, Sec. 4
Chung Hsiao E. Rd
Taipei
Taiwan
Tel: +886 2 2771 5122
Fax: +886 2 2776 9317

Services/Products:
Publisher

Member of:
TDMA

C & D UNIVERSE INTERNATIONAL CO., LTD
6F-1, #276. Sec. 2
Chien Kuo S. Rd
Taipei
Taiwan
Tel: +886 2 2369 5868
Fax: +886 2 2369 3478

Services/Products:
Mail order company

Member of:
TDMA

CHAILEASE MARKETING CO., LTD
6F, #420
Fu Hsing N. Rd
Taipei
Taiwan
Tel: +886 2 2506 3845
Fax: +886 2 2504 7035

Services/Products:
Mail order company

Member of:
TDMA

CITE PUBLISHING CO., LTD
11F, #213, Sec. 2
Hsing Yi Rd
Taipei
Taiwan
Tel: +886 2 2396 5698
Fax: +886 2 2357 0954

Services/Products:
Publisher

Member of:
TDMA

COMMONWEALTH PUBLISHING CO., LTD
4F, #87
Sung Chiang Rd
Taipei
Taiwan
Tel: +886 2 2507 8627
Fax: +886 2 2507 9011

Services/Products:
Publisher

Member of:
TDMA

EASTERN ADVERTISING CO., LTD
7F, #306, Sec. 4
Hsin Yi Rd
Taipei
Taiwan
Tel: +886 2 2707 2141
Fax: +886 2 2705 0709

Services/Products:
Advertising Agency

Member of:
TDMA

FIELD FORCE MARKETING SERVICES CO., LTD
12F, #161, Sec. 2
Min Sheng E. Rd
Taipei
Taiwan
Tel: +886 2 2515 7879
Fax: +886 2 2515 7877
Yi-mei Chen, Manager

Services/Products:
Telemarketing agency; Direct marketing agency

Member of:
DMA (US); TDMA

FORMOSAN MAGAZINE PRESS, LTD
6F, #189
Yen Ping S. Rd
Taipei
Taiwan
Tel: +886 2 2237 5298

Fax: +886 2 2238 1133

Services/Products:
Publisher

Member of:
TDMA

GLOBAL VIEWS MONTHLY
7F, #87
Sung Chiang Rd
Taipei
Taiwan
Tel: +886 2 2507 8627
Fax: +886 2 2508 2941

Services/Products:
Publisher

Member of:
TDMA

GREEN LIFE MAGAZINE CO., LTD
2F #87
Le Yen St
Taipei
Taiwan
Tel: +886 2 2733 5025
Fax: +886 2 2738 2739

Services/Products:
Publisher

Member of:
TDMA

H & H INTERNATIONAL CORP.
5F, #197, Sec. 3
Chung-Hsiao E. Rd
Taipei
Taiwan
Tel: +886 2 2776 2173
Fax: +886 2 2721 7933

Services/Products:
Mail order company

Member of:
TDMA

H.K.G. RECORDS & TAPE CO., LTD
8–2, #1
Kuang Fu N. Rd
Taipei
Taiwan
Tel: +886 2 2746 8818
Fax: +886 2 2760 0465

Services/Products:
Publisher

Member of:
TDMA

HSIN YI FOUNDATION
5F, #75, Sec. 2
Chung Ching N. Rd
Taipei
Taiwan
Tel: +886 2 2396 5303
Fax: +886 2 2396 5015

Services/Products:
Publisher

Member of:
TDMA

INTERSERV INTERNATIONAL INC.
12F-1, #510, Sec. 5
Chung Hsiao E. Rd
Taipei
Taiwan
Tel: +886 2 2346 0121
Fax: +886 2 2346 0242

Services/Products:
Conference/exhibition organiser

Member of:
TDMA

J. WALTER THOMPSON DIRECT
18F, #163, Sec. 1
Keelung Rd
Taipei
Taiwan
Tel: +886 2 2746 9028
Fax: +886 2 2766 1598

Services/Products:
Advertising Agency

Member of:
TDMA

LEE AND LI, ATTORNEYS-AT-LAW
7F, #201
Tun Hua N. Rd
Taipei
Taiwan
Tel: +886 2 2715 3300
Fax: +886 2 2713 3999

Services/Products:
Legal services

Member of:
TDMA

MICROSOFT TAIWAN CO.
10F, No. 6, Sec. 3
Min Chuang E. Rd
Taiwan
Tel: +886 2 2508 7142
Fax: +886 2 2508 7151

Services/Products:
Software supplier

Member of:
TDMA

NETSERVICE DIRECT MARKETING CO., LTD
10F-1, #152, Sec. 1
Chung Shiao E. Rd
Taipei
100
Taiwan
Tel: +886 2 2396 0622
Fax: +886 2 2395 5658

Services/Products:
List services

Member of:
TDMA

OGILVYONE WORLDWIDE
7F, #51, Sec. 3
Min Sheng E. Rd
Taipei
Taiwan
Tel: +886 2 505 5936
Fax: +886 2 506 5936

Services/Products:
Direct marketing agency

Member of:
TDMA

OVERSEAS RADIO & TELEVISION INC.
PO Box 37–3
Taipei
Taiwan
Tel: +886 2 2502 8082
Fax: +886 2 2508 1505

Services/Products:
Publisher

Member of:
TDMA

READER'S DIGEST (EAST ASIA) LTD, TAIWAN BRANCH
3F, #2, Sec. 5
Min Sheng E. Rd
Taipei
Taiwan
Tel: +886 2 2746 1510
Fax: +886 2 2762 8187

Services/Products:
Publisher

Member of:
TDMA

RED INTERNATIONAL MARKETING LTD
11F-1, #63
Jen-Ai Rd
Sec. 4, Ln. 122
Taipei
Taiwan
Tel: +886 2 2709 2958
Fax: +886 2 2709 2950

Services/Products:
Direct marketing agency

Member of:
TDMA

RESPONSE DIRECT MARKETING
149 Sec. 2
Ming Sheng E. Road, 6th Floor
Teipei
Taiwan
Tel: +886 2 516 0700
Fax: +886 2 505 6936
Andrea Hsieh, Vice President

Services/Products:
Database services; Telemarketing agency; Direct marketing agency

Member of:
DMA (US); TDMA

ROCK RECORDS (TAIWAN) CO., LTD
B1, #467, Sec. 6
Chung-Shiao E. Rd
Taipei
Taiwan
Tel: +886 2 2651 8168
Fax: +886 2 2651 1649

Services/Products:
Publisher

Member of:
TDMA

SAATCHI & SAATCHI
20F, #200, Sec. 1
Keelung Rd
Taipei
Taiwan
Tel: +886 2 2345 5700
Fax: +886 2 2345 2557

Services/Products:
Advertising Agency

Member of:
TDMA

SAATCHI & SAATCHI
1/F, N0. 99
Tun Hua South Road
Section 2
Taipei
Taiwan
Tel: 886 22700 3180
Fax: 886 22700 3170
Email: neil_hardwick@saatchi.com.tw
Web: www.saatchi-saatchi.com

Services/Products:
Advertising Agency; Consultancy
services; Direct marketing agency;
Interactive media; Media buying
agency

E-Services:
E-Marketing consultant; Website
design; Online/e-marketing agency

TARGET INTERNATIONAL PUBLISHING CO., LTD
5F, #13, Sec. 2
Chung Chen Rd
Taipei
Taiwan
Tel: +886 2 2833 7460
Fax: +886 2 2833 7480

Services/Products:
Publisher

Member of:
TDMA

TELEDIRECT TAIWAN LTD
6F, #149, Sec. 2
Ming sheng E. Rd
Taipei
Taiwan
Tel: +886 2 516 0700
Fax: +886 2 505 6936

Services/Products:
Telemarketing agency

Member of:
TDMA

UNITED ADVERTISING CO., LTD
10F, #83, Sec. 1
Chung Ching S. Rd
Taipei
Taiwan
Tel: +886 2 2314 3366
Fax: +886 2 2382 0672

Services/Products:
Advertising Agency

Member of:
TDMA

UNITED TASK MARKETING, INC.
8F, Sec. 3
311 Nanking E. Rd
Taipei
Taiwan
Tel: +886 2 2718 4407
Fax: +886 2 2712 5591

Services/Products:
Consultancy services

Member of:
TDMA

UNIVERSAL MAIL SERVICE CO., LTD
4F, #4
Nan-Kang Rd
Sec. 3, Ln. 50
Taipei
Taiwan
Tel: +886 2 2788 4268
Fax: +886 2 2788 2213
Email: rexofc25@ms53.hinet.net

Services/Products:
Call centre services/systems; Database
services; Print services

WARMTH PUBLICATION, INC.
1F-1, 211, Sec. 2
An-Ho Rd
Taipei
Taiwan
Tel: +886 2 2377 0678
Fax: +886 2 2737 3923

Services/Products:
Publisher

Member of:
TDMA

XER INTERNATIONAL INC.
2F, 8, Alley 6, Ln. 235
Pao-Chiao Rd
Taiwan
Tel: +886 2 2918 3319
Fax: +886 2 2912 2640

Services/Products:
Mail order company

Member of:
TDMA

YUANG LIOU PUBLISHING CO., LTD
7–5, #184, Sec. 3
Tingchou Rd
Taipei
Taiwan
Tel: +886 2 2365 1212
Fax: +886 2 2368 4745

Services/Products:
Publisher

Member of:
TDMA

ZUELLIG PHARMA. INC.
10F, Room A, #126 Nanking E. Rd
Sec. 4
Taipei
Taiwan
Tel: +886 2 2577 6438
Fax: +886 2 2578 0662

Member of:
TDMA

SERVICES/PRODUCT LISTING

Advertising Agency
Eastern Advertising Co., Ltd
J. Walter Thompson Direct
Saatchi & Saatchi
Saatchi & Saatchi
United Advertising Co., Ltd

Call centre services/systems
Universal Mail Service Co., Ltd

Conference/exhibition organiser
Interserv International Inc.

Consultancy services
Saatchi & Saatchi
United Task Marketing, Inc.

Database services
Response Direct Marketing
Universal Mail Service Co., Ltd

Direct marketing agency
Asian Lifestyle Database Co., Ltd
Field Force Marketing Services Co., Ltd
OgilvyOne Worldwide
Red International Marketing Ltd
Response Direct Marketing
Saatchi & Saatchi

Interactive media
Saatchi & Saatchi

Legal services
Lee And Li, Attorneys-at-law

List services
Netservice Direct Marketing Co., Ltd

Mail order company
C & D Universe International Co., Ltd
Chailease Marketing Co., Ltd
H & H International Corp.
Xer International Inc.

Media buying agency
Saatchi & Saatchi

Print services
Universal Mail Service Co., Ltd

Publisher
Bacon Cultural Enterprise Co., Ltd
Cite Publishing Co., Ltd
Commonwealth Publishing Co., Ltd

Formosan Magazine Press, Ltd
Global Views Monthly
Green Life Magazine Co., Ltd
H.K.G. Records & Tape Co., Ltd
Hsin Yi Foundation
Overseas Radio & Television Inc.
Reader's Digest (East Asia) Ltd,
    Taiwan Branch
Rock Records (Taiwan) Co., Ltd
Target International Publishing Co.,
    Ltd

Warmth Publication, Inc.
Yuang Liou Publishing Co., Ltd

Software supplier
Microsoft Taiwan Co.

Telemarketing agency
Field Force Marketing Services Co.,
    Ltd
Response Direct Marketing
TeleDirect Taiwan Ltd

E-SERVICES

E-Marketing consultant
Saatchi & Saatchi

Online/e-marketing agency
Saatchi & Saatchi

Website design
Saatchi & Saatchi

THAILAND

Population: 58.7 million
Capital: Bangkok
Language: Thai

GDP: $178 billion
GDP per capita: $3,020
Inflation: 5.8 per cent

Currency: Baht (Bt) = 100 satang
Exchange rate: Bt36.77 : $1

Time: GMT +7 hours

OVERVIEW

Direct marketing in Thailand was pioneered in the early 1980s. The responsiveness of the Thai people to direct mail offers from offshore (using regional and multinational lists) has climbed dramatically over the past few years. This has been largely due to the influx of over US$4 billion a year in tourism and the boom in the stock market and real estate prices. Many wealthy young Thais have also benefited from university education overseas. Direct marketing is expected to grow rapidly as marketers take advantage of the increasing 'Westernization' of consumers.

Mail is currently the dominant direct medium and is well received by business and consumers. Thailand is still a mass-media society, so direct mail is seen as something of a novelty – although this will change rapidly with the growth of DM. Telemarketing is starting to emerge, particularly in financial services.

Phone and fax are popular forms of response and are usually preferred over traditional reply envelopes, so telecommunications capabilities should be an important consideration in planning a campaign.

There are a small number of list brokers, telemarketers, lettershops (manual and automated) and fulfilment houses. Four international agencies are represented in the market. In addition, there are two computer bureaux whose capabilities are quite extensive (for Asia); they develop all their systems in house as turnkey projects. Data security can be a problem, but can be avoided by using a reliable supplier and drawing up an appropriate contract.

LANGUAGE AND CULTURAL CONSIDERATIONS

English is now more widely spoken in Thailand, especially among business people, but any real local roll-out would have to be in the local language.

LEGISLATION AND CONSUMER PROTECTION

The industry is self-regulated and the Thailand Direct Marketing Association (founded in 1996) is preparing codes of practice in areas such as list rental, telemarketing, mail preference, advertising guidelines, etc. There are no laws or regulations specifically restrictive to direct marketing, but rulings of the Food and Drug Association and the Police Regulations relating to lucky draws and sweepstakes must be followed.

THE DIRECT MARKETING ASSOCIATION

Name: Thailand Direct Marketing Association
Address: 4th Floor, Park Avenue Home Office II, 446/40-42 Sukhumvit
             71, Klogntoey, Bangkok 10110 Thailand
Tel: +66 2 381 5270-72
Fax: +66 2 381 5273/4
Contact: Warratada Pattarodom

POSTAL SERVICES

The Communications Authority of Thailand (CAT) is responsible for providing utility services concerning Thailand's communications; postal services, monetary services, telecommunication services, as well as related services (except domestic telephone). The CAT is the sole provider of postal services in Thailand currently running as a state-owned company attached to the Ministry of Transport and Communications. Owing to the fact that the government has announced the plan to privatise the telecommunication business and also to liberalise the market, the telecommunication and postal business of the CAT will be separated in the near future as a consequence.

Services offered:

- Bulk, discounted rates for addressed/unaddressed mail (international only)
- Periodical mailing rates
- Express mail services (EMS)
- Business reply service (BRS)
- International business reply services

- PO Box addresses
- Registered post
- Postal insurance
- Cash on delivery service
- Money order
- Unaddressed mail

For further information contact:

The Communictions Authority of Thailand (CAT)
International Postal Development Division
Postal Planning and Development Department
99 Chaeng Watthana Road
Thung Songhong
Laski
Bankok 10002
Thailand

Tel: +66 2 506 3124
Fax: 66 2 573 1454
Website: www.cat.or.th/post

Domestic service enquiries:
Postal Customer Care Unit
Postal Quality Control Department
Tel: +66 2 982 8887

International service enquiries:
International Post Investigation
Postal Quality Control Department
Tel: +66 2 506 3223

PROVIDERS OF DM AND E-M SERVICES

DIRECT APPROACH
315/582 Fortune Condo Town 1
Sathup adit 19 Chongonotri Rd
Yannawa
Bangkok
10120
Thailand
Tel: +66 2 674 1084
Fax: +66 2 674 1093
Jitana Lertlumying, Managing Director

Services/Products:
Advertising Agency

Member of:
DMA (US)

DIRECT MARKETING SERVICES PUBLIC COMPANY LIMITED
71/25 Borommarajachonnanee Road
Arunamarin
Bangkoknoi
Bangkok
10700
Thailand
Tel: +66 2 436 9000
Fax: +66 2 436 9292

Services/Products:
List services; Lettershop;
Telemarketing agency

INTERACTIVE COMMUNICATIONS CO, LTD
163 Rajapark Building
Sukhumvit 21 (Asoke)
Klong Toey
Bangkok
10110
Thailand
Tel: +66 2 661 7788 94
Fax: +66 2 661 7790
Chusak Dejkriengkraikun, Director,
    Direct Marketing

Services/Products:
Advertising Agency

J WALTER THOMPSON DIALOG UBC
II Building, 20th F
591 Sukhumvit Road (Soi 33)
Klongton, Klongtoey
Bangkok
10110
Thailand
Tel: +66 2 2600820 60
Fax: +66 2 2600606

Services/Products:
Database services

MCCANN DIRECT/MCCANN-ERICKSON THAILAND
5–6F Sethiwan Tower
139 Pan Road
Silom
Bangkok
10500
Thailand
Tel: +66 2 235 6210
Fax: +66 2 237 3009
Shoji Tetsu, Director

Services/Products:
Advertising Agency; Direct marketing
agency

Member of:
DMA (US)

SERVICES/PRODUCT LISTING

Advertising Agency
Direct Approach
Interactive Communications Co, Ltd
McCann Direct/McCann-Erickson
    Thailand

Database services
J Walter Thompson Dialog UBC

Direct marketing agency
McCann Direct/McCann-Erickson
    Thailand

Lettershop
Direct Marketing Services Public
    Company Limited

List services
Direct Marketing Services Public
    Company Limited

Telemarketing agency
Direct Marketing Services Public
    Company Limited

AUSTRALASIA

───── AUSTRALIA ─────

Population: 18.1 million
Capital: Canberra
Languages: English

GDP: $368 billion
GDP per capita: $20,370
Inflation: 2.8

Currency: Australian dollar ($) = 100 cents
Exchange rate: A$1.49 : $1

Time: GMT +8–10 hours

OVERVIEW

Australia is traditionally a production-based economy, and is an important producer and exporter of farm products, as well as minerals, metals and other commodities. However, manufacturing has grown in economic significance, particularly in the small business sector. The main concern of the Australian economy is the level of foreign debts. Australia has the highest debt per capita of any rich industrialized country. All this is likely to have little effect on the direct marketing industry in Australia, whose target audience is mainly consumer and financial and retail businesses.

Direct marketing in Australia has grown to A$7 billion in the last ten years and looks set for further exponential growth in the decade ahead. With the rapidly growing use of direct marketing techniques within organizations, the Australian DMA is strongly positioned to represent the interests of a wide range of companies. Typical member companies' industries are finance and banking, insurance, retailers, major motor vehicle manufacturers as well as traditional mail order traders, advertising agencies and consultants, database consultants, mail processing bureaux and, of course, political parties.

ADMA deals with issues that face the industry and has well-oiled lobbying and PR machinery to deal with problems as they occur and to keep the industry regulation free. By turning out highly trained graduates from its professional education programme, including the highly acclaimed Certificate programme, ADMA ensures the credible growth of the industry.

LANGUAGE AND CULTURAL CONSIDERATIONS

The predominant language used in Australia is, of course, English. However, if a DM campaign is targeted at specific immigrant populations or the native Aboriginal population then a local DM specialist should be consulted about the language and cultural considerations necessary.

LEGISLATION AND CONSUMER PROTECTION

Through the direct marketing industry's Standards of Practice, ADMA improves the status and conduct of direct response advertising and offers consumers comfort when dealing with a member company.

The Advertising Standards Council interprets and applies the self-imposed codes created by advertisers, advertising agencies and the media.

THE DIRECT MARKETING ASSOCIATION

Name:	Australian Direct Marketing Association Ltd (ADMA)
Address:	Suite 1, Level 5, 100 William Street
	East Sydney, NSW 2011
Tel:	+61 2 9368 0366
Fax:	+61 2 9368 0866
Email:	info@adma.com.au
Website:	www.adma.com.au
Year founded:	1966
CEO:	Robert Edwards
Total staff:	7
Members:	500
Contact:	Roslyn Martin, Communications Assistant

DM agencies	75	Telemarketing agencies	33
List brokers	20	DM consultants	30
Mailing houses	32	Handling houses	17
Mail order companies	30	Database agencies	50
Printers	31		

Others: electronic media, financial services, fund raising, loyalty marketing, telecommunications, publishers, recruitment, travel services

Facilities for overseas users of direct mail

Membership: membership fees are determined by Annual Gross Revenue of the company joining. Applications are received by the CEO and need Board approval. Overseas companies can join, but they need an Australian Business Number (ABN).

Newsletter Update is produced every two months for the benefit of members. Advertising is available for non-members.

Library: stocked with books and journals. Research facilities also available on the website.

On-line information service: please see www.adma.co.au

Business liaison service: ADMA's directory of current members, *Who's Who*, is widely considered as the industry bible for leads when it comes to the one-to-one marketplace. Searchable 'Who's Who' information is available online at www.adma.com.au

POSTAL SERVICES

Australia Post has a full range of postal services available. In recent years their direct marketing services have greatly improved, and they now offer the following services:

- *EDIPost*: offers customers an efficient system for handling bulk mailings. Customers lodge mail electronically; it is then transmitted to the processing site closest to its final destination, printed and enveloped, and ready for delivery. *EDIPost* reduces wastage, transport costs and unnecessary processing for the mailer.
- *ePost*: similar to EDIPost, for companies who require speed and security. Letters can be processed overnight for next day delivery.
- *Advertising Mail Discounts*: available on addressed advertising mail, but certain conditions apply. For deliveries within Australia articles must first be registered with Australia Post.
- *Unaddressed Mail Delivery Service*: to use this service a booking must be made with Australia Post by completing an Unaddressed Mail Delivery Service mailing statement.
- *POST Direct*: provides advertising mail solutions plus access to the range of Australia Post advertising mail products and services.
- *Business reply service*: reply paid permits are available from local post offices.
- *Prospecta*: provides Australian marketers with geographical data on potential consumers. By using an existing database of consumers Prospecta identifies a consumer profile, then highlights the area where they are likely to live. The original analysis can either be conducted from the address or probable characteristics of consumers. Australia Post will advise on file formats.

For more information contact:

Australia Post
GPO Box 1777Q
Melbourne Vic 300
Australia
Tel: +61 3 9510 2358
Website: www.auspost.com.au

682

PROVIDERS OF DM AND E-M SERVICES

ABILITY DIRECT MARKETING PTY LIMITED
44 Bay Street
Ultimo
NSW
2007
Australia
Tel: +61 2 9330 7890
Fax: +61 2 9233 7009
Email: sales@ability.com.au
Web: www.ability.com.au
Antony Hing, Director

Services/Products:
List services; Fulfilment and sampling house; Mailing/Faxing services; Telemarketing agency

Member of:
ADMA

ABILITY DIRECT MARKETING PTY LIMITED WA
Suite 5, Subiaco Business Centre
SUBIACO
WA
6008
Australia
Tel: +61 0 8938 08322
Fax: +61 8 9380 8300
Julie Fitzpatrick, Director

Services/Products:
List services; Fulfilment and sampling house; Mailing/Faxing services; Telemarketing agency

Member of:
ADMA

ACCOUNTABLE LIST BROKERS PTY LTD
PO Box 432
Paddington
QLD
4064
Australia
Tel: +61 7 3369 8511
Fax: +61 7 3367 0233
Email: database@powerup.com.au
Web: www.dbase.com.au
Laird Marshall, Director

Services/Products:
List services; Fulfilment and sampling house; Database services; Mailing/Faxing services; Telemarketing agency; Private delivery services; Internet services

Member of:
ADMA

ACTION MAILER COMPANY
3 George Street
Blackburn
VIC
3130
Australia
Tel: +61 1300 656664
Fax: +61 3 9878 1336
Email: print@bvp.com.au
Chris Day, Sales Director

Services/Products:
Labelling/envelope services; Print services

Member of:
ADMA

ADM ACTION DIRECT MARKETING
18 Hotham Street
South Melbourne
Victoria
3205
Australia
Tel: +61 3 9686 9700
Fax: +61 3 9686 9800
Email: stan@aml.com.au
Web: www.aml.com.au
Mr. Stan Gyles, Managing Director

Services/Products:
Consultancy services; Database services; Direct marketing agency; Fulfilment and sampling house; Lettershop; List services

E-Services:
Email list provider; E-Marketing consultant; Online/e-marketing agency

Member of:
ADMA

AMAZING FACES PTY LTD
1/101 Union Street
North Sydney
NSW
2060
Australia
Tel: +61 2 9922 2799
Fax: +61 2 9922 5599
Steven de Vroom, Managing Director

Services/Products:
Print services

Member of:
ADMA

ANISIMOFF DAVENPORT
PO Box 1593
North Sydney
NSW
2059
Australia
Tel: +61 2 9923 2422
Fax: +61 2 9922 1879
Anthony Anisimoff, Principal

Services/Products:
Legal services

Member of:
ADMA

APPLE MARKETING GROUP
Ground Floor, 10 Short Street
Southport
QLD
4215
Australia
Tel: +61 7 5571 2377 Freecall: 1800 811 866
Fax: +61 7 5571 2400
John Appleton, Managing Director

Services/Products:
Fulfilment and sampling house; Database services; Mailing/Faxing services; Telemarketing agency; Print services

Member of:
ADMA

APPROPRIATE SERVICES PTY LTD
PO Box 1078
Box Hill
VIC
3128
Australia
Tel: +61 3 9898 7017
Fax: +61 3 9899 8274
Email: feliciam@appropriate.com.au
Web: www.appropriate.com.au/-feliciam
Felicia Meagher, Managing Director

Services/Products:
Telemarketing agency; Consultancy services

Member of:
ADMA

AT & T EASYLINK SERVICES AUST LTD
PO Box 178
Lane Cove
NSW
2066
Australia
Tel: +61 2 9911 1500
Fax: +61 2 9911 1555
Email: attinfo@att.net.com.au
Web: www.att.net.com.au
Steven McMeechan, Marketing Communications Manager

Services/Products:
Internet services

E-Services:
Website design

Member of:
ADMA

AUSTRALASIAN MEDICAL PUBLISHING COMPANY PTY LTD (AMPCO)
Level 1
76 Berry Street
North Sydney
NSW
2060
Australia
Tel: +61 2 9954 8666
Fax: +61 2 9954 8638
Email: sales@ampco.com.au
Web: www.ampco.com.au
Paul Rippon, Marketing & Sales
  Manager

Services/Products:
List services; Fulfilment and sampling
house; Database services; Lettershop;
Mailing/Faxing services; Publisher

E-Services:
Email list provider

Member of:
National DMA; Australian Direct
Marketin Association (ADMA)

AUSTRALIA POST
GPO Box 1777Q
Melbourne
Victoria
3001
Australia
Tel: +61 3 9204 7407
Fax: +61 3 9639 0445
Email: keed@auspost.com.au
Web: www.austpost.com.au
David Kee, Manager POSTdirect

Services/Products:
Mailing/Faxing services; Postal services

E-Services:
Email list provider; E-Marketing
consultant; Website design

Member of:
FEDMA; DMA (US); DMA (UK)

AUSTRALIAN ENVELOPES
PO Box 76
Mount Waverley
VIC
3149
Australia
Tel: +61 3 9541 0211
Fax: +61 3 9544 8692
Email: pbroom@australianenvelopes.
  com.au

Web: www.australianenvelopes.com.au
Paul Broom, National Business
  Manager

Services/Products:
Envelope manufacturer and marketer

BEELINE SALES SUPPORT
GPO Box 529
Archerfield
QLD
4108
Australia
Tel: +61 7 3274 5133
Fax: +61 7 3275 3658
Noel Teskey, General Manager

Services/Products:
Telemarketing agency; Software
supplier

Member of:
ADMA

BENNETT KEEBLE MARTYN
Level 5, 156 Clarence Street
Sydney
NSW
2000
Australia
Tel: +61 2 9299 7299
Fax: +61 2 9299 7699
Email: bennett@bkm.com.au
Peter Keeble, Partner

Services/Products:
Direct marketing agency

Member of:
ADMA

BERGER SOFTWARE PTY LTD
101 Waterloo Road
North Ryde
NSW
2113
Australia
Tel: +61 2 9870 3000
Fax: +61 2 9870 3099
Email: bsw@bsw.com.au
Web: www.bsw.com.au
Brian Lawrenson, Marketing Manager

Services/Products:
Software supplier

Member of:
ADMA

BERTINI MURRAY & ASSOCIATES
Level 3, 10 O'Connell Street
Sydney
NSW
2000
Australia
Tel: +61 2 9233 7303

Email: bertini@ozemail.com.au
Margie van der Zalm

Services/Products:
Consultancy services

Member of:
ADMA

BLUEPRINT CONCEPT MARKETING PTY LTD
GPO Box 1739
Sydney
NSW
2001
Australia
Tel: +61 2 9223 4911
Fax: +61 2 9223 4040
Email: blueprin@mpx.com.au
David Newton, Marketing Manager

Services/Products:
Telemarketing agency

Member of:
ADMA

BOND DIRECT PTY LTD
Level 6, 100 Mount Street
North Sydney
NSW
2060
Australia
Tel: +61 2 9657 5600
Fax: +61 2 9657 5656
Email: mail@bondirect.com.au
Web: www.bondirect.com.au
Paul McGrath, Managing Director

Services/Products:
Database services; Telemarketing
agency; Direct marketing agency;
Media buying agency; Sales promotion
agency; Data Processing

Member of:
ADMA

BOOMERANG INTEGRATED MARKETING AND ADVERTISING
Old Saint Davids, 17 Arthur Street
Surry Hills
NSW
2010
Australia
Tel: +61 2 9310 3455
Fax: +61 2 9310 3270
Michael Kiely, Managing Director

Services/Products:
Direct marketing agency

Member of:
ADMA

BRETT GOULSTON AND ASSOCIATES
Level 1, 431 Miller Street
Cammeray
NSW
2062
Australia
Tel: +61 2 9460 1888
Fax: +61 2 9460 1988
Email: brett@one.net.au
Brett Goulston, Director

Services/Products:
Advertising Agency; Direct marketing agency

Member of:
ADMA

BRISTOW & PRENTICE PTY LTD RESPONSE ADVERTISING
47 O'Grady Street
Albert Park
VIC
3206
Australia
Tel: +61 3 9682 8199
Fax: +61 3 9682 2575
Email: jan@bristow-prentice.com.au
Jan Mathewson

Services/Products:
Database services; Direct marketing agency; Consultancy services; Direct response TV services; Electronic media; Internet services

E-Services:
Website design

Member of:
ADMA; InterDirect Network

BRISTOW & PRENTICE RESPONSE ADVERTISING
47 O'Grady Street
Albert Park
VIC
3206
Australia
Tel: +61 3 9686 3755
Fax: +61 3 9686 3630
Email: bpresp@labyrinth.net.au
Tony Prentice, Managing Director

Services/Products:
Direct marketing agency

Member of:
ADMA

CALL CENTRE INTEGRITY P/L
PO Box 401
Milsons Point
NSW
1565

Australia
Tel: +61 2 9927 4026
Fax: +61 2 9929 0731
Email: DarleneRichard@
    callcentreintegrity.com
Web:
    www.CallaCentreINTEGRITY.com
Darlene Richard, Managing Director

Services/Products:
Call centre services/systems; Consultancy services; Interactive media; Training/recruitment; Build, rebuild or improve customer response centres for maximum results with integrity; Write workshops/training/white papers/articles/books in industry; Public speaking; Conduct workshops and training for the industry worldwide

E-Services:
E-Marketing consultant

Member of:
DMA (US); National DMA; American & Australian Teleservices Association; National Speakers Association

CAMERON & PARTNERS-INTEGRATED MARKETING SERVICES
5 Mulawa Place
Frenchs Forest
NSW
2086
Australia
Tel: +61 2 9975 2341
Fax: +61 2 9975 4829
Email: dearnec@ip.net.au
Toni Ashley, Senior Account Director

Services/Products:
Direct marketing agency; Consultancy services; Sales promotion agency

Member of:
ADMA

CARLSON MARKETING GROUP
Level 5, 35 Grafton Street
Woollahra
NSW
2025
Australia
Tel: +61 2 9335 5000
Fax: +61 2 9335 5065
Email: mmahoney@carlson.com
Stuart Ford, EVP Sales & Marketing

Services/Products:
Database services; Telemarketing agency; Direct marketing agency

Member of:
ADMA

CARR CLARK RAPP COLLINS
Level 1, 55 Lavender Street
Milsons Point
NSW
2061
Australia
Tel: +61 2 9927 4000
Fax: +61 2 9929 0731
Email: joncla@ccrc.com.au
John Clark

Services/Products:
Fulfilment and sampling house; Database services; Telemarketing agency; Direct marketing agency; Media buying agency

Member of:
ADMA

CARTWRIGHT WILLIAMS PTY LTD
355 Ernest Street
Neutral Bay
Sydney
2089
Australia
Tel: +61 2 9953 8600
Fax: +61 2 9953 8733
Email: centre@cartwill.com.au
Web: www.igenr8.com.au

Services/Products:
Advertising Agency; Call centre services/systems; Mailing/Faxing services; Personalisation; Sales promotion agency; Telemarketing agency

E-Services:
E-Marketing consultant; Website design; Online/e-marketing agency

Member of:
DMA (US); ADMA (Australia)

CDM TELEMARKETING
Suite 2, 15 The Plaza
Lane Cove
NSW
2066
Australia
Tel: +61 2 9936 1900
Fax: +61 2 9418 7571
Phillip Aldwell, General Manager

Services/Products:
Fulfilment and sampling house; Telemarketing agency

Member of:
ADMA

CENTURION MARKETING SERVICES
PO Box 329
Auburn
NSW
2144
Australia
Tel: +61 2 9648 4844
Fax: +61 2 9648 4400
Email: cms@centurion.com.au
Web: www.centurion.com.au
John Edginton, Managing Director

Services/Products:
List services; Database services;
Mailing/Faxing services; Private
delivery services; Data Processing

Member of:
ADMA

CHAMPION PRINT
140 Bourke Road
Alexandria
NSW
2015
Australia
Tel: +61 2 9353 9555
Fax: +61 2 9669 2731
David Dryson, Sales Manager

Services/Products:
Print services; Private delivery services

Member of:
ADMA

CHELSEA IMAGES
PO Box 1142
South Melbourne
VIC
3205
Australia
Tel: +61 3 9646 9555
Fax: +61 3 9646 9566
Email: chelseai@chelseaimages.com.au
Michael Gardner, Director

Services/Products:
Database services; Mailing/Faxing
services; Print services; Data
Processing

Member of:
ADMA

CLEMENGER DIRECT PTY LTD
PO Box 7657
Melbourne
VIC
3004
Australia
Tel: +61 3 9526 2200
Fax: +61 3 9526 2202
Jane Tubb, Managing Director

Services/Products:
Direct marketing agency; Hardware
supplier; Consultancy services

Member of:
DMA (US); ADMA

COHN & WELLS
123 Bouverie Street
Carlton
VIC
3053
Australia
Tel: +61 3 9349 2700
Fax: +61 3 9349 2747
Narelle Allen, Group Account Director

Services/Products:
Database services; Direct marketing
agency; Software supplier;
Consultancy services; Data Processing

E-Services:
Website design

Member of:
ADMA

COMMUNIQUE DIRECT
PO Box 969
Manly
NSW
2095
Australia
Tel: +61 2 9977 3377
Fax: +61 2 9977 3366
David Blythe, Managing Director

Services/Products:
List services; Fulfilment and sampling
house; Mailing/Faxing services;
Telemarketing agency; Direct
marketing agency

COMPRITE DIRECT MARKETING
23 Musgrave Road
Red Hill
QLD
4059
Australia
Tel: +61 7 3839 1866
Fax: +61 7 3839 1966
Email: comprite@ozemail.com.au
Web: www.comprite.com.au
Murray Hopping, Business
Development Manager

Services/Products:
Database services; Direct marketing
agency; Fulfilment and sampling
house; Lettershop; List services;
Mailing/Faxing services; Data
Processing; Internet services

E-Services:
Website design

CONNECT - INTERACTIVE BUSINESS SERVICES
Level 2, 7 Kelly Street
Ultimo
NSW
2007
Australia
Tel: +61 2 9374 3300
Fax: +61 2 9374 3333
Email: joe_tawfic@connect.ibs.com
Web: www.connect-ibs,com
Joe Tawfic, National Business
Development Manager

Services/Products:
Telemarketing agency

Member of:
ADMA

COOMBE TELEPHONE MARKETING PTY LTD
PO Box 4204
Ringwood
VIC
3134
Australia
Tel: +61 3 9830 2553
Fax: +61 3 9830 2333
Email: dorrie_coombe@bigpond.com
Dorothy Coombe, Managing Director

Services/Products:
Telemarketing agency; Training/
recruitment

Member of:
ADMA

CREATIVE MARKETING
Level 4, 21 Goodwood Street
Richmond
VIC
3121
Australia
Tel: +61 3 9426 1126
Fax: +61 3 9426 1215
Email: stephen_carnell@yr.com
Kym McInerney, General Manager

Services/Products:
Direct marketing agency; Consultancy
services; Sales promotion agency

Member of:
ADMA

CUC AUSTRALASIA LIMITED
596 North Road
Ormond
VIC
3204
Australia
Tel: +61 3 9578 5933

Fax: +61 3 9578 5300
Email: cuc@c031.aone.net.au
Web: www.cuc.com.au
Clint Tworney, General Manager -
  Loyalty Services

Services/Products:
Fulfilment and sampling house;
Database services; Telemarketing
agency; Media buying agency;
Consultancy services; Sales promotion
agency; Data Processing

Member of:
ADMA

CURTIS JONES & BROWN DESIGN & PRODUCTION

66 Mullens Street
Balmain
NSW
2041
Australia
Tel: +61 2 9810 5044
Fax: +61 2 9810 5277
Email: mlis@ozemail.com.au
Marek Lis, Director of Direct
  Marketing

Services/Products:
Advertising Agency; Direct marketing
agency

Member of:
ADMA

CW DATABASE SERVICES

355 Ernest St
Neutral Bay
NSW
2089
Australia
Tel: +61 2 9904 1433
Fax: +61 2 9953 8577
Email: alastairm@cwdata.com.au
Web: www.cwdata.com.au
Alastair MacDonald, General Manager

Services/Products:
Database services; Software supplier;
Data Processing

Member of:
ADMA

DATA CONNECTION

264 Normanby Road
South Melbourne
VIC
3205
Australia
Tel: +61 3 9646 4622
Fax: +61 3 9646 5563
Marc Marantz, Managing Director

Services/Products:
Fulfilment and sampling house;
Database services; Mailing/Faxing
services; Telemarketing agency; Print
services; Data Processing

Member of:
ADMA

DATA REFERENCE LIBRARY PTY LTD

14 Valleyfield Court, Unit 1
Wattle Grove
NSW
2173
Australia
Tel: +61 2 9825 6734
Fax: +61 2 9825 4800
Email: drlib@ozemail.com.au
Web: www.ozemail.com.au/-drlib
Darryl Robertson, Managing Director

Services/Products:
List services

Member of:
ADMA

DATABASE CONSULTANTS AUSTRALIA (DCA)

Level 1, 61–63 Wellington Street
Windsor
VIC
3181
Australia
Tel: +61 3 9525 1777
Fax: +61 3 9525 1700
Email: dca@weple.mira.net.au
Web: www.data.com.au
Brendan Morter, Managing Director

Services/Products:
Database services; Hardware supplier;
Software supplier; Data Processing

Member of:
ADMA

DATABASE MARKETING SOLUTIONS PTY LTD

Suite 9
17–19 Knox St
DOUBLE BAY
NSW
2068
Australia
Tel: +61 2 9362 1666
Fax: +61 2 9362 1677
Email: mail@dmsnet.com.au
Web: www.dmsnet.com.au

Services/Products:
Call centre services/systems; Database
services; List services; Mail order
company; Software supplier; Training/
recruitment

E-Services:
Email list provider; Website design;
Email software

Member of:
ADMA

DIBBS CROWTHER & OSBORNE

Level 13, 50 Carrington Street
Sydney
NSW
2000
Australia
Tel: +61 2 9290 8200
Fax: +61 2 9290 2964
Email: mail@dco.com.au
Peter Ludemann, Partner

Services/Products:
Legal services

Member of:
ADMA

DIBSDALL WEEKES & ROSS

PO Box 317
Neutral Bay
NSW
2089
Australia
Tel: +61 2 9957 3876
Fax: +61 2 9955 0739
Email: admin@dwr.www.com.au
Web: www.dwr.www.com.au
Louise Ross, Consultant

Services/Products:
Training/recruitment

Member of:
ADMA

DIRECT CONNECT

Level 2, 35 Chandos Street
St Leonards
NSW
2065
Australia
Tel: +61 2 9936 9988
Fax: +61 2 9936 9999
Email: directconnect@dct.com.au
Bob Westcott, General Manager

Services/Products:
Telemarketing agency; Training/
recruitment; Software supplier

Member of:
ADMA

DIRECT INTENT MARKETING

PO Box 47
Waterloo
NSW
2017
Australia

Tel: +61 130 030 1036
Fax: +61 02 9313 4240
Email: infodial@infodial.com.au
Web: www.infodial@infodial.com.au
Richard Thomas, General Manager

Services/Products:
Fulfilment and sampling house;
Database services; Mailing/Faxing
services; Telemarketing agency; Media
buying agency

Member of:
ADMA

DIRECT MAIL SERVICES PTY LTD
PO Box 284
Mascot
NSW
2020
Australia
Tel: +61 2 9669 3222
Fax: +61 2 9669 5702
Colin Stoffberg, Managing Director

Services/Products:
Fulfilment and sampling house;
Database services; Mailing/Faxing
services; Print services; Labelling/
envelope services; Data Processing

Member of:
ADMA

DIRECT MARKETING SERVICES PTY LTD
Locked Bag No 1
Cremorne Junction
NSW
2090
Australia
Tel: +61 2 9909 2377
Fax: +61 2 9909 8421
Barbie Davis, Director

Services/Products:
Direct marketing agency

Member of:
ADMA

DIRECT MARKETING SOFTWARE
PO Box 1266
Toowong
QLD
4066
Australia
Tel: +61 7 3878 3003
Fax: +61 7 3878 3481
Email: bill@dmsw.com.au
Web: www.dmsw.com.au
Bill Elston, Sales & Marketing Manager

Services/Products:
Consultancy services; Database
services; Software supplier; Service
bureau

Member of:
National DMA

DIRECT MEDIA PTY. LTD.
Level 2
18 Gibbs Street
Miranda
NSW
2228
Australia
Tel: +61 2 9525 5266
Fax: +61 2 9525 5299
Email: lists@directmedia.com.au
Web: www.directmedia.com.au

Services/Products:
Catalogue producer; Consultancy
services; List services; Email
transmissions

E-Services:
Email list provider

Member of:
DMA (US); Australian Direct
Marketing Association

DK MARKETING LTD
4/65 Upton Street
Bundall
QLD
4217
Australia
Tel: +61 7 5539 8911
Fax: +61 7 5539 8903
Email: dk@worldlink.com.au
David Kennedy, Director

Services/Products:
Direct marketing agency

Member of:
FEDMA

DMC DIRECT PRINT SOLUTIONS
Suite 5, 225 Whitehorse Road
Balwyn
VIC
3103
Australia
Tel: +61 3 9888 4522
Fax: +61 3 9888 4359
Email: dmc@dmcprint.com.au
Dino DiPierdomenico, Director

Services/Products:
Print services; Labelling/envelope
services

Member of:
ADMA

DOOLEY DYNAMICS PTY LTD
99 Elanora Road
Elanora Heights
NSW
2101
Australia
Tel: +61 2 9970 7444
Fax: +61 2 9970 7555
Email: dooleydy@ozemail.com.au
Cheryl Dooley, Managing Director

Services/Products:
Telemarketing agency; Consultancy
services

Member of:
ADMA

DOUBLE CLICK
Suite 12, 56–62 Chandos St
St Leonards
NSW
2065
Australia
Tel: +61 2 9906 5111
Fax: +61 2 9906 2718
Clare Plenaar, Director

Services/Products:
Direct marketing agency; Consultancy
services; Design/graphics/clip art
supplier; Catalogue producer;
Electronic media; Internet services

E-Services:
Website design

DRAKE LIST MANAGEMENT
Level 31, 55 Collins Street
Melbourne
VIC
3000
Australia
Tel: +61 3 9245 0343
Fax: +61 3 9245 0217
Email: dlm@drake.com.au
Web: www.drakelist.com.au
Janine Cleaves, Manager

Services/Products:
List services

Member of:
ADMA

DTMS - DESKTOP MARKETING SYSTEMS PTY LTD
87 Willsmere Road
Kew
VIC
3101
Australia
Tel: +61 3 9853 2500
Fax: +61 3 9853 9499
Email: salesin@dtms.com.au
Web: www.dtms.com.au
Debbie Scibor, Administration

Services/Products:
List services; Direct marketing agency;
Software supplier

Member of:
ADMA

DUN & BRADSTREET MARKETING PTY LTD
19 Havilah Street
Chatswood
NSW
2057
Australia
Tel: +61 2 9935 2600
Fax: +61 2 9935 2777
Email:
  information@dbmarketing.com.au
Web: www.dbmarketing.com.au
Chris Pellegrinetti, General Manager

Services/Products:
List services; Database services;
Consultancy services

Member of:
ADMA

E. S. WIGG & SON PTY LTD
79 Port Road
Thebarton
SA
5031
Australia
Tel: +61 8 8416 8888
Fax: +61 8 8352 1905
Tom Davidson, Sales Manager

Services/Products:
Print services; Labelling/envelope
services

Member of:
ADMA

ECHO DIRECT MARKETING
4–16 Yurong Street
East Sydney
NSW
2010
Australia
Tel: +61 2 9332 0150
Fax: +61 2 9332 0151
David Evans, Managing Partner

Services/Products:
Advertising Agency; Direct marketing
agency

Member of:
ADMA

ENVELOPE SPECIALISTS
PO Box 1339, Distribution Centre
Osborne Park
WA
6916

Australia
Tel: +61 8 9445 3077
Fax: +61 8 9445 1627
Email: ismail@ca.com.au
Rodney Chapman, Manager

Services/Products:
Labelling/envelope services

Member of:
ADMA

EURO R S C G PARTNERSHIP
Level 12, 60 Miller Street
North Sydney
NSW
2060
Australia
Tel: +61 2 9963 7711
Fax: +61 2 9922 5864
Email: manager@euroscg.com.au
Web: www.euroscg.com.au
Malcolm Auld, General Manager

Services/Products:
Database services; Telemarketing
agency; Direct marketing agency;
Media buying agency; Sales promotion
agency

Member of:
ADMA

EWA AUSTRALIA PTY LTD
5 Helen Street
Heidelberg
WEST VIC
3081
Australia
Tel: +61 3 9459 4472
Fax: +61 3 9459 9008
Email: ewa@ewa.com.au
Brett Jakes, Managing Director

Services/Products:
Fulfilment and sampling house;
Database services; Mailing/Faxing
services; Telemarketing agency; Data
Processing

Member of:
ADMA

FINEX INTEGRATED COMMUNICATIONS
Level 4, 69 Christie Street
St Leonards
NSW
2065
Australia
Tel: +61 2 9436 2044
Fax: +61 2 9437 5103
Email: ray_aspey@au.finexgroup.com
Web: www.finexgroup.com
Jonathan Knight, Group Account
  Director

Services/Products:
Direct marketing agency; Media
buying agency; Data Processing

E-Services:
Website design

Member of:
ADMA

FNL DIRECT
113 Union Street
North Sydney
NSW
2060
Australia
Tel: +61 2 9922 7611
Fax: +61 2 9922 7889
Web: www.fnl.com.au
Bill Paddis, Account Director

Services/Products:
Direct marketing agency; Sales
promotion agency; Consultancy
services

Member of:
ADMA

FOUR TRADE ONLY DIRECT MAIL & PRINT PTY LTD
Sandown Square - Factory 6, 56 Smith
Street
Springvale
VIC
3171
Australia
Tel: +61 3 9547 4611
Fax: +61 3 9546 1993
Email:
  four_trade_only@cO31.aone.net.au
Chris Glasgow, Managing Director

Services/Products:
Database services; Mailing/Faxing
services; Print services; Labelling/
envelope services; Data Processing

Member of:
ADMA

FOXY ADVERTISING
PO Box 1217
Strawberry Hills
NSW
2016
Australia
Tel: +61 2 9319 1571
Fax: +61 2 9319 6253
Email: foxy@speednet.com
Peter Fox, Director

Services/Products:
Direct marketing agency

Member of:
ADMA

FREEHILL HOLLLINGDALE & PAGE
GPO Box 128a
Melbourne
VIC
3000
Australia
Tel: +61 3 9288 1234
Fax: +61 3 9288 1567
Stephanie Edwards, Marketing
Manager

Services/Products:
Legal services

Member of:
ADMA

GALLAGHERS
Unit 3, 1–3 Burrows Road
St Peters
NSW
2044
Australia
Tel: +61 2 9565 4355
Fax: +61 2 9557 0984
Email: gimg@acay.com.au
Geoff O'Hare, Sales Manager

Services/Products:
Database services; Mailing/Faxing
services; Print services; Private delivery
services; Labelling/envelope services;
Data Processing

Member of:
ADMA

GEORGE PATTERSON BATES
PO Box 941
North Sydney
NSW
2059
Australia
Tel: +61 2 9778 7100
Fax: +61 2 9778 7589
Email: gpbates.com.au
Ian Kennedy, National Director of
Direct Marketing

Services/Products:
Direct marketing agency

Member of:
ADMA

GEOSPEND PTY LTD
Level 4, 123 Lonsdale Street
Melbourne
VIC
3000
Australia
Tel: +61 3 9650 5111
Fax: +61 3 9650 3777
Email: graeme@geospend.ccmail.
compuserve.com
Graeme Neville, Managing Director

Services/Products:
Software supplier; Data Processing

Member of:
ADMA

GMS FULFILMENT SERVICES LIMITED
Private Box 537
Alexandria
NSW
2015
Australia
Tel: +61 2 9381 1555
Fax: +61 2 9381 1550
Email: fulfil@ozemail.com.au
Gavin McCann, General Manager

Services/Products:
Fulfilment and sampling house;
Database services; Mailing/Faxing
services; Telemarketing agency

Member of:
ADMA

GRANTLEY COGZELL BENN
PO Box 556
Brisbane Roma Street Private Boxes
QLD
4003
Australia
Tel: +61 7 3236 2126
Fax: +61 7 3236 2130
Email: ideas@grantley.com.au
Keith Cogzell, Director

Services/Products:
Advertising Agency; Direct marketing
agency

Member of:
ADMA

HEDLEY GARNER PTY LTD
PO Box 188
St Leonards
NSW
2065
Australia
Tel: +61 2 9906 4888
Fax: +61 2 9906 4006
Email: hedley@sbgroup.com.au
Bernard Hedley, Managing Director

Services/Products:
Consultancy services

Member of:
ADMA

HELEN HILL & ASSOCIATES
Level 6, 88 Walker Street
North Sydney
NSW
2060
Australia
Tel: +61 2 9923 2999
Fax: +61 2 9923 2933
Email: hha@tpgi.com.au
Web: www.savel.com.au/
HILL&ASSOC.html
Helen Hill, Managing Director

Services/Products:
Training/recruitment

Member of:
ADMA

HERO COMMUNICATIONS PTY LTD
108 Miller Street
Pyrmont
NSW
2009
Australia
Tel: +61 2 9552 3377
Fax: +61 2 9552 3490
Email: simonf@herocomm.com.au
Web: www.herocomm.com.au
Simon Fitch, Managing Director

Services/Products:
Advertising Agency; Direct marketing
agency; Sales promotion agency

Member of:
ADMA

HOGAN MARKETING SERVICES
Lvl 10
33 Bligh Street
Sydney
NSW
2000
Australia
Tel: +61 2 9207 3600
Fax: +61 2 9207 3500
Email: info@hoganmarketing.com.au
Web:
www.hoganmarketing.com.au

Services/Products:
Call centre services/systems

E-Services:
Online/e-marketing agency

Member of:
National DMA; Australian Telemarke
Association

IBM AUSTRALIA LIMITED
PO Box 400
Pennant Hills
NSW
2120
Australia
Tel: +61 2 9354 7799
Fax: +61 2 9354 4036
Email: willson@au1.ibm.com

Web: www.ibm.com.au
Mark Willson, General Manager Direct
  Marketing

Services/Products:
Database services; Hardware supplier;
Software supplier; Consultancy
services; Data Processing

E-Services:
Website design

Member of:
ADMA

INTEGRATED MAILING
   SERVICES
4 Tullamarine Park Road
Tullamarine
VIC
3043
Australia
Tel: +61 3 9291 5888
Fax: +61 3 9291 5877
Email: mail@integratedmailing.com.au
Buzz Borsitzky, Managing Director

Services/Products:
List services; Fulfilment and sampling
house; Database services; Mailing/
Faxing services; Labelling/envelope
services; Data Processing

Member of:
ADMA

INTEGRATED OPTIONS
71–73 Alexander street
Crows Nest
NSW
2065
Australia
Tel: +61 2 9906 4488
Fax: +61 2 9906 5454
Email: options@options.com.au
Web: www.ioptions.com.au
David Coney, Group Account Director

Services/Products:
Direct marketing agency; Sales
promotion agency

Member of:
ADMA

J. S. MCMILLAN PTY LTD
24 Carter Street
Lidcombe
NSW
2141
Australia
Tel: +61 2 9748 4444
Fax: +61 2 9648 4407
Email: jsm1@hutch.com.au
Web: www.jsmcmillan.com.au
George Collins, Group Sales &
  Marketing Manager

Services/Products:
Consultancy services

E-Services:
Website design

Member of:
ADMA

JMG MARKETING (AUST) PTY
   LTD
PO Box 8489, Perth Business
Centre
Perth
WA
6849
Australia
Tel: +61 9 8422 4224
Fax: +61 9 8227 1968
Email: jim@jmg.com.au
Web: www.jmg.com.au
James Tabor, Direct Marketing
  Manager

Services/Products:
List services; Database services;
Telemarketing agency; Direct
marketing agency; Consultancy
services

Member of:
ADMA

JWT DIALOG
140 Sussex Street
Sydney
NSW
2000
Australia
Tel: +61 2 9394 2222
Fax: +61 2 9394 2299
Email: syd-2000@jwt.com.au
Andrew Linklater, General Manager

Services/Products:
Direct marketing agency; Consultancy
services

E-Services:
Website design

Member of:
DMA (US); ADMA

KDM DIRECT MARKETING
Level 2, 38 Richardson Street
West Perth
WA
6005
Australia
Tel: +61 8 9481 7511
Fax: +61 8 9481 4886
Email: kdmlists@ozemail.com.au
Teresa Kovaloff, Manager

Services/Products:
List services; Database services;
Telemarketing agency; Direct
marketing agency; Market research
agency; Direct response TV services

Member of:
ADMA

KDS PRINT MANAGEMENT
   PTY LTD
10 Lone Pine Place
North Balgowlah
NSW
2093
Australia
Tel: +61 2 9948 8721
Fax: +61 2 9907 6371
Email: kdsprint@compuserve.com
Web: www.ourworld.compuserve.com/
  homepages/kdsprint
Kathryn Shearsby, Director

Services/Products:
Consultancy services

Member of:
ADMA

KENNEDY PACIFIC
PO Box 7700. Gold Coast Mail Centre
Bundall
QLD
4217
Australia
Tel: +61 0 7553 98911
Fax: +61 075 538 9903
Mike Dowling, Business Development
  Manager

Services/Products:
Mailing/Faxing services; Print services

Member of:
ADMA

KORATOR PTY LTD
Ground Floor, 131 Canberra Avenue
Canberra
ACT
2601
Australia
Tel: +61 0 6295 0777
Fax: +61 06 295 1577
Web: www.imageword.com
Richard Melouney, Chief Executive
  Officer

Services/Products:
Software supplier

E-Services:
Website design

Member of:
ADMA

LAVENDER DIRECT
Level 19, 60 Margaret Street
Sydney
NSW
2000
Australia
Tel: +61 2 9240 5580
Fax: +61 2 9240 5588
Web: www.lavender.com.au
Will Lavender, Managing Director

Services/Products:
Direct marketing agency

Member of:
ADMA

LEO BURNETT CONNAGHAN & MAY
73 Miller Street
North Sydney
NSW
2060
Australia
Tel: +61 2 9925 3555
Fax: +61 2 9957 2152
Email:
  jeff_sanders@syd.leoburnett.com.au
Jeffrey Sanders, Head of Direct
  Marketing

Services/Products:
Advertising Agency; Database services;
Direct marketing agency; Media
buying agency; Sales promotion
agency

E-Services:
Website design

Member of:
ADMA

LINDA LOOSE MARKETING & COMMUNICATIONS
50 St Vincent Place North
Albert Park
VIC
3206
Australia
Tel: +61 3 9690 2855
Fax: +61 3 9690 0782
Email: lloose@world.net
Linda Loose, Principal

Services/Products:
Consultancy services

Member of:
DMA (US); ADMA

LINTAS DIRECT
65 Berry Street
North Sydney
NSW
2060
Australia
Tel: +61 2 9925 1700
Fax: +61 2 9957 5222
Email: lintas.linaus.gardnerc@
  linasiap.attmail.com
Christine Gardner, General Manager

Services/Products:
Advertising Agency; Direct marketing
agency; Sales promotion agency;
Consultancy services

Member of:
ADMA

LIST SOLUTIONS – A DIVISION OF APN BUSINESS MAGAZINES PTY LTD
46–50 Porter Street
Prahran
VIC
3181
Australia
Tel: +61 3 9245 7649
Fax: +61 3 9245 7606
Email: sbeitzel@mktg.apnsp.net.au
Stephenie Bietzel, General Manager -
  Marketing Services & Circulation

Services/Products:
List services

Member of:
ADMA

LISTBROKERS AUSTRALIA PTY LTD
PO Box 52
Spit Junction
NSW
2088
Australia
Tel: +61 2 9969 2922
Fax: +61 2 9960 4936
Email: lists@tmlc.com
Web: www.tmlc.com
Caroline Gracie, General Manager

Services/Products:
List services

Member of:
ADMA

M & C SAATCHI DIRECT
131 Macquarie Street
Sydney
NSW
2000
Australia
Tel: +61 2 9270 2732
Fax: +61 2 9270 2731
Email: mercern@mccaatchi.com
Web: www.mcsaatchi.com.au
Nick Mercer, General Manager

Services/Products:
Database services; Telemarketing
agency; Direct marketing agency;
Consultancy services

Member of:
ADMA

MAIL MARKETING WORKS PTY LTD
Building 2, 2 Orion Road
Lane Cove
NSW
2066
Australia
Tel: +61 2 9427 1555
Fax: +61 2 9427 7061
Tony Mineo, Customer Relations
  Manager

Services/Products:
Database services; Mailing/Faxing
services; Print services; Labelling/
envelope services; Data Processing

Member of:
ADMA

MAILCARE SYSTEMS PTY LTD
PO Box 600
Moorabbin
VIC
3189
Australia
Tel: +61 3 9553 5533
Fax: +61 3 9553 5566
Email: mailcare@main.starnet.com.au
Web: www.mailcare.com.au
Mark D. Thompson, General Manager

Services/Products:
Fulfilment and sampling house;
Database services; Mailing/Faxing
services; Data Processing

Member of:
ADMA

MAILING AND PRINT SERVICES PTY LTD
8 Aquatic Drive
Frenchs Forest
NSW
2086
Australia
Tel: +61 2 9451 6433
Fax: +61 2 9451 3338
Email: sales@mailandprint.com.au
Bruce Meers, Managing Director

Services/Products:
Database services; Mailing/Faxing
services; Labelling/envelope services;
Catalogue producer

Member of:
ADMA

MANCHESTER HOLDINGS PTY LTD
GPO Box 1104
Brisbane
QLD
4001
Australia
Tel: +61 73229 6611
Fax: +61 7 3229 6974
Email: michaelt@manchester-holdings.com.au
Web: www.manchester-holdings.com.au
Michael Temperton, Chief Executive Officer

Services/Products:
List services; Fulfilment and sampling house; Database services; Mailing/Faxing services; Direct marketing agency; Data Processing; Internet services

E-Services:
Website design

Member of:
DMA (US); ADMA

MARKET MOVEMENTS (ASIA PACIFIC) PTY LTD
PO Box 382
Northbridge
WA
6865
Australia
Tel: +61 8 9328 8060
Fax: +61 8 9328 8075
Email: lisamoyle@compuserve.com
Lisa Moyle, Customer Service Manager

Services/Products:
Market research agency

Member of:
ADMA

MARKETABILITY
Level 9, 409 St Kilda Road
Melbourne
VIC
3004
Australia
Tel: +61 3 9696 3505
Fax: +61 3 9696 0533
Email: market.net@c031.aone.net.au
Rod Curnow, Managing Director

Services/Products:
Database services; Direct marketing agency; Media buying agency; Media buying agency; Consultancy services

E-Services:
Website design

Member of:
ADMA

MARKETBASE DIRECT SYSTEMS
PO Box R103
Royal Exchange
NSW
2000
Australia
Tel: +61 2 9232 1777
Fax: +61 2 9232 1118
Email: marketbase@s054.aone.net.au
Sharon Belfer, Sales Manager

Services/Products:
Database services; Software supplier; Consultancy services; Data Processing

Member of:
ADMA

MARKETING 1:1 PTY LTD
PO Box 163
New Farm
QLD
4005
Australia
Tel: +61 7 3252 9841
Fax: +61 7 3252 1344
Alana Pelly, Director

Services/Products:
Consultancy services

Member of:
ADMA

MARKETING DATABASE SYSTEMS PTY LIMITED
44 Bay Street
Ultimo
NSW
2007
Australia
Tel: +61 2 9264 3155
Fax: +61 2 9233 7009
Email: sales@mds.com.au
Web: www.mds.com.au
Anthony Hing, Director Business Development

Services/Products:
Fulfilment and sampling house; Database services; Software supplier; Consultancy services; Call centre services/systems; Data Processing

Member of:
ADMA

MARKETING ORIENTATIONS
PO Box 1999
Strawberry Hills
NSW
2012
Australia
Tel: +61 2 9360 5855
Fax: +61 2 9360 5848
Email: 100232.1547@compuserve.com
Web: www.incet@zip.com.au
Tony Johnson, Director

Services/Products:
List services

Member of:
ADMA

MAYNARD'S PROMO MARKETING AUSTRALIA
Level 1, 42–44 Albany Street
St Leonards
NSW
2065
Australia
Tel: +61 2 9438 3755
Fax: +61 2 9906 1424
Email: promo-marketing@maynards.com.au
Roger Maynard, Director

Services/Products:
Direct marketing agency; Media buying agency; Sales promotion agency

Member of:
ADMA

MICHAEL PAGE MARKETING
Level 19, 1 York Street
Sydney
NSW
2000
Australia
Tel: +61 2 9254 0300
Fax: +61 2 9254 0333
Email: mpm.syd@mpage.com.au
Amanda Perille, Director

Services/Products:
Training/recruitment

Member of:
ADMA

MICROMATCH PTY LTD
PO Box 220
Brookvale
NSW
2100
Australia
Tel: +61 2 9941 1111
Fax: +61 2 9905 4638
Email: bevan@micromatch.com.au
Web: www.micromatch.com.au
Terese Alsford, Account Manager

Services/Products:
Fulfilment and sampling house;
Database services; Mailing/Faxing
services; Telemarketing agency; Data
Processing

Member of:
ADMA

MORGAN & BANKS LTD
Level 11, Grosvenor Place, 225 George
Street
Sydney
NSW
2000
Australia
Tel: +61 2 9256 0333
Fax: +61 2 9251 3975
Email:
    b.randall@morganbanks.com.au
Web: www.morganbanks.com.au
Brian Randall, Consultant

Services/Products:
Training/recruitment

Member of:
ADMA

MORRISSEY MALCOLM DIRECT MARKETING
5 Dene Street
Mt Lawley
WA
6050
Australia
Tel: +61 8 9271 2752
Fax: +61 8 9271 2752
Peter Morrissey, Managing Director

Services/Products:
Telemarketing agency

Member of:
ADMA

MOS DATA ASSEMBLY SPECIALISTS PTY LTD
Level 3, 414–418 Elizabeth Street
Surry Hills
NSW
2010
Australia
Tel: +61 2 9211 7155
Fax: +61 2 9211 8362
Email: sales@mosdata.com.au
David Webb, Sales Director

Services/Products:
Advertising Agency; List services;
Database services; Telemarketing
agency; Data Processing

Member of:
ADMA

MULTINET SYSTEMS PTY LTD
PO Box 351
Artarmon
NSW
2064
Australia
Tel: +61 2 9433 5299
Fax: +61 2 9906 3950
Web: www.multinet.com.au
Julie Brook, General Manager

Services/Products:
Fulfilment and sampling house;
Database services; Mailing/Faxing
services; Telemarketing agency;
Hardware supplier; Data Processing

Member of:
ADMA

OFFSET ALPINE PRINTING LTD
42 Boorea Street
Lidcombe
NSW
2141
Australia
Tel: +61 2 9704 4444
Fax: +61 2 9704 4400
Email: sales@offsetalpine.com.au
Ted Brooke, Sales Manager

Services/Products:
Print services; Catalogue producer

Member of:
ADMA

OGILVY & MATHER DIRECT
132 Arthur Street
North Sydney
NSW
2060
Australia
Tel: +61 2 9922 4055
Fax: +61 2 9954 0787
Email: lisa.lee@ogilvy.com
Lisa Lee, General Manager

Services/Products:
Direct marketing agency; Consultancy
services

E-Services:
Website design

Member of:
ADMA

OPTEL RESEARCH
PO Box 252
Dee Why
NSW
2099
Australia
Tel: +61 2 9971 4994

Fax: +61 2 9971 1672
Susan Griffith, Manager

Services/Products:
Telemarketing agency; Training/
recruitment

Member of:
ADMA ·

ORTEGA PUBLISHING PTY LTD
11 Grosvenor Street
Neutral Bay
NSW
2089
Australia
Tel: +61 2 9904 0877
Fax: +61 2 9904 8789
Email: tom@ortega.com.au
Tom Greene, Director

Services/Products:
Catalogue producer; Database
services; Direct marketing agency;
Print services; Publisher

Member of:
National DMA; ADMA

PAC-RIM DIRECT
33 Browns Road
Clayton
VIC
3168
Australia
Tel: +61 3 9544 7733
Fax: +61 3 9543 3613
Trevor Hall, National Sales Manager

Services/Products:
Mailing/Faxing services; Consultancy
services; Private delivery services

Member of:
ADMA

PACIFIC MICROMARKETING
38 Walsh Street
Melbourne
VIC
3000
Australia
Tel: +61 3 9329 6488
Fax: +61 3 9329 6489
Email: pacmic@pacmicro.com.au
Web: www.pmpcomm.com.au
Bronwyn Davie, Group Development
    Manager

Services/Products:
List services; Database services;
Software supplier; Consultancy
services; Data Processing

Member of:
ADMA

PERMAIL PTY LTD
Unit 1/706 Mowbray Road
Lane Cove
NSW
2066
Australia
Tel: +61 2 9424 3200
Fax: +61 2 9427 7400
Email: permail1@mpx.co.au
Sean Burgess, Sales Manager

Services/Products:
List services; Fulfilment and sampling
house; Database services; Mailing/
Faxing services; Private delivery
services; Data Processing

Member of:
DMA (US); ADMA

**PETER HOY & ASSOCIATES
   PTY LTD**
218 West Street
Crows Nest
NSW
2065
Australia
Tel: +61 2 9964 9990
Fax: +61 2 9964 9959
Email: peterhoy@ozemail.com.au
Jennifer Talbot, Snr Account Director

Services/Products:
Advertising Agency; Direct marketing
agency; Media buying agency; Sales
promotion agency

Member of:
DMA (US); ADMA

**PHEONIX CREATIVE
   SERVICES**
3 Ryde Road
Hunters Hill
NSW
2110
Australia
Tel: +61 2 9816 1666
Fax: +61 2 9879 7360
Email: pheonixcs@5054.aone.net.au
Carolina Peters, Principal

Services/Products:
Direct marketing agency; Advertising
Agency

Member of:
ADMA

**POMEROY FRERE THOMAS
   PTY LTD**
Level 1, 2A Glen Street
Milsons Point
NSW
2061
Australia
Tel: +61 2 9959 4705

Fax: +61 2 9925 0092
Email: allpft@ozemail.com.au
Grant Pomeroy, Managing Director

Services/Products:
Direct marketing agency

Member of:
ADMA

POST DATA
46 Frobisher Street
Osborne Park
WA
6017
Australia
Tel: +61 8 9242 3777
Fax: +61 8 9242 2677
Email: postdata@compuserve.com
Peter Milner, Director

Services/Products:
Fulfilment and sampling house;
Database services; Mailing/Faxing
services; Print services; Hardware
supplier; Private delivery services; Data
Processing

Member of:
ADMA

PRIME PROSPECTS PTY LTD
Level 1, 142–144 Gertrude Street
Fitzroy
VIC
3065
Australia
Tel: +61 3 9415 8500
Fax: +61 3 9415 8505
Email: prime@pplm.com.au
Veta Tandora, Director

Services/Products:
List services

Member of:
ADMA

**PROFESSIONAL DIRECT
   MARKETING PTY LTD**
7 Jeays Street
Bowen Hills
QLD
4006
Australia
Tel: +61 7 3252 1180
Fax: +61 7 3252 9841
Email: pdma@powerup.com.au
Web: www.powerup.com.au/pdm
Kevin Hodges, Director

Services/Products:
List services; Database services;
Telemarketing agency; Consultancy
services

Member of:
ADMA

**PROGRESS PRINTERS &
   DISTRIBUTORS**
PO Box 913
Lliverpool
NSW
2170
Australia
Tel: +61 2 9828 1400
Fax: +61 2 9828 1431
Garry Norris, Managing Director
   Distribution

Services/Products:
Print services; Private delivery services;
Mailing/Faxing services

Member of:
ADMA

**QM INDUSTRIES (QLD) PTY
   LTD**
375 Montague Road
West End
QLD
4101
Australia
Tel: +61 7 3844 2244
Fax: +61 7 3844 1829
Email: qmiqid@tpgi.com.au
Richard Sloan, General Manager

Services/Products:
Fulfilment and sampling house;
Database services; Mailing/Faxing
services; Print services; Consultancy
services

Member of:
ADMA

**QUALITY IMAGES AUSTRALIA
   PTY LTD**
23 Leeds Street
Rhodes
NSW
2138
Australia
Tel: +61 2 9743 3499
Fax: +61 2 9743 4078
Paul Canty, Managing Director

Services/Products:
Print services

Member of:
ADMA

**RAPP COLLINS WORLDWIDE
   PTY LTD**
Level 4, 615 St Kilda Road
Melbourne
VIC
3004
Australia
Tel: +61 3 9510 3899
Fax: +61 3 9510 9134
Andrew Hume, General Manager

Services/Products:
Advertising Agency; Direct marketing
agency; Sales promotion agency;
Consultancy services

E-Services:
Website design

Member of:
ADMA

RED-LINE CREATIVE
Level 2, 263 Liverpool Street
East Sydney
NSW
2010
Australia
Tel: +61 2 9380 6055
Fax: +61 2 9380 6181
Email: redline@mypostbox.com
Trevor Hallewell, Managing Director

Services/Products:
Direct marketing agency

Member of:
ADMA

REMARK ASIA PACIFIC PTY LTD
Level 8, 99 Walker Street
North Sydney
NSW
2060
Australia
Tel: +61 2 9955 5488
Fax: +61 2 9955 0525
Email: rfm@ozemail.com.au
Stuart Dickson, General Manager

Services/Products:
Consultancy services

Member of:
ADMA

RETURNITY PTY LTD
#8/44 Bridge Street
Sydney
NSW
2000
Australia
Tel: +61 2 8 213 3000
Fax: +61 2 8 213 3030
Email: info@returnity.com.au
Web: www.returnity.com.au
L Copeland-Smith, Marketing
Director

Services/Products:
Email marketing

E-Services:
Online/e-marketing agency; E-
Marketing consultant

Member of:
ADMA

RGS COMMUNICATIONS
Level 3, Norwich House, 509 St Kilda
Road
Melbourne
VIC
3000
Australia
Tel: +61 3 9820 2755
Fax: +61 3 9821 4404
Email: rgs@rgscomms.com.au
Annie McDonald, Manager-Direct
Marketing

Services/Products:
Advertising Agency; Direct marketing
agency

Member of:
ADMA

RNR INTERNATIONAL MARKETING GROUP
Level 7, 33 Berry Street
North Sydney
NSW
2060
Australia
Tel: +61 2 9937 4567
Fax: +61 2 9937 4500
Email: mail@rnr.com.au
Web: www.mr.com.au
Linda McLean, Account Services
Director

Services/Products:
Fulfilment and sampling house;
Database services; Telemarketing
agency; Direct marketing agency;
Consultancy services; Data Processing

E-Services:
Website design

Member of:
ADMA

ROBE-JOHN & ASSOCIATES PTY LTD
15 Central Boulevard
Port Melbourne
VIC
3207
Australia
Tel: +61 3 9646 0666
Fax: +61 3 9646 0777
Email: robejohn@netspace.net.au
Ray Martin, Account Manager

Services/Products:
Direct marketing agency

Member of:
ADMA

ROBERTSON LEO BURNETT PTY LTD
2F, 99 Frome Street
Adelaide
SA
5000
Australia
Tel: +61 8 8306 0111
Fax: +61 8 8359 2360
Email: arobrib@ozemail.com.au
Serge Petrucco, Marketing Director

Services/Products:
Advertising Agency

Member of:
ADMA

SAATCHI & SAATCHI DIRECT
70 George Steeet
The Rocks
NSW
2000
Australia
Tel: +61 2 9230 0222
Fax: +61 2 9258 3822
Paul Gould, General Manager

Services/Products:
Direct marketing agency

Member of:
ADMA

SALMAT PTY LTD
Head Office, 152 Miller Road
Chester Hill
NSW
2162
Australia
Tel: +61 2 9724 0155
Fax: +61 2 9726 9895
Email: marketing@salmat.com.au
Peter Boyle, General Manager

Services/Products:
Fulfilment and sampling house;
Mailing/Faxing services; Private
delivery services

Member of:
DMA (US); FEDMA; ADMA

SAS INSTITUTE
Private Bag 52
Lane Cove
NSW
2066
Australia
Tel: +61 2 9428 0428
Fax: +61 2 9418 7211
Email: info@oz.sas.com
Web: www.sas.com
Havovi Bonshahi, Marketing
Communications Manager

Services/Products:
Database services; Software supplier

Member of:
ADMA

SG MARKETING PTY LTD
PO Box 7278, St Kilda Road
Melbourne
VIC
3004
Australia
Tel: +61 3 9820 2171
Fax: +61 3 9820 0977
Email:
    simmgroup@onaustralia.com.au
Ian Simm, Managing Director

Services/Products:
Direct marketing agency

Member of:
ADMA

SHARP & ANDERSON PTY LTD
Level 14, 109 Pitt Street
Sydney
NSW
2000
Australia
Tel: +61 2 9223 9322
Fax: +61 2 9223 9388
Email: sa.sydney@s054.aone.net.au
Adrian Ewart, Senior Consultant

Services/Products:
Database services; Consultancy
services

Member of:
ADMA

SHORTER DIRECT (WA)
Suite 42, Plaistowe Mews
West Perth
WA
6005
Australia
Tel: +61 8 9321 8154
Fax: +61 8 9324 1407
Email: email@shorter.com.au
Web: www.shorter.com.au
Tina Agnew, Marketing Manager

Services/Products:
Database services; Telemarketing
agency; Direct marketing agency;
Media buying agency; Consultancy
services

E-Services:
Website design

Member of:
ADMA

SIMON RICHARDS DIRECT
PO Box 261
Port Melbourne
VIC
3207
Australia
Tel: +61 3 9645 2500
Fax: +61 3 9645 2482
Email: ir@srd.com.au
Lois Richards, General Manager

Services/Products:
Direct marketing agency

Member of:
DMA (US); ADMA

SINGLETON DIRECT PTY LIMITED
PO Box 208
Crows Nest
NSW
2065
Australia
Tel: +61 2 9954 4655
Fax: +61 2 9954 4661
Email: sidirect@magna.com.au
Jim Davis, Managing Director

Services/Products:
Direct marketing agency

Member of:
ADMA

SITEL AUSTRALIA
Locked Bag 49
Darlinghurst
NSW
2010
Australia
Tel: +61 2 9273 5000
Fax: +61 2 9273 5001
Email: felicity.mcdonnell@sitel.com.au
Web: www.sitel.com
Felicity McDonnell, Director-Client
    Services

Services/Products:
Database services; Telemarketing
agency; Consultancy services

Member of:
ADMA

STREETFILE
PO Box 456
Cheltenham
VIC
3192
Australia
Tel: +61 3 9532 2020
Fax: +61 3 9532 2020
Email: sfile@ozemail.com.au
Web: www.ozemail.com.au/sfile
Kara Wise, National Marketing
    Manager

Services/Products:
Private delivery services; Mailing/
Faxing services

Member of:
ADMA

SYNCHRO MARKETING AUSTRALIA PTY LIMITED
PO Box 1932
North Sydney
NSW
2059
Australia
Tel: +61 2 9957 1299
Fax: +61 2 9957 1282
Email: synchro@ozemail.com.au
Trevor Barkway, Managing Director

Services/Products:
Database services; Telemarketing
agency; Direct marketing agency; Sales
promotion agency; Consultancy
services

Member of:
ADMA

SYNTAX DIRECT MARKETING SERVICES
PO Box 43
North Melbourne
VIC
3051
Australia
Tel: +61 3 9329 2155
Fax: +61 3 9326 5270
Caroline Inge, Director

Services/Products:
Database services; Mailing/Faxing
services; Data Processing

Member of:
ADMA

TELE MARKETING DIRECT PTY LTD
Suite 12, 899 Whitehorse Road
Box Hill
VIC
3128
Australia
Tel: +61 3 9248 2444
Fax: +61 3 9890 0085
Email: tele@ozonline.com.au
Amanda Buchanan, Manager

Services/Products:
Fulfilment and sampling house;
Database services; Mailing/Faxing
services; Telemarketing agency; Data
Processing

Member of:
ADMA

TELE-SELL MARKETING
PO Box 1199
Windsor
VIC
3181
Australia
Tel: +61 3 9510 4700
Fax: +61 3 9510 8625
Email: ellen@telesell.com.au
Web: www.telesell.com.au
Ellen Richards, Business Development
  Manager

Services/Products:
Fulfilment and sampling house;
Database services; Mailing/Faxing
services; Telemarketing agency;
Software supplier; Data Processing

Member of:
ADMA

TELEMASTERS PTY LTD
Level 19, Plaza Tower 2, 500 Oxford
Street
Bondi Junction
NSW
2022
Australia
Tel: +61 2 9333 8100
Fax: +61 2 9333 8199
Email: tele@telemasters.com.au
Martin Daine, General Manager

Services/Products:
Telemarketing agency

Member of:
ADMA

**TELETECH INTERNATIONAL
  PTY LTD**
PO Box 460
St Leonards
NSW
2065
Australia
Tel: +61 2 9930 1100
Fax: +61 2 9930 1630
Web: www.teletech.com
Michelle Sprod, Marketing Manager

Services/Products:
Fulfilment and sampling house;
Telemarketing agency; Consultancy
services

Member of:
ADMA

TEMPLAR MARKETING
PO Box 1063
Marrickville
NSW
2204
Australia
Tel: +61 2 9582 5711

Fax: +61 2 9557 0700
Email: tdirect@tm.com.au
Web: www.tm.com.au
Rochelle Collis, Sales & Marketing Co-
  ordinator

Services/Products:
Fulfilment and sampling house;
Database services; Mailing/Faxing
services; Telemarketing agency; Data
Processing

E-Services:
Website design

Member of:
ADMA

THE CLARKE GROUP
120 Smith Street
Summer Hill
NSW
2130
Australia
Tel: +61 2 9716 6833
Fax: +61 2 9716 7042
Email: clarke@hutch.com.au
Kevin Clarke, Managing Director

Services/Products:
Database services; Consultancy
services

Member of:
ADMA

**THE DEVINE ALTERNATIVE
  PTY LTD**
Suite 2, 250 Main Road
Toukley
NSW
2263
Australia
Tel: +61 0 43961 000
Fax: +61 0 4396 1010
Email: devine@gogetnetted.com.au
Web: www.gogetnetted.com.au/
  gg0400.html
Gavin Devine, Sales Director

Services/Products:
List services; Database services; Data
Processing

Member of:
ADMA

**THE DIRECT RESPONSE
  COMPANY**
Level 12, 100 Miller Street
North Sydney
NSW
2060
Australia
Tel: +61 2 9955 4878
Fax: +61 2 9955 5332

Email: mail@directresponse.com.au
Doug Browning, Director - Client
  Services

Services/Products:
Direct marketing agency

Member of:
ADMA

**THE GREAT AUSTRALIAN LIST
  COMPANY PTY LTD**
Level 1, Suite 2, 320 West Street
Umina Beach
NSW
2257
Australia
Tel: +61 0 43445120
Fax: +61 0 4344 5299
Email: listinfo@greataussielist.com.au
Web: www.greataussielist.com.au/-
  listinfo
John Melton, Managing Director

Services/Products:
List services

Member of:
ADMA

THE LIST BANK PTY LTD
Level 4, 83 Mount Street
North Sydney
NSW
2060
Australia
Tel: +61 2 9955 6000
Fax: +61 2 9957 1919
Email: info@listb.com.au
Web: www.listbank.com.au
Lloyd Campbell, General Manager

Services/Products:
List services

Member of:
ADMA

THE MAILING LIST CENTRE
PO Box 52
Spit Junction
NSW
2088
Australia
Tel: +61 2 9969 2922
Fax: +61 2 9960 4936
Email: lists@mailinglistcentre.com.au
Caroline Gracie, General Manager

Services/Products:
List services

THE TARGETED APPROACH
368 South Dowling Street
Paddington
NSW
2021

Australia
Tel: +61 2 9332 3222
Fax: +61 2 9360 3401
Email: ttamail@targeted.com.au
David Anstee, Managing Partner

Services/Products:
Direct marketing agency

Member of:
ADMA

THE WORKHOUSE PTY LTD
200 Carlisle Street
St Kilda
VIC
3182
Australia
Tel: +61 3 9537 2244
Fax: +61 3 9537 1863
John Berman, Managing Director

Services/Products:
Advertising Agency; Direct marketing
agency

Member of:
ADMA

THOMAS DIRECT PTY LTD
PO Box 616
Runaway Bay
QLD
4216
Australia
Tel: +61 7 5588 2888
Fax: +61 7 5537 6848
Email: tdirect@pronet.net.au
Douglas Thomas Jnr., General
   Manager

Services/Products:
Fulfilment and sampling house;
Database services; Telemarketing
agency; Direct marketing agency

Member of:
ADMA

**UNIFI COMMUNICATIONS PTY
   LTD**
Level 8, 343 Little Collins Street
Melbourne
VIC
3000
Australia
Tel: +61 3 9670 3199
Fax: +61 3 9670 3199
Nadine Sercombe, Marketing Manager

Services/Products:
Mailing/Faxing services

Member of:
ADMA

VOCAL EDGE PTY LTD
PO Box 785
Willoughby
NSW
2068
Australia
Tel: +61 2 9413 9191
Fax: +61 2 9413 9191
Diana Turner, Director

Services/Products:
Telemarketing agency; Training/
recruitment

Member of:
ADMA

WILKE COLOR
37–49 Browns Road
Clayton
VIC
3168
Australia
Tel: +61 3 9265 8222
Fax: +61 3 9543 3181
Email: robyn.haydon@wilke.com.au
Robyn Haydon, Marketing Manager

Services/Products:
Mailing/Faxing services; Print services

Member of:
ADMA

WUNDERMAN CATO JOHNSON
Level 14, 65 Berry Street
North Sydney
NSW
2060
Australia
Tel: +61 2 9931 6262
Fax: +61 2 9956 7607
Email: david_prentice@wcj.com
Web: www.wcj.com/
Ian MacKelden, Business Manager

Services/Products:
Advertising Agency; Direct marketing
agency; Media buying agency; Sales
promotion agency; Consultancy
services

Member of:
ADMA

YOUNG DIRECT PTY LTD
Unit 5, Norberry Terrace, 177–179
Pacific Highway
North Sydney
NSW
2060
Australia
Tel: +61 2 9957 5465
Fax: +61 2 9954 0023
Email: ydirect@cia.com.au
Janice Young, Managing Director

Services/Products:
Direct marketing agency

Member of:
ADMA

ZEBRA DIRECTION
47 O'grady Street
Albert Park
VIC
3206
Australia
Tel: +61 3 9682 2564
Fax: +61 3 9682 2575
Email: zebra@labyrinth.net.au
Frederic Couturier, Managing Director

Services/Products:
List services; Fulfilment and sampling
house; Database services; Software
supplier; Consultancy services; Data
Processing

Member of:
ADMA

SERVICES/PRODUCT LISTING

Advertising Agency
Brett Goulston and Associates
Cartwright Williams Pty Ltd
Curtis Jones & Brown Design &
   Production
Echo Direct Marketing
Grantley Cogzell Benn
Hero Communications Pty Ltd
Leo Burnett Connaghan & May
Lintas Direct
MOS Data Assembly Specialists Pty
   Ltd
Peter Hoy & Associates Pty Ltd
Pheonix Creative Services
Rapp Collins Worldwide Pty Ltd
RGS Communications
Robertson Leo Burnett Pty Ltd
The Workhouse Pty Ltd
Wunderman Cato Johnson

Build, rebuild or improve customer response centres for maximum results with integrity
Call Centre INTEGRITY P/L

Call centre services/systems
Call Centre INTEGRITY P/L
Cartwright Williams Pty Ltd
Database Marketing Solutions Pty Ltd
Hogan Marketing Services
Marketing Database Systems Pty
   Limited

Catalogue producer
Direct Media Pty. Ltd.
Double Click
Mailing and Print Services Pty Ltd
Offset Alpine Printing Ltd
Ortega Publishing Pty Ltd

Conduct workshops and training for the industry worldwide
Call Centre INTEGRITY P/L

Consultancy services
ADM Action Direct Marketing
Appropriate Services Pty Ltd
Bertini Murray & Associates
Bristow & Prentice Pty Ltd Response Advertising
Call Centre INTEGRITY P/L
Cameron & Partners-Integrated Marketing Services
Clemenger Direct Pty Ltd
Cohn & Wells
Creative Marketing
CUC Australasia Limited
Direct Marketing Software
Direct Media Pty. Ltd.
Dooley Dynamics Pty Ltd
Double Click
Dun & Bradstreet Marketing Pty Ltd
FNL Direct
Hedley Garner Pty Ltd
IBM Australia Limited
J. S. McMillan Pty Ltd
JMG Marketing (Aust) Pty Ltd
JWT Dialog
KDS Print Management Pty Ltd
Linda Loose Marketing & Communications
Lintas Direct
M & C Saatchi Direct
Marketability
Marketbase Direct Systems
Marketing 1:1 Pty Ltd
Marketing Database Systems Pty Limited
Ogilvy & Mather Direct
Pac-Rim Direct
Pacific Micromarketing
Professional Direct Marketing Pty Ltd
QM Industries (QLD) Pty Ltd
Rapp Collins Worldwide Pty Ltd
ReMark Asia Pacific Pty Ltd
RNR International Marketing Group
Sharp & Anderson Pty Ltd
Shorter Direct (WA)
Sitel Australia
Synchro Marketing Australia Pty Limited
TeleTech International Pty Ltd
The Clarke Group
Wunderman Cato Johnson
Zebra Direction

Data Processing
Bond Direct Pty Ltd
Centurion Marketing Services
Chelsea Images
Cohn & Wells
Comprite Direct Marketing
CUC Australasia Limited
CW Database Services
Data Connection
Database Consultants Australia (DCA)
Direct Mail Services Pty Ltd
EWA Australia Pty Ltd
Finex Integrated Communications
Four Trade Only Direct Mail & Print Pty Ltd
Gallaghers
Geospend Pty Ltd
IBM Australia Limited
Integrated Mailing Services
Mail Marketing Works Pty Ltd
Mailcare Systems Pty Ltd
Manchester Holdings Pty Ltd
Marketbase Direct Systems
Marketing Database Systems Pty Limited
Micromatch Pty Ltd
MOS Data Assembly Specialists Pty Ltd
Multinet Systems Pty Ltd
Pacific Micromarketing
Permail Pty Ltd
Post Data
RNR International Marketing Group
Syntax Direct Marketing Services
Tele Marketing Direct Pty Ltd
Tele-Sell Marketing
Templar Marketing
The Devine Alternative Pty Ltd
Zebra Direction

Database services
Accountable List Brokers Pty Ltd
ADM Action Direct Marketing
Apple Marketing Group
Australasian Medical Publishing Company Pty Ltd (AMPCo)
Bond Direct Pty Ltd
Bristow & Prentice Pty Ltd Response Advertising
Carlson Marketing Group
Carr Clark Rapp Collins
Centurion Marketing Services
Chelsea Images
Cohn & Wells
Comprite Direct Marketing
CUC Australasia Limited
CW Database Services
Data Connection
Database Consultants Australia (DCA)
Database Marketing Solutions Pty Ltd
Direct Intent Marketing
Direct Mail Services Pty Ltd
Direct Marketing Software

Dun & Bradstreet Marketing Pty Ltd
Euro R S C G Partnership
EWA Australia Pty Ltd
Four Trade Only Direct Mail & Print Pty Ltd
Gallaghers
GMS Fulfilment Services Limited
IBM Australia Limited
Integrated Mailing Services
JMG Marketing (Aust) Pty Ltd
KDM Direct Marketing
Leo Burnett Connaghan & May
M & C Saatchi Direct
Mail Marketing Works Pty Ltd
Mailcare Systems Pty Ltd
Mailing and Print Services Pty Ltd
Manchester Holdings Pty Ltd
Marketability
Marketbase Direct Systems
Marketing Database Systems Pty Limited
Micromatch Pty Ltd
MOS Data Assembly Specialists Pty Ltd
Multinet Systems Pty Ltd
Ortega Publishing Pty Ltd
Pacific Micromarketing
Permail Pty Ltd
Post Data
Professional Direct Marketing Pty Ltd
QM Industries (QLD) Pty Ltd
RNR International Marketing Group
SAS Institute
Sharp & Anderson Pty Ltd
Shorter Direct (WA)
Sitel Australia
Synchro Marketing Australia Pty Limited
Syntax Direct Marketing Services
Tele Marketing Direct Pty Ltd
Tele-Sell Marketing
Templar Marketing
The Clarke Group
The Devine Alternative Pty Ltd
Thomas Direct Pty Ltd
Zebra Direction

Design/graphics/clip art supplier
Double Click

Direct marketing agency
ADM Action Direct Marketing
Bennett Keeble Martyn
Bond Direct Pty Ltd
Boomerang Integrated Marketing and Advertising
Brett Goulston and Associates
Bristow & Prentice Pty Ltd Response Advertising
Bristow & Prentice Response Advertising

Cameron & Partners-Integrated
  Marketing Services
Carlson Marketing Group
Carr Clark Rapp Collins
Clemenger Direct Pty Ltd
Cohn & Wells
Communique Direct
Comprite Direct Marketing
Creative Marketing
Curtis Jones & Brown Design &
  Production
Direct Marketing Services Pty Ltd
DK Marketing Ltd
Double Click
DTMS - Desktop Marketing Systems
  Pty Ltd
Echo Direct Marketing
Euro R S C G Partnership
Finex Integrated Communications
FNL Direct
Foxy Advertising
George Patterson Bates
Grantley Cogzell Benn
Hero Communications Pty Ltd
Integrated Options
JMG Marketing (Aust) Pty Ltd
JWT Dialog
KDM Direct Marketing
Lavender Direct
Leo Burnett Connaghan & May
Lintas Direct
M & C Saatchi Direct
Manchester Holdings Pty Ltd
Marketability
Maynard's PROMO Marketing
  Australia
Ogilvy & Mather Direct
Ortega Publishing Pty Ltd
Peter Hoy & Associates Pty Ltd
Pheonix Creative Services
Pomeroy Frere Thomas Pty Ltd
Rapp Collins Worldwide Pty Ltd
Red-Line Creative
RGS Communications
RNR International Marketing Group
Robe-John & Associates Pty Ltd
Saatchi & Saatchi Direct
SG Marketing Pty Ltd
Shorter Direct (WA)
Simon Richards Direct
Singleton Direct Pty Limited
Synchro Marketing Australia Pty
  Limited
The Direct Response Company
The Targeted Approach
The Workhouse Pty Ltd
Thomas Direct Pty Ltd
Wunderman Cato Johnson
Young Direct Pty Ltd

Direct response TV services
Bristow & Prentice Pty Ltd Response
  Advertising

KDM Direct Marketing

Electronic media
Bristow & Prentice Pty Ltd Response
  Advertising
Double Click

Email marketing
Returnity Pty Ltd

Email transmissions
Direct Media Pty. Ltd.

Envelope manufacturer and marketer
Australian Envelopes

Fulfilment and sampling house
Ability Direct Marketing Pty Limited
Ability Direct Marketing Pty Limited
  WA
Accountable List Brokers Pty Ltd
ADM Action Direct Marketing
Apple Marketing Group
Australasian Medical Publishing
  Company Pty Ltd (AMPCo)
Carr Clark Rapp Collins
CDM Telemarketing
Communique Direct
Comprite Direct Marketing
CUC Australasia Limited
Data Connection
Direct Intent Marketing
Direct Mail Services Pty Ltd
EWA Australia Pty Ltd
GMS Fulfilment Services Limited
Integrated Mailing Services
Mailcare Systems Pty Ltd
Manchester Holdings Pty Ltd
Marketing Database Systems Pty
  Limited
Micromatch Pty Ltd
Multinet Systems Pty Ltd
Permail Pty Ltd
Post Data
QM Industries (QLD) Pty Ltd
RNR International Marketing Group
Salmat Pty Ltd
Tele Marketing Direct Pty Ltd
Tele-Sell Marketing
TeleTech International Pty Ltd
Templar Marketing
Thomas Direct Pty Ltd
Zebra Direction

Hardware supplier
Clemenger Direct Pty Ltd
Database Consultants Australia (DCA)
IBM Australia Limited
Multinet Systems Pty Ltd
Post Data

Interactive media
Call Centre INTEGRITY P/L

Internet services
Accountable List Brokers Pty Ltd
AT & T Easylink Services Aust Ltd
Bristow & Prentice Pty Ltd Response
  Advertising
Comprite Direct Marketing
Double Click
Manchester Holdings Pty Ltd

Labelling/envelope services
Action Mailer Company
Direct Mail Services Pty Ltd
DMC Direct Print Solutions
E. S. Wigg & Son Pty Ltd
Envelope Specialists
Four Trade Only Direct Mail & Print
  Pty Ltd
Gallaghers
Integrated Mailing Services
Mail Marketing Works Pty Ltd
Mailing and Print Services Pty Ltd

Legal services
Anisimoff Davenport
Dibbs Crowther & Osborne
Freehill Holllingdale & Page

Lettershop
ADM Action Direct Marketing
Australasian Medical Publishing
  Company Pty Ltd (AMPCo)
Comprite Direct Marketing

List services
Ability Direct Marketing Pty Limited
Ability Direct Marketing Pty Limited
  WA
Accountable List Brokers Pty Ltd
ADM Action Direct Marketing
Australasian Medical Publishing
  Company Pty Ltd (AMPCo)
Centurion Marketing Services
Communique Direct
Comprite Direct Marketing
Data Reference Library Pty Ltd
Database Marketing Solutions Pty
  Ltd
Direct Media Pty. Ltd.
Drake List Management
DTMS - Desktop Marketing Systems
  Pty Ltd
Dun & Bradstreet Marketing Pty Ltd
Integrated Mailing Services
JMG Marketing (Aust) Pty Ltd
KDM Direct Marketing
List Solutions – a division of APN
  Business Magazines Pty Ltd
Listbrokers Australia Pty Ltd
Manchester Holdings Pty Ltd
Marketing Orientations

MOS Data Assembly Specialists Pty Ltd
Pacific Micromarketing
Permail Pty Ltd
Prime Prospects Pty Ltd
Professional Direct Marketing Pty Ltd
The Devine Alternative Pty Ltd
The Great Australian List Company Pty Ltd
The List Bank Pty Ltd
The Mailing List Centre
Zebra Direction

Mail order company
Database Marketing Solutions Pty Ltd

Mailing/Faxing services
Ability Direct Marketing Pty Limited
Ability Direct Marketing Pty Limited WA
Accountable List Brokers Pty Ltd
Apple Marketing Group
Australasian Medical Publishing Company Pty Ltd (AMPCo)
Australia Post
Cartwright Williams Pty Ltd
Centurion Marketing Services
Chelsea Images
Communique Direct
Comprite Direct Marketing
Data Connection
Direct Intent Marketing
Direct Mail Services Pty Ltd
EWA Australia Pty Ltd
Four Trade Only Direct Mail & Print Pty Ltd
Gallaghers
GMS Fulfilment Services Limited
Integrated Mailing Services
Kennedy Pacific
Mail Marketing Works Pty Ltd
Mailcare Systems Pty Ltd
Mailing and Print Services Pty Ltd
Manchester Holdings Pty Ltd
Micromatch Pty Ltd
Multinet Systems Pty Ltd
Pac-Rim Direct
Permail Pty Ltd
Post Data
Progress Printers & Distributors
QM Industries (QLD) Pty Ltd
Salmat Pty Ltd
Streetfile
Syntax Direct Marketing Services
Tele Marketing Direct Pty Ltd
Tele-Sell Marketing
Templar Marketing
UNIFI Communications Pty Ltd
Wilke Color

Market research agency
KDM Direct Marketing

Market Movements (Asia Pacific) Pty Ltd

Media buying agency
Bond Direct Pty Ltd
Carr Clark Rapp Collins
CUC Australasia Limited
Direct Intent Marketing
Euro R S C G Partnership
Finex Integrated Communications
Leo Burnett Connaghan & May
Marketability
Maynard's PROMO Marketing Australia
Peter Hoy & Associates Pty Ltd
Shorter Direct (WA)
Wunderman Cato Johnson

Personalisation
Cartwright Williams Pty Ltd

Postal services
Australia Post

Print services
Action Mailer Company
Amazing Faces Pty Ltd
Apple Marketing Group
Champion Print
Chelsea Images
Data Connection
Direct Mail Services Pty Ltd
DMC Direct Print Solutions
E. S. Wigg & Son Pty Ltd
Four Trade Only Direct Mail & Print Pty Ltd
Gallaghers
Kennedy Pacific
Mail Marketing Works Pty Ltd
Offset Alpine Printing Ltd
Ortega Publishing Pty Ltd
Post Data
Progress Printers & Distributors
QM Industries (QLD) Pty Ltd
Quality Images Australia Pty Ltd
Wilke Color

Private delivery services
Accountable List Brokers Pty Ltd
Centurion Marketing Services
Champion Print
Gallaghers
Pac-Rim Direct
Permail Pty Ltd
Post Data
Progress Printers & Distributors
Salmat Pty Ltd
Streetfile

Public speaking
Call Centre INTEGRITY P/L

Publisher
Australasian Medical Publishing Company Pty Ltd (AMPCo)
Ortega Publishing Pty Ltd

Sales promotion agency
Bond Direct Pty Ltd
Cameron & Partners-Integrated Marketing Services
Cartwright Williams Pty Ltd
Creative Marketing
CUC Australasia Limited
Euro R S C G Partnership
FNL Direct
Hero Communications Pty Ltd
Integrated Options
Leo Burnett Connaghan & May
Lintas Direct
Maynard's PROMO Marketing Australia
Peter Hoy & Associates Pty Ltd
Rapp Collins Worldwide Pty Ltd
Synchro Marketing Australia Pty Limited
Wunderman Cato Johnson

Service bureau
Direct Marketing Software

Software supplier
Beeline Sales Support
Berger Software Pty Ltd
Cohn & Wells
CW Database Services
Database Consultants Australia (DCA)
Database Marketing Solutions Pty Ltd
Direct Connect
Direct Marketing Software
DTMS - Desktop Marketing Systems Pty Ltd
Geospend Pty Ltd
IBM Australia Limited
Korator Pty Ltd
Marketbase Direct Systems
Marketing Database Systems Pty Limited
Pacific Micromarketing
SAS Institute
Tele-Sell Marketing
Zebra Direction

Telemarketing agency
Ability Direct Marketing Pty Limited
Ability Direct Marketing Pty Limited WA
Accountable List Brokers Pty Ltd
Apple Marketing Group
Appropriate Services Pty Ltd
Beeline Sales Support
Blueprint Concept Marketing Pty Ltd
Bond Direct Pty Ltd
Carlson Marketing Group
Carr Clark Rapp Collins

Cartwright Williams Pty Ltd
CDM Telemarketing
Communique Direct
CONNECT - Interactive Business
 Services
Coombe Telephone Marketing Pty Ltd
CUC Australasia Limited
Data Connection
Direct Connect
Direct Intent Marketing
Dooley Dynamics Pty Ltd
Euro R S C G Partnership
EWA Australia Pty Ltd
GMS Fulfilment Services Limited
JMG Marketing (Aust) Pty Ltd
KDM Direct Marketing
M & C Saatchi Direct
Micromatch Pty Ltd
Morrissey Malcolm Direct Marketing
MOS Data Assembly Specialists Pty
 Ltd
Multinet Systems Pty Ltd
Optel Research
Professional Direct Marketing Pty Ltd
RNR International Marketing Group
Shorter Direct (WA)
Sitel Australia
Synchro Marketing Australia Pty
 Limited
Tele Marketing Direct Pty Ltd
Tele-Sell Marketing
Telemasters Pty Ltd
TeleTech International Pty Ltd
Templar Marketing
Thomas Direct Pty Ltd
Vocal Edge Pty Ltd

Training/recruitment

Call Centre INTEGRITY P/L
Coombe Telephone Marketing Pty Ltd
Database Marketing Solutions Pty Ltd
Dibsdall Weekes & Ross
Direct Connect
Helen Hill & Associates
Michael Page Marketing
Morgan & Banks Ltd
Optel Research
Vocal Edge Pty Ltd

Write workshops/training/ white papers/articles/books in industry

Call Centre INTEGRITY P/L

E-SERVICES

E-Marketing consultant

ADM Action Direct Marketing
Australia Post
Call Centre INTEGRITY P/L
Cartwright Williams Pty Ltd
Returnity Pty Ltd

Email list provider

ADM Action Direct Marketing
Australasian Medical Publishing
 Company Pty Ltd (AMPCo)
Australia Post
Database Marketing Solutions Pty Ltd
Direct Media Pty. Ltd.

Email software

Database Marketing Solutions Pty Ltd

Online/e-marketing agency

ADM Action Direct Marketing
Cartwright Williams Pty Ltd
Hogan Marketing Services
Returnity Pty Ltd

Website design

AT & T Easylink Services Aust Ltd
Australia Post
Bristow & Prentice Pty Ltd Response
 Advertising
Cartwright Williams Pty Ltd
Cohn & Wells
Comprite Direct Marketing
Database Marketing Solutions Pty
 Ltd
Double Click
Finex Integrated Communications
IBM Australia Limited
J. S. McMillan Pty Ltd
JWT Dialog
Korator Pty Ltd
Leo Burnett Connaghan & May
Manchester Holdings Pty Ltd
Marketability
Ogilvy & Mather Direct
Rapp Collins Worldwide Pty Ltd
RNR International Marketing
 Group
Shorter Direct (WA)
Templar Marketing

NEW ZEALAND

Population: 3.5 million
Capital: Wellington
Languages: English and Maori

GDP: $88 billion
GDP per capita: $24,444
Inflation: 1.7

Currency: New Zealand dollar ($) = 100 cents
Exchange rate: NZ$1.78 : $1

Time: GMT + 12 hours

OVERVIEW

New Zealand has virtually completed a decade of economic reform which has turned a previously highly protected economy into a deregulated, market-driven environment. The Asian market accounts for nearly 40 per cent of total New Zealand exports, and the recent Asian economic problems are causing a temporary recession.

Reliable research indicates that promotional direct mail continues to grow at 10–15 per cent p.a. and the growth in other media looks similarly healthy. Consumer lists are available through traditional direct mail marketers or through broker sources, and business lists which are of a higher quality can be obtained through three or four major sources. There is an efficient DM service and fulfilment structure, and recent advances in communication technology have been the impetus behind much of the recent growth.

New Zealand direct marketers are efficiently served by an active and professional Direct Marketing Association, which provides education, communication, networking and legislative advice.

LANGUAGE AND CULTURAL CONSIDERATIONS

The native Maori have not really been targeted as a market yet, but they would be worth considering for certain campaigns. Their cultural and linguistic differences from the English-speaking New Zealanders would need to be taken into account in any campaign. There are significant Samoan and Tongan populations, particularly in Auckland, and the number of immigrants from Asia has increased markedly over the past five years.

LEGISLATION AND CONSUMER PROTECTION

The DMA requires members to abide by their Code of Ethics and Standards of Practice. Marketers need to be aware of, and implement, Privacy, Fair Trading and Consumer Guarantees laws. The DMA provides an advisory service free of charge.

THE DIRECT MARKETING ASSOCIATION

Name:	New Zealand Direct Marketing Association Inc (DMA)
Address:	PO Box 47681, Ponsonby, Auckland 1034
Tel:	+64 9 303 9470
Fax:	+64 9 303 4787
Website:	www.dma.co.nz
Year founded:	1974
Chief Executive:	Keith Norris
Total staff:	9
Members:	470 (inc 70 individuals)

Direct marketing agencies	48	List brokers	11
Mailing houses	18	Printers/print brokers	23
Handling houses	20	Mail order companies	75
Call centre bureau	15	E-Marketing consulting	34
Database services	25	Software supplier	19
Website development	36		

Facilities for overseas users of direct marketing

Membership: overseas companies can join the DMA on signed acceptance of their Codes of Practice, which include compliance with the laws of New Zealand, such as the Fair Trading Act, Consumer Guarantees Act and the Privacy Act.

Magazine: the DMA publishes a magazine, DLB, six times a year which is free of charge to members.

Library: the DMA does not have a library. It refers enquirers to New Zealand Post's Direct Marketing Centres in Auckland, Wellington and Christchurch.

On-line information service: log on to www.dma.co.nz for current news, the how-to-guide and a supplier Directory. The Reading Room is for members only.

Legal advice: the DMA provides advice on compliance with the laws detailed above.

Business liaison service: the DMA offers help in finding local business venture partners.

Job placements: the DMA assists direct marketers from overseas to find employment in New Zealand. The website also allows members to list situations vacant.

Education services: the DMA runs its Certificate of Direct Marketing and Certificate of Call Centre Management twice each year. The DMA has also introduced a new certificate of E-marketing, which will run twice each year. In addition, they hold business lunches, workshops, seminars, and an annual conference.

POSTAL SERVICES
New Zealand Post Limited
Find 'em Keep 'em Addressing Services

As opposed to most postal administrations, New Zealand Post rates envelopes on size rather than weight. Mail is therefore costed on dimension and certain thickness thresholds. Full information on rates, as for all of New Zealand Post's services, can be obtained from a range of highly informative brochures, mailed to any prospective mailer free on request (see also their website www.nzpost.co.nz). Bulk services do exist, including Kiwimail, a delivery system, with regional selection criteria, for unaddressed mail. Customers can negotiate bulk prices, depending on volumes mailed.

Address list rental services

New Zealand has a very dynamic and mobile population, with upwards of fifteen per cent of households moving home each year. New Zealand Post receives change of address information from most of these households. From the information provided by the householders themselves, they build accurate, up-to-date, privacy compliant, household mailing lists. To help find new customers and keep existing customers, New Zealand Post offers both personalised and non-personalised address lists for rental. There are three specific address list databases available for rental:

1. **New Zealand Movers:** reaches people who have moved home recently. New Zealand Post has captured these addresses since mid-1994. The list also includes up to six previous addresses for each household. The list:

   • targets around 10,000 'new movers' each month, at a time when they are most likely to be seeking new suppliers;

- contains over 300,000 households and almost 700,000 individuals;
- allows identification of households that move within specific time periods;
- includes the following selections: date of move; home ownership; gender; geographical location;
- is continuously growing and updated.

2. **Household Street Address List:** reaches people by their location. There are no names attached to the file, so there are no privacy compliance issues. It is particularly suited to high-volume addressed mailings. The list:

- approaches people using your choice of 'default' address title, such as The Gardener, etc;
- contains over 950,000 unique, non-personalised delivery points;
- includes the following selections: Specific street address ranges; Post codes; and Statistics New Zealand meshblocks;
- is considered highly accurate and highly deliverable;
- is available at a lower cost than 'named' lists, but still retains the strength of containing specific addresses.

3. **Hot Leads List:** reaches people who express an interest in your type of products and services. This list comprises the names and addresses of households that have volunteered information about themselves, including the types of products and services that they are interested in. It is compiled from detailed customer questionnaires which identify 40 interest categories and covers the country. Selections include: gender; age group; occupational group; household demographics; home ownership; and geographical location. The list is growing by approx. 1,000 records per month, with currently over 100,000 records captured since 1987.

'Prospecta', the Geo-demographic Analysis and Mapping Tool

This reaches people by location, lifestyle and behaviour. Prospecta is a geo-demographic market analysis tool, supported by Datamail in New Zealand. New Zealand Movers and Household Street Address Lists can be Prospecta coded for greater targeting and market segmentation.

Privacy Act 1993 compliance

Collection, management and use of all name and address information in the New Zealand Post Addressing Services database is designed to comply with the requirements of the Privacy Act 1993. Approved users of information must agree to comply with New Zealand Post conditions to ensure that individual privacy is respected and legal obligations are met.

For further information on any of the above services, contact:

New Zealand Post Addressing Services
727 Waterloo Quay
P O Box 23
Wellington
NEW ZEALAND
Tel: +64 4 496 4515 or +64 4 576 4249
Fax: +64 4 496 4972 or +64 4 568 8140
Email: addressing.services@nzpost.co.nz
Website: www.nzpost.co.nz

Find 'em Keep 'em Marketing Services

Full consultancy and library service, providing essential local knowledge, and referrals where necessary. Major research projects aside, the consultancy is free, as is the library – a highly innovative direction for a national postal service. Combined with this, Find 'em Keep 'em Direct Marketing Services conduct national direct marketing seminars throughout the country targeting small to medium-sized businesses.

Contact :

Auckland Direct Marketing Services
Level 4
Auckland Mail Centre
167 Victoria Street West
P O Box 93169
Auckland
Tel: +64 9 367 9884
Fax: +64 9 367 9858

Christchurch Direct Marketing Services
5359 Hereford Street
P O Box 83
Christchurch
Tel: +64 3 353 1882
Fax: +64 3 353 1655

Wellington Direct Marketing Services
Level 11
727 Waterloo Quay
Private Bag 39990
Wellington
Tel: +64 4 496 4919
Fax: +64 4 496 4972

PROVIDERS OF DM AND E-M SERVICES

ACTIONMAIL LTD
PO Box 204
Albany
AUCKLAND
1015
New Zealand
Tel: +64 9 4154508
Fax: +64 9 4154509
Email: actionmail@xtra.co.nz
Betsy Duncan

Services/Products:
List services; Database services;
Mailing/Faxing services

Member of:
NZDMA

ADVOC8 ONLINE LTD
PO Box 9112
Greerton
TAURANGA
3030
New Zealand
Tel: +64 7 5411161
Fax: +64 7 5413479
Email: glenn@advoc8.net
Web: www.advoc8.net
Glenn MacLeod

Services/Products:
Electronic media

E-Services:
Website design

Member of:
NZDMA

AIC WORLDWIDE LIMITED
PO Box 5321
Wellesley Street
AUCKLAND
1036
New Zealand
Tel: +64 9 3585566
Fax: +64 9 3585577
Amanda Lennon

Services/Products:
Training/recruitment; Conference/
exhibition organiser

Member of:
NZDMA

AIM DIRECT LIMITED
PO Box 8977
Symonds Street
AUCKLAND
1035
New Zealand
Tel: +64 9 3610100
Fax: +64 9 3610102
Email: billg@aimdirect.co.nz
Web: www.aimdirect.co.nz
Bill Gianotti

Services/Products:
List services; Database services; Direct
marketing agency; Design/graphics/clip
art supplier; Service bureau; Direct
response TV services; Electronic media

E-Services:
Website design

Member of:
NZDMA

AIM DIRECT LIMITED
PO Box 6245
Te Aro
WELLINGTON
6035
New Zealand
Tel: +64 4 3816900
Fax: +64 4 3816901
Email: robertl@aimdirect.co.nz
Robert Limb

Services/Products:
Direct marketing agency

Member of:
NZDMA

AMAZING BUT TRUE
PO Box 207
OREWA
1461
New Zealand
Tel: +64 9 4268239
Fax: +64 9 4244040
Email: jane@amazing.co.nz
Web: www.amazing.co.nz
Jane Francis

Services/Products:
Training/recruitment; Training/
recruitment; Direct marketing agency;
Consultancy services

Member of:
NZDMA

AMMIRATI PURIS LINTAS NEW ZEALAND
PO Box 37530
Parnell
AUCKLAND
1033
New Zealand
Tel: +64 9 3079363
Fax: +64 9 3076426
Email: pearsons@ammirati.co.nz
Stephen Pearson

Services/Products:
Advertising Agency; Direct marketing
agency

Member of:
NZDMA

ARCHIE MASON LTD
PO Box 18266
Glen Innes
AUCKLAND
1130
New Zealand
Tel: +64 9 5288057
Fax: +64 9 5288452
Archie Mason

Services/Products:
Fulfilment and sampling house;
Telemarketing agency; Consultancy
services

Member of:
NZDMA

ARROW LIMITED
Private Bag MBE P305
AUCKLAND
1332
New Zealand
Tel: +64 9 3787900
Fax: +64 9 3787100
Email: steve.duck@xtra.co.nz
Steve Duck

Services/Products:
Consultancy services

Member of:
NZDMA

ATLANTIS MARKETING LIMITED
PO Box 37012
Parnell
AUCKLAND
1033
New Zealand
Tel: +64 9 9809829
Fax: +64 9 9809892
Email: tony@atlantis.co.nz
Web: www.atlantis.co.nz
Tony Bozzard

Services/Products:
List services; Database services;
Telemarketing agency; Direct
marketing agency; Consultancy
services; Electronic media

E-Services:
Website design

Member of:
NZDMA

BOUGHTWOOD PRINTING HOUSE LTD
PO Box 34417
Birkenhead
AUCKLAND

1330
New Zealand
Tel: +64 9 4837649
Fax: +64 9 4834218
Richard Boughtwood

Services/Products:
Print services

Member of:
NZDMA

BOUNTY SERVICES LTD
PO Box 36250
Merivale
CHRISTCHURCH
8030
New Zealand
Tel: +64 3 3386440
Fax: +64 3 3382522
Email: bountynz@xtra.co.nz
Anne Barnett

Services/Products:
List services; Database services

Member of:
NZDMA

CAMPAIGN DIRECT
PO Box 8105
CHRISTCHURCH
8015
New Zealand
Tel: +64 3 3481101
Fax: +64 3 3481109
Email: campaign@xtra.co.nz
Marc Fernandez

Services/Products:
Advertising Agency; Consultancy
services; Direct marketing agency;
Telemarketing agency; Training/
recruitment

Member of:
NZDMA

**CANTERBURY UNIVERSITY
PRESS**
Private Bag 4800
Christchurch
New Zealand
Tel: +64 3 364 2914
Fax: +64 3 364 2044
Email: mail@cup.canterbury.ac.nz
Web: www.cup.canterbury.ac.nz
Mike Bradstock, Managing Editor &
Publisher

Services/Products:
Publisher

Member of:
National DMA; NZ Booksellers
Association; NZ Book Publishers
Association

CARPE DM LTD
PO Box 44083
Point Chevalier
AUCKLAND
1030
New Zealand
Tel: +64 9 8495025
Fax: +64 9 8156585
Email: simon@carpedm.co.nz
Web: www.carpedm.co.nz
Simon Morgan

Services/Products:
Direct marketing agency; Consultancy
services; Electronic media

E-Services:
Website design

Member of:
NZDMA

CHANNEL I LTD
PO Box 37530
Parnell
AUCKLAND
1033
New Zealand
Tel: +64 9 3670304
Fax: +64 9 3076426
Michael O'Sullivan

Services/Products:
Direct response TV services

Member of:
NZDMA

**CIRCULAR DISTRIBUTORS
LTD**
PO Box 33271
Takapuna
AUCKLAND
1332
New Zealand
Tel: +64 9 4890500
Fax: +64 9 4863907
Web: www.circulars.co.nz
Gordon Haynes

Services/Products:
Private delivery services

Member of:
NZDMA

COMIT GROUP LTD
PO Box 90648
AUCKLAND
New Zealand
Tel: +64 9 4156 170
Fax: +64 9 4156 580
Email: info@comitgroup.com
Web: www.comitgroup.com
Craig Pellett, Director Sales and
Marketing

Services/Products:
Consultancy services; Database
services; Labelling/envelope services;
Lettershop; Print services; Service
bureau

E-Services:
E-Marketing consultant; Website
design; Online/e-marketing agency

Member of:
National DMA

**COMMUNICATION GRAPHICS
LIMITED**
PO Box 5859
Wellesley Street
AUCKLAND
1036
New Zealand
Tel: +64 9 6303556
Fax: +64 9 6302457
Brian Spring

Services/Products:
Direct marketing agency; Consultanc
services; Design/graphics/clip art
supplier; Print services

Member of:
NZDMA

**COMPAQ COMPUTER NEW
ZEALAND LTD**
PO Box 6297
Wellesley Street
AUCKLAND
1036
New Zealand
Tel: +64 9 3073969
Fax: +64 9 3099198
Email: belinda.sinclair@compaq.com
Belinda Sinclair

Services/Products:
Hardware supplier

Member of:
NZDMA

**CONSUMERS' INSTITUTE OF
NZ INC**
Private Bag 6996
Te Aro
WELLINGTON
6035
New Zealand
Tel: +64 4 3847963
Fax: +64 4 3858752
David Russell

Services/Products:
Legal services

Member of:
NZDMA

CUMMING ENTERPRISES
PO Box 1199
AUCKLAND
1015
New Zealand
Tel: +64 9 3765700
Fax: +64 9 3600361
David Geary

Services/Products:
Fulfilment and sampling house;
Mailing/Faxing services

Member of:
NZDMA

CURRENT PACIFIC LTD
PO Box 36–536 Northcote
AUCKLAND
1330
New Zealand
Tel: +64 9 480 1388
Fax: +64 9 480 1387

Services/Products:
List services; Lettershop; Mailing/
Faxing services; Direct marketing
agency; Consultancy services;
Publisher

CWFS MCCANN
PO Box 99598
Newmarket
AUCKLAND
1031
New Zealand
Tel: +64 9 3570015
Fax: +64 9 3570017
Robert Munro

Services/Products:
Advertising Agency; Direct marketing
agency

Member of:
NZDMA

DATA MAGIC LIMITED
PO Box 33143
Takapuna
AUCKLAND
1332
New Zealand
Tel: +64 9 4150220
Fax: +64 9 4154565
Roz Vickerman

Services/Products:
List services; Fulfilment and sampling
house; Database services; Consultancy
services; Service bureau

Member of:
NZDMA

DATABASE COMMUNICATIONS
PO Box 27–012
Level 4, Willbank House
57 Willis Street
WELLINGTON
6037
New Zealand
Tel: +64 4 471 6320
Fax: +64 4 471 6321
Email: enquiries@dbc.co.nz
Web: www.dbc.co.nz
Kay Whiteman, Business Development
  Manager

Services/Products:
Lettershop; Database services;
Consultancy services; Software
supplier; Personalisation; Response
analysis bureau

Member of:
NZDMA

DATACOM SERVICES NZ
Private Bag 92630
Symonds Street
AUCKLAND
1035
New Zealand
Tel: +64 9 3575575
Fax: +64 9 3575577
Email: ksarah@mss.co.nz
Sarah-Anne Killpartrick

Services/Products:
List services; Database services;
Software supplier; Electronic media

E-Services:
Website design

Member of:
NZDMA

DATAMAIL LTD
Private Bag 14908
Panmure
AUCKLAND
1134
New Zealand
Tel: +64 9 2700202
Fax: +64 9 2700242
Andrew Corbett

Services/Products:
List services; Fulfilment and sampling
house; Database services; Mailing/
Faxing services; Telemarketing agency

Member of:
NZDMA

DATAMINE LIMITED
PO Box 11452
WELLINGTON
6034
New Zealand
Tel: +64 4 3844153
Fax: +64 4 3841153
Email: simon@datamine.co.nz
Simon Pohlen

Services/Products:
List services; Database services

Member of:
NZDMA

DATAPRINT LTD
PO Box 90501
AUCKLAND
New Zealand
Tel: +64 9 3761 780
Fax: +64 9 3767 205
Email: solutions@dataprint.co.nz
Murray Fitchett

Services/Products:
Lettershop; Fulfilment and sampling
house; Database services; Mailing/
Faxing services; Response analysis
bureau; Service bureau

Member of:
NZDMA

DELTARG DISTRIBUTION SYSTEMS LTD
PO Box 51970
Pakuranga
AUCKLAND
1730
New Zealand
Tel: +64 9 5732280
Fax: +64 9 5732299
Shaun Harkin

Services/Products:
List services; Lettershop; Database
services

Member of:
NZDMA

DIRECT MEDIA (NZ) LTD
PO Box 86
NELSON
7015
New Zealand
Tel: +64 3 5466950
Fax: +64 3 5457950
Email: directmedia@ts.co.nz
Ray Douglas

Services/Products:
List services

Member of:
NZDMA

DMA
PO Box 47681
Ponsonby
AUCKLAND

1034
New Zealand
Tel: +64 9 3039470
Fax: +64 9 3034787
Email: sandra@dma.co.nz
Web: www.dma.co.nz
Sandra Towers

Services/Products:
Training/recruitment

Member of:
NZDMA

DOMINO MARKETING LTD
PO Box 31147
Milford
NORTH SHORE CITY
1330
New Zealand
Tel: +64 9 4798200
Fax: +64 9 4798229
Sandy Harvey

Services/Products:
Labelling/envelope services; Print services

Member of:
NZDMA

DUN & BRADSTREET (NZ) LTD
PO Box 9589
Newmarket
AUCKLAND
1031
New Zealand
Tel: +64 9 3777700
Fax: +64 9 3092050
Email: hallg@mail.dnb.co.nz
Graeme Hall

Services/Products:
List services; Database services; Market research agency

Member of:
NZDMA

DUNHAM BREMMER
PO Box 27041
Te Aro
WELLINGTON
6037
New Zealand
Tel: +64 4 8015200
Fax: +64 4 8024242
Email: angel@dunham.co.nz
Web: www.dunham.co.nz
Angelique Sparnaay

Services/Products:
Design/graphics/clip art supplier; Print services

Member of:
NZDMA

ENERGY MARKETING AND COMMUNICATIONS LTD
PO Box 33463
Takapuna
AUCKLAND
1332
New Zealand
Tel: +64 9 4893229
Fax: +64 9 4893228
Email: energy@wave.co.nz
Paul Bell

Services/Products:
Direct marketing agency

Member of:
NZDMA

EZIBUY WHOLESALE LIMITED
Private Bag 11000
PALMERSTON NORTH
5320
New Zealand
Tel: +64 6 3555478
Fax: +64 6 3510150
Email: michelle@ezibuy.co.nz
Michelle Whitmore

Services/Products:
Mail order company

Member of:
NZDMA

FORTE INTEGRATED MARKETING
PO Box 767
BLENHEIM
7315
New Zealand
Tel: +64 3 5779080
Fax: +64 3 5779080
Email: forte@voyager.co.nz
Web: http://pcmedia.nzl.com/forte
Tony Smale

Services/Products:
Telemarketing agency; Direct marketing agency; Consultancy services; Design/graphics/clip art supplier; Electronic media

E-Services:
Website design

Member of:
NZDMA

FULLWORKS INTERNATIONAL LIMITED
Private Bag 47908
Ponsonby
AUCKLAND
1034
New Zealand
Tel: +64 9 8281500

Fax: +64 9 8281599
Helen Mitchell

Services/Products:
List services; Fulfilment and sampling house; Mailing/Faxing services; Telemarketing agency; Service bureau; Loyalty systems

Member of:
NZDMA

GAINSBOROUGH PRINTING CO LTD
PO Box 71025
Rosebank
AUCKLAND
1230
New Zealand
Tel: +64 9 8284610
Fax: +64 9 8288763
Keith Mackintosh

Services/Products:
Print services

Member of:
NZDMA

GALAXY ENVELOPE MFTG CO LTD
PO Box 51213
Tawa
WELLINGTON
6230
New Zealand
Tel: +64 4 2377785
Fax: +64 4 2379107
Email: envelopes@galaxy.co.nz
Dennis Jones

Services/Products:
Labelling/envelope services

Member of:
NZDMA

GALLAGHER INFO MANAGEMENT GROUP
PO Box 51986
Pakuranga
AUCKLAND
1730
New Zealand
Tel: +64 9 2737367
Fax: +64 9 2735355
Beth Heremaia

Services/Products:
List services; Database services; Mailing/Faxing services; Print services

Member of:
NZDMA

GESTRO HORNE
110 Symonds Street
PO Box 1262
Auckland
New Zealand
Tel: +64 9 379 2370
Fax: +64 9 309 6656
Email: patrickl@gestrohorne.co.nz
Web: www.gestrohorne.com

Services/Products:
Advertising Agency; Consultancy
services; Direct marketing agency;
Interactive media; Media buying
agency; Sales promotion agency

E-Services:
Email list provider; E-Marketing
consultant; Website design; Online/e-
marketing agency

Member of:
National DMA

GILBERT SWAN
PO Box 10530
The Terrace
WELLINGTON
6036
New Zealand
Tel: +64 4 4720165
Fax: +64 4 4720162
Email: swan@gilbertswan.co.nz
John Swan

Services/Products:
Consultancy services; Legal services

Member of:
NZDMA

GO DIRECT MARKETING LTD
PO Box 90095
AUCKLAND MAIL CENTRE
AUCKLAND
1015
New Zealand
Tel: +64 9 3076863
Fax: +64 9 3076790
Rob Cruickshank

Services/Products:
Direct marketing agency

Member of:
NZDMA

**GOLDSACK HARRIS
THOMPSON**
PO Box 3214
WELLINGTON
WE
6015
New Zealand
Tel: +64 4 3846488
Fax: +64 4 3846575
Ross Goldsack

Services/Products:
Advertising Agency; Direct marketing
agency

Member of:
NZDMA

HANDLE WITH CARE LTD
PO Box 33083
Takapuna
AUCKLAND
1332
New Zealand
Tel: +64 9 4159200
Fax: +64 9 4159220
Ross Carpenter

Services/Products:
List services; Fulfilment and sampling
house; Database services; Mailing/
Faxing services; Print services

Member of:
NZDMA

HAVAS MEDIMEDIA NZ LTD
PO Box 31348
Milford
Auckland
New Zealand
Tel: +64 9 488 4278
Fax: +64 9 489 6240
Email: rjackson@havas-
    medimedia.co.nz
Web: www.havas-medimedia.co.nz
Ms Rhonda Jackson, Business Manager

Services/Products:
List services; Fulfilment and sampling
house; Mailing/Faxing services;
Labelling/envelope services; Database
services; Medical database

Member of:
DMA; NZ Chamber of Commerce

**HIGH PERFORMANCE
    SYSTEMS**
PO Box 168
CHRISTCHURCH
8015
New Zealand
Tel: +64 3 3651666
Fax: +64 3 3651665
Email: ajackson@hpsl.co.nz
Andrew Jackson

Services/Products:
Consultancy services

Member of:
NZDMA

HOLLOWAY ADVERTISING
R D 4
DARGAVILLE
300

New Zealand
Tel: +64 9 4394300
Fax: +64 9 4395348
Email: holloway@igrin.co.nz
Mark Holloway

Services/Products:
Consultancy services; Design/graphics/
clip art supplier

Member of:
NZDMA

HYDE AGENCIES LTD
PO Box 37433
Parnell
AUCKLAND
1033
New Zealand
Tel: +64 9 3092413
Fax: +64 9 3022190
Larry Hyde

Services/Products:
List services; Lettershop; Direct
marketing agency; Print services

Member of:
NZDMA

HYPERACTIVE LTD
PO Box 9731
WELLINGTON
6015
New Zealand
Tel: +64 4 8019550
Fax: +64 4 8019560
Email: steve@hyperactive.co.nz
Web: www.hyperactive.co.nz
Steve McMullen

Services/Products:
Electronic media

E-Services:
Website design

Member of:
NZDMA

IBM NEW ZEALAND LIMITED
PO Box 6840
Wellesley Street
AUCKLAND
1015
New Zealand
Tel: +64 9 3588777
Fax: +64 9 3588717
Email: nicolasr@nz1.ibm.com
Web: www.ibm.co.nz
Nicolas Romaniuk

Services/Products:
Hardware supplier; Electronic media

E-Services:
Website design

Member of:
NZDMA

IMAGINE LTD
PO Box 22018
Otahuhu
AUCKLAND
1133
New Zealand
Tel: +64 9 2764939
Fax: +64 9 2768735
Don Merrington

Services/Products:
Design/graphics/clip art supplier; Print services

Member of:
NZDMA

IMPEX PRESS (NZ) LTD
PO Box 8417
Symonds Street
AUCKLAND
1035
New Zealand
Tel: +64 9 3790076
Fax: +64 9 3790458
Bill Van Sambeek

Services/Products:
Print services

Member of:
NZDMA

**INSTITUTE FOR
  INTERNATIONAL RESEARCH**
PO Box 3181
AUCKLAND
1015
New Zealand
Tel: +64 9 3795892
Fax: +64 9 3097986
Email: olad@iir.co.nz
Ola Dabbagh

Services/Products:
Training/recruitment; Conference/exhibition organiser

Member of:
NZDMA

**J WALTER THOMPSON (NZ)
  LTD**
PO Box 2566
AUCKLAND
1015
New Zealand
Tel: +64 9 3799625
Fax: +64 9 3570825
Email: ralfh@jwt.co.nz
Ralf Harding

Services/Products:
Advertising Agency; Consultancy services; Direct marketing agency; Media buying agency

E-Services:
Website design

Member of:
NZDMA

KIWIMAIL LIMITED
PO Box 3140
WELLINGTON
6015
New Zealand
Tel: +64 4 4999331
Fax: +64 4 4999332
Web: www.kiwimail.co.nz
Simon McIver

Services/Products:
Direct marketing agency

Member of:
NZDMA

KPMG
PO Box 996
WELLINGTON
6015
New Zealand
Tel: +64 4 8021768
Fax: +64 4 8021225
Web: www.kpmg.co.nz
Stella Neal

Services/Products:
Consultancy services

Member of:
NZDMA

MACMARKETING LTD
PO Box 68477
Newton
AUCKLAND
1031
New Zealand
Tel: +64 9 3009400
Fax: +64 9 3009401
Email: andy@macmarketing.co.nz
Web: www.macmarketing.co.nz
Andrew McDowell

Services/Products:
Advertising Agency; Consultancy services; Direct marketing agency

E-Services:
Website design

Member of:
NZDMA

MAGNET DIRECT MARKETING
PO Box 47669
Ponsonby
AUCKLAND
1034
New Zealand
Tel: +64 9 3765000
Fax: +64 9 3769913
Email: magnet.direct@clear.net.nz
Craig Smith

Services/Products:
Direct marketing agency

Member of:
NZDMA

MAILSHOP LIMITED
PO Box 18077
Glen Innes
AUCKLAND
1130
New Zealand
Tel: +64 9 5705 775
Fax: +64 9 5705 776
Warwick Lloyd

Services/Products:
Personalisation; Database services; Mailing/Faxing services; Print services; Fulfilment and sampling house; Labelling/envelope services

E-Services:
Email software

Member of:
National DMA

MARKETING IMPACT LTD
PO Box 6364
WELLINGTON
6035
New Zealand
Tel: +64 4 3856618
Fax: +64 4 3858986
Alan Hannay

Services/Products:
List services; Fulfilment and sampling house; Database services; Mailing/Faxing services; Direct marketing agency

Member of:
NZDMA

**MARKETING TECHNOLOGIES
  LTD**
PO Box 37530
Parnell
AUCKLAND
1033
New Zealand
Tel: +64 9 3670300
Fax: +64 9 3670305
Email: robertsonv@brains.co.nz

Web: www.brains.co.nz
Vaughan Robertson

Services/Products:
List services; Database services;
Consultancy services; Software
supplier

Member of:
NZDMA

MARRIOTT SERVICES
PO Box 395
Manurewa
AUCKLAND
1730
New Zealand
Tel: +64 9 2663486
Fax: +64 9 2663486
Email: webmaster@marrserv.com
Web: www.marrserv.com
Jeffrey Marriott

Services/Products:
List services; Database services;
Electronic media

E-Services:
Website design

Member of:
NZDMA

MARSDEN INCH CONSULTING
PO Box 37142
Parnell
AUCKLAND
1033
New Zealand
Tel: +64 9 5202230
Fax: +64 9 5201411
Peter Spencer

Services/Products:
Training/recruitment

Member of:
NZDMA

MASON SEWELL
COMMUNICATIONS
PO Box 47789
Ponsonby
AUCKLAND
1034
New Zealand
Tel: +64 9 3787048
Fax: +64 9 3787050
Email: masewell@iprolink.co.nz
Graham Sewell

Services/Products:
Advertising Agency; Design/graphics/
clip art supplier

Member of:
NZDMA

MAXIM GROUP LTD
PO Box 9417
Newmarket
AUCKLAND
1031
New Zealand
Tel: +64 9 3778890
Fax: +64 9 3778858
Email: johnd@maxim-group.co.nz
John da Silva

Services/Products:
Direct marketing agency; Consultancy
services; Design/graphics/clip art
supplier

Member of:
NZDMA

MAYER CONSULTANTS LTD
2–141 Weatherley Road
Torbay
AUCKLAND
1310
New Zealand
Tel: +64 9 4739240
Fax: +64 9 4738286
Email: annmayer@xtra.co.nz
Ann Mayer

Services/Products:
Telemarketing agency; Training/
recruitment

Member of:
NZDMA

MCLAY & COMPANY
PO Box 10626
WELLINGTON
6036
New Zealand
Tel: +64 4 4995385
Fax: +64 4 4991385
Email: bryan.dunne@eudoramail.com
Bryan Dunne

Services/Products:
Training/recruitment; Training/
recruitment

Member of:
NZDMA

MEDIAPLUS LTD
PO Box 33643
Takapuna
AUCKLAND
1332
New Zealand
Tel: +64 9 4868040
Fax: +64 9 4868020
Email: media@mediaplus.co.nz
Murray Kinsella

Services/Products:
Advertising Agency; Consultancy
services; Direct marketing agency;
Media buying agency

Member of:
NZDMA

MENTAL AS ANYTHING
319 Huia Road
Titirangi
WAITAKERE CITY
1007
New Zealand
Tel: +64 9 3361112
Fax: +64 9 3033530
Clay Bodvin

Services/Products:
Direct marketing agency; Consultancy
services; Design/graphics/clip art
supplier

Member of:
NZDMA

MERCATO COMMUNICATIONS
LTD
PO Box 8218
Symonds Street
AUCKLAND
1015
New Zealand
Tel: +64 9 3660500
Fax: +64 9 3664600
John Albert

Services/Products:
Advertising Agency; Consultancy
services; Direct marketing agency

Member of:
NZDMA

MERCURY DIRECT
MARKETING
PO Box 24013
Royal Oak
AUCKLAND
1030
New Zealand
Tel: +64 9 6253010
Fax: +64 9 6253006
Martine Skinner

Services/Products:
Fulfilment and sampling house;
Mailing/Faxing services

Member of:
NZDMA

METRO CALL CENTRE
PO Box 30654
LOWER HUTT
6315
New Zealand

Tel: +64 800 882222
Fax: +64 800 882223
Email: andrew@metrocall.co.nz
Web: www.metrocallcentre.com
Andrew Lewis

Services/Products:
Telemarketing agency; Software
supplier; Electronic media

E-Services:
Website design

Member of:
NZDMA

MH GROUP
PO Box 7104
Wellesley Street
AUCKLAND
1036
New Zealand
Tel: +64 9 3734926
Fax: +64 9 3097731
Email: sales@mhgroup.co.nz
Garry Browne

Services/Products:
Design/graphics/clip art supplier; Print
services; Publisher

Member of:
NZDMA

MICROSAVE COMPUTER
   SERVICES LTD
PO Box 2102
AUCKLAND
1015
New Zealand
Tel: +64 9 8468554
Fax: +64 9 8468555
Thorsten Sauer

Services/Products:
Hardware supplier

Member of:
NZDMA

MOORE DIRECT MARKETING
   SERVICES
Private Bag 92081
AUCKLAND
1015
New Zealand
Tel: +64 9 5260910
Fax: +64 9 5261144
Email:
    graham.sergent@email.moore.com
Graham Sergent

Services/Products:
List services

Member of:
NZDMA

MOORE GALLAGHER
Private Bag 92 081
AUCKLAND
1020
New Zealand
Tel: +64 9 526 0910
Fax: +64 9 571 1987
Email: custcare.nz@mgnz.co.nz
Web: www.mooregallagher.co.nz
Christine Pennell, Promotions
    Manager

Services/Products:
Database services; Direct marketing
agency; List services; Personalisation;
Print services

Member of:
National DMA

MULLER MARKETING LTD
PO Box 41073
Eastbourne
WELLINGTON
6340
New Zealand
Tel: +64 4 5627221
Fax: +64 4 5627260
Email: theo.muller@clear.net.nz
Theo Muller

Services/Products:
Consultancy services; Market research
agency

Member of:
NZDMA

NEW ZEALAND POST LIMITED
PO Box 23
WELLINGTON
6015
New Zealand
Tel: +64 4 4964100
Fax: +64 4 4964972
Email: lindsay.welsh@nzpost.co.nz
Web: www.nzpost.co.nz
Lindsay Welsh

Services/Products:
List services

Member of:
NZDMA

NEWSNET NEW ZEALAND
200 Victoria St. West
PO Box 90–954
AUCKLAND
New Zealand
Tel: +64 9 307 2405
Fax: +64 9 379 9838
Email: info@newsnetnz.co.nz
Bill Boyle, Manager (New Zealand)

Services/Products:
Mailing/Faxing services;
Personalisation

ONE TO ONE DIRECT
PO Box 991
AUCKLAND
1015
New Zealand
Tel: +64 9 3735278
Fax: +64 9 3005090
Email: rafe@onetoone.co.nz
Web: www.onetoone.co.nz
Rafe Ring

Services/Products:
Direct marketing agency; Electronic
media

E-Services:
Website design

Member of:
NZDMA

ORACLE NEW ZEALAND
   LIMITED
PO Box 6747
Wellesley Street
AUCKLAND
1036
New Zealand
Tel: +64 9 3091946
Fax: +64 9 3778847
Email: sspain@nz.oracle.com
Steve Spain

Services/Products:
Software supplier

Member of:
NZDMA

ORBIT ON-LINE MARKETING
PO Box 37530
Parnell
AUCKLAND
1033
New Zealand
Tel: +64 9 3663947
Fax: +64 9 3076426
Email: linda@orbit.co.nz
Web: www.orbit.co.nz
Linda Geary

Services/Products:
Electronic media

E-Services:
Website design

Member of:
NZDMA

PAGE 1 LIMITED
PO Box 8803
Symonds Street
AUCKLAND

1035
New Zealand
Tel: +64 9 3732604
Fax: +64 9 3021414
Paul Gilbert

Services/Products:
Telemarketing agency

Member of:
NZDMA

PERMARK INDUSTRIES LTD
PO Box 14142
Panmure
AUCKLAND
1134
New Zealand
Tel: +64 9 5287172
Fax: +64 9 5289192
Email: chrisk@permark.co.nz
Chris Kilgour

Services/Products:
Print services

Member of:
NZDMA

PETER GRAHAM MARKETING
PO Box 324
MOTUEKA
7161
New Zealand
Tel: +64 3 5289743
Fax: +64 3 5286509
Email: p.g.marketing@xtra.co.nz
Peter Graham

Services/Products:
Consultancy services

Member of:
NZDMA

**PINPOINT TARGET
   MARKETING SERVICES**
PO Box 33271
Takapuna
AUCKLAND
1332
New Zealand
Tel: +64 9 4890500
Fax: +64 9 4863907
Web: www.circulars.co.nz
Janine Tindale

Services/Products:
List services; Database services;
Consultancy services

Member of:
NZDMA

**PREMIER BUSINESS PRINT
(NZ) LTD**
PO Box 51015
Pakuranga
AUCKLAND
1730
New Zealand
Tel: +64 9 2740421
Fax: +64 9 2742290
Email: tv-orbit@clear.net.nz
Tony Vercauteren

Services/Products:
Labelling/envelope services; Print
services

Member of:
NZDMA

PRESTIGE MARKETING LTD
PO Box 2093
AUCKLAND
1015
New Zealand
Tel: +64 9 5257700
Fax: +64 9 5257710
Paul Meier

Services/Products:
Direct response TV services

Member of:
NZDMA

PROFILE DIRECT
PO Box 5544
Wellesley Street
AUCKLAND
1036
New Zealand
Tel: +64 9 6308940
Fax: +64 9 6301046
Email: jenni@profile.co.nz
Jennifer Batt

Services/Products:
List services

Member of:
NZDMA

PROFILE PUBLISHING LTD
PO Box 5544
Wellesley Street
AUCKLAND
1015
New Zealand
Tel: +64 9 6308940
Fax: +64 9 6304665
Email: info@profile.co.nz
Web: www.profile.co.nz
Toni Myers

Services/Products:
List services; Database services;
Publisher; Translation services

Member of:
NZDMA

**RAINGER DIRECT
   MARKETING LTD**
PO Box 37236
Parnell
AUCKLAND
1033
New Zealand
Tel: +64 9 9141933
Fax: +64 9 9141934
Email: ant@rainger.co.nz
Ant Rainger

Services/Products:
Advertising Agency; Consultancy
services; Direct marketing agency

Member of:
NZDMA

RAPP COLLINS
PO Box 1872
AUCKLAND
1015
New Zealand
Tel: +64 9 3060945
Fax: +64 9 3060974
Email: richardb@rapp.co.nz
Richard Bleasdale

Services/Products:
Direct marketing agency

Member of:
NZDMA

RED CREATIVE LTD
PO Box 105479
AUCKLAND CENTRAL
1030
New Zealand
Tel: +64 9 3770690
Fax: +64 9 3770695
Kerryn Winn

Services/Products:
Fulfilment and sampling house;
Telemarketing agency; Training/
recruitment; Direct marketing agency;
Consultancy services

Member of:
NZDMA

RED ROCKS ADVERTISING
PO Box 27559
WELLINGTON
6015
New Zealand
Tel: +64 4 8017972
Fax: +64 4 8017973
Email: redrocks@actrix.gen.nz
Laura Humphreys

Services/Products:
Direct marketing agency; Electronic media

E-Services:
Website design

Member of:
NZDMA

RESEARCH SOLUTIONS
PO Box 82081
Highland Park
AUCKLAND
1730
New Zealand
Tel: +64 9 5355525
Fax: +64 9 5359627
Email: debra@resolutions.co.nz
Debra Hall

Services/Products:
Consultancy services; Market research agency

Member of:
NZDMA

RESPONSE LIMITED
PO Box 18292
Glen Innes
AUCKLAND
1130
New Zealand
Tel: +64 9 5258688
Fax: +64 9 5258695
Email: norine@response.co.nz
Norine Coles

Services/Products:
List services; Fulfilment and sampling house; Database services; Telemarketing agency; Service bureau; Loyalty systems

Member of:
NZDMA

RESULTS MARKETING LIMITED
PO Box 1361
Shortland Street
AUCKLAND
1015
New Zealand
Tel: +64 9 5253111
Fax: +64 9 3096810
Muir Hamilton

Services/Products:
Telemarketing agency

Member of:
NZDMA

RICHARD P GEE CONSULTANTS LTD
16 Duncansby Road
STANMORE BAY
1463
New Zealand
Tel: +64 9 4243282
Fax: +64 9 4243282
Email:
    100036.1777@compuserve.com
Richard Gee

Services/Products:
Telemarketing agency; Training/recruitment; Consultancy services; Market research agency

Member of:
NZDMA

RISHWORTH HENDERSON CROSS LTD
PO Box 90449
AUCKLAND MAIL SERVICE CENTRE
1030
New Zealand
Tel: +64 9 3583837
Fax: +64 9 3582434
Gary Cross

Services/Products:
Direct marketing agency

Member of:
NZDMA

ROBBINS BRANDT RICHTER LTD
PO Box 105120
AUCKLAND
1030
New Zealand
Tel: +64 9 3799007
Fax: +64 9 3799133
Email: mary@rbr.co.nz
Mary Robbins

Services/Products:
Advertising Agency; Direct marketing agency; Software supplier; Electronic media

E-Services:
Website design

Member of:
NZDMA

ROD SPENCE LTD
PO Box 25122
CHRISTCHURCH
8030
New Zealand
Tel: +64 3 3791475
Fax: +64 3 3650712
Rod Spence

Services/Products:
List services; Telemarketing agency; Consultancy services

Member of:
NZDMA

SAATCHI & SAATCHI LIMITED
PO Box 6540
Te Aro
WELLINGTON
6035
New Zealand
Tel: +64 4 3856524
Fax: +64 4 3859678
Email:
    paul.hackett@wgtn.saatchi.co.nz
Paul Hackett

Services/Products:
Direct marketing agency

Member of:
NZDMA

SALESFORCE LTD
PO Box 4136
AUCKLAND
1015
New Zealand
Tel: +64 9 3551022
Fax: +64 9 3553468
Email: salesforce@xtra.co.nz
Ena Nathan

Services/Products:
List services; Database services; Telemarketing agency

Member of:
NZDMA

SINGLETON, OGILVY & MATHER
PO Box 8735
Symonds Street
AUCKLAND
1035
New Zealand
Tel: +64 9 9148 500
Fax: +64 9 9148 501
John Wilde, Jennifer Hunt

Services/Products:
Advertising Agency; Direct marketing agency; Database services; Media buying agency; Personalisation; Print services

E-Services:
Online/e-marketing agency

Member of:
National DMA

718

SMART MARKETING LTD
PO Box 370
HAMILTON
2015
New Zealand
Tel: +64 7 8390692
Fax: +64 7 8340181
Email: allan@smartbuy.co.nz
Allan Smith

Services/Products:
List services; Database services; Direct
marketing agency; Loyalty systems

Member of:
NZDMA

SOFTWARE IMAGES LIMITED
PO Box 47254
Ponsonby
AUCKLAND
1034
New Zealand
Tel: +64 9 3789790
Fax: +64 9 3789494
Email: jbishop@swimages.co.nz
Web: www.swimages.co.nz
John Bishop

Services/Products:
Electronic media

E-Services:
Website design

Member of:
NZDMA

STARTEL
 TELEPERFORMANCE
Private Bag 92090
AUCKLAND CENTRAL
1030
New Zealand
Tel: +64 9 3039380
Fax: +64 9 3039388
Marshall Taylor

Services/Products:
Telemarketing agency; Training/
recruitment

Member of:
NZDMA

STRATEGIC MEDIA LTD
PO Box 2590
AUCKLAND
1015
New Zealand
Tel: +64 9 3072190
Fax: +64 9 3661570
Email: mail@strategicm.co.nz
Robert Roydhouse

Services/Products:
Media buying agency

Member of:
NZDMA

SULLIVAN THOMSON LIMITED
PO Box 11048
WELLINGTON
6034
New Zealand
Tel: +64 4 3841919
Fax: +64 4 3853397
Email: scottf@stconsult.co.nz
Scott Fuller

Services/Products:
Consultancy services

Member of:
NZDMA

SUMNER DIRECT
 COMMUNICATIONS
40 Bell Road
Remuera
AUCKLAND
1005
New Zealand
Tel: +64 9 5206649
Fax: +64 9 5205218
Email: john@sumnerdirect.co.nz
John Sumner

Services/Products:
Training/recruitment; Training/
recruitment; Direct marketing agency;
Direct response TV services

Member of:
NZDMA

TALKTACTICS
 INTERNATIONAL LIMITED
PO Box 302–263
North Harbour Business Estate
Albany
New Zealand
Tel: +64 9 415 0995
Fax: +64 9 415 0994
Email: theteam@talktactics.com
Web: www.talktactics.com
Katie McFadyen, Sales Director

Services/Products:
Call centre services/systems;
Consultancy services; Interactive
media; Training/recruitment

Member of:
National DMA

TARP AUSTRALASIA PTY LTD
PO Box 11819
WELLINGTON
WELLINGTON
6036
New Zealand
Tel: +64 4 4710166
Fax: +64 4 4710167

Email: dsylvester@tarpaust.com
David Sylvester

Services/Products:
Telemarketing agency; Training/
recruitment; Market research agency

Member of:
NZDMA

TELECOM DIRECTORIES LTD
PO Box 17157
Greenlane
AUCKLAND
1130
New Zealand
Tel: +64 9 5253430
Fax: +64 9 5253900
Email: davidwi@directories.co.nz
Web: www.yellowpages.co.nz
David Williams

Services/Products:
List services

Member of:
NZDMA

TELEFINANCIAL LIMITED
PO Box 331694
Takapuna
AUCKLAND
1332
New Zealand
Tel: +64 9 4881595
Fax: +64 9 4881591
Email: telefin@xtra.co.nz
Richard Johnson

Services/Products:
Telemarketing agency

Member of:
NZDMA

TELELINK LTD
PO Box 6691
Wellesley Street
AUCKLAND
1036
New Zealand
Tel: +64 9 3576680
Fax: +64 9 3794656
Brian Chisholm

Services/Products:
Telemarketing agency

Member of:
NZDMA

TELELINK LTD
PO Box 5109
WELLINGTON
6040
New Zealand
Tel: +64 4 4992 022
Fax: +64 4 4993 033

Email: Telelink@xtra.co.nz
Web: www.telelink.co.nz
Theresa Chang, Wellington Manager

Services/Products:
Telemarketing agency; Database
services; Mailing/Faxing services;
Market research agency; Fulfilment
and sampling house; Call centre
services/systems

Member of:
National DMA

TELETELL CONSULTANTS
PO Box 882
WELLINGTON
WELLINGTON
6041
New Zealand
Tel: +64 4 4994997
Fax: +64 4 4995678
Paul Myers

Services/Products:
Telemarketing agency

Member of:
NZDMA

TELNET SERVICES LIMITED
PO Box 4313
AUCKLAND
1032
New Zealand
Tel: +64 9 3035303
Fax: +64 9 3035300
Email: kateg@telnet.co.nz
John Chetwynd

Services/Products:
Telemarketing agency

Member of:
NZDMA

THE BRIDGE LIMITED
PO Box 6646
WELLINGTON
6015
New Zealand
Tel: +64 4 3853579
Fax: +64 4 3850420
Email: chris@bridge.co.nz
Chris O'Connell

Services/Products:
Direct marketing agency; Electronic
media

E-Services:
Website design

Member of:
NZDMA

THE GREAT ELK COMPANY LIMITED
PO Box 47883
Ponsonby
AUCKLAND
1034
New Zealand
Tel: +64 9 3610888
Fax: +64 9 3610889
Email: stephen.a@greatelk.com
Web: www.greatelk.com
Stephen Andrew

Services/Products:
Database services; Software supplier

Member of:
NZDMA

THE PERSONAL TOUCH
PO Box 65 339
AUCKLAND
1330
New Zealand
Tel: +649 4766 222
Fax: +649 4766 444
Email: cards@thepersonaltouch.co.nz
Web: www.thepersonaltouch.co.nz
Adrienne Bullock, President

Services/Products:
Card pack manufacturer; Design/
graphics/clip art supplier; Direct
marketing agency; Mail order
company; Consultancy services for
CRM

Member of:
NDMA (NZ); SMEI (NZ)

THE WEB LIMITED
PO Box 15175
Miramar
WELLINGTON
6030
New Zealand
Tel: +64 4 3889528
Fax: +64 4 3889588
Email: davem@web.co.nz
Web: www.web.co.nz
Dave Moskovitz

Services/Products:
Electronic media

E-Services:
Website design

Member of:
NZDMA

THE WORKFORCE GROUP
PO Box 6441
Wellesley Street
AUCKLAND
1036
New Zealand

Tel: +64 9 3792308
Fax: +64 9 3792307
Julie Parsons

Services/Products:
Telemarketing agency; Training/
recruitment

Member of:
NZDMA

TIMES COLOUR PRINT
PO Box 33951
Takapuna
AUCKLAND
New Zealand
Tel: +64 9 489 7980
Fax: +64 9 489 7985
Martin Blumberg

Services/Products:
Print services

TOM TOM
PO Box 9307
WELLINGTON
6031
New Zealand
Tel: +64 4 4733100
Fax: +64 4 4733100
Email: greg@tomtom.co.nz
Greg Berge

Services/Products:
Design/graphics/clip art supplier

Member of:
NZDMA

TOUCHSTONE DIRECT
PO Box 99628
Newmarket
AUCKLAND
1031
New Zealand
Tel: +64 9 6236247
Fax: +64 9 6386715
Email: grogan.david@xtra.co.nz
David Grogan

Services/Products:
List services; Database services; Dire
marketing agency; Consultancy
services; Electronic media

E-Services:
Website design

Member of:
NZDMA

TRIO BUSINESS PRINT LTD
PO Box 17103
Greenlane
AUCKLAND
1130
New Zealand
Tel: +64 9 5262333

Fax: +64 9 5262330
Email: graeme@trio.co.nz
Graeme Foster

Services/Products:
Direct marketing agency; Consultancy
services; Design/graphics/clip art
supplier; Print services

Member of:
NZDMA

TRIPS
PO Box 4452
AUCKLAND
1015
New Zealand
Tel: +64 9 3796276
Fax: +64 9 3076889
Email:
    annettee_flexiplan@atlasmail.com
Annette Eltringham

Services/Products:
Loyalty systems

Member of:
NZDMA

URSA MAJOR CONSULTING
Private Bag MBE P381
Ponsonby
AUCKLAND
1034
New Zealand
Tel: +64 9 3768950
Email: ursula@n4b.com
Ursula Hoult

Services/Products:
Electronic media

E-Services:
Website design

Member of:
NZDMA

**VERSARI INTERNATIONAL -
    NEW ZEALAND**
PO Box 98740
South Auckland Mail Centre
AUCKLAND
1730
New Zealand
Tel: +64 9 2688948
Fax: +64 9 2672244
Email: campbell@versari.co.nz
Web: www.versari.co.nz
Campbell Scott

Services/Products:
Consultancy services; Print services

Member of:
NZDMA

WESTERN MAILING LTD
PO Box 48104
Blockhouse Bay
AUCKLAND
1230
New Zealand
Tel: +64 9 8290800
Fax: +64 9 8290850
Web: www.mailing.co.nz
Gary Lewis

Services/Products:
List services; Database services;
Mailing/Faxing services; Service
bureau; Print services

Member of:
NZDMA

**WILSON ADVERTISING AND
    MARKETING LTD**
PO Box 479
CHRISTCHURCH
8015
New Zealand
Tel: +64 3 3775150
Fax: +64 3 3778122
Email: j.wilson@wilsonadvtg.co.nz
Jonathan Wilson

Services/Products:
Direct marketing agency; Consultancy
services; Design/graphics/clip art
supplier; Print services

Member of:
NZDMA

WORDS BY DESIGN
PO Box 87352
Meadowbank
AUCKLAND
1130
New Zealand
Tel: +64 9 5200434
Fax: +64 9 5206877
Email: wordsbydesign@xtra.co.nz
Gary Norris

Services/Products:
Direct marketing agency

Member of:
NZDMA

WUNDERMAN CATO JOHNSON
Private Bag 93234
Parnell
AUCKLAND
1033
New Zealand
Tel: +64 9 3085800
Fax: +64 9 3085801
Email: peter_darroch@wcj.com
Peter Darroch

Services/Products:
Advertising Agency; Direct marketing
agency

Member of:
NZDMA

WYATT & WILSON PRINT LTD
PO Box 4261
CHRISTCHURCH
8015
New Zealand
Tel: +64 3 3661147
Fax: +64 3 3795845
Peter Clarke

Services/Products:
Print services

Member of:
NZDMA

XPO EXHIBITIONS LTD
PO Box 9682
Newmarket
AUCKLAND
1031
New Zealand
Tel: +64 9 3003950
Fax: +64 9 3793358
Email: mblank@xpo.co.nz
Web: www.xpo.co.nz
Marnie Blank

Member of:
NZDMA

**ZEPPELIN DIRECT
    ADVERTISING LTD**
PO Box 8719
Symonds Street
AUCKLAND
1035
New Zealand
Tel: +64 9 3771900
Fax: +64 9 3098605
Email: hamish@zeppelin.co.nz
Web: www.zeppelin.co.nz
Hamish Wilkie

Services/Products:
Direct marketing agency; Direct
response TV services

Member of:
NZDMA

SERVICES/PRODUCT
LISTING

Advertising Agency
Ammirati Puris Lintas New Zealand
Campaign Direct
CWFS McCann

Gestro Horne
Goldsack Harris Thompson
J Walter Thompson (NZ) Ltd
MacMarketing Ltd
Mason Sewell Communications
MediaPlus Ltd
Mercato Communications Ltd
Rainger Direct Marketing Ltd
Robbins Brandt Richter Ltd
Singleton, Ogilvy & Mather
Wunderman Cato Johnson

Call centre services/systems
TalkTactics International Limited
Telelink Ltd

Card pack manufacturer
The Personal Touch

Conference/exhibition organiser
AIC Worldwide Limited
Institute For International Research

Consultancy services
Amazing But True
Archie Mason Ltd
Arrow Limited
Atlantis Marketing Limited
Campaign Direct
Carpe DM Ltd
Comit Group Ltd
Communication Graphics Limited
Current Pacific Ltd
Data Magic Limited
Database Communications
Forte Integrated Marketing
Gestro Horne
Gilbert Swan
High Performance Systems
Holloway Advertising
J Walter Thompson (NZ) Ltd
KPMG
MacMarketing Ltd
Marketing Technologies Ltd
Maxim Group Ltd
MediaPlus Ltd
mental as anything
Mercato Communications Ltd
Muller Marketing Ltd
Peter Graham Marketing
Pinpoint Target Marketing Services
Rainger Direct Marketing Ltd
Red Creative Ltd
Research Solutions
Richard P Gee Consultants Ltd
Rod Spence Ltd
Sullivan Thomson Limited
TalkTactics International Limited
The Personal Touch
Touchstone Direct
Trio Business Print Ltd
Versari International - New Zealand

Wilson Advertising and Marketing Ltd

Consultancy services
Amazing But True
Archie Mason Ltd
Arrow Limited
Atlantis Marketing Limited
Campaign Direct
Carpe DM Ltd
Comit Group Ltd
Communication Graphics Limited
Current Pacific Ltd
Data Magic Limited
Database Communications
Forte Integrated Marketing
Gestro Horne
Gilbert Swan
High Performance Systems
Holloway Advertising
J Walter Thompson (NZ) Ltd
KPMG
MacMarketing Ltd
Marketing Technologies Ltd
Maxim Group Ltd
MediaPlus Ltd
mental as anything
Mercato Communications Ltd
Muller Marketing Ltd
Peter Graham Marketing
Pinpoint Target Marketing Services
Rainger Direct Marketing Ltd
Red Creative Ltd
Research Solutions
Richard P Gee Consultants Ltd
Rod Spence Ltd
Sullivan Thomson Limited
TalkTactics International Limited
The Personal Touch
Touchstone Direct
Trio Business Print Ltd
Versari International - New Zealand
Wilson Advertising and Marketing Ltd

Database services
Actionmail Ltd
Aim Direct Limited
Atlantis Marketing Limited
Bounty Services Ltd
Comit Group Ltd
Data Magic Limited
Database Communications
Datacom Services NZ
Datamail Ltd
Datamine Limited
Dataprint Ltd
Deltarg Distribution Systems Ltd
Dun & Bradstreet (NZ) Ltd
Gallagher Info Management Group
Handle With Care Ltd
Havas MediMedia NZ Ltd
Mailshop Limited
Marketing Impact Ltd
Marketing Technologies Ltd

Marriott Services
Moore Gallagher
Pinpoint Target Marketing Services
Profile Publishing Ltd
Response Limited
SalesForce Ltd
Singleton, Ogilvy & Mather
Smart Marketing Ltd
Telelink Ltd
The Great Elk Company Limited
Touchstone Direct
Western Mailing Ltd

Design/graphics/clip art supplier
Aim Direct Limited
Communication Graphics Limited
Dunham Bremmer
Forte Integrated Marketing
Holloway Advertising
Imagine Ltd
Mason Sewell Communications
Maxim Group Ltd
mental as anything
MH Group
The Personal Touch
tom tom
Trio Business Print Ltd
Wilson Advertising and Marketing L

Direct marketing agency
Aim Direct Limited
Aim Direct Limited
Amazing But True
Ammirati Puris Lintas New Zealand
Atlantis Marketing Limited
Campaign Direct
Carpe DM Ltd
Communication Graphics Limited
Current Pacific Ltd
CWFS McCann
Energy Marketing and Communications Ltd
Forte Integrated Marketing
Gestro Horne
Go Direct Marketing Ltd
Goldsack Harris Thompson
Hyde Agencies Ltd
J Walter Thompson (NZ) Ltd
KiwiMail Limited
MacMarketing Ltd
Magnet Direct Marketing
Marketing Impact Ltd
Maxim Group Ltd
MediaPlus Ltd
mental as anything
Mercato Communications Ltd
Moore Gallagher
one to one direct
Rainger Direct Marketing Ltd
Rapp Collins
Red Creative Ltd
Red Rocks Advertising

Rishworth Henderson Cross Ltd
Robbins Brandt Richter Ltd
Saatchi & Saatchi Limited
Singleton, Ogilvy & Mather
Smart Marketing Ltd
Sumner Direct Communications
The Bridge Limited
The Personal Touch
Touchstone Direct
Trio Business Print Ltd
Wilson Advertising and Marketing Ltd
Words By Design
Wunderman Cato Johnson
Zeppelin Direct Advertising Ltd

Direct response TV services
Aim Direct Limited
Channel I Ltd
Prestige Marketing Ltd
Sumner Direct Communications
Zeppelin Direct Advertising Ltd

Electronic media
Advoc8 Online Ltd
Aim Direct Limited
Atlantis Marketing Limited
Carpe DM Ltd
Datacom Services NZ
Forte Integrated Marketing
Hyperactive Ltd
IBM New Zealand Limited
Marriott Services
Metro Call Centre
one to one direct
Orbit On-Line Marketing
Red Rocks Advertising
Robbins Brandt Richter Ltd
Software Images Limited
The Bridge Limited
The Web Limited
Touchstone Direct
Ursa Major Consulting

Fulfilment and sampling house
Archie Mason Ltd
Cumming Enterprises
Data Magic Limited
Datamail Ltd
Dataprint Ltd
Fullworks International Limited
Handle With Care Ltd
Havas MediMedia NZ Ltd
Mailshop Limited
Marketing Impact Ltd
Mercury Direct Marketing
Red Creative Ltd
Response Limited
Telelink Ltd

Hardware supplier
Compaq Computer New Zealand Ltd
IBM New Zealand Limited
MicroSave Computer Services Ltd

Interactive media
Gestro Horne
TalkTactics International Limited

Labelling/envelope services
Comit Group Ltd
Domino Marketing Ltd
Galaxy Envelope Mftg Co Ltd
Havas MediMedia NZ Ltd
Mailshop Limited
Premier Business Print (NZ) Ltd

Legal services
Consumers' Institute of NZ INC
Gilbert Swan

Lettershop
Comit Group Ltd
Current Pacific Ltd
Database Communications
Dataprint Ltd
Deltarg Distribution Systems Ltd
Hyde Agencies Ltd

List services
Actionmail Ltd
Aim Direct Limited
Atlantis Marketing Limited
Bounty Services Ltd
Current Pacific Ltd
Data Magic Limited
Datacom Services NZ
Datamail Ltd
Datamine Limited
Deltarg Distribution Systems Ltd
Direct Media (NZ) Ltd
Dun & Bradstreet (NZ) Ltd
Fullworks International Limited
Gallagher Info Management Group
Handle With Care Ltd
Havas MediMedia NZ Ltd
Hyde Agencies Ltd
Marketing Impact Ltd
Marketing Technologies Ltd
Marriott Services
Moore Direct Marketing Services
Moore Gallagher
New Zealand Post Limited
Pinpoint Target Marketing Services
Profile Direct
Profile Publishing Ltd
Response Limited
Rod Spence Ltd
SalesForce Ltd
Smart Marketing Ltd
Telecom Directories Ltd
Touchstone Direct
Western Mailing Ltd

Loyalty systems
Fullworks International Limited
Response Limited
Smart Marketing Ltd
TRIPS

Mail order company
EziBuy Wholesale Limited
The Personal Touch

Mailing/Faxing services
Actionmail Ltd
Cumming Enterprises
Current Pacific Ltd
Datamail Ltd
Dataprint Ltd
Fullworks International Limited
Gallagher Info Management Group
Handle With Care Ltd
Havas MediMedia NZ Ltd
Mailshop Limited
Marketing Impact Ltd
Mercury Direct Marketing
Newsnet New Zealand
Telelink Ltd
Western Mailing Ltd

Market research agency
Dun & Bradstreet (NZ) Ltd
Muller Marketing Ltd
Research Solutions
Richard P Gee Consultants Ltd
TARP Australasia Pty Ltd
Telelink Ltd

Media buying agency
Gestro Horne
J Walter Thompson (NZ) Ltd
MediaPlus Ltd
Singleton, Ogilvy & Mather
Strategic Media Ltd

Medical database
Havas MediMedia NZ Ltd

Personalisation
Database Communications
Mailshop Limited
Moore Gallagher
Newsnet New Zealand
Singleton, Ogilvy & Mather

Print services
Boughtwood Printing House Ltd
Comit Group Ltd
Communication Graphics Limited
Domino Marketing Ltd
Dunham Bremmer
Gainsborough Printing Co Ltd
Gallagher Info Management Group
Handle With Care Ltd
Hyde Agencies Ltd
Imagine Ltd
Impex Press (NZ) Ltd
Mailshop Limited
MH Group
Moore Gallagher
Permark Industries Ltd
Premier Business Print (NZ) Ltd

Singleton, Ogilvy & Mather
Times Colour Print
Trio Business Print Ltd
Versari International - New Zealand
Western Mailing Ltd
Wilson Advertising and Marketing Ltd
Wyatt & Wilson Print Ltd

Private delivery services
Circular Distributors Ltd

Publisher
Canterbury University Press
Current Pacific Ltd
MH Group
Profile Publishing Ltd

Response analysis bureau
Database Communications
Dataprint Ltd

Sales promotion agency
Gestro Horne

Service bureau
Aim Direct Limited
Comit Group Ltd
Data Magic Limited
Dataprint Ltd
Fullworks International Limited
Response Limited
Western Mailing Ltd

Software supplier
Database Communications
Datacom Services NZ
Marketing Technologies Ltd
Metro Call Centre
Oracle New Zealand Limited
Robbins Brandt Richter Ltd
The Great Elk Company Limited

Telemarketing agency
Archie Mason Ltd

Atlantis Marketing Limited
Campaign Direct
Datamail Ltd
Forte Integrated Marketing
Fullworks International Limited
Mayer Consultants Ltd
Metro Call Centre
Page 1 Limited
Red Creative Ltd
Response Limited
Results Marketing Limited
Richard P Gee Consultants Ltd
Rod Spence Ltd
SalesForce Ltd
Startel Teleperformance
TARP Australasia Pty Ltd
TeleFinancial Limited
Telelink Ltd
Telelink Ltd
TeleTELL Consultants
Telnet Services Limited
The Workforce Group

Training/recruitment
AIC Worldwide Limited
Amazing But True
Campaign Direct
DMA
Institute For International Research
Marsden Inch Consulting
Mayer Consultants Ltd
McLay & Company
Red Creative Ltd
Richard P Gee Consultants Ltd
Startel Teleperformance
Sumner Direct Communications
TalkTactics International Limited
TARP Australasia Pty Ltd
The Workforce Group

Translation services
Profile Publishing Ltd

E-SERVICES

E-Marketing consultant
Comit Group Ltd
Gestro Horne

Email list provider
Gestro Horne

Email software
Mailshop Limited

Online/e-marketing agency
Comit Group Ltd
Gestro Horne
Singleton, Ogilvy & Mather

Website design
Advoc8 Online Ltd
Aim Direct Limited
Atlantis Marketing Limited
Carpe DM Ltd
Comit Group Ltd
Datacom Services NZ
Forte Integrated Marketing
Gestro Horne
Hyperactive Ltd
IBM New Zealand Limited
J Walter Thompson (NZ) Ltd
MacMarketing Ltd
Marriott Services
Metro Call Centre
one to one direct
Orbit On-Line Marketing
Red Rocks Advertising
Robbins Brandt Richter Ltd
Software Images Limited
The Bridge Limited
The Web Limited
Touchstone Direct
Ursa Major Consulting

SOUTH AFRICA

> *Population*: 42.3 million
> *Capital*: Pretoria
> *Languages*: 11 official languages
> (English widely used as second language)
>
> *GDP*: $141 billion
> *GDP per capita*: $3,329
> *Inflation*: 7.0 per cent
>
> *Currency*: Rand (R) = 100 cents
> *Exchange rate*: R6.61 : $1
>
> *Time*: GMT +2 hours

This report has been prepared by the Direct Marketing Association of Southern Africa.

DIRECT MARKETING IN SOUTH AFRICA

The direct marketing industry has grown considerably over the past years in South Africa. Particular growth has been experienced in the telephone marketing environment, and the country is very well positioned for a boom in electronic commerce.

The direct mail and mail order markets have been aided by the efforts of the South African Post Office to increase access to postal services. Currently almost 3.5 million street addresses and 3.4 million postboxes are serviced, which measures up well with the 8.5 million households and 250 thousand formal businesses.

Although the vast majority of the people have access to facilities whereby they might receive mail, they may not have the experience or sophistication to understand the concepts being sent to them. Only approximately 55 per cent of the adult population have received some form of secondary education. Related to this is the fact that the distribution of income is among the most unequal in the world, with 34 per cent of all households accounting for 72 per cent of total household income. This indicates that Direct Marketing efforts need to be well targeted and well conceptualised.

Telephone marketing is a fast growing and thriving industry, for both in- and outbound calls, although only 30 per cent of households have a telephone. Large financial institutions and retailers have established quite a number of call centres; in addition, there are a number of successful bureaux.

Fax-mail is also becoming popular as a means to get more immediacy into a campaign and save on costs. Another growing direct marketing approach is the use of Internet for response-generating marketing.

Consumer lists

Access to larger databases is rather limited, since many of the institutional list owners have withdrawn the use of their files from general use. On the other hand, private sector list owners are increasingly making their lists available. Due to the fact that databases were not growing as they should, many companies are establishing their own sources.

Larger lists available include account files from a number of major chain stores, mail order responders and cellular phone service providers. Databases are becoming more marketable, with information being gathered and added, and selection in some cases is quite sophisticated.

Business lists

Business-to-business files tend to have a good coverage of larger established businesses, but inappropriate coverage of smaller businesses. However, small business is increasingly being gathered into the net. There are very few providers of major business-to-business files. Many new, smaller commercial databases are becoming available as companies with data are making their lists available to non-competitors. Some of these smaller commercial databases are well constructed and maintained, enabling more specialised marketing.

Ongoing recruitment of lists from owners is taking place, with reasonable effect. It is thought that the introduction of privacy protection legislation in the near future will reassure owners on the security of their files and the protection of their customers. Many of these owners still place onerous restrictions on the use of their files.

List broking

Several hundred lists are available, very few of which are exclusively brokered by one company or another. A number of the larger list owners also act as brokers, and there are a limited number of small list owners who act as brokers. There is one independent list broker who does not own lists, but acts as an agent for almost every available list in the country and offers a service to research new lists where necessary. Local list brokers are increasingly interacting with international clients and list brokers.

Nixies rates and quality

Great variations persist in nixie rates. Nixies on business-to-business files should not be more than 5 per cent, and the accepted limit for consumer files is 7-8 per cent. Some of the list owners offer to buy back the nixies for the ongoing upkeep of their data.

There are wide differences in data quality. Some lists are very basic name and address files, while others have staggering amounts of information though not all are always available to outside users. Sophistication is improving, as owners understand the importance of building relationships within specific markets.

LANGUAGE AND CULTURAL CONSIDERATIONS

South Africa has 11 official languages. Only 12 per cent of the total South African adult population claim English to be their home language, but 92 per cent of all individuals who are into the upper Living Standards Measures Groups (LSM 6–8) read and understand English.

	Home or First Language (% of total adult pop)	Reads and Understands English (% of language group)	LSM 6–8 (% of language group)
Total Adult Population	25.7 million	17.1 million	10.1 million
Percentage of Adult Population	100%	67%	39%
English	12%	96%	92%
Afrikaans	17%	84%	81%
Zulu	24%	53%	22%
Xhosa	16%	54%	19%
North Sotho	9%	65%	17%
South Sotho	9%	62%	29%
Tswana	8%	62%	28%
Tsonga	4%	63%	17%
Venda	2%	56%	15%
Swazi	3%	61%	18%
Ndebele	1%	65%	23%

Source: All Media Product Survey 1997

The LSM grouping system was introduced by the South African Advertising Research Foundation as a 'demographic' measure that did not take race, but rather product usage, into account, to divide the population into eight LSM groups. LSM 1 is the least affluent and most rural; LSM 8 is the most affluent. Most direct mail campaigns will be aimed at the more economically viable LSM 6–8 groups, to which 39 per cent of the total South African adult population belong. English, therefore, remains a convenient language for a direct mail campaign, though there is scope for achieving a more personal note through careful targeting in one of the other official languages. It is advisable to seek guidance from a local agent or translator, so that the appropriate language and cultural nuances can be brought to bear. The above table presents the language usage for the eleven official languages as well as the percentage of the adult population that should be considered as the most appropriate target group for direct marketing.

LEGISLATION AND CONSUMER PROTECTION

The legislative environment has changed quite dramatically in the recent past. In the main this has been enlightened and business friendly, largely due to active lobbying involvement from the Direct Marketing Association.

In particular, the Association has been instrumental in minimising the potential threat of data privacy legislation encompassed in the pending Open Democracy Act. This Act will put in place restrictions on the use and disclosure of information held by public and private entities, and will grant certain rights in terms of access, correction and protection. The Act is expected to become law during 1999 and the Association is optimistic that the direct marketing industry will not be negatively impacted by the legislation.

The Direct Marketing Association of Southern Africa issues a compulsory Code of Practice to all its members. This document details best practice in all aspects of direct marketing, including telemarketing and fax-marketing. A new electronic commerce and infomercial Code is in development. The Code has been published in the *Government Gazette* by the Business Practices Committee of the country's Department of Trade and Industry, and recognises the DMA as the self-regulatory representative of the industry. The DMA maintains close contact with government departments, consumer organizations and trade associations, and deals with complaints received through them or direct from the public. It also offers consumers an industry-wide means to opt out of receiving marketing through the Mail, Telephone and Fax Preference Services.

THE DIRECT MARKETING ASSOCIATION

Name:	The Direct Marketing Association of Southern Africa
Address:	P.O. Box 977, Auckland Park, 2006, South Africa
Tel:	+27 11 482 6440
Fax:	+27 11 482 1200
Email:	dma@dma.org.za
Website:	www.dma.org.za
Year founded:	1984
Executive Director:	Davy Ivins
Total Staff:	6
Membership:	323
Contact:	Davy Ivins, Executive Director

Advertising agencies	35	Mail order companies	73
Consultancies	26	Mailing houses	17
Direct marketing agencies	14	Media/publishers	10
List brokers/owners	42	Printers	4

The DMA is the sole trade body for direct marketers throughout South Africa and represents more than 300 member companies and over 1000 individuals actively involved in the South African DM industry. Membership is strongly representative of both suppliers to the industry and marketers within the industry. Whilst virtually all the major players in the market are active members of the DMA, the Association also has good support from small to medium-size companies. The financial services industry is particularly well represented.

The Association has a very active regional committee infrastructure in Johannesburg and Cape Town, and operates a number of special interest groups. The DMA Postal Affairs and Telebusiness Committees are particularly active, and have proved exceptionally effective on lobbying, service and tariff issues.

POSTAL SERVICES

The South African Post Office offers a wide range of services to direct marketers and business users. A comprehensive discount, rebate and incentive structure has been implemented in negotiation with the DMA. The following definitions apply to services:

- **Registered letter with an insurance option:** Caters for important letters containing something of monetary value. Basic insurance up to R100 is included in the service fee. For valuable letters with a monetary value of over R100, optional insurance for up to R2 000 is available.

- **Signature on delivery:** Allows for letters to be delivered against a signature. No valuables such as cash, share certificates or passports should be sent with this service. No compensation is payable with this service.

- **Fastmail:** Allows for postal articles to be delivered within specific delivery standards. Special pre-paid envelopes have been designed for this purpose and are available from all post offices.

- **Advertising mail:** Ensures that sales, promotional or advertising messages reach target markets cost-effectively. This can be used for recruiting new customers, sending questionnaires to customers, sending out information on special offers, making fund-raising requests and furnishing competition details.

- **Infomail:** Allows for unaddressed mail (pamphlets, brochures, etc.) to be delivered locally and nationally, in private post-boxes, private bags or at mail collection points at more than three million delivery points. It is target market specific and can be adjusted to suit specific needs.

- **Business Reply Service (BRS):** Is a simple and effective way to obtain a response to your direct marketing communication. Using BRS means that you can offer your customer or prospective customer the incentive to reply without having to pay postage. In this regard, two options are available, i.e. you may enclose a business reply postcard or envelope in your mailing, or you may advertise a specified address and freepost number to which the customer may write.
- **Magmail:** Is specifically designed to address the specific needs of the magazine and newspaper industry.
- **Postage paid envelopes:** Make communication through a letter easy and convenient. They are available from all post offices in the following sizes: B4, C4, B5, and DL.

A separate business unit, Securemail, was established in conjunction with financial institutions to dispatch security-sensitive products, such as credit cards, safely. The articles are handled only by assigned Post Office personnel and only the recipient may collect the articles by producing an identity document.

To ensure quick and accurate mail delivery, correct addressing and the use of correct post codes on mail articles are essential. To obviate the use of incorrect postal codes, the Post Office has various services offering the correct post codes to the market. Organisations may obtain the latest postal codes from the Internet (www.sapo.co.za), PostCoder software package (toll-free number is 0800 110 9800) or the ASCII file available from the local sales manager.

Organisations may also have their postal address lists or databases checked and graded in order to benefit from various postage rebates. Members of the Postal Address Management Service Suppliers, an industry body allied to the DMA, assist the Post Office by providing commercial address checking, cleaning and grading services to any organisation interested in receiving rebates. The added benefits of a clean postal address mailing list or database are cost savings with regard to preparation of marketing or advertising material, postage, etc.

For more information, contact:

South African Post Office
International Relations & Customer Services Section
PO Box 10000
Pretoria 0001
South Africa

Tel: +27 12 421 7592
Fax: +27 12 421 7570
Email: sales@sapo.co.za
Website: www.sapo.co.za

PROVIDERS OF DM AND E-M SERVICES

ANALOGUE MIS CC
PO Box 82086
Southdale
2135
South Africa
Tel: +27 11 680 4557
Fax: +27 11 680 4732
Email: interactive@analogue.co.za
Luisa Bozzonetti

Services/Products:
List services; Database services;
Response analysis bureau;
Personalisation

Member of:
SADMA

APPLIED TECHNOLOGY SYSTEMS CC
PO Box 47429
Parklands
2121
South Africa
Tel: +27 11 887 2681
Fax: +27 11 887 1945
Email: lionelf@batec.com
Web: www.batec.com
Lionel Friend

Services/Products:
Database services; Call centre services/
systems; Electronic media;
Relationship marketing

E-Services:
Website design

Member of:
SADMA

B&L DIRECT MARKETING SERVICES
12 Upper Orange Street
Oranjezicht
8001
South Africa
Tel: +27 21 465 0660
Fax: +27 21 465 0664
Email: bldirect@iafrica.co.za
Loriane von Allemann

Services/Products:
List services; Lettershop; Database
services; Telemarketing agency; Direct
marketing agency

Member of:
SADMA

BEHIND THE GREEN DOOR
PO Box 651404
Benmore
2010
South Africa
Tel: +27 11 462 4130
Fax: +27 11 462 4589
Email: greendoo@mweb.co.za
Anthony Hanly

Services/Products:
List services; Database services; Copy
adaptation; Software supplier; Sales
promotion agency

Member of:
SADMA

BREWER'S MARKETING INTELLIGENCE
PO Box 23567
Claremont
7735
South Africa
Tel: +27 21 683 1371
Fax: +27 21 683 1373
Email: brewers@iafrica.com
Chris Brewer

Services/Products:
List services; Database services;
Publisher

Member of:
SADMA

BRIAN PITMAN MARKETING
PO Box 2884
Randburg
2125
South Africa
Tel: +27 11 886 1139
Fax: +27 11 886 2972
Brian Pitman

Services/Products:
Database services; Consultancy
services; Mail order company;
Advertising Agency; Direct Response
Agency

Member of:
SADMA

CAB HOLDINGS (PTY) LTD
PO Box 8182
Johannesburg
2000
South Africa
Tel: +27 11 615 6575
Fax: +27 11 615 1301
Email: cab.holdings@pixie.co.za
Peter Saunders

Services/Products:
Fulfilment and sampling house;
Mailing/Faxing services; Print services

BEHIND THE GREEN DOOR
Member of:
SADMA

CELEBRATIONS AGENCIES
PO Box 411881
Craighall
2024
South Africa
Tel: +27 32 381 011
Fax: +27 11 480 8640
John Browett

Services/Products:
Mail order company; Advertising
Agency; Direct Response Agency

Member of:
SADMA

CHRISTA STEYN AGENCY
PO Box 11179
Bloubergrant
7443
South Africa
Tel: +27 21 557 8703
Fax: +27 21 557 8998
C Steyn

Services/Products:
Advertising Agency; Direct Response
Agency

Member of:
SADMA

COMPUTER FACILITIES (PTY) LTD
PO Box 2191
Randburg
2125
South Africa
Tel: +27 11 789 1921
Fax: +27 11 886 8882
Email: iang@facilities.co.za

Services/Products:
Lettershop; Mailing/Faxing services;
Database services; Personalisation; Call
centre services/systems; Service bureau

Member of:
National DMA

CREATIVE RESPONSE
PO Box 4776
Randburg
2125
South Africa
Tel: +27 11 886 0914
Fax: +27 11 886 0807
Web: www.creativeresponse.co.za
Chris Joseph

Services/Products:
Database services; Telemarketing
agency; Response analysis bureau

731

Member of:
SADMA

CUSTOMER BEHAVIOR DYNAMICS
PO Box 1776
Halfway House
1685
South Africa
Tel: +27 11 265 1400
Fax: +27 11 265 1411
Email: antonettek@abraxas365.com
Web: www.abraxas365.com
Antonette Koen

Services/Products:
Training/recruitment; Training/
recruitment; Direct marketing agency

Member of:
SADMA

CYBERIA (PTY) LTD
PO Box 8220
Roggebaai
8012
South Africa
Tel: +27 21 403 9000
Fax: +27 21 403 9005
Josef Graiser

Services/Products:
Telemarketing agency; Call centre
services/systems; Catalogue producer;
Electronic media

E-Services:
Website design

Member of:
SADMA

DATABASE SOLUTIONS
PO Box 650917
Benmore
2010
South Africa
Tel: +27 11 886 6705
Fax: +27 11 886 6673
Email: andy@listsa.co.za
Web: www.listsa.co.za
Andy Quinan

Services/Products:
List services; Database services;
Mailing/Faxing services; Software
supplier

Member of:
DMA (US); SADMA

DATASHIP MARKETING (PTY) LTD
PO Box 781900
Sandton
2146
South Africa

Tel: +27 11 883 3711
Fax: +27 11 884 3943
Email: admin@pthm.co.za
Andy Hey

Services/Products:
Database services; Consultancy
services; Software supplier; Advertising
Agency; Direct Response Agency

Member of:
SADMA

DATAWORX
Postnet Suite #88
Gallo Manor
Private Bag X23
2052
South Africa
Tel: +27 11 802 4845
Fax: +27 11 802 6957
Email: mike@dataworx.co.za
Mike Esterhuysen

Services/Products:
List services; Fulfilment and sampling
house; Database services; Software
supplier

Member of:
SADMA

DIGITRON
PO Box 542
Eppindust
7475
South Africa
Tel: +27 21 535 1896
Fax: +27 21 535 0642
Email: bgeyser@digitron.co.za
Brad Geyser

Services/Products:
List services; Personalisation; Print
services

Member of:
SADMA

DIMENSION DATA INTERACTIVE
PO Box 56055
Pinegowrie
2123
South Africa
Tel: +27 11 709 1819
Fax: +27 11 709 1818
Email: vanda.dickson@didata.co.za
Web: www.didata.co.za
Vanda Dickson

Services/Products:
Electronic media

E-Services:
Website design

Member of:
SADMA

DIRECT CONCEPTS
Postnet Suite 162
North Riding
Private Bag X3
2162
South Africa
Tel: +27 11 795 3612
Fax: +27 11 795 3648
Shay-Lee Blues

Services/Products:
List services; Consultancy services

Member of:
SADMA

DIRECT MARKETING SERVICES
PO Box 50538
Waterfront
8002
South Africa
Tel: +27 21 434 7781
Fax: +27 21 434 7782
Email: vaughan@vomarketing.co.za
Vaughan Pankhurst

Services/Products:
List services; Fulfilment and sampling
house; Database services; Labelling/
envelope services; Personalisation

Member of:
SADMA

DIRECT RESPONSE MARKETING
PO Box 176
Johannesburg
2000
South Africa
Tel: +27 11 789 2874
Fax: +27 11 789 6637
Email: sueb@drm1997.co.za
Sue Bolton

Services/Products:
Private delivery services

Member of:
SADMA

DODDINGTON DIRECT
PO Box 3939
Honeydew
2040
South Africa
Tel: +27 11794 1918
Fax: +27 11 794 1919
Email: kevan@avspecialist.co.za
Web: www.avspecialist.co.za
Kevan Jones

Services/Products:
List services

Member of:
SADMA

EAGLE TECHNOLOGY
PO Box 4376
Cape Town
8000
South Africa
Tel: +27 21 424 4637
Fax: +27 21 423 4943
Email: eagle@eagle.co.za
Web: www.eagle.co.za
Alan Bearman

Services/Products:
Hardware supplier

Member of:
SADMA

ECNET (PTY)LTD
PO Box 785091
Sandton
2146
South Africa
Tel: +27 11 445 9667
Fax: +27 11 445 9668
Email: genevieve@ecnet.co.za
Web: www.ecnet.co.za
Genevieve Stephenson

Services/Products:
Database services; Electronic media

E-Services:
Website design

Member of:
SADMA

EFFECTIVE INTELLIGENCE
PO Box 663
Rondebosch
7701
South Africa
Tel: +27 21 685 5162
Fax: +27 21 689 7314
Email: info@e-intelligence.com
Web: www.e-intelligence.com
Erica Alma

Services/Products:
List services; Response analysis
bureau; Software supplier

Member of:
DMA (US); FEDMA; SADMA

**EXPRESS MAILING SERVICES
    CC**
PO Box 260761
Excom
2023
South Africa
Tel: +27 11 334 1737

Fax: +27 11 334 3487
Peter Masilo Hutamo

Services/Products:
Mailing/Faxing services

Member of:
SADMA

FCBI
PO Box 78014
Sandton
2146
South Africa
Tel: +27 11 301 1300
Fax: +27 11 301 1364
Nici Stathacopoulos

Services/Products:
Consultancy services; Database
services; Direct marketing agency;
CRM

E-Services:
E-Marketing consultant; Online/e-
marketing agency

Member of:
DMA (US); National DMA

FEDERAL EXPRESS
PO Box 30022
Jet Park
1459
South Africa
Tel: +27 11 923 8000
Fax: +27 11 923 8103
N Freeman

Services/Products:
Private delivery services

Member of:
SADMA

FORBES DIRECT
PO Box 782402
Sandton
2146
South Africa
Tel: +27 11 269 0140
Fax: +27 11 269 1457
Email: dutoits@aforbes.co.za
Web: www.aforbes.co.za
Surika du Toit

Services/Products:
List services; Database services

Member of:
SADMA

GILMARK COMMUNICATIONS
PO Box 16185
Vlaeberg
8018
South Africa
Tel: +27 21 422 2796

Fax: +27 21 422 2799
Email: gilmark@aztec.co.za
Alexander Gilbert

Services/Products:
Advertising Agency; Direct Response
Agency

Member of:
SADMA

GITAM DIRECT
Private Bag x9
Wendywood
2144
South Africa
Tel: +27 11 797 6300
Fax: +27 11 797 6400
Email: fraser@gitam.co.za
Fraser Lamb

Services/Products:
Consultancy services; Advertising
Agency; Direct Response Agency

Member of:
SADMA

**GLOBAL MOUSE
    PRODUCTION CC**
PO Box 3079
Randburg
2125
South Africa
Tel: +27 11 789 4462
Fax: +27 11 789 5380
Glen Roering

Services/Products:
Design/graphics/clip art supplier;
Advertising Agency; Direct Response
Agency

Member of:
SADMA

GLOMAIL
PO Box 6523
Halfway House
1685
South Africa
Tel: +27 11 652 4600
Fax: +27 11 652 4898
Email: info@glomail.co.za
Web: www.glomail.co.za
Andrew Tobias

Services/Products:
Mail order company; Direct response
TV services

Member of:
SADMA

GLOMAIL (LIMITED EDITIONS)
PO Box 6523
Halfway House
1685
South Africa
Tel: +27 11 652 4600
Fax: +27 11 652 4709
Charles Jankelowitz

Services/Products:
Mail order company

Member of:
SADMA

GOLDMAN JUDIN INC
PO Box 78662
Sandton
2146
South Africa
Tel: +27 11 447 8177
Fax: +27 11 447 8122
Web: www.gji.co.za
Michael Judin, Director

Services/Products:
Consultancy services; Legal services

Member of:
National DMA; Advertising Standards
Authority of South Africa

GRINTEK TELECOM
PO Box 11212
Swartkops
51
South Africa
Tel: +27 12 672 8000
Fax: +27 12 665 0081
Email: gt@grintek.com
Web: www.grintek.com
Helen Laurie

Services/Products:
Hardware supplier

Member of:
SADMA

HOME DELIVERY SERVICS
PO Box 276
Bedfordview
2008
South Africa
Tel: +27 11 456 2000
Fax: +27 11 456 2109
Email: ddavies@sun.co.za
Web: www.sun.co.za
D Davies

Services/Products:
Private delivery services

Member of:
SADMA

IAFRICA.COM (PTY) LTD
PO Box 23820
Claremont
7735
South Africa
Tel: +27 21 683 7280
Fax: +27 21 683 7299
Email: robinp@iafrica.com
Web: www.iafrica.com
R Parker

Services/Products:
Database services; Design/graphics/clip
art supplier; Publisher; Advertising
Agency; Electronic media; Direct
Response Agency

E-Services:
Website design

Member of:
SADMA

INCE
PO Box 38200
Booysens
2016
South Africa
Tel: +27 11 241 3000
Fax: +27 11 241 3020
Email: richardm@ince.co.za
Web: www.ince.co.za
Richard Molyneux

Services/Products:
Mailing/Faxing services;
Personalisation; Print services

Member of:
SADMA

INTACT SOLUTIONS
PO Box 70746
Bryanston
2021
South Africa
Tel: +27 11 706 6072
Fax: +27 11 706 6154
Email: keith@intact.co.za
Keith Wiser

Services/Products:
List services; Database services;
Consultancy services; Relationship
marketing

Member of:
SADMA

INTIMATE DATA (PTY) LTD
33 Bell Crescent
Westlake Business Park
Westlake
Cape Town
7800
South Africa
Tel: +27 21 7015 152

Fax: +27 21 7015 153
Email: home@intimatedata.co.za
Web: www.intimatedata.co.za

Services/Products:
List services; Software supplier;
Database services; Personalisation;
Response analysis bureau; Service
bureau

Member of:
National DMA

K&B DIRECT
PO Box 269
Bergvliet
7864
South Africa
Tel: +27 21 797 1628
Fax: +27 21 797 1758
Email: kbdirect@iafrica.com
Belinda Walsh

Services/Products:
List services; Direct marketing agency;
Copy adaptation; Design/graphics/clip
art supplier; Media buying agency;
Electronic media; Relationship
marketing

E-Services:
Website design

Member of:
SADMA

LASER FACILITIES (PTY) LTD
PO Box 2825
Randburg
2128
South Africa
Tel: +27 11 789 1921
Fax: +27 11 886 8880
Email: aaustin@facilities.co.za
Alan Austin

Services/Products:
Mailing/Faxing services; Print services;
Electronic media

E-Services:
Website design

Member of:
SADMA

LEO BURNETT INTERACTIVE
Private Bag X20
Sunninghill
2157
South Africa
Tel: +27 11 235 4200
Fax: +27 11 235 4201
Email: nancy balasar@leoburnett.co.za
Nancy Balasar

Services/Products:
List services; Database services;
Design/graphics/clip art supplier;
Electronic media

E-Services:
Website design

Member of:
SADMA

LIST PERFECT
PO Box 91143
Auckland Park
2006
South Africa
Tel: +27 11 726 2913
Fax: +27 11 726 8284
H Eyre

Services/Products:
List services; Database services

Member of:
SADMA

LISTSEARCH CC
PO Box 13013
Northmead
1511
South Africa
Tel: +27 11 453 2973
Fax: +27 11 453 3668
Email: listsearch@global.co.za
Gill Atkins

Services/Products:
List services; Database services

Member of:
SADMA

LITHOTECH LIMITED
Private Bag X92
Bryanston
2021
South Africa
Tel: +27 11 706 6751
Fax: +27 11 463 7137
Email: lithosaver@icon.co.za
Ben Sachs

Services/Products:
Personalisation; Print services

Member of:
SADMA

LOUISE SINCLAIR DIRECT
PO Box 494
Howard Place
7450
South Africa
Tel: +27 21 531 7071
Fax: +27 21 531 9243
Email: lsd-ct@iafrica.com
Louise Sinclair

Services/Products:
Database services; Advertising Agency;
Direct Response Agency

Member of:
SADMA

MAIL A MILLION
PO Box 1458
Vanderbijlpark
1900
South Africa
Tel: +27 16 982 1384
Fax: +27 16 932 2303
Johan van Vuuren

Services/Products:
Mailing/Faxing services; Labelling/
envelope services

Member of:
SADMA

MAILMASTER
PO Box 1344
Kempton Park
1620
South Africa
Tel: +27 11 970 1498
Fax: +27 11 970 1450
Email: mmsa@pop.onwe.co.za
Steve van Heerden

Services/Products:
List services; Mailing/Faxing services;
Print services

Member of:
SADMA

MAILTRONIC DIRECT
MAILING CC
PO Box 5674
Johannesburg
2000
South Africa
Tel: +27 11 493 9025
Fax: +27 11 493 8880
Email: kkuni@mailtronic.co.za
Kumari Kuni

Services/Products:
Fulfilment and sampling house;
Mailing/Faxing services; Labelling/
envelope services; Print services

Member of:
SADMA

MARKETING LIST SERVICES
8 Timmerman Close
Glenridge
7975
South Africa
Tel: +27 21 713 2058
Fax: +27 21 713 2058

Email: listman@intekom.co.za
Paddy Smith

Services/Products:
List services; Database services

Member of:
SADMA

MARKTEL MARKETING
SERVICES CC T/A INFONET
PO Box 785573
Sandton
2146
South Africa
Tel: +27 11 784 9474
Fax: +27 11 784 9495
Email: info@info-net.co.za
Web: www.info-net.co.za
Piaras Moriarty

Services/Products:
Telemarketing agency; Market research
agency

Member of:
SADMA

MATRIX MARKETING (PTY)
LTD
PO Box 1780
Randburg
2125
South Africa
Tel: +27 11 886 0494
Fax: +27 11 886 9644
Email: matrix@iafrica.com
Web: www.matrixmarketing.com
S Trehair

Services/Products:
List services

Member of:
SADMA

MEDPAGES
9th Floor
Nedbank Building
Adderely Street
Foreshore
8001
South Africa
Tel: +27 21 418 1474
Fax: +27 21 418 1475
Email: info@medpages.co.za
Web: www.medpages.co.za
Andrea Hill, Editor

Services/Products:
Database services; Direct marketing
agency; Labelling/envelope services;
List services; Mailing/Faxing services;
Publisher

E-Services:
Email list provider

Member of:
SADMA

MERPAK ENVELOPES (PTY) LTD
PO Box 39344
Bramley
2018
South Africa
Tel: +27 11 786 7050
Fax: +27 11 885 3174
Deon Joubert

Services/Products:
Labelling/envelope services

Member of:
SADMA

NAMPAK PRODUCTS TRADING AS JIFFY PACKAGING
PO Box 569
Isando
1600
South Africa
Tel: +27 11 974 5538
Fax: +27 11 392 1260
Email: terblanchere@nampak.co.za
Web: www.nampak.co.za
Renier Terblanche

Services/Products:
Protective packaging

Member of:
SADMA

NET TOOLS NETWORK ASSOCIATES
PO Box 70629
Bryanston
2021
South Africa
Tel: +27 11 706 1629
Fax: +27 11 706 1569
Email: admin@syscon.co.za
Brenda Crook

Services/Products:
Database services; Software supplier;
Call centre services/systems

Member of:
SADMA

O'KEEFFE & SWARTZ
2nd Floor Palm Grove
276 Pretoria Street
Frendale
Randburg
2094
South Africa
Tel: +27 11 777 6000
Fax: +27 11 777 6001
Email: seano@intacomm.co.za

Services/Products:
Fulfilment and sampling house; Call
centre services/systems; Response
analysis bureau; Telemarketing agency

Member of:
National DMA; Institute of Marketing
Management South Africa

OGILVY ONE WORLDWIDE
PO Box 70272
Bryanston
2021
South Africa
Tel: +27 11 463 5300
Fax: +27 11 463 5220
Dorothy McLaren

Services/Products:
Advertising Agency; Direct Response
Agency

Member of:
SADMA

ORACLE AIRTIME SALES
Private Bag X10057
Randburg
2125
South Africa
Tel: +27 11 329 5081
Fax: +27 11 329 5040
Email: jeanette@mnet.co.za
Jeanette Honiball van Zyl

Services/Products:
Electronic media

E-Services:
Website design

Member of:
SADMA

PALMER CONSULTING
21 Camilla Steet
Glencairn Heights
7975
South Africa
Tel: +27 21 782 1374
Fax: +27 21 782 1374
Email: csp@cssa.org.za
Colin Palmer, CEO

Services/Products:
Direct marketing agency; Consultancy
services; Training/recruitment;
Facilitator and enabler from meetings
to projects to busines initiatives

E-Services:
E-Marketing consultant

Member of:
National DMA; Computer Society of
SA

PARAGON JHB
PO Box 43078
Industria
2042
South Africa
Tel: +27 11 474 1554
Fax: +27 11 474 3540
Signy Visser

Services/Products:
Mailing/Faxing services; Labelling/
envelope services; Personalisation;
Print services

Member of:
SADMA

PRESTIGE BULK MAILERS (PTY) LTD
PO Box 19803
Pretoria West
117
South Africa
Tel: +27 12 327 3635
Fax: +27 12 327 3668
Andre van Wyk

Services/Products:
Mailing/Faxing services

Member of:
SADMA

PRIMA RESPONSE
PO Box 138
Rondebosch
7701
South Africa
Tel: +27 21 686 0511
Fax: +27 21 685 3858
Email: primares@iafrica.com
Peter Farrell

Services/Products:
Database services; Consultancy
services; Design/graphics/clip art
supplier; Advertising Agency; Direct
Response Agency

Member of:
SADMA

PRINTSOURCE (PTY)LTD
PO Box 1225
Ferndale
2160
South Africa
Tel: +27 11 787 4300
Fax: +27 11 787 2407
Email: printro@global.co.za
Robin Cranna

Services/Products:
Consultancy services; Design/graphics
clip art supplier; Print services; Sales
promotion agency

Member of:
SADMA

**PROFESSIONAL
  MANAGEMENT REVIEW**
PO Box 1200
Parklands
2121
South Africa
Tel: +27 11 880 4720
Fax: +27 11 880 4724
Email: pmr@iafrica.com
Web: www.pmr.co.za
Norman Emdin

Services/Products:
Publisher; Market research agency

Member of:
SADMA

R&R DIRECT MARKETING
PO Box 650814
Benmore
2010
South Africa
Tel: +27 11 883 3520
Fax: +27 11 883 4417
Email: rrdirect@global.co.za
Web: www.rrdirect
Jane Ashburner, Managing Director

Services/Products:
Consultancy services; Direct marketing
agency; List services; Mailing/Faxing
services; Telemarketing agency

E-Services:
Email list provider; E-Marketing
consultant

RAND ENVELOPE (PTY) LTD
PO Box 6204
Johannesburg
2000
South Africa
Tel: +27 11 334 6300
Fax: +27 11 334 4130
Email: Envelope@intekom.co.za
Jennifer Serfontein

Services/Products:
Labelling/envelope services

Member of:
SADMA

RAPP COLLINS SA
PO Box 62116
Johannesburg
2000
South Africa
Tel: +27 11 788 0910
Fax: +27 11 880 2661

Services/Products:
Advertising Agency; Direct Response
Agency

Member of:
DMA

ROCK BOTTOM
PO Box 11133
Tramshed
1026
South Africa
Tel: +27 12 320 1315
Fax: +27 12 320 1313
Email: mail@rockbottom.co.za
Kobus van Rooyen

Services/Products:
Hardware supplier; Software supplier

Member of:
SADMA

SLK WORDS & PICTURES
Postnet Suit 17
Sunninghill
Private Bag X26
2157
South Africa
Tel: +27 11 807 2280
Fax: +27 11 807 3778
Email: candy.slk@pop.co.za
Candy Steyn

Services/Products:
Database services; Direct marketing
agency

Member of:
SADMA

**SOUTH AFRICAN POST
  OFFICE**
PO Box 10000
Pretoria
1
South Africa
Tel: +27 12 421 7036
Fax: +27 12 421 7753
Willie Joubert

Services/Products:
List services; Private delivery services;
Mailing/Faxing services

Member of:
SADMA

SYNERGY AFRICA
PO Box 1921
Durban
4000
South Africa
Tel: +27 31 207 3750
Fax: +27 31 285 907
Email: cebs@iafrica.com
Colin Shepherd

Services/Products:
Advertising Agency; Direct Response
Agency

Member of:
SADMA

SYSTEM PRINT (PTY)LTD
PO Box 281
Mafikeng
2745
South Africa
Tel: +27 18 381 1064
Fax: +27 18 381 0226
Email: n.huber@flashnet.co.za
Norbert Huber

Services/Products:
Print services; Electronic media

E-Services:
Website design

Member of:
SADMA

TELEMESSAGE
PO Box 41353
Craig Hall
2024
South Africa
Tel: +27 11 340 4000
Fax: +27 11 340 4001
Email: Tm@telemessage.co.za
Gareth Tudor

Services/Products:
Telemarketing agency; Consultancy
services; Call centre services/systems

Member of:
SADMA

**THE CUSTOMER
  COMMUNICATION
  COMPANY**
PO Box 595
Sunninghill
2127
South Africa
Tel: +27 11 234 2006
Fax: +27 11 803 3699
Email: ray@thecustomer.co.za
Web: www.thecustomer.co.za
Ray Johnson, CEO

Services/Products:
Call centre services/systems;
Consultancy services; Database
services; Lettershop; Market research
agency; Customer databases;
Communications & loyalty
programmes

E-Services:
Website design

Member of:
DMA (US); National DMA; Institute of Marketing Management; SA Market Research Association

THE DIFFERENCE ENGINE
Building 27
The Woodlands
Woodmead
Johannesburg
South Africa
Tel: +27 11 802 4040
Fax: +27 11 802 6954
Email: michelle@difference.co.za
Michelle Perrow, MD

Services/Products:
Advertising Agency; Database services; Direct marketing agency; Response analysis bureau; Loyalty; DRM; ERM (EnterpriseRelationship Management)

Member of:
SADMA; Institute of Marketing Management, SA

THE FULL SPECTRUM
No 7 6th Street
Parkhurst
2193
South Africa
Tel: +27 11 880 5867
Fax: +27 11 880 5867
Email: fullspec@wweb.co.za
Cheryl Charles

Services/Products:
Advertising Agency; Catalogue producer; Copy adaptation; Database services; Personalisation; Print services; Small below-the-line

E-Services:
Website design

Member of:
SADMA

THE MERCHANTS GROUP SA
PO Box 56055
Pinegowrie
2123
South Africa
Tel: +27 11 709 1412
Fax: +27 11 709 1839
Email: mark.williams@didata.co.za
Mark Williams

Services/Products:
Database services; Training/recruitment; Call centre services/systems

Member of:
SADMA

THE PRESCON GROUP
PO Box 84004
Greenside
2034
South Africa
Tel: +27 11 782 9229
Fax: +27 11 782 2039
Email: prescon@iafrica.com
Belinda Baker

Services/Products:
List services; Fulfilment and sampling house; Direct marketing agency; Publisher

Member of:
SADMA

TNT EXPRESS
PO Box 2185
Johannesburg
2000
South Africa
Tel: +27 11 392 2929
Fax: +27 11 392 2608
Email: rob.ross@netactive.co.za
Web: www.tnt.com
Rob Ross

Services/Products:
Mailing/Faxing services; Private delivery services

Member of:
SADMA

TOTAL COMMUNICATION MANAGEMENT
PO Box 340
Fourways
2055
South Africa
Tel: +27 11 464 1609
Fax: +27 11 464 1085
Email: tcm@iafrica.com
Web: www.virtual1.co.za
Trevor Phillips, Managing Director

Services/Products:
Database services; Interactive media; Media buying agency; Response analysis bureau; Integration and interactive strategist & consultant

E-Services:
E-Marketing consultant; Website design; Online/e-marketing agency

Member of:
SADMA

TS INDUSTRIES CC
PO Box 9136
Edleen
1625
South Africa
Tel: +27 11 791 0410

Fax: +27 11 791 0488
Stephen van Rooyen

Services/Products:
List services; Fulfilment and sampling house; Mailing/Faxing services; Private delivery services; Advertising Agency

Member of:
SADMA

TUNLEY'S CC
PO Box 6446
Johannesburg
2000
South Africa
Tel: +27 11 493 7048
Fax: +27 11 493 0415
Andre de Swardt

Services/Products:
Mailing/Faxing services

Member of:
SADMA

VIRTUAL1 CC
107 Beverley View
Kensington B
Bayswater Road
2194
South Africa
Tel: +27 11 886 5558
Fax: +27 11 781 3159
Email: jurie@virtual1.co.za
Web: www.virtual1.co.za
Jurie Pieterse

Services/Products:
Database services; Electronic media; Relationship marketing

E-Services:
Website design

Member of:
SADMA

WAREHOUSING & DIRECT MAILING (PTY) LTD
PO Box 167
Eppindust
7475
South Africa
Tel: +27 21 54 3261
Fax: +27 21 54 8446
Email: wdm@iafrica.com
Rusty Clement

Services/Products:
Fulfilment and sampling house; Mailing/Faxing services

Member of:
SADMA

**WINSTON TRAVIS &
ASSOCIATES**
PO Box 15065
Vlaeberg
8018
South Africa
Tel: +27 21 683 5258
Fax: +27 21 683 6965
Email: wtaa@iafrica.com
Winston Travis, Proprietor

Services/Products:
Consultancy services; Database
services; List services; Market research
agency

Member of:
National DMA

WUNDERMAN CATO JOHNSON
PO Box 784570
Sandton
2146
South Africa
Tel: +27 11 881 9111
Fax: +27 11 884 1994
Email: matthew_fisher@yr.com
Mathew Fisher

Services/Products:
Advertising Agency; Direct Response
Agency

Member of:
SADMA

YES MARKETING
PO Box 16575
Vlaeberg
8018
South Africa
Tel: +27 21 465 1133
Fax: +27 21 465 1161
Email: yes@new.co.za
Gertrude Smith

Services/Products:
Copy adaptation; Consultancy
services; Design/graphics/clip art
supplier; Catalogue producer;
Advertising Agency; Direct Response
Agency

Member of:
SADMA

SERVICES/PRODUCT
LISTING

Advertising Agency
Brian Pitman Marketing
Celebrations Agencies
Christa Steyn Agency
Dataship Marketing (Pty) Ltd

Gilmark Communications
Gitam Direct
Global Mouse Production CC
Iafrica.com (Pty) Ltd
Louise Sinclair Direct
Ogilvy One Worldwide
Prima Response
Rapp Collins SA
Synergy Africa
The Difference Engine
The Full Spectrum
TS Industries cc
Wunderman Cato Johnson
Yes Marketing

CRM
FCBI

Call centre services/systems
Applied Technology Systems cc
Computer Facilities (Pty) Ltd
Cyberia (Pty) Ltd
Net Tools Network Associates
O'Keeffe & Swartz
Telemessage
The Customer Communication Company
The Merchants Group SA

Catalogue producer
Cyberia (Pty) Ltd
The Full Spectrum
Yes Marketing

Communications & loyalty
programmes
The Customer Communication Company

Consultancy services
Brian Pitman Marketing
Dataship Marketing (Pty) Ltd
Direct Concepts
FCBI
Gitam Direct
Goldman Judin Inc
Intact Solutions
Palmer Consulting
Prima Response
Printsource (PTY)LTD
R&R Direct Marketing
Telemessage
The Customer Communication Company
Winston Travis & Associates
Yes Marketing

Copy adaptation
Behind The Green Door
K&B Direct
The Full Spectrum
Yes Marketing

Customer databases
The Customer Communication Company

DRM
The Difference Engine

Database services
Analogue MIS cc
Applied Technology Systems cc
B&L Direct Marketing Services
Behind The Green Door
Brewer's Marketing Intelligence
Brian Pitman Marketing
Computer Facilities (Pty) Ltd
Creative Response
Database Solutions
Dataship Marketing (Pty) Ltd
DataWorx
Direct Marketing Services
Ecnet (Pty)Ltd
FCBI
Forbes Direct
Iafrica.com (Pty) Ltd
Intact Solutions
Intimate Data (Pty) Ltd
Leo Burnett Interactive
List Perfect
ListSearch cc
Louise Sinclair Direct
Marketing list services
MEDpages
Net Tools Network Associates
Prima Response
SLK Words & Pictures
The Customer Communication Company
The Difference Engine
The Full Spectrum
The Merchants Group SA
Total Communication Management
Virtual1 cc
Winston Travis & Associates

Design/graphics/clip art
supplier
Global Mouse Production CC
Iafrica.com (Pty) Ltd
K&B Direct
Leo Burnett Interactive
Prima Response
Printsource (PTY)LTD
Yes Marketing

Direct Response Agency
Brian Pitman Marketing
Celebrations Agencies
Christa Steyn Agency
Dataship Marketing (Pty) Ltd
Gilmark Communications
Gitam Direct
Global Mouse Production CC
Iafrica.com (Pty) Ltd

Louise Sinclair Direct
Ogilvy One Worldwide
Prima Response
Rapp Collins SA
Synergy Africa
Wunderman Cato Johnson
Yes Marketing

Direct marketing agency
B&L Direct Marketing Services
Customer Behavior Dynamics
FCBI
K&B Direct
MEDpages
Palmer Consulting
R&R Direct Marketing
SLK Words & Pictures
The Difference Engine
The Prescon Group

Direct response TV services
Glomail

ERM (EnterpriseRelationship Management)
The Difference Engine

Electronic media
Applied Technology Systems cc
Cyberia (Pty) Ltd
Dimension Data Interactive
Ecnet (Pty)Ltd
Iafrica.com (Pty) Ltd
K&B Direct
Laser Facilities (Pty) Ltd
Leo Burnett Interactive
Oracle Airtime Sales
System Print (PTY)Ltd
Virtual1 cc

Facilitator and enabler from meetings to projects to busines initiatives
Palmer Consulting

Fulfilment and sampling house
CAB Holdings (Pty) Ltd
DataWorx
Direct Marketing Services
Mailtronic Direct Mailing cc
O'Keeffe & Swartz
The Prescon Group
TS Industries cc
Warehousing & Direct Mailing (Pty) Ltd

Hardware supplier
Eagle Technology
Grintek Telecom
Rock Bottom

Integration and interactive strategist & consultant
Total Communication Management

Interactive media
Total Communication Management

Labelling/envelope services
Direct Marketing Services
Mail A Million
Mailtronic Direct Mailing cc
MEDpages
Merpak Envelopes (Pty) Ltd
Paragon JHB
Rand Envelope (Pty) Ltd

Legal services
Goldman Judin Inc

Lettershop
B&L Direct Marketing Services
Computer Facilities (Pty) Ltd
The Customer Communication Company

List services
Analogue MIS cc
B&L Direct Marketing Services
Behind The Green Door
Brewer's Marketing Intelligence
Database Solutions
DataWorx
Digitron
Direct Concepts
Direct Marketing Services
Doddington Direct
Effective Intelligence
Forbes Direct
Intact Solutions
Intimate Data (Pty) Ltd
K&B Direct
Leo Burnett Interactive
List Perfect
ListSearch cc
Mailmaster
Marketing list services
Matrix Marketing (Pty) Ltd
MEDpages
R&R Direct Marketing
South African Post Office
The Prescon Group
TS Industries cc
Winston Travis & Associates

Loyalty
The Difference Engine

Mail order company
Brian Pitman Marketing
Celebrations Agencies
Glomail
Glomail (Limited Editions)

Mailing/Faxing services
CAB Holdings (Pty) Ltd
Computer Facilities (Pty) Ltd
Database Solutions
Express Mailing Services cc
INCE
Laser Facilities (Pty) Ltd
Mail A Million
Mailmaster
Mailtronic Direct Mailing cc
MEDpages
Paragon JHB
Prestige Bulk Mailers (Pty) Ltd
R&R Direct Marketing
South African Post Office
TNT Express
TS Industries cc
Tunley's cc
Warehousing & Direct Mailing (Pty) Ltd

Market research agency
Marktel Marketing Services cc t/a INFONET
Professional Management Review
The Customer Communication Company
Winston Travis & Associates

Media buying agency
K&B Direct
Total Communication Management

Personalisation
Analogue MIS cc
Computer Facilities (Pty) Ltd
Digitron
Direct Marketing Services
INCE
Intimate Data (Pty) Ltd
Lithotech Limited
Paragon JHB
The Full Spectrum

Print services
CAB Holdings (Pty) Ltd
Digitron
INCE
Laser Facilities (Pty) Ltd
Lithotech Limited
Mailmaster
Mailtronic Direct Mailing cc
Paragon JHB
Printsource (PTY)LTD
System Print (PTY)Ltd
The Full Spectrum

Private delivery services
Direct Response Marketing
Federal Express
Home Delivery Servics
South African Post Office

TNT Express
TS Industries cc

Protective packaging
Nampak products trading as Jiffy
  packaging

Publisher
Brewer's Marketing Intelligence
Iafrica.com (Pty) Ltd
MEDpages
Professional Management Review
The Prescon Group

Relationship marketing
Applied Technology Systems cc
Intact Solutions
K&B Direct
Virtual1 cc

Response analysis bureau
Analogue MIS cc
Creative Response
Effective Intelligence
Intimate Data (Pty) Ltd
O'Keeffe & Swartz
The Difference Engine
Total Communication Management

Sales promotion agency
Behind The Green Door
Printsource (PTY)LTD

Service bureau
Computer Facilities (Pty) Ltd
Intimate Data (Pty) Ltd

Small below-the-line
The Full Spectrum

Software supplier
Behind The Green Door
Database Solutions
Dataship Marketing (Pty) Ltd
DataWorx
Effective Intelligence
Intimate Data (Pty) Ltd
Net Tools Network Associates
Rock Bottom

Telemarketing agency
B&L Direct Marketing Services
Creative Response
Cyberia (Pty) Ltd
Marktel Marketing Services cc t/a
  INFONET
O'Keeffe & Swartz
R&R Direct Marketing
Telemessage

Training/recruitment
Customer Behavior Dynamics
Palmer Consulting
The Merchants Group SA

E-SERVICES

E-Marketing consultant
FCBI
Palmer Consulting
R&R Direct Marketing
Total Communication Management

Email list provider
MEDpages
R&R Direct Marketing

Online/e-marketing agency
FCBI
Total Communication Management

Website design
Applied Technology Systems cc
Cyberia (Pty) Ltd
Dimension Data Interactive
Ecnet (Pty)Ltd
Iafrica.com (Pty) Ltd
K&B Direct
Laser Facilities (Pty) Ltd
Leo Burnett Interactive
Oracle Airtime Sales
System Print (PTY)Ltd
The Customer Communication Company
The Full Spectrum
Total Communication Management
Virtual1 cc

Further Reading
from Kogan Page

Our wide range of marketing titles are available direct from Kogan Page or through good booksellers. Bestselling titles include:

11 Steps to Brand Heaven
Leonard Weinreich
£15.00 ISBN 0 7494 3548 8   March 2001
The ultimate guide to buying an advertising campaign, written by one of the industry's leading figures.

Adding Value to Marketing
David Doyle
£22.50 Paperback ISBN 0 7494 2175 4   1998
How to make the marketing function more profitable and more productive, by adopting a more focused and cost-effective approach.

Business-to-Business Marketing Communications
Sixth Edition
Norman Hart
£22.50 Paperback ISBN 0 7494 2588 X   1997
A practical handbook of business-to-business advertising, promotion and PR.

Commonsense Direct Marketing
Fourth Edition
Drayton Bird
£22.50 Paperback ISBN 0 7494 3121 0   2000
The most authoritative and popular book ever published on direct marketing.

Direct and Database Marketing
Graeme McCorkell
£19.95 Paperback ISBN 0 7494 1960 1   1997
The definitive guide to improving customer knowledge with proper management and analysis of their behaviour.

International Marketing
Second Edition
Roger Bennet
£19.95 Paperback ISBN 0 7494 2272 6   1998
An authoritative textbook covering strategy, planning, market entry and implementation.

Marketing Communications
Second Edition
Paul Smith
£21.95 Paperback ISBN 0 7494 2699 3   1998
A comprehensive framework that enables both students and practitioners to get to grips with the communications mix.

Market Professional Services
Second Edition
Patrick Forsyth
£19.95 Paperback ISBN 0 7494 2982 8   1999
Practical approaches to practice development.

Living the Brand
Nicholas Ind
£18.99 ISBN 0 7494 33663   2001
An essential guide for brand managers and marketing managers on how to create and sustain a long-term brand image.

Mind to Mind Marketing
Harry Adler
£18.99 ISBN 0 7494 3366 3   2001
An essential text written by one of the world's leading practitioners, offers academics and professions insights on how to successfully target their market.

The Handbook of International Market Research Techniques
Robert J. Birn
£60.00 ISBN 0 7494 2616 0   2000
An indispensable textbook equipped with everything you need to know about marketing and advertising research as well as analysis, modelling and report writing.

Key Marketing Skills
Peter Cheverton
£29.95 ISBN 0 7494 3355 8   2000
A step by step action kit by a leading marketing trainer, covering the principal professional concepts, tools and methods.

The Business Enterprise Handbook
Colin Barrow, Robert Brown and Liz Clark
£30.00 ISBN 0 7494 3489 9   2001
A comprehensive handbook offering advice on how to implement marketing strategies and E-commerce in businesses.

The International Dictionary of Marketing
Daniel Yadin
£24.95 ISBN 0 7494 3532   2001
A must-read text that covers all aspects of marketing, making it ideal for students and professionals alike.

It's All About Customers!
John Frazer-Robinson
£16.99 ISBN 0 7494 3073 7   1999
A practical 'Bible', written by the leading master of marketing. Provides a valuable insight on how to promote business growth through marketing, sales and service.

Marketing in Action Series

An accessible series aimed at marketing professionals and students, offering clear and up-to-date analysis on specific marketing topics.

Branding
Geoffrey Randall
£14.99 Paperback ISBN 0 7494 21266   1997

Creative Marketing Communications
Third Edition
Daniel Yadin
£16.99 Paperback ISBN 0 7494 3458 9   2000

Direct Marketing
Margaret Allen
£14.99 Paperback ISBN 0 7494 20529   1997

How to Produce Successful Advertising
Second Edition
A D Farbey
£14.99 Paperback ISBN 0 7494 27019   1998

Introduction to International Marketing
Keith Lewis and Matthew Housden
£14.99 Paperback ISBN 0 7494 2246 7   1998

Introduction to Marketing
Geoff Lancaster and Paul Reynolds
£14.99 Paperback ISBN 0 7494 2095 2 1999

A Practical Guide to Integrated Marketing Communications
Revised Edition
Tom Brannan
£14.99 Paperback ISBN 0 7494 1520 7 1998

Successful Product Management
Second Edition
Stephen Morse
£14.99 Paperback ISBN 0 7494 2702 7 1998

**For further information on these and other titles, please visit our
website at: www.kogan-page.co.uk**

Index of Advertisers